Dictionary of Literary Biography

Dictionary of Literary Biography Documentary Series

Dictionary of Literary Biography Yearbooks

1980 edited by Karen L. Rood, Jean W. Ross, and Richard Ziegfeld (1981)

1981 edited by Karen L. Rood, Jean W. Ross, and Richard Ziegfeld (1982)

1982 edited by Richard Ziegfeld; associate editors: Jean W. Ross and Lynne C. Zeigler (1983)

1983 edited by Mary Bruccoli and Jean W. Ross; associate editor Richard Ziegfeld (1984)

1984 edited by Jean W. Ross (1985)

1985 edited by Jean W. Ross (1986)

1986 edited by J. M. Brook (1987)

1987 edited by J. M. Brook (1988)

1988 edited by J. M. Brook (1989)

1989 edited by J. M. Brook (1990)

1990 edited by James W. Hipp (1991)

1991 edited by James W. Hipp (1992)

1992 edited by James W. Hipp (1993)

1993 edited by James W. Hipp, contributing editor George Garrett (1994)

1994 edited by James W. Hipp, contributing editor George Garrett (1995)

1995 edited by James W. Hipp, contributing editor George Garrett (1996)

1996 edited by Samuel W. Bruce and L. Kay Webster, contributing editor George Garrett (1997)

1997 edited by Matthew J. Bruccoli and George Garrett, with the assistance of L. Kay Webster (1998)

1998 edited by Matthew J. Bruccoli, contributing editor George Garrett, with the assistance of D. W. Thomas (1999)

1999 edited by Matthew J. Bruccoli, contributing editor George Garrett, with the assistance of D. W. Thomas (2000)

2000 edited by Matthew J. Bruccoli, contributing editor George Garrett, with the assistance of George Parker Anderson (2001)

2001 edited by Matthew J. Bruccoli, contributing editor George Garrett, with the assistance of George Parker Anderson (2002)

2002 edited by Matthew J. Bruccoli and George Garrett; George Parker Anderson, Assistant Editor (2003)

Concise Series

Concise Dictionary of American Literary Biography, 7 volumes (1988–1999): *The New Consciousness, 1941–1968; Colonization to the American Renaissance, 1640–1865; Realism, Naturalism, and Local Color, 1865–1917; The Twenties, 1917–1929; The Age of Maturity, 1929–1941; Broadening Views, 1968–1988; Supplement: Modern Writers, 1900–1998.*

Concise Dictionary of British Literary Biography, 8 volumes (1991–1992): *Writers of the Middle Ages and Renaissance Before 1660; Writers of the Restoration and Eighteenth Century, 1660–1789; Writers of the Romantic Period, 1789–1832; Victorian Writers, 1832–1890; Late-Victorian and Edwardian Writers, 1890–1914; Modern Writers, 1914–1945; Writers After World War II, 1945–1960; Contemporary Writers, 1960 to Present.*

Concise Dictionary of World Literary Biography, 4 volumes (1999–2000): *Ancient Greek and Roman Writers; German Writers; African, Caribbean, and Latin American Writers; South Slavic and Eastern European Writers.*

Dictionary of Literary Biography® • Volume Three Hundred Twenty-Seven

Sixteenth-Century French Writers

Dictionary of Literary Biography® • Volume Three Hundred Twenty-Seven

Sixteenth-Century French Writers

Edited by
Megan Conway
Louisiana State University–Shreveport

A Bruccoli Clark Layman Book

THOMSON
GALE

Detroit • New York • San Francisco • New Haven, Conn. • Waterville, Maine • London • Munich

THOMSON
™
GALE

Dictionary of Literary Biography
Volume 327: Sixteenth-Century French Writers
Megan Conway

Advisory Board
John Baker
William Cagle
Patrick O'Connor
George Garrett
Trudier Harris
Alvin Kernan

Editorial Directors
Matthew J. Bruccoli and Richard Layman

LIBRARY OF CONGRESS CATALOGING-IN-PUBLICATION DATA

Sixteenth-century French writers / edited by Megan Conway.
    p. cm. — (Dictionary of literary biography ; v. 327)
    "A Bruccoli Clark Layman book."
    Includes bibliographical references and index.
    ISBN 0–7876–8145–8 (hardcover : alk. paper)
    1. French literature—16th century—Bio-bibliography—Dictionaries. 2. Authors, French—16th century—Biography—Dictionaries. 3. French literature—16th century—Dictionaries. I. Conway, Megan. II. Series.
    PQ231.S59 2006
    840.9'00303—dc22
    [B]   2006014212

Printed in the United States of America
10 9 8 7 6 5 4 3 2 1

To my husband, Calvin Head, with appreciation and thanks for his unflagging patience, encouragement, and technical support. Special thanks also to my sister, Kari Conway Sullivan, for her cheerfulness, to Fred and Sybil Patten for their generosity and friendship, and to all my esteemed colleagues who contributed to this volume.

Contents

Contents

Plan of the Series

. . . Almost the most prodigious asset of a country, and perhaps its most precious possession, is its native literary product—when that product is fine and noble and enduring.

Mark Twain*

The advisory board, the editors, and the publisher of the *Dictionary of Literary Biography* are joined in endorsing Mark Twain's declaration. The literature of a nation provides an inexhaustible resource of permanent worth. Our purpose is to make literature and its creators better understood and more accessible to students and the reading public, while satisfying the needs of teachers and researchers.

To meet these requirements, *literary biography* has been construed in terms of the author's achievement. The most important thing about a writer is his writing. Accordingly, the entries in *DLB* are career biographies, tracing the development of the author's canon and the evolution of his reputation.

The purpose of *DLB* is not only to provide reliable information in a usable format but also to place the figures in the larger perspective of literary history and to offer appraisals of their accomplishments by qualified scholars.

The publication plan for *DLB* resulted from two years of preparation. The project was proposed to Bruccoli Clark by Frederick G. Ruffner, president of the Gale Research Company, in November 1975. After specimen entries were prepared and typeset, an advisory board was formed to refine the entry format and develop the series rationale. In meetings held during 1976, the publisher, series editors, and advisory board approved the scheme for a comprehensive biographical dictionary of persons who contributed to literature. Editorial work on the first volume began in January 1977, and it was published in 1978. In order to make *DLB* more than a dictionary and to compile volumes that individually have claim to status as literary history, it was decided to organize volumes by topic, period, or

*From an unpublished section of Mark Twain's autobiography, copyright by the Mark Twain Company

genre. Each of these freestanding volumes provides a biographical-bibliographical guide and overview for a particular area of literature. We are convinced that this organization—as opposed to a single alphabet method—constitutes a valuable innovation in the presentation of reference material. The volume plan necessarily requires many decisions for the placement and treatment of authors. Certain figures will be included in separate volumes, but with different entries emphasizing the aspect of his career appropriate to each volume. Ernest Hemingway, for example, is represented in *American Writers in Paris, 1920–1939* by an entry focusing on his expatriate apprenticeship; he is also in *American Novelists, 1910–1945* with an entry surveying his entire career, as well as in *American Short-Story Writers, 1910–1945, Second Series* with an entry concentrating on his short fiction. Each volume includes a cumulative index of the subject authors and articles.

Between 1981 and 2002 the series was augmented and updated by the *DLB Yearbooks*. There have also been nineteen *DLB Documentary Series* volumes, which provide illustrations, facsimiles, and biographical and critical source materials for figures, works, or groups judged to have particular interest for students. In 1999 the *Documentary Series* was incorporated into the *DLB* volume numbering system beginning with *DLB 210: Ernest Hemingway*.

We define literature as the *intellectual commerce of a nation:* not merely as belles lettres but as that ample and complex process by which ideas are generated, shaped, and transmitted. *DLB* entries are not limited to "creative writers" but extend to other figures who in their time and in their way influenced the mind of a people. Thus the series encompasses historians, journalists, publishers, book collectors, and screenwriters. By this means readers of *DLB* may be aided to perceive literature not as cult scripture in the keeping of intellectual high priests but firmly positioned at the center of a nation's life.

DLB includes the major writers appropriate to each volume and those standing in the ranks behind them. Scholarly and critical counsel has been sought in deciding which minor figures to include and how full their entries should be. Wherever possible, useful references are made to figures who do not warrant separate entries.

Each *DLB* volume has an expert volume editor responsible for planning the volume, selecting the figures for inclusion, and assigning the entries. Volume editors are also responsible for preparing, where appropriate, appendices surveying the major periodicals and literary and intellectual movements for their volumes, as well as lists of further readings. Work on the series as a whole is coordinated at the Bruccoli Clark Layman editorial center in Columbia, South Carolina, where the editorial staff is responsible for accuracy and utility of the published volumes.

One feature that distinguishes *DLB* is the illustration policy—its concern with the iconography of literature. Just as an author is influenced by his surroundings, so is the reader's understanding of the author enhanced by a knowledge of his environment. Therefore *DLB*

volumes include not only drawings, paintings, and photographs of authors, often depicting them at various stages in their careers, but also illustrations of their families and places where they lived. Title pages are regularly reproduced in facsimile along with dust jackets for modern authors. The dust jackets are a special feature of *DLB* because they often document better than anything else the way in which an author's work was perceived in its own time. Specimens of the writers' manuscripts and letters are included when feasible.

Samuel Johnson rightly decreed that "The chief glory of every people arises from its authors." The purpose of the *Dictionary of Literary Biography* is to compile literary history in the surest way available to us—by accurate and comprehensive treatment of the lives and work of those who contributed to it.

The *DLB* Advisory Board

Introduction

François I's assumption of the French throne in 1515 traditionally marks the beginning of the period that scholars designate as the French Renaissance; the death of Henri IV in 1610 marks its end. Thus, the sixteenth century is nearly, if somewhat arbitrarily, synonymous with the Renaissance in France. While this convention is a useful way to organize a study of a brilliant era in French literary history, it must be remembered that the ideas that characterize the Renaissance had begun to circulate almost a century earlier and that they were starting to fragment by the third quarter of the sixteenth century. For this reason, this volume is titled *Sixteenth-Century French Writers,* referring to an actual historical period, rather than "Writers of the French Renaissance," which would depend on a debatable definition.

It is, perhaps, more useful to describe the Renaissance than to try to define it. The Renaissance in Europe reflects an abrupt break with the past—specifically with the Middle Ages, which fifteenth- and sixteenth-century thinkers who wanted to assert their difference from preceding generations characterized as the "Dark Ages." Medieval culture had been centered on the church, and medieval people generally focused their thoughts and efforts on the next world. This life was to be endured, not enjoyed; therefore, its evils were accepted, and no attempt was made to change them. As the seat of sin and weakness, the body was regarded as shameful. Women were seen as lustful and inferior to men; they needed to be looked after and kept in their place. The reward for a good life was to be found in heaven. Renaissance views were markedly different on all counts. This world was fascinating, various, and wonderful. Life was more than a grueling struggle for survival while one waited for the afterlife. The center of culture migrated from the church to the cities and to the royal courts, and people began to enjoy themselves. New spices delighted the palate, and luxury items softened the rough edges of existence. The body was no longer a thing to be denied but a temple to be worshiped and cared for. Pleasure was not necessarily bad. Nor were women: although they were still not considered the equals of men, during the Renaissance they were taught to read and write.

Economics and history laid the groundwork for this shift. The pyramidal structure of feudal society—serfs at the bottom, God at the top—had broken down in the late Middle Ages, principally because of the rise of the middle class. When the number of merchants grew so large that the private armies of the nobles could not provide them sufficient protection, they began to look to each other, rather than to the lords, for support and security. As the middle class acquired wealth, it also acquired the privileges that wealth makes possible—including educational opportunities and leisure time.

Three additional major factors contributed to the advent of the Renaissance. The first was the introduction of gunpowder to the West from Arab lands and ultimately from China. Gunpowder dramatically altered the way in which wars were fought. With gunpowder came the development of cannons and shot, muskets and bullets. By 1500 most infantries across Europe were carrying the harquebus, a single-shot musket. Although the crossbow had already weakened the institution of chivalry, the cannon and musket sounded its death knell. Armed only with swords and weighed down by heavy armor, knights could be killed as easily as—or even more easily than—common soldiers. The traditional importance of an elite cavalry of knights thus gave way before the increasing value of an infantry equipped with firearms. When knights lost their military superiority, their code of chivalry no longer commanded respect; and as war became bloodier and more brutal, it no longer seemed the genteel and poetic enterprise it was represented to be in knightly romances. Chivalry lived on in literature and art but suffered a rude decline in real life. As war became more democratized with the increased importance of the infantry, the balance of power shifted away from the nobles toward the crown. Gunpowder thus allowed kings to shake off the remaining restraints of the pyramidal social structure. Freed from dependence on their lords to provide knights, kings could use common soldiers to put down rebellious vassals and hold together loosely unified states.

Just as gunpowder had an irrevocable effect on the structure of society, the second factor—the invention of the printing press—changed the way in which society's knowledge was shared and disseminated. Manuscripts on parchment and vellum were reserved for the church or wealthy nobles, as they were labor-intensive to produce and extremely expensive. Because few people outside the clergy could read or write, the Roman Catholic Church dominated medieval intellectual life and education. Reading was not encouraged among the secular members of society, for the church did not favor individual thought. It was better to rely on what the priest said, particularly in regard to interpreting Scripture. The advent of the printing press in the 1450s brought staggering changes. Printing sharply brought down the price of books, making them available to the middle classes. Erudition was no longer the exclusive domain of the clergy and the wealthy. Having books in the home became a status symbol, and more and more people began to read. Would-be scholars no longer had to expend all of their energy memorizing texts but could reread and study them at their leisure. Moreover, scholars in different locations could, for the first time, examine and debate identical copies of a text. The monolithic authority of the Catholic Church was challenged as people began to own Bibles and study them. While the Reformation might have taken place without the invention of the printing press, there is no doubt that the availability of texts and the ability to reach a large audience with printed materials added a driving force to the rise of Protestantism.

The third factor contributing to the advent of the Renaissance was the discovery of new lands, which led to a renewed interest in the applied sciences. Explorers such as Christopher Columbus, Vasco de Gama, Giovanni da Verrazano, and Jacques Cartier brought various kinds of new knowledge from distant parts of the world, instilling Europeans with a desire for yet more. A scientific methodology was developed that used a revolutionary combination of logic, mathematics, and experimentation. The works of scientists of the ancient world, such as Galen and Hippocrates, were rediscovered and emulated. Mathematics gained popularity as a means of understanding the world, for, following the example of the ancients, scientists perceived nature as mathematical in structure. Since printing allowed for the gathering and storage of ideas from all disciplines, it suddenly seemed possible for one person to master all human knowledge. Enthusiasm for science permeated the first half of the Renaissance in France.

During the Renaissance, for the first time in history, people felt a need to disconnect themselves from the immediate past and declare themselves separate from those who had preceded them. Renaissance thinkers preferred to claim kinship with ancient Greece and Rome rather than with the Middle Ages. Medieval theology and philosophy were ridiculed and supplanted by classical doctrines. Latin was retained as the language of scholarship, but the Latin of the church was replaced by that of Cicero and Horace. Greek, which the Catholic Church had long declared a heretical language, regained its esteem as the mother tongue of the ancients. Renaissance scholars prided themselves on their classical studies and, when possible, read primary sources in the original languages. Writers began to eschew traditional medieval forms of verse, preferring to fashion their poetry on classical models and experimenting with rhyme schemes and line lengths.

This combination of attitudes—belief in the limitless potential of human beings, thirst for knowledge, love of the classics, and the notion that people are essentially good—constitutes humanism, the most important intellectual and philosophical movement of the Renaissance. The term comes from the Latin *humanitas,* referring to the development of the higher side of human nature—a combination of noble character (what the Italian Renaissance philosopher Niccolò Machiavelli called *virtù*) and learning. Necessarily a dynamic rather than a static notion, *humanitas* required the continual and rigorous application of logic and reason and an unshakable belief in human freedom and dignity. The word *humanista* (humanist) was used in late-fifteenth-century Italy to designate professors of the liberal arts; it soon evolved to include anyone devoted to the study and promotion of the classics.

Renaissance thinkers came to believe that the restoration of classical culture, language, literature, ideas, and ideals was the best means for developing true *humanitas.* Humanists, therefore, participated in the effort to restore antique culture and circulate ancient texts. This attitude, however, was not adopted at the expense of modern concerns. Latin and Greek—and Hebrew—were studied and venerated but were also translated and imitated in vernacular languages. While most scholarly writing was in classical Latin, the greatest Renaissance works are in the vernacular.

France's participation in this movement was aided in no small part by Louis XII's conquest of Italy and François I's patronage of writers and the arts. The Italian way of life was a startling revelation for the French—particularly for the nobility, who saw there a quite different sort of aristocratic life than the one they led at home. Italian palaces were elegant and designed according to a new architecture. They were decorated with an eye to detail and luxury in furniture and appointments. Paintings, sculpture, fine dishes, silks, gold, and jewelry were not reserved for royalty but were enjoyed by the nobility, as well. Women participated in court life, and men polished their manners and their words to please them. Both sexes took care in their dress and grooming. Art was honored everywhere, and painters, sculptors, and writers held places of esteem at court. French lords carried this new attitude home with them. In 1503 Louis XII began the construction of his château, Blois, in the Italian Renaissance style. Changes in architecture mirrored changes in literary tastes and an openness to new ideas that gained momentum under Louis's successor, François I.

Great popular enthusiasm greeted François's ascension to the throne in 1515 at the age of twenty-one. He was the embodiment of the kingly ideal: young, handsome, gallant, noble in manner, rich, and powerful. He had received a humanist education and had a deep appreciation of culture and the arts. Propelled by a sense of duty and a taste for glory, he set out for Italy almost immediately with the intention of recovering Milan from Duke Massimiliano Sforza, who had overthrown the French there in 1513. Victorious, he returned home determined to encourage and promote French painters, sculptors, and architects. François persuaded Leonardo da Vinci to take up residence not far from Amboise, and the Italian artist lived there until his death in 1519. Although Leonardo produced no masterpieces in France, he brought with him several paintings, including the *Mona Lisa,* that ended up in François's private collection. This collection, housed in his palace at Fontainebleau, came to include works by Titian, Benvenuto Cellini, and Raphael.

The Fontainebleau palace also sheltered the royal library for a time. In 1518 the library, then at Blois, comprised 1,626 volumes; some were in Greek, Hebrew, and Arabic, reflecting François's humanistic leanings. Shortly after Guillaume Budé was given the newly created post of master of the king's library in 1522, François began to send agents abroad to search for rare manuscripts, particularly Greek ones. François's ambassadors in Rome and Venice were also on the alert for Greek manuscripts and were told to have copies made of texts that they were unable to buy. As manuscripts and books flowed into France, François gradually set up a second library at Fontainebleau, to which he added the collection of Charles, Duke of Bourbon, in 1523; the duke's collections were confiscated after he joined forces with Charles V against the French king. The king's favorites included Roman histories and tales of valor, as well as the French medieval classic *Roman de la Rose* (Romance of the Rose). In 1544 François combined the libraries by moving the Blois collection to Fontainebleau. Twenty years after the king's death in 1547, the library, which by then contained 3,650 titles, was moved to Paris. There it eventually evolved into the Bibliothèque nationale, France's foremost library.

François's reign was filled with military campaigns, but the gains and losses ultimately canceled one another out. On the other hand, the importance of François and his sister, Marguerite de Navarre, as patrons of the arts and of letters can hardly be overestimated. While other monarchs kept court poets for entertainment or as historians, François encouraged scholars, poets, painters, sculptors, and architects and conferred a new intellectual and social status on men of letters. Many of the latter enjoyed his patronage and protection, among them Budé; Desiderius Erasmus; Jacques Colin, translator of Baldassare Castiglione's *Il cortegiano* (1528, The Courtier); Clément Marot; and François Rabelais. The king wrote poetry and particularly admired the works of Erasmus, Giovanni Boccaccio, and Petrarch. In 1530, on Budé's advice, François established royal readerships in Greek, Hebrew, and mathematics. These chairs, along with another in Latin established a few years later, formed the nucleus of the Collège des Lecteurs Royaux, which evolved into the Collège Royal and eventually into what is known today as the Collège de France—the first French university not under the direct control of the Catholic Church. In 1539 the king furthered humanist studies by giving scholars at the college permission to examine the Scriptures in the original language despite the disapproval of the Sorbonne (the Faculty of Theology of the University of Paris). That same year, as part of the royal ordinance of Viller-Cotterêts, François ordered that French, rather than Latin, be used in legal documents, and he appointed Robert I Estienne as the royal printer of Hebrew and Latin. Estienne received the same privilege for Greek in 1544, and François personally financed the cutting of three sets of Greek type and provided from the royal collection the manuscripts to be printed. The king's support of and sympathy for the humanist movement infuriated traditional church scholars, even though François remained an ardent Catholic to the end of his life.

Most of the early humanists would have considered themselves faithful Catholics, despite an increasing desire by many of them to reform church practices such as the sale of indulgences. Humanist reformers criticized monkery and ritual and considered the personal study of Holy Writ a necessity. Scholars such as Budé, Erasmus, Jacques Lefèvre d'Etaples, and Jacques Amyot saw no conflict between their scholarly activities and traditional faith. On the contrary, they believed that reading Scripture in Greek promoted a greater understanding of the New Testament, and they valued Jesus Christ as an exemplary classical hero. For humanists, the Christian life was the struggle of an essentially free individual to master his or her passions and control his or her being—a conception fundamentally in opposition to the Protestantism of Martin Luther and Jean Calvin. This open-minded evangelism was embraced by Marguerite de Navarre, Marot, and Rabelais, who got into varying degrees of trouble because of their beliefs. The authority of the Sorbonne was still often as powerful as the royal will, and humanist authors were threatened with imprisonment or even death if they offended too greatly.

Not even the king's sister was immune from church harassment. In 1531 Marguerite's almoner was accused of heresy, and in 1533 her poem *Le Miroir de l'âme pécheresse* (1531, Mirror of a Sinful Soul; translated as *The Glasse of the Synnefoulle Soule,* 1544) was condemned by the University of Paris. That work included a translation by Marot, the best-known French poet of the early sixteenth century, of a psalm from Hebrew into French, putting him on dangerous ground with church authorities. Although mostly remembered for graceful court poetry that shows the early influence of Renaissance ideas, Marot spent much of his life in conflict with the church. Despite the patronage of both François and Marguerite, Marot left France to avoid imprisonment when the "Affair of the Placards" shook Paris in 1534. This incident, in which broadsheets denouncing the Mass were posted around the city and even in the royal apartments, provoked the first widespread reaction against the Reformers, since attacking the Mass was considered clearly heretical. Marot was allowed to return after abjuring his "errors." Nevertheless, he continued translating the Psalms, and the publication of the first collection of the translations in 1541 forced him to leave the country again. He fled to Geneva, where he was first welcomed, then denounced, by Jean Calvin.

Calvin had also been obliged to leave Paris after the Affair of the Placards. In 1536 he published in Basel the first edition of the *Christianæ religionis institutio* (translated as *The Institution of Christian Religion,* 1561), which rejected Catholicism and laid out a stern doctrine for a new church. That same year he moved to Geneva, where he taught theology. His unbending brand of Protestantism soon ran afoul of the ruling faction, and he was banished from the city—only to return as its triumphant master three years later. He controlled Geneva with an iron hand until his death in 1564, whereupon the leadership fell to his disciple Théodore de Bèze.

While Rabelais was a supporter of the early evangelical Reform movement, he opposed the dogmatic rigidity of Calvin. Best known for his entertaining books about the father-and-son giants Gargantua and Pantagruel, Rabelais became a Franciscan monk at an early age. There he learned firsthand to abhor the medieval Scholastic tradition that he later pilloried in his works. When the Franciscans confiscated his Greek books in 1524, Rabelais moved to the Benedictine order, which was more suited to his intellectual pursuits. He studied Latin, Greek, and law until the Sorbonne ordered a halt to Greek studies. In 1530 he abandoned his religious vocation to study medicine at Montpellier, where he became a successful doctor. In 1532 he became a physician at a hospital in Lyon and made a name for himself by publishing an edition of Hippocrates' and Galen's texts with commentaries. In the fall of that same year he anonymously published *Pantagruel. Pantagruel* and *Gargantua* (1534) are quintessential examples of the early humanist spirit—they are filled with enthusiasm, classical allusions and quips, details, and a full consciousness of language. Much of the content of the books is scatological, as well as philosophical, and Rabelais boldly satirizes the monasteries and the educational system supported by the church. Such criticism did not win him favor with the Sorbonne, and the Affair of the Placards convinced him to abandon his religious satire in the *Third Book* (1546), *Fourth Book* (1548, 1552) and *Fifth Book* (1564) of the Pantagruel saga.

Rabelais's bawdy tone is in direct contrast to that of the poets of the so-called School of Lyon. Lyon was the second largest city in France after Paris, which it rivaled in prestige and economic power, and it was a hub of humanist literary activity. Home to a thriving printing industry that for a time outstripped that of the capital, Lyon housed more than a hundred presses by the mid 1520s. By 1528 more than half of Lyon's inhabitants were foreigners, most of them Italians, and many Italian works, including those of Leon Battista Alberti, Ludovico Ariosto, Matteo Maria Boiardo, and Dante, as well as the hugely popular Boccaccio, Petrarch, and Castiglione, found their way to the French public through the efforts of the intellectual elite and printers of Lyon. Editions of Italian and Latin texts were printed, reprinted, translated, and imitated until classical references became commonplace among the literate.

Early Lyonese intellectuals included Symphorien Champier, the first Frenchman to publish translations of Plato's dialogues; Etienne Dolet, a printer and noted Latinist; and Bonaventure des Périers, a classical scholar also known for his creative writings. These men set the stage for the period from 1535 to 1555, when Lyon's intellectual life reached its peak under the influences of Petrarchism and Neoplatonism. Petrarch became the model for the perfect love poet, and Plato—or, at least, the humanists' concept of Plato—became the arbiter of true love and the ideal. These notions are elegantly portrayed in the poetry of Maurice Scève, the leading writer of the School of Lyon, and two female poets: Louise Labé, who puts a gender twist on the Petrarchan tradition, and Pernette du Guillet, who manages to imbue Neoplatonism with humor. Perhaps the best poetic exposition of the Platonic doctrine of love is found in Antoine Héroët's immensely popular *La Parfaicte Amye* (The Perfect Female Friend), published in 1542. Mellin de Saint-Gelais, also associated with the Lyon school, helped to introduce the sonnet and the madrigal to France. All of these poets made their erudition apparent through the many allusions in their works to ancient texts and myths.

Like most early humanists, the School of Lyon admired classical authors such as Horace and Cicero for their linguistic elegance and precision. Renaissance humanists, however, wished not only to emulate the past but also to improve on it. Scholarly writing was still done in Latin, but the vernacular began to take on a special importance. This new attitude was codified in Joachim du Bellay's *La Deffence et Illustration de la Langue Francoyse* (1549; translated as *The Defence and Illustration of the French Language,* 1939). Although he has poetry primarily in mind, Du Bellay contends that French is a worthy language for all literary and scholarly endeavors and that it merely needs to be enriched—"illustrated"—by bringing classical words into the language, creating new ones, and developing classically inspired turns of phrase and rhetorical figures. He urges the abandonment of medieval traditions and encourages experimentation with line length and rhyme. Du Bellay promotes these new trends at the expense of earlier poets such as Marot and Saint-Gelais.

La Deffence et Illustration de la Langue Francoyse was the manifesto of a group of midcentury French poets, the Pléiade. Named after a group of seven Greek tragic poets of Alexandria, who were themselves named after the star cluster Pleiades in the constellation Taurus (which, in turn, was named for the daughters of Atlas who were turned into stars in Greek mythology), the Pléiade comprised seven poets: Du Bellay and Pierre de Ronsard, two of the greatest French poets of the century, and Pontus de Tyard, Jean-Antoine de Baïf, Etienne Jodelle, Rémy Belleau, and Jacques Peletier du Mans. The Pléiade put Du Bellay's ideas into practice by throwing themselves into a passionate study of the ancients and setting out to create a new era in French poetry. Italian poetry—particularly the works of Petrarch and Pietro Bembo—served as their example, and classical mythology began to replace national and Christian images in their writings. The Pléiade manifesto caused a good deal of controversy; but it also fostered many poetic masterpieces, including Du Bellay's dignified and melancholy sonnet collections "Le Premier Livre des antiquitez de Rome" (1558, The First Book of the Antiquities of Rome; translated as "Ruines of Rome," 1591) and "Les Regrets" (1558; translated as "The Regrets," 1984). Ronsard's works display greater variety in both form and content: his odes range from the serious to the lighthearted and imitate a range of models from Pindar to Horace. He is particularly remembered for his sonnets and light odes.

While poetry was the driving force behind the Pléiade, its members were multitalented. Belleau's poetry reflected his extensive knowledge of the natural sciences; Tyard's sonnets gave way to philosophical and astronomical prose; Peletier du Mans was a mathematician, as well as a poet; and Jodelle and Baïf turned their attention to the theater. Jodelle wrote the first French tragedy, *Cléopâtre captive* (Captive Cleopatra), which was produced in 1553. Written partly in decasyllables and partly in alexandrines, the play is based on the works of Plutarch and follows classical models. While prolific, Baïf was not a great poet. He is best known for his extensive experimentation with versification and for the plays he adapted from Plautus, Terence, and Sophocles. His energy and ideas found another outlet in 1570, when, under the patronage of Charles IX, he founded a short-lived academy for poetry and music.

Other dramatists followed the Pléiade's example. Robert Garnier, the most important early tragedian, wrote several works modeled after classical authors—although his best-known play, *Les Juifves* (1583; translated as *The Hebrew Women,* 1978), is based on a biblical theme. Garnier also published the first French tragicomedy, *Bradamante,* in 1582. Jean de la Taille wrote several biblical tragedies, including *Saül le furieux* (1572, The Madness of Saul), in the preface of which he insists on the classical unities of place and time. Like Garnier, La Taille experimented with dramatic form, and his *Les Corrivaus* (1573; translated as *The Rivals,* 1981) is the first French comedy in prose. Their contemporary Pierre de Larivey also wrote comedies in prose. His plays, adapted from Italian models, prefigure the works of Molière and helped to establish the importance of Italian influences on French comedy.

Italian influences were strong in the development of other genres, as well, particularly that of the *conte* (short story). Boccaccio's *Decameron* (circa 1348–1353) made a great impression on French writers, and many used it as a model. Marguerite de Navarre intended to write a "French Decameron" but died in 1548, after completing seventy-two of the intended one hundred tales. The stories were published in 1559 as *L'Heptaméron* (translated as *The Heptameron,* 1894). Marguerite enhances her stories by framing them with discussions among the storytellers that include moral, philosophical, religious, and social commentaries. It is possible that Marguerite's court inspired another posthumously published story collection: *Les Nouvelles Recreations et Joyeux Devis* (1558, Novel Pastimes and Merry Tales; translated as *The Mirrour of mirth, and pleasant conceits,* 1583), by Bonaventure des Périers, who served in a secretarial capacity in Marguerite's household between 1536 and 1538. Written with the stated purpose of providing light entertainment, Des Périers's tales avoid moral and social issues and make little use of framing devices. Borrowing from the works of Marguerite, Des Périers, and Herodotus, Henri II Estienne's popular *L'Introduction au traité de la Conformité des merveilles anciennes avec les modernes, ou, Traité préparatif à l'Apologie pour Herodote* (1566, Introduction to the Treatise on the Conformity of Ancient Marvels with Those of Modern Times, or Preparatory Treatise to the Apology for Herodotus)—generally referred to as the *Apologie* (Apology)—continues the storytelling tradition by combining old tales with contemporary satire of the Catholic priesthood. Jacques Yver's *Le Printemps d'Yver* (1572, The Spring of Yver [Winter]) uses the frame of a house party at which the guests endeavor to prove through their tales which sex is the cause of all of love's suffering. Yver's work reflects the darker side of the Renaissance: his stories are set against the backdrop of the wars between Catholics and Protestants that were then tearing the country apart.

Although the brilliance of François and Marguerite, the wit of Rabelais and Marot, and the economic success of cities such as Lyon outshone the gathering gloom, a storm was brewing. The bright picture of the early sixteenth century began to tarnish under the pressure of economic failures, a heavy national debt, poverty, famine, plague, and rising crime. The uneasy populace vented its uncertainty in food riots and witchcraft hysteria. Religious issues that were deftly handled by François grew beyond the capabilities of Henri II, who succeeded him in 1547. Henri was at best a mediocre king, more interested in hunting and in his mistress than in the affairs of state. When he was killed in a jousting tournament during the celebrations surrounding the signing of the Peace at Cateau-Cambrésis in 1559, the throne passed successively to his sons: François II, Charles IX in 1560, and Henri III in 1574. All three were even more ineffectual than their father had been, and their mother—the Italian Catherine de Médicis, an ardent Catholic—dominated the reign of each. Weakened by factions that had developed during Henri II's years on the throne, France fell into chaos and, in 1562, into civil war based on religion.

In the sixteenth century the notion of the separation of church and state would have been inconceivable. The founders of the Reformation wanted just that: the reformation of the Catholic Church. A powerful element in the Reform movement was the notion that the Bible should be accessible to all: if everyone could read the Scriptures, then no one would need a priest to interpret the Holy Word. Once the question of interpretation was opened, the centuries-old unchallenged authority of the church was undermined. The possibil-

ity of reform crumbled between the rigid stance of the Church and the strengthening protest movement that preferred a total break with Catholicism. Having dispensed with the notion of one inviolable point of view, the Protestant movement inevitably splintered into many sects, each with its own dogma and intolerant of the others. Although the roots of the Reformation are inextricably linked to humanism, by the mid sixteenth century Protestantism had evolved to a distinctly different view of humanity and of everyday life. The Protestant doctrine of predestination stands in direct contradiction to the humanist belief in the freedom and limitless possibilities of the individual. Calvin and his followers loathed the excesses of Rabelais, the tolerance of Erasmus, the frivolity of Marot, and the bawdy cynicism of Des Périers. The enthusiastic optimism of the early humanist movement was eclipsed.

The Reformation, and the Catholic Counter-Reformation that it provoked, cut across class lines and disturbed traditional notions of philosophy, economics, and government. Protestants regarded Catholicism as degenerate and morally lax; Catholics saw the ideas of the evangelicals as threats to the social order. Political unrest added to the tension as nobles began to take advantage of religious strife in an attempt to change the balance of power. Between 1562 and 1598 France was wracked by eight conflicts that are collectively referred to as the Wars of Religion. Neither side could claim much honor during this period of civil war, which was marked by atrocities. The worst, the Massacre de la St. Barthélemy (St. Bartholomew's Day Massacre) in 1572 claimed the lives of as many as three thousand Protestants, among them many nobles who had come to Paris to celebrate the wedding of the Protestant Henri de Navarre to Marguerite de Valois, the daughter of the Catholic king. According to legend, Charles's guilt over the massacre hastened his death two years later. When Henri III made concessions to the Protestants, his reign was threatened by the Catholic League founded in 1576 by Henri, third Duke of Guise. The king was childless, and the death of his brother, François, Duke of Alençon, left the Protestant Henri de Navarre the legal heir to the French throne. The Catholic faction assassinated Henri III in 1589 and refused to acknowledge Navarre as his successor. After more years of war and his conversion to Catholicism, Navarre ascended the throne in 1593 as Henri IV. In 1598 he sought to soothe religious tension with the Edict of Nantes, which allowed Protestants the right to worship with just enough restrictions to pacify the Catholics. But by then France, devastated by years of war, was in ruins economically.

Much of the literature of this period reflects a different mood than that which was created at the courts and under the influence of François I and Marguerite de Navarre. After the death of Saint-Gelais in 1558, Ronsard became the official poet at the court of Henri II. With his assumption of this position, he began writing political pieces—elegies, hymns, and an epic—as well as poems for elegant entertainment. Ronsard defends Catholicism but deplores the violence of war, urging national unity in *Les Hymnes* (1555) and *Discours des miseres de ce temps* (1562, Discourse on the Miseries of This Time). Ronsard's prestige at court was challenged by Philippe Desportes, whose poetry was influenced by the work of the Pléiade as well as by that of Petrarch and his disciples. Although popular because of his easily accessible love poetry, he, too, felt the influence of the times and began to write religious poetry in the late 1580s.

The two writers of the most powerful religious poetry, Guillaume du Bartas and Théodore Agrippa d'Aubigné, were militant Protestants. Du Bartas served in Henri de Navarre's army and was later an ambassador but preferred the life of a country squire. His major work, *La Sepmaine ou Creation du monde* (1578, The Week, or The Creation of the World), is divided into seven cantos, each of which describes in detail one day of the Creation story. Its scope is massive; its intention is didactic; and it is full of current scientific knowledge and verbal excesses. D'Aubigné served as Henri de Navarre's counselor and companion for twenty years, until Henri embraced the Catholic faith. Well educated in the humanist tradition, d'Aubigné began writing poetry fashioned after that of Ronsard. Wounded in a battle in 1575, he turned to more-serious subjects and began work on his long ideological poem, *Les Tragiques* (1616, The Tragic Ones), which took nearly forty years to complete. Although *Les Tragiques* is the quintessential violent expression of French Protestantism, it is also a carefully crafted epic that pays serious attention to form and language. In 1620 d'Aubigné supported an unsuccessful Protestant uprising against Henri's son and successor, Louis XIII. He was forced to flee France for Geneva, where he spent the remainder of his life.

With its convoluted lines, disturbing images, anguished themes, and roiling tumult, *Les Tragiques* is a perfect example of what has come to be known as the baroque. Born out of the loss of the certainty and optimism that had characterized the early sixteenth century, the baroque is distinguished by ostentation, exaggeration, horror, movement, metamorphosis, anguish, illusion, and death and finds some of its best expression in the religious poetry of the late sixteenth century. Jean de Sponde wrote from both sides of the religious divide, for he was raised in a strict Calvinist household but converted to Catholicism late in life. His "Stances sur la Mort" (1588, Stanzas on Death) are often compared to

English metaphysical poetry for their intense spirituality, but they are certainly baroque in their sense of torment, dark images, and movement. Sponde's contemporary Jean de La Ceppède was an ardent Catholic whose *Les Theoremes . . . sur le Sacré Mistere de nostre Redemption, Divisez en trois Livres, Avec quelques pseaumes, et autres meslanges spirituels* (1613, Theorems . . . on the Sacred Mystery of Our Redemption, Divided into Three Books, with a Few Psalms, and Other Spiritual Miscellanies) and *La Seconde Partie des Theoremes . . . sur les mysteres de la descente de Jesus-Christ aux Enfers, de sa Resurrection, de ses apparitions après icelle, de son Ascension, et de la Mission du S. Esprit en form visible, divisée en quatre Livres* (1621, The Second Part of the Theorems . . . on the Mysteries of the Descent of Jesus Christ into Hell, of His Resurrection, of His Appearances Afterward, of His Ascension, and of the Mission of the Holy Spirit in Visible Form, Divided into Four Books)—generally known as the *Théorèmes spirituels*—combine symbolism with rustic realism in sonnets of strange and troubling beauty.

In striking contrast to the tormented violence of the baroque is the work of Michel de Montaigne. Raised in a household dedicated to humanist ideals, Montaigne spoke Latin before he spoke French. He had a brief law career and served as a magistrate in the Parlement of Bordeaux but retired in 1570, two years after the death of his father made him the lord of the family estate. He then devoted himself to reading and writing. Unlike any work that precedes it, Montaigne's *Essais* (1580; enlarged, 1588) covers a myriad of subjects and ranges in philosophical leanings from Stoicism to moderate Epicureanism. Not immune to the horrors of civil war, Montaigne withdrew from the violence of the age to ponder questions of morality and the human condition. Since he is the man he knows best, Montaigne is the principal subject of the *Essais*. Even so, his sincerity evokes more modesty than ego, and the moderation, quiet dignity, and objectivity of the text set it apart from the enthusiasm of the early humanists, as well as from the fanaticism of the later poets. Montaigne does not avoid questions of religion, but rather than take sides he advocates tolerance, the pursuit of self-knowledge, a rational life, and moderation of the passions. His expression of these attitudes had a great influence on seventeenth-century thought.

In poetry the century ended with the deliberate style of François Malherbe, who presages the French classical poets with his harsh criticism of Ronsard and Desportes. Malherbe's "reform" of poetry relied on rules and logic, rejecting the frivolity of Desportes as well as the classical ornamentation and playful metaphors of Ronsard. The exuberance of Rabelais, the optimism of the Pléiade, and the excesses of the baroque all fell out of favor, making way for the highly regimented classicism of the next century.

This volume attempts to give an overview of the most important contributors to the written culture of sixteenth-century France. Therefore, it includes philosophers, historians, evangelists, and men of science, as well as poets, playwrights, and storytellers. It endeavors to provide the reader with a feel for the broad array of intellectual activity alive in France during this incredible century.

–Megan Conway

Acknowledgments

This book was produced by Bruccoli Clark Layman, Inc. George P. Anderson was the in-house editor. He was assisted by Philip B. Dematteis and C. Bryan Love.

Production manager is Philip B. Dematteis.

Administrative support was provided by Carol A. Cheschi.

Accountant is Ann-Marie Holland.

Copyediting supervisor is Sally R. Evans. The copyediting staff includes Phyllis A. Avant, Caryl Brown, Melissa D. Hinton, and Rebecca Mayo. Freelance copyeditors are Brenda Cabra, Jennifer E. Cooper, and David C. King.

Pipeline manager is James F. Tidd Jr.

Editorial associates are Elizabeth Leverton, Dickson Monk, and Timothy C. Simmons.

In-house vetter is Catherine M. Polit.

Permissions editor is Amber L. Coker.

Layout and graphics supervisor is Janet E. Hill. The graphics staff includes Zoe R. Cook.

Office manager is Kathy Lawler Merlette.

Photography editor is Crystal A. Leidy.

Digital photographic copy work was performed by Zoe R. Cook.

Systems manager is Donald Kevin Starling.

Typesetting supervisor is Kathleen M. Flanagan. The typesetting staff includes Patricia M. Flanagan.

Library research was facilitated by the following librarians at the Thomas Cooper Library of the University of South Carolina: Elizabeth Suddeth and the rare-book department; Jo Cottingham, interlibrary loan department; circulation department head Tucker Taylor; reference department head Virginia W. Weathers; reference department staff Laurel Baker, Marilee Birchfield, Kate Boyd, Paul Cammarata, Joshua Garris, Gary Geer, Tom Marcil, Rose Marshall, and Sharon Verba; interlibrary loan department head Marna Hostetler; and interlibrary loan staff Bill Fetty and Nelson Rivera.

Dictionary of Literary Biography® • Volume Three Hundred Twenty-Seven

Sixteenth-Century French Writers

Dictionary of Literary Biography

Jacques Amyot

(29 October 1513 – 7 February 1593)

Ellen Loughran
Gallaudet University

BOOKS: *Le Psaultier des chevaliers ou les prières du St-Esprit* (Paris, 1601)–attributed to Amyot by André Du Saussay in his *Insignis libri de scriptoribus ecclesiasticis, eminentissimi Cardinalis Bellarminini continuatio* (Toulouse: Printed by I. & I. F. les Laurents, 1665);

Projet de l'éloquence royale, composée pour Henry III, Roi de France, par Jacques Amyot, Evêque d'Auxerre, Grand Aumônier de France, etc., edited by Philippe-Denis Pierres (Versailles: Pierres, 1805)–Pierres claims this edition is based on a signed manuscript by the author, but to date the original manuscript has not been found in French libraries.

Edition: *Projet d'éloquence royale de J. Amyot*, edited, with a preface, by Philippe-Joseph Salazar (Paris: Les Belles Lettres, 1992).

OTHER: *Elégie latine sur la mort de Charles IX, In Caroli Noni, Regis christianissimi, immaturum obitum, epicedium*, in Jean Dorat, *Invictis Galliarum Regis Caroli Noni, püssimi iustissimique Principis, et acerrimi Christianae religionis assertoris Tumulus* (Paris: Printed by Federic Morel, 1574);

Oraison pour dire devant (et après) la Communion. Ecrite pour le Roi par feu R. P. Messire Jacques Amyot, Evesque d'Auxerre et grand Aumônier de France, in Jean Chrysostome, *Discours de la verité du S. sacrament de l'autel. Traduit sur l'original grec du sermon de S. Jean Chrysostome . . . sur le XXVI ch. de S. Matthieu, par Fed. Morel* (Paris: Printed by Fédéric Morel, 1596);

Apologie d'Amyot, in Jean LeBeuf, *Mémoires concernant l'histoire civile et ecclésiastique d'Auxerre*, volume 4 (Auxerre: Perriquet / Paris: Dumoulin, 1855), pp. 345–349);

Jacques Amyot et le Décret de Gratien, edited by Pierre de Nolhac, in *Mélanges d'archéologie et d'histoire* (Rome: Cuggiani/L'Ecole Française de Rome, 1885).

TRANSLATIONS: Heliodorus of Emesa, *L'Histoire aethiopique de Heliodorus contenant dix livres traitant des loyales et pudiques amours de Theagenes thessalien et Chariclea aethiopienne: nouvellement traduite de gre cen françois à Paris pour Jean Longis, libraire, tenant sa boutique au Palais, en la gallerie par où l'on va à la Chancelerie* (Paris: Printed by Estienne Groulleau for Vincent Sertenas, 1547; revised, 1559);

Diodorus Siculus, *Sept livres (XI – XVII) des Histoires de Diodore Sicilien, nouvellement traduyts de grec en françoys* (Paris: Printed by Michel Vascosan, 1554; enlarged, with additions, by Regius [Louis Leroy], 1585);

Longus, *Les amours pastorales de Daphnis et de Chloé, escriptes premierement en grec par Longus et puis traduictes en françois* (Paris: Printed for Vincent Sertenas, 1559); revised and enlarged as *Notice sur une nouvelle édition de la traduction françoise de Longus, par Amyot, et sur la découverte d'un fragment grec de cet ouvrage: Daphnis et Chloé, traduction complète d'après le manuscript de l'abaye de Florence. Imprimé à Florence, chez Piatti, 1810* (Paris: Crapelet, 1810);

Plutarch, *Les Vies des hommes illustres grecs ou romains, comparées l'une avec l'autre par Plutarque de Chéronée, translatées de gr. en fr. par maistre J. Amyot*, 2 volumes (Paris: Printed by Michel Vascosan, 1559; revised, 1565; definitive edition, 6 volumes, 1567); translated by Thomas North as *The Lives of the Noble Grecians and Romanes, compared together by . . . Plutarke of Chæronea: translated out of Greeke into French by J. Amyot . . . and out of French into Englishe by T.*

Stamp released in 1963 (from <http://pluq59.free.fr/image/timbresgrandformat/1963/1370.jpg>)

North (London: Printed by Thomas Vautroullier & John Wight, 1579);

Plutarch, *Les Œuvres morales et meslees de Plutarque,* 2 volumes (Paris: Printed by Michel Vascosan, 1572; revised, 1574; revised again, 1575).

Jacques Amyot, one of the most learned men of the French Renaissance, is best known for his translations of Plutarch's *Parallel Lives* and *Moralia* (written in the late first to early second century A.D.) from the original Greek into French. He lived from 1513 to 1593, and during his lifetime he witnessed the reigns of seven French kings. While Amyot is primarily known for his contributions to French letters, he spent almost forty years at court, serving as tutor to Charles IX and Henry III, and becoming the king's chief almoner, a position he held for twenty-nine years, 1560–1589. As a result of his connections at court, Amyot was appointed bishop of Auxerre in 1570. This honor brought him material wealth, but it also made him a target in the religious and civil wars of sixteenth-century France.

Born in the city of Melun on 29 October 1513, Jacques Amyot was among the four children of Nicolas Amyot and Marie Lamour. Nicolas Amyot was in the leather and wool trade; because his wife received a con-

siderable inheritance, the family is believed to have been fairly well off. Between 1528 and 1532 Amyot's father sent him to Paris, where he enrolled at the College of Cardinal Lemoine, which was recognized as one of the finest institutions of learning in France. According to several biographers, Amyot's encounter with Jean Bonchamps de Reims, a professor of Greek, changed the course of his academic life. Bonchamps steered Amyot toward linguistic study, resulting in his lifelong dedication to the task of translating Plutarch's works and his progress toward becoming one of the most celebrated translators of the French Renaissance.

There are several legends surrounding Amyot's student life in Paris that date from the seventeenth century. One of these legends depicts a young Amyot so poor he had to wait each week for a loaf of bread that his mother sent by boat from Melun. Another story describes Amyot's studying by the firelight in one of his classmates' homes. Several of Amyot's biographers, including Alexandre Cioranescu and Auguste de Blignières, attribute these stories to the seventeenth-century writer Abbe Saint-Réal, whose account of Amyot's life in *Usage de l'histoire* (1671), they maintain, was little more than a highly romanticized tale.

In 1532 Amyot received his master of arts degree and began further studies at the newly established Royal College founded by King Francis I. One of his professors was the Greek scholar Pierre Danès, who preceded Amyot as tutor to the king's sons. Amyot and Danès forged a lifelong friendship. Besides Amyot, Danès counted among his students at the Royal College famous sixteenth-century figures such as Jean Calvin, Peter Ramus, Jean Dorat, and Henri Estienne. In addition to languages, Amyot studied the science of the day, a move that prepared him for a university position when he left the Royal College in 1534.

Upon completing his studies in Paris, Amyot took a teaching position at the University of Bourges, probably on the invitation of Jacques Colin, the abbot of Saint-Ambroise and translator of Baldassare Castiglione's *Il Cortegiano* (1528; translated by Colin into French as *Le Courtisan,* 1538; translated as *The Book of the Courtier,* 1561). Scholars debate whether Amyot had to flee Paris for Bourges because of his alleged involvement in the 17–18 October 1534 Affaire des Placards (Affair of the Posters), in which Protestants in Paris posted and circulated denunciations of the Catholic Mass. Records indicate that Bourges had become a refuge for those who subscribed to Protestant thinking, and individuals such as Théodore de Bèze and Melchior Wolmar, friends of Calvin, were already in Bourges when Amyot arrived. The fact that Amyot had become a serious Greek scholar, often associated with the Protestant cause, further cast suspicion on the young professor. However, most of Amyot's biographers agree that these suspicions were laid to rest with his later roles as an ecclesiastic at court and as bishop of Auxerre.

Amyot remained at the University of Bourges from 1536 to 1546, teaching Greek and Latin and enjoying an academic life that afforded time to work on his translations. As tutor first for Colin's nephews, and later for the sons of Guillaume Bochetel, King Francis I's secretary of state, Amyot established an important connection with the royal court, one that eventually led to his appointment as tutor for King Henry II's sons.

During his time at Bourges, Amyot translated Heliodorus's Ethiopian History (third century A.D.). The tale, which comprises ten books, recounts the innocent romance between the Greek Theagenes and the Ethiopian Chariclea. Amyot's translation, *L'Histoire aethiopique,* first appeared in 1547. Five years later, while working in the Vatican Library, Amyot discovered he had been mistaken about the identity of the author of the work. The Heliodorus who composed the *Ethiopian History* had been bishop of Trica during the reign of Theodosius and not, as Amyot had previously thought, the third-century Arab philosopher. Amyot corrected the error in his preface to the 1559 second edition of the translation. *L'Histoire aethiopique* enjoyed many reprintings, and the love story remained a rich source of literary imitation throughout the seventeenth and eighteenth centuries. Blignières explains that Amyot considered his work on *L'Histoire aethiopique* a diversion from the more substantial work he was doing on Plutarch's *Parallel Lives,* but certainly translating *L'Histoire aethiopique* provided him the opportunity to polish his craft as translator and learn from the work of an early Greek writer and Church ecclesiastic.

Amyot was making a vital contribution to the art of translation in the Renaissance. Unlike many of his contemporaries, whose efforts to translate ancient Greek texts into the vernacular depended chiefly on Latin translations, Amyot worked directly from the original Greek, laboring diligently to render each text into French in a fashion that would convey both the substance and style of the original. A sixteenth-century translator was expected by his contemporaries to have a strong background in the history, philosophy, and literature of the ancient culture in question, as well as the ability to write well in one's own language. The last of these tasks was doubly challenging for Amyot because the French language was in the process of freeing itself from the domination of its Latin and Greek roots and building its own lexicon and syntax.

Like many of his Renaissance contemporaries, Amyot was eager to study firsthand the Greek and Latin manuscripts housed in the libraries of Italy. When he embarked for Italy in the spring of 1548, he had already been working for several years on his translation of Plutarch's *Parallel Lives.* His first stop in Italy was Venice, where he remained until the autumn of 1550, under the auspices of his friend and patron, Jean de Morvilliers, now the French ambassador to Venice. While there, Amyot was granted access to St. Mark's Library, and, through the intercession of Morvilliers, he procured an early manuscript of Plutarch's *Moralia.* Amyot also discovered a partial manuscript of the History of Diodorus of Sicily (first century B.C.), which he copied and later translated into French.

In the autumn of 1550 Amyot traveled to Rome, where he remained for the next ten months. There he was able to study and compare the variant texts of Plutarch's works in the Vatican Library, striving always to perfect his own translation of the *Parallel Lives.* While in Rome he made the acquaintance of the well-connected cardinal of Tournon, along with several other erudite Italians. These encounters greatly influenced his literary and ecclesiastical careers.

While Amyot's stay in Italy was productive for him personally, it was a tumultuous time for relations between the Vatican and the French court. Close to war

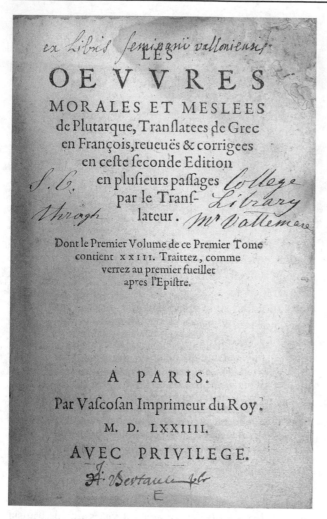

Title page for Amyot's last translation of the writings of Plutarch (Special Collections, Thomas Cooper Library, University of South Carolina)

reading populace. Furthermore, some critics, such as Cioranescu and René Sturel, maintain that Amyot's translation reflects the subtle influence of the Italian language on the French idiom of the time.

The year that Amyot published his translation of Diodorus of Sicily, he was charged with substituting for his former professor, Danès, as tutor to the king's two sons, Charles IX and Henry III. Although it was supposed to be a temporary assignment while Danès recuperated from a brief illness, Amyot assumed the position on a full-time basis in 1557. Several of his biographers view this step as pivotal for his dual career as translator and ecclesiastic at the royal court. Amyot was not only charged with the education of the young princes, but he was also given the task of guarding their Catholicism. Considering the many influential Protestants at court, this assignment was no mean feat, and while Amyot enjoyed a certain amount of success in protecting the faith of the princes while they were still young, his work became increasingly problematic as the tensions and political intrigues between the Huguenots and the Catholic loyalists increased. Nevertheless, the benefits that accrued to Amyot while he was tutor and chaplain to the king's sons enabled him to continue his scholarly work and eventually led to his entry into the episcopate.

In 1559 Amyot published his translation of Longus's *Les amours pastorales de Daphnis et de Chloé* (third century A.D., The Pastoral Love Story of Daphnis and Chloe). Unlike Heliodorus's *Histoire Aethiopique*, this romance between two shepherds was considered too risqué for youthful readers by seventeenth-century translators. Amyot, however, did not work under the same constraints as these later translators, and the elegance and suppleness of Longus's language must have attracted the sixteenth-century writer and translator. Longus's pastoral may have represented a diversion for Amyot from his more serious undertakings, similar to what he had indicated about *L'Histoire aethiopique*. *Les amours pastorales de Daphnis et Chloé* was the only one of Amyot's works not reprinted during his lifetime. In fact, he appeared to distance himself from it in the years that followed its publication, especially after he assumed the spiritual responsibilities of chief almoner to the king.

In 1559 Amyot published his translation of Plutarch's *Parallel Lives*, titled *Les Vies des hommes illustres grecs ou romains* (translated as *The Lives of the Noble Grecians and Romanes*, 1579). In the years immediately following, he continued to work on his text, revising and correcting his first edition, attempting to eliminate archaic words and turns of phrase. In 1565 a second edition of *Les Vies des hommes illustres grecs ou romains* appeared, and in 1567, a third edition, considered by many scholars to be the definitive one. It is reasonable to assume that Amyot

with the king of Spain, Henry II decided to forbid his French prelates from participating in the Council of Trent, the ecumenical council held by the Catholic Church in response to the Reformation. Amyot was called upon to read Henry's declaration at the opening of the Council of Trent, a task that placed him squarely in the middle of an international protest. By all accounts, Amyot performed his mission well, remaining in Italy until 1552, when he returned to France in the company of the cardinal of Tournon.

In 1554 Amyot published *Sept livres (XI – XVII) des Histoires de Diodore Sicilien* (Seven Books [Volumes 11–17] of the Histories of Diodorus of Sicily), his translation of the manuscript that he discovered at St. Mark's Library in Venice. These seven books complemented earlier translations of other books by Antoine Macault and Claude de Seyssel, and they contributed to the dissemination of ancient Greek texts among the French-

was laboring to perfect his translation of Plutarch's work throughout the period he was instructing Charles IX and Henry III in the virtues and wisdom of the men who figured in it.

In 1560 Charles IX, only ten years old and still under the regency of his mother Catherine de Médicis, appointed Amyot his chief almoner. Cioranescu explains that Amyot's duties included supervising many court ecclesiastics; administering the Hopîtal des Quinze-Vingts, the royal hospital for the blind in Paris; and choosing the recipients of scholarships to the Collège Mignon and the Collège de Gervais Chrestien. Amyot's time at court from 1560 to 1570 passed amid intrigues engendered by the larger political and religious struggle between Protestants and Catholics. As chief almoner, Amyot, whose Catholic faith remained central to his life and whose official title entrusted him with preserving the king's faith, was regarded as an enemy by the Protestants at court.

Always mindful of the debt he owed his loyal tutor and spiritual counselor, Charles IX named Amyot bishop of Auxerre in 1570, giving his former teacher a justifiable reason to distance himself from court machinations. Amyot turned his energies to restoring the diocese of Auxerre, one that had already seen its share of destruction and pillaging in the religious and civil wars. Similar to the way he approached his former studies, Amyot dedicated himself to the conscientious study of theology.

Two years after assuming the bishopric of Auxerre, Amyot published his translation of Plutarch's *Moralia*. Although he was now physically distant from the court of Charles IX, Amyot did not forget his former student, preceding his translation with a dedicatory epistle to the king. Encomiastic in tone, Amyot's letter reminded Charles IX that he had been educated to emulate and aspire to all that is virtuous in human behavior. Two years later Charles IX was dead from an unknown malady. Amyot grieved for the young king who had been his student and spiritual charge for almost twenty years.

When Henry III succeeded his brother as king of France, he retained Amyot in the position of chief almoner, thanks in part to the intercession of the king's aunt, Margaret of Savoy. As time went on, Henry III gave Amyot, still bishop of Auxerre, the added responsibility of hiring lecturers for the Royal College. Like his brother Charles IX before him, Henry never lost the respect and esteem he held for his former tutor, often seeking Amyot's counsel and depending on him for honest advice. In 1578 Henry III created l'Ordre du Saint-Esprit (the Order of the Holy Spirit), and appointed Amyot its commander in chief. This new order of knights was an attempt on Henry's part to

gather around him men who were steadfast in their Catholicism, men who might encourage the Protestants at court to leave heresy behind.

Henry also called upon the literary talents of his former teacher, requesting that he prepare a manual to guide the king on the subject of eloquence. This work, known as the *Projet d'éloquence royale* (Program for Royal Eloquence), was first published in 1805 by Philippe-Denis Pierres, who claimed that he had based his edition on a manuscript signed by Amyot. However, this manuscript has never been found. In his preface to his 1995 edition of the *Projet d'éloquence* (based on the text of Pierres's edition), Philippe-Joseph Salazar calls attention to the distinction that Amyot makes between "l'éloquence vulgaire" (the vulgar eloquence) orators have typically used to sway the masses and the "l'éloquence royale" (the royal eloquence) that the great orators of Greece and Rome used to inspire their countrymen to higher standards of action. Salazar then points to three events where Henry III, who fancied himself an orator, demonstrated his knowledge of this distinction. Of these three events, Henry's opening speech at the Estates-General at Blois in 1588 was, in Amyot's estimation, the one in which Henry attained the highest level of eloquence. In that speech, the king attempted to convince the assembly that monarchy is the best form of government and that he, as their monarch, was divinely chosen to rule over France.

While Henry's speech to the Estates-General may have met Amyot's high standards for rhetorical eloquence, subsequent events at Blois would prove to be the king's downfall and a source of serious trouble for his chief almoner. Although Amyot had enjoyed the protection and favor of the king, most of his biographers believe that he typically was not made a party to the scandals at court. However, his presence at the Estates-General at Blois in 1588, where Henry III ordered the assassination of Henry of Lorraine, the Duke of Guise, almost resulted in his ruin as bishop of Auxerre. Members of the Catholic League, led by the Franciscan monk Claude Trahy, were determined to implicate Amyot in the murder. They attempted unsuccessfully to have him excommunicated. During this time Amyot's properties were pillaged, his possessions stolen, and he was forbidden by members of his diocese from entering the cathedral of Auxerre. Through L'Abbé LeBeuf's detailed *Mémoires concernant l'histoire civile et ecclésiastique d'Auxerre* (1743, Memoir Concerning the Civil and Ecclesiastical History of Auxerre) and the records in the Archives of Yonne, one can trace the activity and evolution of this difficult time in Amyot's life. Although some biographers have judged him as weak and treasonous, the dilemma in which Amyot found himself at the end of his life stemmed from his desire to remain loyal to the king he had served for almost thirty-five years while honoring the principles of his conscience and remaining true to his Catholic faith. Seeking to clarify his position, Amyot prepared an official apology (later published in Lebeuf's work as *Apologie d'Amyot* [1855, Apology of Amyot]), in which he denounced the assassination and repudiated the accusations of Trahy and the other zealots. The crossroads at which Amyot had arrived after the assassination of the duke of Guise exemplified the conflict prevalent throughout France between Protestants and Catholics, religious fanatics and moderates, church and state.

In 1590 Amyot was absolved of any wrongdoing by the papal nuncio in Paris, and he reclaimed his status as bishop of Auxerre. In the years that followed he aligned himself with the Catholic League against the Protestant king, Henry of Navarre, but he chiefly sought solace in a quiet life that included books and visiting with loyal friends. Unable to recuperate from a serious illness, Amyot received the last sacraments and died on 7 February 1593.

Jacques Amyot represents the best of the French Renaissance literary tradition. His life spanned the difficulties and turmoil of the French civil and religious wars. As a royal tutor, court ecclesiastic, and bishop, Amyot experienced firsthand the internecine struggles between the French Protestants and Catholics. Yet, amid all of the social and cultural upheaval, he made his mark on French letters, participating in the flowering of humanist thought and the evolution of the French language. Amyot is revered by Renaissance historians and literary scholars alike for his lifelong work of translating ancient Greek texts into French, especially his important and influential translations of Plutarch's *Parallel Lives* and *Moralia*.

Bibliographies:

Ferdinand Brunetière, *Manual of the History of French Literature,* translated by Ralph Derechef (London: Unwin, 1898);

Louis Petit de Julleville, *Histoire de la langue et de la littérature française des origines à 1900,* volume 3: *Seizième Siècle* (Paris: Colin, 1901);

Gustave Lanson, *Histoire de la littérature française* (Paris: Hachette, 1908);

Georges Grente and others, *Dictionnaire des Lettres Françaises: Le Seizième Siècle* (Paris: Fayard, 1951);

Jeanne Giraud, *Manuel de bibliographie littéraire pour les XVI, XVII et XVIII siècles français, 1936–1945* (Paris: Nizet, 1956);

Richard A. Brooks, *A Critical Bibliography of French Literature,* volume 2: *The Sixteenth Century,* edited by Raymond C. La Charité (Syracuse, N.Y.: Syracuse University Press, 1985).

Biographies:

Auguste de Blignières, *Essai sur Amyot, et les traducteurs français au XVI siècle* (Paris: Durant, 1851; reprinted, Geneva: Slatkine, 1968);

René Sturel, *Amyot, traducteur des Vies Parallèles de Plutarque,* Bibliothèque littéraire de la Renaissance, no. 9 (Paris: Champion, 1908 [i.e., 1909]);

Alexandre Cioranescu, *Vie de Jacques Amyot,* preface by Pierre Champion (Paris: Droz, 1941);

André Laurent, *Jacques Amyot, l'Humaniste, 1513–1593* (Etrépilly: Bartillat, 1998).

References:

Robert Aulotte, *Amyot et Plutarque: La Tradition des Moralia au XVI siècle,* Travaux d'humanisme et Renaissance, no. 69 (Geneva: Droz, 1965);

Aulotte, *Plutarque en France au XVI siecle: Trois Opuscules Moraux,* Etudes et commentaires, no. 74 (Paris: Klincksieck, 1971);

Michel Balard, ed., *Les Fortunes de Jacques Amyot: Actes du Colloque International (Melun 18–20 avril 1985)* (Paris: Nizet, 1986);

Camille Bégué, *Les Humanistes français: Amyot, H. Estienne, Etienne Pasquier* (Paris: Larousse, 1937);

Théodore de Bèze, *Histoire ecclésiastique des églises réformées au royaume de France,* volume 1, edited by P. Vesson (Toulouse: Société des Livres Religieux, 1882);

Jean LeBeuf, *Jacques Amyot, XCVI évêque d'Auxerre,* in *Mémoires concernant l'histoire civile et ecclésiastique d'Auxerre,* 4 volumes (Auxerre: Perriquet & Rouillé / Paris: Dumoulin, 1848–1855), II: 160–193; IV: 343–361;

Grace Norton, *La Plutarque de Montaigne: Selections from Amyot's Translation of Plutarch Arranged to Illustrate Montaigne's Essais* (Boston: Houghton, Mifflin, 1906);

Joseph de Zangroniz, *Montaigne, Amyot et Saliat: Etude sur les sources des Essais,* Bibliothèque littéraire de la Renaissance, no. 7 (Paris: Champion, 1906; reprinted, Geneva: Slatkine, 1975).

Théodore Agrippa d'Aubigné

(8 February 1552 – 9 May 1630)

Kathleen P. Long
Cornell University

SELECTED BOOKS: *Les Tragiques* (Au Dézert [i.e., Geneva]: Printed by L.B.D.D., 1616);

L'Histoire universelle du Sieur d'Aubigné, 3 volumes (Maillé: Printed by Jean Moussat, 1616–1620; revised edition, Amsterdam: Printed for the heirs of Hieronymus Commelinus, 1626); translated as *Hell Illuminated, or, Sancy's Roman Catholic Confession, Wherein are Such Lessons, Which if studiously practis'd, 'tis much to be fear'd, the Devil himself will turn Jesuit* (London: Printed for L. Curtis, 1679);

Les Avantures du Baron de Fæneste. Première partie (Maillé: Printed by Jean Moussat, 1617); enlarged as *Les Avantures du Baron de Fæneste. Première partie . . . Plus a esté adjousté la seconde partie* (Maillé: Printed by Jean Moussat, 1617);

Les Avantures du Baron de Fæneste. Troisième partie (Maillé: Printed by Jean Moussat, 1619); enlarged as *Les Avantures du Baron de Fæneste, comprinses en quatre parties* (Au Dézert [i.e., Geneva]: Printed for the author by Pierre Aubert, 1630);

Les Avantures du Baron de Foeneste, par Théodore Agrippa d'Aubigné. Edition nouvelle, augmentée de plusieurs remarques historiques, de l'histoire secrete de l'auteur écrite par luy-même (Cologne: Printed by the heirs of Pierre Marteau, 1729)–includes "Histoire secrete de Théodore Agrippa d'Aubigné, ecrite par luy-même et adressée à ses enfans," translated by John Nothnagle as *His Life to His Children* (Lincoln: University of Nebraska Press, 1989);

Œuvres complètes, 6 volumes, edited by Eugène Réaume and François de Caussade (Paris: Lemerre, 1873–1892)–comprises volume 1 (1873), "Sa Vie à ses enfants," "Son testament," and "Ses lettres"; volume 2 (1877), "Traité sur les guerres civiles," "Du Debvoir mutuel des roys et des subjects"; "Le Caducée ou l'Ange de Paix," "Méditations sur les Pseaumes," "La Confession catholique du Sieur de Sancy," "Le Divorce satirique," and "Lettres diverses"; volume 3 (1874), "Le Printemps," "Poésies diverses," "Poésies religieuses et vers mesurés," "Tombeaux et vers funèbres," "Vers

Théodore Agrippa d'Aubigné (Harlingue/Roger-Viollet/ Getty Images)

funèbres sur la mort d'Estienne Jodelle," and "La Création"; volume 4 (1877), *Les Tragiques,* "Discours par stances avec l'esprit du feu roy Henry IV," "Sonnets et pièces épigrammatiques," "Tombeaux du style de saint Innocent," and "Appendice: Pièces de sources diverses"; volume 5 (1891), "Notice biographique et littéraire" and "Notice bibliographique"; and volume 6 (1892), "Table des noms des personnes" and "Glossaire";

Le Printemps "poème de ses amours." Stances et odes. Publiées pour la première fois d'après un manuscrit de l'auteur, edited by Charles Read, Cabinet du Bibliophile, no. 18 (Paris, 1874).

Editions and Collections: Le Printemps: L'Hécatombe à Diane, edited by Bernard Gagnebin (Geneva: Droz, 1948);

Le Printemps: Stances et odes, edited by Eugénie Droz, introduction by Fernand Desonay (Geneva: Droz, 1952);

Le Printemps: L'Hécatombe à Diane et les Stances, edited by Henry Weber (Paris: Presses Universitaires de France, 1960);

Œuvres, edited by Weber, Jacques Bailbé, and Marguerite Soulié, introduction by Weber (Paris: Gallimard, 1969);

Histoire Universelle, 11 volumes, edited by André Thierry (Geneva: Droz, 1981–2000);

Sa Vie à ses enfants, edited by Gilbert Schrenck (Paris: Nizet, 1986);

Les Tragiques, edited by Armand Garnier and Jean Plattard (Geneva: Droz, 1990);

Les Tragiques, edited by Jacques Bailbé (Paris: Flammarion, 1994);

Les Tragiques, edited by Jean-Raymond Fanlo (Paris: Champion, 1995);

Œuvres complètes, edited by Véronique Ferrer (Paris: Champion, 2004–).

OTHER: "La Confession catholique du Sieur de Sancy," in Recueil de diverses pièces servans à l'Histoire de Henry III (Cologne: Printed by Pierre Marteau, 1663).

Théodore Agrippa d'Aubigné is the most enduring of late-sixteenth-century Huguenot authors. Of all witnesses of his age, he most directly and thoroughly addresses the violence of the Wars of Religion. The psychological and social impact of these conflicts are depicted in d'Aubigné's epic, Les Tragiques (1616, The Tragic Ones), and in his historical work, L'Histoire universelle (1616–1620; revised, 1626; Universal History). Although most of d'Aubigné's writings focus on the Wars of Religion and other aspects of late-sixteenth-century politics, he wrote in diverse forms and touched on many topics. His oeuvre includes a collection of love poetry, Le Printemps (circa 1572–1630, Spring); a satirical novel, Les Aventures du baron de Fæneste (1617–1630, The Adventures of the Baron of Fæneste); polemical pieces such as "La Confession catholique du Sieur de Sancy" (circa 1600, The Catholic Confession of the Lord of Sancy) and "Le Divorce satyrique" (The Satirical Divorce); a political pamphlet, "Du Debvoir mutuel des roys et des subjects" (circa 1620, On the Mutual Obli-

gation of Kings and Their Subjects); and many other epigrams and occasional pieces. Much of d'Aubigné's work, aside from Les Tragiques, L'Histoire universelle, Les Avantures du Baron de Fæneste, and several occasional pieces, remained unpublished during his lifetime.

Over the years d'Aubigné's work has been discovered and disseminated, and it has had an important impact on the literary world. After d'Aubigné's death, the Tronchin family inherited his manuscripts and held them for many years. The English poet John Milton was a friend of the Tronchins, and he occasionally visited them in Geneva and presumably saw their collection. D'Aubigné's portrait of Satan in Les Tragiques may have been an inspiration for Milton's version of that fallen archangel in Paradise Lost (1667).

Also important is d'Aubigné's Sa Vie à ses enfants (translated as His Life to His Children, 1989), which was probably intended as a personal memoir. Its publication was suppressed until after the death of d'Aubigné's granddaughter Françoise, Madame de Maintenon, the second wife of King Louis XIV, and then it appeared in 1729 as "Histoire secrete de Théodore Agrippa d'Aubigné, ecrite par luy-même et adressée à ses enfans" (The Secret History of Théodore Agrippa d'Aubigné, Written by Himself and Addressed to His Children). It has been argued that this work had an impact on the confessional literature that appeared later in the eighteenth century.

Additionally, in 1874 Charles Read discovered the Monmerqué manuscript, which includes two of the three parts of Le Printemps (the Stances and the Odes but not the sonnets). The edition of Le Printemps Read published that year postdates Charles Baudelaire's Les Fleurs du Mal (1857, The Flowers of Evil; translated, 1909), but the resonance between Baudelaire's "Une Charogne" (A Corpse) and the twentieth Stance of Le Printemps, combined with Baudelaire's use of lines from Les Tragiques as the epigraph for the first edition of Les Fleurs du Mal, indicate a strong link between the two poets' works. D'Aubigné and Baudelaire use their versions of the Petrarchan tradition to reflect on the corruption and violence of society. This intertextuality also attests to d'Aubigné's part in influencing major literary works and developing literary trends.

D'Aubigné's life was complicated from the start. His father, Jean d'Aubigné, was the son of a tanner-shoemaker who became a judge and married a well-educated Catholic noblewoman, Catherine de l'Estang. Catherine died giving birth to d'Aubigné on 8 February 1552, which is the reason he was named Agrippa (from aegre partus [difficult birth]). In Sa Vie à ses enfants d'Aubigné writes of his father being given the choice between saving the mother or saving the child. He also describes the ghost of his mother returning to kiss him

François Dubois's Le massacre de la Saint-Barthelemy, *a survivor's rendering of the slaughter of the Huguenots ordered by Charles IX during the festival of the saint in 1572. This event was at the heart of d'Aubigne's epic poem* Les Tragiques, *circa 1577–1616 (Musée cantonal des Beaux-Arts de Lausanne).*

goodnight. Although he never knew her, d'Aubigné's Catholic mother was a significant part of his life. Not only did he imagine her presence, but he also kept in his possession several books in which she had written marginal notes. Furthermore, scholars often have observed that maternal figures dominate d'Aubigné's work, particularly *Les Tragiques*.

D'Aubigné's father was, however, a real and highly influential presence in his life. At some point after Catherine's death, Jean d'Aubigné converted to Protestantism. He had been gradually climbing the social ladder from the artisan class to the nobility, but his newfound religion put his hard-won social status at risk. In 1554 Jean d'Aubigné lost his post as judge at Loudun, and he fled the city to escape persecution. Several years later he played a significant role in the conspiracy of Amboise, which was designed to wrest François II from the grip of the ultra-Catholic Guise family by kidnapping the young king. Jean d'Aubigné did not, however, participate in the attempted abduction in 1560 and therefore escaped the execution that awaited his fellow conspirators. In the spring of 1560 Jean d'Aubigné and his son passed through Amboise on the way to Paris, and there they saw the heads of the executed conspirators hanging from a post and their bodies hanging from the windows of the castle. According to *Sa Vie à ses enfants,* Jean d'Aubigné made his eight-year-old son swear to avenge the deaths of these conspirators, even though they were surrounded by a hostile Catholic mob. Thus began the militant Huguenot career of d'Aubigné.

At ten d'Aubigné was sent to Paris to study with the celebrated humanist Mathieu Béroalde de Verville. Among his fellow pupils were the doomed Richard de Gastines, whose death is featured prominently in "Les Feux" (The Fires), book 4 of *Les Tragiques,* and the moderate Catholic Pierre de l'Estoile, eventual memorialist of the reigns of Henri III and Henri IV. Less than two months later, however, Béroalde was forced to flee Paris with his family, his servants, and four of his pupils. Captured by the chevalier (knight) d'Achon, Béroalde and his little band were threatened with death at the stake. D'Aubigné refused to abjure, expressing greater horror at the possibility of eternal damnation than at the prospect of death. He then charmed his captors with his talent for dancing and for speaking. After enduring many death threats, the group managed to buy its way out of the dangerous situation. They then fled to Montargis, to rest under the protection of Renée de France, the duchess of Ferrara. They next traveled to Gien, and finally to Orléans, where the Protestant presence was strong. Orléans was not a safe place, however: during this time the plague was decimating the population. D'Aubigné watched most of his companions die, and he was himself stricken with the plague, but he survived.

After his recovery, d'Aubigné neglected his studies, much to his father's dismay, and he turned his interest to combats close at hand, tagging along with a group of soldiers. The first great battle of the Wars of Religion took place at Dreux on 19 December 1562. Louis de Bourbon, first Prince of Condé, one of the great Protestant leaders, and Anne, Duke of Montmorency, one of the great Catholic leaders, were each taken prisoner. In January 1563, François, Duke of Guise, brought his forces to Orléans to lay siege to the city. Consequently, d'Aubigné was able to witness the combat firsthand. All seemed lost for the Protestants, but François de Guise was assassinated, and a peace was negotiated. Jean d'Aubigné was wounded in the battle, but he chose to participate in the negotiations rather than rest, and he died shortly afterward.

The orphaned d'Aubigné was sent by a family member to study under the guidance of Théodore de Bèze in Geneva, where he perfected his knowledge of Greek and Hebrew and produced Latin verses. During this time a schoolmate apparently made advances on d'Aubigné and another boy. D'Aubigné testified against this schoolmate after being interrogated, perhaps under torture, an experience that may have fueled the vehement hatred of torture that he later expresses in Les Tragiques. After being forced to witness the schoolmate's execution by drowning, d'Aubigné fled to Lyon. There he studied with Loys d'Arza, an astrologer and alchemist. This opportunity tempted him to study magic, but he eventually renounced the practice. This brief interlude is echoed in the portrait of Catherine de Médicis as a witch in "Misères" (Miseries), the first book of Les Tragiques.

D'Aubigné returned to France just as the Second War of Religion was beginning. Violence had continued even after the Paix de Longjumeau (Peace of Long-

jumeau) in 1568, and after Catherine de Médicis ordered the arrest of Condé and of Gaspard de Coligny, Protestants took refuge at La Rochelle. D'Aubigné longed to join them, and he eventually escaped from his guardian, joined a group of soldiers, and participated in several battles of the Third War of Religion as the Protestant army worked to conquer the region around La Rochelle to create a "safety zone" for their cause. The sixteen-year-old d'Aubigné earned arms and armor from defeated opponents and distinguished himself as an able and fervent warrior. He witnessed the major events of the wars, among them the bloody battles of Jarnac (1569) and Montcontour (1569), both horrific defeats of Protestant forces at the hands of the future Henri III.

D'Aubigné became known for his courage and leadership. Among his many victories, he won back Pons, the town in which he was born, for the Protestant cause. Remorseful for his part in ravaging his own region, he fought his family for control of the family property, Landes-Guinemer, and retired there for a few years. During this time he met Diane Salviati, the object of most of his love poetry. She was the daughter of Bernard Salviati, Seigneur de Talcy, and the niece of Pierre de Ronsard's Cassandre. While there were some mutual feelings that may have led d'Aubigné to believe that promises of marriage had been exchanged, from the beginning this match seemed impossible. She was Catholic, while he was a fiery Huguenot. She was noble and wealthy, while his father had been a magistrate, and his estate was in ruins.

At this time d'Aubigné undoubtedly began to compose some of the poems of Le Printemps, the final version of which includes the Stances, the Odes, and the Hécatombe à Diane (Hecatomb to Diana). The poetry is rarely idyllic or amorous—instead, it is characterized by a violence that echoes the violence of the times. In fact, this poetry can be described as simply a stage in d'Aubigné's maturation as the poet of the Protestant cause, demonstrating the destructive nature of earthly love and of misplaced faith.

D'Aubigné's retreat to Landes-Guinemer was only a brief respite. He was persuaded to join Gaspard de Coligny's planned expedition to Flanders, meant to aid the Protestant uprising, which was experiencing great difficulty. D'Aubigné gathered a company of soldiers and accompanied Protestant leaders to Paris for the marriage of Henri de Navarre to Marguerite de Valois in 1572. D'Aubigné left Paris, however, after participating in a duel and injuring a sergeant at arms who had tried to arrest him. Hence, he was in the Loire region when Catholic mobs began the massacres of St. Bartholomew's Day (24 August 1572), assassinating

Coligny and other Protestant leaders, along with thousands (and eventually tens of thousands) of others.

But the violence soon spread rapidly to other regions of France, including the Loire Valley. D'Aubigné and his men saved one village from the attacks, and then he took refuge in Talcy, where he impressed Diane Salviati's father by burning papers concerning the conspiracy of Amboise, one of which might have compromised the Chancellor Michel de l'Hospital. Eventually, d'Aubigné was caught up in the violence, and he was attacked and nearly murdered in Beauce. He rode twenty leagues on horseback intending to die in the arms of Diane. Contrary to his expectations, she nursed him back to health—according to his account, she even cauterized his wounds. They were apparently betrothed, but her uncle, a fervent Catholic, broke off the engagement because of d'Aubigné's religious affiliation. In *Le Printemps,* d'Aubigné seems to blame this event on Diane, questioning her fidelity and accusing her of pursuing other lovers.

D'Aubigné gives his near-death experience a central role in "Les Fers" (Swords), the fifth book of *Les Tragiques.* This event, combined with the vehement and repeated rejection of his "youthful" and "profane" love poetry in favor of religious poetry and the epic, is an important element of the elaborate portrait d'Aubigné creates of himself as the poet chosen by God to represent the suffering and the superior virtue of the French Protestants.

The massacres drove d'Aubigné to return to military service in support of his religious beliefs. He entered the service of Henri de Navarre, the future Henri IV, in 1573. Henri de Navarre had been a prisoner at the court since the St. Bartholomew's Day Massacres, which had begun the day after his marriage to Marguerite de Valois. D'Aubigné moved freely at court, where Henri de Navarre and the Catholic Henri, Duke of Guise, were constant companions. He observed at close range the corruption of the court, including the luxury and debauchery that he contrasts with the simple but desperate purity of the peasants in *Les Tragiques.*

During this time d'Aubigné was constantly threatened with arrest, as he was almost always involved in court intrigues and Huguenot commando-style raids. He participated in the unsuccessful escape attempt by Henri de Navarre and François, Duke of Alençon, in 1574, which resulted in the capture and execution of the two principal conspirators, Joseph de Boniface, Seigneur de la Môle, and Annibal, Comte de Coconnas, whose deaths are immortalized both in Stendhal's *Le Rouge et le noir, chronique du XIXe siècle* (1830; translated as *Red and Black, A Chronicle of the Nineteenth Century,* 1898) and in Alexandre Dumas *père* and Auguste

Maquet's *La Reine Margot* (1845; translated as *Marguerite de Valois,* 1846).

Next, Henri de Navarre sent d'Aubigné to Normandy to fight in the royal army under Guillaume de Haultemer, Seigneur de Fervacques—and thus against Protestants and against his own cause. Henri de Navarre took this measure in part to restore his reputation at court but also to protect Comte Gabriel de Montgomery, who had fatally injured Henri II in a joust in 1559. Montgomery was returning to France to defend the Protestant cause, and he was vehemently pursued by Catherine de Médicis. D'Aubigné tried to help Montgomery escape, but the count refused his advice, and he was captured and eventually executed. By aiding Montgomery, d'Aubigné earned Catherine's enmity, which was a source of pride for the Protestant soldier-poet.

D'Aubigné soon returned to court, and he was at Charles IX's side at the last stages of the king's illness in 1574. He wanted to observe the death of the monarch responsible for the massacres of St. Bartholomew's Day, but he was struck with pity at Charles's suffering and remorse.

At Charles's death the duke of Anjou and king of Poland was recalled to France as Henri III. Under Fervacques's command, d'Aubigné was still fighting Protestant forces. Meanwhile, Henri de Navarre and other Huguenot leaders were forming plots, but they were betrayed when one fairly extensive plan to take back several important towns from royal control was revealed to the king by Fervacques. On 4 February 1576 d'Aubigné witnessed the betrayal, found Henri de Navarre out hunting, and urged him to escape. On 5 May 1576 the Fifth War of Religion ended with the Treaty of Beaulieu. This treaty conceded so much to the Protestants and their allies, and so greatly angered Catholic partisans, that the extremely militant Catholic League was formed in response, with Henri de Guise, son of the assassinated Duke François, as its leader.

Wounded in a military campaign at Casteljaloux in 1577, d'Aubigné returned to his maternal fiefdom of Landes-Guinemer and began to compose *Les Tragiques.* After proving his aristocratic lineage, and with the support of Henri de Navarre, he married Suzanne de Lezay in 1583. But he did not retreat from military and political life. He continued to defend Henri de Navarre's interests, as well as those of the Protestant cause, whether on the battlefield or in court intrigues.

D'Aubigné's heated defense of the Huguenot cause, however, increasingly distanced him from the man he served. As the presumptive heir to the throne of France after 1584, Henri de Navarre had to demonstrate moderation in his political dealings. At the death in 1584 of François d'Alençon, younger brother of

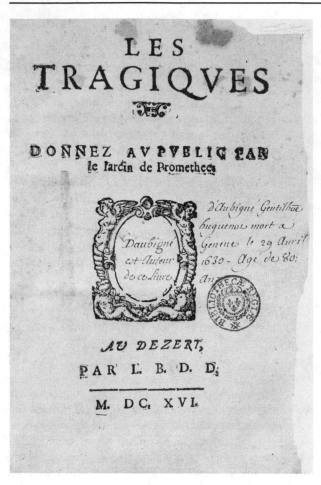

Title page for d'Aubigné's epic poem that treats the sweeping destruction of the Wars of Religion (Roger-Viollet/Getty Images)

he succeeded in conquering or otherwise winning over France. While d'Aubigné witnessed some of these battles, particularly the siege of Paris in 1590, he was not at Henri de Navarre's side as often as he had been in the past. Finally, Henri de Navarre's ascension to the throne was sealed by his abjuration of the Protestant faith on 25 July 1593, and he became Henri IV. This renunciation confirmed the king's separation from the militant ideals that d'Aubigné embraced, and d'Aubigné marked this event with his satirical work, *La Confession catholique du Sieur de Sancy*.

D'Aubigné had become the governor of Maillezais in 1589, and he remained there until 1618, composing both his epic and his history. From here he participated in the reorganization of French Protestants, who were still menaced by Catholic Leaguers and not yet protected by the 1598 Edict of Nantes, which was supposed to afford them rights in "Catholic France." Even after 1598, however, d'Aubigné lived in a sort of exile in his own country, occupied with restoring his property, raising his children–his wife had died in 1596–and composing his greatest works. He visited the court only occasionally, and he always was displeased with the experience. His writings confirmed the force of his faith, and he could never join the conciliatory group of *politiques* (moderates) who now dominated at court. Finally, the assassination of Henri IV in 1610 dissolved any close ties he had there.

D'Aubigné was devastated by Henri's death, but he and other French Protestants felt that there was reason for optimism since Marie de Médicis, who was named regent by the Parliament of Paris, confirmed the Edict of Nantes after the assassination. D'Aubigné bravely called for a meeting of the Estates-General to review this matter. He later came to Paris as a deputy representing the Protestant churches of Poitou, and even met with the queen, who tried to win him over. In 1611 the Protestant churches of France assembled at Saumur, with d'Aubigné once more serving as a deputy from Poitou. The Assembly was determined to demand more concessions, among them a closer adherence to the original Edict of Nantes. They thought the weakened monarchy might make these concessions in return for the political and military support of the Huguenots. D'Aubigné went even further, asking for more *places de sûreté* (safe zones), fortified towns from which Protestants could defend themselves from attack, than granted by the original Edict. Marie ably divided the Assembly between those willing to negotiate with the monarchy, *les prudents* (the prudent ones) and those who would not compromise on their demands, *les fermes* (the zealous ones). Then, *les fermes*, d'Aubigné among them, were excluded from negotiations with the court. It was during these events that d'Aubigné probably composed

Henri III and the only legitimate Valois heir to the throne, tensions between Catholics and Protestants increased. Henri de Navarre, perhaps recognizing the futility of the Protestant cause but certainly seeing the possibility of realizing his ambitions, chose to reconcile with the king. D'Aubigné was ill suited for this conciliatory stance, and he argued for Huguenot independence from royal control. He chose to immerse himself in the Eighth War of Religion, and rose through the ranks of the army, participating as a *maréchal de camp* (field marshal) in the Battle of Coutras in 1587.

In the meantime, the Catholic League became infamous for fomenting violent confrontations between Catholic mobs and the authorities, and targeting any Protestants, open or suspected. After the assassination of the duke of Guise on 23 December 1588, and the assassination of his brother the cardinal of Guise a day later, the kingdom fell into chaos. The Catholic League entered into even more open rebellion against Henri III, who was assassinated on 1 August 1589. Henri de Navarre proved to be a skilled tactician, however, and

Le Caducée ou L'Ange de la paix (1877, The Caduceus or Angel of Peace), which criticizes people with more moderate views than his own. He felt that *les prudents* had been corrupted by gifts and by promises of royal favor.

More than ever, d'Aubigné sought to defend the Protestant cause by insisting on the necessity of military strength. By 1611 this attitude must have seemed too closely linked to the Wars of Religion, and therefore to the conflicts of an older generation. D'Aubigné's time had passed, many believed. Yet, in retrospect, his hardened and militant stance was not so flawed: repeated compromises with the monarchy undermined the Protestants' ability to defend themselves, and they were increasingly coming under attack in France. The situation worsened when Louis XIII reached his majority in 1614. Condé declared a halfhearted war in 1615, and d'Aubigné participated in it, only to be disappointed when the rebels submitted themselves to royal authority.

The first edition of *Les Tragiques* in 1616, with its satirical portrait of the court, further confirmed d'Aubigné's frustration with the politics of his time. He finally began to realize that he could not remain in France. His own son, Constant, father of the future Madame de Maintenon, was converted to Catholicism by Jesuits. He tried repeatedly to take over Maillezais, which d'Aubigné ceded to Henri de Rohan in order to protect his interests. Already in a delicate position, d'Aubigné tried to publish *L'Histoire universelle,* hoping against hope to persuade the king of the justice of the Protestant cause, but he could not obtain royal permission to do so. The first two volumes were condemned by royal authorities in 1620. After supporting Rohan in an uprising in 1620, d'Aubigné found that a warrant for his arrest had been circulated, and he was forced to flee to Geneva. His escape was dramatic: he was pursued by a king's lieutenant who carried his portrait in order better to recognize him. D'Aubigné was apparently betrayed by one of his own servants, but he was later aided by well-wishers, and he crossed France from Poitou to Geneva, where he was warmly welcomed.

In 1623 d'Aubigné married Renée Burlamachi, who encouraged him to gather his work together and also to write his memoirs. The urgency of this work was undeniable. Even under the supposed protection of the Edict of Nantes, Protestants were being massacred and even attacked by royal forces, sometimes led by Louis XIII himself. D'Aubigné was put in charge of the fortifications of Geneva, Bern, and Basel. The French court again condemned d'Aubigné to death, this time on a charge of sacrilege for using stones that had once been part of a Catholic church to repair his property, and he was executed in effigy at the Place de Grève. The French royal authorities demanded that the town

council of Geneva hand d'Aubigné over. Feeling insecure even in Geneva, d'Aubigné built Le Château du Crest, from which he could see enemies approaching, whether from France or from Geneva.

D'Aubigné's son, Constant, became involved in intrigues that drew George Villiers, first Duke of Buckingham to La Rochelle to defend the Huguenots (an event made famous by Dumas *père*'s novel *Les Trois Mousquetaires* [1844; translated as *The Three Musketeers,* 1846]). The English intervention on the Continent incited the people of La Rochelle to revolt. Abandoned by the English as soon as their political interests were in jeopardy, La Rochelle was besieged and lost by the Protestant cause in 1628. Armand-Jean du Plessis, Cardinal and Duke of Richelieu, had been determined to destroy the Protestant party in France, and the revolt of La Rochelle, with its concomitant menace of foreign invasion, gave him the perfect excuse. The city was no longer a *place de sûreté,* and Catholicism was reestablished as the official religion. Only the Cévennes and Languedoc remained under Protestant control. Their power, however, was negligible, and these last pockets of resistance were dealt with by Louis XIV in the second half of the seventeenth century. All that was left to French Protestants was their faith and their history of resistance. D'Aubigné had been a central protagonist and a witness to the major events of this resistance, and his role as chronicler of this period was crucial to the formation of French Protestant identity over the course of the following centuries.

D'Aubigné died on 9 May 1630, having witnessed all of the Wars of Religion and many of the intrigues at the courts of Catherine de Médicis, Charles IX, and Henri III. He also had traversed many regions of France, from Normandy, Brittany, and the Loire Valley to Bordeaux and Languedoc. No better-informed witness to the events of this period existed, and he wrote prolifically and in almost every genre available to him about what he saw and experienced from childhood on, as well as the things he learned secondhand. Although his works are often erudite and complex, the passion he invested in them, especially his angry denunciations of the injustices and cruelties of his time, preserves their power and relevance. For d'Aubigné, the political was always personal, the victims of violence always individuals whose lives were to be cherished and valued. In *Les Tragiques* and in *L'Histoire universelle* he clearly identifies most strongly with the peasants who, having nothing to gain and everything to lose in the Wars of Religion, struggle simply to survive. In d'Aubigné's work French literature turns from the measured humanism of the early sixteenth century to a form of militant humanism that presents every instance of writing as an act of political and social engagement.

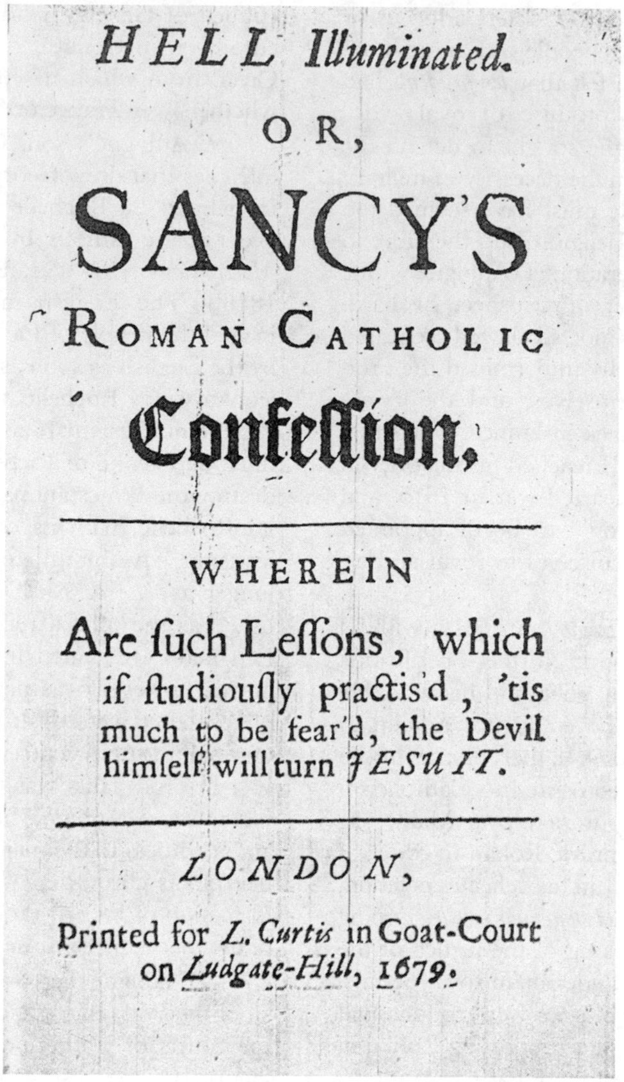

HELL Illuminated.

OR,

SANCY'S

ROMAN CATHOLIC

Confession,

WHEREIN

Are such Lessons, which
if studiously practis'd, 'tis
much to be fear'd, the Devil
himself will turn JESUIT.

LONDON,

Printed for L. Curtis in Goat-Court
on Ludgate-Hill, 1679.

Title page for a translation of d'Aubigné's La Confession catholique du Sieur de Sancy *(1660), a satirical work inspired by Henri de Navarre's abjuration of Protestantism (Thomas Cooper Library, University of South Carolina)*

D'Aubigné's works not only reflect his passionate engagement with his troubled times but also demonstrate his extraordinary intimacy with history and literature. In fact, given d'Aubigné's almost constant engagement in the battles and political affairs of his times, the erudition of his work is astonishing. His learning began early on, if one believes his claim to have translated Plato's *Crito* (early fourth century B.C.) at the age of seven and a half. D'Aubigné continued to be a voracious reader throughout his lifetime. One of his childhood regrets was having to leave behind a roomful of books when he had to flee with the Béroalde family to escape persecution, imprisonment, and possible death. This regret was repeated over and over throughout his life. He was intimately familiar with the Bible, but he was also steeped in classical literature: the works of Ovid, Virgil, Livy, Tacitus, Lucan, Seneca, Horace, and Aeschylus figure prominently in *Les Tragiques*. D'Aubigné was also conversant in contemporary literature. Much of his epic can be seen as a response to Ronsard's *Discours des misères de ce temps* (1562, Discourse on the Misery of This Time). Additionally, his *Le Printemps* echoes Ronsard's *Amours* (1553, Loves) and the work of Philippe Desportes, Maurice Scève, Clément Marot, Estienne Jodelle, René de Birague, Rémy Belleau, and Joachim du Bellay, as well as many Italian poets of the Petrarchan tradition (such as Serafino Aquilano, Jacopo Sannazaro, and Antonio Tebaldeo). Throughout his works d'Aubigné cites Church Fathers, especially St. Augustine. To research

L'Histoire universelle, he read works by Pierre de l'Estoile, Jacques-Auguste de Thou, Simon Goulart, Lancelot-Voisin de La Popelinière, François de La Noue, and Etienne Pasquier, and many documents from churches in France, from the city of Geneva, from other municipal archives, and from friends and acquaintances. He studied the prominent Protestant and Catholic theologians of his time (the works of Cardinal Robert Bellarmine appear in a posthumous inventory of his books), and he also read treatises on witchcraft and the occult, such as Jean Bodin's *De la démonomanie des sorciers* (1580, On Wizards' Love of Demons), as well as political treatises debating the nature and limits of royal authority. His knowledge of the writings of his day seems to have been encyclopedic. Consequently, his works reflect not only the events he witnessed, but also the major theological and political debates of his time, the literary trends of the late sixteenth and early seventeenth centuries, and the contemporary obsessions with, and fear of, the occult.

The three central works of d'Aubigné's oeuvre, *Les Tragiques, L'Histoire universelle,* and *Le Printemps,* seem to be coordinated versions of d'Aubigné's experiences and his knowledge of his times. The purpose of *L'Histoire universelle* was to present the general history of the second half of the sixteenth century, building on the work of Goulart in particular. But d'Aubigné extends the reach of *L'Histoire universelle* back to the eleventh century, using the history of the Waldensians as an example of the potential fate of Protestantism: after many Waldensians were massacred in the Lyon region, they fled and spread their beliefs throughout Europe. The other lesson that d'Aubigné takes from the Waldensians' fate is the necessity of writing history to offer one's perspective on events: "On se plaint que les histoires des Vaudois ont esté toutes falsifiés. Que nous n'avons rien d'eux par leurs mains, mais par celles qui les ont persecutées" (People complain that the histories of the Waldensians are all lies, and that we have nothing about them from their own hands, but from those who have persecuted them). D'Aubigné echoes this idea in a 1616 letter to Goulart, later collected in *Œuvres* (1969): "Il est bien besoin que la posterité sache de [n]os nouvelles par nous-mesmes" (There is a great need for posterity to know our history from us). Agreeing with this agenda, the Synod of Gap authorized d'Aubigné's historical project, which was already under way, and asked Protestant churches in France to gather all information and documentation on significant events of the last fifty years and send this material to d'Aubigné. Thus, *L'Histoire universelle* can be seen as an official project, even if the content is frequently linked to d'Aubigné's personal experience. In fact, the strength of *L'Histoire universelle* lies in the detailed accounts of battles d'Aubigné saw as an eyewitness or heard about from friends or cohorts. The tone of the work is rarely as polemical as that of *Les Tragiques* or of the satirical works, although d'Aubigné is not as evenhanded as Jacques-Auguste de Thou, the *politique* parliamentarian and historian, part of whose work (covering the years 1544 to 1584) d'Aubigné consulted while writing his own history.

The first edition of *L'Histoire universelle,* published in three volumes between 1616 and 1620, covers the period from the birth of Henri de Navarre in 1553 to the end of the Wars of Religion, roughly 1602. The second edition, published in 1626, was also produced in three volumes, but with significant revisions. The basic structure of the work was five books per volume, for a total of fifteen books. D'Aubigné began to prepare a fourth volume before his death, but he started with the years 1620–1622 and never wrote the portion covering the years 1602–1620. André Thierry edited these fragments for his 1981–2000 edition of the history.

D'Aubigné follows a basic pattern for his books that is only sometimes put aside for events of great importance: he describes the situation during the period at hand, recounts the battles of the war, and covers events in neighboring countries, followed by events in "L'Orient" (the Middle East), "Le Midi" (Africa), "L'Occident" (the Americas), and "Le Septentrion" (the North, including Scandinavia and Russia). Each book closes with the peace treaty that ends the war discussed in the book. Although the pattern is not entirely regular, particularly over the course of the first few books, the basic scheme of covering local (mostly French) wars and intrigues thoroughly, offering short summaries of events elsewhere in the world, and ending with a French peace treaty, holds for most of *L'Histoire universelle.* This structure dictates a more geographical than chronological approach to events, and can make *L'Histoire universelle* difficult to follow. When it comes to depicting the sweep of wars and of the many massacres over the course of the second half of the sixteenth century, however, d'Aubigné's presentation can be quite effective: the reader can observe how violence spreads from region to region, eventually taking over the whole country.

The first book begins with the birth of Henri de Navarre and his upbringing. This narrative, along with the author's preface, signals that history will be presented in a highly personal manner. D'Aubigné then quickly reviews the history of pre-Reformation and Reformation movements, as well as the persecution of these movements, throughout Europe. He follows this material with accounts of the wars between Henri II and Charles V, the Holy Roman Emperor (chapters 6–10), and the wars with the English (chapters 11–12).

Then he returns to an account of events in neighboring countries, and finally reviews the other parts of the world (the Middle East, Africa, the Americas, and the North). The book concludes with the peace treaty of Cateau-Cambrésis (1559).

As he begins the second book, d'Aubigné departs somewhat from the pattern established in the first, choosing to focus on religious doctrine and on the history of religious persecution in France. He justifies this project in the first chapter by asserting that it explains the sixty years of religious wars that France has endured. Chapter 2 offers the most complete surviving version of the "Confession of Bordeaux," a confession of faith imposed on Frenchmen who wished to prove themselves good Catholics. He counters this document in chapter 3 with the confession of faith agreed upon by the Reformed Churches of France during a national synod held at Paris in 1559. D'Aubigné then summarizes the beliefs of Catholics (chapter 4) and those of Protestants (chapter 5). He next moves backward in time to discuss the persecution of the Waldensians from the twelfth through the sixteenth centuries (chapter 6), as well as the persecution of the Albigensians (chapters 7–9), who were mostly massacred in a crusade against them in the early thirteenth century. He claims that both groups were precursors of the Reformation in France. D'Aubigné then proceeds to offer an account of pan-European persecution of Protestants before 1560 (chapter 10), which is essentially a version of the fourth book of his epic, *Les Tragiques*. This chapter is enhanced by an account of the strange deaths of some Catholic persecutors (chapter 11), which is followed by a report on Henri II's review of all judges in France in an attempt to tighten the reins of persecution. Subsequent chapters intertwine the prosecution and execution of Anne du Bourg, a prominent member of the Parliament of Paris who refused to participate in religious persecution, and the death of Henri II, which d'Aubigné presents as divine retribution for the death of du Bourg. Chapter 17 details the ill-fated conspiracy of Amboise, after which as many as several thousand Protestants and innocent civilians were executed or simply murdered. Chapters 18 through 26 cover the political maneuverings at court and the general unrest in France, all leading to the Colloque de Poissy. Then, d'Aubigné follows his pattern of covering events elsewhere in the world, but he returns to France for his final chapter, which discusses the January Edict of 1562, often seen as the first edict of tolerance in France.

The structure of each of the following books is more regular. The third book covers the First War of Religion to the Edict of Amboise in 1563, with the usual four chapters on the rest of the world preceding the account of the Edict. The fourth book narrates

events leading up to the Second War of Religion, describes the war itself and events in other major regions of the world, and concludes with the 1568 peace treaty known as the Paix de Longjumeau. The fifth book covers the Third War of Religion to the Edict of St.-Germain (1570). The sixth book tells of events leading up to the St. Bartholomew's Day Massacres, including massacres throughout France in the decades before 1572. Massacres subsequent to St. Bartholomew's Day are also discussed, as is the Fourth War of Religion, which ended with the Edict of Boulogne in July 1573. The seventh book covers the war in Normandy, including the capture and execution of Montgomery, whom Catherine de Médicis blamed for Henri II's death. It also narrates the return of Henri III to France, the Fifth War of Religion, Henri de Navarre's 1576 escape from the Louvre (where he had been a prisoner since the St. Bartholomew's Day massacres), Navarre's leadership in battle, and the peace treaty that ended this round of fighting. The eighth book offers details on the rise of the Catholic League, the Sixth War of Religion, and the Peace of Bergerac. The ninth book covers the Seventh War of Religion, focusing on what d'Aubigné describes as the diabolical maneuverings of Catherine de Médicis and the contrasting valor of Navarre. This book ends with the Treaty of Fleix of 1580. The tenth book focuses on events leading up to the Eighth War of Religion and ends with the disastrous (for French Protestants) July Edict, or the Treaty of Nemours, of 1585.

The eleventh book of *L'Histoire universelle* features what one could argue was still the Eighth War of Religion, since the first July Edict was an attempt by the monarchy to make peace with the Catholic League. This book ends with the second July Edict, the Edict of Rouen, which ceded a great deal of power to the militant Henri de Guise, leader of the Catholic League. In the twelfth book, Protestants wage war elsewhere in France while Henri III and Henri de Guise face off in Paris and Blois. D'Aubigné attempts to convey events on both fronts, eventually narrating the assassination of Henri de Guise and of his brother Louis, the cardinal of Guise, the day after. This book also covers the alliance between Henri III and Henri de Navarre, as well as the assassination of Henri III in August of 1589. Then, to maintain the structure of previous books, he offers one chapter on each of the four major regions of the world that he has designated previously, finally coming back to the treaty between Henri III and Henri de Navarre. Book 13 traces Henri IV's conquest of France, ending with the January 1594 treaty with the Catholic League. D'Aubigné describes this book as "plus herissé de combats qu'aucun autre" (more prickly with battles than any other). Book 14 begins with the surrenders of Lyon and Paris and continues with the surrenders of other major cities and towns in France. The book leaps back and forth in time as discussions of the battles move from region to region, a narrative choice that seems to emphasize the scope of the conflicts and the odds against Henri de Navarre. These wars end with a final treaty with the Catholic League. As he enumerates the various edicts of peace of 1598, d'Aubigné gives little notice to the Edict of Nantes. The fifteenth and last complete book of *L'Histoire universelle* focuses mostly on the wars in Savoie, the remarriage of Henri IV to Marie de Médicis, and the treason of the maréchal de Biron. D'Aubigné ends this book with a brief summary of the Edict of Nantes.

In *L'Histoire universelle* d'Aubigné portrays himself as a central figure in events—and even as the motivating force for some events. For example, in the preface he recounts how Henri de Navarre, having killed a large stag with impressive antlers, tells him to write about this event in his history. D'Aubigné responds scornfully, "Sire, commencez de faire et je commencerai d'escrire" (Sire, begin to do something, and I will begin to write). Then, in every historical event where he places himself at Henri's side, d'Aubigné portrays himself as a goad to action and the conscience of the king. Henri is clearly the protagonist of d'Aubigné's history, but he offers detailed accounts of all of France's leaders, Protestant and Catholic alike. Although the chapters on other parts of the world justify the title *L'Histoire universelle* (a title used at the time to designate a history of the world), their content is sketchy. Most of the accounts of regions beyond France's borders seem like an afterthought, and they are not as insightful and accurate as the passages on France. Still, the material on international events helps to contextualize the strife in France and echoes the sweep of *Les Tragiques*.

D'Aubigné clearly began his work on *L'Histoire universelle* before 1603; hence, he was completing *Les Tragiques* while he was composing his history, and each work enriched the other. While *L'Histoire universelle* covers the history of the Wars of Religion as broadly and in as much detail as possible, *Les Tragiques* presents these events to a literary audience. *Les Tragiques* is an epic in seven books, preceded by a preface, "Aux Lecteurs" (To the Readers), in which the poet identifies himself as "le larron Prométhée" (the thief Prometheus). Here d'Aubigné potrays himself as a man who steals the light of truth so that all of humanity might benefit from it. Also preceding the epic is a verse preface, "L'Autheur à son livre" (The Author to His Book), which presents the work as the author's legacy.

Les Tragiques is written in alexandrine *rime plate* (couplets). Although organized more or less chronologically, the epic is primarily organized according to social

ŒUVRES COMPLÈTES
de Théodore

Agrippa d'Aubigné

publiées pour la première fois
D'APRÈS LES MANUSCRITS ORIGINAUX

*Accompagnées
de Notices biographique, littéraire & bibliographique,
de Variantes, d'un Commentaire, d'une Table
des noms propres & d'un Glossaire,*

Par

EUG. RÉAUME & F. DE CAUSSADE

Tome premier.

FAC ET SPERA

PARIS
ALPHONSE LEMERRE, ÉDITEUR,
27–29, PASSAGE CHOISEUL, 27–29

M. DCCC. LXXIII

Title page for the first volume in a six-volume collection. Despite its title, the collection is not complete: it omits Historie universelle *as well as other works (Thomas Cooper Library, University of South Carolina).*

groups and institutions. The first book, "Misères," describes the effects of religious persecution on the general populace—and peasants in particular. This book presents a general, allegorical portrait of France through a series of good and bad mothers: "Mère France" (Mother France) and her twin sons, who are tearing each other and her apart; Mother Earth, who protects the peasants; a dying peasant mother who tries to save her baby; a mother who eats her baby; and a portrait of Catherine de Médicis as Medea. "Misères" suggests that civil strife destroys society to its very core, down to the family unit, down to the relationship between mother and child.

The second book, "Princes," denounces the corruption of the court and offers satirical portraits of various members of the royal family, including Henri III as a hermaphrodite and as Nero. Incidents of murder, sexual misconduct, infanticide, and sorcery are depicted in detail. These descriptions of the actions of the nobility, coming on the heels of "Misères," underscore just how gratuitous most of the violence of the period was.

The third book, "La Chambre dorée" (The Golden Court), describes parliamentary involvement in the persecution of Protestants. In this allegory the judges of the special chamber for trying "heretics," the Golden Court (also known as the "chambre ardante," or burning court), represent the various sins or evils that fueled the persecution. The fourth book, "Les Feux," describes Protestant martyrs and their fates. Instead of making the death the focal point of each story, however, d'Aubigné focuses on the individuals, giving details that force the readers to see the martyrs in all their humanity rather than as faceless victims of violence. Hence, each story is centered around the martyrs' declarations of faith. By means of this device, d'Aubigné completes the memorial work that Jean Crespin and Goulart undertook in the *Histoire des martyrs* (1554; revised 1619, History of Martyrs), underscoring the lives lost as well as the transcendence of that loss by means of faith. D'Aubigné also depicts the universal nature of the violence by describing different kinds of martyrs: men in their prime, women, children, and the elderly. In this way, he emphasizes that no one is exempt from the cruelty of religious persecution.

The fifth book of *Les Tragiques,* "Les Fers," describes the massacres of Protestants, especially focusing on the deaths of Protestant leaders and the St. Bartholomew's Day massacres. As each town affected by the massacres is named, d'Aubigné makes clear the communal responsibility for the tragic events. He personalizes this violence by drawing detailed portraits of several of the victims. He also portrays himself as a victim in the epic while simultaneously placing himself above everything when he sees, from God's perspective, the tableaux, or paintings, that he has created of the massacres within the context of a greater tableau of all history and all future events. By means of this double perspective—on the one hand, at the center of the violence and a victim of it, and on the other hand, watching it from a distance as a series of artistically rendered scenes composed by God—d'Aubigné conveys both the pain and suffering of individual Protestants and the possibility of the eventual triumph of the Protestant cause in the grand scheme of things. By making his presentation of these two perspectives radically disjointed, each invisible to the other, d'Aubigné avoids the trap of seeming to justify the violence. Instead, he shows that it will not serve the Catholics well. Additionally, d'Aubigné narrates several battles of the Wars of

Religion, showing the Protestants fighting back against their persecutors.

"Vengeances," the sixth book of *Les Tragiques,* depicts biblical and historical examples of faith and faithlessness, injustice and redress, and persecution of the righteous coupled with the divine vengeance visited upon the persecutors. D'Aubigné increasingly attempts to justify the Protestant cause, and comparisons with the Bible dominate the book. Finally, the last book of *Les Tragiques,* "Jugement" (Judgment Day), culminates in God's intervention on behalf of Protestants on the Day of Judgment. In strange countermetamorphoses, the burned, torn, and digested bodies of slain Protestants reform themselves to rise and accuse their horrified persecutors. The final image of the epic is that of the reunion of the saved soul with God as a nurturing mother figure.

Throughout *Les Tragiques* d'Aubigné frames historical material with allegorical and imaginative presentations of violence, cruelty, and strong faith in the face of threats. The core of the epic, represented by "Les Feux" and "Les Fers," is mainly historical, with significant allegorical touches (such as the authorial persona's apotheosis). The first three books, "Misères," "Princes," and "La Chambre dorée," offer highly allegorized versions of historical events and characters, in part to intensify the effects of the violence depicted, and in part to generalize the impact of these descriptions. Then, "Vengeances" associates biblical instances of divine wrath visited upon the persecutors of the faithful with more-recent historical events, while "Jugement," an imaginative rendering of the end of the world, eschews history and places itself outside of time. While history is the ground upon which this epic is placed, *Les Tragiques* reaches beyond history to find a message of hope for the beleaguered Protestant cause.

Both *L'Histoire universelle* and *Les Tragiques* were published under d'Aubigné's supervision, and both of these works were intended for a wide audience. By contrast, *Sa Vie à ses enfans,* so called because it seems to have been intended primarily for d'Aubigné's children, circulated only in several manuscripts over the course of the seventeenth century. This autobiography was meant to present a more personal view of the history of d'Aubigné's times, offering details that were not appropriate to include in *L'Histoire universelle.*

Meanwhile, d'Aubigné's love poetry, *Le Printemps,* was in his personal papers, with a partial version copied in the Monmerqué manuscript and a few poems circulating in seventeenth-century miscellanies. This work consists of three separate sequences of poems: the hundred sonnets of *L'Hécatombe à Diane* (The Hecatomb to Diana), the *Stances,* and the *Odes.* The three sequences are linked by common themes and images, particularly the suffering of the lover, which is often taken to the extreme, including dark and harrowing imagery. In fact, d'Aubigné used the corruption and menace that informs his love poetry to justify his rejection of it. In "Misères" he explains his preference for the religious material of *Les Tragiques*: "Je n'escris plus les feux d'un amour inconu, / Mais par l'affliction plus sage devenue, / J'entreprens bien plus haut" (I write no more of the fires of unknown love, / But made wiser by suffering, / I undertake a much higher task). This professed conversion from profane to sacred poetry has led many critics to believe that *Le Printemps* was merely a youthful work, but the manuscripts in Geneva show that d'Aubigné continued to write and rework this poetry until late in life.

The sonnets of *L'Hécatombe à Diane* are written mostly in alexandrines, but there are a few written in *dizains* (ten-syllable verse) and octosyllabic verse, and there is even a sonnet in seven-syllable verse. D'Aubigné begins the sequence with four sonnets depicting his love as a frail little boat menaced by the storm, but soon the imagery changes to that of war, and the reader is left to wonder whether war is a metaphor for love, as it is in Ovid's *Amores* (circa 10 B.C.–A.D. 1), or love is a metaphor for war. There are, however, moments of peace, as in sonnet 20: "Nous ferons, ma Diane, un jardin fructueux" (We will make, my Diane, a fruitful garden). In fact, sonnets 20–30 reflect more an artist's than a warrior's sensibility. But this stretch of calm is definitively ended in the thirty-fourth sonnet: "Guerre ouverte, et non point tant de subtilitez" (Open war, and not so much subtlety). Sonnet 42 reveals one of d'Aubigné's preferred poetic strategies, which is to take a Petrarchan conceit and twist it into something darker, more menacing. Here he compares the fair skin of the beloved lady to arsenic, which is also white. Meanwhile, sonnet 50 offers an extreme example of d'Aubigné's use of torture in *L'Hécatombe à Diane*: "Quand du sort inhumain les tenailles flambantes / Du milieu de mon corps tirent cruellement / Mon coeur qui bat encor'" (When the flaming pincers / Of inhuman fate cruelly tear from my body / My still beating heart). The poet's hostility toward Diane grows as the sequence progresses, as is evident in sonnet 89: "Diane, ta coustume est de tout deschirer, / Enflammer, desbriser, ruiner, mettre en pieces" (Diane, it is your custom to tear everything / Set it on fire, break it, ruin it, tear it to pieces). The poet sees himself as sacrificed to Diane in sonnet 97: "L'holocoste est mon coeur" (The burnt offering is my heart). As the lovers separate, the poems reflect the torment of a poet's unrequited love. This situation is, of course, the very basis of Petrarchan poetry, but d'Aubigné's emphasis on the torture itself, expressed in the most vivid terms, sets his work apart.

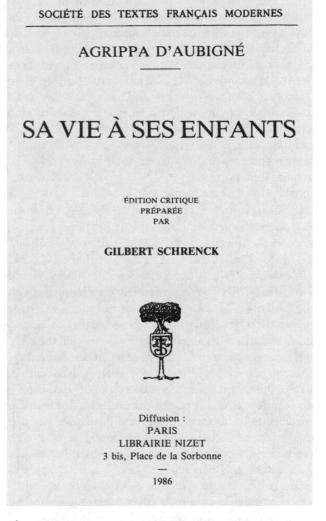

SOCIÉTÉ DES TEXTES FRANÇAIS MODERNES

AGRIPPA D'AUBIGNÉ

SA VIE À SES ENFANTS

ÉDITION CRITIQUE
PRÉPARÉE
PAR

GILBERT SCHRENCK

Diffusion :
PARIS
LIBRAIRIE NIZET
3 bis, Place de la Sorbonne
—
1986

Title page for the modern edition of d'Aubigné's memoir, a work that has contributed to a reassessment of d'Aubigné as an important literary figure (Thomas Cooper Library, University of South Carolina)

The *Stances* begin, thematically at least, where *L'Hécatombe à Diane* ended. The first *Stance* is loaded with images of poison, of wild animals, of piles of bones: "Le lieu de mon repos est une chambre peinte / De mil os blanchissans et de testes de mortz" (My place of rest is a room decorated / With a thousand whitening bones and with skulls). The speaker, a grotesque hermit figure, delights in the death of innocent animals and in demonic rituals. The third *Stance* confirms the violence of the sequence, as the poet portrays himself as a hunted animal. In the sixth *Stance*, the destructive nature of love becomes self-destruction: "J'ouvre mon estomac, une tumbe sanglante" (I open my stomach, a bloody tomb). Throughout the *Stances*, images of delicate flowers stand in sharp contrast to harsh images, such as the rotting corpses of the twentieth *Stance*.

The *Odes* at first echo the violence of the two other sequences of *Le Printemps:* the poet speaks of "Mon sang bouillant de mille endroitz" (My blood bubbling out at a thousand places). While there is violent imagery, and while the word *martyre* recurs throughout the sequence (odes 1, 14, 17, 31, 38), the *Odes* are more traditional than the *Stances* or *L'Hécatombe à Diane.* They especially feature more decorous imagery, classical allusions, and Petrarchan and Ovidian conceits of love (for example, as a little cherub). Nevertheless, a certain perversity subtends the sequence, with horror (ode 51), venom, tumors, vipers (ode 38), and other dark images interrupting delicate moments.

Of his three major works, *Le Printemps* offers the most personal version of d'Aubigné's experiences, as it features the story of his ill-fated love affair with Salviati. Yet, as the Diane addressed in the *Stances,* the *Odes,* and *L'Hécatombe à Diane* demonstrates her infidelity and inconstancy, the poet associates her increasingly with the Catholic Church and its abuses of faith. As Diane rejects the lover outright, she is associated more and more with the authorities who torture and kill the faithful. Hence, similar to Ovid's imagery in the *Amores,* love is compared to war. But Ovid's work is light-hearted, while the graphic details and tone of d'Aubigné's descriptions make his poems disturbing. The lover also participates in his own punishment for having pursued that which is forbidden. Like Actaeon, he is torn to pieces for coming into contact with Diana; but, unlike Actaeon, he also tears himself apart. For d'Aubigné this image, which is typical of later Petrarchan poetry, represents the conscience torn between true religion and an attractive simulacrum of faith. Hence, on the surface this work simply seems to be a collection of Petrarchan love poetry, but the graphic violence of several of the poems signals its connection to *Les Tragiques.* Ultimately, *Le Printemps* is yet another depiction of the Wars of Religion, from yet another perspective, in yet another genre. It completes d'Aubigné's representation of this period by offering insight into the impact of continuous war on the individual psyche, as destruction turns into self-destruction and love turns into hatred. D'Aubigné's insistence on depicting the impact of unrelenting violence at all levels—institutional, social, and personal—and his desire to reach a wide range of audiences in a variety of ways are remarkable, and his works furnish a vital window into the problems of his times.

While d'Aubigné's major works impress scholars with their scope and detail, his minor works also demonstrate a range of knowledge and literary skills. For example, *Les Avantures du baron de Fæneste* forms a strange companion piece to the history and the epic. The first two books of *Les Avantures du baron de Fæneste* appeared in 1617, a year after the first edition of *Les Tragiques.* A continuation of the work appeared in 1619, about the same time as the first edition of *L'Histoire universelle.* The fourth part was published in 1630, shortly before d'Aubigné's death. Part political pamphlet, part Rabelaisian novel, *Les Avantures du baron de Fæneste* offers a satire of the conflict between the duc d'Epernon and the town of La Rochelle, and more generally a satire of the court and the many political intrigues that dominated the landscape of early-seventeenth-century France. In the work, which takes the form of a dialogue, the young *courtisan* (courtier) Fæneste (whose name comes from the Greek word for "to appear" or "to seem") meets an old nobleman, Enay (from the Greek word for "to be"). They discuss the court, religion, love, and other matters. Among other targets, d'Aubigné attacks the use of religion to further personal ambition. The frivolity of court life, also a target in "Princes" of *Les Tragiques,* and excess of all kinds are also satirized. The characters described, often in great detail, are eccentric, even bizarre.

Les Avantures du baron de Fæneste can be seen as a complement to "La Confession catholique du Sieur de Sancy," a satirical work that focuses primarily on religious abuses, particularly the Catholic Church's manipulation of the unstable political situation in France. "La Confession catholique du Sieur de Sancy" was not published until 1663, but it circulated in manuscript well before then. It can be seen as d'Aubigné's foray into theology, although the work takes more of a political perspective on questions of religion.

"Du Debvoir mutuel des roys et des subjects," written around 1620 but not published until the nineteenth century, takes a serious approach to the political issues of the day. This work echoes the debate over royal authority that began after the massacres of St. Bartholomew's Day, best represented by Etienne de la Boétie's *Discours de la Servitude volontaire* (1548, Discourse on Voluntary Servitude) and Philippe DuPlessis-Mornay and Hubert Languet's *Vindiciae contra tyrannos* (1579, The Defense against Tyrants). The idea of a contract between the people and their king that creates mutual obligations informs d'Aubigné's portraits of Henri IV and of the Valois rulers in *Les Tragiques* and the *L'Histoire universelle.*

Passionate, eclectic, and outspoken, Théodore Agrippa d'Aubigné left behind a wide range of work that demonstrates his desire to convey as completely as possible the horrors and the wonders of his time. The discovery and rediscovery of d'Aubigné's work began in the eighteenth century with his autobiography. Major new editions of his works were undertaken in the late nineteenth century, and pieces of his work are still being discovered and published. Thierry's edition of the *L'Histoire universelle,* the first volume of which appeared in 1981, and Gilbert Schrenck's 1986 edition of *Sa Vie à ses enfants* helped to renew scholarly interest in d'Aubigné's work at the end of the twentieth century, and he increasingly has been discussed as a major figure in French literary history. D'Aubigné's bridging of history and literature, and of the personal and the political, makes him an author of particular interest in cultural studies. His work is a credit to his dedication, as well as his remarkable erudition and memory, and it invests passion and pathos, immediacy and force, into historical narratives that might otherwise seem distant to modern readers.

Biographies:

Armand Garnier, *Agrippa d'Aubigné et le parti protestant: Contribution à l'histoire de la réforme en France,* 3 volumes (Paris: Fischbacher, 1928);

Jeanne Galzy, *Agrippa d'Aubigné* (Paris: Gallimard, 1965);

Eric Deschodt, *Agrippa d'Aubigné: Le guerrier inspiré* (Paris: Laffont, 1995);

Madeleine Lazard, *Agrippa d'Aubigné* (Paris: Fayard, 1998).

References:

Jacques Bailbé, *Agrippa d'Aubigné, poète des "Tragiques"* (Caen: Faculté des Lettres et Sciences Humaines de l'Université de Caen, 1968);

Keith Cameron, *Agrippa d'Aubigné* (Boston: Twayne, 1977);

Catharine Randall Coats, *Subverting the System: d'Aubigné and Calvinism,* Sixteenth Century Essays and Studies, no. 14 (Kirksville, Mo.: Sixteenth Century Journal Publications, 1990);

Jean-Raymond Fanlo, *Tracés, ruptures: La composition instable des "Tragiques"* (Paris: Champion, 1990);

Marie Madeleine Fragonard, *La Pensée religieuse d'Agrippa d'Aubigné et son expression* (Paris: Champion, 2004);

Fragonard and Madeleine Lazard, eds., *"Les Tragiques" d'Agrippa d'Aubigné* (Paris: Champion, 1990);

Ullrich Langer, *Rhétorique et intersubjectivité: "Les Tragiques" d'Agrippa d'Aubigné* (Paris & Seattle: Papers on Seventeenth Century Literature, 1983);

Frank Lestringant, *Agrippa d'Aubigné: "Les Tragiques"* (Paris: Presses Universitaires de France, 1986);

Gisèle Mathieu-Castellani, *Agrippa d'Aubigné: Le Corps de Jézabel* (Paris: Presses Universitaires de France, 1991);

Olivier Pot, ed., *Poétiques d'Aubigné: Actes du colloque de Genève, mai 1996* (Geneva: Droz, 1999);

Marie-Hélène Prat, *Les Mots du corps: Un imaginaire lexicale dans "Les Tragiques" d'Agrippa d'Aubigné* (Geneva: Droz, 1996);

Malcolm Quainton, *D'Aubigné: Les Tragiques* (London: Grant & Cutler, 1990);

Richard Regosin, *The Poetry of Inspiration: Agrippa d'Aubigné's Les Tragiques* (Chapel Hill: University of North Carolina Press, 1970).

Papers:

Théodore Agrippa d'Aubigné's papers are in the Archives Tronchin at the Bibliothèque publique et universitaire de Genève, Geneva.

Jean-Antoine de Baïf

(1532 – October 1589)

Thomas L. Zamparelli
Loyola University New Orleans

BOOKS: *Le Tombeau de Marguerite de Valois royne de Navarre. Faict premierement en disticques latins par les trois soeurs princesses en Angleterre. Depuis traduictz en grec, italie, & françois par plusiers des excellentz poétes de la Frãce. Avecques plusiers odes, hymnes, cantiques, epitaphes, sur le mesme subject,* by Baïf and others (Paris: Printed by Michel Fezandat and Robert Granlon for Vincent Sartenas, 1551);

Le Ravissement d'Europe (Paris: Printed by the Widow of Maurice de la Porte, 1552);

Les Amours (Paris: Printed by the Widow of Maurice de la Porte, 1552);

Quatre Livres de l'Amour de Francine (Paris: Printed by André Wechel, 1555);

Remonstrance sur la prinse de Calais (Paris: Printed by Fédéric Morel, 1558);

Chant de joie du jour des espousailles de François roidaufin et de Marie, reine d'Escosse (Paris: Printed by André Wechel, 1558);

Le Premier des Meteores . . . A Caterine de Medicis royne mere du roy (Paris: Printed by Robert Estienne, 1567);

Le Brave, comedie . . . jouee devant le roy en l'hostile de Guise à Paris le XXVIII de janvier M.D.LXVII (Paris: Printed by Robert Estienne, 1567);

Euvres en rime, 4 volumes (Paris: Printed by Lucas Breyer, 1572–1573)—comprises volume 1 (1572), *Poemes;* volume 2 (1572), *Les Amours;* volume 3 (1572), *Les Jeux;* and volume 4 (1573), *Les Passetems;*

Etrénes de poézie fransoêze: An vers mezurés. A Roe. A la Réine mre. A Roe de Polone. A Monséinor Duk D'Alanson. A Monséinor le Grand Prior. A Monséinor de Nevers. & autres (Paris: Printed by Denys du Val, 1574);

Complainte sur le trespas du feu roy Charles IX (Paris: Printed by Federic Morel, 1574);

Premiere salutation au roy sur son avenement à la couronne de France (Paris: Printed by Federic Morel, 1575);

Seconde salutation au roy sur son avenement à la couronne de France (Paris: Printed by Federic Morel, 1575);

Epistre au roy sous le nom de la royne sa mere: Pour l'instruction d'un bon roy (Paris: Printed by Federic Morel, 1575);

Jean-Antoine de Baïf (frontispiece for Les Mimes, Enseignemens et Proverbes, *1576; Center for Research Libraries)*

Les Mimes, Enseignemens et Proverbes (Paris: Printed for Lucas Breyer Marchant Libraire, 1576; enlarged edition, Paris: Printed by Mamert Patisson at the shop of Robert Estienne, 1581); enlarged again as

24

Les Mimes, Enseignemens et Proverbes . . . Reveus & augmentez en ceste derniere edition (Paris: Printed by Mamert Patisson at the shop of Robert Estienne, 1597; enlarged again, Tournon: For Guillaume Linocier, 1619);

Carminum . . . liber I (Paris: Printed by Mamert Patisson at the shop of Robert Estienne, 1577);

Chansonnettes mesurées . . . mises en musiques à quatre parties par Jacques Mauduit, Parisien (Paris: Printed by Adrian le Roy and Robert Ballard, 1586);

Jean Antoine de Baïfs Psaultier: Metrische Bearbeitung der Psalmen mit Einleitung, Anmerkungen und einem Wörterverzeichnis. Zum ersten mal Herausgegeben, edited by Ernst Johann Groth (Heilbronn, Germany: Henninger, 1888);

Le Psautier de 1587, edited by Yves Le Hir, Publication de la faculté des lettres et sciences humaines de Grenoble, no. 31 (Paris: Presses universitaires de France, 1963).

Editions and Collections: *Poésies choisies . . . suivies de Poésies inédites publiées,* edited, with a biographical essay, by Louis Becq de Fouquières (Paris: Charpentier, 1874);

Les Mimes, Enseignemens et Proverbes . . . réimpression complète collationnée sur les éditions originales, 2 volumes, edited, with a preface, by Prosper Blanchemain, Trésor des vieux poétes français, nos. 9–10 (Paris: Willem, 1880);

Euvres en Rime, 5 volumes, edited, with a biographical introduction, by Charles Marty-Lavaux (Paris: Lemerre, 1881–1890; reprinted, Geneva: Slatkine, 1966);

Les Amours de Jean-Antoine de Baïf (Amours de Méline), critical edition, edited by Mathieu Augé-Chiquet (Paris: Hachette / Toulouse: Privat, 1909; reprinted, Geneva: Slatkine, 1972);

J.-A. de Baïf: Poèmes—Les Amours—Les Jeux—Les Passe-temps—Les Mimes—Les Chansonnettes, edited, with a biographical essay, by Alphonse Séché, Bibliothèque des poètes français et étrangers (Paris: Michaud, [1910]);

Chansonnettes mesurees . . . mises en musique à quatre parties par Jacques Mauduit, Parisien, in *Poètes du XVIe siècle,* edited by Albert-Marie Schmidt, Bibliothèque de la Pléiade, no. 96 (Paris: Gallimard, 1953);

Chansonnettes, critical edition, edited, with an introduction, by G. C. Bird (Vancouver: University of British Columbia, 1964);

The Chansonnettes en vers mesurées: A critical edition, edited by Barbara A. Terry, Mississippi State University Studies in Foreign Languages and Literatures, no. 1 (Birmingham: Birmingham Printing, 1966);

Les Amours de Francine, volume 1: *Sonnets,* edited by Ernesta Caldarini, Textes littéraires français, no. 118 (Geneva: Droz / Paris: Minard, 1966);

Les Amours de Francine, volume 2: *Chansons,* edited by Caldarini, Textes littéraires français, no. 139 (Geneva: Droz / Paris: Minard, 1967);

Poems, edited, with an introduction and notes in English, by Malcolm Quainton, Blackwell's French Texts (Oxford: Blackwell, 1970);

Etrénes de poézie fransoeze an vers mezurés; Psautier en vers mesurés (manuscrit B.N. ms. fr. 19140) (Geneva: Slatkine, 1972);

Le Premier Livre des Poèmes, edited by Guy Demerson, Publication de la faculté de lettres de Clermond-Ferrand, second series, no. 35 (Grenoble: Presses Universitaires de Grenoble, 1975);

Le Brave, edited by Simone Maser, Textes littéraires français, no. 265 (Geneva: Droz, 1979);

Mimes, Enseignemens et Proverbes, critical edition, edited by Jean Vignes, Textes littéraires français, no. 411 (Geneva: Droz, 1992);

Antigone, in *La Tragédie de l'époque d'Henri II et Charles IX,* volume 5, edited by Maser (Florence: Olschki / Paris: Presses Universitaires de France, 1993);

Oeuvres complètes, volume 1: *Euvres en rime (première partie): Neuf Livres des Poemes,* critical edition, edited, with an introduction, by Vignes, Textes de la Renaissance, no. 54 (Paris: Champion, 2002).

PLAY PRODUCTION: *Le Brave,* Paris, Hôtel de Guise, 28 January 1567.

TRANSLATIONS: Hermes Trismegistus, *Orpheos e Hermou tou trismegistou. Prognostika peri seismon. Orphei seu Mercurii Termaximi. Prognostica a Terrae motibus* (Basel: Oporinus, 1554);

Giovanni Francesco Pico della Mirandola, *Traitté de l'imagination, tiré du latin de J. François Pic de la Mirandole* (Paris: Printed by André Wechel, 1556);

Terence, *L'Eunuque, traduite . . . en 5. actes en vers de 4. pieds, dédiée à monseigneur le chevalier d'Angoulême, par un sonnet* (Paris: Printed by Robert Estienne, 1567);

Imitations de quelques chans de l'Arioste, adapted by Baïf, Philippe Desportes, Mellin de Saint-Gelais, and Louis d'Orléans (Paris: Printed by Lucas Breyer, 1572);

Sophocles, *Antigone, en vers de 5. pieds, traduite du Grec . . . dédiée à très-auguste princesse Elisabeth d'Autriche royne de France, par un sonnet avec argument en vers, imprimée avec dix-neuf églogues, cinq devis ou dialogues des dieux, pris de Lucian, sous le titre de cinq livres de jeux* (Paris: Printed by Lucas Breyer, 1573).

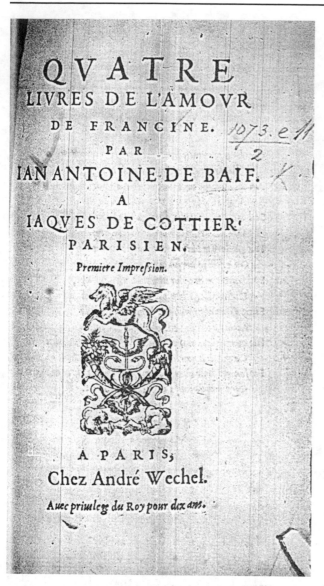

Title page for the volume of poems in which Baïf portrays himself as tortured by his cruel love interest, Francine de Gennes (Center for Research Libraries)

Jean-Antoine de Baïf was a poet, dramatist, and innovator in spelling and versification. He is widely regarded as the most erudite member of the Pléiade group of midcentury poets. A versatile writer, Baïf wrote love lyrics, satire, pastoral, comedy, and didactic, religious, and polemical poetry. He also translated and adapted many Greek and Latin works, and wrote several translations of the Psalms. His genius for literary and linguistic experimentation was superior to his actual talent as a writer; however, toward the end of his life he produced *Les Mimes* (Mimes), a startlingly original work of gnomic poetry published in *Les Mimes, Enseignemens et Proverbes* (1576, Mimes, Lessons, and Proverbs).

Baïf was born in Venice in 1532 to a renowned and influential father, the humanist-diplomat Lazare de Baïf, to whom Jean-Antoine pays homage in his autobiographical *Epistre au roy sous le nom de la royne sa mere* (1575, Letter to the King in the Name of the Queen, His Mother), praising him as "L'un des premiers François qui les Muses embrasse" (One of the first Frenchmen to embrace the Muses). Lazare de Baïf was one of the earliest champions for rewriting classical tragedy in French, and he was particularly known for his French translation of Sophocles' *Electra* (fifth century B.C.), published in 1537. Meanwhile, little is known of Jean-Antoine's mother, a young Venetian woman whom Lazare de Baïf met while serving as François I's ambassador to the Republic of Venice. According to several commentators, this Venetian mistress may have been a member of an illustrious patrician family, perhaps of the House of Morosini or Giustiniani. Because Lazare de Baïf aspired to the clergy, and particularly because he wanted to receive revenues from a future appointment as abbot of Grenetière, any thought of marriage to his son's Venetian mother was out of the question. Jean-Antoine never referred to his mother in any of his writings, and he may have retained no personal memories of her—in fact, he may not have known her at all.

Lazare de Baïf recognized Jean-Antoine as his son and later made him the legal heir to his fortune. In 1534 he brought Jean-Antoine with him when he was recalled to France, where he was first appointed "conseiller clerc," or clerical adviser to the Parlement of Paris, and later "maître des requêtes ordinaires de l'Hôtel du Roi," a receiver of royal petitions and appeals. Lazare de Baïf took an active role in the humanistic education of his son, making sure he acquired in his formative years a deep appreciation for classical languages. For this purpose he chose two distinguished intellectuals and pedagogues of the time, the physician-printer-geographer-translator Charles Estienne, who taught Latin to Jean-Antoine, and the Cretan scholar and calligraphist Ange Vergèce, who taught him Greek and especially Greek calligraphy. Baïf's biographers are inclined to believe that the early proficiency Jean-Antoine achieved in writing the Greek language led him to focus later on the reform of French spelling and writing.

At the beginning of 1540 Lazare de Baïf resumed his travels as official emissary of François I. He traveled with his physician, Estienne, and his secretary, Pierre de Ronsard, to Haguenau, Germany, to mediate a dispute between Catholic and Protestant princes. He later traveled to Blois, Poitou, and the province of Languedoc. Faced with the impracticality of taking his young son with him, Lazare de Baïf entrusted his son to Jacques Toussain, with whom Jean-Antoine studied from 1544 to 1547. A learned and respected teacher of Greek and Latin and described by the humanist Etienne Dolet as a "bibliothèque parlante," or "talking library," Toussain was professor of Greek at the Collège Royal. He was especially noted for his thoroughness and precision in presenting classical texts, and he is said to have trained all the prominent Hellenists of the time, inspiring in his pupils a love of Greek grammar and Latin poetry.

In 1544 Jean-Antoine, still under the tutelage of Toussain, began studying Greek under the guidance of the famous scholar Jean Dorat, who was then residing with the Baïf family in Paris. His fellow pupil was his father's former travel companion and future leader of the Pléiade, Ronsard. The younger and precocious Jean-Antoine, who had grown up surrounded by texts and learned tutors, guided his fellow pupil in mastering the Greek language, while Ronsard in return introduced Jean-Antoine to the intricacies of French versification. Following the death of Lazare de Baïf in November 1547, they continued their humanistic studies over the next three years under the paternal Dorat at the Collège de Coqueret in Paris. They were joined by students from all over Europe, including Maledent, Lambin, Bertrand Berger, Frédéric Jamot, and the noted Joachim du Bellay, who later became the chief theorist of the group of seven poets first known as the Brigade and later dubbed the Pléiade. These pupils, who were drawn to Coqueret because of Dorat's reputation as a prominent classical scholar, acquired not only a firm grounding in Greek and Roman literature but also a profound admiration for Neo-Latin poetry and the Italian masters Dante, Ludovico Ariosto, and Petrarch, and they learned the craft of writing in different forms. Baïf in particular pays tribute to Dorat as the one who initiated him into the "secrets" of the Muses by guiding him, before all others, down the road followed by the Romans and Greeks:

> . . . Il m'aprit vos segrets,
> Par les chemins choisis des vieux Latins et Grecs.
> C'est par luy que sortant de la vulgaire trace
> Dans un nouveau sentier, moy le premier je passe
>
> (. . . He taught me your secrets,
> Leading me down the paths chosen by the Ancient Romans and Greeks.
> It is through him, leaving the path commonly tread,
> Down a new path, I before all others direct my steps)

In 1551 Baïf completed his humanist training, but he continued to deepen his learning. He began his association with Marc-Antoine Muret, a Neo-Latin poet and well-known figure in the humanist coterie, at the Collège de Boncourt. Joining him there were Ronsard, Estienne Jodelle, the painter-poet Nicolas Denisot, and

Rémy Belleau, who together formed the nucleus of the Pléiade. Baïf's circle of humanist colleagues began to widen as he established friendships with poets from the provinces, namely, Olivier de Magny, Imbert de Bordeaux, Claude Turrin, and Etienne de La Boétie. Baïf was a key member of this group and is thought to have played a major role in organizing the famous "pompe du bouc" of 1553—a pseudo-pagan banquet, or goat sacrifice, intended to crown Jodelle's achievement as the first French dramatist to resurrect classical tragedy in French with his production of *Cléopâtre captive* (produced 1553, published 1574, Captive Cleopatra).

Around this time Baïf made his first literary attempts. In 1549 he wrote a sonnet titled "Sonnet prins sur le grec de Claude Rommile" (Sonnet Taken from the Greek of Claude Rommile), a free imitation of several Greek distiches, published with a French translation of a Latin speech by Pierre de Paschal. In 1550 Baïf published a sonnet, "Gentil Ronsard, la mieillère mouche" (Gentle Ronsard, the Honey-Filled Fly), which appeared at the end of Ronsard's first book of love poetry, *Les Quatre Premiers Livres des Odes* (The First Four Books of Odes). Baïf's first work of significant scope and resonance was "Sur la paix avec les Anglois, l'an mil cinq cent quarante-neuf" (1572, On the Peace Treaty with the English), written in 1549. This poem is, however, considered a highly rhetorical but generally amateurish effort, revealing a young poet who has not yet assimilated his vast erudition. Baïf also contributed a variety of poetic pieces, including forty-six quatrains, an elegy, and a series of Greek distiches, to *Le Tombeau de Marguerite de Valois royne de Navarre* (The Poetic Memorial of Marguerite de Valois, Queen of Navarre), a collection of works on the queen's death published in 1551. Although these verses are judged mediocre by scholars, they proved popular and earned for Baïf some name recognition and popularity in literary circles. Three additional pieces round out his miscellaneous early works: a laudatory sonnet he wrote for du Bellay's translation *Le Quatriesme livre de l'Eneide de Vergile* (1552, The Fourth Book of Virgil's *Aeneid*), and two narrative poems, *Le Ravissement d'Europe* (1552, The Abduction of Europa) and *Le Meurier* (1572, The Mulberry Tree).

Baïf next published his first major works: two collections of Petrarchan sonnets and Epicurean lyric verses, *Les Amours* (1552, The Loves) and *L'Amour de Francine* (1555, The Love of Francine). Prior to publishing *Les Amours* in 1552, Baïf was at a turning point in his career and uncertain about which poetic genre to cultivate. In finally settling on love poetry, he was, like many of his contemporaries, consciously following poetic fashion and catering to the demands of a courtly audience passionately interested in hyperbolic, manner-

LES MIMES, ENSELGNEMENS ET PROVERBES DE IAN ANTOINE DE BAÏF.

A MONSEIGNEVR DE IOIEVSE DVC & Pair de France.

A PARIS, Par Mamert Patiſſon Imprimeur du Roy, chez Rob. Eſtienne.

M. D. LXXXI.

Auec priuilege.

Title page for Baïf's volume of poetry, in which he condemns the chaos created by the Religious Wars (Center for Research Libraries)

ist Petrarchan love lyrics. For his models, Baïf chose the Neo-Latin poets Michael Marullus and Joannes Secundus, the major Italian poets Petrarch, Ariosto, Pietro Bembo, and Jacopo Sannazzaro, and a variety of minor Italian poets published in the compilations of Gabriel Giolito de Ferrarii.

Les Amours, Baïf's *canzoniere,* or love-song book, is a substantial collection of poems that assured him a place of honor among the Pléiade poets. The work is divided into two books that describe the trials and tribulations of the disconsolate Petrarchan lover and the charms and cruelty of his almost goddess-like

feminine ideal. In Baïf's case, this archetypal poetic drama of adoration and rejection had no basis in fact. As Baïf himself freely admits in portions of *Les Amours,* Méline is the name of an imaginary mistress, and the love he expresses is counterfeit. The fiction allows him to try his hand at writing love poetry, following in the footsteps of many of his contemporaries, including Mellin de Saint-Gelais, Ronsard, du Bellay, and Belleau.

Baïf's early love lyrics generated more envy and criticism than accolades: "Mastin," a particularly unkind pedant, is known to have defamed the poet, finding fault with his choice of words. Baïf responded in kind, launching a vehement attack on Mastin, although this counteroffensive may have been more rhetorical than heartfelt. During this period Baïf's pride and temper did provoke a genuine falling out with Ronsard, but the two friends were reconciled by the time Baïf published his next major work.

In 1554 Baïf was eager to leave Paris and follow a friend, poet Jacques Tahureau, to Poitiers, where he met Françoise or Francine de Gennes. She became the object of Baïf's praise and affection in *Les Amours de Francine,* which comprises 4 books of love lyrics featuring 248 sonnets and 39 songs. Gennes belonged to a prominent family whose members had served in the judiciary and church hierarchy in Poitiers. As in the poems of Petrarch and his many imitators, the beloved's name leads to wordplay: Baïf exploits the family name "Gennes," a homonym of "gennes" ("gênes" in modern French), which in this case means "torture." Hence, as Baïf confesses to Francine, her family name is appropriate: "Rien que genne et tourment ton nom ne me promet" (Your name holds for me nothing but pain and torment).

Although Baïf was writing about a real person, Francine is cast in the mold of the cruel mistress of Petrarchan sonnets, and the pain and passion the poet expresses are no more than stylized variations of the conventional emotions of this poetic tradition:

Que sen-je dedans moy? quel mal dans moy commance?
Je suis en feu, je croy. Mais, mais ce feu comment
Peut-il estre la source (ô trop divers tourment!)
D'un tel fleuve de pleurs qui de mes yeux s'elance?

(What is going on inside me? What pain do I begin to feel?
I believe I am on fire, but how can it
Be the source—Oh most strange torment!—
Of such a river of tears that springs forth from my eyes?)

For Baïf, form and substance proved inseparable as he continued to draw his models from the sources preferred by the Pléiade poets: Greek, Roman, and

Neo-Latin poets, as well as Petrarch and his Italian imitators. The Italian influence is most evident in the sonnets of unrequited love. However, Baïf often made significant changes to the works that inspired him. He developed the themes and images of the original, sharpened the contrasts, introduced restatement or repetition, and made greater use of adjectives.

It was especially in matters of style and aesthetics that Baïf sought to achieve originality. His goal is evident in his extensive revisions of *Les Amours de Francine,* published in 1572–1573. These editions reveal the efforts of a perfectionist searching for a more euphonic alternation of sounds, greater precision and clarity of poetic language, more expressive variations in poetic rhythm, and more subtle stylistic devices. The two books of *chansons* (songs) that complete *Les Amours de Francine* owe less to Baïf's Italian models, and therefore fewer structural and thematic constraints are imposed on the poet. Consequently, Baïf was free to incorporate some of the more bawdy elements of the Gallic tradition. But in the final analysis, even the *chansons* are essentially Petrarchan and mannerist, demonstrating Baïf's fascination with stylistic ornamentation and elaborate figures of style and patterns of thought.

Meanwhile, the real-life Francine remained aloof when Baïf saw her again in 1560 and attempted to win her affections. He describes their last painful meeting in his *Diverses Amours* (Various Loves), published in volume 3 of *Euvres en rime* (1572, Works in Rhyme). In this work Baïf celebrates other mistresses (Marguerite, Catherine, Janneton, Victoire, and Madeleine) to whom he dedicated several love lyrics.

Despite the support he received from the influential Saint-Gelais, Baïf's love poetry did not bring him the fame and fortune for which he had hoped. He left Paris in 1556 and began to travel extensively. He had a long stay in the Sarthe region at the home of Jacques Morin, a member of the Parlement of Paris. While there Baïf translated Italian philosopher Giovanni Francesco Pico della Mirandola's *De Imitatione,* published as *Traitté de l'imagination* (1556, Treatise on Imagination). He spent the autumn and winter of 1562 in Trent, in northern Italy, with his friend Jean Griffin. Baïf was likely traveling in the entourage of the cardinal of Lorraine or with one of the French bishops representing France at the Council of Trent. He had planned to visit many Italian cities, but when his initial enthusiasm gave way to disillusionment, he cut short his travels and returned to Paris in 1563.

During this period Baïf, finding himself in financial straits, turned to the more lucrative pursuit of writing official or court poetry—intended either to sing the praises of a royal person, patron, or protector, or to celebrate an important public event—in the hope of gaining celebrity, benefices, honors, and material rewards. These celebratory and encomiastic pieces include a poem in honor of the birth of Henri Hurault, an epithalamium celebrating the marriage of François II and Mary Stuart, and several verses full of effusive flattery glorifying the duc d'Anjou and Catherine de Médicis. Baïf's efforts were rewarded, and his fortune changed. He enjoyed the favor at the court of the Valois monarchs, where he participated in the staging of dramatic performances. François II, Charles IX, and Henri III all granted him royal pensions. His appointment as "secrétaire de la Chambre du roi" (secretary of the king's chamber) by Charles IX enabled him to reside in Paris as a member of the king's official entourage. His finances and status were further enhanced because prior to 1543 his father had made him a "clerc à simple tonsure," or tonsured cleric, which meant Baïf was able to collect substantial ecclesiastical revenues from several church properties, including the parishes of Saint-André d'Hargeville in 1564, Saint-Cosme du Vair in 1565 and 1566, Saint-Germain de la Cadre in 1566, and Ormoy in 1567.

Baïf the court poet had not, however, lost interest in what may have been the first love of his youth—the theater. Before all the other members of the Pléiade, he had focused on drama and, according to a sonnet he addressed to Muret, he was already writing tragedies at the age of twenty. Baïf was, in fact, the member of the Pléiade who devoted the most time to dramatic writing or adaptation. He is thought to have translated into French Sophocles' *The Trachinies* (fifth century B.C.), Euripides' *Medea* (431 B.C.), and Terence's comedy *Heauton Timoroumenos* (produced 163 B.C.). However, none of these translations nor any original plays by Baïf have survived. His extant dramatic works include adaptations of Sophocles' tragedy *Antigone* (late fifth century B.C.), Terence's comedy *Eunuchus* (161 B.C., The Eunuch), and especially Plautus's *Miles Gloriosus* (late third–early second century B.C., The Braggart Soldier). Baïf published these works in volume three of *Euvres en rime,* titled *Les Jeux* (Plays), in 1573.

The adaptation of Plautus's comedy, titled *Le Brave* (published and produced 1567), is considered Baïf's best dramatic work, and it is the only one that was actually produced. The first performance, on 28 January 1567 before the royal court at the Hôtel de Guise, marks an important milestone in the history of French comic theater: for the first time the court was able to view a comedy of antiquity performed in French, and Baïf's work heralded the beginning of Plautus's influence in France. *Le Brave* is a play in five acts and in octosyllabic verse. It is a free adaptation of Plautus's comedy of intrigue centering around the character of Taillebras, the braggart soldier who boasts about his

CARMINVM
IANI ANTONII
BAIFII
LIBER I.

LVTETIAE,
Apud Mamertum Patissonium, in
officina Rob. Stephani.
M. D. LXXVII.

Title page for the volume mainly composed of Baïf's translations of Greek epigrams (Center for Research Libraries)

military and love conquests but in the end becomes the gullible victim of the flattery, machinations, and disguises of his wily servant Finet. In the final act, Taillebras is beaten by the other characters, and he loses the young woman he had carried off at the beginning of the play. Without changing the basic structure of the Roman comedy, Baïf succeeds in giving his adaptation a French flavor by setting the play at Orléans and creating distinctly French characters, particularly with Taillebras.

In 1567 Baïf published *Le Premier des Meteores* (The First Book of Meteors), a didactic work on astronomy, celestial phenomena, and atmospheric disturbances dedicated to the queen mother Catherine de Médicis. More fantasy than science, Baïf took the title as well as the subject and general outline from a work, *Meteororum liber* (1490), by the fifteenth-century Italian humanist and diplomat Giovanni Pontano. Baïf's book deals with the four elements of the universe (fire, air, water, and earth), the movements of the heavens, comets, the influence of the stars, and the changing of the seasons. It essentially describes igneous phenomena produced by the earth, and it was intended to be the first book of a larger work. However, civil war and a lack of public interest prevented Baïf from continuing this project.

Over the years Baïf's reputation at court grew as he continued to enjoy the favor of Henri III and Charles IX and the admiration of the intellectual and artistic elite of his generation. Henri III entrusted him with the task of encouraging and rewarding humanists, poets, writers, and musicians. Baïf's home in Paris became a favorite meeting place where concerts, banquets, and discussions were held. In 1570 Baïf, under the patronage of Charles IX and in collaboration with musician Thibaut de Courville, founded an Academy of Poetry and Music that was intended—in keeping with the ideas of the Pléiade—to promote a closer association of the arts. However, the academy was short-lived, ending in 1574 because of the censure of religious and academic authorities and the death of Charles IX. Later, Henri III, adding eloquence and philosophy to the disciplines governed by the academy, transformed it into the Académie du Palais.

In 1572–1573 Baïf published his *Euvres en rime,* a four-volume collection covering approximately twenty years of literary activity, including mythological, amorous, didactic, and pastoral poetry, the epigrams of the *Passetems* (Recreations), theater, and translations from Latin and Greek authors, especially the *Idylls* of Theocritus (circa 270 B.C.). This edition also features examples of one of Baïf's metrical inventions known as baïfin verse, composed of fifteen-syllable lines of feminine rhyming couplets designed to counter the constraints of alexandrine verse. The form was only rarely used by Baïf and had no success with his contemporaries.

In the years that followed, Baïf continued to produce some of his most original and inventive works, such as the *Etrénes de poézie fransoêze: An vers mezurés* (1574, Gifts of French Poetry: In Quantitative Verse). This work features Baïf's system of phonetic spelling, including his use of diacritical signs to represent palatalized consonants, and it also includes his attempts to reform French versification in imitation of Greek and Latin poetry, emphasizing vowel quantity in order to make the verse more compatible with song. During this period Baïf combined quantitative verse and song in his first two translations of the Psalms, his *Psautiers* (Psalters) of 1569 and 1573, published in part in a German edition of 1888, and in his *Chansonnettes mesurées* (1586, Little Songs in Quantitative Verse), which are set to music by Jacques Mauduit.

Baïf's *Les Mimes, Enseignemens et Proverbes,* composed between 1574 and 1587, is considered to be his most original and most important work. It is essentially a complex, multifaceted collection of gnomic and didactic verse, divided into four books, combining traditional lyrics with polemical and satirical pieces. The book includes discourses on religious corruption, virtue, human error, the misfortunes of the period, and the brevity of life, as well as voluminous compilations of adages, maxims, aphorisms, and fables. Scholars now view this collection as an imaginative work in progress, full of abrupt changes in subject, which has no preestablished plan or design.

The remarkable *Les Mimes* champions a type of patriotism founded on peace and tolerance and condemns the excesses and fanaticism of the Religious Wars, which Baïf saw as creating the chaos of a world turned upside down. Baïf develops this image using language reminiscent of Rabelaisian wordplay and fantasy:

> Au feu au feu, nostre puy brûle
>
> Nostre chien brait, nostre asne hûle:
>
> La charrue va devant les beufs,
>
> Les eaux reboursent aux fontaines:
>
> Lon casse les bestes à laines:
>
> Et maintenant lon tond les oeufs.

> (Fire! Fire! Our well is on fire
>
> Our dog is braying, our donkey is howling:
>
> The cart goes before the oxen,
>
> The waters flow backward in the fountains:
>
> We break wool-bearing animals:
>
> And now we shear eggs.)

In his final years, having had little success with either his traditional or his experimental verse, Baïf turned to Neo-Latin poetry. In 1577 he published his *Carminum* (Of Songs), which is, for the most part, a compilation of his translations of Greek epigrams. His third translation of the *Psaumes* in traditional verse, along with his *Prieres* (Prayers) and *Epitafes* (Epitaphs), typify the religious character of his late works. On 3 May 1587, the Jeux Floraux of Toulouse, a literary association and competition dating back to the Troubadours, honored Baïf as a fitting successor to Ronsard in light of his contribution to the enrichment of language and poetry. For his translation of the Psalms he was first awarded a golden Apollo, but because of a lack of funds he instead received a silver David. Yet, when he died from a chronic disease at the end of October 1589, Baïf was in serious financial difficulty. His passing went almost unnoticed in a period of grave national crisis.

Above all, Jean-Antoine de Baïf is regarded as an extremely learned and inventive poet who experimented with language, versification, and music. Most modern critics believe that his poetic and artistic talents were inferior to his great learning, but his poetry is often representative of the major aesthetic and thematic trends of the period, and some of his descriptive and satirical poetry is admired for its vividness and realism. In fact, late-twentieth-century critics such as Jean Vignes have praised his gnomic poetry as an expression of modernity and as an eloquent reflection of the poet's sense of helplessness in the face of a crumbling moral and political order.

References:

Mathieu Augé-Chiquit, *La Vie, les idées et l'œuvre de Jean-Antoine de Baïf* (Paris: Hachette / Toulouse: Privat, 1909; reprinted, Geneva: Slatkine, 1969);

Henri Chamard, *Histoire de la Pléiade,* 4 volumes (Paris: Didier, 1939–1940; reprinted, 1961–1963);

Guy Demerson, *La Mythologie classique dans l'œuvre lyrique de la Pléiade,* Travaux d'Humanisme et Renaissance, no. 119 (Geneva: Droz, 1972), pp. 174–182;

Edelgard DuBrock, "Jean-Antoine de Baïf, Poet of the Absurd," *L'Esprit Créateur,* 12 (1972): 193–204;

Brian Jeffery, *French Renaissance Comedy, 1552–1630* (Oxford: Clarendon Press, 1969);

Raymond Lebègue, *Le Théâtre comique en France de Pathelin à Mélite,* Connaisance des lettres, no. 62 (Paris: Hatier, 1972);

Ann Moss, *Poetry and Fable: Studies in Mythological Narrative in Sixteenth Century France,* Cambridge Studies in French (Cambridge: Cambridge University, 1984);

Marcel Raymond, *L'Influence de Ronsard sur la poésie française (1550–1585),* Bibliothèque littéraire de la renaissance, nos. 14–15 (Paris: Champion, 1927; revised and enlarged edition, Geneva: Droz, 1965);

Albert-Marie Schmidt, *La Poésie scientifique en France au XVIe siècle: Ronsard–Maurice Scève–Baïf–Belleau–Du Bartas–Agrippa d'Aubigné* (Paris: Michel, 1938; reprinted, Paris: Rencontre, 1970);

Jean Vignes, *Des mots dorés pour un siècle de fer—Les Mimes, Enseigemens et Proverbes de Jean-Antoine de Baïf: Texte, contexte, intertexte,* Bibliothèque littéraire de la renaissance, no. 37 (Paris: Champion, 1997);

W. L. Wiley, "Antoine de Baïf and the Ovidian Love Tale," *Studies in Philology,* 33 (1936): 45–54.

François Béroalde de Verville

(1556 – 1626)

Barbara C. Bowen
Vanderbilt University

BOOKS: *Theatrum instrumentorum et machinarum,* by Jacques Besson and Béroalde (Lyon: Barthélemy Vincent, 1578); translated as *Theatre des instrumens mathematiques & mechaniques de Iaques Besson dauphinois, docte mathematicien: avec l'interpretation des figures díceluy par François Beroald* (Lyon: Vincent, 1578);

Les Apprehensions spirituelles, poemes, et autres oeuures philosophiques: avec les Recherches de la pierre philosophale (Paris: T. Jouan, 1583);

Les Souspirs amoureux (Paris: T. Jouan, 1583);

La Muse celeste (Tours: J. Mettayer, 1583);

Dialogue de la vertu (Paris: T. Jouan, 1584);

L'Idée de la republique (Paris: T. Jouan, 1584);

Les Avantures de Floride, Histoire Françoise, En laquelle on peut voir les differens euenements d'Amour, de Fortune & d'Honneur, & combien sont en fin agreables les fruicts de la VERTV (Tours: J. Mettayer, 1592);

De la sagesse, livre premier (Tours: J. Mettayer, 1593);

Seconde partie des Avantures de Floride (Tours: J. Mettayer, 1594);

Troisieme partie des Avantures de Floride (Tours: J. Mettayer, 1594);

Quatriesme partie des Avantures de Floride (Rouen: T. Reinsart, 1596);

Le Cabinet de Minerve (Paris: S. Molin, 1596);

Le Restablissement de Troye (Tours: S. Molin, 1597);

La Pucelle d'Orleans restituee par Beroalde de Verville. Sous le sujet de cette magnanime Pucelle est representée une FILLE vaillante, chaste, sçauante et BELLE (Paris: M. Guillemot, 1599);

Les Tenebres (Paris: M. Guillemot, 1599);

L'Histoire des vers qui filent la soye, des vers qui filent la soy, de leur naturel et gouvernement (Tours: M. Sifleau, 1600);

L'Histoire d'Herodias (Tours: S. Molin, 1600);

L'Histoire veritable, ou Le voyage des princes fortunez (Paris: P. Chevalier, 1610);

Le Palais des curieux. Auquel sont assemblées plusieurs diuersitez pour le plaisir des doctes, & le bien de ceux qui desirent sçauoir (Paris: Veuve M. Guillemot and S. Thibouts, 1612);

Le Moyen de parvenir (N.p., circa 1615–1650); translated by Arthur Machen as *Fantastic Tales, or, the Way to Attain: a Book Full of Pantagruelism Now for the First Time Done in English* (London?: Carbonnek, 1890); translated by Oliver Stonor as *The Way to Succeed: a Work Containing the Reason of All That Was, Is and Shall Be, with Sundry Necessary Evidences and Proofs that Virtue Is Its Own Reward . . .* (London: Hesperides Press, 1930).

Editions: *Le Moyen de parvenir,* edited by Charles Royer (Paris: Lemerre, 1896);

Anthologie poétique de Béroalde de Verville, edited by V. L. Saulnier (Paris: Jacques Haumont, 1945);

Le Moyen de parvenir, edited by H. Moreau and A. Tournon (Aix-en-Provence: Université de Provence, 1984);

Le Moyen de parvenir, edited by I. Zinguer (Nice, 1985);

L'Histoire des vers qui filent la soye, edited by Michel Renaud (Paris: Champion, 2001);

Le Palais des curieux, edited by Véronique Luzel (Geneva: Droz, 2004).

TRANSLATION: Francesco Colonna, *Le Tableau des riches inventions couvertes du voile des feintes amoureuses qui sont représentées dans le Songe de Poliphile* (Paris: M. Guillemot, 1600).

François Béroalde de Verville was one of the most prolific, versatile, and enigmatic authors of his time. He was apparently equally at home composing in prose or verse, or writing fiction, philosophy, or science. He was interested in art and architecture, medicine, the legends of Troy and of Joan of Arc, mathematical instruments, the cultivation of silkworms, and, perhaps especially, alchemy. As Neil Kenny discusses in *The Palace of Secrets: Béroalde de Verville and Renaissance Conceptions of Knowledge* (1991), he is considered an important representative of changing intellectual attitudes toward encyclopedic knowledge at the end of the sixteenth century.

Little is known about Béroalde de Verville's life. He was born in Paris in 1556, the son of Matthieu Béroalde or Bérouart, a well-known Calvinist minister and philosophy professor. He was educated in Geneva. At some point he converted to Catholicism. In 1589 he moved to Tours, where in 1593 he became canon of Saint-Gatien.

What is certain is that Béroalde's publications were many and varied. The first work he was associated with was one of his most popular, an enlarged edition of Jacques Besson's book describing his inventions, which had been originally published as *Instrumentorum et machinarum . . . liber primus* (circa 1571, Instruments and Machines . . . the first book) with only brief captions for its sixty illustrations. Béroalde provided more-detailed descriptions of the machines and instruments when Besson's work was published in Lyon with the title changed to *Theatrum instrumentorum et machinarum . . .* (1578, Theater of Mathematical and Mechanical Instruments . . .). This version of the work was frequently reprinted in the late sixteenth and early seventeenth centuries and translated into Italian (1582), German (1596), and Spanish (1602).

Béroalde's dedication to a prospective patron in his next publication, *Les Apprehensions spirituelles* (1583, Spiritual Understandings), appropriately emphasizes the diversity of the work. The long treatise of the title uses a dream as a narrative frame and features a philosophical mentor called Minerve, a "Palais des Muses" (Palace of the Muses), and much discussion of philosophical and alchemical topics. The work includes two other treatises–"Du bien de la mort commune" (Universal Death as a Good), on ethics, and "Recherches de la pierre philosophale" (Research on the Philosopher's Stone), on alchemy–as well as two long poems and two dialogues: "Les Cognoissances necessaires" (Necessary Knowledge), a poem on the creation of the world that is based on poems by Maurice Scève and Guillaume du Bartas; "De l'ame et de ses facultés" (On the Soul and Its Faculties); "Dialogue de l'honneste amour" (Dialogue on Honorable Love); and the "Dialogue de la bonne grace" (Dialogue on Good Grace).

Béroalde published three more works in the first half of the 1580s. *Les Souspirs amoureux* (The Loving Sighs), a typically baroque anthology of love poems including sonnets, odes, elegies, and a variety of other poetic forms, was published separately in 1583 and reprinted the following year with *Les Apprehensions spirituelles*. Also in 1584 appeared *L'Idée de la republique* (The Idea of the Republic), an epic poem on the ideal state that was influenced by Thomas More's *Utopia* (1518), and *Dialogue de la vertu* (Dialogue on Virtue), a conversation about ethics among ladies and gentlemen compelled to stay indoors because of bad weather.

In the 1590s Béroalde published more–and more varied–works. The first part of *Les Avantures de Floride, Histoire Françoise, En laquelle on peut voir les differens euenemens d'Amour, de Fortune & d'Honneur, & combien sont en fin agreables les fruicts de la VERTV* (The Adventures of Floride, A French Story, in which one can see the different events of Love, of Fortune and of Honor, and how agreeable finally are the fruits of VIRTUE) was printed in 1592 and was followed by a second and third part in 1594 and a fourth in 1596. Floride is the heroine, and the main plot concerns her love for the hero Faramond and the tribulations they endure before achieving a happy ending. There are several dozen minor characters, including other amorous or antagonistic couples, jousting knights, nymphs and shepherds, several magicians, a hermit, the King and Queen, and a learned Fairy. An important secondary character is Minerve, a wisdom figure with a room full of curious and interesting objects and a beautiful garden, who sometimes comments on the action and sometimes becomes part of it; in one of the continuations she marries the knight Barlion. Despite duels, jousts, weddings, a storm at sea, the exploration of mysterious forests and caves, and the use of magic, the pace is slow as narrative alternates with dialogue and with quantities of verse.

Béroalde's concerns and interests are evident in *Les Avantures de Floride* through his emphasis on virtue, which is rewarded in the end after many trials; his descriptions of tapestries, gardens, palaces, and houses, which often have "singularitez" (oddities); and his references to science (Minerve's inventions), magic, and alchemy. In his "Frontispice," or preface, to the *Seconde partie* (Second Part) Béroalde pontificates about the books women ought to read and claims that it would be a good thing if women were "sçauantes" (learned), suggesting that he has a largely female audience in mind. Though little to the taste of modern readers (no critic discusses it in detail), *Les Avantures de Floride* is typical of both Béroalde and his time. It combines fiction of a traditional kind with a rambling discussion of scientific, ethical, and intellectual topics, and thus like many contemporary works, including François Rabelais's *Quart Livre* (1548, Fourth Book), belongs to a genre critics call *philosophical fiction* (an earlier term was *miscellany*).

Other works Béroalde published in the 1590s give further evidence of his intellectual interests. He continues his writings on ethics in *De la sagesse, livre premier* (1593, On Wisdom, First Book), which features a palace of wisdom peopled by allegorical figures. In *Les Tenebres* (1599, Darkness) he provided a verse paraphrase of the lamentations of Jeremiah. In 1599 he also published an extraordinary romanticization of the story of Joan of Arc: *La Pucelle d'Orleans restituee par Beroalde de*

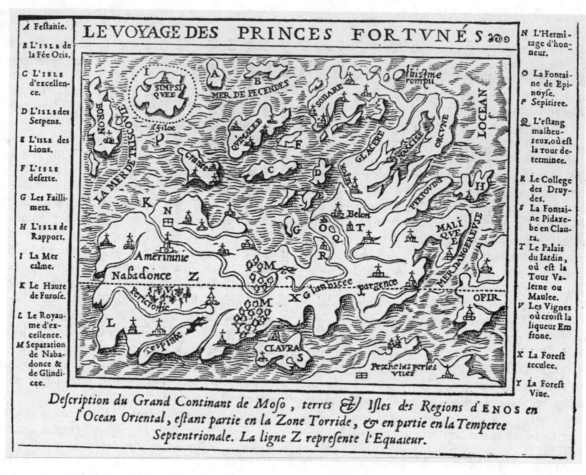

Illustration for François Béroalde de Verville's L'Histoire veritable, ou Le voyage des princes fortunez (1610), *in which a king banishes his sons in order to test their wisdom* (*from Neil Kenny,* The Palace of Secrets: Béroalde de Verville and Renaissance Conceptions of Knowledge, *1991; Thomas Cooper Library, University of South Carolina*)

Verville. *Sous le sujet de cette magnanime Pucelle est representée une FILLE vaillante, chaste, sçauante et BELLE* (The Maid of Orleans restored by Béroalde de Verville. Under the topic of this magnanimous Maid is represented a Girl valiant, chaste, learned and BEAUTIFUL). He presents Joan as having had a knight for a father and a mythical origin–according to Béroalde, she was born on an island called Sympsiquée where an ideal society flourished. Joan's story is interrupted by secondary narratives, flashbacks, and detours into sixteenth-century history; some episodes take place in caverns and in minutely described buildings. Similarities in plot and tone recall the earlier *Les Avantures de Floride*.

A quite different book of these years is *Le Cabinet de Minerve* (The Cabinet of Minerva), the full title of which continues: *Auquel sont plusieurs Singularités. Figures. Tableaux. Antiques. Recherches saintes. Remarques serieuses. Observations amoureuses. Subtilités agreables. Rencontres joyeuses & quelques histoires meslees és auantures de la Sage Fenisse patron du DEVOIR* (1596, in which are numerous Singularities. Figures. Paintings. Antiques. Holy Relics. Seri-

ous Remarks. Loving Observations. Agreeable Subtleties. Cheerful Meetings, and some stories mixed with the adventures of the Wise Fenisse patron of DUTY). As well as Minerve, the book references other protagonists of *Les Avantures de Floride*–including Floride and her son, Cléandre; Isquee; and Yolande–so that it was sometimes assumed to be a continuation of *Floride*. The work is an eccentric mixture of romantic narrative, philosophy, and artistic and architectural description; more than a third of it is comprised of extracts from *Les Apprehensions spirituelles*.

The book is made up of seventeen *rencontres* (encounters), all ostensibly taking place in rooms of the "cabinet" (library) in the garden of Minerve's palace. "Le Curieux" (The Curious Man) and "L'Esprit de contradiction" (The Spirit of Contradiction) are among Minerve's mainly anonymous guests. Each *rencontre* has detailed descriptions of art and/or architecture, including a crucifix (II), a marble Pietà (IV), a remarkable fountain (VIII), a picture of a fool (XV), and a picture of Death (XVI); most also relate philosophical discussion on a variety of subjects: Creation; the composition of the sun (hollow, with a *liqueur* inside which lights it up); the androgyne; the causes of yawning; the nature of salt; the senses; the salamander; whether a vacuum can exist; definitions of love, honor, and beauty; and the analogies between birth and death. There are also many alchemical references and allusions. The architectural descriptions are reminiscent of Francesco Colonna's *Hypnerotomachia* (1499, Strife of Love in a Dream) as well as of previous works by Béroalde, and the book as a whole could be considered one of the *cabinets de curiosité* (curiosity cabinets) so popular in Europe around this time; it can also be viewed as an encyclopedia and as a memory treatise.

The general tone of the work is serious—*vertu* rules in Minerve's house—but there are lighthearted moments. Recontre IV includes a debate in which it is considered whether laughter is the highest pleasure and if it must be combined with thought to be pleasurable. An interest in linguistic correctness and definitions, as when tears are referred to as "les doux-coulans têmoignages de déplaisir" (the sweetly-flowing witnesses of unhappiness), foreshadows the era of the seventeenth-century *Précieuses*. To modern readers *Le Cabinet de Minerve* is a considerably more lively work than *Les Avantures de Floride*.

Béroalde was part of the ongoing campaign to revitalize the silk industry in France, especially in Touraine. Published in 1600, *L'Histoire des vers qui filent la soye* (The Story of Silkworms), sometimes referred to as the *Sérodokimasie,* is a treatise in verse form, comprising three hundred quatrains, and roughly based on Marco-Girolamo Vida's enormously popular *Bombyx,* a Latin-verse work that had more than thirty sixteenth-century editions, including fourteen published in Lyon. Both works treat the origins and history of silk; the habits of silkworms and the cultivation of the mulberry bushes that are their habitat; the techniques of spinning and weaving; and strategies for commercialization. Béroalde, however, replaces Vida's pervasive Classical mythology with Hebrew and Christian references (for instance, the originator of the silk industry is no longer Pamphile but Moses) and employs frequent changes in style.

A more influential work also published in 1600, *Le Tableau des riches inventions couvertes du voile des feintes amoureuses qui sont représentées dans le Songe de Poliphile* (Table of the Rich Inventions disguised under the Veil of Amorous Feigning, which are represented in the Dream of Poliphile) is Béroalde's translation of Colonna's *Hypnerotomachia.* While Béroalde in many respects follows closely a French translation made in 1546, he sometimes significantly modifies characterization or tone. Most importantly, he develops the sugges-

tion, made earlier by author/translator Jacques Gohory, that Colonna's work is an allegory of what alchemists call the Great Work—the attempt to speed up the natural process of perfection, in particular the transformation of base metals into gold. Béroalde's approach is made clear in the preliminary "Recueil Steganographique, contenant l'intelligence du frontispice de ce livre" (Steganographic Collection, containing the explanation of the frontispiece of this book), in which he attributes alchemical significance to every motif of the illustrated title page: Chaos, eagle, cornucopia, myrtle leaves, flames, fountain of youth, and so on.

Béroalde's three last works have been of most interest to modern readers and critics. In 1610 he published *L'Histoire veritable, ou Le voyage des princes fortunez* (The True History, or the Voyage of the Fortunate Princes); the first part of this title recalls Lucian's *The True History,* the common title for his parody of voyage literature in which he describes among many marvels a visit to the moon, but Béroalde uses the voyage as a metaphor for a dynamic quest for knowledge and wisdom. The book, another philosophical fiction, is an adaptation of a popular Italian work, *Peregrinaggio de tre figluoli del re di serendippo* (1557, Pilgrimage of Three Sons of the King of Serendip), itself based on several oriental sources. The three major quests in the book are the journey of the princes whose father, feigning anger, has sent them into exile in order to test their wisdom; the search for the nymph Xyrile by a group of travelers simply called "nous" (we/us); and the Emperor's search for his lost beloved, Etherine. The princes' diversion-filled voyage is circular; the islands they visit—one of which is Sympsiquée, described in *La Pucelle d'Orleans*—may remind the reader of Rabelais's *Quart Livre,* while the frequent detailed description of buildings recalls both Colonna's work and *Le Cabinet de Minerve.*

All three quests end at the "Hermitage d'honneur" (Hermitage of Honor), where the main characters achieve either love or wisdom or both. The Hermitage complex contains seven palaces of the planets, and a "Palais des secrets" (Palace of Secrets) or "Palais de Curiosité" (Palace of Curiosity). Once again there is ample illustration of Béroalde's interest in art, architecture, science, medicine, and alchemy. There are references to previous works by Béroalde, and at one point a character named Verville and his love Mélisse appear before the Emperor. Because its plot is extremely convoluted and the style often even more so, *L'Histoire veritable* is more a work for the scholar than for general readers.

Le Palais des curieux. Auquel sont assemblées plusieurs diuersitez pour le plaisir des doctes, & le bien de ceux qui desirent sçauoir (1612, The Palace of Curious People, in which are assembled numerous diversities for the pleasure of learned people and the profit of those who desire to know) is a more accessible work than *L'Histoire veritable*, largely because it has no narrative framework and consists of eighty short chapters, each identified as an "Obiect" (Object), on a wide variety of subjects in language, science, mathematics, and medicine. Béroalde, who frequently quotes his previous works, presents himself in Obiect 21 as "curieux sectateur de la bonne & iuste curiosité" (a curious member of the sect of good and just curiosity). His discussions are both general—the use of language, musical harmony, time, knowledge in general—and particular, treating such topics as cooked fish (Obiect 9), the beans in the "Cake of the Kings"' baked for Epiphany (Obiect 14), the Salic Law (Obiect 45), the pelican (Obiect 55), the vacuum (Obiect 57), and the herb sage (Obiect 72). Some chapters jump from one subject to another in disconcerting fashion: Obiect 27 is about scientific principles, darkness, odors, and wax.

Sometimes Béroalde asks questions—Why do babies cry when they are born? (Obiect 79)—but usually he simply expresses his own opinion or states contrasting views on the topic or topics in question. He sometimes provides autobiographical asides in a fashion not unlike Michel de Montaigne in his *Essais* (Essays, 1580); for instance, in Obiect 20 he writes, "Qvand ie trouve suiect pour discourir ou disputer ioyeusement, ie le prends, ie m'y attache, & comme si c'estoit iournee à faire ie le retiens à tasche, & m'est aduis que ce faisant ie sauoure ma vie" (When I find a subject [on which] to discourse or dispute joyfully, I take it, I attach myself to it and as if it were a day's work to be done I hold on to it, and it seems to me that thus doing I savor my life). While Béroalde's intellectual preoccupations have not changed since his early publications—Obiect 41 treats alchemy—he seems to have shifted his interest to a degree from physical objects to be described to the language used to talk about them and from a focus on serious encyclopedic instruction to "joyful" intellectual exploration.

The most famous work attributed to Béroalde, *Le Moyen de parvenir* (The Way to Success), was published anonymously, probably between 1615 and 1650. His authorship of the work has not been conclusively proven; it has also been attributed to Rabelais, to T. A. d'Aubigné, and to Henri Estienne. If Béroalde is indeed the author, *Le Moyen de parvenir* is his only work that has been consistently in print from his time to the present.

The extended title of *Le Moyen de parvenir*, Béroalde's longest, continues with a French description: *Oeuvre contenant la raison de tout ce qui a été, est et sera; avec démonstrations certaines et nécessaires, selon la rencontre des effets de VERTU. Et adviendra que ceux qui auront nez à porter lunettes s'en serviront ainsi qu'il est écrit au Dictionnaire à dormir en toutes langues. S.* (Work containing the reason of everything that has been, is and will be; with certain and necessary demonstrations, according to the occurrence of the effects of VIRTUE. And it will happen that those who have noses suitable for wearing glasses will use it as it is written in the Dictionary of sleep in all languages. S.); it is followed by three short phrases in Latin: *Recensuit sapiens ab A. ad Z. Nunc ipsa vocat res. Hac iter est.* (Revised from A to Z by a Wise Man. Now the matter itself summons. This is the way.). These enigmatic words are followed by a reference to Virgil's *Aeneid*, IX. 320.

The first few chapters of this extremely puzzling work set the tone for the whole, being written in the style usually called in French *Coq-à-l'âne*, meaning that the writer jumps about from subject to subject with no logical connection between them. The whole work is apparently some kind of symposium—in which there are a total of 386 discussants instead of the more usual nine—taking place in the house of a certain Madame, never named, who may be Minerve. (In the *Cabinet de Minerve* the title character was referred to as "Madame.") The characters, most of whom are mentioned only once, range from the well known of all historical periods (Socrates, Alexander, Caligula, Savonarola, Rabelais) to characters from previous works by Béroalde (Béroalde, Poliphile, La Pucelle d'Orleans) to characters with made-up names (Le Bon Homme [The Good Man], La Bonne Intention [The Good Intention], Coquefredouille, Cestuici [this one], Chose [thing]). The characters argue, tell stories, and make pronouncements in 111 chapters whose bizarre titles, such as "Mappe-monde" (Map of the World), "Coyonnerie" (Foolishness), and "Calendrier" (Calendar), have nothing to do with their content. Possible sources for the work include Lucian's *Dialogues of the Dead*, Petronius's *Satyricon*, the medieval *Turba philosophorum*, and the works of Rabelais.

Béroalde's highly individual style, marked by constant punning and wordplay, make his work difficult to translate. Nevertheless, the book has been twice translated into English—as *Fantastic Tales, or, the Way to Attain: a Book Full of Pantagruelism Now for the First Time Done in English* (1890) and as *The Way to Succeed: a Work Containing the Reason of All That Was, Is and Shall Be, with Sundry Necessary Evidences and Proofs that Virtue Is Its Own Reward . . .* (1930)—as well as into German (1914), Italian (1989), and Japanese (1988). Critics are sometimes tempted to take phrases out of context and assume that they are important, as when Diogenes says "On doit faire et dire ici tout ce qu'on peut et pense" (one must do and say everything one can and thinks) in the chapter titled "Allegation." In the chapter "Consistoire," Béroalde writes, "les paroles ne sont point sales, il n'y a que l'intelligence" (words are not dirty, only the way they are understood), but he then goes on to discuss specific dirty words at length, as the historical Cicero would not have done.

While critics do not agree on the fundamental purpose of *Le Moyen de parvenir,* Béroalde clearly intends to make fun of the reader's expectations about a book and its structure: the first chapter is "Question I" (there never is a question 2); chapter 11 is titled "'Final Pause" and begins "Now let's begin to conclude"; chapter 13 is "Conclusion"; while in the last chapter, titled "Argument," he writes: "Et afin que je puisse un jour commencer ce volume . . ." (And so that one day I may begin this volume . . .). In chapter 10 he ridicules the cherished humanist distinction between text and gloss (humanists were proud of restoring original ancient texts while rejecting the glosses of medieval commentators). The metaphors used in the text to describe the book are constantly changing, for at different times the book is described as a breviary, a glass, a mold, a globe of infinite doctrine, a monument, and an anamorphosis. From time to time a character makes a pronouncement about the book: chapter 12, "CE LIVRE EST LE CENTRE DE TOUS LES LIVRES" (This Book Is the Center of All Books); chapter 13, "tous les livres qui furent jamais faits, ou seront faits, . . . sont signes ou marques ou paraphrases ou prédictions de cettui-ci" (all the books which were ever made, or will be made, . . . are signs, or marks, or paraphrases, or predictions of this one); chapter 44, "tout ce qui est dit ailleurs est pris d'ici" (everything which is said elsewhere is taken from here).

From the title *Le Moyen de parvenir,* the reader might expect one of the how-to manuals that were popular in the Renaissance. The phrase "le moyen de parvenir" occurs in several other works by Béroalde; for example, Obiect 61 in *Le Palais des curieux* is about, among other things, "aduis touchant le moyen de paruenir" (an opinion about the way to succeed). Béroalde does not explain what his title means, except facetiously: in chapter 34 he writes, "Le moyen de parvenir comprend tout, et est composé des quatres éléments de piperie, avec leur quinte essence" (the way to succeed includes everything, and is composed of the four elements of deception with their quintessence); in chapter 105 he gives unassailable advice, "Le principal mot du guet du MOYEN DE PARVENIR est d'avoir de l'argent" (the main watchword of the WAY TO SUCCEED is to have money).

No narrative action takes place in *Le Moyen de parvenir,* which is written mainly in the form of a dialogue. Béroalde seems to assign speeches to characters more or less at random, and it is rare for Aristotle, Erasmus, or any other historical character to make a remark that could reasonably be ascribed to him (or occasionally, her). The debates and sto-

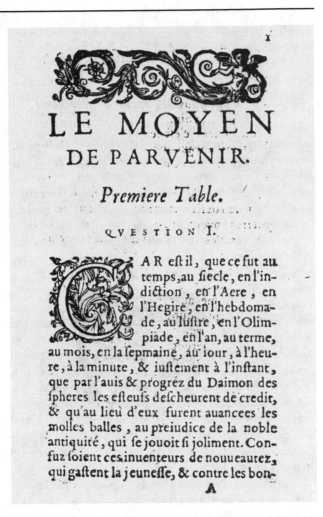

First page of what is believed to be the first edition of Béroalde de Verville's most popular work. It has been translated twice into English as well as into German, Italian, and Japanese (from Michael J. Giordano, ed., Studies on Béroalde de Verville, *1992; Thomas Cooper Library, University of South Carolina).*

ries often deal with scatological or sexual topics—which accounts in large part for the enduring popularity of the book. Some critics in nineteenth-century French strongly disapproved of Béroalde's emphasis, but modern readers usually find his anecdotes delightfully comic. Curiously, scabrous stories—a prostitute who pretends to be breaking wind in bed while actually breaking vials of perfume; an encounter between a penis and a rat-trap—are less common than the discussions about the correct terms, and the most effective metaphors, for sexual organs and for the sexual act. There are also frequent plays on words not readily perceptible in translation; a French reader will at once grasp the comedy in French or Latin words incorporating the syllable *con* (cunt) or *cu* (bottom). For most of its history, the lighthearted, frequently obscene comedy of *Le Moyen de parvenir* has been regarded as its raison d'être.

Modern critical opinion of *Le Moyen de parvenir* can be divided into two camps, with the first camp arguing that the main subject of the book is language. Many chapters include linguistic debate of some kind: the significant fact that *garce* (girl, with pejorative overtones) is an anagram of *grace* (in "Journal"); whether dirty words should be allowed at a banquet ("Sermon VI"); and whether words can be clear, like water ("Commitimus"). Other topics include whether a book has authority; the relationship between the book and the banquet or between reading and eating; whether there is, as Renaissance humanists usually claimed, a fundamental difference between a text and its gloss or commentary; whether the impression left by the book is basically negative (no authority can be trusted and there is no way to succeed) or positive (the spoken word is endlessly creative and fruitful). In the second camp are several critics who take seriously the many references in the text to alchemy and the philosopher's stone. Béroalde knew a great deal about alchemy, wrote a short treatise on it, and inserted references to or discussions of the topic into his previous works. Some critics have read the *Voyage des princes fortunez* as an allegory of alchemical procedure, while the debate continues over whether, in the *Moyen de parvenir*, Béroalde is being sarcastic about alchemy or making a claim for its validity.

Béroalde's publications, even without *Le Moyen de parvenir*, resist any kind of simple analysis. His most basic theme is the quest: for spiritual growth, enduring love, scientific knowledge, religious certainty—or the revival of the French silk industry; but it is possible to see the *Moyen de parvenir* as making fun of the whole concept of quest. Other recurring themes include alchemy (the quest for the philosopher's stone), the wisewoman Minerve, and intellectual curiosity about every aspect of the world. But it is unclear whether Béroalde's work is symptomatic of a gradually lessening confidence, in the course of the sixteenth century, in the possibility of achieving encyclopedic knowledge, or whether he is simply having fun with the various possible ways of talking about knowledge. The only certainty is that François Béroalde de Verville remains one of the most baffling and intriguing authors of the French Renaissance.

References:

Stephen Bamforth, "Béroalde de Verville and the Question of Scientific Poetry," *Renaissance and Modern Studies,* 23 (1979): 104–127;

Béroalde de Verville 1556–1626 (Paris: Ecole Normale Supérieure, 1996);

Barbara C. Bowen, "Béroalde de Verville and the Self-Destructing Book," in *Essays in Early French Literature Presented to Barbara M. Craig,* edited by Norris J. Lacy and Jerry C. Nash (York, S.C.: French Literature Publications, 1982), pp. 163–177;

Bowen, "'Il faut donner dedans': Sexe ou/et rhétori que dans le *Moyen de Parvenir*," in *A French Forum: Mélanges de littérature française offerts à Raymond C. et Virginie A. La Charité,* edited by Gérard Defaux and Nash (Paris: Klincksieck, 2000), pp. 107–114;

Michael J. Giordano, "Reverse Transmutations: Béroalde de Verville's Parody of Paracelsus in *Le Moyen de Parvenir:* An Alchemical Language of Skepticism in the French Baroque," *Renaissance Quarterly,* 56 (2003): 88–137;

Giordano, ed., *Studies on Béroalde de Verville* (Paris: Biblio 17, 1992);

Michel Jeanneret, *Des mets et des mots: Banquets et propos detable à la Renaissance* (Paris: Corti, 1987), pp. 221–246;

Neil Kenny, *The Palace of Secrets: Béroalde de Verville and Renaissance Conceptions of Knowledge* (Oxford: Clarendon Press, 1991);

Lenita Locey, Michael Locey, and Janis L. Pallister, "The Last Days of Béroalde de Verville," *Symposium,* 41 (1987): 42–66;

Michel Renaud, *Pour une lecture du* Moyen de parvenir *de Béroalde de Verville,* revised edition (Paris: Champion, 1997);

André Tournon, "La parodie de l'ésotérisme dans *Le Moyen de parvenir* de Béroalde de Verville," in *Burlesque et formes parodiques dans la littérature et les arts,* edited by Isabelle Landy-Houillon and Maurice Ménard (Seattle: Papers on Seventeenth Century French Literature, 1987).

Théodore de Bèze
(Theodore Beza)
(24 June 1519 – 13 October 1605)

Scott M. Manetsch
Trinity Evangelical Divinity School

BOOKS: *Poemata* (Paris: Printed by Conrad Badius, 1548); revised as *Theodori Bezæ Vezelii Poematum, Editio secunda* (Geneva: Printed by Henri Estienne, 1569); revised again as *Theod: Bezae Poemata* (Geneva: Printed by Henri Estienne, 1576); revised again as *Theodori Bezae Vezelii Poëmata varia* (Geneva: Printed by Henri Estienne, 1597);

Brevis et utilis Zographia Ioannis Cochleæ (Basel: Printed by Johann Oporin, 1549);

Abraham sacrifiant (Geneva: Printed by Conrad Badius, 1550); translated by Arthur Golding as *A Tragedie of Abrahams Sacrifice* (London: Printed by Thomas Vautroullier, 1577);

Epistola magistri Benedicti Passavantii Responsiua ad commissionem sibi datam à venerabili D. Petro Lyseto, nuper Curiæ Parisiensis præsidente: nunc verò Abbate sancti Victoris, prope muros (N.p., 1553);

Response a la confession du feu duc Iean de Northumbelande, n'agueres decapité en Angleterre (Geneva: Printed by Jean Gérard, 1554);

Alphabetum Græaecum (Geneva: Printed by Robert Estienne, 1554);

De Haereticis a civili magistratu puniendis Libellus, aduersus Martini Bellii farraginem, & nouorum Academicorum sectam (Geneva: Printed by Robert Estienne, 1554); translated into French by Nicolas Colladon as *Traitte de l'avthorite du magistrat en la pvnition des heretiques, & du moyen d'y proceder* (Geneva: Printed by Conrad Badius, 1560);

Summa totius Christianismi, sive descriptio et distributio causarum salutis electorum et exitii reprobatorum ex sacris literis collecta (N.p., 1555); translated as *A Briefe Declaracion of the Chiefe Poyntes of Christian Religion, Set Forth in a Table of Predestination* (Geneva: Printed by John Rivery, 1556); translated into French as *Brefve Exposition de la table ou figure contenant les principaus poincts de la religion Chrestienne* (Geneva: Printed by Jean Rivery, 1560);

Théodore de Bèze (Harlingue/Roger-Viollet/Getty Images)

Novum domini nostri Jesu Christi Testamentum . . . a Theodoro Beza versum (Geneva: Printed by Robert Estienne, 1556); revised as *Jesu Christi D. M. Novum Testamentum . . .* (Geneva: Printed by Henri Estienne, 1565); revised again as *Jesu Christi D. N. Novum Testamentum* (Geneva: Printed by Henri Estienne, 1582); revised again as *Jesu Christi domini nostri Novum Testamentum . . . eusdem Th. Beza Annotationes* (Geneva: Printed by J. des Planches, 1598);

Ad sycophantarum quorundam calumnias, quibus unicum salutis nostræ fundamentum, id est æternam Dei Praedestinationem evertere nituntur responsio (Geneva: Printed by Conrad Badius, 1558); translated into French by Conrad Badius in *Response de Jehan Calvin, et Theodore de Besze, aux calomnies & argumens d'un qui s'efforce par tous moyens de renverser la doctrine de la prouidence secrete de Dieu* (Geneva: Printed by Conrad Badius, 1559); translated by William Hopkinson as *An Evident Display of Popish Practices, or Patched Pelagianisme* (London: Printed by Ralph Newberie & Henry Bynnyman, 1578);

De Cœna Domini, plana et perspicua tractatio in qua Joachimi Wesphali calumniæ postremium editæ refelluntur (Geneva: Printed by Robert Estienne, 1559);

Confession de la foy chrestienne, . . . contenant la confirmation d'icelle, & la refutation des superstitions contraires (Geneva: Printed by Conrad Badius, 1559); translated by Robert Fylls as *A Briefe and Pithie Summe of the Christian Faith Made in Forme of a Confession, with a Confutation of All Suche Superstitious Errours, as Are Contrary Thereunto* (London: Printed by Rouland Hall, 1563);

ΚΡΕΩΦΑΓΙΑ sive Cyclops. ΟΝΟΣ ΣΥΛΛΟΓΙΖΟΜΕΝΟΣ sive Sophista. Dialogi duo de vera communicatione corporis & sanguinis Domini, adversus Tilemanni Heshusii somnia (Geneva: Printed by Conrad Badius, 1561); translated into French by Louis des Masures in *Vraye et Droite Intelligence de ces paroles de la Saincte Cene de Jesus Christ, Cecy est mon corps, &c.* (Lyon: Printed by Ian d'Ogerolles, 1564);

Ce qui a este propose par Theodore de Beze au nom de tous ceux qui desirent la reformation de l'Englishe selon la pure doctrine de l'Evangile, en la presence du Roy, de la Royne sa mere, du Roy de Navarre, & des autres Princes, de Messieurs du Conseil, & des Prelats qu'on dit d'Englise (Geneva: Printed by Conrad Badius, 1561); translated as *An Oration Made by Master Theodore de Beze* (London: Printed by Richard Jugge, 1561) and as *Ane Oration Made by Master Theodore de Beze* (Edinburgh: Printed by Robert Lekprewik, 1561);

Responce faite le vingt-quatriesme jour de Septembre mil cinq cents soixante & un, par M. Theodore de Besze, en la presence de la Royne mere, le Roy & Royne de Navarre, les Princes du sang, & Conseil privé sur ce que le Cardinal de Lorraine avoit repliqué, contre ce qui avoit esté proposé en la premiere journée du Colloque par ledit de Besze au nom des Eglises reformées: Avec une autre briefue responce faite par ledit de Besze le vingtsixiéme dudit mois, sur certains articles de replique mis en avant par ledit Cardinal (N.p., 1561); translated as *Ane Answer Made the Fourth* [i.e., Twenty-Fourth] *Day of Septembre a Thousand Fyve Hundreth Syxtie & One, by Maister Theodore de Besza . . . Together with an other Short Answer*

Made by the Said de Besza the 26 Day of the Said Moneth Unto Certein Articles of Replie Set Forth by the Said Cardinall (Edinburgh: Printed by Robert Lekprewik, 1562);

Seconde harangue de M. Theodore de Besze ministre du S. Evangile, prononcée à Poissy en pleine assemblée des Prelats de France. En la presence de la Royne Mere & Princes du Sang. Le vingt-sixiesme jour du mois de Septembre. 1561 (N.p., 1561);

La Troisieme Harangue de M. Theodore de Besze, Ministre du sainct Evangile, prononcee à Poissy devant la Maiesté de la Roine, les Princes du sang, & Seigneurs du Conseil, presens Messieurs les Cardinaux, Prelats, & Docteurs: ledict de Besze assisté de douze Ministres, & douze Deputez des Eglises reformees de ce Royaume. Le vingtsixieme iour du mois de Septembre (N.p., 1561);

Ample discours des actes de Poissy. Contenant le commencement de l'assemblee, l'entree & issue du Colloque des Prelats de France, & Ministres de l'Evangile: l'ordre y gardé: Ensemble la Harangue du Roy Charles IX. Avec les sommaires, poincts des oraisons de Monsieur le Chancelier, Theodore de Besze, & du Cardinal de Lorraine (N.p., 1561);

Ad Francisci Balduini apostatae Ecebolii convicia . . . responsio, & Joannis Calvini brevis Epistola (Geneva, 1563);

Ad defensiones et reprehensiones Sebastiani Castellionis . . . responsio (Geneva: Printed by Henri Estienne, 1563);

Commentaires de M. Jean Calvin, sur le livre de Josué. Avec une preface de Theodore de Besze, contenant en brief l'histoire de la vie & mort d'iceluy (Geneva: Printed by François Perrin, 1564); also printed as *Discours de la vie et trespas de M. Jean Calvin . . . Avec le testament & derniere volonté dudict M. Jean Calvin. Plus, Le Catalogue de ses livres & escrits* (Orléans: Printed by Eloi Gibier, 1564); translated by John Stockwood as *A Discourse Wrytten by M. Theodore de Beza, Conteyning in Briefe the Historie of the Life and Death of Maister Iohn Calvin* (London: Printed by Henry Denham for Lucas Harrison, 1564); original French revised and enlarged as *Commentaires de Jean Calvin, sur le livre de Josué. Avec une preface de Theodore de Besze, contenant en brief l'histoire de la vie & mort d'iceluy: augmentee depuis la premiere edition, & deduite selon l'ordre du temps quasi d'an en an. Il y a aussi deux tables* (Geneva: Printed by François Perrin, 1565); revised and enlarged again, in Latin translation, as *Joannis Calvini Epistolae et responsa . . . Eiusdem J. Calvini Vita* (Geneva: Printed by Pierre de Saint-André, 1575); translated into French by Antoine Teissier as *Les Vies de Jean Calvin, & de Theodore de Beze* (Geneva: Printed by Jean Herman Widerhold, 1681); translated by John Mackenzie as *Memoirs of the Life and Writings of John Calvin;*

Compiled from the Narrative of Theodore Beza, and Other Authentic Documents (London: Williams & Smith, 1809);

Ad D. Io. Brentii argumenta quibus carnis Christi omnipræsentiam nititur confirmare, Theodori Bezæ Vezelii placidum & modestum responsum (Geneva: Printed by Jean Crespin, 1565);

Tractatus tres de rebus gravissimis scripti: Unus de unitate essentiae divinae, & tribus in ea subsistentibus personis, adversus Arianos ịịẽ̃ịõóẽĩõõ. Alter de Hypostatica duarum in Christo naturarum unione adversus D. Iacobi Andreae assertionem. Tertius de sacramentali corporis & sanguinis Christi cum sacris symbolis coniunctione, adversus Matthiae Flaccii Illyrici falsissimas demonstrationes (Geneva: Printed by Jean Crespin, 1565);

De pace christianarum ecclesiarum constituenda, consilium pii & moderati cuiusdam viri (Geneva: Printed by Jean Crespin, 1566);

Psalmorum Davidis paraphrasis poetica, nunc primùm edita, authore Georgio Buchanano, Scoto, poetarum nostri fæculi facilè principe. Eiusdem Davidis Psalmi aliquot à Th. B. V. versi (Geneva: Printed by Henri Estienne & Robert Estienne, 1566); revised as *Psalmorum Davidis et aliorum prophetarum, libri quinque. Argumentis & Latina paraphrasi illustrati, ac etiam vario carminum genere latinè expressi* (Geneva: Printed by Eustace Vignon, 1579);

Apologia . . . ad libellum sorbonici theologastri F. Claudii de Xaintes, cui titulum fecit, Examen Calvinianæ & Bezanæ doctrinæ de Cœna Domini ex scriptis authorum eiusdem collectum (Geneva: Printed by Jean Crespin, 1567);

Græcæ grammatices, in usum genevensis scholæ perscriptæ, pars prima (Geneva: Printed by Jean Durant, 1568);

Graecae grammatices in usum Genevensis scholae perscriptae, pars secunda (Geneva: Printed by Jean Durant, 1568);

Tractatio de polygamia, et divortiis (Geneva: Printed by Jean Crespin, 1568);

Volumen Tractationum Theologicarum, in quibus pleraque Christianæ Religionis dogmata adversus hæreses nostris temporibus renovatas solide ex Verbo Dei defenduntur (Geneva: Printed by Jean Crespin, 1570; revised edition, Geneva: Printed by Eustace Vignon, 1576);

Quaestionum & responsionum christianarum libellus (Geneva: Printed by Jean Crespin, 1570); translated into French as *Questions et responses Chrestiennes* (Geneva: Printed by Jean Crespin, 1572); translated by Arthur Golding as *A Booke of Christian Questions and Answers* (London: Printed by William How for Abraham Veale, 1574);

Ad D. Nicolai Selnecceri et Theologorum Jenensium calumnias, Brevis et necessaria . . . responsio (Geneva: Printed by Jean Crespin, 1571); revised and enlarged as *Ad repititas Jacobi Andreae et Nicolai Selnecceri calumnias responsio* (Geneva: Printed by Eustace Vignon, 1578);

Theodori Bezae modesta et christiana defensio, ad D. Nicolai Selnecceri maledicam et virulentam responsionem (Geneva: Printed by Jean Crespin, 1572);

Epistolarum theologicarum Theodori Bezae Vezelii, liber unus (Geneva: Printed by Eustace Vignon, 1573);

Volumen alterum Tractationum Theologicarum (Geneva: Printed by Eustace Vignon, 1573);

Responsio ad orationem habitam nuper in concilio Helvetiorum: pro defensione caedium & latrociniorum, quae in Gallia commissa sunt: edition & promulgation Germanicè, as Wolfgang Prisbach (La Rochelle, 1573);

Du droit des magistrats sur leurs subjets, anonymous (N.p., 1574); translated into Latin as *De Iure Magistratuum in subditos; et officio subditorum erga Magistratus* (N.p., 1576); translated by H.-L. Gonin as *Concerning the Rights of Rulers over Their Subjects*, edited by A. H. Murray (Cape Town: H. A. V. M., 1956);

Adversus sacramentariorum errorem pro vera Christi præsentia in Cœna Domini, Homiliae duae, as Nathanael Nesekio (Geneva: Printed by J. Stoer, 1574); translated by T. W. as *Two Very Lerned Sermons of M. Beza, Together with a Short Sum of the Sacrament of the Lordes Supper* (London: Printed by Robert Waldegrave for T. Man & T. Gubbins, 1588);

Στοιχειωσις . . . Rudimenta fidei Christianæ, sive Catechismus. Huic adjunctus est Catechismus alius magis compendiarius (Geneva: Printed by Henri Estienne, 1575); translated as *A Little Catechisme, That Is to Say, a Short Instruction Touching Christian Religion* (London: Printed by Hugh Singleton, 1578);

Apologia modesta et Christiana, ad Acta Conventus Quindecim Theologorum Torgæ Nuper Habiti (Geneva: Printed by Eustace Vignon, 1575);

Quaestionum et responsionum christianarum pars altera, quæ est de Sacramentis (Geneva: Printed by Eustace Vignon, 1576); translated by John Field as *The Other Parte of Christian Questions and Answers, Wich is Concerning the Sacraments* (London: Printed by Thomas Woodcocke, 1580); translated into French as *La seconde partie des questions et responses chrestiennes en laquelle est amplement traité des Sacremens* (Geneva: Printed by Jean Crespin, 1584);

Ad repetitionem primam F. Claudii de Sainctes de rebus Eucharistiæ controversis . . . Responsio (Geneva: Printed by Eustace Vignon, 1577);

Lex Dei, moralis, ceremonialis, et politica, ex libris Mosis excerpta, & in certas classes distributa (Geneva: Printed by Pierre Saint-André, 1577);

De corporis Christi omnipraesentia sive ubiquitate, anonymous (Geneva: Printed by Eustace Vignon, 1578);

THEODORI BEZAE VE-
ZELII POEMATA.

PRELVM

ASCENSIANVM

LVTETIAE.

Ex officina Conradi Badii sub prelo Ascensiano, è
regione gymnasij D. Barbaræ.

M. D. X L V I I I.

Cum priuilegio Senatus ad triennium.

*Title page for Bèze's first book, a collection of poems in which he imitates
the style of classic Latin and Greek poets (from Frédéric Gardy,*
Bibliographie des œuvres théologiques, littéraires,
historiques et juridiques de Théodore de Bèze,
*1960; Thomas Cooper Library, University
of South Carolina)*

De hypostatica duarum in Christo naturarum unione & eius effectis, placida & Christiana disceptatio (Geneva: Printed by Eustace Vignon, 1579);

De veris et visibilibus ecclesiæ catholicæ notis, tractatio (Geneva: Printed by Eustace Vignon, 1579); translated as *A Discourse, of the True and Visible Markes of the Catholique Churche* (London: Printed by Robert Waldegrave, 1582); translated into French as *Traicté des vrayes essencielles et visibles marques de la vraye Eglise Catholique* (Geneva: Printed by Jean le Preux, 1592);

De peste quaestiones duae explicatae: una sitne contagiosa: altera, an & quatenus sit Christianis per secessionem vitanda (Geneva: Printed by Eustace Vignon, 1579); translated by John Stockwood as *A Shorte Learned and Pithie Treatize of the Plague, Wherein are Handled These Two Questions: The One, Whether the Plague Bee Infectious, or No: The Other, Whether and Howe Farre It May of Christians Bee Shunned by Going Aside* (London: Printed by Thomas Dawson for George Bishop, 1580);

De Coena Domini, adversus Jodoci Harchii Montensis dogmata . . . Responsio (Geneva: Printed by Eustace Vignon, 1580);

Icones, id est veræae imagines virorum doctrina simul et pietate illustrium, quorum præcipuè ministerio partim bonarum literarum studia sunt restituta, partim vera Religio in váriis orbis Christiani regionibus, nostra patrúmque memoria fuit instaurata (Geneva: Printed by Jean de Laon, 1580); translated into French by Simon Goulart as *Les Vrais Pourtraits des hommes illustres en piete et doctrine, du travail desquels Dieu s'est servi en ces derniers temps, pour remettre sus la vraye Religion en divers pays de la Chrestienté* (Geneva: Printed by Jean de Laon, 1581); translated as *Beza's Icones: Contemporary Portraits of Reformers of Religion and Letters,* edited, with an introduction, by C. G. McCrie (London: The Religious Tract Society, 1906);

Pro Corporis Christi veritate, adversus Ubiquitatis commentum, & Guilielmi Holderi conuitia, responsio (Geneva: Printed by Eustace Vignon, 1581);

Chrestiennes méditations sur huict Pseaumes du prophète David (Geneva: Printed by Jacques Berjon, 1582); translated by John Stockwood as *Christian Meditations upon Eight Psalmes of the Prophet David* (London: Printed in Bacon House by Christopher Barker, 1582);

Volumen tertium tractationes Theologicae . . . (Geneva: Printed by Eustace Vignon, 1582);

De praedestinationis doctrina et vero usu tractatio absolutissima. Ex. Th. Bezae praelectionibus in nonum Epistolae ad Romanos caput à Raphaele Eglino Tigurino Theologiae studioso in schola Genevensi recens excepta. Adiecta sunt aliquot Loca ex libello D. Lutheri de servo arbitrio adversus Erasmum desumpta: ex quibus apparet quae fuerit illius de Praedestinatione sententia, quamque cum nostra consona (Geneva: Printed by Eustace Vignon, 1582);

De Franciae linguæ recta pronunciatione tractatus (Geneva: Printed by Eustace Vignon, 1584);

Responsio ad quaestionum et responsionum Danielis Hofmanni in gravissima de Cœ.na Domini controversia partem primam (Geneva: Printed by Eustace Vignon, 1584);

Responsionis ad Danielis Hofmanni quaestiones et responsiones de Coena Domini, Pars altera (Geneva: Printed by Eustace Vignon, 1585);

Ad Gilberti Genebrardi accusationem. Theodori Bezae defensio (Geneva: Printed by Eustace Vignon, 1585);

Ad Danielis Hofmanni demonstrationes ad oculum (Geneva: Printed by Eustace Vignon, 1586);

Response aux cinq premieres et principales demandes de F. Jean Hay (Geneva: Printed by Jean le Preux, 1586);

Sermons sur les trois premiers chapitres du cantique des Cantiques, de Salomon (Geneva: Printed by Jean le Preux, 1586); translated by John Harmar as *Master Bezaes Sermons upon the Three First Chapters of the Canticle of Canticles* . . . (Oxford: Printed by Joseph Barnes, 1587);

Ad acta colloquii Montisbelgardensis Tubingæ editam . . . *Responsio* (Geneva: Printed by Jean le Preux, 1587);

Ad acta Colloquii Montisbelgardensis Tubingæ edita, Theodori Bezae Responsionis, Pars Altera (Geneva: Printed by Jean le Preux, 1588);

Ecclesiastes. Solomonis concio ad populum habita, de vita sic instituenda, ut ad veram æternamque felicitatem perueniatur (Geneva: Printed by Jean le Preux, 1588); translated as *Ecclesiastes, or the Preacher. Solomons Sermon Made to the People, Teaching Every Man Howe to Order his Life, So As They May Come to True and Everlasting Happiness* (Cambridge: Printed by John Legatt, 1600);

Jobus Theodori Bezæ partim commentariis partim paraphrasi illustratus (Geneva: Printed by Jean le Preux, 1589); translated as *Job Expounded by Theodore Beza, Partly in Manner of a Commentary, Partly in Manner of a Paraphrase* (Cambridge: Printed by John Legatt, n.d.);

Expositio verissima juxta et succincta. De rebus nuper bello gestis inter Allobrogum regulum et helveticas regis Galliarum auxiliares copias . . . (Basel, 1589);

Tractatus pius et moderatus de vera Excommunicatione, & christiano Presbyterio, iampridem pacis conciliande causa, Cl. V. Th. Erasti D. Medici centum manuscriptis thesibus oppositus, & nunc primum, cogente necessitate, editus (Geneva: Printed by Jean le Preux, 1590);

Cato Censorius christianus (Geneva: Printed by J. de Tournes, 1591);

Apologia pro justificatione per unius Christi viva fide apprehensi Justitiam gratis imputatam. Adversus Anonymi scriptoris tractatum, clàm nuper ab Antonio quodam Lescalio editum & publicè postea impudentissimè sparsum (Geneva: Printed by Jean le Preux, 1592); translated into French as *Response . . . pour la justification par l'imputation gratuite de la Justice de Jesus Christ apprehendé par la seule foy* (Geneva: Printed by Jean le Preux, 1592);

Sermons sur l'histoire de la passion et Sepultre de nostre Seigneur Jesus Christ, descrite par les quatre Evangelistes (Geneva: Printed by Jean le Preux, 1592);

Ad tractationem de ministrorum Evangelii gradibus, ab Hadriano Saravia Belga editam . . . *responsio* (Geneva: Printed by Jean le Preux, 1592);

Sermons sur l'histoire de la resurrection de nostre Seigneur Jesus Christ (Geneva: Printed by Jean le Preux, 1593);

De controversiis in Coena Domini, Per nonnullos nuper in Germania partim renovatis, partim auctis Christiana & perspicua disceptatio (Geneva: Printed by Jean le Preux, 1593);

Theodori Bezae ad Joan. Guil. Stuckium Sac. Theologiæ in Ecclesia Tigurina Professorem Epistola, Et Pastorum ac Professorum Genevensium Responsio . . . (Geneva: Printed by Mathieu Berjon, 1597);

Response à la lettre d'un gentilhomme savoisien, ne se nommant point. Par laquelle tres-faussement il charge les Pasteurs de l'Eglise de Geneve, Tant en general qu'en partiulier, de plussieurs tresimpudentes mensonges (Geneva: Printed by Mathieu Berjon, 1598);

Maister Bezaes Houshold Prayers, translated by John Barnes (London: Printed by V.S. for John Barnes, 1603).

Editions and Collections: *Le Passavant de Théodore de Bèze,* translated into French by Isidore Liseux (Paris: Liseux, 1875);

Les Juvenilia de Théodore de Bèze, edited by Alexandre Machard (Paris: Liseux, 1879);

J. Calvini vita a Theodoro Beza, in *Joannis Calvini opera quae supersunt omnia,* volume 21, edited by Johann Wilhelm Baum, August Eduard Cunitz, and Eduard Wilhelm Eugen Reuss (Braunschweig: Schwetschke, 1879), pp. 21–50, 119–172;

Discours du Recteur Th. de Bèze, pronuncé à l'inauguration de l'Académie dans le Temple de Saint-Pierre à Genève le 5 juin 1559, Latin and French edition, translated into French by Henri Delarue (Geneva: Société du Musée historique de la Réformation, 1959);

Réponse à la confession du feu duc Jean de Northumbelande, introduction by Anna-Hélène Chaubard (Lyon: Presses académiques, 1959);

Chrestiennes Méditations, edited by Mario Richter (Geneva: Droz, 1964);

Abraham sacrifiant, edited by Keith Cameron, Kathleen M. Hall, and Francis Higman (Geneva: Droz, 1967);

Du droit des magistrats, edited by Robert M. Kingdon (Geneva: Droz, 1970);

Histoire ecclésiastique des églises réformées au royaume de France, 3 volumes, edited by Baum and Cunitz (Nieuwkoop: Graaf, 1974);

Les psaumes en vers français avec leurs mélodies, by Clement Marot and Bèze, introduction by Pierre Pidoux (Geneva: Droz, 1986);

Les vrais portraits des hommes illustrés, introduction by Alain Dufour (Geneva: Slatkine, 1986);

Epiſtola magiſtri
BENEDICTI PASSAVANTII
Reſponſiua ad commiſſionem ſibi
datam à venerabili D. Petro Ly-
ſeto, nuperCuriæ Pariſienſis præ-
ſidente: nunc verò Abbate ſancti
Victoris, prope muros.

M. D. LIII.

Title page for Bèze's satire in which he responds to Pierre Lizet, an anti-Protestant religious polemicist (from Frédéric Gardy, Bibliographie des œuvres théologiques, littéraires, historiques et juridiques de Théodore de Bèze, 1960; Thomas Cooper Library, University of South Carolina)

Cours sur les Épîtres aux Romains et aux Hébreux (1564–66) d'après les notes de Marcus Widler, edited by Pierre Fraenkel and Luc Perrotet (Geneva: Droz, 1988).

Editions in English: A Tragedie of Abrahams Sacrifice, translated by Arthur Golding, edited, with an introduction, by Malcolm William Wallace (Toronto: University of Toronto Library, 1906);

The Life of John Calvin, translated by Henry Beveridge (Philadelphia: Westminster, 1909);

On the Right of Magistrates, translated by Julian H. Franklin, in Constitutionalism and Resistance in the Sixteenth Century, edited by Franklin (New York: Pegasus, 1969), pp. 97–135;

A Little Book of Christian Questions and Responses, translated by Kirk M. Summers (Allison Park, Penn.: Pickwick, 1986);

The Christian Faith, translated by James Clark (Lewes, East Sussex, U.K.: Focus Christian Ministries Trust, 1992);

A View from the Palatine: The Iuvenilia of Théodore de Bèze, translated by Summers (Tempe: Arizona Center for Medieval and Renaissance Studies, 2001).

SELECTED BROADSIDES: Les vertus de la femme fidèle (Lausanne: Printed by John Rivery, 1556);

"Clarissimo Viro"; "D. Philippi Melanchthonis," (N.p., 1560);

Ad serenissimam Elizabetham Angliæ Reginam Theodor. Beza (London: Printed by George Bishop & Ralph Newberry, 1588).

OTHER: Heinrich Bullinger, La Perfection des chretiens, translated by Bèze (Zurich, 1552);

Les Pseaumes mis en rime françoise, translated by Clément Marot and Bèze (Geneva: Printed by François Jaquy for Antoine Vincent, 1562);

La Confession Helvétique Postérieure, translated by Bèze (Geneva: Printed by François Perrin, 1566);

Athanasii Dialogi V, de sancta Trinitate. Basilii Libri IIII, adversus impium Eunomium. Anastasii et Cyrilli, compendiaria orthodoxae fidei explicatio, translated by Bèze (Geneva: Printed by Henri Estienne, 1570);

Theodori presbyteri Rhæaethensis libellus adversus hæreses quibus iam olim hypostatica duarum in Christo naturarum unio oppugnata est, nunc primum Græcè editus, & Latinus factus, translated by Bèze (Geneva: Printed by Eustace Vignon, 1576);

Histoire ecclésiastique des églises réformées au royaume de France, anonymous, edited by Bèze and others (Anvers [i.e., Geneva]: Printed by J. Rémy [i.e., Printed by Jean de Laon], 1580);

Harmonia confessionum fidei, Orthodoxarum, & Reformatarum Ecclesiarum, quae in praecipuis quibusque Europae Regnis, Nationibus, & Provinciis, sacram Evangelii doctrinam purè profitentur, compiled by Bèze, Jean-François Salvard, and others (Geneva: Printed by Pierre Saint André, 1581);

Canticum Canticorum Solomonis, latinis versibus expressum, translated by Bèze (Geneva: Printed by Eustace Vignon, 1584);

Oratio Bezae in solenni actu inaurationis academiae Genevensis [1564], in Ioannis Calvini Opera Quae Supersunt Omnia, volume 17, edited by Johann Wilhelm Baum and others (Brunswick: Schwetschke, 1877), pp. 542–546.

Théodore de Bèze (or Theodore Beza) was a humanist, Protestant theologian, and minister of the Reformed church in Geneva during the second half of the sixteenth century. In his long career as city minister and professor at the Academy of Geneva, Bèze exercised strategic leadership in his efforts to preserve French Protestantism in Geneva and in his native France, and to defend the theological legacy of John Calvin throughout Europe. Bèze's diverse literary corpus of more than seventy works—including a sacred drama, poems, prayers, satires, theological treatises, French and Greek grammars, political tracts, historical writings, and sermons—shows that he was well versed in classical literature, skilled in biblical exegesis, and adroit in theological controversy. Bèze's ministry of pulpit and pen illustrates the religious convictions and explosive passions that characterized confessional Europe in the early modern period.

Théodore de Bèze was born in Vézelay (Burgundy) on 24 June 1519, the seventh child of Pierre de Bèze and his wife Marie Bourdelot. The family de Bèze was from France's lower nobility: Pierre was the royal bailiff at Vézelay, and his brother Nicholas was the abbot of Cervon, later a counselor of the Parlement of Paris. When Theodore was three years of age, Marie took her son to Paris to live with his uncle Nicholas; she died on the return home. Bereft of maternal influence, possessing a weak constitution and living in fear of physicians' harsh remedies, the boy was miserable and even contemplated suicide. The decisive moment of Bèze's childhood came in December 1528 when Nicholas sent him to Orléans to study in the home of the renowned Hellenist (and secret Lutheran) Melchior Wolmar. In a letter to Wolmar written more than thirty years later (12 March 1560), Bèze likened this event to an "alter natalis" (second birthday). For the next six years, first at Orléans and later at Bourges, Wolmar instructed his pupil in humanistic studies that accented philology and an extensive reading of classical Greek and Latin authors. At the same time, the young man was introduced to the Greek New Testament and to Protestant teaching, including the writing of the Zurich Reformer Heinrich Bullinger. In his 12 March 1560 letter to Wolmar, Bèze acknowledged his debt to his teacher: "Sed hoc est omnium beneficiorum quae a te accepi longe maximum, quod verae pietatis cognitione ex Dei verbo tanquam limpidissimo fonte petita tu me ita imbuisti" (It was you who gave me a knowledge of true piety, drawn from the Word of God as the purest source). As an adolescent Bèze appears to have embraced this vision for Christian renewal and ecclesiastical reform drawn from the Word of God; indeed, he even vowed to leave the Catholic Church when circumstances permitted. This pledge was left unfulfilled—though not forgotten—for more than a decade. Bèze later attributed his long religious hesitation to Satan's three-fold temptation: the youthful lust for carnal pleasure, the ambition for literary glory, and the false security of two "accursed" ecclesiastical benefices.

Religious repression in France in the aftermath of the 1534 *Affaire des Placards* (Affair of the Placards), in which Protestants in Paris posted and circulated denunciations of the Catholic mass, hastened Wolmar's departure for Germany in 1535. When Pierre de Bèze blocked his son's plan to accompany his master to Tübingen, the young man returned instead to Orléans to study civil law. He received his license in law four years later. By that time the love of humanistic letters had conquered him completely. Against the wishes of his family, who intended for him social prominence at court or in the Parlement, Bèze moved to Paris and joined a sodality of gifted young humanists. For the next nine years Bèze lived off two substantial benefices as he wrote poetry, continued his classical pursuits (and the study of Hebrew), and rubbed shoulders with other cultured literati, including Denis Sauvage, Maclou Popon, Jean Dampierre, Jean Martin, and Jacques Peletier. "As for me, my spouse is named Philology," Bèze wrote Popon in a 7 May 1542 letter, "Caeterum, quod ad res meas attinet, una est nobis uxor philologia, quae quidem illud non habet ubi vos mariti gaudia vestra expletis" (My marriage is so happy that I can only wish you equal happiness).

The *Poemata* (1548, Poems) represents the first fruit of Bèze's humanistic studies. In this collection of Latin and Greek poems, epitaphs, and epigrams, Bèze imitates the style of ancient poets such as Virgil, Catullus, and Ovid as he celebrates friendship, praises heroes of the past and present, and even satirizes flaws of the Catholic Church. Several love poems addressed to a young woman named Candida later caused Bèze considerable embarrassment for their erotic content. The *Poemata* firmly situated him as a talented, somewhat precocious Christian humanist well placed among the cultured elite of Paris.

Everything changed in the autumn of 1548. Bedridden with a life-threatening illness, the young poet's conscience was tormented by his long-neglected pledge to leave the Catholic Church. Moreover, he was troubled by the hypocrisy of his clandestine marriage to Claudine Denosse, the daughter of a Parisian merchant, contracted four years earlier. The crisis of body and soul proved to be the crucible of Bèze's public conversion to the Protestant faith. Once his strength returned in late October, he renounced Catholicism and, together with Claudine, fled to Geneva. They solemnized their marriage in a public ceremony several weeks later. The following spring, the Parlement ordered Bèze's arrest, confiscated his goods, and decreed that he be burned in effigy.

During the next decade the young poet matured into a seasoned churchman committed to the Reformed program of Calvin. Through the efforts of Calvin and

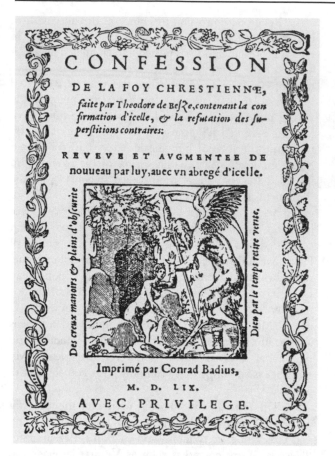 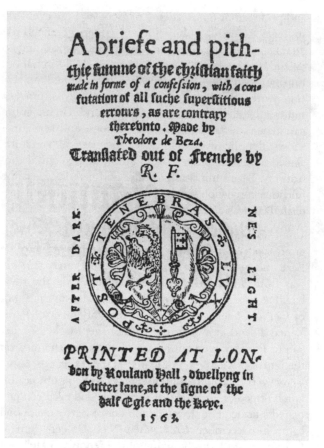

Title pages for the first edition and the English translation of Bèze's summation of Protestantism, which he wrote in part to explain his faith to his Catholic father (from Frédéric Gardy, Bibliographie des œuvres théologiques, littéraires, historiques et juridiques de Théodore de Bèze, *1960; Thomas Cooper Library, University of South Carolina)*

Pierre Viret, Bèze was appointed professor of Greek at the Academy of Lausanne in November 1549. He held this post for the next nine years, lecturing on the great Greek writers (Demosthenes, Homer, Sophocles, and Plato), supervising student pensioners, and (probably) preaching on occasion. Additionally, he gave lectures on the New Testament to other French refugees. His colleagues at Lausanne included the theologian Viret, the famous jurist François Hotman, and the Hebraist Jean Reymond-Merlin. Bèze also established formative relationships with Swiss Protestant leaders such as Guillaume Farel in Neuchâtel and Heinrich Bullinger and Peter Martyr in Zurich. But Calvin was the person who won Bèze's greatest admiration and loyalty. In his extensive correspondence, Bèze regularly defended the reputation and doctrine of the Genevan Reformer, likening him to a second father. Calvin returned his affection, writing in a 30 June 1551 letter, "Equidem inhumanus sim, nisi eum redamem, qui me plus quam fraterne diligit, et colit non secus ac patrem" (I would be remiss if I did not care deeply for

Bèze, who loves me more than a brother and honors me as if I was his father).

Bèze now employed his literary talents in the service of the Reformed faith. In 1550 he published the highly regarded French tragedy *Abraham sacrifiant* (translated as *A Tragedie of Abraham's Sacrifice,* 1577), which wove together elements of Greek tragedy and medieval mystery plays in recounting the story from Genesis 22 of Abraham's sacrifice of his son Isaac. In this work Abraham becomes a type for all those who have resisted Catholic idolatry and sacrificed family and wealth for the sake of the gospel. While admitting his love for the liberal arts, Bèze now changed his focus: "Car je confesse que de mon naturel j'ay tousjours pris plaisir à la poësie, et ne m'en puis encores repentir" (I confess that by nature I have always delighted in poetry, and I am still not able to repent of that). Nevertheless, he explains, "A la verité il leur seroit mieux seant de chanter un cantique à Dieu, que de petrarquiser un Sonnet . . . ou de contrefaire ces fureurs poëtiques à l'antique" (It is far better to know how to sing a song to God than to imitate the passions of the ancient poets). Less refined, but nearly as popular, was Bèze's witty satire *Epistola magistri Benedicti Passavantii* (1553, Letter of Master Benedict Passavant), in which the Reformer deftly answers the anti-Protestant polemic of Pierre Lizet while drawing on the biting humor of François Rabelais's *Pantagruel*. Bèze's most significant literary contributions during his years in Lausanne were, however, in the domain of biblical studies. In 1556 the humanist scholar published *Novum domini nostri Jesu Christi Testamentum . . . a Theodoro Beza versum,* a new Latin translation of the New Testament with theological and exegetical notes that became widely known as the *Annotationes* (Annotations). In subsequent editions of this work Bèze expanded the critical apparatus and added a Greek text based largely upon an early Greek codex (today known as the *Codex Bezae*). Commonly regarded as Bèze's chef d'oeuvre, the *Annotationes* had a crucial influence upon the authorized 1611 English translation of the Bible. Meanwhile, Bèze's translation of the French Psalter was scarcely of less importance. Conceived of by the famous Renaissance poet Clément Marot, but left unfinished at his death in 1544, this metrical version of the French Psalms occupied Bèze's attention throughout his years in Lausanne. Although Bèze's talents as poet did not match Marot's, he approached the project with great determination, completing it in 1562. Published under the title *Les Pseaumes mis en rime françoise* (The Psalms in French Rhyme), the Huguenot Psalter went through more than sixty editions in four years, becoming an identifying mark of Reformed worship, the *cri de coeur* (heart's cry) of embattled Protestants in France.

During this time the French humanist was growing in stature as a theologian. Along with most other Protestant Reformers in Switzerland and Germany, he approved of the execution of the anti-Trinitarian Michael Servetus in Geneva in 1553. One churchman who objected was Sebastian Castellio; he issued an impassioned defense of religious toleration. In response Bèze wrote *De Haereticis a civili magistratu puniendis* (1554, On the Punishment of Heretics by the Civil Magistrate), which provides biblical justification for civil authorities to punish obstinate heretics such as Servetus. If Bèze's attitude toward the persecution of heretics was unoriginal for its time, his oblique suggestion that inferior magistrates might resist cruel princes who attacked pure religion was revolutionary. The following year his *Summa totius Christianismi* (Sum of the Whole of Christianity; also known as *Tabula praedestinationis* [Table of Predestination]; translated as *A Briefe Declaracion of the Chiefe Poyntes of Christian Religion,* 1556) presented a schematized description of the order of salvation in which Calvin's doctrine of double predestination was garnished with Bèze's own supralapsarian twist. During this same period the Lausanne professor completed his *Confession de la foi chrestienne* (1559; trans-

lated as *A Briefe and Pithie Summe of the Christian Faith,* 1563), a comprehensive explanation of Reformed teaching written to convert his Catholic father in old age. This work gained wide popularity during Bèze's lifetime (it was reprinted in thirty editions and five languages before 1600), and it is the best concise summary of his doctrine. Bèze's fidelity to Calvin's theological vision and his emergence as a leader of Reformed Protestantism were evidenced in several diplomatic missions: three times during 1557 and 1558 Bèze was dispatched by Calvin to Germany to consult with Lutheran theologians and princes in an effort to solicit support for the persecuted Protestant churches in France.

By the late 1550s the religious climate in Lausanne had become increasingly difficult for Bèze and his colleagues. Already in 1555 the Bernese magistrates (who governed the Pays de Vaud) had forbidden pastors from preaching the doctrine of predestination from Lausanne's pulpits. Allegiance to Calvin was now viewed with suspicion. In a 23 October 1555 letter to Bullinger, Bèza wrote, "pro Calvinistis habemur, quod crimen multo majus est quam si caetera omnia in unum conjungas." (We are considered to be "Calvinists," which is believed to be a crime far worse than all others put together). In the years that followed, the civil authorities repeatedly blocked efforts of Viret and Bèze to introduce Genevan-style ecclesiastical discipline in the church. Finally, in the fall of 1558, Bèze resigned his professorship in protest and moved to Geneva, where Calvin welcomed him and soon enlisted him as a trusted coworker. Before the end of the year Bèze was elected city preacher; the following spring he was appointed professor of Greek literature; and in June 1559 he was installed rector of the newly founded Genevan Academy. The Reformed city on the shores of Lake Léman was to be Bèze's exile home for the rest of his life.

The urgent needs of Protestants in France soon diverted Bèze from his new responsibilities. Between 1559 (the year of the First National Synod) and 1562, the Reformed church in France grew from a handful of persecuted churches to a powerful religious and political movement of more than 1,200 congregations with as many as two million adherents. Throughout these dramatic months Geneva served as a strategic center for printing Protestant literature as well as recruiting and training missionaries to evangelize the French kingdom. Bèze played a significant role in this effort. Although he probably did not lend explicit support to the 1560 Conspiracy of Amboise, an ill-fated plot to assassinate the duke of Guise and place the young French king François II under the regency of the Bourbon prince Louis de Condé, Bèze did meet privately with the chief conspirator, La Renaudie, beforehand and gave him a translation of an imprecatory psalm calling forth God's

An engraving of the battle of Dreux, 19 December 1562, which Bèze witnessed. During the Wars of Religion he served as the chaplain and adviser for the Huguenot commander Louis de Condé (Roger-Viollet/Getty Images).

vengeance upon the wicked. Several months later, in July 1560, the city's Company of Pastors sent Bèze to Nérac to instruct the noble household of Bourbon in the Reformed faith. During this three-month preaching mission Bèze established friendly—and what proved to be long-standing—ties with Jeanne d'Albret and her son Henri de Navarre, the future king Henri IV. From August to October 1561 the Reformer led a Protestant delegation that included Peter Martyr, Augustin Marlorat, and Nicholas des Gallars to the Colloquy of Poissy where he defended the Reformed churches and their doctrine in the presence of the French royal family and antagonistic Catholic prelates. In the opening session of the colloquy Bèze scandalized the audience by explicitly rejecting the Catholic doctrine of real presence: "Nous disons que son corps est esloigné du pain & du vin, autant que le plus haut ciel est esloigné de la terre" (Christ's body is as far removed from the bread and wine as is heaven from earth). In the end, despite Catherine de Médicis's best efforts to obtain religious reconciliation, the colloquy failed to achieve theological concord or assuage deep-seated distrust between the parties. Never-

theless, at the Queen Mother's insistence, Bèze remained in Paris for the next six months to continue negotiations with Catholic leaders. During these heady months the Reformer solicited noble support for the persecuted churches and on several occasions preached to crowds numbering in the thousands. The Edict of January (1562), which granted Reformed churches and synods legal rights within defined geographical limits, proved to be a final false hope for Bèze and his coreligionists. With the outbreak of the First War of Religion in late March 1562, Bèze threw his support behind the Huguenot commander Louis de Condé, writing to Calvin on 28 March 1562: "Cogar itaque non tantum spectator, sed etiam actor esse tristissimae tragoediae" (I am forced not only to be a spectator, but an actor in this horrible tragedy). For the next eleven months Bèze served as Condé's chaplain and adviser, making secret trips to Germany and Switzerland to raise money and recruit mercenaries for the cause. A week before Christmas he was an eyewitness to the bloody battle of Dreux. The poet Pierre de Ronsard memorialized Bèze—"ce grand soldat, de Baize" (this great soldier de Bèze)—as a dangerous rebel for his complicity in these events. By the time the Peace of Amboise ended hostilities in March 1563, and Bèze returned to Geneva, he had become a well-known controversial champion of French Protestantism.

With Calvin's death in May 1564 the mantle of Calvinist leadership in Geneva fell squarely on Bèze's shoulders. As moderator of the Company of Pastors (an office he held until 1580), he oversaw daily religious life in Geneva and provided theological direction for international Calvinism. For the next thirty-five years Bèze served as the chief minister of St. Pierre's, the city's largest parish church, regularly preaching twice each Sunday and daily every other week. Only eighty-seven sermons are extant from Bèze's extensive homiletic ministry: his sermons on the Song of Songs (published 1586), the Passion of Jesus Christ (published 1592) and the Resurrection of Jesus Christ (published 1593). In these sermons Bèze employs the homiletic method practiced by most other Reformed preachers of his day, preaching successively through the biblical text (the so-called *lectio continua* method), weaving theological instruction with moral injunctions and pastoral consolation. In addition to these preaching duties, Bèze succeeded Calvin as professor of theology at the Academy. His students included Protestant lights such as Kasper Olevianus, François du Jon, Andrew Melville, and Jacob Arminius. Under Bèze's leadership the Academy's curriculum was expanded to include the study of law (and for a brief time the study of medicine), and theological instruction was restructured to employ doctrinal common places *(loci communes)* and Aristotelian logic. By nature, however, the Reformer was not predisposed to innovation. His long ministry in Geneva reflects a religious posture more conservative than creative as he sought to maintain Calvin's theology and institutions. Bèze's brief biography of Calvin titled *Discours de la vie et trespas de M. Jean Calvin* (1564; translated as *Historie of the Life and Death of Maister Iohn Calvin,* 1564) provides clear testimony of the disciple's unwavering loyalty to his spiritual father.

During the next decade, as civil war decimated his homeland, Bèze worked tirelessly on behalf of the churches. From his outpost in Geneva, he recruited and trained pastors for ministry in France. He served as a chief adviser to the Huguenot military commander Gaspard de Coligny and maintained regular epistolary contact with other Protestant notables. Bèze combated theological opponents such as Jean Morély and Pierre de la Ramée (Peter Ramus), who resented Genevan interference and advocated greater congregational control of the French churches. In 1571 Bèze was chosen to preside over the Seventh National Synod of La Rochelle. In the terrible months following the massacres of St. Bartholomew's Day (August 1572), Bèze and the Genevan clergy spearheaded a desperate campaign

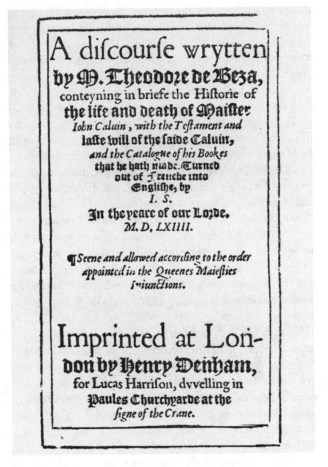

Title page for the first English translation of Bèze's Vie de Calvin *(from Frédéric Gardy,* Bibliographie des œuvres théologiques, littéraires, historiques et juridiques de Théodore de Bèze, *1960; Thomas Cooper Library, University of South Carolina)*

against Charles IX and the Valois monarchy. Once again Bèze secretly raised money and recruited mercenaries for the Huguenots in France. He also wrote his famous (but anonymous) *Du droit des magistrats sur leurs subjets* (1574; translated as *Concerning the Rights of Rulers over Their Subjects,* 1956) in which he defended the right of lesser magistrates to revolt against kings turned tyrants. According to Bèze, magistrates, whether noblemen or city officials, received their authority from the people, not the king, and were responsible to protect the public welfare. If a duly elected monarch violated the fundamental laws of the kingdom and refused to summon an Estates General, lesser magistrates were justified in opposing him with force to defend the true religion. Though written with the French situation in view, this treatise remains a classic in the history of resistance literature.

During his tenure in Geneva, Bèze published several dozen polemical tracts defending Reformed theology and practice from its detractors: "Sed tamen prodenda non est ne silentio quidem veritas, ipsa vita longe pretiosior" (The truth—far more precious than life itself —must never be betrayed to silence). Against the Catholic controversialist Claude de Saincte, Bèze wrote works defending his own Protestant conversion and dismantling the doctrine of transubstantiation (published 1567, 1577). In response to the Jesuit Jean Hay, Bèze wrote to affirm the legitimacy of the Protestant ministry as well as the perspicuity and supreme authority of Scripture (published 1586). He composed equally forceful responses to Bernard Ochino's defense of polygamy (published 1568) and Castellio's dismissal of predestination (published 1563). Additionally, Bèze had protracted disputes over the nature of Christ's presence in the sacramental meal, as well as the communication of the properties of Christ's two natures, with conservative (Gnesio-)Lutheran theologians such as Nicholas Selnecker (including works published in 1571, 1572, and 1578) and Jacob Andreae (including works published in 1565, 1578, 1587, and 1588). These debates became especially acrimonious as Lutheran princes in Germany imposed repressive measures against their Reformed subjects. But not all of Bèze's theological writings from this period were polemical in nature. The Reformer published a brief catechism in 1575. Likewise, employing the commonplace method of the Lutheran theologian Philipp Melanchthon, Bèze composed the *Quaestionum & responsionum christianorum libellus* (1570; translated as *A Booke of Christian Questions and Answers,* 1574) that addressed the central topics of Reformed theology. A second volume, devoted to the sacraments, appeared six years later. The bulk of these theological writings—controversial as well as constructive—were collected and published in three folio volumes titled the *Tractationes Theologicae* (1570–1582, Theological Treatises).

Bèze outlived by several decades all of the first generation leaders of French Protestantism, including Calvin, Viret, Farel, Hotman, Des Gallars, and Antoine de Chandieu. Consequently, it fell to him to preserve and consolidate their legacy while at the same time addressing the urgent needs of embattled churches. Two historical pieces, both published in 1580, illustrate this concern. First, *Histoire ecclésiastique des églises réformées au royaume de France* (Ecclesiastical History of the Reformed Churches in France) is a work for which scholars now recognize Bèze as the chief editor. This partisan history describes the origins and triumphant advance of Reformed Christianity in France over five decades, extolling the courageous men and women who battled superstition and defended true religion at the cost of their lives. The second work, Bèze's *Icones* (translated as *Beza's Icones,* 1906), served a similar purpose, although the scope was more international. This volume included a woodcut print, a eulogy, and brief biographical sketches of more than forty deceased European ministers, martyrs, and princes who had been sympathetic to church reform. The ecumenical sweep of the *Icones* is impressive: one finds in this list of heroes not only magisterial Reformers such as Luther, Calvin, and Huldrych Zwingli, but also Jan Hus of Bohemia, Desiderius Erasmus of Holland, Marguerite d'Angoulême (later Marguerite de Navarre) of France, Jean à Lasco of Poland, Girolamo Savonarola of Florence, Thomas Cranmer of England, and John Knox of Scotland.

Even as Bèze celebrated the past, he was deeply concerned about the future prospects of Reformed churches. The "century of gold" was rapidly degenerating into a "century of iron," he feared. After years of theological wrangling, Auguste of Saxony and other Lutheran princes formally anathematized the "sacramentarian" error of Calvinists and more moderate Philippists (descendants of Melanchthon) in the 1577 Formula of Concord, a document written by the Tübingen theologian Jacob Andreae. Church leaders who did not subscribe to the Formula were to be dismissed or imprisoned. Bèze responded to this crisis by writing two treatises in 1578 that attacked the Formula and its doctrine of ubiquity while defending Christ's spiritual presence in the sacramental meal. Three years later Bèze and several French colleagues compiled the *Harmonia confessionum fidei* (1581, Harmony of Confessions of Faith), which aims to show the basic doctrinal agreement among eleven Protestant confessions drawn from the Reformed, Anglican, and Lutheran churches. The final chapter of this protracted conflict took place at the Colloquy of Montbéliard (1586), where Bèze and Andreae debated sacramental theology, religious images, and predestination in the presence of Count Frederick of Württemberg. By the time Bèze's second written defense of this colloquy was published in 1588, Frederick had embraced the Lutheran position and banished his Protestant subjects unwilling to subscribe to the Formula of Concord.

During the 1580s and 1590s Bèze was also preoccupied with the crisis in France. After initial reservations Bèze threw his full support behind the Protestant prince Henri de Navarre in 1585, agreeing to serve as his spiritual adviser and paid political agent. When Navarre acceded to the French throne as Henri IV in 1589, the Reformer wrote a seventeen-point position paper in which he counseled the king on his personal conduct, the composition of the royal council, and the execution of justice. Bèze's confidence in Henri's good will was shaken, but not completely destroyed, by the king's unexpected conversion to Catholicism in 1593. Bèze continued to support Henri and became a prominent advocate for a political resolution to the French civil wars, which was finally achieved in the Edict of Nantes (1598).

Two years later Henri IV invited Bèze to meet with him in the royal camp at Eluiset outside of Geneva—a final, affectionate interview between the Catholic king and his Protestant subject.

Bèze experienced personal bereavement, poor health, and financial difficulties during the final years of his life. In April 1588 Claudine Denosse died unexpectedly at the age of sixty-six. In a 30 April 1588 letter to his friend Constantine Fabricius, Bèze wrote, "nihil in hac vita accidere mihi potuerit acerbius. . . . Sed benedictum esto Domini Dei nostri nomen" (Nothing more bitter in this life could have happened to me. . . . Yet blessed be the name of the Lord). Four months later the bereaved minister married a widow named Catherine de Piano who cared for him in his old age. Bèze had no children from either marriage. The septuagenarian Reformer was becoming increasingly feeble, afflicted by arthritis, partial deafness, and occasional bouts of vertigo. His preaching duties at St. Pierre's were reduced in 1590 but not suspended entirely until 1599. During this interval, poverty forced Bèze to request financial assistance from Geneva's magistrates and wealthy friends (including Henri IV) and to sell his library to a Czech nobleman. Yet, despite these difficulties, Bèze continued to write: He wrote works defending the practice of ecclesiastical discipline against Thomas Erastus (published 1590), refuting Antoine Lescaille's confused theory of justification (published 1592), and answering Anglican divines' attacks on Presbyterian government (published 1592). During the mid 1590s Bèze also crafted a collection of French prayers, extant only in English translation as *Maister Bezaes Houshold Prayers* (1603). These prayers witness to the Reformer's vibrant spirituality and his pastoral concern to apply the biblical message to daily life as people began a new day, gathered at table, or prepared to die. In 1597 the Catholic controversialist François de Sales visited Bèze for the purpose of winning his conversion. Rumors soon raced through France and Germany that the Genevan minister had abjured the Protestant religion on his deathbed. Bèze silenced these reports in two of his last published works, one addressed to his friend Wilhelm Stucki of Zurich (published 1597), the other to a Catholic apologist named Antoine de Saint-Michel (published 1598). True to form, he promised to battle Catholic error and teach the truth of God to the very last breath. He died on the morning of 13 October 1605 as the bells of St. Pierre's church summoned people to Sunday services.

Historians recognize Théodore de Bèze's strategic leadership in the French political and religious crises during the second half of the sixteenth century. Disagreement remains, however, as to Bèze's fidelity to Calvin's theology and his role in the development of Protestant Orthodoxy. That Bèze departed from Calvin at points is

DV DROIT
DES MAGISTRATS
SVR LEVRS SVBIETS.

Traitté tref-neceffaire en ce temps, pour aduertir de leur deuoir, tant les Magiftrats que les Subiets: publié par ceux de Magdebourg l'an M D L: & maintenant reueu & augmenté de plufieurs raifons & exemples.

PSAL. 2.

Erudimini qui iudicatis terram.

1 5 7 4.

Title page for Bèze's anonymous book in which he argued for the limits of a king's power over his subjects (from Frédéric Gardy, Bibliographie des œuvres théologiques, littéraires, historiques et juridiques de Théodore de Bèze, *1960; Thomas Cooper Library, University of South Carolina)*

beyond question: in the *Tabula praedestinationis* and the *Quaestionum & responsionum christianarum libellus* one encounters a theological system more formal in definition and more scholastic in method than Calvin's. Bèze's commitment to supralapsarian predestination, his presentation of discipline as a "third mark" of a true church, and his willingness to ground the believer's assurance partly in personal experience (the so-called *syllogismus practicus*) were viewpoints not shared by Calvin. So, too, Bèze was more explicit in his defense of limited atonement and fiercer in his opposition to Episcopal government. Whereas scholars once argued that these rationalizing tendencies undermined the biblical and Christological foundations of Calvin's theology, many today affirm the basic continuity between Bèze's theological work and that of his predecessor. Regardless, Bèze clearly played a crucial role in preserving the Reform movement in Geneva and France and in shaping Protestant culture and theology. In fact, in each role he assumed—poet and political activist, humanist and church reformer, biblical exegete and dogged dogmatician—Bèze left a lasting mark on early modern Europe.

Letters:

Correspondance de Théodore de Bèze, 26 volumes, edited by Hippolyte Aubert, Fernand Aubert, Henri Meylan, and others (Geneva: Droz, 1960–2005).

Bibliography:

Frédéric Gardy, *Bibliographie des œuvres théologiques, littéraires, historiques et juridiques de Théodore de Bèze* (Geneva: Droz, 1960).

Biographies:

Johann Wilhelm Baum, *Theodor Beza: Nach handschriftlichen Quellen dargestellt,* 2 volumes (Leipzig: Weidmann, 1843, 1851);

Heinrich Heppe, *Theodor Beza: Leben und ausgewählte Schriften* (Elberfeld: Friderichs, 1861);

Henry Martyn Baird, *Theodore Beza: The Counsellor of the French Reformation, 1519–1605* (New York & London: Putnam, 1899);

Paul Frédéric Geisendorf, *Théodore de Bèze* (Geneva, 1949; reprinted, Geneva: Jullien, 1967);

Alain Dufour, "Théodore de Bèze," in *Histoire Littéraire de la France,* volume 42, part 2 (Paris: Boccard, 2002), pp. 315–470.

References:

Auguste Bernus, *Théodore de Bèze à Lausanne* (Lausanne: Bridel, 1900);

Reinhard Bodenmann, "Le manifeste retrouvé de Théodore de Bèze et de ses collègues contre la Formule de concorde (1578)," *Bulletin de la Société de l'Histoire du Protestantisme Français,* 142 (1996): 345–387;

Natalie Davis, "Peletier and Beza Part Company," *Studies in the Renaissance,* 11 (1964): 188–222;

Michael Jinkins, "Theodore Beza: Continuity and Regression in the Reformed Tradition," *Evangelical Quarterly,* 64 (1992): 131–154;

Robert M. Kingdon, *Geneva and the Coming of the Wars of Religion in France, 1555–1563* (Geneva: Droz, 1956);

Kingdon, *Geneva and the Consolidation of the French Protestant Movement, 1564–1572* (Geneva: Droz, 1967);

Jeffrey Mallinson, *Faith, Reason, and Revelation in Theodore Beza, 1519–1605* (Oxford: Oxford University Press, 2003);

Scott Manetsch, "A Mystery Solved? Maister Beza's Houshold Prayers," *Bibliothèque d'Humanisme et Renaissance,* 65 (2003): 275–288;

Manetsch, *Theodore Beza and the Quest for Peace in France, 1572–1598* (Leiden & Boston: Brill, 2000);

Henri Meylan, "La conversion de Bèze ou les longues hésitations d'un humaniste chrétien," in *D'Erasme à Théodore de Bèze: Problèmes de l'Eglise et de l'école chez les réformés,* preface by Leon R. Halkin (Geneva: Droz, 1976), pp. 145–166;

Richard Muller, *Christ and the Decree, Christology and Predestination in Reformed Theology from Calvin to Perkins* (Durham, N.C.: Labyrinth, 1986);

Jill Raitt, *The Colloquy of Montbéliard: Religion and Politics in the Sixteenth Century* (London & New York: Oxford University Press, 1993);

Raitt, ed., *Shapers of Religious Traditions in Germany, Switzerland, and Poland,* foreword by Kingdon, introduction by Raitt (London & New Haven: Yale University Press, 1981);

Richard Stauffer, "Le calvinisme et les Universités," *Bulletin de la société de l'histoire du protestantisme français,* 126 (1980): 27–51;

David Steinmetz, *Reformers in the Wings: From Geiler von Kayserberg to Theodore Beza,* second edition (Oxford: Oxford University Press, 2001);

Shawn D. Wright, *Our Sovereign Refuge. The Pastoral Theology of Theodore Beza* (Carlisle, U.K.: Paternoster, 2004).

Papers:

The largest archive of Théodore de Bèze's letters and manuscript materials is the Institut d'histoire de la Réformation at the University of Geneva.

Brantôme
(Pierre de Bourdeille)
(1540? – 5 July 1614)

Dora E. Polachek
Binghamton University, State University of New York

BOOKS: *Mémoires . . . contenans les vies des dames illustres de France de son temps* (Leyden: Printed by Jean Sambix, 1665); translated by Katharine Prescott Wormeley as *The Book of the Ladies (Illustrious Dames) . . . with elucidations on some of these ladies by C.-A. Sainte-Beuve* (London: Heinemann, 1899; Boston: Hardy, Pratt, 1899); reprinted as *Illustrious Dames of the Court of the Valois Kings* (New York: Lamb, 1912);

Mémoires . . . contenans les vies des dames galantes de son temps, 2 volumes (Leyden: Printed by Jean Sambix, 1666); translated by A. R. Allinson as *Lives of Fair and Gallant Ladies,* 2 volumes (New York: Carrington, 1901, 1907);

Mémoires . . . contenans les vies des hommes illustres et grands capitaines françois, 4 volumes (Leyden: Printed by Jean Sambix, 1666);

Mémoires . . . contenans les vies des hommes illustres et grands capitaines étrangers (Leyden: Printed by Jean Sambix, 1666; reprinted in 2 volumes, 1666);

Mémoires . . . , 10 volumes in 12 books (Leyden: Printed by Jean Sambix, 1722)–book 10 includes *Anecdotes de la Cour de France sous les rois Henri II, François II, Charles IX, Henri III et Henri IV touchant les duels,* partially translated by George H. Powell as *Duelling Stories of the Sixteenth Century from the French of Brantôme* (London: Bullen, 1904);

Œuvres du seigneur de Brantôme, nouvelle édition considérablement augmentée et accompagnée de remarques historiques et critiques, 15 volumes, edited by Jacob Le Duchat, Antoine Lancelot, and Prosper Marchand (The Hague, 1740)–volume 12 includes the first publication of *Rodomontades;* translated by John Ozell as *Spanish Rhodomontades* (London: Printed by J. Chrichley, 1741); entire collection revised and enlarged (The Hague: 1743)–volume 13 includes the first publication of "Dixseptiesme opuscule: Testament et codicilles de Pierre de Bourdeille, seigneur de Brantôme";

Œuvres complètes de Pierre de Bourdeille, abbé et seigneur de Brantôme, publiées pour la première fois selon le plan de l'auteur, augmentées de nombreuses variantees et de fragments inédits, suivies des œuvres d'André de Bourdeilles et d'une table générale, avec une introduction et des notes, 13 volumes, edited by Prosper Mérimée and Louis Lacour (Paris: Jannet, 1858–1895);

Œuvres complètes, 11 volumes, edited by Ludovic Lalanne (Paris: Renouard for the Société de l'histoire de France, 1864–1882)–volume 10 includes *Poésies inédites de Brantôme* (most of Brantôme's previously unpublished poetry);

Recueil des dames . . . publié d'après les manuscrits originaux, edited by Roger Gaucheron (Paris: Payot, 1926);

Recueil d'aulcunes rymes de mes jeunes amours. Première édition intégrale des autres poésies de l'auteur, edited by Louis Perceau (Paris: Briffaut, 1927)–includes the first publication of poetry considered too risqué by Lalanne for inclusion in his collection.

Editions: *Œuvres complètes du seigneur de Brantôme, accompagnées de remarques historiques et critiques,* 8 volumes, edited by Louis Jean Nicolas Monmerqué (Paris: Foucault, 1822–1823);

Discours sur les colonels de l'infanterie de France, edited by Etienne Vaucheret, De Pétrarque à Descartes, no. 26 (Paris: Vrin / Montreal: Cosmos, 1973);

Recueil des Dames, poésies et tombeaux, edited by Etienne Vaucheret, Bibliothèque de la Pléiade, no. 380 (Paris: Gallimard, 1991).

Before the 1970s only enthusiasts of erotic literature and a small number of Renaissance scholars showed interest in the works of Pierre de Bourdeille, the writer more commonly known as Brantôme. During this time the notoriety of Brantôme's anecdotal recounting of the sexual practices of the Valois court, *Mémoires . . . contenans les vies des dames galantes de son temps* (1666, Memoirs . . . Containing the Lives of Fair and Gallant Ladies of His Time), eclipsed the fact

Pierre de Bourdeille, also known as Brantôme (frontispiece, The Book of Ladies *[New York: Collier, 1899]; Thomas Cooper Library, University of South Carolina)*

maternal families. He was the third son of the baron de Bourdeille, whose noble family name dates back to the days of Charlemagne, and Anne de Vivonne de la Chastaigneraie. The descendants of the house of Bourdeille distinguished themselves with honor at court and on the battlefield. Meanwhile, Bourdeille's maternal grandmother, Louise de Daillon, was a descendant of the great house of Lude; her father, Jean de Daillon, was King Louis XI's chamberlain. Louise de Daillon was raised at court with Anne de Beaujeu, the king's daughter, and she later served as maid of honor at the court of King François I's sister, Marguerite de Navarre.

Bourdeille's father died when he was approximately seven years old, and he and his mother joined his grandmother at court. Surrounded by women, Bourdeille grew up in an environment where conversations revolved around great scandals. When he was older, his grandmother recounted stories of court intrigue to him, providing important material for his later writings. Overall, Bourdeille's recollections give modern readers insights into literary, social, and political facets of court life during the reign of the Valois. For instance, Bourdeille recorded how Marguerite de Navarre composed her novella collection, known today as the *Heptaméron* (1559). He explains that Marguerite formulated her stories while in her carriage, her writing desk held by Bourdeille's grandmother. He also declares that many real-life court intrigues surface in Marguerite's tales, and that his mother, the queen's lady-in-waiting, knew the identity of some of the protagonists and shared this knowledge with him. In fact, Bourdeille's mother claimed to be one of the ten fictionalized storytellers in the *Heptaméron* frame story.

After Marguerite de Navarre's death in 1549, Bourdeille left the court of Navarre to study in Paris, and he completed his education in Poitiers around 1556. He came to be known as Brantôme through the abbacy of Brantôme, which was conferred on him by King Henri II in 1558. This church benefice was a reward for the bravery displayed by his older brother Jean de Bourdeille, who was killed at the siege of Hesdin in 1553. Brantôme was not an abbot, however, and he never took religious orders. He identified himself as *conseigneur de Brantôme*.

Brantôme's career involved travel, military expeditions, and court life, all of which served as material for his voluminous writings. In 1558 he made his first trip to Italy, stopping first in Geneva, where he witnessed the influx of those forced to leave France because of their religious beliefs. Brantôme then proceeded to Milan and Ferrara, finally arriving in Rome during the *sede vacante* (interregnum) period following Pope Paul IV's death. Brantôme was in Rome in 1559 when Pius IV was installed as the new pope, and dur-

that it is but one small portion of a greater work that fills more than eleven volumes. At the end of the twentieth century, however, scholars began to recognize the literary and historical value of Brantôme's extraordinary body of writings. Posthumously characterized as *Mémoires* (Memoirs), his works record and offer special insight into the social and political dimensions of life during a rich and turbulent period of the French court, one that begins with the times of François I and continues through the reign of Catherine de Médicis to the advent of Henri IV.

Pierre de Bourdeille was born circa 1540 in Périgord, a region northeast of Bordeaux. Throughout his writings and in his last will and testament Brantôme emphasizes the illustriousness of both his paternal and

ing this time he met the Cardinal de Guise and François de Lorraine, Duc de Guise, with whom he traveled to Naples. Brantôme was a great admirer and friend of this influential and powerful family. In 1559 Brantôme's link with both the French king, François II, and the Guise clan was strengthened when Marie Stuart, niece of François de Lorraine, married François and became queen of France.

Brantôme's travels included visiting famous military and tourist sights, indulging in what he calls "plaisirs délicieux" (delicious pleasures), and increasing the number of important and influential people that he knew. The blending of the military and the sensual is evident in his recollections. Serving as a volunteer under the Maréchal de Brissac, for example, Brantôme was wounded in the face during a military exercise in Portofino. Blinded for several days, he recounts how a pretty young Genoese woman cured him by infusing his eyes with her breast milk.

Brantôme's journeys included Portugal, Spain, Morocco, England, and Scotland. When François II died in 1560, Brantôme was a member of the party accompanying the young widow back to Scotland in her effort to reclaim the throne there. While in England, he met with Queen Elizabeth and her royal court.

When Brantôme returned to France in 1562, he joined the Catholic side in the French Wars of Religion. He fought at Blois, participated in the siege of Rouen with the duc de Guise, and fought in the battle of Dreux. In 1563 Brantôme was present when Guise was assassinated by the Protestant Poltrot de Méré. That year Brantôme fought with French forces when Le Havre was taken from the English. He next served in Madrid as an intermediary for Elizabeth of Spain, daughter of Catherine de Médicis, and he was instrumental in bringing about the June 1565 Bayonne meeting between the monarchs of France and Spain. In 1568 Brantôme was appointed Gentleman of the Bedchamber of the French king Charles IX, an honor that was also bestowed on him by Charles's successor, King Henri III.

Two unexpected events led to the chronicles Brantôme wrote detailing his thirty-three years of court life. The first was a disagreement with Henri III, and the second was a horse-riding accident. Both events changed the rhythm of Brantôme's active court life, and the latter put an end to his extensive travels.

Brantôme often expressed bitterness about seeing royal favors bestowed on those he considered less worthy than he. Finally, Henri III's failure to honor a promise he had made to Brantôme caused the latter to break with the king. At the 1582 death of Brantôme's elder brother, André de Bourdeille, the king promised

Brantôme his brother's position of seneschal and governor of the Périgord region until his nine-year-old nephew came of age to assume his father's responsibilities. But previous arrangements made by the king overrode this promise made to Brantôme. Brantôme gave public voice to his anger and disappointment. He also removed from his belt the key to the king's bedchamber and tossed it into the Seine River, punctuating his decision to end his ties with the king. Although he claims never to have set foot again into the king's bedroom, he continued to frequent the queen's chamber and the chambers of her entourage of ladies and princesses, as well as those of his good friends among the seigneurs and princes at court. In his writing Brantôme admits that his anger at the king made him consider leaving France in order to serve the more generous king of Spain. If he had done so, he planned to reveal to the king of Spain some strategically important geographical weaknesses on the French coast that would have seriously compromised the French cause. But the economic climate in France made it impossible for Brantôme to sell what he needed in order to establish himself in a new country.

Brantôme's misfortunes increased when a horse reared and fell on him, breaking his lower back. He was bedridden for four years. In the thirty years between this accident and his death, his contact with the outside world was severely curtailed. Brantôme's pen became an important instrument for re-creating the now-inaccessible court that he idolized as a paradise on earth. His writing also served as a means of consoling himself for all that he had lost or all of which he felt unjustly deprived.

That Brantôme held his work in high esteem is evident in the way he describes it in his last will and testament. Written by hand and dated 1609, the will stipulates in great detail what he wants done with his writing. As transcribed by his secretary Mataud, the works comprised five volumes, each covered with a different color velvet. In his will, Brantôme explains that the volumes have been carefully corrected, and that one can be assured of finding there many beautiful things, such as stories, discourses, and histories. He entrusts his niece, Jeanne de Bourdeille, Countess of Durtal, with the publication of his work. He stipulates that the money needed to publish it in beautiful letters and in a large and elegant format be taken from his estate before any inheritance is distributed to anyone. Brantôme's details make it clear that he has approached publishing houses with his work. He mentions that his preliminary inquiries to printers in Paris and Lyon showed that the publication expense would be reasonable. As Brantôme recounts it, once the printers had perused his work, they were willing to publish it without payment, seeing immediately the attention and profit the work would generate for them. In spite of the printers' eagerness to publish, however, he refused, since he did not wish his work to appear in print during his lifetime. He also stipulates that his niece, acting as executor, ascertain that his name and no other appear as author (it was common practice to assign a fictitious author's name to a controversial posthumous work or to publish it anonymously). In this way Brantôme sought to assure that the pains he has taken to produce such a work garner for him the glory due to him alone. He also requests that the first volume printed be a particularly elegant one, well bound and in velvet, and that it be given as a present to the highly esteemed Queen Marguerite de Valois, who had read some of his work and who had praised it.

Despite Brantôme's careful instructions, his work did not appear in published form until 1665. It was published without the guidance of his niece, and fifty years after the death of Marguerite de Valois, his adored dedicatee. Shortly after Brantôme's death on 5 July 1614, what came to be called the "Mémoires de Brantôme" circulated in manuscript form, during which time it was transformed and reshaped by those who had the power to do so. Tallement des Réaux's written remarks from the late 1650s are among the earliest references to Brantôme's work and the changes it underwent. According to Réaux, the cardinal de Retz discovered that a Brantôme manuscript featured anecdotes about the love life of the duchesse de Retz, the Cardinal's grandmother. He succeeded in expunging these stories, which do not appear in the published edition of Brantôme's works. In 1664 Charles Sorel's *Bibliothèque françoise* (French Library) mentions that five or six volumes of Brantôme's memoirs are being hoarded like treasures. But access to the work increased with its fame. Thus, an avid and expanding readership was coming into contact with what Sorel describes as frank and audacious portraits of the temperaments and actions of famous men and women of the last century.

While Brantôme had explored printing possibilities within France, his works were first published in Holland by Dutch publisher Jean Sambix. Appearing in Leyden in 1665, the first volume comprised 407 pages and had as its title *Mémoires de Messire Pierre de Bourdeille, seigneur de Brantôme, contenans les vies des dames de France illustres de son temps* (Memoirs of Messire Pierre de Bourdeille, Seigneur de Brantôme, Containing the Lives of Illustrious Ladies of France of his Time; translated as *The Book of the Ladies [Illustrious Dames],* 1899). In 1666 Sambix published the two-volume, 928-page *Mémoires de Messire Pierre de Bourdeille, seigneur de Brantôme, contenant les vies des dames galantes de son temps* (Memoirs of Messire Pierre de Bourdeille, Seigneur de Brantôme, Contain-

ing the Lives of the Gallant Ladies of his Time; translated as *Lives of Fair and Gallant Ladies,* 1901, 1907). The title of this second volume was not one Brantôme had proposed. In his writing he refers to this part of his work as "Second livre des dames" (Second Book of the Ladies), or "Le second volume que j'ay faict des dames et dédié à M. le duc d'Alençon" (The second volume that I have written on Ladies and dedicated to Monsieur the duc d'Alençon), or he otherwise employed similarly neutral terms. But, as Sorel observed in *Bibliothèque françoise,* given the public's interest for books with "galantes" in the title, it seems that Sambix marketed the work to maximize his sales, and the provocative and economically profitable title has persisted through the ages. *Les vies des dames galantes* remains the most republished edition in French, and the one that is most frequently translated. Sambix published six more volumes of Brantôme's *Mémoires* in 1666, four comprising *Les vies des hommes illustres et grands capitaines françois* (Lives of Famous Men and Great French Military Leaders) and the other two featuring *Les vies des hommes illustres et grands capitaines étrangers* (Lives of Famous Men and Great Foreign Military Leaders).

Because Sambix's nine-volume first edition of Brantôme's *Mémoires* was based on imperfect manuscripts that were in circulation, it was incomplete. Nevertheless, it immediately found favor with readers. Contemporary readers of the work, such as Bonaventure d'Argonne, expressed confidence in its historical validity since they believed the events were witnessed by Brantôme. The many pirated editions that appeared further demonstrate the work's popularity. Madame de Lafayette made use of Brantôme's work for the historical background material for her novels, including *La Princesse de Clèves* (1678; translated as *The Princess of Cleves: The Most Famed Romance,* 1679), which is set in the court of Henri II and Catherine de Médicis. In 1740 a new fifteen-volume edition of Brantôme's *Mémoires* appeared, edited by Jacob Le Duchat, Antoine Lancelot, and Prosper Marchand. The first thirteen volumes feature Brantôme's works, and the rest comprise those of his brother André de Bourdeille. Among eighteenth-century readers, Jean-Jacques Rousseau was particularly struck by Brantôme's *Les vies des grands capitaines* and the exemplary depiction of men of valor.

Nineteenth-century scholars' and readers' fascination with the Renaissance resulted in three new editions of Brantôme's work. Louis Jean Nicolas Monmerqué's eight-volume edition was published in 1822–1823. The second edition of the *Mémoires* was begun in 1858 by the Bibliothèque Elzévirienne. Completed in 1895, it includes 13 volumes compiled and edited under the direction of Prosper Mérimée and Louis Lacour. With all available manuscripts consulted by its editors, and including extensive notes, it is considered the first critical edition of Brantôme's work. Finally, between 1864 and 1882 Ludovic Lalanne's eleven-volume edition was published. Lalanne's edition represents more than twenty years of copious research, and it is the most frequently consulted and respected for its reliability and completeness. The tenth volume features some poetry written when Brantôme was young, published for the first time. Furthermore, Lalanne's 1896 study of Brantôme, *Brantôme: Sa vie et ses écrits* (Brantôme: His Life and His Works), remains an important biographical source. Honoré de Balzac, Alexandre Dumas, and Prosper Mérimée are among the many nineteenth-century readers who found inspiration in Brantôme's work.

In 1904 France's Bibliothèque nationale received from the Baroness James de Rothschild an almost complete set of autograph manuscripts, known as the Bourdeille manuscripts, representing what is believed to be the earliest period of composition of the work, with aspects that vary from later manuscripts. Only two partial editions of Brantôme's work have incorporated these variants: the first is the 1926 Roger Gaucheron edition of the first book of ladies, titled *Recueil des dames* (Compilation of the Ladies). Here Brantôme's late revisions are compared with the text in the Bourdeille manuscript. Additionally, Etienne Vaucheret consulted the Bourdeille manuscript for his 1973 critical edition of Brantôme's *Discours sur les colonels de l'infanterie de France* (Discourse on the Colonels of the French Infantry).

With the exception of *Les vies des dames galantes,* most of Brantôme's work remains accessible only to a French reading public. Only a small portion of Brantôme's work has been translated into English. John Ozell's 1741 translation of the *Rhodomontades* is the only work translated into English before the twentieth century. Katharine Prescott Wormeley's *Lives of Illustrious Ladies* appeared at the turn of the twentieth century and was reissued several times, but no other English translation of this work has appeared. Similar stories surround the few other English translations in print. In fact, the only part of Brantôme's work that has been republished frequently, and translated and retranslated, is *Les vies des dames galantes.* From 1972 to 1995 at least five French editions appeared, and, along with English, it has been translated into German, Hungarian, Korean, Italian, and Polish.

With access to his work long limited, it is perhaps unsurprising that sustained critical interest in Brantôme and his work did not develop until the latter half of the twentieth century. French interest in Brantôme has clearly grown. Historian Anne-Marie Cocula-Vaillières's study, *Brantôme, amour et gloire au temps des Valois* (Brantôme, Love and Glory in the Time of the Valois)

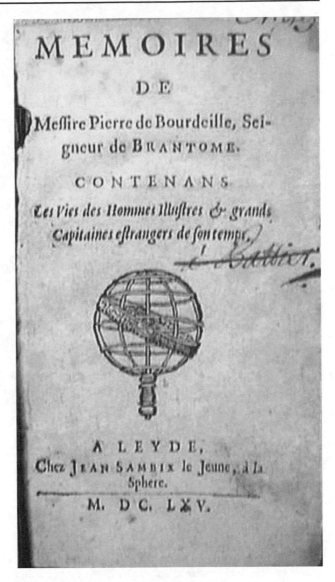

Title page for Brantôme's first work, published more than fifty years after his death (from <http://antikvariat-vintrlik.cz/fotos/ predmety3530.jpg>)

appeared in 1986; another study, literary historian and critic Madeleine Lazard's *Pierre de Bourdeille, seigneur de Brantôme,* was published in 1995. In 1991 Etienne Vaucheret edited and annotated a partial edition titled *Recueil des Dames, poésies et tombeaux* (Compilation of the Ladies, Poetry, and Funerary Writings). More than 1,600 pages in length, this edition includes both books of the ladies and collected shorter pieces by Brantôme. Meanwhile, Robert D. Cottrell's study in English, *Brantôme: The Writer as Portraitist of His Age* (1970), in addition to the English translations of Brantôme in print, have led to wider scholarly appreciation of the work. Finally, a new journal focusing on Brantôme's work, *Cahiers Brantôme* (Brantôme Journal), was launched in 2003. Under the auspices of the Amis de Brantôme (Friends of Brantôme) and with the support of the Université Michel de Montaigne-Bordeaux 3, it appeared with the proceedings of a conference on *Brantôme et les grands d'Europe* (Brantôme and the Great of Europe). The journal plans to continue publishing articles from regularly scheduled conferences on Brantôme.

Brantôme's *Mémoires* provides much for scholars to analyze. For Brantôme, women were a defining feature of court life, which explains why the first volume of his grand oeuvre, *Les vies des dames illustres de son temps,* comprises seven discourses of varying length devoted to the ladies of the court. The first five discourses portray queens of France (respectively, Anne de Bretagne, Catherine de Médicis, Marie Stuart) and French princesses who became queens, such as Elisabeth de Valois, Queen of Spain (daughter of King Henri II and Catherine de Médicis) and Marguerite de Valois, Queen of France and of Navarre. The sixth discourse addresses fourteen renowned princesses of the house of France, including Marguerite de Navarre, sister of King François I; Marguerite de France, Duchesse de Savoie; and Isabelle de France, daughter of King Charles IX. Whereas the first six discourses deal with women Brantôme knew personally, the seventh depicts the two queens Jeanne de Naples of the fourteenth and fifteenth centuries, who are linked to French royal blood through St. Louis.

This book is designed to inspire awe of, and admiration for, the magnificence of court life and of its noble constituents. In the portrait of Catherine de Médicis, for example, more than five pages are devoted to listing the titled names of all the glorious and the grand people who made up the court, with a separate enumeration of those who accompanied the king and queen, and later the king and his mother, during royal entries or celebrations. Using the metaphor of the court as "un vray Paradis du monde" (a true paradise on earth), Brantôme sees the dames and damsels as goddesses– "creatures plustost divines que humaines" (creatures more divine than human).

In his portraits Brantôme is a chronicler more than an historian. He always reveals his bias in favor of the famous women he has chosen to depict. Brantôme's encomiastic sketches abound in hyperbole and flattering metaphors, and they include many anecdotes that buttress the image he aims to create. One of the longest portraits, the fifth, extols Marguerite de Valois, first wife of Henri IV, popularly known as La Reine Margot. All but one of Brantôme's works, *Les vies des dames galantes,* is dedicated to her (and, conversely, Marguerite de Valois dedicated to Brantôme the memoirs she subsequently wrote, memoirs largely inspired as an elabora-

tion of and corrective to Brantôme's depiction of her). Brantôme claims that when compared to Marguerite's physical beauty, all women considered beautiful now, in the future, or in the past, are ugly. Those who doubt God's or Nature's capacity for miracles have only to look at Marguerite to become believers. Brantôme fills pages with examples of distinguished visitors to the court of France and their reactions to her. One Polish ambassador, so overwhelmed by Marguerite's beauty, avows that he has no desire to see anything else after having witnessed such a sight. The ambassador compares his reaction to that of Turkish pilgrims to Mecca, who, after having visited the tomb of the prophet Mohammed, are ready to become blind. The sight of such a beautiful and spectacular monument causes them to become ravished and transported to a higher realm. They claim to have seen the ultimate sight to which nothing else can compare, and insist on having their eyes, now useless, burned out.

That part of the work to which Brantôme referred as the *Second livre des dames* (Second Book of the Ladies) is today commonly called *Les vies des dames galantes.* Though this book deals with the same social class as the first volume, Brantôme refuses to name the famous people involved in bawdy escapades recounted in the more than five hundred pages of the work. Often classified under the category of erotic literature, it has been described by Lazard as "le rapport Kinsey du XVIe siècle" (the Kinsey Report of the sixteenth century). Although this book is different from the first in tone, it nevertheless has many affinities with it. Once again, Brantôme divides his book into seven discourses, and again his focus is solely on the court and the noble class. Additionally, the writing is highly anecdotal: it is based on his personal experiences, travels, readings, and hearsay. How much of what he writes is entirely true, rather than embellished or fantasized, is open to speculation.

Likely begun in the early 1580s and written over a twenty-year period, the second book was published in 1666 with a dedicatory letter to François d'Alençon, son of Henri II and Catherine de Médicis, who was a close friend of Brantôme and his ideal reader. According to the dedicatory letter, the book is meant to entertain and to amuse. In the process, Brantôme ignores the divine and highlights the purely earthy, physical nature of men and women who strive for sexual pleasure in an erotically charged court environment. Characterizing the duc d'Alençon as a lover of "bons mots et contes" (witty sayings and stories), Brantôme formulates the book as a way of maintaining their close rapport through the sharing, now in written form, of the kinds of tales that united them in the past. In the dedicatory letter Brantôme assures his friend that these vignettes, assembled haphazardly, are far from being serious discourses, which will follow at a later date. Here Brantôme is likely referring to the major portion of his work that he devotes to the lives of famous men.

The material that is meant to entertain the sexually mischievous and voyeuristic duc d'Alençon is divided into seven topics: 1) "Discours sur les Dames qui font l'amour et leurs maris cocus" (Discourse on Women Who Make Love and Their Husbands Cuckolds); 2) "Discours sur le sujet qui contente plus en amours, ou le toucher, ou la veue, ou la parole" (Discourse on What Gives the Most Pleasure in Love: Touch, Sight, or Speech); 3) "Autre discourse sur la beauté de la belle jambe, et la vertu qu'elle a" (Discourse on the Beauty of a Pretty Leg, and Its Power); 4) "Discours sur les femmes mariées, les vefves et les filles, à savoir desquelles les unes sont plus chaudes à l'amour que les autres" (Discourse on Married Women, Widows, and Girls, with Reference to Which are Hotter at Love Than Others); 5) "Discours sur l'amour des Dames vieilles et comme aucunes l'ayment autant que les jeunes" (Discourse on the Love of Old Women and How Some Love to Do It as Much as Young Ones); 6) "Discours sur ce qu'il ne faut jamais parler mal des Dames et la consequence qui en vient" (Discourse on Why One Should Never Speak Badly of Women, and the Consequences that Can Result); 7) "Discours sur ce que les belles et honnestes Dames ayment les vaillants hommes et les braves hommes ayment les Dames courageuses" (Discourse on Why Beautiful and Honest Ladies Love Valiant Men, and Brave Men Love Courageous Ladies). Some literary critics believe these topics are based on subjects that humanists of Brantôme's time discussed philosophically with reference to Neoplatonism, which progressively moved love away from the physical toward the spiritual. Here, however, Brantôme always makes love synonymous with desire and locates it strictly in the realm of the senses, and his anecdotes depict the sex drive as equally strong in both men and women.

As the dedicatory epistle to François d'Alençon indicates, Brantôme intended to devote himself to serious discourses after completing *Les vies des dames galantes*. It is believed that he began the more thoughtful phase of his project in the years after his crippling accident. His *Rodomontades*, in which he focuses on Spanish captains, marked the beginning of his interest in exemplary tales of military acts of courage. Dedicated to Marguerite de Valois and presented to her in 1590, these tales seem to have established the organizational structure for his later work: whereas the volumes on ladies comprised the first part of his work, the other, considerably lengthier part would comprise biographical portraits of foreign and French military leaders.

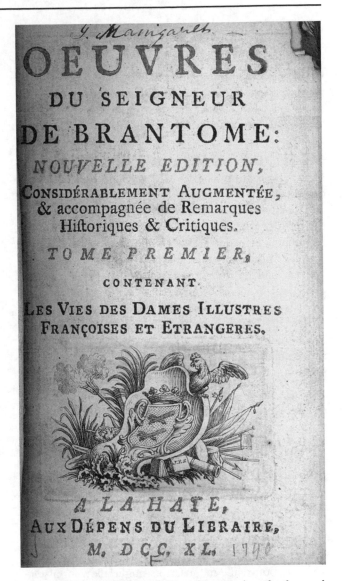

Title page for the fifteen-volume edition of Brantôme's works, the second of two multivolume editions published in the eighteenth century (Special Collections, Thomas Cooper Library, University of South Carolina)

Brantôme's thrust in *Les vies des grands capitaines* (Lives of Great Military Leaders) is the same as in *Les vies des dames illustres,* and he announces this fact at the beginning of the work, where he explains his desire to furnish evidence about the praiseworthiness of the important men he has chosen to describe. His goal is to write *only* about the great, and *only* in order to praise them. Nevertheless, Brantôme's project resists becoming stilted, formulaic, or repetitive because he includes, as he does in virtually all his writings, what he terms "particularités" (particularities)—pertinent details about the personality of, or specific actions of, the luminary in question. These details are often digressive, but they add distinction and power to Brantôme's historiography. For example, Brantôme recounts that during military campaigns, the duc de Guise actively sought soldiers' reactions to certain strategies that had been undertaken and was pleased to receive pertinent advice from those under his command. Guise's military prowess was legendary during the war-torn sixteenth century, but Brantôme adds a detail that both humanizes this venerated figure and underscores his military acumen.

Les vies des grands capitaines accounts for almost 70 percent of Brantôme's work. It is arranged in chronological order, from Charles VIII through Henri III. Out of a total of 274 biographical sketches of varying length, 199 deal with French military leaders. Each begins with the birth of the leader and ends with his death. Those Brantôme considers important in determining the course of history are allotted the most pages. Hence, the account of King François I (whom Brantôme calls "le grand roi François" [the great King François]) spans ninety pages, and Gaspard de Coligny, the commander of the Huguenots during the French Wars of Religion, more than fifty. Because these portraits are arranged chronologically, they offer a collective biography of an important period of time.

As more researchers discover Brantôme, he has become known as more than a minor author of risqué stories, a man who wrote much but thought little. Instead, he is increasingly viewed as an important social commentator. This new perspective may inspire a new generation of scholars to embark on the important work on Brantôme that remains to be done. For example, Henri Omont's extensive analysis of the different manuscripts of Brantôme's work points to the creation of a definitive edition. Furthermore, scholarship such as Omont's and new information that may be gleaned from the Bourdeille manuscripts might allow for a step-by-step study of the creation of the works, as well as a more thorough analysis of the evolution of Brantôme's thought and style.

Brantôme's intimate account of life in the Valois court is extraordinary. His writings are filled with hundreds of portraits of the rich and famous, both French and foreign, who made history in the sixteenth century, most of whom he knew personally. Hence, Brantôme's works provide important insight into the political, cultural, and social changes that took place during a pivotal moment of French history. Additionally, his unusual style raises questions for historians and literary critics about the memoir as genre, and within that context, the relationship between historical writing and literary creation.

Biography:

Ludovic Lalanne, *Brantôme: Sa Vie et ses écrits,* Société de l'histoire de France, no. 280 (Paris: Renouard, 1896).

References:

Françoise Argod-Dutard and Anne-Marie Cocula, *Brantôme et les grands d'Europe: Rencontres de Brantôme en Périgord,* Cahiers Brantôme, no. 1 (Pessac: Editions du Centre Montaigne d'Université de Bordeaux 3, 2003);

Blanchard W. Bates, "Brantôme, the Social Columnist," in *Literary Portraiture in the Narrative of the French Renaissance* (New York: Stechert, 1945), pp. 45–72;

Anne-Marie Cocula-Vaillières, *Brantôme, amour et gloire au temps des Valois* (Paris: Michel, 1986);

Robert D. Cottrell, *Brantôme: The Writer as Portraitist of His Age,* Etudes de philologie et d'histoire, no. 15 (Geneva: Droz, 1970);

Madeleine Lazard, *Pierre de Bourdeille, seigneur de Brantôme* (Paris: Fayard, 1995);

Henri Omont, "Notice sur les manuscrits originaux des oeuvres de Brantôme," *Bibliothèque de l'école des Chartes,* 65 (1904): 5–54;

Dora E. Polachek, "A la recherche du spirituel: L'Italie et les *Dames galantes* de Brantôme," *The Romanic Review,* 94, nos. 1–2 (2003): 227–243;

Charles Sorel, *La Bibliothèque Françoise . . .: Ou le choix et l'examen des livres françois qui traitent de l'éloquence, de la philosophie, de la devotion et de la conduite des moeurs . . . Avec un traité particulier où se trouve l'ordre, le choix, et l'examen des histoires de France* (Paris: Printed by the Compagnie des Libraires du Palais, 1664);

Arthur Tilley, *The Literature of the French Renaissance,* volume 2 (Cambridge: Cambridge University Press, 1904), pp. 191–196;

W. L. Wiley, "Brantôme's Interest in Languages and Literature," *Modern Language Notes,* 65 (1950): 331–336.

Papers:

The most important collection of Brantôme's manuscripts is held by the Bibliothèque nationale in Paris.

Guillaume Budé

(26 January 1468 – 22 August 1540)

Robert B. Rigoulot
University of Illinois at Springfield

SELECTED WORKS: *Annotationes . . . in quattuor et viginti Pandectarum libros* (Paris: Printed by Josse Bade, 1508);

De asse et partibus ejus libri quinque (Paris: Printed by Josse Bade, 1514);

De contemptu rerum fortuitarum (Paris: Printed by Josse Bade, [1520]);

Epistolae Gulielmi Budei regii secretarii (Paris: Printed by Josse Bade, 1520);

De arte svpputandi libri quatuor, by Budé and Cuthbert Tunstall (London: R. Pynsoni, 1522);

Epistolae posteriores (Paris: Printed by Josse Bade, 1522);

Summaire ou epitome du livre de asse (Paris: Printed by Pierre Vidou for Galliot Du Pré, 1522);

Altera editio Annotationum in Pandectas (Paris: Printed by Josse Bade, [1526]);

Latinae linguae flosculi ad operis de reru fortuitaque cõteptu elucidatione collecti (Paris: Printed by Josse Bade, 1526);

Commentarii linguae graecae (Paris: Printed by Josse Bade, 1529);

And. Alciati libellus, De ponderibus et mensuris item, Budæi quædam de eadem re, adhuc non uisa: item, Philippi Melanchthonis, de ijsdem, ad Germanorum usum sententia: Alciati quoq[ue] et Philippi Melanchthonis, in laudem iuris ciuilis, orationes duæ elegantissimæ, by Budé, Andrea Alciati, and Philipp Melanchthon (Haganoæ: J. Sec, 1530);

Epistolarum Latinarum lib. V. annotationibus[que] adjectis in singulas fere epistolas. Græcarum item lib. I. Basilii item Magni Epistola de vita in solitudine agenda, per Budæum latina facta (Paris: Printed by Josse Bade, 1531);

De Philologia (Paris: Printed by Josse Bade, 1532); translated into French by Marie-Madeleine de La Garanderie as *Philologie* (Paris: Belles lettres, 2001);

De studio literarum recte et commode instituendo (Paris: Printed by Josse Bade, 1532); translated into French by La Garanderie *as L'étude des lettres: principes pour sa juste et bonne institution* (Paris: Belles lettres, 1988);

Guillaume Budé (painting by Jean Couet; Metropolitan Museum of Art; from <http://www.wga.hu/html/c/clouet/jean/g_bude.html>)

Georgii Agricolae medici libri quinque De mensuris & ponderibus in quibus plaeraque à Budaeo & Portio parum animaduersa diligenter excutiuntur, by Budé, Georg Agricola, and Simone Porzio (Paris: C. Wechel, 1533);

De transitu Hellenismi ad Christianismum libri tres (Paris: Printed by Robert Estienne, 1535); translated into French by Maurice Lebel as *Le passage de l'hellénisme au christianisme* (Sherbrooke: Editions paulines, 1973);

Fl. Vegetii Renati viri illustris De re militari libri quatuor: Sexti Ivlii Frontini viri consvlaris De strategematis libri totidem: Aeliani De instruendis aciebus liber vnus: Modesti De vocabulis rei militaris liber vnus, by Budé, Flavius Vegetius Renatus, Sextus Julius Frontinus, and others (Paris: Christian Wechel, 1535);

De curandis articularibus morbis commentarius, authore Guillielmo Budaeo disesio doctore medico. . . . (Paris: Pierre Regnault, 1539);

Forensia (Paris: Printed by Robert Estienne, 1544);

De l'Institution du Prince: Livre contenant plusieurs histoires, enseignemens, & saiges dicts des anciens tant Grecs que Latins, edited by Jean de Luxembourg (Troyes: Printed by Nicole Paris, 1547);

Le livre de l'institution du prince (Paris: Printed by Jean Foucher, 1548);

Commentarii linguae Graecae . . . supplicumque libellorum (Paris: Printed by Robert Estienne, 1548);

Omnia Opera Gulielmi Budaei, 4 volumes (Basel: Printed by Nicolaus Episcopius the Younger, 1557; reprinted, Farnborough, U.K.: Gregg, 1966 [i.e., 1967])–volume one also published separately as *Lucubrationes variae;*

Dictionaire françoislatin, auquel les mots françois avec les manières d'user d'iceulx, sont tournez en latin, corrigé & augmenté par Maistre Jehan Thierry avec l'aide & diligence de gens sçavants. Plus ya à la fin un traicté d'aulcuns mots & manière de parler appartenans à la venerie pris du seconde livre de la philologie de Monsieur Budé, translated into French by Louis le Roy from an unpublished Latin work by Budé and Jehan Thierry (Paris: Published by Jacques du Puys, 1564).

Edition in English: Daniel Frank Penham, *De Transitu Hellenismi ad Christianismum: A Study of a Little Known Treatise of Guillaume Budé, followed by a Translation into English,* dissertation, Columbia University, 1954.

OTHER: Anonymous [attributed to Plutarch], *De placitis philosophorum naturalibus,* translated from Greek by Budé (Paris: Printed by Josse Bade, 1503);

Plutarch, *Tria opuscula: De tranquillitate et securitate animi cui accessit epistola Basilii magni de vita per solitudinem transigenda; De fortuna Romanorum; De fortuna vet virtute Alexandri,* translated from Greek by Budé (Paris: Printed by Josse Bade, 1505);

Plutarch, *De tranquillitate & securitate animi. Lib. I.; De fortuna Romanoru[m] ex Plutarcho. Lib. I.; De fortuna uel uirtute Alexandri. Lib. II.; Basilii magni epistola de uira per solitudinem transigenda,* translated from the Latin by Budé (Rome: Jacob Mazochium, 1510);

Sir Thomas More, *Ad lectorem. Habes candide lector opusculum illud vere aureum Thomæ Mori non minus utile quam elegans de optimo reipublicae statu, deque noua insula Utopia . . . ,* prefatory epistle by Budé (Paris: Printed by Gilles de Gourmont, 1517);

Aristoteles De Mundo; Philo De Mundo, translated from Greek by Budé (Paris: Printed by Josse Bade, 1526);

[Demosthenous Logoi duo kai hexekonta]: Habes lector Demosthenis Græcorum oratorum omnium facile principis Orationes duas & sexaginta, & in easdem Vlpiani commentarios, quantum extat: Libanii argumenta, annotations by Budé (Basel: Printed by Johannes Hervagius, 1532).

Guillaume Budé possesses one of the more durable reputations in the history of French letters. Early in his career his countrymen regarded him as one of their nation's brightest lights, and soon contemporaries beyond France also admired him as a Latinist and Hellenist whose research into the literature and history of classical antiquity outstripped that of the admired Italian humanist scholars who preceded him. In the following generation, legal scholars venerated him as the inspiration for a philologically grounded French school of law and legal education. By the nineteenth century Budé was regarded, with only a certain amount of exaggeration, as the founder of France's most prestigious institution of learning, the Collège de France, where his statue still graces the courtyard.

Budé's influence on the growth of French literature was indirect. Only one of his major works (if it qualifies as such) was actually composed in the French language, and his works have never been part of the national curriculum. In fact, no collected edition of his works has appeared since the *Omnia Opera* (Collected Works) of 1557. Only a handful of his Latin works have been translated into French, and all of those have been published since the late 1960s. Nevertheless, in his *Foundations of Modern Historical Scholarship* (1970) Donald R. Kelley proclaimed Budé's scholarship to be the starting point of modern historical sensibility and method, a view that has become commonly accepted in both American and French scholarship. Scholars examining the lengthy digressions in Budé's works have since concluded that he was a political thinker who advanced a program of cultural development based on the alliance of an absolutist monarch with the learned class.

Budé was born 26 January 1468, fourteen years after the end of the Hundred Years' War. His family had provided the French crown with functionaries for three generations. The Budés and the caste of functionaries to which they belonged were members of the urban middle class and were socially and politically ambitious. Most of these men were trained in Roman law or in the *artes dictaminis* (notarial arts), and they provided the administrative service for the monarchy as it reasserted its control over the nation following the departure of the last English occupiers and the collapse of the independent duchy of Burgundy. This new administrative class was essentially unconnected to the traditional elites of the medieval nation: the higher clergy and the hereditary nobility. These groups had served as stumbling blocks to royal ambitions within the kingdom, while the new administrative class gave its loyalty exclusively to the king and, through him, to the state. Budé's father had served as *grand audencier,* or director of the corps of secretaries within the royal chancellery, and as *trésorier des chartes* (keeper of documents) until a series of financial scandals ended his career. During this time Budé absorbed the ideology of this caste of administrators, and it became integral to his vision of literature, national culture, and the state.

Budé's early education was conventional. He was taught grammar at a local parish school in Paris. When he turned fifteen, his father sent him to the University of Orléans to study law. By statute only canon law—not the civil law necessary to an administrator's formation—was taught at the University of Paris. The legal training of the time was more an apprenticeship for a trade than a professional education. No preparation in the liberal arts beyond the schoolboy's introduction was necessary for the prospective law student. Thus, Budé did not pass through the portion of the university's liberal arts curriculum represented in the trivium, additional studies in grammar followed by logic and rhetoric.

To understand the value of Budé's contribution to the study of law, and to the history of scholarship in general, it is necessary to understand how law was interpreted and taught at the time. The basis of the law was the three volumes that made up the *Corpus Juris Civilis,* the sixth-century codification of Roman law accomplished at the directive of the Emperor Justinian. The *Corpus Juris Civilis* made centuries of Roman law manageable by reducing the number of statutes, decrees, and legal decisions accumulated over time into a consistent whole. The first published volume of the *Corpus Juris Civilis,* the *Codex constitutionum,* was a collection in ten books of what is essentially statute law. The commission appointed to carry out Justinian's legal reforms under the chairmanship of his *quaestor* (or Minister of Justice), Tribonian, redacted the body of imperial decrees and edicts (so far as they could be collected). This task was accomplished by eliminating passages from individual decrees when they contradicted the consensus of the whole and by suppressing entire documents when necessary. The second volume of the *Corpus Juris Civilis,* the *Digest,* or in the Greek title preferred by Budé, the *Pandects,* consists of more than nine thousand extracts from treatises on law by thirty-nine jurists of officially recognized authority, divided more or less by topic into fifty books. A third volume of the *Corpus Juris,* the *Institutes,* served for centuries as an authorized introductory text-

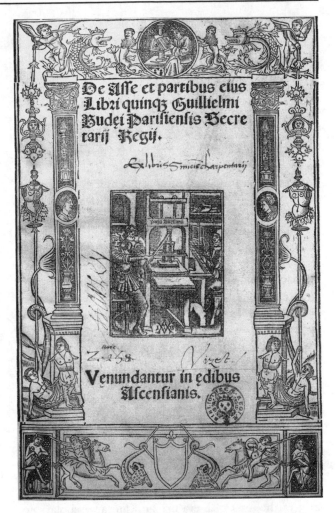

Title page for the work, published in 1514, in which Budé examines the monies, weights, and measures of classical antiquity (Collection Roger-Viollet/Getty Images)

book for law students. Justinian declared all three volumes to be law, superseding all previous law.

Students of Budé's generation invariably encountered civil law through the writings of the thirteenth-century legist Accursius and his followers, the so-called Glossators. The Glossators evolved a highly formalized approach to the study of these texts, similar to that of their scholastic colleagues who taught formal logic and theology in the universities. They labored to turn legal studies into a form of philosophy, systematizing the laws found in the *Digest* and explaining away any conflicts they found. Then, beginning in the fourteenth century, the followers of Bartolus of Sassoferrato, or "post-Glossators," began writing commentary on the commentaries of their predecessors with little reference to the body of Roman law as it appeared in the *Digest.* Consequently, Budé first experienced law as an arid, highly formalized area of study, entirely divorced from its earlier form and substance.

Budé's first experience with the law was fruitless: he left Orléans after three years without earning a degree. For five years he led the leisured life available to a young man of his social class, devoting himself to hunting, riding, and falconry. At the age of twenty-three, for motives that remain unclear, Budé returned to legal studies with new seriousness. He did not return to the university but began to read law on his own, without a master. (Early in his career Budé's status as an autodidact seems to have added to his mystique as a man of letters.) One of the first insights to emerge from his new program of studies was his conclusion that the Glossators and Bartolists were of no use in understanding civil law. He began to look for authors whose methods could help his program. He also extended the range of his classical learning to include large amounts of Roman history and literature. Even more ambitiously, he began to teach himself Greek and to expand his research into that part of the ancient world.

Budé found inspiration in the works of the Italian humanist scholars of the fifteenth century, and particularly in the ideal of *bonae literae* (meaning "good letters or literature," referring to the revival of classical literary forms) they propagated. The terms "humanist" and "humanism" were coined long after this period to designate a set of cultural and intellectual phenomena that centered on the discovery, appreciation, and imitation of the art and literature of classical antiquity. What actually constituted humanistic practice, particularly in the area of literature and literary scholarship, has been a matter of strenuous debate among scholars since at least the mid nineteenth century. This controversy has been particularly important in Budé studies. How scholars assess Budé's place in the history of French intellectual life, and the nature and originality of his contributions to it, is determined in large part by their definitions of humanism and the humanist project.

Budé was one of the first scholars in France to take up the study of classical Greek, and certainly he was the first to do so with any real success. The rising Ottoman threat to the Byzantine Empire had renewed contacts between Constantinople and the West during the first half of the fifteenth century. The fall of the city in 1453 marooned some Greek scholars in Italy, and they and their students decided to pursue their fortunes in the West. The Italian Greek scholar Gregory Tifernus visited Paris and lectured there, as did Andronicos Callistos in 1475. In 1476 the Byzantine copyist George Hermonymus set up shop in Paris and advertised his services as a teacher of Greek and a producer and vendor of manuscripts. The early humanist religious reformer Jacques Lefèvre d'Etaples was one of Hermonymus's earliest students, and he pronounced himself satisfied with the tutor's services, although Lefèvre never mastered more than the basics of the Greek language. Later students, such as the Dutch humanist Desiderius Erasmus, the German Johannes Reuchlin, and Budé, found Hermonymus a shifty character and not a very good teacher, although at least one modern scholar has wondered if he really could have been that bad. However, Budé thought him ignorant and denied having learned anything worthwhile from him. It was not until 1495, when Janus Lascaris came to France and entered the service of Charles VIII, that Budé found a competent teacher. However, Lascaris was away from Paris often enough that Budé could claim to be essentially self-taught. Perhaps, then, Lascaris's greatest contribution to Budé's Hellenist education involved the books he left in Budé's care during his trips away from Paris and the Greek manuscripts he purchased for the king's collection.

After six years devoted to study, Budé secured a position in the college of secretaries within the chancellery, possibly through the intervention of his father's old colleagues. There is little evidence of his early administrative career. It is, however, known that Charles VIII's chancellor, Guy de Rochefort, was a patron of humanist learning and encouraged Budé in his efforts to advance in the king's service. Budé seems to have approached royal service with enthusiasm. Although drafting royal edicts and communications must have interfered with his Latin and Greek studies, there was an air of excitement and optimism during the reign of Charles VIII, and Budé later recalled this period fondly. In 1491 the king reached his majority and began to rule in his own right. His marriage to Anne of Brittany that year firmly secured that frequently rebellious duchy to the realm. In 1494 Charles invaded Italy in pursuit of a claim to the kingdom of Naples and as a first step toward what he announced would be a new crusade against the Turks. His victory at Fornovo the next summer generated much enthusiasm among the French. Although his troops were driven from Naples in 1496, there was every reason to believe that Charles would soon renew his efforts to subdue that kingdom. Hence, during his late twenties Budé was in the employ of an ambitious, dynamic monarch he believed to be committed to culture and learning. During this time he was also developing a scholarly reputation.

Charles VIII died in the spring of 1498 and was succeeded by the duke of Orléans, now Louis XII, who reopened the wars in Italy in pursuit of his own claims to the duchy of Milan. Budé remained in the new king's service for the first few years of his reign and took part in diplomatic missions in Italy in 1501 and 1505. However, he perceived that Louis had less of an interest in learning than had Charles and less of an interest in ostentation as a means of cultivating his own image. The carefulness of the royal treasury, which earned Louis the title "le père du peuple" (father of the people), struck Budé as miserliness and indifference to reputation. He began to spend less time at court and more at his studies.

Soon came the first fruits of Budé's Greek studies: four translations into Latin of works by, or attributed to, Plutarch. The first of these works to be printed, *De placitis philosophorum naturalibus* (1503, On the Doctrines of the Natural Philosophers), comprises five books from an unknown hand (but then attributed to Plutarch) outlining the teachings on natural philosophy of the major figures and schools of classical antiquity. This translation was followed by the publication of *Tria opuscula* (1505, Three Short Works), which includes three ethical treatises taken from Plutarch's *Moralia* (late first century A.D.): *De tranquillitate et securitate animi* (On Tranquility and Composure of the Soul), *De fortuna romanorum* (On the Fortune of the Romans), and *De fortuna vel virtute Alexandri* (On Fortune and Virtue in Alexander the Great).

Budé's decision to work with Plutarch's philosophical works is an early demonstration of his lifelong concern with moral and ethical, as well as historical and jurisprudential, aspects of public life. One ethical dilemma to which Budé returned again and again is the question of the relative values of the active and the contemplative lives. In *De tranquillitate et securitate animi*, Plutarch counseled his readers that tranquility achieved through disengagement from the concerns of the public sphere exacts a high price. Budé returned to this issue in his letters and published writings during those periods in his life when he attempted to balance the demands of public service against those of scholarship and family life.

Budé's translations of Plutarch contributed to his emerging reputation. None of the works had been translated before (although the letter on the solitary life by Basil the Great that Budé appended to the *De tranquillitate et securitate animi* was well known in a previous translation). By modern standards of translation, Budé's works are imprecise and overlong. Where Budé can find in Latin no exact equivalent to a Greek word, he uses several words or a phrase in order to convey his meaning. This practice led some nineteenth-century critics to accuse him of paraphrasing rather than translating. However, Budé's infelicities are shared with many contemporaries who tried their hand at translation. His awkwardness is best attributed to working in what was a relatively new form of liter-

Title page for Budé's last major philological work, published in 1529, which includes some 8,500 notes on ancient Greek and Latin (Collection Roger-Viollet/Getty Images)

ary expression. Furthermore, his translations were highly thought of by their earliest readers, and they brought him status in the world where learning and politics met. In 1505, as part of a French embassy to Julius II led by the Neapolitan humanist Matteo Ricci, Budé presented the Pope with a manuscript copy of *De tranquillitate et securitate animi,* as the dedicatory epistle to the first printed edition later that year indicates.

Through his early translations Budé formed a relationship with the printer Josse Bade, or Badius Ascensius, as he styled himself in humanist circles. The year Badius set up his own press after a long career of correcting texts for others, he printed Budé's version of *De placitis philosophorum naturalibus.* Badius also was responsible for the publication of the three treatises from Plutarch's *Moralia.* Meanwhile, Budé worked as a corrector on Badius's edition of *Rhetoricoru[m] M. Tullij Ciceronis ad C. Herenniu[m] libri quatuor* (1508). Badius was in many ways the ideal printer for a man of Budé's interests. He was well educated and maintained an informed interest in humanistic scholarship. His shop was frequented by men of letters such as Lefèvre d'Etaples, Erasmus, Pierre Danès, and Pierre Vitré. Additionally, Badius became a *libraire juré,* a bookseller licensed by the University of Paris, conferring real prestige on his enterprise and the books that came from his press. Badius and Budé also shared, along with their enthusiasm for *bonae literae,* what can be called a conservative approach to political and religious issues. These similar values may have made it possible for them to continue their collaboration after both had broken with Erasmus, and as François I's monarchy began to harden its stance toward religious innovation and what it saw as political subversion. Almost all of Budé's works were produced by Badius until the printer's death in 1535.

Budé's father died in 1503, and around this time Budé began to suffer from crippling headaches and sleep disturbances that afflicted him for the rest of his life. In his correspondence he complains about his lack of rest and the effect it had on his work. Around 1505 Budé married Roberte Le Lieur, a lawyer's daughter who was much younger than her husband. His friends found her entirely admirable, and she appears to have been regarded as erudite in her own right. Budé now took on responsibilities as a head of family, providing for the twelve children they eventually had. David McNeil quotes him on the subject of their *jucundus quiritatus* (delightful shrieking). Intriguingly, within the household Roberte seems to have served as something of a counterweight to her husband's religious conservatism. After Budé died, she moved to Geneva, the center of the Calvinist movement, with two of their children and converted to Protestantism. Whether this move indicates that there was a gap between Budé's domestic religion and his increasingly draconian attitudes toward public religion can only be a matter for conjecture.

Budé's first major work, *Annotationes . . . in quattuor et viginti Pandectarum libros* (Annotations . . . on Twenty-Four Books of the Pandects), was printed by Badius in 1508. This book, along with *De asse et partibus ejus* (1514, On the "As" and Its Parts) and *Commentarii linguae graecae* (1529, Commentaries on the Greek Language), forms the core of his contribution to technical, philological scholarship. The *Annotationes* is an extensive commentary on the first twenty-four books of Justinian's *Pandectae* (Digest), part 3 of the *Corpus Juris Civilis* (Code), which the emperor commissioned in 533. In 1526 Budé published the *Altera editio Annotationes in Pandectas* (Another edition of the Annotations on the Pendects), which scholars often call the *Annotationes posteriores* (Later Annotations), and it covers an additional nineteen books. The two books on the Pan-

dects, published together in the *Omnia Opera* along with their indices and supporting materials from the *Codex constitutionum* and the *Institutes,* occupy more than four hundred folio pages.

In purpose and appearance the *Annotationes* is not altogether different from the commentaries produced by the Glossators and Bartolists during the later middle ages. For example, all of these commentaries were designed, at least in part, to facilitate the study of Roman law by explaining difficult or misleading terms the student or practicing lawyer encounters in reading the *Pandectae.* However, Budé condemns the content of his predecessors' work, and especially their ignorance both of Latin and of law. He rejects the philosophically oriented, system-building approach they developed. Instead, Budé concentrates on clarifying the sense in which words had originally been used and the historical context in which that sense emerged. His commentaries include substantial discussions, some of them amounting to long essays, on ancient social institutions and practices. Furthermore, Budé reveals a keen interest in ancient daily life over the course of his many digressions on the meaning of various Latin words. But his goals in studying the *Pandectae* go beyond mere antiquarianism to include reforming the ways in which law was practiced in his own society. His ambition, stated clearly at the end of a digression on words that do not appear in the *Pandectae,* is to inaugurate a new era of latinity in French law courts to replace the Accursian barbarity that had reigned for so long. Ironically, many scholars who have spent much time with the *Annotationes* complain of Budé's disorderliness and the impenetrability of his prose.

The *Annotationes* is far too complex to fit into a single category of literature or scholarship. Today, scholars tend to approach the work from one of two perspectives. The first of these approaches emphasizes the technical side of the *Annotationes,* the amalgam of humanist textual criticism, jurisprudence, and historical scholarship that Budé employed in his analysis of Roman law, a style that has come to be called "legal humanism." Scholars interested in this aspect of the *Annotationes,* especially Kelley, have argued that the method Budé created lies at the root not only of most subsequent legal scholarship but also at the very beginning of modern historical consciousness, the mental orientation Kelley calls "historicism." The other scholarly approach to the *Annotationes* emphasizes its many digressions, which deal with social and institutional aspects both of classical antiquity and of Budé's own day. In addition to providing a wealth of information on sixteenth-century France, Gilbert Gadoffre claims that the digressions have ideological importance: in this analysis, Budé's asides on France at the end of

Louis XII's reign are a form of social criticism. They are also, Gadoffre asserts, the outlines of a program for the development of a French national culture, created by the French themselves at the initiative of their kings.

Who inspired Budé's accomplishments? In the *Annotationes* he acknowledges the influence of Italian scholars Lorenzo Valla and Angelo Poliziano on his work. Their influence helps to explain his program and the set of practices he came to call *philologia.* The methods with which Budé approaches the *Pandectae,* the methods that form the basis of his technical accomplishment in the *Annotationes,* emerged from the techniques of humanist textual criticism. Kelley explains that this technique is based on Valla's "revolutionary perception" that the literary style of any given author is in large part the product of the era and culture in which he worked. Sensitivity to style as a function of time and the development of a language provides the critic with a sense of anachronism, an awareness that a document may not be the product of the era to which it is has been assigned by consensus or tradition, or an awareness that a later hand has worked changes into a document.

At the beginning of the *Annotationes,* Budé states that reading Valla's *Elegantiae lingua Latinae* (1471, Elegances of the Latin Language) led him to a reexamination of the *Pandectae.* He explains that the *Pandectae,* as it had come down to the early sixteenth century, was a sadly disfigured thing, full of errors and corruptions because of generations of commentators. Budé traces the greater part of these errors to two sources, the mistakes of Tribonian and his board of editors, and the incompetence of the Accursians and Bartolists. Tribonian had not so much edited as "dissected" the texts that made up the *Pandectae.* The language of the documents had been corrupted, and errors and mutually contradictory statements had crept in. Still worse damage, Budé believed, had been committed by medieval commentators. Ignorant both of good Latin and of ancient history, they had attempted to explain away the errors rather than correct them. Their inaccurate definitions of technical vocabulary, their imaginary etymologies, and their incessant system building had further disfigured the *Pandectae.*

Budé was confident that he could "restore" the text of the *Pandectae* and make its meaning accessible to his contemporaries. This task required clearing away the accretions left by medieval commentators and in some cases those left by the original editors as well. His goal was to reveal the texts as originally left by their authors or to get as close to the original as was humanly possible. He goes about this project in part through the common humanist practice of textual con-

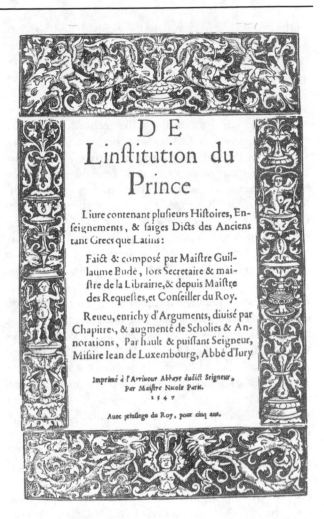

Title page for the only work Budé is known to have written in French, which he had presented as a manuscript to King François I in 1519 (Thomas Cooper Library, University of South Carolina)

jecture, relying on his knowledge of Latin style to sense which word might be an erroneous interpolation by an older commentator or a slip of the pen by a copyist, and then he relies on his ability to supply a replacement more suitable to the author and his era. As Kelley explains, the interpretation or clarification of an obscure or difficult passage requires the combination of Budé's "encyclopedic learning" with his sense of anachronism. In his biography of Budé, Louis Delaruelle indicated that this awareness is what distinguishes Budé's scholarship from that of his predecessors and contemporaries: the sheer number of examples he could deploy to clarify a difficult text distinguishes him from his contemporaries, who generally confined their criticism to the works of a single ancient author at a time. Kelley asserts that Budé differed from the Italian humanists in that he "consciously" evolved a comparative method that could be applied to philology. Budé demonstrated how words and institutions both evolved. He compared medieval and modern French institutions to those of classical antiquity and medieval and modern social mores to those of the ancient world. In his hands humanist textual criticism evolved into a more complex and demanding form of scholarship.

In addition to studying the technical aspects of the *Annotationes,* scholars have become intrigued by the purpose of the digressions Budé scattered throughout the work, disquisitions that can be said only in the broadest sense to bear on their subject matter. The longest of these is an essay on the Roman senate that occupies about fifty pages in the *Omnia Opera.* This essay is intended to demonstrate that the Roman senate in no way resembled the Parlement of Paris, as members of that body liked to claim. Here a diatribe against the Accursians and their vile judicial Latin develops into a defense of eloquence against their modern descendants, the lawyers of the Parlement. These modern barbarians, Budé asserts, amused themselves by arguing that they should "burn poets" and send poetry itself back over the Alps whence it came. More polemical digressions attack lawyers for their ambition and greed, the upper clergy for their lack of learning or religious vocation, courtiers for their venality, and high functionaries of the crown (Budé's own caste) as more devoted to their own interests than to those of the state. The issues that occupy him in these passages clearly have nothing to do with the study of Roman law.

In his 1907 biography of Budé, Delaruelle concluded that these digressions are evidence of defects in Budé's literary style, particularly his inability to reason in a straight line. In this interpretation Budé's digressions merely represent examples of his notoriously difficult Latin prose style. Gadoffre and Jean Céard are among those who have since argued that these passages demonstrate a secondary, unphilological purpose in his work. They remind the reader that Budé began to write the *Annotationes* late in the reign of Louis XII, a period when he was profoundly disillusioned with the king and his servants and when he separated himself from his governmental duties. Many of these digressions record his disenchantment with the French governing classes and the state to which they had brought the kingdom. For these scholars the *Annotationes* form not only a revolutionary treatise on the study of Roman law but also a polemic on the state of French society and culture.

The *Annotationes* were printed ten times in the twenty years following their appearance, but their immediate impact should not be overestimated. It would be decades before French scholarship would absorb the lessons of Budé's methods. Civil law continued to be taught according to traditional scholastic methods in French universities. Not until the 1560s would Budé's followers, led by Andrea Alciato and Jacques Cujas, successfully introduce a *mos docendi gallicus* (French method of teaching) based on Budé's philological approach. Neither did the *Annotationes* introduce, as Budé hoped, an era of elegant latinity to the law courts of his day. And historians did not adopt his methods to their researches until the 1570s. Nevertheless, Budé was becoming famous, and he was aware enough of his audience to tone down the more violently polemical of his digressions in the second edition.

Budé's second great scholarly project, *De asse et partibus ejus,* was printed in 1515. The *as* was a common Roman coin, and Budé proposed to determine its value relative to the other monies of antiquity and to modern French coinage. The attempt required a certain amount of scholarly bravado on his part, since the task had defeated the Italian humanists who had attempted it before him, most notably Flavio Biondo. Budé makes his research on this topic part of a larger investigation: a comparison of the wealth of ancient Rome to that of other empires of the time. He also raises the question of how the wealth, or "magnificence," of the ancients compared to that of France and the other nations of his own day. The finished work was longer than Budé planned, and it amounts to an examination of monies, weights, and measures as they were used throughout classical antiquity.

As in the *Annotationes,* Budé acknowledges the contributions of the humanist scholars who preceded him. Initial research had been accomplished by Biondo, Calderino, Sabellico, and especially Ermolao Barbaro in his work on Pliny the Elder, which made his own work possible. Their works, however, which in many cases had their origin in lecture notes for university courses, were confined to commentary on the writings of individual authors. The relative novelty of *De asse et partibus ejus,* which it shares with the *Annotationes,* is that Budé is able to bring together testimony scattered throughout ancient literature on each of a succession of specialized topics in a methodical way. His attempts at mathematical analysis, modern scholars agree, are not particularly successful. However, Jean-Claude Margolin points out the pedagogical effectiveness of Budé's literary comparisons and the striking examples he uses to bring home to his readers the values of ancient monies, including, for example, the price of a pig sacrificed to the god Sylvanus.

Budé also examines the worth of goods bought and sold in the ancient world by comparing their prices to those of similar items in his own era. Here he is willing to use evidence other than literary. Suspicious of the value assigned by Pliny to a pearl owned by Cleopatra, he arranged a consultation with a Parisian jeweler, who assured him that neither the size nor the price would be impossible. In another case, he went to a baker to find out how much flour went into baking a loaf of bread, how much it cost, and how much bread an ordinary man could eat in a day.

Modern readers of *De asse et partibus ejus* have been impressed by the grasp of the economic and social life of antiquity its author shows. They are usually equally impressed by his realistic view of the ancient Romans. In a famous comment on the sources of Rome's magnificence, Budé remarks that when he examines the material he assembled in his studies, Rome appears to him either as the ancient world's treasury or as the hideout of robbers. His vision of ancient Roman magnificence is an unclouded one.

In 1522 the Parisian bookseller Galliot du Pré marketed an abbreviated French version of the book, the *Summaire ou epitome du livre de asse* (Summary or Abridgement of the Book *De asse*). A small book with large print and generous spacing between the lines, it is clearly a popularization of the original. It summarizes only a small portion of the content of the original book, including such picturesque episodes as Cleopatra's pearl. None of the digressions, which account for as much as one-third of the length of the original, and none of Budé's polemics remain. The need for such a work casts light upon the anomaly of Budé's situation in French culture. Budé was famous, and his scholarly accomplishments had brought prestige to the French nation. *De asse et partibus ejus* was the most famous of his works. Yet, Budé's work remained largely inaccessible to the ordinary, literate Frenchman of the time because of the language in which he wrote. During the reign of François I the proportion of the literate among the population increased greatly, but they were literate not in Latin but in their native language.

Budé's early literary celebrity brought him into correspondence with humanist scholars in Italy and Northern Europe. Much of what is known about Budé's career, indeed, about the careers of many humanist scholars, is to be found in these letters. Humanistic correspondence, conducted in elegant Latin or Greek, had become an important part of learned culture, and Budé enthusiastically carried on the tradition, writing in one ancient language or the other to famous scholars and students alike. His correspondence with Erasmus began in 1516 at the instigation of the Dutch scholar, who made his approach through Budé's childhood friend and fellow university student, François Deloynes. The two scholars were approximately the same age, although Erasmus had achieved fame earlier. In 1516 Erasmus had just pub-

Statue of Budé in the courtyard of the Collège de France, of which he is recognized as the founder (photograph by Ralf Muller; from <http://www.uni-duisbrug.de>)

lished his Latin version of the New Testament. His preface to the *Novum Instrumentum* features warm praise of Budé's learning, while the textual notes make approving use of Budé's opinions in biblical criticism. There were deep similarities in the work being done by the two scholars. Both were humanists who were profoundly influenced by Valla's literary interests and critical methods. What Budé accomplished in the area of Roman law and the study of classical antiquity, many scholars have pointed out, was analogous to Erasmus's achievement in biblical scholarship. To judge from his reply to the Dutch humanist's first communication, Budé was elated by the recognition.

Budé also exchanged letters with English humanists such as Sir Thomas More, Thomas Linacre, Richard Pace, and Cuthbert Tunstall, the Spanish scholar Juan Luis Vives, the Greek refugee scholar Janus Lascaris, and several French humanists and government officials, including Guillaume Petit, Etienne Poncher, Pierre Lamy, and François Rabelais. His surviving correspondence is, for the most part, preserved in three collections published during his lifetime. Counting several previously unedited notes printed by Delaruelle, it consists of 160 letters in Latin and 54 in Greek. His correspondence with Rabelais began in 1521, when the latter was a young Franciscan monk with an unusual interest in Hellenistic studies. About two years later, when Rabelais's suspicious superiors removed his Greek books from his cell, Budé composed a letter of consolation and encouragement, ending it with a passage in Greek. With his younger correspondents, Budé seems to have easily fallen into the role of preceptor. His relationship with Erasmus, however, was more complex.

Budé was completing *De asse et partibus ejus* at the time of the death of Louis and the coronation of François I. The last pages of the book are a panegyric to the new king, whose personality brought hope. François brought with him political and military ambitions in both Italy and the empire and a strong sense of the "magnificence" appropriate to a monarch of the sort he intended to be. He patronized painters, sculptors, and architects. Although by no means an intellectual, he enjoyed the company of men of letters and understood the luster their presence cast on him and on his reign. The advent of the new king, Budé believed, held out hope for the progress of *bonae literis* in France, including greater status and richer rewards for those who practiced them.

Budé corresponded with humanist scholars throughout his life, and this practice greatly contributed to his later reputation as the "founder" of the Collège de France. Early in François's reign, several of his councillors floated a project to enhance the monarchy's prestige by establishing an educational institution based on humanist learning and pedagogical principles. Such institutions already had been founded in Rome, in Spain, and in Venice. Probably the best known was the Collegium Trilingue (College of Three Languages) at Louvain, within the territories of the Holy Roman Emperor. The proposed institution would be independent of the University of Paris, and its faculty would teach Greek, Hebrew, and the Latin of classical letters—as distinguished from the barbarous scholastic Latin still used as the language of instruction in the universities of France. The status brought by such an institution, the king's men believed, would be increased if they could recruit Erasmus, the foremost of Europe's humanist scholars, as its director. Budé was asked to help approach the Dutch scholar about this project at some point in 1517. He dutifully played his role, transmitting the offers made to Erasmus as they were explained to him. However, some scholars believe his letters betray a lack of enthusiasm for the project, possibly because of mixed feelings about establishing someone he must have regarded as a rival in a position in his own country. Regardless, Erasmus decided not to take up the offer, and the king's own enthusiasm for the project began to wane.

Soon after the abortive campaign to recruit Erasmus into French service, Budé began once again to involve himself with official duties and to spend more time at court. In 1519 he presented the king with a manuscript on the subject of kingship garnered from the literature of classical antiquity. This manuscript is unusual among Budé's works because it was composed in French. When it was printed posthumously it was given the title *De l'Institution du Prince* (1547, The Education of the Prince). (The manuscript variant, which differs from each of the printed versions, is often referred to in scholarly literature as the *Receuil d'Apophtegmes* [Collection of Aphorisms].)

De l'Institution du Prince belongs to the literary tradition of the "mirror of princes," a genre whose traditional purpose was to inculcate in the prince the virtues and knowledge necessary to his position. Budé, however, clearly intended the book to win over the new king to the cause of humanistic learning. His purpose emerges most strongly in his preface. Here he predicts to François that he will return "bonnes et élégantes lettres" (good and elegant letters) to France, and that through his generosity he will "fairez [sic] naistre Poëtes et Orateurs" (create poets and orators) just as he now creates counts and dukes. Budé asserts that the nation's happiness depends on peace and that in order to preserve peace the prince must cultivate what the ancients called *sapientia,* or practical wisdom. This wisdom is obtainable through the love of letters and all the liberal arts, and by contemplating and reading about the past.

The body of the book is a collection of anecdotes, taken from ancient writings and especially from Plutarch, intended to illustrate wise rule. Budé emphasizes the authority the prince wields and the scope of his powers. He cites Plutarch's writings on Alexander the Great and endorses Alexander's exercise of his authority unconstrained by anything other than his wisdom. Furthermore, he praises both Alexander's father Phillip and Alexander for having patronized the philosopher Aristotle. Budé goes on to praise history's capacity for inculcating prudence. He believes, not surprisingly, that Plutarch's writings are the finest example of the uses to which history can be put. However, he believes that France has yet to produce an historian or annalist approaching Plutarch's eminence, and he argues that this fault will not be repaired until the kings of France show liberality in supporting writers who are qualified to compose histories of France. (These claims were probably criticisms aimed at Burgundian annalists such as Jean Lemaire, as well as Italian humanists such as Paolo Emili, who were seeking official patronage to write the history of France.) Finally, in emphasizing the crucial importance of humanistic learning to the ruler, Budé claims that of all languages, only Greek and Latin are sufficiently developed to aid in clear thought, and of these languages Greek is far superior. Only he who possesses a command of Greek can have a profound knowledge of either philosophy or governance.

In 1519 Budé served a minor role as part of the French delegation to a conference held at Montpelier in Languedoc with representatives of Charles of Habsburg, king of Aragon, Castile, and Naples, who was François's rival to become Holy Roman Emperor. The conference, called to iron out differences between the two monarchs, was a failure, and it contributed to the decades of Valois-Habsburg struggle after François lost his bid for the imperial throne. In June 1520 Budé took part in the famous meeting between François and English king Henry VIII just outside Calais, at the so-called Field of the Cloth of Gold. François had proposed the meeting in hopes of establishing an English alliance that would isolate his Habsburg rival, now Emperor Charles V. Budé was certainly there to add to the general aura of magnificence surrounding the French king, much like the sumptuous furnishings, decorations, and entertainments with which he attempted to impress his fellow monarch. The famous humanist Thomas More was present as Henry's master of requests and a member of his privy council. Budé admired More, and in 1517 he wrote a prefatory epistle for the first Paris edition of More's *Utopia*. The diplomatic affair would have been the first opportunity for Budé and More to meet.

In 1520 Budé published a short work on moral philosophy, *De contemptu rerum fortuitarum* (On scorn for fortuitous things). This work brings up the issue of the active versus the contemplative life, a question he had treated in his translations from Plutarch. In this text Budé argues in favor of the contemplative life, regretting the time he has lost to the vanities of life at court and lamenting lost opportunities to spend time at his studies and with his family. Scholars have speculated about the sincerity of his commitments to each of these approaches to life. Marie-Madeleine de La Garanderie sees Budé as an essentially philosophical and religious intellect. She asserts that his appointments were essentially sinecures, offered to attach his reputation to the crown while permitting him the time to pursue his research. While his sentiments in the book appear sincere, the remainder of his career points to a real commitment to the ideal of service to the crown.

Frontispiece for Louis Delaruelle's 1907 biography of Budé, Etudes sur l'humanisme français: Guillaume Budé, les origines, les débuts, les idées maîtresses *(Thomas Cooper Library, University of South Carolina)*

By this time Budé was present at the court on a regular basis. Since the courts of Renaissance France were peripatetic, he found himself following his king on his processions throughout the kingdom. The regimen must have been debilitating for anyone of Budé's fragile health. However, during 1523 his labors began to be rewarded. He was appointed one of the king's *maîtres des requêtes* (receivers of petitions). At the time of his appointment, there were a dozen *maîtres des requêtes* within the king's entourage. They were senior officials with a broadly defined range of administrative and judicial functions, including assisting the royal chancellor, participating in the work of various of the king's councils, and participating in certain functions of the Parlement of Paris, the highest law court in the kingdom. Although it is not possible to gauge how involved Budé was in the work of the *maîtres des requêtes* at any given moment, the appointment was a significant gesture of royal regard and trust, and he kept the position for the rest of his life. Later in 1523 Budé was appointed *prevôt des marchands* (provost of merchants) for the city of Paris. Although this appointment was for a term of only one year, he appears to have held several appointments in the municipal administration of the city until his death. He also received the charge of *maître de la librairie du roi* (keeper of the king's books). La Garanderie states that Budé's responsibilities in this position are unclear, but it seems Budé was required to oversee the purchase of books for the new royal library at the château of Fontainebleau, and the position provided him a welcome opportunity to add to the stock of Greek manuscripts in France.

Although they may have been onerous for a scholar, Budé's official duties were serious. In late summer 1523 Charles de Bourbon-Montpensier, Constable of France, the highest ranking among the feudal "great officers" of the crown and the greatest feudal landholder in the kingdom, was accused of treason and fled France to the territory of the empire. The inquiries about how widely Bourbon's conspiracy had spread, and his trial in absentia, introduced Budé to some of the complexities of sixteenth-century dynastic politics and to the ambiguities of his own position as both an administrator and a judicial officer of the crown. There was widespread popular sentiment, even among the legal class, that the constable and his allies had been driven to revolt by the king and his mother because the king's concentration of powers was intolerable to them and their political ambitions. McNeil, who has studied the case, concludes that because of his age and health Budé was one of the less involved of the *maîtres des requêtes* at this time, and he cannot be accused of serving as a "king's inquisitor" in this instance. Yet, Budé did serve on commissions that interviewed and investigated the constable's followers. He sat on the tribunal that in January 1524 condemned Bourbon's fellow conspirator, Jean de Saint-Vallier, to death. (This sentence was later commuted.) Budé also participated in Bourbon's trial in absentia that summer.

While dealing with the realities of political life, Budé seems to have kept up with his scholarly work, at least to the point of publishing two translations in a single volume during 1526. The translations are of the pseudo-Aristotelian *De Mundo* (Of the World) and a similarly titled work by Philo. Both works are dedicated to More.

The literary friendship between Budé and Erasmus, always somewhat fragile as a result of each man's sensitivity about his scholarly reputation, came to an end in 1528. La Garanderie has remarked that the correspondence was driven by a dynamic in which hyperbolic praise was succeeded by criticism, and criticism led to mutual misunderstanding. Erasmus could be caustic and hypercritical in his remarks, while Budé

could be pompous and patronizing. Erasmus was critical of Budé's literary style, especially the many digressions, which he found mystifying. In his turn, the patriotic Budé began to suspect that Erasmus actively disliked the French. (Erasmus's decision not to take up François I's offer of employment, despite his many friendships with French humanists, may in part have been based on unpleasant memories of his student years in Paris, as well as fear of the heresy-hunting members of the Faculty of Theology.) The occasion for the split is generally regarded as the 1528 publication of Erasmus's *Ciceronianus,* a satirical dialogue in which he ridiculed those of his detractors who asserted that the imitation of Ciceronian stylistic norms, and the adoption of an exclusively Ciceronian vocabulary, constituted the only road to elegant latinity. Few among the community of French humanists would have found anything objectionable in the *Ciceronianus* until the last few pages, where they found Budé, the hero of French erudition and culture, lumped with Badius, a mere mechanic in the eyes of many, in a few slighting lines. Apparently, Erasmus had not been able to resist a play on the similarity of the two names. The damage was done. Erasmus became regarded as anti-French in that country, and his correspondence with Budé ended.

In September 1529 Badius printed the last of Budé's three great philological works, the *Commentarii linguae graecae,* a collection of notes on Greek words and usage as explained through comparison to Latin. It consists of 7,000 notes on Greek and 1,500 on Latin. In the *Omnia Opera* it takes up an entire volume of 1,560 columns, with Greek and Latin indices. Budé had been planning the work at least since 1520, and it was impatiently awaited by the learned public. Within days of its appearance in Paris it had been "pirated" by the Basel printer Johann Froben. After Budé's death, his own copy of the work, copiously expanded and corrected, came into the hands of the printer Robert Estienne, and it formed the basis of a second edition, one-third longer than the original, which appeared in 1548. This edition formed the nucleus of Estienne's own monumental *Thesaurus graecae linguae* (Treasury of the Greek Language), which did not appear until 1572.

The *Commentarii linguae graecae* was published with a long prefatory letter addressed to François I. Oddly enough, although the subject matter was important to Budé, he chose to have the letter printed in Greek. Here he begs the king to remember the promises he made years ago to create an institution of humanist studies and instruction in France. He envisions a *museum* in the classical sense of the term, a home for the Muses and a "magnificent building" where languages will be taught (here, for unclear reasons, he counts only two unspecified languages) and where the learned will debate. The tone of the letter is almost hectoring. A contemporary translation into French, believed to have been made for the king's use, is still preserved in the Bibliothèque Nationale.

It is unlikely that Budé's letter alone would have influenced the king to act. Perhaps more than most Renaissance monarchs, François I was chronically short of the cash needed to carry out his cultural and artistic programs. But many of the initial patrons of the idea were still around to add their pleas to those of Budé, and François chose to act at this time. In 1529 Jacques Toussaint, a protegé of Budé, was appointed the first *lecteur royale* in Greek. In 1530 Pierre Danès was also appointed a royal reader (or lecturer) in Greek, and François Vatable and Agathias Guidacerius were appointed readers in Hebrew. At the same time, Oronce Fine was appointed royal reader in mathematics. This discipline had not been considered during the early negotiations over the new institution, but it was unquestionably a study that was beginning to come into its own. Thus, it was deemed as deserving a place in a new and forward-looking institution (as opposed to the universities). A few years later, the humanist Barthélemy le Maçon, called Latomus, became the first reader in Latin. The wages of the readers almost immediately fell into arrears. By the 1570s the "magnificent building" promised the college still had not materialized. Yet, the institution survived to become, in the seventeenth century, the Collège Royale and, after the Revolution, the Collège de France.

The reign of François I, which began with such promise, gradually lost its luster. The revolt of the constable of Bourbon had demonstrated that the king could not count on the unquestioning loyalty of all his subjects. After his early victories in the Italian wars, François was defeated and captured by imperial forces at the battle of Pavia in February 1525. He was taken as a prisoner to Madrid, and he returned to France in March 1526 after allowing his two young sons to take his place as prisoners. Then, with France more or less isolated strategically by the possessions of Charles V, the king scandalized much of Europe and many of his own subjects by forging diplomatic and military relations with a non-Christian power, the Ottoman Turks. The two young princes were not returned until 1529, after the payment of an enormous ransom and certain promises to the emperor which, it soon became clear, François had no intention of honoring.

Budé seems to have absented himself from court for two or three years, beginning at the time of the king's capture. He may have suffered a political eclipse during the king's imprisonment and the regency of the Queen Mother, Louise of Savoy. Perhaps, as some of

Stamp released in 1956 (from <http://www.phil-ouest.com/ Timbre.php?Nom_timbre=G_Bude>)

his letters suggest, age and infirmity led to a return of his distaste for court life. By this time he was in his early sixties, and his health had in no way improved since the onset of his migraines twenty years before.

During this period French society also began to split into religiously defined camps, threatening the unity of the nation. This problem was potentially far more serious for the monarchy than the eclipse of the king's military or personal reputation. Protestantism had been a comparatively unobjectionable phenomenon in France before this time, and some of its practitioners and sympathizers could be found among the nation's elites, the upper nobility, the high clergy, the learned classes, and even the royal family. From time to time, rumors of Protestant sympathies touched even Budé. François was inclined toward tolerance and overlooked those instances of heterodoxy that the theologians of the University of Paris, the Sorbonnistes, insisted on bringing to his attention. While religious schism already had undermined the unity of the German nation, a situation François's agents and diplomats did their utmost to exacerbate, it was not supposed to affect France. However, two events, both of which may have involved Budé, tipped the delicate religious balance: the burning of Louis de Berquin in 1529 and the *Affaire des Placards* (Affair of the Placards) in 1534.

Berquin was a lawyer and member of the minor nobility who was an admirer of Martin Luther and Erasmus, to the latter's great embarrassment. He was arrested three times on charges of heresy involving the possession or distribution of works by German reformers. In the first case, he was released on the orders of the king; in the second, he was released by those of the king's sister Marguerite. In the third instance, the Sorbonnistes and the Parlement took advantage of Berquin's own pugnaciousness, condemning and burning him before the king could intervene again. It has been asserted that Budé took part in these proceedings, or even visited Berquin on the eve of his execution, presumably to attempt to persuade him to recant, but there is no documentary evidence to support this claim.

In late 1532 Budé published two more works through Badius. *De Philologia* (On Philology) appeared along with *De studio literarum recte et commode instituendo* (On the Right Proper Organization of Literary Studies). The first work is a dialogue about eloquence and argues for the cultivation of letters, while the second treats the relationship between the literatures of classical antiquity and Christianity. La Garanderie describes the latter as a link between some of the digressions in *De asse et partibus ejus,* where Budé first raised the issue, and *De transitu Hellenismi ad Christianismum* (1535, On the Transition from Hellenism to Christianity), in which he fully developed his thinking on the subject.

The Affair of the Placards of 1534 finally turned the king, who was already determined to demonstrate his Catholic orthodoxy, against the reformers. During the early morning hours of 18 October, large printed broadsheets attacking the Catholic doctrine of the mass were put up all over Paris. It was even rumored that a copy was nailed on the door to the king's bedchamber. The challenge to François's authority was too much for him. He banned printing throughout France, formed a commission of the Parlement to investigate the crime, and swore to extirpate heresy in his realm. That year John Calvin left France and published the first edition of his *Christianae religionis instiutio* (Institutes of the Christian Religion) in 1536.

Whatever Budé's opinions on religious dissent had been at the time of the Berquin affair, after the Affair of the Placards he was solidly behind the king's program of repression. In the last pages of the dedicatory epistle to his *De transitu Hellenismi ad Christianismum,* Budé praises the decisiveness with which the king moved to investigate these crimes and to punish the guilty. He lauds the king's decision, three months later, to suspend public and private business throughout Paris for a day in order to bring Parisians together for a supplicatory procession and mass intended to turn aside divine wrath at the breach of piety. The ceremonies, he explains, united the nobility who participated and the masses who lined the streets and filled the rooftops of the city. He urges the king to defend his title "Rex Christianissime" (Most Christian King) and prove himself a champion of orthodoxy by defeating the vile sect that perpetrated these outrages.

De transitu Hellenismi ad Christianismum has been described as a valediction, a turning away from philology and the investigation of the world of classical antiquity in favor of the religious concerns of Budé's old age. The book also has been portrayed as an affirmation of the continuity between the moral issues first raised in classical philosophy and the revealed truths of the Christian religion–hence, as an affirmation of humanistic studies. Regardless, *De transitu Hellenismi ad Christianismum* clearly displays strong religious sensibilities. Budé argues that the Bible can, and should, be read as a book of philosophy because philosophy is the search for human salvation. This search was begun by the ancients, particularly Socrates and Plato, who undertook a "speculative" search for truth, and by the Greek Neoplatonists, who first formulated a doctrine of salvation. The doctrines of the ancients, however, have been superseded by the Christian philosophy, which alone is divinely revealed. The Christian philosophy is more sure than the philosophies of the ancients and more complete. Very few among Greek philosophers, for example, went so far as to address the problem of euthemia, the "tranquility of the soul." Moreover, distinct from the philosophies of antiquity, the Christian philosophy offers a doctrine of the immortality of the soul and of the nature of the afterlife, which by virtue of their origin are known to be true.

Although the ancient philosophies have been replaced by revealed truth, Budé argues, they help Christians better understand how their beliefs traditionally have been expressed. The student of philosophy, then, should begin with the basic ideas of the ancient philosophers. Greek philosophers, after all, had striven toward, and in part anticipated, the teachings of the apostles. While some aspects of the ancient philosophies–skepticism, for instance–may be unwholesome in their parts, Budé argues that the scholar who begins his studies with the ancients will almost inevitably be drawn toward religious truth. In addition to discerning purely intellectual connections between ancient philosophy and the doctrines of the Christian faith, Budé recognizes how effective the examples of ancient literature, history, and philosophy are as pedagogical devices for explaining the religious crisis of his time. For example, he demonstrates how serious an affront to religion the placards had been, and how pervasive their sacrilege, by comparing their appearance to the mutilation of the statues of the god Hermes throughout Athens on the eve of Alcibiades' expedition in Sicily. As the ancient sacrilege called into question the deepest certainties of Athenian life, the "new" (Protestant) ideas have called papal authority into question and set the secular clergy and the monastic orders against each other.

Budé uses Homer's reputation among the ancients as the earliest of philosophers to set forth the failings of his contemporaries and to explain how moral shortcomings contribute to the social and religious crises of his time. Christians have been distracted from their true calling by the "sirens" of modern life, voluptuousness, ambition, and greed, as well as by more-Budaean concerns such as the artificialities of life at court and the temptation to misuse eloquence. He calls on the Christian of orthodox belief to struggle, like Ulysses, against the sirens' call and to retain command of his senses. Meanwhile, Budé the philologist is still active, employing elegant expressions and telling examples from ancient literature and using his knowledge of life in classical antiquity to criticize modern institutions and mores, just as he had in the digressions of the *Annotationes* and *De asse et partibus ejus*.

Budé continued in the king's service, but as he traveled to join François in the countryside during the summer of 1540, his fragile constitution succumbed to the heat. He contracted a fever from which he died weeks later, on 22 August. The manner of his death points to one of the central issues of his life and career: Budé seems never to have resolved the matter of the relative worth of the active and contemplative lives. From his writings it seems that he favored the life of study. He praises its virtues in his publications and complains in his letters when he does not have adequate time to devote to his research. Yet, Budé seems to have taken his official duties seriously, so much so that he tried to carry them out even at the risk of his health.

Interest in Budé's writings continued after his death, although the most technical of his works were less frequently printed after the middle of the century. In 1544 his *Forensia* (Of Courts and Laws), a commentary on the origins of the institutions of French governance and law, was printed exactly as he left it by Robert Estienne. The *Adversaria* (Commonplace Books), seven volumes of Budé's reading notes,

remained unprinted. Curiously, three different printers brought out versions of *De l'Institution du Prince* in 1547. Budé's collected Latin and Greek works, the *Omnia Opera,* was first published in four large volumes by Nicolaus Episcopius the Younger at BaselBasel in 1557. The major philological works, *De asse et partibus ejus,* the *Annotationes* (with the *Forensia*), and *Commentarii linguae graecae,* occupy the last three volumes. The printer produced additional copies of the first volume, which includes Budé's translations from Greek into Latin and his correspondence in both languages, as well as his works on education, philosophy, and religion. An alternate title page for this volume identifies it as *Lucubrationes variae* (Miscellaneous Studies)—the Latin implies difficult labors accomplished by lamplight. Traditional scholarship has often used the title *Lucubrationes* to reference these shorter works.

Among his most influential ideas, Budé seems to have envisioned, as Gadoffre asserts, an arrangement between the crown and the practitioners of the new learning in France, in which the king would provide direction for the kingdom's scholars and offer them worldly rewards and status for their labors, and they in turn would carry out his programs and add to his reputation among other monarchs. His conversion to the cause of royal readerships after Erasmus was gone from the scene seems to underline how seriously he took this program. Budé needed to demonstrate to himself and to his king that humanist scholars were useful to the monarchy and that they had a rightful place in its governance.

The historian of classical scholarship R. R. Bolgar may have best summed up Budé's direct contribution to the development of a French literary and intellectual tradition. When Budé first took up the study of Greek, his contemporaries in the French literary community—with the sole possible exception of Lefèvre d'Etaples—were still heavily influenced by medieval standards of learning. Proponents of humanistic studies still used Bartolus to understand the *Digest*. When French humanism came of age in the 1530s, largely through Budé's tutelage, it embraced qualities and methods that Italian and German scholarship had developed over a much longer time. Among the features of this new brand of French humanism were the "zeal" for textual criticism that Budé had introduced to French scholarship and the decidedly religious aspects of his thought. A third quality that Bolgar attributes to Budé's influence, an interest in the development of a vernacular through the imitation of the standards of classical literature, may not be as immediately evident as the first two. If one accepts Gadoffre's claim that Guillaume Budé's cultural program for France was essentially successful, however, then it is possible to see him as one of the progenitors of a continuing classicizing strain in French culture.

Letters:

La Correspondance d'Érasme et de Guillaume Budé, edited and translated by Marie-Madeleine de La Garanderie (Paris: J. Vrin, 1967).

Biographies:

Louis Delaruelle, *Etudes sur l'humanisme français: Guillaume Budé, les origines, les débuts, les idées maîtresses* (Paris: Champion, 1907; reprinted, Geneva: Slakine, 1970);

David McNeil, *Guillaume Budé and Humanism in the Reign of Francis I* (Geneva: Droz, 1975);

Marie-Madeleine de La Garanderie, "Guillaume Budé," *Contemporaries of Erasmus: A Biographical Register of the Renaissance and Reformation,* volume 1: *A–E,* edited by Peter G. Bietenholz and Thomas B. Deutscher (Toronto & London: University of Toronto Press, 1985), pp. 212–217.

References:

R. R. Bolgar, *The Classical Heritage and its Beneficiaries: From the Carolingian Age to the End of the Renaissance* (London: Cambridge University Press, 1954; reprinted, New York: Harper & Row, 1964);

Jean Céard, "Les transformations du genre du commentaire," *L'automne de la renaissance, 1580–1630: XXIIe Colloque international d'études humanistes, Tours 2–13 juillet 1979,* edited by Jean Lafond and André Stegmann (Paris: Vrin, 1981), pp. 101–115;

Louis Delaruelle, *Répertoire analytique et chronologique de la correspondence de Guillaume Budé* (Paris: Cornély, 1907; New York: Burt Franklin, [1962]);

Gilbert Gadoffre, *La révolution culturelle dans la France des humanistes: Guillaume Budé et François Ier* (Geneva: Droz, 1997);

Donald R. Kelley, *Foundations of Modern Historical Scholarship: Language, Law, and History in the French Renaissance* (New York & London: Columbia University Press, 1970);

Marie-Madeleine de La Garanderie, *Christianisme et lettres profanes (1515–1535): Essai sur les mentalités des milieux intellectuels Parisiens et sur la pensée de Guillaume Budé* (Paris: Champion, 1976);

Marie-Rose Logan, "Guglielmus Budaeus' Philological Imagination," *MLN,* 118 (2004): 1140–1151;

Jean-Claude Margolin, "De la digression au commentaire: pour un lecture humaniste du *De asse* de Guillaume Budé," in *Neo-Latin and the Vernacular in Renaissance France,* edited by Grahame Castor and Terence Cave (Oxford: Clarendon Press, 1984), pp. 1–25.

Papers:

Guillaume Budé manuscripts are held by the Bibliothèque nationale de France and the Bibliothèque de la ville de Genève.

Jean Calvin
(10 July 1509 – 27 May 1564)

Karin Maag
*H. Henry Meeter Center, Calvin College and Calvin
Theological Seminary*

BOOKS: *Christianæ religionis institutio* (Basel: Printed by Thomas Platter and Balthasar Lasius, 1536); revised and enlarged as *Institutio christianæ religionis,* as by Alcuinus on some 1939 title pages (Strasbourg: Printed by Wendelin Rihel, 1539; revised and enlarged, 1543; revised again, 1545); translated into French by Calvin as *Institution de la religion chrestienne* ([Geneva]: [Printed by Michel du Bois], [1541]; revised edition, Geneva: Printed by Jean Girard, 1545; revised, 1551; revised edition, Geneva: Printed by Jean Crespin, 1560); original Latin revised and enlarged as *Institutio totius christianæ religionis* (Geneva: Printed by Jean Girard, 1550); revised and enlarged as *Institutio christianæ religionis* ([Geneva]: Printed by Robert Estienne, 1553)—includes the *Catechismus,* the Latin version of *Instruction et confession de foy dont on use en l'Eglise de Geneve;* revised as *Institutio christianæ religionis* (Geneva: Printed by Robert Estienne, 1559); translated by Thomas Norton as *The Institution of Christian Religion* (London: Printed by Reyner Wolffe and Richard Harrison, 1561);

Epistolæ duæ de rebus hoc sæculo cognitu necesariis (Basel: Printed by Balthasar Lasius and Thomas Platter, 1537); first letter translated by Henry Beveridge as "On Shunning the Unlawful Rites of the Ungodly, and Preserving the Purity of the Christian Religion," in *Tracts Relating to the Reformation,* volume 3 (Edinburgh: Calvin Translation Society, 1851), pp. 360–411;

Instruction et confession de foy dont on use en l'Eglise de Geneve, anonymous ([Geneva]: [Printed by Wigand Koeln], [1537]); translated by Ford Lewis Battles in *Calvin's First Catechism: A Commentary,* edited by I. John Hesselink (Louisville, Ky.: Westminster/John Knox, 1997), pp. 1–38;

Jacobi Sadoleti Romani Cardinalis Epistola ad Senatum Populumque Genevensem, qua in obedientiam Romani Pontificis eos reducere conatur. Joannis Calvini responsio (Strasbourg: Printed by Wendelin Rihel, 1539);

Jean Calvin (Harlingue/Roger-Viollet/Getty Images)

translated by Beveridge as "Letter by James Sadolet, a Roman Cardinal, to the Senate and People of Geneva" and "Reply by John Calvin to Letter by Cardinal Sadolet to the Senate and People of Geneva," in *Tracts Relating to the Reformation,* volume 1 (Edinburgh: Calvin Translation Society, 1844), pp. 3–22, 25–68;

Commentarii in epistolam Pauli ad Romanos (Strasbourg: Printed by Wendelin Rihel, 1540); translated by Christopher Rosdell as *A Commentarie upon the Epistle* of Saint Paul to the Romanes (London: Printed by Thomas Dawson for John Harrison and George Bishop, 1583);

Les actes de la journee imperiale tenue en la cité de Reguespourg, anonymous ([Geneva]: [Printed by Jean Girard], 1541);

Petit traicté de la saincte Cene (Geneva: Printed by Michel Du Bois, 1541); translated by Beveridge as "Short Treatise on the Supper of Our Lord," in Tracts Relating to the Reformation, volume 2 (Edinburgh: Calvin Translation Society, 1849) pp. 164–198;

Catechisme de L'Eglise de Geneve: c'est à dire, le Formulaire d'instruire les enfans en la Chrétienté: faict en maniere de dialogue, ou le Ministre interrogue, & l'enfant respond ([Geneva], [1542]), translated as The Catechisme or Manner to Teache Children the Christian Religion (Geneva: Printed by Jean Crespin, 1556);

Exposition sur l'Epistre de sainct Judas ([Geneva]: [Printed by Jean Girard], 1542);

Vivere apud Christum non dormire animis sanctos, qui in fide Christi decedunt, assertio (Strasbourg: Printed by Wendelin Rihel, 1542); revised as Psychopannychia (Strasbourg: Printed by Wendelin Rihel, 1545); translated by Thomas Stocker as An Excellent Treatise of the Immortalytie of the Soule (London: Printed by John Day, 1581);

Advertissement du proffit qui reviendroit à la Chrestienté s'il se faisoit inventaire de tous les corps sainctz, & reliques (Geneva: Printed by Jean Girard, 1543), translated by Stephen Withers as A Very Profitable Treatise . . . Declarynge What Great Profit Might Come to Al Christendome, yf There Were a Regester Made of All Sainctes Bodies and Other Reliques (London: Printed by Rowland Hall, 1561);

Defensio sanæ et orthodoxæ doctrinæ . . . adversus calumnies A. Pighii (Geneva: Printed by Jean Girard, 1543); translated by Graham I. Davies as The Bondage and Liberation of the Will: A Defence of the Orthodox Doctrine of Human Choice against Pighius (Carlisle, U.K.: Paternoster, 1996; Grand Rapids, Mich.: Baker, 1996);

Exposition sur l'Epistre au Romains (Geneva: Printed by Jean Girard, 1543);

Petit traicté, monstrant que doit faire un fidele entre les papistes ([Geneva]: [Printed by Jean Girard], 1543; revised, 1545); translated by Seth Skolnitsky as "A Short Treatise, Setting Forth What the Faithful Man Must Do When He Is Among Papists and He Knows the Truth of the Gospel," in Come Out From Among Them: "Anti-Nicodemite" Writings of John Calvin (Dallas: Protestant Heritage, 2001), pp. 47–95;

Supplex exhortatio ad invictiss. Cæsarem Carolum quintum, anonymous on some title pages ([Geneva]: [Printed by Jean Girard], 1543);

Two Epystles . . . Whether It Be Lawfull for a Chrissten Man To Communicate or Be Partaker of the Masse of the Papystes, by Calvin and Heinrich Bullinger ([Antwerp]: [Printed by Matthias Crom], [1544]);

Advertissement sur la censure de Sorbonne ([Geneva]: [Printed by Jean Girard], 1544);

Articuli facultatis parisiensi cum antidote, anonymous ([Geneva]: [Printed by Jean Girard], 1544; translated into French as Les articles de la sacree Faculté de Theologie de Paris avec le remede contre la poison ([Geneva]: [Printed by Jean Girard], 1544); translated by Beveridge as "Articles Agreed upon by the Faculty of Sacred Theology of Paris, with the Antidote," in Tracts Relating to the Reformation, volume 1 (Edinburgh: Calvin Translation Society, 1844), pp. 71–120;

Brieve instruction pour armer tous bons fideles contre les erreurs de la secte commune des Anabaptistes (Geneva: Printed by Jean Girard, 1544); translated as A Short Instruction for to Arme All Good Christian People agaynst the Pestiferous Errours of the Common Secte of Anabaptistes (London: Printed by John Day and William Seres, 1549);

Epinicion Christo cantatum (Geneva: Printed by Jean Girard, 1544);

Excuse . . . a Messieurs les Nicodémites ([Geneva]: [Printed by Jean Girard], 1544); translated by Skolnitsky as "Answer of John Calvin to the Nicodemite Gentlemen Concerning Their Complaint that He is Too Severe," in Come Out From Among Them: "Anti-Nicodemite" Writings of John Calvin (Dallas: Protestant Heritage, 2001), pp. 97–125;

Contre la secte phantastique et furieuse des Libertins. Qui se nomment spirituelz (Geneva: Printed by Jean Girard, 1545); enlarged as Contre la secte phantastique et furieuse des Libertins qui se nomment spirituelz. Avec une epistre de la mesme matiere, contre un certain Cordelier suppost de la secte: lequel est prisonnier à Roan. ([Geneva]: [Jean Girard], 1547); translated by Benjamin Farley as "Against the Fantastic and Furious Sect of the Libertines Who Are Called 'Spirituals,'" in Treatises against the Anabaptists and against the Libertines, edited by Farley (Grand Rapids, Mich.: Baker, 1982), pp. 187–326;

Pro G. Farello et colleges ejus, adversus Petri Caroli theologastri calumnies, as Nicolas Des Gallars ([Geneva]: [Printed by Jean Girard], 1545);

Admonitio Paterna Pauli III. Romani Pontificis ad invictiss. Caesarem Carolum V. qua eum castigat . . . Cum Scholiis, by Pope Paul III and Calvin ([Basle]: [Printed by Robert Winter], 1545); translated by

Beveridge as "A Paternal Admonition by the Roman Pontiff, Paul III, to the Most Invincible Emperor, Charles V" and "Remarks on the Letter of Pope Paul III," in *Tracts Relating to the Reformation,* volume 1 (Edinburgh: Calvin Translation Society, 1844), pp. 257–286;

Commentarii in priorem epistolam Pauli ad Corinthios (Strasbourg: Printed by Wendelin Rihel, 1546); translated into French as *Commentaire . . . sur la premiere Epistre aux Corinthiens* ([Geneva]: Printed by Jean Girard, 1547); translated by Thomas Tymme as *A Commentarie upon S. Paules Epistles to the Corinthians* (London: Printed [by Thomas Dawson and Thomas Gardiner] for John Harrison and George Bishop, 1577);

Deux sermons . . . faitz en la ville de Geneve (Geneva: Printed by Jean Girard, 1546);

Excuse de noble seigneur Jaques de Bourgoigne, by Jacques de Bourgogne and anonymous ([Geneva]: [Printed by Jean Girard], [1547–1548]);

Acta synodi Tridentinæ. Cum antidoto ([Geneva]: [Printed by Jean Girard], 1547); translated by Beveridge as "Canons and Decrees of the Council of Trent, with the Antidote," in *Tracts Relating to the Reformation,* volume 3 (Edinburgh: Calvin Translation Society, 1851), pp. 18–188;

Commentaire sur la seconde Epistre aux Corinthiens ([Geneva]: Printed by Jean Girard, 1547); original Latin published as *Commentarii in secundam epistolam ad Corinthios* (Geneva: Printed by Jean Girard, 1548); translated by Tymme as *A Commentarie upon S. Paules Epistles to the Corinthians* (London: Printed [by Thomas Dawson and Thomas Gardiner] for John Harrison and George Bishop, 1577);

Commentarii in quatuor Pauli epistolas: ad Galatas, ad Ephesios, ad Philippenses, ad Colossenses (Geneva: Printed by Jean Girard, 1548); translated into French as *Commentaire sur quatre Epistres de S. Paul: aux Galatiens, Ephesiens, Philippiens, Colossiens* (Geneva: Printed by Jean Girard, 1548); commentary on Colossians translated by Robert Vaux as *A Commentarie . . . upon the Epistle to the Colossians* (London: Printed by Thomas Purfoot, [1581]); commentary on Galatians translated by Vaux as *A Commentarie . . . upon the Epistle to the Galathians* (London: Printed by Thomas Purfoot, 1581); commentary on Philippians translated by William Becket as *A Commentarie . . . uppon the Epistle to the Philippians* (London: Printed by John Windet for Nicholas Ling, 1584);

Commentarii in utranque Pauli epistolam ad Timotheum (Geneva: Printed by Jean Girard, 1548); translated by William Pringle as part of *Commentaries on*

the Epistles to Timothy, Titus, and Philemon (Edinburgh: Calvin Translation Society, 1856);

Advertissement contre l'astrologie judiciaire (Geneva: Printed by Jean Girard, 1549); translated by Goddred Gilby as *An Admonicion against Astrology Judiciall* (London: Printed by Rowland Hall, [1561]);

Commentarii in epistolam ad Hebraeos (Geneva: Printed by Jean Girard, 1549); translated into French as *Commentaire . . . sur l'Epistre aux Ebrieux* (Geneva: Printed by Jean Girard, 1549); translated by John Owen as *Commentaries on the Epistle of Paul the Apostle to the Hebrews* (Edinburgh: Calvin Translation Society, 1853);

Interim adultero-germanum ([Geneva]: [Printed by Jean Girard], 1549); translated by Beveridge as "Adultero-German Interim, with Calvin's Refutation," in *Tracts Relating to the Reformation,* volume 3 (Edinburgh: Calvin Translation Society, 1851), pp. 190–239;

Appendix libelli adversus Interim ([Geneva]: [Printed by Jean Girard], 1550); translated by Beveridge as "Appendix to the Tract on the True Method of Reforming the Church," in *Tracts Relating to the Reformation,* volume 3 (Edinburgh: Calvin Translation Society, 1851), pp. 344–358;

Commentarii in epistolam ad Titum (Geneva: Printed by Jean Girard, 1550); translated into French as *Commentaire sur l'Epistre à Tite* (Geneva: Printed by Jean Girard, 1550); translated by William Pringle as "Commentaries on the Epistle to Titus," in *Commentaries on the Epistles to Timothy, Titus, and Philemon* (Edinburgh: Calvin Translation Society, 1856), pp. 275–344;

Commentarii in priorem epistolam Pauli ad Thessalonicenses (Geneva: Printed by Jean Girard, 1550); translated by John Pringle as "Commentary on the First Epistle to the Thessalonians," in *Commentaries on the Epistles of Paul the Apostle to the Philippians, Colossians, and Thessalonians* (Edinburgh: Calvin Translation Society, 1851), pp. 234–306;

Commentarii in posteriorem epistolam Pauli ad Thessalonicenses (Geneva: Printed by Jean Girard, 1550); translated by John Pringle as "Commentary on the Second Epistle to the Thessalonians," in *Commentaries on the Epistles of Paul the Apostle to the Philippians, Colossians, and Thessalonians* (Edinburgh: Calvin Translation Society, 1851), pp. 308–362;

De Scandalis. Quibus hodie plerique absterrentur, nonnulli etiam alienatur a pura Evangelii doctrina (Geneva: Printed by Jean Crespin, 1550); translated into French as *Des Scandales qui empeschent aujourd'huy beaucoup de gens de venir a la pure doctrine de l'Evangile, et en desbauchent d'autres* (Geneva: Printed by Jean Crespin, 1550); translated by Arthur Golding as *A*

Little Book . . . Concernynge Offences, whereby at this Daye Divers Are Feared, and Many also Quight Withdrawen from the Pure Doctrine of the Gospell (London: Printed by [Henry Wykes for] William Seres, 1567);

An Epistle Both of Godly Consolacion and Also of Advertisement . . . to the Right Noble Prince Edwarde Duke of Somerset, translated by Edward Somerset (London: Printed by [William Baldwin and] Edward Whitchurche, 1550);

Commentarii in epistolas canonicas (Geneva: Printed by Jean Crespin, 1551); translated into French as *Commentaires . . . sur les Canoniques* (Geneva: Jean Girard, 1551); partially translated by W.H. as *The Comentaries . . . upon the First Epistle of Sainct Jhon, and upon the Epistle of Jude* (London: Printed by John Kingston [and Thomas East] for John Harrison the younger, [1580]);

Commentarii in Isaiam prophetam (Geneva: Printed by Jean Crespin, 1551; revised and enlarged, 1559); translated by Clement Cotton as *A Commentary upon the Prophecie of Isaiah* (London: Printed by Felix Kingston for William Cotton, 1609);

In omnes Pauli epistolas atque etiam in epistolam ad Hebraeos commentaria (Geneva: Printed by Jean Girard, 1551);

Response a un plaidoyer faict par un certain Advocat de Paris, anonymous ([Geneva]: [Printed by Jean Crespin], 1551);

Commentariorum . . . in Acta Apostolorum, Liber I (Geneva: Printed by Jean Crespin, 1552); translated into French as *Le premier livre des commentaires . . . sur les Actes des Apostres* (Geneva: Printed by Philibert Hamelin, 1552); translated by Christopher Fetherstone in *The Commentaries upon the Actes of the Apostles* (London: Printed by Thomas Dawson for George Bishop, 1585);

De aeterna Dei prædestinatione (Geneva: Printed by Jean Crespin, 1552); translated by Henry Cole as "A Treatise on the Eternal Predestination of God," in *Calvin's Calvinism* (London: Wertheim & Macintosh, 1856–1857), pp. 19–206;

Opuscula omnia in unum volumen collecta (Geneva: Printed by Jean Girard, 1552);

Quatre sermons . . . traictans des matieres fort utiles pour nostre temps ([Geneva]: Printed by Robert Estienne, 1552); translated as *Four Godlye Sermons agaynst the Polution of Idolatries* (London: Printed by Rowland Hall, 1561);

In Evangelium secundum Johannem commentarius ([Geneva]: Printed by Robert Estienne, 1553); translated by Fetherstone as *The Holy Gospel of Jesus Christ, According to John, with the Commentary of M. John Calvine* (London: Printed by Thomas Dawson for George Bishop, 1584);

Commentariorum in Acta Apostolorum liber posterior (Geneva: Printed by Jean Crespin, 1554); translated into French as *Le second livre des commentaires . . . sur les Actes des Apostres* (Geneva: Printed by Philibert Hamelin, 1554); translated by Fetherstone in *The Commentaries upon the Actes of the Apostles* (London: Printed by Thomas Dawson for George Bishop, 1585);

Defensio orthodoxæ fidei de sacra Trinitate, contra prodigiosos errores Michaelis Serveti Hispani ([Geneva]: Printed by Robert Estienne, 1554);

In primum Mosis librum, qui Genesis vulgo dicitur, commentarius ([Geneva]: Printed by Robert Estienne, 1554); translated into French as *Commentaire . . . sur le premier livre de Moyse, dit Genese* (Geneva: Printed by Jean Girard, 1554); translated by Tymme as *A Commentarie . . . upon the First Booke of Moses Called Genesis* (London: Printed by Henry Middleton for John Harrison and George Bishop, 1578);

Vingtdeux sermons auxquels est exposé le Pseaume 119, anonymous ([Geneva]: [Printed by Jean Girard], 1554); as Calvin (Geneva: Printed by Jean Girard, 1554); translated by Thomas Stocker as *Two and Twentie Sermons . . . In which Sermons is Most Religiously Handled, the Hundredth and Nineteenth Psalme of David* (London: Printed by Thomas Dawson for John Harrison the younger and Thomas Man, 1580);

Defensio sanæ & orthodoxæ doctrinæ de Sacramentis ([Geneva]: Printed by Robert Estienne, 1555);

Deux sermons . . . prins de la premiere Epistre à Timothée au second chapitre ([Geneva]: Printed by Jean Girard, 1555);

Harmonia ex tribus Evangelistis composita, Matthæo, Marco & Luca: adjuncto seorsum Johanne ([Geneva]: Printed by Robert Estienne, 1555); translated by Eusebius Pagit as *A Harmonie upon the Three Evangelists, Matthew, Mark and Luke, with the Commentarie of M. John Calvine* (London: Printed by Thomas Dawson for George Bishop, 1584);

Secunda defensio piæ et orthodoxae de sacramentis fidei ([Geneva]: Printed by Jean Crespin, 1556); translated by Beveridge as "Second Defence of the Pious and Orthodox Faith Concerning the Sacraments," in *Tracts Relating to the Reformation,* volume 2 (Edinburgh: Calvin Translation Society, 1849), pp. 246–345;

Brevis responsio . . . ad diluendas nebulonis calumnias (Geneva: Printed by Jean Crespin, 1557); translated by J. K. S. Reid as "Brief Reply in Refutation of the Calumnies of a Certain Worthless Person," in *Calvin: Theological Treatises* (Philadelphia: Westminster, 1954; London: SCM, 1954), pp. 333–343;

In Hoseam prophetam prælectiones (Geneva: Printed by Conrad Badius, 1557);

In librum Psalmorum . . . commentarius ([Geneva]: Printed by Robert Estienne, 1557); translated by Golding as *The Psalmes of David and Others. With M. John Calvins Commentaries* (London: Printed by Thomas East and Henry Middleton for Lucas Harrison and George Bishop, 1571);

Responses à certaines calomnies et blasphemes ([Geneva], 1557);

Sermons . . . sur les dix commandemens de la Loy (Geneva: Printed by Conrad Badius, 1557); translated by John Harmar as *Sermons . . . upon the .X. Commandementes of the Lawe, Geven of God by Moses, Otherwise Called the Decalogue* (London: Printed by Thomas Dawson for George Bishop / John Harrison / Thomas Woodcocke, 1579);

Ultima admonitio . . . ad Joachimum Westphalum ([Geneva]: Printed by Jean Crespin, 1557); translated by Beveridge as "Last Admonition of John Calvin to Joachim Westphal," in *Tracts Relating to the Reformation*, volume 2 (Edinburgh: Calvin Translation Society, 1849), pp. 346–494;

Calumniæ nebulonis cuiusdam, quibus odio & invidia gravare conatus est doctrinam Joh. Calvini de occulta Dei providentia. Johannis Calvini ad easdem responsio ([Geneva]: Printed by Conrad Badius, 1558); translated by Cole as "A Defence of the Secret Providence of God, by Which He Works out his Eternal Decrees," in *Calvin's Calvinism* (London: Wertheim and Macintosh, 1856–1857), pp. 223–350;

Plusieurs sermons . . . touchant la divinité, humanité et nativité de nostre Seigneur Jesus Christ ([Geneva]: Printed by Conrad Badius, 1558)—includes passages on the start of John's Gospel translated by Thomas Wilson in *Three Propositions or Speeches, Which That Excellent Man M. John Calvin, One of the Pastors of the Church of God in Geneva, Had There* (London: Printed by Thomas Dawson for George Bishop, 1580) folios 1–26; entire work translated by Stocker as *Divers Sermons . . . Concerning the Divinitie, Humanitie and Nativitie of Our Lorde Jesus Christe* (London: Printed by Thomas Dawson for George Bishop, 1581);

Sermons . . . sur le dixieme & onzieme chapitre de la premiere Epistre sainct Paul aux Corinthiens, esquels outre plusieurs matieres excellentes ([Geneva]: Printed by Conrad Badius, 1558);

Prælectiones in duodecim Prophetas quos vocant minores (Geneva: Printed by Jean Crespin, 1559)—includes lectures on Jonah, translated by

Nathaniel Baxter as *The Lectures or Daily Sermons . . . upon the Prophet Jonas* (London: Printed by John Charlewood for Edward White, 1578); entire work translated by Owen as *Commentaries on the Twelve Minor Prophets,* 5 volumes (Edinburgh: Calvin Translation Society, 1846–1849);

Dixhuict sermons . . . Ausquels, entre autres poincts, l'histoire de Melchisedec et la matiere de la justification, sont deduites ([Geneva]: Printed by Etienne Anastaise, 1560; [Geneva]: Printed by Jean Bonnefoy, 1560); seven of the sermons translated by Stocker in *Sermons . . . on the Historie of Melchisedech* (London: Printed by John Windet for Andrew Maunsell, 1592);

Sermons . . . upon the Songe that Ezechias Made after He Had Bene Sicke, and Afflicted by the Hand of God, translated by Anne Lok (London: Printed by John Day, 1560); French version published as *Sermons . . . sur le Cantique que feit le bon roy Ezechias* (Geneva: Printed by François Estienne for Etienne Anastaise / Bertrand Bodin / Vincent Brés / Emeran le Melais / Etienne Robinet / Antoine de Véze, 1562);

Traité de la predestination eternelle de Dieu, par laquelle les uns sont eleuz à salut, les autres laissez en leur condemnation. Aussi de la providence, par laquelle il gouverne les choses humaines. Item y sont adjoustez treze sermons, traitans de l'election gratuite de Dieu en Jacob, et de la rejection en Esau ([Geneva]: Printed by Antoine Cercia, 1560; [Geneva]: Printed by Jean Durant, 1560); translated by John Field as *Thirteene Sermons . . . Entreating of the Free Election of God in Jacob, and of Reprobation in Esau* (London: Printed by Thomas Dawson for Thomas Man and Tobie Cooke, 1579);

Two Godly and Notable Sermons Preached . . . in the Yere 1555 (London: Printed by William Seres, [1560]);

Dilucida explicatio sanæ doctrinæ de vera participatione carnis et sanguinis Christi in sacra Cœna (Geneva: Printed by Conrad Badius, 1561); translated by Beveridge as "Clear Explanation of Sound Doctrine Concerning the True Partaking of the Flesh and Blood of Christ in the Holy Supper," in *Tracts Relating to the Reformation*, volume 2 (Edinburgh: Calvin Translation Society, 1849), pp. 496–572;

Gratulatio ad venerabilem presbyterum, dominum Gabrielem de Saconay, anonymous ([Geneva]: [Printed by Conrad Badius], 1561); translated by Douglas Kelly as "Congratulations to the Venerable Presbyter, Lord Gabriel de Saconay," in *Calvin Studies II,* edited by John Leith and Charles Raynal (1984): 109–118;

Impietas Valentini Gentilis detecta, et palam traducta, qui Christum non sine sacrilega blasphemia Deum essentiatum esse

fingit, anonymous ([Geneva]: [Printed by Conrad Badius], 1561);

Prælectiones in librum prophetiarum Danielis (Geneva: Printed by Jean de Laon, 1561); translated by Anthony Gilby as *Commentaries . . . upon the Prophet Daniell* (London: Printed by John Day, 1570);

Responsio ad versipellem quendam mediatorem, anonymous ([Geneva]: Printed by Jean Crespin, 1561); translated into French as *Response à un cauteleux et rusé moyenneur,* anonymous ([Paris]: [Printed by Nicolas Edoard], 1561);

Sermons . . . sur les deux Epistres S. Paul à Timothée et sur l'Epistre à Tite (Geneva: Printed by Conrad Badius, 1561); translated by Laurence Tomson as *Sermons . . . on the Epistles of S. Paule to Timothie and Titus* (London: Printed [by Henry Middleton] for George Bishop and Thomas Woodcoke, 1579);

Trois sermons sur le sacrifice d'Abraham ([Geneva]: [Printed by Jacques Bourgeois], 1561); translated by Stocker as "Three Sermons beginning at the latter end of the 21 Chapter of Genesis, concerning Abraham's sacrificing of his son Izhak," in *Sermons . . . on the Historie of Melchisedech* (London: Printed by John Windet for Andrew Maunsell, 1592), pp. 219–311;

Congregation faite en l'eglise de Geneve . . . En laquelle la matiere de l'election eternelle de Dieu (Geneva: Printed by Vincent Bres, 1562);

Response à un certain Holandois, lequel sous ombre de faire les Chrestiens tout spirituels, leur permet de polluer leur corps en toutes idolatries ([Geneva]: Printed by Jean Crespin, 1562); translated by Seth Skolnitsky as "A Response to a Certain Dutchman Who, under Pretence of Making Christians Really Spiritual, Suffers Them to Defile Their Bodies in All Sorts of Idolatries," in *Come Out From Among Them: "Anti-Nicodemite" Writings of John Calvin* (Dallas: Protestant Heritage, 2001), pp. 241–306;

Sermons . . . sur l'Epistre S. Paul Apostre aux Ephesiens (Geneva: Printed by Jean-Baptiste Pinereul, 1562); translated by Arthur Golding as *The Sermons . . . upon the Epistle of S. Paule to the Ephesians* (London: Printed [by Thomas Dawson and Thomas Gardiner] for Lucas Harrison and George Bishop, 1577);

Soixante cinq sermons . . . sur l'Harmonie ou Concordance des trois Evangelistes, S. Matthieu, sainct Marc, et S. Luc (Geneva: Printed by Conrad Badius, 1562);

Thre Notable Sermones Made . . . on Thre Severall Sondayes in Maye, the Yere 1561, upon the Psalm 46, translated by William Warde (London: Printed by Rowland Hall, 1562);

Responsio ad Balduini convicia, by Calvin and others ([Geneva]: [Printed by Jean Crespin], 1562);

Brevis admonitio . . . ad fratres Polonos, ne triplicem in Deo essentiam pro tribus personis imaginando, tres sibi Deos fabricent (Geneva: Printed by François Perrin, 1563);

Deux congregations . . . du second chapitre de l'Epistre de sainct Paul aux Galatiens, verset onzieme ([Geneva]: Printed by Michel Blanchier, 1563); translated by Thomas Wilcox as *Three propositions or speeches . . . to Which is Added, an Exposition upon that Parte of the Catechisme, Which is Appointed for the Three and Fortieth Sunday in Number* (London: Printed by Thomas Dawson for George Bishop, 1580), folios 27–65;

Mosis libri V, cum . . . commentariis. Genesis seorsum: reliqui quatuor in formam harmoniæ digesti (Geneva: Printed by Henri Estienne, 1563);

Prælectiones: in Librum prophetiarum Jeremiæ, et Lamentationes (Geneva: Printed by Jean Crespin, 1563); translated by Owen as *Commentaries on the Book of the Prophet Jeremiah and the Lamentations* (Edinburgh: Calvin Translation Society, 1850);

Sermons . . . sur l'Epistre S. Paul Apostre aux Galatiens (Geneva: Printed by François Perrin, 1563); translated by Golding as *Sermons . . . upon the Epistle of Saincte Paule to the Galathians* (London: Printed by Henry Bynneman for Lucas Harrison & George Bishop, 1574);

Sermons . . . sur le livre de Job (Geneva: Printed by Jean de Laon [for Antoine Vincent], 1563); translated by Golding as *Sermons . . . upon the Booke of Job* (London: Printed by Henry Bynneman for Lucas Harrison and George Bishop, 1574);

Confession de foy . . . pour presenter à l'Empereur, aux Princes et Estats d'Allemagne en la journée de Francfort (N.p., 1564); translated by Beveridge as "Confession of Faith in Name of the Reformed Churches of France: Drawn up during the War, for Presentation to the Emperor, Princes, and States of Germany," in *Tracts Relating to the Reformation,* volume 2 (Edinburgh: Calvin Translation Society, 1849), pp. 138–162;

In librum Josue brevis commentarius, quem paulo ante mortem absolvit (Geneva: Printed by François Perrin, 1564); translated into French as *Commentaires . . . sur le livre de Josué* (Geneva: Printed by François Perrin, 1565); translated by W.F. as *A Commentarie . . . upon the Booke of Josue* (London: Printed by Thomas Dawson for George Bishop, 1578);

In viginti prima Ezechielis prophetæ capita prælectiones (Geneva: Printed by François Perrin, 1565); translated by Thomas Myers as *Commentaries on the First Twenty Chapters of the Book of the Prophet Ezekiel,* 2 volumes (Edinburgh: Calvin Translation Society, 1849, 1850);

Quarante sept sermons . . . sur les huict derniers chapitres des propheties de Daniel (La Rochelle: Printed by Barthélemy Berton for Pierre Chefdorge, 1565);

Sermons . . . sur le V. livre de Moyse nommé Deuteronome (Geneva: Printed by Thomas Courteau, 1567); translated by Golding as *The Sermons . . . upon the Fifth Booke of Moses Called Deuteronomie* (London: Printed by Henry Middleton for George Bishop / John Harrison / Thomas Woodcocke, 1583);

Joannis Calvini epistolæ et responsa. Quibus interjectæ sunt insignium in ecclesia Dei virorum aliquot etiam epistolæ (Geneva: Printed by Pierre de Saint-André, 1575).

Collections: *Ioannis Calvini noviodunensis Opera omnia: in novem tomos digesta,* 9 volumes (Amsterdam: Printed by J. J. Schipper, 1667–1671);

Ioannis Calvini Opera quae supersunt omnia: Ad fidem editionum principum et authenticarum ex parte etiam codicum manu scriptorum, additis prolegomenis literariis, annotationibus criticis, annalibus Calvinianis indicibusque novis et copiosissmis, 59 volumes, edited by Wilhelm Baum, Edward Cunitz, and Edward Reuss (Braunschweig: C. A. Schwetschke, 1863–1900);

Joannis Calvini Opera selecta, 5 volumes, edited by Peter Barth and Wilhelm Niesel (Munich: Kaiser, 1926–1952);

Supplementa Calviniana: Sermons inédits, 11 volumes, edited by Erwin Mülhaupt (Neukirchen, Germany: Neukirchener Verlag der Buchhandlung des Erziehungsvereins, 1961–);

Ioannis Calvini Opera omnia: denuo recognita et adnotatione, critica instructa, notisque illustrate, 16 volumes, edited by B. G. Armstrong, Helmut Feld, and others (Geneva: Droz, 1992–to date).

Editions in English: *Works,* 52 volumes, Calvin Translation Society Publications (Edinburgh: Calvin Translation Society, 1844–1856);

Institutes of the Christian Religion, 2 volumes, translated by Ford Lewis Battles, edited by John T. McNeill (Philadelphia: Westminster / London: SCM, 1960);

John Calvin: Selections from His Writings, edited by John Dillenberger (Garden City, N.Y.: Anchor/ Doubleday, 1971);

The Best of John Calvin, edited by Samuel Dunn (Grand Rapids, Mich.: Baker, 1981);

The Comprehensive John Calvin Collection, CD-ROM (Albany, Ore.: AGES, [1998]).

OTHER: Nicolas Duchemin, *Antapologia,* preface by Calvin (Paris: Printed by G. Morrhius, 1531);

Seneca, *Libri duo de clementia,* edited by Calvin (Paris: Printed by Louis Cyaneus, 1532; Orléans: Printed by Philippe Loré, 1532); translated by

Ford Lewis Battles and and André Malan Hugo as *Calvin's Commentary on Seneca's De Clementia,* edited by Battles and Hugo (Leiden: Brill, 1969);

La Bible qui est toute la Saincte escriture. En laquelle sont contenus, le Vieil Testament & le Nouueau, translatez en Francoys, edited by Robert Olivétan, preface by Calvin (Neuchâtel: Printed by Pierre de Wingle, 1535).

Centuries after his death, Jean Calvin's reputation among general readers remains that of a harsh and humorless man who founded Calvinism, the branch of the Christian church that bears his name. Yet, his impact from the sixteenth century to the present day stems from his extensive writings, including biblical commentaries, doctrinal works, and polemical tracts. A masterly writer in both Latin and French, he helped to shape the latter as a written language, especially by showing that he had no qualms about using the vernacular for sophisticated theological discourse. At the same time, Calvin's role as a second-generation Reformer, coming after Martin Luther and Huldrych Zwingli, allowed him to build on what earlier Reformers had already accomplished. Although Zwingli and his successors in the Swiss city of Zurich established the branch of Christianity known as the Reformed Church, Calvin's systematic approach to doctrine and scriptural exegesis helped to give Reformation theology more structure, while his ecclesiology offered more leadership roles for laymen. His theological insights and organizational skills helped make Calvinism the dominant form of the Reformed churches across Europe by the later sixteenth century.

Jean Calvin was born on 10 July 1509 in the northern French town of Noyon. His father, Gérard Calvin, was a notary whose main clients included the canons of Noyon Cathedral. Calvin's mother, Jeanne Le Franc, died in 1515, when he was only six years old. In the early 1520s Calvin traveled to Paris to begin his studies in the humanities at the Collège de La Marche and then the Collège Montaigu. His education was funded by church benefices intended for those planning to enter the priesthood. After completing his humanities courses, Calvin should have begun studying theology prior to ordination as a member of the Catholic clergy. However, as a result of his father's quarrel with the cathedral chapter in Noyon, Calvin transferred to the study of civil law at his father's request. Accordingly, Calvin took law courses at Orléans and Bourges, attending the lectures of renowned jurists Pierre de L'Estoile and Andrea Alciati. Indeed, Alciati's lack of respect for de L'Estoile led to Calvin's first published work, a preface to *Antapologia* (1531), a defense of de L'Estoile written by another student, Nicolas Duch-

CHRISTIA

NAE RELIGIONIS INSTI-
tutio, totam ferè pietatis summā, & quic
quid est in doctrina salutis cognitu ne-
cessarium, complectens: omnibus pietatis studiosis lectu dignissi-
mum opus, ac re
cens edi-
tum.

PRAEFATIO AD CHRI
stianißimum REGEM FRANCIAE, qua
hic ei liber pro confeßione fidei
offertur.

IOANNE CALVINO
Noxiodunensi autore.

BASILEAE,
M. D. XXXVI.

*Title page for the first publication of Calvin's summation of Reformed
Protestant doctrine, a work he often revised (from Rodolphe Peter and
Jean-François Gilmont,* Bibliotheca Calviniana: Les Oeuvres
de Jean Calvin publiées au XVIe siècle, *volume 1, 1991;
Thomas Cooper Library, University of South Carolina)*

emin. While in Bourges, Calvin took the opportunity to broaden his fields of knowledge by studying Greek with the Hellenist Melchior Wolmar.

In May 1531 Calvin's father died. To his death he remained embroiled in conflict with the Catholic clergy in Noyon. No longer bound by his father's wishes, Calvin returned to Paris and to the study of the humanities. His interest in the contemporary revival of ancient learning, known as humanism, led him to attempt to make his mark by publishing a commentary on a work by the Roman philosopher Seneca. The *Libri duo de clementia* (1532, Two Books on Clemency; translated as *Calvin's Commentary on Seneca's De Clementia,* 1969) was published in Paris at Calvin's own expense. The work was designed to display his abilities as a humanist scholar and to uphold the superiority of French humanism against other scholars' works,

including those of the Dutchman Desiderius Erasmus, the leading humanist of the early sixteenth century. The commentary attracted little attention, however, and Calvin subsequently returned to Bourges, obtaining his law degree there in the early 1530s.

During this period Calvin experienced a religious conversion, but the specific date of the event is unknown. Some scholars have placed it as early as 1531, while others speculate that it came as late as 1536. Because Calvin was reticent about his personal life, few details about the circumstances surrounding his move away from Catholicism are available; consequently, scholars who have studied Calvin's shift to Protestantism have focused on documented events to trace his passage from one confessional allegiance to another. One such event was a speech given by Nicolas Cop, the rector of the University of Paris, at the opening of the new academic year in November 1533. The speech included Protestant ideas largely taken from Luther, including justification by faith. Cop was a close friend of Calvin, and because a partial copy of the speech survives in Calvin's handwriting, some biographers have suggested that Calvin was the actual author of the speech. However, later scholarship has cast doubt on this claim because of the theological differences between what Cop said and Calvin's writings. Regardless, the reformist character of Cop's address alarmed religious conservatives in Paris. As a result of the investigation for heresy instigated by the Sorbonne, the university's faculty of theology, Cop and Calvin both fled the city to avoid arrest.

By May 1534 Calvin was back in Noyon, where he renounced the Catholic church benefices that had funded his formal education. Although opinions differ as to the significance of the gesture in terms of Calvin's conversion and his inner commitment to Protestantism, the break meant that Calvin needed to find other sources of financial support. He primarily relied on wealthy friends who acted as his patrons. One such friend, Louis du Tillet, offered Calvin an opportunity to spend time in his home in Saintonge in western France, and allowed him access to his library. The ready availability of scholarly works facilitated Calvin's exploration of theological issues. One indication of Calvin's increasing interest in doctrinal matters was a work he wrote in 1534 on what happens to human souls after death, the *Vivere apud Christum non dormire animis sanctos, qui in fide Christi decedunt, assertio* (1542, An Assertion That the Holy Souls, who Die in the Faith of Christ, Do Not Sleep, but Live in Christ; translated as *An Excellent Treatise of the Immortalytie of the Soule,* 1581). Ostensibly directed against the Anabaptists' view that the souls of the dead sleep until the Last Judgment, this polemical work allowed Calvin to hash out several ideas about time, immortality, and the nature of the soul. The work remained in manuscript until 1542, largely at the recommendation of other Reformers, who felt the matter was too sensitive to be printed during the early phases of conflict between the mainline Reformers and their radical critics. In 1545 the work appeared under its better-known title, the *Psychopannychia*.

By January 1535 Calvin had left France and settled in Basel, a Swiss city renowned for its humanist culture and many printing presses. That year a French translation of the Bible edited by Calvin's cousin, Robert Olivétan, appeared in print with a Latin preface by Calvin. This piece emphasizes the need to make God's word accessible to everyone despite the opposition of people who claimed that uneducated readers would become confused or unteachable if they had direct access to the Bible. Calvin argues that those who oppose vernacular Bibles are obscurantists, desperate to retain their hold over the minds of the common people.

A year later Calvin directed his arguments to a more learned audience, publishing the first Latin edition of his most famous work, the *Christianæ religionis institutio* (1536; translated as *The Institution of Christian Religion*, 1561). Frequently revised and enlarged during Calvin's lifetime, this book was intended as a brief overview of Reformed Protestant doctrine. In it Calvin deals with the main theological themes already presented by earlier Reformers, but he structures them into a coherent whole. He lays out the meaning of the Ten Commandments, the Apostles' Creed, the Lord's Prayer, and the sacraments—dealing with the two sacraments accepted by the Reformed churches, baptism and the Lord's Supper, and the five Catholic sacraments that Calvin and other Reformers rejected as unscriptural. His final section outlines the appropriate relationship between church and state. Calvin dedicated *Christianæ religionis institutio* to French king François I in an attempt to show him that accusations of heretical doctrine made against Reformed Protestants in France were unfounded.

A major turning point in Calvin's career occurred in July 1536. While on his way to Strasbourg, where he planned to take up the life of a scholar and writer, he stayed overnight in Geneva. That city had adopted the Reformation only two months earlier, ending the dominance of the ruling duchy of Savoy and sending its Catholic clergy into exile. Guillaume Farel, one of the men who had pushed for the Reformation in Geneva, saw that Calvin could provide much-needed organizational and doctrinal support for the new movement, and he persuaded Calvin to stay in Geneva. Calvin's first role in the city was to provide public exegetical lectures on the Bible. At this early stage of his career, Calvin had no formal theological training and was virtually unknown by his contemporaries, apart from those who had read his *Christianæ religionis institutio*. The Genevan Small Council, the city's highest representative body, was so uninformed about their new lecturer that when Farel came to a meeting on 5 September 1536 to ask for adequate financial provision for Calvin's work, the secretary noted down the request and referred to Calvin in the minutes as "ille gallus" (that Frenchman).

Despite the lack of awareness in Geneva about his work, Calvin played a significant role in helping the message of the Reformation spread to other French-language areas. In October 1536 Calvin served as one of Geneva's delegates to the public disputation against the Catholic clergy held in the neighboring city of Lausanne. The meeting was organized by the Bernese authorities, who had conquered Lausanne and its surrounding territory earlier that year, and who wanted to bring the region into the Reformed fold. As Lausanne's population was largely French speaking, the Genevan Reformation leaders, including Farel, Pierre Viret, and Calvin, proved to be both theologically and linguistically well suited to the task. The Catholic clergy of Lausanne were not strong opponents in the debate. Calvin displayed his knowledge of the Church Fathers' writings, especially when the Reformers were unsuccessfully challenged on their interpretation of the Lord's Supper.

On his return to Geneva after the Lausanne disputation, Calvin helped to draft many of the ordinances needed to help the city function under its new political and religious circumstances. In 1537 he and Farel prepared a catechism in French largely based on the 1536 *Christianæ religionis institutio,* the *Instruction et confession de foy dont on use en l'Eglise de Geneve* (Instruction and Confession of Faith Used in the Church of Geneva; translated as *Calvin's First Catechism: A Commentary,* 1997). That year Calvin also published two letters in Basel directed at his former co-*religionaries* in France, the *Epistolæ duæ de rebus hoc sæculo cognitu necesariis* (Two Letters About Necessary Matters in This Celebrated Century). These polemical texts attack Catholic rites, especially the Mass, and condemn the system of church benefices. The letters were Calvin's first written critique of Catholic practices, and they were also directed against those who chose not to break with Catholicism in spite of personal sympathies toward Protestantism. Calvin's challenge to those he regarded as half-hearted or fearful believers resurfaced in many of his later polemical works as well.

While attacks against Catholic practices helped to define Reformed positions, the Reformation also faced

Title page for Calvin's first work in French, a 1537 catechism based on
Christianæ religionis institutio *(from Rodolphe Peter
and Jean-François Gilmont,* Bibliotheca Calviniana:
Les Oeuvres de Jean Calvin publiées au XVIe
siècle, *volume 1, 1991; Thomas Cooper Library,
University of South Carolina)*

internal debate, some of which entailed larger political considerations. Even in Geneva the pioneers such as Farel and Calvin faced challenges to their ministry. Despite increasing pressure from city magistrates to conform to the Reformed ritual practices in Swiss cities that provided military protection to Geneva, Calvin and Farel refused to comply. Furthermore, Calvin and Farel maintained that the Genevan church, and not civil authorities, should control access to the Lord's Supper and prevent excommunicated members from partaking in the sacrament. The conflict came to a head in the spring of 1538, when Calvin and Farel ignored orders from the magistrates to refrain from preaching, and as a result they were exiled from the city.

After brief stays in Berne, Zurich, and Basel, Calvin spent the next three years in Strasbourg. Under the leadership of Martin Bucer and his fellow pastors, Strasbourg had become a leading center of Reformed thought, and it was particularly welcoming to religious refugees. Calvin remained in the city from 1538 to 1541, working as a pastor for the French refugee church and lecturing in the Strasbourg academy. The leadership role he took among the French refugee congregation allowed him the freedom to develop forms of worship that he later put into practice in Geneva. In particular, the Strasbourg services he led featured congregational unison singing of versifications of the Psalms in the vernacular. Calvin encouraged the use of these metrical settings, many of which were later definitively formulated by the French poet Clément Marot and Calvin's colleague Théodore de Bèze. The use of the Psalms set to music in congregational worship broke with Catholic devotional practice, where congregational singing was virtually unknown, and also with the Reformed church practice as instituted by Zwingli, where no singing of any kind was allowed in congregational worship.

In 1539 Calvin brought out a revised and expanded version of his Latin *Christianæ religionis institutio,* now titled *Institutio christianæ religionis,* in which he altered the ordering of topics in his overview of Christian doctrine. Instead of the traditional Lutheran catechetical approach–Law, Creed, Lord's Prayer, and then sacraments–Calvin begins with the knowledge of God and human self-knowledge, and includes larger sections on providence and predestination. Richard A. Muller's in-depth analysis of the development in Calvin's thought shows that the 1539 edition of his magnum opus features the most significant structural and methodological changes of all the revised versions of the text he brought out during his lifetime. In this edition Calvin strove to integrate the catechetical order and topics featured in the 1536 edition with the order and topics he took from Paul's letter to the Romans. Increasingly, Calvin wanted to make a distinction between his catechetical works intended for a broad, less theologically trained audience and his works of doctrinal instruction, directed primarily at future pastors.

In 1540 Calvin married a widow, Idelette de Bure, who had two children from her first marriage. The couple had no children of their own, apart from a baby boy who died shortly after his birth in 1542. Although by all accounts Calvin found his situation in Strasbourg satisfying, especially because of the support he received from the Strasbourg clergy, his connection to Geneva continued to be strong. In 1539 Calvin had responded to an open letter from Cardinal Jacopo Sadoleto urging the Genevans to return to Catholicism by publishing a polemical reply. In this work, *Jacobi Sadoleti Romani Cardinalis Epistola ad Senatum Populumque Genevensem, qua in obedientiam Romani Pontificis eos reducere conatur. Joannis Calvini responsio* (translated as "Letter by James Sadolet, a Roman Cardinal, to the Senate and People of Geneva" and "Reply by John Calvin to Letter by Cardinal Sadolet to the Senate and People of Geneva," 1844), Calvin opposes the Cardinal's claims about the authenticity of Catholicism by stating that the true church is recognized not by its long tradition but by its faithfulness to God's Word in the Bible. Calvin counters Sadoleto's claim that the Protestant pastors of Geneva had no authority on their side since they had broken with the Pope; he insists on the legitimacy of his vocation, a calling that he says came from God. Calvin also reiterates one of his main points in the *Institutio christianæ religionis:* the main aim of human existence is to glorify God, and not, as Sadoleto argued, to seek eternal salvation. In other words, the focus of human life should be on God rather than on what Calvin characterized as a selfish search for eternal blessedness. Calvin's willingness to respond to the Cardinal's challenge was duly noted by the Genevan authorities.

Calvin's insistence on the centrality of the Bible for the Reformed church led him to begin work on scriptural commentaries designed to illuminate the meaning of the biblical text. These commentaries usually were written in Latin and then translated into French. The first in Calvin's extensive series of biblical commentaries was *Commentarii in epistolam Pauli ad Romanos* (1540; translated as *A Commentarie upon the Epistle of Saint Paul to the Romanes,* 1583). The choice of Romans reflects the centrality of this Pauline epistle for the developing doctrine of the Protestant churches, both Lutheran and Reformed. In the preface Calvin seeks to differentiate his work as an exegetical scholar from that of fellow Reformers, including Philip Melanchthon and Bucer. According to Calvin, Melanchthon omits too many topics while Bucer goes on for too long. Calvin stresses his own concise yet comprehensive approach.

Calvin was asked to participate as one of the delegates at several meetings called by princes and churches to debate and reconcile some of the divisions in the Christian church. One such gathering was the 1541 imperial diet of Regensburg. On his return to Strasbourg, Calvin wrote a report on the proceedings of the diet, *Les actes de la journee imperiale tenue en la cité de Reguespourg* (The Acts of the Imperial Diet Held in the City of Regensburg), and he had it published later that year in Geneva. Ongoing religious controversies over the sacraments led Calvin to publish another polemical

tract in 1541, the *Petit traicté de la saincte Cene* (translated as "Short Treatise on the Supper of Our Lord," 1849). This work deals with the Lord's Supper, one of the most theologically divisive rites of the church at the time; Calvin carefully lays out the purpose and benefits of the Lord's Supper and furnishes a succinct overview of the controversy between Luther and Zwingli on the subject. Calvin's own understanding of Christ's spiritual presence in the sacrament placed him and his followers at a middle point between Luther, who believed that Christ was truly and physically present in the elements, and Zwingli, who believed the Lord's Supper simply reminded the faithful of Christ's sacrifice. In 1541 Calvin also published the French version of the 1539 *Institutio christianæ religionis,* the *Institution de la religion chrestienne* (Institutes of the Christian Religion). According to literary scholars, the impact of this translation on sixteenth-century written French was as significant as the writings of François Rabelais. As with the Latin version of the text, Calvin extensively reworked the French translation during his lifetime.

At the magistrates' invitation, Calvin came back to Geneva in September 1541. Although he returned with reluctance, he made Geneva his home for the rest of his life. One focal point for Calvin when he returned to Geneva was the need to provide better religious instruction for the Genevan population so that they would learn and remember the fundamentals of their faith. Accordingly, Calvin composed a second catechism in 1542, the *Catechisme de L'Eglise de Geneve: c'est à dire, le Formulaire d'instruire les enfans en la Chrétienté* (translated as *The Catechisme or Manner to Teache Children the Christian religion,* 1556); his first Latin translation of this catechism appeared in 1545. In contrast to *Instruction et confession de foy dont on use en l'Eglise de Geneve,* the new catechism follows a question-and-answer format designed to facilitate memorization. Pastors used the catechism during the Sunday afternoon services, which were mandatory for children, servants, and all those who were thought to need more instruction in the basics of their faith: the Lord's Prayer, the Apostles' Creed, and the Ten Commandments.

Another ecclesiastical change Calvin implemented in Geneva was to create the positions of deacons and elders in the Genevan church. Calvin had included these two roles in his presentation of the fourfold ministry (pastors, teachers, elders, deacons) in the *Institutio christianæ religionis.* Elders were laymen, charged with aiding the pastor in the oversight of church discipline. In Geneva they were selected from among the city councillors. Another group of laymen, deacons, were responsible for the collection and disbursement of charitable donations. By giving laymen important responsibilities in church affairs Calvin

GLADIVM. MATT. X.

NON VENI PACEM MITTERE, SED

VENI IGNEM MITTERE LVC XII.

DEFENSIO
SANAE ET ORTHODOXAE
DOCTRINAE DE SERVITVTE
& liberatione humani arbitrii, aduersus calumnias Alberti Pighii Campenfis.

Authore Ioanne Caluino.

GENEVAE,
Per Ioannem gerardum.
1543.

Title page for the work in which Calvin argued that the ability of human beings to choose good has been corrupted by Adam's fall (from Rodolphe Peter and Jean-François Gilmont, Bibliotheca Calviniana: Les Oeuvres de Jean Calvin publiées au XVIe siècle, *volume 1, 1991; Thomas Cooper Library, University of South Carolina)*

strengthened the power of the laity in the Reformed church. This move also made church communities less vulnerable to collapse in times of persecution because leadership was not solely entrusted to the pastor. Among the conditions Calvin laid down for his return was the establishment of a consistory of pastors and elders to oversee church discipline, a decision that over time worsened relations with his Genevan opponents. The consistory was created and dominated by the pastors of Geneva, who were all French, and Calvin's detractors included several leading families who objected to what they saw as foreign censure of their conduct.

Calvin also stirred up controversy outside Geneva with his writings against Catholics, who remained the dominant confessional group in his French homeland. Indeed, a significant proportion of Calvin's polemical writings were directed at the increasingly troubled religious situation in France. His 1543 *Advertissement du proffit qui reviendroit à la Chrestienté s'il se faisoit inventaire de tous les corps sainctz, & reliques* (translated as *A Very Profitable Treatise . . . Declarynge What Great Profit Might Come to Al Christendome, yf There Were a Regester Made of All Sainctes Bodies and Other Reliques,* 1561) targets the Catholic veneration of relics and attacks the authenticity of the relics themselves. In particular, Calvin condemns the popular tendency to honor relics while failing to honor God, a behavior he characterizes as idolatry. He blames the cult of relics both on the avarice of the clergy and on the foolishness of laypeople, whose credulity outweighs their common sense.

That year Calvin went on the offensive against a Catholic theologian, Albert Pigge, also known as Pighius, in his *Defensio sanae et orthodoxae doctrinae . . . adversus calumnies A. Pighii* (1543, A Defence of Pure and Orthodox Doctrine against the Calumnies of A. Pighius; translated as *The Bondage and Liberation of the Will: A Defence of the Orthodox Doctrine of Human Choice against Pighius,* 1996). Here Calvin deals with the nature of the human will, arguing that since the fall of Adam human beings have been unable to choose good of their own accord. Throughout the book Calvin attempts to refute Pighius's arguments by making a distinction between human will before and after Adam's fall. While Pighius argued that Calvin was going against the Church Fathers, Calvin asserts that his opponent had misunderstood their writings and that his own view is supported by both scripture and the writings of the early church.

Calvin also turned his attention to the problems faced by those who held Protestant beliefs but lived in Catholic areas. Was it acceptable for them to hold to their beliefs inwardly but outwardly conform to Catholic rituals? In *Petit traicté, monstrant que doit faire un fidele entre les papistes* (1543; translated as "A Short Treatise, Setting Forth What the Faithful Man Must Do When He Is Among Papists and He Knows the Truth of the Gospel," 2001), Calvin advises those living in Catholic areas not to attend Mass or participate in other rituals, urging them to try to move to Reformed areas instead. Those who could not or would not leave are urged to bear witness to their neighbors regarding their faith, and to be steadfast in their beliefs even if threatened by death. Calvin continues to hold to this high standard of open commitment to one's faith in one of his chief polemical works, *Excuse . . . a Messieurs les Nicodémites* (1544; translated as "Answer of John Calvin to the Nicodemite Gentlemen Concerning their Complaint that He is Too Severe," 2001), a hard-hitting polemical tract laying out two choices for those who favored Protestantism but lived among Catholics: exile or martyrdom. Calvin's use of the term *Nicodemite* refers to the account of Nicodemus, the Jewish leader who came to visit Jesus by night because he feared being seen. Calvin believed that French Protestants who were unwilling to declare their allegiance openly were similar to Nicodemus—or even worse than he was since, according to the biblical account, Nicodemus openly stood with Jesus' followers after his crucifixion.

Calvin's second 1544 work on the subject was a letter published in English together with a letter by the Zurich Reformer Heinrich Bullinger, *Two Epystles . . . Whether It Be Lawfull for a Chrissten Man To Communicate or Be Partaker of the Masse of the Papystes*. Mass was central to Catholic worship, and consequently Reformed Protestants focused most of their attacks on this rite. In fact, the most visible sign that someone in a Catholic country had adopted Protestantism was his or her refusal to attend Mass, even though this rejection was dangerous. The fact that during this period Calvin wrote several works on the issue of right behavior for Protestants in Catholic areas testifies to the real differences of opinion over this matter among the Reformed. The publication of this letter by Calvin in English—without any subsequent French or Latin version—indicates that his reputation was spreading quickly among vernacular readers, even as far as England.

The continued potency of Catholicism was only one of the threats that Calvin addressed. Although the Genevan church did not have many encounters with Anabaptists, Calvin saw the movement as a sufficiently grave threat to compose a work against them in 1544. Together with the Lutherans and other Reformed church leaders, Calvin thought of the Anabaptists as dangerous radicals who threatened civil society because of their rejection of many practices vital for the safety of early modern communities, including bearing arms and swearing oaths. In his *Brieve instruction pour armer tous bons fideles contre les erreurs de la secte commune des Anabaptistes* (1544; translated as *A Short Instruction for to Arme All Good Christian People agaynst the Pestiferous Errours of the Common Secte of Anabaptistes*, 1549), Calvin especially criticizes the Anabaptists for their support for adult baptism. He argues that infant baptism for Christians was similar to the practice of circumcision in the Old Testament: it was a sign of the covenant between God and his people. Calvin's work against the Anabaptists gave him an opportunity to emphasize several of his key points regarding the nature of the church. For Calvin, the church was the covenant community, bound to God through God's promise of faithfulness to believers and their families, expressed through the sacrament of infant baptism.

Calvin also turned his attention to others he perceived as a threat, namely the group he called "the spiritual libertines." According to Calvin, spiritual libertines were those who believed that they were no longer bound to follow the laws and commandments laid out in Scripture because they had been saved by God's grace. In his tract *Contre la secte phantastique et furieuse des Libertins. Qui se nomment spirituelz* (1545; translated as "Against the Fantastic and Furious Sect of the Libertines Who Are Called 'Spirituals,'" 1982), Calvin seeks to condemn their errors and warn the faithful about the dangers posed by this group. He especially links the libertines' beliefs to older but similar heresies within the Christian church.

Calvin continued to challenge the positions of the Catholic church, working to lessen its influence in religious and political affairs across Europe. In *Admonitio Paterna Pauli III. Romani Pontificis ad invictiss. Caesarem Carolum V. qua eum castigat . . . Cum Scholiis* (1545; translated as "A Paternal Admonition by the Roman Pontiff, Paul III, to the Most Invincible Emperor, Charles V" and "Remarks on the Letter of Pope Paul III," 1844), Calvin argues against making any concessions to the Protestants sent by Pope Paul III to Emperor Charles V and rebuts the Pope's arguments. Calvin condemns the Pope for alleging that he alone has the right to call councils and adjudicate religious matters. He also takes this opportunity to criticize the Pope for his failure to live up to the model of a true spiritual leader. According to Calvin, any moral or spiritual authority the Pope might have wielded was lost because of his sins and those of the other princes of the church.

Although Calvin wrote many important and influential polemical works, they are far outnumbered by his commentaries and sermons. In 1546 Calvin published his Latin commentary on Paul's first letter to the Corinthians, *Commentarii in priorem epistolam Pauli ad Corinthios* (translated as *A Commentarie upon S. Paules Epistles to the Corinthians*, 1577). This work was first dedicated to the French nobleman Jacques de Bourgogne, but Calvin changed the dedication in 1556 to honor the Italian nobleman Galeazzo Carraciolo. The change occurred because Bourgogne had broken with Calvin and returned to the Catholic church. In the later dedication Calvin praises Carraciolo for his willingness to leave his home, family, and privileges in Italy to come to Geneva for the sake of his faith.

In 1546 two of Calvin's sermons appeared together in print as *Deux sermons . . . faitz en la ville de Geneve* (Two Sermons . . . Preached in the City of Geneva). These were the first of his sermons to be

Defenſio ſanæ &

orthodoxæ doctrinæ de Sacramētis, eo-
rúmq; natura, vi, fine, vſu, & fructu: quã
paſtores & miniſtri Tigurinæ Eccleſiæ
& Geneuēſis antehac breui Cõſenſionis
mutuæ formula cõplexi ſunt: vnà cum
refutatiõe probrorum quibus eam in-
docti & clamoſi homines infamant.

Iohanne Caluino authore.

Oliua Roberti Stephani.

M. D. LV.

VLTIMA

ADMONITIO

IOANNIS CALVINI

Ad Ioachimum weſtphalũ, cui niſi obtem-
peret, eo loco poſthac habendus erit, quo
pertinaces hæreticos haberi iubet Paulus.

REFVTANTVR ETIAM HOC
ſcripto ſuperbæ Magdeburgenſiũ & aliorum
cenſuræ, quibus cælum & terram obruere
conati ſunt.

APVD IOANNEM CRISPINVM,

M. D. LVII.

*Title pages for the first and last of three treatises that Calvin wrote against the positions of Lutheran pastor Joachim Westphal
of Hamburg (from Rodolphe Peter and Jean-François Gilmont,* Bibliotheca Calviniana:
Les Oeuvres de Jean Calvin publiées au XVIe siècle, *volume 2, 1994;
Thomas Cooper Library, University of South Carolina)*

published, and they represent the earliest attempt by note takers to record Calvin's words as he spoke them. This technique was used for subsequent published sermons and for many of his published lectures. Throughout his career Calvin was reluctant to see his sermons appear in print, largely because he felt that he did not have enough time to revise them as extensively as he would like before publishing them. Yet, the practice of using scribes for his sermons ensured their survival, whereas the countless sermons preached by Calvin's fellow pastors in Geneva and France were rarely written down and have been lost.

In 1547 Calvin returned to his work on Corinthians, publishing the *Commentaire sur la seconde Epistre aux Corinthiens* (translated as *A Commentarie upon S. Paules Epistles to the Corinthians,* 1577). This commentary was one of the few to appear in French translation before the original Latin text was published. In this instance, publication of the Latin version was delayed until 1548

because of the temporary loss of the only copy of the manuscript and Calvin's decision to change printers.

Calvin continued to put considerable time and effort into combating challenges to his theology. His writings to this effect continued to demonstrate his awareness of contemporary events and their impact. For example, Calvin reacted to the decrees of the Catholic Council of Trent that began in 1545. His *Acta synodi Tridentinæ. Cum antidoto* (1547; translated as "Canons and Decrees of the Council of Trent, with the Antidote," 1851) critiques the decisions taken by the Council in its first seven sessions, which occurred between 1545 and 1547. After denying the legitimacy of the Council because of the corruption he saw in the papacy and the Catholic church as a whole, Calvin focuses on the sixth and seventh sessions of the Council and their resulting doctrinal statements, known as Canons. The first set of Canons dealt with justification and salvation, and the second set with the sacraments of the church. In each case Calvin provides the text of the Canons and then proceeds to refute them by contrasting the Catholic church's assertions with the teachings of Scripture.

In the *Advertissement contre l'astrologie judiciaire* (1549; translated as *An Admonicion against Astrology Judiciall*, [1561]), Calvin condemns those people who claimed to convert to the Reformed faith but maintained their ordinary way of life and made no attempt to improve their behavior. Among the practices he criticizes is astrology; he chastises people for believing in the power and influence of the stars and planets over natural phenomena such as storms or outbreaks of disease and over the course of human life, including a person's character, major formative events, and time of death. In the process Calvin carefully distinguishes astrology from the valid scientific disciplines of his day, including mathematics, physics, and astronomy. His principal objection to astrology is that astrologers fail to recognize God's active role in the world and his sovereignty over human affairs.

Calvin's confidence in God's sovereignty was tested in 1549, when his wife Idelette died. In a letter to Viret written on 7 April 1549, Calvin speaks of his profound grief and describes his wife as "optima socia vitae: quae, si quid accidisset durius, no exsilii tantum ac inopiae voluntaria comes, sed mortis quoque futura erat" (the excellent companion of my life, who, if misfortune had come, would have been my voluntary companion, not only in exile and in misery, but even in death).

By the early 1550s Reformed congregations were under threat—especially in France, where Catholic king Henri II enacted repressive measures. Calvin's fear that some of the early supporters of the Reformation might abandon the cause because of the persecutions led him to publish *De Scandalis. Quibus hodie plerique absterrentur, nonnulli etiam alienatur a pura Evangelii doctrina* (1550; translated as *A Little Book . . . Concernynge Offences, whereby at this Daye Divers Are Feared, and Many also Quight Withdrawen from the Pure Doctrine of the Gospell*, 1567). In this work Calvin links the current tribulations of the Reformed church with Christ's suffering and death on the cross, an event that the Bible describes as a scandal and stumbling block in the eyes of the world. Yet, Calvin also strongly criticizes those who created scandals and stumbling blocks in the church, whether through immorality, propensity to quarrel, or false beliefs. Furthermore, he has harsh words for those who took the presence of scandals in the church as a pretext to avoid joining the movement. Instead, Calvin urges the faithful to persevere despite the obstacles. Indeed, he saw the persecutions of his fellow believers as a sign that they were in fact on the right path, since they were following so closely in the footsteps of Christ.

Calvin's series of commentaries on New Testament epistles continued in 1550 with the appearance of his *Commentarii in epistolam ad Titum* (Commentaries on the Epistle to Titus; translated 1856), the *Commentarii in priorem epistolam Pauli ad Thessalonicenses* (Commentaries on Paul's First Letter to the Thessalonians; translated 1851), and *Commentarii in posteriorem epistolam Pauli ad Thessalonicenses* (Commentaries on Paul's Second Letter to the Thessalonians; translated 1851). He also published a new edition of the *Institutio christianæ religionis* in Latin, complete with numbered paragraphs and scriptural and topical indexes, making it easier for readers to use. That year Calvin's letter to Edward Seymour, Duke of Somerset and Lord Protector of England, appeared in print in English, *An Epistle Both of Godly Consolacion and Also of Advertisement*. Calvin intended the letter to serve as encouragement to Somerset in his task of moving England toward a Reformed confession during Edward VI's reign.

Throughout the early 1550s Calvin continued publishing the results of his exegetical work. *Commentarii in epistolas canonicas* (1551, Commentaries on the Canonical Epistles; partially translated as *The Comentaries . . . upon the First Epistle of Sainct Jhon, and upon the Epistle of Jude,* 1580) deals with 1 and 2 Peter, 1 John, James, and Jude. Calvin also published *In omnes Pauli epistolas atque etiam in epistolam ad Hebraeos commentaria* (1551, Commentaries on all the Pauline Epistles and on the Epistle to the Hebrews), which brings together in one convenient volume many of his earlier commentaries on the Pauline epistles and one previously unpublished commentary on Paul's letter to Philemon. Calvin's first printed commentary on the Old Testament was his *Commentarii in Isaiam prophetam* (1551; translated as *A Commentary upon the Prophecie of Isaiah,* 1609). This work was put together by Calvin's fellow pastor Nicolas des Gallars based on notes Des Gallars had taken during Calvin's sermons and lectures. In the preface Des Gallars claims that he read the text back to Calvin to check for accuracy. Although Calvin agreed to this process, he never repeated the experiment, and he issued a complete revision of the Isaiah commentary in 1559.

In 1551 Calvin issued the third edition of *Institution de la religion chrestienne,* based on the Latin revised version published in 1550. He added three paragraphs on Christ's resurrection, additions that found their way into the Latin version only in the 1559 edition. In 1551 Calvin also published a short polemical work, *Response a un plaidoyer faict par un certain Advocat de Paris* (Answer to an Argument Made by a Parisian Lawyer), which rejects the views of a Parisian lawyer, Pierre

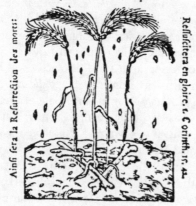

Title page for Calvin's collection of eighteen sermons on Genesis and the synoptic Gospels (from Rodolphe Peter and Jean-François Gilmont, Bibliotheca Calviniana: Les Oeuvres de Jean Calvin publiées au XVIe siècle, volume 2, 1994; Thomas Cooper Library, University of South Carolina)

Séguier, who argued that God punished those who were unfaithful to traditional Catholic religion. In response, Calvin states that God punishes idolatry, but the tribulations endured by the Reformed were not a sign of God's chastisement.

Calvin's sense that the attacks on Reformed Protestants signaled God's favor did not prevent him from making use of both his personal and his written authority to repress any questioning of what he considered key Reformation doctrines. Calvin's polemical work *De aeterna Dei praedestinatione* (1552; translated as "A Treatise on the Eternal Predestination of God," 1856–1857) was intended to be the second part of his 1543 reply to Pighius. He also took the opportunity to respond to the physician Jerome Bolsec's challenge against predestination in 1551. Bolsec had publicly criticized Calvin's doctrine of predestination during a Genevan *congrégation,* one of the weekly gatherings of Genevan pastors and laypeople during which pastors took turns providing exegetical analyses of scriptural passages. According to Bolsec, predestination as articulated by Calvin made God a tyrant and the author of sin. The ensuing debate was adjudicated by the Genevan magistrates, and Bolsec was banished from Geneva in December 1551. Calvin's 1552 treatise on predestination was designed to refute Bolsec's charges for a wide audience. Calvin accuses Bolsec of repeating earlier errors, especially those of Pighius, and he outlines the scriptural foundation for the doctrine of predestination and ascribes God's motivation in electing some and condemning others to "arcanum Dei consilium" (his inscrutable judgement).

The Bolsec affair was eclipsed two years later by a controversy involving Michael Servetus, a Spanish physician and theologian now remembered for being the first to publish a description of the blood's circulation through the lungs. Servetus published several works detailing his antitrinitarian views. Imprisoned under suspicion of heresy in Vienne, France, Servetus managed to escape, but as he was passing through Geneva on his way to Italy, he was recognized and arrested. As in the case of Bolsec, Calvin defended his doctrinal stance against Servetus. The weight of his authority together with the support of the Swiss Reformed cities led to Servetus's execution by burning in October 1553. The Spaniard's death, and particularly Calvin's role in it, was controversial, especially among supporters of a more tolerant approach. In response, Calvin wrote *Defensio orthodoxæ fidei de sacra Trinitate, contra prodigiosos errores Michaelis Serveti Hispani* (1554, Defense of the Orthodox Faith in the Sacred Trinity, against the Prodigious Errors of the Spaniard Michael Servetus), in which he attacks Servetus's antitrinitarian views and justifies his execution for heresy. The work met with mixed reactions—even some of Calvin's supporters in surrounding areas were dismayed by what they saw as his severe tone.

While Servetus had clashed with Calvin over doctrinal matters, others in Geneva focused on issues of church discipline in opposing Calvin. This movement coalesced around Ami Perrin, a member of one of Geneva's leading families. Perrin and his relatives had been on the receiving end of several disciplinary actions because of offenses including dancing, playing games instead of attending church, and being disrespectful toward the consistory and the Genevan pastors, especially Calvin. The Genevan elite's antipathy for what it saw as foreign pastors had been exacerbated by the increasing presence of French religious refugees in the city, many of them wealthy and well connected. The long-standing Perrinist resentment over church discipline, combined with their fear of displacement by the rising tide of French refugees who supported Calvin, led to a riot in May 1555. The aim of the Genevan rioters seems to have been to blame the disturbance on French refugees, but the plan failed and the riot fizzled out. Perrin and his fellow conspirators escaped, but they were judged and condemned to death in absentia, and their property was taken by the city. After 1555 Calvin's situation in Geneva was secure: from then on he had the full support of the Genevan magistrates, and opposition within the city was almost nonexistent.

Meanwhile, external objections to aspects of Calvinist doctrine continued. Beginning in 1555 Calvin produced a set of treatises written against the Lutheran pastor Joachim Westphal of Hamburg. Westphal and others had reacted critically to the publication of the *Consensus Tigurinus* of 1551, the document that articulated the agreement between the Reformed churches of Zurich and Geneva on doctrinal issues, especially on the Lord's Supper. Westphal's support for the Lutheran doctrine of the real and physical presence of Christ in the sacrament led to Calvin's response in the *Defensio sanæ & orthodoxæ doctrinæ de Sacramentis* (1555, A Defense of the Clear and Orthodox Doctrine of the Sacrament). Calvin's polemic against Westphal continued in 1556 with his *Secunda defensio piæ & orthodoxae de sacramentis fidei* (translated as "Second Defence of the Pious and Orthodox Faith Concerning the Sacraments," 1849). Here Calvin addresses Westphal's response to *Defensio sanæ & orthodoxæ doctrinæ de Sacramentis*. Finally, in 1557 Calvin wrote a third pamphlet against Westphal, the *Ultima admonitio . . . ad Joachimum Westphalum* (translated as "Last Admonition of John Calvin to Joachim Westphal," 1849). Although Westphal continued to target Calvin and the Genevans, Calvin never directly intervened in the debate again.

In 1557 Calvin brought out his *Responses à certaines calomnies et blasphemes* (Replies to Certain Slanders and Blasphemies), a brief work written in response to an antipredestinarian tract supposedly written by Sebastian Castellio, one of Calvin's opponents who had settled in Basel. Castellio taught in Geneva until 1545, but he failed to win Calvin's support for advancing to the ordained ministry, and he left Geneva. Castellio's support for Servetus, and his criticism of Calvin's willingness to have Servetus executed for heresy, led Calvin and Bèze to consider him a danger to the cause. Calvin responded to an earlier work that he thought had been written by Castellio in another treatise, *Brevis responsio . . . ad diluendas nebulonis calumnias* (1557; translated as "Brief Reply in Refutation of the Calumnies of a Certain Worthless Person," 1954). In this instance it appears that the work Calvin was attacking was not actually composed by Castellio. In

1558 Calvin published *Calumniæ nebulonis cuiusdam, . . . de occulta Dei providentia* (translated as "A Defence of the Secret Providence of God, by Which He Works Out His Eternal Decrees," 1856–1857). This tract was yet another response to a work thought by the Genevans to be Castellio's, although Castellio firmly denied having written the work in question. In this text Calvin defends the doctrine of Providence and rejects specific criticisms of it. He again received some criticism for his fierce tone.

Calvin continued publishing commentaries in the late 1550s with *In Hoseam prophetam prælectiones* (1557, Lectures on the Prophet Hosea) and *In librum Psalmorum . . . commentarius* (1557; translated as *The Psalmes of David and Others. With M. John Calvins Commentaries*, 1571). The lectures on Hosea were compiled through note taking. Meanwhile, Calvin's sermons continued to appear in print. *Sermons . . . sur les dix commandemens de la Loy* (translated as *Sermons . . . upon the .X. Commandementes of the Lawe, Geven of God by Moses, Otherwise Called the Decalogue*, 1579), published in 1557, features sixteen sermons taken from the two hundred Calvin preached on Deuteronomy between 1555 and 1556. Two more volumes of Calvin's sermons came off the presses in 1558: *Plusieurs sermons . . . touchant la divinité, humanité et nativité de nostre Seigneur Jesus Christ* (translated as *Divers Sermons . . . Concerning the Divinitie, Humanitie and Nativitie of Our Lorde Jesus Christe*, 1581) and *Sermons . . . sur le dixieme & onzieme chapitre de la premiere Epistre sainct Paul aux Corinthiens* (Sermons . . . on the Tenth and Eleventh Chapter of Saint Paul's First Letter to the Corinthians). The sermons in the first volume are those Calvin preached at the quarterly celebrations of the Lord's Supper, and the sermons in the second volume address that particular sacrament.

By the late 1550s Calvin's time was increasingly occupied with new tasks and responsibilities. After years of planning, the Genevan Academy opened its doors in 1559. The academy statutes established an institution in two parts: a Latin school designed for boys and a center of higher learning that offered university-level lectures in humanities, Greek, Hebrew, and theology. Calvin and Bèze taught theology in the Academy on alternate weeks. Although Calvin had given scriptural-exegesis lectures since his first days in Geneva, the more formal structure of the academy allowed him to direct his lectures at an audience of young men ready and eager to make practical use of them. Calvin's classroom lectures yielded publications such as *Prælectiones in duodecim Prophetas quos vocant minores* (1559; translated as *Commentaries on the Twelve Minor Prophets*, 1846–1849). As with his sermons, these lectures were taken down by scribes as Calvin spoke and then transcribed into a clean copy prior to publica-

CONGREGATION
FAITE EN L'EGLISE DE
Geneue par M. Iean
Caluin.

En laquelle la matiere de l'election eternelle
de Dieu fut fommairemēt & clairement par luy
deduite, & ratifiée d'vn commun accord par fes
freres Miniftres : repouffant l'erreur d'vn fe-
meur de fauffe doctrine, qui effrontéement a-
uoit defgorgé fon venin.

Nouuellement mife en lumiere.

A GENEVE,
Par Vincent Bres.
Auec priuilege.
1562.

Title page for the book in which Calvin demonstrated that his doctrine of predestination was endorsed by his colleagues in Geneva (from Rodolphe Peter and Jean-François Gilmont, Bibliotheca Calviniana: Les Oeuvres de Jean Calvin publiées au XVIe siècle, *volume 2, 1994; Thomas Cooper Library, University of South Carolina)*

tion. In 1559 Calvin also published his final revision of the Latin version of the *Institutio christianæ religionis*. He rearranged the topics, added sections, and declared in the preface that he was now finally satisfied with the structure of his work.

In 1560 the majority of Calvin's published works were sermons. His *Dixhuict sermons . . . Ausquels, entre autres poincts, l'histoire de Melchisedec et la matiere de la justification, sont deduites* (Eighteen Sermons . . . In Which, Among Other Matters, the Story of Melchizedek and the Topic of Justification are Dealt With) was printed in Geneva. It featured two parallel sermon series, one on Genesis and the other on the synoptic gospels. Meanwhile, two first editions of Calvin's sermons appeared in English in London: *Sermons . . . upon the Songe that Ezechias Made after He Had Bene Sicke, and Afflicted by the Hand of God* and *Two Godly and Notable*

Sermons Preached . . . in the Yere 1555. Both of these translations were the work of English exiles who had fled their homeland during the reign of the Catholic queen Mary. The books were printed in England upon the exiles' return after the accession of the Protestant queen Elizabeth.

Calvin never lost sight of his role as defender of Reformed doctrine. Indeed, several of his polemical works published in the early 1560s reiterated for broader audiences positions he had defended in earlier texts. For example, in 1560 a compendium volume of Calvin's sermons appeared together with a French translation of Calvin's earlier Latin work on predestination. The book was titled *Traité de la predestination eternelle de Dieu, par laquelle les uns sont eleuz à salut, les autres laissez en leur condemnation. Aussi de la providence, par laquelle il gouverne les choses humaines. Item y sont adjoustez treze sermons, traitans de l'election gratuite de Dieu en Jacob, et de la rejection en Esau* (Treatise on the Eternal Predestination of God, through Which Some are Elected to Salvation, While Others are Left Condemned. Also on Providence, through Which He Governs Human Affairs. Thirteen Sermons Also Added, Dealing with God's Election of Jacob and Rejection of Esau). Among these works, the sermons, taken from the series Calvin preached on Genesis beginning in September 1559, were previously unpublished, and they were translated into English and published in 1579 as *Thirteene Sermons . . . Entreating of the Free Election of God in Jacob, and of Reprobation in Esau*. By linking a treatise on predestination with sermons that explained God's Word to the people, Calvin attempts to show that predestination is not an isolated creation of his, but is in fact grounded in Scripture.

Calvin returned to anti-Catholic polemic when he wrote a satirical work aimed at a Catholic priest, Gabriel de Saconay, who in 1561 had reprinted Henry VIII's 1521 treatise attacking Luther on the subject of the sacraments, *Assertio septem Sacramentorum aduersus Martinum Lutherum* (Defense of the Seven Sacraments against Martin Luther), written prior to the English monarch's break with the Catholic church. De Saconay's edition of Henry's work includes his own preface attacking heretics, including Lutherans, Calvinists, Zwinglians, and Anabaptists. De Saconay had also criticized the late king and Anne Boleyn for England's move to Protestantism. Calvin's response, *Gratulatio ad venerabilem presbyterum, dominum Gabrielem de Saconay* (1561; translated as "Congratulations to the Venerable Presbyter, Lord Gabriel de Saconay," 1984), refutes De Saconay's anti-Protestant charges and suggested that Henry VIII's work against Luther actually had been written by a member of his entourage and simply signed by the king.

Calvin revisited the issue of religious toleration in his *Responsio ad versipellem quendam mediatorem* (1561, Reply to a Sly and Cunning Proponent of a Middle Way), in which he combats advocates of an irenic approach to the conflicts between Catholics and Protestants. In 1561 Catholics and Protestants in France met at the Colloquy of Poissy to try to resolve their differences. Georg Cassander, a German Catholic humanist, wrote *De officio pii viri* (1561, On the Task of a Pious Man), a work intended for the Poissy delegates that strove to mark out common ground between Catholics and Protestants. Calvin saw Cassander's argument as an attempt to appeal to the lowest common denominator and as a cover for Nicodemism. In his response Calvin outlines the dangers he saw in religious compromise and rejects the Catholic writer's view that it was best to work for unity and avoid controversial theological issues such as predestination. In fact, several of the ideas supported by Cassander resembled those that Castellio had presented in earlier years as he promoted a measure of religious toleration.

In *Congregation faite en l'eglise de Geneve . . . En laquelle la matiere de l'election eternelle de Dieu* (1562, Assembly held in the Church of Geneva . . . in Which He Clearly and Briefly Presented the Issue of God's Eternal Election), Calvin returned to the issue that lay at the heart of his conflict with Bolsec. The text is based on the pastors' *congrégation* that had taken place in December 1551 as a result of Bolsec's charges against the doctrine of predestination. While the Bolsec affair had long been resolved, the debates over predestination had continued; consequently, Calvin felt the need to defend his view once more. By publishing the proceedings of a meeting in which the matter was discussed by Genevan pastors, Calvin could show that his view was shared by his colleagues, and that the doctrine of predestination was widely accepted in the Genevan church.

Calvin also returned to the doctrinal issue that had led to Servetus's death, the doctrine of the trinity. This time Calvin addressed the members of the Polish Protestant churches that were being challenged by supporters of antitrinitarianism. In his 1563 work *Brevis admonitio . . . ad fratres Polonos* (Brief Admonition to the Polish Brethren), Calvin attacks the Polish antitrinitarians, especially because of their insistence on three essences rather than three persons in the Trinity. According to Calvin, such a doctrine could lead to a theology of three gods rather than one God in three persons.

Calvin's constant struggles against opponents, both within and outside Geneva, as well as his demanding schedule of preaching, teaching, and writing, took a heavy toll on him. By 1564 his health was

Title page for the biblical commentary that was published after Calvin's death in 1564 (from Rodolphe Peter and Jean-François Gilmont, Bibliotheca Calviniana: Les Oeuvres de Jean Calvin publiées au XVIe siècle, volume 2, 1994; Thomas Cooper Library, University of South Carolina)

deteriorating. Suffering from many ailments, including kidney stones, migraines, intestinal parasites, and a lung condition that was probably tuberculosis, Calvin gradually grew too weak even to be carried to church to preach. After meeting in his home with the magistrates and ministers of Geneva to take his formal farewell, and after urging his fellow pastors not to make any changes to the way the Genevan church was established, Calvin died on 27 May 1564. At his request he was buried in an unmarked tomb.

At the time of his death Calvin was still working on his biblical commentaries. His *In librum Josue brevis commentarius* (translated as *A Commentarie . . . upon the Booke of Josue,* 1578) was published posthumously in 1564. This work is based on Friday *congrégations* that started on the book of Joshua in June 1563. It also includes a Latin translation of the earliest version of

Stamp released in 1964 (from <http://pluq59.free.fr>)

ume features one hundred sermons preached by Calvin between 1555 and 1556, some of which, namely those on the Ten Commandments, had been published in earlier works.

In 1575, in an effort to present another aspect of Calvin's contribution to the Reformation, the Genevans brought out a volume that includes many letters by and to Calvin, *Epistolæ et responsa* (Letters and Replies). The volume includes four hundred documents and Bèze's amplified version of his biography of Calvin. By 1575, then, Calvin's colleagues had published three biographical accounts of Calvin's life: Bèze's in 1564, a second edition reworked and amplified by the Genevan pastor Nicolas Colladon in 1565, and Bèze's final version in 1575. These texts served a dual purpose: they allowed Reformed Protestants to learn more about the life and works of one of the leading figures of the Reformed faith, and they helped refute accounts of Calvin's life written by his opponents.

Since his death, historians and theologians have debated the extent of Calvin's influence over many areas of human endeavor. The spread of his writings across Europe, and the speed at which his works were translated into English, Dutch, Italian, and many other languages, including Polish, Czech, and Hungarian, indicate how significant his impact was in his own day. By 1600 his *Institutio christianæ religionis* had been translated into six languages, many appearing in several editions. Apart from his published works, Calvin's network of correspondents across Europe also testify to his importance for Reformed Christians in the sixteenth century.

The religious movement shaped by Jean Calvin is thought by some scholars to have contributed to capitalism and political-resistance theory. Others contend that Calvin's greatest contribution was his systematic presentation of Reformation doctrine, while still others see him as one of the clearest and most influential biblical commentators of all time. His detractors point to his vehement attacks against those who did not share his doctrinal outlook, and to the condemnation of men such as Bolsec and Servetus in Geneva during Calvin's years of influence. Yet, Calvin's legacy cannot be reduced to one single aspect of his work. Taken together, his sermons, commentaries, and polemical treatises provide a wide range of contributions to Reformed theology, and Western thought in general, both in his own day and in the following centuries.

Bèze's short biography of Calvin. The following year two more works by Calvin appeared in print. The first of these books, *In viginti prima Ezechielis prophetæ capita praelectiones* (translated as *Commentaries on the First Twenty Chapters of the Book of the Prophet Ezekiel,* 1849, 1850), features Calvin's lectures on Ezekiel, which he began in 1562 and ended in February 1564, when his health prevented him from continuing. The next book to appear was a volume of Calvin's sermons, *Quarante sept sermons . . . sur les huict derniers chapitres des propheties de Daniel* (1565, Forty-Seven Sermons . . . on the Final Eight Chapters of Daniel's Prophecies). Calvin began preaching the sermons included in this book in 1552.

In 1567 another set of Calvin's sermons appeared in print, *Sermons . . . sur le V. livre de Moyse nommé Deuteronome* (translated as *The Sermons . . . upon the Fifth Booke of Moses Called Deuteronomie,* 1583). This vol-

Letters:

Letters of John Calvin, 4 volumes, translated by David Constable and Marcus Robert Gilchrist, edited by Jules Bonnet (New York: Burt Franklin, 1973).

Bibliographies:

Alfred Erichson, *Bibliographia Calviniana: Catalogus chronologicus operum Calvini. Catalogus systematicus operum quae sunt de Calvino, cum indice auctorum alphabetico* (Berlin: Schwetschke, 1900);

Joseph Tylenda, Peter DeKlerk, and Paul Fields, "Calvin Bibliography," *Calvin Theological Journal* (1971–);

Rodolphe Peter and Jean-François Gilmont, *Bibliotheca Calviniana: Les Oeuvres de Jean Calvin publiées au XVIe siècle,* 3 volumes (Geneva: Droz, 1991–2000)—comprises volume 1 (1991), *Écrits théologiques, littéraires et juridiques, 1532–1554;* volume 2 (1994), *Écrits théologiques, littéraires et juridiques, 1555–1564;* and volume 3 (2000), *Écrits théologiques, littéraires et juridiques, 1565–1600.*

Biographies:

Paul Henry, *The Life and Times of John Calvin: The Great Reformer,* 2 volumes, translated by Henry Stebbing (London: Whittaker, 1849; New York: Carter, 1851–1852);

Williston Walker, *John Calvin: The Organiser of Reformed Protestantism, 1509–1564* (New York & London: Putnam, 1906);

T. H. L. Parker, *John Calvin, A Biography* (Philadelphia: Westminster, 1975; London: Dent, 1975);

Alexandre Ganoczy, *The Young Calvin,* translated by David Foxgrover and Wade Provo (Philadelphia: Westminster, 1987);

William J. Bouwsma, *John Calvin: A Sixteenth-Century Portrait* (New York: Oxford University Press, 1988);

Alister McGrath, *A Life of John Calvin: A Study in the Shaping of Western Culture* (Oxford & Cambridge, Mass.: Blackwell, 1990);

Theodore Bèze, *The Life of John Calvin: Carefully Written by Theodore Beza,* edited and translated by Henry Beveridge (Milwaukie, Ore.: Back Home, 1996);

Bernard Cottret, *Calvin: A Biography,* translated by M. Wallace McDonald (Grand Rapids, Mich.: Eerdmans / Edinburgh: Clark, 2000).

References:

W. Fred Graham, *The Constructive Revolutionary: John Calvin & His Socio-Economic Impact* (Lansing: Michigan State University Press, 1987);

Wulfert de Greef, *The Writings of John Calvin: An Introductory Guide,* translated by Lyle Bierma (Grand Rapids, Mich.: Baker Books / Leicester, U.K.: Apollos, 1993);

Richard A. Muller, *The Unaccommodated Calvin: Studies in the Foundation of a Theological Tradition* (New York & London: Oxford University Press, 2000);

William G. Naphy, *Calvin and the Consolidation of the Genevan Reformation* (Manchester & New York: Manchester University Press, 1994);

T. H. L. Parker, *Calvin's Preaching* (Edinburgh: Clark / Louisville, Ky.: Westminster/John Knox, 1992);

David Steinmetz, *Calvin in Context* (New York & Oxford: Oxford University Press, 1995).

Papers:

The major collections of Calvin's papers are in the Archives d'Etat de Genève; Institut d'Histoire de la Réformation, Université de Genève; and H. Henry Meeter Center for Calvin Studies, Grand Rapids, Michigan.

Symphorien Champier

(1472? – 1539?)

Judy Kem
Wake Forest University

BOOKS: *Janua logicae et phisicae* (Lyon: Printed by Guillaume Balsarin, 1498);

Dyalogus . . . in magicarum artium destructionem (Lyon: Printed by Guillaume Balsarin, [1500]); translated by Brian Copenhaver and Darrel Amundsen as *A Facsimile and an Annotated Translation Of Champier's Dyalogus . . . In Magicarum Artium Destructionem: "A Dialogue . . . On The Destruction Of The Magical Arts,"* in Copenhaver, *Symphorien Champier and the Reception of the Occultist Tradition in Renaissance France* (The Hague, Paris, & New York: Mouton, 1978), pp. 243–319;

La nef des princes et des batailles de noblesse (Lyon: Printed by Guillaume Balsarin, 1502);

La nef des dames vertueuses (Lyon: Printed by Jacques Arnollet, 1503);

Libelli duo (Lyon: Printed by Jannot de Campis, [1506]);

Liber de quadruplici vita . . . Tropheum gallorum (Lyon: Printed for Stéphane Gueynard and Jacques Huguet by Jannot de Campis, 1507);

De triplici disciplina (Lyon: Printed for Simon Vincent by Claude Davost, 1508);

Le triumphe du treschrestien Roy de France [Loys] *XII* (Lyon: Printed by Claude Davost, 1509);

Le recueil ou croniques des hystoires des royaulmes d'austrasie (Lyon: Printed by Vincent de Portunaris de Trinc, 1510);

Officina apothecariorum seu seplasiariorum pharmacopolarum ac iuniorum medicorum (Lyon: Printed by Simon Vincent, 1511; revised, 1532);

Speculum Galeni ([Lyon]: [Printed by Simon Vincent], [1512]; revised and enlarged, Lyon: Printed by Jean de Jonvelle, dite Piston, 1517);

Rosa gallica ([Paris]: Printed by Josse Bade, 1514);

Periarchon (Paris: Printed by Antoine Bonnemere, 1514);

Symphonia Platonis cum Aristotele: & Galeni cum Hyppocrate (Paris: Printed by Josse Bade, 1516);

Les grans croniques des gestes & vertueux faictz des tresexcellens catholicques illustres & victorieux ducz & princes des pays de Savoye et Piemont (Paris: Printed for Jehan de La Garde, 1516);

Symphorien Champier (Musee d'Histoire de la medicine et de la pharmecie de la Faculte de medicine de Lyon; from <http://fr.wikipedia.org>)

Cathegoriae medicinales . . . in libros demonstrationum Galeni (Lyon: Printed by Jean Marion, 1516);

Epistolae sanctissimorum sequenti codice contentae ([Paris]: Printed by Josse Bade and Joannis Parvi, 1516);

Cribratio lima et annotamenta in Galeni, Avicennae & Conciliatoris opera (Paris: Printed by Ascensus, 1516);

Epithome commentariorum Galeni in libros Hippocratis Cohi (Lyon: Printed by Jean Marion, 1516);

Ars parva Galeni (Lyon: Printed by Jean Marion, [1516]);

Medicinale bellum inter Galenum et Aristotelem gestum (Lyon: Printed by Jean Marion, [1516–1517]);

Mirabilium divinorum humanorumque volumnia quattuor (Lyon: Printed [for Simon Vincent] by Jacques Mareschal, 1517);

Practica nova in medicina (Lyon: Printed by Jean Marion, 1517);

Joannis Herculani (Lyon: Printed by Jacques Myt, 1518);

Pronosticon libri tres quorum primus est de pronosticiis seu presagiis prophetarum ([Lyon]: Printed for Vincent de Portonariis, 1518);

Duellum epistolare, Galliae et Italiae antiquitates summatim complectens ([Venice]: Printed for Jacopo Francesco Giunta by Jean Phiroben and Jean Divineur, 1519);

Arnald de Villanova vita (Lyon: Printed by Guillaume Hoyon, 1520);

Liber canonis totius medicinae ab Avicenna (Lyon: Printed by Jacques Myt, 1522);

Domini Mesuae vita (Lyon: Printed by Francisci de Giunta, 1523);

Les Gestes, ensemble la vie du preulx chevalier Bayard (Paris: Printed by Gilbert de Villiers, 1525);

Symphonia Galeni ad Hippocratem ([Lyon], [1528]);

L'Antiquité de la Cité de Lyon. Ensemble la Rebeine ou rébellion du Populaire (Paris: Printed by St. Denys, 1529);

Du royaume des Allobroges, avec l'antiquité de la très noble et ancienne cité de Vienne sur le fleuve du Rhosne (Paris: Printed by St. Denys, [1530]);

Claudii Galeni, historiales campi (Basel: Printed by A. Cratandrum and J. Bebelium, 1532);

Castigationes seu emendationes pharmacoplarum (Lyon: Printed by Jean Crespin, 1532);

Le Myrouel des appothiquaires et pharmacopoles (Lyon: Printed by Pierre Mareschal, [1532]);

Hortus gallicus (Lyon: Printed by Melchior Trechsel and Gaspar Trechsel, 1533)—includes *Periarchon;*

Campus Elysius Galliae (Lyon: Melchior & Gaspar Trechsel, 1533);

Gallicum Pentapharmacum (Lyon: Printed by Melchior Trechsel and Gaspar Trechsel, 1534);

Cribratio medicamentorum (Lyon: Printed by Sebastien Gryphium, 1534);

Le Fondement et origine des tiltrez de noblesse . . . (Paris: Printed by Denis Janot, 1535);

Libri VII de dialectica, rhetorica, geometria, arithmetica, astronomia, musica, philosophia naturali, medicina et theologia . . . (Basel: Printed by Henri Pierre, 1537);

De Monarchia Gallorum; Galliae Celticae (Lyon: Printed by Melchior and Gaspar Trechsel, 1537).

Editions: *Du royaume des Allobroges, avec l'antiquité de la très noble et ancienne cité de Vienne sur le fleuve du Rhosne* (Lyon: Georg, 1884);

L'Antiquité de la cité de Lyon ensemble la rebeine ou rébellion du populaire contre les conseillers de la cité en 1529, et la hiérarchie de l'église métropolitaine (Lyon: Georg, 1884);

Le myrouel des appothiquaires et pharmacopoles, edited by Paul Dorveaux (Paris: Welter, 1894);

Le livre de vraye amour, edited, with an introduction in English, by James Wadsworth (s'-Gravenhage: Mouton, 1962)—comprises the fourth book of the *Nef des dames;*

"*Condamnation des sciences occultes:* édition critique du *Dyalogus . . . in magicarum destructionem,*" edited by Annie Rijper, *Anagrom,* 5–6 (1974): 1–54;

Le triumphe du tres chrestien roy de France Loys XII, edited by Giovanna Trisolini (Rome: Ateneo & Bizzarri, 1977);

Les gestes ensemble la vie du preulx chevalier Bayard, edited by Denis Crouzet (Paris: Imprimerie Nationale, 1992);

La nef des princes, textkritische und kommentierte Ausgabe der Haupttraktate, edited by Andrea Wilhelmi (Frankfurt am Main: Lang, 2001);

La nef des dames vertueuses, critical edition, edited by Judy Kem (Paris: Champion, 2006).

OTHER: Guy de Chauliac, *Le guidon en françoys,* translated, with commentary, by Champier (Lyon: Printed by Jean de Vingle, 1503).

During his lifetime Symphorien Champier enjoyed a reputation in Lyon and throughout France as a doctor, historian, humanist, and Platonist. He studied, commented on, and translated such ancient and medieval authors as Hippocrates, Galen of Pergamon, Plato, Aristotle, Constantine the African, and Avicenna, and such contemporaries or near contemporaries as Peter of Abano and Arnaldus of Villanova. He published at least 55 works in 100 editions, mostly historical and medical treatises in Latin and French. In 1533 Jérôme Monteux, one of Champier's students, claimed that the Lyonnais physician had written more than 105 volumes, including 35 medical works, 26 histories, 14 pedagogical manuals, 12 theological treatises, 7 tomes on astronomy, 7 collections of correspondence, and 4 apologetic works. This prolific author was the first or at least among the first to introduce Renaissance Platonism, especially the Neoplatonism of the Italian humanist Marsilio Ficino, into the vernacular in France and among the first to use the vernacular in medical writing.

Champier took part in several lively medical and literary debates. He preferred the "Ancient" medical authorities to the "Moderns," whom he often denigrated; he criticized pharmacists for overstepping the bounds of their profession and doing more harm than good; he described syphilis and offered advice on its treatment; he defended women

Title page for Champier's 1503 book in which he presents profiles of famous women (from Le livre de vraye amour, *edited by James Wadsworth, 1962; Thomas Cooper Library, University of South Carolina)*

against their detractors in the *Querelle des femmes* (Debate on Women); and he attacked divinatory astrology and the occult sciences. Although Champier was a celebrated yet controversial figure most of his life, his literary reputation suffered after his death.

Little is known of Champier's early life. He was born around 1472 in a village called Saint-Symphorien-le-Château near Lyon. His father was probably André Champier, a notary and apothecary from whom the young Symphorien probably acquired some Latin and his interest in the medical profession. He studied at the University of Paris where he met fellow humanists Baptista Spagnuoli Mantuanus and Jacques Lefèvre d'Etaples. In *Symphorien Champier and the Reception of the Occultist Tradition in Renaissance France* (1978), Brian Copenhaver, Champier's foremost modern biographer, suggests that Mantuanus probably influenced Champier to treat medicine and theology as interdependent disciplines, while Lefèvre's enthusiasm for Aristotle, Plato, the Church Fathers,

and the Neoplatonists is evident in several of Champier's works.

In 1495 Symphorien enrolled in the medical school in Montpellier. For approximately three years he studied such Arab medical authorities as Razi (Rhazes), Avicenna, and Avenzoar as well as the "Ancients" Galen and Hippocrates. He lived in Lyon, Limousin, and elsewhere before receiving his doctorate from Montpellier in 1504, but as early as 1496, he was already practicing medicine and teaching the liberal arts in Dauphiné. In 1498 Champier published his first known work, *Janua logicae et phisicae* (The Doorway to Logic and Physics), a manual written in Latin that in thirteen tractates taught the basic principles of medical theory under four rubrics: 1) rational psychology, 2) logic, 3) natural science, and 4) medicine. Although not as sophisticated as his later works, the *Janua* demonstrates Champier's predilection for the writings of Ficino and Aristotle, his interest in medical and philosophical controversy, and his dilettantism. In this short work (sixty folios) Champier cites forty different classical authorities, most only once or twice, while he cites Ficino no fewer than twenty times. Most of his citations are marginal glosses without commentary on Ficino's theory of astrological medicine. Champier did not assimilate most of Ficino's thought until he published *Liber de quadruplici vita* (1507, The Book of Fourfold Life) almost ten years later.

Between 1496 and 1498 Champier was also composing his *Dyalogus . . . in magicarum artium destructionem* (1500, A Dialogue . . . about the Destruction of the Magical Arts), a virulent attack on the occult arts. The work, which is divided into three parts, takes the form of a dialogue between Champier and André Botin, a young man he was teaching at the time. The first part defines different forms of divination, such as divinatory astrology, necromancy, geomancy, pyromancy, aeromancy, chiromancy, hydromancy, and divination by dreams, and advises all men to reject such magical arts. The second part summarizes what poets, physicians, astrologers, and theologians think about enchantment and "spell-casters." Champier admonishes Botin to live by God's law and ignore spell casters who will then have no power over him. In the third part Botin asks Champier to explain incubi, succubi, and the "demoniac" disease, or melancholy. In response, Champier describes different forms of demonic possession. While admitting that possession exists, he maintains that it is rare and suggests prayer, obedience to God, and a general cynicism about such matters. In this early work Champier already displays an encyclopedic knowledge, as he cites such sources as Aristotle, Pliny,

Cicero, Virgil, Aulus Gellius, Augustine, Avicenna, Averroes, Albertus Magnus, Thomas Aquinas, and Peter of Abano.

Around 1500 the already prolific Champier met Jacques Robertet, and the two pursued literary, and perhaps Greek, studies together. Robertet was well connected to the Bourbons, and no doubt because of their friendship, Champier began to think of ways to gain Bourbon patronage in order to pursue his writing career. Profiting from the popularity of Sebastian Brant's *Stultifera Navis* (The Ship of Fools), which appeared in several translations and seventeen editions between 1494 and 1520, Champier published *La nef des princes* (1502, The Ship of Princes), a work written during a stay in Limousin and "dediqués et envoyés à divers prelas et seigneurs" (dedicated and intended for diverse priests and lords), and *La nef des dames vertueuses* (1503, The Ship of Virtuous Ladies), a work dedicated to Anne de France and her daughter Suzanne de Bourbon.

La nef des princes is a typical *doctrinal,* or educational treatise, whose aim is to teach "all manner of people to live and die well." It features fifteen short works in both prose and poetry, French and Latin. Some of the titles include "Le Testament de ung vieil prince" (The Old Prince's Will), "Le Gouvernement et regime d'ung jeune prince" (The Governing and Regimen of a Young Prince), "Le Doctrinal des princes" (The Doctrinal of Princes), "Le Doctrinal du pere de famille à son enfant pour le regir et gouverner à toute perfection" (The Doctrinal of a Father to His Child to Rule and Lead Him to Perfection), and "Plusieurs beaux enseignemens utilz et necessaires à tous peres de famille" (Several Beautiful, Useful, and Necessary Teachings for All Fathers). Two interpolated works, "La Nef des batailles" (The Ship of Battles), a how-to book on warfare, and "Le Chemin de l'ospital" (The Path to the Poor House) were written by another physician, Robert de Balsac, who, like Robertet, had connections to the Bourbons.

La nef des princes includes several misogynistic quotes from such classical authors as Plautus, Cicero, Seneca, and Juvenal and from such near contemporaries as Petrarch as well as Champier's own French translation of the misogynist Matheolus's *Liber lamentationum Matheoli* (The Book of Matheolus's Lamentations), composed in Latin by Mathieu de Boulogne in 1295 and first translated into French by Jacques Le Fèvre de Resson around 1371. Champier's antifeminist verse translation is titled "La Malice des femmes" (The Malice of Women). Yet, published a year later, *La nef des dames vertueuses* is a defense of women against their detractors, divided into four

books. In the first book, "Les louenges, fleurs et deffensoir des dames" (The Praise, Flowers, and Defense of Ladies), Champier presents portraits of famous women of Antiquity and the Middle Ages in the style of Giovanni Boccaccio's *De Claris Mulieribus* (1359, Concerning Famous Women). He offers both medical and moral advice on marriage in the second book, "Le gouvernement de mariage" (The Governing of Marriage), and in book 3, "Les propheties, ditz et vaticinations des sibilles" (Prophecies, Sayings, and Predictions of the Sibyls), he juxtaposes sibylline prophecies taken from Lactance's *Institutiones divinae* (Divine Institutions) and other sources to prove that women are just as worthy as men of divine inspiration. The fourth book, "Le livre de vraye amour" (The Book of True Love), is a treatise on Neoplatonic love based on the philosophy of Ficino. Because of this last book Champier has since been recognized as one of the first, if not the first, to introduce Ficino's writings and, thus, Renaissance Platonism into the French vernacular.

Although Champier's efforts to obtain Bourbon patronage failed, the publication of the *La nef des dames vertueuses,* which appeared in two more editions in 1515 and 1531, was wildly popular with the ladies of Lyon and reportedly earned Champier an advantageous marriage with Marguerite de Terrail, cousin of the noble Pierre Terrail, seigneur de Bayard and niece of a powerful Lyonnais abbot. As a result of this favorable match, Champier received the financial aid necessary to pursue his career as a writer. His reputation as a doctor, scholar, and author began to grow. In 1506 he left Lyon to teach medicine in the Lorraine region and published several important works on medicine and Platonism between 1506 and 1509, such as the *Liber de quadruplici vita* and *De triplici disciplina* (1508, On the Threefold Learning). These two works were inspired by Ficino's *De triplici vita* (1489, The Threefold Life) and especially by Giovanni Pico della Mirandola's *Disputationes adversus astrologiam divinatricem* (1495, Arguments Against Divinatory Astrology). In the *Liber de quadruplici vita,* Champier insists that he has not copied Ficino's *De triplici vita* and that he even corrects some of the Italian humanist's errors, such as his belief that the stars and planets influence man. Champier's "fourfold life" nonetheless parallels the first three divisions of Ficino's threefold life: 1) *Liber de vita sana* (The Book of the Healthy Life) outlines medical treatments for the physical ailments of the studious, such as phlegm and black bile; 2) *Liber de vita longa* (The Book of Long Life) proposes ways of prolonging life; and 3) *Liber de vita coelitus comparanda* (On Obtaining Life from the Heavens) describes the astrological theories

Title page for one of the historical works Champier wrote to attract patrons during the last decade of his life (Centre d'Etudes Superieures de la Renaissance, Tours)

and techniques that affect the practice of medicine. To these Champier adds a fourth, *De vita supercelesti* (The Supercelestial Life), which depicts a more Christian afterlife, beyond astrological influences, than the one envisioned by Ficino. Champier's *De triplici disciplina* is comprised of four treatises on natural philosophy, medicine, theology, and moral instruction. As in many of his earlier works, Champier drew from widely varying sources for both of these works: Isocrates, Sextus the Pythagorean, and Pliny the Younger for the *Liber de quadruplici vita;* and Plato, Isidore's *Etymologies,* Hermes Trismegistus, Justin Martyr, and Demosthenes for *De triplici disciplina.* Here Champier displays a familiarity with the works of both Hermes Trismegistus and Ficino while distancing himself from their unorthodox views on divinatory astrology and the occult sciences.

Sometime in 1509 Champier's writing career gave way to his military exploits. He became the *primarius medicus* (primary physician) and adviser to

Antoine de Calabre, Duke of Lorraine, and accompanied him in Louis XII's war with the Venetians, distinguishing himself in the battle of Agnadello. After the war, Champier followed the duke to Nancy and composed *Le recueil ou croniques des hystoires des royaulmes d'austrasie* (1510, A Collection or Chronicle of Histories of the Kingdoms of Austrasia), written half in French and half in Latin. He presented the volume, which praises the duke and attributes a fabled origin to the house of Lorraine, to the duke in 1510.

From 1510 to 1515 Champier stayed mostly in Nancy as part of the duke's large medical household and worked in the library of almost two hundred books. In 1511 he started working on *Rosa gallica* (1514, Gallic Rose), which includes memorable precepts from such authorities as Hippocrates, Galen, Razi, Halyabas, and Avicenna. Shortly afterward Champier followed the duke to Reims for the coronation of François I on 24 January 1515. In the same year Champier received two of his most cherished honors. The duke bestowed upon him the order of chivalry for his courageous deeds in the battle of Marignano, and the well-known Galenist Rustico da Piacenza and others at the University of Pavia, an important center of medical learning, awarded him an *agrégation* (doctorate degree), a distinction never before held by a foreigner.

While still in the service of the duke in Nancy, Champier also wrote another rather curious Neoplatonic work, *Symphonia Platonis cum Aristotele: & Galeni cum Hyppocrate* (1516, The Platonic Symphony with Aristotle and Galen with Hippocrates), in whose four books he tries to reconcile the thought and writings of these four princes of medicine. The four princes appear on the frontispiece, armed with violins and violas, playing a "symphony." The work includes a two-chapter "Philosophia platonica" (Platonic philosophy), which consists of Plato's *Timaeus* with Champier's commentaries, and a collection of proverbial sayings, *Speculum Platonis* (Mirror of Plato). A more clear demonstration of Champier's philosophical syncretism is hard to imagine.

Around 1517 Champier returned to Lyon, where he played an active role in government for more than twenty years. He was chosen by his fellow townsmen at least twice to deliver the oration of St. Thomas Day, an annual ceremony to celebrate the selection of the twelve consuls, the city's governing body. He was elected consul in 1520, and he helped to found the city's first institution of higher education, the Collège de la Trinité, in 1527. By 1529 Champier had become one of Lyon's most prosperous and prominent citizens, which apparently made him a target that year for a local popular uprising known as the Rebeine. In reaction to a proposed tax on wine or wheat, angry citizens rioted and ransacked Champier's house along with those of others. Champier wrote of this rebellion in *L'Antiquité de la Cité de Lyon. Ensemble la Rebeine ou rébellion du Populaire* (1529, The Antiquity of the City of Lyon Together with the "Rebeine" or Popular Rebellion).

Although he was elected consul of Lyon a second time in 1533, Champier apparently refused the honor, as his name does not appear on the list of consul members in 1535. In the last decade of his life he withdrew from public life and increased his literary production, publishing at least a dozen different works, most of them controversial. They can be divided into two categories: historical and medical. One of his most important historical works, *Les Gestes, ensemble la vie du preulx chevalier Bayard* (1525, The Deeds and the Life of the Valorous Knight Bayard), praised his wife's deceased noble cousin Bayard. This popular work was published in more than twenty editions in its first hundred years of existence. Two of its six chapters deal with the knight's valorous deeds under Louis XII and François I, and chapter 4 features several anecdotes attesting to Bayard's moral wisdom. Champier's aims in writing history were not only patriotic and moral but also financial. As he had written many works in praise of various noblemen and noblewomen during his first thirty years, his most likely source of income now was probably the churchmen of Lyon to whom he was connected by birth and marriage. He dedicated his subsequent histories, *Du royaume des Allobroges* (1530, On the Kingdom of the Allobroges) and *De Monarchia Gallorum; Galliae Celticae* (1537, On the Monarchy of the Gauls; Celtic Gaul) to hoped-for patrons.

The medical works he published in Lyon between 1532 and 1534, *Castigationes seu emendationes pharmacoplarum* (1532, Castigations or Corrections of Pharmacists), *Le Myrouel des appothiquaires et pharmacopoles* (1532, The Mirror of Apothecaries and Pharmacists), *Hortus gallicus* (1533, The Gallic Garden), *Cribratio medicamentorum* (1534, A Scrutiny of Medicines), and the *Gallicum Pentapharmacum* (1534, The Gallic Pentapharmacon), all condemned bad pharmacists. Champier preferred "simples," or uncombined medicines, to concoctions, referred to as "multiples," that, he claimed, contained questionable ingredients and often resulted in serious injury or even death. In *Le Myrouel des appothiquaires,* Champier also clearly delineates the superior role of doctors to pharmacists, stating that "les pharmacopoles, dict appothiquaires et chyrurgiens, sont les ministres des

médicins" (pharmacists, known as apothecaries and surgeons, are doctors' assistants).

Champier probably died during the winter of 1539. Much of Champier's reputation as a medical authority died with him; only two or three of his medical treatises appeared in print after his death. His literary reputation suffered as well. Many scholars who had praised him during his lifetime found little to admire or to emulate in the humanist and scholar after his death. His contemporaries and even modern critics accused him of a lack of originality and even plagiarism. However, Copenhaver attributes Champier's posthumous unpopularity more to his "disputatious character," his "fondness for controversy," and the "flood of invective" he poured forth in his writings than to his lack of originality, a fairly common trait of the time. He cites in particular Champier's "anti-Arab dogmatism"; the war he waged against pharmacists, who, he claimed, often overstepped their bounds and poisoned people with their mixed medicines; his anti-Italianism in favor of French superiority, and last, but not least, his attacks on divinatory astrology, magic, and the other occult sciences.

Champier's works have begun to appear in critical editions since the last half of the twentieth century, and a new and more complete bibliography is in preparation. Symphorien Champier will never regain the reputation he enjoyed as an internationally recognized physician, decorated war hero, and celebrated author of the early Renaissance in Lyon, but his work as a prolific historian and propagator of Italian and medical humanism in France merits reevaluation.

Bibliography:

James F. Ballard and Michel Pijoan, "A Preliminary Check-List of the Writings of Symphorien Champier, 1472–1539," in *Bulletin of the Medical Library Association, XXVIII* (1939–1940): 182–188.

Biographies:

Paul Allut, *Etude biographique et bibliographique sur Symphorien Champier* (Lyon: Scheuring, 1859; reprinted, Lyon & Nieuwkoop: De Graaf, 1972);

Brian Copenhaver, *Symphorien Champier and the Reception of the Occultist Tradition in Renaissance France* (The Hague, Paris & New York: Mouton, 1978).

References:

Roland Antonioli, "Un Médecin lecteur du Timée, S. Champier," in *Actes du colloque sur l'humanisme lyonnais au XVIe siècle, mai 1972* (Grenoble: Presses universitaires de Grenoble, 1974), pp. 53–62;

Antonioli, "Songes prophétiques et dames vertueuses," in *Le Songe à la Renaissance: Colloque international de Cannes, 29–31 mai 1987,* edited by Françoise Charpentier (Saint-Etienne: Institut d'Etudes de la Renaissance et de l'Age Classique, Université de Saint-Etienne, 1990), pp. 61–69;

Maurice Boucher, "Champier: Quelques-unes de ses œuvres médicales," in *Conteurs et romanciers de la Renaissance: Mélanges offerts à Gabriel-André Pérouse,* edited by James Dauphiné and Béatrice Périgot (Paris: Champion / Geneva: Diffusion, Slatkine, 1997), pp. 79–89;

Richard Cooper, "Champier et l'Italie," in his *Litterae in tempore belli: Etudes sur les relations littéraires italo-francaises pendant les guerres d'Italie* (Geneva: Droz, 1997), pp. 287–302;

Cooper, "Les dernières années de Champier," *Réforme, humanisme, Renaissance XXIV,* 47 (December 1998): 25–50;

Cooper, "Le roman à Lyon sous François I . . . ," in *Il romanzo nella Francia del Rinascimento: dall'eredità medievale all'Astrea, atti del convegno internazionale di studi, Gargnano, Palazzo Feltrinelli, 7–9 ottobre 1993* (Fasano: Schena, 1996), pp. 109–128;

Cooper, "Symphorien Champier e l'Italia," in *L'Aube de la Renaissance: pour le dixième anniversaire de la dispari-tion de Franco Simone,* edited by Dario Cecchetti, Lionello Sozzi, and Louis Terreaux (Geneva: Slatkine, 1991), pp. 233–245;

Roger Dubuis, "Symphorien Champier pédagogue, moraliste et poète," in *Actes du colloque sur l'humanisme lyonnais au XVIe siècle, mai 1972* (Grenoble: Presses universitaires de Grenoble, 1974), pp. 23–40;

Paule Dumaître, "Le 'Chevalier à la rose': Un médecin contemporain de Rabelais," *Revue alsacienne de littérature,* 50 (2ème trimestre 1995): 54–57;

Christine M. Hill, "Symphorien Champier's Views on Education in the *Nef des princes* and the *Nef des dames vertueuses,*" *French Studies,* 7 (1953): 323–334;

Margaret Holmes, *Italian Renaissance Influence in Lyons in the Early Sixteenth Century, with Particular Reference to the Work of Symphorien Champier,* Ph.D. thesis, King's College, London, 1963;

Giovanni Tracconaglia, *Femminismo e platonismo in un libro raro del 1503: La nef des dames di Symphorien Champier* (Lodi: Dell'Avo, 1922);

Jean Tricou, "Le testament de Symphorien Champier," *Bibliothèque d'humanisme et Renaissance,* 18 (1956): 101–109.

Helisenne de Crenne
(Marguerite de Briet)
(1510? – 1560?)

Megan Conway

Louisiana State University—Shreveport

BOOKS*: Les Angoysses douloureuses qui procedent d'amours* (Paris: Printed by Denis Janot, 1538); edited by Lisa Neal, translated by Neal and Steven Rendall as *The Torments of Love* (Minneapolis: University of Minnesota Press, 1996);

Les Epistres familieres et invectives de ma dame Helisenne composées par icelle dame, De Crenne (Paris: Printed by Denis Janot, 1539); translated by Marianna M. Mustacchi and Paul J. Archambault as *A Renaissance Woman: Helisenne's Personal and Invective Letters* (Syracuse, N.Y.: Syracuse University Press, 1986);

Le Songe de madame Helisenne composé par ladicte dame, la consideration duquel, est apte à instiguer toutes personnes de s'alliener de vice, & s'approcher de vertu (Paris: Printed by Denis Janot, 1540); translated by Lisa Neal as "The Dream," in *Writings by Pre-Revolutionary Women: From Marie de France to Elisabeth Vigée-Le Brun*, edited by Anne Larsen and Colette Winn (New York & London: Garland, 2000), pp. 63 105.

Editions and Collections: *Les Oeuvres de ma dame Helisenne* (Paris: Printed by Charles Langelier, 1543);

Les Oeuvres de ma dame Helisenne, edited by Claude Colet (Paris: Estienne Groulleau, 1551);

Les Angoysses douloureuses qui procedent d'amours, première partie, critical edition, edited by Paule Demats (Paris: Les Belles Lettres, 1968);

Les Angoisses douloureuses qui procèdent d'amours, première partie, edited by Jérôme Vercruysse (Paris: Lettres Modernes, 1968);

Le songe de madame Hélisenne de Crenne: 1541, edited by Jean-Philippe Beaulieu (Paris: Indigo & Côté-femmes éditions, 1995);

Les épistres familières et invectives de ma dame Hélisenne, critical edition, edited by Beaulieu and Hannah Fournier (Montreal: University of Montreal Press, 1995);

Les Epistres familieres et invectives, critical edition, edited by Jerry C. Nash (Paris: Champion, 1996);

Helisenne de Crenne (Marguerite de Briet) (Bibliothéque royale de Bruxelles; from Les Angoisses douloureuses qui procèdent d'amours, première partie, *edited by Jérôme Vercruysse, 1968; Thomas Cooper Library, University of South Carolina)*

Les Angoysses douloureuses qui procedent d'amours, critical edition, edited by Christine de Buzon (Paris: Champion, 1997);

Les angoisses douloureuses qui procèdent d'amour, edited by Beaulieu (St.-Etienne: Université de St.-Etienne, 2005).

TRANSLATION: Virgil, *Les quatre premiers livres des Eneydes du treselegant poete Virgile, Traduicte de Latin en prose Francoyse, par ma dame Helisenne* (Paris: Printed by Denis Janot, 1541).

Helisenne de Crenne is best known for writing the first sentimental novel—and, some would argue, the first psychological novel—in French. She was immensely popular during her lifetime: nine editions of her novel, *Les Angoysses douloureuses qui procedent d'amours* (translated as *The Torments of Love*, 1996), appeared between 1538 and 1560, seven of them in editions of her collected works. Her writing is unique for the period in its introspective intensity and its occasional use of a female narrator. At the same time, it embodies much of what is considered characteristic of the Renaissance: classical allusions, mythological references juxtaposed to Christian symbols and ideas, philosophical debate, a latinized vocabulary, and an elaborate style. She borrows freely from the fashionable literary traditions of the time, combining elements from Spanish romances of chivalry, Giovanni Boccaccio's *Elegia di Madonna Fiammetta* (1343–1344, Elegy of Lady Fiammetta), Jacopo Caviceo's *Il Peregrino,* (1508, The Wanderer), and *Les Illustrations de Gaule et Singularitez de Troie* (1510–1513, The Illustrations of Gaul and the Excellencies of Troy), by Jean Lemaire de Belges. Other elements are drawn from medieval theology, astrology, Bible stories, and Ovid's tales. Like most writers of the time, she also makes use of arguments borrowed from the "Quarrel of Women," a literary debate over the relative merit of the sexes that began in the late Middle Ages and continued into the mid seventeenth century. Her main themes are the constraints of marriage and the suffering caused by illicit, obsessive love.

Two hundred years of controversy over the identity and even the existence of Crenne came to an end in 1917, when the scholar Louis Loviot discovered in old archival records a Latin chronicle briefly stating that in May 1540 a learned woman from Abbeville named Marguerite de Briet, but popularly known as Helisenne de Crenne, had become famous in the noble town of Paris. The revelation of the name behind the pseudonym allowed scholars to uncover other pertinent facts in extant documents, from which a rudimentary biography can be pieced together.

Briet was born in Abbeville in Picardy, probably between 1500 and 1515; this conjecture is based primarily on a document, dated 9 August 1548, stating that her husband gave their eighteen-year-old son, Pierre, an allowance to support him during his studies at the University of Paris. A birth year of 1500 would make her thirty when her son was born; given the social norms and average life spans of the day, a date nearer 1510 or even 1515 would be more likely. The Briet family was rich, powerful, and socially and politically active and provided Abbeville with several magistrates and mayors. Paul J. Archambault and Marianna M. Archambault speculate that she was the daughter of Daniel Briet, a municipal magistrate; Paule Demats, the editor of a critical edition of *Les Angoysses douloureuses qui procedent d'amours* (1968), postulates a connection with a woman named Jeanne Briet because of repeated mentions in Crenne's work of a town called Gorenflos. Gorenflos is a village near the lands that in 1510 belonged to Jeanne Briet, the wife of the king's adviser in the region of Ponthieu, and several properties in Ponthieu formed part of Marguerite de Briet's inheritance.

Nothing is known for certain concerning Briet's education; as a young woman of the lower nobility, she was probably privately tutored. From the evidence of her works, which show the influence of various Continental writers and are full of mythological allusions and imagery, she was widely read in both contemporary and classical literature. For the modern reader an encyclopedia of mythology and a biographical dictionary of historical figures of the ancient world are often necessary to identify her myriad references. Her style is cultivated and deliberately shows off her knowledge of literature, philosophy, and the Bible.

Given the age of their son in 1548, Briet may have married Philippe Fournel, a country squire, around 1530. It seems that she brought significant wealth to the union in terms of land holdings and residences; the earliest extant official document mentioning her, dated 1539, relates to the rental of property belonging to the wife of Philippe Fournel. She took the pen name Crenne from her marriage: Fournel was the lord of Crasnes, an ancient holding near Coucy; alternate archival spellings of Crasnes include Cresnes and Crennes. Helisenne seems to be a name of her own creation. While some critics point to a resemblance to the name of a pastoral heroine, it seems more likely that she picked the name to accord with the fate of the protagonist of her novel, who ascends to the Elysian Fields: Helisenne is the femininized form of Helisien (Elysian).

All of Briet's works appeared between 1538 and 1541. Her initial publication was *Les Angoysses douloureuses qui procedent d'amours,* a long prose romance in three books. Book 1, narrated in the first person by the heroine, is often thought to be semi-autobiographical, although the basis for that judgment is slight. The character shares the author's pseudonym, and she is endowed with more worldly goods than her husband, which was true in Briet's case. Also like Briet, Helisenne has a troubled marriage. These similarities are reinforced in Briet's second publication. But whether the author's marriage was threatened by Briet falling in love with another man is unknown, and verifiable parallels between the author and her creation evaporate at this point.

Book 1 is prefaced by a letter addressed to "honestes dames" (honest women), in which Helisenne asks for their pity and sympathy and urges them to avoid vain and immodest love. She then begins her story. At a young age she married a young gentleman who is never named. Incredibly beautiful—"au treizieme an de mon aage, j'estois de forme elegante, et tout si bien proportionée, que j'excedois toutes autres femmes en beauté de corps" (at thirteen years of age, I had an elegant form, and was so well proportioned that I exceeded all other women in bodily beauty)—she is pursued by many men; but she never wavers in her love for her husband until she accompanies him into town, where he must attend to a lawsuit. There she falls passionately in love at first sight with a handsome young man she sees from the window of their lodgings. Her interest in the young man, whose name is Guenelic, is immediately apparent to her husband, who, in a manner more like that of a lover than a spouse, declares his concern and affection for her. Unmoved, Helisenne transfers her love completely to Guenelic, who turns out to be a disreputable character of low degree. When they finally meet, Helisenne agrees to accept a letter from him and promises one in return. Guenelic exposes his unheroic character by telling her how fearful he is of her husband. Terrified that Guenelic's fear will be stronger than his love, Helisenne lies to him, telling him that her husband suspects nothing. In his letter Guenelic declares his passion in physical terms. In her reply Helisenne insists that he must not "persister en telle amours: lesquelles ne consistent en vertu" (persist in such a love which is not virtuous) but ends by stating, "mais croyez que si amour de la doree sagette m'avoit ataincte, qu'autre que vous de ma benevolence ne seroit possesseur" (but believe me, if Cupid had hit me with his golden dart, no one but you would be the possessor of my benevolence). She takes delight in rereading copies of both letters and is so preoccupied that she fails to hide them when her husband enters her chamber. Beside himself with hurt and anger, he knocks her down "outre ma coustume" (against my custom) and forbids her to leave her room or approach the window without his permission.

Guenelic takes his revenge by singing under their windows until they are forced to change lodgings because the noise is disturbing the neighbors. As a result of the move, Helisenne does not see Guenelic for three weeks, and her health suffers. When she finally sees him in church, she stares at him immoderately. Furious, her husband takes her home and hits her again. Helisenne screams, throws herself against the

walls and furniture of her bedroom, and tries to kill herself. Her husband, "epris d'angoisseuse douleur, à cause de l'excessif amour qu'il me portoit" (struck with anguished pain because of the excessive love he felt), restrains her from harming herself and begs her to "imposer fin à mes extremes tristesses, soit par separation, ou par vous reduire, en vivant en plus grand honesteté" (put an end to my extreme sadness either by separation or more honest living). He takes her to a religious hermit, who uses reason to try to dissuade her from her passion; more and more comfortable with deceit, she pretends to acquiesce, while stubbornly clinging to her illicit love.

The cycle of furtive meetings, threats, illness, and anxiety continues until Guenelic accuses Helisenne of making fun of him and tells her, "quand au deviser je m'en content" (as for conversation, I've had enough). He demands to be rewarded for his time, his love, and his service. Having little confidence in his character, Helisenne is afraid that she will lose him if she denies him but will be ruined if she does not; but she still cannot renounce her love. His public behavior grows increasingly spiteful; rumors begin to circulate; and Helisenne falls ill from grief. Her suffering is increased when a servant betrays her and shows her letters to her husband. Furious and hurt, he tries to kill her, but the servants intervene. When his anger cools, he decides to exile her to her favorite château, Cabasus, in the company of two of her servants. The book ends with the older servant consoling Helisenne by telling her that if Guenelic loves her, he will surely find her.

In the prefatory letter to book 2 Helisenne declares that Guenelic's social status is not as base as she had described it in book 1; on the contrary, it is high enough for him to pursue the knightly arts. Book 2 itself is narrated by Guenelic, who takes responsibility for his troubles because of his "follie et indiscretion" (folly and indiscretion). When he met Helisenne, he was twenty-two and undecided as to whether to devote himself to the military arts or continue the literary work he had begun writing. Distracted by his passion for Helisenne, he followed neither course but devoted himself to her pursuit. Not realizing that Helisenne's husband has sent her away, Guenelic believes that she is ignoring him. He confides his troubles to Quezinstra, a young man he meets while walking in the woods. Wellbred, levelheaded, and trained in the knightly arts, Quezinstra tries to talk Guenelic out of his love; failing to do so, he proposes that they embark on a quest to discover Helisenne's whereabouts.

Guenelic and Quezinstra are attacked near the outset of their journey by brigands who steal their horses. They take shelter with a hermit, who treats their wounds. They board a ship bound for Cyprus, but the wind takes them in a different direction. They end up in the city of Gorenflos, whose lord welcomes them and bids them to stay. This idea suits Quezinstra, who wishes to try out his knightly skills in the upcoming tournament, but Guenelic wants to continue his quest and complains at length. The two friends are knighted on the second day of the tournament; Quezinstra tries to make Guenelic see the value of this distinction and exhorts him to show himself worthy of his lady. Guenelic responds with a long discourse on love and concludes that Quezinstra is totally ignorant of that emotion. After sailing to Cythera, where Guenelic visits the temple of Venus, they set out for Troy but are again blown off course to the coast of Africa. They visit Rhodes, Cyprus, Syria, and Damascus and finally arrive at Troy, where they see the tombs of Hector, Ajax, and Achilles. Passing the Hellespont, they are welcomed to the city of Eliveba by a beautiful princess. When the city is attacked by a rogue admiral, they lend their aid and witness her marriage to the admiral. Resuming their search, they look for Helisenne in Athens, Thebes, and Mycenae. The book ends with a speech by Guenelic on loyal service in the name of love.

In the short prologue to book 3 Helisenne tells her readers that while the previous book concentrated on the "discipline de l'art militaire" (discipline of the military arts), the final book will provoke the reader to resist the temptations of sensual love. Guenelic again takes over the narration. The two friends sail to ports that include Carthage, Valencia, Barcelona, and Marseilles. Finally, they reach Genoa, where Guenelic falls gravely ill. When he recovers, Quezinstra takes him to an island to recuperate. The island's only inhabitant, a wise hermit, hears Guenelic's confession of passion and exhorts him to give up his lascivious obsession and return to God's will. Guenelic tells the old man that true love is the source of all virtue. Their next port of call is an inhospitable town where no one will give them shelter. As they are leaving, they are insulted by a woman. At a nearby château a gentleman explains that the evil-tongued woman is the sister-in-law and guardian of a "noble & gratieuse dame" (noble and gracious lady) imprisoned in a château called Cabasus. The captive lady's name is Helisenne.

Under cover of darkness Guenelic brings a ladder to Helisenne's barred window in the tallest tower of the château. They exchange protestations of love, and Helisenne tells Guenelic that her sister-in-law discovered the book she had written about her love for him and her misfortunes. Guenelic and Quezinstra bribe the château's forester, who helps them to effect Helisenne's escape. The three have ridden only a few miles when they hear the sounds of pursuit. Helisenne, weakened by sorrow, illness, and captivity, is left under a tree

while the two knights go to fight off their pursuers. When they return to Helisenne, she is dying. Having no desire to outlive his beloved, Guenelic wills himself to die, as well. They commend their souls to God and breathe their last.

Quezinstra finishes the tale in the following section, titled "Ample Narration faicte par Quezinstra, en regrettant la mort de son compagnon Guenelic, et de sa Dame Helisenne après leurs deplorables fins ce qui se declarera avec decoration du stille poetique" (Ample Narration Made by Quezinstra, Regretting the Death of His Companion Guenelic and of His Lady Helisenne after Their Sad Ends Which Will Be Told with the Adornment of Poetic Style). Mercury arrives and takes the souls of the lovers for judgment in the underworld. They are admitted to the Elysian Fields, and Quezinstra returns to the world to erect a suitable tomb. The gods decide that Helisenne's book should be published in Paris. Quezinstra accepts this task, for it will help others to "delaisser les choses transitoires, pour les choses perpetuelles acquerir" (forsake transitory things in order to obtain things that are everlasting).

Helisenne's turbulent marriage is the subject of part of Briet's second work, *Les Epistres familieres et invectives de ma dame Helisenne composées par icelle dame, De Crenne* (The Familiar and Invective Letters of My Lady Helisenne, Composed by that Lady, De Crenne; translated as *A Renaissance Woman: Helisenne's Personal and Invective Letters,* 1986), which appeared the year after *Les Angoysses douloureuses qui procedent d'amours*. As was the case with the novel, Helisenne de Crenne is listed on the title page as the author. While Helisenne the character appears to write the letters that discuss incidents from the novel, Helisenne the author is responsible for the letters that refer to the publication of the novel. Other letters do not mention any particular detail that would link the letter to either persona; and still others, particularly those that refer to Helisenne's marital difficulties, seem to identify Helisenne the author with Marguerite de Briet. The title evokes the classical tradition with its echo of Cicero's *Epistolae ad familiares* (Letters to My Friends), and Cicero's influence can be seen in the style and content of the letters. Classical genres also included letters of invective, and the humanist revival of classical erudition gave rise to manuals on epistolary style that included descriptions of invective writing. Helisenne's letters, however, are far from a simple imitation of classical models.

The work comprises eighteen letters with no connecting material; the thirteen personal letters are followed by five invective letters. Each section has its own preface, and neither has any conclusion other than the lines "Fin des Epistres Familieres" (End of Familiar Letters) and "Fin des Epistres invectives de ma dame Helisenne" (End of invective Letters of my lady

Helisenne), respectively. While the Archambaults perceive the letters as a sort of self-constructing story, this interpretation can only be achieved through a diligent effort on the part of the reader. The five invective letters form a cohesive unit, but the personal letters display a diffuse and sometimes bewildering variety; the preface to the personal letters promises diversity of character and content, and Helisenne keeps the promise.

The personal letters are addressed to a wide assortment of people, male and female, and suggest a wide and colorful network of correspondence of which they offer merely a glimpse. The first thanks an abbess at whose convent Helisenne had been a guest for her kindness and that of all of the sisters. Helisenne says that a sense of "filiale obedience" (filial duty) led to her "forcé et non voluntaire retour" (forced and involunary departure); if it were up to her, she would take up permanent residence at the convent. Although the details of Helisenne's situation are obscure, it is apparent that she is unhappy with her life and depends on intellectual pursuits for satisfaction. Filial duty also plays a role in the second letter, in which Helisenne regretfully declines an invitation to the wedding of a relative's daughter because she has to look after her mother, who is slowly recovering from a serious illness. For the same reason she will also be absent at the birth of the relative's grandchild, to which she has also been invited. No mention is made of a husband in either letter. The first two letters are intimate in tone and devoid of references to literature or philosophy.

The next seven letters are replete with criticism and advice, with Helisenne as the voice of virtuous authority. In the third letter she consoles a cousin who has been the victim of malicious gossip, adjuring the woman to have patience and courage and follow the example of Plato ("de resister contre les excessive passions; afin qu'elles ne superent la vertu" [to resist against excessive passion in order that they not overcome virtue]). She also advises patience in the next letter, written to a friend who has lost his prince's favor and been expelled from court because of the envy and slander of others. Here she refers to Socrates, some French philosophers, St. Paul, David, and the Psalms.

Letters 5 and 6 are distinctly less sympathetic. Letter 5 is a reply to Galazia, a friend who has written to Helisenne about an affair she is having. Accusing Galazia of losing her reason, Helisenne launches into a long lecture on the unfaithful nature of men that is studded with examples from mythology. She urges her friend to "efforce toy, contre la violence d'amour" (arm yourself against the violence of love) and to follow "la droicte voye de raison" (the straight path of reason). Her lack of sympathy for Galazia and a hint that her own knowledge of love is purely academic–"certes amour, comme nous lisons est un songe plein d'erreur, de follie" (certainly

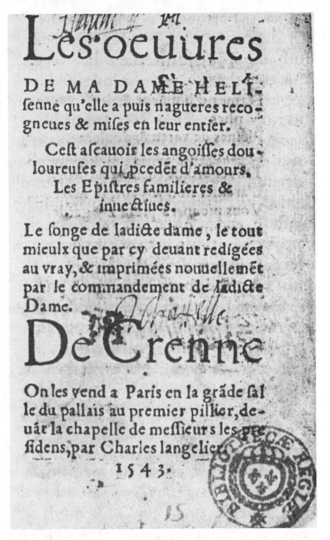

Title page for the first collected edition of Briet's works (from A Renaissance Woman: Helisenne's Personal and Invective Letters, translated by Marianna M. Mustacchi and Paul J. Archambault, 1986; Thomas Cooper Library, University of South Carolina)

love, as we read, is a dream full of error and folly)–indicate that the letter was composed before Helisenne herself fell in love. The sixth letter chides a friend who is in despair over the loss of his wealth. Helisenne decries his inability to bear misfortune and orders him to act his age.

Letters 7, 8, and 9 recapture some of the intimate tone of the first two letters, primarily because of their subject matter. The seventh letter reprises the theme of shared troubles as Helisenne commiserates with a friend, Guisnor, over the death of his wife. In contrast to her scathing characterization of men in her letter to Galazia, she praises Guisnor for the true and perfect love he and his wife shared. The eighth letter urges filial duty to a friend whose feelings for her old lover prevent her from following her father's wish that she marry someone else.

A departure from conventional virtue occurs for the first time in the letters when Helisenne urges her friend to use deception by feigning indifference to her old lover. In the next letter Helisenne encourages the friend to keep up her successful deception and suggests that she also profess a desire to become a nun: to avoid this outcome, the friend's father might be amenable to the suit of her old lover.

In the tenth letter, which is devoid of any literary allusions, a humbled Helisenne confesses to Galazia that she, too, has fallen in love. The man she describes does not, however, resemble the Guenelic of book 1 of *Les Angoysses douloureuses qui procedent d'amours:* this man's "modestie, grace, faconde, benignité & parfaite doulceur" (modesty, grace, eloquence, gentleness and perfeect sweetness) stand in contrast to Guenelic's craven self-centeredness. Nor are the flutterings of jealousy, fear, and hope she recounts reminiscent of the committed and obstinate passion depicted in the novel. The next letter, also to Galazia, is on the same subject but sounds more like the Helisenne of the novel. She no longer wavers between fear and hope but sadly relates the lack of Fortune's favor. She has been the victim of vicious gossip, which caused her to fall ill. When she recovered, she learned that her lover had left town; as a result, she is uncertain of his devotion.

The last two personal letters are addressed to Quezinstra and an unnamed gentleman admirer, presumably Guenelic. In the former she praises friendship in general and Quezinstra's in particular, thanking him for defending her against gossip and for trying to reason with her husband. Letter 12 is a love letter set with classical examples. The reader is tempted to believe that it is a copy of one of the letters written by Helisenne to Guenelic in *Les Angoysses douloureuses qui procedent d'amours,* although there Helisenne told the reader that she never completely declared her love for Guenelic for fear that he would lose interest in her.

The invective letters are a succinct summary of the feminist and antifeminist attitudes of the day. The preface gives no warning of the shift in subject matter but merely alerts the reader to a change of style. It also states that Fortune has persecuted Helisenne and used her cruelly. In the first invective letter, written to her husband, Helisenne makes it clear that he is the instrument of Fortune and the cause of most of her sufferings. She decries his anger at the publication of *Les Angoysses douloureuses qui procedent d'amours,* chastises him for believing that the book was written to commemorate an illicit love rather than to pass the time, and skillfully protests her innocence. The second letter is unique in that it is not from Helisenne but to her: it is ostensibly her husband's angry reply to the preceding epistle. Here Briet sets up traditional misogynist arguments—that women are prey to

unbridled lust, that they are cunning and deceitful, that they avoid good and seek evil, that their beauty is wicked, and that men should think carefully before marriage—that Helisenne proceeds to tear down in the following letter, addressed to her husband. In the fourth letter Helisenne continues her championship of women and demolishes the arrogant presumption of a man named Elenot that women should not write. Her examples of intelligent and literate women include a long list of classical and Christian figures, ending with the illustrious Marguerite de Navarre. She further discredits his judgment by citing his poor opinion of the poet Clément Marot, "duquel les oeuvres sont tant excellentes et elegantes, qu'en icelles souverainement se delectent Roys et princes" (whose works are so excellent and elegant that they are enjoyed by kings and princes). The last invective letter is sent to the ill-bred inhabitants of "une petite ville" (a small town) who have objected to what she has written about them; she is probably referring to the malicious residents of the village near Cabasus described in book 2 of *Les Angoysses douloureuses qui procedent d'amours.*

A virtue of the letters is their seeming realism. It would be easy to confuse the character Helisenne with the author and to believe that the latter spent time at a convent, took care of her sick mother, gave advice to friends, and fell under the spell of a handsome man. It is equally believable that Briet's real husband took exception to the publication of her novel. While the relationship of autobiographical fact to fiction in Briet's writing remains in question, the strategy of referring to actual events lends credibility to both of her works and helped to boost the popularity and sales of the novel. That sales were excellent is indicated by the printer's note at the front of the first edition of the letters, in which the printer and book dealer Denis Janot asks the provost of Paris to award him exclusive rights to publication of both *Les Angoysses douloureuses qui procedent d'amours* and the letters. The inscription at the bottom of the page indicates that Janot's request was granted for a period of two years. His worries seem to have been justified: as soon as the special permit expired in 1541, another Parisian printer brought out an edition of *Les Angoysses douloureuses qui procedent d'amours.*

Janot also published the first editions of Briet's other two works. *Le Songe de madame Helisenne composé par ladicte dame, la consideration duquel, est apte à instiguer toutes personnes de s'alliener de vice, & s'approcher de vertu* (1540, The Dream of Madame Helisenne Composed by the Said Lady, the Consideration of Which Is Apt to Incite All People to Turn Away from Vice and to Draw Closer to Virtue; translated as "The Dream," 2000) recounts a dream Helisenne experiences while residing at her favorite château, Cabasus. The prologue states that the work was written in imitation of Cicero's "Somnium Scipionis"

(Dream of Scipio), the last book of *De Republica* (54–51 B.C., On the Republic). Briet notes that Cicero's text deals with "the immortality of the soul," while her own is about the renunciation of sexual passion and the morality of men and women. For all the humanist education—literary, philosophical, and religious—exhibited within *Le Songe,* its exposition of love is much more reminiscent of the medieval *Roman de la Rose* (Romance of the Rose) than anything written in the new Neoplatonic or Petrarchan conventions.

The dream is a debate on the respective merits of sensual love and virtue among a lady in love, her lover, Venus, Athena, Cupid, Shame, and Lady Reason. Helisenne says that when she woke up, her soul "fut de tant vehemente tristesse agitee" (was agitated by such vehement sadness) at the thought of "chose digne de si grand memoire ne me tournast en oblivion" (something worthy of so great a memory fading in oblivion) that she decided to set the debate down in writing. She places herself into the dream as narrator and commentator, interrupting the text after each character speaks. The speeches of the lady in love and her lover and Helisenne's commentaries take up the first third of the text, after which the goddesses are introduced. The speeches of the lady in love and Helisenne are rich in mythological references; the goddesses' words include fewer such references; and the lover's includes only a mention of Cupid. Although *Le Songe* has been called an allegory, the allegorical characters Shame and Lady Reason do not appear until two-thirds of the way through the work; at that point allegory and Christianity supercede mythology. Shame has one speech; Lady Reason occupies center stage, quoting at length from the Bible and St. Thomas Aquinas. Shame directs one long argument at Sensuality, who is mentioned as a character but—like Equity and Justice, who help to indict her—never speaks. The rest of Lady Reason's remarks are addressed to the lady in love, who is allowed a final reply, in which she refers to Dame Chastity to show that she has been rehabilitated by Lady Reason.

Briet's last work, *Les quatre premiers livres des Eneydes* (1541, The First Four Books of the Aeneid), carries the distinction of being the first published French prose translation of Virgil's work. This book was published in a more elegant physical format than her previous works—no doubt a reflection of the status of its dedicatee, King François I. Following current literary conventions, Briet embellishes the text with her own additions and with passages from other versions of the story. Unlike her other publications, the translation went through only one edition.

Given the popularity of her original works, it is a mystery why Briet quit writing. Popular tastes, however, were apparently beginning to change. Although book 1 of *Les Angoysses douloureuses qui procedent d'amours* is written in relatively ordinary language, Briet's vocabulary becomes more arcane in book 2 and with each successive work. This stylistic device is not unique to Briet: François Rabelais latinized his texts, as did Briet's models Caviceo and Lemaire de Belges. What sets Briet's writing apart is her excessive use of erudite embellishments. While that style held appeal for a large audience, some readers voiced their dismay over her vocabulary. Briet apparently realized that the language posed difficulties, for she allowed the poet and translator Claude Colet to simplify the text in his edition of her collected works. In a letter dated 15 March 1550 and included in the edition, printed by Estienne Groulleau in Paris in 1551, Colet states that he put "en nostre propre et familier langage les motz obscurs, et trop aprochans du Latin, a fin qu'elles vous fussent plus intelligibles" (into our own and familiar language the obscure words too close to Latin so that the work would be more intelligible). He goes on to say that French is as good as Latin and that women writers are equal to men and denies making any stylistic changes. Nothing is known of Briet's reaction to the edition.

While Briet and her husband did not reside permanently in Paris, that they spent a good deal of time in the capital is attested by the fact that a suit was brought against them in 1550 by a baker for nonpayment of a large sum of money. Their marriage was not happy. A legal document issued in Paris, dated 25 August 1552, indicates that their possessions had been divided up, and it is possible, given the several residences that the couple owned, that they were also living separately. The 1552 document has the tone and wording of a will. Briet leaves to Christophe Le Manyer, a squire living in Paris, an annual income of 213 livres and half ownership of the two houses she owns in the Paris suburb of St. Marcel, of which she is to have usufruct until her death. This gift to him and his heirs is a reward for his "services" and the rooms that he has given her. Nothing more is known about Le Manyer or the nature of the services he rendered.

The 1552 document is the last official record of Briet. In 1555 François de Billon dedicated a paragraph to her and her works in his *Le Fort inexpugnable de l'honneur du sexe Femenin* (The Impregnable Fortress of the Honor of the Feminine Sex). No record exists giving—or even suggesting—the date of her death. Since the last edition of her work before its twentieth-century rediscovery appeared in 1560, that year has been arbitrarily proposed by critics, including the Archambaults, as the year in which she died.

Modern criticism has focused primarily on book 1 of *Les Angoysses douloureuses qui procedent d'amours* because of the unusual heroine and female narrator. Books 2 and 3, with their male narrators and adventure stories, seemed more traditional and less interesting. This view has begun to shift as Marguerite de Briet and her work have become more widely known, and more attention is being given to the novel as a whole. New editions of *Les Angoysses douloureuses qui procedent d'amours, Le Songe,* and *Les Epistres familieres et invectives* make Briet's writings available to modern readers, who continue to be fascinated by this unusual author and her tale of obsessive, undeniable passion.

Biography:

Paul J. Archambault and Marianna Mustacchi Archambault, "Helisenne de Crenne," in *French Women Writers: A Bio-bibliographical Source Book,* edited by Eva Martin Sartori and Dorothy Wynne Zimmerman (New York: Greenwood Press, 1991), pp. 99–107.

References:

Mary J. Baker, "*Fiammetta* and the *Angoysses Douloureuses qui procedent d'amours,*" *Symposium,* 27 (1973): 303–308;

Baker, "France's First Sentimental Novel and Novels of Chivalry," *Bibliothèque d'humanisme et renaissance,* 36 (1974): 33–45;

Cathleen Bauchatz, "'Hélisenne aux Lisantes': Address of Women Readers in the *Angoisses douloureuses* and in Boccaccio's *Fiammetta,*" *Atlantis,* 19 (1993): 59–66;

Jean-Philippe Beaulieu, "Erudition and Aphasia in Helisenne de Crenne's *Les Angoysses douloureuses qui procedent d'amours,*" *L'Esprit Créateur,* 29 (1989): 36–42;

Beaulieu and Diane Desrosiers-Bonin, eds., *Hélisenne de Crenne: L'Ecriture et ses doubles* (Paris: Champion, 2004);

François de Billon, *Le Fort inexpugnable de l'honneur du sexe Femenin* (Paris: Ian d'Allyer, 1555; Wakefield, U.K.: S. R. Publishers / New York: Johnson Reprint / The Hague: Mouton, 1970);

Tom Conley, "Feminism, *Ecriture,* and the Closed Room: The *Angoysses douloureuses qui procedent d'amours,*" *Symposium,* 27 (1973): 322–332;

Megan Conway, "Christianity and Classicism in Helisenne de Crenne's *Les Angoysses douloureuses qui procedent d'amours,*" *Journal of the Rocky Mountain Medieval and Renaissance Association,* 18 (1997): 111–131;

Robert D. Cottrell, "Hélisenne de Crenne's Le Songe," in *Women Writers in Pre-Revolutionary France: Strategies of Emancipation,* edited by Colette Winn and Donna Kuizenga (New York: Garland, 1997), pp. 189–206;

Luce Guillerm, "La Prison des textes ou *Les Angoysses douloureuses qui procedent d'amours* d'Hélisenne de Crenne, 1538," *Revue de Sciences Humaines,* 196 (1984): 9–23;

Anne Larsen, "The Rhetoric of Self-Defense in *Les Angoysses douloureuses qui procedent d'amours* (Part One)," *Kentucky Romance Quarterly,* 29 (1982): 235–243;

Louis Loviot, "Hélisenne de Crenne," *Revue des livres anciens,* 2 (1917): 137–145;

Jerry Nash, "The Fury of the Pen: Crenne, the Bible and Letter Writing," in *Women Writers in Pre-Revolutionary France,* pp. 207–225;

Nash, "Renaissance Misogyny, Biblical Feminism, and Helisenne de Crenne's *Epistres familieres et invectives,*" *Renaissance Quarterly,* 50 (1997): 379–410;

Nash, "The Rhetoric of Scorn in Hélisenne de Crenne," *Strategies of Rhetoric,* 19 (1992): 1–9;

Gustave Reynier, *Le roman sentimental avant l'Astrée* (Paris: Librairies Armand Colin, 1908), pp. 99–121;

Kittye Delle Robbins-Herring, "Helisenne de Crenne: Champion of Women's Rights," in *Women Writers of the Renaissance and Reformation,* edited by Katharina M. Wilson (Athens: University of Georgia Press, 1987), pp. 177–218;

Verdun L. Saulnier, "Quelques nouveautés sur Hélisenne de Crenne," *Bulletin de l'Association Guillaume Budé,* 4 (1964): 459–463;

Jérôme Vercruysse, "Hélisenne de Crenne: Notes bibliographiques," *Studi Francesi,* 11 (1967): 77–81;

Colette H. Winn, "La Symbolique du regard dans *Les Angoysses douloureuses qui procedent d'amours* d'Hélisenne de Crenne," *Orbis Litterarum,* 40 (1985): 207–221;

Diane S. Wood, "The Evolution of Hélisenne de Crenne's Persona," *Symposium,* 45 (1991): 140–151;

Wood, *Hélisenne de Crenne: At the Crossroads of Renaissance Humanism and Feminism* (Madison, Wis.: Fairleigh Dickinson University Press / London: Associated University Presses, 2000).

Bonaventure des Périers

(1510? – 1543?)

Emily Thompson
Webster University

BOOKS: *La Prognostication des Prognostications, non seulement de ceste presente annee M.D.XXXVII. Mais aussi des aultres a venir, voire de toutes celles qui sont passees, composee par Maistre Sarcomoros, natif de Tartarie, et secretaire du tresillustre et trespuissant roy de Cathai, serf de vertus* (Paris: Morin, 1537);

Cymbalum Mundi, en francoys, Contenant quatre Dialogues Poétiques, fort antiques, joyeux, & facetieux, anonymous (Paris: Morin, 1537); translated by Prosper Marchand as *Cymbalum mundi. Or, Satyrical dialogues upon several subjects . . . To which is prefix'd a letter containing the history, apology, &c. of that work* (London: A. Baldwin, 1712);

Recueil des Oeuvres de feu Bonaventure Des Periers, vallet de chambre de Treschrestienne Princesse Marguerite de France, Royne de Navarre, edited by Antoine du Moulin (Lyon: De Tournes, 1544);

Les Nouvelles Recreations et Joyeux Devis de feu Bonaventure Des Periers valet de chambre de la Royne de Navarre (Lyon: Granjon, 1558); translated by T.D. as *The Mirrour of mirth, and pleasant conceits* (London: Roger Warde, 1583).

Collections and Editions: *Cymbalum Mundi en françoys, contenant quatre Dialogues Poétiques, fort antiques, joyeux et facetieux,* anonymous (Lyon: Bonnyn, 1538);

Oeuvres françoises de Bonaventure Des Periers, edited by M. Louis Lacour (Paris: Jannet, 1856);

Cymbalum Mundi, edited by Félix Frank (Paris: Lemerre, 1873);

Cymbalum Mundi, edited by Peter Hampshire Nurse (Oxford: University of Manchester Press, 1967);

Nouvelles Récréations et Joyeux Devis I-XC, edited by Krystyna Kasprzyk (Paris: Champion, 1980);

"La Prognostication des Prognostications, non seulement de ceste presente annee M.D.XXXVII. Mais aussi des aultres a venir, voire de toutes celles qui sont passees," edited by Trevor Peach, *Bibliothèque d'humanisme et renaissance,* 52, no. 1 (1990): 109–121;

Cymbalum Mundi, edited by Max Gauna (Paris: Champion, 2000).

Editions in English: *The Mirrour of Mirth, and Pleasant Conceits,* edited by James Woodrow Hassell Jr. (Columbia: University of South Carolina Press, 1959);

Cymbalum Mundi, four very ancient joyous and facetious poetic dialogues, translated by Bettina L. Knapp (New York: Bookman Associates, 1965);

Novel Pastimes and Merry Tales, translated by Raymond C. and Virginia A. La Charité (Lexington: University Press of Kentucky, 1972).

OTHER: Interpretive table and notes, in *La Bible, qui est toute la Saincte escripture. En laquelle sont contenus / le Vieil Testament & le Nouueau / translate en Francoys. Le Vieil / de Lebrieu & le Nouueau / du Grec. Aussi deux amples tables / l'une pour l'interpretation des propres noms: lautre en forme Dindice / pour trouuer plusieurs sentences et matieres,* translated by Pierre Robert Olivétan (Neufchastel: Pierre de Wingle, 1535);

"Pour Marot absent contre Sagon" and "Eiusdem Bonaventurae de eodem epigramma," in *Les disciples et amys de Marot contre Sagon, La Hueterie et leurs adherentz* (Paris: Morin, 1537);

"Cantique de Moyse" in *Cinquante Pseaumes de David, traduictz en rithme françoise selon la verité hebraïque par Clement Marot, avec plusieurs compositions tant dudict autheur que d'autres, non jamais encore imprimées* (Paris: Ambroyse Girault, 1545).

Bonaventure des Périers's name recurs at significant moments in the religious and literary debates of early sixteenth-century France while remaining only tentatively linked to actual literary works. Nearly everything that has been suggested about his life has been just as quickly contested: the date and the location of his birth, the date and manner of his death, his religious convictions, his relationships with Marguerite of Navarre and Clément Marot, and most important, his authorship of several texts. The works that have been at one time or another attributed to him include poetry, dialogues, *nouvelles* (short stories), and translations from

*Title page for the anonymous work, attributed to Bonaventure des Périers,
that was condemned by King Francis I, Protestant reformers, and the
Sorbonne (Collection Roger-Viollet/Getty Images)*

Greek and Latin. Although not a well-known figure among twenty-first-century students of French literature, Des Périers provoked vehement condemnations from prominent Renaissance writers for his supposed libertine beliefs while enjoying a rare legal immunity, probably resulting from the patronage of the queen of Navarre. His fragmented and incoherent biography reflects some of the tensions in the quickly evolving religious, literary, social, and political contexts in which he lived, giving his life particular significance to historians and literary critics of the French Renaissance.

Most scholars agree that Des Périers was born in Bourgogne, although they do not all believe there is enough evidence to claim he was from the small town of Arnay-le-Duc, where municipal records reveal a sixteenth-century family named Des Périers. The author Estienne Tabourot linked Des Périers for the first time in print with this town in his collection *Les Bigarrures du Seigneur des Accords* (1583, Odds and Ends). Nothing definite can be concluded about his family's social status. If indeed Des Périers was born in Arnay-le-Duc, town records suggest that his relatives held positions as town magistrates and apothecaries but were

probably not wealthy. In *Bonaventure Des Périers: sa vie, ses poésies* (1886, Bonaventure des Périers: His Life, His Poetry) biographer Adolphe Chenevière proposes a birth year around 1510 as consistent with Des Périers's ensuing professional life and friendships. Philipp Becker in *Bonaventure Des Périers als Dichter und Erzähler* (1924, Bonaventure des Périers as Poet and Storyteller) and Lionello Sozzi in *Les Contes de Bonaventure Des Périers* (1964, Tales of Bonaventure des Périers) likewise find this year plausible. A key piece in what modern readers know about Des Périers's life is his relationship with Robert Hurault, a familiar of King François I's sister, Marguerite de Navarre, and member of the Parlement of Paris. Chevenière convincingly uses references in Des Périers's poetry to identify Hurault as the man Des Périers describes thus:

Qui me congnoist mieulx que ne fais moy même,
Qui ha esté et est mon precepteur;
Qui m'a monstré quel est mon Redempteur;
Qui m'a monstré rhythmes, grec et latin;
. . . .
C'est monseigneur monsieur de Sainct Martin

(Who knows me better than I know myself,
Who was and is my tutor;
Who showed me who my Redeemer is;
Who showed me rhymes, Greek and Latin;
. . . .
It's My Lord, Mister Saint Martin.)

Hurault came to the town of Autun in Burgundy as abbot of Saint Martin in 1529. Des Périers, studying in Autun, probably met Hurault there. Not only the poetic references and the geographic proximity but also Hurault's connections in Paris render compelling the hypothesis that he served as Des Périers's mentor. Hurault's influence would explain Des Périers's later success in becoming *valet de chambre* (manservant or, in this context, secretary) to Marguerite de Navarre. Hurault's known sympathies with the Reformation could help trace the evangelical influence detectable in Des Périers's early work.

Between the end of his studies and 1535, Des Périers left no trace for biographers. He may well have traveled to Lyon, an intellectual center where he could have interacted with many of the people to whom he later dedicated poems. In any case, he resurfaced in 1535 in Switzerland as a collaborator of Jean Calvin's cousin Pierre-Robert Olivétan, who was responsible for one of the earliest translations of the Bible into French. In his acknowledgments Olivétan thanks "Eutychus Deperius" (a Latinized version of Des Périers's name) for his work on the interpretative table of Greek, Chaldean, and Hebrew names and for assistance with the summaries in the margins of the translated Bible. As the member of the Olivétan group who went on to become a well-known poet, Des Périers most likely composed the Latin verses that follow the biblical translation and perhaps two poems in French that frame the table of names. Some contemporary testimonies refer to Des Périers as a fellow translator of this Bible, but there is no strong evidence that his participation exceeded that of interpreting the table of names and writing the marginal summaries. How he earned his reputation as poet and translator before meeting Olivétan is unknown. Regardless of the minor significance of his contribution to the Olivétan Bible, this work linked Des Périers with an innovative linguistic and religious project. He remained associated with similar undertakings for the rest of his literary life.

Shortly after his work in Switzerland with Olivétan, Des Périers went to Lyon and entered into another scholarly collaboration, assisting Etienne Dolet, an unorthodox humanist writer and printer whose circle of intimates included prominent writers such as Guillaume Budé, François Rabelais, and Clément Marot. Dolet used Des Périers as a proofreader for the first volume of his *Commentariorum linguae latinae* (1536, Of Commentaries of the Latin language). In the printed acknowledgments of the second volume of the *Commentariorum linguae latinae* (1538), Des Périers's name appears for what amounts to clerical work. His interactions with other humanists in Lyon at the time appear to have been restricted. Of the many recipients of poetic dedications or references in Des Périers's oeuvre, only Mellin de Saint-Gelais and Marot can be counted among the most famous writers at the time. Jean de Tournes, the prominent printer, also knew Des Périers well enough to merit a poem. Des Périers never mentions Rabelais or Maurice Scève, nor do either of these well-known writers ever allude to him.

By 1536 Des Périers was interested in making more-powerful connections than with his humanist contemporaries. He had met Marguerite of Navarre in Lyon and was requesting, via poems dedicated to her, a position in her service and among the group of evangelical sympathizers whom she supported. He names the abbot of Saint Martin as a common acquaintance in some of the poems he wrote to the queen while beseeching her to employ him. These poems were published for the first time in *Recueil des Oeuvres de feu Bonaventure Des Periers, vallet de chambre de Treschrestienne Princesse Marguerite de France, Royne de Navarre* (1544, Collection of the Works of the Late Bonaventure des Periers, Secretary to the Most Christian Princess Marguerite of France, Queen of Navarre) by his friend Antoine du Moulin after Des Périers's death. A record in the queen's accounts attests to Des Périers's continued association with her in 1541, but no similar record permits an accurate dating of the beginning of his royal employment. His employment probably began in 1536 since the royal court had been present in Lyon much of the year, and by the end of that year Des Périers was writing poems that suggest a familiarity with the people and the Neoplatonism of Marguerite's entourage.

Des Périers was eventually granted the position of *valet de chambre*–a title that was noted in Marguerite's accounting books in 1541 and that was used to identify him in the poetry of François Sagon. Among his duties would have been the copying and translation of texts and the transcription of Marguerite's dictated works. Marguerite also integrated some of Des Périers's verse into her play *L'Inquisiteur* (The Inquisitor), as Verdun L. Saulnier noted in his edition of Marguerite's dramatic works, *Théâtre profane* (1946, Secular Plays). Before Des Périers, Marot had held the position of Marguerite's *valet de chambre*. For a person of no distinguished genealogy like Des Périers, the post was a major coup that implied financial security and interaction with the leading evangelical thinkers in France.

Perhaps emboldened by this new status, Des Périers quickly acquired notoriety by jumping to the defense of his fellow court poet Marot. The Affaire des Placards (Affair of the Placards) of 1534 had by this time altered the religious atmosphere in Paris. King François I's previous indulgence toward evangelical thought and to his sister's protégés had turned to anger when belligerent attacks on the Catholic Mass appeared on placards in various strategic locations throughout France. Marot, whose sympathies with the Reform were well known, had fled to Italy to escape the violent retributions led by the Sorbonne. Another court poet, Sagon, took advantage of Marot's absence to criticize him in verse. Des Périers wrote a poem in response, "Pour Marot absent contre Sagon" (In Favor of the Absent Marot Against Sagon), defending Marot's talent and decrying the cowardice and the jealousy inherent in Sagon's attack. In his poem Des Périers asks the king to forgive the exiled Marot and urges other French poets to come to the aid of Marot's reputation. Des Périers thus sparked an exchange of colorful and hostile poems addressing the rivalry between Sagon and Marot and became the subject of Sagon's dismissive responses in verse and a single cursory expression of gratitude in one of Marot's poems. Part of this exchange (including two poems by Des Périers) was printed in 1537 by the printer Jean Morin as *Les disciples et amys de Marot contre Sagon, La Hueterie, et leurs adherentz* (The Disciples and Friends of Marot against Sagon, La Hueterie and Their Followers).

Another 1537 publication, *La Prognostication des Prognostications* (The Prognostication of Prognostications), written under the pseudononym Maistre Sarco-

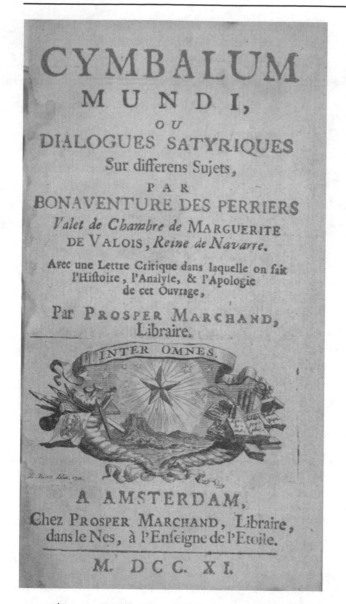

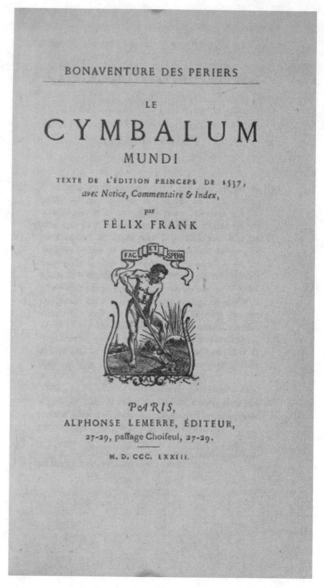

Title pages for later editions of the Des Périers's work in which Mercury mocks theologians and dogs consider the wisdom of revealing their gift of speech to humans (Douglas H. Gordon Collection, University of Virginia Library)

moros, was attibuted to Des Périers by Moulin when he included it in the posthumous *Recueil des Oeuvres* with a hitherto unpublished preface addressed to Marguerite. The 290-verse poem belongs to a literary type of parodic attack on almanacs and on those who wrote them. The humanist writer Rabelais, for example, denounced prophesizing in a similar text, the 1533 *Pantagrueline Prognostication* (Pantagruelian Prognostication). Des Périers targets the self-interested liars who sell their inaccurate almanacs, but he reserves his principle criticism for the credulous readers of these books. Those who abuse and those who are abused become one and the same, equally guilty of falling prey to the seduction of empty words and of neglecting the Word of God.

The concluding section of the poem echoes Marguerite's evangelical lexicon in its juxtaposition of an imperfect world of lies with a perfect God of Truth. Throughout this poem of evangelical piety Des Périers uses characteristic wordplay, proverbial language, and apostrophes to the reader. These traits recur in his other poems as well as in the collection of short stories later attributed to him.

While the prose works that have kept Des Périers's name alive are the same ones that made him notorious in the sixteenth century, his reputation as a poet has suffered from the test of time. The poems that modern critics dismiss are probably the very works that earned him his place in Marguerite's service. His poetry was also praised in two significant Renaissance treatises: Thomas Sebillet's *Art poétique français* (1548, The French Art of Poetry) and Jacques Peletier du Mans's *Art Poétique* (1555, Art of Poetry). Although not named as often as Marot, Saint-Gelais, or Maurice Scève in these treatises, Des Périers did receive recognition as an innovative poet whose compositions brought honor to the French language. Sebillet credited Des Périers with originality and poetic courage in composing verse without rhyme. Peletier du Mans chose to praise Des Périers's integration of regional words into his French poetry. In yet another sixteenth-century commentary on poetry, *Replique aux furieuses defenses de Louis Meigret* (1551, Reply to the Furious Defenses of Louis Meigret), the Pléiade poet Guillaume des Autelz named Des Périers as the first Frenchman to use the ode correctly.

In many ways Des Périers's poetic style recalls that of Marot, the poet he so publicly admired. In a note in the seccond volume of *Oeuvres Poétiques Complètes* (1990, Complete Poetic Works) of Marot, editor Gérard Defaux characterizes Des Périers's poems as "le plus pur style 'marotique'" (the purest "marotic" style). Like Marot, Des Périers could convey philosophical and religious ideas in simple words and personal anecdotes, giving an impression of effortless verse. He too excelled in satire and infused his court poetry with humor. While he used short poetic forms Marot mastered, such as the epigram and rondeau, Des Périers also experimented with original forms and rhymes and displayed his own style of wordplay.

Des Périers's poetic works address varied themes. He wrote few love poems, preferring instead poetry celebrating the events and people in his immediate vicinity. Poems praising the moral qualities of friends and patrons and thanking them for past favors recur frequently among his works. He also wrote verse commentaries on the poetry and language of his contemporaries and translated verse from classic authors. References to Des Périers's own life and character figure prominently in his poetry.

Most of what scholars have been able to reconstitute of Des Périers's life comes from information he shares through his poems. Although it is important to treat these poems as artistic works and not as straightforward biographical data, they nonetheless provide the only light to be shed on many specific incidents in Des Périers's life, particularly on the stages of his professional relationship with Marguerite. He memorializes these significant moments by capturing them in poems he dedicates to his patron. Unfortunately for modern readers, these poems were published only after his death and any attempt at giving them a fixed chronology remains tentative.

In 1537, for example, several members of the royal family suffered from a severe fever. This occurrence suggests a likely time of composition for some poems that Des Périers wrote concerning his own illness and the consolation he received from the king's daughter. A reference in one of Sagon's poems also places Des Périers at court and in favor during 1537, the year of the anonymous publication of *Cymbalum Mundi* attributed to him.

The most well-known work associated with Des Périers, *Cymbalum Mundi* (1537, Cymbal of the World; translated as *Cymbalum mundi. Or, Satyrical dialogues upon several subjects . . . To which is prefix'd a letter containing the history, apology, &c. of that work,* 1712), has also elicited the most controversy. Morin, who had previously published *Les disciples et amys de Marot contre Sagon, La Hueterie et leurs adherents* and *La Prognostication des Prognostications,* published the *Cymbalum Mundi* as an anonymous work in Paris. Some scholars believe that Morin used an older way of dating in which the new year began at Easter. If so, then the book would have been published before Easter 1538. The *Cymbalum Mundi* consists of four dialogues modeled after those of the Greek satirist, Lucian, combining irreverent comedy and philosophical debates using mythological figures, most notably Mercury, as characters. In style the dialogues of the *Cymbalum Mundi* recall the wit and popular tone of Des Périers's poetry although no clear linguistic pattern convincingly connects this prose to Des Périers's poetic language. The twin targets of credulity and vain language recall the themes of *La Prognostication des Prognostications.*

The *Cymbalum Mundi* is a short text with loosely related dialogues. The first dialogue pits Mercury, the divine messenger, against a tavern maid and two common thieves. Mercury has descended among mortals in order to have Zeus's book of life rebound. The two thieves recognize Mercury and decide to rob the god of theft himself. They substitute a book of mythology for Zeus's book before leaving Mercury to debate faith and skepticism with the tavern maid.

Mercury reappears in the second dialogue. Here it is he who mocks mortals, in this case theologians who waste their time seeking bits of the shattered philosopher's stone he has thrown to them. Disguising himself, he converses with them, testing their faith, questioning their claims to possess truth, and accusing them of failing to make significant social reform.

In the third dialogue Mercury complains of his divine superiors who have sent him on futile errands. He encounters Cupid, and they speak of love and desire. As Cupid departs to continue his erotic conquests, Mercury once again amuses himself at the

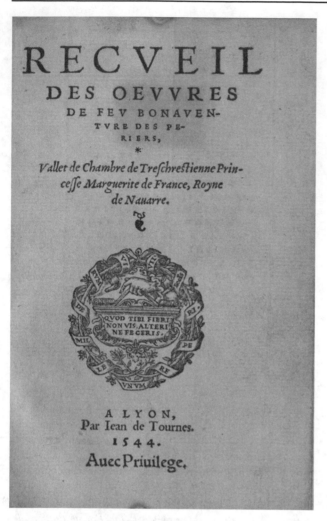

RECVEIL
DES OEVVRES
DE FEV BONAVEN-
TVRE DES PE-
RIERS,

*

*Vallet de Chambre de Treschrestienne Prin-
cesse Marguerite de France, Royne
de Nauarre.*

QVOD TIBI FIERI
NON VIS, ALTERI
NE FECERIS.

A LYON,
Par Iean de Tournes.
1544.
Auec Priuilege.

*Title page for the collection of Des Périers's works published a year after
his death by Antoine du Moulin (Douglas H. Gordon Collection,
University of Virginia Library)*

expense of mortals by enabling a horse to speak. The horse uses its new talent to accuse its master of abusive treatment.

The fourth dialogue returns to the theme of animals and speech. Two dogs have acquired the ability to speak. One of them dreams of the glory that will follow the revelation of his gift to humans. The other counsels silence, preferring the freedom of a natural dog's modest existence and warning against the capriciousness of humans. The dialogue ends with the discovery of a pack of letters from mysterious inhabitants on the other side of the world seeking to initiate a conversation with humans but threatening violence if rejected. The dogs hide these letters, thus deferring once again an act of communication with the Other.

The authorship of these strange dialogues has never been definitively established. The *Cymbalum Mundi* was published twice anonymously (the original

printing in Paris in 1537 and another in Lyon in 1538), and no document from the 1530s identifies Des Périers as the author. Only in the 1560s did several writers explicitly name Des Périers as the libertine author of the *Cymbalum Mundi.* However, two earlier references, one to the *Cymbalum Mundi* and one to Des Périers, suggest links between the author and the work. In the surviving summary of a 1538 letter from the Swiss reformer André Zébédée to Charles de Candeley, Zébédée rejects the supposed religious sincerity of an unnamed assistant to Olivétan who, he adds, later wrote the *Cymbalum Mundi.* In his 1541 work *Des Scandales* (1541, Concerning Scandals), Calvin accused Des Périers of having replaced faith with mockery. Des Périers's supposed authorship of *Cymbalum Mundi* would provide plausible cause for Calvin's otherwise surprisingly sudden and intense repudiation of him. Des Periers's poetry, heavily imbued with pre-Reformist sentiment, and his participation in the translation of the Bible into French suggest no earlier evidence of antipathy toward Calvin and his followers.

The *Cymbalum Mundi* provoked condemnation from Reformers and from the king as well as the disapproval of the Catholic authorities at the Sorbonne, the powerful faculty of theology at the University of Paris. In 1538 King François I brought the book to the Parlement of Paris and requested that it be condemned as heretical and that both the author and the publisher be punished. The parlement proceeded to arrest and sentence Morin. After Morin's appeal, the parlement deferred the verdict on the *Cymbalum Mundi* to the Sorbonne, which, a bit more tentatively, found the book "pernicious" while agreeing that all copies should be burned. In his request for clemency, Morin claimed that he had innocently published the book without understanding it. Scholars know from a letter Morin wrote to Chancellor Antoine du Bourg that he had revealed the name of the author to his interrogators, although that identity was apparently never made public. While the parlement condemned Morin to exile, there is no record of an author having been arrested. Scholars who support the theory that Des Périers wrote the *Cymbalum Mundi* assume that Marguerite's protection explains the immunity of the author.

Beyond the identification of the author, the underlying religious message of the *Cymbalum Mundi* poses the most difficult challenge to the modern scholar. Influenced by the resounding condemnations of the work by Reformers as well as by later Catholic writers, many literary scholars have interpreted the *Cymbalum Mundi* as espousing a spiritual skepticism. Some scholars, notably Lucien Febvre, Henri Busson, Max Gauna, and Malcolm Smith, have seen in this work evidence of Renaissance atheism. Michael A. Screech, on the other hand, argues that the *Cymbalum Mundi* expresses an orthodox Catholic position. Some critics believe that the work was not intended as a serious commentary on religion at all, whereas Saulnier and Peter Hampshire Nurse have tried to recuperate the *Cymbalum Mundi* as a mystical evangelical work in harmony with the beliefs of Marguerite. Even for an era of paradox like the Renaissance, the ability of a text to support such starkly opposing interpretations is unusual. The underlying religious message, if any, is too deeply entangled with lost references and deliberately disguised historical allusions for modern readers ever to recapture a comprehensive or definitive Renaissance reading.

The violence of the reaction against the *Cymbalum Mundi* at the time it was published may, in fact, have stemmed as much from the perception that it encoded a slanderous subtext as from its suspicious theology. The king's animosity and his unusual intervention, for example, would be more easily understandable as a response to a suspected personal attack on someone close to him. The targets of the *Cymbalum Mundi*, however, continue to resist identification. The names of the characters in the dialogues form anagrams that critics have tried to decipher in order to shed light on the religious significance of the text. In the fictional dedication that precedes the dialogues, a Thomas du Clevier claims that the dialogues that follow are a translation for his friend Pierre Troycan S. of a mysterious text found in a monastery. In 1841 Eloi Johanneau decoded these anagrams as "Thomas Incredule" (Doubting Thomas) and "Pierre Croyant" (Pierre the Believer). In 2002 Trevor Peach suggested that these two names hide the name of the author: *Lucian Samo.Rhet. de simonia, Periers Auctor* (Lucian of Samosate, rhetor; about simony; Periers author). Critics have found references to such figures as Martin Luther, Martin Bucer, Erasmus, Girard Roussel, and Dolet in the names of the characters in the *Cymbalum Mundi*. Textual allusions and critical consensus support only the identification of Bucer (Cubercus) and Luther (Rhetulus) with any certainty.

Although the meaning of the *Cymbalum Mundi* continues to defy literary critics and historians, the controversial history and themes of the text make it a vital piece in the study of changing religious thought and the history of belief and faith. The seemingly disproportioned impact of these four satirical dialogues offers clues to the delicate balance between political and religious power in France at this critical moment before the Religious wars. The dialogues also allow scholars to seek evidence of religious skepticism in France at this early date.

After the publication of the *Cymbalum Mundi*, Des Périers virtually disappears from the records. He published nothing more although he continued to write poetry and dedicate it to contemporaries. He remained in the service of the queen of Navarre at least until 1541, when she noted that he had not been paid for the year. This oversight combined with poems complaining of rumors estranging the queen from him could imply a cooling of their relationship after the publication of the *Cymbalum Mundi* and the ensuing scandal. On the other hand, since the poems cannot be convincingly dated, it is impossible to reconstruct the events of this supposed distancing or to hypothesize as to its resolution. Therefore, the nature of the queen's support, both intellectual and financial, after 1537 remains uncertain.

Des Périers is believed to have died in 1543. The printer Henri Estienne in his 1566 *Apologie pour Hérodote* describes Des Périers's death as a suicide. Estienne, however, was an ardent critic of the author he believed responsible for the scandalous and irreligious *Cymbalum Mundi*. The year 1566 is early enough to lend some credibility to Estienne's version of Des Périers's death. Suicide, however, was believed to be the inevitable outcome for atheists at the time, so the symbolic temptation of imagining Des Périers's death as a suicide may have outweighed Estienne's concern with factual confirmation. The suicide theory directly contradicts an allusion to Des Périers's death in the 1544 edition of his works, published by Du Moulin, *Recueil des Œuvres de feu Bonaventure Des Periers, vallet de chambre de Treschrestienne Princesse Marguerite de France, Royne de Navarre* (Collection of the Works of the Deceased Bonaventure des Périers, Valet de Chambre of the Most Christian Princess, Marguerite of France, Queen of Navarre). Although Du Moulin's friendship would have provided sufficient motive to deny a suspect death, it is difficult to believe that he would have used the expression "l'homme propose et Dieu dispose" (man proposes and God disposes) had Des Périers taken his own life.

Du Moulin also laments Des Périers's death in the preface dedicated to Marguerite de Navarre:

Mort implacable, implacable Mort l'a surpris au cours de sa bonne intention, lorsqu'il estoit après à dresser et à mettre en ordre ses compositions, pour les vous offrir et donner . . .

(Death implacable, implacable Death surprised him in the midst of his good intentions, while he was preparing to put his compositions in order so as to offer and give them to you.)

This literary tribute could have been Du Moulin's attempt to repair Des Périers's reputation in the queen's eyes or may instead suggest that she had never formally separated from him. In either case, by publishing Des Périers's often self-referential poetic work and by estab-

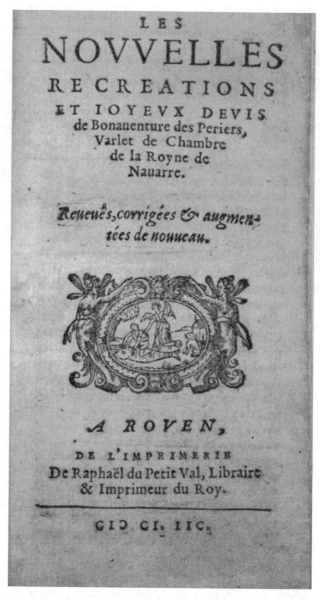

Title pages for sixteenth-century editions of the collection of short stories Des Périers left unpublished at his death (Douglas H. Gordon Collection, University of Virginia Library)

lishing his death as prior to August 1544, Du Moulin provided most of the biographical information about Des Périers that is known today. In the same dedication Du Moulin promised to publish more of Des Périers's works. He claimed that a friend of his as well as Marguerite herself possessed as yet unpublished texts by the author. Du Moulin does not allude to or include the *Cymbalum Mundi* in his collection. Nor does he explicitly mention another work that was published fourteen years later in Des Périers's name: *Les Nouvelles Recreations et Joyeux Devis* (1558, Novel Pastimes and Merry Tales; translated as *The Mirrour of mirth, and pleasant conceits*, 1583).

Despite the fact that this collection of ninety *nouvelles* was published with his name on the title page, the authorship of *Les Nouvelles Recreations* has not been formally proven. More than twenty-five years after the collection was published, two separate critics proposed Jacques Peletier du Mans as a more likely author. Most modern scholars, however, accept the authorship of Des Périers.

The publishing history of the work sheds little light on the question of authorship. The publisher Robert Granjon had connections to Du Moulin and to Jean De Tournes, the publisher of *Recueil des Oeuvres*, and could have acquired the manuscript and decided to publish it following Du Moulin's death in 1550. The *nouvelle* genre was selling well at the time; Marguerite's own collection of short stories, *L'Heptameron,* was also published in 1558. Des Périers probably assisted Marguerite in writing *L'Heptameron,* most likely by copying what she dictated but also possibly by contributing story ideas.

Although it made less of an initial impact than the *Cymbalum Mundi, Les Nouvelles Recreations* was reprinted more than twenty times during the sixteenth and seventeenth centuries and also provides significant insight into sixteenth-century literary France. The author rejected the Boccaccian frame story structure that Marguerite had chosen, preferring instead the looser collection of tales from the French popular tradition. The strong narrative voice and the frequent apostrophes to the implied readers, however, reconstitute a different kind of frame, one in which the narrator and the implied readers bring attention to certain characteristics commonly associated with prose fiction and debate their importance to the reading experience. The relationship established by the narrator with his imagined readers thus elucidates expectations sixteenth-century readers had of the *nouvelle* genre.

The narrator of *Les Nouvelles Recreations* systematically evokes elements common to prefaces of sixteenth-century *nouvelle* collections only ultimately to discard them. He refers, for example, to the different implications of the term *nouvelle.* But whereas other narrators claim that their stories are both historically true and contemporary as well as newly recorded in written form, Des Périers's narrator makes light of all these concerns, suggesting that his stories comply with none of them. Furthermore, he assumes an ambivalent position on the worthiness of his stories for the purpose of the edification of his readers, another typical claim on the part of sixteenth-century narrators. Lionello Sozzi suggests that the narrator of *Les Nouvelles Recreations,* in fact, reflects the agenda of the sixteenth-century French *nouvelle* authors who, far from adhering to the literary formalism of their narrators, were attempting to redefine their type of fiction and to free themselves from the constraints of older narrative forms. By flaunting each of the anticipated expectations of the reader of *nouvelles,* Des Périers's narrator simultaneously defines the *nouvelle* genre and defies any type of imposed formalism, proposing instead a new contract with the implied readers of fiction.

In his two-volume work *Sources and Analogues of the Nouvelles Récréations et Joyeux Devis of Bonaventure des Périers* (1957, 1969), James Woodrow Hassell Jr. finds traces of the fifteenth-century Italian writer of facetiae, Poggio, and references to the Italian Renaissance best-

seller, Baldassare Castiglione's *Il Libro del Cortegiano (The Book of the Courtier),* but concludes that Des Périers was also strongly influenced by the French popular tradition. The author of *Les Nouvelles Recreations* constructed many of his stories around French proverbs or lines from traditional songs. *Les Nouvelles Recreations* thus provides a rare published source of sixteenth-century popular French language and culture.

The themes of the collection recall those of the *Cymbalum Mundi* and of *La Prognostication des Prognostications.* The laughable credulity of all humans, from pedantic men of the church to simplistic village women, constitutes the primary target of the *nouvelles.* Nor does the narrator spare his implied readers. They too are mocked for their desire for verifiable truths. The rhetorical verve of certain characters elicits admiration from the narrator and other characters but fails to protect its practitioners from falling prey to the verbal manipulation of others. As in the *Cymbalum Mundi,* animals are granted speech to comment both on the hubris of humans and the deceptive and frivolous nature of dialogue itself.

The literary importance of *Les Nouvelles Recreations* has interested critics such as Gaston Paris and Becker less than the supposed historical realism of the tales. The introductions to many of the ninety *nouvelles* provide explicit historical references, and many of the characters are fifteenth- and sixteenth-century court or legal personalities. Unlike Marguerite's short stories, those attributed to Des Périers depict characters from a variety of socioprofessional groups and include dialogue that mimics regionalisms and professional idioms. The stories depict interactions between people of different classes and are set in intimate settings such as bedrooms or kitchens as well as in public settings such as courtrooms or in the streets.

Other critics of the *nouvelle* genre such as Sozzi, however, have warned against excessively literal readings of these stories. The pretense of presenting stories that were based on true and recent events is one of the literary devices that Des Périers's narrator highlights through his constant taunting of the implied readers. Many of the historical and geographical references that lend a sense of historicity to the *nouvelles* form part of the introduction to the individual *nouvelles* and do not prove central to the stories themselves. The events alluded to in some of these stories would appear to evoke events that occurred and people who lived after Des Périers's presumed death. For critics such as Paris these historical anachronisms throw into question the authenticity of Des Périers's authorship. Others, notably Charles Nodier and later, Sozzi, interpret these introductions as inconsequential to the stories themselves and therefore possibly later editorial additions irrelevant to determining authorship of the collection.

Like the two better-known writers who were influential in his life, Marguerite de Navarre and Clément Marot, Des Périers is credited with comic, secular works as well as writings of a deeply evangelical nature. The contrasting character and varied genres of his oeuvre suggest an attempt at assimilating diverse influences: a popular French tradition, classic and Italian literary models, contemporary religious debates, and an evolving French language as well as Latin and Italian. As a man of modest origins, Des Périers needed to be wary of religious censorship while trying to court patrons and write works for a growing readership. The preface to the *Cymbalum Mundi* reveals an author who consciously translated foreign models into a form of French literature that could be appreciated by many readers.

The limited information the modern reader has about Bonaventure des Périers and the requisite caution with which he wrote about religious matters render it impossible to determine his religious convictions. Nonetheless, the works attributed to him provide insight into other beliefs: moral and linguistic. Des Périers's writings depict a world of deception, presumption, and rivalry. Only an underlying sense of playfulness offsets this grim picture of human nature. Des Périers's most significant contributions lie in the treatment of the theme of language. *Les Nouvelles Recreations* uses discourse in innovative ways. Through his regionally and socially diverse settings and his characteristic use of proverbial language, Des Périers illustrates the richness of the sixteenth-century language before Joachim du Bellay published his famous *Deffence et Illustration de la langue francoyse* (1549, Defense and Illustration of the French Language). Besides its ability to connote in varied ways, language also interested Des Périers for its resistance to communication. His writings repeatedly address the themes of linguistic deception, miscommunication, verbal aggression, and the meaninglessness of words. His own words, in the form of his surviving texts, continue to defy facile interpretation to this day.

Biography:

Adolphe Chenevière, *Bonaventure Des Périers: sa vie, ses poésies* (Paris: Plon, 1886).

References:

Philipp Becker, *Bonaventure Des Périers als Dichter und Erzähler* (Vienna & Leipzig: Hölder-Pichler-Tempsky, 1924);

Wolfgang Boerner, *Das "Cymbalum Mundi" des Bonaventure des Périers: Eine Satire auf die Redepraxis im Zeitalter der Glaubenspielung* (Munich: Wilhelm Fink Verlag, 1980);

Lucien Febvre, "Une histoire obscure: la publication du *Cymbalum Mundi*," *Revue du seizième siècle,* 17 (1930): 1–41;

Félix Frank and Adolphe Chenevière, *Lexique de la langue de B. Des Périers* (Paris: L. Cerf, 1889);

Max Gauna, "The Cymbalum Mundi," in *Upwellings: First Expressions of Unbelief in the Printed Literature of the French Renaissance* (Rutherford, N.J.: Fairleigh Dickinson University Press, 1992), pp. 108–204;

Franco Giacone, ed., *Le Cymbalum Mundi: Actes du Colloque de Rome (3–6 novembre 2000)* (Geneva: Droz, 2003);

James Woodrow Hassell Jr., *Sources and Analogues of the Nouvelles Récréations et Joyeux Devis of Bonaventure des Périers,* 2 volumes (volume 1, Chapel Hill: University of North Carolina Press, 1957; volume 2, Athens: University of Georgia Press, 1969);

Eloi Johanneau, "Clef du Cymbalum Mundi," in *Le Cymbalum Mundi, et autres oeuvres* (Paris: C. Gosselin, 1841);

Charles Nodier, *Bonaventure Desperiers. Cirano de Bergerac* (Paris: Techener, 1841);

Trevor Peach, "*The Cymbalum Mundi:* An Author in Anagram," *French Studies Bulletin: A Quarterly Supplement,* 82 (2002): 2–4;

V.-L. Saulnier, "Le sens du *Cymbalum Mundi*," *Bibliothèque d'humanisme et renaissance,* 13 (1951): 42–69, 137–171;

Michael A. Screech, preface to *Cymbalum Mundi,* edited by Peter Hampshire Nurse (Geneva: Droz, 1983), pp. 3–17;

Malcolm Smith, "A Sixteenth-Century Anti-Theist," *Bibliothèque d'humanisme et renaissance,* 53 (1991): 593–618;

Lionello Sozzi, *Les Contes de Bonaventure Des Périers* (Turin: G. Giappichelli, 1964).

Philippe Desportes
(1546 – 1606)

Russell Ganim
University of Nebraska–Lincoln

BOOKS: *Imitations de quelques chansons de l'Arioste,* by Desportes, Mellin de Saint-Gelais, Antoine de Baïf, and others (Paris: Lucas Breyer, 1572);

Les Premieres Œuvres de Philippes Des Portes (Paris: Robert Estienne, 1573; revised and enlarged, Paris: Mamert Patisson, imprimeur du Roy, au logis de Robert Estienne, 1583); enlarged as *Les Œuvres de Phillipes Des Portes* (Paris: Mamert Patisson, 1600);

Soixante psaumes de David (Rouen: Raphael Du Petit Val, 1591); enlarged as *Les CL Pseaumes de David, mis en vers français par Ph. Des-Portes Abbé de Thiron* (Paris: A. L'Angelier, 1603).

Editions: *Les Premieres Œuvres de Philippes Des Portes. Au Roy de France et de Pologne. Reveues, corrigees et augmentees outré les precedents impressions* (Lyon: Benoist La Caille, 1615);

Œuvres choisies dans Annales poétiques, ou Almanach des Muses depuis l'origine de la poésie françoise, volume 11 (Paris: Delalain, 1779);

Œuvres choisies de Desportes, Bertaut, et Reginer, edited by M. Pellissier (Paris: Firmin Dodot, 1823);

Œuvres de Philippe Desportes, edited by Alfred Michiels (Paris: Adolphe Delahays, 1858);

Cartels et Masquarades, Epitaphes, edited by Victor E. Graham (Geneva: Droz, 1958);

Les Amours de Diane, 2 volumes, edited by Graham (Geneva: Droz, 1959);

Les Amours d'Hippolyte, edited by Graham (Geneva: Droz, 1960);

Elégies, edited by Graham (Geneva: Droz, 1961);

Cléonice, Dernières Amours, edited by Graham (Geneva: Droz, 1962);

Diverses Amours et Autres Œuvres Meslées, edited by Graham (Geneva: Droz, 1963).

As a poet and courtier in the service of three kings, Philippe Desportes enjoyed one of the most varied careers among literary figures of the French Renaissance. Not the most gifted poet of his age, Desportes nonetheless made the most of his talent and political connections to become one of the most noted authors

Philippe Desportes (from <http://gallica.bnf.fr/themes/LitXVII.htm>)

of the late sixteenth and early seventeenth centuries. Known for both his secular and religious poetry, Desportes's work illustrated many of the main currents of lyric poetry in his era.

Desportes was born in Chartres in 1546 to a wealthy bourgeois family. His father, Philippe, and mother, Marie Edeline, made their fortunes as clothing merchants. His mother's family also had strong ties to civil administration. Desportes received a rigorous classical education at the Cathedral school in Chartres and

123

was tonsured at a relatively early age. He was well versed in Latin, Greek, Italian, Hebrew, philosophy, and theology. In 1564 Desportes went to Paris to pursue an ecclesiastical career and came under the protection of Antoine de Senecterre, Bishop of Puy. The bishop named Desportes his secretary and took him to Rome for three years. During this stay in Rome, Desportes became familiar with Italian language and culture, steeping himself in the lyric of Ariosto and Petrarch as well as the courtly manners of Castiglione. These figures, as well as the general influence of Medici Renaissance culture, played a large role in shaping the poet's artistic endeavors.

Upon his return to Paris in 1567, Desportes applied what he had learned of art and politics in Italy to the court of King Charles IX in France. He began a deep friendship with the influential Claude de Laubespine, who was soon to inherit the title of "Secrétiare d'Etat" (Secretary of State) from his father. The intense relationship lasted only three years because of Laubespine's death. His friend's passing provided significant artistic inspiration for a few sonnets and other lyric offerings. Equally important was Desportes's alliance with Laubespine's sister, Madeleine de Villeroy. While some critics insist that the relationship was platonic, most believe that the two became lovers. Whether or not she was his lover, Madame de Villeroy was the subject of dozens of Desportes's secular love poems. Through the Laubespines the poet was able to penetrate the highest echelons of court society. During the late 1560s Desportes ingratiated himself with the king's brother, the duke of Anjou, who later became Henri III.

At the time Desportes met Duke Henri, Pierre de Ronsard—the leading poet of the Pléiade—was firmly ensconced as Charles IX's royal poet. Desportes, however, was confident he could make a name for himself with the right combination of skill and luck because the lyric and the arts in general were flourishing under the Valois dynasty. Like other poets of the day, Desportes became the lyric spokesperson for important noblemen wanting to impress current or potential mistresses. In addition to the future monarch, among those availing themselves of Desportes's services were luminaries such as Pierre de Brantôme and Bussy d'Amboise. Though such verse—Desportes's and others'—is often perceived as flat and impersonal, it nonetheless is indicative of a key aspect of the role of poetry in society during this era.

Desportes's literary and social reputation advanced a step further when he became a favorite at the salon of the Maréchale de Retz. Her salon, considered to be the most respected in France during the late Renaissance, became a haven to poets such as Desportes,

Pontus de Tyard (also a member of the Pléiade), and Amadis Jamyn. These poets were trained in the Petrarchan tradition, in which the poet celebrated his lady but saw her as distant, silent, and unmoved by his declarations. Love was to be avowed but remained as chaste as it was intense. The only consolation for the long-suffering poet was to seek a kind of Platonistic transcendence in which physical desire was transposed to a divine plane. Love for a woman transformed into love for God, the incarnation of real beauty and perfection.

Desportes's reputation as a poet grew, and in 1572 he published his *Imitations de quelques chansons de l'Arioste* (Imitations of Some Songs of Ariosto), a volume that included the work of selected poets. Desportes's contribution is part translation, part paraphrase, and part free adaptation of Ariosto's *Orlando Furioso,* first published in 1516. A lyric epic that combines the legends of Arthur and Charlemagne, Desportes's text is noted for three major poems: "Roland Furieux" (known also in English as *Orlando Furioso*), "La Mort de Rodomont" (The Death of Rodomont), and "Angélique" (Angelica). Both Ariosto and Desportes portray Roland—the noble knight of the twelfth-century poem *La Chanson de Roland* (The Song of Roland)—as a character in conflict between his duties as a Christian knight and his passion for a woman, Angelica. What Desportes adds to the portrayal of Roland is a psychological depth that underscores the moral ambiguity of his character while questioning the codes of conduct upon which medieval chivalry is based. "La Mort de Rodomont" and "Angélique" stand out for their depiction of the clash between the Christian and Muslim cultures. Rodomont, the king of Algiers, is known as the "Mars of Africa" who helps lay siege to Paris. His defeat and subsequent descent into hell reinforce the triumph of the Western worldview in the face of a pagan threat. In the battle between East and West, Angélique, the princess of Cathay, represents the temptations of the Orient. Roland falls desperately in love with her, only to have Angélique reject him for Medoro, a Moor solider from the lowest ranks of society. Muslim civilization thus represents a danger to be confronted on both a military and emotional level.

Desportes's contribution in *Imitations de quelques chansons de l'Arioste* consists not only of amplifying the psychological, moral, and cultural dimensions of the Roland saga, but also in establishing a "classical" sense of clarity and coherence with respect to language, structure, and style. In addition, Desportes sanitizes certain passages in Ariosto in order to render the erotic aspects of the epic less passionate. Consequently, one sees in Desportes a kind of *bienséance* (decorum) that was to define neoclassical French literature well into the seventeenth century.

In 1573 Desportes published *Les Premières Œuvres* (First Works), dedicating it to the duke of Anjou. Allusions to Greek and Latin mythology abound, especially in this first edition of *Les Premières Œuvres,* which primarily consists of two books titled "Amours de Diane" (Loves of Diane) and "Amours d'Hippolyte" (Loves of Hippolyta*)*. Both books were addressed to Marguerite de Valois–the infamous Queen Margot–the first wife of Henri de Navarre. Diane was the Roman equivalent of Artemis, the goddess of the hunt, while Hippolyta bore the title of queen of the Amazons. The theme of the hunt figures prominently in both texts, and the poet depicts himself as a lover inescapably tormented by both the beloved and by the personified god of love. In typical Petrarchan fashion, the beloved is impenetrable, with the poet/lover languishing in silence, his agony deepened by the cruelty of the gods who impose the affliction of desire upon him. Grief and despair often dominate the work as the poet's distress causes a reversal of his world where "La nuict es mon soleil, le discord est ma pais" (The night is my sunlight, discord is my peace). Frequently, the poet compares himself to the Greek figure of Icarus, thereby emphasizing the tragedy of his aspirations. In many cases, however, the anguish is attenuated by either strong countervailing images of human or natural beauty or by a sense of irony that evokes a kind of grace or even glory in suffering. Moreover, the delicate balance of pain and loveliness lends an elegance to the story that underscores Desportes's deftness, if not his originality, as a poet.

Of note is the fact that the *privilège,* or royal authorization for publication, for *Les Premières Œuvres* identifies Desportes as the "Secrétaire de la chambre du Roi" (Secretary of the Royal Chamber). While Desportes had not displaced Ronsard as the "poète des princes" (poet of princes), the leader of the Pléiade did start to view Desportes as a rival. However, just as Desportes began to make a name for himself in Paris, his protector was summoned by the Polish Diet to assume that country's throne. The poet accompanied Henri to Poland and stayed with him during what was a short but difficult reign in eastern Europe. Henri's return to France in 1574 was necessitated by the death of his brother Charles IX. The third son of Henri II then became the third Henri to rule the country.

Although the historical view of Henri III has been mixed because of the Wars of Religion as well as his presumed personal indiscretions, there can be no doubt as to his support of humanist endeavors. The son of Catherine de Médicis, Henri III continued the tradition of Valois patronage begun by his grandfather François I and his father, Henri II. Academies flour-

TEXTES LITTÉRAIRES FRANÇAIS

PHILIPPE DESPORTES

ÉLÉGIES

Edition critique
suivie du Commentaire de Malherbe
publiée par
VICTOR E. GRAHAM

GENÈVE
LIBRAIRIE DROZ
8, Rue Verdaine

PARIS
LIBRAIRIE MINARD
73, Rue Cardinal Lemoine

1961

Title page for one of several critical editions of Desportes's works edited by scholar Victor E. Graham (Thomas Cooper Library, University of South Carolina)

ished during his reign, and intellectual and artistic activity dominated much of the court's agenda. Under Henri's patronage, *Les Premières Œuvres* was reedited and republished on various occasions. The most notable example is the 1583 edition that included collections titled "Elégies" (Elegies), "Meslanges" (Miscellany), "Diverses Amours" (Various Loves), as well as "Dernières Amours" (Last Loves), of which the "Amours de Cléonice" (Loves of Cléonice) are the best known. The "Meslanges" include Desportes's "Bergeries" (Pastoral Poems) that were modeled in part after the Pléiade poet Rémy Belleau's *La Bergerie* (1565–1572, The Shepherd's Song). While Desportes's work is often not as bold or as imaginative as that of the Pléiade poets, his poetry does show a technical skill and subtlety that indirectly advances the Pléiade philosophy that the French language should be considered the artistic rival of classical Greek and Latin.

Although Desportes wrote in various genres—elegies, stanzas, ballads, epitaphs, and "dialogues"—the sonnet is his preferred mode of expression. By and large, the sonnets are intended to be read as discrete units rather than as part of a narrative sequence. At the same time, there is a continuity between the sonnets, not simply through variations on the theme of desperate love but through the interrogative style of a personable narrator with whom the reader comes to identify. Desportes is able to express the loss of self with a pathos and nostalgia that strike the reader's own sense of vulnerability.

With Henri III's assistance, Desportes's prominence increased, and upon Ronsard's death in 1585, he was officially recognized as the court's chief poet. He came into possession of several Church holdings, among them the Abbey of Tiron. (In later years Desportes went by the title Abbot of Tiron.) With his newly acquired wealth, the poet himself became a benefactor, extending protection to the convert Jacques Davy Du Perron as well as to his nephew, the satirist Maturin Régnier. His followers also included several religious poets called the "Louvre poets," whose members included Guy le Fèvre de la Boderie, Joachim Blanchon, Guillaume Du Peyrat, and Isaac Habert. Given the political troubles in France, however, stability was far from assured, and with Henri III's assassination in August 1589, Desportes temporarily allied with the Catholic League before reconciling with the crown under the new Bourbon king Henri IV, formerly Henri de Navarre. Among other things, Desportes acted as intermediary for the new king in settling religious disputes. In return the monarch rewarded the poet by conferring upon him a luxurious retreat in Vanves as well as an additional abbey in Bonport. As Desportes turned to religious poetry later in life, he played host to devotional poets at these sites.

In 1591 Desportes published his first religious work, *Soixante psaumes de David* (Sixty Psalms of David), a book mainly of psalm paraphrases. For several years afterward, more religious lyric appeared. In 1600 the *Cent pseaumes de David* (One Hundred Psalms of David) was published, followed by the *CL Pseaumes de David, mis en vers français* (One Hundred Fifty Psalms of David, Put into French Verse) in 1603. Desportes's "Prieres et meditations chrestiennes" (Christian Prayers and Meditations) were included in the *CL Pseaumes* and mark the culmination of his devotional efforts. To an extent, the questions of weakness and doubt raised in Desportes's secular poetry find an answer in the devotional works that dominated the latter part of his career, but for the most part, his religious poems represent a break with his secular beginnings.

Desportes's complete turn toward the religious adds an intriguing dimension to his work. One might argue that his move to the devotional is hardly surprising given his ecclesiastical background and the tendency of secular poets to compose devotional works, sometimes announcing a "conversion" in which they renounced their former work in favor of their latter. He may, too, have had practical reasons to reinvent himself artistically. With the civil and spiritual battles of his time, religious poetry—both Catholic and Protestant—came into vogue. Clearly a man adept at gauging the trends of his era, Desportes no doubt wanted to make his contribution to the Catholic revival that helped shape the French Baroque. Also, it is a distinct possibility that criticism of Desportes's secular writings as *précieux* (precious) or even banal prompted him to compose works that would be read more seriously by the literate public.

Whatever his motivation, Desportes wrote sonnets, prayers, and paraphrases of the psalms that give a rich portrait of a poet/meditant trying to find God's grace, though his poetic and spiritual zeal does not often match that of contemporaries such as Claude Chappuys, Antoine Favre, or Jean-Baptiste Chassignet. Much of Desportes's religious lyric falls under the rubric of the *vanitas* or penitential traditions in which the poet shamefully admits the vanity of his sins and asks for God's absolution. As in his secular poetry, Desportes's narrator is racked by doubt, guilt, and desperation. At times the depiction of God resembles that of the unyielding lady in that Desportes portrays a cold, angry Old Testament deity not inclined to dispense favor upon a wayward mortal. Yet, the distant, if not vengeful, God is tempered by the poet's depiction of Christ. Desportes's interpretation of the New Testament focuses on the Passion and its redemptive power. Like many other poets, Desportes internalizes Christ's suffering and derives from it both poetic and spiritual inspiration. Undergoing a contemplative examination himself, he encourages self-examination in the reader, thereby linking the literary and devotional processes.

While it would be inaccurate to call Desportes's meditative peregrinations superficial, his religious poetry does not often contain the analytical dimension of other noted texts of the same epoch. Largely absent is the extended theological debate and biblical exegesis that characterizes the work of a poet such as Jean de la Ceppède. Many of Desportes's biblically related themes and motifs are commonplaces readily identifiable to the general public and are not expounded upon at any great length. If one agrees that devotional poetry is organized in a tripartite structure consisting of description, interpretation, and prayer, then Desportes's work frequently seems to skip the middle phase. While

Desportes conveys a wide range of imagery and feeling, the imbalance between the intellectual and affective components of his work leaves a gap that the readers may close either by consulting other poets or by contemplation of their own.

The final indication of Desportes's success is illustrated by Henri IV's desire that he oversee the education of the Dauphin, the future Louis XIII. However, Desportes's death at Bonport in 1606 precluded this plan. Because of the influence he achieved in royal circles, Desportes had many detractors who saw him more as an opportunist than as a bonafide poet.

Desportes's poetry cannot be read outside the context of his life, and the question of how to judge his corpus remains a difficult one. Within the chronology of the Renaissance lyric, Desportes occupies a middle space between Ronsard and François de Malherbe, who both acknowledged Desportes's contributions but also saw him as a threat. Malherbe took an especially adversarial posture toward Desportes. He is reputed to have insulted Desportes while having dinner at the poet's home, and his hostile commentaries on Desportes's poetry are often considered the points of departure for what were to become the stylistic guidelines for French neoclassical poetry and prose. From a general standpoint, however, what one repeatedly sees in both Desportes's secular and religious lyrics are clever juxtapositions of seemingly contradictory images and themes as well as a vivid depiction of personal experience and the role of poetry in rendering that experience more intense.

Though Philippe Desportes's legacy is mixed, he was an important figure. He influenced not only French poets of his era but also Elizabethan writers such as Henry Constable, William Drummond, Thomas Lodge, and Sir Walter Ralegh. In addition, contemporary scholars have expressed an increasingly favorable view of Desportes, suggesting that in the future the poet's status will continue to rise and that his work will merit further close attention.

References:

Wendy Ayres-Bennett, "From Malherbe to the French Academy on Quinte Circe," *Seventeenth-Century French Studies,* 19 (1999): 1–9;

Jean Balsamo, *Philippe Desportes, 1546–1606: Un poète presque parfait entre Renaissance et classicisme* (Paris: Klincksieck, 2000);

Yvonne Bellenger, "Rupture dans la poésie française de la fin du XVIe siècle: l'example de Desportes," in *Tourments, doutes et ruptures dans l'Europe des XVIe et XVIIe siècles,* edited by Claude Arnould and Pierre Demarolle (Paris: Champion, 1995), pp. 95–105;

Ferdinand Brunot, *La Doctrine de Malherbe* (Paris: Librairie Picard, 1891);

Robert M. Burgess, *Platonism in Desportes* (Chapel Hill: University of North Carolina Press, 1954);

Terence Cave, "Desportes and Maynard: Two Studies in the Poetry of Wit," in *The Equilibrium of Wit: Essays for Odette de Mourgues,* edited by Peter Bayley and Dorothy Gabe Coleman (Lexington, Ky.: French Forum), pp. 86–94;

Cave, *Devotional Poetry in France c. 1570–1613* (Cambridge: Cambridge University Press, 1969);

Paul A. Chilton, *The Poetry of Jean de La Ceppède: A Study in Text and Context* (Oxford: Oxford University Press, 1977);

Jonathan Gibson, "French and Italian Sources for Ralegh's, 'Farewell False Love,'" *Review of English Studies,* 50 (1999): 155–165;

Jacques Lavaud, *Les Imitations de l'Arioste* (Paris: Droz, 1936);

Lavaud, *Philippe Desportes (1546–1606): Un poète au temps des derniers Valois* (Paris: Droz, 1936);

François de Malherbe, *Commentaire sur Desportes,* edited by Arthur Sideleau (Montreal: Editions Chantecler, 1950);

Susan K. Silver, "'And the Word Became Flesh,' Cannibalism and Religious Polemic in the Poetry of Desportes and d'Aubigné," *Renaissance and Reformation/Renaissance et Réforme,* 24 (2000): 45–56;

Rosalind Smith, "The Sonnets of the Countess of Oxford and Elizabeth I: Trans-Lations from Desportes," *Notes and Queries,* 41 (1994): 446–450;

Frank Warnke, *European Metaphysical Poetry* (New Haven & London: Yale University Press, 1961).

Papers:

The vast majority of Philippe Desportes's manuscripts and papers are in the Bibliothèque Nationale de France (National Library of France) in Paris.

Madeleine des Roches

(1520?– November 1587?)

and

Catherine des Roches

(December 1542–November 1587?)

Anne R. Larsen
Hope College

BOOKS: *Histoire et Amours pastoralles de Daphnis et de Chloe escrite premierement en grec par Longus et maintenant mise en françois. Ensemble un debat judiciel de Folie et d'Amour, fait par dame L. L. L. (Loyse Labé Lyonnoise). Plus quelques vers françois, lesquels ne sont pas moins plaisans que recreatifs, par M.D.R., Poictevine (Madame des Roches)* (Paris: Jean Parent, 1578);

Les Oeuvres de Mes-dames des Roches de Poetiers, Mere et Fille (Paris: Abel l'Angelier, 1578); enlarged as *Les Oeuvres de Mes-dames des Roches de Poetiers, Mere et Fille. Seconde edition, corrigée et augmentée de la Tragi-comedie de Tobie et autres œuvres poëtiques* (Paris: Abel l'Angelier, 1579);

La Puce de Madame des Roches. Qui est un recueil de divers poemes Grecs, Latins et François, composez par plusieurs doctes personnages aux Grands Jours tenus à Poitiers l'an M.D.LXXIX, by the Dames des Roches, Estienne Pasquier, and others (Paris: Abel l'Angelier, 1582; enlarged, 1583);

Les Secondes œuvres de Mes-dames des Roches de Poictiers, Mere et Fille (Poitiers: Nicolas Courtoys, 1583);

Les Missives de Mes-dames des Roches de Poitiers, Mere et Fille, avec le ravissement de Proserpine prins du Latin de Clodian. Et autres imitations et meslanges poëtiques (Paris: Abel l'Angelier, 1586).

Editions: *Les Premieres œuvres de Mes-dames des Roches de Poitiers, Mere et Fille, corrigées et augmentées de six dialogues. Avec une Tragicomedie de Tobie et autres œuvres poëtiques. Troisieme edition* (Rouen: Nicolas Hamillon, 1604);

Les Secondes œuvres de Mes-dames des Roches de Poitiers, Mere et Fille, corrigées et augmentées de deux dialogues: le premier traicte de Placide et Severe, le deuxiesme traicte d'Iris et Pasithée, avec la Puce et la chanson de Sincero, et de Charite. Troisieme edition (Rouen: Nicolas Hamillon, 1604);

Les Oeuvres, edited by Anne R. Larsen (Geneva: Droz, 1993);

Les Secondes œuvres, edited by Larsen (Geneva: Droz, 1998);

Les Missives, edited by Larsen (Geneva: Droz, 1999).

Edition in English: *From Mother and Daughter: Poems, Dialogues, and Letters of Les Dames Des Roches,* translated by Anne R. Larsen (Chicago: University of Chicago Press, 2006).

Madeleine des Roches and her daughter Catherine des Roches rank among the most prolific French women writers of the sixteenth century. Celebrated for their learning and for their collaborative mother-daughter bond, they distinguished themselves as well for boldly asserting women's right to *auctoritas* (authority) in the realm of belles lettres. The Dames des Roches, as they were commonly called, took pride in counting themselves among the few published women of their time. Their literary coterie, among the first in France, paved the way for the flowering of the salon in the next century. Catherine's deliberate refusal to marry, so as to continue writing and publishing with her mother, inspired future women writers such as Madeleine de Scudéry.

Little is known of Madeleine des Roches's birth and early life. Born Madeleine Neveu into a bourgeois family of notaries in about 1520, she inherited the name Des Roches from a family property some seven kilometers east of Châtellerault. She was married twice. André Fradonnet, whom she married in 1539, was a public prosecutor and the father of her three children: Nicolles, baptized on 17 March 1540; Catherine, baptized on 15 December 1542; and Lucrèce, baptized on 22 October 1547. Only Catherine survived infancy. After the death of André Fradonnet in 1547, Madeleine married François Eboissard, seigneur de la Villée, in 1550. An appeals-court lawyer originally from Brittany, Eboissard had a distinguished career and a good income; he was elected to the council at Poitiers's city hall, where he participated in the "Mois et Cent," a municipal council consisting of seventy-five councilmen and twenty-five aldermen. Upon his death from an upper respiratory disease during the summer of 1578, Des Roches wrote an epitaph lauding his nobility, learning, and love for her. Their marriage, founded upon mutual respect and a deep friendship, was unusual for the time.

Madeleine des Roches's education is a matter of speculation. She was probably a studious young woman, for in ode 1 of *Les Oeuvres de Mes-dames des Roches de Poetiers, Mere et Fille* (1578, The Works of Mesdames des Roches of Poitiers, Mother and Daughter), she admits that she had to cut short her studies once she married. According to the humanist scholar Joseph-Juste Scaliger in his *Prima Scaligerana* (1595, First Collection of Items by Scaliger), she was a Latinist. She probably continued learning in her spare time by making use of private libraries, including the library of her erudite husband Eboissard. In his study of Parisian private libraries, *Vernacular Books in Parisian Private Libraries of the Sixteenth Century* (1955), A. H. Schutz indicates that more than half of the 220 libraries he documented belonged to lawyers and parliamentarians. In the libraries likely open to her, Des Roches would have had ready access not only to legal works but also to the Church Fathers and translations of the Bible, humanists such as Desiderius Erasmus, Giovanni Boccacio, Petrarch, and Ludovico Ariosto, Plato's works as interpreted by Marsilio Ficino and Pico della Mirandola, historians such as Herodotus, Sallust, and Suetonius, as well as poets such as Hesiod, Horace, Ovid, and Hyginus. The Dames des Roches demonstrate ample knowledge of these texts.

While mothers in the sixteenth century were charged with the care of infants and the young, in directing Catherine's education Madeleine went much further than the majority of mothers of her social class. She inspired her daughter to follow the lead of well-known Italian learned women who aspired to fame and literary immortality. In her prefatory letter to Catherine that opens *Les Oeuvres,* Madeleine urges her daughter to "faire ton devoir / Envers la Muse et le divin sçavoir" (do your duty / Toward the Muse and divine learning) so that "Tu sois un jour par vertu immortelle, / Je t'ay tousjours souhaitée estre telle" (You may some day become immortal through your virtue, / It is thus that I have always wanted you to be). Catherine likely had private tutors in several languages. She mastered Latin, even translating two complete Latin classical texts that

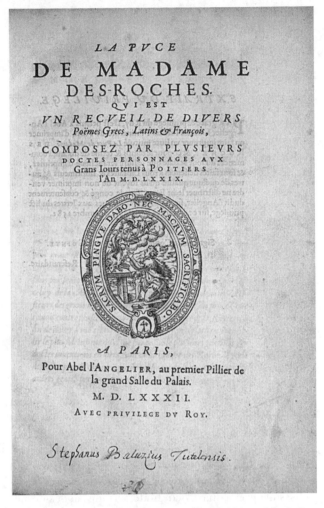

Title page for the book of witty, punning verse by Madeleine and Catherine des Roches and others that was inspired by the sighting of a flea on Catherine des Roches's bosom (Douglas H. Gordon Collection, University of Virginia Library)

had never been translated into French, Pythagoras's *Symbola* (Symbols) in *Les Secondes œuvres de Mes-dames des Roches de Poetiers, Mere et Fille* (1583, Second Works of Mesdames des Roches of Poitiers, Mother and Daughter), and Claudian's *De raptu Proserpinae* (On the Rape of Proserpina) in *Les Missives de Mes-dames des Roches de Poetiers, Mere et Fille* (1586, Missives of Mesdames des Roches of Poitiers, Mother and Daughter).

From 1560 to 1570 the Dames des Roches had legal and financial problems. Madeleine refers four times in *Les Œuvres* to a thirteen-year lawsuit and in *Les Missives* to legal wrangling on other occasions. To these concerns were added the ransacking of Poitiers by Protestant troupes in May 1562 and the siege of the city in 1569 by Admiral Gaspard de Coligny's Protestant army that led to the destruction of two of her town houses on the outskirts of the city. Madeleine's outspoken poem to King Henri III in which she requests an indemnity for her properties that "pouvoient bien valoir deux mille livres, / Plus que ne m'ont valu ma plume ny mes livres" (may well have been worth two thousand pounds, / More than the worth of my pen and my books combined) finally bore fruit years later in February 1587. Another striking piece written during this period, Madeleine's ode 8 in *Les Oeuvres,* gives a dramatic account of the 1569 siege of Poitiers that highlights incidents and heroic feats also described by historians Marin Liberge, François de La Noue, Lancelot de La Popelinière, and Agrippa d'Aubigné. Her epitaph on the death of Timoléon de Cossé, count of Brissac and a favorite at the court, who was killed at the age of twenty-six at the siege of Mussidan in Périgord in 1569, attained a certain fame since it was included in a court manuscript collection.

The Dames des Roches's publications first appeared in the 1570s when they were establishing their literary coterie. In 1571 Caye-Jules de Guersens, a distinguished member of their salon and a suitor of Catherine, published the play *Panthée* that he dedicated to Catherine in the hope of marrying her. The mathematician and musician Claude Pellejay, another suitor of Catherine, dedicated to her love sonnets and a "Hymne de la Beauté" (Hymn to Beauty). Catherine's sonnet sequence "Sonets de Sincero à Charite" (Sonnets from Sincero to Charite) and "De Charite à Sincero" (From Charite to Sincero), as well as her "Dialogue de Sincero, et de Charite" (Dialogue of Sincero and Charite), can be dated to this salon romance. Catherine refused Pellejay's suit, preferring to continue writing alongside her mother.

In 1574 Catherine wrote an ode, "Au Roy" (To the King), to Henri III, who, on his return to court on 30 May from a brief sojourn in Poland, was crowned king following the death of his brother Charles IX. Scévole de Sainte-Marthe and Scaliger translated this ode, the former into Latin in 1575 and the latter into Greek. In this striking ode belonging to the genre of the advice manual or the "miroir des princes" (mirrors for princes), Catherine reminds the king of his duties and praises him for his filial devotion to Queen Mother Catherine de Médicis. By participating in the flurry of publications lauding the newly appointed king, Catherine expressed her desire to become better known among literary circles in the capital.

In 1577 Poitiers hosted the ambulatory royal court for three months, from 2 July to 5 October, to enable Henri III to negotiate the Peace of Bergerac, marking a temporary truce to the hostilities between the Catholic and Protestant armies. Catherine wrote at that time several sonnets in honor of the king; "Hymne de l'Eau à la Roine" (Water Hymn to the Queen) in honor of Queen Louise of Lorraine; and "Imitation de la mere de Salomon" (An Imitation of the Mother of Solomon), addressed to Queen Mother Catherine de Médicis. Madeleine, for her part, wrote a sonnet in honor of the Queen Mother that found its way into an elegant court manuscript. Catherine might also have then composed "Pour une Mascarade des Amazones" (For a Mascarade of the Amazons) and her "Chanson des Amazones" (Song of the Amazons) in memory of court entertainments favored by Henri III. These two poems by Catherine des Roches celebrate the defiance of the mythical Amazons who refused to submit to love and male control of their lives.

These and other poems were collected in 1578 in *Les Oeuvres de Mes-dames des Roches de Poetiers, Mere et Fille,* which the Dames des Roches elected to publish in Paris rather than their native Poitiers. Abel l'Angelier, a rising star in the Parisian book market, likely contacted them first. Their manuscript works were known among the king's entourage and in Parisian literary society; an early version of Catherine's "Hymne de l'Eau à la Roine" had appeared earlier in 1578 in *Histoire et Amours pastoralles de Daphnis et de Chloe escrite premierement en grec par Longus et maintenant mise en françois* (The Story and Pastoral Loves of Daphne and Chloe first written in Greek by Longus and now put into French), a volume that included a translation of Longus's *Daphne and Chloe* and Louise Labé's *Débat de Folie et d'Amour* (Debate of Folly and Love).

Les Oeuvres de Mes-dames des Roches de Poetiers, Mere et Fille is made up of two sections, one including the mother's works prefaced by a dedicatory epistle to her daughter, the other her daughter's prefaced by a dedicatory epistle to her mother. This pattern is repeated in each subsequent published volume, thereby emphasizing their devotion to each other and the collaborative nature of their works. This strategy of dedicating their writings to each other invokes the convention of the female "chaperon" so frequently seen in works by Renaissance women as a cautionary way to protect their reputation. Madeleine's part includes nine odes, thirty-six sonnets, and epitaphs to her deceased husband Eboissard, the count of Brissac, and to the baron of Anguervaques. Catherine chose for her portion six dialogues; a sonnet sequence of twenty-six poems exchanged between Sincero to Charite as well as several songs and a blazon concerning the couple; the two poems on the Amazons; the sonnets "A ma quenouille" (To My Distaff) and "A mes escrits" (To My Writings); "Chanson de la musique" (Song of Music); poems written for the king's entourage; "La Femme Forte descrite par Salomon" (The Strong Woman described by Solomon), a paraphrase of the Song of the Valiant Woman in Proverbs 31 that Catherine dedicates to her mother; "L'Agnodice" (Agnodice); and epitaphs translated from the Italian for Medea, Clytemnestra, Lucretia, and Niobe.

This first volume was soon followed in 1579 by a second edition that added more sonnets, Madeleine's request for an indemnity from the king for her two destroyed town houses, and Catherine's "Un acte de la tragicomedie de Tobie" (One act of the Tragicomedy of Tobias). In her preface "Aux Dames" (To the Ladies) to both the 1578 and the 1579 editions, Madeleine des Roches appeals for the patronage of two different groups of women readers: the first group consists of Parisian women possibly contemptuous of this provincial mother-daughter team seeking fame in the capital; the second consists of more lowly and disapproving Poitevine bourgeoises who admonish their peers to remain "silent" and not meddle with publishing. "Le silence," Madeleine reminds them, "peut couvrir les fautes de la langue et de l'entendement, . . . il peut bien empescher la honte, mais non pas accroistre l'honneur, aussi que le parler nous separe des animaux sans raison" (silence can cover errors of the tongue and of understanding, . . . it may well prevent shame but cannot increase honor, and speech distinguishes us from the reasonless beasts).

The Dames des Roches's informal coterie acquired prestige when from 10 September to 18 December 1579, the "grands jours," or assizes, brought to Poitiers influential jurists from the Paris Parlement commissioned by the king to relieve the congestion of the local courts caused by property damages resulting from the civil wars. Upon their arrival, two of these legists, Etienne Pasquier and Antoine Loisel, headed for the Des Roches's home. Their conversation with the Des Roches produced one of the best-known episodes in social literary history. Pasquier, upon sighting a flea on Catherine's bosom, suggested a contest of versified wit. No sooner had both complied than some of the Parisian legists and local habitués of the salon began to produce innumerable blazons punning in Latin, Greek, French, Spanish, and Italian on the peregrinations of the "puce" (flea) over the body of the fair "pucelle" (maiden). These poems were later collected and published by Abel l'Angelier in a ninety-three–folio collection *La Puce de Madame des Roches* (The Flea of Madame des Roches) in 1582, enlarged in 1583.

Catherine des Roches's nine poems or "responses" included in the collaborative volume of *La Puce* (The Flea) appear, along with another seven of her responses on the flea, in *Les Secondes œuvres*. This volume was published in 1583 by Nicolas Courtoys, the newly appointed editor in chief for the University of Poitiers. Madeleine had asked l'Angelier to publish this second volume, but he refused, thinking perhaps that the collection was too focused on Poitiers. The volume includes many poems on the siege of Poitiers in 1569,

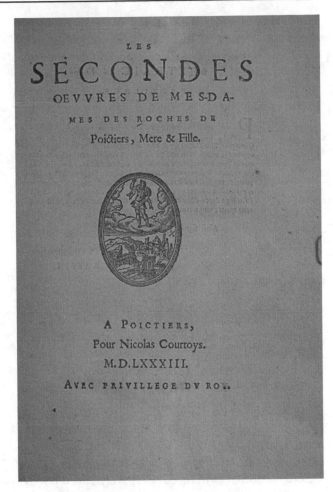

Title page for the second of three collections of poetry by the Dames des Roches (Douglas H. Gordon Collection, University of Virginia)

its "grands jours," and the flea contest. In her portion of the volume, Madeleine praises the guests of her salon, the city of Poitiers for its institutions and its resistance during the 1569 siege, and pleads with the king to reestablish a parliament in Poitiers. Catherine includes in her portion two pedagogical dialogues on the education of girls, translations of Pythagoras's "Vers dorez" (Golden Verse) and "Egnimes" (Symbols), epitaphs and sonnets, a pastoral drama, songs and blazons, and forty-six "Responses." In the first of the two dialogues, "Dialogue de Placide et Severe" (Dialogue of Placide and Severe), Placide, the father of a well-read daughter, converses with his neighbor Severe, the misogynist father of a flighty and ignorant daughter, on the merits of educating girls. Placide presents the educational views of Erasmus, Juan Luis Vives, and Thomas More, who defended female education as a means of transforming a young girl into a sweet-tempered wife and companion. Placide ends with a catalogue of ten exemplary women, five from antiquity and five from contemporary times, that patterns itself on the canonical ten Attic Orators. Then, rather than raising up the women worthies of the past, as in most compilations of the period, he emphasizes the contributions of Italian, Portuguese, and French intellectual women of the present, known not so much as wives and mothers but as the most learned women of their age. This list of luminaries reveals Catherine des Roches's pride in women who overcame marital and social obstacles to win renown for themselves.

In 1586 the Dames des Roches had their last work, *Les Missives,* published in Paris by l'Angelier. They were the first women in France to publish their private letters, rewritten for publication, to be sure. They adapted two epistolary conventions: the humanist letter intended to influence public opinion and make a name for oneself, and the "lettre mondaine" (courtly letter) modeled by such court secretaries as Etienne du Tronchet, whose *Lettres missives et familieres* (1569, Familiar Letters and Missives) dominated the epistolary market into the next century. The Des Roches's last volume contains ninety-six letters, Catherine's 590–lined verse translation of Claudian's *De raptu Proserpinae,* and several "responses," epitaphs, and "Imitations" by both mother and daughter.

In the summer of 1587 the plague reached Poitiers. Upon becoming ill, the Dames des Roches dictated their last testament on 8 October and both died before the end of November. They were buried not in a church chapel but in an unmarked common grave. Posthumous *elogia* (eulogies) all claim that they died together on the same day. Scévole de Sainte-Marthe, a close relative of the Dames des Roches, concludes in his *Eloges des hommes illustres* (1644, In Praise of Illustrious Men) that just as life had united the mother and her daughter, so they were united in death: "la mort mesme toute sourde et toute inexorable qu'elle est, n'a peu resister aux ardans et nobles desirs de ces deux genereuses Dames, qui ne souhaittoient rien plus passionnément que de vivre et de mourir ensemble" (death itself, as deaf and inexorable as she is, could not refuse the ardent and noble desire of these two generous Ladies who sought nothing more passionately than to live and die together).

Madeleine and Catherine des Roches were noted throughout their lives for their uncommon ability to combine the life of the mind with the tasks of their *ménage* (household). They were considered exemplary in aligning themselves with the interests of their class, the Crown, and a reformed Catholicism. As part of the newly emerging class of the *noblesse de robe* (nobility of the robe), they sought in their writings to strengthen the national consciousness and the glory of the weak monarchy. They belonged to the party of the Moderns, which defended the superiority of French culture. They were staunch Catholics, critics of the Reform movement, and pacifists. They were linked, as Italian learned women before them, to the civic pride of their native city. Exceptionally learned, they rank high in catalogues of illustrious women before the nineteenth century. Their writings provide a glimpse into the development of early modern feminism and abundant evidence of the vitality of humanist learning among members of the provincial upper bourgeoisie.

Biography:

George E. Diller, *Les Dames des Roches. Etude sur la vie littéraire à Poitiers dans la deuxième moitié du XVIe siècle* (Paris: Droz, 1936).

References:

Evelyne Berriot-Salvadore, *Les femmes dans la société française de la Renaissance* (Geneva: Droz, 1990);

Susan Broomhall, *Women and the Book Trade in Sixteenth-Century France* (Aldershot, U.K. & Burlington, Vt.: Ashgate, 2002);

Ann Rosalind Jones, *The Currency of Eros: Women's Love Lyric in Europe 1540–1620* (Bloomington: Indiana University Press, 1990);

Anne R. Larsen, "The French Humanist Scholars: Les Dames des Roches," in *Women Writers of the Renaissance and Reformation,* edited by Katharina Wilson (Athens: University of Georgia Press, 1987), pp. 232–259;

Madeleine Lazard, "Les Dames des Roches: une dévotion réciproque et passionnée," *Papers on French Seventeenth-Century Literature,* 105 (1997): 9–18;

Todd Olson, "'La Femme à la Puce et la Puce à l'Oreille': Catherine des Roches and the Poetics of Sexual Resistance in Sixteenth-Century French Poetry," *Journal of Medieval and Early Modern Studies,* 32, no. 2 (2002): 327–342;

Tilde Sancovitch, "Catherine des Roches's *Le Ravissement de Proserpine:* A Humanist/Feminist Translation," in *Renaissance Women Writers; French Texts/American Contexts,* edited by Larsen and Colette Winn (Detroit: Wayne State University Press, 1994), pp. 55–66.

Papers:

The major collection of Madeleine and Catherine des Roches's papers is in the Médiathèque François Mitterrand in Poitiers.

Etienne Dolet

(3 August 1509 – 3 August 1546)

James Herbert Dahlinger, S.J.
Le Moyne College

and

Megan Conway
Louisiana State University–Shreveport

BOOKS: *Orationes duae in Tholosam* (Lyon: Gryphe, 1534; revised edition, Neapoli: M. de Ragusia, 1535);

Dialogus de imitatione Ciceroniana, adversus Desiderium Erasmum Roterodamum, pro Christophoro Longolio (Lyon: Gryphe, 1535); republished as *L'Erasmianus d'E. Dolet,* edited by Emile V. Telle (Geneva: Droz, 1974);

Commentariorum linguae Latinae. Tomus primus (Lyon: Gryphe, 1536);

De re Navali Liber ad Lazarum Bayfium (Lyon: Gryphe, 1537);

Commentariorum linguae Latinae. Tomus secundus (Lyon: Gryphe, 1538);

Cato Christianus (Lyon: Dolet, 1538);

Carminum libri quatuor (Lyon: [Gryphe for] Dolet, 1538);

Genethliacum Claudii Dolet (Lyon: Dolet, 1539); translated as *L'Avant naissance de Claude Dolet fils de Estienne Dolet premièrement composée en Latin par le pere et maintenant par ung sien amy traduicte en langue Francoyse. Oeuvre très utile et necessaire a la vie commune: contenant, comme l'homme se doibt gouverner en ce monde* (Lyon: Dolet, 1539);

Formulae latinarumlocutionum illustriorum (Lyon: Dolet, 1539);

Francisci Valesii Gallorum Regis Fata (Lyon: Dolet, 1539);

La Manière de bien traduire d'une langue a une aultre (Lyon: Dolet, 1540; revised 1541, 1542, 1543);

De imitatione Ciceroniana adversus Floridum Sabinum (Lyon: Dolet, 1540);

Observationes in Terentii comoedias Andriam et Eunuchum (Lyon: Dolet, 1540);

Les Gestes de Françoys de Valois roy de France (Lyon: Dolet, 1540; revised and enlarged, 1543);

Etienne Dolet (frontispiece from Joseph Boulmier, Etienne Dolet, sa vie, ses oeuvres, son martyr, *1857; Howard Tilton Memorial Library, Tulane University)*

De officio legati, de Immunitate legatorum, et de Joannis Lemmmovicensis episcopi legatioibus (Lyon: Dolet, 1541);

Le second enfer (et Deux dialogues de Platon. L'ung intitulé Axiochus. Ung intitulé Hipparchus) (Lyon: Dolet, 1544);

La forme et la maniere de la poinctuation et accents de la langue françoise (Paris: Thibout et Denise, 1556; revised edition, Paris: Regnault, 1560; revised again, Lyon: Gros, 1577);

Les préfaces françaises de Dolet, edited by Claude Longeon, (Geneva, Droz, 1979).

Editions: *La manière de bien traduire d'une langue en aultre* (Geneva: Slatkine Reprints, 1972);

Le second enfer de Dolet, edited by Claude Longeon (Geneva: Droz, 1978);

Correspondance: répertoire analytique et chronologique, suivi du texte de ses lettres latines, edited by Longeon (Geneva: Droz, 1982);

Orationes duae in Tholosam d'Etienne Dolet, edited by Kenneth Lloyd-Jones and Marc van der Poel (Geneva: Droz, 1995).

OTHER: Four Poems, *Recueil de vers latins et vulgaires sur le trepas de Monsieur le Dauphin* (Lyon, Gryphe, 1536);

Le Courtisan de Messire Baltazar de Castillon, edited by Dolet (Lyon: François Juste, 1538);

Clément Marot, *Oeuvres,* edited by Dolet (Lyon: Gyphe, 1538; revised and enlarged, Lyon: Dolet, 1542, enlarged, 1543);

Le Guydon des Practiciens, edited by Dolet (Lyon: Gabiano, 1538);

Galen, *Le Troisiesme Livre de la Thérapeutique,* edited by Dolet (Lyon: Jean Barbou for Guillaume de Guelques, 1539);

Terence, *Comeodiae,* edited by Dolet (Lyon: Dolet, 1540);

Marot, *L'Enfer,* edited by Dolet (Lyon: Dolet, 1542; revised, 1542);

Psalmes, du royal prophete David: Opuscule de Sainct Athanase sur les psalmes de David, translated by Dolet and Pierre-Robert Olivétan (Lyon: Dolet, 1542);

Exhortation à la lecture des sainctes Lettres: avec suffisantes probation des docteurs de l'Eglise, qu'il est licite et nécessairey-celles estre translatees en langue vulgaire, et mesmement en la francoyse, edited by Dolet (Lyon: Dolet, 1542);

Le Manuel du chevalier chrestien, traduit du latin d'Erasme (Lyon: Dolet, 1542);

Le Vray Moyen de bien et catholiquement se confesser; opuscule faict premierement en latin par Erasme (Lyon: Dolet, 1542);

Les Epistres familiaires de Marc Tulle Cicero, pere d'eloquence latine, translated by Dolet (Lyon: Dolet, 1542); revised as *Les Epistres familieres de M. T. Ciceron, latin-francois, par E. Dolet et F. de Belleforest* (Paris: Gilles Beys, 1587);

François Rabelais, *Pantagruel,* edited by Dolet (Lyon: Dolet, 1542);

Rabelais, *Gargantua,* edited by Dolet (Lyon: Dolet, 1542);

Les Questions tusculanes de M. T. Cicéron, translated by Dolet (Lyon: Dolet, 1543).

Etienne Dolet is one of the most paradoxical and tragic figures of the first half of the French Renaissance. He was a devoted humanist and ardent admirer of Cicero as well as an important printer of scholarly and religious texts. Although he was not personally deeply interested in the religious debates of his time, he was combative and imprudent and drawn to controversy. His ambiguity toward Christian doctrine made him a focus for opponents and left him open to censorship and persecution. He was imprisoned five times in his life. It was his ultimate condemnation and execution for heresy, perhaps more than his highly erudite philological works, that gave him the impact he always sought to have on the world of learning and ideas.

Dolet is believed to have been born on 3 August 1509 in Orléans into a poor but respectable middle-class family. The only evidence to support the day 3 August comes from the work of Jean le Laboureur, who in his *Additions aux Mémoires de Messire Michel de Castelnau* (1659, Additions to the Memoires of Sir Michel de Castelnau) included several poems about Dolet's tragic end. After quoting a Latin epitaph by the Calvinist leader Theodore de Bèze, who at first admired Dolet and later repudiated him, Le Laboureur added the lines: "Stephanus Doletus, Aurelius, Gallus, die sancto Stephano sacro, et natus et Vulcano devotus, in Malbertina area, Lutetiae, 3 augusti 1546"—which Joseph Boulmier in *Etienne Dolet, sa vie, ses oeuvres, son martyr* (1857, Etienne Dolet: His Life, His Works, His Martydom) translates: "Etienne Dolet, of Orleans, born the day of the feast of St. Etienne and delivered to the fire the same day, in Paris, at the Place Malbert, 3 August 1546."

In his collection of poems titled *Carminum libri quatuor* (Poems in Four Books), which he published himself in 1538, Dolet declares his love for his native city and writes that Orléans is his home. So little is known of his family that one legend has it that Dolet was an illegitimate son of François I, a romantic but unlikely notion since François would have been only fifteen years old in 1509. Although Boulmier speculates that Dolet's relative silence concerning his family indicates some sort of estrangement, Richard Copley Christie in *Etienne Dolet, the Martyr of the Renaissance, His Life and Death* (1899) quotes a passage from Dolet in which the author cites the "honorable station" and prosperity and happiness of his parents. However, given Dolet's tendency to exaggerate his own merit, it is difficult to draw any certain conclusions. Like other men of letters of the time, Dolet complained in his correspondence about his financial dependence on wealthy patrons and presumably had little or no support from his family. Whatever the case, from an early age he was able to commit himself to a liberal education rather than worry over earning a living. No details remain of Dolet's life in Orléans, but several times in his writings he praised the education he received there.

In 1521 the young Dolet arrived in Paris, where he remained for five years. There he acquired what would be a lifelong enthusiasm for the study of the Latin language and oratory and a passion bordering on obsession for the eloquence and style of Marcus Tullius Cicero. In addition to his studies of Cicero, in 1525 he began to study rhetoric and oratory under Nicolas Bérauld, also from Orléans, who was among the greatest Latin scholars of the time. Bérauld was a friend of the famous humanist Desiderius Erasmus and had been tutor to several members of the Coligny family. Learned in Greek as well as Latin, Bérauld was also an ardent Ciceronian, a passion that undoubtedly contributed to the lasting friendship he formed at this time with Dolet.

Inspired by his love of Cicero and a desire to further his education, Dolet traveled to Italy in 1527. There he spent three years at the University of Padua, which was then at the height of its brilliance and reputation. Christie asserts that at Padua, Dolet acquired the heretical opinions that later caused his enemies to label him an atheist and ultimately contributed to his death. Less than a decade earlier, Pietro Pomponazzi, the university's most noted professor of philosophy, had published a treatise in which he attacked the doctrine of the immortality of the soul. Pomponazzo died in 1525, but during Dolet's three years in Padua his influence and celebrity, carried on by a group of his devoted disciples, were at their peak. Dolet found Pomponazzo's daring theories intriguingly modern and attractive.

Far more than Pomponazzo, Simon Villanovanus (or de Villeneuve), a humanist and Ciceronian, had the greatest impact on Dolet. Although Villanovanus did not hold an official position at the university, he seems to have been its leading professor of Latin when Dolet came to Padua. Dolet attributes the perfection of his oratory and the purity of his Latin to the teaching of Villanovanus. More than master and student, the two became fast friends. When Villanovanus died in 1530 at age thirty-five, Dolet was grief stricken. He expressed his loss and sadness in the epitaph he wrote and had engraved on the tomb of his friend:

STEPHANI
DOLETI ORATIO-
NES DVAE IN
THOLOSAM.

Eiufdem Epiftolarum libri I I.
Eiufdem Carminum libri I I.
Ad eundem Epiftolarum ami-
corum liber.

Title page for Dolet's 1534 work, which included two speeches delivered in Toulouse that had led to his banishment from the city (Claude Longeon, Bibliographie des œuvres d'Etienne Dolet, *1980; Thomas Cooper Library, University of South Carolina)*

Salve viator
et animvm hvc paulvm adverte.
Qvod miservm motales dvcvnt.
Felicissimvm cito mori pvto qvamobrem.
Et mihi mortvo mortem gratvlare.
Et qvestv abstine.
morte enim mortalis esse desii.
vale.
Et mihi qviescenti bene precare.

(Hail, traveler, and pause a moment before this tomb. What you mortals regard as misfortune, to die young, for me is supreme happiness. Congratulate me on being dead, therefore, and do not grieve for me, for, by my death, I am no longer mortal. Hail and farewell! And wish me a happy repose.)

Notably, there is an absence of any overt reference to Christian salvation or the soul in this epitaph. Dolet also composed three Latin odes commemorating his friend and mentor, all of which were included in his first published work, *Orationes duae in Tholosam* (1534, Two Speeches in Toulouse).

After Villanovanus's death Dolet thought about returning to France but was persuaded to go to Venice in the capacity of personal secretary to Jean de Langeac, bishop of Limoges, who was passing through Padua on his way to assume his duties as ambassador of France to the Italian city-state. An intrepid traveler who had served his country as ambassador to Poland, Portugal, Hungary, Switzerland, Scotland, and England,

Langeac was also a man of culture and a patron of letters. Dolet remained in Venice for most of a year under the patronage of Langeac, availing himself of the city's educational opportunities and cultivating a relationship with the bishop that afforded him future financial assistance when the need arose. Dolet was able to attend the public lectures of Giovanni Battista Egnazio, who had been appointed by the senators of Venice as the city's Professor of Eloquence. Egnazio's special lectures that year were on Cicero's *De Officiis* (On Duties) and Lucretius's *De Rerum Natura* (On the Nature of Things).

While in Venice, Dolet met a young Venetian woman, Elena, whom he calls by the Latin form of her name, Helena. Nothing is known for sure about the young lady, but in one poem Dolet playfully records his attitudes about wanting a mistress:

> Amicam volo non nimis decoram,
> Ne vultu moveat procos salaces;
> Eamdem volo sat tamen decoram,
> Ne me a se arceat, et fuget coactum
> Deformi nimium et nigrante vultu.
> Eamdem volo comitate plenam,
> Facundam, improbulam in toro: at modestam
> Torum extra. Sit et illa tota facta
> Ad meum ingenium: quod ipse nolim,
> Nolit; sed velit id, velim quod ipse.
> Talem, blanda Venus, volo, da amicam.

(A mistress? Yes, I would like one, but not too pretty as to attract the local lads. But I want her pretty enough, that a hideous visage, or a blackened and deformed one not send me running with fright! I would also like her to be amicable, charming in conversation, wild when alone with me, but reserved with others. She should be suited to my own character, wanting what I want, leaving aside what I leave aside. Sweet Venus! Give me such a mistress and I will be content!)

Dolet seems to have found some measure of happiness with Elena, though the youthful romance was cut short when she died suddenly. Dolet composed three poems in her memory and henceforth devoted himself to Minerva—his studies, poetry, and book-publishing trade—rather than to Venus.

Dolet returned to France before the end of 1530. He continued gathering models and materials for his great project, a commentary on the Latin language, which he had been planning since the age of sixteen. However, Dolet heeded the advice of Langeac, who no doubt wanted him to have a reliable profession, and decided to pursue a career in law. In 1532 he entered the University of Toulouse, an internationally prestigious center for the study of both civil and canon law. In a letter to the great Hellenist Guillaume Budé, dated 22 April 1534 and written after two years

of studying civil law, Dolet gives a frank appraisal of Toulouse and its inhabitants, finding both rude and barbarous. This opinion was perhaps influenced by his freethinking experience at Padua. By comparison, many of the professors at Toulouse must have seemed steeped in medieval Scholasticism. In a university that seems to have been divided into two camps, Dolet naturally gravitated toward the humanist element and particularly to Jean de Pins, bishop of Rieux, who became both his friend and his patron.

By the early 1530s the country's religious questions were echoed in Toulouse. The city, which had a history of religious intolerance, had become a bastion of orthodoxy in the early sixteenth century. The university, with its contingent of humanist professors and students, was a natural target for the religious authorities. Those suspected of heresy were arrested and subjected to public humiliation. In 1532 the eminent scholar Jean Caturce was burned as a suspected Lutheran. That same year the humanist Jean de Boysonné, professor of law and friend of François Rabelais, was arrested and imprisoned on charges of heresy and forced to recant his "errors" in public. Even Dolet's benefactor, the bishop of Rieux, was accused of heresy.

Unrest over philosophical and religious questions came to a head at the university when the civic parlement (parliament) became concerned with student comportment and prohibited the giving of annual speeches by representatives of the *nations* (student associations based on national or regional affinity groups) on the feast day of their particular patron saint. These annual speeches included the funeral oration for members who had died during the preceding year as well as a discussion of events of the previous year that in some way affected student life at the university. Competition among the *nations* was fierce and often led to fights and riots, hence the city's desire to avoid such destructive unrest. However, this and other curtailments angered the French students. Dolet, twenty-four and keen to make himself noticed as widely as possible as an orator, soon caught the attention of his fellow students of the French *nation* and was named their official spokesman. Indignant at the refusal of parlement to rescind its ban on student orations, the French students decided that Dolet should speak.

Dolet delivered his first oration to the French *nation* and various listeners on 9 October 1533. By all accounts, it was a brilliant imitation of Ciceronian style, and the overwhelming response on the part of his fellow students gave Dolet a heady moment of success. According to fellow student and faithful friend, Simon Finet, Dolet's delivery was eloquent, and his voice and gestures most expressive. In addition to treating traditional subjects such as friendship and social union, Dolet displayed the fiery temper and violent nature for which he became well known. He denounced the parlement for depriving honest people of their ordinary rights of assembly, rights that he notes were enjoyed ordinarily in all the great developed cities of Europe. He declared the city backward and corrupt and the government repressive. He also attacked other *nations,* stirring up a great deal of animosity among the factions, particularly the Gascon *nation.* The ill feeling led to a general strike, which continued until December 1533, when the parlement ordered the professors to return to their duties.

This climate of unrest forms the backdrop for Dolet's second oration, delivered sometime in December 1533 or January 1534, probably on the occasion of his election as prior. His audience was much larger than it had been for his first speech. In this oration, far longer than the first and regarded as superior in eloquence and power, Dolet personally attacked the orator of the Gascon *nation* and decried the barbarity of Toulouse, in his view a particularly depraved city where learning and culture were despised. He denounced the execution of Caturce as proof of the city's intolerance and superstitious religious practices: "Dixisset multa audacter, pleraque esset non moderate locutus, omni scelere coopertus esset, haereticorum supplicio plectenda admisisset, quem vivum comburi in hac urbe vidistis nimen mortui praeterio, igne quidem consumpti, sed hic adhuc invidiae flamma flagrantis" (You have all seen burned alive, in this very spot, in this city, an unhappy soul whose name will go without mention. The fires of the stake devoured his mortal remains, but the flames of envy still burn in your memory of him). He then furiously accused the town officials of branding anyone of superior intellect as a heretic. At the same time he was careful to draw attention to his own belief in traditional religious "doctrines and practices." His invective, however, outweighed his earnestness, earning him the enmity of many and providing ample material for a charge of heresy. In March he was arrested and imprisoned with six other students. Dolet was luckier than the others. His friends, including the bishop of Rieux, interceded on his behalf and procured his release after only three days.

Perhaps encouraged by the praise of his oratory by critics such as Jules-César Scaliger, Dolet was undeterred by his early brush with authorities. He continued to antagonize highly placed members of the community and insisted on participating in the yearly "Floral Games," an annual poetry contest in Toulouse dating from the Middle Ages. When he did not win the prize, Dolet issued scathing statements ridiculing

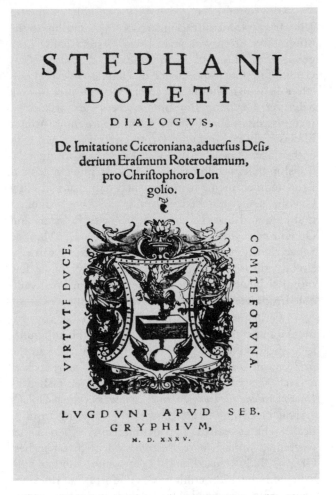

Title page for Dolet's second volume, in which his treatment of Desiderius Erasmus infuriated the latter's followers (Claude Longeon, Bibliographie des œuvres d'Etienne Dolet, 1980; Thomas Cooper Library, University of South Carolina)

his competitors. At about this time Dolet wrote to Budé, soliciting his friendship and support and receiving his approval in writing—a sign of favor desired by every rising scholar of the day. But Dolet had also made fierce enemies. He was forced to leave Toulouse in late May or early June in order to avoid being arrested a second time, and in June 1534, the parlement decreed his banishment from Toulouse.

Both illness and uncertainty apparently beset the scholar as he departed from Toulouse. The prospect of continuing his legal career was questionable, and he entertained the notion of returning to Italy—but the state of his health prevented a lengthy voyage. Furthermore, he desired to see his work published before leaving France. Accompanied by his friend Finet, Dolet arrived in Lyon on 1 August 1534 ill, exhausted, and depressed.

Boysonné exercised his considerable clout as a scholar and humanist to insure Dolet's welcome to the progressive literary circle in Lyon. Critic Claude Longeon, the editor of *Corrrespondance de Claude Dolet* (1982, The Correspondence of Claude Dolet), cites a letter in which the older scholar urges Dolet to visit Sébastien Gryphe, Boysonné's "very dear friend," a recently nationalized German and the foremost printer of classical texts in Lyon. Gryphe received Dolet with enthusiasm, and the two developed a working relationship that lasted nearly a decade despite Dolet's difficult temperament. In the learned circle surrounding Gryphe, Dolet mingled with many of Lyon's intellectual elite and became close friends with Rabelais and Guillaume Scève, the cousin of the poet Maurice Scève. Dolet initially worked for Gryphe as an occasional editor and proofreader but only for a few months. Nevertheless, this time gave him an invaluable inside view of the printing world.

Guillaume Scève is believed to have been instrumental in persuading Gryphe to publish the inflammatory speeches Dolet had given in Toulouse when the printer was initially unwilling to do so. The speeches, as well as some of Dolet's poetry, were published as *Orationes duae in Tholosam* only six weeks after Dolet's arrival in Lyon. As Dolet was still suffering from ill health, Finet edited the manuscript. When Dolet wished to publish a revised version of the speeches, Gryphe flatly refused, and Dolet sought another publisher for the 1535 edition. Gryphe's refusal does not seem to have affected their relationship, however, for he printed five more of Dolet's works over the next four years.

In October 1534 Dolet left for Paris to obtain royal permission to publish his commentary on the Latin language, on which he had been doggedly laboring. While in Paris he composed the controversial *Dialogus de imitatione Ciceroniana, adversus Desiderium Erasmum Roterodamum, pro Christophoro Longolio* (1535, A Dialogue Concerning the Imitation of Cicero in Defense of Christopher Longolius against Desiderius Erasmus of Rotterdam). Arguably the best known of the humanists, Erasmus had in 1528 published *Ciceronianus,* in which he had argued against a too-slavish imitation of Cicero. He insisted that a wider classical culture was desirable for the educated person and that a perfect Latin prose style was unnecessary and probably unattainable. Erasmus declined to answer Scaliger, who had employed invective when he sought to engage him in a debate on the usefulness of imitation. Without regard to how his supporter Scaliger might react, Dolet decided to try to engage Erasmus himself.

Dolet also employed invective against Erasmus in *Dialogus de imitatione Ciceroniana,* attacking him as a poor stylist who wrote merely for a popular readership. He further questioned why Erasmus paid so much attention to religious and theological matters when these disciplines lay outside his competence. Beyond the personal abuse, however, *Dialogus de imitatione Ciceroniana* is considered one of the best contemporary analyses and justifications for Ciceronian imitation. The work recounts a supposed conversation between Sir Thomas More, Erasmus's defender, and Villanovanus, who expresses Dolet's views, recorded as if it took place in Padua during Dolet's time there as a student. In substance, Dolet agreed with Erasmus that exposure to a wide array of classical authors was of value, though he affirmed the preeminence of Cicero as the best comprehensive model of both style and personal conduct. The prefatory letter included with the work, however, is particularly scathing and abusive, and when the book appeared from Gryphe's press in mid 1535, close to the time when Dolet returned to Lyon, it caused a good deal of comment. Admirers of Erasmus were scandalized, and many of Dolet's friends, including Boysonné, were dismayed by the violence of his expression. Though Erasmus himself remained publicly silent, several authors replied in print, a circumstance that added to Dolet's reputation as a scholar and infuriated Scaliger, who became Dolet's bitter enemy.

After Dolet's return to Lyon he resumed his editing and copyreading duties for Gryphe, spending much of his time editing his own writing for the printer. In April 1536 Gryphe printed the first volume of Dolet's great work, *Commentariorum linguae Latinae* (Commentaries on the Latin Language). The second volume appeared in 1538. (A third volume was proposed but never realized.) Both volumes include two dedications; to François I and to Budé. While Christie calls the work "one of the most important contributions to Latin scholarship which the sixteenth century produced," it has been of little interest to modern scholars. Dolet comments on Latin nouns, verbs, adjectives, and other parts of speech, giving examples from a range of authors. In the first volume especially, Dolet manages to work in scathing commentaries on Erasmus and other contemporaries. The second volume is less vitriolic, the death of Erasmus having stopped Dolet's pen on that subject. The work did not garner the critical acclaim Dolet might have expected, principally because he had already offended most of the influential thinkers of the day. Supporters of Erasmus despised him; traditional religious leaders, including the professors of the Sorbonne, had not forgotten his ridicule of Toulouse and his defense of the "heretic" Caturce; and proponents of Martin Luther and, later, of Jean Calvin considered him an atheist.

Meanwhile, Dolet had fallen prey to other misfortunes. On 31 December 1536 he was attacked in the street by a painter named Compaing. While defending himself against what appeared to be a mortal attack, Dolet had the misfortune to kill his assailant. Compaing seems to have been in the company of a band of ruffians, who immediately tried to stir up a mob against Dolet. Through the offices of his friends, Dolet escaped the city and fled during the night to Paris, where he hoped to gain the sympathy and pardon of the king. Although Dolet denies any such assistance, it is because of the efforts of his friends that he did obtain a pardon on 19 February 1537, an event celebrated by a banquet that counted Clément Marot and Rabelais among the attendees. On Dolet's return to Lyon, however, city officials refused to ratify the royal pardon, and he was arrested and put in prison until mid April. As Dolet continued to insist he had no support from his friends, several of his intimates began—with some justification—to withdraw their support. Boysonné remained faithful and took Dolet's side when Charles Estienne accused him of plagiarism, charges Dolet answered in his *De re Navali Liber ad Lazarum Bayfium* (The Book About Naval Affairs to Lazare de Baif), published in May 1537. Dolet was still working at this time for Gryphe but was also editing and reading copy for other Lyon printers not specializing in Latin works. In 1538 he edited and corrected *Le Courtisan de Messire Baltazar de Castillon,* Jacques Colin's French translation of Baldassare Castiglione's immensely popular *Il libro del cortegiano* (1528, The Book of the Courtier). That same year he edited a book of legal procedures for notaries and lawyers for yet another printer.

The year 1538 was pivotal in Dolet's life. Through the influence of his friends he was able to meet François I, who accepted *Commentariorum linguae Latinae* as a gift and granted Dolet the privilege to become a printer. Scholars speculate that Dolet wanted to become a printer—a more financially rewarding profession than writing—because he desired to marry. The marriage took place sometime in early 1538. Little is known of his wife besides her name, Louise Giraud, discovered by Longeon on a promissary note in notarial archives, and the fact that Dolet seems to have been quite happy with his married life. By the end of 1538 Dolet's press was up and running. Gryphe evidently gave aid to his former employee, as Dolet used not only Gryphe's press at times but also his woodcut capitals and print blocks. In the next six years Dolet printed at least sixty-seven works, several of them in multiple editions. Fifteen of these books were composed or translated by Dolet himself; many of the others were edited by him.

Title page for the first of two volumes Dolet wrote on the Latin language (from <http://classes.bnf.fr/page/grand/003.htm>)

The first work issued from Dolet's press was his own short treatise titled *Cato Christianus* (1538, Cato the Christian), which he wrote in part as a response to Cardinal Sadolet's suggestion that he ought to try writing on religious themes. Writing in Latin dystichs, Dolet discusses the Lord's Prayer and the creed, concluding with two odes to the Virgin Mary. Scholars speculate that the next work that appeared with Dolet's name listed as printer was actually issued from Gryphe's press. *Carminum libri quatuor* is composed of 195 of Dolet's Latin poems (all of which had previously been published with the *Orationes duae in Tholosam*) divided into four books, each with its own dedication, plus some commendatory poems by other authors.

In 1539 Dolet's son, Claude, was born, an event that he marked with the publication of *Genethliacum Claudii Dolet* (Birthday Ode of Claude Dolet), which was shortly thereafter translated into French and published as *L'Avant naissance de Claude Dolet fils de Estienne Dolet premièrement composée en Latin par le pere et maintenant par ung sien amy traduicte en langue Francoyse. Oeuvre très utile et necessaire a la vie commune: contenant, comme l'homme se doibt gouverner en ce monde* (Before the Birth of Claude Dolet, son of Etienne Dolet First Composed in Latin by the Father Now by His Friend Translated in the French Language. A Very Useful Work Necessary to Everyday Life Containing How a Man Must Act in This World). Christie calls this book "the most interesting and admirable" of Dolet's works.

In the first volume of the *Commentariorum linguae Latinae,* Dolet had expressed his interest in writing a history of contemporary France. Although he envisioned a great work requiring the financial assistance of the king and the cooperation of his ministers, he settled for a less ambitious work. Dedicated to François, *Francisci Valesii Gallorum Regis Fata* (1539, The Destiny of François of Valois, King of France) was written in Latin verse. He published a French prose version the next year under the title *Les Gestes de Françoys de Valois roy de France* (1540, The Heroic Deeds of François of Valois, King of France). Although both books were successful—the French version was revised in 1543 and reprinted twice by others—they did not bring him the attention of the king, which Dolet had no doubt anticipated.

Being a publisher afforded Dolet the opportunity to comment, translate, and theorize about language. He addresses the contemporary preoccupation with translation and language in his *La Manière de bien traduire d'une langue a une aultre* (1540, How to Translate Well from One Language to Another), in which he also expresses the desire to develop French as a language of intellectual and poetic expression. Dolet notes that the translator ought to have a thorough knowledge of both languages and that the translation should not be literal but instead should convey the sense of the original as faithfully as possible. Intended to be part of a larger work titled "l'Orateur françoys" (The French Orator), which was never completed, *La manière de bien traduire d'une langue a une aultre* was the most immediately successful of all of Dolet's writings; it was reissued three times by Dolet and several times by other presses during the sixteenth century.

Just as Dolet was establishing himself as a printer, Franciscus Floridus Sabinus, another scholar and admirer of Erasmus, again raised the accusation of plagiarism and charged Dolet with ignorance, irreligion, immorality, and gluttony as well. Dolet answered the vitriolic, personal attack in *De imitatione Ciceroniana adversus Floridum Sabinum* (1540, On the Imitation of Cicero against Floridus Sabinus). The first part of the book is an intellectual defense of Ciceronian discourse; the second and last part is a personal attack on Sabinus. Sabinus refused to let the matter rest and replied with another round of invective in his *Adversus Doleti calumnias* (1541, Against Dolet's Lies), accusing Dolet of denying the immortality of the soul, an issue that later had grave consequences.

Like his literary career, Dolet's life as a printer and bookseller was not without controversy. A rift between the workmen and journeymen printers and the master printers escalated until a royal edict settled the matter in favor of the master printers in December 1541. Workmen were forbidden to form unions and were ordered to accept the same wages as before. In addition, no book was to be printed without a royal license. Dolet, who had taken the side of the workmen in the dispute, made many enemies among the master printers, several of whom considered him an interloper.

Besides printing a variety of classical works, including Cicero's *Letters,* Aesop's *Fables,* and Sophocles' *Antigone,* and five different works by his former foe Erasmus, Dolet also published some of the best work being written in sixteenth-century France. He issued Bertrand de la Borderie's *L'Amie de Court* (Lady Friend of the Court), a malicious attack on women, in May 1542 and Heroet's Neoplatonic riposte, *La Parfaicte Amye* (The Perfect Lady Friend), the following month. The pairing was successful, as both works were reissued the next year. Dolet's friendships with Marot and Rabelais continued into the 1540s, though both relationships came to sudden ends. Dolet published three editions of Marot's *Oeuvres* (Works) in 1538, 1542, and 1543, and two editions of his *L'Enfer* (Hell) in 1542 and 1544. The details are unknown, but something occurred between publication of the last edition of Marot's works and the poet's death in 1544 that abruptly ended the friendship. Dolet's friendship with Rabelais ended in 1542 when he published editions of *Gargantua* and *Pantagruel* without the author's permission. Fearing for his safety, Rabelais had prudently decided to revise the two volumes by deleting or modifying passages to which the Sorbonne and its doctors of theology could charge with heresy. The revised versions were published by François Juste in 1542, but Dolet put Rabelais's life at risk by issuing unauthorized editions of both books that claimed to be revised and augmented by the author but were in fact based on the unexpurgated texts of 1537 and 1538.

Although the publication of *Gargantua* and *Pantagruel* might have been a good financial decision, it only added fuel to a fire Dolet's enemies, particularly his fellow master printers, were intent on starting. Dolet's careless manner, vicious tongue, and bad temper earned him the enmity of many, and his questionable attitudes toward traditional religion troubled the authorities. His own writings were critical of the clergy and of the faculty of theology of the University of Paris, the Sorbonne, and the works he published certainly made him guilty by association. Many of his friends—notably Marot, Rabelais, and Boysonné—were suspected of heresy. For a man seemingly uninvolved with the Church, Dolet brought out many religious works from his press. Longeon points out that a full 25 percent of works Dolet published dealt with religion; his publications include an edition of the New Testament in Latin and in French, an exposition on the Gospel of St. Matthew, a translation of the Psalms, a summary of the Old and New Testaments, and Lefèvre d'Etaples's *Epistres & Evangiles pour les cinquante & deux sepmaines de l'an* (Epistles and Gospels for the Fifty-Two Weeks of the Year).

In July or August 1542 Dolet was arrested on suspicion of heresy and thrown into prison. After his house and shop were searched and his books confiscated, he was officially charged. Dolet's trial lasted for more than two months, and on 2 October 1542 he was pronounced guilty and condemned to be burned at the stake. Dolet immediately appealed the case, thus delaying his execution and giving him time to petition the king. François granted a royal pardon sometime in June 1543. The pardon required that Dolet abjure his errors and that all of the books mentioned in the trial be burned. Dolet gratefully complied and went back to Lyon determined to tread carefully.

His enemies, however, were not content. In January 1544 two bundles of books with "Dolet" written in capitals on the wrapping were seized at the gates of Paris and found to contain books from the forbidden Genevan press as well as Dolet's own works and those he published. Dolet maintained that he had no connection with the packages and that the whole matter was a ruse perpetrated by his enemies. He was arrested once again and imprisoned but tricked his jailers into letting him return to his house, from whence he fled to the Piedmont, where he remained for several months. From there he prepared an edition of poems about his time in prison, titled *Le second enfer* (The Second Hell) after Marot's work in which that author had described his own imprisonment. Unable to stay away, Dolet quietly returned to Lyon in May 1544 and prepared the book, intended to garner the sympathy of François, for publication. Along with his poems, the book included Dolet's translations of two dialogues attributed to Plato, the *Axiochus* and the *Hipparchus*. Not long after his return, he was again arrested and taken to Paris, where he was imprisoned in the Conciergerie.

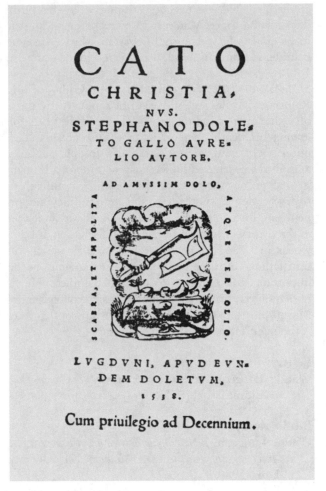

Title page for the first book Dolet published from his own press (from Claude Longeon, Bibliographie des œuvres d'Etienne Dolet, *1980; Thomas Cooper Library, University of South Carolina)*

In November 1544 Dolet was formally accused by the Sorbonne of having denied the immortality of the soul in his translation of "a certain book of Plato," the *Axiochus*. Dolet had appended "rien du tout" (nothing at all) to the phrase "après la mort tu ne seras plus" (after death you will be no longer). These three words not found in the original (nor in the Latin translation) formed the grounds on which the judges found him guilty of blasphemy. The entire trial lasted nearly two years. His *Le second enfer* seems to have garnered no sympathy from the monarch, and the few friends he had remaining did not dare raise their voices in his defense.

His sentence was finally pronounced 2 August 1546. Deemed guilty of blasphemy, sedition, and selling prohibited books, he was condemned to be tortured, hanged, and burned and his property confiscated. He was executed the next day–his birthday–on the Place Maubert in Paris after asking the forgiveness of God and the Virgin Mary. A statue commemorating his death was erected in the square in 1889.

Because he had offended both Catholics and Reformers, Dolet's death was not mourned by those on either side of the religious debate. In the years following his death, men of letters–most notably Theodore Beza, and later biographers Joseph Boulmier and Christie–painted Dolet as something of a humanist martyr, but the facts of his life make it difficult to support such a simple characterization. Beyond his penchant for controversy, Etienne Dolet was a pioneer in the theory of translation, and his discussion of Latin words in *Commentariorum linguae Latinae* as well as his translations of Cicero justify his reputation as an important contributor to classical studies. He is remembered primarily, though, as a publisher of Marot and Rabelais, and Dolet as a humanist printer is the main focus of recent scholarship.

Letters:

Claude Longeon, ed., *Corrrespondance de Claude Dolet* (Geneva: Droz, 1982).

Bibliography:

Claude Longeon, *Bibliographie des œuvres d'Etienne Dolet, Travaux d'humanisme et renaissance,* 174 (Geneva: Droz, 1980).

Biographies:

Jean-François Née de la Rochelle, *Vie d'Etienne Dolet, imprimeur à Lyon dans le XVIe siècle* (Paris: Chez Gogué & Née de la Rochelle, 1779; Geneva: Slatkine Reprints, 1970);

Richard Copley Christie, *Etienne Dolet, the Martyr of the Renaissance, His Life and Death,* revised edition (New York: Macmillan, 1899).

References:

Jacques Alary, *Estienne Dolet et ses luttes avec la Sorbonne* (Paris, 1898; Geneva: Slatkine Reprints, 1970);

Joseph Boulmier, *Etienne Dolet, sa vie, ses oeuvres, son martyr* (Paris: A. Aubry 1857; Geneva: Slatkine Reprints, 1969);

John Charles Dawson, *Toulouse in the Renaissance: The Floral Games; University and Student Life; Etienne Dolet* (New York: Columbia University Press, 1923);

Lucien Febvre, *Le problème de l'incroyance au 16e siècle* (Paris: Editions Albin Michel, 1942; second edition, 1968);

Cahiers V. L. Saulnier, *Etienne Dolet* (Paris: Centre National des Lettres, 1986);

Valerie Worth, *Practising Translation in Renaissance France: The Example of Etienne Dolet* (Oxford: Clarendon Press, 1988).

Jean Dorat

(1508 – 1 November 1588)

James Herbert Dahlinger, S.J.
Le Moyne College

BOOKS: *Triumphales Odae* (Paris: R. Estienne, 1558);

Epitaphes sur le tombeau de haut et puissant seigneur Anne duc de Montmorancy, pair et connestable de France (Paris: P. G. de Roville, 1567);

Paeanes sive Hymni in triplicem victoriam, felicitate Caroli IX Galliarum Regis (Paris: Charron, 1569);

Epithalame ou chant nuptual sur le mariage de tres-illustres prince et princesse Henry de Lorraine duc de Guyse, et Catarine de Cleve contesse d'Eu (Paris, 1570);

Novem cantica de pace ad Carolum Nonum Galliae regem, Ioanne Aurato auctore; Neuf cantiques ou sonetz de la paix a Charles neufiesme roy de France (Paris: Extra Portam diui Victoris, sub Signo Fontis, 1570);

Ad Deum pro sanitate sibi restituta . . . ode latina et graeca (Paris: P. L'Huillier, 1571);

Tumulus reverendiis: domini Claudii Espencaei (Paris: Bienné, 1571);

Magnificentissimi spectaculi, a regina regum matre in hortis suburbanis editi, in Henrici regis Poloniae inuictissimi nuper renunciati gratulationem, descriptio, by Dorat, Pierre de Ronsard, and others (Paris: F. Morel, 1573);

Ad amplissimos Polonorum legatos, Parisiorum urbem ingredientes, Io. Aurati . . . prophonetici versus (Paris: F. Morel, 1573);

Elogium Francisci Balduini, cum epitaphio (Paris: D. du Pré, 1573);

Inuictiss: Galliarum Regis Caroli Nonitumulus: Jo. Aurato et alijs clarissimis et doctissimis viris auctoribus (Paris: F. Morel, 1574);

In Henrici III: Regis Galliae. Et Poloniae, foelicem reditum, versus, in fronte domus publicae Lutetiae urbis ascripti, quo die supplicationes et ignes solenes publico conuentu celebrati sunt: qui dies fuit mensis Septembris XIIII anno M.D. LXXIIIIY (Paris: F. Morel, 1574);

Ad diuam Caeciliam musicorum patronam (Paris: F. Morel, 1575);

Octo cantica sacra e Sacris Bibliis latino carmine expressa (Paris: F. Morel, 1575);

Sur la cosmographie d'André Thevet (Paris: L'Huilier, 1575);

Jean Dorat (from Geneviève Demerson, Dorat et son temps, *1983; Thomas Cooper Library, University of South Carolina)*

Ad Beatiss. Virginem Mariam, laetitae nomine apud gallos consecratam Ouatio (Paris: F. Morel, 1576);

Psalmo Davidis ex Hebraïca veritate Latinis versibus expressi a Io. Matthaeo Toscano Quibus praefixa sunt argumenta singulis distichis comprehensa (Paris: F. Morel, 1576);

Martialis Campani medici Burdegalensis è latronum manibus diuintus liberati, monadia tragica, ad Henricum III: Galliae et Poloniae regem: Item Paraenesis as eundem de iuris administratione in meliorem statum restituenda (Paris: Bienné, 1576);

Eclogue latine et françoise avec autres vers . . . Ensemble l'oracle de Pan (Paris: F. Morel, 1578);

Ioannis Avrati Lemovicis Poetae et Interpretis Regii Poëmatia (Paris: Linocier, 1586);

Sibyllarum duodecim oracula (Paris: J. Rabel, 1586);

Poëmatia (Paris: Linocier, 1586);

Psalmi Davidis ex Hebraîca veritate lat. versibus expressi cum octo canticis sacris (Paris: F. Morel, 1598).

Editions: *Œuvres Poétiques de Jean Dorat, poète et interprète du roy,* edited, with a biographical note, by Charles Marty-Laveaux (Paris: A Lemerre, 1875; Geneva: Slatkine, 1974);

Œuvres Poétiques de J. Dorat (Paris: Librairie des Bibliophiles, 1888);

Les odes latines, edited by Geneviève Demerson (Clermont-Ferrand: Association des Publications de la Faculté des Lettres et Sciences Humaines, 1979);

Mythologicum, ou Interprétation allégorique de l'Odyssée, X-XII et de l'hymne à Aphrodite, edited by Philip J. Ford (Geneva: Droz, 2000).

Edition in English: *The Latin Odes of Jean Dorat,* edited and translated by David R. Slavitt (Washington: Orchises, 2000).

OTHER: *Hymne de Bacus de Pierre de Ronsard avec la version latine de Jean Dorat* (Paris: A. Wechel, 1555);

Ronsardi exhortatio ad milites Gallos Latinis versibus de Gallicis expressa à Io Aurato Lemouice, translated by Dorat (Paris: A. Wechel, 1558).

Jean Dorat was a celebrated poet in French, Latin, and Greek and a renowned classical scholar in Paris in the mid to late sixteenth century. Though entitled to sign his name as the *poète du roi* (king's poet)—a much coveted honor—his chief contribution to French literature is as a teacher and scholar. As a professor and then principal of the Collège de Coqueret in Paris he nurtured Pierre de Ronsard, one of France's greatest poets, as well as other young artists who became known as the *Pléiade.* Dorat's reputation as a brilliant teacher spread throughout Europe, and students came to him from Germany, Italy, and England. Scholars, particularly in the nineteenth century, have tried to reconstruct his teaching methods by analyzing the content of his students' writings. Dorat, however, left no printed documents that describe his teaching or detail his innovative approaches to the classics.

Dorat was born Jean Disnematin or Dinemandi, according to local dialect, in Limoges, France, in 1508. The actual day and month of his birth are uncertain, and no parish records survive that provide the details of his family lineage. He affirms in one of his Latin poems that his mother belonged to a respected merchant family and that his father was a nobleman. Critics have sometimes named the De Bermondet family as that of his mother, though this is uncertain since the only indication of her name is the initial "N." There are two hypotheses concerning his father. One maintains that his first name was Jean, and that he was guardian of the civic mint. He had two sons, Jean and

Pierre, the latter of which became lord of the Chavalade and lieutenant general of Limoges. The other hypothesis suggests that the father's name was Martial Dinemandi the Younger, councilor of Limoges. In either case, critics give credence to Dorat's assertion that his father was a nobleman.

Few details are known of Dorat's youth or the schools he attended. He apparently was sociable by nature and made friends and exchanged ideas easily. He was observant, adventurous, and ambitious and enjoyed reading and reflection. He worked assiduously at his studies and was attracted to reading poetry of national and regional reputation, notably the *Roman de la Rose* (Romance of the Rose) and the works of Rutebeuf and François Villon. Even as a boy he liked to compare poets and find common elements in their works as well as trace their sources. In his late teens he began to frequent local circles of poets and intellectuals who were drawn to the ideas of the Italian Renaissance and greatly interested in the study of classical antiquity and classical poetry. Like many other intelligent young Frenchmen, Dorat was receptive to this new attitude. He was also fascinated by Greek studies that were becoming popular in France. This attraction was probably strengthened by Dorat's encounter as a young man with Guillaume Budé whom François I had recently installed as professor of Greek at the Collège Royal. Dorat applied himself to learning Greek and Latin and began to write verse in those languages as well as in French. His eventual mastery of Latin was so perfect that many scholars believe he was more comfortable writing in Latin than in French.

Dorat's interests in the exegesis and translation of classical texts led him to correspond with outstanding Hellenists and Latin scholars of the period. He wrote letters and exchanged poetry with Germain de Brie, a poet of neo-Latin and Greek verse, as well as the renowned Hellenist Jacques Toussain of the Collège des Lecteurs Royaux in Paris, who accepted Dorat as a student.

Dorat left Limoges for Paris in 1538 accompanied by Marguerite de Laval, with whom he had fallen in love two years earlier. Devoting himself to the study of literature, philosophy, and history under Toussain, Dorat continued to refine his poetry. He read the ancient poets and imitated them daily in voluminous verse. Dorat met other men of letters, most notably Robert Breton d'Arras, a teacher at the Collège of Guyenne, who became a close friend and engaged in discussions of social, political, and religious questions. Breton published a collection of letters in 1541 in which he included a letter thanking Dorat for a poem he had written to him and praised his friend as one of the greatest lyric poets of the day. Dorat was thus quickly establishing his reputation in the capital as a great poet in Latin.

Dorat's literary ambitions led him to be dissatisfied with the name *Dinemandi,* which means "dining in the morning" and seemed common to contemporaries because of the reference to eating. He decided to change it—probably when he moved to Paris, though the date of the change is not known. He preferred Dorat or Daurat, D'Aurat, or D'Auratus in Latin. (Orthography, even of proper names, was still rather unstable in the sixteenth century, when a writer might spell his own name in different ways on the same page of his manuscript.) According to Charles Marty-Laveaux, the editor of an 1875 edition of Dorat's works, the poet's friend Jean Papyre Masson speculated that Dorat chose "Auratus" after the river Aurence in his native Limoges. Gilles Ménage explains that he chose "Daurat" or "Aurat" since this was the name of one of Dorat's ancestors who had blond or golden hair. Ronsard styles him "Daurat" and "Dorat," and plays on these names and "Orence" (the Aurence River).

Dorat began giving private instruction sometime after his arrival in Paris, undoubtedly to support himself. In 1542 his teaching ability was recognized by François I, who accorded him the post of tutor to his pages, a task that Dorat performed in addition to giving private lessons. Dorat became friends with the king's son, the dauphin Henri, who soon acceded to the throne. While Dorat was intrigued by court life, he was also critical of the moral laxness he found there. Nevertheless, his desire for renown and royal favor kept him at his post, and he benefited from the acquaintances he made there. In court circles he met the eighteen-year-old Ronsard, who became his student two years later. His court associations and standing led Robert Breton to introduce Dorat to his friend Lazare de Baïf, the French ambassador to England. In 1544 the ambassador employed Dorat as the tutor to his twelve-year-old legitimized son Jean-Antoine de Baïf, the first of Dorat's star pupils.

Later in 1544 Ronsard joined Antoine de Baïf as Dorat's student. Rémy Belleau soon followed. In a poem addressed to Belleau, Ronsard celebrates their friendship and the time spent with Dorat: " . . . disciple je vins estre/De Daurat, à Paris, qui sept ans fut mon maistre/En Grec et en Latin: chez luy premierement/Nostre ferme amitié print son commencement" (I came to be the disciple of Dorat in Paris who was my master in Greek and Latin for seven years: at his house our firm friendship first took its beginning). Although Ronsard admits to spending seven years under Dorat's tutorship, scholars speculate that he

counted time in which he was more a friend than a student.

Despite his commitment to his students, Dorat did not ignore his duty as a loyal servant of the crown. To judge from allusions made in his poetry, he enlisted in the army of the dauphin Henri sometime in 1544 when Charles V was approaching Paris. He apparently managed somehow to keep up his teaching responsibilities, for his students make no mention of his absence. Though evidence indicates that he served the prince's cause more as a poet than as a soldier, he was wounded in the shoulder and unable to write for some time. He probably left the army shortly after the dauphin's coronation as Henri II in July 1547. Because of his service to the crown and his talent for teaching, evident in his efforts with the royal children and many students at court, he was rewarded with an appointment as principal of the Collège de Coqueret in 1547—his only appointment to a college of which there remains a written record. In *Histoire de la Pléiade* (1961, History of the Pleiad), critic Henri Chamard suggests that the former principal Dugast had been suspended and that Dorat was offered his place. When Dugast returned, Dorat ceded many administrative duties to him while preferring to spend his time working with students. He also maintained a full schedule of translation and verse composition and worked assiduously at establishing correct texts and variants of manuscripts for which he searched exhaustively.

In 1548 Dorat married Marguerite de Laval at the parish church of Saint-André-des-Arcs in Paris. The record of the marriage notes official intervention, indicating that Dorat was legally compelled to marry. Earlier that year Marguerite had given birth to twin girls, and this circumstance may have forced Dorat to act. Nevertheless, the marriage seems to have been happy.

Dorat transferred his students, including Baïf, Ronsard, and Belleau, with him to Coqueret. These three gifted students were later joined by Estienne Jodelle, Joachim du Bellay, Jean de la Péruse, Guillaume des Autels, and Pontus de Tyard, forming the poetic circle known as the Brigade and, later, the Pléiade. Dorat had a deep affection for his students, whose poetic testimony shows that they regarded him as a father. In *Le Second livre des hymnes* (1556, The Second Book of Hymns), Ronsard credits Dorat with having taught him the poet's craft: to "déguiser la vérité des choses avec des fables" (disguise the truth of things with fables) and ornamentation, and to render the great immortal in verse. He declares further that he owes his fame to Dorat's instruction.

Ronsard's friend Claude Binet describes more fully what Dorat imparted to his students in *La Vie de*

P. de Ronsard (1586, The Life of P. de Ronsard). They studied Greek and Latin, philosophy, and other "doctes sciences" (worthy sciences). Dorat introduced them to Greek tragedy, notably the *Prometheus* of Aeschylus, which they cooperatively translated into French in order to appreciate its nuances. He instinctively recognized their talents and potential and saw in Ronsard a future French Homer.

Dorat's special approach to classical languages was to teach Greek and Latin comparatively, letting the students see that Latin literature often comprised an imitation of a Greek original. For example, he showed his students what Virgil's *Aeneid* owed to Homer's *Iliad*. Dorat's profound knowledge of Greek language and literature thus increased his students' understanding of the roots and structures of the Latin language and the themes of its literature. He gave a moral interpretation to the *Odyssey* and introduced his students to Hesiod and Aeschylus, Aristophanes, and Pindar, as well as to Plato. They also read the Romans that were familiar to all schoolboys of the period: Horace, Ovid, and Catullus. The effect of such readings are clear in the students' poetry. Chamard asserts that Dorat's initiation of his students into Hellenism was his greatest gift to them.

Critics generally believe that Dorat's attitudes informed those of his students. From Dorat the members of the Brigade doubtless learned to find fault with older forms of French poetry, including the writings of Clément Marot, so popular earlier in their own century. His students' work with classical poets inspired in them a desire to reform and change French poetry. In 1548 the magistrate and literary critic Thomas Sébillet codified traditional views of French poetics in his *Art Poétique* (The Art of Poetry), the first such treatise to appear in France. Sebillet's book gave advice that borrowed heavily from the style and taste of Marot and his imitators, the Marotiques. In response, Du Bellay composed *La Défense et Illustration de la Langue Francoyse* (1549, Defense and Illustration of the French language), a work that summarized the revolutionary ideas and feelings Dorat had inculcated in his students. Although Dorat never wrote on the art of poetry directly, he had introduced his students to some of the chief Roman rhetorical sources called upon by Du Bellay in *La Défense et Illustration de la Langue Francoyse:* the orator Quintilian, the stylist Cicero, and the poet Horace, the latter particularly in his own *Ars Poetica* (Art of Poetry). All three of these Roman authors were staples of sixteenth-century education, and Dorat used them as he used the Greek writers—to challenge and sharpen his own and his students' poetical works. As Chamard notes, Dorat and his followers understood that if a knowledge of Greek could strengthen the appreciation and understanding of Latin, then the classical languages could be used similarly to strengthen and enhance their French, eventually allowing it to rival Latin as a language both of ideas and artistic beauty. *Imitatio* (imitation) of the ancients, therefore, was in order as were the creation of French words invented from Greek or Latin roots. Ronsard led the other members of the Pléiade in imitation of the especially difficult Pindaric ode. Dorat had acquainted his students with the Homeric and Virgilian epics, and Ronsard also made an attempt at that genre with his unfinished *La Franciade,* a narrative of the founding of the French monarchy by Francus, a mythical prince of Troy. Dorat's teaching of Greek theater was almost certainly instrumental in leading Jodelle to write *Cléopâtre Captive* (1553, Cleopatra Imprisoned), the first theater piece in French to follow the principles of Greek tragedy.

Dorat in his teaching also addressed the contemporary interest in and resentment of Italianism in French political and cultural life. The Pléiade sought to make French literature the rival of Italian literature. Dorat, Ronsard, Du Bellay, Tyard, Belleau, and Jodelle all produced sonnet cycles in imitation of the Italian poet Petrarch and explored Neoplatonic themes and images, notably those of poetic inspiration, war, virtue, and unrequited love. Tyard translated Neoplatonic dialogues of Marsilio Ficino and Leon Hebraeus in his philosophical works, *Solitaire premier* (First Solitary Treatise) and *Solitaire Second* (1555). Dorat favored the epigram and the epitaph forms as well.

Dorat's followers also imitated his routine of writing about daily events in verse. His own poetry often reads as a verse diary of his life. No doubt much of this work was produced as a self-discipline or exercise, a daily practice of his poet's craft. He wrote about his family, his colleagues, his likes and dislikes.

Dorat's life was marred only by financial worries. His future seemed assured when he was called back to service at the court of the new king in 1549. Dorat instructed King Henri's illegitimate children, Henri, duke of Angoulême, and his three sisters, the princesses Elizabeth, Claude, and Marguerite. The post was not to his liking, however, and he left the court after a year, seemingly poorer than ever, to reestablish his private students at his home. He complains in verse that he received few advantages from the year he spent at court. Moreover, his own home had been violated in his absence, and his belongings had been rifled and stolen. His teaching duties at court had resulted in his forced neglect both of his poet's craft and of his Greek studies.

After spending the next few years reading and studying and making whatever money he could by

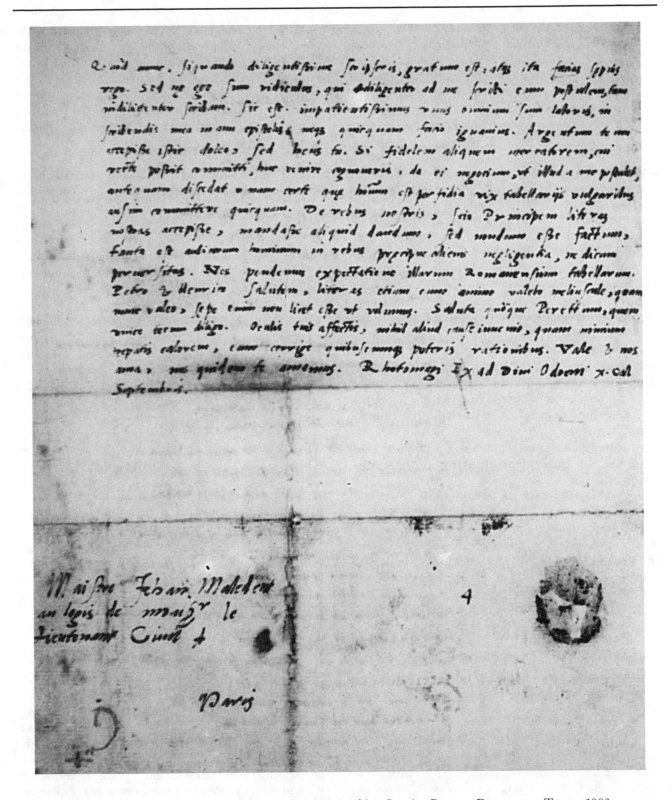

Page from a letter written by Dorat to the humanist Jean Maledent (from Genevieve Demerson, Dorat en son Temps, *1983; Bibliotheque nationale, Paris)*

teaching privately, Dorat in 1556 was appointed to the distinguished post of royal reader at the Collège des Lecteurs Royaux (College of Royal Lecturers), the forerunner of the Collège de France (College of France). Dorat devoted himself to the teaching of Greek and is credited with inspiring a love of the classics in some of the best minds of the day. This felicitous situation did not last long because of political and social instability. In 1562 both the religious wars and the plague shook Paris. As a result, students at the college numbered in the fifties where there had been hundreds, and the professors went unpaid for three years. Dorat left the city for a short time but returned after a few months to pursue his studies. His fortune was to improve, however. Dorat had paid poetic tribute to King Charles IX and his mother, the dowager queen Catherine de Médicis, as well as a host of other prominent figures, and was honored in turn. Many of his tributes and other short poems were collected in *Ioannis Avrati Lemovicis Poetae et Interpretis Regii Poëmatia* (1586, Brief Poems of Jean Dorat, of Limoges and Poet Royal). In 1563 his friend Denis Lambin dedicated the sixth book of his edition of Lucretius to Dorat, praising his expertise in establishing correct editions of ancient texts and his intimate knowledge of their authors.

Dorat's family was doubtless a continuing concern, especially during years that were stressful to the nation as well as personally. After the death of his son Louis, who had been born around 1550, Dorat lavished his attention on his daughter Madeleine (the fate of her twin sister is unknown). According to her epitaph, she was adept at languages and knew Greek and Latin as well as Spanish and Italian. In 1567 at age nineteen she married Nicolas Goulu, a fine Hellenist and probably one of her father's students, who was twice her age. Dorat was not happy with his new son-in-law's name—which in French means "greedy" or "glutton"—but he apparently felt warm affection for him and respected him as a poet. Dorat provided the couple a place to live by giving them the half of his house in which he had formerly received his students. He also named Goulu his successor when he gave up his position at the college in November 1567.

Earlier that year Dolet had become embroiled in a quarrel with Pierre de La Ramée (Peter Ramus), the renowned anti-Aristotelian scholar and another royal reader at the Collège des Lecteurs Royaux. Although Dorat decried La Ramée's arrogance in his letter of complaint to the cardinal of Lorraine, it seems that Dorat was more outraged that La Ramée was lecturing at the college in French rather than in Latin. Although Dorat and his students championed the development and use of the vernacular in the arts and in learning, Dorat found La Ramée's use of French in the classroom offensive. Despite the fact that François I had established French as the official language of the law courts more than two decades earlier, Dorat still believed in the scholarly superiority of the language of Cicero and called for its retention for public academic lectures. His protests went unheeded and, having already chosen his successor and been named "poète royal," he resigned his post.

When the Catholic duke Anne de Montmorency fell in battle at Saint-Denis in 1567, the admiring Dorat wrote one of his best long poems in the duke's honor: *Epitaphes sur le tombeau de haut et puissant seigneur Anne duc de Montmorancy, pair et connestable de France* (1567, Epitaphs on the Tomb of Anne of Montmorency, Peer and Constable of France). The poem is a moral portrait of a great man, and while it is heavily ornamented with the conventional topoi of heroism, Dorat's genuine affection for his hero can be discerned. The poet is dismayed "Quand le peuple François par rebelle fureur recommençoit iouer son Tragique malheur" (When the French people began to play out again their tragic misfortune), which has brought about the especially tragic forfeit of the duke's life. In battle this "chef de l'armée" (chief of the army), though "de vieillesse cassé" (broken by the years), "gardant d'un jeune encore la chaleur intestine" (still possessed a youthful fire). When the noble leader falls, Dorat almost regrets even his compatriots' victory bought by the loss of "un gouverneur si brave" (so worthy a governor).

The poem reveals Dorat's desire for bloody revenge against the Protestants. In the last verse the poet insists that Montmorency died disappointed not to have exacted more vengeance for the disturbance of the peace: "de grand regret d'estre occis par outrance, n'ayant parfaict du païs la vengeance" (regretted so dying by mishap, not having fully sated his country's [desire for] revenge). The violence of the sentiments seem surprising from a man who incarnated the benefits of peace, education, and civilized refinement. Dorat seems to have felt that the Reformers threatened all that was good in France. His implacable opposition to the Protestant cause is also evident in the Latin poem "Elegia in te Deum laudamus" (Elegy: In Thee Oh God We Give Thanks), one of the most enthusiastic verse endorsements of the general nationwide slaughter of Protestants known as the St. Bartholomew's Day massacre that began on 24 August 1572. The poem is a hymn of praise for divine intervention against "the enemy"—the Huguenots—and a celebration of vengeance. It caught the attention and favor of Charles IX, who sent Dorat £ 250 and augmented his pension.

As was also true of his students, Dorat wrote occasional poetry to honor the great and the powerful of his time. His dedicated his long poem "In Originem Nominis, Et Matrimonii Henrici Regis Navarrae et Margaritae Valesiae, Eius Vxoris" (Of the Origins and Celebrating the Marriage of Henry, King of Navarre with Margaret of Valois) to the royal couple, whose wedding took place just a few days before the St. Bartholomew massacre. Many of Dorat's pieces honor the queen mother, Catherine de Médicis, and are filled with mythological detail. One such example, titled "Sur le retour de la royne" (On the Queen's Return), was apparently written contemporaneously in 1579 to commemorate Catherine's return from a political visit to Navarre. Dorat likens Catherine to Ceres in this poem and praises her maternal care for her son Henri III. He depicts the king as protective of his people and his lands: "nostre soleil en sa splendeur divine Henri assez nos champs de ses rais n'enlumine" (our sun in its/his splendor, divine Henry, sheds his rays on our fields). In the role of Ceres, Catherine is the great "nourisiere"(nurturer), an augur of hope who sustains the State. As mother of the king, she is "la paix–des loix la mere" (peace, mother of the laws).

Chamard notes that Dorat overornaments his poems with predictable, academic, conventional allusion. Thus, the king is likened to the sun god: "Phebus, quand par tristesse amere, sa face il va couvrant d'un voile nubileux" (Phoebus, in bitter distress, covers his face in a veil of clouds). Catherine is compared to the great and fertile earth goddess: "ô nostre Ceres si ton plaisir s'adonne a revenir vers nous, ensemble reviendra sa lumiere au soleil, et soudain reprendra tout astre qui le suit sa lumiere sereine, et la lune on verra en sa figure pleine" (O Ceres if your good pleasure persuades you to return to us, the sun also, and the stars will shine once again, and we shall again see the full moon). Thus, Ceres restores brilliance to Phebus. While Dorat's mythological ornamentation seems somewhat overdone to modern tastes, it was at that time a fashionable way of expressing France's greatness.

In his epigram "Au Roy" (To the King), Dorat shows a courtier's style and charm. After congratulating himself on having served five kings and teaching for fifty years, he manages to praise his own poetry while deferring to the greatness of the king, making a wordplay on his own name as a variation on the French word for gold, *or:* "Si par ma Muse j'ay mon siecle doré, ne sousrés que par vous D'Aurat soit dedoré" (If by my Muse I have rendered my times brilliant [golden], only you [sire], can outshine [tarnish] me). "Epitaphe de Paiot," another epitaph in the same collection, is dedicated to a dutiful treasurer. In four verses Dorat describes a life of virtue rewarded. The poet plays on the treasurer's age and vocation and declares his renown and destiny among the blessed. Duquel "comptant des ans soixante et deus, Le corps ici, l'esprit soit mis és cieus" (. . . counting some sixty-two years, the body [remains] here, the spirit must be raised on high).

Although Dorat's pension reached the sum of £1,200 in 1577, he often had difficulty in getting paid at all. For several years his major preoccupation besides writing poetry seems to have been writing pleas, threats, and letters begging friends and patrons for financial support. His monetary worries were eased a bit in 1580 when an epidemic of influenza hit Paris. Because his students decamped, his house was empty and had therefore been commandeered to shelter the sick. Dorat demanded restitution and, supported by the doctors involved, was evidently amply rewarded. Once the danger had passed, the students returned to the capital and Dorat's reputation as a professor reached its apogee. Masson noted that young men came from Germany, Italy, Scotland, England, and even Greece to study Greek under his tutelage.

In his declining years Dorat continued to revise his work and record his impressions of contemporary conditions in verse. The best of his Greek and Latin poems appeared in a Parisian edition titled *Poëmatia* (Brief Poems) in 1586. His widening interest in the rustic life is evident in the pleasure he took reading his friend Claude Gauchet's *Plaisirs de la vie rustique selon les quatre saisons de l'année* (1583, Pleasures of Rustic Life During the Four Seasons of the Year). He still enjoyed his reputation as a great teacher, but as the years passed he began to have fewer and fewer students—a circumstance that caused him concern. Sometime after the death of his first wife, Dorat at the age of seventy-seven or seventy-eight astonished his friends by marrying a second time. The identity of his new wife is unknown, but scholars speculate that she was the nineteen-year-old daughter of a Parisian pastry chef. The couple had a son, Polycarpe, whose birth gave the elderly poet great joy. According to one of Dorat's early biographers, Polycarpe's education was put into the care of his brother-in-law Goulu after Dorat's death, but the boy was no scholar. He became a cloth merchant and died extremely rich.

Not long after his son's birth, Dorat died at Saint-Jean de Latran on 1 November 1588. His final words to those attending his deathbed were a verse from the Gospel of Saint Mark, "Let us go and cross over to the other shore." He was buried in the church of Saint-Benoît in Paris. He had composed more than fifty thousand Latin and French verses in his lifetime.

The critical consensus is that a great deal of the Latin and vernacular verse of the sixteenth century is not of high quality and not worth reading today. This judgment is true for the most part in Dorat's case. Chamard comments that much of Dorat's Latin verse is "merely the exercises of a virtuoso." Indeed, Dorat's legacy as a great pedagogue and humanist far outstrips his talent as a poet. He earned a reputation as a specialist in ancient languages and manuscripts, and other scholars profited from his editions of classical manuscripts, for he had a critic's intuition and could glean the main lines of meaning from an incomplete, poorly copied, or poorly preserved text. His easy familiarity with Greek and Latin and innate understanding of classical authors made him one of the foremost professors of his time. But beyond his vast knowledge of his chosen subjects, Dorat had the ability, the gift, of passing on his appreciation and love of the works of the ancient authors to his contemporaries and to his students. Jean Dorat's greatest contribution to the development of the French language and poetry was as a passionate teacher and mentor to some of France's most gifted poets.

Biography:

Henri Demay, *Jean Dorat (1508–1588)* (Paris: L'Harmattan, 1996).

References:

Grahame Castor, *Pléiade Poetics* (Cambridge: Cambridge University Press, 1964);

Henri Chamard, *Histoire de la Pléiade,* volumes 1, 4 (Paris: Didier, 1961);

Geneviève Demerson, *Dorat et son temps* (Clermont-Ferrand: Adosa, 1983);

Joachim du Bellay, *Défense et Illustration de la Langue Francoyse,* edited by Chamard (Paris: Didier, 1966);

Pierre de Nolhac, *Ronsard et l'humanisme* (Paris: Champion, 1966), pp. 52–83;

Walter J. Ong, *Ramus Method and the Decay of Dialogue* (Cambridge, Mass.: Harvard University Press, 1958);

Timothy J. Reiss, *Tragedy and Truth: Studies in the Development of a Renaissance and Neoclassical Discourse* (New Haven & London: Yale University Press, 1980);

Arthur Tilley, *Studies in the French Renaissance* (Cambridge: Cambridge University Press, 1922), pp. 219–232.

Guillaume du Bartas

(1544 – 1590)

Russell Ganim
University of Nebraska–Lincoln

BOOKS: *La Muse Chrestiene* (Bordeaux: Printed by Simon Millanges, 1574)—comprises *La Judit, L'Uranie, Le Triomfe de la foi,* and sonnets; revised as *Les Œuvres . . . Reveues et augmentees par l'autheur, et divisees en trois parties* (Paris: Printed by Gabriel Buon, 1579)—includes "Poeme pour l'accueil de la Royne de Navarre" in place of the sonnets; *La Judit,* translated by Thomas Hudson as *The Historie of Judith in Forme of a Poem* (Edinburgh: Printed by Thomas Vantrouillier, 1584); *L'Uranie,* translated by James VI as *The Urania or Heavenly Muse,* in *Essayes of a Prentice in the Divine Art of Poesie, with the Rewlis and Cauteles to be Pursued and Avoided* (Edinburgh: Printed by Thomas Vantrouillier, 1584); *Le Triomfe de la foi,* translated by Joshua Sylvester as *The Triumph of Faith,* in *The Triumph of Faith; The Sacrifice of Isaac, the Ship-Wracke of Ionas, with a Song of the Victorie Obtained by the French King at Yvry* (London: Printed by Richard Yardley & Peter Short, 1592);

La Sepmaine ou Creation du monde (Paris: Printed by Michel Gadoulleau, 1578; Paris: Printed by Jean Feburier, 1578); revised as *La Sepmaine ou Creation du monde . . . Reveue, augmentee, & embellie en divers passages par l'auteur mesme. En ceste Quinzieme Edition ont esté adjoustez l'argument general, & amples sommaires au commencement de chasque livre, annotations en marge, & indices propres pour l'intelligence des mots & matieres de tout l'œuvre,* commentary by Simon Goulart (Geneva: Printed by Jacques Chouet, 1581);

Hymne de la Paix . . . Avec Les Neuf Muses Pyrenées, presentées au Roy de Navarre (Antwerp: Printed by Gaspard de la Romaine, 1582);

La Seconde Sepmaine ou Enfance du monde (Paris: Printed by Pierre L'Huillier, 1584); revised as *Le Second Sepmaine . . . Reveuë, augmentee & embellie en divers passages par l'autheur mesme. En ceste nouvelle Edition ont esté adioustez l'argument general, amples sommaires au commencement de chaque livre, annotations en marge, & explications continuelles des principales difficultez du*

Guillaume du Bartas (Corbis)

texte, commentary by Goulart (Geneva: Printed by Jacques Chouet, 1589);

Cantique de la victoire d'Ivry (Caen: Printed by Jacques le Bas, 1590); translated by Joshua Sylvester as *A Song of the Victorie, Obtained by the French King at Yvry,* in *The Triumph of Faith; The Sacrifice of Isaac,* the Ship-Wracke of Ionas, with *A Song of the Victorie Obtained by the French King at Yvry* (London: Printed by Richard Yardley & Peter Short, 1592);

Les Œuvres Poetiques . . . Le tout nouvellement r'imprimé, avec argumens, sommaires & annotations, commentary by Goulart (Paris: Printed for Michelle Nicod, 1608; Geneva: Printed for Samuel Crespin, 1608)–includes *Quelques Epitaphes.*

Editions and Collections: *Les Œuvres . . . Reveües corigees, augmentees de nouveaux, commentaires, annotations en marge, et embellie de figures, sur tous Les Jours de la sepmaine. Plus a esté adjouste, la premiere et Seconde partie de la suitte, avecq l'argument general et amples sommaires au commencement de chacun livre . . . Derniere Edition,* commentary by Simon Goulart (Paris: Printed by Claude Rigaud, 1611; Paris: Printed by Jean de Bordeaulx, 1611; Paris: Printed by Toussainctz du Bray, 1611);

The Works of Guillaume de Salluste Sieur du Bartas, 3 volumes, edited by Urban Tigner Holmes Jr., John Coriden Lyons, Robert White Linker, and others (critical apparatus in English) (Chapel Hill: University of North Carolina, 1935–1940);

La Sepmaine, edited by Kurt Reichenberger (critical apparatus in German) (Tübingen: Niemeyer, 1963);

La Judit, edited by André Baïche (Toulouse: Publication de la Faculté des Lettres et Sciences Humaines de Toulouse, 1970);

La Sepmaine, edited by Yvonne Bellenger (Paris: Société des Textes Française Modernes/Nizet, 1981);

La Sepmaine ou Creation du Monde, edited by Victor Bol (Arles: Actes Sud, 1988);

La Seconde Semaine, 2 volumes, edited by Bellenger and others (Paris: Société des Textes Française Modernes/Klincksieck, 1991, 1992);

Les Suittes de La Seconde Semaine, edited by Bellenger (Paris: Société des Textes Française Modernes/Klincksieck, 1994.

Edition in English: *Bartas: His Divine Weekes and Workes,* translated by Joshua Sylvester (London: Printed by Humphrey Lownes, 1605–1606).

OTHER: *La Lepanthe de Jaques VI. Roy D'Escosse,* translated into French by Du Bartas (Edinburgh: Printed by Robert Waldegrave, 1591).

Guillaume du Bartas's epic *La Sepmaine ou Creation du monde* (1578, The Week, or The Creation of the World) was one of the most influential texts of the late sixteenth century. Some intellectuals in France and on the European continent considered Du Bartas to be a great luminary of French literature, and this reputation lasted a few decades after his death. Although he fell into virtual obscurity in subsequent years, a small revival of interest in Du Bartas occurred in the nineteenth century, and scholars began to show significant interest in his contributions to Renaissance literature in the twentieth century. Du Bartas's life and works provide a window into the political and religious turmoil of sixteenth-century France and a deeper understanding of the literary trends that influenced major writers in France and the rest of Europe.

Du Bartas–a name that came with a title he received when his father died–was born in 1544 as Guillaume de Salluste (also Salustre). His wealthy merchant family lived in the small town of Montfort, France, in what is now the Department of Gers. As a child he may have been sent to Bordeaux to study, but he certainly received traditional training in sciences and letters. In 1564 Du Bartas was sent to Toulouse to pursue a degree in law. At this time Du Bartas, a Calvinist, formed a strong friendship with the Catholic poet Pierre de Brach, an intimate of Michel de Montaigne. De Brach's assistance was of value to Du Bartas both professionally and personally. While in Toulouse, both Du Bartas and Brach participated in the annual poetry competition known as the Jeux Floraux (Floral Games). Du Bartas first entered the competition in 1564, and he captured the top prize the following year. The award-winning poem was secular, as were most of Du Bartas's lyric efforts during these early years. Although he earned his *docteur en droictz* (doctor of laws) in 1567, Du Bartas mainly employed his legal training to oversee and enrich family properties. His chief calling was poetry, and it was primarily through this endeavor that he made a name for himself in artistic, and later political, circles.

As was true of almost any profession in the late 1500s, poets with a title had a better chance of succeeding than those without one. In 1565 the young poet's father, François Salluste, bought a farm from a local bishop. The land, referred to as "Bartas" (meaning "evil forest" in the Gascon dialect), was deeded with minor nobility, conferring upon its owner the title sieur du Bartas (lord of Bartas). The following year, François Salluste died, and he passed to his son membership in the minor nobility and several small but valuable estates in Gascony. The chateau at Bartas became the poet's principal residence. Improvements to this property and others occupied much of the poet's time but enhanced his wealth and standing in court society. The rise of the Du Bartas name aided the arrangement of Du Bartas's marriage around 1570 to Catherine de Manas, daughter of the Sieur d'Homps. This union seems to have been Du Bartas's only marriage; it produced four daughters, none of whom were married when Du Bartas died.

While Du Bartas's title and marriage led to a certain prominence in various Gascon social circles, his literary and political ascendancy was marked by his close relationship to the family of Henri, king of Navarre, who later became Henri IV of France. Henri's mother, the queen of Navarre, was aware of Du Bartas's award for poetry in Toulouse and suggested that he tackle the subject of the Old Testament figure of Judith. The result was *La Judit* (translated as *The Historie of Judith in Forme of a Poem,* 1584), a relatively short epic poem that was first published in Bordeaux in 1574 in a volume titled *La Muse Chrestiene* (The Christian Muse) and later revised in *Les Œuvres* (1579, The Works). The other significant poems in this collection are *L'Uranie* (translated as *The Urania or Heavenly Muse,* 1584) and the *Le Triomfe de la foi* (translated as *The Triumph of Faith,* 1592). While Du Bartas was not satisfied with these works, they established him as a religious poet.

Of the works published in *La Muse Chrestiene, La Judit* has received the most critical attention. Portrayals of Judith slaying the Assyrian general Holofernes abounded in Renaissance art, including a sculpture by Donatello and paintings by Michelangelo and Caravaggio. Judith was appropriated by both Catholics and Protestants in France to embody elements of their respective political agendas. It can be argued that Du Bartas's depiction of Judith is both reactionary and radical; while he was neither a protofeminist nor a militant, the depiction of regicide in a time of civil strife carries obvious political overtones. Whatever Du Bartas's intentions may have been, in his preface to the work he readily admits his preference for imitating Homer's *Iliad* (circa eighth century–seventh century B.C.), Virgil's *Aeneid* (circa 19 B.C.), and Ludovico Ariosto's *Orlando Furioso* (1516) rather than following "l'ordre ou la frase du texte de la Bible" (the order or the words of the biblical text). Hence, Du Bartas says his desire to reflect epic scale and drama is greater than his desire to reproduce accurately a biblical event. Here Du Bartas claims to model his efforts after those of illustrious predecessors, both Ancient and "Modern." He clearly wants his work to achieve the status of "literature" in the highest sense of the term. Although Du Bartas remained unsatisfied with *La Judit,* it and the other works published in *La Muse Chrestiene* indicate an artistic ambition that was to come to fruition later in the poet's career.

While Du Bartas's talent was chiefly responsible for his success, there is no doubt that Du Bartas's renown benefited from his close association with Navarre. From the return of Navarre from captivity in 1576 until Du Bartas's death in 1590, the poet faithfully served the House of Navarre in a variety of functions. A member of the king's court at Nérac, Du Bartas held the positions of *écuyer trenchant* (squire), *gentilhomme ser-* *vant* (gentleman servant), *gentilhomme ordinaire* (ordinary gentleman), and most notably the title of ambassador to Scottish king James VI. In this last post Du Bartas's mission was to secure money and soldiers while attempting to arrange a marriage between James VI and Henri's sister, thereby solidifying the alliance between the Scottish throne and French Protestants. Du Bartas's affinity for Navarre went beyond shared regional origins and religious convictions. Like many of his era, Du Bartas saw in Navarre a kind of progressive, humanistic leadership that could benefit society culturally and spiritually. Navarre and/or his family provided inspiration for several occasional poems, among them a work dedicated to Navarre's first wife, the infamous Reine Margot, titled "Poeme pour l'accueil de la Royne de Navarre" (1578, The Welcome of the Queen to Navarre), as well as the *Hymne de la Paix* (1582, Hymn of Peace), written to celebrate Henri's skill in concluding the 1580 Peace of Fleix that nominally ended the Seventh War of Religion. Additionally, just before his death, Du Bartas wrote and published his *Cantique de la victoire d'Ivry* (1590, Song of the Victory at Ivry), which lauded the king's decisive victory over the Catholic League on the outskirts of Paris in March 1590. While legend has it that Du Bartas fought in and later succumbed to wounds suffered in that battle, he actually died in August near the chateau of Bartas.

Although he was loyal to his king and his religion, Du Bartas was viewed as a moderate who more than once sought to reconcile differences between Protestants and Catholics. Indeed, his poetry was read and respected by noted Catholic poets of the royal court in Paris. While documents indicate that Du Bartas was awarded funds to raise troops for the Huguenot cause, he was seemingly a reluctant combatant, and his poetry and military career show little of the aggressiveness that characterized the other renowned Huguenot poet-commander of the day, Théodore Agrippa d'Aubigné. Still, some scholars have plausibly suggested that had Du Bartas lived longer, he would have broken with Henri over the latter's conversion to Catholicism on assuming the French throne.

In his literary works, Du Bartas's Protestant orientation is certainly present, but more striking is his use of other traditions that render his work among the most distinctive of the late Renaissance and early Baroque periods. His most noted works, the *La Sepmaine ou Creation du monde* and the *La Seconde Sepmaine ou Enfance du monde* (1584, The Second Week, or the Childhood of the World), mix literary forms and themes in ways typical of humanistic literary efforts. *La Sepmaine* is based on the events of Genesis and is divided into seven *jours* (days). Originally, *La Seconde Sepmaine* was also to have consisted of seven days, but because of Du Bartas's ill

Title page for the first collected edition of Du Bartas's works (from The Works of Guillaume de Salluste Sieur du Bartas, 1935; Thomas Cooper Library, University of South Carolina)

health, as well as his diplomatic and domestic obligations, the poet was able to complete only four of these segments. *La Seconde Sepmaine* is also structured differently from the first in that each *jour* is divided into sections that might be called "chapters." The titles of these chapters—including "Eden," "L'Arche" (The Arc), "Les Peres" (The Fathers), and "Histoire de Jonas" (The Story of Jonas)—deal with Old Testament events and cast them in light of humanity's sinful nature and God's redemptive plan for the universe. While Du Bartas chooses not to focus either on the New Testament or on the portrait of Christ nearly as much as some of his Protestant and Catholic contemporaries, it is clear that if the Old Testament is to make sense to Renaissance readers, it is only within the context of the New. Du Bartas's purpose in extrapolating voluminously on the figures and events of the Old Testament is to educate his readers in the historical and spiritual continuum that constitutes human and divine existence as recounted in the Bible.

Du Bartas's "educational project" is in part characterized by long descriptions and catalogues of natural phenomena such as flora, fauna, and celestial bodies. In fact, Du Bartas's portrayal of the natural world is extremely vivid, and traditionally such poetry has been categorized as "scientific." Several prominent Renaissance poets, including Peletier du Mans, Pierre de Ronsard, and Maurice Scève, wrote scientific works of this kind. What distinguishes Du Bartas's descriptions, however, is that they occur within the context of lyric poetry, and the descriptions are closely tied to the poet's religious convictions. In some respects, Du Bartas's exhaustive listing of birds, plant life, and the movement of the stars finds its origin in antiquity with the Latin author Lucretius's *De Rerum Natura* (mid first century B.C., On the Nature of Things). For Lucretius, the goal of such "encyclopedic" or "didactic" poetry was to instruct the reader on the marvels of the universe, especially those of the natural world. However, Lucretius's project was secular in design and the author portrays the gods as indifferent to human concerns. Lucretius also made no effort to hide his distrust of organized religion. Sometimes called a "Christian Lucretius," Du Bartas aimed to illustrate the intricate totality of the universe in order to highlight the majesty of God's creation. In Du Bartas's world, the great and small are interconnected by design and embody the perfection that is the godhead itself. The author's goal is to increase readers' knowledge of the deity's earthly and celestial domains in order to enhance awareness of the Creator. For Du Bartas, greater knowledge of the physical world and of God's role in it does not guarantee salvation, but it does strengthen the reader's intellect and puts him or her in a better position to make spiritual progress, if not to receive grace.

Most critics rightfully view the *Sepmaines* as relatively free of partisan Huguenot discourse. Yet, the works do represent, at least indirectly, the Protestant tenet of individual interpretation of the Bible or other religious literature. The poet sees himself as an intermediary between God and the reader, but at the same time, he presents the world as a kind of book from which believers (and perhaps nonbelievers) have the freedom to draw their own inspirations and conclusions. Implicit in the text is the idea that individuals, once informed and motivated, can become responsible for their relationship with God. In Du Bartas's work—unlike other, more sectarian literature of the period, whether Reformist or Catholic—the role of religious institutions and their officials is diminished. Within the intellectual climate of the Renaissance, "scientific" and "encyclopedic" works such the *Sepmaines* were consistent with humanistic aims of cultivating the mind and spirit through the discovery of what were believed to be universal and interdependent truths about the world and human nature. This synthetic, if not syncretic, dimension of the *Sepmaines* is reinforced by the work of Simon Goulart, a Calvinist pastor whose annotations to early editions of Du Bartas's poetry aided readers in understanding the historical, literary, and theological frames of reference embedded in the text.

The *Sepmaines* represent, in France at least, the most successful effort to revive the epic genre during the sixteenth century. While the epic was still highly regarded, its French incarnations during the period before Du Bartas left much to be desired. Among the predecessors of the *Sepmaines* was a failed effort by Ronsard, *La Franciade* (1572), which recounts the founding of the French nation by Francus, the presumptive Gallic equivalent of Aeneas. Unlike Ronsard's work and other traditional epics, which are organized around the exploits of a warrior-hero, the *Sepmaines* form a conceptual epic whose conflicts between existence and the void, and between mortality and immortality, are played out in the natural and cosmic worlds. If there is a traditional hero in Du Bartas's works, it is God himself, who through the essence of his perfection is able to engender all life. While Du Bartas's ambitious project found success with readers, some critics have described it as soporifically long, impersonal, and pedantic. Du Bartas has been criticized for not imbuing his text with an adequate sense of the mystery—if not the *frisson* (shivers)—typical of many devotional texts, and his style has been criticized as bulky with awkward rhyme schemes.

Among Guillaume du Bartas's contemporaries in France, reaction to his works was mixed. While some in French literary circles valued Du Bartas's works as highly as Ronsard's, the leader of the Pléiade viewed Du Bartas as a rival and critiqued his work harshly. Meanwhile, Ronsard's mentor Jean Dorat defended Du Bartas's poetry, and many French humanists such as Pierre Charron, Frédéric Morel II, and Henri II Estienne either drew inspiration from Du Bartas or contributed Latin or Greek lyrics to the *La Seconde Sepmaine*. Outside France, Du Bartas's poetry was quickly embraced in Northern Europe. Many translations of the *Sepmaines* and other works appeared in English, German, and Dutch. Josuah Sylvester's *Bartas his Divine Weekes and Workes* (1605–1606) is the most noted of the many English translations. Du Bartas's popularity in Britain is evident in his influence on Sir Philip Sidney, Edmund Spenser, and John Milton. His reputation also extended into Southern Europe, as Italian and Spanish versions of his major works were published shortly after the poet's death. Further aiding the dissemination

of Du Bartas's works, several Latin translations appeared in the late sixteenth and early seventeenth centuries. In the years following Henri IV's assassination in 1610, however, Du Bartas's influence began to wane. The poet is mentioned in some literary histories published in the seventeenth and eighteenth centuries, but it is not until the Romantic period that interest began to increase, especially with Johann Wolfgang von Goethe's favorable assessment of Du Bartas as well as with Charles-Augustin Sainte-Beuve's negative evaluation of the poet. Finally, a twentieth- and twenty-first-century revival of interest in Du Bartas's narrative, linguistic, and rhetorical strategies has led to heightened awareness of his genius and enriched scholars' understanding of the ideological and literary landscape of sixteenth-century France.

Bibliography:

Yvonne Bellenger and Jean-Claude Ternaux, *Du Bartas: Ouvrage préparé avec le concours du Centre national du livre,* Bibliographie des écrivans français, no. 12 (Paris: Memini, 1998).

References:

Michel Braspart, *Du Bartas, Poète Chrétien* (Neuchâtel & Paris: Delachaux & Niestlé, 1947);

Bruno Braunrot, *L'Imagination poétique chez Du Bartas: Elements de sensibilite baroque dans la Creation du monde* (Chapel Hill: University of North Carolina Department of Romance Languages, 1973);

Terence C. Cave, *Devotional Poetry in France, c. 1570–1613* (Cambridge: Cambridge University Press, 1969);

James Dauphiné, ed., *Du Bartas, poète encyclopédique du XVIe siècle: Colloque International, Faculté des letters et sciences humaines de Pauet des pays de l'adour, 7, 8 et 9 mars 1986* (Lyons: La Manufacture, 1988);

Jan Miernowski, *Dialectique et connaissance dans La Sepmaine de Du Bartas* (Geneva: Droz, 1992);

Michel Prieur, *Le Monde et l'homme de Du Bartas* (Paris: Sedes, 1993);

Albert-Marie Schmidt, *La Poésie scientifique en France au seizième siècle: Ronsard—Maurice Scève—Baïf—Belleau—Du Bartas—Agrippa d'Aubigné* (Paris: Michel, 1938);

Paula Sommers, "Gendered Readings of The Book of Judith: Guillaume du Bartas and Gabrielle de Coignard," *Romance Quarterly,* 48 (2001): 211–220.

Papers:

Important collections of Guillaume du Bartas's manuscripts and papers are at the Société Archéologique du Gers and the Bibliothèque Municipale in Auch, France.

Joachim du Bellay

(1522? – 1 January 1560)

Eric MacPhail
Indiana University

BOOKS: *L'Olive et quelques autres œuvres poëtiques,* as J.D.B.A. (Paris: Printed for Arnoul l'Angelier, 1549)—comprises *L'Olive,* "Anterotique de la vieille et de la jeune amye," and *Vers lyriques;* revised and enlarged as *L'Olive . . . augmentee depuis la premiere edition* (Paris: Printed for Gilles Corrozet and Arnoul l'Angelier, 1550)—includes *L'Olive* in 115 sonnets, "La Musagnoeomachie," and "Contre les envieux poetes";

La Deffence et Illustration de la Langue Francoyse, as J.D.B.A. (Paris: Printed for Arnoul l'Angelier, 1549); translated by Gladys M. Turquet as *The Defence and Illustration of the French Language* (London: Dent, 1939);

Recueil de Poesie (Paris: Printed by Guillaume Cavellat, 1549)—includes the "Prosphonematique au Roy Treschrestien Henry II" and seventeen new "Vers Liriques"; revised and expanded as *Recueil de Poesie . . . reveu et augmenté depuis la première édition* (Paris: Printed by Guillaume Cavellat, 1553)—includes "A une Dame";

Le Quatriesme livre de l'Eneide de Vergile . . . Autres œuvres de l'invention du translateur, as J.D.B.A. (Paris: Printed by Vincent Certenas, 1552)—comprises *Le Quatriesme livre de l'Eneide,* "La Complainte de Didon à Enée," "Sur la Statue de Didon," and the "Œuvres de l'invention de l'Autheur";

Le Premier Livre des antiquitez de Rome contenant une generale description de sa grandeur, et comme une deploration de sa ruine . . . Plus un Songe ou Vision sur le mesme subject (Paris: Printed by Federic Morel, 1558); translated by Edmund Spenser as "Ruines of Rome" and "Visions of Bellay," in *Complaints: Containing Sundrie Small Poemes of the Worlds Vanitie* (London: Printed for William Ponsonbie, 1591);

Les Regrets et autres œuvres poëtiques (Paris: Printed by Federic Morel, 1558); translated by C. H. Sisson as *The Regrets* (Manchester, U.K.: Carcanet, 1984);

Joachim du Bellay (Harlingue/Roger-Viollet/Getty Images)

Divers Jeux Rustiques et autres œuvres poëtiques (Paris: Printed by Federic Morel, 1558);

Poematum libri quator (Paris: Printed by Federic Morel, 1558)—includes *Amores,* translated by Hubert W. Hawkins as *The Amores of Faustina,* edited, with an introduction, by Hawkins (Manquin, Va.: Uppingham House, 2004);

Discours au Roy sur la trefve de l'an M.D.LV (Paris: Printed by Federic Morel, 1558);

Hymne au Roy sur la prinse de Callais . . . avec quelques autres œuvres . . . sur le mesme subject (Paris: Printed by Federic Morel, 1558);

Entreprise du Roy-Daulphin pour le tournoy, soubz le nom des chevaliers advantureux . . . (Paris: Printed by Federic Morel, 1559);

Epithalame sur le mariage de tresillustre Prince Philibert Emanuel, Duc de Savoye, et tresillustre Princesse Marguerite de France . . . (Paris: Printed by Federic Morel, 1559);

Tumulus Henrici secundi, Gallorum regis christianiss (Paris: Printed by Federic Morel, 1559);

Antonii Minarii Tumulus Latinogallicus (Paris: Printed by Federic Morel, 1559);

Louange de la France et du Roy Treschrestien Henry II (Paris: Printed by Federic Morel, 1560)–includes "Discours au Roy sur la Poesie";

Ode sur la naissance du petit Duc de Beaumont, as J.D.B.A. (Paris: Printed by Federic Morel, 1561)–includes the "Sonnets à la Royne de Navarre" and a "Hymne chrestien";

Ample Discours au roy sur le faict des quatre estats du royaume de France (Paris: Printed by Federic Morel, 1567);

Œuvres françoises de Joachim Du-Bellay, edited by Guillaume Aubert (Paris: Printed by Federic Morel, 1568)–includes the "Amours de I. du Bellay," which is a sequence of twenty-nine love sonnets, and other poems;

Xenia seu illustrium quorundam nominum allusiones (Paris: Printed by Federic Morel, 1569)–includes "Elegia ad Ianum Morellum, Pyladem suum."

Collections: *Œuvres françoises de Joachim Du Bellay,* 2 volumes, edited by Charles Marty-Laveaux, La Pléiade françoise, nos. 1–2 (Paris: Lemerre, 1866, 1867);

Œuvres poétiques, 6 volumes, edited by Henri Chamard (Paris: Cornély / Hatchette / Droz for Société des Textes Français Modernes, 1908–1931)–comprises volume 1 (1908): *Recueils de sonnets, part 1;* volume 2 (1910): *Recueils de sonnets, part 2;* volume 3 (1912): *Recueils lyriques, part 1;* volume 4 (1919): *Recueils lyriques, part 2;* volume 5 (1923): *Recueils lyriques, part 3;* and volume 6 (1931): *Discours et traductions;*

Œuvres poétiques, volumes 7–8, edited by Geneviève Demerson (Paris: Nizet for Société des Textes Français Modernes, 1984, 1985)–comprises volume 7: *Œuvres latines: Poemata* and volume 8: *Autres œuvres latines;*

Œuvres complètes, edited by Olivier Millet and others (Paris: Champion, 2003–   )–comprises volume 1: *La Deffence, et illustration de la langue françoyse,* edited by Francis Goyet and Olivier Millet; and volume 2: *L'Olive et quelques autres œuvres poétiques (1549); Recueil de poesie; L'Olive augmentée (1550),* edited by Marie-Dominique Legrand and others.

Edition in English: *Antiquitez de Rome,* translated by Edmund Spenser, edited by Malcolm C. Smith (Binghamton, N.Y.: Center for Medieval and Early Renaissance Studies, 1994).

OTHER: "A la ville du Mans," in Jacques Peletier du Mans's, *Œuvres poëtiques* (Paris: Printed by M. de Vascosan for himself and G. Corrozet, 1547) folio 103, verso;

"Tombeau de Marguerite Royne de Navarre," "Imitation de l'ode latine de Jean Dorat," and "Les deux Marguerites," in *Le Tombeau de Marguerite de Valois, Royne de Navarre* (Paris: Printed by Michel Fezandat & Robert Granlon for Vincent Sartenas, 1551);

Adrien Turnèbe, *La Nouvelle Maniere de faire son profit des Lettres,* translated into French by Du Bellay, as I. Quintil du Tronssay en Poictou (Poitiers, 1559)–includes Du Bellay's "Le Poëte courtisan";

Michel de L'Hospital, *Discours sur le sacre du Treschrestien Roy Francoys II,* translated into French by Du Bellay (Paris: Printed by Federic Morel, 1560);

Virgil, *Deux livres de l'Eneide,* translated by Du Bellay (Paris: Printed by Federic Morel, 1560)–includes Du Bellay's "Le Sixiesme Livre de l'Eneide."

Joachim du Bellay was one of the most important lyric poets of the European Renaissance. With Pierre de Ronsard, he founded the influential poetic movement known as La Pléiade. In his brief career Du Bellay created an enduring legacy with his sonnet sequences, his translations, his neo-Latin verses and occasional poems, and his prose manifesto in defense of the French language. He championed the renovation of French poetry through the imitation of classical and humanist models, and in the process he contributed to the distortion of French literary history through his repudiation of previous generations of French poets. In his imitative dialogue with the ancients, Du Bellay both celebrates and interrogates a Renaissance that depends on continuity with antiquity. He also creates a haunting voice of exile, both from his native land and from his humanist ideals, and this characteristic more than any other defines Du Bellay's place in the poetic tradition.

Du Bellay was born either in 1522 or 1524 in the castle of la Turmelière in Liré, near Angers. His native province is an important motif in his verse, and he regularly signed his works "J.D.B.A" for Joachim du Bellay Angevin. Du Bellay came from a family of illustrious statesmen and prelates who distinguished themselves in the service of the French kings François I and Henri II in the first half of the sixteenth century. Du Bellay, however, was born into a minor branch of the family and never enjoyed the status of his more exalted cousin, Jean du Bellay, who was appointed Bishop of Paris and Archbishop of Bordeau before being named Cardinal in 1535. Du Bellay's parents, Jean and Renée, died when he was just a child, leaving him to the indifferent care of his older brother René, whom he held responsible for

**≫LA DEF-
FENCE, ET IL-
LVSTRATION DE LA
Langue Francoyse.**

Par I. D. B. A.

Imprimé à Paris pour Arnoul l'Angelier,
tenât sa Bouticque au second pillier
de la grand' sale du Palays.

1549.

AVEC PRIVILEGE.

Title page for Du Bellay's book that came to be regarded as the poetic manifesto for the Pléiade (Frédéric Boyer, Joachim du Bellay, 1958; Thomas Cooper Library, University of South Carolina)

the neglect of his education in a poem of uncertain veracity (the Latin elegy to Jean Morel). In his own estimation, Du Bellay spent the better part of his youth and adolescence "rather uselessly," and to aggravate matters, he suffered from delicate health right from his birth. There are no documentary traces of Du Bellay's youth until he entered law school at the University of Poitiers in 1545, where he began to engage with literary and humanist circles for the first time. At Poitiers he met Marc Antoine de Muret, later to become one of the most distinguished scholars and teachers of the Renaissance, and Jacques Peletier du Mans, in whose *Oeuvres poëtiques* (1547, Poetic Works) Du Bellay published his first poem, a ten-verse stanza in honor of the city of Le Mans. In Poitiers, Du Bellay is thought to have met Ronsard, whom he followed to Paris in 1547 in order to study with the Hellenist Jean Dorat at the Collège de Coqueret.

At Coqueret, Du Bellay found his vocation as a poet through an arduous regimen of study and the emulation of his fellow students Ronsard and Jean-Antoine de Baïf, who formed the nucleus of the Pléiade. Their preceptor Dorat, whom biographer Guillaume Colletet describes as "the father of all our most excellent poets," taught the allegorical interpretation of ancient poets and encouraged the vernacular imitation of Greek and Latin models. In addition to receiving a

solid humanist foundation, Du Bellay was strongly influenced by the vogue for Italian poetry and poetic forms that flourished at the court of Henri II and Catherine de Médicis. He avidly studied Petrarch's *Il Canzoniere* (circa 1336–1347) as well as the anthologies of contemporary Petrarchan love poetry published in Venice by Gabriel Giolito in the late 1540s. These anthologies furnished the models for many of Du Bellay's and Ronsard's earliest love poems.

An important stimulus or provocation for Du Bellay's literary career was the publication in 1548 of Thomas Sebillet's *Art Poétique François* (French Art of Poetry). Sebillet's manual of French poetry champions the work of Clément Marot and of his followers, known as the Ecole Marotique (Marot School), while expressing an exalted and even hieratic view of poetry that anticipates many of the cherished themes of the Pléiade. To answer this work, Du Bellay composed a manifesto of the new poetic movement, published in 1549 under the title *La Deffence et Illustration de la Langue Francoyse* (translated as *The Defence and Illustration of the French Language,* 1939). Dedicated to Cardinal Jean Du Bellay, *La Deffence et Illustration de la Langue Francoyse* is a major prose work in its own right, distinguished as much for its provocative opinions as for its tortuous logic. The first book, which consists of twelve chapters, purports to defend the French language as a medium of literary expression against neo-Latin chauvinists who derided all vernaculars as barbaric. Du Bellay also implicitly responds to the cultural chauvinism of Italian humanists, who from Petrarch to Baldassare Castiglione regularly denounced the French as barbarians. As a defender of the vernacular, Du Bellay appeals to a sort of linguistic relativism that challenges the hierarchical relationship of human languages at the same time as he appeals to the principle of historical supersession. Chapter 9 especially, where the author recognizes the superiority of modern inventions such as printing and firearms, is often cited in surveys of the idea of progress and in the historiography of the quarrel of the ancients and the moderns.

The defense of the vernacular entails the question of how to render the national language illustrious and how to confer upon it the same status and prestige as the classical languages. In response to this problem, Du Bellay advocates the imitation of classical and humanist models to the exclusion of native literary models. He also rejects poetic translation and discourages neo-Latin composition, two positions he later retracted both in theory and in practice. The shifting series of images that Du Bellay evokes in the first book to describe the imitative process—a form of digestion, transplantation, and architectural reconstruction—have fascinated critics for their instability as well as for their rich intertextual associations. They remind the reader that Du Bellay's vaunted theory of imitation is much more a poetic impulse than a coherent discursive argument.

Book 2, also divided into twelve chapters, elaborates on the importance of imitation while offering a succinct defamatory survey of French poetic tradition, all under the pretense of advising aspiring French poets on which genres to select and which models to emulate. Chapter 2 considers French poets, both ancient and modern, and finds them wanting. In the very first sentence, Du Bellay sets the polemical tone of the chapter when he declares that of all the old French poets, only two are still worth reading: the authors of the *Roman de la Rose* (circa 1237–1277), Jean de Meun and Guillaume de Lorris. As for the moderns, he disdains even to name them, but he does level indirect and veiled attacks, a technique of defamation that has entertained readers from his own time to the present. Purporting to challenge anonymous critics of modern poetry, he reports the judgment that one poet lacks knowledge and would have been twice as famous if he had written only half as much, a description that seems to target Marot. Another person is described as more philosopher than poet, which may implicate Antoine Héroët's Neoplatonic love poetry. Another seeks fame through others' verses and fears to publish under his own name. This indictment fits Mellin de Saint-Gelais, Ronsard's great rival as court poet in the reign of Henri II. Finally, through excess of erudition, another poet has achieved such obscurity that his works are as impenetrable to the learned as they are to the ignorant. This description seems to suit Maurice Scève, author of the *Délie* (1544), although one sixteenth-century reader of *La Deffence et Illustration de la Langue Francoyse* found the portrait adequate to Du Bellay himself. Employing dismissive comments attributed to unnamed critics but certainly representative of his own views and aims, Du Bellay prepares his main thesis that French poetry is capable of a more exquisite form if French poets only turned away from their French predecessors and imitated the ancient Greeks and Latins: "mais aussi diroy-je bien qu'on pouroit trouver en notre Langue (si quelque scavant homme y vouloit mettre la main) une forme de poësie beaucoup plus exquise, la quele il faudroit chercher en ces vieux Grecz et Latins, non point és aucteurs Francoys" (but I would also maintain that one could find in our language [if some learned man would set his hand to it] a much more exquisite form of poetry, which would have to be sought for among the old Greeks and Latins, and not among the French authors). By insisting at every turn on the importance of imitating non-French literary models, Du Bellay means to parry Sebillet's canonization of Marot as the model French poet.

In chapter 3 of book 2, the topic of imitation leads Du Bellay to rehearse the question of whether art or nature contributes more to the success of a poet. His answer is the familiar compromise between nature, associated with inspiration, and art, identified with imitation. Having dutifully acknowledged that talent without learning surpasses learning without talent, the author insists that his project of enhancing the French language will never be realized "sans doctrine et sans crudition" (without learning and study). Consequently, he advocates a comprehensive program of literary imitation of models drawn from both the classical and the vernacular languages: "je veux bien avertir ceux qui aspirent à cette gloire, d'immiter les bons aucteurs Grecz et Romains, voyre bien Italiens, Hespagnolz et autres, ou du tout n'ecrire point, si non à soy (comme on dit) et à ses Muses" (I must warn those who aspire to this glory, to imitate the approved Greek and Roman authors, indeed the Italians, Spanish and others, or else not to write at all, if not to himself [as the saying goes] and to his Muses). Among the potential literary models, the French are conspicuous in their absence.

In chapter 4 Du Bellay addresses the issue of genre. He advocates the cultivation of classical and Italian genres, such as the ode and the sonnet, in lieu of native forms such as the ballade, rondeau, and chanson, which he dismisses as "episseries qui corrumpent le goust de nostre Langue, et ne servent si non à porter temoingnaige de notre ignorance" (spices which corrupt the taste of our language and only serve to testify to our ignorance.) The author encounters some embarrassment in this section of his work, since many of the genres that he advocates had already been cultivated by Marot, including the sonnet, of which Marot is the acknowledged pioneer in French poetry. Du Bellay is even compelled to recognize Marot's precedence in the eclogue, the only favorable mention Marot receives in the work.

Book 2, chapter 6 of *La Deffence et Illustration de la Langue Francoyse* addresses a contentious question of literary usage by authorizing a moderate use of neologisms and archaisms, two categories of *verba inusitata* (unusual words). Erasmus similarly had endorsed this approach in keeping with the Quintilian tradition of rhetoric. Subsequent chapters deal with the technical aspects of versification, a topic readers might expect to be prominent in an *art poétique* but in which Du Bellay seems to have taken only a meager interest as a theoretician. One notable feature of this section is that Du Bellay admits the possibility of blank verse, which he calls "vers libre." In fact, he later furnished one of the rare examples of blank verse in French Renaissance lyric poetry in sonnet 114 of *L'Olive*.

La Deffence et Illustration de la Langue Francoyse concludes with an exhortation to the French to write in their own language and encomiastic praise of France. Du Bellay's militant nationalism rings somewhat hollow, however, in the wake of his wholesale rejection of French literary tradition. Following the last chapter, there is a

L·OLIVE
ET QVELQVES
AVTRES OEVVRES POE-
TICQVES.

Le contenu de ce liure.

Cinquante Sonnetz à la louange de l Oliue.

L'Anterotique de la vieille,& de la
ieune Amye.

Vers Lyriques.

I. D. B. A.

CAELO MVSA BEAT

Imprimé à Paris pour Arnoul l'Angelier
tenant sa Bouticque au second pillier de
la grand' sale du Palays.

1549.

Auec priuilege.

Title page for Du Bellay's first collection of poems, recognized as the first French sonnet sequence (from Frédéric Boyer, Joachim du Bellay, *1958; Thomas Cooper Library, University of South Carolina)*

"Conclusion de tout l'Oeuvre" (Conclusion of the Whole Work), a "Sonnet à l'ambitieux et avare ennemy des bonnes lettres" (Sonnet to the Ambitious and Avaricious Enemy of Good Literature), and a paragraph "Au Lecteur" (To the Reader). This prolonged conclusion betrays the author's unease and anxiety to defend his own dubious arguments. Du Bellay's problem is that he wants to pose not only as the champion of the vernacular but also as the first valid French poet, as if he could enrich the French language by evacuating French literary history at one stroke. The tensions and even the incoherence of this project managed to convince Barthélemy Aneau that Du Bellay's purpose was not the defense and illustration but rather the "offense et denigration" (offense and denigration) of his native language.

According to the standard chronology of his works, Du Bellay published a collection of sonnets and odes, *L'Olive et quelques autres oeuvres poëtiques* (The Olive and Other Poetic Works), at the same time as *La Deffence et Illustration de la Langue Francoyse,* as if to offer a practical demonstration of his theory of imitative enrichment of the vernacular. The fifty sonnets of *L'Olive,* recognized as the first sonnet sequence in French, appear to offer a poor vindication of the theory, in part because so many of the poems merely translate Italian verses from the Giolito anthologies. Ironically, Du Bellay expressly condemns

poetic translation in *La Deffence et Illustration de la Langue Francoyse,* where he strives to maintain a tenuous distinction between translation and imitation, both of which are admitted as legitimate practices by Sebillet in his *Art poétique.* To compound the dilemma, literary history has conclusively demonstrated that many of the arguments Du Bellay advances in defense of the vernacular are actually translations of passages written in defense of Italian from Sperone Speroni's *Dialogo delle lingue* (1542, Dialogue of the Languages). Du Bellay later recanted his hostility to poetic translation in 1552, when he dedicated his 1552 translation of book 4 of Virgil's *Aeneid* (circa 29–19 B.C.) to his friend Jean Morel.

For its polemical tone and infuriating self-promotion, *La Deffence et Illustration de la Langue Francoyse* provoked a wave of controversy, particularly among those who resented Du Bellay's comprehensive dismissal of the native poetic tradition. The most petulant and tenacious attack was launched by the humanist pedagogue Barthélemy Aneau, writing under the pseudonym of Le Quintil Horatien, a name derived from Quintilius, the figure who exemplifies the uncompromising critic in Horace's *Ars poetica* (circa 23–8 B.C.). Posing as a linguistic nationalist, Quintil describes the author of *La Deffence et Illustration de la Langue Francoyse* as a "peregrineur" (foreigner, or perhaps foreign agent) for his advocacy of Greek, Latin, and Italian models. Du Bellay responded to his critics in the preface to the revised edition of *L'Olive,* published in 1550, where he disavows "superstitious imitation" in favor of "natural invention" or originality. He also proclaims his intention to enrich the vernacular with a "new or rather ancient renewed poetry." This oxymoronic description goes to the heart of the problematic identity of the Renaissance, whose greatest novelty is its renewal of antiquity.

In late 1549, between the treatise on literature and the attack it provoked, Du Bellay published a lyric collection titled *Recueil de Poesie* (Poetry Anthology), dedicated to Marguerite of France, the sister of King Henri II. The first poem in the collection is the "Prosphonematique," an address to King Henri II on the occasion of his royal entry into Paris on 16 June 1549. Here Du Bellay, like his colleague Ronsard in a contemporary poem, seizes on the occasion of this public ceremony in order to claim his role in enhancing the cultural prestige of the kingdom at the outset of a new reign, and thus a new competition for royal patronage. Another piece in this collection is addressed to the poet's relative Cardinal Jean du Bellay, to whom *La Deffence et Illustration de la Langue Francoyse* is also dedicated. Through his strategic dedications, Du Bellay sought to define his relationships to power and patronage at the outset of his career and at the beginning of a poetic revolution he helped to initiate.

Du Bellay's intense efforts in poetry, prose, and propaganda in the first year of his celebrity are generally thought to have taken a severe toll on his health. More-over, in 1551 the death of Du Bellay's older brother René left the poet with custody of his nephew Claude and also placed him at the center of a series of intrafamily lawsuits resulting from René's shady real-estate transactions. As a result of this convergence of events, Du Bellay's literary production slackened noticeably from 1550 to 1553.

Nevertheless, the poetry Du Bellay did compose during this period took some interesting new directions. The expanded *L'Olive* appeared in 1550, with the number of sonnets increased from 50 to 115. The most remarkable additions are the final poems, which combine Neoplatonic motifs with Christian themes. The best-known sonnet of the collection is number 113, known as "the sonnet of the Idea," where the poet exhorts his imprisoned soul to escape from the body and to ascend to the pure realm of Ideas:

Que songes-tu, mon âme emprisonnée?
Pourquoi te plaît l'obscur de notre jour,
Si pour voler en un plus clair séjour
Tu as au dos l'aile bien empennée?
Là est le bien que tout esprit désire,
Là le repos où tout le monde aspire,
Là est l'amour, là le plaisir encore.
Là, ô mon âme, au plus haut ciel guidée,
Tu y pourras reconnaître l'Idée
De la beauté qu'en ce monde j'adore.

(What are you thinking of, my imprisoned soul?
Why do you prefer the darkness of our day
When to escape to a clearer stay
You have wings well affixed to your back?
There is the good that every mind desires,
There is the rest to which the whole world aspires,
There is love, there is pleasure too.
There, my soul to the highest heaven guided,
You will know the Idea
Of the beauty which in this world I adore.)

Critics have disputed whether the final movement of the poem represents spiritual transcendence or a return to material reality. Nevertheless, they have remarked that the sound patterns of the poem strive to enact the Platonic theme of eternal return.

Another important milestone in Du Bellay's career came in 1552 when he published *Le Quatriesme livre de l'Eneide de Vergile . . . Autres oeuvres de l'invention du translateur,* which, as the title indicates, is a French translation of the fourth book of Virgil's epic poem the *Aeneid* together with some original works by the translator. The original works include several explicitly religious poems, including "Hymne Chrestien" (Christian Hymn), "La Lyre Chrestienne" (The Christian Lyre), and a miniature biblical epic titled "La Monomachie de David et de Goliath" (The Combat of David and Goliath). The collection also includes a sequence of "XIII sonnetz de l'honneste amour" (Thirteen Sonnets of Chaste Love) that develops the themes and images of Christian Platonism introduced in the second edition of *L'Olive*. The book concludes with "L'Adieu aux Muses" (Farewell to the Muses), which echoes the disillusionment of the opening "Complainte du desesperé" (Complaint of Despair). Overall, the collection seems to enact a conversion from classicism to Christianity—or at least to announce a new orientation toward the sacred that would continue to preoccupy the poet for the rest of his career.

In 1553 Du Bellay demonstrated further versatility with a brilliant satire of Petrarchanism in "A une Dame" (To a Lady), one of four new poems included in the second edition of the *Recueil de Poesie*. Here Du Bellay deplores the vogue for Petrarchan love poetry tinged with Neoplatonic philosophy, a style of which he had been a pioneer. In a series of thirty-one eight-verse stanzas, the poet catalogues all the antithetical images and mythological allusions that characterize this predictable style, concluding with a brilliant self-parody that echoes some of the most famous verses of *L'Olive*. With this poem Du Bellay anticipates the shift away from a high or grandiose style of poetry to the natural simplicity popularized by Ronsard in his *Continuation des Amours* (1555, Continuation of Loves).

Du Bellay's career entered a new phase in 1553. Early that year King Henri II decided to recall Cardinal Jean du Bellay from his enforced political retirement and to dispatch him on a diplomatic mission to Pope Julius III. The cardinal invited Du Bellay to accompany him to Rome in the capacity of secretary, and he eventually appointed him "intendant" (steward) of his many households in the city. The voyage to Rome afforded Du Bellay the opportunity to realize not only his humanist ideals but also to further his more worldly ambitions by undertaking a sort of pilgrimage to the source of humanist culture while under the protection of a powerful and generous patron.

Du Bellay left France in April 1553 and arrived in Rome in June. He wrote sonnets to commemorate the vicissitudes of the journey, including one that comprises a propitiatory vow to a fever that disabled him, and one addressed to the bleeding that cured him. Du Bellay also wrote an eloquent homage to the poet Scève, whom he is supposed to have met in Lyon in May 1553 while en route to Rome. The poet's first impressions of the eternal city are recorded with genuine enthusiasm in a Latin elegy titled "Romae descriptio" (Description of Rome). His subsequent impressions of Roman mores and monuments are less panegyrical. During the four years he spent in Rome in the cardinal's service, Du Bellay composed, in uncertain order and perhaps simultaneously, four major poetic collections: *Le Premier Livre des antiquitez*

not have been eligible without taking holy orders and joining the clergy at some point during his stay in Rome. Hence, Du Bellay prospered from his Roman exile.

In Rome the spectacle of ancient ruins juxtaposed with modern decadence inspired Du Bellay to compose the thirty-three sonnets of his *Premier Livre des antiquitez de Rome* followed by the fifteen sonnets of the enigmatic *Songe ou Vision*. For their profound meditation on Roman history and their poignant images of the corrosive power of time, these works have earned for their author the recognition as a "poet of destiny." In fact, certain sonnets seem to portend a tragic coincidence of French and Roman destiny: the powerful evocation of dusty ruins and collapsing monuments undermines the imperial ambitions of the present and call into question the Renaissance's cherished ideal of rebuilding classical antiquity. Sonnet number 3, the best-known sonnet of *Le Premier Livre des antiquitez de Rome,* develops the theme of looking for Rome in Rome, following the model of the neo-Latin poet Janus Vitalis. Du Bellay addresses the visitor to Rome:

> Nouveau venu, qui cherches Rome en Rome
> Et rien de Rome en Rome n'aperçois,
> Ces vieux palais, ces vieux arcs que tu vois,
> Et ces vieux murs, c'est ce que Rome on nomme.

> (Thou stranger, which for Rome in Rome here seekest,
> And nought of Rome in Rome perceiv'st at all,
> These same old walls, old arches, which thou seest,
> Old palaces, is that which Rome men call.)

Statue of Du Bellay at the Musée Joachim du Bellay in Lire (from <http://musee.du.bellay.chez_alice.fr>)

For many readers of these verses, the echoing name of Rome, through its hollow repetition, suggests the futility of all ambitions to renew the past.

Exile is the defining theme of Du Bellay's masterpiece, *Les Regrets,* a heterogeneous collection of 191 sonnets preceded by a long poem in quatrains dedicated to Cardinal Jean d'Avanson and a preliminary sonnet in which the poet speaks to his book. The dedicatory verses set the tone of the work by releasing a flood of sighs and tears that purport to be all the more authentic because they replace the conventional sighs of the lover with the laments of the unwilling traveler banished from his home. In his exile, the poet's only companion is the Muse, and poetry is his sole consolation. His model is Ulysses, who wandered for ten years before being reunited with his family. Du Bellay develops these themes in several of the sonnets located at the beginning of the collection. One example is a sonnet addressed to the Motherland, the "France mère des arts, des armes et des lois" (France mother of arts, arms and laws), in which the poet compares himself to a lamb separated from the flock and wandering among cruel wolves. Another example is a sonnet in which the poet likens himself to Ovid composing his verses in exile on the

de Rome . . . Plus un Songe ou Vision sur le mesme subject (1558, The First Book of the Antiquities . . . Plus a Dream Vision on the Same Subject), *Les Regrets et autres œuvres poëtiques* (1558; translated as *The Regrets,* 1984), *Divers Jeux Rustiques et autres œuvres poëtiques* (1558, Various Rustic Games and Other Poetic Works), and a collection of neo-Latin poems, the *Poematum* (1558), which is divided into elegies, epigrams, epitaphs, and love poems. The widely divergent character of these four books testifies not so much to the shifting fortunes of the poet as to the tremendous flexibility of his poetic voice. From these works, especially their plaintive aspects, biographers have sought to reconstruct a narrative of Du Bellay's Roman sojourn. But the poems are not the only biographical resource. Archival research has unearthed a series of legal documents showing the poet's administrative duties in the cardinal's household and contradicting his hyperbolic claims of poverty and distress. Du Bellay seems to have been engaged in negotiations with the cardinal's bankers and creditors, and he seems to have been rewarded with several rich benefices for which he would

shores of the Black Sea. The most famous sonnet of the collection, "Heureux qui comme Ulysses" (Fortunate Who Like Ulysses), evokes a series of images and classical literary allusions to convey a powerful sense of longing for the simplicity of home.

While the early sonnets of *Les Regrets* sound the clearest notes of regret or nostalgia, subsequent poems offer a satirical panorama of the papal city with its characteristic alliance of cardinals and courtesans and its elaborate rituals of courtesy and betrayal. Some of these satirical poems target the paganism of Pope Julius III, while others portray the octogenarian bellicosity of his successor Paul IV. When Paul was elected in 1555, his nephew Carlo Caraffa negotiated a military alliance with France against Spain, and the following year a war broke out that periodically threatened to disturb the decadent complacency of the Romans. Du Bellay evokes this situation in the dedicatory verses to Jean d'Avanson, in which he declares, "J'estois à Rome au milieu de la guerre" (I was in Rome in the midst of war.) He goes on to express the fear and expectation that engulfed Rome when a Spanish army led by the duke of Alba laid siege to the city in September 1556 and again the following year. Du Bellay's Roman poetry bears privileged testimony to the public and private hardships of life in Renaissance Rome.

Perhaps the most notorious of the Roman adventures Du Ballay recorded was his liaison with a married woman, celebrated under the name of Faustina in his Latin love poetry or *Amores* (Loves) in the *Poematum*. In elegiac couplets, Du Bellay describes how he had resisted the charms of Roman beauties for three years before he finally became enamored of Faustina. Faithful to the conventions of elegiac poetry, the *Amores* include poems on the door of Faustina's house, which excludes the tormented poet; Faustina's jealous husband; the poet's dream; the poet's votive offering to Venus; and the kisses Faustina yields the poet ("Basia Faustinae"). These poems follow the tradition of Catullus and of the Renaissance neo-Latin poet Janus Secundus, famous for his collection of *Basia* (1541, Kisses). Biographers often have discussed Du Bellay's poems as grounded in experience and sincere, but nothing guarantees that Faustina ever existed outside the pages of the *Amores*. Whether fiction or confession, these poems remain a favorite of readers and translators.

Divers Jeux Rustiques, the least studied of Du Bellay's Roman collections, is an approximation of the humanist genre of the *silva,* or poetic miscellany. In this collection of forty pieces, many of which are adaptations or translations of classical and humanist Latin poetry, Du Bellay shows a strong affinity for paradox and the seriocomic tradition. The second poem in *Divers Jeux Rustiques* is a translation of the *Moretum* (Rustic Salad) from the *Appendix Virgiliana* (circa first century B.C.–first century A.D.), a work Erasmus had mentioned as a precedent for his *Moriae encomium*

(1509, Praise of Folly) in his dedicatory epistle to Thomas More. The last poem in *Divers Jeux Rustiques* is a "Hymne de la surdité" (Hymn of Deafness) that functions both as a paradoxical encomium of his deafness and as a paradoxical vindication of his parity with Ronsard. In this context Du Bellay has placed a variety of elegies, epitaphs, love songs, and rustic vows adapted from the neo-Latin poet Andrea Navagero, who in turn imitated the model of the votive epigrams from the *Greek Anthology,* a giant collection of verse written and pulled together between the fourth century B.C. and the tenth century A.D. Here Du Bellay revised his satiric poem "A une Dame" under the more polemical title "Contre les Pétrarquistes" (Against the Petrarchan Poets). Also of note are the three Courtesan poems: "La Courtisanne Repentie" (The Repentant Courtesan), "La Contre-Repentie" (The Counter-Repentant), and "La Vieille Courtisanne" (The Old Courtesan). The first two are translated from now-lost Latin originals by Du Bellay's contemporary and compatriot Pierre Gilbert, who visited Rome during Du Bellay's stay there. The third courtesan poem is an original composition which revisits the satiric themes of *Les Regrets* by celebrating prostitution as the most enduring monument of Roman grandeur. In all, the brief, evanescent pieces of *Divers Jeux Rustiques* demonstrate the spontaneity and freedom of inspiration associated with the *silva* since the time of the Silver-Latin poet Statius. Similarly, the diversity announced in the title of the work constitutes an important element in Renaissance aesthetics and an important dimension of Du Bellay's own poetic achievement.

Archival evidence indicates that Du Bellay was still in Rome on 20 September 1557, and he is presumed to have returned to France shortly afterward. The poet recounts his homeward journey in a sequence of sonnets from *Les Regrets,* which first describe a sea voyage and then a land journey from Urbino to Venice, through the Swiss Alps to Geneva, to Lyons, and finally to Paris. The sonnet on Geneva is particularly interesting for its portrayal of the somber hypocrisy of the Calvinist city, which counterbalances the antipapal satire of *Les Regrets* and confirms Du Bellay's independence from any sectarian spirit. So effective was Du Bellay's diatribe against Geneva that he provoked a counterattack from an anonymous author, to whom Du Bellay responded with a further sequence of sonnets justifying his original satire. These sonnets are sometimes reproduced as an appendix to editions of *Les Regrets.*

The last two years of Du Bellay's life are well documented by the poet's personal correspondence, discovered and published in the late nineteenth century, and by some notarized documents conserved in the French National Archives. In 1558 Du Bellay published his four collections of Roman poetry with the bookseller Federic Morel in Paris, and these seemed to have earned him immediate

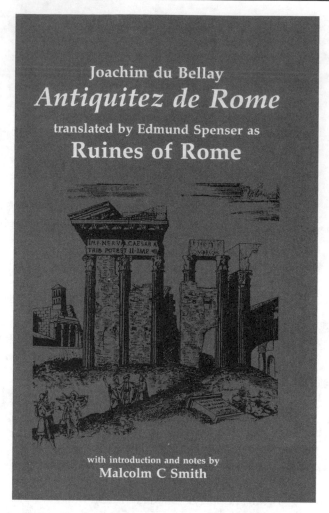

Joachim du Bellay
Antiquitez de Rome
translated by Edmund Spenser as
Ruines of Rome

with introduction and notes by
Malcolm C Smith

Cover for the 1994 edition of the first English translation of Du Bellay's 1558 work, originally published in 1591 (Thomas Cooper Library, University of South Carolina)

notoriety and hostility. For example, that year Du Bellay included with the *Poematum* a letter from the Chancellor François Olivier to Jean Morel praising Du Bellay's vernacular poetry and confessing that having reread the poet's verses three or four times there were still things in them that escaped him: "sunt in iis nonnulla quae me fugiunt." Scholars generally take this phrase as referring to the obscurity of the *Songe ou Vision* that accompanied *Le Premier Livre des antiquitez de Rome*. In this reading, the passage suggests that Du Bellay was already acquiring a reputation as a hermetic poet like Scève before him. Meanwhile, *Les Regrets* were causing difficulties between the poet and his patron Cardinal Du Bellay. In a letter to the cardinal dated 31 July 1559, Du Bellay refutes accusations (apparently circulated by his own cousins) that the satirical sonnets of the *Regrets* were defamatory and heretical and meant to discredit or compromise the cardinal. Du Bellay had already seen a letter from the cardinal giving credence to these accusations and castigating the author of *Les Regrets*

for his indiscretion. Du Bellay naturally protests his innocence and invokes the authority of King Henri II, who had supposedly read the collection in manuscript and encouraged its publication. The scandal of *Les Regrets* did not provoke a complete rupture between poet and patron, but it does show how Du Bellay's Roman poetry earned him a dubious celebrity from the moment of its publication.

Du Bellay continued to compose new verses, including occasional poems that respond to the political events of 1558 and 1559. His *Hymne au Roy sur la prinse de Callais* (Hymn to the King on the Capture of Calais), written in January 1558, records a rare French military success in the geopolitical rivalries of the European Renaissance. Henri II's recovery of Calais was a major event: the English had occupied Calais since the outset of the Hundred Years War. However, the most important public event of Du Bellay's last year of life was the Peace Treaty of Cateau-Cambrésis between France and Spain. This document was signed on 3 April 1559 and consecrated by the double marriage of Elisabeth, the eldest daughter of Henri II, to Philip II of Spain, and of Emanuel-Philibert, Duke of Savoy, to Henri's sister and Du Bellay's patroness Marguerite. These weddings were celebrated with a lavish chivalric tournament held in Paris in June. During this time Du Bellay and his colleagues wrote a deluge of occasional poems, culminating in the funeral laments for Henri II, who was killed while jousting in his own tournament on 30 June 1559. The coronation of his son and successor François II on 18 September 1559 was the occasion for Du Bellay's final works, including one of his more serious and successful pieces, an eight-hundred-verse foray into political theory titled *Ample Discours au roy sur le faict des quatre estats du royaume de France* (1567, The Ample Discourse to the King on the Four Estates of the French Kingdom). This work is widely recognized as a precursor of Ronsard's more famous discourses on the Wars of Religion.

During the time he was cultivating his standing as a poet of national events, Du Bellay continued to write love poetry, satire, and translations. In 1558 Du Bellay collaborated with the philosopher and Hellenist Louis Le Roy to translate into French a variety of Greek and Latin verses cited by Le Roy in the commentary to his 1559 French translation of Plato's *Symposium* (circa 380–360 B.C.). Le Roy rewarded Du Bellay with a generous recognition of his talents in the preliminary epistle to his work, where he speaks of their project in terms of the original ambition of the Pléiade's to enrich the vernacular. In 1559 Du Bellay composed a new sonnet sequence of twenty-nine love poems that—much to the chagrin of critics invested in the evolutionary theory of literature—seem to revert back to the Petrarchan themes and motifs of *L'Olive*. (These poems were published as "Amours de I.

du. Bellay" in *Œuvres françoises de Joachim Du-Bellay* in 1568.) In several of the sonnets the poet acknowledges that for the past ten years he has forsaken love poetry, and he is returning to the task burdened with age and its infirmities, especially deafness. The idea of the deaf poet who communicates with his eyes and who relies on a kind of "spiritual hearing" is nimbly exploited by Du Bellay in these undervalued poems. In the satirical vein, Du Bellay's last triumph was his portrayal of the courtier-poet, "Le Poëte courtisan," which he published under a pseudonym in 1559 together with his translation of a Latin satire by Adrien Turnèbe titled *La Nouvelle Maniere de faire son profit des Lettres* (The New Way to Profit from Literature). With "Le Poëte courtisan," Du Bellay aimed a parting shot at the adversaries of his youth, the court poets in the line of Marot and Saint-Gelais.

Du Bellay's very last poetic undertaking seems to have been the collection of Latin epigrams published posthumously under the title *Xenia seu illustrium quorundam nominum allusiones* (1569), the subtitle of which refers to the etymological wordplay in which the poet indulges while interpreting the proper names of his addressees. A model for this type of game, which Du Bellay takes care to echo in the epigram addressed to Jean Morel, is Erasmus's play on the name Thomas More in his *Moriae Encomium*. On 1 January 1560, however, before Du Bellay could prepare these epigrams for publication, he died of an apoplexy in his house in Paris near the Notre Dame Cathedral, where he had served as canon. Du Bellay was no older than thirty-seven at the time of his death, yet his health was fragile at birth and had steadily declined over the years. He was buried in a chapel of the Cathedral on 4 January. Later that year his friend and collaborator on the *Xenia*, Charles Utenhove, put together a bilingual collection of poetic epitaphs in Du Bellay's honor. The jurist Guillaume Aubert became the poet's literary executor. In 1568, after eight years of patient effort, Aubert and Federic Morel published the first edition of Du Bellay's collected poetry, *Œuvres françoises de Joachim Du-Bellay* (French Works of Joachim Du Bellay), widely known as the *Recueil Aubert* (Aubert Anthology).

Joachim Du Bellay remains for posterity the poet of exile, the failed Ulysses, the lost sheep of the national flock, the very persona which he so carefully elaborates in his most enduring monument, *Le Regrets*. In addition, his reflections on imitation, translation, and language change in the *La Deffence et Illustration de la Langue Francoyse* continue to fascinate students of the Renaissance, while English literature specialists explore Du Bellay's influence on the lyric works of Edmund Spenser. In his time, Du Bellay exerted an immediate influence on a generation of French poets who satirized Rome and deplored, during the French Wars of Religion (1562 to 1598), the unhappy convergence of French and Roman destiny. Du Bellay has much to teach the modern reader about Renaissance self-consciousness and about the role of poetry in mediating between tradition and change. Perhaps his most haunting achievement is to have proposed a disillusioned meditation on Rome in which he makes the reader hear both the presence and the absence of ancient voices in modern lyric.

Letters:

Lettres de Joachim Du Bellay, edited by Pierre Nolhac (Paris: Charavay, 1883).

Biographies:

Henri Chamard, *Joachim du Bellay, 1522–1560* (Lille: Université de Lille, 1900);

Guillaume Colletet, "Vie de Joachim du Bellay," in *Divers jeux rustiques et autres oeuvres poétiques de Joachim du Bellay,* edited by Adolphe van Bever (Paris: Sansot, 1912), pp. 11–72;

Frédéric Boyer, ed., *Joachim du Bellay: Un tableau synoptique de la vie et des oeuvres de Joachim du Bellay et des événements artistiques, littéraires et historiques du XVIe siècle* (Paris: P. Seghers, 1958).

References:

Henri Chamard, *Histoire de la Pléiade,* 4 volumes (Paris: Didier, 1939), I: 85–95, 160–241, 274–304; II: 32–47, 208–351;

Richard Cooper, "Nouveaux documents sur le séjour italien de Joachim du Bellay," in his *Litterae in tempore belli: Etudes sur les relations littéraires italo-françaises pendant les guerres d'Italie* (Geneva: Droz, 1997), pp. 367–392;

Gilbert Gadoffre, *Du Bellay et le sacré* (Paris: Gallimard, 1978);

Eric MacPhail, *The Voyage to Rome in French Renaissance Literature,* Stanford French and Italian Studies, no. 68 (Saratoga, Cal.: ANMA Libri, 1990);

François Rigolot, "Du Bellay et la poésie du refus," *Bibliothèque d'humanisme et renaissance,* 36 (1974): 489–502;

Verdun L. Saulnier, *Du Bellay,* enlarged edition (Paris: Hatier, 1951);

George Hugo Tucker, *The Poet's Odyssey: Joachim du Bellay and the Antiquitez de Rome* (Oxford: Clarendon Press; New York: Oxford University Press, 1990);

Henri Weber, *La création poétique au XVIe siècle en France de Maurice Scève à Agrippa d'Aubigné* (Paris: Nizet, 1955), pp. 399–462.

Pernette du Guillet

(1520? – 17 July 1545)

Megan Conway
Louisiana State University—Shreveport

BOOK: *Rymes de Gentile, et Vertueuse Dame D. Pernette du Guillet Lyonnoise* (Lyon: Jean de Tournes, 1545; enlarged, 1552).

Editions: *Les rithmes et poesies de gentile, et vertueuse Dame D. Pernette du Guillet Lyonnoise. Auecq' le Triumphe des Muses sur Amour: Et autres nouuelles composicions* (Paris: Jeanne de Marnef, 1546);

Poésies de Pernette du Guillet, Lyonnaise, edited by Claude Breghot du Lut (Lyon: Louis Perrin, 1830);

Rymes de gentile et vertueuse dame D. Pernette du Guillet, Lyonnoise, edited by Jean Baptiste Monfalcon (Lyon: Louis Perrin, 1856);

Rymes de gentile et vertueuse dame (Lyon: Nicolas Scheuring, 1864);

Poètes du XVIe siècle, edited by Albert-Marie Schmidt (Paris: Gallimard, 1953), pp. 227–264;

Rymes, critical edition, edited by Victor E. Graham (Geneva: Droz, 1968);

Oeuvres poétiques, by Du Guillet and Louise Labé, edited by Françoise Charpentier (Paris: Gallimard, 1983), pp. 35–89.

Although largely forgotten in succeeding centuries, Pernette du Guillet enjoyed the esteem of her contemporaries, and her poetry was widely read during the decade that followed her death. Her collection *Rymes de Gentile, et Vertueuse Dame D. Pernette du Guillet Lyonnoise* (Rhymes of the Gentle and Virtuous Lady D. Pernette du Guillet of Lyon) went through four editions between 1545 and 1552. Along with Maurice Scève, Louise Labé, Mellin de Saint-Gelais, and Antoine Héroët, Du Guillet was one of the central figures of the so-called *Ecole de Lyon* (School of Lyon), a group of poets who wrote according to the literary traditions of Petrarchism and Neoplatonism that had recently been introduced into France from Italy. Du Guillet's poetry shows an excellent grasp of these traditions, as well as a knowledge of classical mythology and a concern for variety of form and rhyme. While Du Guillet cannot be labeled a feminist, her work and the circumstances of its publication shake the modern stereotype of the oppressed

Renaissance woman in several ways: Du Guillet makes it clear in her poems that the lovers are equals; her male editor addressed the work to a female audience and urged them to follow Du Guillet's example; and the second and third editions of the collection were published by a woman, Jeanne de Marnef.

No contemporary portrait of Du Guillet is known to survive, nor have any contemporary archival records that include her name been uncovered. According to convention, she was born in 1520, but 1518 and 1521 are also possible years of her birth. Although scholars have suggested several likely relatives, nothing is known for certain about her family. Even her social standing is questionable: she appears to have belonged either to the lower nobility or to the upper bourgeoisie. In 1537 or 1538 she married a Monsieur du Guillet. The date of her death, 17 July 1545, is recorded in the title of a series of four poems written in memoriam by fellow poets including Scève and Jean de Vauzelles; she probably died of the plague.

Du Guillet died before she had prepared her poems for publication as a collection. After her death, her husband enlisted the aid of Antoine du Moulin, a respected translator and editor. They sorted through Du Guillet's papers, finding, as Du Moulin notes in his preface, "Epygrammes, Chansons, et autres diverses matières de divers lieux, et plusieurs papiers confusément extraits" (Epigrams, Songs and other diverse materials in diverse places and several papers confusedly collected). The information in this four-page preface provides virtually all that is "known" about Du Guillet. Even allowing for some embellishment of the truth, Du Moulin's description is impressive:

Vue le peu de temps, que les Cieulx l'ont laissée entre nous, il est quasi incroyable comme elle a peu avoir le loisir, je ne dy seulement de se rendre si parfaitement asseurée en tous instrumenz musiquaulx, soit au Luth, Espinette, et autres, lesquelz de soy requierent une bien longue vie à se y rendre parfaictz, comme elle estoit, et tellement, que la promptitude, qu'elle y avoit, donnait cause d'esbahissement aux plus experimentez: mais encores à si bien dispencer le reste de ses bonnes heu-res, qu'elle l'aye employé à toutes bonnes lettres, par lesquelles elle avoit eu premierement entière et familiere congnoissance des plus louable vulgaires (oultre le sien) comme du Thuscan, et Castillan . . . avait jà bien avant passé les Rudimentz de la langue Latine aspirant à la Greque . . . quand les Cieux . . . la nous ravirent.

(Seeing the short time that the heavens left her among us, it is almost unbelievable how she could have had the leisure, I say, not only to render herself so perfectly assured in all musical instruments—be it the lute, spinet and others, which require a very long life to become perfect like she was, and how her aptitude caused the astonishment of the most accomplished; but also to spend the rest of her good hours so well that she had them employed in all good letters by which she had an entire and familiar knowledge of the most praiseworthy vulgar tongues—besides her own—like Tuscan and Castilian . . . and had already passed the rudiments of Latin and was aspiring to Greek . . . when the heavens took her.)

Only some of these claims can be verified in the poems themselves, but Du Moulin clearly intends that the information be taken as fact; near the beginning of his paean and at several other points in the preface he uses the first person singular *je* (I) to remind the reader that he knew Du Guillet personally. He says that her "petit amas de rymes" (little pile of rhymes) bears wit-ness to "la dexterité de son divin esprit" (the dexterity of her divine *esprit* [mind, spirit, or wit]). Toward the end of the preface he declares that had he not availed himself of the opportunity to publish Du Guillet's col-lection, it would have been similar to a theft of the honor and public praise of the female sex.

The audience Du Moulin had in mind for the collection is indicated in the title of the preface: "Autoin du Moulin aux dames Lyonnoizes" (Antoine du Moulin to the Women of Lyon). The preface is an exhortation to these women to follow Du Guillet's example and finish what she has begun—"à sçavoir de vous exerciter, comme elle, à la vertu" (to know, like her, how to deal very much with virtue). *Vertu* in this context is used in the original Italian sense of *virtù*, meaning strength rather than moral qualities, and the strength to which Du Moulin refers is that of literary talent. Du Guillet has shown the way; now it is up to other women to follow so that "la memoire de vous puisse testifier à la Posterité de la docilité et vivacité des bons espritz, qu'en tous artz ce Climat Lyonnois a tousjours produict en tous sexes" (for posterity, your memory can attest to the sweetness and liveliness of the good minds that in all the arts this Lyonese climate had always produced in all sexes). Du Moulin seems to take the artistic ability of the women of Lyon as an accepted fact; he is merely urging them to let them-selves be inspired by Du Guillet's work. He hopes that by reading the poems, which were, he says, so much enjoyed by everyone when they were read at private gatherings during her lifetime, the Lyonese ladies will be "incited" and "animated" to study letters "pour participer de ce grand et immortel los, que les Dames d'Italie se sont aujourd'huy acquis, et tellement, que par leurs divins escrits elles ternissent le lustre de maints hommes doctes" (in order to participate in the great and immortal praise acquired by the women of Italy whose divine writings have tarnished the luster of many learned men). Frenchwomen are doing the same, but Du Guillet's collection will "poulser à plus hault bien" (push them to a higher good).

The confused state of her papers is not an indi-cation that Du Guillet never intended to publish her work. Several years before her death, four of her poems were set to music and appeared in song collec-tions: Pierre Attaingnant included what became her Epigrams XLIII and XLIV in a collection he pub-lished in Paris in 1540 and, with alterations, in another collection in 1543; Jacques Moderne included Epigrams XII and XIV in a popular compilation of songs he published in 1540 and 1541 in Lyon. Had Du Guillet lived, she might have put together a much different collection from the *Rymes;* in any event, it seems reasonable to conclude that she would not have opposed the presentation of her work to the reading public.

The *Rymes* is a collection of lyric love poems that reflect the philosophy of Neoplatonism with an under-current of Petrarchism. The first three editions com-prise seventy-four poems; seven more thought to be authentic were added to the 1552 edition. They include ten *chansons* (songs), five elegies, two *epîtres* (epistles), and sixty epigrams of four to twelve lines. Only a few incidental pieces stray from the theme of love: Epigram XXII is about the weather; Epigram LX describes humanity as a microcosm of the uni-verse; and *Epîtres* I and II concentrate on humor and rhyming games. Some poems relate mythological or allegorical stories in which love plays an important part; in other poems the poetic voice belongs to a detached, experienced observer who makes general remarks about love and its universal problems, such as jealousy, distrust, and infidelity. Most often, however, the speaker is a particular lover who addresses or talks about a particular beloved. This pair of lovers has sev-eral distinguishing characteristics that make them easy to recognize whenever they appear in the *Rymes*. The beloved is called *Jour* (Day) and described in meta-phors and images such as Apollo and the sun; he is the representative of enlightenment, knowledge, and virtue and the opponent of vice and ignorance. The lover recognizes and honors his wisdom, casting herself in the role of worthy pupil while the beloved figures as *maître* (master or teacher). Knowledge and virtue are the preoccupations of this couple. Many scholars have identified the pair as Du Guillet herself and Scève, who celebrates Du Guillet as the beloved in his poetic masterpiece, *Délie, Objet de plus haulte vertu* (1544, Delie, Object of Highest Virtue). While this identification is probably correct, it is not crucial to an understanding of the *Rymes*.

In Du Guillet's version of Neoplatonism, lovers must achieve and sustain a delicate balance between physical and intellectual passion. Reason is at the core of Du Guillet's theory of love; at no point does physical desire take the upper hand. Yet, the poems never suggest that the speaker's physical passion is inhibited; instead, the rational impulse is so strong that it dominates the physical with no hint of repression. Physical passion is not absent from the *Rymes,* but it is of less importance than reason because it occupies a lower part of the soul. For Renaissance Neoplatonists, love was too exalted a matter to leave to the undependable and indiscriminate whims of the heart and the senses; a diligent application of one's rational faculties was required.

Love demands a careful, intellectual approach, because it involves much more than a mere amorous attraction between two people. In accordance with Neoplatonic precepts, Du Guillet's theory of love involves an ascent toward the ideal realm of the Good that is made possible by the lovers' mutual perception of goodness in each other and the resultant striving for self-improvement. To approach the ideal realm requires much effort and, occasionally, pain and suffering. The lovers must analyze and purify their feelings, sharpen their perceptions, and increase their knowledge.

According to Neoplatonic doctrine, recognition of the beloved's physical beauty is the first step toward the perception of his or her inner beauty—that is, virtue and wisdom—and, ultimately, of the Good. While this step is referred to in the *Rymes,* the collection reflects a more advanced stage in the lover's ascent toward the Good: her passion is fired by her perception of the beloved's virtue and wisdom, which fills her with the desire to equal his merits. Of paramount importance to the Neoplatonic relationship is that this passion not be unrequited: the lover's virtues must equally provide inspiration for the beloved to strive for improvement, for both must participate in the progressive ascent toward the ideal realm. The reciprocal alliance of lover and beloved is presented as a matter of honor and free will in *Chanson* IV:

O amytié bien prise
Que j'ay voulu choisir
Par vraye foy promise
Qui mon cueur vint saisir
Quand honnor s'allia
Au bien qui nous lia.

(O friendship well received
That I wanted to choose
By true faith promised
Which came to seize my heart
When honor allied itself
To the good that bound us together.)

Du Guillet celebrates the emotional involvement of both parties in several places in the collection, including Epigram XXVIII:

Et toutes fois, vous voyant tousjours pris
En mon endroit, vostre ardeur me convye
Par ce hault bien, que de vous j'ay compris
A demeurer vostre toute ma vie.

(And all times, seeing you always taken
In my vicinity, your ardor invites me
By this glorious good which I have understood through you
To remain yours all my life.)

A key word in both passages is *bien* (good). Du Guillet's use of the term confirms that her persona has advanced beyond the perception of inner goodness through external beauty and has reached the point where the goodness perceived in the beloved will lead her to the perception of "ce hault bien" (the ideal Good). *Bien* functions both as a noun and an adverb and in both senses carries overtones of the Good, the highest of the Platonic Ideas or Forms. This meaning is the one that Du Guillet intends in Epigram XVI when she speaks of "le bien du bien" (the greatest good) that the lovers are seeking. Leaving aside casual uses of *bien,* Du Guillet employs the word with direct or implied Neoplatonic overtones in twenty-eight poems, conditioning the reader to hear her special meaning. When, in Epigram XXVIII, the lover speaks of "ce hault bien, que de vous j'ay compris" (this glorious good, that I have understood through you), the reader knows that she is talking about the reciprocal relationship that leads the lovers toward the ideal.

Contentement (happiness) is a distinctive element in Du Guillet's personal Neoplatonic system. It is a complicated creation that she crafts through her use of humor, the speaker's joyful persona, and a specific vocabulary. *Contentement* is the logical extension of Du Guillet's conception of true love and the ultimate realization of the Good. Her lovers' perception of true beauty in the attributes of virtue and knowledge allow them to love deeply, rarely troubled by physical desires. The joy and satisfaction that they experience as they share their knowledge result in a mutual happiness filled with spiritual pleasure. As the earthly goal of Du Guillet's Neoplatonism, *contentement* represents a spiritual achievement and an intense satisfaction that the lovers experience together. In this respect Du Guillet's version of Neoplatonism is unique among her French contemporaries, none of whose speakers arrive at such a positive goal.

Although the *Rymes* are not essentially Petrarchan in form, and Petrarchist themes are central to few of the pieces, mythological references and other classical allusions reflect Petrarchan conventions and Renaissance humanism. Although Du Guillet does not make a point of displaying her erudition in the manner of writers such as Helisenne de Crenne, eleven poems include some "classical" element: Apollo, the Graces, Venus, Ceres, Bacchus, Danae (or Daphnes), the Muses, nymphs, Parnassus, Psyche, Adonis, Diana, or Acteon. Elegy II provides an example of Du Guillet's use of mythology. The poem describes the lover's daydream of gaining power over her beloved and employs the myth of Diana and Acteon from Ovid's *Metamorphoses* (A.D. 8) to illustrate her fantasy. A much-used Petrarchan setting of a fountain combined with thoughts of Diana creates in the speaker the desire to rule the beloved; such a power, however, would deprive Apollo and the nine Muses of the beloved's service. To avoid their displeasure, the lover quickly renounces her wish.

The suffering of lovers is an essential part of the Petrarchan tradition. This theme is found in Elegy IV, "Desespoir traduict de la prose du parangon italien" (Despair Translated from the Prose of the Italian Paragon). It is the most Petrarchan piece in the collection, probably because it is a translation; Du Guillet even retains the masculine gender of the speaker. In this poem, love is equated with death, pain, sorrow, and war; the lover's torment is expressed through eye imagery and the use of the antitheses of love and hate and fire and water. Du Guillet employs a vocabulary of suffering, intensifying the effects of love's pain. She also uses the common Petrarchan trope of the amorous wound. By showing her mastery of the standard Petrarchan tradition in this translation, Du Guillet demonstrates that her decision to use Petrarchan elements to ornament her other poems is a conscious one.

Du Guillet also follows Petrarchan tradition when she describes the *innamoramento* (birth of love). This theme is best exemplified in the piece Du Moulin chose to be the first poem in the collection, a *dizain* (a ten-line epigram with lines of ten syllables). Life was

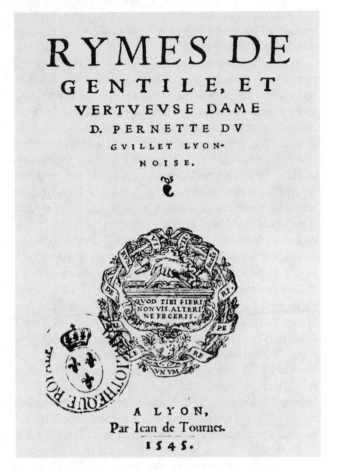

Title page for Pernette du Guillet's only book (from Paul Ardouin, Maurice Scève, Pernette du Guillet, Louise Labé: L'Amour à Lyon au temps de la Renaissance, 1981; Thomas Cooper Library, University of South Carolina)

nothing before the advent of the beloved, who gives it meaning and form; love began the moment the speaker perceived the beloved's divine qualities and was "reborn" into a new life. The *innamoramento* brings about a significant change in the speaker. Whether the change is a new awareness, as in Epigrams I and II; the gaining of new knowledge, as in Epigram XXVIII and *Chanson* III; or a new perspective and vision, as in Epigrams II and VIII, all provide new ways to praise the beloved.

Du Guillet's identification of the beloved as *maître* operates on the levels of both love and learning. On the one hand, the beloved is her "master" in the sense of the lover's will being subject to that of the beloved; on this interpretation the term is the masculine equivalent of the Petrarchan *maîtresse* (mistress) in poems with a female beloved. On the other hand, Du Guillet also uses the word's meaning of "teacher," which casts the speaker into the role of a student seeking wisdom. Both meanings are appropriate, and the linking of love and learning in a single word fits into her Neoplatonic scheme.

As the speaker's teacher, the beloved is superior to the lover in wisdom and in knowledge. His wisdom comes from experience and his knowledge from study. On the other hand, the lover's ignorance results from inexperience and inadequate study, not lack of intelligence; the equality of their intelligence is never brought into question. The lover accepts the role of student because the beloved can teach her and she desires to learn. A defense of such a relationship in terms of Neoplatonic doctine is given in Epigram LIII. The content of the poem resembles Socrates' argument in Plato's dialogue *Lysis* that it is better to aspire to win the affection of one who is superior than to settle for someone as ignorant and untried as oneself. By this reasoning the speaker's love for the wiser, more experienced, and, perhaps, older beloved is right and appropriate. No inferiority is attached to the lover's role in the relationship. Occasionally, the speaker appears humbled before the teacher-beloved; such humility is, however, as much a matter of Petrarchan rhetorical convention as it is a Platonic praise of the beloved's wisdom and knowledge and, more often than not, it is contradicted in the same poem. This situation is reflected in the first five lines of Epigram VI:

Par ce dixain clerement je m'accuse
De ne sçavoir tes vertues honnorer,
Fors du vouloir, qui est bien maigre excuse:
Mais qui pourroit par escripts decorer
Ce qui de soy se peult faire adorer?

(With this dizain I clearly accuse myself
Of not knowing how to honor your virtue
Although I wish to, which is a pretty thin excuse:
But who could adorn with writing
He who just by being makes himself adored?)

The speaker complains that her literary efforts—at least in this *dizain*—are unable to praise the beloved adequately. She contrasts her desire with her ignorance: she simply does not know how to honor him properly. She acknowledges that ignorance is a poor excuse but then dismisses personal responsibility for her inability—and abandons the pose of humility—by asking who could properly praise such a beloved. The implication is that no one could, since the beloved is so wonderful.

Although the speaker freely admits the superiority of the beloved's learning, she establishes their essential parity in poems such as Epigram XVI: "Dieu / . . . m'a donné raison, qui a pouvoir / De bien juger ton heur, et ton sçavoir" (God / . . . gave me reason,

which has the power / To judge well your happiness and your knowledge). The use of *"juger"* (to judge) implies that they are peers. Epigrams XVI, XXVIII, and XLVIII, and *Chansons* VIII and IX all reflect the Neoplatonic notion that the lovers must be on equal footing because their ascent toward the ideal is made together.

Because the frame of reference is both Petrarchan and Neoplatonic, the beloved possesses a vast quantity of virtues—although, contrary to the usual Petrarchan practice, Du Guillet devotes no lines to the beloved's physical charms. Instead, she characterizes him by repeated references to his knowledge and eloquence. Although Du Guillet ranks these qualities higher than physical beauty, the latter is never denigrated; it is simply unimportant in regard to the beloved. The beloved's virtue has captured the heart of the speaker. In Epigram XVII she contrasts virtue with beauty:

Par sa vertu, qui à l'aymer m'attire
Plus que beauté; car sa grace, et faconde
Me font cuyder la première du monde.

(By his virtue which drew me to love him
More than his beauty; for his goodness and eloquence
Make me believe [I am] number one in the world.)

Virtue, in the sense of "good qualities," is of primary importance, as is the insinuation that the lover—"number one in the world"—is equally worthy of being loved.

Du Guillet's repeated praise of the beloved's virtue represents a convergence of Petrarchism and Neoplatonism, which complement each other. Petrarchism sets the precedent for lengthy and repeated praises; Neoplatonism provides attributes more worthy of that praise than flashing eyes or alabaster skin. The two traditions are well blended in Epigram III, which begins with the acknowledgment that an appreciation of the beloved's knowledge is not limited to the speaker but is perceived by all:

Ce grand renom de ton meslé sçavoir
Demonstre bien, que tu es l'excellence
De toute grace exquise, pour avoir
Tous dons des Cieulx en pleine jouyssance.

(This great renown of your varied knowledge
Shows quite plainly that you are the excellence
Of every exquisite virtue, having
The full enjoyment of all the gifts of Heaven.)

Du Guillet's use of *jouyssance,* with its undertones of sexual fulfillment, is a reminder that the lovers' relationship is far from stiff and sterile but, rather, full of joy and satisfaction.

Although physical passion occupies a minor role in the *Rymes,* Du Guillet neither denies nor ignores it. Three of the poems are openly erotic. While this eroticism might appear at first to contradict Du Guillet's Neoplatonism, it serves a definite purpose in the collection. To win the beloved—and the reader—to her point of view on spiritual love, the speaker has to make her perspective believable and possible, not artificial and superhuman. If she were to suppress all physical desire and passion, and lesser emotions such as jealousy, her credibility would suffer. Consequently, her sensual poems help to disarm both the beloved's and the reader's prejudices. Knowing that the lover is not inhuman or frigid but feels passion as much as the beloved does, he—and the reader—can more readily give credence to the lover's assertions of the superiority of spiritual love.

The first half of Elegy II is full of erotic suggestion. Du Guillet describes the speaker's recurring desire to be together with her scholarly beloved by a fountain in the heat of summer. To distract him from his philosophizing, she contemplates throwing herself "toute nue" (completely naked) into the water. Having caught his attention, she would entice him with a song and tease him when he tried to touch her by splashing him with the clear water. Epigram XIV playfully combines Neoplatonic terminology with an allusion to sexual gratification:

Le grand desir du plaisir admirable
Se doit nourrir par un contentement
De souhaicter chose tant agreable,
Que tout esprit peult ravir doulcement.
O que le faict doit estre grandement
Remply du bien, quand pour la grand envie
On veult mourir, s'on ne l'a promptement:
Mais ce mourir engendre une autre vie.

(The great desire of admirable pleasure
Must nourish itself by a contentment
To wish something so agreeable,
That every spirit can sweetly ravish.
O that the fact must be greatly
Filled with good, when for this great desire
One wants to die, if one does not have it quickly:
But this death engenders another life.)

In Du Guillet's poetry, the reader becomes accustomed to associating *bien* and *contentement* with Neoplatonism. In this poem, however, Neoplatonic interpretation of these two words is arrested by the poet's use of *desir* (desire) and *plaisir* (pleasure) and put in question by the modifying presence of *admirable* and *tout esprit* (every spirit). In the second quatrain Du Guillet resolves the reader's uncertainty, for the death

to which she refers in the last line is easily interpreted as the accepted metaphor for orgasm.

Physical passion is also the subject of the first half of Epigram XII. In this poem the exact nature of the "good" that the lover receives is open to question, particularly when one considers the variations of the poem as it was published by Moderne in his 1541 song collection:

Le corps ravy, l'Ame s'en esmerveille
Du grand plaisir, qui me vient entamer [Moderne: que tu me peut donner],
Me ravissant d'Amour, qui tout esveille
Par ce seul bien, qui le faict Dieu nommer [Moderne: il se faict Dieu nommer].

(The body ravished, the soul wonders at
The great pleasure, which comes to wound me [that you can give me]
Ravishing me with love which stirs up everything
With this single good, which makes itself called God [he makes himself called God]).

The position of "body ravished" at the opening of the poem immediately checks a spiritual interpretation of "great pleasure," and line 2 of the 1541 text explicitly defines that ravishing pleasure as a gift from the beloved. The speaker's enthusiasm in this poem and in Epigram III and Elegy II is obvious, but there is no conflict between sexual desire and reason. In the elegy the fantasy is never realized; the speaker abandons her desires in favor of the claims of the Muses. The two epigrams avoid the use of a first-person subject and other characteristics that mark Du Guillet's Neoplatonic couple and seem to comment on the nature of love in general. Their presence in the collection informs the reader that despite Du Guillet's insistence on the superiority of ideal love, she is aware of the joys of sex.

That awareness does not lead to conflict in Du Guillet's work, as it does in Scève's. After all, Neoplatonic intellectual love begins in the love of external beauty; consequently, the speaker's love must have been located initially on the sensual level. Since Du Guillet's speaker has progressed to a higher plane in the ascent toward perfect love, it is not surprising that she has moved away from descriptions of physical pleasure, but nowhere in the collection does she repudiate it. The speaker still appreciates sensual pleasures, and they represent no threat to her Neoplatonic beliefs. Desire is not the speaker's personal obstacle in the *Rymes;* jealousy is.

Jealousy disturbs the day-to-day course of love only superficially, not at the core, and poses no real danger to the speaker's love; yet, the collection is probably stronger for its admission of weak moments on the part of the lover. None of the seven poems that deal with jealousy (Epigrams XXXI, XXXII, XXXIII, XXXIV, XXXVII, XL, and XLI) betrays torment or anguish. Most often the speaker admits that she is jealous and proceeds to postulate why she should not be. Thus, while jealousy is non-Platonic, its appearance in her work does not contradict or interfere with Du Guillet's Neoplatonism. The speaker can write of seeing her beloved talking to another woman without being driven to despair, because the same reason that allows her to perceive the beloved's goodness also allows her to explain his lapses from ideal behavior. Moreover, the speaker's steadfast belief in her own worth and virtue reassures her of the beloved's love.

Du Guillet places a great deal of emphasis on virtue as the basis of the continuing attraction between the lovers. Much of the success of the collection is owed to the fact that she manages to make virtue charming, rather than tedious or prudish. In Du Guillet's Neoplatonic system, virtue has no negative side; it never demands sacrifice or denial. Virtue is dynamic, not sterile; an increase in virtue represents progress toward the Ideal and benefits both the lover and the beloved: virtue itself is a pleasure and a reward. In the *Rymes* virtue has nothing to do with the denial of physical love; instead, it is part of the affirmation of spiritual love.

Several elements in the collection demonstrate that Du Guillet was committed to the progressive attitudes of the early Renaissance. Her attention to style is conscious; unlike Scève, who concentrated on the dizain, and Labé, whose favorite form was the sonnet, Du Guillet explores various poetic forms: more than fifty combinations of form and rhyme occur among the seventy-seven poems. The variety of rhyme and line length among her poems places her at the forefront of early Renaissance poets who experimented with strophic and metric forms. Du Guillet shunned medieval genres in favor of more "modern" forms, although she did not employ the sonnet, as Labé did a few years later. Like her more learned humanist contemporaries, Du Guillet was apparently interested in classical languages. While the extent of her knowledge of Greek is not known, Epigrams XL and XLI each include a single Greek word. In Epigram XL, *callimera* (hello) is used in a play on words: the speaker overhears the beloved greeting another woman with this word, which sounds like the French *qu'il l'aymera* (that he will love her), and suspects the worst. *Imera* (Day) in Epigram XLI is the Greek equivalent of the name the speaker uses for the beloved in her poems.

Du Guillet might also have used a Greek source as the model for her tenth song, "Conde Claros de Adonis"; it is usually referred to by its first line, "Amour avecques Pysches" (Love with Psyche), since scholars have been unable to decipher the meaning of the title. The *chanson* is a reworking of the traditional Venus and Adonis motif and seems to have been written in response to a poem by Saint-Gelais on the same subject. (Du Guillet's poem was included as a companion piece to Saint-Gelais's in the 1547 edition of Saint-Gelais's poetry.) While Saint-Gelais imitated an idyll of Bion readily available in Latin, Du Guillet probably used the *Eis nekron Adonin* (On the Death of Adonis) of the pseudo-Theocritus as her model; she embellishes her poem with a few details borrowed from Saint-Gelais, whose work she seems to have seen in manuscript. Line comparisons show that Du Guillet's poem is closer to the Greek text than to the Latin version. While these considerations do not prove Du Guillet's familiarity with Greek, they support Du Moulin's assertion of her interest in the language and illustrate her Petrarchan attitude toward the classics.

Although Du Guillet is little known today outside scholarly circles, the four editions of her work in the seven years following her death and the inclusion of her poems in popular songbooks attest to her appeal in her own time. "Amour avecques Psyches" was included in several poetry collections and in songbooks printed in Paris in 1557 and in Anvers in 1578. It was so well known by 1549 that Joachim Du Bellay mentions it in his *Deffense et llustration de la langue francoyse* (translated as *The Defence and Illustration of the French Language,* 1939). By that time new ideas in poetry were beginning to take hold, and Du Bellay cites Du Guillet's poem as an example of an old-fashioned form to be avoided.

Pernette du Guillet was all but forgotten until three editions of the *Rymes* appeared in the mid nineteenth century. After Joseph Buche identified her in 1904 as the beloved in Scève's *Délie, Objet de plus haulte vertu,* critical attention focused on her relationship to that poet. Du Guillet's poetry was not considered on its own merits until a landmark article by Verdun-Louis Saulnier appeared in 1944. Scholarship on Du Guillet remained scarce until the last decades of the twentieth century, when some feminist critics were drawn to her. Gender issues aside, Du Guillet's poetry is worthy of attention because of her manipulation of the major poetic traditions of her day and her emphasis on a serene Neoplatonic love shared by two equally meritorious lovers.

References:

Paul Ardouin, *Maurice Scève, Pernette du Guillet, Louise Labé: L'Amour à Lyon au temps de la Renaissance* (Paris: Nizet, 1981);

Ardouin, *Pernette du Guillet: L'Heureuse Renaissante. Miracle de l'Amour, de la Lumière et de la Poésie* (Paris: Nizet, 1991);

Joseph Buche, "Pernette du Guillet et la 'Délie' de Maurice Scève," in *Mélanges de philologie offerts à Ferdinand Brunot* (Paris: Société nouvelle de librairie et d'édition, 1904), pp. 33–39;

Robert Cottrell, "Pernette du Guillet's *Rymes*," *Bibliothèque d'humanisme et renaissance,* 31 (1969): 553–571;

Lance Donaldson-Evans, *Love's Fatal Glance: A Study of Eye Imagery in Poets of the Ecole Lyonnaise* (University, Miss.: Romance Monographs, 1980), pp. 51–61;

Donaldson-Evans, "The Taming of the Muse: The Female Poetic Voice in Pernette du Guillet's *Rymes*," in *Pre-Pléiade Poetics,* edited by Jerry C. Nash (Lexington, Ky.: French Forum, 1985), pp. 84–96;

Robert Griffen, "Pernette du Guillet's Response to Scève: A Case for Abstract Love," *L'Esprit Créateur,* 5, no. 2 (1965): 110–116;

Karen Simroth James, "Pernette du Guillet: Spiritual Union and Poetic Distance," *French Literature Series,* 16 (1989): 27–37;

Gillian Jondorf, "Petrarchan Variations in Pernette du Guillet and Louise Labé," *Modern Language Review,* 71 (1976): 766–778;

Anne Rosalind Jones, "Pernette du Guillet: The Lyonnais Neoplatonist," in *Women Writers of the Renaissance and Reformation,* edited by Katerina Wilson (Athens: University of Georgia Press, 1987), pp. 219–233;

Theodore Anthony Perry, "Pernette du Guillet's Poetics of Love and Desire," in his *Erotic Spirituality: The Integrative Tradition from Leone Ebreo to John Donne* (University: University of Alabama Press, 1980), pp. 53–67;

Verdun-Louis Saulnier, "Etude sur Pernette du Guillet et ses *Rymes*," *Bibliothèque d'humanisme et renaissance,* 4 (1944): 7–119.

Henri II Estienne
(Henricus Stephanus)
(1531 – 1597)

Barbara C. Bowen
Vanderbilt University

BOOKS: *Ciceronianum lexicon Graecolatinum* (Geneva: Printed by H. Estienne, 1557);

In M. T. Ciceronis quamplurimos locos castigationes (Geneva: Printed by H. Estienne, 1557);

Dictionarium Medicum (Geneva: Printed by H. Estienne, 1564);

Traicté de la conformité du language françois avec le grec (Geneva: Printed by H. Estienne, 1565);

Alphabetum hebraicum (Geneva: Printed by H. Estienne, 1566);

L'Introduction au traité de la Conformité des merveilles anciennes avec les modernes, ou, Traité préparatif à l'Apologie pour Herodote (Geneva: Printed by H. Estienne, 1566);

Advertissement de Henri Estienne, pour son livre intitulé l'Introduction au traité de la conformité (Geneva: Printed by H. Estienne, 1567);

Artis typographiae querimonia: De illiteratis quibusdam typographis, propter quos in contemptum venit (Paris: Printed by H. Estienne, 1569);

Epistola qua ad multas multorum amicorum respondet de suae typographiae statu nominatimque de suo Thesauro linguae Graecae (Geneva: Printed by H. Estienne, 1569);

Glossaria duo, è situ vetustatis eruta: Ad vtrisqve lingvae coditionem & locupletationem perutilia. Item, De atticae linguae seu dialecti idiomatis (Geneva: Printed by H. Estienne, 1573);

Francofordiense Emporium (Geneva: Printed by H. Estienne, 1574); edited and translated by Isidore Liseux as *The Frankfort Book Fair* (Paris: Liseux, 1875);

Parodiae morales (Geneva: Printed by H. Estienne, 1575);

De Latinitate falso suspecta (Geneva: Printed by H. Estienne, 1576);

Pseudocicero, Dialogus Henr. Stephani: In hoc non solùm de multis ad Ciceronis sermonem pertinentibus, sed etiam quem delectum editionum eius habere & quam cautionem in eo legendo debeat adhibere, lector monebitur (Geneva: Printed by H. Estienne, 1577);

Henri II Estienne (Collection Roger-Viollet/Getty Images)

Deux dialogues du nouveau langage françois italianizé et autrement desguizé, principalement entre les courtisans de ce temps (Geneva: Printed by H. Estienne, 1578);

Nizoliodidascalus siue, Monitor Ciceronianorum Nizolianorum, dialogus (Geneva: Printed by H. Estienne, 1578);

Project du livre intitulé, De la precellence du langage françois (Paris: Printed by Mamert Patisson, 1579);

Hypomneses de gallica lingua (Geneva: Printed by H. Estienne, 1582);

De criticis vet. Gr. et Latinis, eorúmque variis apud poetas potissimùm reprehensionibus (Paris: Printed by H. Estienne, 1587);

De bene instituendis Graecae linguae studiis Henr. Stephani Dialogus (Geneva: Printed by H. Estienne, 1587);

Principum Monitrix Musa (Basel, 1590);

Les premices, ou le i livre des proverbes épigramatizéz, ou des épigrammes proberbializéz. C'est à dire, signez et seellez par les prouerbes françois: Aucuns aussi par les grecs & latins, ou autres, pris de quelcun des langages vulgaires. Rengez en lieux communs. Le tout par Henri Estienne (Geneva: Printed by H. Estienne, 1593);

De J. Lipsii latinitate (vt ipsimet antiquarii antiquarium Lipsii stylum indigitant) palaestra I Henr. Stephani, Parisiensis, nec Lipsiomimi, nec Lipsiomomi, nec Lipsiocolacis, multóque minus Lipsiomastigis (Frankfurt am Main: Printed by H. Estienne, 1595);

Henr. Stephani Carmen De Senatulo foeminarum (Strasbourg: Printed by Antonius Bertramus, 1596).

Editions: *Traicté de la conformité du language françois avec le grec,* edited by Léon Feugère (Paris: J. Delalain, 1853);

L'Introduction au traité de la Conformité des merveilles anciennes avec les modernes, ou, Traité préparatif à l'Apologie pour Herodote, 2 volumes, edited by Paul Ristelhuber (Paris, 1879);

Deux Dialogues du nouveau langage François italianize, 2 volumes, edited by Ristelhuber (Paris: Lemerre, 1885);

Project du livre intitulé, De la precellence du langage françois, edited by Edmond Huguet (Paris: Armand Colin, 1896);

Deux Dialogues du nouveau langage François italianize, edited by Pauline M. Smith (Geneva: Slatkine, 1980);

Hypomneses de Gallica lingua, edited and translated by Jacques Chomarat (Paris: Champion, 1999);

La France des Humanistes: Henri II Estienne éditeur et écrivain, edited by Judit Kecskeméti, Bénédicte Boudou, and Hélène Cazes (Turnhout, Belgium: Brepols, 2003).

Edition in English: *The Frankfort Book Fair: The Francofordiense Emporium of Henri Estienne,* edited and translated by James Westfall Thompson (Chicago: Caxton Club, 1911).

OTHER: Dionysius of Halicarnassus, *Responsio,* edited by Estienne (Paris: Printed by Charles Estienne, 1554);

Anacreon, *Teii Odae,* edited by Estienne (Paris: Printed by H. Estienne, 1554);

Moschus, Bion, and Theocritus, *Idyllia aliquot,* edited by Estienne (Venice: Printed by Paulo Manuzio, 1555);

Davidis Psalmi aliquot Latin carmine expressi, edited by Estienne (Geneva: Printed by H. Estienne, 1556);

Ctesias and Agatharchides, *Memnone excerptae historiae,* edited by Estienne (Geneva: Printed by H. Estienne, 1557);

Aeschylus, *Tragoediae VII,* edited by Estienne (Geneva: Printed by H. Estienne, 1557);

Aristotle and Theophrastus, *Scripta quaedam,* edited by Estienne (Geneva: Printed by H. Estienne, 1557);

Athenagoras, *Philosophi Christiani Apologia,* edited by Estienne (Geneva: Printed by H. Estienne, 1557);

Maximus of Tyre, *Philosophi Platonici Sermones,* edited by Estienne (Geneva: Printed by H. Estienne, 1557);

Justinian I, Marcus Junianus Justinus, and Pope Leo I, *Autokratoron Ioustinianou, Ioustinou, Leontos Nearai diataxeis; Ioustinianou Edikta = Impp. Justiniani, Justini, Leonis novellae Constitutiones,* edited by Estienne (Geneva: Printed by H. Estienne for Ulrich Fugger, 1558);

Desiderius Erasmus, *Adagiorum Chiliades,* edited by Estienne (Geneva: Printed by Robert I Estienne, 1558; revised edition, Paris: Printed for Joannes Charron by Michel Sonnius, 1572);

Diodorus Siculus, *Bibliothecae historicae libri quindecim,* edited by Estienne (Geneva: Printed by H. Estienne, 1559);

Appian of Alexandra, *Hispanica et Annibalica,* edited by Estienne (Geneva: Printed by H. Estienne, 1560);

Athenagoras, *De mortuorum resurrectione,* edited by Estienne (Zurich: Printed by A. Gesner, 1560);

Pindar, *Olympia, Pythia,* edited by Estienne (Geneva: Printed by H. Estienne, 1560);

Xenophon, *Omnia quae extant opera,* edited by Estienne (Geneva: Printed by H. Estienne, 1561; revised, 1581; revised, 1596);

Genesis, cum Catholica expositione, edited by Estienne (Geneva: Printed by H. Estienne, 1562);

Liber Psalmorum Davidis, edited by Estienne (Geneva: Printed by H. Estienne, 1562);

Sextus Empiricus, *Philosophi Pyrrhoniarum hypotypose in libri III,* edited and translated by Estienne (Geneva: Printed by H. Estienne, 1562);

De abusu linguae graecae, edited by Estienne (Geneva: Printed by H. Estienne, 1563);

Jean Calvin, *Rudimenta fidei Christianae,* translated by Estienne (Geneva: Printed by H. Estienne, 1563);

Fragmenta poetarum veterum latinorum, edited by Estienne (Geneva: Printed by H. Estienne, 1564);

Thucydides, *De bello Peloponnesiaco libri octo,* edited by Estienne (Geneva: Printed by H. Estienne, 1564; revised, 1588; revised edition, Frankfurt am

Main: Printed by the heirs of Andreas Wechel, 1594);

Colloquiorum seu Dialogorum Graecorum specimen Henrici Stephani, edited by Estienne (Lyon: Printed by Thomas de Straton, 1564);

Florilegium diversorum epigrammatum veterum, edited by Estienne (Geneva: Printed by H. Estienne, 1566);

Herodotus, *Historiae libri IX,* edited and translated by Estienne (Geneva: Printed by H. Estienne, 1566); revised as *Historia* (Geneva: Printed by H. Estienne, 1570); revised as *Historiarum libri IX* (Geneva: Printed by H. Estienne, 1592); enlarged as *Historiae libri IX et de Vita Homeri libellus* (Frankfurt am Main: Printed by the heirs of Andreas Wechel, 1595);

Poetae Graeci principes heroici carminis, edited by Estienne (Geneva: Printed by H. Estienne, 1566);

Medicae artis principes, edited by Estienne (Paris: Printed by H. Estienne, 1567);

Aulo Giano Parrasio, *Liber de rebus per epistolam quaesitis,* edited by Estienne (Geneva: Printed by H. Estienne, 1567);

Antonius Polemo, *Himerii et aliorum declamationes, Graece, nunc primum editae,* edited by Estienne (Geneva: Printed by H. Estienne, 1567);

Varii historiae Romanae scriptores, 4 volumes, edited by Estienne (Geneva: Printed by H. Estienne, 1568);

Plutarch and Diogenes Laertius, *Apophthegmata Graeca,* edited by Estienne (Geneva: Printed by H. Estienne, 1568);

Sophocles and Euripides, *Annotationes in Sophoclem et Euripidem: Tractatus de orthographia quorundam vocabulorum Sophocli cum caeteris tragicis communium. Dissertatio de Sophoclea imitatione Homeri,* edited by Estienne (Geneva: Printed by H. Estienne, 1568);

Comicorum Graecorum sententiae, edited by Estienne (Geneva: Printed by H. Estienne, 1569);

Epigrammata Graeca, selecta ex Anthologia, edited by Estienne (Geneva: Printed by H. Estienne, 1570);

Diogenes Laertius, *De vitis, dogmatis et Apophthegmatis eorum qui in philosophia claruerunt, libri X,* edited by Estienne (Geneva: Printed by H. Estienne, 1570; revised, 1593);

Conciones sive orationes ex Graecis Latinisque historicis excerptae, edited by Estienne (Geneva: Printed by H. Estienne, 1570);

Thesaurus graecae linguae, 5 volumes, edited by Estienne (Geneva: Printed by H. Estienne, 1572);

Plutarch, *Extant opera,* 13 volumes, edited by Estienne (Geneva: Printed by H. Estienne, 1572);

Virtutum encomia sive Gnomae de virtutibus, edited by Estienne (Geneva: Printed by H. Estienne, 1573);

Poesis philosophica, edited by Estienne (Geneva: Printed by H. Estienne, 1573);

Homer and Hesiod, *Homeri et Hesiodi certamen,* edited by Estienne (Geneva: Printed by H. Estienne, 1573);

Apollonius Molon, *Argonauticon libri IIII,* edited by Estienne (Geneva: Printed by H. Estienne, 1574);

Oratorum veterum Orationes, edited by Estienne (Geneva: Printed by H. Estienne, 1575);

Horatio, *Quinti Horatii Flacci Poemata,* edited by Estienne (Geneva: Printed by H. Estienne, 1575);

Virgil, *Publii Virgilii Maronis poemata,* edited by Estienne (Geneva: Printed by H. Estienne, 1575);

Novum Testamentum: Obscuriorum vocum & quorudam loquendi generum accuratas partim suas partim aliorum interpretationes margini adscripsit, edited by Estienne (Geneva: Printed by H. Estienne, 1576);

Epistolia, Dialogi breves, Oratiunculae, Poematia, edited by Estienne (Geneva: Printed by H. Estienne, 1577);

Dionysius of Alexandria and Pomponius Mela, *Situs orbis descriptio,* edited by Estienne (Geneva: Printed by H. Estienne, 1577);

Callimachus of Cyrene, *Hymni (cum suis scholiis Græcis) et Epigrammata,* edited by Estienne and Nicodemus Frischlin (Geneva: Printed by H. Estienne, 1577);

Cicero, *Epistolarum volumen,* edited by Estienne (Geneva: Printed by H. Estienne, 1577);

Homer, Virgil, and Nonnus of Panopolis, *Homerici centones, a veteribus vocati Homerokentra. Virgiliani Centones. Utrique in quaedam historiae sacrae capiti scripti. Nonni paraphrasis Evangelii Ioannis, Graece & Latine,* edited by Estienne (Geneva: Printed by H. Estienne, 1578);

Plato, *Opera quae extant omnia,* 3 volumes, edited by Estienne, Latin translation by Jean de Serres (Geneva: Printed by H. Estienne, 1578);

Henr. Stephani Schediasmatum variorum, id est observationum, emendationum, expositionum, disquisitionum libri tres, 2 volumes, edited by Estienne (Geneva: Printed by H. Estienne, 1578, 1579);

Theocritus, *Aliorumque Poetarum Idyllia,* edited by Estienne (Geneva: Printed by H. Estienne, 1579);

Juris Civilis Fontes et Rivi, edited by Estienne (Geneva: Printed by H. Estienne, 1580);

Pierre Bunel and Paulo Manuzio, *Epistolae,* edited by Estienne (Geneva: Printed by H. Estienne, 1581);

Herodian, *Histor. Lib. VIII,* edited by Estienne (Geneva: Printed by H. Estienne, 1581);

Paralipomena Grammaticarum Gr. linguae Inst., edited by Estienne (Geneva: Printed by H. Estienne, 1581);

Pliny the Elder, *Epist. Libri IX,* edited by Estienne (Geneva: Printed by H. Estienne, 1581);

Marcus Terentius Varro, *Operae quae supersunt,* edited by Estienne (Geneva: Printed by H. Estienne, 1581);

Virgil, *Poemata,* edited by Estienne (Geneva: Printed by H. Estienne, 1583);

Aulus Gellius, *Noctes Atticae,* edited by Estienne (Paris: Printed by H. Estienne, 1585);

Ambrosius Aurelius Theodosius Macrobius, *In somnium Scipionis libri II,* edited by Estienne (Paris: Printed by H. Estienne, 1585);

Seneca, *Lectionem Proodopoeia,* edited by Estienne (Geneva: Printed by H. Estienne, 1586);

Dicaearchus, *Geographica quaedam,* edited by Estienne (Geneva: Printed by H. Estienne, 1589);

Dio Cassius, *Romanarum Historiarum libri XXV,* edited by Estienne (Geneva: Printed by H. Estienne, 1591);

Pliny the Younger, *Epist. lib. IX,* edited by Estienne (Geneva: Printed by H. Estienne, 1591);

Varro, *Assertiones analogiae sermonis Latini,* edited by Estienne (Geneva: Printed by H. Estienne, 1591);

Appian of Alexandria, *Rom. Historiarum Punica,* edited by Estienne (Geneva: Printed by H. Estienne, 1592);

De Martinalitia Venatione sive, de therophonia segetum et vitium alexicaca, edita ab illustriss. principe Friderico IIII palatino electore. Epigrammata H. Stephani, edited by Estienne (Heidelberg: Abraham Smesmann, 1592);

Dio Cassius, *E Dione Excerptae historiae ab Joanne Xiphilino,* edited by Estienne (Geneva: Printed by H. Estienne, 1592);

Isocrates, *Orationes et Epistolae,* edited by Estienne (Geneva: Printed by H. Estienne, 1593);

Memnon of Heraclea Pontica, *Ex Memnone excerptae historiae de tyrannis Heracleæ Ponticæ,* edited by Estienne (Geneva: Printed by H. Estienne, 1594);

Concordantiae Testamenti Novi Graecolatinae, edited by Estienne (Geneva: Printed by H. Estienne, 1594).

Henri II Estienne—who often used the Latin version of his name, Henricus Stephanus—has been called the last of the overlooked giants among French humanists. There is less excuse for such neglect in his case than in that of his celebrated predecessor Guillaume Budé: the latter published only Latin works, whereas Estienne's books in French, while far fewer than those in Latin, were well known and influential. He was also the most distinguished member of a distinguished printing dynasty that was founded in Paris by his grandfather Henri I Estienne around 1502. Reliable information about his life is difficult to obtain; the long-standard authorities, Antoine-Augustin Renouard (1837, 1838) and Louis Clément (1899), have been shown to be inaccurate and should be consulted with caution. Much information has, however, become available in a 2003 edition of Estienne's prefaces by Judit Kecskeméti, Bénédicte Boudou, and Hélène Cazes.

In 1526 Henri I Estienne's oldest son, Robert I, became the head of the printing firm. Henri II Estienne was born in 1531. In 1539 King François I made Robert Estienne the official king's printer for Hebrew and Latin works. Robert and his wife, Perrette, née Bade, who also came from a family of printers, gave Henri a thorough classical education with one variation: he studied Greek before Latin, although he already spoke Latin as a child; his Greek tutor was the renowned Pierre Danès. In 1544 Robert Estienne became the king's printer for Greek, but in 1551 he moved to Geneva because of the hostility of the Sorbonne (the theology faculty of the University of Paris) to some of his publications; under the rule of Jean Calvin, Geneva had been a refuge for Reformers since 1541. Robert's younger brother Charles, author of *La guide des chemins de France* (1552, Guide to the Roads of France) and *Praedium rusticum* (1554, The Country Estate), took over the Paris press. From this time onward the Estienne family was split, with those who lived in Paris remaining Catholics and those in Geneva converting to Protestantism.

After traveling in Italy, Henri Estienne seems to have settled in Geneva in 1555. That year he married Marguerite Pillot and set up his own printing firm alongside his father's; when Robert Estienne died in 1559, Henri took over his father's press. In the preface to his Ciceronian lexicon of 1557—a work that is still useful today—Estienne pays homage to the editorial achievement of his father, whom he hopes, with some trepidation, to imitate; explains his editorial procedure in great detail; and sneers at the "servum pecus" (slave herd) of would-be imitators of Cicero. In the same year he published some *castigationes* (objections) to those overzealous followers of Cicero, for whom he coins derogatory names such as *Ciceroniastri, Ciceronicolae,* and *Ciceronipetae.* Between 1557 and 1568 he edited works by Aeschylus (1557), Aristotle and Theophrastus (1557), Pindar (1560), and Xenophon (1561); a book of Roman law (1558); the adages of Desiderius Erasmus (1558); the books of Genesis (1562) and Psalms (1562); a medical dictionary (1564); and a collection of Greek dialogues for schoolboys (1564). Probably his most important publication of these years was his 1562 translation of the *Hypotyposes* of Sextus Empiricus; the work crucially influenced skeptical thought in France, particularly that of Michel de Montaigne. In the preface Estienne says that he fell ill and into a temporary state of disgust with literature; the condition was cured by reading the Pyrrhonians (skeptics), who made him laugh.

The breadth of Estienne's expertise and interests, from Greek and Roman classics to law, medicine, and education, is astonishing. Each edition of a work by a classical author is accompanied by comments about the state of the text, previous editions, and Estienne's editorial procedures, as well as attacks on other ancient or modern scholars and confidences about his private life. Thirty-one of the books he printed between 1558 and 1568 were financed by the banker Ulrich Fugger.

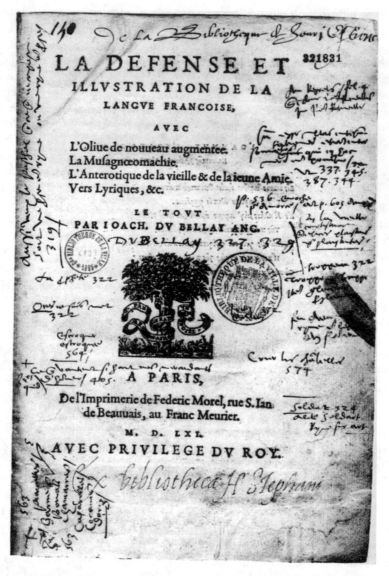

Title page for an edition of Joachim du Bellay's book on the French language, originally published in 1549, with notes in Estienne's hand (Bibliothèque de la Ville de Lyon; from Louis Clément, Henri Estienne et son oeuvre française, 1899; Thomas Cooper Library, University of South Carolina)

In 1565 Estienne published his first work in French: *Traicté de la conformité du language françois avec le grec* (Treatise on the Conformity of the French Language with Greek), usually referred to as the *Conformité*. In this book, in which the word *critique* is used for the first time, he states two convictions that he never abandoned: that French has more in common with Greek than with Latin, and that among languages French ranks next to Greek in superiority. He thus modified a common humanist topos of the hierarchy of languages: that Hebrew was the "best" language, because it was given to Adam by God and because in Hebrew there is no gap between word and thing; the next best language

was classical Greek, then Latin, and then, much lower on the scale, the vernacular languages. (Estienne left Hebrew at the apex of the hierarchy.) Estienne's main subject is "la remonstrance du desordre & abus qui est auiourdhuy en l'vsage de la langue Françoise" (a protest against the contemporary disorder in and misuse of the French language). The French of which he approves is not that of the king's court or the lawyers, but that which is "Du pur & simple, n'ayant rien de fard, ni d'affectation" (Pure and simple, having no makeup or affectation); elsewhere in the book he says that languages, like women, are more attractive without cosmetics. He characterizes the kind of French he does not like as "desguisé, masqué, sophistiqué, fardé & affecté" (disguised, masked, adulterated, made up and affected), or, in summary, as "Italianizé & Espagnolizé" (Italianized and Spanished). Linguistic perfection, he says, consists of ease of pronunciation, gratification to the ear, and a copious vocabulary. Borrowing of words from other languages is occasionally permissible. He advocates the use of proverbs and sayings and tells a sarcastic tale about a seigneur who invited some local gentlemen to dinner, promising them "un bon epigramme à l'entree de table" (a good epigram as prologue to the meal); one of the gentlemen becomes furious with his cook, who has never prepared epigrams for his dinner. Estienne argues with tremendous energy but little formal organization and piles up examples at great length.

In 1566 Estienne published his translation of Herodotus's history into Latin; he also published his second work in French, *L'Introduction au traité de la Conformité des merveilles anciennes avec les modernes, ou, Traité préparatif à l'Apologie pour Herodote* (Introduction to the Treatise on the Conformity of Ancient Marvels with Those of Modern Times, or Preparatory Treatise to the Apology for Herodotus), which modern scholars call the *Apologie* (Apology). The title is typical of Estienne: he designates an enormous volume—855 pages in the modern edition—an "introduction" and a "preparatory treatise." Readers have objected to Herodotus's historical writings on the grounds of lack of verisimilitude, saying that the "marvels" he recounts are too improbable; but, says Estienne, they are as nothing compared to the "marvels" of the modern world: the wickedness of humanity in general and of the Catholic priesthood in particular. After contrasting the biblical Golden Age to his own period, he embarks on a seemingly endless litany of the vices preachers have castigated; he often quotes the celebrated fifteenth-century preachers Michel Menot and Olivier Maillard. There is little structure in this tirade, and the principal vices—lust, incest, sodomy, blasphemy, theft, murder, cruelty, greed, and drunkenness—are mentioned many times. Estienne makes no secret of his prejudices: sodomy came to France from Italy; more aristocrats than ordinary people commit incest; François Rabelais and Bonaventure des Périers were mockers of religion. Nineteen of the forty chapters are devoted to the vices of the Roman Catholic clergy, whose greed, immorality, and ignorance are no different from those of the rest of the population.

The *Apologie* has always been Estienne's most-read book, in large part because of his energy and verve as a storyteller. He borrows *contes* (stories) from Erasmus, Des Périers, Gian Francesco Poggio Bracciolini, and Marguerite de Navarre and retells them with a mix-

ture of indignation and satisfaction so that the old chestnuts, familiar since the Middle Ages, about immoral priests and lubricious wives seem fresh and amusing. In chapter 21, "De la lubricité et paillardise des gens d'église" (On the Lewdness and Lechery of Churchmen), a series of comic and some tragic anecdotes about the misdeeds of Franciscan monks includes one that all of his readers already knew: a friar has to leave his mistress's bed in such haste on the return of her husband that he leaves his *brayes* (underpants) behind; the wife convinces her husband that they are a precious saint's relic. Estienne is hostile to the clergy not only because of their vices but also because they are stupid: they make basic mistakes about theological matters and worry about trivialities. In chapter 35 he castigates stupidly "curieuses" (curious) theological questions:

> A-sçavoir-mon si Dieu pourroit pècher s'il vouloit. A-sçavoir-mon si Dieu peut faire maintenant tout ce qu'il a pu faire par le passé. . . . A-sçavoir-mon si Dieu pouvoit prendre la nature humaine en sexe féminin. . . . A-sçavoir-mon qu'eust consacré S. Pierre s'il eust consacré alors que le corps de Jésus Christ estoit pendu en la croix.

> (Item, whether God could sin if he wanted to. Item, whether God can do today everything he was able to do in the past. . . . Item, whether God could have taken human nature in feminine form. . . . Item, what St. Peter would have consecrated if he had consecrated [a communion wafer] while the body of Jesus Christ was hanging on the cross.)

Estienne notes that someone once asked what God was doing before the creation of the world; the ironic reply was that he was building hell for the askers of such questions.

This book is partly responsible for Estienne's reputation as a bitter, disillusioned misanthrope, but laughter is discussed and illustrated several times in the work. The last item on the title page is a quatrain stressing not bitterness but laughter and pleasure:

> Tant d'actes merueilleux en cest oeuvre lirez,
> Que de nul autre apres esmerueillé serez.
> Et pourrez vous sçauans du plaisir ici prendre,
> Vous non sçauans pourrez en riant y apprendre.

> (You will read in this work of so many astonishing acts,
> That afterwards you will not be astonished by anything.
> And you, learned men, will be able to take pleasure here,
> While you the nonlearned can learn while laughing.)

Estienne affects to despise Rabelais as an author of "escrits brocardans toute sorte de religion" (writings mocking any kind of religion), but Rabelais is an obvious and constant influence on his style. Estienne's stories about unfaithful wives and lecherous priests were stock fare in the short stories and theatrical farces of the time, but the book offended the Geneva authorities, who accused him of being "a new Rabelais" and insisted on the deletion of some passages.

During the next few years Estienne published an astonishing variety of books: editions of classical works, including the influential Greek Anthology, *Florilegium diversorum epigrammatum veterum* (1566, Anthology of Varied Epigrams by Classical Authors); selections from the works of Plutarch and Diogenes Laertius (1568) and from Sophocles and Euripides (1568); and speeches, epigrams, and heroic verse. He also produced another medical book (1567); a poem on printing, *Artis typographiae querimonia: De illiteratis quibusdam typographis, propter quos in contemptum venit* (1569, Complaint of the Typographic Art: About Certain Illiterate Typographers on Account of Whom It Comes to Be Despised); and a lighthearted hyperbolic tribute to the Frankfurt book fair, *Francofordiense Emporium* (1574; translated as *The Frankfort Book Fair,* 1875), which has been translated into English, French, and German. He praises Frankfurt for its housing, citizens, magistrates, and consideration for foreigners, especially if they are merchants. He describes the fair at length—not just the great variety of books, which, he says, would entitle Frankfurt to be called Athens, but also its extremely varied merchandise, including wine, hams, horses, precious metals, technological advances, artistic masterpieces, and pottery. In 1575 appeared the notorious *Discours merveilleux de la vie et déportements de la reine Catherine de Médicis* (Marvelous Discourse on the Life and Doings of Queen Catherine de Médicis); long thought to be by Estienne, it has been shown not to be his work.

Estienne's money troubles probably began with the cessation of Fugger's patronage in 1568, but they were exacerbated by the *Thesaurus graecae linguae* (1572, Greek Thesaurus). *Thesaurus* means treasure, and Estienne quotes Hesiod's comment that there is no more beautiful treasure than the Greek language. But alas, Estienne says in his preface, this thesaurus has stripped him of his own treasure. He recounts falling in love with Greek as a child, his struggles to learn it, and the loss of his personal fortune to the thesaurus. He explains the organizational problems posed by such a work and his solutions to them, daring to criticize the great Budé. He is interested in the relationships among languages and their borrowings from each other. As usual, he satirizes enemies, especially plagiarists who might hope to profit from his work, and gives examples of egregious linguistic errors. Two themes here are common to many of his prefaces: he says that the work as it stands is unfinished, and that he, Estienne, is the Hercules of philologists. The thesaurus was apparently his

favorite work: the project had been begun by his father years earlier; Estienne announced it in 1557, published it in 1572, and reworked it throughout the rest of his life. It is still consulted by scholars.

Alongside the serious scholarship are some works in a lighter vein, such as the *Parodiae morales* (1575, Ethical Parodies). By "parody" Estienne means textual adaptation and manipulation not for comic effect but for moral instruction. The parodies make up the first part of the book, while the second part is devoted to centos: patchworks of fragments from various texts—for instance, a line from Homer and a line from Virgil applied to a context unrelated to either poet. The following year Estienne published an edition of the New Testament in Latin and Greek, with linguistic comments in the margin and a preface dedicated to his friend Sir Philip Sidney, and his own *De latinitate falso suspecta* (On Latin, Unfairly Suspected [of borrowing from French]), in which he argues that expressions and turns of phrase used in Latin by French writers are not Gallicisms but correct classical usage.

A work that is ignored by modern critics takes humor as its subject: *Pseudocicero, Dialogus Henr. Stephani: In hoc non solùm de multis ad Ciceronis sermonem pertinentibus, sed etiam quem delectum editionum eius habere & quam cautionem in eo legendo debeat adhibere, lector monebitur* (1577, Pseudo-Cicero, a Dialogue by Henri Etienne: In Which the Reader Will Be Advised Not Only about Many Things That Pertain to Cicero's Style, but Even What Choice of Editions of Cicero He Should Have, and What Caution He Should Take in Reading Him). Three erudite friends, Paulus, Antonius, and Dionysius, discuss the comic in general (Latin *facetiae,* Greek *geloios*), the terms used by Cicero in particular, and the stylistic qualities and defects of contemporary writers. They praise Angelo Poliziano, Pietro Bembo, and Carlo Sigonio and discuss many others who have emended Cicero, including Jacques Cujas, Adrien Turnèbe, Robert and Henri Estienne, and Julius Caesar and Joseph Justus Scaliger. The longest discussion concerns the adjective *facetosus,* found in one edition of Cicero's works; they finally decide that it is a scribal or printing error. The conversation illuminates the concerns of late-sixteenth-century intellectuals but is also witty and even playful—two qualities not often associated with Estienne.

A 1578 publication insured Estienne's lasting fame. In his three-volume edition of the complete extant works of Plato, each page is divided into two columns; the right column is the Greek text, the left a Latin translation by Jean de Serres. Between the columns, letters from *a* to *e* divide the columns into five sections. These "Stephanus numbers" are still used to identify quotations from Plato: the name of the dialogue is followed by the page number in Estienne's edition and the letters of the sections that include the quotation.

Estienne's next French work was *Deux dialogues du nouveau langage françois italianizé et autrement desguizé, principalement entre les courtisans de ce temps* (1578, Two Dialogues of the New French Language, Italianized and Otherwise Disguised, Mainly by the Courtiers of Today). The courtiers in question are those of King Henri III, and the large volume—more than four hundred pages in Pauline M. Smith's 1980 edition—satirizes them unmercifully, beginning with four long poems apostrophizing them. The speakers are Celtophile (Lover of France or of the French), who represents Estienne's ideas; Philausone (Lover of Italy or of Italian); and Philalethe (Lover of Truth), to whom Celtophile and Philausone appeal, late in the dialogue, to settle their dispute. Philausone claims that to be accepted at court one must speak Italianized French, which he does; Celtophile objects strongly on the grounds that Italian is inferior to French, which has no need of borrowed terms. (Estienne was unaware of the existence of Vulgar Latin, from which both Italian and French developed.) He says that it is permissible to borrow Italian words where no equivalents exist in French, as is the case with character traits unknown in France such as *charlatano* (charlatan), *bofone* (buffoon), *poltrone* (poltroon), and *forfante* (braggart); he claims that there are no borrowings from Italian for words related to virtue. Many linguistic and cultural points are made, some in passing and others at considerable length. Celtophile and Philausone discuss formulas for expressing gratitude and the correct definition of "le langage courtisan." Celtophile objects to the current pronunciation of the adjective for "French" in its feminine plural form as *franceses* instead of *françoises* (the former pronunciation has, however, become the standard one in modern French). Philausone compares languages to dishes of meat stuffed with herbs: different appetites like different "farces" (stuffings). They argue at length over misuses of Latin, the superlatives popular at court, military terms, polite formulas of refusal, courtly periphrases, Greek as the most perfect language, and much, much more. Sometimes many pages are devoted to one phrase or even one word. As in many of Estienne's works, other books by him are mentioned; at one point Celtophile reports in detail on a conversation he had with Estienne. But the main aim of the book is to satirize courtiers, not just for their Italianate language but also for their lack of culture—one of them refers to "les apostumes" (abscesses) rather than "les Apophtegmes" (the Apothegms) of Plutarch; their overelaborate dress; and, implicitly, their effeminacy. To succeed at court, says Philausone, one needs impudence, hypocrisy, dissimulation, flattery, and a false face. The book appears to have no structure, but the satire of courtiers constitutes a leitmotif to which, much as in an essay by Montaigne, Estienne returns every so often after excursions elsewhere. Estienne's anger is genuine, but there is a good deal of humor: Celtophile often laughs at Philausone, and sometimes they laugh together; courtiers, on the other hand, are good at repressing their laughter. Estienne's language often recalls that of Rabelais, and he is fond of quoting the best-known French farce of the period, the anonymous fifteenth-century *Maistre Pierre Pathelin* (translated as *Master Pierre Pathelin,* 1914). The book concludes with Celtophile's promise to persuade Philausone that French is as beautiful a language as Italian, a promise Estienne attempted to fulfill in *Project du livre intitulé, De la precellence du langage françois* (1579, Project of the Work Entitled On the Preeminence of the French Language).

Deux Dialogues does not strike a modern reader as in any way dangerous, but the work got Estienne into trouble again with the Geneva authorities. He avoided prosecution by escaping to France. He was promised a pension by Henri III, for whom he wrote *Project du livre intitulé, De la precellence du langage françois*—once again, a long book is merely the "project" of a presumably even longer book that was never written. In *Principum Monitrix Musa* (1590, The Muse Adviser of Princes) Estienne explains that he wrote *Project du livre intitulé, De la precellence du langage françois* at the king's urging, completing it in three months without the notes that he had left behind in Geneva. Estienne asserts that French can prove that it is more "grave" (serious), more "gentil et de meilleure grace" (graceful), and more "riche" (copious) than Italian. The third attribute is developed at much greater length than the other two; like the poet Pierre de Ronsard, Estienne wants French to be enriched from a variety of sources—but not from Italian. He notes that Greek and French proverbs have much in common. He charges that Italian stole the French *connestable* (constable) and deformed it into *connestabole*—not realizing that both words derive from the Vulgar Latin *comes stabuli* (count of the stable). The book ends with a playful proposition. If Italian will admit the superiority of French, then French will defend Italian against the claims of the obviously inferior Spanish:

Mais je ne leur feray point d'avantage la guerre touchant les mots de la guerre: m'asseurant qu'ils se rendront à composition, quand ils auront consideré que leur fort n'est aucunement tenable: et qu'ils seroyent malavisez d'attendre qu'ils fussent battus d'un beaucoup plus grand nombre de pieces: veu que si peu ont desja faict une telle breche. . . . La composition donc sera que leur langage avouera la superiorité et precellence du nostre, sans jamais contrevenir à cest aveu, par voye directe ne oblique. Moyennant lequel aussi, le nos-

Title page for the influential anthology of classical Greek literature, edited by Estienne (Thomas Cooper Library, University of South Carolina)

second rank; and if ever Spanish wanted to dispute this, French will take Italian under its protection, to maintain it in this position. Giving Italian, however, six days to accept these terms. During which time, if new support comes to their aid, we grant them lightheartedly the cancellation of these terms.)

After a year at the French court, Estienne returned to Geneva, where he was briefly imprisoned. His second wife, Barbe de Wille, died in 1581; he pays touching tribute to her in one of the prefaces to his 1585 edition of Aulus Gellius's *Noctes Atticae* (translated as *The Attic Nights,* 1795). In 1582 he published *Hypomneses de Gallica lingua* (Recollections of the Gallic Tongue), a treatise in Latin for foreigners who want to learn French. He discusses phonetics, etymology, the parts of speech, writing, and pronunciation. As in other works, he stresses that the best French is that of Paris; though here, while still anticourt, he accepts the usage of the parlement.

As religious strife in France increased, Estienne spent much of his time traveling in Switzerland and Germany. In 1586 he married Abigail Poupart. Despite constant financial problems, he continued to edit classical works and to publish his own writings, including *De criticis vet. Gr. et Latinis, eorúmque variis apud poetas potissimùm reprehensionibus* (1587, Dissertation on the Ancient Greek and Latin Critics, and Their Varied, Most Powerful Objections to Poets), in which the critic is defined as a talented and prudent person who, like the poet, is endowed with furor and enthusiasm; a dialogue on the right way to study Greek (1587); and the *Principum Monitrix Musa,* a verse treatise that has been called a systematic refutation of the ideas of Niccolò Machiavelli. Estienne treats all aspects of the prince as military commander and civil governor; he also expresses at length his affection for Henri III, who had been assassinated in 1589 by a Dominican monk, and his love of France.

tre le declarera digne du second lieu; et au cas que l'Espagnol le voulust quereler, le nostre prendra l'Italien en sa protection, pour le maintenir en ce droit. En luy donnant toutesfois six jours de terme pour s'en resoudre. Pendant lesquels si leur venoit nouvelle aide et secours, nous leur ottroyons de gayeté de cueur que la presente composition soit nulle.

(But I will not make war against them any longer over military terminology, since I am confident that they will come to terms when they consider that their fortress is by no means impregnable, and that they would be ill advised to wait until they are vanquished with a much greater number of guns, seeing that so few have already made such a breach. . . . The peace terms will be, then, that their language will admit the superiority and preeminence of ours, without ever going back on this admission, directly or indirectly. It will follow that our language will declare theirs worthy of occupying the

Estienne's last French work is *Les premices, ou le i livre des proverbes épigramatizé, ou des épigrammes proberbializé. C'est à dire, signez et seellez par les prouerbes françois: Aucuns aussi par les grecs & latins, ou autres, pris de quelcun des langages vulgaires. Rengez en lieux communs. Le tout par Henri Estienne* (1593, First Fruits, or The First Book of Epigrammatized Proverbs, or Proverbialized Epigrams. That Is to Say, Signed and Sealed by French Proverbs; Some Also by Greek and Latin Proverbs, or by Others, Taken from One of the Vernacular Languages. Arranged by Commonplaces. The Whole by Henri Estienne). Clearly, the same old Estienne is at work here: "The First Book," never followed by a second; the fondness for proverbs and epigrams; the facility in switching languages; and the emphasis on commonplaces can all be found in earlier works. Even the structure of the book, if it can be so called, is typical: of the six commonplaces, the first, God, takes up 128 pages; the second, Man, 18 pages; the third, Life, 16 pages; and the last three, Youth, Old Age, and Death, 16, 9, and 10 pages, respectively. Each section is a series of short verse adaptations of proverbs related to the commonplace, beginning with 32 on "En peu d'heure Dieu labeure" (God works in a short time), with occasional prose commentaries. Of the total of 243 epigrams, 50 are variations on "Man proposes and God disposes." Estienne still hates Italianizing courtiers and is still correcting misuses of words and phrases: the idiom for mocking God, for example, is "faire gerbe de paille à Dieu" (give God a bale of straw), not "barbe de paille" (a straw beard).

Estienne had fourteen children by his three wives; his daughter Florence married the scholar and theologian Isaac Casaubon in 1586. He was clearly a sincere Christian; though only a few of the works he published are specifically religious, he refers frequently to God and religion, in the *Premices* reproaching French poets for attributing to fortune what should be attributed to God. Although he spent much of his life outside of France, he was, as he tells his readers in the preface to the Greek Thesaurus, proud of being French. For most of his life Estienne was harassed by money troubles and by the intolerance of the Geneva authorities; yet, he retained his courage and energy and sense of humor. He can hardly have been the irascible curmudgeon of tradition, since his friends included Sidney, Conrad Gesner, Joachim Camerarius, Théodore de Bèze, and Philipp Melanchthon. And his achievements both as printer and as author are astonishing: his printing record amazes both for its quantity and for its variety. His main passion was for Greek and Roman authors, and he produced first editions of works both of the famous—Anacreon (1554; Ronsard wrote a poem to salute the edition) and Plutarch (1572)—and of those who today are barely remembered: Dionysius of Halicarnassus (1554), Ctesias (1557), Maximus of Tyre (1557), Diodorus Siculus (1559), and Dicaearchus (1589). He edited and reedited the works of his favorite ancient poets, historians, orators, and philosophers. He also produced a large number of anthologies of highly varied natures: ancient historians (1557 and 1568), Roman poets (1564), ancient epigrams and heroic verses (1566), apophthegms (1568), sayings from ancient Greek literature (1569 and 1570), oratory (1570, 1575, and 1593), works of Church Fathers (1570), praises of virtue (1573), philosophical poetry (1573), geographical writings (1577), centos from Homer and Virgil (1578), Greek idylls (1578), ancient laws (1578), and some that defy summary, such as *Epistolia, Dialogi breves, Oratiunculae, Poematia* (1577, Letters, Brief Dia-

logues, Small Orations, Poems) by writers in both Greek and Latin.

While a large majority of the works Estienne printed were classical, he also edited books of the Bible and theological texts, including one by Calvin (1563); legal and medical works; texts for schoolboys; and Hebrew primers. He also showed his interest in printing in two 1569 works, *Artis typographiae querimonia* and *Epistola qua ad multas multorum amicorum respondet de suae typographiae statu nominatimque de suo Thesauro linguae Graecae* (Epistle That Responds to the Objections of Many Friends about the State of His Typography and Specifically about His Thesaurus of the Greek Language). In the latter he expands on his future editing plans, justifies the arrangement of the thesaurus, and lists at enormous length—as usual—examples of errors and stupidities committed by other printers.

Estienne was not only a printer but also a scholar, and a combative one at that. He does not hesitate to criticize the greatest of his predecessors—Budé, Erasmus, Poliziano, and Lorenzo Valla—and to affirm that his view or interpretation is the correct one. Today he would be called a philologist, though he was hampered by an imperfect knowledge of the history of the French language and its relationship to Latin. He is occasionally inconsistent; in several works he claims the "conformité" of French and Greek; yet, in *De latinitate falso suspecta* he makes the same claim for Latin. But his knowledge of both Latin and Greek was enormous, and his dictionaries are still used by scholars. In 1578 he contributed to the quarrel of the Ciceronians that raged throughout the century with *Nizoliodidascalus siue, Monitor Ciceronianorum Nizolianorum, dialogus* (Instruction for Nizzoli, or the Admonisher of Ciceronian Nizzolians, Dialogue), a satirical attack on the ultra-Ciceronian Mario Nizzoli and Nizzoli's followers. One of his final works (1595) is an attack on the scholar Justus Lipsius and Lipsius's disciples, for whom he makes up facetious names reminiscent of those he had used for overenthusiastic admirers of Cicero. Estienne died in Lyon while on a visit to France in 1597.

Thus, unlike many Renaissance humanist scholars, Henri II Estienne was also a creative writer. He was equally at home, and equally prolix, in Greek, Latin, and French; in prose and poetry; in dialogue and invective; and in the elaboration of scholarly minutiae and in virulent satire. He is almost always mentioned when sixteenth-century short stories are discussed, mainly because of the scabrous anecdotes of the *Apologie;* but he also tells stories in many other works. He was, no doubt, fond of the dialogue partly because it was the most popular literary genre of the century, but also because he relished argument and its satirical possibilities. As a poet he is undistinguished but—as witnessed by the apparently inexhaustible variations on a single theme in the *Prémices*—extraordinarily versatile. Finally, he has not been sufficiently recognized as one of the major comic writers of the sixteenth century.

Biographies:

Antoine-Augustin Renouard, *Annales de l'imprimerie des Estienne, ou Histoire de la famille des Estienne et de ses éditions,* 2 volumes (Paris: J. Renouard, 1837, 1838);

Louis Clément, *Henri Estienne et son oeuvre française* (Paris: Picard, 1899).

References:

Bénédicte Boudou, *Mars et les Muses dans l'Apologie pour Hérodote d'Henri Estienne* (Geneva: Droz, 2000);

Hélène Cazes, "Les mille et une pages d'Henri Estienne et de ses lecteurs: le recueil infini," *Etudes Françaises,* 38 (2002): 71–80;

Henri Estienne: Actes du Colloque organisé à l'Université de Paris-Sorbonne, le 12 mars 1987 par le Centre V. L. Saulnier, Université de Paris Sorbonne et l'Ecole normale supérieure de jeunes filles (Paris: Presses de l'Ecole normale supérieure, 1988);

Jean Jehasse, *La Renaissance de la Critique: L'Essor de l'humanisme érudit de 1560 à 1614* (St.-Etienne: Publications de l'Université de St.-Etienne, 1976), pp. 71–141;

Kenneth Lloyd-Jones, "'La grécité de notre idiome': *Correctio, Translatio* and *Interpretatio* in the Theoretical Writings of Henri Estienne," in *Translation and the Transmission of Culture between 1300 and 1600,* edited by Lloyd-Jones and Jeannette Beer (Kalamazoo: Medieval Institute Publications, Western Michigan University, 1995), pp. 259–304;

Silvia Longhi, "*Propagata voluptas*: Henri Estienne et la parodie," *Bibliothèque d'Humanisme et Renaissance,* 47 (1985): 595–608;

Winfried Schleiner, "Linguistic 'Xenohomophobia' in Sixteenth-Century France: The Case of Henri Estienne," *Sixteenth-Century Studies,* 34 (2003): 747–760.

Robert Garnier

(1545? – 20 September 1590)

Gillian Jondorf
University of Cambridge

BOOKS: *Plaintes amoureuses de R. Garnier, Manceau, contenans Elégies, Sonetz, Epîtres, chansons. Plus deux Eglogues, la première apprestée pour réciter devant le Roy et la seconde récitée devant la Magesté du Roy* (Toulouse: Printed by J. Colomiès, 1565);

Hymne de la Monarchye à G. du Faur, Seigneur de Pibrac, Avocat Du Roy au Parlement de Paris, par R. Garnier (Paris: Printed by Gabriel Buon, 1567);

Porcie: Tragédie françoise, représentant la cruelle et sanglante saison des guerres civiles de Rome, propre et convenable pour y voir depeincte la calamité de ce temps (Paris: Printed by Robert Estienne, 1568);

Hippolyte: Tragédie (Paris: Printed by Robert Estienne, 1573);

Cornélie: Tragédie (Paris: Printed by Robert Estienne, 1574); translated by Thomas Kyd as *Cornelia* (London: Printed by James Roberts for Nicholas Ling & John Busbie, 1594);

M. Antoine: Tragédie (Paris: Printed by Mamert Patisson, 1578); translated by Mary Sidney Herbert, Countess of Pembroke, as *Antonius: A Tragœdie*, in *A Discourse of Life and Death, Written in French by Ph. Mornay; Antonius: A Tragœdie, Written Also in French by Ro. Garnier* (London: Printed for William Ponsonby, 1592); translation republished as *The Tragedie of Antonie* (London: Printed by P. Short for William Ponsonby, 1595);

La Troade: Tragédie (Paris: Printed by Mamert Patisson, 1579);

Antigone, ou la Pieté: Tragédie (Paris: Printed by Mamert Patisson, 1580);

Bradamante: Tragecomédie (Paris: Printed by Mamert Patisson, 1582);

Les Juifves: Tragédie (Paris: Printed by Mamert Patisson, 1583); translated by Michael C. Zoltak as *The Hebrew Women*, in *Four French Renaissance Plays*, edited by Arthur P. Stabler (Pullman: Washington State University Press, 1978).

Editions and Collections: *Les tragédies de Robert Garnier* (Paris: Printed by Mamert Patisson, 1585);

Robert Garnier (from <http://en.wikipedia.org>)

Œuvres complètes, 4 volumes, edited by Raymond Lebègue (Paris: Les Belles Lettres, 1949–1975);

Les Juifves (Menston, U.K.: Scolar Press, 1972);

Two Tragedies: Hippolyte and Marc Antoine, edited by Christine M. Hill and Mary Morrison (London: Athlone Press, 1975);

Les Juifves, edited by Keith Cameron (Exeter, U.K.: Elm Bank, 1977);

185

Antigone, ou la Pieté, edited by Jean-Dominique Beaudin, Textes de la Renaissance, volume 17 (Paris: Champion, 1997);

La Troade, edited by Beaudin, Textes de la Renaissance, volume 27 (Paris: Champion, 1999);

Porcie, edited by Jean-Claude Ternaux, Textes de la Renaissance, volume 28 (Paris: Champion, 1999);

Les Juifves, edited by Sabine Lardou, Textes de la Renaissance, volume 29 (Paris: Champion, 1999);

Cornélie, edited by Ternaux, Textes de la Renaissance, volume 53 (Paris: Champion, 2002).

OTHER: "Sonnet sur la mort du feu Roy Charles IX" and "Aultre sonnet du mesme auteur," in *Tombeau du feu Roy Tres-Chrestien Charles IX* (Paris, 1574);

"Sonet *[sic]* à l'auteur" and "Autre sonnet du mesme auteur," in Arnaud Sorbin, *Le Vray discours des derniers propos memorables, et trespas du feu Roy de tres-bonne memoire Charles neufiesme* (Paris: Printed by Le Sieur, 1574).

Robert Garnier was the most prolific French playwright of the second half of the sixteenth century. Responding to the call of the Pléiade poets for a vernacular but classicizing theater, he composed seven tragedies in a style much influenced by the Roman Stoic philosopher and poet Seneca the Younger. He also wrote the first French tragicomedy, a genre that became highly successful in the next century.

Garnier was born in La Ferté-Bernard, Sarthe, probably in 1545, to Loys Garnier and Anne Guillon. His family was mainly bourgeois but had links to country nobility. He seems to have been orphaned when he was quite young. He presumably went to school in La Ferté-Bernard and then, perhaps, in Le Mans or Paris before beginning the study of law. It took five years to achieve a *baccalauréat* and then a *licence* in law; it is known only that Garnier spent the last three of these years, 1563 to 1566, at the University of Toulouse, which was considered by many to be the best law school in France. He may have acquired his *baccalauréat* at the University of Angers, which was much favored by young men from Le Mans, or at the University of Poitiers.

Toulouse held an annual poetry competition, the Jeux floraux (Floral Games), in which the prizes were gold and silver flowers. (The contest is mentioned contemptuously by Joachim du Bellay in his *La Deffence et Illustration de la Langue Francoyse* [1549; translated as *The Defence and Illustration of the French Language,* 1939].) In 1564 no prize was awarded on the first day of the competition, 1 May, so it was renewed two days later. This time the first prize was awarded, but there was a runoff for the second and third prizes among seven competitors, including Garnier, who were given the task of composing a *huitain* (eight-line poem) on a set refrain. Garnier won the second prize, the *violette* (violet), and the privilege of writing some of the celebratory verses for a visit to Toulouse by King Charles IX in early 1565. His prizewinning poem was "Chant royal allégorique des troubles passés de la France" (Allegorical *chant royal* on the Past Troubles of France)—a bold choice, since poems entered for the competition were traditionally on religious subjects. The *chant royal* had a one-line refrain at the end of each stanza and of the envoi; it was longer than a *ballade* and on a serious subject. Built around the refrain "La mer n'est pas toujours bouillonnante en oraige" (The sea is not always seething and stormy), Garnier's poem shows the influence of Pierre de Ronsard in its language and versification. The president of the judges of the competition was Guy du Faur de Pibrac, and Garnier's friendship with Pibrac probably began at this time. Pibrac and another friend, Etienne Potier de la Terrasse, became Garnier's patrons and received dedications of his works. In 1566 Garnier won the first prize in the competition, the *eglantine* (wild rose), for another political allegory in which he deplored the horrors of civil war and praised the young king in the refrain as "L'Hercule qui dompta les monstres de son aige" (The Hercules who overcame the monsters of his age). Meanwhile, he had published his prizewinning poem from 1564, his commissioned verses for the king, and some love poems addressed to a woman he calls Agnette in a collection, now lost, titled *Plaintes amoureuses* (1565, Lover's Laments). He may also have composed his first tragedy, *Porcie* (Portia), dedicated to Potier de la Terrasse, although it was not published until 1568.

Having completed his studies, Garnier went to work as a lawyer attached to the Parlement of Paris. In 1567 he contributed a sonnet to Ronsard that appears at the beginning of the second book of the latter's *Les Amours* (The Loves) and published the long *Hymne de la Monarchye* (Hymn of Monarchy), dedicated to Pibrac, which shows a strong Ronsardian influence in both form and content. The poem claims that monarchy is the source of the arts of civilization and is the best and most natural form of government; it is exemplified in nature by bees, which offer a perfect model of the monarchic state.

The title page of Garnier's first play indicates not only its subject but also its contemporary relevance: *Porcie: Tragédie françoise, représentant la cruelle et sanglante saison des guerres civiles de Rome, propre et convenable pour y voir depeincte la calamité de ce temps* (Portia: Tragedy in French, Portraying the Cruel and Bloody Period of the Roman Civil Wars, Where One May Aptly and Fitly See

Depicted the Disaster of the Present Time). Like all of Garnier's plays, *Porcie* follows what was perceived as the classical model of five acts accompanied by choric odes. Also, like many humanist plays of the period, *Porcie* has a slight plot: Porcie, the daughter of Cato and wife of Brutus, commits suicide after receiving the news of her husband's suicide after his defeat at Philippi by the forces of Mark Antony and Octavian in 42 B.C. But the work includes many references to the horrors of civil war–a recurrent theme in Garnier's work–and raises serious questions about liberty and repression. As in all of Garnier's tragedies, the language is rhetorically elaborate; his gift for lyrical verse is displayed in the choric lamentations for Porcie and for Rome, which has cast off the tyranny of Julius Caesar only to succumb to that of Augustus and his successors.

In 1569 Garnier moved to Le Mans to become *conseiller au présidial*, an officer of a tribunal that heard both criminal and civil cases. In 1573 he published the tragedy *Hippolyte* (Hippolytus), in which the skillful use of imagery creates an "atmosphere" for each of the principal characters. For example, the athletic huntsman Hippolyte, whose appropriate setting is outdoors in sunlight, recounts a nightmare that links him with the foul atmosphere of hellish darkness and monsters evoked by the ghost of his grandfather Egée (Aegeus). The latter opens the play with a 284-line speech describing the horrors of the underworld and predicting the doom about to befall his beloved Athens. There is less political material in this work than in any of Garnier's other plays, but a passage about rich people being drawn to unnatural and forbidden pleasures might be a reference to the rumor that the future King Henri III and his sister, Marguerite de Valois, had committed incest.

In the dedication of *Cornélie* (1574; translated as *Cornelia*, 1594) to "Monsieur de Rambouillet" (Nicolas d'Angennes), Garnier points out that his play is "propre aux malheurs de nostre siècle" (suitable for the miseries of our age) because it deals with a "grande Republique rompue par l'ambicieux discord de ses citoyens" (great state shattered by the ambitious discord of its citizens). The work deals with an episode in the Roman civil wars that occurred in 46 B.C., before the incidents portrayed in *Porcie*. Cornélie is the daughter of Metellus Scipio, leader of the senatorial forces battling Caesar in Africa, and the widow of the consul Pompey the Great. Scipio's defeat by Caesar at Thapsus and his suicide are reported in act 5, leaving Cornélie to mourn both her father and her husband. Powerful and horrible descriptions of bloodshed in the play may reflect the violence in various parts of France that followed the St. Bartholomew's Day Massacre in 1572.

Charles IX died in 1574, and Garnier contributed two sonnets to his *Tombeau* (poetic memorial). One of these sonnets also appeared, along with a third by Garnier, in an edifying account of the king's death prepared by his chaplain, Arnaud Sorbin, to counter Huguenot rumors that the king was tormented on his deathbed by guilt about the St. Bartholomew's Day Massacre. Also in 1574 Garnier was promoted to deputy president of the town assembly of Le Mans and chief justice for the Maine region.

By late 1575 Garnier was married to Françoise Hubert, whose family was from Nogent-le-Rotrou. She must have been unusually well educated for a woman of the bourgeoisie, since she was able to write verses for her husband's works. The couple had two daughters: Diane, born in 1579, and Françoise, born in 1582.

In 1578 Garnier published *M. Antoine* (Mark Antony). Based mainly on Plutarch's life of Antony, the play deals with the title character's defeat by Octavian at the battle of Actium in 31 B.C. and his subsequent suicide and that of Cléopâtre (Cleopatra). Mark-Antoine's distinguished ancestry, past heroism, and destruction by his passion for Cléopâtre and the extravagant and dissipated life into which she has lured him have parallels with the life of Henri III, who had been a popular military hero before his accession but, once on the throne, was the object of vituperative abuse in pamphlet literature. If Garnier's play is meant as criticism of Henri, it is restrained and even sympathetic. Garnier dedicates the play to Pibrac, who is distressed by the "dissentions domestiques et malheureux troubles" (internal strife and wretched troubles) of contemporary France, and asks: "à qui mieux qu'à vous se doivent adresser les représentations tragiques des guerres civiles de Rome?" (who better than you to receive the tragic representation of Rome's civil wars?).

In each of his next two plays, *La Troade* (1579, The Story of Troy) and *Antigone, ou la Pieté* (1580, Antigone, or Piety), Garnier combines the subjects of several classical works; as a result, they are unwieldily long. The most prominent themes in *La Troade* are the aftermath of war and the need for compassion and restraint on the part of conquerors if destruction and suffering are not to continue. In his dedicatory note to Renaud de Beaune, bishop of Mendes (later archbishop of Bourges), Garnier, as usual, draws attention to the topical relevance of such a subject; but he does so in a more optimistic vein than in his earlier dedications, pointing out that the example of such ancient misfortunes should be a consolation at the present time, since the outcome of the fall of Troy was, first, the Roman Empire (because Aeneas was a refugee from Troy), and then, after the collapse of that "orgueilleux empire" (proud empire), the rise of the flourishing French monarchy (it was a frequent French claim, especially by the

*Title page for Garnier's play about the Trojan War (from <http://
lelouptheatre.free.fr/TERMOR/text.html>)*

HÉMON: Plustost l'ondeux Triton sur la terre naistra,
Et le mouton laineux dedans la mer paistra,
Que j'esteinde l'ardeur que j'ay dans la moüelle
Pour aimer saintement vostre beauté trop belle.
Le jour, quand Phébus marche, et la nuit, quand les cieux
Monstrent pour ornement mille astres radieux,
Je vous ay dans mon âme, et tousjours vostre image
Errant devant mes yeux me fait un doux outrage.

ANTIGONE: Et je vous aime aussi. Mais mon affection
Se trouble maintenant par trop d'affliction.
Je n'ai dedans l'esprit que mort et funerailles.

HÉMON: Moi j'ay tousjours l'amour cousu dans mes
entrailles.

(HAEMON: Sooner shall wave-tossed Triton be born on
land
And the woolly sheep graze in the sea
Than shall I extinguish the passion that burns in my mar-
row
From my pure love of your too-lovely loveliness.
By day, when Phoebus moves over the sky, and by night,
when the heavens
Are decked with countless bright stars,
I have you in my soul, and always your image,
Moving before my eyes, causes me sweet pain.

ANTIGONE. And I love you, too. But my affection
Is clouded now by too much sorrow.
I have nothing in my mind but death and funerals.

HAEMON. But I still have love sewn into my belly.)

Such a passage could never appear in the works of the
tragedians of the seventeenth century: it would have
been considered indecorous for a woman–particularly
a young, unmarried woman–to make such a frank declaration of love, and the physicality of Hémon's last line
would have been equally shocking. But the use of love
as a theme in tragedy, introduced by Garnier, became
widespread in the seventeenth century.

Garnier's next play, *Bradamante* (1582), is the first
tragicomedy in French. Based on an episode in Ludovico Ariosto's *Orlando Furioso* (1516), it combines heroic
adventure with scenes of homely and amusing dialogue–particularly that between the parents of the warrior maiden Bradamante, who will marry only a man
who can defeat her in single combat. The characters
include the emperor Charlemagne, whose presence
leads to much discussion of topics Garnier developed in
earlier plays: kingship, law, and the aftermath of war.

Around this time–possibly in late 1583, and probably while visiting Paris–Garnier and his wife escaped
an attempt by their servants to poison them. The servants presumably intended to rob them and hoped that
the deaths would be attributed to the plague, which was
widespread at the time. The plot was discovered when

Pléiade poets and those close to them, that France
rather than Italy was the cultural heir of Rome).

Antigone is 2,740 lines in length; it combines the
subject matter of Seneca the Younger's *Phoenissae* (The
Phoenician Women), section 9 of Statius's epic poem
Thebaid, and Sophocles' *Antigone.* The play touches on
many aspects of kingship and ambition, but its subtitle,
la Piété, directs the reader's attention both to Antigone's
loyalty to her father in the first act and to her obedience
to religious duty rather than to political authority when
she buries her brother Polynice (Polynices). Garnier has
added to his source material some amorous exchanges
between Antigone and her lover, Hémon (Haemon).
One such exchange is typical of Garnier in its wealth of
epithets, rhetorical figures, rich rhyme, and direct
expression of physical passion:

Garnier's wife tasted the poisoned drink and became suspicious.

In 1583 Garnier published his last play, generally considered his best. Named for the chorus, like many plays of classical antiquity (such as Seneca's *Phoenissae*), *Les Juifves* (translated as *The Hebrew Women*, 1978) is based on an episode recounted in 2 Kings 24:18–25:7 and 2 Chron. 36:11–14. A tragedy on a biblical subject by a Catholic author is unusual for the period, but several notable biblical plays had been written by Protestants. Garnier must have read one of these plays, André de Rivaudeau's *Aman* (1566, Haman), for he imitates one of its choric poems. Garnier describes his play as representing "les souspirables calamitez d'un peuple, qui a comme nous abandonné son Dieu" (the lamentable misfortunes of a nation which, like us, abandoned its God). Sédécie (Zedekiah), the last king of Judah, swears an oath of allegiance to Nabuchodonosor (Nebuchadnezzar), the king of Babylon, but then rebels against him. Nabuchodonosor's revenge is brutal. He besieges and destroys Jerusalem and has the Jewish royal family brought to Antioch, where the children are killed in front of their father before Sédécie's eyes are put out. Nabuchodonosor is a cruel, boastful tyrant modeled on Atreus in Seneca's *Thyestes* and Nero in the pseudo-Senecan *Octavia;* Sédécie is a rebellious subject but a model monarch, concerned for his people, whom he has led into disaster, and a prototypical Christian king sustained by his faith in God. Equally impressive is Sédécie's mother Amital (Hamital), a Hecuba-like figure who mourns the destruction of her city and pleads for the lives of her son and grandchildren. Nabuchodonosor is opposed by his gentle and compassionate queen and his lieutenant Nabuzardan (Nebuzaradan), who argues against vindictive cruelty. A Jewish prophet narrates the deaths of the children and the torture of their father and foretells that Nabuchodonosor, having been used by God to punish the backsliding Jews, will in his turn be punished for his pride and inhumanity. The prophet's account includes gruesome descriptions of suffering and free use of pathos. Even more striking, however, are the elegiac choric odes based on Old Testament texts, particularly the psalms of exile. For example, at the end of act 3 Amital, duped by Nabuchodonosor into false optimism, asks the Jewish women to sing a hymn of praise to God. Their ode begins:

> Comme veut-on que maintenant
>   Si desolees
> Nous allions la flute entonnant
>   Dans ces valees?
>
> Que le luth touché de nos dois
>   Et la Cithare

> Facent resonner de leur voix
>   Un ciel barbare?
>
> Que la harpe, de qui le son
>   Tousjours lamente
> Assemble avec nostre chanson
>   Sa voix dolente?
>
> Trop nous donnent d'affliction
>   Nos maux publiques,
> Pour vous reciter de Sion
>   Les saints cantiques.

> (How can we be asked,
>   Desolate as we are,
> To sound the flute now
>   In these valleys?
>
> How can the lute touched by our fingers,
>   And the lyre,
> Make a barbarian sky
>   Echo with their voices?
>
> How can the harp, whose sound
>   Is always mournful,
> Blend its grieving voice
>   With our singing?
>
> Our common ills afflict us
>   Too greatly
> For us to sing you
>   The holy hymns of Zion.)

The meter of this poem—8, 4, 8, 4, rhyming ABAB—gives it a gentle but slightly halting rhythm, appropriate to its theme of regret and reluctance. For modern readers, the psalms of exile deal with long-ago miseries; here Garnier offers the genesis of such a poem. It is as though the audience of *Les Juifves* is being privileged to hear the first rendering of Psalm 137, "By the rivers of Babylon, there we sat down, yea, we wept. . . . How shall we sing the Lord's song in a strange land?" This effect gives an exceptional poignancy to the poem.

Garnier's last published work was a contribution to the *Tombeau* for Ronsard in 1586. Surprisingly, in 1589 he seems to have joined the Catholic League, an extremist movement formed in 1584 when the death of Henri III's younger brother left the Protestant Henri de Navarre as heir presumptive; the Catholic League hoped to remove Henri III from the throne, or at least deprive him of power, and wipe out Protestantism in France. Garnier's political views, as suggested by the plays, do not seem to have been of this kind. In play after play he gives eloquent descriptions of the sufferings of war, particularly civil war. Although in *Porcie* he shows sympathy with republican ideals and criticizes tyrannicide for its unsatisfactory results rather than on principle, in his last two plays, written when the French

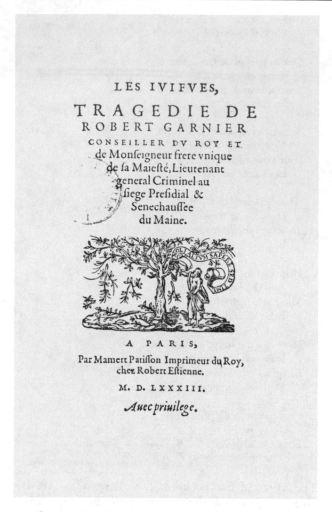

Title page for the facsimile of Garnier's play (translated as The Hebrew Women, *1978) based on the Old Testament story of the conflict between Zedekiah and Nebuchadnezzar (from* Les Juifves [sic] 1583, *1972; Thomas Cooper Library, University of South Carolina)*

never put on at court. They may have been performed in colleges or private homes. There has been much inconclusive debate as to whether the choric poems in humanist tragedies such as Garnier's were intended to be spoken or sung. A musical setting has come to light of a choric passage from *Porcie;* but there is no evidence that it was used in performance, and the text has been slightly altered to make it less specific to its original context. *Antigone* has three choruses—of Theban citizens, of old men, and of Theban girls associated with Antigone—and it is not clear whether any or all of these groups are supposed to remain visible throughout the play or even to speak or sing together when a choric passage is simply labeled "Choeur" (Chorus) rather than being attributed to one of the three groups.

Garnier's plays were admired by his contemporaries, and the great tragedians of the seventeenth century, Pierre Corneille and Jean Racine, clearly read at least some of them. The repertory of the acting troupe in Paul Scarron's *Le Roman comique* (1651–1657; translated as *The Comical Romance; or, A Facetious History of a Company of Stage-Players,* 1665) includes *Bradamante.* The tragedies went through frequent editions until well into the seventeenth century but fell from favor as dramatic and poetic fashions changed. Their language was too heavily ornamented, too obviously rhetorical, and at times too earthy and physical, and the action too limited to suit seventeenth-century tastes, and the use of a chorus made the plays look old-fashioned.

In the twentieth century, in the context of a revival of interest in sixteenth-century French literature and a better understanding of the part played by rhetoric in education and literary creation in early modern France, Garnier's plays came to be seen as more than imperfect models that later dramatists improved on by adding greater plot interest and fuller characterizations. His powers of lyrical and eloquent composition came to be admired for their own sake; his most impressive characters, such as Nabuchodonosor and Amital, were acknowledged to have dramatic power; and his passages of clashing argument between characters were related not only to their models in the tragedies of Seneca but also to controversial political topics of the day concerning kingship and war—particularly civil war. Many sixteenth-century French tragedies were written by young men who tried their hand at playwriting before moving on to other things; in some cases they abandoned literature altogether. Robert Garnier was unusual in continuing to write plays while pursuing his legal career, and he created a substantial body of work that justifies his reputation as the leading French sixteenth-century dramatist.

monarchy was at its weakest after two decades of intermittent civil war, he stresses the sanctity of kingship and shows the audience several good kings. He may have joined the Catholic League under duress, as did many others, or he may have felt that he could no longer support the troubled monarch after Henri III had Henri, third Duke of Guise, a leader of the league, assassinated in 1588. Whatever Garnier's motive for joining the league, he left it within a year.

Garnier's financial situation deteriorated during the last four years of his life, owing to the gap in time between his last two appointments, the cost of purchasing his last appointment, some unpaid debts, and the loss of revenue from his lands during the civil war. His wife died in 1588, and he died on 20 September 1590.

Nothing is known about the staging of Garnier's plays except that, to his disappointment, they were

Biographies:

Henri Chardon, *Robert Garnier: Sa vie, ses poésies inédites, avec son véritable portrait et un fac-simile de sa signature* (Paris: Le Mans, 1905);

Marie-Madeleine Mouflard, *Robert Garnier, 1545–1590,* volume 1: *La Vie* (La Ferté-Bernard: R. Bellanger, 1961).

References:

Françoise Charpentier, *Pour une lecture de la tragédie humaniste: Jodelle, Garnier, Monchrestien* (St.-Etienne: Publications de l'Université de St.-Etienne, 1979);

Maurice Gras, *Robert Garnier: Son art et sa méthode,* Travaux d'Humanisme et Renaissance, volume 72 (Geneva: Droz, 1965);

Richard Griffiths, *Garnier: Les Juifves,* Critical Guides to French Texts, no. 52 (London: Grant & Cutler, 1986);

Griffiths, "The Influence of Formulary Rhetoric upon French Renaissance Tragedy," *Modern Language Review,* 59 (1964): 201–208;

John Holyoake, *A Critical Study of the Tragedies of Robert Garnier,* American University Studies, Series 2: Romance Languages and Literature, no. 57 (New York: Peter Lang, 1987);

Gillian Jondorf, *French Renaissance Tragedy: The Dramatic Word,* Cambridge Studies in French (Cambridge: Cambridge University Press, 1990);

Jondorf, *Robert Garnier and the Themes of Political Tragedy in the Sixteenth Century* (Cambridge: Cambridge University Press, 1969);

Raymond Lebègue, *Les Juives de Robert Garnier,* revised edition (Paris: Centre de Documentation Universitaire et Société d'Edition d'Enseignement Supérieur Réunis, 1979);

Frank Lestringant, "Pour une lecture politique du théâtre de Robert Garnier: Le commentaire d'André Thevet en 1584," in *Parcours et rencontres: Mélanges de langue, d'histoire et de littérature françaises offerts à Enea Balmas,* 2 volumes, edited by Paolo Carile and others (Paris: Klincksieck, 1993), I: 405–422;

Marie-Madeleine Mouflard, *Robert Garnier, 1545–1590,* 3 volumes (volume 1, La Ferté-Bernard: R. Bellanger; volumes 2 and 3, La Roche-sur-Yon: Imprimerie Centrale de l'Ouest, 1961–1964);

Donald Stone Jr., *French Humanist Tragedy: A Reassessment* (Totowa, N.J.: Rowman & Littlefield / Manchester, U.K.: Manchester University Press, 1974), pp. 84–154;

Alexander Maclaren Witherspoon, *The Influence of Robert Garnier on Elizabethan Drama* (New Haven: Yale University Press, 1924).

Marie de Gournay

(6 October 1565 – 13 July 1645)

Marie-Thérèse Noiset
University of North Carolina at Charlotte

BOOKS: *Le Proumenoir de M. de Montaigne, par sa fille d'alliance* (Paris: Abel L'Angelier, 1594); republished as *Le Proumenoir de Monsieur de Montaigne, par sa fille d'alliance* (Paris: Abel L'Angelier, 1595); enlarged as *Le Proumenoir de M. de Montaigne, par sa fille d'alliance. Edition troisiesme, plus correcte et plus ample que les précédentes* (Paris: Abel L'Angelier, 1599); revised as *Alinda. Histoire tragique* (Paris: Toussainct du Bray, 1623);

Bienvenue de Mgr le duc d'Anjou, desdiée à la sérénissime Republique ou Estat de Venise, son parrain designé, par Mademoiselle de G. (Paris: Fleury Bourriquant, 1608);

Adieu de l'Ame du Roy de France et de Navarre, Henry le Grand à la Royne, avec la Defence des Peres Jesuistes, par la damoiselle de G. (Paris: Fleury Bourriquant, 1610);

Version de quelques pièces de Virgile, Tacite et Saluste, avec l'Institution de Monseigneur, frere unique du Roy, par la Damoiselle de Gournay (Paris: Fleury Bourriquant, 1619);

Egalité des hommes et des femmes (Paris, 1622);

Remerciement au Roy, harangue du tres illustre et tres magnanime Prince François, duc de Guise, aux soldats de Mets, le jour de l'assault, à Charles illustrissime Cardinal de Lorraine, son frere (Paris, 1624);

L'Ombre de la Damoiselle de Gournay. Oeuvre composé de meslanges (Paris: Jean Libert, 1626); revised as *Les Advis ou les presens de la Demoiselle de Gournay* (Paris: Toussainct du Bray, 1634; revised again, Paris: Jean du Bray, 1641).

Editions: *Le Proumenoir de M. de Montaigne par sal fille d'alliance (1594), A Facsimile Reproduction with an Introduction by Patricia Cholakian* (New York: Delmar, 1985);

"Preface de Marie de Gournay à l'édition de 1595 des *Essais*," with a preface by François Rigolot, *Montaigne Studies,* 1 (1989): 7–60;

Marie Le Jars de Gournay, Les Advis ou les presens de la Demoiselle de Gournay 1641, 2 volumes, edited by

Marie de Gournay (from <http://homepage.mac.com/gujacqu/dico/gournay.html>)

Jean-Philippe Beaulieu and Hannah Fournier (Atlanta, Ga. & Amsterdam: Rodopi, 1997–2002);

Marie de Gournay. Oeuvres complètes, 2 volumes, edited by Jean-Claude Arnould, Evelyne Berriot, Claude Blum, Anna Lia Franchetti, Marie-Claire Thomine, and Valerie Worth-Stylianou (Paris: Champion, 2002).

Edition in English: *Apology for the Woman Writing and Other Works,* translated by Richard Hillman and Colette Quesnel (Chicago: University of Chicago

Press: 2002)—includes "Apologie pour celle qui escrit," *Le Proumenoir*, "L'Egalité des hommes et des femmes," and "Le Grief des Dames."

OTHER: "Préface sur les Essais de Michel de Montaigne par sa Fille d'Alliance," in Montaigne, *Essais* (Paris: Abel L'Angelier, 1595); translated by Richard Hillman and Colette Quesnel as *Preface to the Essays of Michel de Montaigne by His Adoptive Daughter, Marie Le Jars de Gournay* (Tempe, Ariz.: Center for Medieval and Renaissance Studies, 1998).

Marie de Gournay has always been known for her association with Michel de Montaigne, who affectionately called her his "fille d'alliance" (chosen daughter), but she has only been recognized as a writer in her own right since the 1950s. She was the original editor of Montaigne's *Essais* (1595, Essays) after the philosopher's death. The long preface she composed for the posthumous edition of *Essais* was one of her first published works. Gournay was principally a moralist who severely condemned the frivolity of her times. She wrote many treatises and pamphlets that show her effort to mold and reform society. She also played an active role in political controversies, including the reform of the French language at the end of the sixteenth century and the defense of the Jesuits after the assassination of Henri IV. At a time when women were not expected to speak on serious topics, her strong opinions often cost her dearly. She constantly revised her writings, including a novel titled *Le Proumenoir de M. de Montaigne* (1594, The Promenade of M. de Montaigne), and offered them as her collected works under the title *L'Ombre de la Damoiselle de Gournay* (The Shadow of the Damoiselle de Gournay) in 1626. She revised this collection twice more during her lifetime, in 1634 and 1641, as *Les Advis ou les presens de la Demoiselle de Gournay* (The Advice or Presents of the Demoiselle de Gournay).

Gournay was born in Paris on 6 October 1565. Her father, Guillaume le Jars de Gournay, belonged to the landed gentry. He was lord of Neufvi and Gournay-sur-Aronde and also exercised several public functions in Paris. Her mother, Jeanne de Hacqueville, was a member of an aristocratic family from Picardy. Gournay's father died when she was only eleven years old. Her mother, who was left with six young children (Marie was the oldest), decided to raise her family at the castle of Gournay-sur-Aronde. The scant details that are known concerning Gournay's childhood come from three separate pieces she wrote about herself at different times of her life, the main one being "Apologie pour celle qui escrit" (Apology for She Who Writes).

Gournay was a mature woman when she wrote this piece, but the exact date of its composition is unknown.

Gournay did not receive much formal schooling. Her mother simply wanted to initiate her into the womanly arts in order to have her marry well. Gournay writes that she taught herself Latin by comparing Latin texts to their French translations. When she was about eighteen years old she came upon the first edition of *Essais* (1580). In "Préface sur les Essais de Michel de Montaigne, par sa Fille d'Alliance" (1595; translated as *Preface to the Essays of Michel de Montaigne by His Adoptive Daughter, Marie Le Jars de Gournay*, 1998), she recalls her first encounter with the *Essais* in the following terms: "*Ils me transsissoient d'admiration*" (They made me numb with admiration). From that time on, Gournay's dearest wish was to meet Montaigne in person. Her wish came true in 1588 when her mother took her to Paris with the intention of finding a suitable match for her. Montaigne was in Paris as a representative of the States-General. Gournay was far more interested in meeting the author of the *Essais* than in finding a husband, and Montaigne was obviously impressed by her. He subsequently made several trips from Paris to Gournay-sur-Aronde, where he spent three months. He also gave Gournay the title of "fille d'alliance" that she cherished all her life.

Upon Montaigne's return to Gascony, Gournay on 26 November 1588 sent him her first piece of writing, *Le Proumenoir de M. de Montaigne*, asking him for advice. The letter that accompanied her novel later served as an introduction to *Le Proumenoir*. Montaigne's reaction to Gournay's work remains a mystery. Gournay's correspondence, except for a few letters to Justus Lipsius, has not been found, and Gournay never mentions in her subsequent writing what happened to her novel before Montaigne's death in 1592. At that time, however, *Le Proumenoir* was returned to Gournay by Montaigne's wife, Françoise de Montaigne. Gournay was established in Paris then, and she published her novel in 1594.

Le Proumenoir is a complex text that has been hailed by twentieth-century critics as a forerunner of modern feminism. The novel tells the story of Alinda, the niece of a Persian king. When her uncle is defeated in battle and held prisoner by another king, Alinda is sent to the enemy king in exchange for her uncle. During her journey the innocent Alinda is seduced by Léontin, a handsome young man. Unable to resist him, she forgoes her duty and flees with him to an island. When he betrays her, she kills herself. Gournay took the story line for *Le Proumenoir* from a tale by Claude de Taillemont, but while Taillemont wanted to show women's constancy in love, Gournay's purpose is to warn young girls about the dangers of ignorance. *Le*

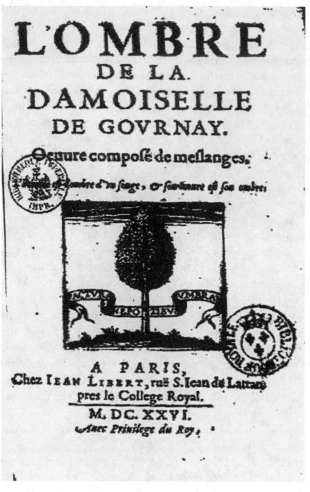

Title page for the first edition of Gournay's collected works, which she twice revised (Bibliothèque nationale de France)

Proumenoir not only makes the case for the education of young women but also encompasses topics that Gournay later developed in her treatises. Among other subjects, the novel discusses in much detail the burdensome responsibilities of a monarch toward his or her subjects. It also explores the damage done to people's reputations by calumny. Often republished during Gournay's lifetime, the novel can be regarded as her entry into the world of moralistic literature.

When Gournay's mother passed away in 1591, civil war was still raging in France, and her fortune had dwindled considerably. As the eldest in the family, Gournay was left with the task of dividing her parents' inheritance between her five siblings and herself. She was twenty-seven years old at the time and inexperienced in financial matters. Her "Apologie pour celle qui escrit" describes at length the financial difficulties that she encountered. She first had to pay the considerable debts of her mother, who had engaged in elaborate new

constructions. She had to settle the matter of a sister's dowry, which had not been completely paid. Several times during the liquidation of family property, Gournay's ignorance of money matters was exploited, and she was swindled by unscrupulous people. Gournay kept little for herself and was left with few resources after ensuring that her younger brothers and sisters were established. When the family affairs were finally in order, she went to live in Paris, determined to add to her meager resources with her pen.

Shortly after Montaigne's death, Madame de Montaigne, backed by her husband's friends from Gascony, wrote to ask Gournay to oversee the publication of a new edition of *Essais*. She sent Gournay a copy of the work with the many *allongeails* (additions) that Montaigne had scribbled in the margins of his 1588 edition. Gournay states in her preface that hers was an arduous task, but that she accomplished it with the utmost care. The long preface for the 1595 edition of *Essais* was only Gournay's second publication.

The preface to *Essais* is an important yet controversial document. Gournay gave her preface an intimate tone that probably displeased the critics, and in her 1599 edition of *Essais* she replaced her long preface with a ten-line introduction. At the same time, she must have believed that her comments on Montaigne's work were valuable, since she revised her original preface, giving it a much more impersonal tone, and appended it to the 1599 edition of *Le Proumenoir*. This revised preface, with minor revisions, graced her subsequent editions of Montaigne's *Essais* in 1617, 1625, and 1635.

In her revised preface Gournay joins in the evolving critical debate over Montaigne's *Essais* after his death. In addition to her own positive personal evaluation of *Essais,* she discusses and refutes the negative criticism the 1595 edition encountered and in so doing opens an interesting window on the reception of Montaigne's work by his contemporaries. From Gournay's preface, one gathers that Montaigne's last revision of his grand work, with its greater emphasis on his own self-portrait, was not received with the same general acclamation that had greeted the pervasive stoicism of his earlier versions of *Essais*. Some critics evidently regarded Montaigne's insistence on the self-portrait as pure vanity; some questioned his religion; and some complained of his Gasconisms. Indeed, these are the points that Gournay addresses at length in her preface as she vigorously defends Montaigne's writing.

It is only in the second half of the twentieth century that critics started paying attention to Gournay's works in their own right, beyond her connection to Montaigne. Her *Proumenoir,* her autobiographical pieces, and two of her treatises, *Egalité des hommes et des femmes* (1622, Equality of Men and Women) and "Grief des dames" (Women's Complaint), attracted the attention of researchers because these works plead for the recognition of women. Gournay focuses her interest on the plight of the intellectual female scorned by her male counterparts. In her long autobiographical piece "Apologie pour celle qui escrit," she describes her personal struggle to assert herself in a world dominated by men. In *Egalité des hommes et des femmes,* she recalls the achievements of famous women of antiquity to give weight to her thesis that women can be the intellectual equals of men. Following the sixteenth-century custom, she makes frequent use of examples to defend her cause.

Gournay's other treatises, which for the most part have not been studied in depth, encompass a vast array of interests: moral, political, and philological. Many of these pieces were only first published as part of her collected works, so it is not always possible to tell in what period of her life they were written. Gournay is a stern moralist. She grew up during the civil wars that ravaged France, witnessed the scandalous reigns of Charles IX and Henri III, and disapproved of the frivolous behavior of the aristocracy during Henri IV's tenure.

Gournay regarded education as the most powerful remedy for the problems of her time. The four treatises that she wrote for the future Louis XIII–"De l'éducation des Enfans de France" (On the Education of the Princes of France), "Naissance de Messeigneurs les Enfans de France" (The Birth of My Lords, the Princes of France), and "Institution du Prince, deux traittez" (Education of the Prince, Two Treatises)–bear comparison with the earlier works of Budé and Erasmus on the education of a crown prince. Finding no contemporary examples, Gournay proposes to educate her prince by offering him the heroes of antiquity as models for his conduct. She asserts that only ancient literature can give the crown prince the integrity and strength of character that he needs to govern.

Most of Gournay's other moral/political treatises, such as "De la neantise de la commune vaillance de ce temps, et du peu de prix de la qualité de Noblesse" (Of the Worthlessness of the Common Bravery of Our Time, and of the Little Value of Being an Aristocrat), denounce the aristocracy for its superficiality, arrogance, cowardice, and lack of judgment and wisdom. They condemn the courtly practices of flattery and hypocrisy. They castigate the damaging gossip and calumny that pervade the aristocracy and plead for a return to the values of the ancient Greek and Roman models of stability, courage, and integrity. Because as a woman Gournay did not enjoy the privileges reserved for male nobility, she was well placed to criticize the king's entourage. She attacked the so-called birthrights of the noble and reproved the degrading treatment of common people by the aristocracy. She condemned some of the most cherished practices of the nobility, such as the duel. She even reproached the king for

letting this custom endure. Gournay also berated the clergy for its special treatment of the aristocratic sinner. In her treatise "Advis à quelques gens d'Eglise" (Advice to Members of the Clergy), she begged the church to put a stop to its hypocrisy and to treat all its members equally as sinners.

Intent on keeping intact the reputation of the great writers of the recent past, Gournay threw herself into the quarrel over language that raged at the beginning of the seventeenth century. She fiercely defended the richness of Montaigne's and Ronsard's language and opposed the dry technicality imposed on poetry by Malherbe and his disciples. She wrote more than ten treatises to expose the harshness of the new rules. In the first of these, "Deffence de la Poësie et du langage des Poëtes" (Defense of Poetry and of the Language of Poets), probably written around 1600, Gournay compares the weak poets of the beginning of the seventeenth century to the great ones of the recent past. She indicts the frivolous contemporary society for being unable to produce anything but "*des poetes grammairiens*" (grammarian poets), devoid of inspiration. In another essay written at the turn of the century, "De la façon d'escrire de Messieurs l'Eminentissime Cardinal du Perron et Bertault, Illustrissime Evesque de Sees, qui sert d'advis sur les Poesies de ce volume" (Of the Writing Style of Their Excellencies, Most Distinguished Cardinal Du Perron and Very Illustrious Bishop of Sees, Bertault, Which Serves as Guide to the Poems of This Volume), Gournay argues that Montaigne and Ronsard were models for Du Perron and Bertault, admired poets who had recently died. Like their models, she maintains, these two revered poets recognized the importance of inspiration, used an abundant and colorful vocabulary, and imitated the classical writers praised by the Pleiade.

Gournay was not alone in her effort to preserve the language of the great works of the recent past. Jean-Pierre Camus, Mathurin Régnier, and many other writers also fought against reforms that seemed too restrictive and were taking place too fast. Gournay, however, seems to have been the most vocal defender of the language of her most cherished authors. Most of her philological treatises are full of humorous remarks on the lexical rejections of Malherbe's school and give the modern reader a taste of the preciosity that had invaded the French language at the beginning of the seventeenth century. Gournay was mocked for her opinionated points of view in a few plays, such as Gilles Ménage's *La Requête des dictionnaires* (1638, The Dictionaries' Request), written several years after the quarrel had subsided. Later, however, Sainte-Beuve recognized the wisdom of her protests in *Tableau historique et critique de la poésie et du théâtre français* (1869, Historical and Critical Survey of French Poetry and Theater).

In spite of her strong defense of the philological canon, Gournay realized that a living language must necessarily evolve with the passing of time. She constantly revised her own work, sometimes, as in the case of her preface to *Essais,* to modify her content, but most of the time to modernize her use of the language. Her often entertaining but powerful jabs at the new way of speaking praised by the court seem to have been more a result of the sudden severity of the reforms demanded by Malherbe and his followers than an uncompromising desire to retain the status quo.

While Gournay was appreciated by many intellectuals, such as Marolles, who was her neighbor, and Baudius, who praised her wisdom, the misogynistic current of the era worked against her, and she complained of being made light of because she was a woman. Her strong opinions apparently often aroused the anger of her contemporaries and at the same time made her an easy target for mockery. She herself tells of a hoax that occurred in 1616. She was asked for her biography by a man posing as an English canon representing the king of England. Flattered by the request, she hastened to write her "Vie de la demoiselle de Gournay" (The Life of the Demoiselle de Gournay) which is included in *Les Advis ou les presens de la Demoiselle de Gournay.* A little later, a falsified and insulting biography was disseminated throughout Paris by a group of aristocratic jokers. Anecdotes about Gournay's irascibility, her uncompromising opinions, and her lack of feminine charm are repeated in several dictionaries of biographies of the seventeenth and eighteenth centuries.

The only works of Gournay that did not find a place in *Les Advis ou les presens de la Demoiselle de Gournay* were her preface to *Essais* and a long political treatise titled "La Deffence des Peres Jesuistes" (The Defense of the Jesuit Fathers), which was published in *Adieu de l'Ame du Roy de France et de Navarre, Henry le Grand à la Royne* (1610, Farewell of the Soul of Henry the Great, King of France and Navarre, to the Queen). Alone among Gournay's works, "La Deffence des Peres Jesuistes" was never reworked or republished, perhaps because it caused her too much trouble. In this treatise, addressed to Marie de Médicis and written soon after the assassination of Henri IV in 1610, Gournay takes on the popular suspicion that the Jesuits played a role in the king's murder. She carefully examines the arguments for and against the involvement of the Catholic order and concludes that the Jesuits were innocent. Gournay's reasoned defense, with which modern historians concur, was an act of courage, but it was vilified in the most vulgar manner by an anonymous pamphlet full of the basest insults, *Remerciements des Beurrieres de Paris au sieur de Courbazon ou l'Anti Gournay* (1610, The Many Thanks of the Parisian Butter Makers to the Lord of Courbazon or the Pamphlet Against Gournay).

In 1634 Gournay allowed the title of her collected works to be changed from *L'Ombre de la Damoiselle de Gournay* to *Les Advis ou les presens de la Demoiselle de Gournay* at the request of an editor who found the original title obscure. Gournay preferred her first, far more poetic title; but she complied, giving in, she explained, to the shallowness of her epoch, which could only fathom the literal. The last edition of her collected works, published in 1641 when she was seventy-six, included translations of passages from *The Aeneid,* a collection of poems addressed to famous people, and several pieces written to honor the powerful and win their favor.

Gournay strove all her life, just like her male counterparts, to supplement her meager resources by her writing. She managed to obtain a small pension from Henri IV, and later Cardinal de Richelieu, charmed by her wit, also granted her a pension. When she died on 13 July 1645, she was far from rich, but she had earned the success she had achieved and the respect of many. Because of her preface to *Essais* and her writings on the treatment of the learned woman in society, Marie de Gournay remains one of the most intriguing figures of her era.

References:

Jean-Claude Arnould, ed., *Marie de Gournay et l'Edition de 1595 des* Essais *de Montaigne* (Paris: Champion, 1996);

Patricia Francis Cholakian, *Le Proumenoir de Monsieur de Montaigne (1594)* (New York: Delmar, 1985);

Elyane Dezon-Jones, *Marie de Gournay. Fragments d'un discours féminin* (Paris: José Corti, 1988);

Marjorie Henry Ilsley, *A Daughter of the Renaissance. Marie le Jars de Gournay. Her Life and Works* (The Hague: Mouton, 1963);

Marie-Thérèse Noiset, *Marie de Gournay et son oeuvre* (Namur: Presses Universitaires de Namur, Editions Namuroises, 2004);

Mario Schiff, *La fille d'alliance de Montaigne. Marie de Gournay* (Geneva: Slatkine Reprints, 1978);

Anne Uildriks, *Les Idées littéraires de Mlle de Gournay. Réédition de ses traités philologiques des* Advis *et* Presens. *Avec les variantes de 1626 et 1634; et réédition de sa Préface des* Essais *de Montaigne, édition de 1635 avec les variantes de 1595 et 1599* (Groningen: Der Kleine, 1972).

Antoine Héroët

(1490? – 1567?)

Danielle Trudeau
San José State University

BOOK: *La Parfaicte Amye Nouvellement composée par Antoine Heroet, dict la Maison neufve, Avec plusieurs aultres compositions dudict Autheur* (Lyon: Estienne Dolet, 1542).

Editions: *Opuscules d'amour par Heroet, La Borderie, et autres divins poëtes* (Lyon: Jean de Tournes, 1547);

Opuscules d'amour par Heroet, La Borderie, et autres divins poëtes, edited by M. A. Screech (New York: Johnson Reprints / The Hague: Mouton, 1970);

Œuvres poétiques, edited, with a biographical note, by Ferdinand Gohin (Paris: Droz, 1909);

"Complaincte d'une dame surprise nouvellement d'amour," edited by Valéry Larbaud, *Commerce,* 9 (1926): 171–194;

Blason de l'œil, in *Poètes du XVIe siècle,* edited by Albert-Marie Schmidt (Paris: Bibliothèque de la Pléiade, 1953), pp. 311–312;

La Parfaicte Amye, with introduction and notes by Christine Marie Hill (Exeter, U.K.: Exeter University Press, 1981);

Complaincte d'une dame surprise nouvellement d'amour in *Mille et cent ans de poésie française,* edited by Bernard Delvaille (Paris: R. Laffont, 1991), pp. 437–443.

OTHER: Epitaphs of Louise de Savoie, in *In Lodovicae Regis matris mortem, Epitaphia Latina et Gallica. Epitaphes a la louenge de ma Dame Mere du Roy faictz par plusieurs recommendables Autheurs* (Paris: Printed and sold by Geoffroy Tory, 1531);

"Blason de l'œil," in *Hecatomphile* (Paris: Sold by Pierre Sergent, 1539);

Fray Antonio de Guevara, *Le Mespris de la court avec la vie rusticque. Nouvellement traduict Despagnol en françoys. Lamye de court La Parfaicte Amye La Contreamye L'androzyne de Platon Lexperience de lamye de court, contre la contreamye,* translated by Héroët (Paris: Printed by Galiot du Pré, 1544);

Plato, *Le Sympose de Platon, ou de l'Amour et de Beauté, traduit de Grec en Françoys, avec trois livres de Commentaires, extraictz de toute Philosophie,* translated by

Héroët (Paris: Printed by Jean Longis & Robert Le Mangnyer, 1558).

The poet Antoine Héroët, known by his contemporaries as "La Maison Neuve," is often associated with the *Ecole lyonnaise,* or the School of Lyon, although he was born in Paris during the last decade of the fifteenth century into an ancient and illustrious family that served in the royal administration. Throughout his life Héroët enjoyed the protection of affluent individuals, such as Louise de Savoie, King François I, Marguerite de Navarre, Connetable Anne de Montmorency, King Henri II, and Chancellor François Olivier. Often mentioned as one of the best writers of the reign of François I, he is commended for translating Plato into French. He may have provided the model of Dagoucin, one of the storytellers in Marguerite de Navarre's *Heptaméron* (1559). His most famous works are *La Parfaicte Amye* (The Perfect Lady Friend), *L'Androgyne de Platon* (The Androgyne by Plato), and *Aultre invention extraicte de Platon* (Second Invention Taken from Plato)—all of which were first published as *La Parfaicte Amye Nouvellement composee par Antoine Heroet, dict la Maison neufve, Avec plusieurs aultres compositions dudict Autheur* (The Perfect Lady Friend Recently Invented by Antoine Héroët, Known as la Maison Neufve, along with Several Other Poems by This Author) in 1542. Joachim du Bellay and Pierre de Ronsard saluted him as a precursor, one who was concerned with the "illustration," or consciously showing the power and grace, of the French language through poetry. His reputation as a *poète philosophe* (philosophic poet) and learned writer survived until the beginning of the seventeenth century.

Both sides of Héroët's family belonged to the rising Parisian *noblesse de robe* (nobility of the robe), the circle of high-ranking administrators, notaries, secretaries, and treasurers that contributed so much to spread humanism at the king's court and in the French upper class. Louis XI had ennobled Antoine's mother's grandfather for his service in the king's administration. Antoine's father, Jean Héroët—or "Herouet" as the

Title page for Antoine Héroët's only book, which features the title poem that celebrates the ideal woman (from Œuvres poétiques, edited by Ferdinand Gohin, 1943; Thomas Cooper Library, University of South Carolina)

name was then spelled—may have come from Normandy. He was one of Louis XII's treasurers and accompanied him in Italy. Despite suspicions of complicity in an embezzlement case, Jean Héroët was still in the administration after his return to France and does not seem to have suffered much from this accusation. In addition to a house he owned in Paris, Jean Héroët held the fief of Carrières west of Paris between Saint-Germain-en-Laye and the river Seine. This fief included the rear-fief of La Maison Neuve, which Antoine Héroët later shared with his younger brother, and whose name he added to his surname, to be known as "Antoine Héroët, dict (called) La Maison neufve." After his father's death in 1511 his mother married Jean Bal-

lue, nephew of Cardinal de La Balue. Jean Ballue became *maistre d'hostel* (major domo) of Marguerite de Navarre and *écuyer tranchant* (esquire trenchant) of the dauphin. This alliance brought the family close to the future François I and even closer to François's mother and sister.

Although the exact date of Héroët's birth cannot be found in the archives, his friendship with Jean Salmon Macrin, who was born in 1490, suggests that he was born near the beginning of the 1490s. Jean Salmon's father, of modest origins, sent his son to Paris to be educated by the best professors of the time. Apparently, the Héroët family played a part in Macrin's integration into the Parisian milieu. Most probably through the Héroëts—Georges, the elder, as well as Antoine—Macrin met Antoine Bohier, who later hired him as his secretary. Antoine Héroët and Macrin both received the same humanist education, which stressed Latin and included the study of Greek. They may have both studied with Jérôme Aléandre and may have met Lefèvre d'Etaples as early as the 1510s.

In 1515 Héroët, who would have been about twenty-five that year, wrote a prefatory poem for Macrin's third volume of religious *Elegies*. In the title of this piece, "Antonii Heroici Malingrii hexasticon" (Six-Line Poem by Antoine Héroët Malingre), one can recognize the surnames of Héroët's father and mother (Malingre). By translating his patronym into *Heroici*, the poet defined himself as *héroïque*, that is writing in the higher style, whereas *Malingrii—malingre* (skinny, famished)—carries the same connotations as "Macrin," the name François I used for Jean Salmon because he was very thin. In other words, Héroët was introducing himself as the "famished heroic poet." The witty play on words made him a twin brother of Macrin, the other notorious "famished" poet, while the other adjective indicated his poetic orientation toward higher subjects.

If Héroët could present himself as a "heroic" poet in a Latin piece as early as 1515, he was perhaps already writing in this language and following the example of the thriving neo-Latin poets of the day. However, except for this short poem, no other work by him in Latin has survived. Moreover, his name is so attached to French poetry that only recently have modern critics turned their attention to this piece and proved with certainty that he was the author. Indeed, during the sixteenth century Héroët was praised by his fellow French poets for his contribution to the "illustration" of the French language, never for his Latin poetry. His choice of French over Latin seems to be tied to his appointment, in the 1520s, to the court of Marguerite de Navarre and her mother, Louise de Savoie, where he joined his stepfather and his relatives the Robertets and the Oliviers.

At that time the promotion of the French language—though not the formal doctrine it later became—was common and had already stimulated an abundant literary and scientific production. At Marguerite's court Héroët was in regular contact with poets, humanists, and religious thinkers. Here he discovered Neoplatonism, perfected his knowledge of Greek, and prepared himself to "illustrate" Plato in French. Although some critics have questioned Héroët's knowledge of Greek, claiming that he did not actually translate from the original but adapted passages of Ficino's *Symposium* in the poems *L'Androgyne de Platon* and *Aultre invention extraicte de Platon,* the Hellenists who knew him during his lifetime, and those who came after him—such as Louis Le Roy, who saluted him as the "first interpreter" of Plato in French—all suggest he was as well versed in Greek, and probably also in Italian, as in Latin. How well he could read and write Greek may never be known, but his ability in this regard has little significance compared to his choice of French over Latin early in his career. This decision is what led to his fame.

In 1524 Héroët appears in Marguerite de Navarre's account book with a pension of 200 livres, a comfortable annuity at the time. Five years later the book lists him as *Pensionnaire extraordinaire* (pensioner extraordinary) of Marguerite and Louise de Savoie. In 1538, when he was made prior of the Abbey of Cercanceaux, he was designated as *Maistre des requestes ordinaires* (Master of ordinary requests) of the queen of Navarre. This legal title, perhaps more than merely nominal, suggests that Héroët had studied law. A few facts support this hypothesis. In 1527 an Antoine Héroët is mentioned as an auditor (judge hearing small-claims cases) at the Châtelet (Paris main police station). If this auditor was in fact the poet, then he may well have earned the credentials to hold a legal position at the queen of Navarre's court. In 1532, when Héroët rented a house in the quartier des Blancs-Manteaux in Paris, the lease was registered to "noble homme maistre Anthoine Herouet," which again suggests that he may have had the status of a legal professional. During his ecclesiastical career Héroët took part in many negotiations, mostly as an administrator to legal disputes and contract signing. He is also mentioned as *Maistre des requestes* of King Henri II. The law, however, does not seem to have occupied him much during the 1530s, since then there are only few traces of his involvement with the law in the record. Thus, it is legitimate to think that the queen of Navarre's generosity was directed to the intellectual and poet rather than the lawyer. Indeed, as a courtier with many connections with brillant intellectuals, Héroët helped make Marguerite's court the most progressive of the time.

The 1530s was the most productive of Héroët's literary career, although most of his work was not yet in print. Only two epitaphs for Louise de Savoie were included in a collection published by Geoffroy Tory in 1531. These are the first of his poems in French that can be dated with certainty. The longer poem, 132 lines, unfolds as a touching prosopopoeia of Louise's soul speaking from beyond and telling the passerby about her transitory passage in a human body. After explaining that death finally brought her the freedom she had longed for, she sends the passerby off with a message for her daughter Marguerite, her son François, and all those who grieved for her, that they should be rejoicing since God has called her back to him.

This epitaph is an early illustration of Héroët's application of Neoplatonism and Christianity to human feelings, which also characterize Marguerite's poetry. In fact, the same year Marguerite published a book deeply inspired by Neoplatonism and evangelism, her *Miroir de l'âme pécheresse* (1530, The Mirror of the Sinful Soul), which the Sorbonne censored in 1533. The condemnation had a devastating effect on Héroët's protector. From then on, Marguerite practiced self-censorship in order to keep some intellectual and political influence on the king, which she much needed for her protegés. In 1534, after the *Affaire des Placards* when anti-Catholic placards were posted everywhere in Paris, even on the king's bedroom door, the crackdown on the "heretics" made it dangerous to be identified as a member of her progressive entourage. This context may explain why most of Héroët's works were not printed and did not circulate except within the small circle of his friends: Héroët, who drew most of his inspiration from Neoplatonism, may have feared raising the suspicions of the religious authorities.

His reluctance to publish is implied in *Panegyric des Damoyselles de Paris* (Panegyric of the Maids of Paris), a text composed in 1535 in which the anonymous author presses Héroët to resume his literary activities. A year later, probably during the short stay François I made in Paris between the end of December 1536 and the end of January 1537, Héroët presented *L'Androgyne de Platon,* the work that sealed his reputation as a learned man, to François I in manuscript rather than in print. In the beginning of his dedicatory epistle to the king, Héroët admitted that he had kept his poems "longuement en silence" (silent for a long time) because he did not deem them worthy enough for the king. He then wrote he was showing them privately to the king in obedience to his wishes since he had expressed interest in them. The excuse of perfectionism may be read as a discrete voicing of concern, as Héroët probably wondered if he could count on the king's support if his works were attacked by the censors. He likely had less cause for concern at the time, however, since the king in 1536 had just ended Clément Marot's exile and was allowing his sister to intervene in favor of writers who were victims of censorship.

After the preamble, Héroët's epistle turns into a panegyric on François I's commitment to the arts and letters: the time is gone, says Héroët, when the court was mostly composed of ignorant individuals who took pride in their lack of knowledge. Rather than a remote period of history, though, Héroët may well be alluding to the state of pervasive censorship that Marot the same year described as "ce mauvais vent qui court" (this bad wind that blows) poets away from the court. Héroët's epistle can be read as a plea to François I to continue supporting artists and writers and not to give in to the censors lest the barbarians come back and destroy his achievements. In dedicating *L'Androgyne de Platon* to François I, Héroët was not only displaying his talent but also cleverly positioning himself among the group of intellectuals commissioned by the king to enlighten the court and the nation.

Perhaps Héroët had reason to fear *L'Androgyne de Platon* might be found unorthodox. First, the title and contents referred to Plato, which indicated that the author knew Greek, a language linked at that time to freethinking and heresy. Second, the poem began with a retelling of the creation of the human species that blended ideas from Plato's *Symposium* with Christian perspectives, a combination not likely to please some sensitive theologians. Héroët warded off both dangers by presenting his work as translated from the Latin, which implied that he was following Ficino—a Christian author—rather than Plato. Also, the main purpose of the poem was not to contend any religious dogma but to spiritualize human love. *L'Androgyne de Platon* was indeed an elegant fable that introduced the idea of "perfect friendship" that Héroët later elaborated in his *Parfaicte Amye*. The success of *L'Androgyne de Platon* motivated the poet to write a second fable based on the myth of Anteros. This piece, *Aultre Invention extraicte de Platon,* amplifies the theme of platonic, disembodied love. Both poems are in harmony with Baldassare Castiglione's *Il libro del cortegiano* (1528, The Book of the Courtier) in their focus on love as the highest expression of human life. The first analyzes love as an attraction between two exceptional individuals who used to be united in one soul. The second praises chastity as the means to transform and refine *eros* into his brother *anteros,* an elitist form of love that increases rather than decreases as does physical love. The poems must have circulated, if not outside the court then at least within it, because from then on his colleagues saluted Héroët. Etienne Dolet called him "the fine interpreter of Plato's high meaning."

Héroët was indeed present on the literary scene during the last years of the decade even though his works had still not been published separately. In 1535 or 1536 he entered in the *Blasons* contest initiated by Marot. His "Blason de l'œil" (Blason of the Eye) was praised by Marot as written "in learned fashion," but the poem was not included in the first edition of the blasons collection and would not be published until the 1539 edition of *Hécatomphile.* Considered by some critics to be his weakest poem, "Blason de l'œil" is an attempt to bring together the traditions—classical, alexandrine, allegorical, and Neoplatonic—in which the "eye" is a central concept since, as explained by Ficino in his commentary on the *Banquet* by Plato, love results from a glance that, like an arrow or a ray, penetrates the lover's eyes and reaches his heart. Between 1535 and 1540 Héroët's name is linked to Mellin de Saint-Gelais and Clément Marot. For example, in the *Panegyric des Damoyselles* he was praised as the French "Horatius" while Marot and Saint-Gelais were respectively saluted as the French "Ovid " and "Virgil," meaning they were the best poets of the country. During the same period Marot mentioned Héroët in three poems, once referring to him with the nickname "Thony," which indicates that they were friends rather than acquaintances; elsewhere, he links Héroët to Jean de Selve and Saint-Gelais.

Between 1535 and 1538, when religious conservatives and progressives were already clashing at the king's court, Héroët's discretion ensured his survival; furthermore, he accumulated enough support eventually to advance his ecclesiastic career. He was appointed *recteur* (lay or ordained rector) of three parishes between 1533 and 1538. Then he became prior commendatory of the abbey of Cercanceaux in 1538. Critics assume he was ordained between 1533, the date of his first appointment to an office that did not require ordination, and 1538, when he was made abbot of Cercanceaux, a position that required full ordination and membership in the Cistercians, the order of the abbey. In 1538, in addition to the abbey of Cercanceaux, Héroët was receiving benefits from at least three other places: two from Saint-Germain de Villepreux and Sainte-Geneviève de Lindry, of which he was priest, and one from Nesles-la-Gilberte, where he was named prior commendatory.

Because Héroët was attached to the court of Marguerite de Navarre, where he often had contact with prominent reformers, some historians have suggested he was for a time attracted to the Reform or the Evangelist movement. Yet, his pursuit of ecclesiastical benefits shows that he had chosen the Roman Church as early as 1533. After that date he did not change course. In fact, without taking a position either for or against the new religion, Héroët built around himself a complex network of alliances that served him the rest of his life. He made friends with Marguerite's protegés, including Marot and D'Etaples; far from alienating the most important figures among the counterreformers, he sought and earned their favor. For instance, at the end of the 1530s he grew closer to Claude Chappuys and Saint-Gelais, two poets who, like him, had friendly ties with both parties and were more interested in advancing their careers than in promoting the new religion. Together the three poets composed "L'Amour de Cupido et Psyché" (Love of Cupid and Psyche), a thirty-stanza poem that explicated a tapestry based on the same story. The tapestry is lost, but the poem is extant in a manuscript offered in 1540 to Anne de Montmorency, Connetable (constable) of France, who took such a fancy to the story that he had it reproduced along with the poem on stained-glass windows at his castle at Ecouen (the windows were eventually moved to the Chantilly castle).

Héroët's participation in writing "L'Amour de Cupido et Psyché" and his name no longer appearing in Marguerite's account book could be indications that the poet had switched loyalty from the queen of Navarre to Montmorency. The connetable, who was then at the height of his power, had greater influence on the king and the dauphin and on the country in general than did Marguerite. But the truth could be that Marguerite had decided to sever herself from Héroët as she was slowly distancing herself from politics and spending more time in Béarn. Was Héroët courting Montmorency as a result of being cast aside by Marguerite? Did he seek the connetable's favor in order to distance himself from her? Or was he simply hoarding benevolence the same way he was then accumulating clerical benefits? These questions will probably always remain open. Certainly, when Héroët started living exclusively off his ecclesiastical appointments in 1538, the favor of the connetable had to be a precious asset to him and explains his participation in the "L'Amour de Cupido et Psyché" project. Even though Montmorency eventually lost his position and was forced into exile from the court, Héroët's connection to him eventually paid off. When Montmorency came back after François I's death to have a second career under Henri II, Héroët also received the king's favor.

After 1538 Héroët resided mainly in Paris or at the abbey of Cercanceaux, which he seems to have preferred over all the other places to which he was appointed. He had by then written the major part of his poetry but his most accomplished poem, *La Parfaicte Amye,* was still to come. Perhaps it was at Cercanceaux that he composed it between 1540 and 1542.

Title page for an anthology of love poems that features Héroët's work (Douglas H. Gordon Collection, University of Virginia Library)

Héroët's manuscripts include several other pieces he wrote before 1540, among them: *Complaincte d'une dame surprise nouvellement d'amour* (Lament of a Lady Newly Surprised by Love), "Douleur et volupté" (Sadness and Voluptuousness), "Description d'une femme de bien" (Description of a Woman of Wealth), and a few songs that were also published in collections around the same time. Composed during his years in the service of Marguerite de Navarre, these poems reflect the queen's concerns of the time—life after death, the nature of human love, control of the passions. They also have a distinct moral and exemplary objective. Héroët probably invented the stories in verse for Marguerite, or for her daughter or her niece, whose educations she carefully supervised.

The Parisian Héroët is often associated with the *School of Lyon* in large part because of the many points he has in common with Maurice Scève and Pernette du Guillet, the most important being that both Scève's *Délie* (1544) and Du Guillet's *Rymes* (1545) promoted an ideal love that resembled the exemplary friendship of the *Parfaicte Amye* and her lover. Both Lyonnais poets, like Héroët, introduced philosophy in love poetry. That Héroët met either or both poets is possible, perhaps through fellow poet Charles Fontaine, editor Antoine du Moulin, or through the Lyonnais publishers Etienne Dolet and Jean de Tournes. Even though it is not known for certain when Héroët visited Lyon, it seems reasonable to conclude that he must have accompanied either the king or Marguerite there on one or more of their occasional lengthy stays in that city.

Héroët's ties to Lyon certainly go through Dolet, who in 1542 published *La Parfaicte Amye,* including with the new work the two poems for which the poet was already famous in court circles, *L'Androgyne de Platon* and *Aultre invention extraicte de Platon,* as well as *Complaincte d'une dame surprise nouvellement d'amour,* a monologue centered on the discovery of love. A big success, *La Parfaicte Amye* was republished in several editions in Lyon and other cities during the decade. De Tournes featured the whole book in first position of *Opuscules d'amour,* an anthology of love poems published in 1547.

The protagonist of *La Parfaicte Amye* is an ideal woman—wise, literate, and able to discuss philosophy. Although she is unhappily married, she has found her "other half" in the person of her lover, and together they enjoy the pleasures of a perfect, chaste friendship: a gift for a few selected souls. She remains loyal to her husband by not giving herself physically to her lover, but she will not renounce the rare chance she is given of enjoying real love. All this is narrated in the first person, as if the character were addressing an audience. The immediate success of the book, however, does not rest only on the invention of this ideal character. It derives from a clever marketing coup by Dolet who, a few weeks apart, published Héroët's poem and Bertrand de La Borderie's *L'Amie de court* (The Court's Lady Friend). Dolet stated his intention of pairing them in the preface he wrote for each book. *L'Amie de court* had stirred up a controversy because the main female character advocated the cynical manipulation of male desire for narcissistic and monetary profit. Héroët's poem offered a wholly opposite treatment of the question of love, as well as an idealized depiction of women, one that refuted the blunt statements of La Borderie's character. In contrast with the frivolous and immoral *Amie de court,* in which the lady only sought material satisfactions, *La Parfaicte Amye* represented a woman who carried on an intellectual and affectionate relationship with a man who respected her and discussed the highest subjects with her. Héroët's poem appeared to respond to La Bor-

derie's defense of coquetry by proposing a disembodied and idealistic way of life. In fact, it was probably not so much intended to be a response to La Borderie as to promote humanistic values and a vision of the world for women who, without them, would be easy prey for adulterous lovers. While Héroët justified love outside the bonds of marriage, he maintained that such a love had to remain spiritual, in the tradition of courtly love.

La Parfaicte Amye emphasized a kind of love that required restraint and austerity, while *L'Amie de court* advocated hedonism and sensuality: both, however, despised marriage. Someone had to take the stage to defend marriage. In 1543 Charles Fontaine published *La Contre-Amye* in which he represented a pragmatic and socially conscious woman who believed in the sanctity of marriage. Several other poems followed, also centered on the issue of love and marriage. This body of texts formed "La Querelle des Amyes" (The Quarrel of the Lady Friends), the main literary episode of the 1540s. The texts were often published together throughout the decade, composing a modern "Judgment of Paris." In this context the heroine of *La Parfaicte Amye* stood out as the modern Pallas-Athena.

Héroët's poem occupies the first or second place in the anthologies of love poems published during the 1540s. One of these collections, last reprinted in 1568, includes the poems of the "Querelle des Amyes" together with a translation of Fray Antonio de Guevara's *Le Mespris de la Court* (The Contempt of the Court). One may wonder what the connection may be between an essay that praises retirement over active life and the "Querelle des Amyes." The link may be that a few years before the publication of *La Parfaicte Amye* in 1542 Héroët had stopped writing, left the court, and was devoting himself to his ecclesiastical duties. La Borderie and perhaps some other authors of the "Querelle des Amyes" also disappeared from the literary scene after 1542. Indeed, many of the intellectuals who flocked around François I during the 1530s had fled for fear of religious persecution. Marot died in 1544 and Dolet was executed in 1546. Montmorency had withdrawn in disgrace to his castle at Ecouen, where he occasionally enjoyed the company of the small group of intellectuals still loyal to him; Héroët may have been among those, along with Claude Chappuys and Saint-Gelais.

The Dolet publication of Héroët's works probably signified the conclusion of a period of his life rather than a beginning, since he did not write anything significant after that. He certainly enjoyed seeing his book become so successful at convincing other writers to pursue a Neoplatonic perspective on love. Indeed, *La Parfaicte Amye* may have helped inspire Du Guillet's and Scève's concepts of love, as well as the character of the Wise

Woman in Marguerite de Navarre's *Comédie des quatre femmes* (Comedy for Four Women). Héroët's life after 1542 exemplifies the ideal of the courtier and writer become a clergyman, as he was freed from the urge to pursue worldly success. He had gained notoriety in the circle that meant the most to him at a certain time, but he did not aspire to a higher position as a court poet. Still, he did not completely abandon the court. Under Henri II he was granted the titles of *conseiller et aulmônier du roi* (adviser and confessor of the king), titles that were far from being exclusive but that do indicate that he still enjoyed connections in court, mainly Montmorency and Chancellor Olivier.

Héroët's ecclesiastic career culminated with Henri II's appointment of him as bishop of Digne in 1551 and the Pope's confirmation of him in this position in 1553. Meanwhile, in 1552 Héroët was appointed prior at Longjumeau, a position held before by Théodore de Bèze, who had sold it to a Protestant lord in 1548. Héroët may well have been charged to help recover this ecclesiastical fief for the Catholic Church—a circumstance that would explain the favor he enjoyed with Henri II, who needed men who could negotiate with the Protestants. Once confirmed as bishop of Digne, Héroët resigned from his other appointments, keeping only his position at the abbey of Cercanceaux. No evidence exists to show that he ever resided in Digne, and there are several indications that he administered his diocese from Paris. As with his birth, there is no direct record of Héroët's death. However, since a new bishop was invested at Digne in the early months of 1568, Héroët probably died during the last quarter of 1567.

Antoine Héroët's major works were kept alive thanks to the many reprintings of Guevara's *Le Mespris de la court,* three of which came out in 1568, a few months after his death. Hellenist scholars still celebrated him as the first "translator of Plato," but Héroët's aesthetics were soon superseded by Petrarchism and the Pleiad doctrine. A learned poet and promoter of the French language in his own time, Héroët should also be remembered as one of the few men of his era who devoted most of his literary talent to defining a form of humanism that recognized the intelligence and worth of women.

References:

Guillaume Colletet, "Ms. Bibl. Nat., n. acq. fr. 3073, f. 241 r°," in Antoine Héroët, *Œuvres poetiques,* edited by Ferdinand Gohin (Paris: Droz, 1943), pp. 147–155;

André Gendre and Loris Petris, eds., *Par Elévation d'esprit: Antoine Héroët, le poète, le prélat et son temps. Actes du colloque de Cercanceaux (26–27 septembre 2003)* (Paris: Champion, 2006);

Claude-Pierre Goujet, *Bibliothèque françoise,* volume 11 (Geneva: Slatkine Reprints, 1966), pp. 141–148;

Lucien Grou, "La Famille d'Antoine Heroet," *Revue d'Histoire littéraire de la France* (1899): 277–282.

Estienne Jodelle
(1532? – 1573)

Julia A. Nephew
Elmhurst College

BOOKS: *Le Receuil des Inscriptions, Figures, devises, et masquerades, ordonnees en l'hostel de ville à Paris, le Jeudi 17 Fevrier 1558. Autres Inscriptions en vers Heroïques Latins pour les images des Princes de la Chrestienté* (Paris: Wechel, 1558);

Les Œuvres et Meslanges Poëtiques d'Estienne Jodelle, Sieur du Lymodin, premier volume, with a preface by Charles de la Mothe (Paris: Nicolas Chesneau & Mamert Patisson, 1574); revised and enlarged as *Les Œuvres et Meslanges Poëtiques d'Estienne Jodelle, Sieur du Lymodin. Reveues et augmentees en ceste derniere edition* (Paris: Robert Le Fizelier, 1583)–includes *L'Eugene,* translated by Arthur Phillips Stabler (Pullman: Washington State University Press, 1978).

Collections and Editions: *Les Œuvres et Meslanges Poëtiques d'Estienne Jodelle, Sieur du Lymodin. Avec une Notice biographique et des Notes par Charles Marty-Laveaux* (Paris: A. Lemerre, 1868–1870);

L'Eugène, edited by Enea Balmas (Milan: Cisalpino, 1955);

Les œuvres et meslanges poétiques d'Estienne Jodelle, sieur du Lymodin, avec une notice biographique et des notes par Charles Marty-Laveaux (Genève: Slatkine Reprints, 1965?);

Etienne Jodelle: Œuvres complètes, 2 volumes, edited, with an introduction and chronology, by Enea Balmas (Paris: Gallimard, 1965, 1968);

Le recueil des inscriptions, 1558; a literary and iconographic exegesis, edited by Victor E. Graham and W. McAllister Johnson (Toronto: University of Toronto Press, 1972);

Cléopâtre captive, edited, with an introduction, by Kathleen M. Hall (Exeter: Exeter University Printing, 1979);

L'Eugène, critical edition by Michael Freeman (Exeter: University of Exeter, 1987);

Cléopâtre Captive, edited, with introduction and notes, by Françoise Charpentier, Jean-Dominique Beaudin, and José Sanchez (Mugron, France: Editions José Feijóo, 1990).

Estienne Jodelle (portrait by Leonard Gaultier; from frontispiece, Jodelle, Les amours et autres poesies *[Paris: E. Sansot, 1907]; Thomas Cooper Library, University of South Carolina)*

PLAY PRODUCTIONS: *Eugène,* Paris, Collège de Boncourt, September 1552?;

Cléopâtre captive, Paris: Hôtel de Reims, February or March 1553; Paris, Collège de Boncourt, February or March 1553; Paris: Hôtel de Clermont, 1972.

OTHER: "Epitaphe de Clément Marot," in Clément Marot, *Œuvres* (Paris: Jean de Tournes, 1546);

"A Madame Marguerite de France" and "Au Roy Henry en ses mascarades," in *Le Parnasse des Poètes Francois Modernes, contenant leurs plus riches et graves sentences, discours, descriptions et doctes enseignements, Recueillis par feu Gilles Corrozet, Parisien* (Paris: Galiot Corrozet, 1571), f.11 v° and f. 67 v°;

"Sans estres esclave," "Amour n'est point," "Les vers des amans," "J'ay sans nulle occasion," and "Je suis parmi le trouble," in *Le recuil [sic] de chansons d'amours, composees par Daniel Drouin Lodunoys, joinct à icelles plusieurs autres chansons de divers poötes François,* put to music by Daniel Drouin Lodunoys (Paris: N. Bonfons, 1575);

"Ha! Je le disois bien qu'elle a la cuisse molle," in *Le second livre de la muse folastre. Recherche des beaux esprits de ce temps* (Rouen: Le Vilain, 1603);

"En quelle nuict de ma lance d'ivoire," "Douce lancette à la couleur vermeille," and "Touche ma main mignonne, frétillarde," in *La Quintessence satyrique, ou la seconde partie du Parnasse des Poètes satyriques de nostre temps* (Paris: A. de Sommaville, 1622);

"Il faut qu'un cours du ciel estrangement contraire" and "Piquez d'une acre humeur, n'ayans de quoy se plaire," in *Recueil des plus belles pieces des poètes françois depuis Villon jusqu'à Benserade* (Paris: Claude Barbin, 1692).

Estienne Jodelle—poet, playwright, musician, painter, architect, orator, and soldier—is remembered as the first writer in the French language to compose tragedies and comedies in the classic style. His short life remains mostly a mystery despite many poems and other short works about him by his contemporaries. None of his manuscripts has survived, and most of what he wrote went unpublished. The "premier volume" (first volume) of *Les Œuvres et Meslanges Poëtiques d'Estienne Jodelle* (1574, The Works and Selected Poetry of Estienne Jodelle)—a collection projected to be four or five volumes—was published a year after his death, but no other volumes were forthcoming. Jodelle was the only Parisian member of the Pléiade, a group of seven poets—including Pierre de Ronsard, Joachim du Bellay, Pontus de Tyard, and Jean Antoine de Baïf—whose goal was to write works in the French language comparable to the great works of Greek and Latin. He also stood out among Pléiade members as an admirer of the poet Clément Marot. His most important published works are the comedy *Eugène* (Eugene) and the tragedy *Cléopâtre Captive* (Captive Cleopatra).

Jodelle, Sieur du Lymodin, was born circa 1532 to Estienne Jodelle and Marie Drouet, both from rich bourgeois merchant families whose members included humanists and notaries. He had a sister, Marie, who married Jean Habert, collector of fines for the court of parliament in Paris. Jodelle's cousin, Jean Drouet, was a counselor to King Henry II. Jodelle's grandmother's maiden name was Passavant, and members of that family were famous as tapestry merchants. Jodelle's great-great-grandfather, Jean de Passavant, was a humanist who knew Greek. In *Un poeta del Rinascimento francese: Etienne Jodelle* (1962, A Poet of the French Renassaince: Etienne Jodelle) biographer Enea Balmas suggests that the young Jodelle probably had access to a large collection of books and manuscripts at the Passavant family home in Paris.

Jodelle grew up on the Left Bank in Paris. His father died between 1532 and 1535, and after his death legal documents and wills indicate that the writer's mother had some financial difficulties and was aided by family members. The first known publication of Jodelle's work is an epitaph to the poet Marot that appears at the beginning of a 1546 edition of Marot's *Œuvres* (Works). Charles de la Mothe, the contemporary of Jodelle who wrote the preface to the first and only volume of *Les Œuvres et Meslanges Poëtiques d'Estienne Jodelle,* declares that the writer began his literary career with several poems written in 1549.

Jodelle's literary fame evidently grew quickly. In "Au seigneur de Lymodin, Parisien, excellent Poëte" (To Lord Lymodin, Parisian, Excellent Poet), a long poem published in 1553 in *Epitome de la corographie d'Europe* (Synopsis of the Chorography of Europe), Guillaume Guéroult complains of Jodelle's "silence" and urges him not to be beaten by his misfortunes and to continue to write. Balmas concludes that Guéroult's poem was written before Jodelle's trip to Lyon for performances of his tragedy, *Cléopâtre captive,* 1551–1552. At about that same time, Jodelle also traveled to Italy and Switzerland. Balmas writes that Jodelle was a Protestant and supported the cause with his writings when he stayed in Geneva. Later in 1552 Jodelle published an ode in *Cantiques du premier advenement de Jésus Christ* (Hymns of Christ's First Coming) that condemned modern poets for their use of pagan mythology and for their neglect of moral and religious inspiration.

Jodelle's first comedy, *Eugène,* was probably staged in 1552 in the courtyard of the Collège de Boncourt, where the famous humanist Marc-Antoine Muret taught. (Critics know of a second comedy by Jodelle, *La Rencontre* [The Meeting], but that play is lost.) The prologue of the play *Eugène,* which Balmas describes as its most innovative part, is written in ten-syllable lines instead of the eight-syllable lines of traditional farces and denigrates medieval farce while lauding the use of the French language and French characters. The end of the prologue introduces the main character, the abbot Eugène.

The action of the play, which revolves around Eugène's intrigues, takes place during an interlude of the military activities of late 1552: King Henry II has recently returned from Germany with his armies after aiding Protestant German princes against Emperor Charles V. The king intends to lead his troops to battle again later in the year at Metz, and the play is set in between the two campaigns. During the play Jodelle contrives to mention two real-life Collège de Boncourt students, the brothers Antoine and Saladin d'Anglure, relatives of the royal constable Anne de Montmorency, who had died in the recent battles in Germany at Montmédy and Trelon. Balmas maintains in both his edition of the play and the *Œuvres complètes* (1965, 1968, Complete Works) that their deaths were the reason that Jodelle wrote the play for an audience that included soldiers just returned from the expedition to Germany.

The first act begins with the abbot Eugène explaining to his chaplain that his life's goal is personal pleasure. The description of his epicurean philosophy leads to a discussion of his mistress, Alix, for whom he arranged a marriage with Guillaume, "le bon lourdaut" (the good dullard), so as to cover up his affair. In order to ensure his happiness and preserve his life, Eugène in the course of the play must contend with Florimond, a vengeful "gentleman" who has returned to Paris after the first campaign with the hope of recommencing his own liaison with Alix; the creditor Mathieu, who threatens to have Guillaume put in debtors' prison at Châtelet; and his own sister, Hélène, whom he must convince to take back Florimond, a man she had previously rejected. The abbot manages a conclusion in which Guillaume allows him to continue his affair with Alix, and then Florimond and Hélène go to bed without the marriage sacraments.

Tilde Sankovitch, the author of "Folly and Society in the Comic Theatre of the Pléiade," is one of several modern critics who condemn the ending of *Eugène* as "immoral and cynical." Eugène, she argues, is a detestable character, a narcissistic manipulator who even uses his own sister to further his adulterous plans. Sankovitch does not agree with critics who argue that Eugène is a type found in contemporary and medieval farces and instead sees in the character's madness a Renaissance invention. Sankovitch explains that the last lines of the play, which Balmas attributes to Guillaume, are attributed to Eugène in the first edition of the play by Charles de la Mothe and by most modern editors:

Eugène: Sus entrons, on couvre la table,
Suivons ce plaisir souhaitable
De n'estre jamais soucieux:

Tellement mesme que les Dieux
A l'envi de ce bien volage,
Doublent au Ciel leur sainct breuvage.

(Eugene: Ho, let's go in; the table is being set;
Let us follow this pleasant course
Of banishing all worry:
Even as the Gods themselves,
Pursuing this elusive goal,
In Heaven quaff deep of their ambrosia,
Let us do likewise.)
                    —translation from Arthur P. Stabler,
                    Four French Renaissance Plays

For Sankovitch, these last lines show that Eugène remains corrupt and unrepentant for his actions.

Jodelle's *Cléopâtre captive* was performed at the Hôtel de Reims in Paris for King Henry II in February or March 1553 as part of the celebrations for the return of Duke François de Guise from military success at Metz and to fete the marriage between Diane d'Angoulême (illegitimate daughter of Henry II) and Horace Fornèse. The five-act tragedy in rhymed verse was a huge success and was praised by many contemporary writers. The king gave the playwright five hundred écus, an enormous payment. The play was also performed in the courtyard at the Collège de Boncourt and led Pierre de Ronsard to declare Jodelle the inventor of humanist theater. Estienne Pasquier, a contemporary whose journals were published, wrote that the courtyard of the school where the play was staged overflowed with students and famous guests. The tragedy was performed several times in the twentieth century, including in 1972 at the Hôtel de Clermont.

The classical inspiration for *Cléopâtre captive* is evident. In *La prima tragedia di Etienne Jodelle* (1919, The First Tragedy of Etienne Jodelle), Italian critic Ferdinando Neri argues that Jodelle imitated Cesare de Cesari's Italian tragedy *Cleopatra* (1552). Marie Delcourt in her 1934 essay "Jodelle et Plutarque" (Jodelle and Plutarch) shows that Jodelle was inspired by Plutarch's *Life of Antony*. Jodelle clearly followed the three unities of classical theater of time, place, and action—rules followed by later playwrights, especially Racine. The play takes place in half a day, and the audience is often reminded of the passage of time. The setting is Egypt, and the scenes take place in Cleopatra's quarters, although the decor is not specified.

Jodelle's prologue is similar to the one he wrote for *Eugène,* in that he makes a claim for the first work of its kind, here the first tragedy in French. Jodelle also praises King Henry II and mentions recent military victories—the Scottish naval campaign, the retaking of Boulogne in 1550, and the victory at Metz in 1553—and alludes to the king's future triumphs, possibly in Italy. In the first act Jodelle presents the conflict that is the

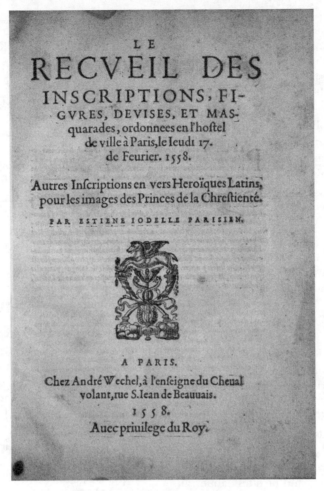

Title page for the only work by Jodelle published during his lifetime, which he wrote to explain the failure of a theatrical entertainment he organized (Douglas H. Gordon Collection, University of Virginia Library)

focus of the play: following the death of Antony, Cleopatra fears capture by Octavian, the Roman emperor who defeated Antony, because it could include her transportation to Rome where she would be paraded in the streets. The first act ends with the chorus—an element from ancient theater—deploring the vicissitudes of fortune. The most dramatic act of the drama is the third, in which Octavian and Cleopatra meet face to face. The queen tries every ploy to convince the emperor to free her and her children, blaming love and even Antony. But her offer of royal treasure is undermined when her servant, Seleuque, reveals that the queen has hidden most of the fortune from the emperor. She attacks Seleuque in a dramatic rage, pulling his hair and pulling him to the ground and beating him. The fourth act describes Cleopatra's preparations for death—her suicide occurs off stage—and the last act announces her death.

Critics have accused *Cléopâtre captive* of lacking a plot because there is so little action or surprise since the audience knows from the beginning that the queen will die. In the second volume of his edition of *Etienne Jodelle: Œuvres complètes* (1968), Balmas contends that the real subject of the play is the message delivered by the chorus: that human beings are powerless to control their fortunes. Françoise Charpentier argues in her introduction to the 1990 edition of *Cléopâtre captive* that the question is not if Cleopatra will die but if she will die a captive. Will Octavian be able to take his revenge on her, and by association, on Antony, by parading her triumphantly as his captive through the streets of Rome? Cleopatra, thus, actually triumphs at the end by succeeding in killing herself, thereby preventing Octavian from carrying out his plan to expose her to ridicule.

Charpentier also describes the role in the play of stoic philosophy, in which death is viewed as a kind of liberty. From the stoic perspective, passionate love is an illness, a defect, a poison. Jodelle, Charpentier argues, believed that tragedy should propose a moral lesson about the danger of passion. Charpentier also compares the tragedy to a musical piece or opera whose crescendo is Cleopatra's physical attack on her unfaithful servant Seleuque, then a brusque decrescendo ending with the description of the queen's death. The chorus ends the play by declaring Cleopatra's glory.

As a result of *Cléopâtre captive,* the Pléiade poets discovered Jodelle, counting him as a member of their group and praising him frequently in published collections. Pierre de Ronsard was particularly congratulatory, publishing a poem in his *Livret des folastries* (1553, Little Book of Gaieties) that describes the famous "cérémonies du bouc" (ceremonies of the goat) at which Jodelle was celebrated by his compatriots with a fete inspired by the ancient Greek tradition of sacrificing a goat and singing before the performance of a tragedy (hence the meaning of the word *tragedy:* "goat song"). The ritual for Jodelle was called "la Pompe du bouc" (The Adulation of the Goat).

Jodelle's celebrity was further shown when one of his sonnets was placed at the beginning of the second edition of Ronsard's *Amours* (1553, Love Poems). This collection also included a Ronsard poem titled the *Iles fortunées* (The Fortunate Islands), in which Jodelle is portrayed as sailing away on the ship of the Pléiade, heading toward "les îles bienheureuses de la grande poésie" (the Happy Poetry Islands). Baïf wrote another dithyramb "Dithyrambes à la pompe du bouc d'Etienne Jodelle," to celebrate the ceremony of the goat. Renaissance writers enjoyed anagrams and Jacques Tahuereau used the letters of Jodelle's name for the refrain of an ode, "A Estienne Jodelle se jouant sur son nom retourné" (To Estienne Jodelle playing on his name) in *Poésies* (1554). His famous phrase is: "Jo, le Délien est né!" (Jodelle, the fine spirit is born!). Jodelle's importance among the Pléiade poets as even rivaling that of Ronsard is evident in Olivier de Magny's placing Jodelle's ode before Ronsard's in his collection titled *Amours* (1552 or 1553, Love Poems). Many poets in their collections exhorted Jodelle to publish his works.

Jodelle's sister Marie signed her will in 1555, which indicates that she probably passed away that year. Legal papers show that Jodelle was continually seeking money, often from relatives. A few months after his sister's death, he borrowed money by using his five inherited properties—an estate at Lymondin, two houses in Paris, and a house and vineyards near Bagneulx—as surety. His excessive loans suggest that Jodelle lived beyond his means, but his constant indebtedness was in large part a result of his not having a patron to fund his literary work—a lack lamented by Baïf in the poem "Les Muses" (The Muses), written in 1555, in which he writes that the soul of the author of *Cléopâtre captive* was being left to die. Yet, Jodelle courted favor and was compensated to some extent by many nobles, such as Marguerite, sister of King Henry II, and later Catherine de Médicis and her son, King Charles IX.

In about 1558 Jodelle wrote a second tragedy, *Didon se sacrifiant* (Dido Sacrifices Herself), which was based on the fourth book of Virgil's *Aeneid.* Balmas argues that the main conflict in the five-act drama is between human will—the desire of Dido, the Queen of Carthage, and Aeneus, hero of the Trojan War, to remain together—and God's will, as Aeneus must leave Carthage and Dido to fulfill his destiny of founding Rome. The play did not achieve the fame of *Cléopâtre captive,* and there is no record of any productions. In *Etienne Jodelle: Œuvres complètes,* however, Balmas contends that Jodelle's second tragedy is superior to his first.

Jodelle's great decline in fortune, by his own telling, began 17 February 1558 when the theatrical entertainment that he had organized was presented at the Hôtel de Ville as part of a reception hosted by the city of Paris for the king and the duke of Guise in celebration of the military victory against the English at Calais. Chosen as the playwright because of his reputation for producing brilliant work quickly, Jodelle had only four days to write his play. Jodelle himself took the role of Jason in his play about Jason and the Argonauts. His only collection published during his lifetime is a pamphlet that seeks to explain the failure of this entertainment: *Le Receuil des Inscriptions, Figures, devises, et masquerades, ordonnees en l'hostel de ville à Paris, le Jeudi 17 Fevrier 1558. Autres Inscriptions en vers Heroïques Latins pour les images des Princes de la Chrestienté* (Collection of Inscriptions, Illustrations, Mottos, and Masquerades Organized at City Hall, Paris, Thursday, 17 February 1558. Other Inscriptions in Heroic Latin Verse for Images of the Christian Princes).

In *Le Receuil,* Jodelle includes descriptions of the festivities, room decorations, and the text of the play of Jason and the Argonauts as well as *Icones* (Inscriptions), or laudatory poems about members of the royal family, in particular, Marguerite de France, sister of King Henry II. He also details with great bitterness how his production was plagued by actors who did not know their lines and could not be heard above the immense crowd and by machines that malfunctioned. In his 1995 essay "From Mascarade to Tragedy: The Rhetoric of Apologia in Jodelle's *Recueil des incriptions,*" François Cornilliat characterizes *Le Receuil* as "a remarkable piece of rhetoric, a dark, aggressive apology whose peculiar brand of whining has no equivalent in French sixteenth-century literature." By publishing *Le Receuil,* Jodelle was trying to clear his reputation. Short as it is, it was an important endeavor for a renowned poet who had never before published his work.

While Jodelle left Paris for a time after the failed entertainment, he continued to receive the support of contemporary poets. In three laudatory sonnets about him in his 1558 collection *Regrets* (Regrets), Du Bellay writes of Jodelle's "Dæmon," or poetic inspiration. Other poets echo Du Bellay's praise. Ronsard was one of the writers who continued to mention Jodelle's genius and misfortune, although much later, after Jodelle's death, he praised the playwright Robert Garnier at Jodelle's expense. Théodore Agrippa d'Aubigné, however, staunchly supported Jodelle against his detractors and plagiarists, including an ode to Jodelle in his unpublished collection *Le Printemps* (Spring).

In 1559 Jodelle turned to a military career, although he continued to write. Philippe de Boulanvilliers was Jodelle's protector and was therefore the subject of admiring verses by the poet. Jodelle was living in Paris in early 1564, and court papers show that he was condemned to death that year. A legal document from 1566 indicates that the poet's Lymodin estate was impounded as part of the sentence. There is no indication of why he was judged or how he escaped execution, but it may have had to do with his interest in the Reformation. He probably left the city for several years.

As the religious wars between Catholic and Protestant nobles were beginning, Jodelle sought the patronage of King Charles IX and his mother Catherine de Médicis by writing anti-Protestant poetry. He indicates in his writings in 1567 that he had fallen ill, during which time he wrote a satire against the chancellor Michel de L'Hospital, who had failed in his efforts to reconcile the warring factions. Jodelle took a hard line against Protestants and supported the edict of 28 September 1568 that banished all Protestant ministers and administrators working for the state and led to the third religious war. Jodelle also composed various poems that celebrated Catholics who had died, some of them in battle during the Wars of Religion.

By 1569 Jodelle was frequenting the salon of Claude Catherine, Maréchale de Retz, and writing love poetry, though his collected poems give little indication of their chronology. One of his sonnets, "A Madamoyselle de Surgières" (To Miss Surgières), was written for Hélène de Surgières, who also often visited the salon and was made famous by Ronsard by his *Sonnets pour Hélène* (1578, Sonnets for Helen). Some of Jodelle's love poems are considered to rank among the most beautiful in the French language. Many critics consider his poems—a mixture of sonnets, odes, songs, elegies, and other forms—Jodelle's best work.

By 1571 Jodelle's star had waned, and he was no longer considered one of the great poets of his era. He continued to have financial difficulties, failing to make payments on debts. After the St. Bartholemew's Day Massacre of 24 August 1572, Jodelle wrote sonnets in support of the mass murder of Protestants. Although these sonnets resulted in a monetary gift from King Charles IX, Jodelle's property at Lymodin was still seized in July 1573 to pay his debts. A few weeks later, on 23 July 1573, the poet signed his will in his sickbed in a house at the Jeu de Paume on the corner of the rue Neuve-Saint-Paul in Paris. He named De la Mothe his executor and died a few days later. The exact date of his death is uncertain. His nephew, Jean II Habert, a lawyer at the Court of Parlement and the son of his sister Marie and Jean Habert, was the author's closest living relative. Balmas reports in his biography of Jodelle that Pierre L'Estoile, a contemporary of Jodelle, wrote in his *Registre-Journal de Henri III* an unflattering account of Jodelle's death, in which he says that the poet lived a godless life and death. His death was reportedly miserable, as described by this detractor, with him blaspheming and crying out in pain. He left behind a long list of creditors that included relatives. Jodelle's last sonnet, intended for King Henry III, ends with this accusatory phrase: "Qui se sert de la lampe au moins de l'huile y met" (One who uses a lamp at least puts oil in it).

Jodelle was not forgotten, but most of his life's work was not brought to the press. The protestant poet Agrippa d'Aubigné, despite Jodelle's support of the Catholic cause, published *Vers funèbres sur la mort d'Etienne Jodelle Parisien Prince de Poètes Tragiques* (1574, Funeral Verses on the Death of Etienne Jodelle, Parisian, Prince of Tragic Poets), in which he deplored the idea that the poet's unpublished works would be forgotten. De la Mothe and a group of Jodelle's friends published *Les Œuvres et Meslanges Poëtiques d'Estienne Jodelle,* including *Cléopâtre captive* and *Didon se sacrifiant,* in November 1574, but even in the preface in which he promises to publish more volumes of Jodelle's work, De la Mothe concedes that most of Jodelle's work had already been lost.

In his preface to the 1574 edition of Jodelle's works, De la Mothe wrote about Jodelle: " . . . nous ne croirons jamais qu'aucune autre nation de tout le temps passé ait eu un esprit naturellement si prompt et adextre en ceste science. . . . tant que les François se souviendront de leur vieil honneur, et merite vers les Muses . . . ils ne devront estre ingrates à la memoire de cestuy leur nourisson . . . et qui tousjours ses œuvres n'a dressé qu'à la gloire de la France" (We will never believe that any nation from the past ever had a mind naturally so agile and skilled in this science [of poetry as Jodelle's]. . . . as long as the French remember their old honor and credit owed the Muses . . . they should never be ungrateful to the memory of this their infant . . . who always raised his works to the glory of France). Estienne Jodelle continues to be remembered for his genius and innovation as a poet as well as for his groundbreaking dramatic works that introduced classical tragedy and comedy to the French public. While much of his life was unhappy, he experienced many years as the premier poet and playwright of France.

Biographies:

Enea Balmas, *Un poeta del Rinascimento francese: Etienne Jodelle. La sua vita. Il suo tempo,* Biblioteca dell'Archivium Romanicum, Serie 1, volume 66 (Florence: Olschki, 1962);

Jean Perrin, *Etienne Jodelle: poète, sieur du Lymodin, 1532–1573* (La Houssaye-en-Brie: Centre culturel de la Brie, 1963).

References:

Francois Cornilliat, "From Mascarade to Tragedy: The Rhetoric of Apologia in Jodelle's *Recueil des incriptions,*" *Renaissance Quarterly,* 48 (Spring 1995): 82–108;

Marie Delcourt, "Jodelle et Plutarque," *Bulletin de l'Association Guillaume Budé,* 42 (1934): 36–56;

Agrippa d'Aubigné, *Le Printemps. Stances et Odes* (Geneva: Droz, 1952), pp. 171–173;

D'Aubigné, *Vers funèbres sur la mort d'Etienne Jodelle Parisien Prince de Poètes Tragiques* (Paris: Lucas Breyer, 1574);

Joachim du Bellay, *Regrets* (Paris: Gallimard, 1975);

Michael Freeman, "Florimond face aux Badauds Parisiens: L'homme d'armes dans *L'Eugène* de Jodelle," in *L'homme de guerre au XVIᵉ siècle, Actes du Colloque de l'Association RHR Cannes,* edited by Gabriel-André Pérouse, André Thierry, and André Tournon (Saint-Etienne: Publications de l'Université de Saint-Etienne, 1992), pp. 267–276;

Freeman, "Jodelle et le théâtre populaire: Les sabots d'Hélène," in *Aspects du théâtre populaire en Europe au XVIᵉ siècle,* edited by Madeleine Lazard (Paris: Centre National des Lettres, 1989), pp. 55–68;

Guillaume Guéroult, "Au seigneur de Lymodin, Parisien, excellent Poëte," in *Epitome de la corographie d'Europe* (Lyon: Balthazar Arnoullet, 1553);

Ferdinando Neri, *La prima tragedia di Etienne Jodelle* (N.p.: Giornale Storico della Letteratura Italiana, 1919);

Tilde Sankovitch, "Folly and Society in the Comic Theatre of the Pléiade," in *Folie et Déraison à la Renaissance* (Bruxelles: Editions de l'Université de Bruxelles, 1976), pp. 99–108;

Sankovitch, *Jodelle et la création du masque: Etude structurale et normative de* L'Eugène (York, S.C.: French Literature Publications, 1979);

Arthur P. Stabler, *Four French Renaissance Plays* (Pullman: Washington State University Press, 1978);

Donald Stone Jr., *French Humanist Tragedy* (Manchester: Manchester University Press, 1974).

Papers:

Published works are available at the Bibliothèque de France in Paris. Some of Estienne Jodelle's poetry exists in manuscript form as parts of anthologies, which can be found at the Bibliothèque nationale.

Louise Labé

(1520? – 1566)

Lance K. Donaldson-Evans
University of Pennsylvania

BOOK: *Euvres de Louïze Labé Lionnoize* (Lyon: Printed by Jan de Tournes, 1555; revised, 1556).

Editions: *Euvres de Louïze Labé Lionnoize* (Lyon: Printed by Durand & Perrin, 1824);

Œuvres de Louise Labé, edited by Prosper Blanchemain (Paris: Librairie des Bibliophiles, 1875);

Œuvres de Louise Labé, 2 volumes, edited by Charles Boy (Paris: A. Lemerre, 1887);

Œuvres de Louise Labé, 2 volumes, edited by Boy (Paris & Geneva: Slatkine, 1981);

Œuvres complètes, edited by Enzo Giudici (Geneva: Droz, 1981);

Œuvres complètes, edited by François Rigolot (Paris: Flammarion, 1986).

Editions in English: "The Debate betweene Follie and Loue," translated by Robert Greene, in his *Gwydonius: The Carde of Fancie, Wherein the Folly of Those Carpet Knights Is Decyphered, Which Guyding Their Course by the Compasse of Cupid, Either Dash Their Ship against Most Dangerous Rocks, or Els Attaine the Hauen with Paine and Perill. Wherein Also Is Described in the Person of Gwydonius, a Ciuell Combat betvveene Nature and Necessitie* (London: Printed for William Ponsonby, 1584), pp. 69–79;

The Debate between Folly and Cupid, translated by Edwin Marion Cox (London: Williams & Norgate, 1925);

Love Sonnets, translated by Frederic Prokosch (New York: New Directions, 1947);

Sonnets of Louise Labé "La Belle Cordière," translated by Alta Lind Cook (Toronto: University of Toronto Press, 1950);

The Twenty-four Love Sonnets, translated by Frances Lobb (London: Euphorion, 1950);

Sonnets, edited by Peter Sharratt, translated by Graham Dunstan Martin (Austin: University of Texas Press, 1972; Edinburgh: Edinburgh University Press, 1973);

Louise Labé's Complete Works, edited and translated by Edith R. Farrell (Troy, N.Y.: Whitson, 1986);

Louise Labé (engraving by Pierre Woeiriot, used as the frontispiece for Euvres de Louïze Labé Lionnoize, *1555; from <http://en.wikipedia.org>)*

Debate of Folly and Love: A New English Translation with the Original French Text, translated by Anne-Marie Bourbon (New York: Peter Lang, 2000);

Complete Poetry and Prose: A Bilingual Edition, edited by Deborah Lesko Baker, translated by Annie Finch (Chicago: University of Chicago Press, 2006).

Although her literary production is relatively slight—a single volume, *Euvres de Louïze Labé Lionnoize* (1555, Works of Louise Labé of Lyon) comprising one prose work, "Débat de Folie et d'Amour" (translated as

"The Debate betweene Follie and Loue, 1584); three lyric poems characterized as "elegies"; and twenty-four sonnets—Louise Labé is the most widely read female poet of the French Renaissance. The sensuality, vigor, and immediacy of her poems have attracted both extravagant praise and harsh criticism. On the one hand, the first edition of her works included twenty-four anonymous poems of varying genres, comprising an extraordinary panegyric that exceeds Labé's own poetic production in length. On the other hand, Labé was attacked for what were deemed her loose morals, as illustrated by Jean Calvin's famous condemnation of her in a 1560 pamphlet as a "meretrix plebeia" (common whore).

Labé's father, Pierre Charly, was an apprentice rope maker in Lyon when, probably around 1493, he married Guillemette Decuchermois; she was the widow of a prosperous rope maker, Jacques Humbert, who was also known as Labé. No record exists of any children from the marriage. When his wife died around 1514, Charly, who had added Labé to his name, inherited her previous husband's rope-making workshop, as well as a large house and garden. Around 1515 he married Etiennette Roybet; through her he acquired several properties, including a small estate, la Gela. This marriage produced five children, including Louise, who may have been born anytime between 1516 and 1523 but was probably born around 1520. Her mother died around 1523, and Pierre Charly Labé married for a third time.

Nothing more is known of Labé's early years, including how a young woman of her social class acquired the excellent education to which her writings bear testimony. Karine Berriot notes that Labé's apparently illiterate father was interested in education, since he contributed to the foundation of the Collège de la Trinité, a coeducational establishment catering to students of aristocratic and bourgeois origin; Louise may have been educated there. The dedication of her book to Clémence de Bourges, a young noblewoman and therefore of a social class far higher than her own, suggests an alternative scenario. François Rigolot speculates that Labé may have been sent to the convent school of La Déserte when her mother died. The convent, to which some of her relatives had made contributions, was in the same neighborhood as la Gela, and De Bourges attended its school. In any case, it is clear that in Renaissance Lyon the social hierarchy was becoming relatively flexible and that a humanistic education was available, at least in exceptional cases, to women whose social status would have previously precluded such a possibility.

In the intellectual ferment of Lyon—a center of trade and printing, home to a large Italian expatriate colony, birthplace of the poet Maurice Scève, and temporary abode of such Renaissance luminaries as François Rabelais, Clément Marot, and Olivier de Magny, with whom Labé had a literary and personal relationship and, perhaps, a liaison—Labé was able to flourish intellectually and hone her poetic talents. According to Antoine Du Verdier's literary chronicle, *La bibliothèque d'Antoine Du Verdier* (1585, The Library of Antoine Du Verdier), and Guillaume Aubert, a Paris lawyer to whom the longest poem in the "Hommage à Louise Labé" section of her book is attributed, Labé was instructed in swordsmanship by her brother François and, dressed as a man, participated in the siege of Perpignan in 1542. According to Du Verdier, she used the name Captain Louis; Aubert calls her "La Pucelle Lionnoize" (The Maid of Lyon), suggesting a comparison with Joan of Arc, "La Pucelle d'Orléans" (The Maid of Orléans), another female warrior who fought in male garb. But Labé's involvement in the siege is disputed by Charles Boy in his 1887 edition of Labé's *Œuvres*. Boy speculates that Labé participated in a tournament held in Lyon when the French army, commanded by the future King Henri II, passed through the city on the way to do battle with the Spaniards at Perpignan.

Sometime between 1543 and 1545 Labé married the rope maker Ennemond Perrin. In 1551 they bought a house with a garden near what is now Place Bellecour in Lyon. Labé most likely began writing her sonnets the following year.

In 1554 the Greek poet Sappho was rediscovered by European humanists when Longinus's treatise *Peri hypsous* (On the Sublime), including Sappho's "Ode to a Loved One," was published. The ode became one of the most imitated poems of the time, and in one of her elegies Labé claims Sappho as a predecessor and exemplum of female-authored love poetry. That same year Labé received from Henri II a *privilège* for the publication of her works; the book was brought out by the renowned Lyonnais printer Jan (or Jean) de Tournes the following year, and a revised edition was published by the same printer in 1556. The ancestor of copyright, the *privilège* gave exclusive rights to an author or printer for a limited number of years. The language of a *privilège* was usually matter-of-fact and objective; the *privilège* to Labé's *Œuvres* is unusually warm and quite personal in tone:

Henri, par la grace de Dieu Roy de France. . . .

Reçue avons l'humble supplicacion de notre chère et bien aymée Louïze Labé Lionnoize, contenant qu'elle auroit dés long temps composé quelque Dialogue de Folie et d'Amour: ensemble plusieurs Sonnets, Odes et Epistres qu'aucuns ses Amis auroient souztraits et iceus encore non parfaits publiez en divers endroits. Et doutant qu'aucuns ne les vousissent faire imprimer en cette sorte, elle les ayant revus et corrigez à loisir, les mettroit volontiers en lumiere . . . mais elle doute que les Imprimeurs ne se vousissent charger de la despence sans estre asseurez qu'autres puis apres n'entreprendront sur leur labeur. POURCE EST IL: que nous inclinans liberalement à la requeste de ladite suppliante luy avons . . . donné Privilege . . . de pouvoir faire imprimer sesdites Euvres . . . dans le temps de cinq ans consecutifs, faits et accomplis: commençans au jour et date que ledit livre sera achevé d'imprimer. . . .

(Henri, King of France by the Grace of God. . . .

We have received the humble request of our dear and beloved Louise Labé, stating that a long time ago she wrote the Dialogue of Folly and Love together with several sonnets, odes and epistles, which some of her friends published in a number of different places without her knowledge before these works were ready for publication. But doubting that anyone would want to print her works in the imperfect state they were in, she has reviewed and corrected them and would willingly publish them . . . but she doubts that printers will be willing to undertake this expense unless they are assured that others will not be able to do the same. It is for this reason that we favorably receive the request of the said supplicant and accord her the Privilege to have her works printed . . . for a period of five consecutive years from the time of its first publication. . . .)

The dedicatory epistle to De Bourges, which follows the privilège, is couched in protofeminist terms. Labé declares that until this time "les sévères loix des hommes" (the repressive rules of men) have prevented women from applying themselves to learning and literature, and she calls on women to renounce jewelry and fine clothing and adorn themselves instead with their writings so as to show themselves the intellectual equals of men. Labé notes that just as women are discouraged from going out alone in public, it is considered less than seemly for a woman to publish her works, and she closes the epistle by asking De Bourges to accompany her symbolically as she ventures out in public as an author.

Most studies of Labé's work have dealt with her poetry, but her sole prose work, the "Débat de Folie et d'Amour," has also begun to receive critical attention. The piece is a combination of a medieval-style debate and the kind of paradoxical mock encomium that became popular in the Renaissance largely as a result of the influence of Desiderius Erasmus's Encomium Moriae (1511; translated as The Praise of Folie, 1549). Labé's work is a dramatized fable in which Folly, who is here included in the Roman pantheon, and Cupid are on their way to a banquet hosted by Jupiter and begin to argue about their respective importance in the universe.

The quarrel turns violent when Cupid shoots an arrow at Folly; she eludes it by making herself invisible, then retaliates by gouging out Cupid's eyes and covering the empty sockets with a blindfold that is impossible to remove. Cupid complains to his mother, Venus, who appeals the dispute to Jupiter. Each side is assigned an advocate: Cupid and Venus are represented by Apollo, Folly by Mercury. Apollo begins the debate by crediting Cupid with everything that is good and admirable in the world; in his summation he asks Jupiter to restore Cupid's sight and place Folly under Cupid's authority. Mercury finds as much to say in Folly's favor as Apollo had said in praise of Cupid; according to Mercury, Folly makes the world go round and is at the root of all the advances of civilization. He goes on to maintain that the two form an inseparable union and that Cupid would lose his sway over the human race if he were not aided by Folly's handmaidens: Ignorance, Nonchalance, Hope, and Blindness. The gods and goddesses of Olympus are divided in their opinions as to the respective importance of love and folly. Jupiter finally announces that he is postponing judgment; in the meantime, he orders the two to live peaceably together and commands Folly to lead Cupid, who will be given back his sight if the Fates so ordain.

The debate is lively and amusing, reminiscent not only of Erasmus but also of the ironic praise of debts Rabelais has his character Panurge undertake at the beginning of the Tiers livre des faits et dits héroïques du noble Pantagruel (1546, Third Book of the Heroic Deeds and Words of the Noble Pantagruel; translated as The Third Book of the Works of Mr. Francis Rabelais, Doctor in Physick Containing the Heroick Deeds of Pantagruel the Son of Gargantua, 1693). The debate also introduces the theme of folly as a component of the type of passion bordering on madness that Labé describes in her verse. Finally, the debate is a testimony to Labé's erudition, demonstrating that she has assimilated and taken full advantage of the "sciences et disciplines" (knowledge and learning) that she encourages women to acquire in the dedicatory epistle.

Labé opens the poetry section of her works with three elegies. During the French Renaissance this genre comprised lyrical poems concerned with love, usually unrequited, in the neo-Petrarchan tradition. Labé's elegies include some autobiographical (or pseudo-autobiographical) details and recount, in mythological terms, her awakening to poetry and her use of this medium as both a record of her past love and a consolation for its loss.

In Elegy I, lines 14–15, Labé identifies her poetic endeavor with that of Sappho, who was seen by European intellectuals as the archetypal example of a woman poet writing about romantic love. Referring to

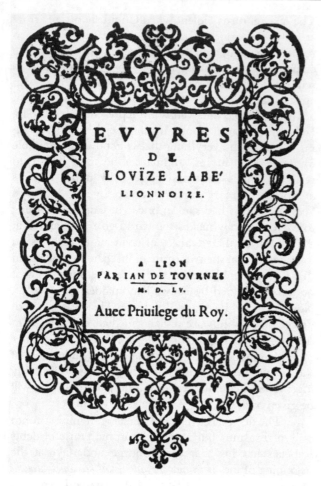

medieval romances—the link between the two is clearly implied.

One of the main themes of Labé's poetry is that of absence: the absence of the speaker's beloved, the remembrance of things past, and the hope for a future that might reconstitute the happiness the speaker once knew. In Elegy II she imagines possible reasons why the beloved has not returned, including illness and a new love. Labé's persona presents both herself and her beloved as poets and expresses confidence that even if the beloved is courting a woman more beautiful than she, her reputation as a poet will be certain to bring him back. But confidence gives way to despair as the poem concludes by depicting the speaker's precarious state in the absence of her beloved: she is hovering between life and death, a malady for which the only cure is the prompt return of the beloved. If he tarries, the tears of regret he will shed over her grave will come too late and will not quench the destructive fire of her love for him.

The third elegy begins with a direct appeal to "Les Dames Lyonnaises" (The Women of Lyon) for their understanding. Labé refers to her participation in jousting and remarks that an observer of her youthful activities in this domain might have taken her for a Bradamante or a Marphise, the popular warrior heroines in Ludovico Ariosto's narrative poem *Orlando furioso* (1516). The speaker represents herself as a devotee of Mars, the god of war; this reference and Labé's participation in the tournament in 1542 probably account for the legend of her involvement in the siege of Perpignan. The speaker states that she was fifteen when she felt the first pangs of love and that the suffering has now lasted for thirteen years. This possibly autobiographical reflection leads to the exploitation of a literary theme: the cruelty of time, whose passage usually heals all wounds but seems only to increase hers. In the final lines Eros is entreated to cause the speaker's negligent beloved to experience the same all-consuming love for her that she feels for him, since she cannot bear the burden of love alone.

The three elegies lay out the principal themes of the sonnets that follow, as well as define the nature of the love that the speaker experiences. In the sonnets, as critics such as Lawrence E. Harvey have shown, Labé masterfully uses the economy of the form to distill this passion to its quintessential and most eloquent purity.

The first sonnet, written in Italian, begins by comparing the speaker's beloved to the hero of the *Odyssey*. Such a comparison presents a somewhat ambiguous picture of him. Although it suggests the exemplary and mythical nature of her love experience, during the Renaissance Ulysses was viewed not only as a symbol of heroism but also as an incarnation of cunning and—as demonstrated by his dalliance with the enchantress

Phoebus-Apollo, she declares: "Il m'a donné la lyre, qui les vers / Souloit chanter de l'Amour Lesbienne" (He gave me the lyre / The instrument which sings of Lesbian love). "Amour Lesbienne" refers not to homosexual love but to love poetry written by a woman. Sappho lived on the island of Lesbos, and in Labé's time it was assumed that her love poetry was addressed to a man.

Like that of most other women writers of the period, Labé's presumed audience was female, and her poetry includes several apostrophes to these readers. Labé's appeal is both a call for female solidarity in the face of unhappy love and also a means to deflect possible moral criticism, since love, represented as an irresistible force, is capable of inflicting the same or even worse suffering on her readers. Love is unpredictable, cruel, and vindictive and causes its victims to behave in foolish and uncharacteristic ways. Although folly is not explicitly mentioned as a component of this type of love—a descendant of the *fol'amour* (mad passion) of

Circe, for example—of infidelity. Even if the delay was not entirely his fault, the length of time—ten years—it took him to return to his wife, Penelope, after the Trojan War also makes him the symbol of the absent beloved. Describing the handsome face of her beloved, the speaker notes that his beauty is what causes her suffering; his eyes were the weapons by which the wound of love was inflicted on her heart—a traditional theme that is further developed in subsequent sonnets. He is next depicted as a scorpion, an animal whose venom was believed to be curable only by using the same venom as antidote. She begs the god of love to put an end to her suffering; yet, she asks that her love may outlast the torture of Eros. In spite of the almost unbearable pangs of love she is enduring, she is not willing to relinquish desire.

The rest of the sonnets are in French. The change in language signals the subversion that the Petrarchan tradition will undergo in Labé's sonnets. Labé has shown that she is capable of writing a Petrarchan sonnet in excellent Italian; but she chooses instead the idiom of her own country, which was struggling to assert the worth of its language in the face of the prestige of Greek, Latin, and the one Romance language that had established its nobility in the eyes of Europeans of the sixteenth century, Italian. Labé's poetry also subverts the traditional Petrarchan model of the cruel woman dominating a helpless, passive male victim who attempts to woo her with his poetic skills: here the woman suffers at the hands of an indifferent male whom she tries to persuade to return her love, and she does so through the traditionally male activity of writing poetry.

Sonnet II, while drawing on some aspects of typical Petrarchan diction, is a highly original treatment of this theme. As Nicolas Ruwet points out, the first lines of the poem create an intense emotional and erotic climate with their succession of exclamations punctuated by the vocative "o," their lack of transitive verbs leaving the reader in suspense as to precisely what is happening. Until one reads the subsequent sonnets, it is not certain whether the other member of the couple is male or female—a feature reminiscent of some of the poetry of Sappho, whom Labé invoked as a kind of muse in Elegy I. As in the elegies, the beloved is associated in the sonnets with poetry and music: "O lut pleintif, viole, archet et vois" (O plaintive lute, viola, bow and voice) are among the many weapons used by him to kindle love in the heart of the speaker. The accusatory line 11, "Tant de flambeaux pour ardre une femmelle!" (So many torches to inflame the passion of a female!), is striking in its directness, which eschews the often oblique and somewhat mannered style of Petrarchan verse in exchange for a more down-to-earth parlance.

Sonnet III at first appears to be a continuation of its predecessor, since it begins with another series of exclamations marked by the vocative "o." In this poem, however, the accent is on the aftermath of the intense erotic experience hinted at in the previous sonnet. Sonnet III describes the speaker's pitiful present state, which is attributed as much to the cruelty of the gods—in particular, Eros—as to the indifference of the beloved. Throughout Labé's poetry, in fact, there is a constant shifting of blame, now pointing to the beloved, now attributing everything to the malevolence of Eros. Here the intensity of the suffering engendered by unrequited love is expressed in the form of a challenge to the god of love to do his worst, since her body and soul have sustained so many wounds from the arrows of love that there is no more room for any more.

The following sonnet continues the recital of the speaker's torment, which is again attributed to Eros: "Tousjours brulay de sa fureur divine, / Qui un seul jour mon cœur n'abandonna" (I continued to burn, a prey to the flame of love / Which gave me not a single day of rest). She bitterly concludes that this suffering is a deliberate strategy of the god to prove his superiority over men and women, who, in their pride, believe that it is possible to resist him.

Sonnet V renews a traditional conceit of Petrarchan love poetry: that of the suffering lover who hopes that the pangs of love felt during the daylight will be alleviated by night's restful sleep; of course, love's victim soon discovers that he or she will be denied such a respite, since love's torments are so intense that they provoke insomnia. Labé gives new life to this hackneyed theme by addressing a prayer to Venus, invoked not just as the goddess of love but also as a planet and as a fellow woman who becomes both confidante and witness of the speaker's intense suffering.

The return of the absent and recalcitrant beloved is the subject of Sonnet VI; but, as in most of Labé's poems, the ruling verb tense is either the conditional or the future, indicating a wish rather than an actual situation. Here the beloved is compared to the Sun: "ce cler Astre" (this bright [or famous] Star). The adjective *cler* creates a link with the preceding poem, where it was used in the feminine form to refer to Venus, thus establishing a relationship between the two heavenly bodies and between the goddess of love and the beloved. Although Labé uses the hyperbole typical of Petrarchan rhetoric, the tone here is ironic. While in the first quatrain the beloved is compared with the Sun, a not unusual image in Petrarchan verse, the second quatrain feminizes him by stating that the woman lucky enough to kiss him would be kissing "le plus beau don de Flore" (Flora's most beautiful gift), a common periphrasis for the rose. The rose, of course, is almost always used to refer to a female rather than a male beloved, and this unusual comparison can be seen as one of many examples of ironic mockery of the beloved. In the concluding lines of the poem the verb tense becomes the future. With uncharacteristic confidence the speaker predicts that when the beloved returns, she will win back his love, thanks to the power emanating from her eyes—the same eyes that have been shedding such an abundance of tears because of his absence.

Sonnet VII returns to a more usual pleading mode with a rhetorical strategy designed to persuade the beloved that his return is not only desirable but also essential for both of them. The sonnet turns on the definition of death that was still current during the Renaissance: the departure of the soul from the body. This notion is translated into the realm of love, where the speaker and her beloved each have a role in the soul-body duo. In contradistinction to the model proposed by Neoplatonism, in which the partners are (in theory, at least) equal, and a mutual exchange occurs in which each soul leaves its body to take up residence in the body of the other, Labé designates the man as soul—and, therefore, superior ("toy la meilleure part" [you the better part])—while the speaker takes the humbler role of body. Since he, her soul, is absent, she, the body, is in danger of dying; and she appeals to the self-interest of the soul not to allow his body to suffer such a fate because of his absence.

Sonnet VIII returns to an analysis of the strange condition of love and is an exercise in Petrarchan antithesis and hyperbole, given freshness by a strong rhythm created by repetitions and parallelisms. It charts the highs and lows of the experience of passion, which, in the quatrains, resembles a violent illness or fit of madness. The peaks and valleys of this emotional progression are seen not as successive states but rather as coexistent: when the speaker cries "Je vis, je meurs . . ." (I live, I die. . .), it is obvious that she is living and dying simultaneously—a situation repeated throughout the quatrains. The tercets regain a relative calm as they reflect on this highly volatile emotional state, but finally they come to the same conclusion: at the apparent height of ecstasy ("au haut de mon desiré heur"), the speaker is engulfed in her original unhappiness ("Il me remet en mon premier malheur").

The following sonnet treats another common theme of Renaissance love poetry: the vision of the beloved in a dream. No longer plagued by insomnia, the speaker goes to sleep. In this state her spirit leaves her, and in her dream her love is reciprocated. She realizes that it is an illusion, but an imagined consolation is preferable to none at all: "Et si jamais ma povre ame amoureuse / Ne doit avoir de bien en verité, / Faites au moins qu'elle en ait en mensonge" (And if my poor lovesick soul can never enjoy what it desires in real life, / Let it at least enjoy happiness in its own illusion).

In Sonnet X the beloved's association with poetry is once again stressed, and he is compared both to Apollo, god of poetry and father of the Muses, and to Orpheus, the archetypal poet of antiquity. This sonnet is a further exercise in persuasion, since it suggests that, given all his virtues and the praise they evoke, the beloved should be willing to add one more laurel to his crown: that of loving the speaker. In Sonnet II the beloved was apparently impervious to the fire of love he had awakened in her; here he is asked to "De mon amour doucement t'enflamer" (Let the fire of my love set you gently aflame).

The eyes, the messengers and receptors of love in Renaissance imagery that were evoked in the elegies, are the subject of Sonnet XI, which deals with their conflict with the heart. As in Sonnet II, the first line comprises two apostrophes: "O dous regard, ô yeus pleins de beauté" (O sweet look, o eyes so full of beauty). They refer to the beloved's eyes, the source of Eros's arrows; the speaker's eyes are attracted to those of the beloved, allowing love to come into her body and penetrate her heart and thereby introduce torment and suffering into her life. Her eyes continue to be so entranced by his that they do not consider the havoc they are wreaking by allowing his gaze to infect her body with the malady of love. The eyes are betraying the heart by allowing the enemy, Eros, entrance into the body.

The speaker's only consolation for her suffering is the music of her poetry; her lute, the symbol of this activity, provides solace. But in Sonnet XII the lute, although capable of playing a joyful song, refuses, as a faithful companion, to express anything but sadness.

In Sonnet XIII the speaker imagines herself happily in the beloved's arms. Here Labé has recourse to two images that often appear in the love poetry of the period: the ivy that holds a tree in its firm embrace and the kiss that joins the bodies of the lovers and allows their souls to flow into each other's bodies. The kiss results in a kind of death, since when the soul (which, in the Renaissance, is equated with the breath) leaves the body, a form of death results. This death is desirable, since it involves a permanent union with the beloved.

Whereas Sonnet XIII represented the conditional, fantasy world, the following sonnet brings the speaker back into the real world, where she has only her lute and her poetry to console her. Yet, while she still draws breath, she will continue to sing of her love until she can sing no more and no longer can play the role of lover. At the end of Sonnet XIV she asks that death may end her days once her eyes run dry of tears, her voice cracks, and her hand becomes impotent: "Prirary la Mort noircir mon plus cler jour" (I will pray for Death to darken my brightest day).

Sonnets XV, XVI, and XVII continue the speaker's lament and beg for the beloved's return. The first does so in the context of the natural phenomenon of the return of the Sun after each night as the speaker asks the morning breeze *(le Zéphyr)* to persuade her personal Sun, the beloved, to emulate the real Sun, which each morning favors nature with its light and makes the natural world beautiful again. Sonnet XVI, using a combination of meteorological and mythological imagery, evokes a time in the lovers' past when the beloved had reproached the speaker for being tepid in the expression of her feelings for him. Now that her love is in full bloom, the tables are turned, and he is the one who is cold and unresponsive. Sonnet XVII describes how she flees from all the places and activities that remind her of her beloved, but in vain; the memory of his love fills every corner of her being: "Mais j'aperçoy, ayant erré maint tour / Que si je veus de toy estre delivre, / Il me convient hors de moymesme vivre" (But I realize, after attempting to escape, that if I wish to be free of you, / I will have to live outside myself). This possibility could only be realized in death, when her soul would definitively leave her body; but unlike the death of Sonnet XIII, this death would be a separation from the beloved—a solution that she can only reject.

Of course, the ideal way out of her dilemma, and one that she has already evoked, depends on the cooperation of the beloved. This solution is expressed in apparently Neoplatonic terms at the end of Sonnet XVIII, Labé's most often quoted poem: "Baise m'encor, rebaise moy et baise" (Kiss me once again, kiss me once more, kiss me). In Renaissance French *baiser* means simply "to kiss" and does not have its modern sexual connotation. The poem is one of the most sensual examples of the "Kiss" poetry that proliferated at the time and of which the Neo-Latin poet Jean Second, with some two hundred such poems to his credit, was the most prolific exponent. The theme was already present in antiquity—Labé's poem is a partial rewriting of a poem by Catullus dedicated to Lesbia—and in the Bible (the Song of Songs, in particular). In quatrains of this sonnet the sensual rhythms created by alliteration and repetition, and the fact that the speaker appears to be addressing the beloved directly in conversational style—"Las, te plains tu? ça que ce mal j'apaise" (Come now, you're complaining? Come here so that I can make it all better)—give the reader the illusion of viewing an actual love scene. The union seems assured in line 8: "Jouissons nous l'un de l'autre à notre aise" (Let us enjoy one another at our leisure), where the verb *jouir* (to enjoy) suggests much more than mere social enjoyment of each other's company.

The blatant sensuality of the quatrains is somewhat mitigated in the tercets, where the Neoplatonic myth of double death followed by double resurrection resurfaces. Deborah Lesko Baker points out that the spiritual nature of the Neoplatonic reference is considerably muted here; the implication is that the desired union is corporeal and of this world, rather than spiritual and of the world of Ideas. The union of love and folly in line 11 is a perfect echo of the "Débat de Folie et d'Amour": "Permets m'Amour penser quelque folie" (Allow me, my Love, to imagine something that is quite crazy). The speaker imagines leaving her body, as in Sonnet XIII; but whereas the previous departure would have been the equivalent of death, here she images a *saillie* (sallying forth) that will implicitly result in her continuing to live in her beloved's body, into which her spirit will have gained entry through the power of a kiss.

Classical mythology is the basis of Sonnet XIX. The huntress Diana is in a forest surrounded by her nymphs, who are presumably armed, as she is, with bows and arrows. Wandering lovesick and distracted in the forest, the speaker is mistaken for one of Diana's nymphs and told to return to her mistress. The unidentified interlocutor, noting that she has neither bow nor quiver, assumes that she has had an unusually successful hunt. The speaker replies that she had attacked a passerby (the beloved), shooting all her arrows at him but missing each time. He had counterattacked by picking up the arrows and firing them back at her, gravely wounding her. The arrows are figures of the speaker's glance; they are ineffectual against the impervious beloved, whereas his glances are deadly accurate when used against her.

The beloved's ingratitude is the subject of Sonnet XX. The speaker was predestined to fall in love with her beloved and console him after he experienced an unhappy love affair. Whereas she at first saw this scenario as an example of good fortune, she now understands that Eros's malevolence was responsible for her falling in love. She uses the image of a ship foundering in a storm to characterize her present condition, brought about by the departure of the beloved, who apparently feels no gratitude for the consolation she gave him after his rejection by another woman.

A striking feature of female-authored love poetry of the period is that little physical description is given of the male objects of female desire. In direct contrast, in male-authored poetry the description of the woman, even if highly stylized and conventional, is extensive, with the poet lingering longingly and lovingly over every detail of the female body. Ann Rosalind Jones

Title page for the first modern edition of Labé's work (Thomas Cooper Library, University of South Carolina)

pointless for her to try. What she can say—and in this respect the poem is quite anti-Petrarchan—is that no description of the beauty of the beloved could increase her desire, since it is already at its zenith; the power of poetry and rhetoric can have no further effect on her except as a source of consolation.

This comment leads the speaker in Sonnet XXII to deplore once more her beloved's absence and to remark bitterly that if the famous couples of the past had experienced her fate, the whole order of the cosmos, ruled as it is by Love, would have been thrown into jeopardy. Just as the previous sonnet can be seen as an anti-*blason,* the speaker's experience in love is here presented as an antiexemplum; and she herself becomes something of an antiheroine in her own love drama, since she is not in harmony with the natural order of the cosmos.

The penultimate sonnet returns to the *blason* theme, ironizing the beloved's use of traditional male hyperbolic rhetoric in his praise of her: "Las! que me sert qui si parfaitement / Louas jadis et ma tresse dorée" (Alas! what does it avail me now / That you once so perfectly praised my golden locks). She castigates his duplicity now that he has abandoned her. Her only remaining consolation is a vengeful one: she fervently hopes that he is suffering the same martyrdom at the hands of another that he has inflicted on her.

The final sonnet is addressed to the speaker's female readers. She asks for comprehension and compassion and begs to be spared their reproaches for her folly, which has come upon her not of her own choosing but because of the overwhelming power of Eros. The sonnet takes up again the opening theme of the first elegy, while at the same time reprising in a kind of coda her appeal to the "Dames Lyonnaises" in Elegy 3. Baker sees in these appeals an attempt to create a sympathetic community of women readers. But the speaker's appeal for understanding includes a threat: it implies that her female readers should beware of casting the first stone by criticizing her behavior, the power of Eros being so great that even those who think themselves impervious to his charms could fall under his spell at any moment and could endure a fate even worse than that of the speaker. Thus, the last sonnet harks back not only to the initial elegies of the *Euvres* but also recalls implicitly the conclusion of the "Débat de Folie et d'Amour": that folly is an integral part of love and can no more be resisted than can the bonds of Eros himself.

In 1557 Labé purchased a country house near Parcieux-en-Dombes, some twelve miles from Lyon. That same year an anonymous song was published that describes a liaison between her and a Florentine banker. The banker was almost certainly her friend Thomas

suggests that the lack of description in female-authored poetry may result from the fact that there was no model of canonical male beauty for a women poet to adopt; or it may be a way of expressing independence from—and, perhaps, even revolt against—the objectification of woman in male-authored verse. Sonnet XXI has been read as a parody of the *blason,* a genre of sixteenth-century poetry dedicated to singing the praises of the female body. The quatrains pose a series of ironic questions: "Quelle grandeur rend l'homme venerable? / Quelle grosseur? quel poil? quelle couleur?" (How tall does a man have to be to be venerated? / How corpulent? What sort of hair should he have? What color?). In the tercets of this anti-*blason* the speaker gives the reason for her refusal to indulge in lavish physical description of the beloved: love has so clouded her judgment that she is incapable of doing so accurately, and so it is

Fortini, who was a member of the Italian colony in Lyon and invested money for Labé. The song alleges that Labé engaged in the liaison for purely mercenary motives.

Labé's husband died between 1555 and 1557; De Magny's *Odes,* published in Paris in 1559, include a mocking and rather scurrilous reference to him. In 1560 and 1562 Labé bought more land in Parcieux-en-Dombes. The dedicatee of the *Euvres,* De Bourges, probably died in 1562. In 1565 Labé fell ill and moved in with Fortini, who witnessed the will she made on 28 April of that year. She died the following year and was buried on her property in Parcieux-en-Dombes.

Labé's life and work present a fascinating vignette of the possibilities and limitations of women in Renaissance France. On the one hand, in spite of her relatively lowly social situation she was able to obtain an education that in many ways was the equal of what most men received at the time. The social hierarchy was fluid enough to enable her to move in literary, intellectual, and even aristocratic circles, where the high esteem in which she was held is evidenced by the fact that one of the most important publishers in Lyon published and republished her work and that the book included an extraordinary number of laudatory poems. On the other hand, in spite of the relative ease with which Labé moved in the various social circles of Lyon, she remained within her own class by marrying a rope maker. She was also the butt of much criticism, which undoubtedly stemmed more from the fact that she, a woman, dared to write and publish passionate love poetry than from her alleged immoral behavior. Whatever the truth about her lifestyle may be, Labé left a dense, yet remarkably accessible, collection of prose and poetry that includes some of the most striking expressions of female desire in the canon of French literature.

A provocative 2006 book by the French Renaissance specialist Mireille Huchon claims that much of what is "known" about Labé's work is fiction. Huchon does not question Labé's existence but hypothesizes, with the support of a wealth of contemporary documents, that the *Euvres* is the creation of a group of male poets from the Lyon region, including Scève and De Magny, who wrote the texts as a literary hoax to imitate Petrarch's desire to "laudare Laure" (praise Laura) by "louer Louise" (praising Louise). A major objection to Huchon's often convincing demonstration is that the poems in the *Euvres* are far superior to anything that these men–with the exception of Scève–produced in their own works. While Scève's poetry can bear comparison with Labé's, the style of his verse is completely different; it is hard to imagine him writing anything as down-to-earth and as sensual as the poems attributed to her. In any case, Huchon sees him as the presumed author of the prose "Débat de Folie et d'Amour," not of the poems. Whether or not readers find Huchon's arguments persuasive, any subsequent study of Louise Labé will have to take her book into account.

Biography:
Dorothy O'Connor, *Louise Labé: Sa vie et son œuvre* (Paris: Presses françaises, 1926).

References:
Paul Ardouin, *Pernette du Guillet, Louise Labé: L'Amour à Lyon au temps de la Renaissance* (Paris: Nizet, 1981);

Deborah Lesko Baker, *The Subject of Desire: Petrarchan Poetics and the Female Voice in Louise Labé* (West Lafayette, Ind.: Purdue University Press, 1996);

Karine Berriot, *Louise Labé: La belle rebelle et le françois nouveau* (Paris: Seuil, 1985);

Natalie Zemon Davis, *Society and Culture in Early Modern France: Eight Essays* (Stanford, Cal.: Stanford University Press, 1975), pp. 73–86;

Antoine Du Verdier, *La bibliothèque d'Antoine Du Verdier* (Lyon: B. Honorat, 1585), p. 822;

Lawrence E. Harvey, *The Aesthetics of the Renaissance Love Sonnet: An Essay on the Art of the Sonnet in the Poetry of Louise Labé* (Geneva: Droz, 1962);

Mireille Huchon, *Louise Labé une créature de papier* (Geneva: Droz, 2006);

Ann Rosalind Jones, *The Currency of Eros: Women's Love Lyric in Europe 1540–1620* (Bloomington & Indianapolis: Indiana University Press, 1990), pp. 155–200;

Daniel Martin, *Signe(s) d'Amante: L'agencement des Euvres de Louize Labé Lionnoize* (Paris: Champion, 1999);

François Rigolot, *Louise Labé Lyonnaise ou la Renaissance au féminin* (Paris: Champion, 1997);

Nicolas Ruwet, "Un sonnet de Louise Labé," in his *Langage, Musique, Poésie* (Paris: Seuil, 1972), pp. 176–199.

Papers:
Louise Labé's will is in the Archives Départementales du Rhône, Lyon.

Jean de la Ceppède

(1550? – 1623)

Russell Ganim
University of Nebraska–Lincoln

BOOKS: *Imitation des Pseaumes de la Penitence de David* (Lyon: Printed by Jean Tholosan, 1594); revised and enlarged as *Imitation des Pseaumes de la Penitence de David. . . . Seconde édition, reveüe & augmentée de quelques paraphrases d'autres Pseaumes, & pieces de devotion* (Toulouse: Printed by Jacques Colomiez, 1612);

Les Theoremes . . . sur le Sacré Mistere de nostre Redemption, Divisez en trois Livres, Avec quelques pseaumes, et autres meslanges spirituels (Toulouse: Printed by Jacques Colomiez and Raymond Colomiez, 1613);

La Seconde Partie des Theoremes . . . sur les mysteres de la descente de Jesus-Christ aux Enfers, de sa Resurrection, de ses apparitions après icelle, de son Ascension, et de la Mission du S. Esprit en form visible, divisée en quatre Livres (Toulouse: Printed by Colomiez, 1621).

Editions: *Les Theoremes sur le sacré Mystere de nostre Redemption: Reproduction de l'édition de Toulouse de 1613–1622,* preface by Jean Rousset (Geneva: Droz, 1966);

Les Theoremes sur le sacré Mystere de nostre Redemption, 3 volumes, edited by Yvette Quenot (Paris: Société des Textes Français Modernes/Nizet, 1988–1989);

Les Théorèmes sur le sacré Mystere de nostre Rédemption, edited by Jacqueline Plantié (Paris: Champion, 1996).

Edition in English: *From the Theorems of Master Jean de La Ceppède: LXX Sonnets—A Bilingual Edition,* edited and translated, with an introduction, by Keith Bosley (Ashington, U.K.: Mid Northumberland Arts Group / Manchester, U.K.: Carcanet, 1983).

Renewed interest in the lyric of Jean de la Ceppède began in the 1920s with Henri Bremond's discussion of the poet and his work in his *Histoire littéraire du sentiment religieux en France depuis la fin des Guerres de religion jusqu'à nos jours* (1920–1936, Literary History of Religious Sentiment in France from the End of the Wars of Religion to Our Times). While not as well known as his friend and colleague François Malherbe, La Ceppède was nonetheless one of the principal figures in the circle of poets supported by Henri d'Angoulême, governor of Provence from 1576 to 1586. Joining Malherbe and La Ceppède in this literary coterie were authors such as Louis Gallaup de Chasteuil, François du Périer, and César de Nostredame. Based in Aix, this group contributed to a revival of the lyric form that coincided with the Wars of Religion and the other civil strife wracking France at the end of the sixteenth century. In many respects, La Ceppède's life and work represent a call to order in the face of this upheaval.

Born in approximately 1550 in Marseille and descended from a long line of jurists and financial administrators, La Ceppède made law his profession, officially receiving the title of "Conseiller au Parlement d'Aix" (Counsel to the Aix Parlement) in 1578. Eight years later he was named the president of the Cour des Comptes, Aides et Finances de Provence (Court of Revenue, Expenditures, and Finance of Provence), cementing his place among the most influential men in the region.

During this period of relative calm La Ceppède's first poetic work, a short text titled *L'Idée de la Beauté* (1582, The Idea of Beauty), was published, although no copies have survived. All that is known about this publication is that it was dedicated to Henri d'Angoulême and that its title alludes to poem CXIII of Joachim du Bellay's *L'Olive et quelques autres oeuvres poëticques* (1549, The Olive and Other Poetic Works), a fact that probably suggests La Ceppède's Neoplatonism. Three years later La Ceppède married his first wife, a wealthy widow named Madeleine de Brancas. The match assured his financial well-being and produced two daughters: Angélique, born in 1587, followed by Claude, in 1588.

Soon, however, a series of assassinations threw Provence and the rest of France into a state of prolonged turmoil: in 1586 Henri d'Angoulême was murdered, while Henri I de Lorraine, Duke of Guise, and his brother Louis II, Cardinal of Guise, were assassinated in December of 1588. The following year King Henri III was killed, and Henri de Navarre eventually acceded to the throne as Henri IV. This period is characterized by the prolonged struggle for power between the Royalists, the radical Catholic League, which was headed by the

Guise clan, and the Huguenots. Much of southern France, including the cities of Aix, Marseille, and Toulouse, announced allegiance to the Guises.

Meanwhile, La Ceppède consistently sided with the Crown (whether Valois or Bourbon), even at great personal peril. Because of his loyalty to the monarchy, La Ceppède was held captive by members of the Catholic League for part of 1589. He escaped to Avignon, however, and spent much of the early 1590s in that city, frequenting lay and ecclesiastical groups dedicated to a rekindling of the Catholic faith through renewed emphasis on spirituality and religious fervor.

La Ceppède's continuous support of the royal cause can be explained by his belief that the Crown offered the most stability in a time of crisis. Although he sympathized with its hard line against Protestants, the poet felt the Catholic League was too disruptive and unpredictable in the promotion of its agenda. Consequently, La Ceppède remained in the camps of the Valois and the Bourbon dynasties despite the presumably dubious nature of Henri IV's conversion to the Catholic faith.

La Ceppède wrote from Avignon to Henri IV in March 1594. In the letter he reaffirmed his loyalty to the monarchy and asked to regain his former position as president of the Cour des Comptes. By this time the parlement in Aix had recognized the newly converted Henri as king. La Ceppède's request was granted, and he returned for a second administrative term in June 1594.

That year *Imitation des Pseaumes de la Penitence de David* (Imitation of the Psalms and the Penitence of David) was published. The bulk of this work likely was composed during La Ceppède's exile in Avignon. While not specifically political in concept or message, *Imitation des Pseaumes de la Penitence de David* frequently refers to the poet's inner turmoil. This anguish partially reflects the personal and social upheaval the poet experienced during the Wars of Religion. The work features, among other items, lyrical paraphrases of selected Psalms that are followed by meditative commentary the poet calls *penitentiaux* (penitentials). The penitential is a kind of prose continuation of the psalm that reveals the poet's sinful nature and beseeches God's forgiveness. In these pieces La Ceppède sometimes directly lifts images and phrases from the original Psalms, but he often extends his poetic license to create variations on the themes elucidated in the Bible. To a large extent the 1594 edition of *Imitation des Pseaumes de la Penitence de David* attempts to underscore humankind's vulnerability in the face of divine wrath. The promise of redemption exists, but it is often overshadowed by Old Testament notions of punishment and vengeance. In addition to the psalm paraphrases and commentaries, *Imitation des Pseaumes de la Penitence de David* includes Latin hymns and twelve sonnets that serve as a template for his principal work, *Les*

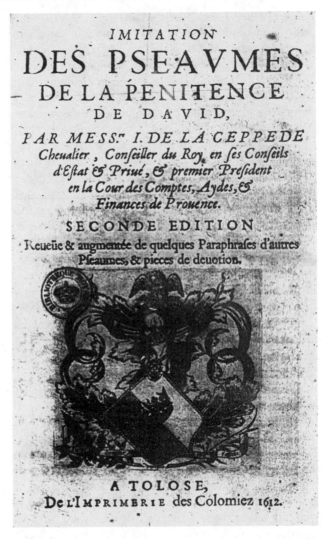

Title page for Jean de la Ceppède's revised version of his first work, published eighteen years earlier (Center for Research Libraries)

Theoremes . . . sur le Sacré Mistere de nostre Redemption (Theorems on the Sacred Mystery of our Redemption), which was published in two parts in 1613 and 1622.

In 1594 La Ceppède returned to Aix and formed an important friendship with Guillaume du Vair, who was named president of the Aix parlement in 1599. A man of letters as well as a skilled politician, Du Vair encouraged the work of the Aixois poets who had flourished under Henri d'Angoulême. Du Vair also assisted La Ceppède in resolving several social and economic issues affecting the region in the early 1600s. The long friendship with Du Vair enhanced La Ceppède's standing as both a literary and a political figure in Provence and in France as a whole.

La Ceppède's status as a landowner increased in 1600 when he purchased an estate at Aygalades, a rich parcel of land between Marseille and Aix. His literary and political reputation was enhanced in November of that year when La Ceppède, along with Du Vair, Malherbe, and others, was selected to speak in honor of Queen Marie de Medici's arrival in Marseille and Aix. In fact, *Les Theoremes . . . sur le Sacré Mistere de nostre Redemption* open with a dedication to Marie, underscoring La Ceppède's fervent support of the monarchy despite the vulnerability of the Crown at this point in French history.

Unexpectedly, however, La Ceppède's long-standing loyalty to the Crown went unrewarded when Henri IV named Jean de Rolland first president of the Cour des Comptes in 1601. Nevertheless, La Ceppède's professional and domestic responsibilities continued to grow. He dealt with persistent instability in Provence while he developed Aygalades, arranged the marriage of his first daughter, Angélique, and secured the entrance of his second daughter, Claude, into a religious order. Then in 1608 Rolland died, precipitating La Ceppède's appointment to the post he had long coveted.

In 1610 Henri IV was assassinated. That year La Ceppède's first wife died, and the following year he married Anne de Faret. During this time he was finishing the first part of the *Les Theoremes . . . sur le Sacré Mistere de nostre Redemption* and beginning the second part. In 1612 a new version of the *Imitation des Pseaumes de la Penitence de David* appeared, published in Toulouse by Jacques Colomiez, known primarily as a printer of religious materials. This second version of the Psalms basically follows the format of the first, but the general message signals redemption over contrition. The more assured mood of the second *Imitation des Pseaumes de la Pénitence de David* probably reflects both the relative political calm that had returned to France after the civil wars and the poet's growing confidence as an artist. Stylistically, the work conforms more to Malherbian standards of clarity and coherence with respect to language and structure. New Testament promises of salvation are reinforced through references to the Holy Trinity, the Virgin Mary, and the Saints. The overall effect is to recontextualize the Psalms and their meaning for a Christian audience.

La Ceppède's second version of the *Imitation des Pseaumes de la Penitence de David* is also included in the 1613 publication of the first part of the *Les Theoremes . . . sur le Sacré Mistere de nostre Redemption*. The works complement each other in their emphasis on self-exegesis and the quest for grace. *Les Theoremes,* however, represents a much more ambitious effort to bring a sense of consistency and totality to the devotional experience.

The two parts of *Les Theoremes* comprise 515 sonnets and more than 2,500 annotations, all precisely and systematically organized. The first part of *Les Theoremes* features three books of 100 sonnets each. In a brief section titled "Cet œuvre est divisé en trois livres" (This Work is Divided into Three Books), La Ceppède provides the reader with an overview of each book. Then each book is preceded by an "Argument," a prose outline of the coming narrative. The first book recounts Christ's departure from Jerusalem, his capture by the Romans, and his subsequent agony in the garden. The second book describes Christ's return to Jerusalem, his trials by both the Sanhedrin and by Pilate, and his eventual condemnation. The third book deals primarily with Christ's suffering and death on the Cross.

Colomiez was also responsible for publishing the second part of *Les Theoremes*. This book was dedicated to Louis XIII, whom La Ceppède received during a royal visit to Provence in 1622. Part 2 follows much the same format as part 1 although it features fewer sonnets. Book 1 consists of 50 poems that describe Christ's descent into hell, the Resurrection, and the emergence from the tomb. Book 2 features 100 sonnets about the apparition from the tomb, the role of the Marys—especially Mary Magdalene—in announcing and verifying Christ's return, and the reaction of the Apostles to the Resurrection. It closes with Christ's order that the Disciples preach the gospel upon his ascent to heaven. The 35 sonnets of book 3 focus on the future arrival of the Holy Spirit and the meaning of the Word in light of the Ascension. The fourth and final book features 30 sonnets describing the descent of the Holy Spirit to Earth and the importance of Holy Scripture and the Church to human life now that Christ has departed for the kingdom of God. Somewhat more ethereal in style and substance than the first part, the second part of *Les Theoremes* complements its better-known predecessor because it further develops many of the prominent images, motifs, and themes. Cross-references—implicit or explicit—abound between the two parts, lending unity to the work and underscoring the totalistic nature of La Ceppède's project.

Throughout the work La Ceppède draws from the Bible and the Church Fathers both to create and defend his interpretation of Christ's Passion, Resurrection, and Ascension. Given his focus on the Passion, consultation of the Bible naturally focuses on the Gospels. However, La Ceppède's interpretation of Matthew, Mark, Luke, and John is often part of a typological construct in which the Old Testament serves as a precursor for the New Testament. Events and personages in the Hebrew Bible not only prefigure the coming of Christ but also find fulfillment in Christ's life and death. Within the Christian dispensation, divine logic dictates that Christ unifies the Bible and therefore all of human history. La Ceppède then reinforces the scholarly dimension of his theodicy through his study of patristic writing. Among the Church Fathers most commonly cited are St. Augustine, St. Jerome, St. John Chrysostom, and Pope Leo the Great.

While biblical narrative and patristic writing form the primary sources of La Ceppède's discourse, he also strengthens the authenticity of his poetry by incorporating allusions to classical mythology, philosophy, and rhetoric, as well as to secular literature. These references, cited in the poems and duly explained in the annotations, demonstrate the totality of God's redemptive plan by underscoring how all erudite expression—whether expository or aesthetic, pagan or Judeo-Christian—finds its ultimate meaning in Christ's death and resurrection. Human thought and art, regardless of their supposed original purpose, find real value only in terms of the contribution they make to a pan-Christian worldview.

From an historical and theological perspective, the most important event that influenced *Les Theoremes* was the Counter-Reformation. The Council of Trent (1545–1563), with its reaffirmation and reform of Catholic doctrine, inspired many Catholic poets, artists, and theologians to underscore their faith in tradition and dogma. In the process they often added a decidedly humanistic dimension that stressed the power of human thought, emotion, and morality in spiritual matters. During the Renaissance the increased importance of religion in the development of a cultural identity for both Catholics and Protestants led to an explosion of artistic and intellectual activity focusing on the human soul and its salvation. Hence, La Ceppède's lyric mirrors not only that of Catholic poets such as Antoine Favre, Philippe Desportes, Jean-Baptiste Chassignet, Lazare de Selve, and Jean Auvray, but also that of contemporary Calvinist poets such as Agrippa d'Aubigné, Théodore de Bèze, Guillaume du Bartas, and Jean de Sponde (a later convert to Catholicism). All of these poets make little distinction between poetic and religious endeavor: literature emerges as an instrument of faith and vice versa. The result is a reinvigoration and redefinition of the poetic enterprise in which the aims of poetry become much higher and the level of reader participation becomes much greater.

La Ceppède considers the reader of *Les Theoremes* to be a *dévot* (devout person) whose task it is to meditate on the poems, internalize them, and when possible, apply their meaning in order to enhance spiritual growth. His work owes much to a revived interest in meditative technique that occurred during the Middle Ages and early Renaissance. Initially, this interest was spurred by widespread reading of St. Augustine, whose writings on the subject focused on a systematic approach to fixating on external objects and investing them with spiritual significance. *Meditationes vitae Christi* (circa 1300, Meditations on the Life of Christ), a work often attributed to St. Bonaventure, also played a key role in popularizing the contemplative method. During La Ceppède's lifetime, meditative practice became more detailed and refined in works such as St. Ignatius Loyola's *Exercitia spiritualia* (1548, Spiritual

Title page for La Ceppède's collection of three hundred sonnets that describe Christ's life from his departure from Jerusalem and capture by the Romans to his death (Thomas Cooper Library, University of South Carolina)

Excercises) and St. François de Sales's *Introduction à la vie dévote* (1609, Introduction to a Devout Life). Loyola's emphasis on the imagination and its importance in helping the *exercitant* to envision and dramatize the significance of various religious stimuli is crucial to defining the reader's role in *Les Theoremes*.

While the writings of Loyola and de Sales give form to La Ceppède's poetry, other meditative treatises, such as those by Antonio de Guevara, Vincent Bruno, Francesco Panigarola, Pierre Crespet, and Francisco Suarez, contribute to the content of *Les Theoremes* by posing theological questions that La Ceppède also raises either in the sonnets or in the many annotations that accompany the lyric text. From both a structural and a thematic perspective, La Ceppède's annotations are his contribution to the meditative genre of the era, featuring his perspective on certain devotional issues and additional material for the reader/ *dévot* to contemplate. The annotations range from simple explanations of literary references to essay-like treatises on the significance of biblical events. The purpose of the annotations is to broaden the artistic and intellectual context of *Les Theoremes* and give the work more authority both with the literate public and with specialists in devotional literature and theology. Consequently, La Ceppède lists his poetic, mythological, historical, and biblical sources in exhaustive detail while providing substantial interpretations of Christ's redemptive act. Such cross-referencing highlights the continuity between *Les Theoremes* and the highest examples of philosophical and spiritual endeavor. They also contribute to the reader's religious and humanistic education.

Because *Les Theoremes* is based on the incidents that occurred in Christ's final days, the narrative is highly episodic. Most of the episodes are presented as sonnet sequences that take the reader through levels of understanding. Scholars generally agree that these levels include a descriptive phase, an interpretive phase, and a spiritual phase. The descriptive phase refers to the account of the primary actions or images; the interpretive phase is an elaboration of the emotional and intellectual significance of the event; and the spiritual phase represents the internalization of the experience on a spiritual–if not mystical–level. Depending on their capacity to apprehend these stages of meaning, meditators are able to develop a progression of cognitive, affective, and sacred states of mind that help them identify with Christ and recognize the need for self-exegesis and personal improvement as members of God's true following.

While it can be assumed that those who actually read *Les Theoremes* were members of the literary and social elite to which La Ceppède himself belonged, the poet states in the *Avant-Propos* (Preface) that his work is written "dedans pour les doctes, & dehors pour les ignorans" (inward for the learned, & outward for the ignorant). This passage indicates that the descriptive passages, which emphasize graphic imagery and outline basic events of the Passion, are primarily aimed at the less cultivated members of his audience. Accordingly, the interpretive and spiritual phases are designed for a sophisticated public able to apprehend the nuances, if not the moral and theological problems, associated with Christ's sacrifice. In other words, *Les Theoremes* should appeal to a wide array of readers who will benefit according to their degree of comprehension. One of La Ceppède's goals was to raise, where possible, the ignorant to the level of the learned. The fact that La Ceppède dedicates the *Avant-Propos* "à la France" (to France) lends a democratic element to the work.

From an intellectual and emotional standpoint, the reader/meditator is prompted to apply biblical examples–especially the example of Christ–to his or her own circumstance in an effort to improve the self. Because it stresses that the faithful can enhance their condition not merely through grace but through learning and discipline, La Ceppède's work clearly reflects the "devout humanism" of the late Renaissance. While belief in God represents a "mystery" for La Ceppède, it is also part of an "education" in which devotion is built as much on knowledge of the divine as it is on those elements of religious experience that remain inscrutable. The etymology of the title of the work, *Les Theoremes,* suggests a heuristic exercise. The notions of "theory" and "contemplation" are supplemented by a process in which incidents in the Passion effectively become "problems" that are explored, if not in some cases resolved, in order to heighten the meditator's cognitive and affective awareness of Christ's sacrifice.

La Ceppède attempts to draw his readers in by creating a sense of intimacy so strong that the *je* (I) of the poet becomes at times indistinguishable from the *je* of the reader or the *je* of the characters. This high degree of identification between the reader and the poet, and between the reader and Christ, enhances the drama of the narrative and engages readers fully in the meditative process. La Ceppède effectively transforms his audience from readers into *dévots* by making them participants in Christ's suffering, death, and Resurrection. The overall result is a fusion of personal, literary, and biblical experience that underscores the comprehensive nature of God's plan for redeeming humanity. The Christian experience is internalized, making the Passion more accessible, while La Ceppède's use of the first-person pronoun emphasizes consciousness of the self as part of the contemplative act. An awareness of the self as an independent moral agent who may choose to accept or reject Christ, a characteristic of modernity, extends and deepens the reader/meditator's role in *Les Theoremes.* Reflecting the spirit of the Counter-Reformation, the self seeks a closer relationship with God while still respecting the teachings and practices of the Church that give the relationship a meaning beyond the self.

La Ceppède's use of the first-person pronoun to develop the voice and persona of the poet situates *Les Theoremes* firmly within the lyric tradition, and the desire to create a sense of intimacy partially explains his choice of the sonnet as his chief mode of expression. La Ceppède exploits the formal rigor of the sonnet and its thematic emphasis on love to produce a discourse that is structurally consistent and able to reflect deep emotional and intellectual change in the poet and reader. Additionally, the form is useful for the meditative format of the work, as sonnets, or parts of sonnets, may be contemplated individually or within the context of a sequence, allowing meditators flexibility in approaching the work.

In *Les Theoremes,* poetry is designed to provide a conduit to the divine. La Ceppède's *Avant-Propos* is crucial to understanding his aesthetic and religious aims: it outlines his desire to save poetry from those who devote the lyric to "folastres & lascives amours" (foolish and lascivious love). While neither a critique of the *Pléiade* nor of the early-seventeenth-century Libertines (known for, among other things, the lewdness of their lyrics), La Ceppède's denunciation of secular love poetry demonstrates a zeal to restore poetry to its former glory as an instrument of celestial communication. Describing poetry as "l'agréable compagne du bel Apollon" (the pleasant companion of beautiful Apollo), La Ceppède expects *Les Theoremes* to win "L'irreprochable tesmognage de ceux, qu'on estime avoir divinement philosophé, appele les espris de la Poësie sacrez & divins" (The irreproachable testimony of those, that one esteems to have divinely philosophized, calls great lovers of sacred and divine poetry). The idea that *Les Theoremes* embody a mission on the part of the author is intriguing because the mission is at once political and artistic. Although the work does not explicitly inveigh against Calvinists or other Protestants, there can be no doubt about its call to reinvigorate the Catholic faithful in the face of the Reform movement. The work not only reaffirms Church teaching but also functions as an example of the theory and practice of a Counter-Reformation literary aesthetic. While not a militant, La Ceppède is a missionary whose objective is to return order to a social and artistic world he sees as chaotic.

The fact that *Les Theoremes* consist of a complete narrative recounted in more than five hundred sonnets has led to questions about the genre to which the work belongs. The text certainly corresponds to the lyric traditions of Renaissance Baroque and Metaphysical poetry, with their characteristic sensuality, spirituality, and theological mystery. Additionally, the Neoplatonic language and imagery of the sonnets have much in common with the works of the *Pléiade,* and references and allusions to the work of Pierre de Ronsard, Bellay, and Remy Belleau can be found in the annotations. But the length of the work, its episodic format, the scale of the combat between God and Satan, and the many comparisons between Christ and the heroes of Homer and Virgil, all give the work an epic quality that adds to its generic complexity. Furthermore, Christ's journey to hell to rescue Hebrew Fathers such as Noah, Abraham, and Isaac is clearly reminiscent of the epic tradition of the *nekuia,* where the protagonist visits the underworld in order to receive instruction or to deliver the stranded from eternal torment. The fact that each sonnet is written in alexandrines also underscores the heroic tenor of the text. In fact, *Les Theoremes* represent a kind of "internal epic" where the readers follow the exploits of the warrior/hero, applying the protagonist's experience to their own. In this way, meditators become characters in the epic as well. Finally, La Ceppède employs a mixed-voice format, typical in the epic tradition, in which the action is recounted by a (presumably) omniscient narrator and the characters themselves. Since La Ceppède's poet-narrator relates his reaction to events, he, like the reader, is involved in the epic as it unfolds.

The generic breadth of *Les Theoremes* is enhanced by the poet's frequent use of the terms *tragique* (tragic) and *tragédie* (tragedy) to describe Christ's final hours. Additionally, the Passion is often referred to as a "triste spectacle" (sad spectacle) with the Virgin, Apostles, and the reader

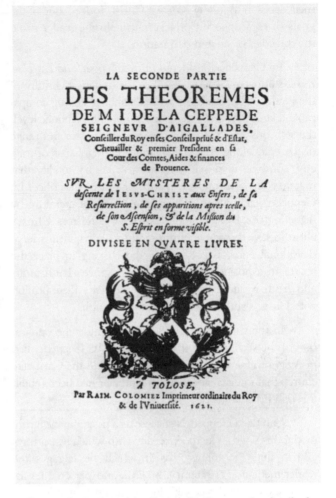

Title page for La Ceppède's collection of 215 sonnets that describe the aftermath of Christ's crucifixion, from his descent into Hell through the advent of the Holy Spirit (from François Ruchon, Essai sur La Vie et L'oeuvre de Jean de La Ceppède, 1953; Thomas Cooper Library, University of South Carolina)

described as witnesses or spectators. In broad, modern terms, *Les Theoremes* are "tragic" in that they evoke a sense of what the seventeenth-century playwright Racine later called "tristesse majestueuse" *(majestic sadness)* in action, character, and tone. At the same time, *Les Theoremes* may be understood as a tragic text in a more classical sense because key Aristotelian elements such as *hamartia* (error in judgment), and catharsis are crucial to the narrative and reading experience. In La Ceppède's work, *hamartia* cannot be committed by characters such as Christ or Mary because they are perfect. But figures such as Judas and Peter are guilty of *hamartia* in their betrayal of Jesus. Peter recognizes his error and finds redemption while Judas does not. Identification with Peter and Judas's betrayals leads to the arousal and purgation of pity and fear in readers who recognize that they could meet either fate depending on their decision to follow or leave Christ. Indeed, one of the goals of La Ceppède's project is to help the reader avoid the tragedies of sin and damnation.

La Ceppède considered himself a poet, and *Les Theoremes* is above all a lyric text, but the generic hybridity of the work is what renders it truly distinctive among comparable texts of the era. On a conceptual and symbolic level, the self-conscious nature of the sonnet, the size and range of the epic, along with the calamity and catharsis of tragedy, combine to provide a sense of literary totality that matches the consummate nature of Christ's sacrifice. La Ceppède's attempt to redeem the whole of literature by depicting the Passion and Resurrection mirrors Christ's effort to save the whole of humanity. Literary means serve devotional ends, with the final goal being to place the reader in a position to receive God's grace. Truth in art and truth in life are found in the reader's identification with Christ's suffering and eventual triumph.

In the summer of 1623, not long after the publication of the second part of *Les Theoremes,* La Ceppède died in Avignon. He was buried at Aygalades in the Carmelite church that initially stood on his land and had been rebuilt through his generosity.

Jean de la Ceppède's success as a poet may be attributed to his vivid style, the intimacy with which he portrays Christ, and the intensity with which he engages the reader/meditator on literary, biblical, and personal levels. His work was well received during his time, as evidenced by the number of laudatory poems published in *Les Theoremes* by counterparts such as Malherbe, Gallaup, and Du Périer. However, it is difficult to determine La Ceppède's influence on the devotional poetry in the period following his death because the genre was in decline. In France religious lyric continued to be written into the mid-to-late seventeenth century but did not flourish. Poets such as Claude Hopil, Martial de Brive, Georges de Brébeuf, and Antoine Godeau achieved a certain amount of recognition, but their work was displaced in favor of Jean de La Fontaine and Nicolas Boileau-Despréaux, whose emphasis on satire, rhetorical dexterity, and literary history was more consonant with the secular mind-set that dominated the beginning and middle of Louis XIV's reign. Furthermore, poetry as a whole was eclipsed by theater and by moralist writing. While devotional poetry in France did not disappear after the seventeenth century, its popularity declined considerably and its composition was often limited to ecclesiastical milieus. In subsequent decades, any hope of reviving the religious lyric died with the French Revolution and the wave of anticlericalism it inspired. In many ways then, La Ceppède and his contemporaries represent the high point in the production of the genre. For critics and students, the legacy of La Ceppède lies in his ability to personalize the language, themes, and conflicts of devotional experience and his efforts to redeem poetry so that humanity may find salvation through literary and spiritual truth.

Biography:

François Ruchon, *Essai sur La Vie et L'oeuvre de Jean de La Ceppède* (Geneva: Droz, 1953).

References:

Henri Bremond, *Histoire littéraire du sentiment religieux en France depuis la fin des Guerres de religion jusqu'à nos jours,* 12 volumes (Paris: Bloud & Gay, 1920–1936);

Terence C. Cave, *Devotional Poetry in France c. 1570–1613* (Cambridge: Cambridge University Press, 1969);

Bernard Chédozeau, *Le Baroque* (Paris: Nathan, 1989);

Paul A. Chilton, "Jean de La Ceppède," in *La poésie française du premier 17ᵉ Siècle: Textes et contextes,* edited by David Lee Rubin (Tübingen: Narr, 1986), pp. 65–96;

Chilton, *The Poetry of Jean de La Ceppède: A Study in Text and Context* (Oxford: Oxford University Press, 1977);

Lance K. Donaldson-Evans, *Poésie et méditation chez Jean de La Ceppède* (Geneva: Droz, 1969);

Russell Ganim, *Renaissance Resonance: Lyric Modality in La Ceppède's Théorèmes* (Amsterdam & Atlanta: Rodopi, 1998);

Ganim, "Rewriting for Redemption: Adapting the Epic in La Ceppède's *Théorèmes*," *EMF: Studies in Early Modern France,* 8 (2002): 43–73;

Myron P. Gilmore, *The World of Humanism, 1453–1517* (New York: Harper, 1952);

Julien Gœury, *L'Autopsie et le théorème: Poétique des Théorèmes spirituels (1613–1622) de Jean de La Ceppède* (Paris: Champion, 2001);

Louis Martz, *The Poetry of Meditation: A Study in English Religious Literature of the Seventeenth Century* (New Haven: Yale University Press, 1954);

Yvette Quenot, *Les Lectures de La Ceppède* (Geneva: Droz, 1986);

Jean Rousset, *La littérature de l'âge baroque en France: Circé et le paon* (Paris: Corti, 1954);

Frank J. Warnke, *European Metaphysical Poetry* (New Haven: Yale University Press, 1961).

Papers:

The library of the Musée Arbaud in Aix-en-Provence has a special archive related to Jean de la Ceppède.

Pierre de La Ramée
(Petrus Ramus, Peter Ramus)
(1515 – 26 August 1572)

Robert B. Rigoulot
University of Illinois at Springfield

BOOKS: *Dialecticae partitiones: Ad celeberrimam & illustrissimam Lutetiae Parisorum Academiam* (Paris: Printed by Jacques Bogard, 1543); enlarged as *Dialecticae institutiones; Aristotelicae animadversiones* (Paris: Printed by Jacques Bogard, 1543);

Oratio de studiis philosophiae et eloquentiae coniungendis (Paris: Printed by Jacques Bogard, 1546);

Brutinae quaestiones in Oratorum Ciceronis (Paris: Printed by Jacques Bogard, 1547); translated by Carole Newlands as "The Questions of Brutus," in *Peter Ramus's Attack on Cicero: Text and Translation of Ramus's* Brutinae Quaestiones, edited by Newlands and James J. Murphy (Davis, Cal.: Hermagoras Press, 1992);

Rhetoricae Distinctiones in Quintilianum (Paris: Printed by Matthieu David, 1549); translated by Murphy and Newlands as *Arguments in Rhetoric against Quintilian Translation and Text of Peter Ramus's* Rhetoricae Distinctiones in Quintilianum (De Kalb: Northern Illinois University Press, 1986);

Pro philosophica Parisiensis Academiae disciplina oratio (Paris: Printed by Matthieu David, 1551);

Oratio initio suae professionis habita (Paris: Printed by Matthieu David, 1551);

Arithmetica (Paris: Printed by André Wechel, 1555); translated by William Kempe as *The Art of Arithmeticke in Whole Numbers and Fractions in a More Readie and Easie Method Then Hitherto Hath Bene Published* (London: Printed by Richard Field for Robert Dextar, 1592);

Dialectique de Pierre de la Ramee (Paris: Printed by André Wechel, 1555); republished as *Dialecticae libri duo* (Paris: Printed by André Wechel, 1556); translated by Roland MacIlmaine as *The Logike of the Most Excellent Philosopher P. Ramus Martyr: Newly Translated, and in Diuers Places Corrected after the Mynde of the Author* (London: Printed by Thomas Vautroullier, 1574; edited by Catherine M.

Pierre de La Ramée (from <http://en.wikipedia.org>)

Dunn, Northridge, Cal.: San Fernando Valley State College Renaissance Editions, 1969);

Audemari Talaei Admonitio ad Turnebum, by La Ramée and Omer Talon (Paris: Printed by André Wechel, 1556);

Quod sit unica doctrinae instituendae methodus (Paris: Printed by André Wechel, 1557);

Ciceronianus (Paris: Printed by André Wechel, 1557);

Oratio de legatione (Paris: Printed by André Wechel, 1557);

Liber de moribus veterum Gallorum (Paris: Printed by André Wechel, 1559);

Liber de Caesaris militia (Paris: Printed by André Wechel, 1559);

Grammatica (Paris: Printed by André Wechel, 1559); translated as *The Latine Grammar of P. Ramus* (London: Printed by Robert Waldegrave, 1585; Amsterdam: Theatrum Orbis Terrarum / New York: Da Capo Press, 1971);

Rudimenta grammaticae (Paris: Printed by André Wechel, 1559); translated as *The Rudimentes of P. Ramus his Latine Grammar* (London: Printed by Robert Waldegrave, 1585 / New York: Da Capo Press, 1971);

Scholae grammaticae (Paris: Printed by André Wechel, 1559);

Algebra, anonymous (Paris: Printed by André Wechel, 1560);

Grammatica Graeca (Paris: Printed by André Wechel, 1560);

Liber de syntaxi Graeca (Paris: Printed by André Wechel, 1560);

Rudimenta grammaticae Graecae (Paris: Printed by André Wechel, 1560);

Gramere, anonymous (Paris: Printed by André Wechel, 1562);

Prooemium reformandae Parisiensis Academiae (N.p., 1562); republished as *Advertissements sur la réformation de l'Université de Paris* (Paris: Printed by André Wechel, 1562);

Oratio de professione liberalium artium (Paris: Printed by André Wechel, 1563);

Libri duo de veris sonis (Paris: Printed by André Wechel, 1564);

Scholae physicae (Paris: Printed by André Wechel, 1565);

Scholae metaphysicae (Paris: Printed by André Wechel, 1566);

Actiones duae habitae in Senatu, pro regia mathematicae professionis cathedra (Paris: Printed by André Wechel, 1566);

Proemium mathematicum (Paris: Printed by André Wechel, 1567);

La Remonstrance de Pierre de la Ramée, faite au Conseil privé, en la chambre du Roy au Louvre, le 18 de Ianvier 1567, touchant la profession royalle en mathematique (Paris: Printed by André Wechel, 1567);

Scholae mathematicae (Basel: Printed by E. Episcopius, 1569);

Petri Rami et Iacobi Schecii epistolae (Basel, 1569);

Defensio pro Aristotle adversus Iacobum Schecium (Lausanne: Printed by Joannes Probus, 1571);

Basilea (Lausanne: Printed by Joannes Probus, 1571);

Testamentum (Paris: Printed by Joannes Richerius, 1576);

Commentariorum de religione Christiana libri quatuor (Frankfurt am Main: Printed by André Wechel, 1576).

Editions in English: *Elementes of Geometrie. Written in Latin by That Excellent Scholler, P. Ramus, Professor of the Mathematicall Sciences in the Vniuersitie of Paris: And Faithfully Translated by Tho. Hood, Mathematicall Lecturer in the Citie of London* (London: Printed by John Windet for Thomas Hood, 1590);

The Art of Logick Gathered out of Aristotle, and Set in Due Forme, According to His Instructions, translated by Samuel Wotton (London: Printed by I. Dawson for Nicholas Bourne, 1626);

Peter Ramus of Vermandois, the Kings Professor, His Dialectica in Two Bookes. Not Onely Tr. into English, but Also Digested into Questions and Answers for the More Facility of Understanding, translated by R. Fage (London: Printed by W. L., 1632);

Via regia ad geometriam: The Way to Geometry. Being Necessary and Usefull, for Astronomers. Geographers. Land-meaters. Sea-men. Engineres. Architecks. Carpenters. Paynters. Carvers, &C. Written in Latine by Peter Ramus, and Now Translated and Much Enlarged, translated by William Bedwell (London: Printed by Thomas Cotes, to be sold by Michael Sparke, 1636);

"That There Is but One Method of Establishing a Science," translated by Eugene J. Barber and Leonard A. Kennedy, in *Renaissance Philosophy: New Translations,* edited by Kennedy (The Hague: Mouton, 1973), pp. 109–155.

OTHER: "Oratio de studiis mathematicis," in *Tres orationes a tribus liberalium disciplinarum professoribus* (Paris: Printed by Jacques Bogard, 1544);

Cicero, *Scipiones Somnium,* commentary by La Ramée (Paris: Printed by Jacques Bogard, 1546);

Cicero, *De fato liber explicatus,* commentary by La Ramée (Paris: Printed by Michel Vascosans, 1550);

Cicero, *Epistola nona ad Publicum Lentulum illustrata,* commentary by La Ramée (Paris: Printed by Michel Vascosans, 1550);

Cicero, *Pro Caio Rabiro oratio illustrata,* commentary by La Ramée (Paris: Printed by Matthieu David, 1551);

Cicero, *De lege agraria orationes illustrata,* commentary by La Ramée (Paris: Printed by Ludovicus Grandinus, 1552);

Cicero, *In Catilinam orationes illustratae,* commentary by La Ramée (Paris: Printed by Ludovicus Grandinus, 1553);

Cicero, *De legibus liber primus illustratus,* commentary by La Ramée (Paris: Printed by Michel Vascosans, 1554);

Virgil, *Bucolica exposita, una com poetae vita,* commentary by La Ramée (Paris: Printed by André Wechel, 1555);

Virgil, *Georgica illustrata,* commentary by La Ramée (Paris: Printed by André Wechel, 1556); republished as *Praelectiones in Virgilii Georgicorum Libros III* (Frankfurt am Main: Printed by the heirs of André Wechel, 1584);

Cicero, *De optimo genere oratorum praefatio illustrata,* commentary by La Ramée (Paris: Printed by André Wechel, 1557);

Préface de Pierre de la Ramée sur le Proëme des mathématiques, in *Lettres patentes du roy, touchant l'institution de ses lecteurs en l'Université de Paris* (Paris: Printed by André Wechel, 1567).

TRANSLATIONS: Plato, *Epistolae Latinae factae et expositae,* translated, with commentary, by La Ramée (Paris: Printed by Matthieu David, 1549);

Aristotle, *Politica,* translated, with commentary, by La Ramée (Frankfurt am Main: Printed by André Wechel, 1601);

Euclid, *Euclides,* translated, with commentary, by La Ramée (Paris: Printed by Thomas Richard, n.d.).

Pierre de La Ramée–known as Petrus Ramus in Latin and as Peter Ramus in English–was one of the most celebrated, and in some circles notorious, of sixteenth-century academicians. A professor at the University of Paris and the principal of one of its colleges who also held a chair in the Collège Royal (the ancestor of today's Collège de France), La Ramée was a proponent of educational reform and a critic of the French university's institutions and curriculum. He published, in Latin and later in French, on a remarkably broad range of topics associated with universities and learning, including all seven of the traditional liberal arts and the literature and philosophy of antiquity. He was a controversialist in an age of great controversies, regularly taking part in scholarly disputes. Some of his contemporaries conjectured that his taste for disputation may have lead to his violent death in the aftermath of the St. Bartholomew's Day Massacre.

At the heart of La Ramée's program of educational reform lay his attempt to reform the discipline of logic. His *Dialectique de Pierre de la Ramee* (1555, Dialectic of Peter de La Ramée; translated as *The Logike of the Most Excellent Philosopher P. Ramus Martyr,* 1574) was intended to free students from the complexities of Scholastic logic so that they could pursue more-practical or rewarding studies. By no means a formal logic in the sense that its predecessors had been, the *Dialectique* was embraced by several generations of writers and orators who were intrigued by its promise of generating and

organizing arguments for any occasion; it had appeared in around three hundred editions by the end of the century and has been called the only work of technical philosophy in French before René Descartes. Its influence extended to Germany, to England, and finally to colonial New England. "Ramism" has become a catchword for several approaches derived from La Ramée's logical writings, which promised, through the application of a "single method," to make the most abstruse arts or sciences comprehensible. Ramism's failures as a system of logic have long since been exposed, but Ramism and its relations to the intellectual currents of the sixteenth century continue to inspire scholarly inquiry.

La Ramée was born in Cuts, a small town in Picardy, in 1515. Much of what is known about his family and childhood comes from his conversations with students. According to the memoirs they left of their teacher, La Ramée's ancestors were of the nobility; but his grandfather had been reduced in status and wealth and had become a charcoal burner. La Ramée's father, Jacques, was a laborer who died when La Ramée was quite young. La Ramée was raised by his mother, Jeanne, née Charpentier, whom he faithfully supported after he became a successful academic.

La Ramée learned the rudiments of grammar– that is, reading and writing–from the local schoolmaster. He began his studies at the Collège de Navarre of the University of Paris when he was twelve, which was a rather advanced age for that era. To support himself he became the servant of a wealthy student; he later regaled his own students with stories of how he had balanced his conflicting duties as servant and scholar by getting by with less sleep than his fellows. Doing without sleep remained a habit for the rest of his life and may help account for La Ramée's astonishing productivity and his success as a university administrator.

The University of Paris traced its origins to the twelfth century, when teachers such as Peter Abelard established their own schools outside the cathedral schools and monasteries. It was organized into four faculties: Liberal Arts and the professional schools of Theology, Medicine, and Law. Students were housed, fed, and for the most part taught in the colleges, foundations much like those that were then emerging in the English universities. Teaching at the university was still rooted in medieval Scholastic philosophy, in which Aristotelian logic, especially the syllogism and dialectic, was considered the basis of all knowledge. The Liberal Arts, especially those of the Trivium–grammar, logic, and rhetoric–were taught according to the conventions of instruction in dialectic. These conventions included the *lectio* (reading and commentary on a text): professors carried on scheduled courses of readings to the students of their colleges in which they elucidated the assigned text page by page and phrase by phrase. From time to time they engaged in public disputations with their colleagues over textual interpretation; the disputations were conducted and judged according to dialectical standards.

La Ramée rebelled against this traditional method of teaching, which he considered "poisonous" and unproductive. He found antidotes to Scholasticism in humanistic educational theory and in the philosophy of Plato. Humanists had begun exploring alternatives to Scholastic logic in the fourteenth century; in the fifteenth century, humanist teachers had challenged Scholastic teaching methods. Humanism proposed a logic that would be of practical, everyday use to students: a method that would facilitate rapid mastery of the subjects that confronted them on their way to academic and worldly success. Around 1529 La Ramée began attending courses on logic offered by the humanist Johann Sturm. Sturm's teaching methods, particularly his use of literary ornament and examples to illustrate philosophical points, intrigued La Ramée as an alternative to the Scholastic style of teaching. Around the same time, he read the works of the second-century Greek physician Galen, which led him to read Plato's dialogues. What attracted him most about the dialogues, he claims in the *Dialectique,* was the "spirit" in which Socrates refuted false opinions while lifting his auditors above the level of their own prejudices.

Also during this period La Ramée established a relationship with Charles de Lorraine, a fellow student at the Collège de Navarre. Lorraine's importance for La Ramée's career cannot be overestimated. A member of the powerful and ambitious Guise family, he went on to achieve prominence in the Church hierarchy and the French court as archbishop of Reims in 1538, cardinal of Guise in 1547, and cardinal of Lorraine and bishop of Metz in 1550. Lorraine's friendship and appreciation of La Ramée's intellectual goals brought the poor scholar the first preferments of his career, provided him with a platform to publicize his ideas, and protected him from his academic rivals.

La Ramée was granted the master of arts degree, which permitted him to teach at the university, in early 1536. This presumably unexceptional achievement became the basis for one of the dramatic legends about his life: candidates for the master's degree were tested by disputing a thesis in the presence of the faculty; according to the legend, La Ramée chose to defend the statement "quaecumque ab Aristotele dicta essent, commentitia esse" (that all that Aristotle said was falsehood) and successfully maintained it through a day of argumentation, brilliantly turning the weapons of the dialecticians against them. The tale, which exists in several versions, is no more outrageous than Voltaire's claim

that La Ramée was murdered as a result of a debate between the humanists of the Collège Royal and the obscurantist theologians of the Sorbonne over the pronunciation of the words *quisquis* and *quamquam.* Such stories reinforce La Ramée's posthumous reputation as the rebellious champion of academic integrity who could not be intimidated by the forces of intellectual authoritarianism.

La Ramée taught first at the Collège du Mans and then at the Collège de l'Ave Maria, where he organized and taught his courses after the example of Sturm. He made friendships and established collaborative relationships that served him well in his writing projects and his controversies. One lengthy collaboration, with a professor of rhetoric named Omer Talon (Audomarus Talaeus), was so close that scholars have in some cases despaired of telling their work apart.

La Ramée scandalized the university community in 1543, when his first two works, "Dialecticae institutiones" (Training in Dialectic) and "Aristoteles animadversiones" (Remarks on Aristotle), were published in one volume by the printer Jacques Bogard. It seems unlikely that the first of these works, a brief outline of a system of logic in the humanistic tradition, by itself would have attracted such immediate attention in the Paris academic community. "Dialecticae institutiones" was La Ramée's first attempt to reform dialectic according to humanistic principles. This approach, first laid down by Lorenzo Valla in the fourteenth century and further developed by Rodolphus Agricola in the late fifteenth, sought to replace Scholastic logic with a logic derived from rhetoric. Their aim, according to Paul Oskar Kristeller, was clarity of expression in teaching and literary composition, rather than the scientific precision that had been the goal of the Scholastics. In "Dialecticae institutiones" La Ramée turns the concepts of "invention" and "disposition," borrowed from traditional rhetoric, into a system for defining and organizing the terms of a discourse and transforming them into meaningful statements about the subject at hand. The second work, however, was clearly intended to incite controversy. In "Aristotles animadversiones" La Ramée claims that Aristotle and his followers corrupted the older and truer dialectic of Socrates and Plato. Charles Waddington and Walter J. Ong, who agree on little else, characterize the tone of the work as one of unrestrained invective. The Aristotelians are obscurantists; their logic is ineffective and confused and should be replaced by one that combines the best elements of philosophy and eloquence.

The reaction to La Ramée's provocation was quick. Two members of the Liberal Arts faculty, Joachim de Perion and Antonio de Gouveia, rushed into print to attack him. After their pamphlets appeared, the rector of the university asked the Faculty of Theology to issue a judgment on La Ramée's two works. He also asked the Parlement of Paris, the supreme court of the realm, to issue an *arrêt* suppressing both texts as false and contrary to good public order. The affair was brought to the attention of King François I, who had become sensitive to the subversive potential of print and had instituted a form of censorship. He ordered a debate between La Ramée and Gouveia, to be judged by a university commission. After the accusations against La Ramée were upheld by the panel in March 1544, the king forbade him to lecture from his works or to have them copied or distributed, and printers and booksellers were prohibited from publishing or selling them. La Ramée was further forbidden to lecture on dialectic or any form of philosophy without royal permission. In an aside in his *Scholae mathematicae* (1569, Lectures on Mathematics) La Ramée compares his situation to that of his hero Socrates: "I lacked nothing but the hemlock."

For the remainder of François's reign La Ramée's conduct was relatively discreet. He and Talon continued their program of combining the teaching of philosophy and eloquence at the Collège de l'Ave Maria; but it appears that in deference to the royal order, Talon taught philosophy while La Ramée lectured on poets and orators. In early 1545 La Ramée accepted an invitation to take over the direction of the Collège de Presles from its ailing principal.

When François I died at the end of March 1547, La Ramée's academic fortunes began to change for the better. Lorraine, who had accepted La Ramée's dedication of his first two works and remained loyal to him through his difficulties, persuaded the new king, Henri II, to lift the ban on La Ramée's philosophy. In 1551 Lorraine successfully lobbied Henri to create the chair of Regius Professor of Philosophy and Eloquence at the Collège Royal for La Ramée, providing him an academic base where he was safe from his rivals at the university.

With the ban on his teachings lifted, La Ramée was free to proceed with his reforms. First, he returned to the campaign against the ancient authorities on logic and rhetoric he had launched in "Aristoteles animadversiones." In 1547 he published *Brutinae quaestiones in Oratorum Ciceronis* (Brutus's Problems on the Oration of Cicero; translated as "The Questions of Brutus," 1992); dedicated to Henri II, the work is an attack on the Roman orator's theory of rhetoric in *De Oratore* (55 B.C., On the Orator). In *Rhetoricae Distinctiones in Quintilianum* (1549; translated as *Arguments in Rhetoric against Quintilian,* 1986) he condemns Quintilian's *Institutio oratoria* (circa 92–94, Training in Oratory) as illogical and unmethodical. James J. Murphy shows that in La

Ramée's eyes the chief sin of both authors was having been misled by "Aristotelian" theories.

In 1555 Wechel published *Dialectique de Pierre de la Ramee;* he followed it the next year with the Latin version, *Dialecticae libri duo* (Dialectic in Two Books). In terms of both number of editions and influence, it is the most significant of La Ramée's works. La Ramée's logic is an elaborate and continually evolving procedure for creating discourse, the central purpose of which is to simplify a subject so that it can be easily apprehended. "Invention" classifies the arguments, which are the elements of a discourse; defines them; and places them within an organizing scheme. "Judgment" examines their relationships and produces axioms—self-evident statements that La Ramée considers more reliable than the syllogism—and other related statements about the subject.

To his contemporaries, the most attractive aspect of La Ramée's logic may have been his concept of "method." His concept is not the modern one of a series of steps to investigate phenomena that are not yet understood; instead, it is a way to learn an already extant discipline. Method emerges from invention as the means of organizing or classifying arguments. Each art or discipline has its own rules, which will reveal themselves to methodical investigation. As early as the "Dialecticae institutiones," La Ramée had taken advantage of the potential of typography to present method visually. A printed chart shows, beginning on the left margin of the page, how by means of progressive divisions—usually, bifurcations—a subject can be reduced to groups of smaller parts until, at the right margin, one is left with its most basic elements. Most later works in the Ramist tradition feature elaborate and visually striking dichotomizing tables that summarize their content and major points spatially.

Although the *Dialectique* was soon overtaken in number of editions by the *Dialecticae libri duo,* it marks a new interest on La Ramée's part in French as an artistic and scholarly language. In furtherance of his program of combining philosophy with eloquence, La Ramée recruited writers of the most elegant modern French he could find, Pierre de Ronsard and the other members of the Pléiade, to translate his citations from classical Greek and Latin into the vernacular. He discusses the potential of French in *Ciceronianus* (1557, The Ciceronian)–which, paradoxically, is written in Latin. Marc Fumaroli shows that La Ramée believed that French would develop into a literary language by imitating the languages of classical antiquity, just as Latin had developed through imitation of Greek, and by searching the works of its own poets and authors for examples of *bona consuetudo* (good usage); examples of the best French oratory, he thought, could be found among the judges of the *parlements* and in the "sacred eloquence" of the preaching clergy. La Ramée's own learning remained almost exclusively Latin, but he believed that French would inevitably be taught in the schools and that it should be the subject of a methodical program of teaching. His French grammar appeared in 1562. Later, he arranged for several of his Latin works to be translated into French.

What sort of orator La Ramée himself was remains a matter of debate. The university chose him to speak on its behalf in matters of importance. Ong discerns in some of his printed orations a histrionic tendency to play to the lowest common denominator in his audience; yet, Ong also describes a 1551 oration before the university body as both personal and eloquent. After scouring the literature of the period for references to La Ramée's speaking style, Waddington concludes that his language was directed to the man of affairs and that he was perceived as speaking *en seigneur* (in a lordly manner). As a teacher, he was criticized by other faculty members for training his students to debate, pose, and gesture in a manner that was too mature for their years.

Ramist method became popular because it brought results, as La Ramée himself showed in his reading of Julius Caesar's memoirs of the Gallic wars—first according to a Socratic understanding of the human virtues, then according to the topics of military art. *Liber de moribus veterum Gallorum* (1559, Book on the Customs of the Ancient Gauls) is a portrait of the life of the Gauls at the time of their conquest by Caesar; *Liber de Caesaris militia* (Book of Caesar's Military Science) lays out the principles of Roman military technique. Published in a French translation, *Traicte des façons et coustumes des anciens Galloys,* by the diplomat Michel de Castelnau at the same time the Latin version appeared, *De moribus veterum Gallorum* shared in the popular esteem that other works on the nation's origins enjoyed during that era.

In January 1557 Henri II had named La Ramée to a commission charged with the reform of studies at the University of Paris. Henri died in 1559; in 1562 La Ramée submitted a report, apparently his work alone, to Henri's widow, Catherine de Médicis, and son, King Charles IX. It was printed that same year as *Prooemium reformandae Parisiensis Academiae* (Notes on the Reform of the University of Paris). As a member of the humanist movement, La Ramée recommended that the works of medieval authors be replaced in the curriculum by those of classical authors. He also recommended that student fees be lowered by reducing the number of lecturers in the colleges, that the Trivium be taught entirely within the colleges, and that a corps of state-paid professors be entrusted with higher and professional instruction. There was no opportunity to implement the recommendations: the Wars of Religion virtually destroyed the university and drove off its students.

With the outbreak of the first war in March 1562, La Ramée's position at the university and in the city of Paris became tenuous at best. For much of his career he had been rumored to be a Protestant, but he seems to have converted to Calvinism only in 1561. When La Ramée fled the city for Fontainebleau near the end of 1562, he was replaced as principal of the Collège de Presles; he had to sue to get his place back when he returned after the war ended in March 1563. While La Ramée was away, his friend Talon died, and his relationship with his protector, Lorraine, ended because of his conversion to Protestantism. During the second War of Religion (1567–1568), La Ramée again fled Paris, taking refuge with the Protestant army of Louis de Bourbon, Prince of Condé. When he returned to his college, he discovered that he had again been replaced and that his library had been burned. He solicited Charles IX for permission to make an extended tour of the learned institutions of Germany and Switzerland. Equipped with a royal *laissez-passé,* he and two companions went to Strasbourg, where he was received by his old professor, Sturm. He spent the next two years abroad, visiting scholars and teaching at various institutions, and began to write his only religious work, *Commentariorum de religione Christiana libri quatour* (1576, Commentary on the Christian Religion). He also engaged in a controversy over method with the philosopher-physician Jacobus Schegk. By this time his projects for curriculum reform were well advanced. He and his colleagues had written on all three subjects in the Trivium and arithmetic and geometry, half of the subjects in the Quadrivium. He returned to Paris in 1570.

Although he resumed his chair as Regius Professor at the Collège Royal, Pierre de La Ramée did not regain the right to teach after his return. Nevertheless, under the protection of the king and queen mother, La Ramée had every reason to believe that he was safe when the St. Bartholomew's Day Massacre of Protestants occurred on 24–25 August 1572; but on 26 August he was murdered in his room by men who had deliberately sought him out. Some contemporaries argued the men had been hired by Jacques Charpentier, a rival whose candidacy for a chair in the Collège Royal had been opposed by La Ramée; most modern scholars discount this theory and believe that he was simply a victim of the massacre because of his religious sentiments. To his Protestant admirers, especially in England, he became "Peter Ramus Martyr," a victim of papist intolerance. Others, such as Voltaire and Pierre

Bayle, saw him as a victim of obscurantism and a martyr to freedom of thought.

Bibliography:

Walter J. Ong, S.J., *Ramus and Talon Inventory: a Short-Title Inventory of the Published Works of Peter Ramus (1515–1572) and of Omer Talon (Ca. 1510–1562) in Their Original and in Their Variously Altered Forms. With Related Materal: 1. The Ramist Controversies: A Descriptive Catalogue. 2. Agricola Check List: a Short-Title Inventory of Some Printed Editions and Printed Compendia of Rudolph Agricola's* Dialectical Invention (De inventione dialectica) (Cambridge, Mass.: Harvard University Press, 1958).

Biographies:

Charles Waddington, *Ramus: Sa vie, ses écrits et ses opinions* (Paris: Meyrueis, 1855);

Charles Desmaze, *P. Ramus: Savie, ses écrits, sa mort* (Paris: Cherbuliez, 1864).

References:

Nelly Bruyère, *Méthode et dialectique dans l'œuvre de La Ramée: Renaissance et Age Classique* (Paris: Vrin, 1984);

Philippe Desan, *Naissance de la méthode: Machiavel, La Ramée, Bodin, Montaigne, Descartes* (Paris: Nizet, 1987);

Mordechai Feingold, Joseph S. Freedman, and Wolfgang Rother, eds., *The Influence of Petrus Ramus: Studies in Sixteenth and Seventeenth Century Philosophy and Sciences* (Basel: Schwabe, 2001);

Marc Fumaroli, *L'Age de l'éloquence: Rhétorique et "res literaria" de la Renaissance au seuil de l'époque classique* (Geneva: Droz, 1980);

Neal Gilbert, *Renaissance Concepts of Method* (New York: Columbia University Press, 1960);

Frank Pierrepont Graves, *Peter Ramus and the Educational Reformation of the Sixteenth Century* (New York: Macmillan, 1912);

Lisa Jardine, "Humanism and the Teaching of Logic," in *The Cambridge History of Later Medieval Philosophy,* edited by Norman Kretzman and others (Cambridge: Cambridge University Press, 1982), pp. 797–807;

Paul Oskar Kristeller, "Renaissance Philosophy and the Medieval Tradition," in his *Renaissance Thought and Its Sources,* edited by Michael Mooney (New York: Columbia University Press, 1979), pp. 106–133;

Kees Meerhoff, *Rhétorique et poétique au XVIe siècle en France: Du Bellay, Ramus et les autres,* Studies in Medieval and Reformation Thought, volume 36 (Leiden: Brill, 1986);

Norman Edward Nelson, *Peter Ramus and the Confusion of Logic, Rhetoric, and Poetry,* University of Michigan Contributions in Modern Philology, no. 2 (Ann Arbor: University of Michigan Press, 1947);

Guido Oldrini, *La disputa del metodo nel Rinascimento: Indagini su Ramo e sul ramismo* (Florence: Le lettere, 1997);

Walter J. Ong, S.J., *Ramus, Method, and the Decay of Dialogue: From the Art of Discourse to the Art of Reason* (Cambridge, Mass.: Harvard University Press, 1958);

Ramus et l'université (Paris: Rue d'Ulm, 2004);

André Robinet, *Aux sources de l'esprit cartésien: L'Axe La Ramée-Descartes. De la* Dialectique *des 1555 aux* Regulae (Paris: Vrin, 1996);

Peter Sharratt, "The Present State of Studies on Ramus," *Studi Francesi,* 26, fascicle 2–3 (1972): 1–13;

Sharratt, "Ramus 2000," *Rhetorica: A Journal of the History of Rhetoric,* 18 (2000): 399–455;

Sharratt, "Recent Work on Petrus Ramus (1970–1986)," *Rhetorica: A Journal of the History of Rhetoric,* 5 (1987): 7–58;

James Veazie Skalnik, *Ramus and Reform: University and Church at the End of the Renaissance* (Kirksville, Mo.: Truman State University Press, 2002).

Pierre de Larivey

(20 July 1541 – 12 February 1619)

Catherine E. Campbell
Cottey College

BOOKS: *Les Six Premieres comedies facecieuses de Pierre de Larivey, Champenois: A l'imitation des anciens Grecs, Latins, et modernes Italiens. A sçavoir: Le Laquais. La Vefve. Les Esprits. Le Morfondu. Les Jaloux. Les Escolliers* (Paris: Printed by Abel L'Angelier, 1579)—*La Vefve* translated by Catherine E. Campbell as *The Widow (La Veuve)* (Ottawa: Dovehouse, 1992); *Les Esprits* translated by Jean-Charles Seigneuret as *The Spirits,* in *Four French Renaissance Plays,* edited by Arthur P. Stabler (Pullman: Washington State University Press, 1978), pp. 109–214;

Trois comedies des six dernieres de Pierre de Larivey Champenois: A l'imitation des anciens [sic] *Grecs, Latins et Modernes italiens. A sçavoir: La Constance. Le Fidelle. Et les Tromperies* (Troyes: Printed by Pierre Chevillot, 1611);

Almanach, 6 volumes, as Claude Morel (Troyes: Printed by Jean Oudot, 1611–1616, 1618).

Editions: *Les Esprits: Comédie, adaptation en trois actes,* edited by Albert Camus (Paris: Gallimard, 1953);

Les Esprits, edited by Donald Stone Jr. (Cambridge, Mass.: Harvard University Press, 1978);

Les Esprits, edited by Michael J. Freeman (Exeter, U.K.: University of Exeter Press, 1978);

Le Laquais: Comédie. Edition critique, edited by Madeleine Lazard and Luigia Zilli (Paris: Nizet, 1987);

Le Fidèle, edited by Zilli (Paris: Cicéro, 1989);

Les Tromperies: Edition critique, edited by Keith Cameron and Paul Wright (Exeter, U.K.: University of Exeter Press, 1997).

PLAY PRODUCTION: *Le Fidelle,* Paris, Théâtre du Chaillot, 1989.

TRANSLATIONS: Giann francesco Straparola, *Les Facétieuses nuits* (N.p., 1576);

Anton Francesco Doni, Ibn al-Muqaffa', and Agnolo Firenzuola, *Deux Livres de Filosofie fabuleuse: Le premier prins des discours de M. Ange Firenzuola Florentin. Par lequel soubs le sens allegoric de plusieurs belles fables, est monstree l'enuye, malice, & trahison d'aucuns courtisans. Le second, extraict des Traictez de Sandebar Indien Philosophe moral, traictant soubs pareilles alegories de l'Amitié & choses semblables* (Paris: Printed by Abel L'Angelier, 1577);

Alessandro Piccolomini, *L'Institution morale* (Paris: Printed by Abel L'Angelier, 1581);

Lorenzo Capelloni, *Les Diuers discours de Laurent Capelloni, sur plusieurs examples & accidens meslez, suiuis, & aduenuz* (Troyes: Printed by Michel Sonnius / Paris: Printed by Jean le Noble, 1595);

Pietro Aretino, *Trois Livres de l'humanité de Jesuchrist* (N.p., 1604);

Barthélemy Arnigio, *Les Veilles* (Troyes: Printed by P. Chevillot, 1608).

Pierre de Larivey was the most prolific author of comedies during the French Renaissance. Some scholars dispute this title, since all of his plays are adaptations of contemporary Italian comedies; yet, his versions are better known than their sources. Larivey's translations contributed to the establishment of Italy's literary influence on the French Renaissance. Larivey wrote his plays in prose, the language of the common people he depicted; this choice was not repeated in French comedy until Molière in the following century.

Larivey was born in Troyes on 20 July 1541. Little is known of his early life. Some sources indicate that his family was of Florentine origin and named Giunti (The Arrived), which was originally translated into French as L'Arrivé. He published his first work, *Les Facétieuses nuits* (Facetious Nights), in 1576; it is a translation of the second book of Giann francesco Straparola's *Piacevoli notti* (1550–1553; translated as *The Nights of Straparola,* 1894). The following year he published *Deux Livres de Filosofie fabuleuse* (Two Books of Fabulous Philosophy), based on Anton Francesco Doni's *La moral filosofia* (1552, Moral Philosophy) and on *Kalila wa Dimna* (Kalila and Dimna), a collection of fables translated into Arabic from a fourth-century Sanskrit source by Ibn al-Muqaffa' in the eighth century and into Italian by Agnolo Firenzuola (pseudonym of Michelangelo Giovannini) as *La prima veste dei discorsi degli animali* (The First Appearance of the Discourses of the Animals) in 1548. The volume includes a sonnet by Guillaume Le Breton. The Arabic version features a gentle and reasonable jackal, Kalila, and his mean and jealous brother, Dimna. After various translations into languages lacking a word for jackal, by the time Larivey tells the story the animals have been transformed into sheep.

In 1581 Larivey published *L'Institution morale* (Moral Institution) his translation of Alessandro Piccolomini's *Della Institutione morale* (1560). The greatest problem Larivey confronted in his translation was the imprecision of French in contrast with Italian in the expression of philosophical ideas. Larivey dedicated the volume to a Monsieur de Pardessus, a member of the Parlement of Paris, counselor to the king, and canon of Paris. Jean Balsamo, in his article in Yvonne Bellenger's 1993 collection, says that this work marked the beginning of philosophy in French; but it is ignored by most Larivey scholars, who concentrate on his plays, and by historians of French philosophy, who regard Larivey as a playwright and translator.

Larivey is the only dramatist of the French Renaissance who wrote comedies exclusively. Pietro Toldo notes that in adapting his source plays for the French stage, Larivey changed the settings from Italy to Paris and Troyes; removed or altered allusions to historical events and customs; changed characters' names from Italian to French; shortened or deleted scenes and abridged long speeches; and eliminated characters—especially women, whose roles were usually played by boy actors. He did not hesitate to translate the greatest obscenities, but he suppressed religious jibes as much as possible. Finally, he did freely changed or commented on passages where the original text was unclear or the motivations for actions unconvincing.

Larivey published his first six plays in a single volume in 1579: *Le Laquais* (The Lackey), adapted from Lodovico Dolce's *Il Ragazzo* (1541); *La Vefve* (translated as *The Widow*, 1992), from Nicolo Buonaparte's *La Vedova* (1568); *Les Esprits* (translated as *The Spirits*, 1978), from Lorenzino de Medici's *Aridosia* (1536); *Le Morfondu* (The Frozen Man), from Anton Francesco Grazzini's *La Gelosia* (1568, Jealousy); *Les Jaloux* (The Jealous Men), from Vincenzo Gabbiani's *I Gelosi* (1551); and *Les Escolliers* (The Students), adapted from Girolamo Razzi's *La Cecca* (1563, The Magpie). In each case Larivey transposes the action from Italy to Paris, gives French names to the main characters, and eliminates some lesser characters; but he leaves the plots almost entirely intact. Most of the plays have the same basic plot: two young people are in love; a parent or guardian does not want them to marry; an older man is foolishly in love with the girl; love triumphs; and the young couple ends up together.

In *Le Laquais* the servant Jacquet is disguised as a girl, and the old man, Symeon, spends the night with him instead of with the girl both he and his son love. Meanwhile, the son and the girl are together; Symeon's daughter

elopes with her beloved; and Symeon's servant robs his master. In the end Symeon agrees to the marriages and forgives everyone for deceiving him. The prologue to the play presents a moral lesson: old men should learn to be more moderate and less given to the pleasures of Venus.

In *La Veuve* Bonaventure, a stranger in Paris, wants to marry Madame Clemence, who is supposedly a widow but is actually Bonaventure's wife, who was believed drowned in a shipwreck; why he does not recognize her is not explained. A courtesan, also named Clemence, tries to convince Bonaventure that she is his wife. In the end Bonaventure picks the right woman, and their reunion is happy. Subplots involve an old man, Ambroise, who is also in love with Madame Clemence but ends up in bed with the procuress Guillemette; and Constant, a young man who is in love with one girl but ends up with her cousin, who is better suited to him.

Considered Larivey's best play, *Les Esprits* is about three young men in love: Urbain and Fortuné, the sons of Severin, and Désiré, who loves Severin's daughter. The obstacle to the accomplishment of the various pairings is Severin, the most miserly man in Paris. To help the young people, Severin's servant, Frontin, distracts the old man: at one point he tries to keep Severin from entering his house by telling him that it is haunted; later, he brings in a sorcerer to exorcize the house in exchange for Severin's ring, which Urbain needs to pay his debts. At the end Severin discovers that his purse, which he had buried to keep it from being stolen, has been stolen anyway and that his children have disobeyed him. He forgives them, stating that avarice serves no purpose. The play may have served as the model for Molière's *L'Avare* (1668; translated as *The Miser*, 1672).

In *Le Morfondu* an old man, Lazare, is so jealous of the girl he loves that he nearly freezes to death while spying on her one night. She is in love with someone else, with whom she is spending that cold night. *Les Jaloux* includes several jealous characters and involves tricks, disguises, inventions, and lies, all devised by a clever valet. More interesting than the plot, however, is a secondary character, the braggart soldier Captain Fierabras (the name means "Proud of His Arm"), who has mounted a guard to protect his sister but lets her lover enter when the young man disguises himself as a valiant soldier being pursued by the law. In this play Larivey takes special care that each character's dialogue accurately reflect his or her station in life.

Les Escolliers is set in Paris's Latin Quarter. The students Lactance and Hippolite are more interested in tricks and love than in their studies; their victims are an overly zealous father intent on protecting his daughter and a ridiculed husband trying to protect his wife. Critics have noted that the last part of the play involves elements—disguises, overheard conversations, and consideration of throwing one of the characters into the river—for which no groundwork has been laid and that seem to have been added merely to bring the drama to a conclusion.

Larivey was named canon of Troyes in 1586 and ordained a priest in 1587. In 1611 he published *Trois comedies des six dernieres de Pierre de Larivey Champenois: A l'imitation des anciens* [sic] *Grecs, Latins et Modernes italiens* (Three Comedies of the Last Six by Pierre de Larivey of Champagne: Imitating the Ancient Greeks, Latins and Modern Italians). The volume comprises *La Constance* (Constancy), *Le Fidelle* (The Faithful One), and *Les Tromperies* (Tricks), adaptations of Razzi's *La Costanza* (1565), Luigi Pasqualigo's *Il Fedele* (1576), and Niccolo Secchi's *Gl'Inganni* (1547, The Deceived), respectively. In a prefatory letter to his patron, François d'Ambroise, Larivey confirms what the title of the volume indicates: that these three plays are the first of six. If the remaining three were ever written, they have been lost. The three comedies in the volume are set in Troyes. They are considered inferior to Larivey's earlier plays. *La Constance* is slow, moralistic, and loaded down with boring speeches; the prologue even warns the audience that it may find the story unbelievable. The main character is the pedant Fidence, who is full of jargon, in love, credulous, and finally humiliated. Constance was in love with Leonard but was forced to marry Anthoine, who never consummated the relationship. When Leonard returns at Mardi Gras, disguised as a Spanish soldier, Anthoine consents to their marriage, and fun is made of Fidence's pedantry.

Le Fidelle also has problems: it is long, the plot is overstuffed, and the style and language are heavy. Fidelle is in love with his tutor, Victoire, who reveals his infatuation to her husband, Cornille. But Victoire is not blameless: she is in love with Fortuné. Fidelle denounces her to her husband and wants to kill her rather than let someone else have her. Neither the pedant Josse nor the soldier Brisemur ("Wall-breaker") can change Fidelle's mind. Victoire knows of Fidelle's betrayal and stages a false death to win back his loyalty. Cornille forgives her, and she and Fidelle end up as friends. *Le Fidelle* was staged by the director Jean-Marie Villégier in Paris in 1989.

In *Les Tromperies* Genièvre's father disguises her as a young man named Robert to protect her virginity. Another girl falls in love with "Robert"; she is passed off to Fortunat, the brother of "Robert," and becomes pregnant by him. "Robert" is in love with another man but cannot declare her love. The courtesan Dorothée and the procuress Gillette try to resolve the situation through ruses involving a doctor and a captain before the father of "Robert" and Fortunat returns to Troyes and straightens everything out. Although this situation would seem fertile ground for comedy, the humor is spoiled by the greed shown by some of the characters and the malice displayed by some of the women toward the men.

Like the models on which they are based, Larivey's comedies include the standard comedy character types: the old men in love with a young woman; the young lovers; the braggart soldier, who is usually Spanish or Italian; and the crafty servant. Other types are less common: the procuress, the procurer, the sorcerer, the parasite, the student, and the pedant. And each of the nine plays introduces a character unknown in comedy until then: the pedant in *La Constance* and the valet in *Les Jaloux,* for example. Larivey's true genius, however, lies in his dialogue, where he employs a vocabulary and tone appropriate to each character.

An almanac for 1611 published in Troyes and presumably written by Claude Morel has been proved to be by Larivey. It inaugurated a series of such volumes, all signed "Morel" but probably by Larivey, for 1612 to 1616 and 1618; they are printed in red and black and illustrated with woodcuts representing historical, astrological, and mythological figures. In general, these volumes are pessimistic in their predictions. It has been suggested, but never established, that Larivey had a role in the publication in Troyes in 1611 of the prophecies of Nostradamus.

Confusion existed for several hundred years about Larivey's dates and writings, for, as Louis Morin has pointed out, three men shared the name: the playwright; his nephew, Pierre de Patris, who was called Pierre de Larivey *le jeune* (the Younger); and the playwright's grand-nephew. The confusion was augmented by the fact that the playwright gave the nephew a volume of astrological verses one month before the former's death on 12 February 1619; in 1623 a volume titled *Centuries* was published in Lyon, dedicated to the Duc de Nevers and consisting of six hundred prophetic quatrains, with the author's name given as Pierre de Larivey. It was not correctly attributed to the nephew until Morin did so in 1937.

Of the sixteen writers of comedies during the French Renaissance, Pierre de Larivey was the most prolific: his nine comedies form the largest body of works in this genre. Although the last three show a decline in quality, Larivey's contribution to the theater cannot be overlooked. His influence on later comic playwrights, including Molière, is significant, and some of his plays continue to be studied and performed today.

References:

Yvonne Bellenger, ed., *Pierre de Larivey, Champenois: Chanoine, traducteur, auteur de comédies et astrologue (1541–1619)* (Paris: Klincksieck, 1993);

Jacques Brémond, "'Les Esprits' de Pierre de Larivey," M.A. thesis, Université de Grenoble, 1971;

René Doumic, "Les 'Esprits' de Pierre de Larivey," *Revue des Cours et Conférences* (1893): 183–191;

Louis Morin, *Les Trois Pierre de Larivey: Biographie et bibliographie* (Troyes: J.-L. Paton, 1937);

Pietro Toldo, "La Comédie française de la Renaissance," *Revue d'Histoire littéraire de la France,* 5 (1898): 588–603.

Jean de la Taille

(1534? – 1611?)

Thomas L. Zamparelli
Loyola University New Orleans

BOOKS: *Remonstrance pour le roy, à tous ses subjects qui ont pris les armes* (Paris: Printed by Fédéric Morel, 1562);

Saül le furieux: Tragedie prise de la Bible. Plus une remonstrance faicte pour le roy Charles IX. à tous ses subjects à fin de les encliner à la paix. Avec hymnes, cartels et autres oeuvres d'un mesme autheur. Recueil des inscriptions, anagrammatismes et autres oeuvres poëtiques de Jaques [sic] *de La Taille* (Paris: Printed by Fédéric Morel, 1572);

La Famine, ou les Gabéonites: Tragedie prise de la Bible, et suivant celle de Saül (Paris: Printed by Fédéric Morel, 1573);

La Geomance abregée . . . : Pour sçavoir les choses passées, presentes et futures. Ensemble le blason des pierres précieuses, contenant leurs vertuz et proprietez, abridged and translated by La Taille (Paris: Printed by Lucas Breyer, 1574);

Histoire abrégée des singeries de la Ligue, Familière description des états de la Ligue, Les chardons de la Ligue ou sentences des poètes de notre temps, attributed to La Taille (N.p., 1595);

Les Œuvres Poëtiques de Jean de la Taille, seigneur de Bondaroy (Paris: Printed by R. Fouet, 1602);

Discours notable des duels (Paris: Printed by C. Rigaud, 1607);

Œuvres de Jehan de la Taille, edited by René de Maulde (4 volumes, Paris: Léon Willem, 1878–1882; 2 volumes, Geneva: Slatkine, 1968).

Editions: *La Famine; Saül le furieux* (Paris: Printed by Fédéric Morel, 1598);

Saül le furieux (Rouen: Printed by Raphaël du Petit-Val, 1601);

La Famine, ou les Gabéonites: Tragedie prise de la Bible, et suivant celle de Saül (Rouen: Printed by Raphaël du Petit-Val, 1602);

"Le Courtisan retiré," in *Les Satires françaises du XVIe siècle,* 2 volumes, edited by Fernand Fleuret and Louis Perceau (Paris: Garnier, 1922);

Jean de la Taille (frontispiece to La Famine, ou les Gabéonites, *1573; from* De l'Art de la Tragédie, *edited by Frederic West, 1939; Thomas Cooper Library, University of South Carolina)*

De l'Art de la Tragédie, edited by Frederic West (Manchester, U.K.: Manchester University Press, 1939);

"De l'Art de la Tragédie," in *Critical Prefaces of the French Renaissance,* edited by Bernard Weinberg (Evanston, Ill.: Northwestern University Press, 1950);

Saül le furieux, in *Four Renaissance Tragedies,* edited by Donald Stone Jr. (Cambridge, Mass.: Harvard University Press, 1966);

Saül le furieux; La Famine ou les Gabéonites, critical edition, edited by Elliott Forsyth (Paris: Marcel Didier, 1968);

Dramatic Works, edited by Kathleen M. Hall and C. N. Smith (London: Athlone Press, 1972);

Les Corrivaus, critical edition, edited by Denis L. Drysdall (Paris: Didier, 1974);

Les Corrivaus, edited by G. Macri (Galatina, Italy: Salentina, 1974);

Saül le furieux, edited by Laura Kreyder, in *Théâtre français de la Renaissance,* series 1, volume 4: *La Tragédie à l'époque d'Henri II et de Charles IX* (Florence: Olschki / Paris: Presses universitaires de France, 1992);

La Famine, edited by Kreyder, in *Théâtre français de la Renaissance,* series 1, volume 5: *La Tragédie à l'époque d'Henri II et de Charles IX* (Florence: Olschki / Paris: Presses universitaires de France, 1993);

Le Negromant, edited by François Rigolot, in *Théâtre français de la Renaissance,* series 1, volume 9: *La Comédie à l'époque d'Henri II et de Charles IX* (Florence: Olschki / Paris: Presses universitaires de France, 1997).

Edition in English: *The Rivals (Les Corrivaus),* edited and translated by H. Peter Clive (Waterloo, Ont.: Wilfrid Laurier University Press, 1981).

PLAY PRODUCTIONS: *Saül le furieux,* Amiens, 1584; *Gabéonites (La Famine?),* Béthune, 1601.

Jean de la Taille, Seigneur of Bondaroy in Gâtinais, is considered by many scholars to be the best playwright of the French Renaissance. He is especially known for his two biblical tragedies and one original comedy that reveal a strong sense of theatricality and a talent for creating dramatic situations and dialogue. He also wrote a treatise on the nature of tragedy that many commentators view as a significant affirmation in French of the importance of Aristotle's unities of time and place. Although he had little influence on contemporary dramatists, his plays exemplify the transition that developed in France in the sixteenth and seventeenth centuries from medieval popular drama to plays directed at a learned or aristocratic audience and based on classical and Italian models.

The few details that are known about La Taille's life come from a handwritten genealogy by his son, Lancelot; this document, now lost, served as the basis for biographies of the author by René de Maulde, included in his edition of La Taille's works (1878–

1882), and Gustave Baguenault de Puchesse (1889). Both biographers also made use of Guillaume Colletet's seventeenth-century manuscript "Histoire des poètes françois" (History of French Poets), which is also lost. Relying especially on the documents published by De Maulde and the "Epistre au lecteur" (Letter to the Reader) that La Taille wrote as a preface to his brother Jacques's "Recueil des inscriptions" (1572, Collection of Inscriptions), critics and commentators have established that he was the eldest son of Louis de la Taille, a member of the minor Beauceron nobility of modest means, who married Jacqueline de l'Estendart de Heurteloup in 1539. The family's domain was in the Gâtinais region south of Paris. The exact date of Jean de la Taille's birth remains unknown; but 1533 or 1534 are regarded as the most likely years, on the assumption that he was probably at least seven years older than Jacques, who was born in 1542. Jacques, who regarded Jean as paternal figure, and another brother, Pascal, died of the plague in 1562. Their only sister, Angélique, died at fourteen in 1571. Valentin, the youngest brother, outlived all of his siblings and devoted his life to military pursuits. Jean de la Taille was profoundly affected by Angélique's death and expressed his grief in the *epithaphe* (1572, epitaph) and *cantique* (1573, hymn) he wrote in her memory.

Although he himself was not a cultivated man, Louis de la Taille sent his three oldest sons to be educated in Paris. In the preface to Jacques's "Recueil des inscriptions" Jean de la Taille maintains, albeit unconvincingly, that their father was motivated by his love for learning and culture rather than by a desire to prepare them for legal or ecclesiastical careers. Jean spent six years at the celebrated Collège de Boncourt, which had become a center of humanistic studies and literary experimentation, as a nonresident student working independently with a tutor: the influential humanist Marc-Antoine Muret, author of the Latin tragedy *Julius Caesar* (1553) and a leading promoter of classical drama in French. Two other noted dramatists of the period, George Buchanan and Jean de La Péruse, also taught at Boncourt. La Taille probably saw Estienne Jodelle's *Cléopâtre captive* (Captive Cleopatra), which was performed at Boncourt in 1553; during his stay in Paris he is known to have attended performances of Jodelle's *Eugène* and two comedies by Jacques Grévin at the Collège de Beauvais.

La Taille went on to study law in Orléans under Anne du Bourg, who taught there from 1549 to 1557. He was, however, more interested in literature, especially the poetry of Pierre de Ronsard and Joachim du Bellay. Much to the chagrin of his father, he neglected his legal studies and began to devote himself to writing. Around 1557 he returned to Paris to live with his brothers Jacques and Pascal. Jacques, who had begun writing poetry, comedies, and tragedies at sixteen, was a student of the humanist Jean Dorat. He may have inspired Jean, who composed several works prior to 1562; they include his two best-known plays, the tragedy *Saül le furieux* (1572, The Madness of Saul) and the comedy *Les Corrivaus* (1573; translated as *The Rivals,* 1981), as well as official or court poetry. He also produced a free translation of Ludovico Ariosto's comedy *Il Negromante* (1520, The Necromancer) as *Le Negromant* (1573).

Although La Taille was a Huguenot from birth, and his father's house in Bondaroy was a meeting place for the Protestants of the region, at the outbreak of the first War of Religion in 1562 he took up arms at Blois for the Catholic monarch Charles IX. Scholars have speculated that he must have felt a sense of duty to the king and may also have hoped to find in Charles's mother and regent, Catherine de Médicis, a mediator capable of preserving national unity. La Taille's religious and political opinions are difficult to assess. Some of his poetry, such as "La Religieuse contre son gré" (1572, The Reluctant Nun), reveals clear Protestant leanings; but in 1562 he published *Remonstrance pour le roy, à tous ses subjects qui ont pris les armes* (Remonstrance for the King to All His Subjects Who Have Taken Up Arms), in which he assumes the voice of the Catholic king. La Taille's speaker exhorts his rebellious subjects to avoid further bloodshed:

Combien que je vous puis, mes subjects, commander,
J'useray toutefois envers vous de priere,
Pour vous faire jecter les armes en arriere,
Vous disant la pitié que c'est d'ainsi mesler
Par vos seditions le ciel, la terre & l'air.

(As much as I am able to command you, my subjects,
I will instead entreat you
To lay down your arms
Telling you how unfortunate it is to trouble
Heaven and earth by your rebellious acts.)

The *Remonstrance* was La Taille's most popular and successful work and was republished eight times during his lifetime. In December 1562 he fought in the Battle of Dreux, a victory for Charles IX.

Thanks to the Treaty of Amboise, the period from 1563 to 1568 was one of relative peace and stability. During this time La Taille resided at court and in Gâtinais and composed a variety of minor works, ranging from court poetry to love lyrics. He wrote verses exhorting Marguerite de Valois to marry and epitaphs for François de Clèves, Duke of Nevers, and Anne, first Duke of Montmorency. In addition, he tried his hand at Petrarchan love poetry celebrating the charms and cruelty of a certain Jeanne du Plessis and the beauty of a woman he calls Marguerite and compares to the flower of that name:

J'auray tousjours en la bouche & au cueur
La MARGUERITE estant des fleurs la fleur:
Et pour la rendre en sa beauté parfaitte,

Je voudroy tant l'arroser quelque jour,
Qu'estant entré au beau jardin d'Amour
Cueillir je puisse une fleur si tendrette!

(I will always have on my lips and in my heart
The Marguerite, the flower of flowers
And to capture it in its perfect beauty

I shall so much like to water it so that one day
Having entered the beautiful garden of love
I may be able to pluck such a delicate flower!)

La Taille did not take part in the second War of Religion in 1568; some scholars see his absence as an indication that he and his family officially converted to Protestantism around this time. In the third War of Religion of 1568 to 1570 he joined the Protestant forces of Louis I de Bourbon, first Prince of Condé, and Henri de Navarre, perhaps in reaction to the increasing influence of the extremist Catholic Guise family. He took part in skirmishes in Poitou, and in 1568 he wrote the pacifist "Sonnets satyriques du camp de Poictou" (1573, Satirical Sonnets from the Camp of Poitou). He probably witnessed the battles of Jarnac and Moncontour. On 26 June 1570 he was wounded at Arnay-le-Duc; Henri de Navarre ordered La Taille to be tended by his own physician and is said to have embraced La Taille on the battlefield. Shortly afterward, La Taille was robbed. He decided to retire from military service and devote himself to literary pursuits and family matters.

La Taille spent 1570–1571 restoring his health, taking care of financial matters, and preparing editions of his works and those of his brother Jacques that were published between 1572 and 1574. Although written much earlier, his *Saül le furieux* was published in 1572; it is preceded by his treatise "De l'art de la tragedie" (On the Art of Tragedy). In the treatise, which is dedicated to his protectress, Henriette de Clèves, Duchess of Navarre, the niece of Antoine de Bourbon, the king of Navarre, La Taille advocates the Horatian-Aristotelian-Senecan model for French tragedy; the Italian theorist Lodovico Castelvetro also influenced him. According to La Taille, the principal aim of tragedy is to inspire sorrow and pity. Thus, a suitable plot must deal with calamitous subjects such as war, famine, tyranny, plague, banishment, the downfall of ancient personages, and the vagaries of fortune, but it must avoid subjects of a topical nature and religious subjects that are merely pretexts for preaching dogma. The tragic hero must be

De l'Art de la Tragédie.

A

Treshaulte Princesse Henriette De Cleues, Duchesse de NEVERS,

Ian De la Taille de Bondaroy.

MADAME combien que les piteux desastres aduenus nagueres en la France par nos Guerres ciuilles, fussent si grãds, & que la mort du Roy HENRY, du Roy son Fils, & du Roy de Nauarre, vostre Oncle, auec celle de tant d'autres Princes, Seigneurs, Cheualiers & Gentils-hommes, fust si pitoiable qu'il ne faudroit ia d'autre chose pour faire des Tragedies: ce neátmoins pour n'en estre du tout le propre subiect, & pour ne remuer nos vieilles & nouuelles douleurs, volótiers ie m'en deporte, aimant trop mieux descrire le malheur d'autruy que le nostre: qui m'a fait non seulement voir les deux rencheutes de nos folles guerres, mais

A ij.

First page of the treatise in which La Taille advocates the Horatian-Aristotelian-Senecan model for French tragedy. It was included in the 1572 edition of his play Saül le furieux *(from* De l'Art de la Tragédie, *edited by Frederic West, 1939; Thomas Cooper Library, University of South Carolina).*

critics see in it the first statement in French of the classical unities of time, place, and action.

While not faithful to all of the dramatic principles La Taille outlines in his treatise, *Saül le furieux* is a complex, action-oriented drama. Inspired by the biblical books of Samuel and by Seneca's *Hercules furens* (The Madness of Hercules), it is a vivid portrayal of a ruler pursued by ill fortune and the mysteries of divine providence. A hallucinating Saul attempts to kill his sons, whom he mistakes for his enemies, while they are discussing plans for war against the Philistines. A sense of impending doom weighs on the characters as omens foretell disaster. An increasingly deranged and abandoned Saul rails against the injustice of divine punishment, but his first squire reminds him of his act of disobedience toward God: despite God's commandment, Saul had refused to put Agag, king of the Amalekites, to death. In act 3 Saul has a sorceress conjure up the spirit of the prophet Samuel, who announces David's victory and the destruction of Saul and his family:

> Sçaches doncques, que DIEU est ja tout resolu
> De Bailler ton Royaume à un meilleur Esleu,
> C'est David dont tu as par ta maligne envie
> Tant de fois aguetté la juste et droitte vie
> Mais tes faicts sur ton chef à ce coup recherront,
> Car ton Regne et ta vie ensemble te lairront.
>
> (Know then that God is completely resolved
> To give your kingdom to a better-chosen one,
> It is David whose just and honest life
> So often you have plagued
> But your misdeeds will fall on your own head
> For your reign and your life will both be forfeit.)

With the death of his sons in battle and the victory of the Philistines, all seems lost for the Israelites. Saul contemplates suicide but then asks to die at the hand of his first squire, who refuses to grant his wish. Keeping violence offstage, as he recommended in "De l'art de la tragedie," La Taille has the second squire tell of Saul's bravery in the final battle and his self-sacrifice over the body of his son Jonathe (Jonathan). The volume also includes a republication of the *Remonstrance,* some poems, and the "Recueil des inscriptions" and other pieces by Jacques.

In 1573 a volume of La Taille's works appeared; it comprises the plays *La Famine, ou Les Gabéonites* (Famine, or The Gibeonites), *Les Corrivaus,* the translation *Le Negromant,* and many poems. Dedicated to Marguerite de Valois, *La Famine* is set in Jerusalem and deals with the plight of Saul's descendants. Borrowing from the books of Kings and Seneca's *Troades* (The Trojan Women), La Taille develops the notion of a just but

neither a paragon of virtue nor an abject villain. The play should begin in the middle–or, preferably, toward the end–of the tragic events and need not portray the hero's good fortune before showing the onslaught of adversity. The plot should be tightly knit and divided into five acts; only necessary and relevant events, culminating in an inevitable tragic conclusion, should be depicted. All characters should exit the stage at the end of each act, and, in keeping with Horace's dramatic principles, violent actions should occur offstage. The chorus is relegated to passive commentary on the action between acts. Though somewhat fragmentary and ambiguous in places, "De l'art de la tragedie" remains an important document in French literary history; some

vengeful God. David and his family are shown facing the ravages of hunger; the scene then shifts to the widow and daughter of Saul, who learn from Saul's ghost that it is God's will that the children of Saul's concubine Resefe (Rizpah) and those of Saul's eldest daughter, Merobe (Merah), be sacrificed. These sacrifices will placate the Gibeonites, who had been wronged by Saul, and will end the famine. The mothers attempt to save their children, but Joabe, David's counselor, exhorts the children to sacrifice themselves for God. The children are crucified and die stoically before the eyes of their anguished mothers. This drama differs from *Saül le furieux* in several respects. The element of individual struggle against metaphysical forces is absent, as is the focus on the fate of a single character, and greater use is made of the structures of formal lament associated with Senecan and humanist tragedy. Also, the dramatic language tends to be more ornate and varied in *La Famine* than in *Saül le furieux,* which, except for the choruses, which are in seven- and eight-syllable verse, and the fifth act, which is in ten-syllable verse, is composed in alexandrine verse; in *La Famine,* La Taille uses alexandrine verse in the first, third, and fifth acts and ten-syllable verse in the second and fourth acts. *La Famine* is considered a less successful drama than *Saül le furieux* but is admired for the moving depiction of Resefe.

Literary historians regard *Les Corrivaus,* written in early 1562, as the earliest surviving original French comedy in prose based on classical and Italian sources. La Taille draws inspiration from Terence; tale V.5 of Giovanni Boccacio's *Decameron* (circa 1348–1353); Ariosto's *I suppositi* (1509, The Pretenders); *Gl'ingannati* (1531, The Deceived), a collective work by the Accademici Intronati of Siena; and also, perhaps, Jacopo Nardi's *I due felici rivali* (1513, The Two Fortunate Rivals) and Girolamo Parabosco's *Il Viluppo* (1547, The Imbroglio). In the prologue he echoes Du Bellay's recommendations in *La Deffence et illustration de la langue françoyse* (1549; translated as *The Defense and Illustration of the French Language,* 1939) for defending French against its detractors and cultivating a contemporary literature based on classical and Italian models. He thus advocates a complete break with the French medieval comic tradition; some scholars have suggested, however, that traces of medieval farce remain in the language and conduct of the servants. The play is praised as an entertaining comedy of intrigue and character with a complex, skillfully developed plot full of symmetrical or parallel structures, suspense, and surprising coincidences; witty, natural, and engaging dialogue; and vividly drawn characters. Unbeknownst to each other, the rivals Philadelfe and Euvertre hatch plots to abduct Fleurdelys, the object of their affections, on the same day. A secondary story line concerns Restitue, who was made pregnant by Philadelfe before he abandoned her for Fleurdelys. The distraught Restitue reveals her secret to her *nourrice* (nurse), whose flippant, matter-of-fact reaction provides the first of many comic moments: "Mais quoy Restitue? Si n'en faut-il pourtant pleurer, ny se desconforter ainsi: Et bien, c'est un enfant que vous aurez, Dieu mercy, le monde aumoins sera certain de ne faillir point de vostre costé" (But what, Restitue? It's not necessary to cry and be so sad. So, you are going to have a child, thank God, the world at least will be certain not to be disappointed on your side). All ends well when Philadelphe's father, Bernard, recognizes Fleurdelys as his long-lost daughter; he proclaims that Euvertre will marry Fleurdelys; and Philadelphe's father declares that Philadelphe will marry Restitue. A triple wedding will be celebrated, since Bernard also decides to marry Restitue's mother. Along with the dramas, the volume includes poems written in the 1560s and early 1570s: *elégies* (elegies) of plaintive and love poetry; *chansons* (songs); "Cantique sur la mort de sa soeur" (Hymn on the Death of His Sister); "Sonnets d'amour" (Love Sonnets); the "Sonnets satyrques du camp de Poictou," depicting the rigors and hardships of military life; "La Mort de Pâris, Alexandre et d'Oenonne" (The Death of Paris, Alexander and Oenone), written in ten-syllable verse; "Combat de fortune et de pauvreté" (The Battle of Fortune and Poverty); and "Le Courtisan retiré" (The Retired Courtier), a long satirical poem exposing the vices and follies of court life.

In 1574 La Taille published *La Geomance abregée* (Short Handbook on Divination), an abridged version of the Italian Christoforo Cattan's 1558 work on divination and the occult. Although, according to his preface, La Taille views astrology and occultism not as serious pursuits but as welcome distractions during the third War of Religion, he showed an interest in the occult in his translation of *Le Negromant* and in the conjuration scene of *Saül le furieux.* The volume includes La Taille's "Blason de la marguerite et des autres pierres précieuses" (Blazon of the Marguerite and Other Precious Stones), dedicated to Marie de Clèves and Marguerite de Navarre, and several satirical *epigrammes,* such as "D'un devin" (About a Soothsayer) and "A un prelat inutile" (To a Useless Prelate).

During this period La Taille wrote "Le Prince nécessaire" (The Ideal Prince), a long political poem on government, military affairs, and the education of rulers addressed to Henri de Navarre, which remained unpublished until it appeared in 1882 in De Maulde's *Œuvres de Jehan de la Taille* (Works of Jean de La Taille). "Le Prince nécessaire" documents La Taille's reaction to the ravages of civil war. He pleads for tolerance and attacks fanaticism, arguing that religious differences do not have to bring turmoil and destruction to the state and that citizens who belong to different sects can find a way to live together in peace. If these efforts toward compromise are not successful, the blame lies with the unbridled ambitions of leaders; the latter must be held in check and forced, under pain of death or exile, to accept the beliefs of the dominant sect. La Taille's work is less a statement of Machiavellian political pragmatism than an expression of faith in divine providence and the power of a Christian monarch to restore peace and to further God's plan for improving humanity. Despite his Calvinist leanings, La Taille places his desire for public tranquility above sectarianism.

In 1575 La Taille married Charlotte Dumoulin de Rouville in a Catholic ceremony. Of their three children, only Lancelot survived infancy; he was brought up in the Protestant faith. In his final years La Taille occasionally composed works of a polemical nature. In 1584 he wrote two satirical sonnets on "l'etat corrompu de la France" (the corrupt state of France). A pamphlet in three parts denouncing the Catholic League appeared in 1595: *Histoire abregée des singeries de la Ligue, Familière description des états de la Ligue, Les chardons de la Ligue ou sentences des poètes de notre temps* (A Short History of the Antics of the League, Familiar Description of the States of the League, The Thistles of the League or Aphorisms of Poets of Our Time); although some critics question La Taille's authorship of the work, it is included in De Maulde's edition. La Taille's final work, *Discours notable des duels* (A Notable Discourse on Duels), appeared in 1607, shortly after Lancelot killed his daughter's fiancé in a duel. A collection of anecdotes drawn from French history, from the works of authors such as Jean Froissart and Symphorien Champier, and from La Taille's reminiscences, the book both celebrates and criticizes the practice of dueling.

The exact date of La Taille's death remains uncertain; legal documents relating to the settlement of his estate indicate that he probably died either in the last months of 1611 or in 1612. La Taille seems to have made little impression on his contemporaries; in an article in a 1998 collection edited by Yvonne Bellenger, Raymond Lebègue speculates that he may have been overshadowed as a tragedian by Robert Garnier. His plays were rarely, if ever, performed; La Taille was eager to have *Saül le furieux* staged for Charles IX, but it is not known whether such a performance ever took place. A sketchy record exists of possible performances of his tragedies: on 19 July 1584 the aldermen of Amiens granted permission to the players of the parish of St. Jacques to perform *Saül le furieux;* in 1599 the Jesuit students of Pont-à-Mousson put on a production of a play titled *Saül le furieux;* and in 1601 students at Béthune staged a tragedy titled *Gabéonites.* His comedies—*Les Corrivaus* and the translation *Le Negromant*—were not republished until the late nineteenth century. Nevertheless, many modern critics regard Jean de la Taille as the Renaissance playwright with the strongest dramaturgical instincts. They admire his skillful use of dramatic conventions, his talent for exposition, and his flair for creating believable characters. The critical consensus is that he possessed a genuine sense of theater that enables him to involve the spectator—or, at least, the reader—in the dynamics of his plays.

Biography:

Gustave Baguenault de Puchesse, *Jean et Jacques de La Taille: Etude biographique et littéraire sur deux poètes du XVIe siècle* (Orléans: Herluison, 1889).

References:

Yvonne Bellenger, ed., *Le Théâtre biblique de Jean de La Taille: Etudes sur "Saül le furieux," "De l'Art de la tragédie," "La Famine ou les Gabéonites,"* Collection Unichamp, no. 72 (Paris: Champion, 1998);

Françoise Charpentier, ed., *Les Tragédies de Jean de La Taille,* Cahiers textuels, no. 18 (Paris: UFR "Sciences des textes et documents," Université Paris 7, 1998);

Tatham Ambersley Daley, *Jean de La Taille (1533–1608): Etude historique et littéraire* (Paris: J. Gamber, 1934);

Elliott Forsyth, *La Tragédie française de Jodelle à Corneille (1533–1640): Le thème de la vengeance* (Paris: Nizet, 1962);

Brian Jeffery, *French Renaissance Comedy, 1552–1630* (Oxford: Clarendon Press, 1969);

Gillian Jondorf, *French Renaissance Tragedy: The Dramatic Word* (Cambridge: Cambridge University Press, 1990);

Gustave Lanson, *Esquisse d'une histoire de la tragédie française* (Paris: Champion, 1927);

H. W. Lawton, *Handbook of French Renaissance Dramatic Theory* (Manchester, U.K.: Manchester University Press, 1949);

Kosta Loukovitch, *L'Evolution de la tragédie religieuse classique en France* (Paris: Droz, 1933);

Maria A. Thiel, *La Figure de Saül et sa représentation dans la littérature dramatique française* (Amsterdam: H. J. Paris, 1926).

Jacques Lefèvre d'Etaples

(1460? – 1536)

E. Bruce Hayes
University of Kansas

BOOKS: *Introductio in metaphysicorum libros Aristotelis* (Paris: Johann Higman, 1494);

De Maria Magdalena & triduo Christi disceptatio (Paris: Henri Estienne, 1517);

De tribus et unica Magdalena disceptatio secunda (Paris: Henri Estienne, 1519);

Epistres & Evangiles pour les cinquante & deux sepmaines de l'an (Paris: Simon Dubois, 1525);

Epistres et Evangiles des cinquante et deux dimenches de l'an (Neuchâtel?: Pierre de Vingle, 1534?).

Editions: *Epistres & Evangiles pour les cinquante & deux sepmaines de l'an,* edited by M. A. Screech (Geneva: Droz, 1964);

Epistres et Evangiles pour les cinquante et deux dimanches de l'an, edited by Guy Bedouelle and Franco Giacone (Leiden: Brill, 1976).

OTHER: Aristotle, *Totius Aristotelis philosophicae naturalis paraphrases,* paraphrased by Lefèvre (Paris: Johann Higman, 1492);

Pseudo-Dionysius, the Areopagite, *Theologia vivificans. Cibus solidus. Dionysii Celestis hierarchia,* edited by Lefèvre (Paris: Johann Higman and Wolfgang Hopyl, 1499);

Raymon Lull, *Opera quaedam,* 4 volumes, edited by Lefèvre (Paris: Guy Marchant, 1499);

Aristotle, *Libri logicorum,* edited by Lefèvre (Paris: Wolfgang Hopyl & Henri Estienne, 1503);

John of Damascus, *De orthodoxa fide,* edited by Lefèvre (Paris: Henri Estienne, 1507);

Quincuplex Psalterium. Gallicum. Romanum. Hebraicum. Vetus. Conciliatum, edited by Lefèvre (Paris: Henri Estienne, 1509);

S. Pauli Epistoae XIV ex Vulgate, adiecta intelligentia ex graeco, cum commentariis, edited by Lefèvre (Paris: Henri Estienne, 1512);

Liber trium virorum et trium spiritualium virginum, edited by Lefèvre (Paris: Henri Estienne, 1513); translated by Carolyn Osiek as *The Shepherd of Hermas: A Commentary,* edited by Helmut Koester (Minneapolis: Fortress Press, 1999);

Nicholas of Cusay, *Opera omnia,* 3 volumes, edited by Lefèvre (Paris: Josse Bade, 1514);

Aristotle *Metaphysica,* edited by Lefèvre (Paris: Henri Estienne, 1515);

Commentarii initiatorii in quartuor Evangelia, edited by Lefèvre (Meaux: Simon de Colines, 1522).

TRANSLATIONS: *Nouveau Testament: Les quatre Evangiles* (Paris: Simon de Colines, 1523);

Nouveau Testament: Les epistres, les actes et l'apocalypse (Paris: Simon de Colines, 1523);

Le psaultier de David (Paris: Simon de Colines, 1523);

L'Ancien Testament (Antwerp: Martin de Keyser, 1528);

La Saincte Bible en Francoys (Antwerp: Martin de Keyser, 1530; revised, 1541).

Edition: *Nouveau Testament: Les epistres, les actes et l'apocalypse; Fac-similé de la première édition Simon de Colines, 1523,* 2 volumes, edited by M. A. Screech (East Ardsley, U.K.: S.R.; New York: Johnson, Reprint, 1970).

A renowned and celebrated humanist during his life, Jacques Lefèvre d'Etaples (Jacobus Faber Stapulensis is the Latinized form) became a leading figure of Christian humanism in the early sixteenth century and was one of the scholars whose work led from the Renaissance to the Reformation. He was nearly as famous as Desiderius Erasmus, and the two were frequently compared, leading many, including the king of France, François I, to confuse the two scholars. Lefèvre is credited with translating the Bible into French (1523–1530) and with contributing to one of the most important successes of the Renaissance: a modern, scientific approach to texts. Lefèvre broke with the medieval tradition of glossing—a practice that neglected the original text—but unlike other humanists who called for a rejection of medieval scholastic thought, he proposed a correction based on updated Aristotelian ideas.

No records exist concerning the birth of Lefèvre. When he died in 1536, many contemporaries believed that he was about one hundred years old. Based on a

Title page for a later edition of Jacques Lefèvre d'Etaples's 1525 book, one of several of his works that revealed his sympathy with Protestant reformers (from M. A. Screech, ed., Epistres & Evangiles pour les cinquante & deux sepmaines de l'an, 1964; Thomas Cooper Library, University of South Carolina)

debates never tired of emphasizing his lack of formal training in theology.

After graduating, Lefèvre became a professor of philosophy at the same college where he had been a student, the college of Cardinal Lemoine. This institution was attended by students who, like Lefèvre, came from Picardy. He remained a professor there until 1508. His reputation as a teacher was one of uncompromising thoroughness, but despite the demands he made of his students, many of them later acclaimed him for his compassion as well as his erudition. Much of the work he produced during this period was primarily pedagogical in nature, providing difficult texts with indexes and glossaries of important terms, which he placed at the beginnings of chapters. He began to move away from medieval scholastic glossing, the practice of inserting into the text questions and answers that often obscured the original text. Lefèvre's methodology as well as the clarity of his translations and commentaries were highly innovative for the time.

In 1490 Lefèvre produced *Introductio in metaphysicorum libros Aristotelis* (Introduction to Aristotle's Metaphysics), which was published in 1494. His first publication was *Totius Aristotelis philosophicae naturalis paraphrases* (1492, Paraphrases of all of Aristotle's Natural Philosophy), in which he presented a selection of Aristotelian texts. These first two treatises underscore Lefèvre's profound interest at the beginning of his career in Aristotle's writings; in both he sought to preserve the original Aristotelian thought with as little editorial interference as possible.

Lefèvre was also influenced by his reading of the thirteenth-century Spanish philosopher Raymon Lull. Lull believed that because God possesses an infinite nature and humans are finite creatures, all attempts to define God are impossible because of humans' limited nature. He argued that one can come to understand God only by reaching a synthesis of opposites, through a unity of all knowledge, comparable to the harmony of the cosmos. Mystical and hermetic ideas such as these profoundly influenced Lefèvre until he later turned to strict biblical exegesis and translation.

A trip to Italy in 1492 proved extremely beneficial for Lefèvre. At this time humanism was just beginning to gain a foothold in France, and for a scholar such as Lefèvre, a pilgrimage to meet with the great Italian humanists was essential. While in Florence he met Marcilio Ficino, the leader of Italian Neoplatonist thought, as well as Giovanni Pico della Mirandola, a scholar whose eclecticism encouraged Lefèvre's desire to combine Platonic and Aristotelian thought. Perhaps Lefèvre's most important contact in Italy was Ermolao Barbaro, who at the time was preparing notes on the various manuscripts of Pliny, applying a strict scientific

comment Lefèvre made in a letter to a fellow scholar about his age, as well as University of Paris records (a Jacobus Fabri is recorded as having received his degree in 1479), it is likely that Lefèvre was born between 1450 and 1460. He was born in Etaples in Picardy, the same northern French province where Jean Calvin and Guillaume Farel, two future leaders of the Reformation, were born. He pursued his classical studies at the University of Paris, graduating as a master of arts in 1480. Although he was ordained to the priesthood and was actively engaged in theological debates throughout his life, Lefèvre did not study theology at the University of Paris nor become a doctor of theology for reasons that remain unknown. His later adversaries in theological

method to produce a Latin translation more faithful to the original Greek. Barbaro was also interested in Aristotle's writings, particularly in recovering the authentic Aristotle, unencumbered by the "barbaric" commentaries of medieval scholastics. As Bernd Renner has noted in an article on Lefèvre in *Great Lives from History* (2005), these Italian scholars introduced him to ideas and concepts that guided his future work, with its emphasis on the study of original texts, including the Bible, coupled with an interest in hermeneutics and contemplation.

Upon his return to France, Lefèvre's knowledge of Florentine Platonism, along with his focus on the interior life, led to his placing greater emphasis on mystical theology rather than rational philosophy. He became interested in hermetic writings and in Dionysius the Areopagite, or Pseudo-Dionysius, whose work, *Theologia vivificans* (Life-giving Theology), he published in 1499. According to Robert D. Cottrell in his essay "Lefèvre d'Etaples and the Limits of Biblical Interpretation," Lefèvre considered this apocryphal work to be the most sacred work after the gospels because he believed the author was the Areopagite converted by St. Paul referred to in Acts and because it included visions not included in the Pauline epistles. Even after Erasmus established in 1505 that the document was inauthentic, Lefèvre maintained his conviction of its sacredness. Along with *Theologia vivificans,* Lefèvre began to publish works by medieval mystics such as Lull.

At the beginning of the sixteenth century, Lefèvre engaged in a variety of intellectual activities that represented a continuation and completion of his previous writings on Aristotle. In 1503 he published *Libri logicorum* (Books of Logic), a single volume comprised of a selection of Aristotle's writings. He divided the volume into three parts, with the first two parts made up of his annotations and paraphrases, but chose to present the writings in the third section without any scholarly apparatus. While Lefèvre begins each section with his own prefatory epistle—a practice he followed in many of the works and translations he published—the volume demonstrates Lefèvre's pedagogical concern in producing works such as Aristotle's: his commentaries are limited to explanations of difficult passages. The early years of the century were also important as Lefèvre developed important ties with students and scholars, such as the publisher Josse Bade, who collaborated with him on various works of Aristotle as well as many other books, and Charles de Bovelles, who became a devoted disciple and later introduced him to the work of Nicholas of Cusa.

Lefèvre's publication of the treatise *De orthodoxa fide* (1507, The Orthodox Faith), by the eighth-century author John of Damascus, is a marker of his growing interest in a strictly biblical theology. The work, which outlines the main doctrines of the Christian faith and is a model for Catholic orthodoxy, shows Lefèvre's interest in patristic writing and led to his increasing participation in debates over Catholic doctrine. Lefèvre had read and greatly appreciated Erasmus's *Enchiridion militis christiani* (1503, A Handbook for the Christian Soldier), one of the most influential books during the so-called pre-Reformation, in which Erasmus insists on the purification of the Christian faith through a return to the Bible. Catholics such as Erasmus and Lefèvre sought a reform of practices and doctrines of the church from within. Like future Reformation leaders such as Martin Luther and Calvin, both Erasmus and Lefèvre favored a return to a purer form of Christianity, one that was more in harmony with the New Testament. However, as Philip Edgcumbe Hughes observes in *Lefèvre: Pioneer of Ecclesiastical Renewal in France* (1984), Lefèvre used John of Damascus's work to support the justification of the practice of saint worship, a matter of orthodoxy for the Catholic faith that departed from the antisaint-worship position of Erasmus and others.

In 1508 the abbot of St. Germain-des-Prés, Guillaume Briçonnet, invited Lefèvre to be the librarian at the Parisian monastery. A leading reform-minded leader, Briçonnet was a close adviser to Marguerite de Navarre, the sister of François I. Lefèvre's move to the monastery allowed him to devote more of his time to reformist endeavors as a translator and commentator of Scripture. Lefèvre soon produced the *Quincuplex Psalterium* (1509, Fivefold Psalter), one of his most important works, whose complex format presented the text of each psalm in five columns, providing the Gallic, Roman, and Hebraic versions, followed by the Old Latin text and his own harmonized version in the last two columns. Providing a harmonized Latin version opened Lefèvre to attacks from conservative theologians who balked at his efforts to provide a superior version of the Psalms. Along with the translations, Lefèvre also included commentary on the theme of each psalm, an expository overview of the first two dozen or so psalms, and other annotations on topics ranging from vocabulary to patristic opinions. The *Quincuplex Psalterium* represented an important advance in the realm of hermeneutics and exegesis and became an important model for the scriptural interpretation of reformers.

In the preface for *Quincuplex Psalterium,* Lefèvre proposed monastic reforms and posited the notion of a *duplex sensus literalis* (twofold literal sense), where two literal senses exist, the first governed by human reason and the second by divine inspiration. He noted that monks were guilty of following the former while ignoring the latter. Lefèvre's insistence on the primacy of the literal sense of Scripture directly contradicted the four-fold method of the scholastic tradition, which started with the literal sense and moved on to more important tropological, allegorical, and finally anagogical meaning of a given biblical passage. The *Quincuplex Psalterium* created great interest well beyond France and solidified Lefèvre's reputation as one of the leading French humanists. Luther, unknown at the time, took a keen interest in the work, especially in its hermeneutical principles. Hughes notes that a copy of the first edition of the work was found in the library of Dresden in 1885 containing copious notes and annotations in Luther's handwriting. The *Quincuplex Psalterium* marked a turning point in Lefèvre's intellectual career; from then on, more and more of his energies were devoted to the translation of and commentary on Scripture.

Early during his stay at St. Germain-des-Prés, Lefèvre met the future Protestant leader Guillaume Farel. According to Farel's account written some twenty years later, Lefèvre was a model of devotion and spirituality. He recalled that Lefèvre had encouraged him to become a preacher and expressed gratitude for Lefèvre's spiritual guidance. Farel decried those who criticized Lefèvre because of his lack of formal training. During his stay with Lefèvre, Farel experienced an evangelical conversion that became a defining moment in his life.

Lefèvre's popularity and renown increased further with his translation of and commentary on the epistles of St. Paul, *S. Pauli Epistoae XIV ex Vulgate, adiecta intelligentia ex graeco, cum commentariis* (1512, The Fourteen Epistles of St. Paul taken from the Vulgate, with Annotations from the Greek, with Commentary). This massive work of 530 folio pages is an important advance in the methods Lefèvre employed three years previously with the *Quincuplex Psalterium*. The commentaries are Lefèvre's own, and the Church Fathers are quoted infrequently. Lefèvre avoids the abstract language of scholastic theologians, opting instead for clarity and simplicity of expression. Rather than the tedious divisions and subdivisions of commentary commonly found in scholastic glosses, Lefèvre stays close to the text and focuses exclusively on explaining St. Paul's thought. The work contains both the Latin of the Vulgate Bible and his own Latin revision, based on a comparison with the Greek text. A monumental step toward modern exegesis and New Testament textual criticism, Lefèvre's work became a cornerstone for evangelical humanists, but at the time Lefèvre was attacked by scholastic theologians, notably those of the Sorbonne, for offering corrections to the Vulgate. Anticipating such attacks, Lefèvre prefaced his work with an apologia pointing out that St. Jerome's Vulgate Bible of the fourth century similarly constituted a critical revision of the preexisting Latin version.

The following year Lefèvre published *Liber trium virorum et trium spiritualium virginum* (1513, The Book of Three Men and Three Spiritual Virgins; translated as *The Shepherd of Hermas,* 1999). The six figures of the title were five medieval mystics—Hatto, Robert of Uzés, Hildegard of Bingen, Elizabeth of Schönau, and Mechthild of Hackeborn—and the Shepherd of Hermas, an apocryphal figure. Lefèvre explained in his dedicatory epistle that he chose these writings because of the simplicity and sincerity of their sacred visions. As was the case with the Pseudo-Areopagite work, Lefèvre mistakenly relied upon a biblical reference, assuming that the Hermas mentioned in Rom. 16:14 was the author even as he acknowledged the apocryphal nature of the text. The so-called Vulgate version of *The Shepherd of Hermas,* which had been accorded a near canonical status by Church Fathers, actually dated from the late second century. For Lefèvre, the text presented a mystical, visionary experience directly connected to the apostolic authority of St. Paul. He was deeply influenced by the writings included in this work of female medieval mystics such as Hildegard von Bingen of the twelfth century and Mechthild von Hackeborn of the thirteenth century.

Lefèvre enthusiastically studied the works of the fifteenth-century hermetic writer Nicholas of Cusa and in 1514 produced a three-volume edition of his works, *Opera omnia* (Complete Works). Interest in the mystical properties of mathematics, Cusa insisted on a seemingly contradictory *docta ignorantia* (learned ignorance), identifying God as the synthesis of all worldly contradictions and positing an abstract metaphysics replete with mathematical symbols. Cusa put forward a model of three levels of understanding, the sensual, the rational, and the intellectual, each representing an improvement over the previous. He taught that it is through the hermetic journey from senses to rational thought, then from reason to pure intellect, that one grasps the simplicity of the divine mind. Cusa maintained that positive theology, or making positive assertions about the nature of God, was ultimately limiting. He believed that it was only through negative theology, which consists of defining God's nature by addressing and eliminating what God is not, that one could come to understand more fully the nature of God. Works such as those of Cusa allowed Lefèvre to reconcile Aristotelian scientific thought and his Christian beliefs.

The publication of Aristotle's *Metaphysica* (Metaphysics) in 1515 was a significant milestone for Lefèvre. The version he based his edition on was the Bessarion translation he had received from Pico della Mirandola during his trip to Italy. At this point Lefèvre had gone full circle, producing an edition for which he had written an introduction more than twenty years earlier,

Introductio in metaphysicorum libros Aristotelis. This edition was the last of an impressive list of publications that included all of the philosopher's works. Until 1515, Lefèvre was known primarily among scholars, including Thomas More, for giving them the true Aristotle.

Lefèvre then began to devote his efforts exclusively to the Bible, publishing in 1517 and 1519 two critical essays on Mary Magdalene, *De Maria Magdalena & triduo Christi disceptatio* (1517, Dispute on Mary Magdalene and the Three Days of Christ) and *De tribus et unica Magdalena disceptatio secunda* (1519, Second Debate on the Three and One Magdalene). In these writings he endeavored to prove that Mary, sister of Lazarus, Mary Magdalene, and the penitent woman who anointed Christ's feet were three distinct persons. This opinion, novel at the time, gave rise to a violent controversy. He was attacked by Noël Béda, syndic of the University of Paris, and his ideas were condemned by the Sorbonne in 1521, the same year that this faculty excommunicated Luther. Lefèvre had the good fortune of being protected by King François I and his sister, Marguerite de Navarre, and the Sorbonne was therefore blocked from prosecuting him.

In 1521 Lefèvre left to follow his friend Briçonnet, who had just been appointed bishop of the city of Meaux. In 1523 Bishop Briçonnet appointed Lefèvre as his vicar-general. Lefèvre became a member of the Circle of Meaux, a group of evangelical humanists who used the diocese of Meaux to institute liturgical reforms that they believed were more in harmony with the Christianity of the New Testament. Encouraged by Briçonnet's leadership and Marguerite de Navarre's protection, the Circle of Meaux engaged in a period of bold experimentation in reform-minded practices. Saint worship was diminished, greater portions of the mass were done in French, and preaching, including that of Lefèvre, focused on the need to study directly the holy Scriptures. The Circle became an important force driving institutional reforms based on the evangelical, humanistic ideas.

Lefèvre continued his biblical studies, publishing the *Commentarii initiatorii in quartuor Evangelia* (Initial Commentary on the Four Gospels) in 1522. The following year he published French translations of the New Testament and the Psalms: *Nouveau Testament: Les quatre Evangiles* (New Testament, The Four Gospels), *Nouveau Testament: Les epistres, les actes et l'apocalypse* (New Testament: The Epistles, Acts, and the Apocalypse), and *Le psaultier de David* (The Psalter of David). In 1525 he published *Epistres & Evangiles pour les cinquante & deux sepmaines de l'an* (Epistles and Gospels for the Fifty-two Weeks of the Year). As these works revealed the author's sympathies for the doctrines of the reformers, they again brought him into conflict with the Sorbonne.

Title page for the volume of Lefèvre's philosophical works that was published four years after his death (from <http://www.ucm.es/BUCM/foa/exposiciones/01BulaCisneriana/lefebre43.htm>)

Lefèvre's commentary on the Gospels was condemned in 1523, and only the interposition of the king shielded him temporarily from further attack. After Luther made it more difficult to be neutral, the Sorbonne denounced the Circle of Meaux as heretical in 1525. Some members recanted; others became avowed Protestants; and still others fled into exile or to the shelter of Marguerite de Navarre's court. During the Spanish captivity of François I after the battle of Pavia (1525), further proceedings were instituted against Lefèvre for his seemingly subversive doctrines, and he was forced to seek safety in Strasbourg, along with Gérard Roussel, a future Protestant leader. After the king's release, Lefèvre was recalled from exile in 1526. During his return journey he passed through Basel, where he had the pleasure of meeting Erasmus.

François I appointed Lefèvre royal librarian and tutor of his youngest son, a four-year-old, at the royal residence in Blois (1526). This position gave Lefèvre the time he needed to complete his work on the translation of the Bible, and he published *L'Ancien Testament* (The Old Testament) in Antwerp in 1528. The fact that his Old Testament translation had to be published in Holland is significant. The continuation of his translation of the Bible into French proved more and more dangerous, and with each new translation his position became more precarious. In 1530 he had to leave Blois, accompanying Marguerite de Navarre to Nérac, where he spent the last years of his life under her protection. During these years he met Calvin and the poet Clément Marot, both of whom fled Paris in 1534 when the Affair of the Placards greatly increased the persecution of evangelical humanists and made Paris a particularly dangerous place. Lefèvre died at Nérac in 1536, the same year as Erasmus.

Best known as the first person to translate the entire Bible into French, Jacques Lefèvre d'Etaples was only an average Latin scholar and a rather mediocre Greek scholar. He began as a commentator; then he became a translator; and he found some of his greatest satisfaction as a preacher at Meaux, sympathetic to reform. Although advocating some of the ideas that later became integral to the Reformation, Lefèvre, like Erasmus, believed in reform from within and refused to break with the church. As Hughes has observed, while it is true that Lefèvre never deserted the Catholic church, it is also true that he wholeheartedly dedicated himself to the cause of biblical doctrine and felt a deep affinity of mind and purpose with those who promoted the reform of the church. Both Catholics and Protestants have claimed him as their own.

Biographies:

Guy Bedouelle, *Lefèvre d'Etaples et l'Intelligence des Ecritures* (Geneva: Droz, 1976);

Philip Edgcumbe Hughes, *Lefèvre: Pioneer of Ecclesiastical Renewal in France* (Grand Rapids, Mich: Eerdmans, 1984).

References:

Irena Backus, "Renaissance Attitudes to New Testament Apocryphal Writings: Jacques Lefèvre d'Etaples and His Epigones," *Renaissance Quarterly*, 51 (1998): 1169–1198;

Robert D. Cottrell, "Lefèvre d'Etaples and the Limits of Biblical Interpretation," *Oeuvres et Critiques*, 20 (1995): 79–95;

Eugene F. Rice Jr., "The Humanist Idea of Christian Antiquity: Lefèvre d'Etaples and His Circle," *Studies in the Renaissance*, 9 (1962): 126–160;

Rice, *The Prefatory Epistles of Jacques Lefèvre d'Etaples and Related Texts* (New York: Columbia University Press, 1972);

Richard Stauffer, "Lefèvre d'Etaples, artisan ou spectateur de la Réforme," in his *Interprètes de la Bible* (Paris: Editions Beauchesne, 1980), pp. 11–25.

Jean Lemaire de Belges
(1473 – ?)

Frederic J. Baumgartner
Virginia Polytechnic Institute and State University

BOOKS: *Petit Livret Sommaire,* by Lemaire and others (N.p., 1498);

Le Temple d'Honneur et de Vertus (Paris: Antoine Vérard, 1503);

La pompe funeralle des obsequies du feu Roy dom Phelippes, filz vnique de lempereur Maximilian cesar auguste (Antwerp: Guillaume Voserman, 1508);

La Concorde du gendre humain (Brussels: Thomas de La Nooe, 1509);

La Légende des Vénitiens (Lyon: Jean de Vingle, 1509);

Les illustrations de Gavle et singvlaritez de Troye avec les deux epistres de Lamant Vert (Lyon: Etienne Baland, circa 1510);

Le traictie intitule de la difference des scismes et des concilles de leglise (Lyon: Etienne Baland, 1511);

Le second liure des Illustrations de Gaule et singularitez de Troye (Lyon: Etienne Baland, 1512);

Le tiers liure des Illustrations de Gaule et singularitez de Troye (Paris: Geoffroy de Marnef, 1513);

Lepistre du Roy a Hector de Troye (Paris: Geoffroy de Marnef, 1513).

Editions and Collections: *Lepistre du roy a Hector de Troye. Le traicte de la difference des scismes* (Paris: P. Le Noir, 1528);

Le promptuaire des conciles de leglise catholique, auec les scismes & la differece diceulx (Lyon: Romain Morin, 1532); translated by John Gowgh as *The abbreuyacyon of all general councellys holden in Grecia, Germania, Italia, et Gallia* (London: John Gowgh, 1539);

Les illustrations de Gavle et singvlaritez de Troye, auec la Couronne Margaritique, & plusieurs autres œuures de luy, non iamais encore imprimees (Lyon: Jean de Tovrne, 1549);

Oeuvres, edited by Auguste Jean Stecher (Hildesheim: G. Olms, 1882);

La concorde des deux langages, edited by Jean Frappier (Paris: Libraire Droz, 1947);

Les épitres de l'amant vert, edited by Frappier (Geneva: Libraire Droz, 1948);

Jean Lemaire de Belges, seated, as portrayed by an unknown artist (Bildarchiv, Österreichische Nationalbibliothek, Vienna)

Le temple d'honneur et de vertus, edited by Henri Hornik (Geneva: Libraire Droz, 1957);

La concorde des deux langages, et Les épîtres de l'amant vert, edited by Marcel Françon (Cambridge, Mass.: Schoenhof's, 1964);

La concorde du genre humain, edited by Pierre Jodogne (Brussels: Palais des Académies, 1964);

Traité de la différence des schismes et des conciles de l'Eglise, edited by Jennifer Britnell (Geneva: Librairie Droz, 1997);

La légende des Vénitiens (1509), edited by Anne Schoysman (Brussels: Académie royale de Belgique, 1999);

Epistre du roy à Hector et autres pièces de circonstances (1511–1513), edited by Adrian Armstrong and Britnell (Paris: Société des textes français modernes, 2000);

Chronique de 1507, edited by Anne Schoysman Zambrini and Jean-Marie Cauchies (Brussels: Académie royale de Belgique, 2001);

Des Anciennes pompes funerailles, edited by Marie Fontaine (Paris: Sociéte des Textes Français Modernes, 2001).

Jean Lemaire de Belges was a Walloon poet, historian, and pamphleteer who, writing in French, was one of the last and perhaps the best of the school of poetic Rhétoriqueurs (rhetoricians). He was also the chief forerunner, both in style and in thought, of the Renaissance humanists in France and Flanders.

Lemaire was a native of Bavay in Hainault (then in the Burgundian Netherlands, now in the French department of Nord). The year of his birth, 1473, to which he attested by writing that he was twenty-seven years old in 1500, is more certain than that of his death, something highly unusual for persons of his era. He was born into a bourgeois family that was well connected to the noted author Jean Molinet, who was either Lemaire's godfather or an uncle, or perhaps both. He introduced Lemaire to writing poetry and took an active role in furthering his career. Lemaire's early education took place in Valenciennes, where Molinet resided. Lemaire called himself a disciple of Molinet in one of his first works.

During Lemaire's teenage years he received a benefice from the bishop of Cambrai, which allowed him to study at the University of Paris, according to an autobiographical sketch found in the first of the three volumes he published under the general title *Les illvstrations de Gavle et singvlaritez de Troye* (Illustrations of Gaul and Singularities of Troy). It is not known what degrees if any he took from the university, but he may have had the humanist Robert Gaguin as a teacher, as later he often praised him highly. By 1498 Lemaire was serving as clerk for finances for Pierre de Bourbon, whose wife, Anne de Beaujeu, had served as guardian for King Charles VIII, her younger brother. Lemaire spent most of his time in that position at the Burgundian court in Beaujolais, where he made contact with the large Italian colony in nearby Lyon and met Symphorien Champier, the scholarly physician; Jean Per-

réal, the noted artist and architect; and Guillaume de Cretin, one of the more respected poets of the time, regarded as the leader of the Rhétoriqueurs.

The term Rhétoriqueurs was used for a dozen or more poets from the late fifteenth and early sixteenth centuries, including Cretin, Jean Bouchet, André de La Vigne, Jean d'Auton, Jean Marot (father of Clément), Octovien de Saint-Gelais, and eventually Lemaire. The term was coined as an insult by Guillaume Coquillart, a somewhat older poet who objected to their obsession with style over content and called them *les grands rhétoriqueurs.* They invented new words from Latin and used complicated rhyming and elaborate word games. For example, Jean Marot wrote a poem dedicated to Queen Anne of Brittany in which the first letter of each line spelled out her name and title, a device called an acrostic. Later generations of French poets and modern literary scholars have been scathing in their criticism of them, although Lemaire was sometimes excluded or less harshly criticized. In *The Dawn of the French Renaissance* (1918) Arthur Tilley wrote, "No school or *cenacle* [coterie] was ever so foolish, so dull, or so pretentious as that school of *grands rhétoriqueurs.*" Later literary critics, studying their works as serious literary texts, have been less severe.

The Rhétoriqueurs had much in common, including a strong interest in classical Latin, even if their knowledge of it was mediocre, an interest in history, especially of the realm of France, and an active involvement in the literary life of the French court of their era. Louis XII served as an inspiration for several Rhétoriqueurs, including Lemaire, with his statement that the Greeks had done mediocre deeds in war but had had great writers to embellish them, while the Romans had done great deeds and wrote of them with dignity; the French also had been great in war but lacked great writers to tell about it. Like Lemaire, several Rhétoriqueurs were natives of lands held by the Burgundian dukes and sought patronage at the Burgundian court as well as at the French court.

Lemaire published his first verses in Latin and French in 1498 in a compilation of poems from Ovid, Virgil, Seneca, several contemporary poets, and himself, which he called *Petit Livret Sommaire* (Little Handbook). He modeled the book after the Song of Songs and gives even the works by the pagan authors a Christian flavor. His poem "Une Oraison composée par Jehan Le Maire" (A Prayer Composed by Jean Lemaire), which he wrote in honor of the Virgin Mary, demonstrates the wordplay for which the Rhétoriqueurs were famous. An acrostic, "Salve Regina misericordia" (Hail, Queen of Mercy!), runs both vertically and diagonally through the poem.

In 1500 he began writing the fabulous narratives that make up his *Illustrations de Gaule et singularitez de Troye,* which were eventually published in three volumes (n.d. [1510?], 1512, 1513) and became his best-known work. The death of Pierre de Bourbon in 1502 resulted in Lemaire leaving the Bourbon court at Moulins. He later expressed his regret at having to leave the delightful vineyard of Moulins. Seeking patronage elsewhere, he presented his *Le Temple d'Honneur et de Vertus* (n.d., Temple of Honor and Virtue), his first major work, to Louis of Luxembourg, Comte (Count) de Ligny. Cretin, whom Lemaire later credited with helping him define his vocation as a poet, wrote a dedicatory poem for the collection, which, like many of the works of the Rhétoriqueurs, combined verse and prose. Lemaire later claimed that in *Le Temple d'Honneur et de Vertus* he introduced terza rima, in which the first and third lines of each triplet end in the same vowel sound, to French poetry.

Lemaire's lifelong bad luck in choosing patrons manifested itself again when Louis of Luxembourg died in December 1503. He quickly wrote "La plaincte du desire" (1509, The Complaint of Desire) in Louis's honor and dedicated it to Anne of Brittany. The plot of the poem involves the poet being awakened by the sound of women weeping to find Dame Nature, with her two handmaidens Painting and Rhetoric, inconsolable at Louis's death. The two handmaidens call on their disciples to help comfort Dame Nature, thus providing the poet with the opportunity to link the great painters and poets of his era with those of the past. Among the great painters he included his friend Perréal with Italians such as Leonardo da Vinci and Giovanni Bellini, and among the great poets such as Virgil and Catullus he lists most of the Rhétoriqueurs. Rhetoric's task is convincing the readers of the poem that they should not lament Louis's death but honor him for his surpassing worth.

Lemaire's next source of patronage was Margaret of Austria, daughter of Emperor Maximilian I and aunt of future emperor Charles V. Her accounts reveal that he received a generous pension of ten *écus* (gold crowns) in the money of Piedmont while at her court in Turin in 1504. She was married to Philibert of Savoy, and when he died in September 1504, Lemaire wrote "La Couronne margaritique" (1549, The Crown of Pearls) for her. Both verse and prose, this work presents Dame Virtue taking pity on the grieving widow. To make a crown for Margaret, she summons a renowned goldsmith, who uses as his model ten nymphs arranged in a circle with a stone on each of their foreheads. Ten philosophers then explain the meaning of the stones. For example, Lemaire has Gaguin provide the explanation of the first gem, a pearl. Lemaire may have coined the term *urbanité* (urbanity) in this work.

Another death, that of Margaret's pet green parrot devoured by a dog, was the occasion for one of his best-known works, *Les epîtres de l'amant vert* (Letters from the Green Lover), written in 1505 and published in 1510. The poem took the form of two letters the parrot writes to his mistress. The first has the parrot still alive but in despair over Margaret's absence on a political mission. He declares his intention of killing himself by throwing himself into the jaws of a dog. The second has the parrot writing to her from the grave to describe the afterlife. Lighthearted and whimsical, the poem shows Lemaire's talent for humor and inventiveness.

Margaret secured for him the position of secretary and historiographer to her brother, Philip of Castile, Charles V's father, replacing Molinet in those offices, who took the same positions with Margaret. Philip sent Lemaire to Venice and Rome to collect books and antiquities, but Lemaire's bad luck with his patrons continued when Philip died in 1506. He returned to Margaret's service, accompanying her when she became the governor of the Netherlands for her nephew and securing a position as canon in the church of Notre Dame in Valenciennes, where he had studied as a child. Margaret made him her secretary and historiographer when Molinet died in 1507 and also involved him in designing and constructing a church to house the tomb for her brother at Bourg-en-Bresse. Perréal was the principal architect for the project. Lemaire eventually lost his commission for the tomb when he chose marble that Margaret found unsatisfactory. In 1508 he wrote a description of Philip's funeral at Malines, "Les pompes funerailles" (1549, The Funeral Ceremony).

Meanwhile, Lemaire was also seeking patronage from Louis XII. In 1509, while he was residing at Dole in the Franche-Comté, he wrote *La légende des Vénitiens* (The Legend of the Venetians), for which he received a royal privilege to print, dated 30 July 1509, which gave him a three-year copyright on the work. The work was intended as propaganda for the French cause in a brief war with Venice that had broken out in 1509 largely at the instigation of Pope Julius II, *il papa terribile* (The Awesome Pope), for the purpose of recovering several towns in the papal states that Venice had seized. It detailed all of the crimes that Venice had allegedly committed since Charlemagne's time.

The next year the publication of *Les illvstrations de Gavle et singvlaritez de Troye avec les deux epistres de Lamant Vert* (1510, The Illustrations of Gaul and Singularities of Troy with Both Letters of Lamant Vert) became part of his quest for patronage from the French king. This

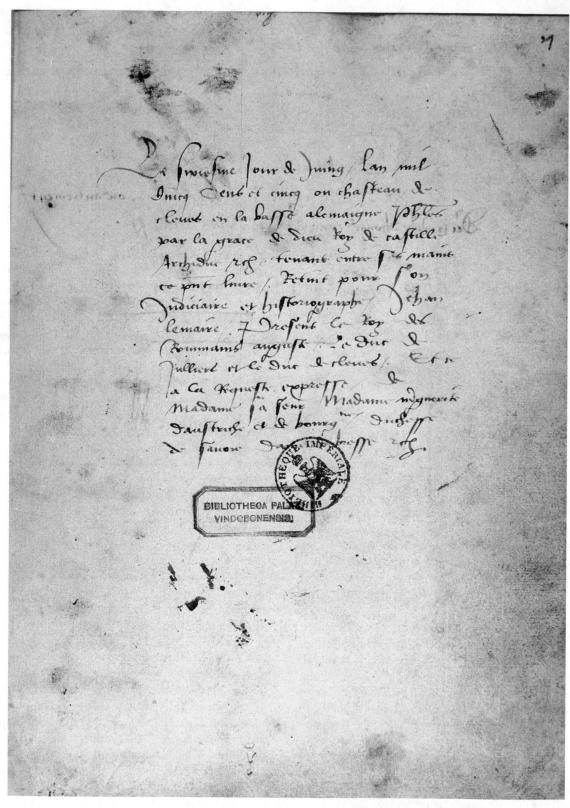

Lemaire's dedication for the manuscript "La Couronne margaritique" (Bildarchiv, Österreichische Nationalbibliothek, Vienna)

work was largely responsible for popularizing the myth that the Gauls, based on the presence of the Galatians or Celts in Asia Minor, had founded Troy and that after the fall of the city, led by Francus, the son of Hector, they had fled back to Gaul to create French culture, society, and monarchy. Pharamond, the legendary founder of the Frankish Merovingian dynasty, was supposedly a descendent of Francus, who gave his name to the Franks; thus, the Gauls and the Franks were tied together in a common legacy bound up in the realm of France and its monarchy. As a direct descendant of both Hector and Aeneas, the French king was thus believed to be the rightful sovereign of both Asia Minor and Rome, founded by the Trojans. Hence, the French king was the proper leader of any crusade to recover Constantinople and Asia Minor from the Turks. By tracing in his first two volumes the genealogy of European kings from Noah to Priam and then in *Le tiers liure des Illustrations de Gaule et Singularitez de Troye* (1513, The Third Book . . .) the line of Frankish kings from Hector to Charlemagne, Lemaire proclaimed that the Trojan ancestry was the common patrimony of all European monarchs, especially the Holy Roman Emperors, who also claimed their origin in Charlemagne. He thereby expressed his desire for a unified realm of France and Brittany, the original homeland of the Gauls, with Germany, Austria, and Hungary, the lands of the east Franks, surely with an eye toward retaining the favor of his former Habsburg patrons.

The myth of the Trojan origins of the French monarchy was not original with Lemaire. He drew heavily from Gaguin's *Compendium de origine et gestis Francorum* (1495, Compendium of the Origin and Deeds of the Franks) and even more so from Giovanni Nanni's edition of Berosus the Chaldean's history, *Antiquitatum libri quinque* (Five Books of Antiquities), which had been published in 1489. Berosus's pseudohistory conjured up a past in which Noah, the ancestor of the Trojans, chose to be buried at Rome. Lemaire's own pseudohistory included the idea that Celtic was the ancestral language of Greek, which in turn engendered French. Hoping to flatter Anne of Brittany, he spoke of her natural Breton tongue, calling it the true Trojan language, although she could not speak Breton. Since one of Louis XII's mottos was *Ultius avos Torjae* (Avenge our Trojan ancestors), it is easy to see how Lemaire expected *Les Illustrations de Gaule* to secure patronage from the French crown, as it did.

After his victory over Venice in 1509, Louis XII found himself the object of Julius II's wrath and cunning, when the league the Pope had organized against Venice suddenly turned against France. At a time when the Pope personally commanded the papal army in the field, the French king used a religious weapon against him by summoning a general council of the church to declare Julius an antipope. In the context of Louis's poorly attended council at Pisa, Lemaire wrote *Le traictie intitule de la difference des scismes et des concilles de leglise* (Treatise on the Difference between Schisms and Councils of the Church), which was printed at Lyons in 1511. After giving a long history of both church councils and schisms and citing Lorenzo Valla's demonstration that the Donation of Constantine was a forgery, he concluded that not only was Louis's council a true one but also that the papacy had created most schisms. Lemaire had strong words in favor of the Pragmatic Sanction of 1438, which had removed the papacy from any role in appointing bishops in the French church, as vital for the "grand bien honneur de nostre religion chrestienne" (great good honor of our Christian religion). Julius, he proclaimed, was planning his own schism through the Fifth Council of Lateran that he had summoned. Lemaire's position as revealed in his book is that of a staunch Gallicanist, unwilling to grant the papacy more than a token authority over the French church. The treatise proved to be immensely popular, as six thousand copies were sold, an astounding number for that era. Protestants later gleefully annexed Lemaire's blistering attack on the papacy and saw to it that a Latin translation of it was reprinted as late as 1627. Both the Sorbonne and the papal Index of Forbidden Books included it on their lists of banned works in the 1550s.

Lemaire had not abandoned poetry entirely for his polemical prose works. In 1511 he finished his *La concorde des deux langages* (Concord of the Two Languages), which was printed with his *Lespistre du Roy a Hector de Troye* (Letter from the King to Hector of Troy) under the latter title in 1513. Again combining prose and poetry, Lemaire presents himself as overhearing a debate over the value of the French and the Tuscan languages. The pro-French speaker names Jean de Meung, the "Dante de la langue française" (Dante of the French language), and many of the Rhétoriqueurs as proof of the superiority of French, with Cretin labeled "le prince des poëtes" (the prince of poets). The pro-Italian speaker has Dante, Petrarch, and Boccaccio along with several contemporaries to make the case for his language. They ask the author to suggest how they can reach a conclusion in the debate, since they agree that both have a strong case. Moved by a desire to bring about a perpetual peace between the two nations, Lemaire states that he cannot achieve it in the Temple of Venus, where he had spent his youth, for Venus is associated with Mars, the god of war. Rather he must be admitted to the Temple of Minerva, the goddess of study and learning. The heart of the work is made up of the descriptions of the two temples, but he devotes three times as much space to the Temple of Venus. According to Arthur Tilley in *The Dawn of the French Renaissance,* "The description of the Temple of Venus . . . is inspired by the Renaissance in its most pagan mood." Lemaire concludes the work with a dream in which an historian, an old man with a long white beard, promises to lead him to Repose and Reward, who will reveal to him the concord of the two languages.

In 1512 Lemaire's dispute with Margaret of Austria over his choice of marble for her brother's tomb, along with his increasingly pro-France stance in his works, cost him his positions with her. He received 70 *écus* from her as back pay and entered the service of Anne of Brittany as her *indiciaire* (chronicler). Lemaire spent much of the year 1512 in Brittany searching for sources for a history of the duchy, which was never written. He dedicated *Le second liure des Illustrations de Gaule et singularitez de Troye* (The Second book . . .) to her daughter Claude and the third to Anne herself. He was present at Anne's funeral in the abbey church of St-Denis in 1514 and dedicated his *Pompes funebres d'Anne de Bretagne,* a poem not published until the 1882 edition of *Oeuvres* (Works), to Claude. Anne's husband Louis XII died on 1 January 1515, and the last piece of evidence that exists for Lemaire's life appeared that year in the form of his translation of a poem, *La Description des roses* (Description of the Roses), wrongly attributed to Virgil, which was dedicated to the new king François I and his queen Claude. At that point Lemaire disappeared from history. His biographers generally agree that he probably did not die in 1515 or the next several years, because the demise of a noted author as close to the royal family as he had been should have occasioned some notice. If he had stopped writing in 1515, however, he would have slipped out of the public eye, and his death some years later might not have been noted. In February 1526 Galiot du Pré published *Traictez singuliers,* a collection of poems from several deceased poets, which referred to him as the "late" Jean Lemaire, and it is assumed that he had died before then.

Lemaire's reputation remained high for some four decades after his last work appeared. Clément Marot, whose father was Lemaire's friend, was fifteen when he met the older poet and received advice on his first verses, for which he was always grateful. Joachim du Bellay in his *Deffense et Illustration de la langue francoyse* (1549, Defense and Illustration of the French Language) praised Lemaire as the first to give luster to the French language and drew heavily from his work. Literary historians regard Pierre de Ronsard as Lemaire's truest disciple among the Pléïade, all of whom he influenced. Ronsard's *La Françiade* (1572) was based largely on *Illustrations de Gaule et singularitez de Troye.* Among later French authors, however, none owed as much to him as did François Rabelais. In *Pantagruel* (1532) especially, Rabelais seems to draw descriptions, phrases, and ideas from Lemaire's works and satirizes the papacy by portraying Lemaire dressed as a pope and accepting homage from kings and emperors. In 1549 an edition of most of Lemaire's works was printed, indicating a strong interest in them at mid sixteenth century. After 1560, however, the contempt that the Pléïade had for the Rhétoriqueurs was extended to Lemaire as well.

Like most of his contemporaries, Jean Lemaire de Belges produced his works either on commission or with the hope of impressing a powerful person who would grant him patronage. His success in finding patronage indicates that his tastes coincided well with those at the highest levels of French and Burgundian societies. His patrons—Louis XII, Anne of Brittany, and Margaret of Austria—laid the foundation for the French Renaissance that François I would so successfully build upon after 1515. William Calin in his essay "Jean Lemaire de Belges: Courtly Narrative at the Close of the Middle Ages" states that Lemaire, who was "equally divided between North and South, Middle Ages and Renaissance, Burgundy and France, is the perfect model for the problems brought about by this sort of periodization. He belongs to all of the categories and none of them." One would be hard put to find a better description of this transitional figure.

Biographies:

Philipp Becker, *Jean Lemaire, der erste humanistische dichter Frankreichs* (Strassburg: Karl J. Trübner, 1893);

Pierre Jodogne, *Jean Lemaire de Belges, écrivain franco-bouguignon* (Brussels: Académie royale de Belgique, 1972).

Bibliography:

Kathleen Mum, *A Contribution to the Study of Jean Lemaire de Belges: A Critical Study of Bio-bibliographical Data, Including a Transcript of Various Unpublished Works* (Southdale, Penn.: Mennonite Publishing House, 1936).

References:

James Beard, "Letters from the Elysian Fields: A Group of Poems for Louis XII," *Bibliothèque d'humanisme et renaissance,* 31 (1969): 27–38;

Jennifer Britnell, "The Antipapalism of Jean Lemaire de Belges' *Traité de la Difference des Schismes et des Con-*

ciles," *The Sixteenth Century Journal,* 24 (1993): 783–800;

Britnell, "La mort de Jean Lemaire des Belges, l'édition de 1517 du *Traité des schismes et des conciles,* et les impertinences d'un éditeur," *Bibliothèque d'humanisme et renaissance,* 56 (1994): 27–33;

Cynthia Brown, "Jean Lemaire's *La Concorde des deux langages:* The Merging of Politics, Language, and Poetry," *Fifteenth-Century Studies,* 3 (1980): 29–39;

Brown, "The Rise of Literary Consciousness in Late Medieval France: Jean Lemaire and the Rhétoriqueur Tradition," *Journal of Medieval and Renaissance Studies,* 13 (1983): 51–74;

Brown, *The Shaping of History and Poetry in Late Medieval France* (Birmingham, Ala.: Summa, 1985);

William Calin, "Jean Lemaire de Belges: Courtly Narrative at the Close of the Middle Ages," in *The Nature of Medieval Narrative,* edited by Minette Grunman-Gaudet and Robin Jones (Lexington, Ky.: French Forum, 1980), pp. 205–216;

Michael Jenkins, *Artful Eloquence: Jean Lemaire de Belges and the Rhetorical Tradition* (Chapel Hill: University of North Carolina Department of Romance Languages, 1971);

Judy Kem, *Jean Lemaire de Belges's* Les illustrations de Gaule et singularitz de Troyes (New York: Peter Lang, 1984);

Michael Randall, *Building Resemblance: Analogical Imagery in the Early French Renaissance* (Baltimore: Johns Hopkins University Press, 1996), pp. 72–102;

Marian Rothstein, "Jean Lemaire de Belges 'Illustrations de Gaule et singularitez de Troye': Politics and Unity," *Bibliothèque d'humanisme et renaissance,* 52 (1990): 593–609;

Michael Sherman, "Political Propaganda and Renaissance Culture: French Reactions to the League of Cambrai, 1509–1510," *Sixteenth Century Journal,* 8 (1977): 97–128.

Papers:

The major archive for Jean Lemaire de Belges's manuscripts is the Bibliothèque nationale, Paris.

Pierre de L'Estoile

(1546 – 11 October 1611)

Frederic J. Baumgartner
Virginia Polytechnic Institute and State University

BOOKS: *Iournal des choses memorables advenues durant le règne de Henri III. roi de France et de Pologne,* anonymous, edited by Pierre Dupuy (N.p., 1621);

Mémoires pour servir à l'histoire de France: Contenant ce qui s'est passé de plus remarquable dans ce royaume depuis 1574 jusqu'en 1611. Avec les portraits des Rois, Reines, Princes, Princesses & autres personnes illustres dont il y est fait mention, 2 volumes, edited by Jean Godefroy (Cologne [i.e., Brussels]: Printed by the heirs of Herman Demen, 1719);

Mémoires-journaux de Pierre de L'Estoile: Edition pour la première fois complète et entièrement conforme aux manuscrits originaux, 11 volumes, edited by Gustave Brunet, Aimé Louis Champollion-Figeac, Eugène Halpen, P. L. Jacob, Charles Alexandre Read, Philippe Tamizey de Larroque, and Eduoard Tricotel (Paris: Librairie des bibliophiles, 1875–1883).

Editions and Collections: *Journal du regne de Henry IV, roi de France et de Navarre,* 4 volumes (The Hague: Vaillant, 1741);

Mémoires pour servir à l'histoire de France, et Journal de Henri III et de Henri IV, 5 volumes, edited by Claude-Bernard Petitot, Collection complète de mémoires relatifs à l'histoire de France, series 1, volumes 45–49 (Paris: Foucault, 1819–1826);

Journal de L'Estoile pour le règne de Henri III (1574–1589), edited by Louis Raymond Lefèvre (Paris: Gallimard, 1943);

Journal de L'Estoile pour le règne de Henri IV, 3 volumes, edited by Lefèvre and André Martin (Paris: Gallimard, 1948–1960);

Registre-journal du règne de Henri III, 6 volumes published, edited by Madeleine Lazard and Gilbert Shrenck (Geneva: Droz, 1992–).

Edition in English: *The Paris of Henry of Navarre, as Seen by Pierre de l'Estoile: Selections from His Mémoires-Journaux,* edited and translated by Nancy Roelker (Cambridge, Mass.: Harvard University Press, 1958).

OTHER: *Fragment des Recueils de Pierre de l'Estoile: Edition critique originale,* collected by L'Estoile, edited by Isabelle Armitage (Lawrence: University of Kansas Publications, 1976).

Pierre de L'Estoile's journal and the pamphlets, broadsides, and books he collected are the most valuable sources of information about life in Paris during the last phases of the French Wars of Religion and the reign of Henri IV. His descriptions are among the most vivid to come out of the sixteenth century, and his observations of the political events through which he lived continue to provide historians with insights into the anarchy of the religious wars and the recovery under Henri.

There is little mention of L'Estoile in late-sixteenth-century documents beyond his presence on payrolls of the chancery and some entries in the records of the Paris notaries. What is known about him comes largely from his journal, and it provides little information about his life until his final years. He was born in Paris in 1546 into a bourgeois family with a long tradition of service in the judicial courts. The L'Estoiles were from Orléans, where they had held high offices under the dukes of Orléans. Pierre de L'Estoile's grandfather, also named Pierre, was a prominent legal scholar and a supporter of the Gallican method of teaching law; so called because of its popularity in sixteenth-century French universities, the method was based on the application of humanist techniques to the study of law and held that a thorough knowledge of Roman culture and of Latin was necessary for a proper understanding of Roman law. Among L'Estoile's grandfather's students at the University of Orléans were Jean Calvin and Théodore de Bèze. L'Estoile's father, Louis de L'Estoile, held several high royal offices, including one of the seven presidencies of the Parlement of Paris. L'Estoile's mother, Marguerite de Monthalon, came from another judicial family with many offices in the royal courts. Her father was a president of the Parlement of Paris and was *garde des sceaux* (keeper of the royal seals) during the reign of François I. Through her L'Estoile was related to several prominent parlementaire families, including the De Thous.

L'Estoile studied liberal arts at the University of Orléans; Matthieu Béroalde, who later became a Calvinist minister in Geneva, taught him ancient languages. Among his fellow students was the Huguenot author Theodore-Agrippa d'Aubigné. He then studied law briefly at Bourges, where he was tutored by Alexander Arbuthnot, who, after returning home to Scotland, became noted as a poet and played a role in the Scottish Reformation. These connections help to explain the tolerance L'Estoile later exhibited. The most noted of his law professors at Bourges was Jacques Cujas, an advocate of the Gallican method.

L'Estoile returned to Paris around 1566 and never left again for any extended period. In February 1569 he married Anne de Baillon; she was the daughter of Jean de Baillon, head of the Epargne (royal treasury). They had seven children, six of whom survived infancy. During the year of his marriage L'Estoile purchased the office of *grand-audiencier* in the royal chancery, which carried the title of royal secretary. The *grand-audiencier* presented the chancellor with documents to be sealed and cases for Parlement to hear; in addition to a good salary, he received fees from those for whom the documents were drawn up. L'Estoile accumulated a small fortune from his four decades of service in the office. It is not clear why he never secured a higher position, since he demonstrated his loyalty to the monarchy over the years and was wealthy enough to afford one.

L'Estoile began the journal on which his fame rests in 1574. He revised it late in life, so that it exists in two manuscript versions. The changes mostly involve adding precise dates to the loose chronology of the first version. The manuscripts have the title "Registre-journal d'un curieux" (Register-Journal of a Curious Man). L'Estoile constantly uses some variant of *curieux* (curious) to explain how he came to see or to hear of something that he wrote down. Nothing escapes his attention, whether it concerns war, politics, crime, processions, festivals, religious services, marriages, funerals, duels, the behavior of gentlemen and ladies, or popular gossip in the streets. His writing style is that of a well-educated but not pedantic Parisian: he rarely uses Latinisms, and his language reflects popular usage—in part because he is often paraphrasing or quoting street gossip. In addition to the major figures of the French court, he frequently mentions foreign leaders such as Queen Elizabeth, Mary Stuart, Francis Drake, Philip II, and Sultan Selim II. L'Estoile was also interested in natural events, noting epidemics, extreme cold and heat, and flooding in Paris, and unusual phenomena such as the births of deformed babies or the appearance of fiery objects in the sky. In his entry for 12 August 1595 he describes a wolf swimming across the Seine and eating a child as "a monstrous thing and a bad omen."

L'Estoile was a compulsive collector of coins and of printed works, including books, pamphlets, placards,

and broadsides; he copied many of the shorter pieces into his journal. His collection was passed on to his heirs and eventually to the Bibliothèque Nationale; his copies of many of these works are the only ones known to exist. He was also compulsive about recording the prices of the pieces he collected. As he aged, he spent more time seeking out books and paid more for them. He often notes the publication of books, even when he has not purchased a copy, and he sometimes provides commentaries on books he has bought. For example, he describes *Memoires d'estat et religion sous Charles IX* (Memoirs of State and Religion under Charles IX), which was published anonymously in October 1574, as "a jumble, too quickly published to contain the truth. . . . But there are many things worth knowing about in these volumes, and some singular treatises that will be useful in writing the history of our times."

L'Estoile's journal begins with the statement that Charles IX died on 30 May 1574 at three o'clock in the afternoon at Vincennes, after a long illness that had led many to predict his death for months. L'Estoile describes the funeral; the establishment of the regency of Queen Mother Catherine de Médicis until Charles's younger brother Henri could return to France from Poland, of which he had been elected king a year earlier (Catherine had persuaded Charles to bribe the Polish nobles to choose Henri, and he had taken the throne five months before Charles's death); and the defeat of a conspiracy led by the youngest of the royal brothers, François, Duke of Alençon, to take the throne before Henri could get home.

L'Estoile's entry for 12 June 1574 includes a copy of a poem attacking the memory of the dead king:

> More cruel than Nero, than Tiberius, more scheming,
> Hated by his subjects, mocked abroad,
> . . . .
> His entire reign was a horrible carnage,
> And he died like a mad dog locked in a cage.

L'Estoile notes that the author of this piece of doggerel is alleged to be a Huguenot, but he is certain that it was a "very Catholic lawyer in the Parlement of Paris."

The new king was crowned Henri III at Reims on 11 February 1575; L'Estoile takes as a bad omen that Henri complained that the crown was so heavy that it hurt his head and that it almost fell off twice. Although he did not fail to note the monarch's character flaws, constant demands for higher taxes, and bad decision making, L'Estoile remained a supporter even as Henri became probably the most vilified king in French history. As opposition to Henri increased after 1584, L'Estoile became even more supportive of him.

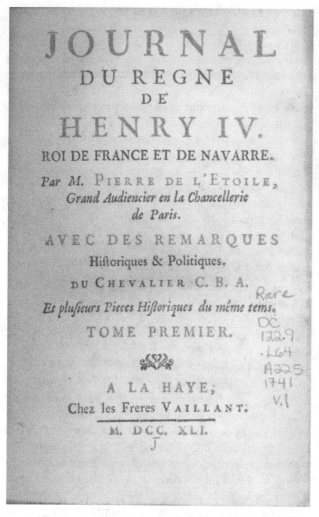

Title page for an eighteenth-century edition of Pierre de L'Estoile's journal of the reign of King Henri IV, written between 1589 and 1610 and first published in 1719 (Thomas Cooper Library, University of South Carolina)

Like most Frenchmen of his era, L'Estoile was convinced that the presence of so many Italians in France and at the court, especially Catherine de Médicis, was a major cause of the ills of the kingdom. After noting the execution of a man in July 1575 for saying that the Italians must be chased from France or have their throats cut, he copies a bitterly anti-Italian poem into his journal:

> When these cowardly rascals came to France,
> They were thin as sardines, empty, save of evils,
> But by their fat pickings, and not by chance,
> They've become as rich and fat as boll weevils.

One of the most frequent complaints about Henri III was that he dressed in Italian fashion; L'Estoile reports in November 1575 that the king wears his collar reversed in the Italian style. He also mentions that the king visited all of the churches of Paris, "murmuring prayers to himself as he walked." Afterward, the king and queen went out to add to their collection of lapdogs. The king often indulged in these sorts of incongruous acts and was routinely criticized for them. His public piety also contrasted with his behavior after dark and gave rise to accusations of gross hypocrisy. L'Estoile mentions in January 1576 that the king had been outside of Paris visiting brothels when his coach broke down; he was forced to walk more than a league back to the city in a terrible storm, arriving at the Louvre Palace after midnight.

By far the most damaging to Henri III's reputation was his relationship with his *mignons* (darlings), young noblemen who received large pensions and titles from the king. L'Estoile comments in July 1576: "These fine darlings wear their hair long, curled and recurled artificially; on top they wear little velvet bonnets like those of the girls in the brothels. . . . Their occupations are gambling, blaspheming, jumping, dancing, quarreling, fornicating, and following the king around." The journal is filled with the misbehavior of the *mignons* and the king's extravagance in paying for their marriages and for their funerals when they fought duels to the death with the retainers of other major figures at the court. From the first, Henri's relationship with them gave rise to gossip and obscene verses about homosexuality. The king's taste for cross-dressing at masquerades, "where he usually dressed as a woman, with a low-cut collar which showed his throat, hung with pearls," added to the suspicion that sodomy was common at the court. L'Estoile copied and collected many verses and other pieces that skewer the king. One from 1583, for example, contrasts Henri's public piety with his presumed private behavior:

> He has chosen Our Lady
> For the patron of his vows,
> But he prefers, on my soul,
> A young lad with blonde hair.

Many of the verses L'Estoile collected are important sources for sixteenth-century attitudes toward homosexuality.

Henri's failure to lead his army in the field added to the sense that he was effeminate and not worthy of being king, but the most serious problem was that he had no children. For many of his critics the lack of offspring proved the truth of the accusation of homosexuality, but L'Estoile records several occasions when the king and queen went to shrines believed helpful to infertile couples. He also takes notice of the times when the king took his pleasure with nuns in the convents of Paris.

Henri's personal foibles might have not have mattered so much had it not been for the political situation in which he found himself on becoming king. The sectarian violence that had wracked France since 1560 destroyed much of its infrastructure, and the king received only a small portion of the taxes collected in his name. L'Estoile refers often to the sacking of cities by one side or the other, in which murder, pillage, and the violation of women left the communities miserable and desolate. He also frequently comments on troops ravaging and destroying the countryside. He reports on severely cold weather, as when the grapevines in the region around Paris froze on 24 May 1587—extraordinarily late in the spring for such an occurrence—and the price of wine shot up in Paris. Flooding of the Seine must have occurred unusually often during L'Estoile's lifetime, as he frequently mentions it. In 1596 a flood brought down a bridge over the river, drowning about 160 people. The bad weather caused high grain prices, which L'Estoile duly records.

Henri III's never-ending demands for money from the Paris bourgeoisie especially caught L'Estoile's attention: it not only affected him personally but also had a severe impact on the class with which he identified. In May 1576, for example, he writes that the king seized the interest that was due on the bonds issued by the Hôtel de Ville of Paris. He does not mention whether he held any of the bonds, but his circle had invested heavily in them and were harmed by the king's refusal to pay. Making matters worse for all Parisians, not just the parlementaires, was the blatant extravagance of the royal court in these times of severe economic distress.

For L'Estoile, the worst aspect of the religious wars was the sedition that they created against the monarchy. While he remained a Catholic to the end, he expresses sympathy for "those of the Religion," as he usually refers to the Huguenots, and understands why they would be reluctant to trust the king after the St. Bartholomew's Day Massacre of 1572. He often expresses himself in ways that have a Protestant ring, such as: "I confine myself simply to the words of Jesus Christ, which are of themselves so clear and intelligible, and admit no figure of speech." L'Estoile criticizes the Catholic practice of invoking the saints and frequently writes disrespectfully of the popes. When he thought he was dying in 1610, the priest who came to give him last rites told him that he had to declare that he believed in the unerring Roman Catholic and Apostolic faith. L'Estoile balked, saying that he was not certain that the church of his time conformed to the primitive church. He was thoroughly Gallican, strongly opposed to allow-

ing the Pope any control over the French church beyond a limited authority in matters of doctrine and morality, and few things annoyed him as much as papal attempts to interfere in French affairs.

What angered L'Estoile the most, however, was the Catholic League. It arose in 1576 to resist the Peace of Beaulieu, in which Henri III, hoping to end the fifth War of Religion, granted the Huguenots public exercise of their religion except in Paris and allowed them to garrison eight towns as places of security. Henri, Duke of Guise, was the head of the Catholic League. L'Estoile describes the league as "nothing more than a rebellion against the state." He was convinced that the leaders were using religion as a cover for their political ambitions: "The truth is that these people would be willing for the whole world to be Huguenot provided that they could rule, and make their League and conspiracy against the state successful," he writes in September 1576, soon after hearing of the league's formation. L'Estoile never conceded that religious zeal might have motivated many members of the league.

The king tried to deal with the opposition by calling a meeting of the Estates-General at Blois in December 1576. The league dominated the meeting and pressed Henri into declaring that there was a "law of Catholicity" that required that the king be Catholic. This maneuver was intended to prevent the Huguenot Henri de Bourbon, King of Navarre, a distant cousin who stood second in the line of succession behind Henri III's youngest brother, François, from becoming king of France. L'Estoile unwaveringly supported Henri de Navarre's right of succession for the next eighteen years. For him, there were only two fundamental laws of the kingdom of France: the Salic law and the law that the king could not alienate any part of the royal patrimony; there most certainly was no "law of Catholicity." If the Salic law admitted the possibility of a Protestant becoming the French king, then that was God's will, and it was not permitted to humans to resist it. Those who held this point of view became known as *politiques*, a word L'Estoile uses for the first time in 1586 but that had appeared early in the religious wars to describe Catholics who were willing to tolerate the Huguenots to prevent the greater evil of civil war; after 1576 it referred to Catholics who accepted Henri de Navarre's right of succession to the throne. L'Estoile was the epitome of a *politique* in both senses of the term.

A major factor in L'Estoile's support of Henri de Navarre's right of succession was his admiration of the man. L'Estoile expresses respect for Henri's courage, ability as a commander, and political acumen—and his sense of humor: L'Estoile's journal is the best source for Henri's many puns and jokes. L'Estoile also recognized Henri's flaws, especially the constant womanizing that frequently distracted him from politics and war and often led to bad decisions.

Failing to gain anything from the meeting of the Estates-General 1576, Henri III reduced his concessions to the Huguenots, issuing an edict in 1577 that limited their right of worship to the places that they controlled. This change satisfied the Catholic League without drawing the Huguenots back into war, and for the next seven years France was largely at peace. In 1580 L'Estoile's wife died, leaving him with six children under the age of twelve. In 1582 he married Colombe Marteau, from another parlementaire family. They had ten children together, all of whom survived into adulthood.

In 1584 Henri III's brother Francis died childless, leaving Henri de Navarre as the royal successor. The Catholic League reappeared on the scene; this time it included not only the Catholic nobility but also many ordinary citizens, especially in Paris. Supported by Spain's Philip II, the league persuaded Henri to declare the law of Catholicity again. L'Estoile found the league's alliance with the Spanish especially treasonous. His journal rings with denunciations of the league and its leaders, the Guises. He is also sharply critical of Pope Sixtus V, whom he accuses of promoting destruction instead of instruction. When Sixtus excommunicated Henri de Navarre as a heretic in September 1585, L'Estoile included in his journal a vehement response accusing the Pope of tyranny and usurpation; it is designated as "written by the author of the present memoirs" instead of the usual "copied."

In response to the papal bull, Henri de Navarre took up arms, leading to the "War of the Three Henrys"–the king, Henri de Navarre, and Henri, Duke of Guise. In late 1587 Guise defeated a Protestant army in eastern France. While regarding Guise as a traitor, L'Estoile is willing to admit that he is a fine commander and gives him proper credit for his victory. (On the other hand, L'Estoile utterly despised Guise's sister, Catherine, Duchess of Montpensier, for her zeal for the league and her success in stirring up the Parisians against the king.) Guise's victory so elevated his standing among Paris's Catholics that the king, terrified of a Guise-led rebellion, barred him from coming to Paris. He came anyway, and on 12 May 1588 the league set up barricades in the streets, isolating the royal troops and forcing them to surrender. Henri III fled from Paris. L'Estoile's journal is the most complete source of information about this event, which has become known as the Day of the Barricades. It is clear that he wrote his account sometime after 12 May; but his rage at the king for allowing the rebellion to succeed, at Guise for leading it, and at the "asses of Paris"–the radical members of the league–for bringing it about is still palpable.

Humiliated but unable to strike back, Henri III agreed to the league's demand that he call a meeting of the Estates-General for the purpose of barring Henri de Navarre from the throne. When the meeting ended in December, Henri III ordered the assassinations of Guise and his brother Louis II, Cardinal of Guise. Catholic rage at the king was uncontrollable. The Pope excommunicated him, and league preachers and pamphleteers denounced him as a tyrant whose killing would be a holy deed. L'Estoile collected some three hundred such pamphlets, along with many woodcuts and placards. In the journal he calls his collection "Les Belles Figures et Drolleries de la Ligue" (The Pretty Pieces and Oddities of the League): "They fill four large volumes . . . besides a great folio of pictures and placards, which I should have thrown into the fire, as they deserved, except that they may serve in some way to show and expose the abuses, impostures, vanities and furies of this great monster of the league."

By this time, despite his prudence in confining his views to his journal, L'Estoile had become known as a *politique,* and his house was one of the first to be searched by the league-controlled municipal government. He began collecting satires directed against the league, copied them, and "let them fall into many good hands, more boldly than prudently."

Many parlementaires escaped to Tours, where a royalist parlement was established, but L'Estoile remained in Paris despite the threat to his life and property. Henri III and Henri de Navarre reconciled, and as their combined armies approached Paris on 31 July 1589 the league put three hundred *politiques,* including L'Estoile, into prison to prevent them from aiding the royalist forces when they assaulted the city. The next day Jacques Clément, a young Dominican, gained entrance to Henri III's camp at St.-Cloud and stabbed him. Before dying, the king recognized Henri de Navarre as his successor. L'Estoile eulogizes Henri III as having had the potential to be a good king if he had lived in a good century and expresses astonishment that a little monk with a vile little knife could kill the king of France in his camp, surrounded by bodyguards. He has no hesitation in recognizing Henri de Navarre as Henri IV, calling him the king and His Majesty within days of Henri III's death.

A week after the king's death, the imprisoned *politiques* were released. In November, L'Estoile's eldest son, Louis, went to fight for the league, paining L'Estoile greatly. In May 1590 Henri IV's army placed Paris under siege; L'Estoile records the suffering of the people, which extended to cannibalism. His pregnant wife and two of their children left the city on 15 August, and L'Estoile was preparing to flee when a Spanish army forced Henri to lift the siege. L'Estoile's wife returned in October. In November 1591 he learned of a league list of *politiques;*

next to each name was printed a letter signifying "hang," "stab," or "chase out." His name had the letter for "stab."

The situation in France was stalemated, and L'Estoile amused himself by recording the rabid sermons of the league preachers; he says that one of them "did not have enough brains to fry an egg." The stalemate broke in July 1593, when Henri declared that he would become Catholic. He is reputed to have said, "Paris vaut bien une messe" (Paris is worth a mass), but although L'Estoile especially admired Henri's wit, the journal does not mention this quip. Soon after Henri's conversion, L'Estoile records league charges that he is a hypocrite. On 22 March 1594 Henri entered Paris in triumph. L'Estoile's admiration for him increased even more because of his clemency: a handful of league members were banished from Paris, and a great bonfire purged the city of league works. This destruction of much of the era's historical record makes L'Estoile's collection, which he refused to give up, so valuable.

In 1595 Louis de L'Estoile, having switched to the royalist cause, was killed in battle. As Pierre de L'Estoile passed age fifty, he became interested in collecting information about the deaths of prominent people: he believed that good ones had good deaths, calling on God for mercy, while evildoers had the horrible deaths that their deeds merited. In 1601 he sold his office, expecting to retire to his library; but he found himself in financial difficulties and faced with lawsuits and had to sell many of his books and coins. Until the end of his life he was quick to go to see anything "curious." Twice, he records, he was so ill that he thought he was dying. Henri IV's assassination in 1610 by a fanatical Catholic, François Ravaillac, came as a shock to L'Estoile, though he indicates in the journal that he had a premonition of it. L'Estoile died on 11 October 1611.

None of L'Estoile's sons followed their father in a career in the magistracy, which may explain the cynicism about offspring that one detects in the entries for the last years of the journal. One son became a monk, to his father's disgust. The youngest son, Claude, was disfigured in a fire, turned to writing, and became a charter member of the Académie française in 1634. Six daughters, however, married into parlementaire families and carried on the family tradition. The husband of one of them, Anne, agreed to have their children take the name L'Estoile, and Pierre de L'Estoile's journal and collections passed to them. In 1621 they published the part of the journal covering the reign of Henri III. The second part, on Henri IV's reign, was not published until 1719. Most of the placards and pamphlets that were included with the manuscript of the journal were published for the first time, except for those the editors regarded as obscene, in the 1875–1883 edition by Gustave Brunet and others. An edition that was in progress in 2006 will include all of these pieces, as well as the variants in the two manuscript versions.

Biography:

Eugène Vallée, *Notice sur Pierre de L'Estoile* (Paris: Lemerre, 1888).

References:

Joseph Cady, "The 'Masculine Love' of the 'Princes of Sodom': The Homosexuality of Henri III and His Mignons in Pierre de L'Estoile's *Mémoires-Journaux*," in *Desire and Discipline: Sex and Sexuality in the Premodern West,* edited by Jacqueline Murray (Toronto: University of Toronto Press, 1996), pp. 123–154;

Michel Chopard, "En marge de la grande érudition, un amateur éclairé, Pierre de l'Estoile," in *Histoire et Littérature: Les écrivains et la politique,* edited by Alain Pomeau (Paris: Presses universitaires de France, 1877), pp. 205–235;

Chopard, "Entre Rome et Genève: L'individualisme religieux de P. de l'Estoile," in *Humanisme et Foi chrétiene,* edited by Yves Marty and others (Paris: Beauchesne, 1976), pp. 193–201;

Louis Dufour, *Événements météorologiques anciens d'après les Registres-Journaux de Pierre de l'Estoile* (Brussels: Académie royale, 1978);

François Marin, "The Editorial Fortunes of the *Registres-journaux des règnes de Henri III et Henri IV* by Pierre de L'Estoile," *Nouvelle Revue du Seizième Siècle,* 20 (2002): 87–108;

William McCuaig, "Paris/Jerusalem in Pierre de L'Estoile, the *Satyre Menipée,* and Louis Dorléans," *Bibliothèque d'humanisme et renaissance,* 64 (2002): 295–315;

M. McGowan, "Lestoile, Pierre–Amateur Collector of Medals and Coins," *Seventeenth-Century French Studies,* 15 (1993): 115–127;

Nancy Roelker, "French News of Great Britain, 1574–1603," *Renaissance News,* 8 (1955): 90–101;

Gilbert Shrenck, "Pierre de L'Estoile devant ses manuscripts: La Fadaise et la sagesse," *Travaux de Littérature,* 11 (1998): 95–105;

P. M. Smith, "Réalisme et pittoresque dans le *Journal* de Pierre de L'Estoile," *Bibliothèque d'humanisme et renaissance,* 29 (1967): 153–156.

Papers:

Pierre de L'Estoile's manuscripts are in the Bibliothèque nationale, Paris.

François de Malherbe
(1555 – 6 October 1628)

Bernd Renner
Brooklyn College and the Graduate Center, The City University of New York

BOOKS: *Les Larmes de Saint Pierre, imitées du Tansille* (Paris: P. Ramier, 1587);

Consolation à Monsieur du Périer (N.p., 1590–1599);

Ode du Sieur de Malherbe. A la Reine. Pour sa bienvenue en France (Aix: J. Tholosan, 1601);

Ode sur l'attentat commis en la personne de Sa Majesté, le 19 décembre 1605 (N.p., 1606);

Vers du Sieur de Malherbe à la Reine (Paris: A. Beys, 1611);

Lettre de consolation à Madame la Princesse de Conty sur la mort de M. le chevalier de Lorraine de Guise, son frère (Paris: Toussaint du Bray, 1614);

Récit d'un berger sur les alliances de France et d'Espagne fait devant leurs Majestez au ballet de Madame (Paris, 1615);

Pour le marquis de la Vieuville, superintendent des finances (N.p., 1623–1624);

Œuvres (Paris: Ch. Chappelain, 1630);

Les Poésies de M. de Malherbe, avec les Observations de M. de Menage (Paris: Th. Jolli, 1666);

Les Œuvres de François de Malherbe avec les observations de M. Menage et les remarques de M. Chevreau sur les poesies, 3 volumes (Paris: Coustelier, 1722);

Poésies de Malherbe, rangées par ordre chronologique avec un Discours sur les obligations que la langue et la poésie françoise ont à Malherbe, et quelques remarques historiques et critiques (Paris: J. Barbon, 1757).

Editions: *Œuvres de Malherbe,* edited by L. Lalanne, 5 volumes (Paris: L. Hachette, 1862);

Les Premiers vers de F. de Malherbe, traduction de l'épitaphe de Geneviève Rouxel, publiés d'après le manuscript de Jacques de Cahaignes par F.-G. S. Trébutien. (Caen: F. Le Blanc-Hardel, 1872);

Les Poésies de M. de Malherbe, edited by J. Lavaud, 2 volumes (Paris: Droz, 1936);

Malherbe. Œuvres poétiques, edited by R. Fromilhague and R. Lebègue, 2 volumes (Paris: Collection des Universités de France, 1968);

Œuvres, edited by A. Adam (Paris: Gallimard-Pléiade, 1971).

Editions in English: "Consolation to M. du Perrier," "On the Departure of Viscountess D'Auchy," and

François de Malherbe (from Albert duc de Broglie, Malherbe *[Paris: L. Hachette et cie, 1897]; Thomas Cooper Library, University of South Carolina)*

"On Marie de Bourbon" in *Anthology of French Poetry,* edited by H. Carrington (London & New York: H. Froude, 1900);

"Imitation of a Psalm" and "On the Death of Mlle. de Conty," in *Limits of Art,* edited by H. Cairns (New York: Pantheon, circa 1948);

"Consolation to M. Du Périer" and "To Louis XIII," in *Renaissance and Baroque Lyrics; an Anthology of Translations from Italian, French, and Spanish,* edited by H. M. Priest (N.p.: Northwestern University Press, 1962);

"Stanzas from Malherbe," in Alexander Pope, *Poetical Works,* edited by H. Davis (London & New York: Oxford University Press, 1966).

OTHER: Sonnets, in *Les Muses gaillardes, recueillies des plus beaux esprits de ce temps, par A.D.B.* (Paris: Antoine du Brueil, 1609?);

Poems, in *Les Délices de la poésie française, ou Recueil des plus beaux vers de ce temps, recueillis par François de Rosset,* 2 volumes (Paris: Toussainct du Bray, 1615);

Twelve poems, in *Le Second livre des Délices de la poesie françoise, ou nouveau Recueil des plus beaux vers de ce temps* (Paris: Toussainct du Bray, 1620);

Forty-nine poems, in *Les Delices de la poesie françoise, ou dernier Recueil des plus beaux vers de ce temps, corrigé de nouveau par ses autheurs et augmenté d'une eslite de plusieurs rares pièces non encore imprimées, dédié à madame la princesse de Conty* (Paris: Toussainct du Bray, 1621);

"Au Roy" (N.p., 1624);

"Amphion au Roy" (Aix, 1624);

"A Monseigneur le Cardinal de Richelieu" (N.p., 1624);

"Pour Monseigneur" (N.p., before 1626);

Sixty-two poems, in *Le Recueil des plus beaux vers de messieurs de Malherbe, Racan, Maynard, etc.* (Paris: Toussainct du Bray, 1626);

"A Monsieur de Verdun sur le mort de Madame sa femme" (N.p., 1626–1627);

"Pour le Roi allant châtier la rebellion des Rochelois" (Paris, 1628);

"Commentaire sur Desportes," in *Œuvres de Malherbe,* volume 4, edited by L. Lalanne (Paris: L. Hachette, 1862), pp. 249–273.

TRANSLATIONS: *Le XXXIII livre de Tite-Live* (Rome, 1616; enlarged and completed, Paris: Toussainct du Bray, 1621);

Les Epistres de Sénèque (Paris: A. de Sommaville, 1637);

Sénèque. Des Bienfaits (Paris: A. de Sommaville, 1639).

François de Malherbe is hard to classify as a literary figure. Although he was born in the middle of the sixteenth century, virtually an exact contemporary of Théodore-Agrippa d'Aubigné (1552–1630), he has never been designated as a writer of the Renaissance. On the contrary, he has generally been considered the "père du classicisme" (father of classicism), a somewhat radical generalization that has been at the center of scholarly discussions ever since. "Enfin Malherbe vint" (Finally Malherbe arrived) famously wrote Nicolas Boileau in his *Art Poétique* (1674, The Art of Poetry), which contributed largely to Malherbe's reputation as the instigator of neoclassicist principles. Malherbe is chiefly remembered in Boileau's phrase even though he never published a formal theory of his doctrine. His translations and poetry, largely omitted from the canon today, were meant to be a sufficient illustration of the proper way to write in French.

Malherbe was born in 1555 at Caen in Normandy, the first of nine children of François de Malherbe, sieur de Digny, a royal magistrate at the Presidial of Caen, and Louise Le Vallois. Except for a year spent in Paris, he attended boarding school in Caen, where he was aware of circles interested in the Reformation, before leaving for Switzerland and Germany with his preceptor Richard Dinoth in 1571. He enrolled that same year at the University of Basel, and in 1573 attended the University of Heidelberg. From 1574 until 1576 he continued his education in Caen, where he was introduced to the city's Catholic circles, especially Jean Rouxel's literary group, which included Vauquelin de la Fresnaie and Le Fèvre de la Borderie. In 1575 he composed his first known poem, "Larmes du sieur de Malherbe" (Tears of the Sieur of Malherbe), as well as a French translation of Jacques de Cahaignes's Latin epitaph deploring the death of Geneviève Rouxel on 27 May 1575. (Both texts were first published in F.-G. S. Trébutien's 1872 edition of Malherbe's early works.) In August 1576 Malherbe left Caen for Paris, where he was introduced at the royal court and became secretary of Henri d'Angoulême, great prior of France. In 1577 Henri was sent to Provence, where he settled first in Marseilles and then in 1578 in Aix as royal governor. Malherbe followed his protector and became an integral part of the civilized court society in that provincial capital, where he frequented, among others, the poets César de Nostredame and Jean de la Ceppède. On 1 October 1581 he married Madeleine de Carriolis, daughter of the president of the provincial parliament. Their first child, Henri, was born on 21 July 1585 in Aix.

In spring 1586 Malherbe returned to Caen. The assassination of Henri d'Angoulême in Aix on 2 June of the same year led Malherbe to try to reaffirm the king's favor and possibly a royal appointment by presenting HenriHenri III with his first published poem, *Les Larmes de Saint Pierre, imitées du Tansille* (Tears of Saint Peter, Imitated from Tansillo), in March 1587. The poet later dismissed the poem as a youthful error, as its debts to the baroque tradition severely clashed with his later development, especially in the first decade of the new century. The king granted Malherbe a monetary award of 500 crowns but no other favors.

In the next several years Malherbe suffered through personal tragedies—including the deaths of two of his sons, Henri in fall 1587 and his second son, François, at the end of 1589—as he developed his craft. Despite becoming municipal magistrate of Caen on 23

Malherbe's home in his native Caen (from Œuvres de Malherbe, recueillies et annotées par m. L. Lalanne
[Paris: L. Hachette et cie, 1869]; Thomas Cooper Library, University of South Carolina)

February 1594, the poet returned the following year to Aix, where he met Guillaume du Vair and through him was introduced to Claude Nicolas Fabry de Peiresc, one of the most distinguished French scholars of the period. In summer 1598 Malherbe was at Caen to see his daughter Jourdaine, who lived there with her grandparents. A year later, on 23 June 1599, she died of the plague, and Malherbe returned to Aix in December of that year to join his wife. During this period he was evidently liberating his poetry from the baroque elements that had distinguished it before. The "Consolation à M. du Périer" (Consolation to M. du Périer), for example, first composed under the title "Consolation à Cléophon" (Consolation to Cléophon) in Caen before 1595, is remarkable for its stylistic rigor. Malherbe also ventured into lyrical poetry when he celebrated Henri IV's capture of Marseilles in two odes written during his stay in Provence from 1595 to 1598.

As he brought the classical ideals of clarity, vigor, and harmony to his poetry, Malherbe started to become better known around the turn of the century,

and his poems were included in several collections that were published in Rouen and Paris between 1597 and 1603. On 17 November 1600 Marie de Médicis arrived in Aix, and Malherbe had the privilege—most likely thanks to Du Vair, president of the parliament of Provence—to read a poem that he composed in her honor. In the first years of the new century the poet stayed in Aix and primarily worked on translating Seneca.

The year 1605 proved pivotal for Malherbe's career. He accompanied Du Vair to Paris, where he was introduced to Henri IV. The king commissioned him to write an ode on the campaign that he was about to undertake in the recently pacified Limousin region. Using biblical and Virgilian imagery, Malherbe composed an enthusiastic lyric in which he prayed for a divine benediction on the king's mission and sang the benefits of peace. Henri was so pleased with the poem that he put Malherbe in the service of M. de Bellegarde, royal equerry—a court position the poet had coveted for many years. Malherbe was also named squire of the king's chamber and thus had access to the inner circles of the royal court. As court poet, his poetry, religious as well as political in nature, celebrated official events, as befitted his prestigious position as court poet.

Also in 1605, Malherbe's conflict with Philippe Desportes began. Not only did Malherbe consider Desportes his rival at court, but also he saw him as the incarnation of the preceding century's "unruly" poetry that needed to be reformed and purified. To put forward his own ideas on poetry as well as to discredit his rival, Malherbe annotated a volume of Desportes's poetry, which he intended to publish. Desportes's death in 1606, however, rendered such an aggressive measure unnecessary, and the volume was not published in its entirety until 1757 as *Poésies de Malherbe, rangées par ordre chronologique avec un Discours sur les obligations que la langue et la poésie françoise ont à Malherbe, et quelques remarques historiques et critiques.* (Poetry of Malherbe, arranged in alphabetical order with a Discourse on the debt that the French language and poetry have contracted toward Malherbe and some historical and critical comments). The annotations underline Malherbe's reputation as a blunt and brutally honest critic. He offered corrections to Desportes's grammar and vocabulary and was severe in stylistic questions, describing qualifying verses or even entire stanzas time and again as "superflu" (superfluous), "cela ne veut rien dire" (meaningless), as well as "bourre" (useless). Even though Malherbe's annotations were not published at the time, Mathurin Régnier, Desportes's nephew, felt compelled to defend his uncle in his *Satire à M. Rapin* (1608, Satire to M. Rapin).

Malherbe evidently felt no need to write a formal treatise covering his doctrine, whose main tenets had already been articulated in Du Vair's 1594 treatise *De l'Eloquence française* (Of French eloquence). He began to attract a circle of disciples in his modest Parisian apartment on the rue Croix-des-Petits-Champs, continuing his practice of encouraging and advising aspiring poets that he had begun at the end of the preceding century in Caen, where the effects of his suggested stylistic corrections to Antoine de Montchrestien's tragedy *Sophonisbe*—the progressive eliminations of archaisms, neologisms, and repetitions in the name of clarity—were evident in the editions of the play between 1596 and 1601. In Paris, the nightly gatherings included two famous admirers: François Mainard, secretary of Marguerite de Valois, whose poetry was more rigorous than his mentor's (he became a founding member of the Académie française in 1635), and Honorat de Bueil, Seigneur de Racan, whom Malherbe considered his most [disc]iple. In 1610, Pierre de Deimier, a dedi[catee] of Malherbe, published *Académie de l'Art*

poétique (The Academy of the Art of Poetry), another treatise that advanced Malherbe's teachings.

Malherbe's doctrine is essentially a reaction against his predecessors, especially the Pléiade poets and the baroque and mannerist currents of the late sixteenth century. Discrediting preceding generations also serves to underline the notion of the progress of civilization, so essential to the time, especially after the decades of turmoil that France had been through. In large part, Malherbe's rules are not inventions but codifications of the changing literary tastes of the times. Du Vair's treatise and the poetry of most late-sixteenth-century poets, especially during the last two decades of the century, had been moving in the direction of the rules that Malherbe formulated so forcefully. Even Desportes, Malherbe's main target, had simplified his vocabulary in an attempt to adapt his poetry to the general demands of the times.

Malherbe's doctrine originates in his belief that to restore order to a country shaken by four decades of religious wars, one must restore order to the language itself—hence his emphasis on logic and reason over inspiration. In concrete terms, his project of purifying the French language calls for a suppression of archaisms, neologisms, and involuntary repetitions, amounting thus to a relative linguistic impoverishment in the name of clarity of expression. Moreover, the critic demands respect for *les bienséances* (the rules of etiquette), a diminished and more careful use of metaphors and images, which, no longer ornamental, are to serve the ideas being conveyed. He argued against stylistic devices such as hiatus and enjambment and for the enforcement of simple rhyme schemes, in which the rhymes are pleasing to the eye and the ear. He holds that the language used must be accessible to a common reader and that grammar and syntax must be straightforward and governed by logic. He advocates the use of general and abstract terms to confer an impersonal, even philosophical character to the teachings that can be extracted from the poet's work. Among Malherbe's preferred lyrical forms are the *ode,* which he restored to a prominent position, and the *stance.* Malherbe in a way returned to older notions of poetry by defining poetry virtually as an *art de seconde rhétorique* (art of second rhetoric), an expression that was used explicitly for the genre before the efforts of poets and theoreticians such as Thomas Sebillet and Joachim du Bellay—their poetic treatises were published in 1548 and 1549 respectively—strove to assert the genre's independence from rhetoric.

Even with his position at the royal court and his growing number of disciples, Malherbe also had his critics. In addition to Régnier, the admirers of Ronsard and Guillaume du Bartas—poets who prized inspiration

A poem in Malherbe's hand (from Œuvres de Malherbe, recueillies et annotées par m. L. Lalanne [Paris: L. Hachette et cie, 1869]; Thomas Cooper Library, University of South Carolina) over logic and artifice—were among his most important adversaries. For Régnier, Malherbian poetry was characterized by a lack of imagination and persnickety linguistic and stylistic formalism.

Malherbe's attempt to adhere strictly to a set of rules resulted in his diminished poetic production during the remainder of his life. The austere image that the idea of a rule-governed man might evoke is at odds with Malherbe's private life. Known as "Père Luxure" (Father Lust) among his acquaintances, Malherbe allowed the publication of some of his obscene sonnets in various contemporary collections. His turbulent relationship with the Viscountess d'Auchy toward the end of the new century's first decade is manifest in his love poetry, especially his contributions to the *Nouveau Recueil* (1609, New Collection).

From 1605 until 1610—the year of Henri IV's assassination on 14 May—Malherbe was consumed by the tasks of his position as a court poet, following the court to Fontainebleau and Burgundy and on many of its sojourns in the provinces. During the regency, 1610–1614, Malherbe was near the summit of his influence at court, as Marie de Médicis, whom he frequently celebrates in his poetry, appreciated and supported his work. Malherbe received a onetime gift of 10,000 crowns in the summer of 1610, and in 1612 his pension was raised from 400 crowns to 500—quite a considerable amount at the time. Even without counting his other sources of income, this pension amounted to about six times the sum necessary to pay for his valet. In 1613 he had to fight for his pension, however, as he was omitted from the payroll by accident. He thereafter regularly complained about delays and other irregularities in securing his pay. Having failed to obtain a landed pension on a bishopric, Malherbe nonetheless saw his remuneration raised to 1,500 livres by Louis XIII in the fall of 1615, most likely because of the queen's support. By 1627 it reached 2,000 livres.

While most of his poems celebrated official occasions and enriched royal ballets, Malherbe also began to pay more attention to religious poetry, composing *Stances spirituelles* (Spiritual Stanzas) and paraphrases of the Psalms. He seemed to turn toward religion out of a certain disappointment in the powerful patrons that he had served for so long and whose promises proved empty more often than not. His religious poetry may have served as a reminder to these patrons that their power and status were ephemeral. "Et rien que Dieu n'est permanent" (Nothing but God is permanent), as the poet put it in his 1625/1626 inscription composed for the fountain of the Hôtel de Rambouillet. For the remainder of his career his poems were published in anthologies, the number of which attests to his unbroken influence and popularity: *Les Délices de la poésie française* (1615, The Delights of French Poetry), dedicated to one of his most faithful patrons and most important protector, the Princess of Conty; *Le Second livre des Délices* (1620, The Second Book of the Delights), with twelve new poems; *Les Delices de la poesie françoise, ou dernier Recueil* (1621, The Last Collection of the Delights of French Poetry), including forty-nine of his poems; and *Le Recueil des plus beaux vers* (1626, The Collection of the Most Beautiful Verses), including sixty-two of his poems. More and more, though, Malherbe turned to prose translations, publishing in 1616 *Le XXXIIIe livre de Tite-Live,* a partial translation of book 33 of Titus Livy's *History of Rome*. The complete version of the translation, which served as a model of French prose writing, followed in 1621. That same year he sold his house in Caen, an indication of his continuing financial troubles.

Although Malherbe generally remained in the favor of Louis XIII and of Cardinal Richelieu, named the new head of the king's council in 1624, his last years were marked by tragedy and disappointment because of the fate of his last-born son, Marc-Antoine. In summer 1624 his son killed a citizen of Aix, Raymond Audebert, in a duel and was sentenced to death. Fleeing the city, Marc-Antoine managed to find refuge in Normandy, out of the jurisdiction of the courts of Provence. Malherbe worked for two years to obtain an official pardon for his son, and his efforts were finally rewarded in June 1626. A little over a year later, on 13 July 1627, Marc-Antoine was killed outside Aix. Although his murderers, Gaspard Cauvet and Paul de Fortia, were sentenced to death, both were supported by the archbishop of Aix. Malherbe wrote to the archbishop on 2 February 1628 to demand that he withdraw his support. Around the same time, Malherbe sent the king and Cardinal Richelieu the poems that he had composed to celebrate the campaigns of La Rochelle and the Isle of Ré—"Pour le Roi allant châtier la rebellion des Rochelois" (For the King going to chastise the rebellion of the citizens of La Rochelle)— along with a long letter imploring the king for justice. Richelieu replied with a letter thanking him for his ode on 15 March. As he saw no progress in the matter, Malherbe decided to go to La Rochelle himself in July 1628, one year after his son's murder. On 24 September a letter sent from the court attested to the fact that Malherbe's adversaries, despite Louis XIII's personal promise to the contrary, had obtained their letters of remission, which meant that the matter of his son's killing would end up before the Parlement of Toulouse. Disappointed yet again, Malherbe left La Rochelle and returned to Paris, where he arrived ill. He died on 6 October 1628 and was buried at Saint-Germain-l'Auxerrois the following day.

Malherbe's influence on literature was considerable, even if it is ultimately Boileau's overly enthusiastic assessment of this influence that cemented Malherbe's position in literary history. He bears a large share of the responsibility for Renaissance poetry falling out of favor for two centuries, until its "rediscovery" by nineteenth-century romantic poets. Touching on the domains of language, versification, style, and the preceding generations of poets, Malherbe's doctrine is essentially an inventory of the changing tastes and poetic practices of his time, which he recorded, illustrated, and, through his teachings, attempted to summarize, put into order, and spread. His combining the aspiration to create poetry that conforms to a complex set of new rules with the effort to formulate and teach those rules truly sets him apart from his contemporaries. François de Malherbe was a highly ambitious writer, convinced of the value of his work. In his sonnet "Au Roi" (To the King), which he composed around 1624 to remind Louis XIII of his loyal services and the power of his pen, he writes: "Ce que Malherbe écrit dure éternellement" (What Malherbe writes is eternal). But while Malherbe's poetry has been largely forgotten, his doctrine has had an influence that confirms the high opinion that he had of his importance.

References:

Claude K. Abraham, *Enfin Malherbe: The Influence of Malherbe on French Lyric Prosody, 1606–1674* (Lexington: University Press of Kentucky, 1971);

Ferdinand Brunot, *La doctrine de Malherbe d'après son commentaire sur Desportes* (Paris: Colin, 1969);

René Fromilhague, *Malherbe: Technique et création poétique* (Paris: Colin, 1954);

Fromilhague, *La vie de Malherbe, les luttes (1555–1610)* (Paris: Colin, 1954);

Michel Jeanneret, *Poésie et tradition biblique au XVIe siècle. Les paraphrases des Psaumes de Marot à Malherbe* (Paris: José Corti, 1969);

Francis Ponge, *Pour un Malherbe* (Paris: Gallimard, 1965);

Catherine Randall, "Possessed Personae in Early Modern France: Du Bellay, d'Aubigné, and Malherbe," in *Signs of the Early Modern 2: Seventeenth Century and Beyond,* edited by David Lee Rubin (Charlottesville, Va: Rockwood, 1997), pp. 1–16;

Marie-Odile Sweetser, "The Art of Praise from Malherbe to La Fontaine," in *The Shape of Change,* edited by Anne Birberick and Russell Ganim (Amsterdam: Rodopi, 2002), pp. 119–139;

Sweetser, "Les Pierres et les mots: Du Bellay, Malherbe, Saint-Amant," *Travaux de Littérature,* 12 (1999): 351–364.

Papers:

The major collection of François de Malherbe's manuscripts is in the Bibliothèque nationale de France.

Marguerite de Navarre

(11 April 1492 – 21 December 1549)

Régine Reynolds-Cornell
Agnes Scott College

BOOKS: *Miroir de l'âme pécheresse,* anonymous (Alençon: Simon du Bois, 1531); enlarged as *Le Miroir de tres chrestienne princesse Marguerite de France, Royne de Navarre, Duchesse d'Alençon et de Berry; auquel elle voit & son neant, & son tout* (Paris: Augereau, 1533); translated by Princess Elizabeth Tudor as *The Glasse of the Synnefoulle Soule* (Marburg? 1544);

Dialogue en forme de vision nocturne (Alençon: Simon du Bois, 1533);

Marguerites de la Marguerite des princesses, tresillustre Royne de Navarre and *Suyte des Marguerites de la Marguerite des Princesses, tresillustre Royne de Navarre,* 2 volumes (Lyon: Jean de Tournes, 1547)—comprises volume 1, "Marguerite de France, par la grâce de Dieu Reine de Navarre, aux lecteur," *Le Miroir de l'ame pécheresse,* "Discord étant en l'homme par la contrariété de l'esprit et de la chair, et paix par vie spirituelle," "Oraison de l'ame fidèle à son Seigneur Dicu," "Oraison à notre Seigneur Jésus-Christ," *Comédie de la Nativité de Jésus-Christ, Comédie de l'adoration des Trois Rois à Jésus-Christ, Comédie des Innocents, Comédie du Désert, Le Triomphe de l'Agneau, Complainte pour un détenu prisonnier, Chansons spirituelles,* "L'Esprit de Vie en corps de Mort mussé"; and volume 2, "L'Histoire des Satyres et Nymphes de Diane," "Epître de la Reine de Navarre au Roi François, son frère," "Epître II envoyée par la Reine de Navarre, avec un David au Roi François, son frère, pour ses étrennes," "Réponse envoyée par le Roi François à ladite Dame, avec une Sainte-Catherine, pour ses étrennes," "Epître III de la Reine de Navarre au Roi François, son frère," "Epître de la Reine au Roi François son frère," "Epître de la Reine au Roi de Navarre, malade," "Les quatre Dames et les quatre gentilshommes," *Comédie. Deux Filles, Deux Mariées, La Vieille, Le Vieillard, et les Quatre Hommes, Farce, de Trop, Prou, Peu, Moins, La Coche, L'Umbre, La Mort et Résurrection d'Amour,* "Chanson faite à une Dame, sur laquelle la Reine a fait la

Marguerite de Navarre, as painted by Jean Clouet, circa 1530
(Walker Art Gallery, Liverpool)

réponse suivante," "Les Adieux des Dames de chez la Reine de Navarre, allant en Gascogne, à ma Dame la Princesse de Navarre," deux Enigmes;

L'Heptaméron, edited by Claude Gruget (Paris: Cavelier, 1559); translated by John Smith Chartres as *The Heptameron of the Tales of Margaret, Queen of Navarre: Newly Translated into English from the Authentic Text of M. Le Roux de Lincy,* 5 volumes, with an essay by George Saintsbury (London: Society of English Bibliophilists, 1894);

Les dernière poésies, edited by Abel Lefranc (Paris: Armand Colin, 1896);

Oeuvres de Marguerite de Navarre: Comédies, edited by F. Schnegans (Strasbourg: Biblioteca Romanica, 1924);

Théâtre Profane, edited by V. L. Saulnier (Geneva: Droz, 1946; revised and enlarged, 1963); translated by R. Reynolds-Cornell as *Marguerite de Navarre, Théâtre Profane* (Ottawa: Carleton Plays in Translation, 1992);

La Navire, edited by Robert Marichal (Paris: Champion, 1956);

Petit Oeuvre dévot et contemplatif, edited by Hans Sckommodau (Frankfurt: Analecta Romanica, 1960);

Chansons spirituelles, edited by Georges Dottin (Geneva: Droz, 1971);

Les Prisons, edited by Simone Glasson (Geneva: Droz, 1978); translated by Claire Lynh Wade as *Margueite de Navarre: Les Prisons, A French and English Edition* (New York: Peter Lang, 1995);

Les Comédies bibliques, edited by Barbara Marczuk (Geneva: Droz, 2000).

Editions: *Dialogue en forme de vision nocturne,* edited by Pierre Jourda, *Revue du Seizième Siècle* (1926): 1–49;

Heptaméron, edited by Michel François (Paris: Garnier, 1943);

Les Marguerites de la Marguerite des princesses, tresillustre Royne de Navarre and *Suyte des Marguerites de la Marguerite des Princesses, tresillustre Royne de Navarre,* 2 volumes, edited by Ruth Thomas (The Hague: Mouton, 1970);

La Coche, edited by Robert Marichal (Geneva: Droz, 1971); translated by Hilda Dale as *The Coach* in *The Coach; & and the Triumph of the Lamb* (Exeter: Elm Bank Publications, 1999);

Heptaméron, 2 volumes, edited by Renja Salminen (Helsinki: Annales *Heptaméron* Academiae Scientiarum Fenicae, 1991, 1997);

Heptaméron, edited by Gisèle Mathieu-Castellani (Paris: Librairie Générale Française, 1999);

Heptaméron, edited by Nicole Cazauran (Paris: Folio, 2000).

Editions in English: *The Mirror of the Sinful Soul,* edited by Percy Ames (London: Asher, 1897);

The Mirror of the Sinful Soul, edited by Renja Salminen (Helsinki: Suomalainen Tiedekademia, 1979);

The Heptameron, translated by Paul Chilton (London & New York: Penguin, 1984);

Les Prisons: A French and English Edition, edited and translated by Claire Wade (New York: Peter Lang, 1989);

Secret Memoirs Of Marguerite De Valois: Queen of Navarre (Honolulu: University Press of the Pacific, 2004).

Marguerite de Navarre was not the only educated woman to write and publish verse during the first half of the sixteenth century, but she was the first woman of the French nobility who carefully compiled from her complete works a selection of poems, prayers, religious meditations, songs, biblical and secular (without biblical characters) plays, and other works that she felt worthy to appear in print. She was also the first woman to play an active role in the efforts of the Evangelical Circle of Meaux and to promote the study and the publication in French of Scriptures translated from Aramaic, Hebrew, and Greek, seeking the way to personal salvation only in the Bible rather than in the less reliable Latin translations and the often confusing interpretations of Scriptures by the Roman Church. Her belief that eternal salvation could only be received, if given, from the sincerity of one's faith and true repentance for one's sins rather than from rote prayers, pilgrimages, good works, or religious rites antagonized the Faculty of Theology of the University of Paris as well as members of the court who condemned her proselytism as damaging to the stability of the crown.

The only daughter of Charles de Valois, Comte d'Angoulême, and Louise de Savoie, Marguerite was born on 11 April 1492 in Angoulême but raised in Cognac, where her brother François was born two years later. Jean and Octavien de Saint-Gelais resided at the Cognac castle as cultural advisers if not teachers of the young countess d'Angoulême, who was both intelligent and ambitious. The Angoulême court at Cognac was known for the artists, painters, and scholars who frequented it, the musicians who played at its concerts and dances, and its superb library of illuminated manuscripts and printed volumes to which were added richly bound works written or translated by contemporary authors.

Unexpectedly widowed on 1 January 1496, nineteen-year-old Louise and her children remained in Cognac, with Romorantin as a second residence. Upon the sudden death of King Charles VIII in April 1498, his cousin Louis, son of Charles d'Orléans, became king, as the four children born to Charles VIII and Anne, Duchess of Brittany, had died in infancy. In compliance with the Treaty of Rennes, Queen Anne was soon married to her husband's cousin, King Louis XII. Although the young count d'Angoulême, being the only male offspring of the Valois dynasty, would inherit the crown if Queen Anne failed to give the new king a son, such an event seemed a remote possibility because Louis was thirty-six years old and she but twenty-two when she became queen of France for the second time. However, as heir presumptive, the nearly four-year-old François, his mother, and his six-year-old sister were invited to move to Blois, and by the end of the year or in early 1499 they had joined the court in Amboise.

Less than a year after her marriage to Louis, the queen was delivered of a girl, Princess Claude. The second royal offspring was a much desired male, but as Louise noted in her journal, he was stillborn or died soon after birth. The third and last royal child, Princess Renée of France, was born in Blois in 1510. Louise and her children lived for about nine years in the small château of Cloux (now Clos Lucé), linked to the Amboise castle, which became the residence of Leonardo da Vinci from his arrival in France in 1515 until his death.

A voracious but sophisticated reader, Louise had surrounded herself in Cognac with scholars. In Amboise she chose for her children highly respected scholars open to new ideas who provided a solid education of remarkable breadth to both François and his sister. In addition to the indispensable Bible and the New Testament, the edifying texts compiled for them by their teachers included readings of philosophers and poets such as Sallust, Socrates, Juvenal, Cicero, and Virgil. They read Ovid's *Epistles,* translated for Louise by Octavien de Saint-Gelais, rather than his *Ars Amatoria* (The Art of Love), and not only Giovanni Boccaccio's *De casibus mulieribus* (Concerning Famous Women) and *De casibus illustrium virorum* (The Fates of Illustrious Men), as pragmatic exempla, but also Petrarch's *Triumphs* and Dante Alighieri's *Canzoniere* in French.

Beyond the trivium of grammar, rhetoric, and logic, Marguerite not only was given a humanist appreciation of poetry but also was expected to follow the strict moral guidelines for the ideal ruler that Louise applied to her son. Louise commissioned Jean Thénaud to write the *Triomphe des Vertus* (The Triumph of Virtues), a daunting two-volume allegory of Prudence, Fortitude, Justice, and Temperance that was presented to her son when he became king, but Marguerite, less likely to reign, does not seem to have been given a copy.

In addition to reading the poems of Petrarch, Dante, and more nearly contemporary authors, Marguerite immersed herself in the study of philosophy, and it may be through Marsilio Ficino's works on Plato and particularly his translation of Plotinus's *Enneads* that she later acquired her lasting affinity for Neoplatonism. Ficino succeeded in harmonizing the doctrine of Plotinus with Christianity, which probably explains why a translation of his philosophical essays was among the books that accompanied Marguerite when she traveled.

While Louise enjoyed playing the virginal, music was not part of her children's curriculum: court musicians performed during dinners, dances, and pageants, and court members who played or sang usually did so for more private entertainment. Unshakable as she was in her belief that her son would be king, Louise may have felt that excellence in all martial arts should have precedence for a future ruler over a pleasurable pastime such as playing the lute. For Marguerite, she chose calligraphy and needlework, for the sister of a king need not play an instrument to enjoy music performed by others. Indeed, with the exception of the work she later titled *Chansons spirituelles* (1547, Spiritual Songs), music as such is rarely mentioned in Marguerite's writings and the visual arts not at all. Marguerite loved reading and particularly enjoyed poetry. As young adults, she and her brother exchanged rhyming notes, but she is unlikely to have written verse as a child. The charming "Recipe For a Happy Life"—"written by Margaret of Navarre in the year Fifteen Hundred" and printed in various modern publications—has been generally dismissed as apocryphal, and the original text in French has so far not been found among her papers.

Marguerite was sixteen years old and still unmarried when she left Amboise in 1508 with her brother François d'Angoulême, who had been officially engaged to Princess Claude since 1506, to join the court in Paris. King Louis XII had offered Marguerite to the prince of Wales in 1500, to Henry of York two years later, and to the duke of Calabria in 1503, but Marguerite's dowry may have been found paltry. In 1505 Henry VII, king of England, asked for Marguerite's hand for himself or for his second son Henry. The king of France had other plans: his own marriage to Anne had given him Brittany, and he wanted to add part of other provinces to the royal domain.

On 9 October 1509, and clearly not by choice, Marguerite d'Angoulême was formally engaged to Charles, Duke of Alençon. The duke, who owned a large part of Normandy, had inherited a claim to the county of Armagnac, and when the king offered the stunning dowry of 60,000 crowns for Marguerite, Charles agreed to the match. When the marriage was celebrated on 2 December 1509, King Louis XII led Marguerite to her seat, a great honor usually reserved for royal daughters. A courtier nevertheless reported that the bride "pleurait a fendre le caillou" (wept enough tears to hollow out a stone) during the entire ceremony. The new duchess and her retinue moved to the medieval castle of Alençon, which boasted of splendid stables but had neither a library nor court musicians. At Marguerite's request, books were soon sent from the libraries of Amboise, Blois, and Cognac, followed by others ordered from printers' shops in France and in other European countries. She also invited scholars and poets to dinners or evenings of music and conversation that became more frequent a few years later during visits from court members.

The duke of Alençon spent most days at the hunt, and his mother, who dressed as a nun long before she

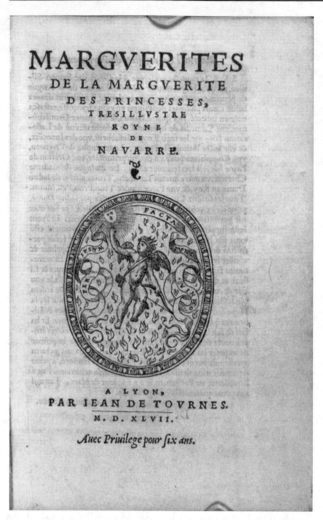

Title page for Marguerite's selection of her works, which includes poems, prayers, religious meditations, songs, and plays (Douglas H. Gordon Collection, University of Virginia Library)

cent, rape, incest, child abandonment, and infanticide. At Marguerite's request her brother founded in Paris the Hôpital des Enfants Rouges (Red Children Hospital)—so called because the children were provided with red clothing—for abandoned or orphaned children who until then had been sheltered with sick and dying adults. Far from losing interest in such projects once they were put into effect, she sent observers and acted at once if and when they reported that the original rules of hygiene, diet, and safety were not strictly respected.

Queen Anne, who had been strongly opposed to Princess Claude's marriage to François, died on 9 January 1514. The distressed Louis XII named Louise, Countess d'Angoulême, as guardian of his two young daughters and, against all rules of court etiquette, decreed the celebration of the marriage of Princess Claude and François d'Angoulême. The lavish ceremony took place on 18 May, while the court was still in mourning.

When Louis XII, who had married Mary Tudor in October, died at the end of 1514 without a male heir, François d'Angoulême became the monarch, and the life of Marguerite, Duchess of Alençon, changed drastically as she became "La mignonne du roi de France" (the Sweetheart to the King of France). Their more affluent lifestyle greatly pleased the duke of Alençon, and Marguerite, suddenly much in the public eye, began spending a good deal of time at court, where she often assumed the duties of her sister-in-law Claude, the frail queen of France. Reports from ambassadors who conversed with Marguerite praised her wit, charm, intelligence, and ability to converse on a variety of subjects, but none described her as beautiful.

Marguerite was familiar with the controversial ideas of Desiderius Erasmus by 1511 at the latest, with the publication in Paris of *Moriae Encomium* (The Praise of Folly) and of the *Adagia* as well as *Institutio Christiani Principis* (The Education of a Christian Prince). Four years later the scholar's 1516 translation of the New Testament was of particular interest to Marguerite, but although Erasmus expressed his admiration and paid homage to Marguerite in writing, his influence on her was short-lived. She read his later works, and one of the three *Colloquia* that Clément Marot, who became her secretary and court poet in 1519, had translated into French for her was erroneously published under her name in the nineteenth century. Erasmus's religious works were perhaps too lukewarm to inspire her.

Martin Luther, however, had a deep and lifelong spiritual impact on Marguerite's thought. She eagerly accepted and made her own his three-pronged approach to faith and salvation: man must recognize and confess that he is a sinner when he compares himself to the immensity and the holiness of God's love; he

took the veil, showed little interest in the world at large. Marguerite, however, chose to become involved in the lives of her subjects, particularly the poor. She embarked on a lifelong effort to eliminate begging from the lands over which she held any control, beginning with the city of Alençon. She involved upper-class and bourgeois women in collecting funds for hospices and almshouses where orphans, abandoned children, the old, and the sick could find shelter. She also initiated reforms in convents and hospices, insisting on hygiene and a healthy diet. Turning to the problems of abortion, abandonment, and infanticide, she demanded that poor or abandoned unmarried mothers be provided food and shelter several days or weeks before and after giving birth. In towns and villages as well as in monasteries and nunneries where such scandals occurred, she made it known to culprit and victim alike that she would act promptly when informed of willful deceit of the innois righteous when he knows that the only way to the divine grace of salvation is his absolute and total faith in God's love through his son Jesus; and he is repentant when he stands humbly before God, aware that he has nothing to offer to God, who has given him everything but whom he offends daily. Marguerite was to use in her religious writings throughout her life Luther's metaphor of *le Tout et le Rien* (the All and the Naught)—"All" being the Creator and "Naught" the faithful Christian aware of his sins and of his being unworthy of his grace.

Luther's posting of the Ninety-Five Theses in which he denounced and condemned the practice of indulgences caused much turmoil in 1517 and later. His text was widely commented on and translations soon circulated, and Luther's "new" religion acquired adepts long before it had a name. At Marguerite's request, Luther's writings and those of European Reformist theologians were translated and regularly sent to her, strengthening her belief that the Scriptures, unburdened from confusing glosses, must be written in a language that common people, literate or not, could understand. An increasing number of scholars translated newly found or rediscovered manuscripts of the Scriptures, and their work revealed more than superficial discrepancies with those texts and commentaries currently used in faculties of theology. They also raised unexpected and disturbing questions about some of the Roman Church rites and sacraments.

To Marguerite, reform seemed inevitable, but she believed that such a monumental task could only be undertaken from within the church and by the clergy. She found it difficult to reconcile the teachings of reformers and her desire to remain within the Roman Church in which she was raised but in which dissension was strictly forbidden. The threat of excommunication was real and terrifying. In 1521, the year Luther was condemned for heresy and excommunicated, she sought spiritual guidance from a theologian whom she could trust.

By seeking help from Jacques Lefèvre d'Etaples, Marguerite demonstrated that she had already parted, not from the Roman Church but from its orthodoxy. As early as 1500, Lefèvre was known as one of the most erudite and respected professors of philosophy in Paris. After "ayant redécouvert Aristote" (discovering a new Aristotle) when he studied Greek authors in their original language in Italy, he had eschewed the rigid scholastic school of thought for a more humanist tradition. He and a few others were committed to the printing and circulation in French of all biblical exegeses and commentaries as well as the Bible itself. In 1512 he had published *S. Pauli Epistoae XIV ex Vulgate, adiecta intelligentia ex graeco, cum commentariis* (The Fourteen Epistles of St. Paul taken from the Vulgate, with Annotations from the Greek, with Commentary), his Latin translation that Luther much admired and saw as a source of inspiration.

Lefèvre introduced Marguerite to Guillaume Briçonnet, bishop of Meaux, who had served her brother as ambassador to the papal court in Rome and who was engaged in reforming church abuses. Under his influence the Circle of Meaux became the center of French evangelism. For three years Marguerite became his dedicated and conscientious student. She unwittingly imitated Briçonnet's convoluted style when she answered his letters between 1521 and 1524, later quoting him from memory in some of her works.

When he returned to Meaux, Briçonnet left Gérard Roussel with her for spiritual guidance, and although Roussel was repeatedly accused of heresy, he remained by her side until her death. The serenity she gained from a faith in which all doubts were answered in Scriptures became both the source and the message of her own writings, even when she adopted a rhetoric of silence and a self-imposed censorship in painful and sometimes dangerous circumstances. In 1524 she was already playing a major role in the Circle of Meaux, providing spiritual as well as financial support for the printing and distribution of evangelical and Reformist texts, all written in or translated into French. Letters from reformers such as Calvin and Erasmus mention her support and some have indicated that she contributed a few of her own writings among those published anonymously at the time.

Briçonnet, Lefèvre, and other erudite theologians of various nationalities who translated Scriptures into French from Greek, Hebrew, and Aramaic incurred the wrath of the Faculty of Theology of the University of Paris. Their writings were examined and usually ruled to be "in error," an offense as serious as blasphemy, if not heresy. When theologians such as those of the Circle of Meaux tampered with the Roman dogma and suggested modifying the text of prayers, they were threatened with excommunication; their homes and those of their friends were searched; and their works were judged to be of a heretical nature and were confiscated and burned in public. On 8 August 1523 Marguerite's protégé Louis de Berquin's *Briefve admonition de la manière de prier: Selon la doctrine de Jesuchrist* (A Brief Admonition on the Manner to Pray According to the Doctrine of Jesus Christ), from which the cult of the Virgin and of the Saints was conspicuously absent, was condemned by the Faculty of Theology. Several of his works were later burned in front of Notre Dame Cathedral in Paris, and he was executed on 17 April 1529.

King François I was at first open to the new ideas, and he usually complied with his sister's pleas for leniency or pardon when her protégés or their friends were arrested and found guilty of blasphemous writings, of straying from the Roman tradition, or simply of failing to observe Lent. But the pressure to prosecute those believed to be enemies of the Church was great. Among Marguerite's associates who were eventually executed were Berquin, Etienne Dolet, several clerics and lay members of the Circle of Meaux, her almoner Jean Michel—all burned at the stake—and Antoine Augereau, one of her printers, who was hanged.

All persons found in possession of condemned works were liable to prosecution, but this rule was not systematically enforced. Marguerite, because of her privileged status, continued to order banned works. One of the works she ordered was a subject of great interest to her, the translation of Luther's treatise on monastic vows of celibacy.

While she was reading forbidden texts, Marguerite was also beginning to write. As early as 1522 or 1523 she aspired to expand the scope of her skills beyond those of didactic or proselytizing poetry. From Marot, she learned prosody, from rhymed couplets to terza rima and Alexandrine verse forms. During the many years he was in her service she practiced all forms of versification and explored other literary genres as well. Until he went into exile in the 1530s, he was also involved in editing her works before publication.

For years Marguerite refrained from committing to print her own work, such as her prose translation of prayers in which Christ's name is substituted for that of Mary. Her *Petit Oeuvre dévot et contemplatif* (Brief Devout and Contemplative Work), a work that was not published until 1960, circulated in manuscript through the evangelical network as early as 1525 where it was praised by lay reformers and by theologians. Wolfgang Capito, a former Benedictine professor of theology and provost of St. Thomas at Strasbourg, praised her in the Latin preface to a 1528 manuscript copy of the text. A supporter of Luther, he formally declared for the Reformation.

In *Petit Oeuvre dévot et contemplatif,* Marguerite, the narrator, seems lost as to which spiritual road to follow—a situation that strongly recalls that of Dante in his *Divinia Comedia* (Divine Comedy), where the author seems lost until an unnamed traveler, an "homme honorable" (honorable man) tells him what he needs to hear but must not reveal. Only after the distressed Marguerite has followed the path in which she, too, had been led and pauses to pray and meditate, does she notice an olive tree in the shape of a cross. She prostrates herself at its base in a mixture of joy and grief —an emotional state that she finds impossible to describe and that is more fully developed later in her religious poems and in her theater. After having regained her strength and her

courage at the foot of the cross, she rejoices at being able to pray in French in the simple and sincere words that come from her heart.

Marguerite then confesses her sins and weeps with pity and love for Christ, who suffered the ultimate sacrifice. In a supreme act of contrition she prays for "la divine ignorance" (divine ignorance)—the surrender of her intellect, her memory, and her willpower—to be one with him, free from sin. Her contrition and her true faith lead her into prayer, and she hears his message of love and of forgiveness for the humble and sincere believers. She resolves that as penitence for her sins, she will carry three crosses: the black cross of repentance, the white cross of patience, and the cross of compassion, red from the blood of Christ. In the final verses she invites others to accompany her on the path of the cross for the love of Christ, *nunc et semper* (now and always).

Many of Marguerite's religious writings circulated only in manuscript form in her lifetime and were not transcribed and published until the late nineteenth century and later. Because what she wrote at the time would have been judged controversial, she did not wish to place her brother or especially her mother, who served as regent during her son's Italian expeditions in 1515–1516 and 1525–1526, in the position of having to either protect or silence her. None of her writings were published until after her mother's death in 1531.

Louise's personal beliefs are not fully known, but her public and official acts as the king's mother and defender of the faith are unequivocal. In 1523 she asked the Faculty of Theology of the University of Paris what would be the most effective means to "extirper l'hérésie luthérienne" (extirpate the Lutheran heresy) from France. In 1525, as regent, she gained the approval of Pope Clement VII to create a permanent inquisitorial tribunal, which was used to dismantle the Circle of Meaux. When Briçonnet appeared before the tribunal, he recanted and denounced all his previous writings. Lefèvre was arrested and refused to recant, but with Marguerite's help he went into exile in Strasbourg. Marguerite's own chaplain was summoned to appear before this tribunal.

After Queen Claude died on 24 July 1524, Marguerite moved to Blois to oversee the education and the pastimes of her six nephews and nieces. In late August the royal children became ill with a virulent form of measles. All but the eldest recovered, and Marguerite was deeply affected by the death on 8 September of her favorite niece, seven-year-old Princess Charlotte.

Briçonnet's 15 September 1524 letter of condolences and consolation to Marguerite is the source and inspiration of the *Dialogue en forme de vision nocturne* (Dialogue in the form of a nocturnal vision)—which she wrote before the end of that year and became her second published work in 1533. Briçonnet understood that though Marguerite lamented the death of Queen Claude, she was truly distressed by the passing of her niece. In his letter he culled from Scriptures examples of grief at the death of an innocent child and then sternly leads her, through many quotations from the Bible, to accept God's will with gratitude and even to rejoice for the dead.

A strongly evangelical work, *Dialogue en forme de vision nocturne* presents a colloquy between Marguerite and "l'âme de Madame Charlotte" (Madame Charlotte's soul). Princess Charlotte exhorts her aunt to cease grieving and repeats in her own words the admonition of Briçonnet's letter. Her voice is that of the stern adult and Marguerite's is that of the student who sees herself as *pis que morte* (worse than dead). She tells Marguerite that tears such as those she is shedding offend her and God, for death is nothing for the Christian strong in his faith, whose soul it liberates from its prison on Earth for its mystical union with God through Christ. On the theme of salvation, she repeatedly invokes Briçonnet's belief: God chooses among the innocent and among sinners those who will know the infinite bliss of divine love, and none will be saved but by the grace of God, through Christ; it is not in religious works or ritual acts of piety but in Christ only that one may hope for divine grace. In the final tercets, after Marguerite pleads to be allowed to join her niece in death, the soul of Princess Charlotte, before soaring to heaven, tells her that she must wait until God opens the door to her, leaving her in the world of tribulations, still living and, repeating the earlier line, "pis que morte" because she remains overwhelmed by "le rein" (her nothingness).

Dialogue en forme de vision nocturne was at the time of its compostion Marguerite's most ambitious and longest religious work, running to 1,293 lines in terza rima. She did not then consider publishing the poem because it would have appeared in print while her brother after his failed Italian campaign was held prisoner by Emperor Charles V. In the king's absence, the Faculty of Theology of the University of Paris and the Parlement (Parliament) of Paris could have reacted at once against the poem—which stresses that without the sinner's sincere faith in God, such Roman practices as morning or evening mass, good works, fasting and pilgrimages are but a worthless fraud—and placed Louise in an impossible position.

With her brother and the best of his men held in Spain for exorbitant ransom after their defeat at Pavia in February 1525, Marguerite assumed the functions of the late queen and of surrogate mother to her brother's children. When the duke of Alençon, who was in part responsible for the capture of King François, returned to Lyon with his men, he begged Louise for forgiveness, but the regent remained implacable and left the room, ordering her daughter to follow her. Marguerite ignored her mother's command and stayed by her husband's bedside, reading from Scriptures to him daily until he died on 11 April 1525, her thirty-third birthday.

Marguerite was involved in the negotiations for the release of her brother and met Charles V in Madrid on 26 October 1525. When the emperor's terms proved unacceptable and additional mediations took longer than expected, François suspected that Charles was trying to keep Marguerite in Spain long enough for her safe-conduct to expire and thus hold two royal hostages instead of one. He ordered his sister to leave, and she returned to France through the most direct northern passage. Her entourage crossed the snow-covered Pyrenees Mountains on horseback, reaching the French border on 25 December with a few days to spare.

On 14 January 1526 François signed the Treaty of Madrid. Two months later, two boats left opposite banks of the Bidassoa River, one carrying the eight-year-old Dauphin François and Prince Henri as hostages and the other their father, king again as he reached France. Marguerite's life at court resumed, and so did her interest in the Reformist cause.

On 26 December 1526, Marguerite, Duchess of Alençon, was formally engaged to Henri II d'Albret, King of Navarre, eleven years her junior, who had escaped from the emperor's jail after being made prisoner at Pavia. Whether this marriage was her choice or that of her brother, she clearly liked and most likely loved Henri, to whom she wrote loving letters and poems. Less than a month later she became queen of Navarre, and by the end of October she arrived in the part of Béarn north of the Pyrenees that was Henri's kingdom. Except for frequent and often lengthy visits to the French court or extensive official journeys of a diplomatic nature, she resided until the last year of her life at the large castle of Pau or the smaller castle at Nérac. On 16 November 1528 she was delivered in Fontainebleau of a daughter, Princess Jeanne (future queen of Navarre), and on 14 July 1530 in Blois, of a son, Prince Jean, who died on 25 December of the same year. Between these births Marguerite served as a hostage during the negotiation in 1529 of the Paix des Dames (Peace of the Ladies) by the two most powerful women in Europe: Marguerite of Austria, representing her nephew Charles V, and Louise, representing her son the king. The treaty resulted in the return of François's sons and his marriage to Eleanor, dowager queen of Portugal and the emperor's sister, on 7 July 1530.

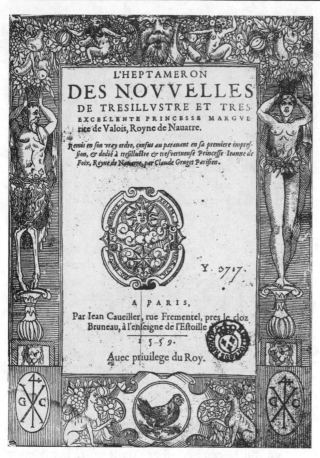

Title page for Marguerite's unfinished work that was inspired by Giovanni Boccaccio's Decameron
(Collection of Roger-Viollet/Getty Images)

Between 1525 and 1531 Marguerite wrote several important works: *Miroir de l'âme pécheresse* (The Mirror of the Sinful Soul), her first published book; "Oraison à notre Seigneur Jésus-Christ" (Prayer to Our Lord Jesus Christ) in which she addresses to Christ the traditional invocation to the Virgin Mary; the lyrical *Oraison de l'âme fidèle à son Seigneur Dieu* (Prayer of the Faithful Soul to Our Lord), attesting that before the creation of man God decided on the election of some of his creatures and that the gift of faith is a divine decision; and the *Discord étant en l'homme par la contrariété de l'esprit et de la chair* (Discordance Caused in Man by the Conflict between the Spirit and the Flesh), a commentary on chapters 7 and 8 of Paul's Epistles to the Romans, fundamental to the doctrine of grace and justification by faith. Other works composed during these years include "Récit de sa conversion" (Account of Her Conversion), a personal introspection that is also an early draft or the seed of *Les Prisons* (1978, Prisons; translated as *Marguerite de Navarre: Les Prisons, A French and English Edition,* 1995) that she completed in 1549 as she prepared for death. She also translated the Lord's Prayer—

"Le Pater Noster faict en translation et dialogue par la Royne de Navarre" (The Lord's Prayer, translated as a dialogue by the queen of Navarre)—and requested the translation of Baldassare Castiglione's *Il libro del Cortegiano* (The Book of the Courtier), undoubtedly because it heaped lavish praises on her brother. Her *L'Heptaméron* (1559; translated as *The Heptameron of the Tales of Margaret, Queen of Navarre,* 1894), however, shows that the Italian work had more than a passing influence on her own prose.

After Louise died on 22 September 1531, Marguerite returned to court to take her mother's place near her brother. The same year her *Miroir de l'âme pécheresse* was first printed in Alençon, where Simon du Bois had moved his shop after the 1529 execution for heresy of Berquin, whose work he had published. Seven printings followed in 1533.

Marguerite had honed her skills in the more than ten years she had been writing when she published *Miroir de l'âme pécheresse,* a 1,434-line poem in decasyllabic couplets. After minor textual changes in 1533, she revised it further when she included it in 1547 in her two-volume collection *Les Marguerites de la Marguerite des princesses* (Pearls from the Pearl of Princesses). The female narrator is the sinful soul who offers to the readers the mirror in which they can see their own souls because all are sinners since Adam. Too weak to shake off the yoke of her sins or to seek help, the sinful soul suffers from offending God. Her transgressions are such that she is "trop moins que rien" (much less than nothing), mud before life, dung after death. No human can change her, and nothing can deliver her but the gift of divine grace through Christ.

The major part of the poem is a long monologue to Christ, her constant and forgiving intercessor, and is divided among the four roles of mother, daughter, sister, and wife in which she sees herself in her relationship with Christ. These roles are then used as exempla in biblical events in which she was unworthy and betrayed him, yet remained welcome in the eyes of immortal, invisible, and incomprehensible God. The poem shows a remarkable use of both the Old and New Testaments within the text and of silence as a rhetorical device. Silence, in Briçonnet's and of Lefèvre's apologia, is present in its most subtle and abstract forms: silence as praise, silence as an act of pure love, silence as meditation, silence in confession to God as an act of faith, silence as an act of humility as it reflects the failure of man's own words and of his capacity to understand the immensity of God's love and grace, and more particularly the silence of religious ecstasy. Silence is used in a mystical union with God, and the material world ceases to exist.

In the early 1530s the king was tolerant of his sister's proselytizing, and he allowed her spiritual adviser, the controversial Roussel, to preach the sermon for Lent in 1532 at the Louvre, to the dismay of the Sorbonne. In defiance of the Faculty of Theology, Marguerite included in the new editions of the popular *Miroir de l'âme pécheresse* the sixth psalm of David, translated from Hebrew into French by Marot, valet de chambre to the king. Even a superficial reader of this psalm could not have missed its Reformist orientation, its emphasis on the primacy of faith, and its exclusive use of the French language for all biblical quotations.

Marguerite's *Miroir de l'âme pécheresse* was soon condemned and listed by the Faculty of Theology among works judged to be tainted with heresy. King François intervened, and on two different occasions the Sorbonne officially rescinded its condemnation and removed *Miroir de l'âme pécheresse* from the list of blacklisted works. The censors of the Faculty of Theology nevertheless took their revenge on Antoine Augereau, who had printed the offending volume, and he was hanged in 1535.

Marguerite and King Henri were returning to their kingdom when the Affaire des Placards compromised Marguerite's relationship with her brother. On the night of 17 October 1534 pamphlets that decried the abuses of the papal Mass were nailed on the doors of various churches in Paris, Orléans, Tours, Rouen, and, making it a case of lèse-majesté, on the doors of the king's chamber. It has since been determined that the sacrilegious leaflets, printed in Switzerland, were posted by conservative members of the Roman Church who found the king's attitude toward Reformers too lenient.

Repression was swift and harsh. A list was made of suspected religious dissenters; many were jailed, and some, mostly lower- or middle-class men unknown at court, were executed. Among those who found refuge or aid in the kingdom of Navarre were Jean Calvin, Marot, and Lefèvre d'Etaples. The court of Navarre seems to have been particularly open to religious freedom, as many who adhered to the teachings and the dogma of the Roman Church also resided there.

From around 1534 or 1535 until 1546 Marguerite wrote four biblical comedies based in part on Medieval plays: *Comédie de la Nativité de Jésus-Christ* (Comedy on the Nativity of Jesus Christ), *Comédie de l'adoration des Trois Rois à Jésus-Christ* (Comedy on the Adoration of the Three Kings to Jesus Christ), *Comédie des Innocents* (Comedy of the Holy Innocents), and *Comédie du Désert* (Comedy in the Desert). While Marguerite scrupulously followed Scripture, the simplicity of her language, the realism of the characters, the serenity of the Virgin despite her awareness of danger, and the sobri-

ety of the mise-en-scène enhanced the power of her deeply personal evangelical message. During the same period she also wrote four of her seven secular comedies, plays that were short and lively enough to be performed: *Le Malade* (The Patient), *L'Inquisiteur* (The Inquisitor), *Comédie des quatre femmes* (Comedy for Four Women), *Trop Prou Peu Moins* (Too Much, Much, Little, and Less). (The first complete edition of her secular works, *Théâtre Profane* [1946; translated as *Marguerite de Navarre, Théâtre Profane*, 1992], included plays that had not been previously published.)

In *Le Malade,* written in 1535, a man in excruciating pain who begs his wife to fetch a doctor symbolizes the Christian Church or a Christian. The doctor attempts a diagnosis while the wife suggests all sorts of amusing remedies that include amulets or a mass, but when the doctor leaves the room to write a prescription, the young servant girl tells her master to put his faith in God and in God alone. When the doctor returns he finds his patient cured and immediately suspects witchcraft, but the girl boldly holds her own in the subsequent colloquy. The doctor leaves while the patient praises God.

L'Inquisiteur, written in 1536, presents an obvious caricature of Noël Béda, the overzealous censor of the Sorbonne, who is shown as stingy, power-thirsty, devious, and cruel. The Inquisitor is irritated by a group of innocent young boys who play in the snow without feeling cold, particularly by their happiness and the fact that they show no fear of him. The names of the children are loosely based on those of Marguerite's protégés, all under suspicion of heresy. The dialogues are cleverly built on two levels: the language of the interrogator, who tries to trap young children with questions that evoke those of the Inquisition, and the language of the children, whose witty repartee and plays on words show that they know Scripture better than the Inquisitor. The Inquisitor's manservant tries to protect the children and is converted. The evil Inquisitor also hears God's message, which comes as in a flash of lightning. All leave the stage together, singing a psalm that had been translated into French.

As an effective means to proselytize, particularly to those who could not read or write, Marguerite began work on her *Chansons spirituelles,* in which new religious verses were written to the melody of popular—and occasionally naughty—songs, easily recognized and retained. Handwritten copies of these songs circulated as far as Geneva, thereby avoiding religious censorship. Marguerite included them in *Marguerites de la Marguerite des princesses.*

In late 1535 the king relented in his anger and invited his sister to join him in Lyon, where they stayed for nearly a year. The eighteen-year-old Prince

François, heir to his father's throne, died in Lyon, perhaps of pleurisy. Poison, however, was suspected and was found in the belongings of an Italian page, who was condemned. All members of the court, including Marguerite, witnessed the public execution.

The king, whose health had been adversely affected by his son's death, deliberately tried to show that his rift with his sister had been healed, but she subsequently had less influence over the king and less power at court than she had enjoyed in the past. Eager to regain the closeness and the warmth of their previous relationship, Marguerite avoided religious issues. During her stay in Lyon she met with scholars and poets who exemplified the humanist spirit of the city, including François Rabelais, Maurice Scève and his siblings, Dolet, and Bonaventure des Périers, all of whom recognized Marot as their uncontested master. Like Marguerite, several of these Lyonnais writers were under suspicion of evangelical if not Lutheran leaning and were cautious about publishing religious works.

In late 1536, a few months after the death of the dauphin François, Marguerite helped her niece Princess Madeleine convince her reluctant father to give his permission for her marriage to King James V of Scotland. The marriage took place in January 1537. Madeleine was not yet seventeen when she died less than six months after her arrival in Scotland, whose climate was too harsh for her delicate constitution. Marguerite increasingly mentioned death, "la dame tant noire" (the lady so black), as shadowing her to take those she loved. Nevertheless, she did not curtail her official activities, and for several years she was seen at court during lengthy stays and at important political events such as the 1538 Conference of Nice and Aigues-Mortes, an attempt at conciliation with Charles V, where she met Pope Paul. Among various poems that she wrote between 1535 and 1540, "Le Triomphe de l'Agneau" (The Triumph of the Lamb) and "Complainte pour un detenu prisonnier" (Complaint of One Held Prisoner), probably alluding to Marot, who had suffered imprisonment for heresy, remained in manuscript form.

Marguerite had long eschewed the cult of the saints, but eager to please her brother or at his command, she attended a feast in the honor of St. Martin in Lyon as a public display of orthodoxy in 1539. She was accompanied by her secretary Des Périers, suspected of heresy, to indicate that he remained in her protection. This event was followed by her required presence on 16 July 1540 at the signing of a contract of marriage between Princess Jeanne and the duke of Cleves. Marguerite and her husband were stunned and hurt by the arbitrary decision of the king who, disregarding their well-known wishes, had imposed his choice of a husband for their daughter. They submitted to the king's will, and their humiliation was compounded when their retinue was stopped during their journey back to the castle of Pau, and they were denied permission to take their daughter with them.

In December 1541 Marguerite completed *La Coche* (The Coach), a 1,400-line poem that avoids the subject of religion. According to her precise directions, woodcuts were interpolated in an elegantly bound volume that she presented in person to Mme. d'Etampes, her brother's mistress, most likely to seek her help to bring her back into her brother's favor. In the poem she writes of herself in the third person as a kind, caring, but disillusioned middle-aged woman looking back sadly on the past events in her life. She meets and listens to the complaints of two unhappy women of her entourage, comforts them and encourages them to move from the nonverbal language of tears to put in writing their debate on the suffering caused by those one loves.

In 1541 Calvin's *Christianae religionis institutio* (1536, Institution of the Christian religion), which had been dedicated to King François, was published in French as *Institution de la religion chrétienne*. Marguerite's relationship with Calvin had deteriorated over the years, and they grew estranged when she found his dogmatism excessive. In 1545 Marguerite broke all contacts with Calvin after his writings criticized and ridiculed her spiritual advisers.

In June 1541 twelve-year-old Princess Jeanne was married to the duke of Cleves, though she refused to walk down the aisle and had to be carried to the altar. The marriage was not then consummated as the princess had not reached puberty, and for the next two years Marguerite nearly exhausted all excuses to postpone her daughter's departure for Germany. When the duke finally agreed to desist from the union in 1543, Marguerite initiated the procedure of annulment. Two years later Pope Paul III, a few weeks before his death, honored her request and annulled the marriage.

Following the marriage of the princess to the duke, François had invited Marguerite and her husband to join the court. Once more in high favor, she wrote a comedy to entertain important guests, her first secular play in six years. Eager to avoid controversy, she chose the safe subject of love and marriage in the *Comédie des quatre femmes*.

In spite of its title, *Comédie des Quatre Femmes* features five female characters. Two young, happy girls are engaged in a debate about love. One refuses to love because she argues that men cannot be trusted, and the other contends that love is the source of supreme and everlasting happiness. Two sad married women join them: one has an insanely jealous husband who mistreats her without reason, and the other has a husband she loves but who is in love with another woman. They ask for an old woman's opinion. She tells the girls that whether they want to or not, they will both love and suffer, and she advises the women that the only way they can overcome their grief is by taking a lover. When they refuse to take her advice, she concludes that time will solve their problem: the jealous husband will no longer love her when she is old and ugly and will stop tormenting her; the unfaithful husband will be too tired to stray and too ugly for her to care. While Marguerite more than hints that women too can play the game of infidelity, she clearly points to the double standards of male and female roles in love and in marriage. This comedy, already anticipating the debates of the storytellers in *L'Heptaméron,* was played before King François and the cardinal of Tournon.

In February 1542 Marguerite left the court to return to Béarn, where she stayed for two years. In December of that year King François, accompanied by Prince Henri and Prince Charles, traveled to Nérac on his way to La Rochelle, where a rebellion was threatening to spread. It was his only visit to the the kingdom of Navarre. Marguerite was then fifty years old and pregnant but this last chance at giving Navarre a king ended when she miscarried in April 1543.

When she returned to the court at her brother's invitation in 1544, Marguerite brought *Trop Prou Peu Moins,* a complex comedy in which Trop (Too Much) and Prou (Much), easily recognized as the Pope and Emperor Charles V, are given donkey's ears that they are unable to hide under their caps, hats, miters, or crowns. Both are rich, giddy with power, greedy, and cruel. They decide to make fun of Peu (Little) and Moins (Less), two simple shepherds in rags whose small horns pierce through their hats. While Trop and Prou complain about their embarrassing ears, they are puzzled by the blissful laughter of the men of faith. The replies of Peu and Moins to their pointed questions are simple yet ambiguous and seemingly nonsensical. Trop and Prou scream with pain and refuse to hear, even for a brief moment, the message of pure faith when Peu and Moins offer their help. By 1544 Marguerite understood that the alliance of the emperor with the Roman Church was unbreakable. She also knew that Rome would neither hear nor listen to the evangelical message of reform within the church. Suggesting that silence or exile are the only solutions left to Reformists, Marguerite's Peu and Moins leave the stage, aware of the danger but eager to proselytize wherever the roads take them.

Marguerite suffered a painful loss in September 1544, when Marot whom she had long protected when she was able, died in exile in Turin. The following year, on 9 September, Charles, Duke of Orléans, her favorite nephew, died from the plague in less than two days at age twenty-three. Of the king's seven children, only two were left: the heir apparent Prince Henri and the youngest, Princess Marguerite, neither of whom was close to their aunt. Religious repression continued, and in 1546, after returning to the kingdom of Navarre, she learned that Dolet, another of her protégés, had been hanged and then burned at the stake in Paris.

In 1546 Marguerite helped Rabelais, an evangelical scholar and prominent physician who had refrained from publishing for nearly ten years because of the threat of excommunication, to obtain a license to print *Le Tiers Livre des faicts et dicts héroïques du bon Pantagruel* (1546, The Third Book of the Heroic Deeds and Sayings of Good Pantagruel), a work he dedicated to Marguerite with a poem in which he alluded to her faith and encouraged her to come out of her own imposed silence. She then decided to collect and edit a selection of her writings, published and unpublished, that she considered worthy of her talent as an author. Her selection was cautious, as except for a few amusing poems, enigmas, and letters, she chose many didactic or proselytizing works. Several of her secular comedies as well as many religious poems were omitted. The two volumes, *Marguerites de la Marguerite des Princesses, tresillustre Royne de Navarre* (Pearls of the Pearl of Princesses, Most Illustrious Queen of Navarre) and *Suyte des Marguerites de la Marguerite des Princesses, tresillustre Royne de Navarre* (Continuation of Pearls of the Pearl of Princesses, Most Illustrious Queen of Navarre) were published in Lyon in 1547 (with privilege to reprint for six years) by Jean de Tournes.

Marguerite was traveling to see her brother when she learned of his death on 31 March 1547. She stopped in Tusson, where she wrote *La Navire* (1956, The Ship), a 1,464-line poem in terza rima that recalls the poet's dialogue with Princess Charlotte in the *Dialogue en forme de vision nocturne.* In the poem the apparition of her brother admonishes Marguerite for persisting in her grief, describing the delightful experience of the beatific light that he encourages her to seek. Far from soothing her pain, the words deepen her sense of loss, and she praises the incomparable virtues of the king. While the soul of her brother insists on the vanity of regrets, she rejects in horror the idea that her love for him could offend God, refusing to cease grieving because she finds in it a blend of joy and of despair. He urges her to contemplate the greatness of God and God alone, telling her that her own death will come soon and that she must throw herself into the open arms of Christ. At dawn the sunlight dissolves the king's ghost. Dazzled, filled with indescribable joy, she expresses the hope that she will be among the chosen. More so than in her earlier work, the poem captures the complexity and the

Statue of Marguerite in the Luxembourg Gardens
(<http://www.insecula.com>)

depth of her emotions, confirming that Marguerite had become a far better poet in the twenty-three years since she had written about the death of her niece.

La Comédie sur le Trespas du Roy (Comedy on the Passing of the King), a pastoral lamentation written shortly after *La Navire,* is neither a comedy nor an eclogue nor a dirge. Similar to the later developed genre of the Oratorio, the work includes songs of varying meters interpolated in the decasyllabic rhymed text and sung by the characters as solos, duets, trios, and a quartet. Among them are several of the *Chansons spirituelles* that she wrote before and after her brother's death. The roles in the poem are clear: Pan, ruler and shepherd to his flock, is François; Amarissima is the expression of Marguerite's grief; Securus is her devoted husband, Henri de Navarre; the shepherd Agape is her nephew Henri, the new king. The role of Paraclesis, the paraclete or great intercessor, is unexpectedly played by a woman. Marguerite leads the reader from her original feelings of anger toward fate and her resentment when others try to stop her tears and pull her from her self-imposed solitude to reconciliation and finally to acceptance.

Marguerite gave much thought to the details of this carefully crafted work, imagining a two-level stage and a backdrop of a painted cloth showing a steep downward path with a crossroad at which stood a large cross. The poem was a personal memorial to her brother, but in giving her characters names taken from antiquity or from Scriptures, dressing them in traditional shepherd clothes and staging it in a bucolic setting that precludes any suggestion of time and place, Marguerite created a timeless and universal reflection of the healing process of catharsis that transcends personal pathos.

In late December or early January 1548, Marguerite traveled to Mont-de-Marsan, where she wrote or completed the best of her secular plays, *The Comedy de Mont-de-Marsan,* a 1,015-line work that was performed on Shrove Tuesday, 15 February 1548. The opening monologue of each of the four female protagonists reveals their religious attitudes. La Mondaine (The Worldly), well-to-do, carefree and superficial, cares only for her body and what makes it more beautiful. She lives for the present. La Superstitieuse (The Bigot), ignorant of Scriptures, is obsessed by rituals, orations that she meticulously counts by the hundreds, pilgrimages, and fasting. She believes that punishing one's body is the only way to earn salvation and condemns others for not following her example. La Sage (The Wise Woman), secure in her faith, whose reading of Scriptures gives peace and serenity, gives each of them a Bible. She cares for her body because it has been entrusted to her, and she tries to keep her soul pure. For her, grace means union with the perfect friend, father, brother, and spouse. Finally, La Ravie (Enraptured by the Love of God) is a young shepherdess blissfully oblivious of the physical world and its traditions. She scorns all material possessions and, unlike the other three, she does not ask herself questions about redemption anymore than she would be interested in Scriptures, for she enjoys a total and joyful faith in God.

Temporarily baffled by La Ravie's behavior, the other women are briefly united in reproaching her for ignoring her sheep and singing passionate love songs to the lover she is going to meet. She answers their questions with parts of songs, incomplete sentences, and much laughter. The three women fail to understand her and leave. She remains alone on stage to deliver an inspired paean to God. The most moving moment in the play is a space left blank between lines 1,011 and 1,012: it is an illumination from God, an ecstatic moment of silence in which the soul is temporarily a separate entity from the body. No words can reflect the mystical and voluptuous possession by divine grace that La Ravie experiences. After this pause she states "Tu l'as fait et je t'en mercie" (Thou hath so done and I thank Thee). The last three lines of the play, a metaphor on death as resurrection, impress upon the audience that one must break the shackles of the material world and surrender one's being with absolute faith to live in the spiritual world of God's love.

King Henri II, ignoring the wishes of Marguerite and King Henri de Navarre, arranged the marriage of Princess Jeanne and Antoine de Bourbon-Vendôme, a son of Charles, Duke of Vendôme, of the second House of Bourbon. Marguerite and her husband postponed their departure from Béarn as long as they could but were told that the marriage would take place in Moulins on 20 October 1548 whether or not they were present. They soon reconciled themselves to the union, and when the newlywed couple traveled to Pau in January 1549 for a visit, Marguerite wrote the charming but far from polished 186-line poem "Le Parfait Amant" (On Perfect Love), praising selfless love and faithfulness.

Marguerite may have begun writing *Les Prisons* in 1548, though the 4,928-line epistle generally seen as her spiritual autobiography was not completed until 1549. In works such as *La Coche*, in several tales included in *L'Heptaméron*, and the *Récit de sa conversion*, she had shown an autographical impulse, but *Les Prisons*, which is written as a letter from a male narrator to a lady he had loved in the past but who had been unfaithful to him, is a far more developed spiritual work. The narrator describes for her his moral, intellectual, and religious triumph over the temptations and pleasures of her love whose prisoner he had once been. The work is divided into three books that might be titled, the "Prison of Human Love," the "Prison of Worldly Pleasures," and the "Prison of the Written Word."

At the end of the first book (1–618), after a lyrical description of how deeply the narrator had desired the prison in which his love for her had kept him, how he cherished the pain that it caused him and had prolonged his suffering before conquering it, his second and last farewell to the lady is far from affectionate. He coldly concludes that he no longer cares for her. The second book (1–1,096) follows the author's progress as, freed from the prison of love that had blinded him to natural beauty, he is seduced first by nature itself and then by the desire to acquire material possessions. At the point when he has achieved every goal that he had set for himself, he meets an elderly scholar who tells him that he is now as much a prisoner of worldly pleasures as he had been of love. He understands that what he had long sought is another prison from which he can escape through knowledge and the world of ideas. Immensely grateful, he asks for his benefactor's name, but the scholar simply replies that he is a lover of learning and that the narrator should emulate him. The narrator follows his advice and begins at once to read the books that liberate him from his second prison.

In the 3,214-line third book, by far the longest of the three, the narrator eagerly accumulates the books he must study, beginning with the Bible. He divides his time between reading the books, conversing with scholars about them, listening to sermons, and attending mass. Books become his reality and his prison.

He begins to experience doubts, but as he studies Scriptures as well as other books, he remains in the prison of the written word and cannot find his way to pure and simple faith for several years. God finally enlightens him, and the mystical ecstasy that he experiences is similar to that of Moses with the burning bush and to that of shepherdess in Mont-de-Marsan. Marguerite is inspired to devote nearly 2,600 lines to the jubilation and the euphoria of this vertiginous "tomber en Dieu" (fall into God). Liberated from his last prison, the narrator does not destroy his books but will henceforth read them in a different light. He knows and understands that none of his prisons would have been destroyed without God's intervention.

The last sixteen lines of *Les Prisons* rejoice in man's redemption, for it is through Christ, whose gentle loving spirit is fire, that man, who is "naught," can be "all" in a mystical union with God, for only where the divine spirit can soar can there be freedom. Marguerite and her ladies-in-waiting embroidered this same message—the *ubi spiritus, ibi libertas* (where the spirit is there is freedom) of St. Paul's second letter to the Corinthians—panels displayed at the castle of Pau. Ten of these panels, in Latin, were placed on the walls of the antechamber leading to the room where she met those to whom she had granted an audience. In this formal room where she sat under a canopy of black and crimson satin, however, the message on the ten identical wall panels was in French because many of those who sought her help did not know Latin.

L'Heptaméron, an unfinished work first published a decade after Marguerite's death, has made her a reputation as a well-known but often misquoted author of a naughty book. She and those around her had gathered for several years anecdotes and gossip to include in a French version of Boccaccio's *Decameron*. But while Marguerite acknowledges her model and praises Boccaccio in her prologue, her intent is more dynamic than that of the Italian author, as she did far more than interpolate dialogues and anecdotes. While the circumstance she contrives to isolate her storytellers—a flood that washes away bridges and confines them to a monastery for ten days—is less dramatic than the devastating plague Boccaccio conceives, Marguerite improves upon her model by having her characters react to the tales. Their conversations and debates are more meaningful than the stories on which they are based because they reflect Marguerite's preoccupation with ethics and her analytical interest in topics such as love and friendship, marriage, faithfulness, and the conflict between faith and religion.

Like their Italian counterparts, the French aristocrats decide to while away the hours by telling stories, each relating one story per day on a chosen topic. However, unlike Boccaccio, whose storytellers include three men and seven women who declare their need for male support, Marguerite's cast is equally divided among the sexes. There is a clear parallel between the five women, single, married, or widowed, representing three generations of distinct personalities, and those of *Comédie des quatre femmes*, but in her brief earlier work the one-dimensional characters had no room to evolve. Age, social status, and education play an equally important role for her five male characters, who rarely reach a consensus.

Marguerite's multifaceted characters are fascinating in their own right because what they are and what they think, what they say and how they react, often supersede who they are. The intricacy of the relationships between the ten narrators who know but do not necessarily like one another yet are forced to spend ten days in a sort of *huis-clos* (closed space) is shown in their observations and reactions to one another's words and gestures. The reader, like the monks hidden behind the hedge, becomes a spectator and must attempt to decipher the true emotions and feelings of the characters, the depths of their relationships, and what goes on behind the scenes.

The tales and conversations alike reveal Marguerite's appreciation of a good joke and the sense of humor for which she was well known. By creating characters who could speak their minds, she dared make critical statements that she would have been otherwise unable to put in writing about customs, traditions, social mores, and religion. Having placed her stranded *devisants* (storytellers) in a monastery where the chaplain or a priest would be in charge of the daily religious service, she boldly chose to have a woman, Oisille, fill the role of religious leader, reading Scriptures in French to them every day and giving a sermon based on the text she has selected.

Marguerite's *L'Heptaméron* remained incomplete, and she did not live long enough to publish it herself. About twenty manuscripts, some with marginal additions, were found after her death. The earliest published text, edited by Pierre Boaistuau in 1558, was not divided into days and comprised sixty-seven tales in random order. In 1559, at the request of Jeanne, Princess of Navarre, Claude Gruget edited a text

divided into eight days that included prologues and debates between the narrators, "in which," according to the editor, "the seventy-two tales were put back into their proper order." Different manuscripts have been used as the basis for modern editions of *L'Heptaméron* because it is impossible to know whether a single manuscript among those containing seventy-two tales was revised by Marguerite herself. It is doubtful that she devoted much time after August 1549 to the manuscript for which she had not yet chosen a name.

In September, Marguerite stopped all audiences, relinquished to the king of Navarre all her official duties, and moved to the castle of Odos. In December she became ill with a high fever, and when pleurisy set in, she was told that she must face death. Roussel, her spiritual adviser since 1521, was not summoned in time, and Brother Gilles Caillau, a Franciscan monk, gave her the last rites. She had been unable to speak for three days, but on 21 December 1549, between 3:00 and 4:00 A.M., she shouted the name of Jesus three times. Brother Gilles then put the crucifix to her lips and she died.

Marguerite's selected collection, *Marguerites de la Marguerite des princesses,* was her main literary legacy until the late nineteenth century, when more of her unpublished works were discovered and brought to print, leading to a new respect for her versatility as a writer. Nevertheless, the depth and the multifaceted talent of Marguerite was not fully acknowledged until the twentieth century, when her incomplete *L'Heptaméron* was read more closely and with greater appreciation. All of Marguerite's discovered works have now been published in French and are increasingly being translated into other languages. While many studies and theses have explored her work, scholars and critics are still coming to terms with Marguerite de Navarre's rich legacy, in all its literary, historical, philosophical, religious, and social dimensions.

Bibliography:

H. P. Clive, *Marguerite de Navarre, An Annotated Bibliography* (London: Grant & Cutler, 1983).

Biographies:

Pierre Jourda, *Marguerite d'Angoulême, Duchesse d'Alençon, Reine de Navarre (1491–1549), étude biographique et littéraire* (Paris: Champion, 1930);

Samuel Putnam, *Marguerite of Navarre* (New York: Coward-McCann, 1935);

Raymond Ritter, *Les solitudes de Marguerite de Navarre* (Paris: H. Champion, 1953);

Jean-Luc Déjean, *Marguerite de Navarre* (Paris: Fayard, 1987).

References:

Nicole Cazauran, "Les citations bibliques dans l'Heptaméron" in *Prose et Prosateurs de la Renaissance, Mélanges Robert Aulotte* (Paris: SEDES, 1988), pp. 153–163;

Cazauran and J. Dauphiné, eds. *Marguerite de Navarre, 1492–1992. Actes du colloque international de Pau (1992)* (Mont-de-Marsan: Editions interuniversitaires, 1995);

R. D. Cottrell, *The Grammar of Silence: A Reading of Marguerite de Navarre's Poetry* (Washington, D.C.: Catholic University of America Press, 1986);

Lucien Febvre, *Amour sacré, amour profane: Autour de l'Heptaméron* (Paris: Gallimard, 1944);

Gary Ferguson, *Mirroring Belief: Marguerite de Navarre's Devotional Poetry* (Edinburgh: Edinburgh University Press, 1992);

Jules Gelernt, *World of Many Loves: The Heptameron of Marguerite de Navarre* (Chapel Hill: University of North Carolina Press, 1966);

Christine Martineau and Michel Veissière, eds., *Guillaume Briçonnet-Marguerite d'Angoulême, Correspondance (1521–1524)* (Geneva: Droz, 1975–1979);

Gabriel-André Pérouse, *Nouvelles françaises du XVIe siècle, images de la vie du temps* (Geneva: Droz, 1977);

Régine Reynolds-Cornell, *Les Devisants de l'Heptaméron, dix personnages en quête d'audience* (Washington, D.C.: University Press of America, 1977);

Reynolds-Cornell, "Silence as a Rhetorical Device in Marguerite de Navarre's Théâtre Profane," *Sixteenth Century Journal*, 17, no. 1 (1986): 17–32;

Reynolds-Cornell, ed., *International Colloquium Celebrating the 500th Anniversary of the Birth of Marguerite de Navarre* (Birmingham, Ala.: Summa, 1995);

Eva Martin Sartori, ed., *The Feminist Encyclopedia of French Literature* (Westport, Conn.: Greenwood Press, 1999);

Paula Sommers, *Celestial Ladders: Readings in Marguerite de Navarre's Poetry of Spiritual Ascent* (Geneva: Droz, 1989);

Marcel Tetel, *Marguerite de Navarre's* Heptaméron: *Themes, Language and Structure* (Durham, N.C.: Duke University Press, 1973).

Papers:

The major collection of Marguerite de Navarre's manuscripts and papers is held by the Bibliothèque nationale de France.

Clément Marot

(1496 – September 1544)

Ehsan Ahmed
Michigan State University

BOOKS: *Le Temple de Cupido* (N.p., 1515?);

Epistre de maguelonne a son amy pierre de prouvance elle estant a lhospital (N.p., circa 1517–1520?);

Lepistre et ordonnance du camp de monseigneur Dalençon ayant la charge du roy nostre sire, et aussi les noms des capitaines estant en la compagnie du dit seigneur (N.p., 1521);

Sensuyvent les Regretz messire Jaques de beaulne chevalier seigneur de sainct Blancay (N.p., after 12 August 1527);

Deploration sur le trespass de feu messire Florimont Robertet seigneur Dalluys. Jadis Chevalier, Conseiller du Roy, Tresorier de France, Secretaire des finances du dict seigneur (Lyon: Printed by Claude Nourry, after 29 November 1527);

Les opuscules et petitz Traictez de Clement Marot de Quahors, Varlet de chambre du Roy. Contenans Chantz royaulx Ballades Rondeaulx Epistres Elegies avec le Temple de Cupido & la plaincte de Robertet, ensemble plusieurs aultres choses joyeuses & recreatives redigees en ung & nouvellement Imprimees (Lyon: Printed by Olivier Arnoullet, 1531);

Ladolescence clementine. Autrement, les Oeuvres de Clement Marot de Cahors en Quercy, Valet de Chambre du roy, composees en leage de son Adolescence. Avec la Complaincte sur le Trespas de feu Messire Florimond Robertet. Et plusieurs autres Oeuvres faictes par ledict Marot depuis leage de sa dicte Adolescence. Le tout revu, corrige & mis en bon ordre (Paris: Printed for Pierre Roffet by Geofroy Tory, 1532; enlarged, 1532); enlarged as *Ladolescence clementine. Ce sont les oeuvres de Clement Marot nouvellement imprimez* (Lyon: Printed by Francoys Juste, 1533);

Petit traicte contenant plusieurs chantz royaulx: Ballades et Epistres faictes et composees par Clement Marot de Quahors en quercy, varlet de chambre du Roy, Ensemble le Temple de Cupido avec la Deploration sur le trespas de feu messire Florimond Robertet iadis chevallier Conseillier du Roy, Tresorier de France, Secretaire des finances dudict seigneur, Seigneur Dalluye faicte par ledict Marot (N.p., 1532?);

Clément Marot (from <http://en.wikipedia.org>)

La Suite de L'adolescence clementine, dont le contenu s'ensuyt, Les Elegies de l'autheur, Les Epistres differentes, Les Chantz divers, Le Cymetiere, Et le Menu (Paris, late 1533 or early 1534);

Les Oeuvres de Clement Marot de Cahors, Valet de chambre du Roy. Augmentees de deux Livres d'Epigrammes: Et d'ung grand nombre d'aultres Oeuvres par cy devant non imprimees. Le tout songneusement par luy mesme revue, & mieulx ordonné (Lyon: Printed by Estienne Dolet, 1538); republished as *Les Oeuvres de Clement Marot de Cahors, Valet de Chambre du Roy. Desquelles le contenu sensuit. . . . Le tout par luy autrement & mieulx ordonné, que par cy devant. La Mort n'y mord* (Lyon: Printed by Sebastianus Gryphius, 1538);

Recueil des dernieres oeuvres de Clement Marot non imprimées. Et premierement Celles quil fit Durant son exil Et depuis son retour. 537 En Mars (N.p., 1538);

Les Oeuvres de Clement Marot de Cahors, Valet de chambre du Roy. Augmentées d'ung grand nombre de ses compositions nouvelles, par cy devant non imprimées (Lyon: Printed by Estienne Dolet, 1542);

Oeuvres de Clement Marot, de Cahors, vallet de chambre du Roy. Plus amples, & en meilleur ordre que paravant (Lyon: Printed by Rocher, 1544).

Collections: *Oeuvres complètes,* 6 volumes, edited by Claude Albert Mayer (London: Athlone Press, 1958–1970);

Oeuvres poétiques, 2 volumes, edited by Gérard Defaux (Paris: Classiques Garnier, 1990, 1993).

OTHER: Guillaume de Lorris and Jean de Meun, *Le Rommant de la Rose: Nouvellement reveu et corrige oultre les precedentes Impressions,* edited by Marot (Paris: Sold by Galliot du Pré, 1529);

François Villon, *Oeuvres,* edited by Marot (Paris: Galliot du Pré, 1533).

TRANSLATIONS: Ovid, *Le Premier Livre de la Metamorphose d'Ovide. Item Certaines oeuvres qu'il feit en prison, non enocore imprimez* (Paris: Printed by Estienne Roffet, 1534);

Aulcuns pseaulmes et cantiques mys en chant (Strasbourg, 1539);

Psalmes de David, Translatez de plusieurs Autheurs, & principallement de Cle. Marot. Veu recongneu et corrigé par les theologiens, nommeement par nostre M.F. Pierre Alexandre, Concionateur ordinaire de la Royne de Hongrie, translated by Marot and others (Antwerp: Printed by Antoine des Gois, 1541);

Trente pseaulmes de David, mis en francoys par Clement Marot, valet de chambre du Roy (Paris: Printed for Estienne Roffet, 1541);

Cinquante pseaumes en francois par Clem. Marot. Item une Epistre par luy nagueres envoyée aux Dames de France. Psal. 9. Chentez en exultation Au Dieu qui habite en Syon (N.p., 1543); republished as *Cinquante pseaumes, mis en françoys selon la vérité hébraïque,* edited by Gérard Defaux (Paris: Champion, 1995);

Trente deux Pseaulmes de David, translatez et composez en rythme francoyse par Clement Marot, veuz et visitez oultre les precedentes editions par ledit Marot, etaultres gens scavans, avec arguments sur chascun Pseaulme. Plus vingt aultres Pseaulmes Nouvellement envoyez au Roy par ledit Marot (Paris: Printed by Estienne Roffet, 1543).

Though eclipsed by poets such as Joachim du Bellay and Pierre de Ronsard in histories of French Renaissance literature, Clément Marot remains one of the most intriguing poets of the sixteenth century because he wrote during the volatile times of the early Reform and was implicated in several of its controversies. His poetry is a testimony to the life of a humanist writer during that turbulent period, and it reveals the challenges Marot confronted to survive as a poet.

Scant documentation exists about Marot's life; most of the information one might garner from the poetry is not completely reliable, since the speaker is often a fictive persona. He was born in 1496 in Cahors, in the province of Quercy; scholars have deduced the year of his birth based on evidence from his poem "L'Enfer" (Hell), written in 1526, and from *Ladolescence clementine* (Clementine Adolescence), published in 1532. His father, Jehan Marot (born Des Mares or Des Marets), came from the village of Mathieu near Caen; his mother was from Quercy, but nothing more is known of her. Unlike his father, she is never mentioned in his verse. For that matter, there is no account in Marot's poetry of his wife and hardly any of his children.

Marot's father worked in the hat business in Cahors during the last third of the fifteenth century. He was also a member of the first generation of Renaissance poets in France, known as the Grands Rhétoriqueurs. In 1506, with the help of Michelle de Saubonne, Baronne de Soubise, he obtained a position in the court of Anne de Bretagne in Paris.

Marot is believed to have served as a page in the Paris home of Nicolas de Neufville, Seigneur de Villeroy, a highly placed civil servant, between 1510 and 1519. One of the last and best of the Grands Rhétoriqueurs, Jean Lemaire de Belges—who, like Marot's father, attended the court of Anne de Bretagne—taught Marot the "feminine caesura." Marot put the technique to effective use around 1512 in translating Virgil's first eclogue. The poem, which first appeared in the *Adolescence clementine,* is a dialogue between two shepherds. Melibée and his flock have encountered bad fortune; without a protector he has been forced into exile, and his prized ewe is weakened and must abandon her newborn lambs. In contrast, Tityrus has robust animals and a rich pasture. Tityrus attributes his good fortune to a beneficent god, the emperor Augustus. Marot's career, as far as one can judge from his poetry, resembled at various times the situations of both Melibée and Tityrus. He was keenly aware that his success as a poet depended on having a powerful patron.

Marot composed *Le Temple de Cupido* (1515?, Temple of Cupid) at De Neufville's request, probably in 1513 or 1514. The dedicatory epistle is addressed to the heir apparent to the French throne, François de Angoulême, and his wife, Claude de France. The poem recounts the speaker's quest to find the goddess ferme

Amour (constant Love), who is tied intimately to the royal couple. He finds her, accompanied by François and Claude, residing in the *choeur* (choir or chancel) of an orchard designed as a temple; the temple is ruled by the pagan god Cupid and contains sacred Catholic items such as relics, fonts, psalters, and breviaries that refer ironically to worldly desires. In creating a religion of profane love instilled with Catholic elements, Marot is using the commonplaces of love poetry found in earlier works such as Guillaume de Lorris and Jean de Meun's *Le Roman de la Rose* (1225–1280, The Romance of the Rose), Lemaire's *Temple de Venus* (1511, Temple of Venus), Jean Molinet's *Temple de Mars* (1475, Temple of Mars), and Martial d'Auvergne's *Arrêts d'Amour* (circa 1460, Love's Decrees); traces of Ovid's *Ars amatoria* (Art of Love) are evident, as well. Marot plays on the word *choeur,* which inevitably recalls its homophone, *coeur* (heart). The poem not only praises the love of the future king and queen but also initiates Marot's quest to obtain their patronage.

Another of Marot's earliest poems, "Des Enfans sans soucy" (Children without Worry), takes its name from a fraternity of palace clerks who performed theatrical farces. Placed first among the ballads in the 1538 edition of the *Adolescence clementine,* this poem—along with "Ballade IV" of the *Adolescence clementine* and "Epître XIV" (Epistle XIV) of *La Suite de L'adolescence clementine* (late 1533 or early 1534, Continuation of the Clementine Adolescence)—confirms that Marot worked in the palace chancellery during this period and might have participated in the fraternity.

The epistle, a poetic form cultivated in the fifteenth century by Christine de Pisan, François Villon, and Charles d'Orléans and later by the Grands Rhétoriqueurs, became more personalized in Marot's hands. The difference between the contrived and impersonal style of the earlier poets and the intimate tone adopted by Marot is apparent by contrasting his *Epistre de maguelonne a son amy pierre de prouvance elle estant a lhospital* (Epistle from Maguelonne to Her Friend Pierre of Provence, She Being at the Hospital) to his "Petite Epistre au Roy" (Short Epistle to the King) and "Epistre du despourveu" (Epistle of the Destitute One), all of which were composed between 1517 and 1519. The *Epistre de maguelonne* draws on the prose story, popular in the fifteenth and sixteenth centuries, of Pierre de Provence and the beautiful Maguelonne, the daughter of the king of Naples. Poetic epistles by Octavien de Saint-Gelais and Andry de la Vigne based on Ovid's *Heroides* probably inspired Marot to undertake this type of epistle, which is called "artificial" because it is addressed by a mythological or fictive woman to an absent man. Maguelonne relates her forbidden love for Pierre, their flight from her father, and her unintentional abandonment by her lover

when he is captured by Moorish pirates while trying to retrieve her necklace, which was stolen by a raven while she was asleep. She takes refuge at the court of Provence and founds a hospital. Maguelonne is converted from profane to sacred love when she turns her attention from Pierre to the sick.

Probably written in 1518, the "Petite Epistre au Roy" begins, "En m'esbatant je faiz Rondeaux en rime" (While frolicking I make rondeaux in rhyme). The poem is a tour de force built on *rimes équivoques* (rhymes formed with more than one word); it displays Marot's flair, wit, and what Nicolas Boileau-Despréaux in *L'Art poétique* (1674, Poetic Art) called his "élégant badinage" (elegant banter). His ostensible subject is poetry, but another theme looms large in this deceptively light epistle: the poet's need for patronage. "Des biens avez et de la rime assez" (You have necessities and rhyme enough), he tells the king; "Mais moy, à tout ma rime et ma rimaille, / Je ne soutiens (dont je suis marry) maille" (But I, with all my rhyme and rhyming, / Do not have [for which I'm sorry] a penny). Yet, "si je ne rimoys / Mon pauvre corps ne seroit nourry moys, / Ne demy jour" (if I weren't rhyming / My poor body would not be fed a month, / Or even a half a day). The poem ends with a plea that the king grant him "heur" (happiness) so that he may continue rhyming and know "quel bien par rime on a" (what good one has through rhyme).

Marot composed the "Epistre du despourveu" when he was seeking employment by François's sister Marguerite d'Alençon, the future queen of Navarre. Again, the tone is noticeably personal. He tells of a dream in which Mercury, the god of eloquence, descended from the heavens to encourage him to become a poet and to ask for the patronage of the duchess of Alençon, because "elle peult te garder d'endurer/ Mille douleurs" (she can prevent you from suffering a thousand pains). He had to overcome Crainte (Fear) that his poetry was not worthy of being presented to Marguerite. Fortunately, Bon Espoir (Good Hope) appears, banishes Crainte, and inspires the poet to compose new verse. Comforted by Bon Espoir, he asks Marguerite to allow him "D'estre le moindre, & plus petit servant / De vostre hostel" (To be the least, and the smallest, servant / In your house). He also recognizes the help given to him by François, who serves as an intermediary between him and the duchess.

The "Epistre au Roy, du temps de son exil à Ferrare" (Epistle to the King, at the Time of His Exile in Ferrara), composed during the summer of 1535, indicates that Marot entered Marguerite's service in 1519. While he claims in the poem to have been "secrétaire de la reine Navarre" (secretary to the queen of Navarre), he is listed in her financial records under "Autres pensionnaires" (Other members of the household). Marguerite, who protected humanist writers such as François Rabelais and Bonaventure des Périers, exposed Marot to the new evangelical religious ideas; Marot often refers to her in his poetry as "Pallas" (Athena, the Greek goddess of wisdom). During his service in Marguerite's household Marot attended the meeting in 1520 of François and King Henry VIII of England–the Field of the Cloth of Gold–and documented it in his poetry. He accompanied Marguerite's husband, Charles d'Alençon, on a military campaign to Hainaut in 1521 and included that experience, too, in his work. Scant testimony is, however, available concerning Marot's activities from late 1521 to the spring of 1526.

In addition to the epistle, Marot cultivated such other poetic forms cherished by the Grands Rhétoriqueurs as the complaint, epitaph, ballad, *chant royal,* rondeau, and chanson (song), all of which appear in *Ladolescence clementine*. Notable among the ballads in *Ladolescence clementine* is "D'ung qu'on appeloit Frere Lubin" (Of Somebody Called Friar Lubin), a caricature of a vile, dishonest, and debauched monk whose name, according to Randle Cotgrave's *A Dictionarie of the French and English Tongues* (1611), signifies "a certaine Monke, who loved a neighbors house better than his own Covent." This humorous portrait stems from Marot's dismay with church practices, which he also voices in other works. Rabelais later used Lubin in *Gargantua and Pantagruel* (1532–1542) to mock the hypocritical lifestyle of clerics.

In 1521 Marot presented his "Chant Royal de la Conception nostre Dame" (Royal Song of the Conception of Our Lady) at the Puy de la Conception (Contest of the Conception) in Rouen. Though Du Bellay later declared in *La Deffence et Illustration de la Langue Françoyse* (1549; translated as *The Defence and Illustration of the French Language,* 1939) that the contest showcased poetic "episseries, qui corrumpent le goust de nostre Langue, & ne servent si non à porter temoingnage de notre ignorance" (trivial spices, which corrupt the taste of our language and serve only to attest to our ignorance), it was, in fact, an erudite event. Marot's *chant royal* reveals the complexity of his religious beliefs, which were critical of some of the dicta of the church and faithful to others. Marot did not win the competition, as his later nemesis, François Sagon, reminded him in an acerbic poem, "Le rabais du caquet Frippelippes" (1537, The Fall of the Prattling Frippelippes)–Cotgrave defines *frippelippes* as "a lickoros slave, a saucie companion."

Love is a major topic in Marot's rondeaux and chansons. The rondeaux, most of which were written before 1527, are based on those of the fifteenth century and those by his father and other Grands Rhétoriqueurs. They include such topoi as "la belle dame sans

Title page for Marot's edition of Guillaume de Lorris and Jean de Meun's thirteenth-century poem (Thomas Cooper Library, University of South Carolina)

merci" (the beautiful lady without pity) and the martyred lover, along with motifs borrowed from the Italian Petrarchist poets. The Petrarchist influences entered France through François's court, which welcomed Italian courtiers, and they can be detected in the poetry of Jehan Marot. From the late-fifteenth-century Italian Petrarchists Antonio Tebaldeo and Serafino dell'Aquila and from d'Orléans and De Pisan he learned the use of antitheses such as the bitter and sweet and the intense focus on the heart, on being burned or wounded by love, on suffering, on the kiss, and on solitude. Like the rondeaux, his chansons are borrowed from the popular love tradition; many were set to music.

In the spring of 1526 Marot was arrested and incarcerated in the Châtelet prison. Because of the lack of documents and the unreliability of Marot's account, the cause of his arrest remains clouded. He claimed in "Contre celle qui fut s'amye" (1526, Against the One Who Was His Girlfriend) that a mistress denounced him to the authorities for having "mangé le lard" (eaten meat) during Lent. The expression, which in sixteenth-century colloquial French signified a theft or crime of any sort, could, of course, have had its literal meaning and referred to Marot's flouting of fasting laws, which would have been seen as a heresy. But, he says, coupled with this denunciation was the accusation that the poet was a "lúthérien" (Lutheran), a term loosely used to suggest heretical beliefs. His accuser, he says, sought retribution after he castigated her inconstancy in the ballad "Contre celle qui fut s'amye" (Against the One Who Was His Love) and the rondeaux "De l'inconstance de Ysabeau" (Of the Inconstancy of Ysabeau) and "A ses Amys après sa delivrance" (To His Friends after His Deliverance). The notion that an amorous quarrel could lead to such grave consequences makes Marot's account questionable. Claude Albert Mayer in *Clément Marot* (1972) wonders whether the attribution of the poet's incarceration to a mistress was simply a fiction imitated from Villon, who also claimed that his tribulations with the law were caused by a lover.

According to Marot's epistle "A Monsieur Bouchart, Docteur en theologie" (To Mr. Bouchart, Doctor in Theology), written in March 1526, he was put in jail by a theologian at the Sorbonne, Nicolas Bouchart, who was involved in persecutions of heretics instigated by the Faculty of Theology of Paris from 1523 to 1525. Marot vehemently denies having any heretical beliefs—"Point ne suis Lutheriste, / Ne Zuinglien, & moins Anabatistes" (I am not a Lutheran, / Nor a Zwinglian, and even less an Anabaptist)—swears his adherence to "La saincte, vraie, & catholique Eglise" (The holy, true, and Catholic Church), and demands his freedom. When Bouchart did not respond, Marot composed the better-known "A son amy Lyon" (To His Friend Lyon), in which he asks Lyon Jamet to secure his release. The epistle is a rewriting of Aesop's fable of the lion and the rat: the rat (Marot), caught in a trap for having "mangé le lard, & la chair toute crue" (eaten meat and completely raw flesh), implores his lion friend (Jamet) to free him, and the lion does so. When the lion is later trapped, the rat comes to his aid. As a result of Jamet's efforts, the bishop of Chartres, Louis Guillard, transferred Marot to an inn in that city.

Marot began to compose his satirical masterpiece, "L'Enfer," in Chartres in March 1526. Writing to his "treschiers Freres" (very dear brothers), he looks back on the "grand chagrin, & recueil ord, & laid, / Que je trouvay dans le Chastellet" (great suffering, and the foul and ugly welcome / That I found in Châtelet). He attributes his miserable descent into the abyss, redolent of sulfur, to his former mistress, Ysabeau, whom he calls "Luna." After passing Cerberus, the many-headed dog who guards the entrance to Hades, he meets Minos, one of the three judges of Hades; Minos is a mask for Gabriel d'Allègre, the *prévot* (provost marshal) of Paris. Trials are compared to long, convoluted, venomous snakes; they exist through "faulte de charité / Entre Chrestiens" (lack of charity / Among Christians). The prisoner is brought before Rhadamantus, another of the judges of Hades; he is a disguise for Gilles Maillart, a justice of the *prévôté* (judicial district) of Paris. Rhadamantus is "plus enflammé, qu'une ardente fournaise" (more inflamed than a burning furnace) and has a predilection for torture. Interrogated about his birth, name, and condition, the poet informs the judge of his friendship with the gods of the upper world—the royal family, who will rescue him. He connects his first name with that of the Pope, Clement VII, and his last with that of Virgil (Publius Vergilius Maro), who was Dante's guide in the *Inferno,* in an effort to prove that he is not a heretic Lutheran. Finally, he explains that his patron, Marguerite d'Alençon, has gone to Spain with her mother to seek the freedom of the king, who was captured in Pavia in 1525 by the forces of the Holy Roman Emperor Charles V and imprisoned in Spain. On being liberated, François, like Christ, will descend to hell to deliver souls such as the poet's. In the Treaty of Madrid of 14 January 1526 François agreed to exchange his two sons for his own release. Marot was freed from Chartres on 1 May, shortly after François's return from Madrid.

In 1527 Marot began to neglect the poetic forms drawn from the vernacular tradition, replacing them with more-refined ones of Latin origin such as the elegy, the epithalamium, and the eclogue. The elegies, published in *La Suite de L'adolescence clementine,* nevertheless retain traditional themes and medieval commonplaces. The form that Marot called the *épître* (epistle) treated matters quite apart from love, but the elegies are, in essence, letters about love inspired by Ovid's *Heroides.* At this point in his career Marot was looking to the ancients so dear to Renaissance humanists.

On 13 January 1527 Jacques de Beaune, Seigneur de Semblançay and treasurer of the kingdom, was arrested for misuse of royal funds. He was convicted, condemned to death, and hanged on 12 August on Montfaucon, a hill northeast of Paris that was used as a place of execution from the twelfth to the seventeenth centuries. (Villon had evoked the place in his "La Ballade des pendus" [1489, Ballad of the Hanged Men].) Semblançay's execution prompted Marot to write "Le vingttroisieme elegie du riche infortuné messire Jacques de Beaune, seigneur de Semblançay" (The Twenty-third Elegy of the Unlucky and Wealthy Sir Jacques de Beaune, Seigneur of Semblançay) and the epigram "Du

Lieutenant Criminel de Paris, & de Samblançay" (Of the Lieutenant of Criminal Justice of Paris, and of Semblançay). Public opinion was divided over Semblançay, and Marot does not deny the former treasurer's guilt in either work. Instead, he highlights Semblançay's constancy in the face of death and sees the execution as the result of the vicissitudes of fortune and the transience of worldly values. The epigram underscores Semblançay's dignified air at Montfaucon; in an ironic twist, Marot describes the expression of Gilles Maillard, the officer who presided at the execution, as that of one going toward a disgraceful death, while Semblançay has the mien of a stern executioner.

In October 1527 Marot was arrested again; the reason is unclear. In the witty epistle "Marot, Prisonnier escript au Roy pour sa delivrance" (Marot, a Prisoner, Writes to the King for His Deliverance) he says that he has been made a brother in the diocese "De sainct Marry en l'Eglise sainct Pris" (Of Holy Sorrow in the Church of the Holy Arrest). He was picked up in front of the royal palace by guards and carried off like a bride to the prosecutor, who took from him "une Becasse, / Une Perdrix, et ung Levrault aussi" (a woodcock, / A partridge, and a young hare, too). The matter was referred to the king for adjudication. François sent a letter to the Parlement of Paris on 1 November, and Marot was released four days later.

On 29 November 1527 Marot's friend and patron Florimond Robertet died and was buried in Blois. Marot memorialized Robertet, who was known for his open mind, in the longest poem he ever wrote. "Deploration sur le Trespas de Messire Florimond Robertet" (Lament on the Death of Sir Florimond Robertet) is the first piece in *La Suite de l'Adolescence clementine* and is remarkable for its evangelical and Pauline tones. Influences on the poem traced by scholars include the sermons on the Pauline epistles of Thomas Malingre, a Dominican preacher in Blois at the time of Robertet's death; a 15 September 1524 letter to Marguerite d'Alençon from Guillaume Briçonnet, the archbishop of Meaux; and Marguerite's "Dialogue en forme de vision nocturne" (Dialogue in the Form of a Nocturnal Vision), marking the death of her niece Charlotte and probably composed at the end of 1524. "Deploration sur le Trespas de Messire Florimond Robertet" begins with a reflection on the nature of mourning that is consistent with the evangelical emphasis on the inner state of the believer: it is "Non point ung deuil, qui dehors apparoist, / Mais qui au coeur (sans apparence) croist" (Not a mourning that appears on the outside / But one that grows [invisibly] in the heart). The simplicity of the pained heart in the opening verses contrasts with the Catholic Church's demonstrative and complex expression of mourning. Death appears on a cart in a trium-

phal procession, a portrayal no doubt inspired by Petrarch's *Trionfi* (Triumphs). In "Gothic" style, Marot describes her as "hydeuse, & redoubtée" (hideous and dreaded). She stands with her foot on a corpse and holds an arrow tinged with the blood of the deceased as an old crow intones a dirge of evil predictions. In front of the cart walks a fairy; she is richly dressed and wields temporal power but hides the signs of her worldliness behind a humble cloak: "Ceste grand Dame est nommée Rommaine" (This great Lady is called Roman). On the right side of the fairy is "Republique françoyse" (French Republic) and on the other side the "bon hommeau Labeur" (good man Labor). Two speeches are given. The French Republic's discourse of 103 verses eulogizes Robertet and curses Death. Death's 167 verses attempt in an evangelical manner to enlighten the "Peuple seduict, endormy en tenebres / Tant de longs jours par la doctrine humaine" (People seduced, lulled asleep in darkness / For so long by human doctrine). Death seeks to turn the people to an inner faith in God's grace, which alone brings salvation. She attributes the people's scorn of Death to their excessive self-love and exhorts them: "Prie à Dieu seul que par grâce te donne / La vive Foy, dont Sainct Paul tant escrit" (Pray to God alone that through grace he may give you / Living faith of which Saint Paul has written so much). Such "vive Foy" will cause the people to desire "Mourir, pour estre avecques Jesuchrist" (To die, in order to be with Jesus Christ). Marot removes the traditional Gothic mask of Death to unveil it in its evangelical light as a welcome liberation from the prison of the body. The people, however, are deaf to Death's speech, and they continue the funeral in the accustomed ways.

Marot became a member of the royal household after his father's death in late 1526. But it is evident from the epistle "Au Roy" (To the King), composed at the end of 1527, that he had still not been placed on the royal payroll a year later. Describing himself as a poor sheep, the least of the flock, he refers to the roster of royal accounts in telling François: "Et ne falloit, Sire, tant seulement, / Qu'effacer Jan, & escrire Clement. / Or en est Jan par son trespas hors mis, / Et puis Clement par son malheur obmis" (All you had to do, Sir, / Was to erase Jan, and write Clément. / Now Jan is removed by his death, / And still, Clément, through his misfortune, is omitted). His poetic talent, he asserts, is his spiritual inheritance from his father, and now he would like to receive his temporal inheritance—that is, the salary once provided by the king, who had hired Jehan after Anne de Bretagne died in 1514. After a concerted effort that is documented in his poetry, he was finally placed on the royal payroll as *valet de chambre* at the beginning

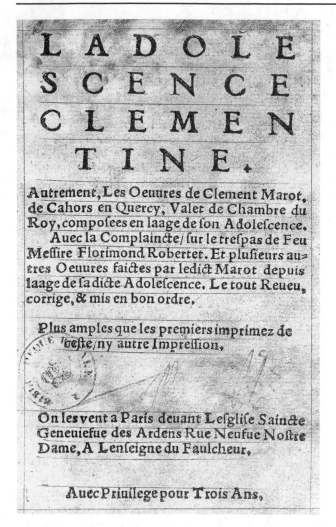

*Title page for the enlarged second edition of Marot's collection of poems
published in 1532, the same year as the first edition
(Collection Roger-Viollet/Getty Images)*

of 1528. He was, moreover, able to recoup his salary for the prior year.

In 1528 Marot composed a "Chant nuptial" (wedding song) for the marriage of the queen's sister, Renée de France, to Ercole d'Este, Duke of Ferrara. The poem has a distinctive evangelical bent. Marot combines elements from Catullus's wedding songs 61 and 62 with a loose imitation of Desiderius Erasmus's colloquy "Proci et puellae" (The Suitor and the Young Girl), which was condemned by the Sorbonne between 1526 and 1528 because it favors married life over celibacy. Marot urges Renée not to lament the loss of her virginity: "Fille de Roy, Adieu ton Pucellage: / Et toutesfoys tu n'en doibs faire pleurs, / Car le Pommier, qui porte bon fructage, / Vault mieulx, que cil, qui ne porte que Fleurs" (Daughter of a king, say good-bye to your virginity: / But you must not cry about it, / For the apple tree that bears good fruit / Is worth more than the one that bears only

flowers). For Marot, as for Erasmus, one should not ignore nature. Yet, a few lines earlier, Marot refers to the couple's "chaste Lict" (chaste bed). Like Erasmus, Marot recognizes the role of nature in joining a couple in marriage but envisions the union's developing into a more spiritual bond.

The Treaty of Cambrai was signed on 3 August 1529. Also called "La Paix des Dames" (The Peace of the Ladies), because it was negotiated by Louise de Savoie, Marguerite de Navarre (the former Marguerite d'Alençon, who had married the Protestant Henri d'Albret, King of Navarre, in 1527, two years after the death of her first husband), and Marguerite d'Autriche, it marked the end of hostilities between France and Spain. Among the conditions were that Charles V send his sister Eleanor to France to marry the widowed king—Claude had died in 1524—and that he return François's two sons, whom François had agreed, in the Treaty of Madrid of 14 January 1526, to exchange for his own release. Marot marked the "Paix des Dames" with a rondeau, "De la Paix traictée à Cambray par trois Princesses" (Of the Peace Arranged in Cambray by Three Princesses), a parody of the Judgment of Paris in which the three women are portrayed as goddesses who sow "paix, & accord" (peace and accord) rather than "guerre, & discord" (war and discord) and tender an olive branch, the symbol of peace, instead of the golden apple offered by the goddess of discord.

Scholars attribute to Marot the creation of the *coq-à-l'âne* (parody or satire; literally, the rooster to the ass). He addressed the first one to Jamet sometime before the winter of 1531–1532–probably in March or April 1530. Derived from the medieval *sottie* and *fatrasie,* the *coq-à-l'âne* is a biting letter, replete with illogicalities and non sequiturs, whose subject matter, as Thomas Sebillet wrote in his *Art Poétique François* (1548, The Art of French Poetry), is "les vices de chacun" (the vices of each of us). Reason is displaced by a folly that is not completely empty of wisdom. Sebillet and the poetic theoreticians of the Renaissance–Du Bellay, Barthélemy Aneau, and Jacques Peletier du Mans–concur that it is the French form of the satire.

The king's sons were surrendered on 1 July 1530, and Marot commemorated the event in the "Chant de joye composé la nuict qu'on sceut les nouvelles de la venue des Enfans de France retournant des Hespaignes" (Song of Joy Composed the Night We Learned the News That the Children of France Were Returning from Spain). The refrain conveys a Pauline message often repeated by humanists of the time: "Gloire à Dieu seul, Paix en Terre aux Humains" (Glory to God alone, Peace on Earth to humans).

Marot captures the joy in France caused by the simultaneous arrival of Eleanor and the king's sons in

1530 in the epistle "A la Royne Elienor nouvellement arrivée d'Espaigne avec les deux enfans du Roy, delivrez des mains de l'Empereur"(To the Queen Eleanor Recently Arrived from Spain with the Two Children of the King, Delivered by the Hands of the Emperor). He observes that the return of the two princes happened "par le vueil de Dieu, qui tout prevoit" (by the will of God, who foresees all). And since François is his king and patron, Eleanor will be his queen and patron: "Voylà pourquoy mes escriptz je t'adresse" (That is why I address my writings to you).

François and Marguerite's mother, Louise de Savoie, died of the plague on 24 September 1531; Marot memorialized her in *Eglogue sur le Trespas de Ma Dame* (Eclogue on the Death of My Lady), written toward the end of the year. Gérard Defaux in his edition of Marot's *Oeuvres poétiques* (1990, 1993, Poetic Works) identifies Virgil's fifth eclogue, a close imitation of the Greek pastoral poet Theocritus's first idyll, as Marot's principal source. The poem is a dialogue between Colin and Tenot that begins with Tenot suggesting a poetry contest between Colin and the god Pan (François). Colin, who evidently represents Marot, calls Louise the mother of the "grand Berger" (great shepherd) François, of Margot (Marguerite), and of the other poets (nous aultres), who are also shepherds. The poets and the royal court are united under Louise. At the end of the poem Colin asks Pan to carry on "avec meilleure grâce" (with more grace) the lament of Louise that he started; but the distracted Pan sings to his beloved Syrinx, lending a slightly comic effect to an otherwise grave poem.

In perhaps his best-known epistle to François, "Au Roy, pour avoir esté desrobé" (To the King, Because I Have Been Robbed), composed at the end of 1531, Marot bemoans the doubling of his misfortune: while he slept, his valet pilfered from his purse the money the king had given him, donned his most elegant garments, and escaped on his most dependable steed; then he contracted the plague. He details the ravaging effects of the disease and appeals to François for financial help. He recounts the events with mordant humor, painting his tragedy in riotous hues, then concludes with a characteristically abrupt shift in tone: declaring that "mon stile j'enfleray" (my style I will inflate), he extols François as if the king were a divinity. Levity and gravity thus conjoin, as they so often do in Marot's poems, to create greater complexity and to keep his reader alert and interested. The king eventually gave Marot the money he requested. Scholars have shown Marot's debt in this poem to the profane poetic tradition of the Middle Ages and the early Renaissance, and he draws equally on a "rhetoric of misfortune" shared by such poets as Villon, Molinet, Rutebeuf, Eustache Deschamps, and Michault

Taillevent. Nonetheless, Marot's account is not devoid of truth: he was a victim of the plague.

The first edition of Marot's works was published by the Lyon printer Olivier Arnoullet at the end of 1531 or the beginning of 1532. It was so successful that another edition was printed between February and June 1532 by the widow of Jean Saint Denis in Paris. The inclusion of works by other poets in these editions point to the absence of Marot's knowledge and consent. During Lent in 1532 Marot was again accused of having "mangé le lard" with other evangelical friends; this time he was saved from imprisonment by Marguerite's secretary, Etienne Clavier. He voices his dismay over the unauthorized editions of his works in the preface to a 12 August 1532 edition prepared by Pierre Roffet and printed by Geofroy Tory. *Ladolescence clementine* appears for the first time in this edition. Twenty-two known editions of *Ladolescence clementine* up to the publication of Marot's *Oeuvres* in July 1538 attest to its success.

In September 1533 Marot published an edition of Villon's works that includes glosses of Villon's language; it was an important contribution to French literary history. At the end of 1533 or beginning of 1534 Roffet's widow published *La Suite de l'Adolescence clementine* with preliminary poems by Salmon Macrin, Antoine Macault, and Nicolas Bourbon that testify to Marot's celebrity. Marot's translation of the first book of Ovid's *Metamorphoses* followed shortly thereafter. The second edition of this translation, published later in 1534, includes the poems pertaining to Marot's first arrest in 1526, but "L'Enfer" was excluded from it.

A lengthy quarrel between Marot and a minor Rhétoriqueur from Normandy, François Sagon, secretary to the abbot of St.-Evroult, began with a conversation on 16 August 1534, the wedding day of Marguerite's niece Ysabeau d'Albret and René, Vicomte de Rohan. The subject of the debate was religion; in his *Défense de Sagon contre Clément Marot* (Sagon's Defense against Clément Marot), Sagon claims that Marot tried to turn him against the church:

Apres souper eusmes noise & tenson
Pour la leçon de la foy catholicque,
Où tu voullus faindre l'Evangelique,
Quant tu me dictz (o bon prince des cieulx)
Qu'encore estoit au devant de mes yeulx
L'obscure nuict & vele de Moyse,
Pource qu'estoye adherent à l'esglise.

(After supper we had an argument and conflict
Concerning the lesson of the Catholic faith,
In which you wanted to play the evangelical,
When you said to me [o good prince of the heavens]
That the obscure night and the veil of Moses
Were still before my eyes,
Because I was an adherent to the church.)

Religious fanaticism coupled with jealousy probably caused Sagon to become Marot's unrelenting nemesis. A victory for the new religious thinkers at the court during the summer of 1534 had likely emboldened Marot to criticize Sagon's orthodox beliefs, but the favor that the evangelicals enjoyed did not last long. On the night of 17–18 October 1534 copies of a placard denouncing the Catholic Mass were posted throughout Paris; in Orléans, Tours, and Rouen; and on the door of the king's bedchamber in Amboise. It had been composed by Antoine Marcourt, a pastor in Neuchâtel printed there by Pierre de Vingle; and stealthily brought into France, where unidentified schismatics distributed it. The placard, printed in Gothic letters with the title *Articles veritables sur les horribles, grandz, et importables abuz de la Messe papalle* (True Articles on the Horrible, Great, and Insupportable Abuses of the Papal Mass), espoused a Zwinglian position on the Eucharist: Christ's sacrifice occurred only once and can never be repeated, and other sacrifices are "inefficient, insufficient and imperfect"; Christ resides with God, so that the Real Presence does not exist in the wine and the host; the notion of the transubstantiation of the body and blood of Christ is untenable; and Communion is a simple commemoration of the Passion of Christ. The Affaire des Placards led to extensive persecutions of the dissidents, and by the end of November five people had been burned at the stake.

A second campaign in Paris against the Mass took the form of a booklet by Marcourt, *Petit Traicté de la Sainte Eucharistie* (Short Treatise on the Holy Eucharist), against which the king and the principal corporations rallied on 21 January 1535. On 25 January a list was presented to the assembly naming seventy-three "luthériens" who, if they ignored the summons to appear before a tribunal, would be banished, have their possessions confiscated, and be burned at the stake. On an incomplete list that has been preserved, Marot's name is seventh.

In the "Epistre au Roy, du temps de son exil à Ferrare," Marot says that he was in Blois on the night of the Affaire des Placards. He then went to the court of Marguerite de Navarre in Nérac, where he remained until March. He arrived in Italy in April and took refuge at the court of Renée de France in Ferrara. Renée's court, like Marguerite's, favored the new ideas. Also there were Michelle de Saubonne, who had protected Marot's father at the court of Anne de Bretagne, and her three daughters.

The epistle from Ferrara serves not only as a defense against accusations of Marot's participation in the Affaire des Placards but also as an argument for the rights of the poet. He criticizes the Sorbonne (the Faculty of Theology of the University of Paris) and the

Parlement, the protectors of Catholic orthodoxy in France and the institutions that were persecuting the schismatics. The motives of the Sorbonne cannot be founded on justice, because the faculty has continuously reprimanded the humanist Collège des Lecteurs Royaux (College of Royal Readers, the future Collège de France) that the king himself founded in 1530: the Sorbonne is "ignorante . . . ennemye / De la trilingue, & noble Academie / Qu'as erigee" (ignorant . . . an enemy / Of the trilingual and noble Academy / That you built). While the theologians live in darkness, the humanists bring light to France. Outraged that the Parlement ordered the confiscation of his possessions, particularly his books and papers, Marot denounces the judge: "Juge sacrilege, / Qui t'a donné ne loy, ne privilege / D'aller toucher, & faire tes massacres / Au cabinet des sainctes Muses sacres?" (Sacrilegious judge, / Who gave you either the legal right or privilege / To touch and make a massacre / Of the study of the holy and sacred Muses?). The private space of the poet is sacrosanct; Marot demands the right of complete intellectual and artistic freedom. In response to the accusation of Lutheranism, Marot writes: "De Lutheriste ilz m'ont donné le nom: / . . . je leur reponds, que non" (They have given me the name Lutheran: / . . . I answer that I am not one). Marot mentions Martin Luther, denying that he bears any similarity to Christ. M. A. Screech, who believes that Marot was a Lutheran, points out that the devaluation of Luther was a commonplace among Lutherans and employs Luther's own rhetoric. But Marot's abjuration may indicate the weakness of his Lutheranism—if, indeed, he was a Lutheran. One might also argue that Marot aims to separate himself from the Reformers when he identifies the participants in the Affaire des Placards as "certains folz" (certain madmen). Marot's religious attachments remain a matter of controversy. The epistle, published in 1536, elicited virulent responses from Sagon, another by a General Chambor, and Jean Leblond, a jurist in the Parlement of Rouen. Each defends the authorities criticized by Marot and repeats the accusations of criminal acts committed by the poet.

During his stay in Ferrara, Marot completed his well-known "Blason du beau tetin" (*Blason* on the Beautiful Breast). The *blason,* which dates from the fifteenth century, is a descriptive poem that praises its subject. Marot entered his *blason* in a competition judged by Renée de France; among the many French poets who participated were Antoine Héroët, Victor Brodeau, and Maurice Scève. Each poem focused on one part of the female body. Scève won with his "Blason du sourcil" (*Blason* on the Eyebrow). Marot attempted to initiate a contest of *contre-blasons* (counter-*blasons*) with his "Blason du laid tetin" (*Blason* on the Ugly Breast), but the poetic joust was preempted by Marot's departure from Ferrara in the spring of 1536. The French exiles who had gathered at the court to escape persecution had begun to compromise the relations of Renée's husband, Ercole d'Este, with the Holy Roman Emperor and with Rome, and he joined forces with the Inquisition. Marot fled to Venice, an independent and tolerant republic. There he composed an epistle to Renée that denies the renewed accusations that he held heretical beliefs and attributes his departure to the xenophobia of the people of Ferrara. He also wrote "A Madame de Ferrare," which is probably the first sonnet in French.

Though the Edict of Coucy of 16 July 1535 that allowed for the release of prisoners and the return of exiles who abjured heresy was extended by an edict issued on 31 May 1536, Marot sought special permission to return to France in epistles to François, the dauphin, and Marguerite. In writing these epistles, Marot is inspired by the exiled Ovid's *Tristia* (Sad Things) and *Epistulae ex Ponto* (Letters from the Black Sea). In the melancholy poem to François he waxes nostalgic about France, conveys his longing to return home to see his children, and asks for a grace period of six months in France. In the second epistle he attempts to enlist the aid of the dauphin in persuading François to grant him permission to reenter France. In the poem to Marguerite, whom he considers "plus mere que maistresse" (more mother than patron), Marot tells of his tribulations following the Affaire des Placards: his brief stay in Nérac and his flight to Ferrara and then to Venice. He compares himself to the hunted stag and the frightened lamb, both figures of Christ. He recalls the friendship they shared and the times when Marguerite would have him sing the "Pseaulmes divins" (divine psalms), her favorite songs, in her room. He says that he is as desirous of his homeland as Ulysses was of Ithaca. Marguerite secured permission from Anne de Montmorency for Marot to reenter the country. Marot abjured before Cardinal de Tournon, the governor of Lyon, in December 1536.

Marot returned to the French court in early 1537. There he wrote a poem celebrating the 1 January 1537 marriage of King James VI of Scotland and François's daughter Madeleine de Valois and a love epistle—a rare subject for an *épître* by Marot—to an unnamed "Nymphe de pris" (prized nymph). Marot refers to her as a noble woman and as a goddess, comparing her love for him to that of Cybele for the mortal Attis, of Diana for the equally human Endymion, and of Venus for Adonis. He equates this felicitous encounter with his newly restored freedom. In the late winter or early spring he wrote "Le Dieu Gard de Marot à la Court" (May God Protect You, from Marot to the Court), which is both a hymn filled with prayers of hope for members of the royal court and an elegy that begins with the plaint of the former exile and continues with an expression of gratitude for his return to his motherland. In an apostrophe to Ovid, Marot compares his fate to that of the exiled Roman poet who never returned home and attributes his own good fortune not to his poetic talent—which, he concedes, cannot excel Ovid's—but to "ung Prince humain plus, que le tien" (a prince more human than yours). He ends with a wish to mend relations with past antagonists.

In spite of Marot's plea, the quarrel with Sagon began again in early summer 1537 when the two attended a celebration hosted by Marguerite in the park of St. Cloud. From this meeting issued a strident epistle, "Le Valet de Marot Contre Sagon, Frippelippes" (Marot's Valet, Frippelippes, against Sagon). Frippelippes, Marot's fictional secretary, treats his adversary like a "Sagouyn" (monkey) and an ass. He also attacks General Chambor and a friend of Sagon's, Charles de la Huetterie, who tried to take Marot's place as the king's *valet de chambre* during his exile. Sagon responded in a long-winded poem in which he disguises himself as a page named Mathieu de Boutigny. Many more written attacks by Sagon followed.

Shortly after his return, Marot probably met Etienne Dolet in Paris at a banquet that Dolet gave after receiving a pardon from François for killing a painter named Compaing in a duel. Dolet exerted an immense influence on Marot, particularly on the latter's cultivation of the epigram, and Marot probably discovered Martial through Dolet. On 31 July 1538 Dolet published a volume of Marot's *Oeuvres*, excluding works not intended for the public. Because Marot participated in this publication, it is an edition of paramount importance. He included the *Adolescence clémentine*, *La Suite de l'Adolescence clementine*, and *Le Premier Livre de la Metamorphose d'Ovide* as sections of the volume, added "Deux livres d'epigrammes" (Two Books of Epigrams), and moved the "dixains, blasons et envoys" (of the *Adolescence clementine* and the "menu" (short) section of *La Suite de l'Adolescence clementine* to the first book of epigrams. In the second book of epigrams he included poems written during his exile and immediately after his return to France, as well as those he had prepared for Anne de Montmorency in March 1538 following Montmorency's being named Constable of France on 10 February. Marot's second book of epigrams dedicated to Anne established the unified pattern of a *canzoniere* (songbook) that Scève imitated in his *Délie, Objet de plus haulte vertu* (1544, Delie, Object of Highest Virtue).

In the summer of 1538 Dolet and Marot had a dispute; the cause is unknown. Another 1538 edition of Marot's *Oeuvres* was printed in Lyon by Sebastianus Gryphius (Sébastien Gryphe). In the preface Dolet,

Renée de France, Duchess of Ferrara, at whose court Marot took refuge from April 1535 until the spring of 1536 after being accused of heresy (drawing by François Clouet, Bibliothèque de Knowsley; from Pierre Bennezon, Gérard Sablayrolles, and François Zerluth, Seizième siècle, 1963; Thomas Cooper Library, University of South Carolina)

tion of Virgil's first eclogue, is central to this poem. François will be Marot's benefactor whose name the poet will make reverberate throughout the "montz, & boys, / Rocz, & Estangs" (hills and woods, / Rocks, and ponds). Although Robin assures his god that his poetic vocation aims to give his patron "plaisir à [son] chant escouter" (pleasure by listening to [his] song) rather than "pour emporter le pris" (to garner the prize), the praise seems dependent on Pan/François's recognition of the poet's craft. Robin closes the poem with joyous remarks; Pan has acknowledged his lowly shepherd. The eclogue was written around the time that François gave Marot a house in Paris, and there is some debate as to whether it was composed to seek benefits from the king or to thank him after they were tendered.

The crowning achievement of Marot's career is his verse translations of forty-nine psalms. More than five hundred editions of the translations appeared between 1539, the year the first collection was published, and the end of the century. Marot's decision to undertake the translations had probably been inspired by Marguerite and her circle in 1527. He had translated his first psalm, Psalm 6, between 1527 and 1531, and it was published in 1533 in Antoine Augereau's edition of Marguerite's *Miroir de l'âme pécheresse* (translated as *The Glasse of the Synnefoulle Soule,* 1544). His translation of Psalm 3 was incorporated into Marguerite's play *L'Inquisiteur* (The Inquisitor), written circa 1536. And Marot's 1536 epistle to Marguerite from Venice not only recalls how Marguerite would have him sing the Psalms to her but also includes unmistakable echoes of the Psalms, particularly images of David's persecution by his enemies.

The first collection of Marot's psalm translations, *Aulcuns pseaulmes et cantiques mys en chant* (Some Psalms and Canticles Put into Song), appeared in Strasbourg. Another edition was printed by Antoine des Gois in Antwerp in 1541; it included a dedicatory epistle to François by Marot, as well as some psalm translations by other poets. Later the same year the Paris printer Etienne Roffet published a collection of thirty translations by Marot that incorporated most of the psalms from the des Gois edition along with the dedicatory poem to François. In 1543 Roffet republished, with an erroneous title, the thirty psalm translations, augmented by nineteen more and the "Cantique de Siméon" (Canticle of Simeon). The dedicatory epistle to François continued to be included. Thus, François appears as the dedicatee of a work more likely inspired by Marguerite.

The complex 170-verse epistle to François discusses many topics, such as the equality between the King David and François, the truth of the Psalms, the spiritual figures of Christ in the songs, and the humanist efforts to restore the Hebraic texts. He states that his

who was praised in the preface to his edition of Marot's works, is condemned.

Between 1538 and 1542 Marot translated six sonnets by Petrarch, the *Histoire de Leander et de Hero* (Story of Leander and Hero) by Museus, the second book of Ovid's *Metamorphoses,* and three colloquies by Erasmus. He was also certainly working on his psalm translations.

In 1539 Marot composed his third eclogue, "L'Eglogue au Roy, soubs les noms de Pan, & Robin" (Eclogue to the King, under the Names of Pan and Robin). The image of François as Pan, god and poet, had already been developed in Marot's eclogue on the death of Louise de Savoie. Here Marot, disguised as the shepherd Robin, tells Pan how he was guided by the Muses and fortune to serve him. Janot (Jehan Marot) had explained to Robin that only good would come through this most sacred god of shepherds and had admonished him to master the art of the flute to win the god's favor. The importance of having a beneficent protector, to which Marot had alluded in his early transla-

translation of the thirty psalms is derived from the texts of the Hebrew scholars, but he does not identify the scholars. Defaux in his 1995 edition of Marot's *Cinquante pseaumes* (Fifty Psalms) says that reports by Florimond de Raemond and Etienne Pasquier that Marot received help with the translations from François Vatable, the Hebraic reader of the Collège des Lecteurs Royaux, are not completely accurate.

Marot reiterates his claim to have drawn his psalms from the Hebraic text in the title of the 1541 edition: *Les Trente Premiers Pseaumes de David, mis en françoys selon la Vérité Hébraïque* (The Thirty First Psalms of David, Rendered in French according to the Hebraic Truth). But during the first half of the sixteenth century, "la vérité hébraïque" referred to the Latin translation of the Hebrew by St. Jerome, and Defaux concludes that Jerome was Marot's source. Elaborating on Defaux's finding in his contribution to the symposium *Clément Marot: "Prince des poëtes françois" 1496–1996* (1997), edited by Defaux and Michel Simonin, Bernard Roussel specifies that Marot worked with Jerome's text as it appeared in Jacques Lefèvre d'Etaples's *Quincuplex Psalterium* (1509, Fivefold Psalter) and with Martin Bucer's Latin rendition of the original Hebrew, published in 1529.

François issued four edicts against Lutherans from December 1538 to June 1540, but the evangelicals reasserted themselves between 1540 and August 1542. In the latter year fourteen new evangelical works were published by Dolet in Lyons, but his success provoked Catholic authorities and led to his death. After François issued two new edicts against the evangelicals in August 1542, the response of the Catholic authorities intensified. Between Christmas 1542 and March 1543 the Sorbonne drew up a list of heretical works; among them were four by Marot, including the psalm translations and a poem of dubious authenticity, the *Sermon du bon pasteur* (Sermon of the Good Pastor). By early December, Marot had fled to Jean Calvin's Geneva. Calvin wanted Marot to help with the completion of the Huguenot Psalter, but efforts to secure money for the exiled poet from the Geneva Consistory proved futile.

The two most important editions of Marot's psalm translations were published in 1543 by the Geneva printer Jean Gérard as *Cinquante pseaumes*. One edition was intended for external use in Catholic France and the other for internal use in Geneva. For the "external" edition Marot added to the lengthy dedicatory epistle to François an epigram to the king, an epistle to the "Dames de France" (Ladies of France), and a collection of prayers under the title "L'Instruction et foy d'un chrestien" (The Instruction and Faith of a Christian). At the request of the Geneva Council, the "Salutation angelique" (Ave Maria) was removed from the "inter-

nal" edition because it denied the cult of the Virgin, an issue that divided the orthodox from the Reformed.

Scholars have drawn from Marot's poetry various conclusions about his religious beliefs. Paulette Leblanc considers him a Catholic, while Screech sees him as Lutheran. Michel Jeanneret senses a pronounced influence of Calvin, particularly in the psalm translations, and Defaux detects that of the evangelicals Erasmus and Lefèvre. It remains difficult to attribute to Marot a fixed religious stance.

At the end of 1543 Clément Marot left Geneva for the Savoy. He died in Turin in September 1544. He was buried in the Ospidale San Giovanni Battista by his friend Jamet, who composed the epitaph for his tomb:

> Icy devant, au giron de sa Mere,
> Gist des François le Virgile & Homere
> Cy est couché & repose à l'envers
> Le nompareil des mieux disans en Vers
> Cy gist celuy qui peu de terre coeuvre
> Qui toute la France enrichit de son oeuvre
> Cy dort un mort qui toujours vif sera
> Tant que la France en François parlera
> Brief gist, repose & dort en ce lieu cy
> Clement Marot de Cahors en Quercy.

> (Here before us, in the bosom of his Mother,
> Lies the Virgil and Homer of the French
> Here lies and rests on his back
> The one incomparable voice among the best speakers in verse
> Here lies the one who now occupies little ground but
> Who enriched all of France with his work
> Here sleeps a dead man who will always be alive
> As long as France speaks French
> In sum, here lies, rests, and sleeps in this place
> Clément Marot of Cahors in Quercy.)

Bibliography:

Claude Albert Mayer, *Bibliographie des oeuvres de Clément Marot,* 2 volumes (Geneva: Droz, 1954).

References:

Randle Cotgrave, *A Dictionarie of the French and English Tongues* (London: Printed by Adam Islip, 1611; Columbia: University of South Carolina Press, 1950);

Gérard Defaux, *Marot, Rabelais, Montaigne: L'Ecriture comme présence* (Paris: Champion, 1987);

Defaux, "Marot, traducteur des psaumes: Du nouveau sur l'édition anonyme (et genevoise) de 1543," *Bibliothèque d'humanisme et renaissance,* 56 (1994): 59–82;

Defaux, *Le Poète en son jardin: Etude sur Clément Marot et l'Adolescence clementine* (Paris: Champion, 1997);

Defaux and Frank Lestringant, "Marot et le problème de l'évangélisme: A propos de trois articles récents de C. A. Mayer," *Bibliothèque d'humanisme et renaissance,* 54 (1992): 125–130;

Defaux and Michel Simonin, eds., *Clément Marot: "Prince des poëtes françois" 1496–1996. Actes du Colloque international de Cahors en Quercy, 1996* (Paris: Champion, 1997);

Jean-Luc Déjean, *Clément Marot* (Paris: Fayard, 1990);

Robert Griffin, *Clément Marot and the Inflections of Poetic Voice* (Berkeley: University of California Press, 1974);

Michel Jeanneret, *Poésie et tradition biblique au XVIe siècle* (Paris: José Corti, 1969);

Charles Kinch, *La Poésie satirique de Clément Marot* (Paris: Boivin, 1940);

Paulette Leblanc, *La Poésie religieuse de Clément Marot* (Paris: Nizet, 1955);

Lestringant, *Clément Marot: De* L'Adolescence *à "L'Enfer"* (Padua: Unipress, 1998);

Claude Albert Mayer, *Clément Marot* (Paris: Nizet, 1972);

Mayer, "Evangélisme et Protestantisme," *Studi francesi,* 88 (1986): 1–12;

Mayer, *La Religion de Marot* (Geneva: Droz, 1960);

Christine Scollen-Jimack, "Marot and Deschamps: The Rhetoric of Misfortune," *French Studies,* 42 (1988): 21–32;

M. A. Screech, *Clément Marot: A Renaissance Poet Discovers the Gospel. Lutheranism, Fabrism, and Calvinism in the Royal Courts of France and of Navarre and in the Ducal Court of Ferrara* (Leiden & New York: Brill, 1994);

Annwyl Williams, *Clément Marot: Figure, Text and Intertext* (Lewiston, N.Y.: Edwin Mellen Press, 1990).

Papers:
The most important collections of Clément Marot's manuscripts are held by the Château de Chantilly and the Bibliothèque nationale de France.

Michel de Montaigne
(28 February 1533 – 13 September 1592)

Virginia Krause
Brown University

BOOKS: *Les Essais de Messire Michel Seigneur de Montaigne, Chevalier de l'Ordre du Roy, & Gentil-homme ordinaire de sa Chambre, Livre Premier & Second* (Bordeaux: Printed by Simon Millanges, 1580; revised and enlarged, 1582); revised and enlarged as *Essais de Michel Seigneur de Montaigne* (Paris: Printed by Abel L'Angelier, 1588); revised and enlarged as *Les Essais de Michel seigneur de Montaigne,* edited by Marie de Gournay (Paris: Printed by Abel L'Angelier, 1595); translated by John Florio as *The Essayes, or, Morall, politike and millitarie discourses of Lo. Michaell de Montaigne* (London: Printed by Valentine Simmes for Edward Blount, 1603);

Journal de voyage de M. de M. en Italie, par la Suisse et l'Allemagne, edited by Anne-Gabriel Meusnier de Querlon (Rome & Paris: Le Jay, 1774); translated by Donald M. Frame as *Montaigne's Travel Journal* (San Francisco: North Point Press, 1983);

Œuvres complètes de Michel de Montaigne, 12 volumes, edited by Arthur Armaingaud, Reinhold Dezeimeris, and Jeanne Duportal (Paris: L. Conard, 1924–1941).

Editions and Collections: *Les essais de Michel, seigneur de Montaigne,* edited by Marie de Gournay (Paris: Printed by Toussainct Du Bray & Pierre Rocolet, 1635);

Essais: Reproduction phototypique de l'exemplaire de Bordeaux, edited by Fortunat Strowski (Paris: Hachette, 1912);

Œuvres complètes, edited by Albert Thibaudet and Maurice Rat (Paris: Gallimard, 1962);

Les Essais, 3 volumes, edited by Pierre Villey and Verdun L. Saulnier (Paris: Presses Universitaires de France, 1965);

Essais: Reproduction photographique de la deuxième édition, Bordeaux, 1582, edited by Marcel Françon (Cambridge, Mass.: Harvard University Press, 1969);

Essais: Réproduction photographique de 1'édition originale de 1580, avec une introduction et des notes sur les modifications apportées ultérieurement au texte en 1582, 1587, 1588 et sur l'exemplaire de Bordeaux, 2 volumes,

Engraved by J.W. Steel

Frontispiece to The Works of Montaigne, *edited by William Hazlitt (1849); Thomas Cooper Library, University of South Carolina*

edited by Daniel R. Martin (Geneva: Slatkine, 1976);

Les Essais: Reproduction photographique du livre troisième de l'édition originale de 1588: Avec une introduction, des notes et des additions faites par Montaigne entre 1588 et

1592, année de sa mort, edited by Martin (Geneva: Slatkine, 1988);

Journal de voyage, edited by François Rigolot (Paris: Presses Universitaires Françaises, 1992);

Corpus des œuvres de Montaigne (CD-ROM), edited by Claude Blum (Paris: Champion, 1997).

Editions in English: *The Works of Michael de Montaigne: Comprising His Essays, Letters, and Journey through Germany and Italy. With Notes from All the Commentators, Biographical and Bibliographical Notices &c., &c.,* edited by William Hazlitt (Philadelphia: J. W. Moore, 1849);

The Essays of Montaigne, translated by George Burnham Ives (Cambridge, Mass.: Harvard University Press, 1925);

Complete Works: Essays, Travel Journal, Letters, translated by Donald M. Frame (Stanford, Cal.: Stanford University Press, 1957);

The Essays, translated by Frame (Stanford, Cal.: Stanford University Press, 1958);

Essays, translated by John M. Cohen (Harmondsworth, U.K. & Baltimore: Penguin, 1959);

An Apology for Raymond Sebond, translated by Frame (London & New York: Penguin, 1987);

The Complete Essays, translated by M. A. Screech (London & New York: Penguin, 1993).

OTHER: Raymond Sebond, *La Théologie naturelle,* translated by Montaigne (Paris: Printed by Michel Sonnius, Gilles Gourbin & Guillaume Chaudière, 1569; revised edition, Paris: Printed by Gilles Gourbin, 1581);

La Mesnagerie de Xenophon: Les Regles de mariage de Plutarque: Lettre de consolation de Plutarque à sa femme: Le tout traduict de Grec en François, translated by Etienne de La Boétie, edited by Montaigne (Paris: F. Morel, circa 1570–1572);

Le Livre de raison de Montaigne sur l'Ephemeris historica de Beuther, edited by Jean Marchand (Paris: Arts Graphiques, 1948);

"Annotations inscrites en Marge des Commentaires de César," edited by André Tournon, in his *Montaigne: La glose et l'essai* (Lyon: Presses Universitaires de Lyon, 1983), pp. 311–351;

Montaigne's Annotated Copy of Lucretius, edited by M. A. Screech (Geneva: Droz, 1998).

In literary histories and anthologies the name Michel de Montaigne is often associated with the rise of private life. His famous tower study has come to be almost synonymous with the "ivory tower" and Montaigne himself with the introspective intellectual. He led most of his adult life amid the long and bloody Wars of Religion, a time when militants on both the Protestant and Catholic sides sought alliances with foreign powers and fought ruthlessly. At a time when both sides proclaimed the truth of their cause and took up arms, Montaigne proclaimed his ignorance and—so the story goes—retreated to his ivory tower: "En un temps où le meschamment faire est si commun, de ne faire qu'inutilement il est comme louable." ("In a time when it is so common to do evil, it is practically praiseworthy to do what is merely useless" [III, 9]; translations throughout from Donald M. Frame's 1958 edition of *The Essays*). In fact, however, Montaigne composed his roughly one-thousand-page masterpiece, *Les Essais* (1580; translated as *The Essayes,* 1603), translated a theological treatise into French, and edited his friend Etienne de La Boétie's works, in addition to leading a busy and prominent public life. He performed delicate diplomatic service, held important public office, entertained great lords at his château, and oversaw production in his vineyards. Despite repeated claims to be "useless" and "retired" from active life, Montaigne played an important role as counselor and negotiator for the preeminent princes of his day—a role he played not only in Bordeaux and at the royal court but also in his famous tower study through composing his *Essais* and through his correspondence. And despite his claims of ignorance, no figure better embodies the twilight of French humanism, thoroughly steeped in the poetry and philosophy of the ancients, but despairing of reaching the encyclopedic knowledge envisaged by early humanists such as Marsilio Ficino and Guillaume Budé.

Montaigne occupies a place among the great figures in French literature in part because the modern essay genre may be attributed to his literary and philosophical experiment. Montaigne was the first to give his work the title *Essais.* More importantly, he elaborated a practice of the essay as a method of analysis as well as a literary form. In the *Essais* Montaigne's literary and philosophical preoccupations converge. His sustained skepticism contributed to the development of what is today termed "critical thinking," at the heart of the humanities. At the same time, the *Essais* took shape as a self-portrait, as Montaigne wrote about himself in unprecedented ways. He scrutinized his opinions and his reactions to a variety of circumstances while reporting traits ranging from the most prosaic personal habits to sexual tastes. Making the self the object of his writing set him apart from his predecessors. The centrality he accorded to the self earned him illustrious imitators such as the eighteenth-century philosopher and writer Jean-Jacques Rousseau. But Montaigne's pursuit of self-knowledge also drew sharp criticism from others, including Blaise Pascal, the seventeenth-century religious philosopher who denounced Montaigne's decision to write about himself, proclaiming "le moi est haïssable" (the self is contemptible). By opposing torture unequivocally and by defending freedom of conscience, Montaigne also became an early spokesman for principles now considered to be fundamental human rights. Finally, the *Essais* have come to occupy an important place in the history of the book, with their complex editorial history drawing renewed critical attention.

The first surviving child of Pierre Eyquem de Montaigne and Antoinette de Louppes de Villeneuve, Montaigne was born in 1533 at his family's château, thirty miles west of Bordeaux. In this region, Gascon, not French, was the lingua franca, and Montaigne maintained that his own spoken and written French reflected certain Gascon expressions and turns. For the standards of the time, Montaigne's nobility was established but not illustrious. According to legal criteria, an originally nonnoble family could lay claim to nobility after three generations had "lived nobly" by residing on a noble estate while the head of the family led the life of a gentleman, which entailed refraining from commerce and other activities associated with commoners.

The fortune amassed by Montaigne's paternal great-grandfather, Raymond Eyquem, allowed the family to begin its social ascension to nobility, beginning with the purchase of a noble estate (Montaigne). Montaigne's grandfather Grimon Eyquem remained a Bordelais businessman, but the essayist's father led a life in keeping with conceptions of nobility. Pierre Eyquem de Montaigne was the first in the line to be born in the family château and further bolstered the family's noble status by his distinguished military service during the Italian Wars, for arms were still considered to be the most perfect vocation of a nobleman, as Montaigne observes in the *Essais*: "La forme propre, et seule, et essencielle, de noblesse en France, c'est la vocation militaire" ("The proper, the only, the essential, form of nobility in France is the military profession" [II, 7]). In Bordeaux, Pierre also served as mayor—a position traditionally reserved for nobles. Michel was the first in his family officially to drop the name Eyquem—thereby shedding the last traces of his family's roots in commerce and becoming simply Michel de Montaigne. As for the maternal side of his family, it is possible that Antoinette de Louppes came from a family of converted Spanish Jews *(conversos)*, although this hypothesis has been disputed.

Pierre Eyquem de Montaigne took great care in planning his son's education. The infant was first placed under the care of a nurse in a nearby village, a practice presumably intended to promote good health as well as to develop strong ties early on between the future lord of Montaigne and the local peasants. Montaigne's formal education, which began soon thereafter, was in accordance with Erasmian ideals. His father brought in a German doctor, who spoke little or no French, and several assistants to begin Montaigne's instruction in Latin, which thus constituted his true "maternal tongue." Greek lessons were to be as amusing as possible, and the child was to be awakened only by the sound of musical instruments, as he relates in his chapter "De l'institution des enfans" ("On the education of children" [I, 26]). Although Montaigne never became much of a Hellenist, his Latin was impeccable—so impeccable that during his first years in the famous Collège de Guyenne he was given not translation from French into Latin like the other students but exercises in transforming bad Latin into good Latin.

In "De l'institution des enfans" Montaigne paints a dark picture of the conditions ostensibly presiding over the life of students in Renaissance *collèges,* where tutors seem never to cease bellowing into the ears of their pupils, applying the same method to all students regardless of individual differences, or spouting prefabricated precepts that the class is presumably required to memorize. This account should not be taken literally, however, for it does not do justice to the methods used in these *collèges,* and certainly not in the Collège de Guyenne, one of the best schools in France at the time. Montaigne received the careful attention of private tutors, chosen among the best of a faculty of illustrious scholars. Rather than imposing readings in the classics, one of these tutors proved particularly astute in leaving works in Latin, seemingly by mistake, within the reach of the young Montaigne. Ovid, Virgil, Terence, and Plautus thus constituted his pleasure reading, rather than *Amadis de Gaule* and other popular romances of knight-errantry, at which the essayist later scoffs in the *Essais.*

Few archival documents or specific comments in his *Essais* elucidate Montaigne's activities from ages fourteen to twenty-one. He might have attended an academy for noblemen to learn military arts, politics, heraldry, and other subjects suited to the life of a gentleman. According to another hypothesis, Montaigne studied law in Toulouse. It is known from the *Essais* that Montaigne was present in Toulouse for the famous case of Martin Guerre in 1560, a dramatic trial hinging on accusations of impersonation and witchcraft. Montaigne later observed that the sentence that condemned the accused impersonator to death was rash because the evidence in the trial did not allow one to distinguish the real Martin Guerre from his impersonator. Roger Trinquet rejects what he terms the "myth" of Montaigne's studies in Toulouse and contends that Montaigne must have pursued his humanist education by studying in Paris. Another hypothesis is that after studying grammar and rhetoric, Montaigne remained at the Collège de Guyenne, where he took courses in the *faculté des arts.*

Wherever he was studying, Montaigne was also apparently engaging in amorous adventures, if the intimate confessions about his romantic and sexual involvements in "Sur des vers de Virgile" ("On some verses by Virgil" [III, 5]) can be applied to this part of his life. As Hugo Friedrich observes in *Montaigne* (1991), the essayist's manner of talking about love bears no trace of the platonizing idealization typical of Renaissance lyric poetry. Next door to the Collège de Guyenne was a bordello, and Montaigne claims to have visited the prostitutes. He attributes the two minor bouts of venereal disease he contracted to his infrequent commerce with prostitutes. Claiming to have written his share of love letters, he apparently indulged in romantic seduction and, while never revealing the identity of any of his mistresses, writes frankly about his sexual tastes in *Les Essais*: "Jamais homme n'eust ses approches plus impertinemment genitales. . . . Il est à cette heure temps d'en parler ouvertement" ("Never was a man more impertinently genital in his approaches . . . it is time now to speak of it openly" [III, 5]).

In 1554 Montaigne began his career in law at la Cour des Aides, one of the high courts in his region. In 1557 this court was absorbed into the Parlement of Bordeaux, where he held a seat until 1570. The Parlement of Bordeaux was one of eight bodies constituting the Parlement, the highest court of law in France. In the *Essais* Montaigne passes over in silence his time as a magistrate, though these years had great impact on his life. It was during his years as a magistrate that Montaigne met La Boétie, a colleague in the Parlement, thus beginning the friendship made famous by Montaigne's chapter "De l'amitié" ("Of friendship"). An eminent Hellenist of his generation, La Boétie translated Plutarch's *Rules of Marriage* and *Letter of Consolation to His Wife* into French. His translation of Xenophon's *Œconomicus* was the first French rendering of the work.

In "De l'amitié" Montaigne describes meeting La Boétie after having read the manuscript for his *De la Servitude volontaire* (On Voluntary Servitude), an ardent attack on the tyranny of princes that was published posthumously in its entirety in 1577. The two men evidently enjoyed from the beginning the kind of friendship so rare that it is hardly ever found in life or even in books. Underlying Montaigne's account of his friendship with La Boétie is the classical ideal closely associated with virtue and, in particular, Cicero's definition of perfect friendship as the opposite of tyranny. In light of this notion of friendship, Montaigne's anecdote seems to assume an almost prophetic coloration: before meeting the man who would become his sole true and perfect friend, Montaigne knew of his opposition to tyranny expounded in *De la Servitude volontaire*, as

though writing against tyranny announced La Boétie's potential to realize perfection in friendship.

Their friendship of four or five years was cut short when La Boétie contracted an intestinal ailment. Montaigne hardly left his friend's bedside, even though both men feared that La Boétie had the plague and might be contagious. La Boétie died on 18 August 1563, leaving his impressive library to Montaigne, who gave an account of La Boétie's last hours in a published letter that he wrote to his own father. In the throes of a fever, La Boétie apparently became delirious, entreating Montaigne again and again to "give him a place." Montaigne relates his enigmatic last words: "Mon frere, mon frere, me refusez-vous doncques une place?" (My brother, my brother, do you refuse me a place?)

The question of the "place" Montaigne ultimately granted his deceased friend is closely tied up with the genesis of the *Essais*. One of the ways Montaigne gave La Boétie a place was by arranging in his tower study the some one thousand volumes that his friend had bequeathed to him seven years earlier. These books, a cherished component of La Boétie's identity, helped to transform his study into what Alain Legros terms "a temple of friendship." Second, Montaigne edited La Boétie's works, thereby formalizing his place among humanist men of letters. Finally, Montaigne decided to give his friend a place at the heart of the *Essais* by publishing one of La Boétie's works within his own. As he relates in "De l'amitié," his original intention was to publish La Boétie's *De la Servitude volontaire* in chapter 28, near the center of the first book. He abandoned this project because part of the treatise had been published in a Protestant pamphlet in 1574 and instead chose to include his friend's twenty-nine sonnets.

In his chapter on friendship Montaigne uses the analogy of the painter at work to describe his intention to publish La Boétie's work in the *Essais*. The painter, Montaigne explains, chooses the most beautiful spot in the middle of a wall to put "un tableau élabouré de toute sa suffisance" ("a picture labored over with all his skill"). He then fills in the space all around it with grotesques "qui sont peintures fantasques, n'ayant grace qu'en la varieté et estrangeté" ("which are fantastic paintings whose only charm lies in their variety and strangeness"). Montaigne concludes that being unable to create "a rich polished picture" himself, he chose to place La Boétie's work in the center instead: "ma suffisance ne va pas si avant que d'oser entreprendre un tableau riche, poly et formé selon l'art" ("my ability does not go far enough for me to dare to undertake a rich, polished picture, formed according to art.") His own writing surrounding the twenty-nine sonnets thus functions as grotesques—charming by virtue of their "variety and strangeness." The early chapters of *Les Essais* resemble Renaissance *lectiones* (miscellanies), a contemporary genre defined by its variety, but as his project developed, Montaigne departed from this model. His skepticism and his intention to compose a self-portrait placed *Les Essais* well outside reigning conventions. In this sense, part of the charm of *Les Essais* did lie in their "strangeness."

La Boétie's twenty-nine sonnets appeared in all of the editions of the *Essais* published during Montaigne's lifetime. But among the editorial changes he made in his last years was the decision to remove the sonnets, noting in the margins of the 1588 edition "Ces vers se voient ailleurs" (These poems can be found elsewhere). As François Rigolot observes in *Les Métamorphoses de Montaigne* (1988, Montaigne's Metamorphoses), this change in effect displaced La Boétie, as Montaigne's own writing moved from the periphery to the center.

During the two years following La Boétie's death, Montaigne embarked upon more amorous adventures. In 1565 Montaigne married Françoise de La Chassaigne, who was from a distinguished Bordelais family. Between 1570 and 1583 they had six children, all girls; only one survived to adulthood: Léonor, born in 1571. What sort of a marriage Montaigne may have had remains the object of speculation. Despite his reputation as a libertine, he acknowledges that "j'ay en verité plus severement observé les loix de mariage que je n'avois ny promis ny esperé" ("I have in truth observed the laws of marriage more strictly than I had either promised or expected" [III, 5]). Montaigne says little about his wife in the *Essais,* at least partly out of discretion. He does, however, speak about marriage as an institution, describing the ideal roles for husband and wife. But even his praise seems lacking in enthusiasm. For instance, he claims that he was more hostile to marriage before he tried it. In another passage he refers to "Ung bon mariage, s'il en est" ("A good marriage, if such there be").

Montaigne, like most of his contemporaries, believed that the expression of passion was best reserved for outside of marriage. Friends but not lovers: such was the appropriate role for spouses. For Montaigne, however, the kind of friendship to which a married couple should aspire was not the same kind that he enjoyed with La Boétie. Rather, in accordance with the Ciceronian understanding of different kinds of friendship, he argued that marriage could at best realize only the more banal sort—a friendship based on an exchange of services. "C'est une douce societé de vie, pleine de constance, de fiance et d'un nombre infiny d'utiles et solides offices et obligations mutuelles" ("It is a sweet association in life, full of constancy, trust, and an infinite number of useful and solid services and mutual obligations" [III, 5]).

The tower at Montaigne's château that housed his study on the third floor (Collection Roger-Viollet/Getty Images)

Montaigne's marriage is another example of how closely his life was tied up with the world of the Parlement of Bordeaux. Like Montaigne, Françoise had strong family connections to the Parlement. Montaigne's father-in-law, Joseph de La Chassaigne, and his brother-in-law, Geoffroy de La Chassaigne, Sieur de Pressac, both held seats in the Parlement of Bordeaux. Many of Montaigne's other relatives also had ties to the world of magistrates. He counted among his friends other *parlémentaires,* including, of course, La Boétie but also Pierre de Brach and Florimond de Raemond, both of whom served on the Parlement of Bordeaux, as well as Etienne Pasquier and Jacques Auguste de Thou, eminent magistrates of the day.

Montaigne's thirteen years in the Parlement of Bordeaux left their mark not only on his personal life but also on his writing. André Tournon reveals the extent to which Montaigne's legal training shaped the literary form of the *Essais* by informing his method of analysis and exposition. When a case too complex to receive an initial judgment came before the Parlement, it was passed on to the Chambre des Enquêtes (Chamber of Inquests), where Montaigne held a seat. Difficult civil law cases were thus assigned to a single magistrate, thereby designated as "rapporteur" for the case. The rapporteur then prepared a dossier to be delivered to his colleagues. After closely examining the case from all possible angles, he selected excerpts while preparing an exposition of the argumentation from differing points of view. This entailed generating the sort of multiple perspectives the reader encounters in the *Essais,* for just as the rapporteur defended the point of view of each side in turn, so too does the essayist examine questions from different—and often opposing—perspectives.

Montaigne's approach is evident in "Des Cannibales" ("Of cannibals"). The essayist begins by reporting and scrutinizing European condemnations of New World anthropophagy. He first examines the label "barbare" (barbarous)—its linguistic use, etymology, and cultural assumptions. He then applies it to European cultural practices, concluding that the cannibals—the Tupinamba (Tupi) residing in what is today Brazil—are ultimately no more "barbarous" than his European contemporaries. Then, in a final perspectivist twist, the essayist reports the Tupi point of view on European society, particularly its institutionalized social injustice. In his eyes, the Europeans' Christianity does not necessarily make them morally superior to the Tupi or to the ancients, who upheld high ethical standards while leading noble lives. Montaigne was one of the first European writers to praise the "noble savage" living in accordance with the laws of nature in contrast to the corrupt European. According to the essayist, the cannibals are loving toward their wives and ferocious toward their enemies; they also cultivate refined aesthetic practices, and he likens their poetry to that of the Greek lyric poet Anacreon. Finally, he maintains that the social injustice rampant in European society is foreign to them. Speculating on Plato's reaction to New World peoples, Montaigne concludes that the philosopher would have recognized the superiority of their societies to the utopia he described in his *Republic*. Montaigne asserts that the true impact of European culture on the New World has been one of "corruption." The campaign of massacres and pillaging carried out by Spanish conquistadors is the subject of "Des Coches" ("Of coaches").

From his professional experiences as a rapporteur, Montaigne also assimilated techniques of commentary, as well a particular understanding of the relationship between text and gloss, or commentary for the sake of explanation, interpretation, or paraphrase. Influenced by figures such as Andrea Alciat and Jacques Cujas, his generation of jurists was marked by a desire to return to the source. These jurists believed that the layers of gloss obscured as much as they elucidated the original source. This habit of mind finds its corollary in the humanists' will to return to the original ancient texts and contexts as well as in the parodies of medieval commentaries one finds in the works of writers such as François Rabelais. Such is the context of Montaigne's lamentations when it comes to the proliferation of commentaries in "De l'experience" ("Of experience"), the final chapter of *Les Essais*. "Il y a plus affaire à interpreter les interpretations qu'à interpreter les choses, et plus de livres sur les livres que sur autre subject: nous ne faisons que nous entregloser. Tout fourmille de commentaires" ("It is more of a job to interpret the interpretations than to interpret the things, and there are more books about books than about any other subject: we do nothing but write glosses about each other. The world is swarming with commentaries; of authors there is a great scarcity" [III, 13]).

Although Montaigne's century may be characterized by its longing for direct access to the source, in practice jurists and humanists recognized the legitimacy of having recourse to commentaries. Maligned in many cases, the commentaries of Franciscus Accursius and Bartolus of Saxoferrato were, nevertheless, considered to be indispensable in some instances, as Tournon observes. Besides, in a paradox that did not escape contemporaries, any attempt to understand the law inevitably results in the production of more "gloss" on the legal corpus. In the *Essais* Montaigne applies methods of commentary to the humanist corpus of Greek and especially Latin letters. Moreover, his *Essais* then became the object of his close scrutiny and commentary as he returned to reevaluate and reinterpret his thought and expression. In the *Essais,* however, while every statement is subject to reinterpretation (and thus to commentary), Montaigne's commentaries question more than they purport to explain, as Tournon notes.

During his years as a magistrate, and particularly between 1559 and 1565, Montaigne frequented the royal court. During these six years there were four different rulers: Henri II, who died in 1559; François II, who died the next year; Catherine de Médicis, regent during the minority of her son; and Charles IX, who came of age in 1563. In October 1562 Montaigne followed the court to the siege of Rouen where he was able to interview a cannibal, a discussion that he evokes in "Des cannibales."

Royal courts in Renaissance France were competitive social environments in which aristocrats performed before the jealous or scornful eyes of rivals while pursuing royal favor. Although the condemnation of sycophant courtiers was a popular theme in literature of the time, courtliness remained an important social ideal. The perfect courtier was the subject of Baldasarre Castiglione's *Il Libro del Cortegiano* (1528; translated as *The Book of the Courtier,* 1561), which he dedicated to the French monarch François I. According to remarks he makes in the *Essais,* Montaigne seems to have had many of the qualities that were valued at court. He was apparently an excellent horseman. He also liked conversation with both sexes, engaged in gallantry, and was unusually erudite. At the same time, Montaigne confesses to being too small to cut a dashing figure at court. He also expresses his distaste for the stereotypical courtier's shameful use of flattery, claiming to prefer to be as frank as possible with princes who ask for his opinion. Finally, Montaigne expresses strong reservations regarding the aristocratic pastime of the hunt. Although he participated in such events, and arranged for at least one hunting party to entertain guests, in the *Essais* he confesses to being moved by the spectacle of a cornered stag or hare whose eyes seem to plead for pity. He claims that when possible he let the prey go free rather than allowing it to be torn apart by the dogs—a degree of empathy out of place at a sixteenth-century aristocratic hunt.

Growing political strife and religious repression led in 1562 to the outbreak of the first of the Wars of Religion, which continued—with interruptions for treaties and peace accords—for the next thirty-six years. The 1570s were characterized by the rise of a new league for the defense of the Catholic faith. The Catholic League *(La Ligue)* opposed attempts made by the crown to accommodate Protestants. While in the first part of the century Protestants called for the overthrow of the king, the Catholic League began to challenge the king's authority during this period. The Protestants, the Catholic League, and the crown each sought alliances and pursued military, political, and ideological objectives. The political terrain was further complicated by the continuation of feudal alliances and machinations for power. These feudal agendas were thus superposed over religious beliefs. Montaigne's allegiance seems closest to the *politique* party, composed largely of magistrates such as his friend Pasquier. Montaigne writes in praise of the French chancellor Michel de L'Hôpital, whose name is closely associated with the religious toleration favored by the *politiques* in the name of stability. The *politiques* remained Catholic but, most of all, firmly loyal to the throne. They resisted imposing religious uniformity at the cost of domestic peace, toleration being a political necessity more than a moral imperative.

In the *Essais* Montaigne repeatedly affirms his loyalty to the throne and expresses opposition to any new ideas that threaten domestic stability, be they Protestant or Catholic. His political line helps explain his decision not to publish La Boétie's *De la Servitude volontaire* in his book, for this treatise had been used by Protestant advocates of tyrannicide. But neither did Montaigne side against the Huguenots. In the *Essais* he offers praise for the leaders of both the Huguenot cause and the Catholic League. For the essayist, moral virtue is independent of religious faith, as Marcel Conche points out. The essayist praises great men who lived before Christ or even, like Julian the Apostate, rejected Christianity.

Montaigne's is the only voice in his century raised to praise the Roman emperor Julian, who reinstated paganism in 360. In "De la liberté de conscience" ("Of freedom of conscience") the essayist concedes that in "En matiere de religion, il estoit vicieux par tout" ("in the matter of religion, he [Julian the Apostate] was bad throughout"). Yet, the rest of the chapter offers praise for the emperor Julian's many virtues. Montaigne further states unequivocally: "C'estoit, à la vérité, un tres-grand homme" ("He was, in truth, a very great and rare man" [II, 19]).

Montaigne does not judge Julian the Apostate, pagan philosophers of antiquity, or his contemporaries on the basis of religion. When it came to the contemporary political turmoil, Montaigne condemned both the Catholic League and the Reformation for their "harmful effects": "Je suis desgousté de la nouvelleté, quelque visage qu'elle porte, et ay raison, car j'en ay veu des effets tres-dommageables" ("I am disgusted with innovation, in whatever guise, and with reason, for I have seen very harmful effects of it" [I, 23]). For Montaigne, both sides share responsibility. "Celle qui nous presse depuis tant d'ans, elle n'a pas tout exploicté" ("The one that has been oppressing us for so many years is not the sole author of our troubles"). The Protestants may have initiated what Montaigne perceives as the downward slide into violence and instability, but the Catholic League soon followed suit, unleashing an era of unprecedented brutality on the land: "Mais si les inventeurs sont plus dommageables, les imitateurs sont plus vicieux, de se jetter en des exemples, desquels ils ont senty et puny l'horreur et le mal" ("But if the inventors [the Protestants] have done more harm, the imitators [the League] are more vicious in that they wholeheartedly follow examples whose horror and evil they have felt and punished" [I, 23]).

The *Essais* include Montaigne's public profession of faith. He writes in "Des Prieres" ("Of prayers"), "tenant pour execrable, s'il se trouve chose ditte par moy ignorament ou inadvertament contre les sainctes prescriptions de l'Eglise catholique, apostolique et Romaine, en laquelle je meurs et en laquelle je suis nay" ("I hold it as execrable if anything is found which was said by me, ignorantly or inadvertently, against the holy prescriptions of the Catholic, Apostolic, and Roman Church, in which I die and in which I was born" [I, 56]). How one should interpret such statements remains open to debate. At least some of Montaigne's professions of Catholic faith may have fulfilled first and foremost a social and political function. For Montaigne, to be a moderate Catholic was to preserve the social and political fabric; to be Protestant or even ultra-Catholic was to risk tearing this fabric apart.

In the Bordeaux region the changes under way were brought home in 1562 when Jeanne d'Albret, mother of Henri de Navarre (the future Henri IV), instituted the Reformation in Navarre, a kingdom in the southwest near Montaigne's estate. Civil war broke out around Bordeaux in this same year. The city was divided, and Montaigne's family reflects some of the religious division in the region as both his brother Thomas de Beauregard and his sister Jeanne de Lestonnac converted to Protestantism. The municipal administration was also divided. The first president of the Parlement of Bordeaux at the time, Jacques Benoist de Lagebaston, defended the *politique* line of L'Hôpital. In opposition to this policy of religious toleration, the Parlement reinstated a decision from 1543 requiring all of its members to profess the Catholic faith. Reactionary tendencies within the Parlement may have been inflamed by the activities of Protestants in the area, which included image breaking and church burning. In response to the civil war in Bordeaux, Blaise de Monluc, leader of the king's army in the southwest, imposed a "pacification" on the region. This campaign took the form of a bloody repression.

In 1568 Pierre Eyquem de Montaigne died, leaving Michel the new lord of Montaigne. Apparently out of a sense of filial duty, Montaigne undertook the translation into French of a Catalan theologian's treatise, *Liber Creaturarum* (The Book of Creatures), that his father had requested. Montaigne's translation, *La Théologie naturelle* (Natural Theology), appeared in 1569, but Montaigne dated the dedication to his father 18 June 1568–the date of his father's death. Raymond of Sabunde (Raimondo Sabunde)–or Raymond Sebond, as Montaigne gallicized his name–taught in Toulouse around 1430 and died in 1436. In the last years of his life Raymond Sebond composed the *Liber Creaturarum,* which was printed for the first time in Lyon in 1484 and translated into French in 1519. Raymond Sebond argued for the truth of Christianity without having recourse to theology or even Scripture: nature itself could prove Christian doctrine; one simply had to exercise reason in reading "the book of Nature" to arrive at these truths.

Montaigne's translation marked his first tangible step toward becoming a writer. During the Renaissance, translation was considered an appropriate training ground, the occasion to perfect one's style and gain recognition. In the first edition of Montaigne's translation, his name did not appear in the title. When the second edition was published in 1581 by Gilles Gourbin, Montaigne's name was prominently displayed. By then he was no longer a newcomer to the world of Renaissance letters, for the first edition of his *Essais* had appeared in 1580.

Raymond Sebond's treatise is the subject of the longest chapter in the 1580 *Essais*. Montaigne's "Apologie de Raymond Sebond" ("Apology for Raymond Sebond") is less an apology or defense than a critical reassessment of Raymond Sebond's theology. Montaigne challenges Raymond Sebond's conception of the hierarchical structure of Creation with humanity clearly positioned above all animals and thus nearer to the divine. He also mounts a skeptical attack on reason, implicitly undermining Raymond Sebond's contention that one can prove the Christian dogmas by observing nature using only human reason.

Regarding the ostensible superiority of humans over animals, Montaigne devotes some thirty pages—roughly one-fourth of the length of the chapter—to reflections on a wide range of animals, from magpies to elephants. Montaigne finds examples of the most cherished human qualities and faculties in the animal kingdom. Animals live in well-ordered societies (honeybees); they exercise judgment (swallows); they are able to communicate among themselves (birds); they are able to reason (foxes); they display noble sentiments and respect for one another (lions); they enjoy music, one of the liberal arts (elephants); they participate in religious worship (elephants); they are able to learn (parrots, monkeys, dogs, to name a few)—in fact animals have in turn taught humans many things (spiders taught man to weave, swallows taught man to build . . .). Why, then, is humanity so certain of its superiority? It is a matter of presumption, the essayist concludes. For Montaigne, presumption is to be consistently unmasked and resisted not only for moral reasons such as the sin of pride but also for philosophical reasons. He holds that presumption blinds, making one too willing to think one knows what one does not know. He shares Socrates' belief that the most important step toward wisdom is acknowledging one's ignorance.

Montaigne's list of animal stories prepares the way for the second part of the "Apologie de Raymond Sebond," which seeks to deflate the presumption of human reason by demonstrating its "vanity." He sets out to show that it is vain presumption to believe that human reason can by its own means arrive at certain truths. His primary tool in this attack on reason is Pyrrhonism, or Greek skeptical thought. Derived from the philosophy of Pyrrho and Sextus Empiricus, Pyrrhonism is a practice of questioning, doubting, and searching. It is a philosophy without doctrine: it questions but does not assert. The idea of a doctrine, even a negative doctrine such as "there is no truth," is contrary to the spirit of skepticism. For one can be no more certain of falsehood than of truth.

The importance of skepticism in the *Essais* has led some critics to question Montaigne's faith. Although in the *Essais* Montaigne professes to be unwavering in his Catholic faith, he also questions fundamental aspects of the Catholic dogma. For instance, at a time when the Church was emphasizing the importance of confession, the essayist seems to brush aside sacramental confession. In "Du Repentir" (Of Repentance) he claims to be almost without repentance; he also relies on his own conscience to such an extent that spiritual guidance from a confessor or spiritual director is eclipsed from the picture: "J'ay mes loix et ma court pour juger de moy, et m'y adresse plus qu'ailleurs" ("I have my own laws and court to judge me, and I address myself to them more than anywhere else" [III, 2]). For critics such as Donald M. Frame and Pierre Villey, Montaigne was a sincere Catholic. For others, such as Géralde Nakam, he was Catholic by culture, but Calvinist by intellectual inclination. On the other end of the spectrum, some readers and critics, including Arthur Armaingaud, see Montaigne as a nonbeliever. In *Les Essais* one can find support for all three of these mutually exclusive claims, but the modern consensus among critics allows for Montaigne's questioning attitude toward religion to be compatible with Catholic faith rather than seeing these positions as mutually exclusive.

The death of his father in 1568 may partly elucidate Montaigne's decision to resign from the Parlement of Bordeaux two years later. As George Hoffmann suggests, his new duties as lord of Montaigne may have required his presence on the family estate where he assumed new responsibilities. One finds in *Les Essais* direct allusions to his vineyards, to the climate in his region, to the winemaking process. Such remarks constitute reminders of the agricultural production on which his livelihood depended. In a passage in "De la phisionomie" ("Of physiognomy"), the essayist observes that when the family had to flee their property for several months they had to leave the harvest. "Les raisins demeurerent suspendus aux vignes" ("The grapes remained hanging from the vines" [III, 12]), a statement that, as Hoffmann points out, evokes what would have been for Montaigne a financial disaster for the year.

Another event in Montaigne's life that occurred shortly after his father's death may also have played a role in his decision to step down from the Parlement. Montaigne was involved in a horseback riding accident in 1569 or 1570—during the second or third civil war, as he states. He relates this accident in "De l'exercitation" ("Of practice"), describing how he was riding near his house, thinking himself perfectly safe, when another horseman came crashing into him at full speed. As he explains, one of his men sought to impress him by spurring his large and powerful workhorse to race past the other members of the party: the man "vint à le pousser à toute bride droict dans ma route, et fondre comme un colosse sur le petit homme et petit cheval" ("spurred his horse at full speed up the path behind me, came down like a colossus on the little man and the little horse, and hit us like a thunderbolt with all his strength and weight" [II, 6]). The collision left Montaigne unconscious—or dead, as he narrates the story. Indeed, his attendants thought him to be so. As he explains, he was "plus de deux grosses heures tenu pour trespassé" ("taken for dead for two full hours" [II, 6]) while he was being carried back to the château. Finally, he regained consciousness, though remaining weak and still "dead"—for the essayist continues to describe his state not as unconscious, but rather as "dead." In relating in detail his first experiences during this encounter with death, Montaigne describes feeling a sweetness like that of sleep.

Whatever his reasons, Montaigne decided to change his course of life. On 24 July 1570 he sold his seat on the Parlement of Bordeaux. Several weeks before his official departure, Montaigne was at his château completing dedications to L'Hôpital and Henri de Mesmes to accompany his edition of La Boétie's works, published about seven years after his friend's death.

Sometime during this period Montaigne refurbished the third floor of one of the towers of his château to accommodate his library. Symbolically isolated from the rest of the château, this building consisted of three floors. On the ground level was the chapel; on the second floor were his sleeping quarters; and the third floor he made his study. The tower study was closely tied to the meditative world of *Les Essais,* but it also served as a post of observation, for the tower's windows afforded a good view of the courtyard and main building of the château. Removed from the world of work below him, the essayist was nevertheless able to oversee his servants and peasants engaged in the activities on which his livelihood depended, as Hoffmann points out.

The third floor of the tower consisted of two rooms. Montaigne made the large circular room his study. The books that La Boétie had bequeathed to him were arranged in an arc. Adjoining the large round room that held his books was a small rectangular room—a secluded alcove that Montaigne terms his *cabinet*. Both rooms were given elaborate decoration on the walls, ceilings, and perhaps furniture. While much of this decoration has been lost over the centuries, Legros has used the accounts of tourists visiting the tower beginning in the seventeenth century to reconstruct a clearer picture of both spaces.

The decoration given to each room seems to emphasize two quite different spaces. In the study Mon-

Inscriptions in Greek and Latin painted on the ceiling of Montaigne's tower study (Collection Roger-Viollet/Getty Images)

taigne had *sententiae* painted in black paint, some in Greek, most in Latin. Seventy-three inscriptions were painted on the beams and joists of this room. Although most of Montaigne's château was destroyed by a fire in 1885, the tower is still standing, and many of the ceiling inscriptions are still legible. Examples of these inscriptions include Terence's "Homo sum humani a me nihil alienum puto" (I am human and nothing human is foreign to me), Lucretius's "Humanum genus est avidum nimis auricularum" (The human ear is avid for stories), and from the Book of Ecclesiastes, "Per Omnia Vanitas" (All is vanity). During the Renaissance adages or pithy statements were collected in commonplace books, orga-

nized together thematically with some commentary. Montaigne took at least some of the inscriptions in his study from one or several such books.

The inscriptions in Montaigne's tower study provided a source of meditation always available to the essayist, who had only to look up at the ceiling. Some inscriptions were painted in one direction (north-south) and others in the opposite direction (south-north), suggesting that they were meant to be read as Montaigne walked back and forth in the study. In the *Essais* Montaigne describes his existence in the study: "Là, je feuillette à cette heure un livre, à cette heure un autre, sans ordre et sans dessein, à pieces descousues; tantost je resve, tantost j'enregistre et dicte, en me promenant, mes songes que voicy" ("One moment I muse, another moment I set down or dictate, walking back and forth, these fancies of mine that you see here" [III, 3]). This passage serves also as a reminder to the modern reader that Montaigne was not necessarily alone in his tower. He would sometimes have been accompanied by his secretary, to whom he dictated part of the *Essais*. (As Montaigne relates, he once lost a part of the manuscript for the *Essais* when his secretary stole the only copy.)

While the study was large and drafty, Montaigne's second room, his *cabinet,* was small and well heated. The walls of the *cabinet* were covered with paintings of Roman scenes, but the warm colors and subjects represented emphasized the more sensual side of Roman civilization. Among the scenes represented were what may have been a banquet, the burning of Troy, and episodes from Classical mythology such as the lovers Venus and Mars surprised by Vulcan. One painting had a maritime theme, with four verses from Horace that served as its legend: "me tabula sacer / votiva paries indicat uvida, / suspendisse potenti, / vestimenta maris Deo" (The painting that I hung on the temple indicates that I consecrated to the powerful God of the sea my clothes still damp from the shipwreck). He quotes these same verses in his chapter "Sur des vers de Virgile," in which he suggests that he survived the "shipwreck" of his amorous adventures. Since, he claims, he no longer has anything to lose, he can now write openly about sex in general and about his own sexual being in particular, as though he had stripped away his clothing and were standing naked. In the *Essais* Montaigne uses nakedness as a metaphor for speaking frankly about himself.

Montaigne also had painted on the wall of his *cabinet* a Latin inscription commemorating his retirement on the day of his thirty-eighth birthday, some six months after his departure from the Parlement. A kind of manifesto, this inscription proclaimed his intention to dedicate what remained of his life to *libertas* (freedom), *tranquillitas* (tranquility), and *otium* (idleness). After years of public service, he here declared his intention to retire to *otium* and the muses. Montaigne's exaltation of *otium* was an articulation of the persistent dream of literary idleness among erudite magistrates, whose lives were characterized at once by an active daily life and an elaborate idealization of leisure. In Montaigne's milieu literary idleness was an art practiced in the shadow of the *vita activa* but that in reality constituted its complement, for neither letters nor leisure were entirely disinterested pursuits. To display erudition and gain recognition through writing was to earn prestige—a valuable form of symbolic capital. Similarly, idleness was an art to master, a mark of culture and nobility, and thus a sign of

distinction. Despite his desire to liberate himself from the public sphere, Montaigne's declared intention to practice idleness in earnest thus remained firmly attached to the realm of social practices in his world.

While Montaigne probably began composing the first chapters of the *Essais* around 1572, he had not entirely forsaken public service for letters. Montaigne's military service probably took place between 1573 and 1577. Increasingly, the modern court was redefining the aristocrat's role as courtier rather than soldier. The old social order ruled by an aristocratic warrior class was being replaced by the modern state's reliance on a corps of elite functionaries, the so-called *robe* nobility. Nevertheless, Montaigne and many of his contemporaries continued to exalt the noble life of arms over more-modern careers with the bureaucratic state. For Montaigne, Spartans were infinitely more noble than Athenians.

While he was composing the early chapters of the *Essais,* Montaigne was also called upon to act as a negotiator during a period of intermittent civil war. The fourth war of religion took place between 1572 and 1573 and the fifth between 1575 and 1576. From 1572 to 1576 Montaigne served as a negotiator between Henri de Navarre, leader of the Protestant armies, and Henri duc de Guise, the charismatic leader of the Catholic League. Although he does not address his diplomatic service directly in the *Essais,* the art of negotiation is a theme running through the early chapters of the first book, as some of their titles suggest: "Si le chef d'une place assiégée doit sortir pour parlementer" ("Whether the governor of a besieged place should go out to parley" [I, 5]); "On est puny pour s'opiniastrer à une place sans raison" ("One is punished for defending a place obstinately without reason" [I, 15]); "Un traict de quelques ambassadeurs" ("A trait of certain ambassadors" [I, 17]); "Divers evenemens de mesme conseil" ("Various outcomes of the same plan" [I, 14]). The full title of the first English translation of the *Essais* emphasized its political dimension: *The Essayes, or Morall, politike and millitarie discourses of Lo. Michaell de Montaigne.*

Amid his military and diplomatic service, Montaigne became gentleman of King Charles IX's chamber in 1571. In 1577 he became gentleman of Henri de Navarre's chamber. Montaigne recorded both events in his family's *livre de raison* (household record). In a Renaissance *livre de raison* the head of the family registered the dates of important public and private events, such as births, deaths, and marriages, as well as distinctions received and public offices held. Montaigne's family's *livre de raison* was Michael Beuther's *Ephemeris historica,* a small book published in 1551. The format of this book accommodated its intended function as both an agenda and a household record. One page was devoted to each day of the year: at the top of the page was a brief text relating events that happened on that day, but the rest of the page was blank, leaving room for the owner's personal records. Never intended for publication, this book has been an invaluable source of information on Montaigne's life. Montaigne's *livre de raison* contains many entries made in his own hand over the years, in addition to those made by his father and by his daughter Léonor.

The early chapters of the *Essais* were composed in the immediate wake of the massacre of St. Bartholomew's Day, 24 August 1572. The massacre took place when the Huguenot Henri de Navarre married Marguerite de Valois, the sister of Charles IX. With so many prominent Huguenots attending the Paris wedding, the king authorized a massacre of the sleeping Protestants, hoping to strike a decisive blow to their cause by eliminating many of their leaders. In Paris the bodies of the slain were thrown into the Seine, which was said to turn red with blood. By the end of the night, there were 3,000 victims out of a total Parisian population of about 300,000. The same scenes of horror followed in other cities in the kingdom: Orleans, Lyon, Rouen, and Toulouse. On 3 October, Protestants in Bordeaux were massacred. Following the massacre in Paris, Henri de Navarre was forced to abjure and held as a prisoner at court for the next few years.

L'Hôpital is said to have cried, "excidat illa dies!" (let this day be obliterated). Indeed, royal legislation that followed the events imposed a silence covering the horror of the massacres. Montaigne, for his part, seems to attempt to obliterate their memory. Several pages from his *livre de raison,* including that specific date, have been torn out. In the *Essais* Montaigne never refers directly to the St. Bartholomew's Day Massacre.

The pages of the *Essais,* however, do not gloss over human brutality or rationalize royal policies. The first chapter in book 1 concludes with the spectacle of Alexander the Great massacring the inhabitants of Thebes. The last words of the chapter are: "Dura ce carnage jusques à la derniere goute de sang qui se trouva espandable, et ne s'arresta que aux personnes desarmées, vieillards, femmes et enfans, pour en tirer trente mille esclaves" ("This slaughter went on to the last drop of blood that could be shed, and stopped only at the unarmed people, old men, women, and children, so that thirty thousand of them might be taken as slaves" [I,1]). In "De la phisionomie" Montaigne evokes the dangers of using religious sentiment to justify inhumanity: "Je doubte souvent si, entre tant de gens qui se meslent de telle besoigne, nul s'est rencontré d'entendement si imbecille, à qui on aye en bon escient persuadé [qu'en] desmembrant sa mere et en donnant à ronger les pieces à ses anciens ennemis, remplissant des haines parricides les courages fraternels, appellant à son ayde les diables et les furies, il puisse apporter secours à la sacrosaincte douceur et justice de la parole divine" ("I often doubt whether among so many men who meddle in such a business a single one has been found of so feeble an understanding as to have been genuinely persuaded that . . . by dismembering his mother and giving the pieces to her ancient enemies to gnaw on, by filling the hearts of brothers with parricidal hatreds, by calling the devils and the furies to his aid, he could bring help to the sacrosanct sweetness and justice of the divine word" [III, 12]).

Such was the political and religious climate as Montaigne was beginning the as-yet-untitled *Essais.* Evidence suggests that Montaigne was reading Seneca at the time. The *Epistles to Lucilius* was one of his favorite books, and the early chapters cite and paraphrase it abundantly. For example, in "De la solitude" ("Of solitude") there are at least thirty quotations and allusions. With its lessons of self-mastery in the face of adversity, Seneca's Stoic philosophy must have seemed well suited to the times. At roughly the same time as Montaigne was composing the *Essais,* his brother-in-law, Pressac, had undertaken the first French translation of Seneca's epistles (1580), which Montaigne never mentions in the *Essais.* In his dedication to Henri III, Pressac emphasized the usefulness of Seneca's lessons for the beleaguered ranks of the nobility in dire need of the constancy taught by Stoic philosophy. Finally, beyond any question of their philosophical content, Seneca's epistles influenced the literary form Montaigne was elaborating. In his *Essais* Montaigne often expresses admiration for the epistolary form. Several chapters in the *Essais* are prefaced with dedications to friends, and while he professes little esteem for Cicero, he has abundant praise for the Roman orator and statesman's *Letters to Atticus.* The familiar letter seems to have partly shaped the nascent essay, as Rigolot observes.

On a more general level, the *Essais* grew almost organically out of Montaigne's notes on Seneca and, indeed, on many other books. The practice of marginalia (writing commentary in the margins) was an important factor shaping the genesis of his text. Several of Montaigne's annotated books have been recovered and edited, including his annotations on Nicole Gilles's *Annales* (Annals), Julius Caesar's *Commentarii* (Commentaries), and Lucretius's *De rerum natura* (On the Nature of Things). These annotations shed light on the genesis of the *Essais,* which in some ways resemble a compendium of ancient philosophy and history. Montaigne frequently quotes and paraphrases such ancients as Seneca, Plutarch, Sextus Empiricus, Aristotle, Cicero, Lucretius, and Caesar. The *Essais,* however, diverge from the tradition of the compendium in two important ways. First, Montaigne rarely identifies his sources. (In the editions published during his lifetime, almost none of the quotes are identified—they are italicized, but Montaigne gives neither the author's name nor the title of the work.) More important, the wisdom of the ancients is not presented as a continuous whole in the *Essais*. Montaigne's references bring out discrepancies and discord rather than continuity. He weighs the Stoics against the Epicureans, the academics against the skeptics, Socrates against Alexander the Great. As critics have pointed out, this movement of weighing one idea or one author against another defines the essay as practiced by Montaigne (*essai* comes from *exagium* [weighing]).

Growing partly out of Montaigne's comments on the authors he read, the *Essais* themselves came to serve both as text and commentary, for Montaigne also wrote comments and additions in the margins of his own text. The addition of these comments and editorial changes—Montaigne commenting on Montaigne—produced the raw material for the 1595 edition. "Nos opinions s'entent les unes sur les autres. La premiere sert de tige à la seconde" ("Our opinions are grafted upon one another. The first serves as a stock for the second, the second for the third" [III, 13]); he comments about himself and his era in the final chapter of the *Essais*.

Montaigne's brief preface, "Au Lecteur" ("To the Reader"), was among the last parts of the *Essais* he composed for the first edition. During the Renaissance it was common to leave the prefatory texts such as the dedicatory epistle to the end. They were often printed last to allow an author who might have been working for years on the text to make last-minute changes in the dedicatee or overall presentation of the text. Montaigne signs and dates his preface "de Montaigne, ce premier de Mars mille cinq cens quatre vingts" ("from Montaigne, this first day of March, fifteen hundred and eighty"). Given the delays that came with getting a manuscript published, Hoffmann estimates that most of the chapters published in 1580 were completed before the end of 1578.

Hoffmann also describes the active role Montaigne played in getting his manuscript published. He and his Bordelais printer Simon Millanges had what was a common arrangement at the time to print *à compte partiel* (splitting costs). Montaigne bore the responsibility for procuring from a mill the paper to be used (approximately 200 reams). Beyond the costs of publication, there remained the legal question of rights. To protect the rights to a published work one had to receive a *privilège,* which conferred both legal permission to print and a commercial license to sell copies. As was common practice, the *privilège* for the *Essais* went not to Montaigne but to his printer.

Montaigne left his château on 22 June 1580 with bound copies of his *Essais* in hand. This first edition consisted of two books (the third book was added for the 1588 edition). The full title—*Les Essais de Messire Michel Seigneur de Montaigne, Chevalier de l'Ordre du Roy, & Gentil-homme ordinaire de sa Chambre, Livre Premier & Second* (Essays of Sir Michel de Montaigne, Knight of the Order of the King and Gentleman of the King's Chamber, First and Second Books)—emphasizes the aristocratic credentials of the author by citing his three honorific titles: lord of a noble estate, knight of the Order of Saint-Michel, and gentleman of the king's chamber.

Montaigne's first official act after publishing his work was to present one of the bound copies to the king. This exchange is related by François de La Croix du Maine. After Henri III complimented Montaigne on his *Essais,* the latter replied, "il faut donc nécessairement que je plaise à Vostre Majesté puisque mon livre lui est agréable, car il ne contient autre chose qu'un Discours de ma vie et de mes actions" (I must therefore be equally pleasing to Your Majesty, since my book is pleasing to Him, for it contains nothing else than an examination of my life and my actions). Montaigne followed the king's army, which had begun to lay siege to La Fère in what was ultimately a successful attempt to retake it from the Protestants. The siege began on 7 July 1580. In his *livre de raison* Montaigne writes that his friend and neighbor Philibert de Gramont was wounded and died four days before Montaigne arrived at the siege.

With a few companions and servants, including an anonymous personal secretary, Montaigne then set out on a seventeen-month trip through France, Switzerland, Germany, Austria, and Italy. A few years earlier, in 1579, Montaigne had suffered his first attack of kidney stones. After witnessing his father suffer from this painful illness that finally killed him, Montaigne had long dreaded getting it himself. Part of his trip was thus apparently intended to be therapeutic—he visited mineral baths along the way and experimented with self-medication by drinking various quantities of different mineral waters. But mainly Montaigne seems to have traveled for the pleasure of traveling. He kept a journal of his trip that he never intended for publication but that was rediscovered in 1770 and published for the first time in 1774 with the title *Journal de voyage de M. de M. en Italie, par la Suisse et l'Allemagne* (M. de M.'s Travel Journal in Italy and through Switzerland and Germany; translated as *Montaigne's Travel Journal,* 1983). The first part of his *Journal de voyage* was written by his secretary (it was apparently not dictated, since the author uses the third person to refer to Montaigne). The second part, however, is in Montaigne's own hand. He wrote in Italian while he remained in Italian-speaking regions and later in French.

Montaigne apparently enjoyed almost all aspects of traveling, from horseback riding and tasting local cuisine to conversing with a wide variety of people he encountered along the way. His *Journal de voyage* reflects his curiosity about the religious practices he observed. He attended synagogues and Protestant churches and engaged many people from different faiths in conversation about religion. Montaigne's interest in religion as an anthropological phenomenon is manifest in the pages of his *Journal de voyage* as well as in the *Essais*.

Montaigne's European tour was also an occasion to visit the Roman ruins–a trip to Rome was a kind of humanist pilgrimage during the Renaissance. His secretary reported Montaigne's reaction to the ruins, which he proclaimed to be "plus rien que son sépulchre" (nothing but its sepulcher). The only thing remaining from ancient Rome was the sky above, Montaigne reportedly concluded. As for modern Rome–the site of pomp and political intrigue rather than of the philosophy and poetry humanists associated with ancient Rome–as Madeleine Lazard points out, Montaigne did not express bitterness at what Rome had become, as Joachim du Bellay had in *Le Premier Livre des antiquitez de Rome* (1558, The First Book of the Antiquities of Rome; translated as "Ruines of Rome" and "Visions of Bellay," 1591) and "Les Regrets" (1558; translated as *The Regrets*, 1984). Unlike Du Bellay, Montaigne did not feel "exiled" in Rome. He enjoyed the cosmopolitan dimension of the city and its constant activity. He visited Michelangelo's *Moses*, the Pope's painting gallery, and la Villa D'Este's famous gardens.

While he was in Rome, Montaigne had an audience with Pope Gregory XIII, who greeted him courteously and helped him obtain Roman citizenship. In the concluding pages of the chapter "De la vanité" ("Of vanity") in the *Essais* (III, 9) he transcribes the bull granting him citizenship–though he does so with no small irony, pointing to its pompous language and gilt letters. He also visited the Vatican Library, which must have been a sign of favor, since even the French ambassador was not allowed to do so. Montaigne also describes submitting the *Essais* to the papal censor, a professor of theology at the University of Rome who did not speak French and so relied on help from a French friar. When he arrived in Rome, his books were confiscated at customs, which was at the time a common practice. All of his books were returned to him aside from a Swiss history, which was kept because its translator was a heretic. When the *Essais* were returned

to him, he learned that six things had been criticized by the censor: his use of the word "fortune" instead of God or Providence, his praise of heretic poets such as Théodore de Bèze, his praise of Julian the Apostate, his assertion that prayer required that one have no wicked intentions while praying, his position against torture, and his opinion that children should be exposed to diverse experiences as part of their education. During the interview that followed, the explanations for each of the objections that Montaigne offered satisfied the censor. It was left up to Montaigne to redress what was seemingly "in bad taste." In future editions, however, the essayist never cut the offending passages or words to align the *Essais* with orthodoxy.

In 1581 Montaigne received word that he had been elected mayor of Bordeaux in absentia, which prompted him to cut short his trip. On returning to his château, he discovered a letter from the king. In his *livre de raison* he records that "Le Roy m'écrivit de Paris qu'il avoit eue et trouvée très agréable la nomination que la ville de Bourdeaus avoit faict de moi pour leur maire & me comandoit de m'en venir à ma charge" (The king wrote me from Paris that he had learned that the city of Bordeaux had nominated me for their mayor and was very pleased by this nomination and commanded me to assume the office). He was reelected two years later, which he also noted in his *livre de raison*.

Montaigne thus served as mayor of Bordeaux from 1581 to 1585. Jacques de Goyon-Matignon arrived in Bordeaux in 1581 to serve as the king's lieutenant general in Guyenne. Matignon's was a delicate position to occupy, since the lieutenant general was also responsible to the Protestant Henri de Navarre. Matignon was a zealous Catholic but also known for having saved the lives of Protestants during the St. Bartholomew's Day Massacre. He had already acquired the reputation of being a talented and experienced negotiator and had been made Maréchal de France in 1579. As for his relationship with the new mayor–whom he had encountered at least once before, at the siege of La Fère–their correspondence suggests that over the next few years Montaigne and Matignon established a collaborative working relationship. Since Montaigne was the friend of Henri de Navarre, the basis was laid for effective negotiation between Navarre and the French crown via Matignon and Montaigne.

Montaigne's first term as mayor was relatively tranquil thanks to the Peace of Fleix, which had been concluded in 1580. During this time Montaigne made an official visit to court on behalf of the city of Bordeaux. Although the exact reason for his visit is not known, he was able to negotiate the repeal of a tax on commerce entering and leaving the city. Another of

Montaigne's actions as mayor concerned a Jesuit orphanage whose minimal budget left the children in dire conditions near starvation. Montaigne intervened to bring the orphanage under municipal administration and insure that it had adequate funding. This action was characteristic of a broader movement in both Catholic and Protestant cities during the Renaissance to establish charitable institutions run by city administrations. Poor relief had previously been left to private charity and to religious institutions.

Although he had assumed what must have been a demanding and absorbing public office, Montaigne did not abandon his literary endeavors. In 1582 a second edition of the *Essais,* with some additions, was published by Millanges in Bordeaux.

During Montaigne's second term as mayor the fragile peace was threatened, first by unrest in southwest France and later by the death in 1584 of the king's younger brother, François, Duke of Alençon and of Anjou, which left Henri de Navarre the heir presumptive to the French throne. The perspective of a Protestant king of France enraged the Catholic League. Moreover, although the Peace of Fleix allowed the Huguenots to keep their surety towns, aside from Cahors, for another six years, tensions mounted as these concessions were slow in coming. In 1583 Navarre took by force one such location that had been granted to him but not yet turned over: Mont-de-Marsan. Matignon responded by establishing garrisons in Bazas near Nérac, one of the two capitals of Navarre. Lazard observes that despite these mounting hostilities, neither Henri de Navarre nor Henri III wished for war; indeed, Henri III supported Navarre as his successor. During this crisis Montaigne was called on to mediate between Navarre and Matignon. Letters exchanged between Navarre and Montaigne show the former explaining his intentions and entreating Montaigne to plead his case with Matignon. The mounting tensions were deflated in early 1584, as Navarre was allowed to retain Mont-de-Marsan with Matignon reducing the garrisons at Bazas. Over the coming years Montaigne continued to mediate between the French monarch and the Protestant Navarre. In 1584 Henri de Navarre and his company of noblemen, including Henri de Bourbon, Prince of Condé, stayed at Montaigne's château and in the nearby village. In his *livre de raison* Montaigne notes that he released a stag in his forest to entertain his royal guests with a hunt.

Near the end of Montaigne's second term the political context degenerated rapidly in Bordeaux. In July 1585 Henri III gave in to the Catholic League's militant anti-Protestantism. A large League army under Charles de Lorraine, Duke of Mayenne joined Matignon's troops in Bordeaux to lay siege to Castillon.

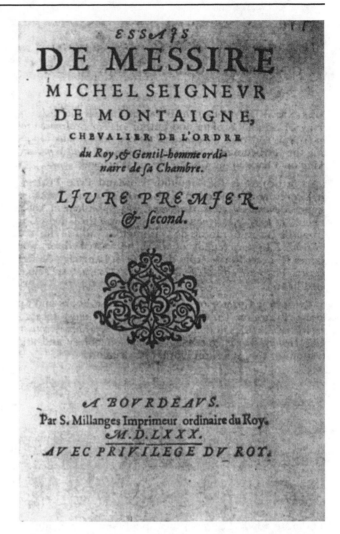

Title page for the first edition of Montaigne's major work (from Dikka Berven, ed., Montaigne: A Collection of Essays, *1995; Thomas Cooper Library, University of South Carolina)*

This turn of events came at the end of a series of crises within the city. In March 1585 the Catholic League sympathizer Louis Ricard Gourdon de Genouillac, baron de Vaillac, governor of the Château-Trompette and long hostile to Montaigne, mounted an unsuccessful coup in Bordeaux. In May, assassination plots were uncovered against Matignon and Montaigne, who were both accused of being sympathetic to Henri de Navarre by members of the Catholic League. Henri de Navarre wrote Montaigne a letter full of anxiety for the security of the city as well as for Montaigne's own safety. At the same time the city prepared for its annual muster—when all inhabitants able to bear arms were required to turn out for a general review. The presence of so many armed men was potentially explosive, with tensions high and conspiracies afoot. Municipal authorities foresaw a riot, and Montaigne had cause to fear for his life.

The essayist writes of this event in the 1588 edition of the *Essais*. In "Divers evenemens de mesme conseil" ("Various outcomes of the same plan") he describes the debate among the city councillors over what course of action to pursue. The general consensus was to allow only a limited display of artillery fire, thereby limiting occasions for assassination or rioting. Montaigne, however, defended a counterintuitive course. Any sign of fear would be disastrous, he argued. Instead, he pleaded in favor of sending out word that captains should tell their troops to "advertir les soldats de faire leurs salves belles et gaillardes en l'honneur des assistants, et n'espargner leur poudre" ("make their volleys fine and lusty in honor of the spectators, and not spare their powder" [I, 24]). Further, he asserted that the municipal authorities should not try to protect themselves from the armed men but should instead walk confidently among them, with their heads held high and an open demeanor. Underlying Montaigne's plan was a strategic use of confidence based on the idea that behaving with one's potential enemies as though they were friends invites them in turn to behave as friends rather than enemies. Montaigne's strategy was adopted, and it proved successful. As he observes: "Cela servit de gratification envers ces troupes suspectes, et engendra dés lors en avant une mutuelle et utile confience" ("This served to gratify the suspected troops, and engendered from then on a useful mutual confidence" [I, 24]).

During these dangerous times no defense was apparently Montaigne's consistent line of defense. The moderate Catholic views he openly expressed along with his friendship with Henri de Navarre made him suspect to both the Protestants and Catholic League sympathizers in the region. With potential enemies on all sides, Montaigne claims to have promoted "mutual confidence" by refusing to move to defend himself and by refusing to transform his family château into a fortress, as did his neighbors. Anyone could gain access to his château, he claims, for it had only a doorman rather than a guard at its entry. According to the essayist, this lack of defense proved to be the best strategy for protecting his château during the hostilities.

Montaigne's *Essais* reveal traces of his sustained reflection on diplomatic survival strategies to be employed when in a position of weakness. Throughout the *Essais* he reflects on ethical and political choices in various circumstances, evoking not only his own experiences but also episodes from the lives of great generals, diplomats, and statesmen culled from ancient and recent history. Montaigne went back and inserted an account of his actions as mayor in the midst of an analysis of Caesar's way of handling potential mutiny in the chapter "Divers evenemens de mesme conseil," ini-

tially published in the 1580 edition—before Montaigne became mayor. In his addition the essayist observes that as mayor of Bordeaux he behaved much as Caesar had done under comparable circumstances. "A ses legions, mutinées et armées contre luy, Cæsar opposoit seulement l'authorité de son visage et la fierté de ses paroles; et se fioit tant à soy et à sa fortune, qu'il ne craingnoit point de l'abandonner et commettre à une armée seditieuse et rebelle" ("To his legions, mutinous and in arms against him, Caesar opposed only the authority of his countenance and the pride of his words, and he trusted himself and his fortune so much that he did not fear to abandon his person and commit his fate to a seditious and rebellious army" [I, 24]). As the essayist observes, "la crainte et la deffiance attirent l'offence et la convient" ("fear and mistrust attract and invite attack" [I, 24]).

This last example is emblematic of Montaigne's practice of the essay. The essayist's self-portrait—here, of himself as mayor in a situation of crisis—is inextricably linked to a process of rereading and rewriting. Rereading the analysis he wrote of Caesar prior to 1580, Montaigne later scrutinizes his own actions during the crisis of May 1585 in this light. And in adding the account of his own actions in Bordeaux to the analysis of Caesar's actions, the essayist not only imagines Montaigne and Caesar adopting the same course of action when faced with the same situation but also captures himself in the act of contemplating himself contemplating Caesar. The account of his own actions and thoughts thus emerges in the midst of an ongoing dialogue with his culture and with his own text. His self-portrait is not figured as an attempt to get at the "deepest self," the most profound being in isolation from all exterior influences and all other points of comparison. The *Essais* are not intended to represent its author as a still life. Instead, they attempt to capture him in motion—thinking, comparing, acting. "Je ne peints pas l'estre. Je peints le passage" ("I do not portray being; I portray passing" [III, 2]), writes Montaigne.

The 1588 edition was published in Paris by Abel L'Angelier with a nine-year *privilège*. It included substantial additions to existing chapters, as well as a third book of thirteen new chapters. The emphasis on self-portraiture is clearly apparent in this edition, in which Montaigne accumulates prosaic details—how he likes to sleep, dine, ride horseback—from his daily life. In the chapter "Sur des vers de Virgile" he speaks openly about his sexual preferences, stating that he hopes that this chapter will make his *Essais* intimate reading for women: "Ce chapitre me fera du cabinet" ("This chapter will put me in the boudoir" [III, 5]). Yet, the third book also continues to develop Montaigne's critical gaze on his world. According to Nakam, half of the

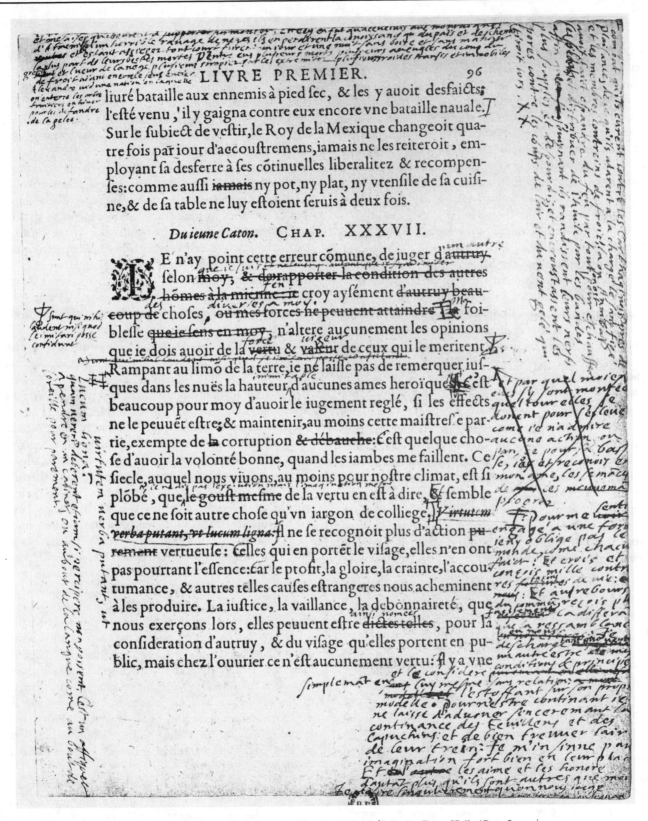

Page from Les Essais *with annotations in Montaigne's hand (Collection Roger-Viollet/Getty Images)*

third book could be considered "Advice to a Prince." For instance, in chapter 11, "Des boyteux" ("Of cripples"), Montaigne reflects critically on the Renaissance witch-hunts on the eve of the worst period of persecution, which extended from 1590 to 1640. The persecution in France was carried out by secular courts under the authority of the king. Montaigne attacks his former colleagues in the magistrature, while couching his critique in terms that would not offend a royal interlocutor. He uses humor and wit, as well as a salacious anecdote—the legend that lame women make the best sexual partners—as though to mirror the style of conversation at court. But despite its light tone, the chapter offers an informed critique of the logic used to defend the witch-hunts as well as a denunciation of the inhumanity of the persecution. Montaigne advances a skeptical view of demonology, the so-called science of demons that provided the rationale for the witch-hunts. He writes against royal policies as well as against the work of magistrates engaged in the persecution. He does not challenge the existence of supernatural occurrences but rather the capacity of human reason to reliably apprehend them. "Inanité" (inanity), "songes" (dreams), "opinions" (conjectures), and "l'erreur" (error) are among the terms used by the essayist to deflate the pretension of demonology to describe reality. Montaigne attacked the demonologists' claims and denounced the inhumanity of the witch-hunts at a time when skepticism was a dangerous position to defend. In his treatise *De la démonomanie des sorciers* (On the Demon-Mania of Witches), published in 1580, Jean Bodin, a major thinker of the time, wrote that if a magistrate mocked witchcraft, it was a sign that he was himself guilty of witchcraft.

In "Des boyteux" Montaigne relates his observations bearing on the case of a condemned witch. He describes passing through the territory of a prince who tried to persuade him of the reality of the threat posed by witches by showing him a dozen or so prisoners accused of witchcraft, including an old woman who was widely held to be a witch. Montaigne notes that he was allowed to interview this "witch," study the evidence against her, read the recorded confessions, and examine the would-be "mark of the devil" found on her body. He concluded that the woman—a confessed witch sentenced to be burned at the stake—was mad, not guilty of witchcraft. Further, in "De la conscience" ("Of conscience" (II, 5) he criticizes the reliance in trials on torture to extract confessions, because he understands that pain can push a person to even the most extravagant and fantastic admissions. Montaigne insists that what is said under torture can just as easily be false as true. Indeed, Montaigne stands as the only

major figure of his time to oppose judicial torture unequivocally.

When Montaigne went to Paris in June 1588 for the publication of his revised and expanded *Essais,* the capital was in turmoil. Sympathy for the Catholic League and hostility to the king were at their peak. On the Day of the Barricades, 12 May, when crowds erected barricades surrounding the king's troops, the king and his immediate entourage fled the capital to take refuge in Rouen. On 20 July, having recently returned from Rouen, Montaigne was taken prisoner in Paris. He narrates the event in some of the most detailed entries in his *livre de raison,* explaining that he was taken from his sickbed and sent to the Bastille, where he learned that he was being held in retribution for the king's arrest of a Catholic League member in Rouen. Learning of his plight, Catherine de Médicis petitioned the duke of Guise and obtained Montaigne's release in the evening of the day he was captured. Montaigne observes in his *livre de raison* that this day in the Bastille was the first day of imprisonment he had known.

The last few years of Montaigne's life were marked by further political instability. Following the assassination of Henri III in 1589, Henri de Navarre's ascension to the throne was contested by the Catholic League. Although the Salic law dictated that Navarre should be king of France, members of the Catholic League advanced their own choice for king. In July 1593 Navarre abjured his Protestant faith, claiming, according to legend, that "Paris is worth a mass." His conversion to Catholicism rendered the league's main argument against him null and void. In 1594 Navarre was crowned king of France in Chartres. The new King Henri IV soon arranged for reconciliation with some of the leaders of the Catholic League while defeating others in battle, thereby bringing to an end the prolonged period of civil war in France. The Edict of Nantes finally put an end to the wars in 1598 when Protestants were granted some measure of religious freedom. Under the Edict of Nantes, Protestant worship was tolerated only on noble estates with tenurial rights of justice; specific places to be designated by royal commissioners; and finally wherever Protestants could prove that their faith had been openly practiced in 1596 and 1597. Montaigne, however, did not live to see peace restored.

Montaigne worked intensely on the *Essais* in his final years, making substantial additions as well as some editorial changes to the existing 107 chapters of the 1588 edition—the last one published during his lifetime. During this time he also received visits to his château from friends such as Pierre Charron. His most important relationship in his last years—at least as concerned the future of the *Essais*–was his friendship with Marie de Gournay, whom he met while he was overseeing the printing of the 1588 edition. Although self-taught, Gournay was highly erudite. At the age of twenty she discovered the *Essais* and was so impressed that two years later she went to Paris to meet their author. She and Montaigne became close during his last years, with Montaigne apparently dictating parts of the *Essais* to her. He visited her several times at her estate in Picardy, and they cultivated a correspondence.

Montaigne died on 13 September 1592. Although there are no eyewitness accounts of his death, Pasquier wrote of Montaigne's last hours in a letter. According to his description, Montaigne's tongue was paralyzed for the last three days, leaving him unable to speak. Knowing that he was dying, he wrote a request that a few neighbors be summoned to his bedside. He then had mass said in his room. Pasquier notes that when the priest came to the elevation of the Corpus Domini, Montaigne lifted himself up from his bed with hands clasped and then expired; Pasquier suggests that this last gesture was a fine mirror of his inmost soul. Pasquier's telling of Montaigne's last hours reflects his century's ideal of the exemplary death, death being the ultimate philosophical test.

After Montaigne's death, Gournay undertook the task of preparing an edition of the *Essais* that included the changes and additions he had made since 1588. The edition was printed in Paris by L'Angelier in 1595. Gournay also presided over the editorial fortunes of the *Essais* in the first part of the seventeenth century. For instance, while Montaigne rarely cited his sources, Gournay added to her 1635 edition references for the many Latin and occasional Greek quotations, a practice twentieth-century editors continued. She also made some editorial changes to accommodate Montaigne's language to the taste of seventeenth-century readers in the 1635 edition. She made these changes reluctantly, for she saw herself as Montaigne's advocate and the guardian of his *Essais* rather than their modernizer.

The history of the *Essais* has a final, surprising chapter. In the eighteenth century a copy of the 1588 edition with Montaigne's notes in his own hand was found. It was clearly Montaigne's personal copy, and it included changes and additions written in the margins, between the lines, and on top of the printed text. This copy is now commonly referred to as *l'Exemplaire de Bordeaux* (the Bordeaux Copy). Although it is close to Gournay's 1595 edition, there are differences between the two versions. There were, thus, at least two different copies: the Bordeaux Copy, which was lost sometime after Montaigne's death and recovered in the eighteenth century, and a later working copy of the Bordeaux Copy with additional annotations by Montaigne that was sent

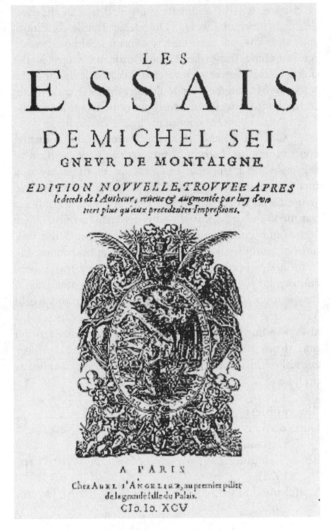

Title page for the edition of Montaigne's work edited by Marie de Gournay on the basis of his annotations in the 1588 edition. It was published three years after his death (Ministere de l'Education nationale, de l'Enseignement superieur et de la Recherche Direction de la technologie-SDTICE; from <http://www.educnet.education.fr>).

to Gournay, who used it to constitute the 1595 edition. Further complicating the picture, the Bordeaux Copy is incomplete. Montaigne wrote some of his additions on separate pieces of paper that are now lost, and a bookbinder carelessly cut off part of the margins with Montaigne's notes which were then thrown out. Scholars wishing to ascertain Montaigne's final intentions as expressed on the Bordeaux Copy have thus used Gournay's 1595 edition, based on the other copy–probably Montaigne's final copy–as a basis to reconstruct the missing parts of the Bordeaux Copy.

Today the Bordeaux Copy belongs to the French government and is under the jurisdiction of the minister of culture. It is in a climate-controlled box in the Bordeaux Municipal Library. Despite its fragile condition, specialists can still occasionally consult it, although without touching the pages. The Bordeaux Copy is the object of this degree of reverence because it contains the traces of Montaigne's scrupulous reworking and editing of his text; he was not nearly as nonchalant about the task of writing as his comments in the *Essais* suggest.

One of Michel de Montaigne's most enduring contributions to literature remains the new medium of the essay he fashioned. His practice of the essay is a method of inquiry, of searching and questioning. He wrote as part of a continuing dialogue with a tradition that he knew to be fraught with dissension. In the *Essais* Montaigne cites, paraphrases, and challenges the wisdom of antiquity while pointing to its contradictions. He fashioned a bookish world in which every text invites commentary, and every commentary is potentially a new text eliciting yet another commentary. In this world Montaigne's critical gaze is brought to bear on his always-unfinished self-portrait and on the reality around him, from peasants laboring in the fields to princes enmeshed in the religious, political, and social conflicts of the end of the French Renaissance.

Biographies:

Donald M. Frame, *Montaigne: A Biography* (New York: Harcourt, Brace & World, 1965);

Roger Trinquet, *La Jeunesse de Montaigne* (Paris: Nizet, 1972);

Madeleine Lazard, *Michel de Montaigne* (Paris: Fayard, 1992).

References:

Dikka Berven, ed., *Montaigne: A Collection of Essays,* 5 volumes (New York: Garland, 1995);

Marcel Conche, *Montaigne ou la conscience heureuse* (Paris: Seghers, 1964);

Philippe Desan, ed., *Dictionnaire de Michel de Montaigne* (Paris: Champion, 2004);

Hugo Friedrich, *Montaigne,* translated by Dawn Eng (Berkeley: University of California Press, 1991);

George Hoffmann, *Montaigne's Career* (Oxford: Clarendon Press, 1998);

François de La Croix du Maine, *Premier volume de la bibliotheque du sieur de la Croix-du Maine* (Paris: Printed by Abel L'Angelier, 1584);

Alain Legros, *Essais sur poutres: Peintures et inscriptions chez Montaigne* (Paris: Klincksieck, 2000);

Géralde Nakam, *Les Essais de Montaigne, Miroir et Procès de leur Temps* (Paris: Nizet, 1984);

Paul Porteau, *Montaigne et la vie pédagogique de son temps* (Paris: Droz, 1935);

François Rigolot, *Les Métamorphoses de Montaigne* (Paris: Presses Universitaires Françaises, 1988);

André Tournon, *Montaigne: La glose et l'essai* (Lyons: Presses Universitaires de Lyon, 1983).

Papers:

Michel de Montaigne's personal copy of the 1588 edition of the *Essais* is at the Bibliothèque municipale de Bordeaux. His correspondence is part of the Collection Payen at the Bibliothèque nationale in Paris.

Bernard Palissy
(1510? – 1590?)

Isabelle Fernbach
University of California, Berkeley

BOOKS: *Architecture, et Ordonnance, de la grotte rustique de Monseigneur le Duc de Montmorancy, Pair & Connestable de France* (La Rochelle: Barthelemy Berthon, 1563);

Recepte veritable par laquelle tous les hommes de la France pourront apprendre à multiplier et augmenter leurs thrésors. Item, ceux qui n'ont jamais eu cognoissance des lettres, pourront apprendre une philosophie nécessaire à tous les habitans de la terre. Item, en ce livre est contenu le dessein d'un jardin autant délectable et d'utile invention qu'il en fut oncques veu. Item, le dessein et ordonnance d'une ville forteresse, la plus imprenable qu'homme ouyt jamais parler (La Rochelle: Barthelemy Berthon, 1563); excerpts translated as *A Delectable Garden*, edited by Helen Morgenthau Fox (New York: The Watch Hill Press, 1931);

Discours admirables, de la nature des eaux et fonteines, tant naturelles qu'artificielles, des métaux, des sels et salines, des pierres, des terres, du feu et des émaux, avec plusieurs autres excellens secrets des choses naturelles. Plus un traité de la marne, fort utile et nécessaire pour ceux qui se mellent de l'agriculture. Le tout dressé par dialogues, esquels sont introduits la théorique et la praticque (Paris: Martin le Jeune, 1580); translated by Aurèle La Rocque as *Admirable Discourses* (Urbana: University of Illinois, 1957).

Editions and Collections: *Le moyen de devenir riche, et la maniere veritable, par laquelle tous les hommes de la France pourront apprendre à multiplier & augmenter leurs thresors & possessions. Avec plusieurs autres excellens secrets des choses naturelles, desquels iusques à present l'on ouy parler* (Paris: R. Foüet, 1636)—comprises revised editions of the *Recepte veritable* and the *Discours admirables*;

Architecture & ordonnance de la grotte rustique de Monseigneur le Duc de Montmorancy. Premier livre du célèbre potier demeuré inconnu, réimprimé d'après l'édition de La Rochelle, 1563 (Paris: D. Morgand, 1919);

Oeuvres de Bernard Palissy: Recepte véritable, edited by Charles Corbière (Strasbourg: Heitz; New York: G. E. Stechert, 1921);

Bernard Palissy; detail from a bronze statue in the courtyard of the National Ceramics Museum in Sèvres (Le Musée national de Ceramique)

Recepte veritable, edited by Keith Cameron (Geneva: Droz, 1988);

Recepte veritable, edited by Frank Lestringant and Christian Barataud (Paris: Macula, collection Argô, 1996);

Discours admirables: de la nature des eaux & fontaines tant naturelles qu'artificielles, des métaux, des sels & salines, . . . le tout dressé par dialogues lesquels sont introduits la théorie & la pratique (Clermont-Ferrand: Paleo, 2000).

Edition in English: *The Admirable Discourses of Bernard Palissy,* translated by Aurèle La Roque (Urbana: University of Illinois Press, 1957).

Bernard Palissy was a protean artist, writer, and naturalist. Celebrated for having rediscovered the lost secret of making enamels and for having brought the art of pottery to perfection, he is best known for the creation of the *rustiques figulines* (rustic ceramics), extravagant glazed potteries representing animals cast from life. His fame as a virtuoso was established by the 1550s, during a period in which he benefited from the protection of two prestigious patrons, the Constable Anne de Montmorency and the queen mother Catherine de Médicis. In his books *Recepte veritable par laquelle tous les hommes de la France pourront apprendre à multiplier et augmenter leurs thrésors* (1563, True Formula, through which all Frenchmen May Learn How to Multiply and Increase Their Treasures; excerpts translated as *A Delectable Garden,* 1931) and *Discours admirables, de la nature des eaux et fontaines, tant naturelles qu'artificielles, des metaux, des sels et salines, des pierres, des terres, du feu et des emaux* (1580, Admirable Discourses on the Nature of Waters and Fountains, Natural as well as Artificial, of Metals, Salts and Salt Marshes, Soils, Fire and Enamels; translated as *Admirable Discourses,* 1957) he places his artistic achievements and naturalistic observations in dialogue with the intellectual debates of his time. These works, which provide rich information about Palissy's life, have also been considered to be precursors of the autobiographical novel in France.

An engaged Huguenot in the turbulent period of the Wars of Religion, Palissy's artistic and literary production is a testimony to the progress of Protestantism in sixteenth-century France. Immortalized by Théodore Agrippa d'Aubigné in his epic poem *Les Tragiques* (1616, The Tragic Ones), Palissy embodied for centuries the romantic figure of a misunderstood genius and martyr of the Catholic repression. His art continues in the twenty-first century to attract the interest of scholars of different disciplines, such as art history, literature, history of science, and archeology.

According to François de Lacroix du Maine in the first volume of his *Les bibliothèques françoises* (1584), Palissy was born around 1510, probably in Agen. Little is known about the first thirty years of his life. The style of his writing indicates a modest social background; Ernest Dupuy in *Bernard Palissy: l'homme, l'artiste, le savant, l'écrivain* (1902, Bernard Palissy: Man, Artist, Savant, Writer) places him among the ranks of the

bourgeoisie, while Leonard N. Amico in *Bernard Palissy: In Search of Earthly Paradise* (1996) characterizes him as a peasant. Palissy spent his youth traveling in southwestern France between the Garonne River, the region of the Landes, and the Basque country. During Palissy's youth, this territory was controlled by Henri d'Albret and Marguerite d'Angoulême, rulers of Navarre, whom Jeanne d'Albret and her son Henri de Bourbon, the future Protestant branch of the royal family, succeeded.

Palissy began working as a glass painter and as a land surveyor. He seems to have become interested in the art of pottery between 1536 and 1539. According to Palissy, his passion for pottery resulted from the glimpse of a cup in majolica, probably brought back from Italy by his friend Antoine de Pons after a stay at the court of Ferrara. Amico has suggested that his earlier work as a land surveyor, and more specifically his later interest in the opulent fauna and flora of the Saintonge region, might have inspired his famous ceramics of animal shapes. The artist settled down in the city of Saintes, on the banks on the Charente River, known for its ceramic trade, and opened a workshop inside the city walls, where he is assumed to have started working in the late 1530s. During this first period of activity, as the artist recalls in his *Discours admirables,* he rediscovered the art of enameling after having burnt his own floor and part of the workshop in 1546.

Palissy's early production included pottery medals copied after metal originals, dinner services, and various portable objects. The year 1556 marks the beginning of a second type of production, the animal-shaped *rustiques figulines,* as the artist named them. Following the life-cast technique of goldsmiths, Palissy deposited a dead animal on the clay mold, from which he made a mold in plaster. He applied the same process to small-sized subjects such as ferns and insects. Palissy's mastery of the art of pottery is confirmed by the purchase of his first rustic basin by Henri II of France. In the same year, the potter began work on the ceramic grotto of the duke Anne de Montmorency, one of the most ambitious commissions of the time. The grotto garden, probably destined for the castle at Ecouen, was left unfinished.

Palissy probably converted to Protestantism during his first period of activity. Although his conversion is not documented, it is known that the potter was acquainted with leading figures of the Reformed religion from the time of his arrival in the Saintonge region. He was particularly close to the printer and minister Philibert Hamelin, to the local Protestant noble Antoine de Pons, and to a group of defrocked priests, whose martyrdom he records in the *Recepte veritable.* According to the same book, Palissy gave his first sermon in 1558 at Saintes in front of a small crowd. His

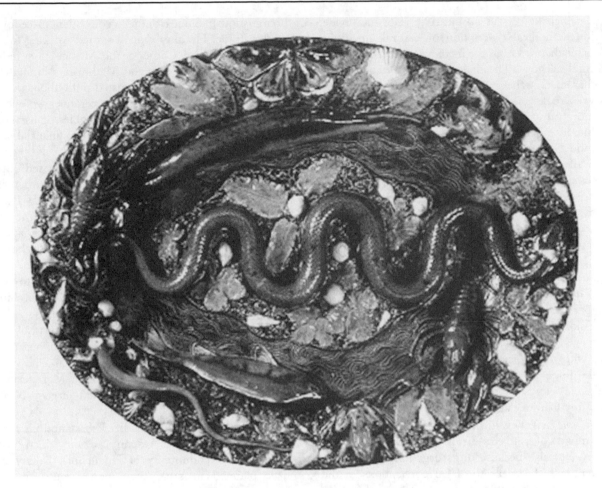

A ceramic plate by Palissy showing how he incorporated molds of natural objects, such as snakes, in his pottery
(Musée national de la Renaissance-Chateau d'Ecouen)

ministry quickly ended, however, after a warrant was issued in 1559 by the Parlement of Guyenne that led to many arrests in the Saintonge region.

Nonetheless, the Catholic repression had not prevented the expansion of Protestantism in the Saintonge where, as Palissy recalls, psalms were sung in streets and fields. The Protestant idyll lasted until the outbreak of the first War of Religion in October 1562, when the troops of Louis II de Bourbon, Duke of Montpensier, took the city. Consequently, the potter was thrown into the prison of Bordeaux, accused of heresy and of having destroyed the paintings of St-Pierre, one of the two churches of Saintes. During his imprisonment he wrote a letter to his patron and protector Montmorency, in which he begged to be set free in order to finish the commission of the grotto garden. Thanks to the intervention of his patron, Palissy was soon released from prison, but his workshop had been sacked and his reputation tarnished.

Immediately after his return to Saintes he published a dialogue: *Architecture, et Ordonnance, de la grotte rustique de Monseigneur le Duc de Montmorancy, Pair & Connestable de France* (1563, Architecture, and Disposition of the Rustic Grotto of His Lordship the Duke of Montmorency, Peer & Constable of France). In this twenty-page booklet, Palissy praises his own enameling talents and describes in great length the project of the grotto garden for the constable. This first work, probably written in his cell, is remarkable for at least three reasons: it is the first work published by the great Protestant printer Barthélémy Berthon; it constitutes the most detailed description of a Renaissance grotto garden; and it illustrates the dependence of a Protestant artist on his Catholic patron.

The same year, right after the Edict of Amboise had marked the end of the first War of Religion, Berthon published what remains Palissy's best-known work, the *Recepte veritable,* a heterogeneous work in which he consecutively adopts the point of view of a teacher, a landscape architect, and an historian. The body of the text is organized in a question-answer form, methodically developing Palissy's observations on nature, which he sees as an incarnation of the divine. Yet, the methodical description of natural life distinguishes his theories from the medieval view of nature as a spiritual allegory. The dialogue takes place between two characters, where "Responce" (Answer) is constantly correcting the mistaken beliefs of "Demande" (Question) on various agricultural matters. The debate is essentially a demonstration of the superiority of practical knowledge over book learning, as well as an illustration of how the Bible and the Book of Nature complement one another. The first part of the *Recepte veritable* deals with the author's considerations on nature, supposedly addressing the peasants and providing them with some basic knowledge of agriculture. The second part describes the plan of an ideal grotto garden, inspired by Psalm 104 and modeled on an Italian garden, intended for the protection of the persecuted Huguenots as well as a pleasure garden for his noble patrons. The third part, "Histoire," recounts the progression of the Reformation in the Saintonge region on the eve of the first War of Religion. The book concludes with the project of a city fortress, or a "plan et modelle d'une Ville la plus imprenable" (plan for an imprenable city), to protect the Huguenot citizens against any Catholic aggression.

Recepte veritable is a complex work not only for its wide range of subjects—from the lazy clerics to alchemy—but also because of its organization into one argument, which recalls the legal conventions of the times. With its militant account of the spread of Calvinism in Saintonge and its focus on the persecutions against the Protestant community, the *Recepte veritable* is traditionally viewed as a pamphleteering work against Catholic authorities. More particularly, different scholars have offered a wide range of interpretations about the specific purpose of the work: to encourage and organize the Huguenot resistance (Amico); to promote Calvinism and project a utopian haven for persecuted Huguenots (Frank Lestringant); to re-create an original golden age following the teaching of nature, whose authority Palissy put next to that of the Bible (Jean Céard).

Tired of living among detractors and enemies, whom he called "mes haineux" (my hateful people), Palissy, in his mid fifties, eventually left Saintes between 1564 and 1567 for Paris, after a short stay in La Rochelle. He seems to have brought his entire family to the French capital except for one of his daughters, Marguerite. Little is known about Palissy's family, other than he did not get along with his wife, to whom he referred as his "second persecution" (the first being his continuous misfortunes at the workshop). He had at least twelve children, six of whom died in childhood. In Paris, Palissy settled outside of the city walls, in the fau-

bourg (suburb) Saint-Honoré, a convenient place for his pottery trade. He immediately started working for the Tuileries grotto of Catherine de Médicis, assisted by two of his sons, Nicolas and Mathurin. Although the queen mother's commission lasted until about the late 1570s and various *rustiques figulines* ceramics were found in the inventory of some Parisian nobles, Palissy does not seem to have enjoyed a satisfactory financial situation.

The new project for the queen was based in part on the plans of the Montmorency grotto garden, but the remnants of the Paris atelier showed that Palissy had made some radical changes to it, such as the addition of figures in classical dress, in order to adapt the garden to a courtly taste, influenced by the school of Fontainebleau as well as the German goldsmith tradition. At the Tuileries workshop Palissy had to work with Philibert Delorme, the queen mother's architect, for whom he had little respect. In the autobiographical passages of his various works, Palissy seems oblivious to the artistic life in Paris. Instead, he was extremely interested in the scientific environment, and he was in close contact with François Choisnyn, Marguerite de Valois's physician, and the renowned surgeon Nicolas Rasse des Noeuds.

In 1573, records show that Palissy and his family moved to Sedan in the Ardennes region, which hosted an important community of Huguenots. Palissy may have planned to settle there permanently since he bought a house near Sedan, which he called "Montpalissy." When and why Palissy left Paris remains a mystery, but the St. Bartholomew's Day Massacre (23–24 August 1572) was an obvious reason for the potter to seek refuge far from the French capital. Palissy continued working on the Tuileries grotto from Sedan, where he opened another studio and worked with members of his family, including his two sons-in-law. Registers of the consistory of Sedan show that the Palissy family was constantly agitated by rather violent quarrels, requiring the intervention of civil authorities.

Leaving the workshop in Sedan to his son-in-law Charlemagne Moreau, Palissy eventually returned to Paris, supposedly in the early 1580s, moving to Saint-Germain-des-Prés, rue de Vaugirard, where he had maintained a base for his activities. Besides his workshop at the Tuileries, he had started in 1575 what he called a "Little Academy," where scientists, physicians, surgeons (such as the famous Ambroise Paré), and even lawyers attended his public lectures on various matters of natural history, medicine, and alchemy. According to Palissy the experience was a success, and he kept lecturing until at least 1584. The content of many of these lectures was summarized in his second book, the *Discours admirables,* which shows Palissy's familiarity with the work of scientists such as Avicenna, Gerolamo Cardano, Raymond Lully, and Guillaume Rondelet. Although published in 1580, part of the *Discours admirables* was probably written in the same year as the *Recepte veritable*.

A detailed account of Palissy's natural theories, the *Discours admirables* can be compared to a manual combining physics, chemistry, geology, agriculture, and alchemy. The discourses recall the *Recepte veritable* since they adopt the form of a dialogue between "Practice" and "Theory," in order to demonstrate with clarity the primacy of empirical knowledge over theory. They also present Palissy's "natural philosophy," based on five principles. The first of these claimed that the natural phenomena of the earth were independent from the other celestial bodies. The second principle holds that the quantity of earthly substances—such as minerals or metals—was fixed by God and could not be altered by human beings, a belief that opposed the alchemists who claimed that gold could be produced from another metal. The third principle proposes that every natural element was subject to a movement of change that, for instance, led the rocks to "grow," without modifying the fixed quantities. The fourth principle posits Palissy's theory of the "womb" of the earth, which he saw as an enclosed and moist place similar to the human uterus. Finally, the potter believed in a "fifth" element, in addition to earth, water, air, and fire, which was a kind of aqueous salt called "generative" water and was compared to man's semen. The book is organized into eleven treatises, among which "Des Sels divers" (On the Different Kinds of Salts), "De l'Art de terre" (On the Art of Earth), and "Des Pierres" (On Stones) are the most famous.

Once again, this period of relative prosperity was interrupted because of Palissy's religious beliefs. After ignoring the 1585 Edict of Nemours, which stated that all Protestants had to abjure their faith or leave the kingdom, Palissy was arrested in December 1586, alongside other refugees of the faubourg Saint-Germain-des-Prés. The Huguenots were ordered to leave France immediately, but because of Palissy's failure to obey, he was arrested again in 1588 and jailed under the accusation of heresy. He was to have been hanged and burnt, but the sentence was appealed against Palissy's will, probably because of the fame he had gained after his former commissions for the queen mother and Montmorency.

The memorialist and court historian Pierre de L'Estoile, who was also Palissy's friend, reports a trick played on the potter, who was unaware of the appeal. Determined to test the faith of his prisoner, Bussy le Clerc, captain of the Bastille, gave Palissy the choice of either walking into the fire or abjuring Protestantism. As Palissy had undressed "tout gaiement" (cheerfully)

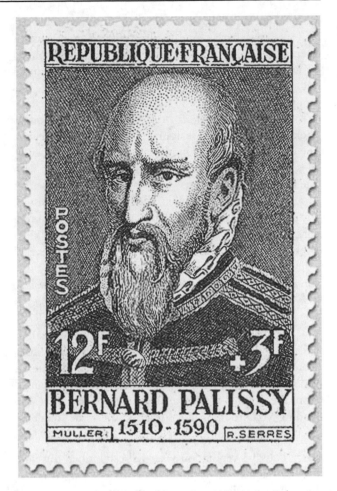

Stamp honoring Palissy (from <http://pluq59.free.fr>)

and was about to set himself on fire, the captain stopped him and, full of respect for the integrity and strength of such a believer, had food and wine sent to his cell until the end of his detention. Palissy appears to have spent another two years in prison at the Bastille, where he died "of misery, need, and poor treatment" at the age of eighty. His corpse was thrown to the dogs.

In the seventeenth century Palissy became a legendary figure. His memory was immortalized by his co-religionist Théodore Agrippa d'Aubigné, first in his *La Confession catholique du Sieur de Sancy* (circa 1600, The Catholique Confession of the Lord of Sancy), and then in *L'Histoire universelle* (1616–1620; revised, 1626; Universal History), in which the author altered the account of the encounter between Palissy and Bussy le Clerc, substituting King Henri III of France for the captain. According to this anecdote, the king visited Palissy in his cell in the Bastille to ask him to abjure, for he could not save a heretic from the stake. Palissy answered the king with the courage of the martyr: "Vous m'avez dit plusieurs fois que vous aviez pitié de moi; et moi j'ai pitié de vous qui m'avez dit ces mots: 'Je suis contraint.' Ce n'est pas parler en roi, sire; et c'est ce que vous-même . . . ne pourrez jamais sur moi; car je sais mourir" (You told me several times that you pitied me; and I pity you who said these words to me: I am forced. It is not to speak as a king, my lord, and it is what you yourself . . . could never do for me; because I know how to die). A third allusion is found in *Les Feux* (The Fires), the fourth book of the *Tragiques,* where d'Aubigné reiterates the comparison between Palissy and Henri III with the famous verse: "France avoit metier que ce potier fût Roy, que ce Roy fût potier" (It was in the interest of France that this potter be a king, that the king be a potter), commenting on the poor political state of the kingdom during the Wars of Religion. In 1636 a revised edition of Palissy's two books appeared under the title *Le moyen de devenir riche, et la maniere veritable, par laquelle tous les hommes de la France pourront apprendre à multiplier & augmenter leurs thresors & possessions* (How to Become Rich, and the True Way for French People to Increase their Wealth and Possessions). All allusions to Protestantism were suppressed, in accordance with the climate of ardent Catholicism under Louis XIII. What remained from the original work was a focus on material wealth, leading Voltaire in 1768 to describe the Little Academy as a "pure quackery."

Palissy's reputation was well established throughout the eighteenth century, and his *Discours admirables* held the scientific interest of René-Antoine Ferchault de Réaumur, the French physicist who invented the alcohol thermometer. The scientist Georges Cuvier even claimed the embryo of geology was to be found in Palissy's works. Since the eighteenth century the intermittent revivals of interest in the artist have stemmed primarily from a romantic curiosity about his life and creations. In the 1850s his rustic ceramics inspired various artists such as Charles-Jean Avisseau, Victor Barbizet, and Georges Pull, known as the Palissystes, who produced creations based on aquatic animals, reptiles, insects, and shells, all traditional subjects used by Palissy for his *rustiques figulines*. More generally, a cult of Palissy developed in the nineteenth century, focusing on the most symbolic aspects of his life, such as the burning of the wooden floor of his house for the making of enamels and his heroic response to the challenge of his warden in the Bastille. Eventually, Palissy became a lay hero and a pioneer of experimental science under the influence of the naturalist movement. In the twentieth century the romanticized image of Palissy began to change thanks to the discovery of new documents on his architectural work, as well as some grotto fragments attributed to the master. Finally in 2002, a pleasure garden identified as the earthly paradise of the *Recepte veritable* was discovered at the castle of Troissereux near Beauvais. These recent discoveries are conjectural, but they keep attracting a growing interest in the potter in the various fields of art history, literature, and theology.

Biographies:

Ferdinand de Lasteyrie, *Bernard Palissy: étude sur sa vie et sur ses oeuvres* (Paris: Pillet Fils Aîné, 1865);

Ernest Dupuy, *Bernard Palissy: l'homme, l'artiste, le savant, l'écrivain* (Paris: Lecène, Oudin et cie, 1894; revised edition, 1902);

Leonard N. Amico, *Bernard Palissy: In Search of Earthly Paradise* (New York & Paris: Flammarion, 1996).

References:

Jean Céard, "Relire Bernard Palissy," *Revue de l'Art,* 78 (1987): 77–83;

Nathalie Z. Davis, "The rites of violence: religious riot in sixteenth-century France," *Past and Present,* 59 (1973): 51–91;

Martin Kemp, "Wrought by No Artist's Hand: The Natural, the Artificial, the Exotic, and the Scientific in Some Artifacts from the Renaissance," in *Reframing the Renaissance: Visual Culture in Europe and Latin America 1450–1650,* edited by Claire Farago (New Haven: Yale University Press, 1995), pp. 176–196;

Frank Lestringant, "Le Prince et le Potier: introduction à la 'Recepte veritable' de Bernard Palissy (1563)," in *Nouvelle revue du seizième siècle,* 3 (1985): 5–24;

Lestringant, ed., *Actes du colloque Bernard Palissy (1510–1590): l'écrivain, le réformé, le céramiste* (Amis d'Agrippa d'Aubigné: Mont-de-Marsan, 1992);

Frank Rolland, "Le Château et le jardin de Troissereux," in <http://thierry.jouet.free.fr/Sommaire/troissereux.htm>.

Ambroise Paré

(1510 or 1517? – 20 December 1590)

Marie-Thérèse Noiset
University of North Carolina at Charlotte

BOOKS: *La Methode de traicter les playes faictes par hacque-*
butes et aultres bastons à feu: Et de celles qui sont faictes
par fleches, dardz, et semblables: Aussy des combustions
specialement faictes par la pouldre à canon (Paris:
Printed by Vivant Gaulterot, 1545); revised as *La*
Maniere de traicter les playes faictes tant par harquebutes,
que par fleches: Et les accidentz d'icelles, comme fractures
et caries des os, gangrene et mortification: Avec les pourtra-
ictz des instrumentz necessaires pour leur curation. Et la
methode de curer les combustions principalement faictes par
la pouldre à canon (Paris: Printed by Veuve Jean de
Brie, 1551); revised as *Dix livres de la chirurgie, avec*
le magasin des instruments necessaires à icelle (Paris:
Printed by Jean le Royer, 1564); translated by
Walter Hammond as *The Method of Curing Wounds*
Made by Gun-shot. Also by Arrowes and Darts, with
Their Accidents (London: Printed by Isaac Jaggard,
1617);

Briefve collection de ladministration anatomique: Avec la maniere
de conjoindre les os: Et d'extraire les enfans tant mors que
vivans du ventre de la mere, lors que nature de soy ne
peult venir à son effet (Paris: Printed by Guillaume
Cavellat, 1549); revised by Paré and Isnard Rostan de Binosque as *Anatomie universelle du corps*
humain, composée par A. Paré Chirurgien ordinaire du
Roy, et juré à Paris: Reveuë & augmentee par ledit
autheur avec I. Rostaing du Bignosc Provençal aussi chi-
rurgien juré à Paris (Paris: Printed by Jehan le
Royer, 1561);

La Methode curative des playes, et fractures de la teste humaine:
Avec les pourtraicts des instruments necessaires pour la
curation d'icelles (Paris: Printed by Jehan le Royer,
1561);

Traicté de la peste, de la petite verolle et rougeolle: Avec une
bresve description de la lepre (Paris: Printed by André
Wechel, 1568); translated as *A Treatise of The Plague,*
Contayning the Causes, Signes, Symptomes, Prognosticks, and
Cure thereof. Together with sundry other remarkable pas-
sages (for the prevention of, and preservation from the Pes-
tilence) never yet published by anie man (London:
Printed by R. Y. & R. C., 1630);

Ambroise Paré *(from* <*http://en.wikipedia.org*>*)*

Cinq livres de chirurgie: I. des bandages; II. des fracteures; III.
des luxations, avec une apologie touchant les Harque-
bousades; IV. des morsures et picqueures venimeuses; V.
des goustes (Paris: Printed by Chr. Wechel, 1572);

Deux livres de chirurgie: I. De la generation de l'homme, et
maniere d'extraire les enfans hors du ventre de la mere,
ensemble ce qu'il faut faire pour la faire mieux, et plus tost
accoucher, avec la cure de plusieurs maladies qui luy peu-
vent survenir. 2. Des monstres tant terrestres que marins,
avec leurs portrais. Plus un petit traité des plaies faites aux
parties nerveuses (Paris: Printed by André Wechel,
1573);

Les Oeuvres de M. Ambroise Paré Conseiller et Premier Chirurgien du Roy: Avec les figures et portraicts tant de l'anatomie que des instruments de chirurgie et de plusieurs Monstres. Le tout divisé en vingt-six livres, comme il est contenu en la page suyvante (Paris: Printed by Gabriel Buon, 1575); revised and enlarged as *Les Oeuures d'Ambroise Paré Conseiller et Premier Chirurgien du Roy, divisées en vingt sept Liures, auec les figures & portraicts, tant de l'anatomie que des instruments de chirurgie & de plusieurs monstres. Reueuz & augmentez par l'autheur, pour la seconde edition* (Paris: Printed by Gabriel Buon, 1579); enlarged as *Les Oeuvres d'Ambroise Paré, conseiller et premier chirurgien du roy, divisées en vingt-huict livres, avec les figures et portraicts, tant de l'anatomie, que des instruments de chirurgie, et de plusieurs monstres. Reveuës et augmentees par l'autheur. Quatriesme edition* (Paris: Printed by G. Buon, 1585); revised and enlarged as *Les Oeuvres d'Ambroise Paré* (Paris: Printed by G. Buon, 1585); translated by Thomas Johnson as *The Workes of that famous Chirurgion Ambrose Parey translated out of Latine and compared with the French* (London: Printed by T. Cotes & R. Young, 1634);

Responce De M. Ambroise Paré, premier chirurgien du roy, aux calomnies d'aucuns medecins, & chirurgiens, touchant ses oeuvres (Paris, 1575?);

Discours D'Ambroise Paré, Conseiller et Premier Chirurgien du Roy: A sçavoir, de la mumie, de la licorne, des venins, et de la peste. Avec une table des plus notables matieres contenues esdit discours (Paris: Printed by Gabriel Buon, 1582);

Replique D'Ambroise Paré, Premier Chirurgien du Roy, a la response faicte contre son Discours de la licorne (Paris: Printed by Gabriel Buon, 1584).

Collection: *Oeuvres complètes d'Ambroise Paré revues et collationnées sur toutes les editions, avec les variantes; ornées de 217 planches et du portrait de l'auteur; accompagnées de notes historiques et critiques; et précédées d'une introduction sur l'origine et les progrès de la chirurgie en occident du sixième au seizième siècle, et sur la vie et les ouvrages D'Ambroise Paré,* edited by Joseph-François Malgaigne (Paris: J. B. Baillière, 1841).

Editions in English: *Journeys in Diverse Places,* translated by Stephen Paget (New York: Putnam, 1897);

The Apologie and Treatise of Ambroise Paré, Containing the Voyages Made into Divers Places with Many of His Writings upon Surgery, edited by Geoffrey Keynes (Chicago: University of Chicago Press, 1952).

Called the "Father of Modern Surgery," Ambroise Paré is particularly recognized for the techniques that he pioneered to treat battlefield wounds. One of his main innovations was the ligature of arteries to prevent hemorrhages after amputations, a procedure

that was known in theory but had never been implemented. As official surgeon to four kings of France, Paré wrote many surgical and medical treatises that were highly esteemed in his time. In 1575 he published his collected works under the title *Les Oeuvres de M. Ambroise Paré Conseiller et Premier Chirurgien du Roy: Avec les figures et portraicts tant de l'anatomie que des instruments de chirurgie et de plusieurs Monstres. Le tout divisé en vingt-six livres, comme il est contenu en la page suyvante* (The Works of Mr. Ambroise Paré, Counselor and First Surgeon of the King, with Drawings and Pictures of Anatomy as Well as of Surgical Instruments and of Several Monsters. The Entire Work is Divided into Twenty-Six Books, as Described on the Following Page; translated as *The Workes of that famous Chirurgion Ambrose Parey translated out of Latine and compared with the French,* 1634). His works were translated into Latin, English, German, and Dutch; parts of them were even translated into Japanese. They remained popular until the end of the seventeenth century.

Little is known about Paré's childhood and adolescence; even the date and place of his birth are shrouded in mystery. Joseph-François Malgaigne, the editor of an 1841 edition of his works and his most reliable biographer, believes that Paré was born in Bourg-Hersent in 1517. But the chronicler Pierre de L'Estoile, who lived in Paré's time, says that he died on 20 December 1590 at the age of eighty, which would make 1510 his year of birth. Paré himself gives Laval as his hometown at the beginning of his collected works.

According to some early sources, Paré's father was a jewel-case maker; according to others, he was a barber-surgeon attached to the house of the Count of Laval. Paré had at least two brothers: one was a jewel-case maker in Paris, the other a surgeon in Vitré, Brittany. He also had a sister, who was married to a Paris surgeon.

An unconfirmed anecdote relates that as a youth Paré was entrusted to a chaplain to learn Latin but only learned to care for the chaplain's mule and garden. Another story reports that Paré decided on his vocation after witnessing a successful surgical operation in Laval. Paré says that he studied surgery for nine or ten years, four of them in Paris. He arrived in Paris in 1532 or 1533 and probably worked for a time as a barber's apprentice and attended public lectures that doctors from the Faculté de Médecine (School of Medicine) of the University of Paris gave for apprentice surgeons. The apprentices could not read medical textbooks, which were in Latin; but the doctors lectured in French, basing their teachings on Galen's books on surgery, as well as on the popular treatises of Guy de Chauliac. Medical books were beginning to appear in French, and Paré says that he read Jean de Vigo's work in French

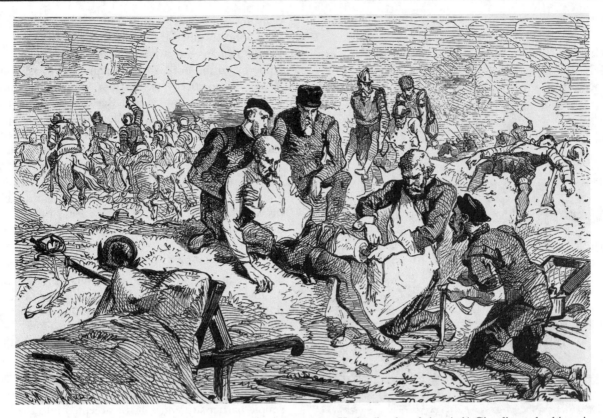

Paré on the battlefield, inventing the ligature of arteries after an amputation. He describes the technique in his Cinq livres de chirurgie
(Five Books on Surgery), published in 1572 (Jacques Boyer/Roger-Viollet/Getty Images).

during his early days in Paris. Soon after his arrival in Paris, Paré began working at the Hôtel-Dieu, the old hospital for indigent patients. In "Avis au lecteur" (To the Reader) in his collected works he proudly recalls that his internship at the hospital allowed him to see every sort of ill that can befall the human body. His stay at the Hôtel-Dieu also gave him, he says, ample opportunities to dissect human bodies, thus allowing him to learn the finer points of anatomy. After passing an examination given by doctors of the Faculté de Médecine, Paré was officially received as a master barber-surgeon around 1536.

In 1537 Paré accompanied Marshal of France René de Montjean to northern Italy, where the French king François I was battling Holy Roman Emperor Charles V. During that campaign he proved erroneous the medical belief that gunshot wounds were poisoned by gunpowder and had to be cauterized with boiling oil. He describes the discovery in his first book, *La Methode de traicter les playes faictes par hacquebutes et aultres bastons à feu: Et de celles qui sont faictes par fleches, dardz, et semblables: Aussy des combustions specialement faictes par la pouldre à canon* (1545, Method of Treating Wounds Inflicted by Harquebuses and Other Firearms: And of Those Made by Arrows, Spears, and Similar Weapons: Also about Burns Made by Gunpowder): the battle had created so

many victims that he ran out of cauterizing oil. Fearing that his patients whose wounds had not been cauterized would be dead in the morning, he could hardly sleep, but he was pleasantly surprised to find them faring better than those who had received the agonizing oil treatment. The book is the first monograph ever written on the treatment of gunshot wounds.

Paré married Jeanne Mazelin in 1541. They had several children, but only one, Catherine, lived to adulthood. In 1543 Paré accompanied René, Viscount of Rohan, to the battle of Perpignan. During that campaign Paré found a way to locate a bullet in a victim's body by asking the patient to assume the position he was in when he was hit.

Between 1543 and 1551 Paré performed dissections for the physicians of the Faculté de Médecine who taught anatomy. This experience led him to write *Briefve collection de ladministration anatomique: Avec la maniere de conjoindre les os: Et d'extraire les enfans tant mors que vivans du ventre de la mere, lors que nature de soy ne peult venir à son effet* (1549, Short Exposé on Anatomy: With the Way to Put Bones Back Together: And to Extract Children Dead as Well as Alive from the Mother's Womb, When Nature by Herself Is Not Effective). The book includes an elaborate discussion of anatomy based on Paré's own observations, as well as on Jehann Canappe's 1541 translation of

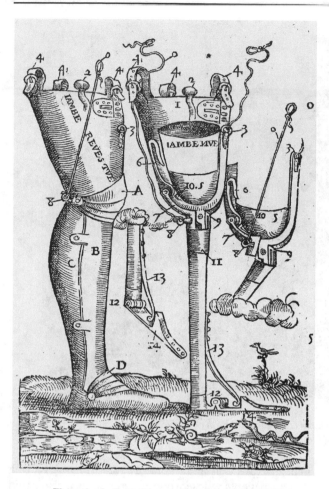

Illustration by Paré of the operation of an artificial leg
(Jacques Boyer/Roger-Viollet/Getty Images)

the works of Galen and on a 1545 book on anatomy by Paré's fellow surgeon Etienne de La Rivière. Paré notes that although much of his discussion is derived from the two earlier works, everything he says was tested with his own scalpel. The book also sketches a treatise on birth that Paré completed later. The volume had just been sent to the printer when he was called to the siege of Boulogne.

Paré was sought out in 1551 by Antoine de Bourbon, Duke of Vendôme, the future king of Navarre, to accompany him on a campaign against Spain in Picardy. Afterward, on the duke's recommendation, Henri II named Paré one of his regular surgeons. The king sent Paré to treat the wounded troops of François, second Duke of Guise, at the siege of Metz in 1552.

In 1552 Paré published a revised edition of his treatise on wounds. Dedicated to King Henri II, it discusses the damage done by bullets not only to flesh but also to bones. The new edition includes a treatise on gangrene, as well as illustrations of the various tools used by the surgeon and of prostheses—many of Paré's

own invention—that could replace amputated body parts. Shortly after the publication of the book, Paré joined Rohan on two swift campaigns against the emperor on the border of Germany and Luxembourg. There he practiced for the first time the ligature of arteries after an amputation. Recounting the outcome of this treatment in his "Apologie touchant les playes faites par harquebuzes" (Apology on the Subject of Wounds Inflicted by Harquebuses), included in his *Cinq livres de chirurgie* (1572, Five Books on Surgery), he says, "Je le pensay, et Dieu le guarist" (I dressed his wounds, and God cured him). He repeats this phrase throughout his works, practically every time he tells of his care of a desperately wounded man bringing about a happy resolution.

In 1553 Paré was taken prisoner by the imperial army at the siege of Hesdin in northern France. Citing his loyalty to his king, he rejected a tempting offer from the emperor's surgeon to work for the enemy. Paré's successful treatment of an important member of the imperial army bought him his freedom while Henri II was negotiating to pay his ransom.

Le Collège de St. Côme was a brotherhood of surgeons who considered themselves superior to the simple barber-surgeons. To be accepted into the brotherhood, surgeons had to meet strict requirements, one of which was to know Latin. But they were eager to count among their members a surgeon who enjoyed the favor of the king; therefore, in spite of his rudimentary knowledge of Latin, Paré was inducted as Master in Surgery on 18 December 1554. The king sent him to treat wounds at the battle of St.-Quentin in 1557 and at the siege of Amiens in 1558.

After Henri II died from a wound to the eye in a jousting tournament in 1559, Paré became the regular surgeon of his son, François II and of Charles IX, who succeeded his brother François in 1560. *La Methode curative des playes, et fractures de la teste humaine: Avec les pourtraicts des instruments necessaires pour la curation d'icelles* (1561, The Curative Method of Wounds and Fractures of the Human Head, with Drawings of the Instruments Used in Their Treatment), the first book to carry Paré's title of *Chirurgien ordinaire du Roy et juré à Paris* (Regular Surgeon of the King, Sworn in Paris), discusses the anatomy of the head, fractures of the skull, and wounds of the face, ears, eyes, nose, and mouth. Also in 1561 Paré and his friend and colleague Isnard Rostan de Binosque revised *Briefve collection de ladministration anatomique* as *Anatomie universelle du corps humain* (Universal Anatomy of the Human Body). Paré acknowledges in the introduction that the work owes much to Andreas Vesalius's *De Corporis Humani Fabrica* (1543, On the Structure of the Human Body), which had been translated into French in 1559. *Anatomie universelle du corps humain* was widely used by surgeons well into the seventeenth century.

After caring for many wounded noblemen at the siege of Rouen in 1564, Paré was named first surgeon of the king. That same year he published a third revised edition of his treatise on gunshot wounds, *Dix livres de la chirurgie, avec le magasin des instruments necessaires à icelle* (Ten Books on Surgery, with a Collection of Surgical Instruments), which includes three new books on urology and Paré's first description of the use of the ligature in amputations. This volume borrows from the writings of the physician Laurent Colot, as well as from the works of Paré's fellow surgeons Thierry de Hery—his closest friend—and Pierre Franco. Paré acknowledged his debt to them in the 1575 edition of his collected works.

Paré spent most of the next two years accompanying the young king on a trip through his provinces, during which they developed a lasting friendship. When they returned to Paris, syphilis was ravaging the population. Paré's experiences treating the victims led him to write *Traicté de la peste, de la petite verolle et rougeolle: Avec une bresve description de la lepre* (1568, Treatise of the Plague, Syphilis and Measles: With a Brief Description of Leprosy; translated as *A Treatise of The Plague, Contayning the Causes, Signes, Symptomes, Prognosticks, and Cure thereof. Together with sundry other remarkable passages [for the prevention of, and preservation from the Pestilence] never yet published by anie man*, 1630). Difficulties he encountered on the publication of this book gave the first hint of the problems that later multiplied because of Paré's unusually successful career: the Faculté de Médecine, led by Etienne Gourmelen, was envious of Paré's enormous popularity and began scrutinizing his work and objecting to his discussions of topics that they said were the domain of physicians, rather than of surgeons. In 1569 a member of the Faculté de Médecine, Julien Le Paulmier, published a book that plagiarized Paré's work while at the same time attacking his method of treating wounds and blaming him for the loss of many men on the battlefield. This accusation prompted Paré to write "Apologie touchant les playes faites par harquebuzes," in which he defends his methods of treating the wounded, denounces Le Paulmier's plagiarisms, and condemns the latter's antiquated therapeutics. The remainder of the volume *Cinq livres de chirurgie* discusses tumors, wounds, and dislocations.

In 1569 civil war was raging in France between Catholics and Protestants, and Paré dressed wounds and repaired limbs at the Battle of Moncontour. For a time he was suspected of being a Huguenot, and the memoirs of Pierre de Bourdeille, Seigneur de Brantôme, affirm that Charles IX spared his surgeon from the St. Bartholomew's Day Massacre in 1572; but the claim

has never been proven. The doctors' hatred of Paré became more intense, and a pamphlet bearing the initials of a barber's apprentice but obviously written by Le Paulmier heaped insults and criticisms on him. Paré chose not to respond to the attacks, and the pamphlet was soon forgotten.

In 1573 Paré began putting together his collected works. He also published *Deux livres de chirurgie* (Two Books on Surgery), which includes the chapters "De la génération de l'homme" (Of Human Conception) and "Des Monstres" (Of Monsters). That same year his wife died, and he married again. The second marriage, to Jacqueline Rousselet, produced five children, of whom only two daughters survived to adulthood.

When Charles IX died in 1574, Paré became first surgeon to Henri III, who elevated him to even higher honors as a personal counselor. At that time Paré's refusal to take part in certain dishonest dealings of the surgeons to improve the status of their profession made him enemies among his colleagues. The success of his collected works in 1575 aroused the envy of several doctors, who again accused Paré of discussing subjects that belonged to medicine alone. He replied in the pamphlet *Responce De M. Ambroise Paré, premier chirurgien du roy, aux calomnies d'aucuns medecins, & chirurgiens, touchant ses oeuvres* (1575? Response of Mr. Ambroise Paré, First Surgeon of the King, to the Calumnies of Certain Doctors and Surgeons, Concerning His Writings). In 1579 a revised edition of the *Oeuvres* included an added treatise, "Des animaux et de l'excellence de l'homme" (Of Animals and of the Excellence of Man).

In 1582 Paré published *Discours D'Ambroise Paré, Conseiller et Premier Chirurgien du Roy: A sçavoir, de la mumie, de la licorne, des venins, et de la peste. Avec une table des plus notables matieres contenues esdit discours* (Discourse of Ambroise Paré, Counselor and First Surgeon of the King: On the Mummy, on the Unicorn Horn, on Venoms, and on the Plague. With a Table of Contents of the Most Worthy Subjects Included in this Discourse), in which he refutes the age-old beliefs in the healing properties of mummies and unicorn horns. Based on the works of the Italian physicians Andrea Marini and Andrea Bacci, Paré's text is written in simple language for the general public. In his dedication to Christophe Jouvenel des Ursins, the governor of Paris, Paré says that he wrote the work after a nobleman he had successfully treated for a complicated injury asked him why he had not prescribed mummy: the dried skin and flesh of mummies mixed with water was widely believed to be a powerful remedy against many injuries; Paré vigorously opposed this notion. Even at that late date Paré's authority was still questioned, but without success. An anonymous pamphlet, *Response au discours d'Ambroise Paré, touchant l'usage de la licorne* (Response to

Postage stamp honoring Paré (from <http://pluq59.free.fr>)

Journeys Made into Diverse Places) in the 1585 edition of the *Oeuvres* is Paré's definitive response to his detractors. He demonstrates the validity of his techniques and shows once and for all that his experience on the battlefield, combined with his copious reading, makes him much better suited to write about medical matters than his armchair colleagues who know Latin. Ambroise Paré's collected works were published in four separate editions during his lifetime, were translated into Latin in 1582, spread throughout Europe in vernacular translations, and became, as Malgaigne puts it, "le code de la chirurgie" (the code of surgery).

Bibliographies:

Stephen Paget, *Ambroise Paré and His Times 1510–1590* (London: Putnam, 1899);

Janet Doe, *A Bibliography of the Works of Ambroise Paré*, (Chicago: University of Chicago Press, 1986).

Biographies:

Jeanne Carbonnier, *A Barber-Surgeon: A Life of Ambroise Paré, Founder of Modern Surgery* (New York: Pantheon, 1965);

Wallace Hamby, *Ambroise Paré: Surgeon of the Renaissance* (St. Louis: Warren H. Green, 1967);

Paule Dumaître, *Ambroise Paré: Chirurgien de quatre rois de France* (Paris: Perrin, 1986).

References:

Pierre de Bourdeille, Seigneur de Brantôme, *Mémoires*, 8 volumes (Leiden: Printed by J. Sambix, 1665–1666);

Pierre de L'Estoile, *Mémoires pour servir à l'histoire de France: Contenant ce qui s'est passé de plus remarquable dans ce royaume depuis 1574 jusqu'en 1611. Avec les portraits des Rois, Reines, Princes, Princesses & autres personnes illustres dont il y est fait mention*, 2 volumes, edited by Jean Godefroy (Cologne [i.e., Brussels]: Printed by the heirs of Herman Demen, 1719);

Francis R. Packard, *Life and Times of Ambroise Paré (1510–1590) with a New Translation of His Apology and an Account of His Journeys in Divers Places* (New York: P. B. Hoeber, 1921; London: Oxford University Press, 1922).

the Discourse of Ambroise Paré, Concerning the Use of Unicorn Horn) sought to discredit him, but to no avail. In 1584 Paré published a brilliant *Replique D'Ambroise Paré, Premier Chirurgien du Roy, a la response faicte contre son Discours de la licorne* (Reply of Ambroise Paré, First Surgeon of the King, to the Response Given against His Unicorn Treatise).

Paré's adversaries were unable to stifle the success of the *Oeuvres*. A book by Gourmelen published in 1580 criticized the use of the ligature in amputations. The revised "Apologie, et Traité contenant les voyages faits en divers lieux" (Apology, and Treatise Containing the

Jacques Peletier du Mans

(25 July 1517 – July or August 1582)

Mary Santina

BOOKS: *Arithmeticae practicae methodus facilis, per gemmam frisium, medicum et mathematicum* (Paris: Printed by Jean-Louis Tiletan & Thomas Richard, 1545);

Les Œuvres poetiques de Jacques Peletier du Mans (Paris: Printed by Michel de Vascosan, Galiot du Pré & Gilles Corrozet, 1547);

L'Arithemetique de Jacques Peletier du Mans departie en quatre livres à Theodore Debesze (Poitiers: Printed by Jean & Enguilbert de Marnef, 1549);

Dialogue de l'Ortografe e Prononciation francoese, departi an deus livres par Jacques Peletier du Mans: Moins e Meilheur (Poitiers: Printed by Jean & Enguilbert de Marnef, 1550);

L'Algèbre de Jaques Peletier du Mans, departie an deus livres (Lyon: Printed by Jean de Tournes, 1554);

Enseignemens de vertu au petit seigneur Timoléon de Cossé (Lyon: Printed by Jean de Tournes, 1554);

L'Amour des Amours et Vers liriques (Lyon: Printed by Jean de Tournes, 1555);

L'Art poetique de Jacques Peletier du Mans departi an deus livres (Lyon: Printed by Jean de Tournes & Guillaume Gazeau, 1555);

Exhortation pacificatoria ad christianos principes Carolum V et Henricum II (Lyon: Printed by Jean de Tournes, 1555); translated into French by Peletier as *Exhortation à la paix* (Paris: Printed by André Wechel, 1558);

Discours non plus mélancoliques que divers de choses mesmement qui appartiennent à notre France, et à la fin la manière de bien et justement entoucher les lucs et les guiternes (Poitiers: Printed by Enguilbert de Marnef, 1556 or 1557);

Jacobi Peletarii Cenomani in Euclidis Elementa Geometrica Demonstrationum Libri sex (Lyon: Printed by Jean de Tournes & Guillaume Gazeau, 1557);

Jacobi Peletarii Cenomani De occulta parte numerorum quam Algebram vocant libri duo (Paris: Printed by Guillaume Cavellat, 1560);

Jacobi Peletarii Cenomani De Conciliatione Locorum Galeni sectiones duae (Paris: Printed by André Wechel, 1560);

Jacobi Peletarii Medici et Mathematici De Peste compendium (Basel: Printed by Johannes Oporinus, circa 1563);

De Contactu linearum commentarium, suivi De constitutione Horoscopi commentarium (Basel: Printed by Johannes Oporinus, 1563);

Jacobi Peletarii Medici et Mathematici Disquisitiones Geometricae (Lyon: Printed by Jean de Tournes, 1567);

La Savoye de Jacques Peletier du Mans: A Très illustre Princesse Marguerite de France Duchesse de Savoye et de Berry (Annecy: Printed by Jaques Bertrand, 1572);

Jacobi Peletarii Medici et Mathematici de usu Geometriae liber unus (Paris: Printed by E. Gourbin, 1572);

De L'usage de Geometrie, par Jaques Peletier, Medecin et Mathematicien (Paris: Printed by E. Gourbin, 1573);

Jacobi Peletarii Medici et Mathematici Oratio Pictavii habita in praelectiones Mathematicas (Poitiers: Printed by J. & G. Bouchet, 1579);

Jacobi Peletarii Medici et Mathematici in Christophorum Clavium de Contactu Linearum Apologia: Ejusdem demonstrationes tres (Paris: Printed by Hiérosme de Marnef & Guillaume Cavellat, 1579);

Jacobi Peletarii Medici et Mathematici In Mauricium Bressium Apologia (Paris: Printed by J. Richer, 1580);

Euvres poetiques, intituleez Louanges avec quelques autres ecriz du meme non encore publiés (Paris: Printed by R. Coulombel, 1581);

De Contactu linearum Commentarius (Paris: Printed by R. Coulombel, 1581).

Editions and Collections: *L'Algèbre de Jaques Peletier du Mans, departie an deus livres* (Lyon: Printed by Jean de Tournes, 1609);

Œuvres poetiques de Jacques Peletier du Mans, publié d'après l'édition originale de 1547, edited by Léon Séché and Paul Laumonier (Paris: Revue de la Renaissance, 1904);

"Discours de J. Peletier du Mans, 1579," edited by Laumonier, *Revue de la Renaissance*, 5 (October–December 1904): 281–303;

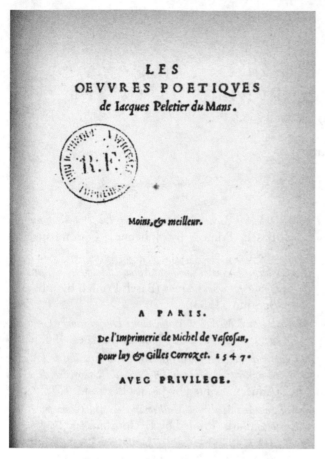

LES
OEVVRES POETIQVES
de Iacques Peletier du Mans.

Moins, & meilleur.

A PARIS.

De l'Imprimerie de Michel de Vascosan,
pour luy & Gilles Corrozet. 1 5 4 7.

AVEC PRIVILEGE.

Title page for the first collection of the poems of Jacques Peletier du Mans (from Les Œuvres poetiques de Jacques Peletier du Mans: Reproduction photographique, *edited by Marcel Françon, 1958; Thomas Cooper Library, University of South Carolina)*

L'Art Poëtique de Jacques Peletier du Mans (1555), edited by André Boulanger (Paris: Société d'Edition Les Belles Lettres, 1930);

Les Œuvres poetiques de Jacques Peletier du Mans: Reproduction photographique, introduction by Marcel Françon (Rochecorbon: Charles Gay, 1958);

Dialogue de l'ortografe e prononciation françoese, departí an deus liures par Iacques Peletier du Mans (Geneva: Slatkine, 1964);

L'Amour des Amours, edited by Jean-Charles Monferran (Paris: Société des Textes Français Modernes, 1996).

TRANSLATIONS: Horace, *L'Art poëtique d'Horace translaté de latin en rithme françoyse* (Paris: Printed by Jean Granjehan, 1541);

Horace, *L'Art Poëtique d'Horace, traduit en vers François* (N.p., 1544); republished as *L'Art Poëtique d'Horace, traduit en vers François par Jacques Peletier du Mans,*

recongnu par l'auteur depuis la première impression (Paris: Printed by Michel de Vascosan, 1545);

Homer, *Premier et second livre de l'Odissée d'Homère* (Paris: Printed by Claude Garnier, 1571); revised in *Homère, Les XXIV livres de l'Iliade . . . trad. H. Salel et A. Jamyn et Premier et Second Livre de l'Odyssée d'Homère par Jacques Peletier du Mans, reveu et corrigé de nouveau depuis la dernière édition* (Paris: Printed by Brayer, 1577);

Euclid, *Euclidis Elementorum Libri XV: Graece et Latine* (Paris: Printed by Hiérosme de Marnef & Guillaume Cavellat, 1573);

Carmen de moribus, cum ex distichis Catoni vulgo tributis, tum ex aliis probatioribus poetis collectum: Vers moraux recueillis en partie des distiques vulgairement attribuez à Caton et principallement des autres poëtes plus approuvez (Paris: Printed by R. Coulombel, 1583).

As evidenced by his interest in many diametrically opposed topics, the diversity of his published works, his strong desire to travel, and his passion for learning, Jacques Peletier (or Pelletier) du Mans was representative of the many inquisitive and creative scholars who appeared in Renaissance France. He was a poet, a student of law, a grammarian of Latin and French, a physician, and a mathematician. He is not regarded as a key literary figure, nor was his talent as a poet particularly admired during his lifetime; but he did have a strong influence on several major Renaissance figures and did contribute to sixteenth-century French humanist endeavors. Despite a sulky and solemn personality, he was well liked and counted among his friends Pierre de Ronsard and other Pléiade poets, several poets of L'Ecole Lyonnaise (the School of Lyon), and the essayist Michel de Montaigne.

Peletier was born to a prosperous and respected family in Le Mans, the capital of the Maine region, on 25 July 1517. He was the ninth of fifteen children of Pierre Peletier, a lawyer, and Jeanne Peletier, née Le Royer. Three of his brothers (two of whom were named Jean) became clergymen; two others became lawyers; little is known about his sisters. When he was twelve, Peletier went to Paris to study religion under his older brother Jean, a renowned theologian and professor of mathematics and philosophy at the College of Navarre. He then left Paris and completed more than five years of legal studies—perhaps with his brother Victor, a lawyer and seneschal of Maine. But he decided against a legal career and undertook several other academic projects, including his first studies of mathematics and Greek. In 1536, with Jean's assistance, he obtained a post teaching philosophy at the College of Navarre. At this time he began studying medicine; he continued these studies until 1540 but did not complete his degree

until twenty years later. While teaching at the College of Navarre he became a visitor at court and met Marguerite de Navarre, sister of King François I of France; there he also met such prominent figures as Clément Marot, Mellin de Saint-Gelais, and Théodore de Bèze.

In 1540 Peletier became secretary to Bishop René du Bellay in Le Mans. While serving in this position, he became interested in orthography and created a system of spelling that he used for much of the rest of his life, even though it received much criticism and scorn, and he had a difficult time finding publishers who would print his works in his unique orthography. The negative reaction did not deter him, although it did add to his bitter nature. Also during this time he began writing essays and translating Horace's *Ars poetica* (The Art of Poetry), Homer's *Odyssey,* and Virgil's *Georgics* into French verse. His first published work was *L'Art poëtique d'Horace translaté de latin en rithme françoyse* (1541, Horace's Art of Poetry Translated from the Latin into French Verse).

On 5 March 1543 Peletier met Ronsard, a relative of the bishop, at the funeral of another relative, Captain Guillaume du Bellay; Ronsard was tonsured by Bishop Du Bellay the following day. Peletier may also have met the poet Joachim du Bellay at the funeral. Ronsard, who was seven years younger than Peletier, adopted many of Peletier's poetic principles and included Peletier in his list of excellent French poets. Ronsard became significantly better known than Peletier, but the disparity in their fame did not prevent their friendship from enduring throughout their lives.

On 6 November 1543 Peletier was named director of the College of Bayeux in Paris. In 1544 he published another verse translation of the *Ars Poetica;* in the preface to this translation, of which the earliest known extant edition is dated 1545, he enunciates the tenets that are at the core of Joachim du Bellay's *Deffence et Illustration de la Langue Francoyse* (1549; translated as *The Defence and Illustration of the French Language,* 1939). In 1545 he published *Arithmeticae practicae methodus facilis, per gemmam frisium, medicum et mathematicum* (Practical and Easy Method of Arithmetic Based on That of Gemma Frisius, Physician and Mathematician).

Peletier may have met Joachim du Bellay for the first time in 1546, and not at the funeral of Captain Du Bellay. In any case, at this time they established a lifelong friendship. In the preface to the second edition (1550) of his *L'Olive et quelques autres oeuvres poëticques* (1549, The Olive and Other Poetic Works), Du Bellay notes that Peletier persuaded him to write sonnets and odes, forms that were not widely used by French poets at the time.

Les Œuvres poetiques de Jacques Peletier du Mans (The Poetic Works of Jacques Peletier du Mans) appeared in

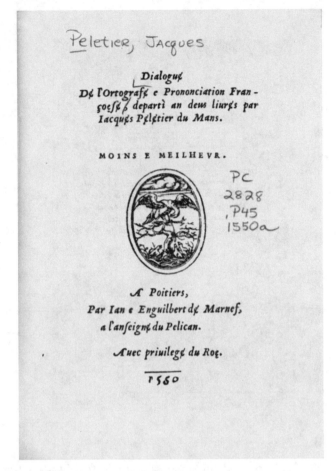

Title page for the book in which Peletier defended his unconventional system of French spelling, which was widely criticized and was rejected by all but one of the printers of his works (from Dialogue de l'ortografe e prononciation françoese, departían deus liures par Iacques Peletier du Mans, *1964; Thomas Cooper Library, University of South Carolina)*

1547. Peletier's use of the sonnet form and of a variety of meters, from hexasyllables to alexandrines, as well as his stanza combinations, were echoed on a grand scale a few years later by the poets of the Pléiade. His sonnets inaugurated the ABBA ABBA CCD EDE scheme that is still prevalent in French poetry. In addition to Peletier's own sonnets, epigrams, and odes, the collection includes the first published verses of Ronsard and Du Bellay.

In February 1547 Peletier delivered an elegy at Notre Dame Cathedral for King Henry VIII of England. On 18 March he resigned as director of the College of Bayeux. He later explained in his *Dialogue de l'Ortografe e Prononciation francoese, departi an deus livres* (1550, Dialogue on French Spelling and Pronunciation, Divided into Two Books) that he had decided that the teaching profession was undignified and paid only a pittance, and he also wanted to travel. Nevertheless, in

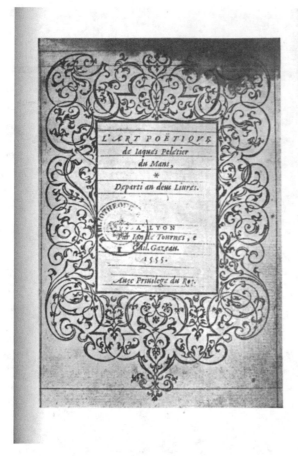

Title page for Peletier's collection of poems that includes an ode to his fellow poet Louise Labé of Lyon (from L'Art Poëtique de Jacques Peletier du Mans *[1555], edited by André Boulanger, 1930; Thomas Cooper Library, University of South Carolina)*

Labé, critics believe that she is the lady celebrated in his Petrarchan sonnets in *L'Amour des Amours et Vers liriques* (Love of Loves and Lyrical Verses); the work was published in Lyon in 1555 by Jean de Tournes, the only printer who agreed to publish Peletier's works in his unconventional French spelling. Peletier includes an ode to Labé by name in *L'Art poetique de Jacques Peletier du Mans departi an deus livres* (The Poetic Art of Jacques Peletier Divided into Two Books), printed by De Tournes and Guillaume Gazeau in the same year. Also in 1555 De Tournes printed Peletier's Latin *Exhortation pacificatoria ad christianos principes Carolum V et Henricum II* (Plea for Peace to the Christian Kings Charles V and Henri II); the work is addressed to the Holy Roman Emperor and the king of France, who were at war from 1547 to 1556.

Before leaving Lyon in 1557, Peletier wrote letters to many of his friends. In the letter to Tyard, Peletier complained about not being appreciated and about the inadequacies of the written French language and declared that he would henceforth write in Latin; he did so, with only a few exceptions, until 1572. In a letter to his brother Jean he complained about being away from Parisian life, not finding long-term patrons, and not being able to maintain personal relationships in Lyon. He traveled to Rome but soon returned to France, after which he seems to have regarded his country more favorably than he had before. Later in 1557 he moved back to Paris, where in 1558 he published a bilingual French and Latin edition of his *Exhortation pacificatoria ad christianos principes Carolum V et Henricum II* as *Exhortation à la paix* (Plea for Peace); no copies of this edition are known to exist.

Peletier spent the next three years in Paris completing his studies in medicine. After receiving his medical degree in 1560, he abandoned poetry and devoted himself to medicine and mathematics; the title pages of many of his publications after 1560 refer to the author as Jacobi Peletarii Medici et Mathematici (Jacques Peletier, Physician and Mathematician). In 1563 he traveled to Basel and published *De Peste compendium* (Compendium on the Plague), in which he recommends a potion that he believes will cure the disease, and *De Contactu linearum commentarium, suivi De Constitutione horoscopi commentarium* (Comments on Linear Contacts, Followed by Comments on the Constitution of the Horoscope), in which he recounts some of the misfortunes that befell him earlier in the year: he was robbed of his money and clothing by thieves who tried to kill him but failed; a month later, a potion he was heating exploded in his face and left him blind for three days.

Little is known of Peletier's activities for the next several years. In 1567 De Tournes printed his *Disquisitiones geometricae* (Geometrical Studies), in which Peletier refers to four years of solitude and travel; the solitude

1548 he accepted a position as professor of mathematics at the College of Guyenne in Bordeaux. On arriving, however, he learned that someone else had been given the post while he was en route. In 1549 he took a job teaching mathematics in Poitiers. That same year he published *L'Arithemetique de Jacques Peletier du Mans departie en quatre livres à Theodore Debesze* (For Theodore Debesze, the Arithmetic of Jacques Peletier du Mans Given in Four Books), which appeared in many editions over the next twenty years.

Peletier left Poitiers in 1552, probably to travel. He reappeared at Lyon in 1553 as a member of Marshal of France Charles de Cossé-Brissac's entourage—perhaps as the marshal's personal physician (even though he was not yet officially licensed), or perhaps as tutor to Cossé-Brissac's son Timoléon. In Lyon, Peletier became acquainted with the well-known poets Maurice Scève, Pontus de Tyard, and Louise Labé. While there is no evidence that Peletier was deeply enamored of

made him increasingly depressed and bitter. In 1569 he began practicing medicine in Annecy in the Savoy region. In 1572 he composed a lengthy poem to Marguerite, Duchess of Savoy and of Berry, the daughter of King François I, in his unusual French spelling; but the Annecy printer Jacques Bertrand's press could not reproduce his orthography, and he had to rewrite the work in standard French. It is generally considered to be one of his better poems.

In mid 1572 Peletier returned to Paris, where he published another treatise on geometry. Before the end of the year he accepted a position as director of the College of Aquitaine in Bordeaux. He planned to stay in the job for only a short time but was forced to remain for seven years because of the political instability, religious persecutions, and civil war following the St. Bartholomew's Day Massacre in August 1572. While in Bordeaux, he lost a lawsuit in which he tried to recover money he believed he was owed for his teaching; the transcript of the case exists and is titled *Contra Sexuiros Burdegalenses defensio in senatu* (Defense in the Senate against Burgundy Judges). He also became friends with Montaigne and spent time at the latter's château in Perigord. His explanation to Montaigne of Euclid's postulates that parallel lines do not meet in infinity is mentioned in "Apologie de Raimond de Sebonde" (Apology for Raymond Sebonde) Book II, chapter 12 of Montaigne's *Essais* (1580; translated as *The Essays*, 1603). Peletier is also mentioned in Book II, chapter 21, "De la force de l'imagination" (The Force of Imagination).

Peletier returned to teaching mathematics in Poitiers in 1579, but by 1580 he was back in Paris. That year a defamatory manuscript about him was circulated by Mauritius Bressius, who held a prestigious mathematical post founded by Pierre de La Ramée (Peter Ramus). A competition was held for the position every three years, and Bressius feared that Peletier would win the upcoming contest. In the manuscript, now presumed lost, Bressius claimed that Peletier was too old for the position, questioned his credibility, and even suggested that he was a heretic. Peletier rebutted the charges in *In Mauricium Bressium Apologia* (1580, Defense against Mauritius Bressius), in which he insisted that he was not interested in the post. Shortly afterward, he was named director of the College of Le Mans in Paris. He published a few more works on scientific and literary topics before he died in July or August 1582. He had never married and had no known offspring.

Jacques Peletier du Mans was not a major literary figure, but he influenced some of the greatest French poets. His first collection of verse shows a conscious effort at innovation in form and rhyme. Many of his thoughts on French poetry in the introduction to his 1544 translation of Horace were reiterated in Du Bellay's *Deffence et Illustration de la Langue Francoyse*. Shortly after his *Exhortation à la Paix* appeared in 1558, Ronsard published an almost identical poem on the same subject. Peletier's translations of the works of Euclid into French were used in schools for many years. His belief that words should be written as they are pronounced is a precursor to modern phonetics. In his promotion of Horace and Petrarch, his interest in antiquity and Italy, his use of the sonnet and ode, his devotion to language reform, and his passion for mathematics, Peletier is a prime example of the Renaissance humanist; and, to a much greater extent than that for which he is given credit, he helped foster the celebrated love poetry of the era.

Biography:

Clément Jugé, *Jacques Peletier du Mans (1517–1582): Essai sur sa vie, son œuvre, son influence* (Geneva: Slatkine, 1970).

References:

Sophie Arnaud, *La voix de la nature dans l'oeuvre de Jacques Peletier du Mans (1517–1582)* (Paris: Champion, 2005);

Joseph Axelrod, "A Phonemic Analysis of the Speech of Jacques Peletier (1517–1582) with a Facsimile of His Dialogue de l'ortografe," dissertation, University of Chicago, 1945;

Giovanna Cleonice Cifoletti, "Mathematics and Rhetoric: Jacques Peletier, Guillaume Gosselin and the Making of the French Algebraic Tradition," dissertation, Princeton University, 1992;

Robert J. Fink, "Les premières oeuvres de Jacques Peletier du Mans," dissertation, University of Chicago, 1971;

Stéphane Goyette, "Le système verbal de Jacques Peletier du Mans, XVIe siècle," M.A. thesis, University of Montreal, 1994;

Yves-Charles Morin, "Peletier du Mans et les normes de prononciation de la durée vocalique au XVIe siècle," in *Les normes du dire au XVIe siècle: Actes du colloque de Rouen, Université de Rouen, 15–17 novembre 2001*, edited by Jean-Claude Arnould and Gérard Milhe-Poutingon (Paris: Champion, 2004), pp. 421–434.

Papers:

Some manuscripts for works by Jacques Peletier du Mans are in the Bibliothèque nationale in Paris, including "Oraison funèbre du Roy Henry VIII par Le Peletier" and "De Ciceroniana Lectione."

François Rabelais
(1494? – 1553)

Elizabeth Chesney Zegura
University of Arizona

BOOKS: *Pantagruel. Les horribles et espoventables faictz et prouesses du tresrenomme Pantagruel Roy des Dipsodes, filz du grand geant Gargantua,* as Alcofrybas Nasier (Lyon: Claude Nourry, [1532?]; revised and enlarged, Lyon: François Juste, 1533); revised as *Pantagruel, Roy des Dipsodes, restitue a son naturel* (Lyon: François Juste, 1542); translated by Sir Thomas Urquhart as *The Second Book of the Works of Mr. Francis Rabelais, Doctor in Physick* (London: Printed for Richard Baddeley, 1653);

Pantagrueline Prognostication certaine veritable & infalible pour Lan mil.D.XXXIII (N.p.: [1532?]); revised as *Pantagrueline Prognostication, certaine, veritable et infallible pour Lan perpetuel* (Lyon: François Juste, 1542); translated by Democritus Pseudomantis as *Pantagruel's Prognostication: Certain, True, and Infallible for the Year Everlasting,* as Alcofribas (London, 1660);

Almanach pour l'an 1533, calculé sur le Meridional de la noble Cité de Lyon, et sur le climat de royaume de France. Composé par moy François Rabelais, Docteur en Medecine, et Professeur en astrologie (Lyon: François Juste, 1532?);

Pantagrueline Prognostication certaine veritable & infalible pour Lan mil.D.XXXIIII (Lyon, François Juste, 1533?);

Pantagrueline prognostication, certaine, veritable, et infalible, pour l'an M.D.XXXV (Lyon: François Juste, [1534?]);

Almanach pour l'An 1535, calculé sur le noble Cité de Lyon, à l'elevation du Pole, par xlv. Degrez xv. Minutes en Latitude et xxvi. En longitude (Lyon: François Juste, 1534);

Gargantua, as Nasier (Lyon: François Juste, [1534]); revised as *La vie treshorrificque du grand Gargantua, pere de Pantagruel,* as Nasier (Lyon: François Juste, 1542); translated by Urquhart as *The First Book of the Works of Mr. Francis Rabelais, Doctor in Physick* (London: Printed for Richard Baddeley, 1653);

Almanach pour l'an 1536 (N.p., 1535?);

Pantagrueline prognostication, certaine, veritable, et infalible, Pour l'an M.D.XXXVII (Lyon: François Juste, 1537);

François Rabelais (anonymous portrait; Musée national du château et des Trianons, Versailles)

Pantagrueline prognostication, certaine, veritable et infallible, Pour l'an M.D.XXXVIII ([Lyon: Denis de Harsy], 1537–1538);

Stratagemata . . . Domini de Langeio, militis, in principio tertii belli Caesarei ([Lyon: Sebastian Gryphius, 1539?]); translated by Claude Massuau as *Stratagemes, c'est à dire proesses et ruses de guerre du preux et tres celebre chevalier Langey, on commencement de la tierce guerre Cesarienne* (Lyon: Sebastian Gryphius, 1542).

Almanach pour lan M.D.xli.calcule sus le meridien de la noble cite de Lyon ([Lyon: François Juste, 1540?]);

Tiers livre des faictz et dictz Heroïques du noble Pantagruel (Paris: Chrestien Wechel, 1546); translated by

334

Urquhart as *The Third Book of the Works of Mr. Francis Rabelais, Doctor in Physick Containing the Heroick Deeds of Pantagruel the Son of Gargantua* (London: Printed for Richard Baldwin, 1693);

Almanach pour l'an 1546, compose par Maistre Françoys Rabelais, Docteur en Medecine (Lyon: Pierre de Tours, [1546?]);

Le quart livre des faictz et dictz Heroiques du noble Pantagruel (Lyon: Pierre de Tours, 1548); revised and enlarged as *Le quart livre des faicts et dicts Heroiques du bon Pantagruel* (Paris: Michel Fezandat, 1552); translated by Peter A. Motteux in *Pantagruel's Voyage to the Oracle of the Bottle Being the Fourth and Fifth Books of the Works of Francis Rabelais, M.D., with the Pantagruelian Prognostication, and Other Verse and Prose by That Author, also his historical letters . . . , never before printed in English* (London: Printed for Richard Baldwin, 1694);

La sciomachie & festins faits a Rome au Palais de mon seigneur reuerendissime Cardinal du Bellay, pour l'heureuse naissance de mon seigneur d'Orleans (Lyon: Sebastian Gryphius, 1549);

Almanach et Ephemerides pour l'an de Nostre Seigneur Jesus Christ, 1550, compose & calculé sur toute l'Europe, par maistre François Rabelais, medecin ordinaire de Monseigneur le Reverendissime Cardinal du Bellay (N.p., [1549?]);

L'Isle Sonante, par M. Francoys Rabelays, qui n'a point encores esté imprimee ne mise en lumiere: en laquelle est continuee la navigation faicte par Pantagruel, Panurge et autres ses officiers. Imprimé nouvellement (N.p., 1562);

Le cinquiesme et dernier livre des faicts et dicts Heroiques du bon Pantagruel, compose par M. François Rabelais, Docteur en Medecine. Auquel est contenu la visitation de l'Oracle de la Dive Bacbuc, et le mot de la Bouteille: pour lequel avoir, est entrepris tout ce long voyage. Nouvellement mis en lumière (N.p., 1564); translated by Motteux as *The Fifth Book of the Works of Francis Rabelais, M.D., Containing the Heroic Deeds and Sayings of the Great Pantagruel* (London: Printed for Richard Baldwin, 1694).

Editions and Collections: *Grands Annales tresveritables des Gestes merveilleux du grand Gargantua & Pantagruel son filz, Roy des Dipsodes* (Lyon: Pierre de Tours, 1542–1543);

La Plaisante, & joyeuse histoyre du grand Geant Gargantua (Valence: Claude La Ville, 1547)–includes *Second Livre de Pantagruel, Roy Des Dipsodes, Restitué a son naturel* and *Tiers Livre Des Faictz, et Dictz Heroiques du noble Pantagruel*;

Les oeuvres de M. Francois Rabelais Docteur en Medicine (N.p., 1553)–includes *Gargantua, Pantagruel, Tiers livre des faicts et dicts Heroïques du noble Pantagruel,* and *Le quart livre des faicts et dicts Heroiques du noble Pantagruel;*

Les oeuvres de M. François Rabelais, docteur en medecine (Lyon, 1566);

Les oeuvres de François Rabelais, illustrated by Gustave Doré (Paris: J. Bry aîné, 1854);

L'isle Sonante, edited by Abel Lefranc (Paris: H. Champion, [1905?]);

Une réimpression ignorée du Pantagruel de Dresde, edited by Pierre-Paul Plan and Léon Dorez (Paris: *Mercure de France,* 1910);

Le quart livre de Pantagruel, edited by Jean Plattard (Paris: H. Champion, 1910);

Oeuvres de François Rabelais, 6 volumes, edited by Abel Lefranc and others (Paris: H. Champion, 1912–1955);

L'isle Sonante, facsimile reproduction of the first edition (Paris: Editions des Bibliothèques Nationales de France, 1931);

Pantagruel, edited by Verdun-Louis Saulnier (Paris: Droz, 1946);

Le quart livre, edited by Robert Marichal (Geneva: Droz, 1947);

Le cinquiesme livre, edited by Plattard (Paris: Société Les Belles Lettres, 1948);

Oeuvres complètes, 5 volumes, edited by Plattard (Paris: Société Les Belles Lettres, 1948–1961);

Oeuvres completes, 2 volumes, edited by Pierre Jourda (Paris: Garnier Frères, 1962);

Le tiers livre, edited by Michael A. Screech (Geneva: Droz, 1964);

Gargantua, edited by Ruth Calder, Screech, and Saulnier (Geneva: Droz, 1970);

Pantagruéline prognostication pour l'an 1533 avec Les almanachs pour les ans 1533, 1535 et 1541, La grande et vraye pronostication nouvelle de 1544, edited by Screech (Geneva: Droz, 1974);

Le tiers livre, edited by Françoise Joukovsky (Paris: Garnier-Flammarion, 1993);

Pantagruel, edited by Gérard Defaux (Paris: Livre de poche, 1994);

Le quart livre, edited by Defaux and Marichal (Paris: Livre de poche, 1994);

Oeuvres completes, edited by Mireille Huchon and François Moreau, Bibliothèque de la Pléiade, no. 15 (Paris: Gallimard, 1994);

Gargantua, edited by Floyd Gray (Paris: H. Champion, 1995);

Le tiers livre, edited by Jean Céard (Paris: Librairie générale française, 1995);

Le cinquiesme livre, edited by Joukovsky (Paris: Flammarion, 1995);

Oeuvres complètes, edited by Guy Demerson, Michel Renaud, and Geneviève Demerson (Paris: Editions du Seuil, 1995);

Pantagruel, edited by Guy Demerson, Michel Renaud, and Geneviève Demerson (Paris: Editions du Seuil, 1996);

Le quart livre, edited by Demerson, Renaud, and Demerson (Paris: Editions du Seuil, 1997).

Editions in English: *The Works of Francis Rabelais, M.D., or, The Lives, Heroic Deeds and Sayings of Gargantua and Pantagruel,* translated by Thomas Urquhart and Peter Anthony Motteux (London: Printed for Richard Baldwin, 1694);

The First Edition of the Fourth Book of the Heroic Deeds and Sayings of the Noble Pantagruel, translated by William F. Smith (London: Private printing, 1899);

The Fourth Book of the Heroic Deeds and Sayings of the Good Pantagruel, His Voyages and Wonders, based on the translation of Urquhart and Motteux (London: Gibbings, 1901);

All the Extant Works of François Rabelais, translated by Samuel Putnam (New York: Covici-Friede, 1929);

The Urquhart-Le Motteux translation of the works of Francis Rabelais: Five Books of the Gargantua and Pantagruel, the Pantagruelian Prognostication, Letters from Italy, and Minor Writings, 2 volumes, edited, with an introduction and notes, by Albert Jay Nock and Catherine Rose Wilson (New York: Harcourt, Brace, 1931);

The Five Books of Gargantua and Pantagruel, translated by Jacques LeClercq (New York: Random House, 1944);

The Histories of Gargantua and Pantagruel, translated by James M. Cohen (Harmondsworth, U.K.: Penguin, 1955);

Gargantua and Pantagruel, translated by Burton Raffel (New York: Norton, 1990);

The Complete Works of Rabelais, translated by Donald Frame (Berkeley: University of California Press, 1991);

Pantagruel: King of the Dipsodes Restored to His Natural State with His Dreadful Deeds and Exploits Written by the Late M. Alcofribas, Abstractor of the Quintessence, translated by Andrew Brown (London: Hesperus, 2003);

Gargantua, translated by Brown (London: Hesperus, 2003).

OTHER: Dedication to André Tiraqueau, in Giovanni (Jean) Manardi, *Epistolarum medicinalium Tomus Secundus* (Lyon: Sebastian Gryphius, 1532);

Hippocrates and Galen, *Hippocratis ac Galeni libri aliquot, ex recognitione Francisci Rabelaesi,* edited by Rabelais (Lyon: Sebastian Gryphius, 1532);

Ex reliquiis venerandae antiquitatis Lucii Cuspidii Testamentum, edited by Rabelais (Lyon: Sebastian Gryphius, 1532);

Giovanni Bartolomeo Marliani, *Topographia Antiquae Romae,* edited by Rabelais (Lyon: Sebastian Gryphius, 1534).

Described as "the miracle of the sixteenth century" by Anatole France and often considered the French equivalent of William Shakespeare and one of the half-dozen or so giants of world literature, François Rabelais was a master of prose fiction, a humanist and physician, and a *uomo universale* (Renaissance Man) whose versatility rivaled that of Leonardo da Vinci. In addition to taking religious orders, first as a Franciscan and later as a Benedictine, Rabelais supplemented his medical and literary career with work as an editor, translator, botanist, naturalist, and secretary. A major reason for his continuing appeal more than five centuries after his birth results from the window on Renaissance civilization that Rabelais provides: voyages of discovery, advances in printing, fascination with Greek and Roman culture, utopian currents, and religious ferment all figure in his works, which—underneath their veneer of fantasy—offer paradoxical praise of the "new learning" and a scathing satire of military opportunism, petty tyrants, religious abuses, social injustice, and the darker side of the era. Rabelais's classical studies and his ongoing criticism of the Sorbonne (the Faculty of Theology at the University of Paris), the official Catholic arbiter of right thinking in sixteenth-century France, landed him in difficulty on several occasions while his irreverent humor and satire also drew the wrath of the Protestant Jean Calvin, who objected to his impiety and obscenity.

While the controversies surrounding his life add to the historical interest of Rabelais's work, his stature as a literary giant hinges upon the writings themselves: *Pantagruel. Les horribles et espouentables faictz et prouesses du tres-renomme Pantagruel Roy des Dipsodes, filz du grand geant Gargantua* (1532?; Pantagruel. The Horrific and Frightful Deeds and Heroics of the Very Famous Pantagruel, King of the Dipsodes and Son of the Great Giant Gargantua; translated as *The Second Book,* 1653), *Gargantua* (1534; translated as *The First Book,* 1653), *Tiers livre des faicts et dicts Heroïques du noble Pantagruel* (1546; Third Book of the Heroic Deeds and Sayings of the Noble Pantagruel; translated as *The Third Book,* 1693), and *Le quart livre des faicts et dicts Heroiques du noble Pantagruel* (1548, 1552; Fourth Book of the Heroic Deeds and Sayings of the Noble Pantagruel; translated as *The Fourth Book,* 1694), as well as an inauthenticated *Le cinquiesme et dernier livre des faicts et dicts Heroiques du bon Pantagruel* (1564; The Fifth and Last Book of the Deeds and Sayings of Good Pantagruel; translated as *The Fifth Book,* 1694) that was published posthumously in 1564. Building upon the ternary structure of medieval chivalric romances, which typically chronicle the hero's nativity, education, and feats, Rabelais narrates the marvelous births, encyclopedic learning, and larger-than-life adventures of Gallic giants named Gargantua and Pantagruel, whose unbridled appetite for knowledge and food figuratively identifies them as Renaissance Men. In addition to refurbishing these folkloric giants—archetypally associated with evil—as humanistic heroes, Rabelais deviates from his models by introducing a rapscallion sidekick whose escapades rival the protagonist's heroics: in *Pantagruel* this roguish upstart, Panurge, shares stage center with the giant, but in the *Tiers livre* and *Le quart livre,* Panurge's quandary over whether he should marry supplants the hero's prowesses and motivates the intellectual and geographical journeys that drive the plot.

Rabelais's grotesque imagination and idiosyncratic style of writing reinforce these innovations. His ribald humor, love of paradox, penchant for carnivalesque hyperbole and invective, shifts between learned and popular discourse, affinity for the *coq-à-l'âne* (a primarily satiric genre in the Renaissance, literally meaning "from rooster to ass," that is characterized by cock-and-bull nonsense and rapid jumps in subject matter) and non sequitur, and odd mixture of Latinisms, neologisms, and archaic elements give his text a macaronic quality that at times eludes interpretation. While some readers see in his works an apology for evangelism, an early-sixteenth-century movement that sought to reform the Catholic Church from within, others explain his writings as a form of Menippean satire, a genre borrowed from Lucian that couches serious social commentary in levity; and while some scholars see in the Pantagrueline tales an "altior sensus" (higher meaning) informed by Platonism and intended for initiates, others believe that Rabelais's goal is purely ludic or playful, an effort to bamboozle his readers. This interpretive debate, set in motion by Rabelais himself in the prologue to *Gargantua,* adds to the importance of his work, by posing questions about the nature of signs and meaning, language and truth, that have perplexed scholars for centuries.

Much like his message, the details of Rabelais's birth are obscure. That he was born toward the end of the fifteenth century in or near the hillside town of Chinon in southern France, to the wife of a well-to-do lawyer named Antoine Rabelais, is fairly certain. Since women of the upper middle class and noblesse de robe (administrative and judicial nobility) rarely gave birth in their town homes, it is likely that Rabelais was born in or on the way to his family's stone farmhouse in Seuilly, known as "La Devinière," a location to which he refers several times in *Gargantua.* This historic building, which remains standing, was acquired by the

Title page for Rabelais's first book, which chronicles the adventures of the prince of Utopia, the son of Gargantua (Collection Roger-Viollet/Getty Images)

department of Indre-Loire in 1948 and opened as a museum in 1951. Records indicate that the author had two older brothers, Antoine and Jamet, as well as a sister named Françoise, but the date of his birth remains unknown. An eighteenth-century manuscript of epitaphs, which indicates that Rabelais died in 1553 at the age of 70, seems to establish the year of his birth as 1483; but other documents, including the author's own claim in 1521 to be an "adulescens" (adolescent), a Latin term designating young adults between the ages of 14 and 28, suggests an alternative birth date as late as 1494. No matter which scenario one chooses, Rabelais was no longer a young man when his first burlesque epic, *Pantagruel,* was published in 1532.

Information about Rabelais's youth is scarce. Many scholars believe he spent much of his childhood at La Devinière, a theory based on child-rearing practices of the era and on the assumption that *Gargantua,* with its fond references to Seuilly, is semi-autobiographical. His familiarity with canon and civil law, as well as a reference in 1521 by the humanist jurist Guillaume Budé to Rabelais's legal studies, suggest that François may initially have followed in his father's footsteps, studying law at Angers or Bourges or even several universities, in the manner of his character Pantagruel. Other accounts place Rabelais provisionally in the abbey of La Baumette, near Angers where he may have studied with the Franciscans as early as 1510 or 1511.

The first reference to Rabelais in the historical record dates from a letter he wrote to Budé in 1521 at the behest of his friend and fellow humanist Pierre Amy. This epistle, written from the Franciscan monastery of Le Puy Saint-Martin in Fontenay-le-Comte in Poitou, establishes that Rabelais was already a monk and a priest interested in Hellenistic studies. During his stay at the cloister, Rabelais made friends with Amaury Bouchard and André Tiraqueau, contemporary humanists and jurists whose polemics on the nature of women and marriage anticipate both the Querelle des Femmes (Woman Question) of the 1540s and the *Tiers livre*. Rabelais probably translated the second book of *The Histories* of Herodotus and one or more works by Lucian into Latin during this period. The future author remained at Fontenay-le-Comte until shortly after the seizure and return of his Greek books by Franciscan authorities in 1523 and 1524, following a ban on Hellenic studies by the Sorbonne. By 1525 he had obtained a papal indult allowing him to move to the Benedictine monastery at Saint-Pierre-de-Maillezais, where he enjoyed the protection of his first patron, Bishop Geoffroy d'Estissac, whose nephew he may have tutored. Either implicitly or explicitly, the abbot appears to have sanctioned Rabelais's decision to abandon the monastic life for that of a layman sometime between 1526 and 1528. During this time Rabelais may have studied medicine in Paris; and it is likely that two of his three children, Junie and François, were born from his liaison with a Parisian widow sometime prior to 1530.

On 17 September 1530 Rabelais's name appears again in the historical record, this time in the matriculation list of new enrollees at the faculty of medicine in Montpellier. While this career change seems abrupt, preparing Rabelais for a vocation radically different from his priestly calling, in fact there were close parallels between the author's medical pursuits and his earlier life as a Franciscan, Benedictine, and humanist. Medicine in the sixteenth century was grounded in philosophy and religion, which meant that Rabelais had already prepared for his career while poring over ancient texts and aiding the needy. The course of study during the Renaissance at the University of Montpellier, one of the oldest and most distinguished medical colleges in Europe, focused less on experimental anatomy or clinical practice than on the explication of medical treatises from antiquity, a bias that served Rabelais well. Within six weeks of his enrollment, on 1 November 1530, he was received as a bachelor of

medicine. His public commentaries on the writings of Hippocrates and Galen, which date from around this time, were considered groundbreaking: not only was Rabelais the first scholar to explicate the original Greek texts, which he translated into Latin and eventually published as *Hippocratis ac Galeni libri aliquot* (1532, Some Books of Hippocrates and Galen), but his success apparently revived interest in Hellenistic medical practices. In his *Tiers livre* Rabelais also reveals that during his stay in Montpellier, in October 1531, he and some of his fellow physicians acted in a medical farce, *La comédie de celui qui épousa une femme muette* (The Comedy of the Man Who Married a Dumb Wife).

Although Rabelais may have practiced medicine in the provinces surrounding Montpellier prior to leaving the area, the earliest official record of his activities as a doctor dates from November 1532, when he was named primary physician at one of France's most important hospitals, the Hôtel-Dieu de Notre-Dame de Pitié in Lyon. Situated at the confluence of four rivers, Lyon during the Renaissance was a center of intellectual ferment, bustling international trade, and a flourishing printing industry. The atmosphere there was more open and favorable to humanistic inquiry than in Paris, where the Sorbonne and the Parlement (parliament) of Paris used heavy-handed tactics, ranging from the seizure of banned texts to the burning of accused heretics, to quell intellectual freedoms that thrived in Lyon.

Almost immediately upon his arrival in Lyon, Rabelais formed important associations with printers such as Sebastian Gryphius and Claude Nourry; his first significant publications date from the months before his official start date at the Hôtel-Dieu. In 1532 alone he edited and wrote a preface for a volume of Giovanni (Jean) Manardi's Latin letters on medicine, which he dedicated to his friend Tiraqueau; finished the preface to a translation of Hippocrates' *Aphorisms,* which he had corrected and annotated the previous year; edited the apocryphal *Ex reliquiis venerandae antiquitatis Lucii Cuspidii Testamentum* (1532, Will of Lucius Cuspidius), believed at the time to be a document from Roman times; and completed the first volume of his magnum opus, *Pantagruel,* which was published in the fall under the anagrammatic pseudonym Alcofrybas Nasier by Nourry. Notwithstanding his literary commitments, which increased with the publication of *Pantagrueline Prognostication* in 1533 and *Gargantua* a year later, Rabelais remained active as a physician at the Hôtel-Dieu until 1535, instituting reforms that seem to have lowered the rate of mortality during his tenure.

Little exists in Rabelais's early writings, with the possible exception of his lost translation of Lucian, that explains the bawdy, mock-serious *Pantagruel*. Like many fellow humanists, the author had heretofore exhibited an affinity for classical scholarship, religion, medicine, and the law; but while each of these interests is evident in *Pantagruel,* their humorous treatment, the satirical and fanciful contexts in which they appear, and the borrowings from popular as well as learned culture result in a new type of work. For a model, one must look to the successful *Chroniques gargantuines* (Gargantuan Chronicles), an anonymous work in the oral tradition that had enjoyed enormous popularity in Lyon earlier that year. Some scholars hypothesize that Rabelais was the author of the roughly hewn *Chroniques gargantuines,* which recounts the fabulous and burlesque adventures of Arthurian giants. While he borrows characters from the earlier work, including Gargantua and his parents Grandgousier and Gargamelle, both *Pantagruel* and its prequel, *Gargantua,* are far more complex, suggesting that Rabelais and his publisher merely sought to capitalize on the chapbook's success.

Rabelais's correspondence holds a key to the new direction his writing was taking. On 30 November 1532, probably just after the publication of *Pantagruel,* Rabelais sent a letter to Desiderius Erasmus acknowledging the older man as his intellectual father. Parallels between the two humanists, even in Rabelais's first novel, are many. Gargantua's letter on learning in chapter 8 of *Pantagruel* echoes Erasmus's belief that education should be pleasurable, and Rabelais's satire of Scholasticism and the clergy recalls the Dutchman's battles with the Sorbonne, his abandonment of monastic life, and his distaste for clerical hypocrisy and empty formalism. Rabelais later borrowed his famous allegory of the Sileni, used in his prologue to *Gargantua,* from the Dutch scholar's *Adagiorum collectanea* (1500, Adages). More importantly, Erasmus's tone and techniques in *Moriae Encomium* (1511, The Praise of Folly), a fast-paced satirical work narrated by Folly herself, anticipate the unreliable narrator, shifting tonalities, paradoxical discourse, and irreverent humor of the Pantagrueline tales.

Many contend that *Pantagruel* first appeared at the Lyon fairs of 1532. At the very least, Rabelais's pseudonymous narrator Nasier, who doubles as an alchemist, carnival barker, and patent-medicine peddler, conjures up a sideshow atmosphere in the prologue by using the hyperbole and invective typically associated with hawkers at the fair to market his new and peerless ("sans pair") product. Alternately flattering, cajoling, and browbeating the public, Alcofrybas expresses doubts about the long-term viability of printing, vaunts the therapeutic powers of both his own chronicles and other books with "propriétés occultes" (occult properties), and threatens readers who doubt the veracity of his discourse with a host of colorful ailments.

Marketed as an oddity, *Pantagruel* fulfills the promise of its advance billing. Structurally and generically, the work is a hybrid that combines traits of the epic, romance, dialogue, and Menippean satire within a framework of loosely connected, often burlesque, episodes. Ostensibly devoted to the "horrific" adventures of the great giant Pantagruel, son of Gargantua, the work chronicles the young prince's illustrious origins and genealogy, his marvelous birth and education, and his intellectual and physical prowesses. Despite Rabelais's claim to "newness," his protagonist's name preexisted *Pantagruel.* In Simon Gréban's *Actes des Apôtres* (Acts of the Apostles), a mystery play of the fifteenth century, Penthagruel was a small, thirst-producing demon who poured salt down the throats of drunkards. The character's ready-made association with drinking was timely during the drought of 1532, and Rabelais added a figurative, humanistic dimension, along with several other new twists, to the traditional figure of Pantagruel: no longer demonic, he is a hero who thirsts and hungers after knowledge as well as food, a fact that at once derives from and explains his gigantic physical and intellectual stature.

In keeping with the Renaissance fascination with origins and antiquity, Rabelais opens *Pantagruel* with a creation story and genealogy that trace the race of giants back to Cain's slaying of Abel. At that time, according to the narrator, Abel's spilled blood fertilized the soil and produced an abundant crop of medlar trees that triggered extraordinary growth among those who ate the fruit. In contrast to the biblical account in the sixth chapter of Genesis, which associates giants, the progeny of miscegenation between human women and the gods, with the wickedness that prompted God to flood the earth, Rabelais portrays fundamentally good giants descended from the "sang du juste" (blood of the just) and thus sets the stage for Pantagruel to function, symbolically or parodically, as a Christ-like Redemptor. The giant's lineage, which playfully emulates both biblical genealogies and the Renaissance nobility's own penchant for family trees, as exemplified by Jean Lemaire de Belges's *Illustrations de Gaule et singularitez de Troye* (1510–1513, Illustrations of Gaul and Singularities of Troy) and Ludovico Ariosto's *Orlando furioso* (1532), includes a syncretic combination of classical, biblical, medieval, and completely fictional ancestors. Consisting of both victors and the vanquished, good and bad giants, inventors and tipplers, the genealogy establishes the parodic tone of the book and lays the groundwork for Pantagruel's own thirst, inventiveness, and mock-epic adventures.

The episode also introduces, through the description of Pantagruel's ancestor Hurtaly, both the possibility of authorial unreliability and the shifting physical dimensions that characterize Rabelais's fictional world, in which the size ratio between giants, other humans, the landscape, and natural or man-made objects is both unexpected and fluid, reflecting the destabilizing effect of New World discoveries on the *terra firma* of medieval geography. Too large or "trop grand" to fit into Noah's

Woodcuts facing title pages from 1537 editions of Rabelais's first novels (Bibliotheque nationale Impremes, Reserve; Collection Roger-Viollet/Getty Images)

ark, the narrator contends, Hurtaly was able to survive and continue his line by sitting astride the massive Old Testament ship in child-like fashion, as if it were a toy boat or hobbyhorse. While spatial distortions and oversized characters are commonplaces of folklore and fantasy, this playful enlargement of Hurtaly and miniaturization of the ark are not just comic but distinctly humanistic as well, as Rabelais metaphorically subordinates Noah's piety to the young giant's resourcefulness. Although the narrator slyly claims the example will strengthen the credibility of his narrative, it actually does the opposite, at once alerting the audience to his unreliability and launching what many scholars believe is a more serious project: the formation of a critical thinker. Most evident in the prologue to *Gargantua,* where he urges his audience to dig beneath the surface of the text, Rabelais's attempt to generate a discerning reader is already present in the prologue and first chapters of *Pan-*

tagruel, where his unreliability forces the audience to ask questions, not just about the truthfulness of his own fictional text but also about the veracity of authoritative discourse in general.

The actual birth of Pantagruel, whose name means "tout altéré" (all athirst), takes place in Utopie, a term borrowed from Sir Thomas More's *Utopia* (1519). Despite the positive connotations of this setting, the giant's nativity is steeped in ambivalence.

On the one hand, the infant is so large that he suffocates his mother Badebec, one of many events some scholars view as revealing Rabelais's antipathy for women. Scholars such as Abel Lefranc point to Gargantua's short-lived grief over his wife's death, whose funeral he declines to attend, as further evidence of the author's antifeminism. On the other hand, the festive atmosphere and prodigious nature of the birth, which is preceded by the emergence of a caravan of thirst-producing banquet provisions from the womb of Badebec, including a mule laden with salt, dromedaries carrying bacon and meat tongues, camels loaded with sausages and chitterlings, and horses pulling wagons of onions, garlic, and leeks, support a more positive interpretation. Heralded by prophecies and prodigies, the nativity of Pantagruel is at once messianic and humanistic in its connotations, thus encouraging readers to interpret Badebec's death symbolically as the death of an old world that gives way to a new civilization. Uncertain whether to laugh or cry, whether to rejoice in the birth of his son or lament the passing of his wife, whom he loved like a "savate" or "pantofle" (old shoe), Gargantua is the emblem of the temporal ambivalence of the Renaissance, vacillating between past and future. By attempting to resolve his emotional distress with formal logic, in a burlesque parody of the *pro et contra* methods of medieval Scholasticism, the giant king at once reinforces the tension between tradition and invention triggered by the birth of his son and suffuses the entire scene in comedy.

While his parody of Scholasticism recurs in the mock-serious episodes devoted to Pantagruel's upbringing and education, particularly in the list of vacuous books with Latin titles at the library of Saint-Victor in chapter 7, Rabelais looks at learning from multiple angles. As a father, Gargantua is exemplary for the nurture, guidance, and protection he offers his gifted but irrepressible son, who in a frenzy of humanistic hunger, and a whimsical twist on the myth of Romulus and Remus, happily devours the udder and stomach of the cow that suckles him before eating his father's pet bear. For the child's own well-being Gargantua chains the infant giant to his cradle, an action that initiates the back-and-forth struggle between patriarchal authority and filial independence that subtends Rabelais's discourse on education. In a sequence of chapters comprising lists, correspondence, games, travel, university studies, and encounters with other students, the youth finds educational models and antimodels.

Among the negative educational models are the useless library books and a pretentious Limousin schoolboy, whose affected Latinisms introduce the "language question" that figures throughout Rabelais's work, nearly causing Pantagruel to strangle the aspiring sophist. "Parle-tu naturellement" (Speak naturally), the giant commands, announcing a linguistic principle that many experts ascribe to Rabelais. Yet, Pantagruel's own erudite speech, Panurge's polyglotism, and the author's macaronic discourse are by no means transparent, suggesting either that the comment is partly ironic or that Rabelais's target is not learned speech per se, but rather the inappropriate use of fractured Latin in oral discourse, particularly by self-serving academics and theologians bent on obfuscating the truth and ensuring their own power rather than communicating with or educating the people.

As for positive models of learning, the most important example is Gargantua's letter to Pantagruel in chapter 8, where the young prince's father outlines an ambitious humanistic curriculum covering both the Trivium and the Quadrivium, urging his son to become an "abîme de science" (abyss of knowledge). While the letter features other progressive elements, including Gargantua's emphasis on the pleasure to be derived from studies, it is also conservative in places: despite admitting that the youth of his son's generation are far more knowledgeable than those of his own era, for example, the older giant repeatedly voices the hope that Pantagruel will be an "image" or clone of himself rather than forging an independent identity. For these reasons and because of the patriarch's pompous Ciceronian style, scholars such as Gérard Brault and Gérard Defaux view the letter not as a serious manifesto of Renaissance pedagogy but instead as a parody of both sophistic and humanistic hubris.

The introduction of Panurge, the giant prince's roguish companion, in chapter 9 contributes to Pantagruel's education in a different way, moreover, by exposing him to a behavioral model diametrically opposed to that of his father. Panurge, whose name means "jack of all trades," asks for food in thirteen languages before finally speaking French to Pantagruel. Medium-sized and middle-aged, he is experienced, resourceful, and wily rather than erudite; and far from adhering to Gargantua's dictum that "science sans conscience n'est que ruine de l'âme" (knowledge without conscience leads to ruin), his accomplishments for the most part are not heroic but illegal.

Together Panurge and Pantagruel, along with their companions Epistemon (the wise), Carpalim (the swift), and Eusthenes (the strong), embark on a course of feats that diverge markedly from chivalric models. In keeping with epic tradition, many of these odd heroics are military and take place during a war between the Amaurotes (from "Amaurote," the capital of More's Utopia) or residents of a large Utopian city, and the neighboring Dipsodes (meaning "gens altéréz" or "thirsty people") who attack them. Far from dominating the action, this military subplot is preceded and interrupted by verbal and intellectual feats. While the prince resolves a legal dispute by speaking gibberish, and defeats Loup Garou (Werewolf), captain of the attacking Dipsodian forces, by throwing salt in his face and swinging him around in the air like a scythe, thus mowing down the surrounding troops, his roguish sidekick tells stories, debates and defeats an English scholar named Thaumaste with sign language, and humiliates the Haughty Parisian Lady who refuses his advances by showering her with the urine of dogs in heat.

The growing identification between the prince and knave is dramatized by Panurge's last-minute substitution for Pantagruel in the gesticulatory duel with Thaumaste, a burlesque encounter in which Rabelais both parodies epic contests and offers a new variation on the "language question;" and by the giant's abandonment of his own Parisian lady, who sends the prince a ring and a coded message that the prince and his friends Panurge and Epistemon attempt to decipher. Not only courageous, Pantagruel proves to be almost as cunning as Panurge when he uses a mendacious prayer, deliberately crafted to mislead an enemy spy about the Amaurotes' troop movement, to achieve victory over the Dipsodes. The mock epic concludes with not one but three netherworld journeys: one into hell, where the pedagogue Epistemon discovers a world upside-down in which great lords and ladies toil and suffer, while the poor and oppressed finally rule; the second into Pantagruel's mouth, where the narrator takes shelter during a storm; and the final one into the giant's stomach, where miners go to relieve an obstruction.

Although reactions to *Pantagruel* were polarized, it was an enormous popular success. The Sorbonne characterized the work as "obscène" (obscene) but apparently the theologians did not censor the volume. No doubt encouraged by the positive reception of his book, Rabelais followed it later the same year with *Pantagrueline Prognostication certaine veritable & infalible pour Lan mil.D.XXXIII* (1532; translated as *Pantaguel's Prognostication,* 1660), a collection of irreverent and humorous predictions that is laced with evangelical undercurrents. Traditionally viewed as an effort to capitalize without delay on the popularity of *Pantagruel, Pantagrueline Prognostication* appears to counter astrological writings in vogue at that time that supported Charles V's claim to a pan-European empire. One theory is that Rabelais composed his *Pantagrueline Prognostication* at the behest of his patron Jean du Bellay, at that time the bishop of Paris. If this is true, Rabelais and Du Bellay must have known each other a good deal earlier than their first recorded meeting in 1534, when Rabelais accompanied the prelate to Rome as his personal physician.

The political climate in France became increasingly tense in 1533 as Rabelais published an expanded edition of *Pantagruel* and prepared his *Pantagrueline Prognostication* for 1534. In spring 1533 the Sorbonne condemned Marguerite de Navarre's *Miroir de l'âme pécheresse* (1531, Mirror of the Sinful Soul), in part because of her role, as sister of King François I and a Reformist sympathizer, in inviting Evangelicals such as Gérard Roussel to preach in the Louvre. Also that year Du Bellay, whom François I dispatched to England as his liaison to Henry VIII during his divorce from Catherine of Aragon, was criticized by Catholic zealots for his lenient attitude toward heresy.

The English king's divorce, with its potential consequences for church-state relationships, was the reason for Du Bellay's journey to Italy in 1534, when he appealed to the Pope in vain for a compromise solution that would stop short of excommunicating Henry.

During his trip to Rome with Du Bellay, Rabelais also petitioned the papal court unsuccessfully, seeking absolution for his abandonment of monastic life. He had planned to construct a topography of Rome based on his firsthand observations of the city, but upon discovering that the Italian naturalist Giovanni Bartolomeo Marliani had already written on the subject, he decided to have Marliani's volume reprinted in Lyon. Like other humanists, Rabelais considered Rome the capital of the world, and his correspondence indicates that he relished the opportunity to engage in intellectual commerce with other scholars and to study the flora and fauna of the region. In his letter to Du Bellay dated 31 August 1534, several months after his return to France, Rabelais expressed disappointment that "Plantas autem nullas, sed nec animantia ulla habet Italia, quæ non ante nobis & visa essent & nota" (Italy has no plant, no animal, that I had not seen previously).

In addition to editing Marliani's *Topographia Antiquae Romae* (1534, Topography of Ancient Rome), Rabelais published three more works in 1534: *Almanach pour l'an 1535* (Almanac for 1535), containing advice and predictions for the upcoming year; the *Pantagrueline Prognostication* for 1535, of which only fragments survive; and *Gargantua,* a prequel to *Pantagruel.* In *Gargantua* Rabelais reprises the birth-education-adventures structure of the previous chronicle while focusing on the childhood and adolescence of Pantagruel's father, whose companions include the humanist preceptor Ponocrates; a well-mannered page named Eudemon, who first appears in chapter 15 as a role model for young Gargantua; and the squire Gymnaste, known for his agility on horseback and in battle.

Like *Pantagruel, Gargantua* includes lists, correspondence, battle scenes, shifting dimensions, and sheer nonsense, but Rabelais adds new elements: formal orations, a heightened focus on color symbolism, wardrobe inventories, the transcript of a half-eaten manuscript fragment, an enigmatic prophecy, and a utopian treatise. In mock-serious fashion the narrator contends in the prologue that the book holds "mystères horrificques" (dreadful mysteries) about religion, politics, and the economy. This suggestion that *Gargantua* is a coded work, meant to be deciphered by Rabelais's fellow humanists or Evangelicals, has intrigued readers for centuries; but many view his "symboles Pythagoricques" (Pythagorean symbols) not as an esoteric code but rather as an elaborate game intended to mystify the public and mock the exegetical process. Whether his intention is to frustrate or to impart hidden wisdom, Rabelais challenges his readers as few other writers do, reinforcing at the narrative level his central theme in *Gargantua*—the importance of education and the formation of judgment.

Despite being addressed to drinkers and syphilitics, the prologue to *Gargantua,* with its invocation of Plato's *Symposium* and its references to drink dignified by allusions to divine frenzy or Bacchic furor, is more overtly learned than the preface to *Pantagruel.* The narrator Alcofrybas opens the prologue with four container metaphors, likening the book to a Silenus box, frivolous on the outside but filled with "fines drogues" (fine drugs); to Socrates, who was ugly but wise; to an onion, with its many layers; and to a dog bone, which yields precious marrow when gnawed. Having persuaded the reader that his "fôlastries" (foolish antics) are in fact serious, Alcofrybas immediately reverses himself and mocks those who seek allegorical meanings in such narratives as the *Iliad* and the *Odyssey.* Because it both promises and withholds meaning, this prologue is the key to both traditional and postmodernist approaches to Rabelais.

Far from being resolved in the prologue, the tension between deep and surface meaning persists throughout *Gargantua.* The notion that reading is an archaeological process in which truth must be excavated informs the opening chapters in particular. The giant's genealogy, the narrator reveals, was found buried in a field along with cryptic texts—possibly of a prophetic nature—half eaten by moths and rats. Alcofrybas develops the inner-outer motif further in the chapters on Gargantua's livery, which focus not only on the material abundance of fabrics and jewels used to make the prince's clothing but also on the symbolism of his emblem (the androgyne) and his colors (blue and white). By exploring and questioning the way in which colors, emblems, and devices signify, Rabelais encourages his reader to rethink the relationship between signs and their meanings and challenges his reader to think critically.

Rabelais's creation of a thinking reader parallels and reinforces young Gargantua's education, which pits the rote memorization advocated by his first Sophist preceptors against the field trips, discussions, and educational games introduced by his tutor Ponocrates. Jobelin Bridé and Thubal Holoferne, the two Scholastic pedants initially charged with Gargantua's training, are caricatures of monachal sloth who actually cause the child to regress. Through them, Rabelais condemns the Sorbonne theologians who thwarted humanistic inquiry and intellectual freedom in Renaissance France. Ponocrates, however, balances book learning with observation, hands-on experience, physical education, and visits to local artisans.

Beyond the half-dozen chapters addressed specifically to pedagogy, the theme of education, maturation, and the formation of judgment underlie the entire plot of

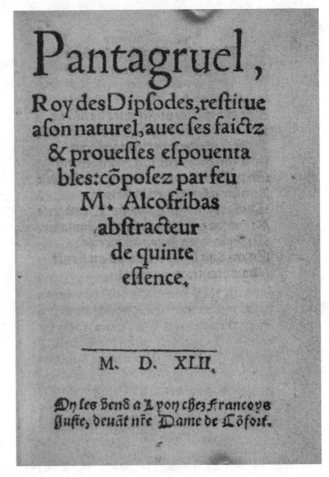

Title page for the last edition of Pantagruel *revised by Rabelais (Douglas H. Gordon Collection, University of Virginia Library)*

Gargantua, but Rabelais camouflages these serious concerns with scatology, paradoxical encomia, and burlesque humor. Through trial and error, or the experimental method, the young giant discovers a soft and efficient arsewipe. Showing his scorn for Sorbonne theologians, he drowns countless Parisians when he urinates, and impulsively steals the bells from the tower of Notre Dame. The prince is even instrumental in creating La Beauce, France's fertile plain or breadbasket, when his oversized mare razes a forest while flicking flies from her back with her tail.

Even the epic conflict in the book stems from lowly rather than lofty origins: a petty squabble between bakers and grape producers (symbolically associated with liturgical bread and wine) over the bakers' right to buy raisins escalates into a war between old friends and neighboring kingdoms, ruled by Gargantua's father Grandgousier and the tyrant Picrochole, respectively. The episode is rich with historical and literary associations: scholars have linked it to the world-conquest motif in literature, to a real-life dispute between Antoine Rabelais and a neighbor at La Devinière, to the hostilities between France and Holy Roman Emperor Charles V, to the development of a market economy in Europe, and to arguments between Catholics and Reformers over the mass. The Picrocholine War also introduces an important new character, Frère Jean des Entommeures (Friar John of the Hashes), who reappears in Rabelais's later chronicles. In contrast to his lethargic colleagues, Frère Jean is a lusty, good-natured, and proactive soldier of Christ, who repels Picrochole's men and protects his order's vineyards with burlesque heroics, using the cross as a stick to mow down his foes.

The episode of the Picrocholine War figures most importantly as a cautionary tale about judgment. Picrochole, a negative behavioral model whose name means "quick to anger," rushes to judgment and prepares for war upon hearing his grape growers' biased account of their roadside altercation with the bakers. In striking contrast, Grandgousier, the Utopian king, questions his bakers carefully to ascertain what really happened, seeks counsel from his advisers, and sends reparations to the grape growers in an attempt to avoid bloodshed. His temperate and reasoned response, the result of weighing and balancing multiple viewpoints, serves as a decision-making model for Gargantua, who, after returning home to help win the war for his father, rounds out his humanistic education at the end of hostilities with a practical lesson in humane governance. Drawing upon examples from antiquity, the prince absolves and frees the defeated Lerneans, or followers of Picrochole, opting to build living memories—and a model of liberality—in the hearts of the vanquished rather than triumphal arches on their soil.

Gargantua rewards Frère Jean by constructing a utopian monastery for him, the Abbaye de Thélème. In this utopia, which resembles a Renaissance court more than a cloister, young men and women who are "bien néz" (well born) and "bien instructz" (well educated) live together in harmony, free from monastic rules and austerity. Garbed in satin, velour, feathers, and lace and well versed in music and art, the Thelemites adhere to the provocative motto "Fais ce que vouldras" (Do What You Will). While such a sentiment might seem to encourage hedonistic, amoral behavior, the underlying premise is quite the opposite: the narrator explains that good, rational, and educated people "ont par nature un instinct et aguillon, qui tousjours les poulse à faicts vertueux et retire de vice" (have a natural instinct that drives them to avoid vice and act virtuously). This assumption is borne out in the display of reciprocity informing the Thelemites' behavior: they "entrèrent en louable émulation de faire tous ce que à un seul voyoient plaire" (all tried to do what they saw pleased one of them) rather than making unilateral decisions or acting solely out of self-interest. While Rabelais perhaps questions the viability of this behavioral ideal by writing of Thélème in the past tense, the episode nonetheless provides a fitting conclusion to Gargantua's education and the war he experiences. Armed with a liberal education and a willingness to consider the needs of others, Rabelais implies, humans should be able to coexist peacefully, happily, and productively.

Paris, however, was not peaceful in 1534 as Sorbonne theologians continued to protest the teaching of Hebrew and Greek and decried the presence of evangelical preachers at court. Reform sympathizers in turn escalated their own campaign against Catholic practices. On the night of 17 October, a group of Evangelicals, perhaps led by Antoine Marcourt, affixed incendiary pamphlets denouncing the mass to doors all over Paris, perhaps even to the Chambre du Roi (chamber of the king), and in neighboring cities. This action, called the Affaire des Placards (Affair of the Placards), led to demonstrations and wide-scale arrests, including that of the poet Clément Marot. Many scholars trace the erosion of King François I's benevolent attitude toward Reformers and humanists to this date. Following a reprise of the Affaire des Placards in January 1535, the king forbade all printing for a brief time, until the Du Bellay brothers—Guillaume, the Sieur de Langey, and Jean, newly installed as a cardinal—apparently persuaded him otherwise.

Rabelais apparently weathered this crisis in Lyon, which in general was more tolerant of dissenting ideas than Paris during the sixteenth century. His abrupt resignation of his post at the Hôtel-Dieu in February 1535, however, has given rise to speculation that he sought refuge elsewhere, fearful that his status as an apostate monk made him vulnerable to arrest and imprisonment. Rabelais's prospects improved in the spring and summer, in the wake of Jean du Bellay's election as a cardinal and as a result of renewed contacts between François I and German Reformers. In July, Rabelais left Lyon for Rome with the newly elected cardinal, stopping in Ferrara at the court of Anne de France—a known protector of dissidents—where he likely saw Marot.

During his sojourn in Rome, Rabelais finally succeeded in gaining absolution for his unauthorized departure from the cloister. His correspondence with his former patron Geoffroy d'Estissac provides insight into the behind-the-scenes maneuvering that led to the granting of his petition as well as showing his continuing interest in botany and in gossip about the Pope's family, legitimate and illegitimate. Given the birth in 1536 of his own illegitimate son, Théodule, Rabelais's contention that Pierluigi Farnese, the most famous of Paul III's natural sons, was "veritablement bastard" (really a bastard) is particularly intriguing. Most noteworthy are Rabelais's extensive commentaries on international politics, including his reflections on hostilities in Florence between the Médicis and republican forces; on antagonism between the duke of Ferrara and the Pope; on rumors that Henry VIII would be excommunicated; and, most frequently, on movements of the Turks and Emperor Charles V, the archenemy of King François I.

Upon his return to France late in 1535 or early the next year, Rabelais received authorization to resume his practice of medicine and was admitted to Du Bellay's Benedictine Abbey of Saint-Maur-les-Fossés, which was secularized in February 1536. He was allowed to cast aside his monachal habit permanently and enter the world—with the church's blessing—as a secular priest. Rabelais probably followed Du Bellay when he was summoned to Lyon later in February and then to Paris as lieutenant-general of the city in July, taking part in the defense of France against the forces of Charles V, who invaded Provence that summer and threatened to overrun the country from multiple fronts, including Picardy, the Alps, and the Pyrenees.

Amid his many other activities, Rabelais's renown as a physician continued to flourish. In February 1537 he joined such humanist luminaries as Marot, Budé, Salmon Macrin, and Nicolas Bourbon at a banquet held in Paris for Etienne Dolet, who had recently been pardoned for killing a man in self-defense. In verses written to commemorate the occasion, Dolet paid tribute to Rabelais's "honos et gloria" (honor and glory) as a physician, claiming that he could bring the dead back to life. Shortly thereafter Rabelais returned to Montpellier, where he received his master's degree in medicine in April, prior to becoming a doctor of medicine on 22 May 1537. As a fully established medical authority, Rabelais performed dissections of the bodies of hanged men during the summer of 1537 in Lyon, taught a course in Montpellier on Hippocrates's *Prognostics* (October 1537–April 1538), and on 17 November 1537 received one gold *écu* for conducting a public demonstration of the proper techniques for performing an autopsy.

The one known troubling event of 1537 for Rabelais occurred in August, when he was interrogated at the behest of Cardinal François Tournon, the king's lieutenant-general in southwest France. Although details about the case are uncertain, Rabelais apparently had written letters to a correspondent in Italy that included indiscreet comments about public affairs. Tournon, a reactionary as well as an avowed enemy of Jean and Guillaume du Bellay, intercepted the correspondence and chose to pursue the case. Rabelais appealed to King Henri and Queen Marguerite de Navarre. Through their influence, Rabelais was acquitted of any wrongdoing by the liberal magistrate Anne du Bourg.

Rabelais may have written *Stratagemata . . . Domini de Langeio, militis, in principio tertii belli Caesarei* (Stratagems . . . of the Soldier Lord Langey, at the Beginning of the Third Caesarean War), as early as 1539, the year it was probably published, as proposed by scholar Charles Perrat in his essay "Le *Polydore Virgile* de Rabelais." Now lost, the Latin work was translated into French by Claude Massuau and published by Sebastian Gryphius in 1542. Rabelais was inspired to write the book by the successful political strategy Guillaume du Bellay, Seigneur de Langey, employed in Italy, Switzerland, and England. Late in 1539 or early the next year Rabelais traveled to Turin, joining Du Bellay, the new governor of Piedmont, during the French occupation of the region. Although information about this period is scarce, Rabelais likely served as Du Bellay's physician, secretary, librarian, and botanist, studying and classifying local plants with an eye toward their medicinal properties.

According to Rabelais's friend Jean de Boysonné, another indiscreet letter by the author was intercepted by authorities in 1540, which caused him to take an alternative route through Chambéry when he returned to France from Italy. Boysonné also reports the death of Rabelais's son Théodule. His two surviving natural children, François and Junie, were legitimized in 1540.

In November 1541 Rabelais returned with Du Bellay to Lyon, where during the following months he helped prepare the definitive edition, with corrections, of his novels: *La vie treshorrificque du grand Gargantua, pere de Pantagruel* (The Most Horrific Life of the Great Gargantua, Father of Pantagruel) and *Pantagruel, Roy des Dipsodes, restitue a son naturel* (Pantagruel, King of the Dipsodes, Restored to His Natural State). In these editions Rabelais and his editor, François Juste, removed some of his more incendiary jibes at the Faculty of Theology, including references to "Sorbillans" and "Sorbonagres," and they toned down other pejorative allusions to the Sorbonne. For example, Rabelais replaced the word "théologien" (theologian) with the more generic "sophiste" (sophist). The emendations did little to protect the author against the Sorbonne censors, however, especially after Etienne Dolet, acting without Rabelais's permission, republished the unexpurgated version of the mock epics shortly after the more politically orthodox revision appeared. Despite vehement protests by Rabelais and Pierre de Tours, the successor to Juste, against Dolet's pirated editions of *Gargantua* and *Pantagruel,* the Sorbonne in 1543 condemned Rabelais's works without making any distinction between the expurgated and unexpurgated editions.

As the drama surrounding his fiction unfolded, Rabelais returned to Turin in May with Guillaume du Bellay, who, in a will dated 13 November 1542, settled upon Rabelais a benefice of up to 300 *livres tournois* yearly—a sum substantially more than an artisan would have received per year but far less than a nobleman's income. (As it turned out, this money was almost entirely consumed by Du Bellay's extensive debts.) The next

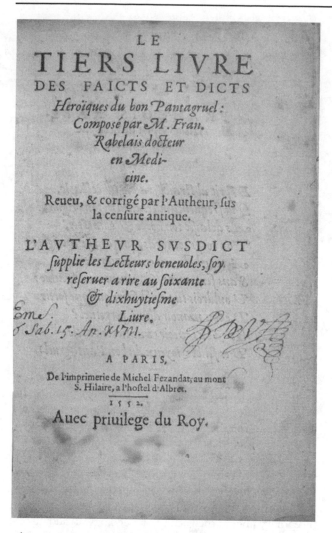

LE
TIERS LIVRE
DES FAICTS ET DICTS
Heroïques du bon Pantagruel:
Composé par M. Fran.
Rabelais docteur
en Medi-
cine.

Reueu, & corrigé par l'Autheur, sus
la censure antique.

L'AVTHEVR SVSDICT
supplie les Lecteurs beneuoles, soy.
reseruer a rire au soixante
& dixhuytiesme
Liure.

A PARIS,
De l'imprimerie de Michel Fezandat, au mont
S. Hilaire, a l'hostel d'Albret.
1552.
Auec priuilege du Roy.

Title page for an edition of Rabelais's 1546 novel in which Pantagruel's companion Panurge faces the question of marriage (Douglas H. Gordon Collection, University of Virginia Library)

month Rabelais accompanied an ailing Du Bellay to France, where on 9 January 1543 the seigneur de Langey died, near Tarare and with Rabelais in attendance.

The experience of Guillaume du Bellay's death may have contributed to the increasing darkness of Rabelais's later works, in which he alludes to his passing. Panurge visits the dying poet Raminagrobis in the *Tiers livre,* for example, on the assumption that humans close to death communicate directly with angels and other heavenly beings, who share with them "art de divination" (art of divination): "Les troys et quatre heures avant son décès" (During the three or four hours before he died), says Pantagruel, the dying man "employa en parolles viguoureuses, en sens tranquil et serain, nous prædisant ce que depuys part avons veu, part attendons advenir" (spoke vigorously, yet with tranquility and serenity, predicting things we have either already seen or

expect to happen). And in the "le trépas des héros" (death of heroes) espisode in *Le quart livre,* Epistemon, Pantagruel's teacher and companion, remarks that France was envied by the whole world while the "docte" (learned) and "preux" (courageous) Du Bellay was alive, and that "portentes" (portents) and "prodiges" (prodigies) announced his death.

Rabelais's early protector d'Estissac also died in 1543, leaving the author doubly bereft and potentially vulnerable, both to attacks from conservatives and to the "faute d'argent" (lack of money) that plagues Panurge. Some scholars hypothesize that Rabelais found favor with the king during the months that followed, citing the contention of the court poet Claude Chappuys that the physician was named *maître des requêtes* (Master of Requests) during the summer of 1543. Rabelais may also have returned to his vocation as a popular writer with *La grande et vraye Pronostication nouvelle pour lan Mil.CCCCC.xliiii* (1544?, The Great and True New Prognostication for the Year 1544), a work published under the pseudonym Seraphino Calbarsy that many scholars consider spurious. A cross between a farmer's almanac and a horoscope, the prognostication–if it is authentic–bears witness to Rabelais's career-long fascination with portents, predictions, and prophecy: while Gargantua, in his letter to Pantagruel (*Pantagruel,* chapter 8), may balk at reading the stars, Rabelais alternatively mocks, shares, and responds to his contemporaries' thirst for predictive literature.

Throughout the early and mid 1540s *Gargantua* and *Pantagruel* remained on the index of works proscribed by the Sorbonne. In an effort to circumvent the ban on sales and private possession of his fiction, Rabelais applied for and was granted a royal privilege from François I in 1545, which authorized the publication of his works and provided an early form of copyright protection, ostensibly with the king's imprimatur. In addition to praising Rabelais's writing, the privilege castigates the incompetent and malicious printers who have "corrompuz" (corrupted) and "pervertis" (perverted) the text in "en plusieurs endroictz" (several places), laying the blame for objectionable passages squarely on the shoulders of publishers such as Dolet, who failed to respect his wishes. The document even suggests that Rabelais's frustration with unauthorized editions prompted him to abandon the Pantagrueline chronicles after writing *Gargantua,* despite public demand for another installment in the adventures of the Utopian giants.

The royal privilege of 1545 authorized the publication of Rabelais's *Tiers livre* the following year. He dedicated his new installment, written more than a decade after his last full-length chronicle, to Marguerite de Navarre. While many of the characters introduced in the first two books continue to figure in the *Tiers livre*–not only Pantagruel, Panurge, and Gargantua, whom Rabelais resurrects despite his demise in *Pantagruel,* but also Frère Jean (now spelled Jan), Epistémon, Carpalim, Gymnaste, Ponocrates, and Eudemon–Rabelais departed in important ways from the models that originally brought him success. Gone is the feisty narrator Alcofrybas, the author's unreliable alter ego, with his carnivalesque banter. In his place readers discover the noted physician François Rabelais, writing popular fiction under his own name and making no attempt to camouflage his erudition. Many of the mock-epic trappings that distinguished the earlier books are no longer present: the burlesque battle scenes, outlandish nativities, apocryphal genealogies, and satiric feats. Gone also in the *Tiers livre* is Rabelais's focus on the prodigious physical stature of Gargantua and Pantagruel, an important source of comedy in the first two books, and his fascination with the size differential between giants and other characters.

While the new installment takes up where *Pantagruel* left off, at the end of the Dipsodian War, the plot differs markedly from the preview Alcofrybas provided back in chapter 34 of his first novel. The *Tiers livre* does not show "comment Panurge fut marié, et cocqu dès le premier moys de ses nopces" (how Panurge got married and was cuckolded in the first month of his marriage), or "comment Pantagruel trouva la pierre philosophale" (how Pantagruel found the Philosopher's stone) and "visita les régions de la lune" (visited the regions of the moon). Instead, the *Tiers livre* focuses primarily on Panurge's effort to determine whether he should marry, a decision he is loathe to make without resolving a secondary question: will his wife be unfaithful and beat him?

Addressed to both drinkers and the gouty, Rabelais's prologue to the *Tiers livre* opens with an extended discussion of Diogenes of Sinop. This account of the cynical philosopher, who purportedly lived in a tub to demonstrate his scorn for material possessions, recalls the classical flavor of the prologue to *Gargantua* and offers a new allegory of reading, writing, and judging that builds upon the model of the Silenus box. Diogenes Laërtius tells us that Alexander the Great, who greatly admired the Sinopian cynic, offered to grant Diogenes any favor he might desire. Instead of asking for wealth, the philosopher reportedly demanded only that Alexander move aside so as not to block his sunlight. Rabelais invokes this legend at both the beginning and end of his prologue, shouting "Hors de mon soleil" (Out of my sun) to hypocrites seeking to disparage his work. Reinforcing this reference to sunlight with repeated allusions to "la veue" and clear-sightedness, Rabelais reprises the theme of judgment that dominated *Gargantua.* This opening focus on insight foreshadows Panurge's investigation into marriage in the body of the text, which is both a contribution to the Querelle des Femmes and a book-long exercise in

judgment and decision making. The author's emphasis on seeing also challenges readers to closely examine his text, which on the outside, he implies, in an anecdote borrowed from Lucian, may seem just as "monstrous" and "ridiculous" as the Bactrian camel and two-toned slave Ptolemy presented to the Egyptians in hopes of securing their affection. Instead, the Egyptians condemned the general's offering as an "erreur de nature" (error of nature), says Rabelais, who fears his own work will suffer the same reception if readers fail to see beyond its oddity.

Mentions of both war and censorship in the prologue lend political resonance to Rabelais's insistence upon seeing clearly. In a veiled attack upon both Sorbonne theologians and Calvinists, the author implicitly urges readers to look critically rather than blindly at "cagotz" (hypocrites) who pretend to be pious. Rabelais also combines references to current events with some of his classical allusions. Most notably, the author's lengthy enumeration of the Corinthians' defensive efforts during an attack by Philip of Macedonia, an endeavor in which Diogenes participated by rolling his tub or barrel, echoes sixteenth-century accounts of measures taken by Parisians under the direction of Jean du Bellay, in an attempt to fortify the city in 1544 following the victory of Charles V at Saint-Dizier in August.

Diogenes's tub furnishes Rabelais one of his best-known metaphors. He likens his own writing to the cynic's tub rolling, an activity undertaken as a gesture of solidarity, and perhaps futility, in time of war. Like the platonic Silenus box, but refurbished with Christian connotations as well, Diogenes's tub doubles as a "tonneau" (barrel of wine), whose "source vive" (living waters) will never run dry. Because of their New Testament association with the Word and their classical identification with poetic inspiration, water and wine serve as metaphors for the text, which Rabelais describes as "un vray cornucopie de joyeuseté et raillerie" (a cornucopia of fun and merriment). In keeping with Christian theology and Pantagruelism, a term coined by Rabelais that he defines as a willingness to look positively at whatever springs from an honest, loyal heart, the narrator uses wine and water symbolism in part to articulate in evangelical terms the humanistic optimism evident in *Pantagruel,* claiming that his font offers hope rather than despair to those who drink deeply.

The body of the *Tiers livre,* which consists primarily of interviews with sages, seers, and other experts on marriage, is framed by two mock encomia: first, the Praise of Debts, in which Panurge justifies his spendthrift ways; and second, the Praise of the Pantagruelion, a hemp-like plant that Pantagruel has used in dozens of inventions. Set just after the Dipsodian conflict, the book initially chronicles the Utopians' transition from war to peace, a

Gargantua, as drawn by Gustave Doré (Collection Roger-Viollet/Getty Images)

period that is typically characterized by a shift from conquest to conciliation and by an increased focus on love, marriage, and rebirth. This backdrop, along with Panurge's discovery that married men are exempted from military service, provides the narrative logic behind the rogue's sudden fixation on matrimony. Invested by Pantagruel with a title, an estate, and revenues that he promptly depletes, Panurge announces his readiness to marry with a change of costume. Abandoning his *longue braguette* (massive codpiece), which Pantagruel describes as the warrior's principal piece of armor in time of war, the rogue has his right ear pierced and inserts a single gold earring inlaid with a flea. He completes his sartorial makeover by tying a pair of spectacles to his cap and by replacing his breeches with five yards of coarse brown cloth draped loosely around him.

Despite his elaborate show of nubility, Panurge's doubts about the advisability of marriage prevent him from moving forward with his project. Realizing that any change entails some degree of risk, the prospective bridegroom worries that he may be happier as he is, particularly if he should inadvertently marry an emasculating wife disposed to beat and cuckold him. When Panurge puts the question to Pantagruel, asking whether he should marry given all the variables involved, the Utopian prince advises his friend to look inward and examine his own "vouloir" (wishes). If after this soul-searching he still wants to marry, Panurge should entrust himself to God and chance, knowing full well that marriage is a gamble: some couples, observes Pantagruel, enjoy wedded bliss that embodies "les joyes de paradis" (the joys of paradise), while others experience the misery of frustrated devils "qui tentent les hermites par les déserts de Thébaïde et Monserrat" (who tempt hermits in the deserts of Thebaid and Monserrat).

Declining to follow the Delphic and Socratic directive to "know thyself" or to accept uncertainty as a condition of marriage, Panurge, in the company of his Utopian companions, embarks on a series of consultations intended to resolve his matrimonial conundrum. In an attempt to divine the future, he first seeks an answer in the works of Virgil, through a practice known as the "sors virgilianes" (Virgilian Lottery) that involves opening the book to a random page, choosing a passage on the basis of its line number, and scouring the excerpt for portents and omens. Somewhat skeptically, Panurge observes that the method promises to be less effective than throwing dice, a form of divination that Gargantua forbids as diabolical. As a compromise, the companions use dice to determine which lines of Virgil they will read. Ultimately, however, the lottery fails as a method of prophecy, in part because the characters disagree over how to interpret the texts.

Decoding potential signs proves to be a stumbling block for Panurge and his friends throughout their exegetical journey. When the reluctant bridegroom engages in dream analysis, his vision of a pretty wife making horns on his forehead suggests two opposing interpretations. Pantagruel and Frère Jan both contend that Panurge's bride will betray him, causing him to wear the figurative horns of cuckoldry, but Panurge associates the horns in his dream with a cornucopia, or horn of plenty. The companions' interpretive quagmire deepens in the course of subsequent consultations, many of which are burlesque or punctuated with obscenities. The first experts consulted by Panurge hold the promise of occult wisdom that is veiled in everyday discourse. They include the Sibyl of Panzoust, who inscribes her prophecy on sycamore leaves, tosses the leaves in the air, and then bares her buttocks while the companions try to reconstruct her cryptic message, as well as a deaf-mute named Nazdecabre, whose elaborate sign language—believed by many to be purer than written or spoken discourse—consists primarily of obscene gestures. The companions also visit a dying French poet named Raminagrobis, often identified with the author's friend and patron Guillaume du Bellay, in hopes that his deathbed utterances will reveal glimpses of the future; and the astrologer Herr Trippa, a character loosely based on the Renaissance magus Cornelius Agrippa of Nettesheim, who upon one glance at Panurge predicts that he will be cuckolded.

The group's dialogue with more traditional sages, including the theologian Hippothadée, an antifeminist physician named Rondibilis, the doublespeaking philosopher Trouillogan, and the dice-throwing judge Bridoye, prove no more enlightening. Panurge's last visit is with the fool Triboullet, in whose ravings the group hopes to discover transcendent wisdom, traditionally associated with divine frenzy and the "fool in Christ." Instead Triboullet slaps Panurge in the nose with a pig's bladder, and the companions abandon their philosophical banquet for a different project. They decide to undertake a sea voyage to the Dive Bouteille (Oracle of the Divine Bottle) in Cathay, a plan that announces *Le quart livre* and *Le cinquiesme et dernier livre*.

While the *Tiers livre* is virtually devoid of anti-Scholastic satire and in many ways is more moderate than its predecessors, the Sorbonne included it in a list of censored books that was published in December 1546. Little is certain about Rabelais's situation as the suppression of dissent deepened. His reliance in the *Tiers livre* upon André Tiraqueau's *De legibus connubialibus* (1524, On the Laws of Marriage), a work originally dedicated to Rabelais, and Tiraqueau's subsequent excising of references to Rabelais in his 1546 revision of his treatise have given rise to speculation that even mentioning Rabelais was impolitic. Rabelais's decision to move to Metz in 1546, where he practiced medicine for a year or two during the unrest at home, may have been made because he sought religious and political asylum in this relatively independent imperial town, which did not come under French control until 1552. While there, Rabelais resided with Étienne Lorens, a connection of the Du Bellay family, which has led some scholars to hypothesize that he went to Metz—a city of considerable strategic importance for relations between the Empire, the German States, and France—at the behest of Cardinal Jean du Bellay, perhaps on a diplomatic or information-gathering mission. Rabelais's sole surviving letter from this period, addressed to Cardinal du Bellay and dated 6 February 1547, indicates that he was in dire straits economically: "Monseigneur, si vous ne avez de moi pitié" (My lord, if you do not take pity on me), Rabelais implores, "je ne sçache que doibve faire sinon, en dernier désespoir, me asservir à quelqu'un de par deçà" (I do not know what I will do, unless I become the servant of someone here out of desperation).

Later that year, or perhaps in 1548, Rabelais either accompanied Cardinal du Bellay to Rome or joined his patron there, after depositing an almanac or prognostication for 1548, as well as an incomplete version of *Le quart livre*, with the printer Pierre de Tours in Lyon. This partial edition, divided into eleven chapters that correspond loosely to the first twenty-five chapters of the complete fifty-seven-chapter edition of 1552, ends abruptly after the tempest scene. While in Italy, Rabelais composed *La sciomachie & festins faits a Rome au Palais de mon seigneur reuerendissime Cardinal du Bellay, pour l'heureuse naissance de mon seigneur d'Orleans* (1549, The Simulated Combat and Festivals Held in Rome at the Place of My Most Reverend Lord Cardinal du Bellay, for the Joyous Birth of My Lord of Orléans) to honor the birth on 3 February 1549 of Louis d'Orléans, the short-lived son of Henri II. The thin volume, which holds more historical than literary interest, describes the elaborate festivities replete with nymphs and fireworks that Jean du Bellay organized in Rome on 14 March 1549 to celebrate the prince's nativity. Originally composed as a series of letters to Cardinal de Guise, the *Sciomachie* provided Rabelais an excellent opportunity to affirm his loyalty—and that of his patron—to the crown. In addition to honoring the infant prince, Rabelais's text implicitly pays tribute to the king as well by recalling the pageantry that greeted Henri II the preceding fall, when he made his triumphant entry into Lyon. Upon Rabelais's own return to Lyon late in 1549, he arranged for the *Sciomachie* to be published by Sebastian Gryphius.

Because of his increasing prominence as a writer, physician, and humanist and the heightening of religious tension in France, Rabelais was a natural target of criticism. In 1549 the Sorbonne-trained doctor Gabriel de Puy-Herbault, a monk at Fontevrault, condemned Rabelais as an enemy of religion in his *Theotimus sive de tollendis et expungendis malis libris* (Theotimus, or On Evil Books to be Seized and Expunged). Catholic theologians were not alone in their objections to the humanist physician and author. The next year Calvin labeled Rabelais a "chien enragé" (mad dog) in his *De Scandalis* (1550, Treatise on Scandals), vilifying him for the scatological content and language of his work. These and other attacks clearly troubled Rabelais, who responded heatedly to the charges against him in the dedicatory epistle that opens his completed *Le quart livre*.

Notwithstanding the storm of criticism surrounding him, Rabelais continued to enjoy the support of highly placed protectors. In the second half of 1550, while attending the ailing Cardinal du Bellay at Saint-Maur, Rabelais met Cardinal Odet de Châtillon, who arranged for the author to obtain a new royal privilege. Issued by Henri II and dated 6 August 1550, the privilege ostensibly shielded Rabelais from both rogue publishers and religious censors, guaranteeing and protecting his right to publish all his writings. The next year, probably through the efforts of Cardinal du Bellay, Rabelais became curate of Saint-Martin Meudon, a benefice he seems to have consigned to other priests on a yearly basis, rather than residing there himself. The same probably holds true for the curacy of Saint-Christophe-du-Jambet, although the chronology of Rabelais's tenure there is less certain. Du Bellay may have arranged the appointment for him in 1551, along with the post at Meudon; but some scholars speculate that Rabelais held the position as early as 1545, when he reputedly used his title and referred to his position at Saint-Christophe-du-Jambet as a witness for a legal document.

Despite his powerful patrons and the king's authorization of his works, Rabelais's *Gargantua, Pantagruel,* and *Tiers livre* appear in a list of censored works that the Sorbonne published in 1551, the same year he completed *Le quart livre.* Published by Michel Fezandat in January, 1552, the new chronicle begins with a dedicatory letter to Odet de Châtillon, in which Rabelais—perhaps already ill—expresses his weariness and indignation at the unfounded attacks against his works. Insisting that his writings are in no way heretical, Rabelais takes the offensive and challenges the logic of his detractors. His chronicles, he contends, bring "soulaigement" (relief) to the "affligéz et malades" (sick and unhappy), by raising their spirits in a manner approved by Hippocrates. By the same token, the detractors of Rabelais who would force him "plus . . . escrire un iota" (not to write another word) emerge in this letter as mean-spirited hypocrites, who use the rhetoric of righteousness as a weapon to inflict pain and as a mask to camouflage their lack of charity. In further defense of his writings, Rabelais points out that King François I had the chronicles read to him and found nothing objectionable, and that Henri II has given his special protection to the current volume, promising to shield the author from slanderers who "make perverse interpretations," "twist plan statements," and find heresy in typographical errors. In the last instance, Rabelais is referring to the uproar caused by the substitution of "asne" (ass or donkey) for "ame" (soul) in two instances in the *Tiers livre.*

The prologue of the *Le quart livre,* addressed only to "Gens de bien" (good people), continues the *Tiers livre* theme of seeing and emphasizes the importance of good health and moderation. Rabelais illustrates the value of moderation in an extended parable about the woodcutter Couillatris, whose name refers to his "ballocks" (testicles). Having lost his axe, Couillatris implores Jupiter to return the blade, which is essential for his identity as a man and his livelihood. Through the intermediary of Mercury, a classical deity as well as a common treatment for syphilis in the Renaissance, Jupiter tests the woodcutter, to whom he offers a gold axe, a silver axe, or the wooden axe that he had lost. Should the woodcutter prove greedy and claim the gold or silver axe, Jupiter has instructed Mercury to cut off the man's head. Because Couillatris refuses the gold and silver axes and unhesitatingly reclaims his own axe, Jupiter rewards him for his

moderation and honesty by giving him the other tools as well. Other woodcutters who do not practice moderation pay a high price for their greed: upon the orders of Jupiter, Mercury kills each of them, in a cautionary tale about material and, symbolically, sexual excess. Rabelais's advocacy of moderation also has political and religious ramifications: his warnings against excess reflect critically on the religious fanaticism of both counter-Reformers and intolerant Protestants.

Combining echoes of such authors as Homer, Virgil, Lucian, and Folengo, *Le quart livre* begins by chronicling the Utopians' ceremonious departure in twelve sailing vessels, which bear insignias related either to drinking or to the oracular *mot* (word) that Panurge seeks from the divine bottle, Bacbuc, to end his matrimonial dilemma. The sailors' first port of call is Medamothi, or Nowhere Land, where they buy exotic, mythical animals such as unicorns and the chameleonic tarand, as well as paintings and tapestries that represent such ephemeral subjects as "les Idées de Platon" (Ideas of Plato) and "les Atomes de Epicurus" (Atoms of Epicurus). After exchanging letters by carrier pigeon with Gargantua and sending exotic gifts back home, the crew encounters another French sailing vessel carrying a pretentious sheep merchant named Dindenault. In a tragicomic scene the trader falls overboard and drowns in an attempt to save his sheep, which he had refused to sell to Panurge. Subsequent episodes include visits to Ennasin (the Island of Alliances); Cheli (the Island of Compliments), where inhabitants ceremoniously bow and kiss their guests; to Procuration, where hairy process servers earn their livelihood by being beaten; and to the islands of Tohu and Bohu, where the windmill-eating giant Bringuenarilles recently died from indigestion.

In addition to the archetypal tempest and encounter with a sea monster, other key episodes of the *Le quart livre* include visits to the Island of Macraeons, where dead heroes are buried; a sighting of Tapinois or Sneak's Island, ruled by the austere King Lent (Quaresmeprenant), whose subjects engage in battle with carnivalesque Andouilles; and a stopover at the Island of Ruach, where the inhabitants dine on wind. Following visits with the impoverished Papefigues, who scorn the Pope, and with their enemies, the Decretal-worshiping Papimanes (papal maniacs), the sailors encounter the Parolles gelées (Frozen Words), one of the most provocative episodes in the book. In this elaboration of an allegory previously treated by Celio Calcagnini and Baldassare Castiglione, the companions thaw sounds produced during a battle at sea that took place months earlier, regenerating the voices of the dead. The book concludes with a philosophical banquet, in which Pantagruel promises an answer to "toutes questions" (all questions),

Rabelais's signature (from Jean Plattard, Anthologie Du XVI Siecle Français *[London & New York: Thomas Nelson, 1927];*
Thomas Cooper Library, University of South Carolina)

and with a foray into the lower bodily strata by Panurge, who soils himself upon mistaking a cat for the devil.

In the body of *Le quart livre* Rabelais reprises many of the themes outlined in the prologue: the importance of health emphasized in the prologue provides a backdrop for the threat of death that looms over the sea voyage; the theme of religious moderation recurs in Rabelais's attacks on Calvin and the monsters of Anti-Physie, as well as in references to the Council of Chésil or Trent and in the tension between Carnival and Lent; and the Andouilles or Chitterlings echo the phallic and sexual imagery of the liminary text. Despite these threads of continuity, many consider the *Le quart livre* to be Rabelais's most intriguing work, a cross between an epic quest and a Renaissance voyage of discovery. Such episodes as the storm and the battle with a whale are staples of the epic, as is the presence of other monsters that figure as obstacles the protagonists must overcome. Furthermore, Rabelais's realistic nautical vocabulary, his lively descriptions of exotic flora and fauna similar to accounts found in travel journals, and the topographical detail of his characters' itinerary show that he was familiar with sixteenth-century geographical exploration.

At the same time, however, Rabelais's almost surrealistic blend of fantasy, allegory, anthropology, and topical satire makes *Le quart livre* a subject of ongoing debate. For some readers the unity of the work resides in its parade of monsters, ranging from the windmill-eating giant Bringuenarilles to the flying pig Mardigras. Others believe Rabelais's recurring focus on wind, which not only propels ships but also feeds the people of Ruach, powers windmills, and fuels the tempest, ties the disparate episodes together. Because so many of these exotic societies and rulers are dysfunctional, their striking contrast with the model evangelical community of sailors on Pantagruel's ship, the *Thalamège,* further suggests that Rabelais is using foreign locales in *Le quart livre* to caricature divisive groups within European society. Scholars have also interpreted the work as a linquistic quest, as religious allegory, as a dreamscape or journey through the psyche, and as Rabelais's nightmarish descent into hell.

Despite the royal privilege that protected *Le quart livre,* the Parlement de Paris condemned the volume at the Sorbonne's request in early March 1552, little more than a month after its publication, and temporarily banned its sale in April, during the king's absence from Paris. The ban was apparently lifted when Henri II returned. Rumors that Rabelais had been imprisoned, based on the speculation of a friend of his in Lyon, surfaced late in the year; but scholars today question the truth of this report, given the friend's own doubt about its accuracy. Records show that Rabelais resigned his two benefices at Meudon and Saint-Christophe-du-Jambet on 9 January 1553, and that his brother, Jamet Rabelais, a merchant in Chinon, was listed as his only legatee or beneficiary on 14 March, suggesting that the author died at the beginning of the month. Yet, his epitaph from Saint-Paul's Church, near the cemetery where he was purportedly buried, listed the date and place of Rabelais's death as 9 April 1553, in the Rue des Jardins in Paris. Thus, the details of his death and of his final resting place remain the subject of much debate.

After Rabelais's death, a new chronicle attributed to him, *L'isle Sonante* (Ringing Island), was published in 1562. *L'isle Sonante* satirizes the church and the papacy in particular, and it also targets the veniality and corruption of the justice system as the Utopians continue their sea journey. Composed of two long episodes (eight chapters on Ringing Island and five devoted to the Chatz fourrez) or "Furry Lawcats" and three shorter episodes (Ferrements, or Toolmaking Island; Cassade, or the Island of Lying Illusions; and Apedeftes, or Island of the Ignorant), *L'isle Sonante* may have been written by Rabelais at the same time as *Le quart livre,* particularly if the last chapter is excluded for stylistic reasons.

L'isle Sonante, without the chapter on the Apedeftes, opens the *Cinquiesme et dernier livre,* which was published in 1564. Composed of thirty-two additional chapters and a prologue, this new work focuses more on hermeticism and on Panurge's initiation by Queen Quinte and the priestess Bacbuc, than on religious and judicial satire, which is limited primarily to the episode of the Frères Fredons (Quavering Friars). In this work replete with alchemical symbolism, Panurge and his companions arrive at the Oracle of the Divine Bottle and finally hear its prophecy, which is "Trinch," meaning "Drink!" Despite the similarity between this advice and Panurge's words at the conclusion of *Le quart livre* ("Sela, beuvons," or "Let's drink"), many scholars doubt the authenticity of the full-length *Cinquiesme et dernier livre,* believing instead that it is a compilation of fragments by opportunistic editors and humanists who attempted to profit from Rabelais's success.

Scores of editions of Rabelais's writings have appeared since 1532, including almost a hundred during that first century alone; and while the specific historical context that polarized his early readers has disappeared, his works have continued to fuel controversy, eliciting passionate responses from both admirers and detractors. In the seventeenth century his writings found particular favor with libertine authors such as Cyrano de Bergerac and Paul Scarron, but classical writers, with the exception of Molière and Jean de La Fontaine, were generally less enthusiastic. In his *Caractères* (1688, Characters) Jean de La Bruyère called Rabelais's works "un monstreux assemblage d'une morale fine et ingénieuse, et d'une sale corruption" (a monstrous assemblage of fine and ingenious morality and filthy corruption). Voltaire criticized his "misérable usage" (miserable use) of his wit. Rabelais's critical fortunes improved dramatically in the nineteenth century, when Romantic writers and critics—enamored of the past, and with a penchant for verbal excess and the grotesque imagination—came to recognize his literary genius. This view has endured in modern times, as evidenced by the wealth of scholarship focused on his texts, and by his influence on authors as diverse as Louis-Ferdinand Céline, Raymond Queneau, and James Joyce. Much earlier than Joyce and before Thomas Urquhart's first translations in 1653, English-speaking readers discovered and came to love Rabelais. According to the *Old English Dictionary,* the terms "Gargantuist" (Gabriel Harvey, *Pierce's Supererogation,* 1593) and "gargantuan" (Thomas Nashe, *Have with You,* 1596) date from the end of the sixteenth century. Early-modern writers including Sir Philip Sidney, Francis Bacon, Ben Jonson, and John Donne either refer to or quote Rabelais, and his influence on Laurence Sterne's *Tristram Shandy,* and on *Gulliver's Travels* by Jonathan Swift, is well known.

Rabelais's texts have also inspired a variety of non-literary adaptations. In addition to the famous illustrations associated with his work, most notably those of Gustave Doré, Rabelais's characters and subjects have provided the inspiration for dozens of musical and theatrical productions. Included in the list are royal masquerades (*Naissance de Pantagruel,* 1622), ballets (*Ballet des Andouilles,* 1628; *Boufonnerie rabelésique,* 1638), comedies (André Grétry's *Panurge dans l'île des lanternes,* 1785), and opera (*Pantagruel* by Alfred Jarry and Eugène Demolder, 1910; *Panurge, haute farce en trois actes* by Jules Massenet, 1913), as well as the spectacular and carnivalesque *Rabelais,* a "jeu dramatique" (dramatic game) by Jean-Louis Barrault that was staged in May 1968 during a time of student protests and social unrest. Although Rabelais's primary sphere of influence is learned culture, moreover, both Barrault's production and Mikhail Bakhtin's theories point out his ties with popular culture. Inoshiro Honda's *War of the Gargantuas,* released in 1966, as well as an American monster movie titled *Gargantua* (1998), attest to Rabelais's contributions to the industrialized world's collective imagination. In contemporary society, organizations ranging from restaurants to popular bands to student newspapers have borrowed the name "Gargantua," bearing witness to François Rabelais's continuing and wide-ranging legacy to modern culture, more than five centuries after his birth.

Letters:

Les epistres de Maistre Francois Rabelais . . . escrites pendant son voyage d'Italie, nouuellement mises en lumiere. Auec des obseruations historiques. Et l'abregé de la vie de l'autheur, edited by Louis de Saint-Marthe (Paris: Chez Charles de Sercy, 1651);

Les lettres de François Rabelais, escrites pendant son voyage d'Italie (Brussels: François Foppens, 1710);

Lettres écrites d'Italie par François Rabelais, edited by Victor-Louis Bourrilly (Paris: H. Champion, 1910).

Bibliographies:

Pierre-Paul Plan, *Bibliographie Rabelaisienne: Les éditions de Rabelais de 1532 à 1711* (Paris: Imprimerie nationale, 1904);

Stephen Rawles and M. A. Screech, *A New Rabelais Bibliography. Editions of Rabelais before 1626* (Geneva: Droz, 1987);

Bruno Braunrot, *François Rabelais: A Reference Guide, 1950–1990* (New York: G. K. Hall, 1994).

Biography:

Jean Plattard, *The Life of François Rabelais,* translated by Louis P. Roche (New York: Knopf, 1931).

References:

Erich Auerbach, "The World in Pantagruel's Mouth," in his *Mimesis: The Representation of Reality in Western Literature,* translated by Willard Trask (Princeton: Princeton University Press, 1953), pp. 262–284;

Mikhail Bakhtin, *Rabelais and His World,* translated by Hélène Iswolsky (Cambridge: MIT Press, 1968);

Alice Fiola Berry, *The Charm of Catastrophe. A Study of Rabelais's* Quart Livre (Chapel Hill: University of North Carolina Press, 2000);

Barbara Bowen, *The Age of Bluff. Paradox and Ambiguity in Rabelais and Montaigne* (Urbana: University of Illinois Press, 1972);

Gérard Brault, "'Un Abysme de Science': On the Interpretation of Gargantua's Letter to Pantagruel," *Bibliothèque d'Humanisme et Renaissance,* 28 (1966): 615–632;

Nan Cooke Carpenter, *Rabelais and Music* (Chapel Hill: University of North Carolina Press, 1954);

Terence Cave, *The Cornucopian Text: Problems of Writing in the French Renaissance* (Oxford: Clarendon Press, 1979), pp. 183–222;

Carol Clark, *The Vulgar Rabelais* (Glasgow: Pressgang, 1983);

Dorothy Gabe Coleman, *Rabelais: A Critical Study in Prose Fiction* (Cambridge: Cambridge University Press, 1973);

Edwin Duval, *The Design of Rabelais's* Pantagruel (New Haven & London: Yale University Press, 1991);

Duval, *The Design of Rabelais's* Quart Livre de Pantagruel (Geneva: Droz, 1998);

Lucien Febvre, *The Problem of Unbelief in the Sixteenth Century: The Religion of Rabelais,* translated by Beatrice Gottlieb (Cambridge: Harvard University Press, 1982);

Donald Frame, *François Rabelais: A Study* (New York: Harcourt Brace Jovanovich, 1977);

Carla Freccero, *Father Figures. Genealogy and Narrative Structure in Rabelais* (Ithaca, N.Y.: Cornell University Press, 1991);

Thomas M. Greene, *Rabelais: A Study in Comic Courage* (Englewood Cliffs, N.J.: Prentice-Hall, 1970);

Samuel Kinser, *Rabelais's Carnival: Text, Context, Metatext* (Berkeley: University of California Press, 1990);

Deborah Losse, *Rhetoric at Play. Rabelais and Satirical Eulogy* (Bern: Peter Lang, 1980);

Mallary Masters, *Rabelaisian Dialectic and the Platonic Hermetic Tradition* (Albany: State University of New York Press, 1969);

John Parkin, *Interpretations of Rabelais* (Lewiston, N.Y.: Edwin Mellen Press, 2002);

Charles Perrat, "Le *Polydore Virgile* de Rabelais," *Bibliothèque d'Humanisme et Renaissance,* no. 11 (1949): 203–204;

François Rigolot, *Les langages de Rabelais,* Etudes Rabelaisiennes, no. 10 (Geneva: Droz, 1972);

Jerome Schwartz, *Irony and Ideology in Rabelais. Structures of Subversion* (Cambridge: Cambridge University Press, 1990);

Michael A. Screech, *Rabelais* (Ithaca, N.Y.: Cornell University Press, 1979);

Paul J. Smith, *Voyage et écriture: Etude sur le "Quart Livre" de Rabelais,* Etudes Rabelaisiennes, no. 19 (Geneva: Droz, 1987);

Leo Spitzer, "Rabelais et les 'rabelaisants,'" *Studi Francesi,* 4 (September–December 1960): 401–423;

Walter Stephens, *Giants in Those Days: Folklore, Ancient History, and Nationalism* (Lincoln: University of Nebraska Press, 1989);

Marcel Tetel, *Etude sur le comique de Rabelais* (Florence: L. Olschki, 1964);

Florence M. Weinberg, *The Wine and the Will: Rabelais's Bacchic Christianity* (Detroit: Wayne State University Press, 1972);

Elizabeth Chesney Zegura, ed. *The Rabelais Encyclopedia* (Westport, Conn.: Greenwood Press, 2004);

Zegura and Marcel Tetel, *Rabelais Revisited* (New York: Macmillan/Twayne, 1993).

Pierre de Ronsard

(11 September 1524 – 28 December 1585)

Roberto E. Campo
University of North Carolina–Greensboro

BOOKS: *Epithalame d'Antoine de Bourbon et Janne de Navarre* (Paris: Printed by Michel de Vascosan, 1549);

Avantentrée du Roi Treschrestien à Paris (Paris: Printed by Gilles Corrozet, 1549);

L'Hymne de France (Paris: Printed by Michel de Vascosan, 1549);

Les Quatre Premiers Livres des Odes de Pierre de Ronsard, Vandomois. Ensemble son Bocage (Paris: Printed by Guillaume Cavellat, 1550); revised with new preface as *Les Quatre Premiers Livres des Odes* (Paris: Printed by Guillaume Cavellat, 1553; enlarged, Paris: Printed by the widow of Maurice de la Porte, 1555);

Ode de la Paix, au Roi (Paris: Printed by Guillaume Cavellat, 1550);

Les Amours de P. de Ronsard Vandomoys. Ensemble Le cinquiesme de ses Odes (Paris: Printed by the widow of Maurice de la Porte, 1552); enlarged as *Les Amours de P. de Ronsard Vandomois, nouvellement augmentées par lui, & commentées par Marc Antoine de Muret. Plus quelques Odes de L'Auteur, non encor imprimées* (Paris: Printed by the widow of Maurice de la Porte, 1553); revised and enlarged as *Le Cinquiesme des Odes . . . augmenté. Ensemble La Harangue que fit monseigneur le Duc de Guise, aus Soudars de Metz le jour qu'il pensoit avoir l'assaut, traduite en partie de Tyrtée poëte Grec: et dediée à monseigneur le Reverendissime Cardinal de Lorraine son frère* (Paris: Printed by the widow of Maurice de la Porte, 1553);

Livret de folastries. A Janot Parisien. Plus quelques Epigrames grecs: et des Dithyrambes changés au bouc de E. Jodelle Poëte Tragiq (Paris: Printed by the widow of Maurice de la Porte, 1553);

Le Bocage . . . , dedié à P. de Paschal, du bas païs de Languedoc (Paris: Printed by the widow of Maurice de la Porte, 1554);

Les Meslanges . . . dediées à Jean Brinon (Paris: Printed by Gilles Corrozet, 1555; enlarged, 1555);

Continuation des Amours (Paris: Printed by Vincent Sertenas, 1555);

Pierre de Ronsard (Hutton Archive/Getty Images)

Les Hymnes (Paris: Printed by André Wechel, 1555);

Le Second livre des Hymnes (Paris: Printed by André Wechel, 1556);

Nouvelle Continuation des Amours (Paris: Printed by Vincent Sertenas, 1556); enlarged as *Continuation des Amours de P. de Ronsard Vandomois* (Paris: Printed by Vincent Sertenas, 1557);

Exhortation au Camp du Roy pour bien combatre le jour de la bataille (Paris: Printed by André Wechel, 1558);

Exhortation pour la pais (Paris: Printed by André Wechel, 1558);

L'Hymne de tresillustre Prince Charles Cardinal de Lorraine (Paris: Printed by André Wechel, 1559);

Chant de liesse au Roy (Paris: Printed by André Wechel, 1559);

Chant pastoral sur les Nopces de de Monseigneur Charles duc de Lorraine et de Madame Claude (Paris: Printed by André Wechel, 1559);

La Paix. Au Roy (Paris: Printed by André Wechel, 1559);

Discours à treshault et trespuissant Prince Monseigneur le Duc de Savoye. Chant pastoral à Madame Marguerite, Duchesse de Savoye. Plus XXIIII inscriptions (Paris: Printed by Robert Estienne, 1559);

Suyte de l'Hymne de tres-illustre Prince Charles Cardinal de Lorraine (Paris: Printed by Robert Estienne, 1559);

Le Second livre des meslanges (Paris: Printed by Vincent Sertenas, 1559);

Les Œuvres de P. de Ronsard gentilhomme vandomois (4 volumes, Paris: Gabriel Buon, 1560; revised and enlarged, 6 volumes, 1567–1573; revised and enlarged, 7 volumes, 1578–1584; revised and enlarged, 10 volumes, 1587);

Elegie sur le despart de la Royne Marie retournant à son royaume d'Escosse (Lyon: Printed by Benoist Rigaud, 1561);

Institution pour l'adolescence du Roy treschrestien Charles neufviesme de ce nom (Paris: Printed by Gabriel Buon, 1562);

Discours des miseres de ce temps. A la Royne mere du Roy (Paris: Printed by Gabriel Buon, 1562);

Continuation du discours des miseres de ce temps (Paris: Printed by Gabriel Buon, 1562);

Remonstrance au peuple de France (Paris: Printed by Gabriel Buon, 1563);

Responce de P. de Ronsard Gentilhomme Vandomois, aux injures et calomnies, de je ne sçay quels Predicans, et Ministres de Geneve. Sur son Discours et Continuation des Miseres de ce Temps (Paris: Printed by Gabriel Buon, 1563);

Elegie de P. de Ronsard Vandomois, sur les troubles d'Amboise, 1560 (Paris: Printed by Gabriel Buon, 1563);

Les Trois Livres du Recueil des nouvelles Poësies (Paris: Printed by Gabriel Buon, 1564);

La Promesse . . . à la Royne (N.p., 1564);

Elegies, Mascarades et Bergeries (Paris: Printed by Gabriel Buon, 1565);

Le Proces. A tresillustre Prince Charles, Cardinal de Lorraine (Paris, 1565);

Abbregé de l'Art poëtique François (Paris: Printed by Gabriel Buon, 1565);

Le Fourmy de P. de Ronsard à R. Belleau: Le Papillon de R. Belleau à P. de Ronard. Mis en latin par P. Est. Tabourot (Paris, 1565);

Le Sixiesme Livre des Poëmes (Paris: Printed by Jean Dallier, 1569);

Le Septiesme Livre des Poëmes (Paris: Printed by Jean Dallier, 1569);

Quatre premiers livre[s] de la Franciade (Paris: Printed by Gabriel Buon, 1572);

Le Tombeau du feu Roy Tres-Chrestien Charles IX. Prince tres-debonnaire, tres vertueux & tres-eloquent. Par Pierre de Ronsard Aumosnier ordinaire de sa Majesté, et autres excellens Poètes de ce temps (Paris: Printed by Federic Morel, 1574);

Discours au Roy, après son retour de Pologne en l'année LMDLXXIIII (Lyon: Printed by Michel Jove and Jean Pillehotte, 1574);

Estreines au Roy Henry III. Envoyees à sa Majesté au mois de decembre (N.p., 1574);

Les Estoilles à Monsieur de Pibrac (Paris: Printed by Gabriel Buon, 1575);

Le Tombeau de tres-illustre Princesse Marguerite de France, Duchesse de Savoye (Paris: Printed by Gabriel Buon, 1575);

Panegyrique de la Renommée (Paris: Printed by Gabriel Buon, 1579);

Les Derniers vers de Pierre de Ronsard, Gentilhomme Vandomois (Paris: Printed by Gabriel Buon, 1586).

Editions and Collections: *Œuvres complètes de Pierre de Ronsard,* 8 volumes, edited by Prosper Blanchemain (Paris: P. Jannet, 1857–1867);

Œuvres de Pierre de Ronsard, gentilhomme vandômois, 6 volumes, edited by Charles Marty-Laveaux (Paris: A. Lemerre, 1887);

Œuvres complètes, 20 volumes, edited by Paul Laumonier, Isidore Silver, and Raymond Lebègue (volumes 1–7, Paris: Hachette; volumes 8–10, Paris: Droz; volumes 11–20, Paris: Didier, 1914–1975);

Le Second livre des amours, edited by Hugues Vaganay and Margaret de Schweinitz (Lyon: M. de Schweinitz, 1914);

Livret de folastries, à Janot parisien. Edition conforme au texte original de 1553, collationnée sur l'exemplaire de la Bibliothèque de l'Arsenal; augmentée d'une bibliographie de chaque pièce de toutes les variantes, d'un glossaire et d'un notice, edited by Fernand Fleuret and Louis Perceau (Paris: Bibliothèque des curieux, 1920);

Œuvres Complètes, 7 volumes, edited by Vaganay (Paris: Garnier, 1923–1924);

Ronsard et sa province: Anthologie régionale, edited by Laumonier (Paris: Presses Universitaires de France, 1924);

Discours des miseres de ce temps (Paris: Le Fuseau chargé de Laine, 1930);

Œuvres complètes de Ronsard, texte de 1578, 7 volumes, edited by Vaganay and Pierre de Nolhac (Paris: Garnier, 1944);

Sonnets pour Hélène, edited by Jacques Lavaud (Paris: Droz, 1947);

Discours des misères de ce temps, edited by Jean Baillou (Paris: Société les Belles Lettres, 1949);

Œuvres complètes de Ronsard, edited by Gustave Cohen (Paris: Gallimard, 1950; revised, 1958);

Le Second livre des Amours, edited by Alexandre Micha (Geneva: Droz, 1951);

Les Amours, edited by Henri Weber and Catherine Weber (Paris: Garnier, 1963);

Poésies choisies de Ronsard, edited by Nolhac (Paris: Garnier, 1963);

Œuvres complètes, 8 volumes, edited by Silver (Chicago: University of Chicago Press, 1966–1970);

Poésies choisies de Pierre de Ronsard, edited by Françoise Joukovsky (Paris: Garnier, 1969);

Sonnets pour Hélène, edited by Malcolm Smith (Geneva: Droz, 1970);

Selected Poems, edited by Christine M. Scollen (London: Athlone Press, University of London, 1974);

Ronsard, I: Poems of Love, edited by Grahame Castor and Terrence Cave (Manchester, U.K.: Manchester University Press, 1975);

Ronsard, II: Odes, Hymns and Other Poems, edited by Castor and Cave (Manchester, U.K.: Manchester University Press, 1977);

Hymnes, edited by Albert Py (Geneva: Droz, 1978);

Discours des misères de ce temps, edited by Smith (Geneva: Droz, 1979);

Les Amours (1552–1584), edited by Marc Bensimon and James L. Martin (Paris: Garnier-Flammarion, 1981);

Œuvres complètes de Ronsard, 2 volumes, edited by Jean Céard, Daniel Ménager, and Michel Simonin (Paris: Gallimard, 1994).

Editions in English: *Songs & Sonnets of Pierre de Ronsard,* translated by Curtis Hidden Page (Boston & New York: Houghton Mifflin, 1924);

Pierre de Ronsard: Sonnets pour Hélène, parallel translations by Humbert Wolfe (New York: Macmillan, 1934);

Poems of Pierre de Ronsard, translated by Nicholas Kilmner (Berkeley: University of California Press, 1979);

Lyrics of the French Renaissance: Marot, Du Bellay, Ronsard, translated by Norman R. Shapiro, introduction by Hope Glidden (New Haven: Yale University Press, 2002);

Pierre de Ronsard: Selected Poems, translated by Malcolm Quainton and Elizabeth Vinestock (London: Penguin, 2002).

OTHER: "Elegie . . . à J. Grevin," in *Théâtre de J. Grévin* (Paris: Printed by Vincent Sertenas & Guillaumne Barbé, 1561);

"Sonet de Pierre de Ronsard à l'Autheur," "À la porte S. Denis," and "Sonet de Pierre de Ronsard," in *Bref et sommaire recueil de ce qui a esté faict . . . à la joyeuse . . . Entrée de . . . Charles IX,* compiled by Simon Bouquet (Paris: Printed by Denis du Pré for Olivier Codoré, 1572);

"Il me souvient, Garnier. . . ," in *Hippolyte,* by Robert Garnier (Paris: Printed by Robert Estienne, 1573);

"La Nymphe de France parle," in *Magnificentissimi spectaculi, a Regina Regum Matre in hortis suburbanis editi, In Henrici Regis Poloniae invictissimi nuper renunciati gratulationem, Descriptio,* by Jean Dorat (Paris: Printed by Federic Morel, 1573);

"Ode, par Monsieur de Ronsard: 'Homere, il suffisoit assez,'" in *La Continuation de l'Iliade d'Homere,* by Amadis Jamyn (Paris: Printed by Lucas Breyer, 1574);

"Le vieil cothurne d'Euripide," in *Cornélie,* by Garnier (Paris: Printed by Robert Estienne, 1574);

"Si doctement ta muse assemble," in Louis Le Jars, *Lucelle, tragi-comedie en proze françoise Disposée d'actes & scenes suivant les Grecs & Latins* (Paris: Printed by Robert le Mangnier, 1576);

"Heureux tu jouïs de ta peine," in *Les Œuvres poetiques,* by Jamyn (Paris: Printed by Mamert Patisson, 1577);

"Ne taillez, mains industrieuses," in *Remigü Bellaquei Poetae Tumulus* (Paris: Printed by Mamert Patisson, 1577);

"En fance," "La Puerilitá," "Adolessance," "Jeunesse," "Le Viril," "Viellesse," and "Le Caduc," in *Les Figures et Portraictz des sept Ages de l'homme, Avec le subject sur chacun diceux, Faictz tailler et graver, Par N[icolas] L[e] C[amus]. Sur les principaux enluminez de Feu B[aptiste] P[ellerin]* (Paris: Printed by Nicolas le Camus, 1580).

SELECTED PERIODICAL PUBLICATION–UNCOLLECTED: "'De la joie et de la tristesse,' Un discours inédit de Ronsard," edited by Roger Gaucheron, *Mercure de France,* no. 636 (December 1924): 604–613.

Pierre de Ronsard is unquestionably the greatest poet of the French Renaissance. His famous appellation speaks broadly to the reasons for this renown: "prince des poètes, poète des princes" (prince of poets, poet of princes). On the one hand, he founded and led a small group of like-minded writers known first as the Brigade and later as the Pléiade, a name derived from the cluster of seven stars in the constellation Taurus that was first used in a literary sense for the seven most prominent Greek tragic poets of the reign of Ptolemy II. On the other hand, by assuming that leadership he transcended his rank as the tonsured son of a Vendôme country gentleman to gain a place in the service of four

Renaissance French kings, a queen regent, and many of the foremost lords, ladies, and officials of their courts.

Central to Ronsard's eminence are his literary and intellectual achievements. Not only did he go farthest to implement the principles for invigorating the French language laid out by his friend and colleague Joachim du Bellay in his *La Deffence et illustration de la langue françoyse* (Defense and Illustration of the French Language, 1549), but also, in accord with the tenets of the treatise, Ronsard stretched the formal and expressive bounds of his art while exalting the status of poetry and the "Poète" (true poet). Inspired by the lessons of contemporary classicists such as Jean Dorat, Ronsard set out to break away from the stale conventions of his contemporaries by infusing his verse with the spirit, wisdom, and mythological legacy of antiquity. That influence fueled experiments with major and minor ancient genres ranging from the ode to the dithyramb; moreover, supported by the theories of poets such as Horace and Virgil, it emboldened him to ascribe a potential prophetic quality to verse. Antiquity was not the only source of Ronsard's creative flow. He also drew upon the writings of early modern Italian and neo-Latin poets such as Francesco Petrarch and Michael Marullus. The result was a voluminous corpus of poetry as diverse as the worlds Ronsard aspired to represent—a body of literary works that shaped French poetry for decades after his death, gave direction to the idealistic voices of the nineteenth-century Romantics, and provides literary critics and cultural historians of today with insight into the dominant aesthetic, philosophical, and social concerns of France during the second half of the sixteenth century.

It is generally agreed that Pierre de Ronsard was born near the little Vendôme town of Couture-sur-Loir, during the early morning hours of Sunday, 11 September 1524. He was the youngest of the four surviving children of Louis de Ronsard and Jeanne Chaudrier. Jeanne was the daughter of a Poitevin family with ties to several prominent bloodlines of sixteenth-century France; Louis was a country gentleman whose distinction as a knight in the Italian campaigns of Charles VIII and Louis XII earned him the position of royal diplomat and maître d'hôtel of the two elder sons of François I, the dauphin François and Henri of Orléans, future Henri II. Louis was a man of considerable culture as well—a quality that found expression both in the Italian-style elements he added to the family domain, La Possonnière, around 1515 and in his affection for letters, which inspired his own efforts at rhyming and motivated the protection he offered to poets such as Jean Bouchet, of the school known as the Grands Rhétoriqueurs. Because of his father's frequent absences, Ronsard was also strongly influenced by his relation

Cassandre Salviati, the daughter of a Florentine banker, who inspired many of Ronsard's lyrics (Harlingue/Roger-Viollet/Getty Images)

with his cleric uncle, Jean de Ronsard. Thought to have played an important role in his nephew's earliest education, Jean de Ronsard was likewise a writer of verses, and he possessed a substantial library to which Ronsard became heir upon his uncle's death.

In fall 1533 Ronsard left his home to receive formal instruction in Paris. Recognizing his son's intellectual promise, Louis enrolled his nine-year-old son at the academically and religiously conservative Collège de Navarre in the Latin Quarter of the capital. Here Ronsard met Charles of Lorraine-Guise, a classmate of his own age who would one day become an influential cardinal, minister, and advocate of the poet in the court of Henri II. In spring 1534, after only one semester of study, the boy was peremptorily withdrawn from the school and returned to the paternal manor. This departure has been ascribed both to the young Ronsard's homesickness and to his father's fear that his son might become associated with the position taken by the college against the Reformist leanings of the king's sister, Marguerite de Navarre.

Nearly two years later, on 4 August 1536, Louis took advantage of his office in the royal household to secure his son a position as page to the dauphin François. A mere six days after joining François in the Rhône Valley, the dauphin died, and Ronsard, not yet twelve years old, found himself attending the prince's autopsy—an event he recalled, some thirty-nine years later, among the verses of his *Le Tombeau de tres-illustre Princesse Marguerite de France, Duchesse de Savoye* (1575, Tomb for the Most Illustrious Princess, Marguerite de France, Duchess of Savoie):

Je vey son corps ouvrir, osant mes yeux repaistre
Des poulmons & du coeur & du sang de mon maistre.
Tel sembloit Adonis sur la place estendu,
Apres que tout son sang du corps fut respandu.

(I saw his body being opened, daring to feast my eyes
on the lungs, and the heart and the blood of my master.
Thus was Adonis spread out on the ground
after all of the blood was spilt from his body.)

This shocking experience was followed by others. While in Lyon on 7 October 1536, Pierre was witness, on orders from a vengeful Charles V, to the quartering of the dauphin's foreign-born squire, wrongly convicted of poisoning his master; on 2 July 1537, barely a month and a half after arriving in Scotland as a page in the service of the deceased prince's sister and the newly crowned queen of that country, Madeleine de France, he watched as the ravaging effects of pulmonary consumption extinguished the lady's life before she reached her seventeenth birthday. Biographers and literary critics have speculated that these encounters with human mortality at an early age account for the themes of cruel Fortune and the inevitability of death throughout Ronsard's poetry.

After his initial sojourn in Scotland, which lasted until fall 1538, Ronsard reentered France and rejoined the household of François I's youngest son, Charles d'Orléans, to whom he had been briefly attached after the death of the dauphin. By winter, however, Ronsard was on his way back to Scotland as a member of his first diplomatic mission, one involving a voyage on storm-battered seas that nearly cost the lives of the entire French delegation. By March 1539 he was once more in France. Then almost fourteen, Ronsard was promoted from page to squire and assigned to military training at the royal stables of the Hôtel des Tournelles in Paris. There Pierre met Claudio Duchi, a young Italian scholar nicknamed the "seigneur Paul" who introduced him to the works of Virgil and Horace. This interlude lasted until May 1540, when the squire resumed the role of assistant diplomat at the Diet of Haguenau, having been assigned to join the distinguished humanist Lazare de Baïf, leader of the French embassy that endeavored (unsuccessfully) to convince the Lutheran princes of Germany to support François I's continuing campaign against Charles V.

Ronsard's life took a different path after his return to France in August 1540. Struck by a high fever that permanently impaired his hearing, he was obliged to abandon his previous pursuits and retreat to La Possonnière. The ensuing three-year convalescence afforded him an opportunity to deepen his admiration for the natural beauty of the Vendôme countryside and to peruse his uncle Jean's library while reflecting on the lessons of life and art learned in the company of Lazare de Baïf, the "seigneur Paul," and his previous royal masters. The result was an awakening to the inspirational possibilities of the nearby Gastine forest and the Bellerie fountain, as well as a renewed understanding of the precariousness of human fortune and a conviction, crystalized by his readings of Horace and Virgil, that the poet enjoys a special relation with the divine that enables him to immortalize the merely human. These discoveries evidently led to his decision to write and became central themes in early poems such as his "Les louanges de Vandomois" (The Praises of the Vendôme) and the two odes "A la fontaine Bellerie" (To the Bellerie Fountain).

By the beginning months of 1543 Ronsard had recovered from his fever and was confronted with supporting himself in his new vocation. The surest option for a gentleman of the day in his situation—a third-born son with rights to inherit only a minor share of the paternal estate who had no further interest in a military or diplomatic career—was to enter the church. With his father at his side, he did just that by receiving the simple tonsure of a cleric in minor orders on 6 March 1543, a day after attending the funeral mass dedicated to Guillaume de Langey du Bellay, a distant cousin of the Ronsard family and a relative of his future Pléiade comrade, the Angevin poet Joachim du Bellay. Ronsard aspired to obtain income from both the church and the crown, the latter having acquired substantial control over the disposition of ecclesiastical revenues and property since the Concordat of 1515. Ronsard's future thereby became vulnerable to the whims of courtiers who granted such benefices, a dependency he at once cultivated and regretted throughout his life.

The tonsuring was likewise the occasion of Ronsard's encounter with the next significant figure in his literary career, the rising humanist and poet Peletier, who read several of the neophyte's early pieces and exhorted him to pursue his poetic calling. Moreover, as a scholar and translator of Horace, Virgil, Ovid, and

Homer, Peletier was first to cultivate Ronsard's appreciation for those ancient authors.

Ronsard's poetic career took another step forward when he returned to Paris in spring 1543. Still attached to the household of Charles d'Orléans, he again took up residence at the Tournelles where his renewed vigor and athleticism caught the eye of the dauphin Henri who, if the poet's later friend and biographer Claude Binet is to be believed, wanted Ronsard on his side in every game he played. Of greater importance to Ronsard, however, was the opportunity to renew his acquaintance with Lazare de Baïf, with whom he enjoyed an almost father-son relation. At Ambassador Baïf's luxurious townhouse near the Parisian Latin Quarter, the young poet was able to join his host's son, Jean-Antoine de Baïf, another future principal of the Pléiade, in the study of Greek and Latin letters. The Hôtel Baïf brought Ronsard into contact with many dignitaries whose praises were subsequently sung in the third book of the *Quatre Premiers Livres des Odes . . . Ensemble son Bocage* (First Four Books of Odes . . . Along with His Grove).

With the deaths of his father in June 1544 and his mother in January 1545 and the attainment of his majority at age twenty the intervening September, Ronsard found the independence to devote greater attention to his poetic ambitions. Especially valuable was the time he began dedicating to his studies under the eminent Hellenist, Dorat, the latest addition to the team of Baïf preceptors and a scholar whose analyses of Homer captured the imagination of Ronsard and his fellow pupils. Beginning in fall 1544 these lessons included an examination of Greek mythology that complemented the study of Roman myths Ronsard had undertaken while reading Ovid's *Metamorphoses* at the urging of Peletier. Among the works of this period that inscribe his fascination with the lore of antiquity are the "Chant de folie à Bacchus" (Song of Folly to Bacchus), "La defloration de Lède" (The Deflowering of Leda), and "Le ravissement de Cephale" (The Rape of Cephalus), all of which were published in *Ode de la Paix, au Roi* (1550, Ode of Peace to the King).

The next five years, during which Ronsard continued to expand his poetic portfolio, were important to his developing career. A signal event was his first sighting of Cassandre Salviati, the beautiful fourteen-year-old daughter of a Florentine banker, during a ball held at the royal castle in Blois on 21 April 1545. No alliance apparently came of this encounter, but the poet's resulting sentiments—as much imaginary as real—inspired hundreds of lyrical pieces over the following decade. The same year Ronsard began his search for a reliable source of patronage. François I's sister, Marguerite de Navarre, a prolific author in her own right, was among

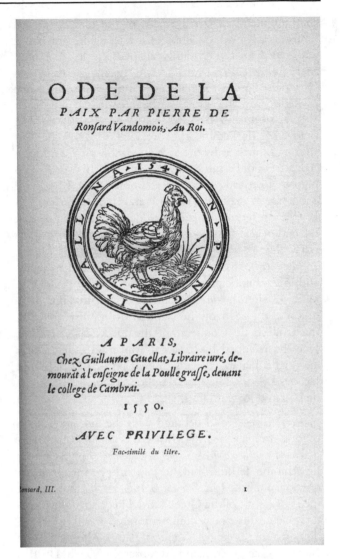

Title page for the poem in which Ronsard announces his intention to write "La Franciade," a heroic national epic to celebrate the mythical founder of France (from Œuvres complètes, edited by Paul Laumonier, Isidore Silver, and Raymond Lebègue, 1914–1975; Thomas Cooper Library, University of South Carolina)

those from whom he sought favor. He offered her his "Consolation à la Royne de Navarre sur la Mort de Charles de Valois duc d'Orléans, son neveu" (Consolation to the Queen of Navarre on the Death of Charles de Valois, Duke of Orleans, Her Nephew), a Horatianesque ode memorializing the queen's beloved nephew, his former master, who had died at age twenty-three in September. This solicitation proved as unsuccessful as the others he made at the time.

Two years later, as Henri II acceded to the throne on 31 March 1547, Ronsard turned for support to his former royal teammate and the notables of the new court. Although again unsuccessful, he had the fortune that summer to cross the path of Joachim du Bellay. The meeting was the start of a friendship and poetic association that profoundly shaped the lives of both men. In September, Ronsard had the added satisfaction of witnessing, for the first time, the publication of one of his poems, the ode "Des beautez qu'il voudroit en s'amie" (On the Beauties He Would Wish in His Beloved). Marked by the precious style of Clément Marot as much as by the love poetry of Ovid, Ludovico Ariosto, and Petrarch, the poem, which was written before Ronsard became enamored of Cassandre Salviati, was dedicated to his literary counselor Jacques Peletier. In return, Peletier included Ronsard's poem at the end of *Les Œuvres poetiques de Jacques Peletier du Mans* (1547, The Poetic Works of Jacques Peletier du Mans), a collection of verses whose ancient and Italian forms and themes anticipated those of the coming Pléiade. In fall 1547, after the death of Lazare de Baïf and the dissolution of the academy he inspired, Ronsard enrolled in the Collège de Coqueret of the University of Paris. Here he resumed his classical education under Dorat and made valuable friends such as Nicolas Denisot and Jacques Bouju while renewing bonds with Jean-Antoine de Baïf and Joachim du Bellay.

The year 1549 debuted with the first publication of a pamphlet bearing Ronsard's name: *Epithalame d'Antoine de Bourbon et Janne de Navarre* (Epithalamium for Antoine de Bourbon and Janne de Navarre), subsequently published in *Ode de la Paix, au Roi*. Written in the idyllic style of the Greek bard Theocritus (third century B.C.), this poem commemorated the recent wedding of the duke of Vendôme and Marguerite de Navarre's daughter, Jeanne d'Albret. In March, Du Bellay's *La Deffence et illustration de la langue françoyse* and *L'Olive* (The Olive) were published. Notwithstanding its logical inconsistencies, the *Deffence* promotes the French language and the calls for its poets to transcend the conceptual and lexical limits of the medieval past by emulating the most worthy writings of Greek and Roman antiquity and early modern Italy. Although Ronsard's contribution to Du Bellay's discourse remains unclear, few dispute that it represents the inaugural declaration of the new poetics espoused by Ronsard and his followers among the elite alumni of the Hôtel Baïf and Collège de Coqueret. This group, then known as the "Brigade," was to be described in his 642-verse poem *Les Bacchanales ou le folastrissime voyage d'Hercueil pres Paris* (The Bacchanals or the Most Wanton Voyage in Arcueil Near Paris), published in 1552. The printing of Du Bellay's sequence of Petrarchan-style love sonnets, *L'Olive,* was also significant to Ronsard, albeit primarily as a motive to hasten the assembly of his own collection of poems.

In summer 1549 Ronsard made the important acquaintance of the king's sister, Marguerite de France, and her entourage. Among the brightest beacons of learning in the court of Henri II, the princess quickly became the poet's "Pallas" and one of his staunchest defenders against the "vilain monstre Ignorance" (villainous monster Ignorance): the official royal poet, Mellin de Saint-Gelais, and the partisans of both the Grands Rhétoriqueurs and the Marot school who had mounted a campaign to discredit the innovations of Ronsard and his fledgling Brigade.

In January 1550 the twenty-five-year-old Ronsard published his first major work, *Les Quatre Premiers Livres des Odes de Pierre de Ronsard, Vandomois. Ensemble son Bocage.* The first part of the collection is made up of ninety-four odes unevenly partitioned into four books and strongly influenced by the styles of two ancient authors: Pindar, the Greek lyric poet famous for odes honoring the victors of the Panhellenic games, and Horace, the Roman author of odes treating a range of philosophical, political, and personal topics. The Pindaric style dominates the initial thirteen poems, distinguished (with one exception) by their triadic organization into strophes, antistrophes, and epodes; by a gravity of tone suitable for praising both rulers and friends; and by a quality, proudly promoted in the poet's prefatory "Au lecteur" (To the Reader), distinguished by a topical variety inspired by the infinite diversity of Nature. The Horatian style marks the majority of odes that remain. These pieces vary considerably in length, meter, and tone. Several odes affirm the poet's role as a mystical prophet and the power of his rhymes to immortalize any subject, while often suggesting the superiority of poetry to other arts. Other verses exhibit Ronsard's fondness for esoteric mythological references as well as for the natural beauty of the Vendôme. The second part of the volume, the *Bocage,* is comprised of fourteen poems of irregular form and caliber, variously inspired, and generally gleaned from Ronsard's earliest writings.

Les Quatre Premiers Livres des Odes was attacked in the highest circles of the court. Saint-Gelais and the old-guard poets were especially offended by Ronsard's audacious preface, wherein he claims to be "le premier auteur Lirique François" (the first French author of lyric) and declares his intention to seek models among "étrangers" (foreigners) such as Pindar and Horace because he failed to find a "chose qui fust suffisante d'imiter" (thing that was worth imitating) in the poetry of his compatriots. Marguerite de France came to his defense, seconded by her powerful chancellor Michel de l'Hospital, both of whom were familiar with Ronsard's sources and recognized the ability of the poet to revitalize the French language and verse of the day.

Ronsard's next work was published in April 1550 in pamphlet form, *Ode de la Paix, au Roi*. Conceived to gain royal favor by applauding Henri II for bringing an end to the recent wars with England, this ode—written in the style of Pindar—fell short of its goal but is noteworthy for its announcement of the poet's career-long ambition to write the first French *Iliad*, a heroic national epic in twenty-four books celebrating the king's legendary ancestor and the mythical founder of France, Francus (or Francion, known originally as Astyanax), son of Homer's Trojan hero, Hector. Ronsard subsequently titled the poem "La Franciade," but, failing to secure financial support from the king, he did not begin to compose it until many years later.

Within a few months Ronsard left Paris and his critics at court for the calm of the family estates in the Vendôme and environs. The poet pursued two main projects during this bucolic retreat, which lasted until spring 1552. To begin, he composed three odes and a hymn for inclusion in the *Tombeau de Marguerite de Valois royne de Navarre* (1551, Tomb for Marguerite de Valois, Queen of Navarre), the poetic memorial for Marguerite de Navarre, who had died in 1549, that was organized by his Coqueret colleague Denisot. Among Ronsard's contributions, "Hymne triumphal" (Triumphal Hymn) is noteworthy for the counterattack it launches against Saint-Gelais.

Ronsard then focused on preparing the majority of pieces destined for *Les Amours de P. de Ronsard Vandomoys. Ensemble Le cinquiesme de ses Odes* (1552, The Loves of P. de Ronsard, along with the Fifth Book of Odes). Consisting of 183 sonnets, a "Chanson" (song), and an "Amourette" (infatuation), the *Amours* collection represents the tumultuous emotional and psychological consequences of unreciprocated love in the case of a poet who vainly pursues the affections of Cassandre, an aloof, brown-eyed, blonde beauty whose name links her at once with the cursed prophetess of Greek myth and the Florentine damsel who had captured Ronsard's heart at Blois seven years earlier. When Ronsard first addressed Cassandre in ten of the 1550 odes, his sources were the sensual verses of Latin authors such as the ancients Gaius Catullus and Valerius Marullus and his contemporary Johannes Secundus. For the *Amours* poems, however, he took primary inspiration from the Italian sonnets of Petrarch's *Rima Sparse* (Scattered Rhymes), the *canzoniere* (songbook) portraying the poet's quest to win the spiritual love of his sublime lady, Laura. Ronsard not only demonstrated his ability to emulate the Tuscan laureate (thereby enacting a central principle of Brigade poetics) but also aspired to win back favor at court, where Petrarch's writings enjoyed considerable popularity. A different spirit distinguishes the twelve-poem *Cinquiesme de ses Odes*. Beyond including

the four pieces originally submitted for Marguerite de Navarre's *Tombeau* and *Les Bacchanales* that introduced the band of Brigade comrades, this diverse collection delivered additional blows to Ronsard's detractors as it extolled his defenders, Marguerite de France and Michel de l'Hospital. It also afforded the context for further theoretical reflections on the poet's privileged relation with the Muses and the divine. In an ode titled "A Madame Marguerite," for instance, he simultaneously praises the "Vierge tresbonne" (most-kind Virgin) who supported him when his work was "Mellinisé" ("Mellinized," or attacked by Mellin de Saint-Gelais), and he promises to apply his sacred poetic gifts to immortalize her virtues. Similarly, in his longest and most important Pindaric poem, "Ode à Michel de l'Hospital," which was probably written during the second half of 1550, Ronsard glorifies Marguerite's chancellor as "L'ornement de nostre France" (ornament of our France) while presenting an explanation of the role of divine poets such as the author himself.

The year 1553 began auspiciously with a reconciliation between Ronsard and Saint-Gelais brokered by L'Hospital and Jean de Morel, master of the king's household. A general condemnation of "Anger" completes a proclamation of the resulting new friendship in his ode "A Melin de Saint-Gelais," written in early January. Soon after, Ronsard approved the second edition of *Les Quatre Premiers Livres des Odes,* which omitted the contentious preface that had enraged the old-guard poets at court. Next to appear was the *Livret de folastries. A Janot Parisien. Plus quelques Epigrammes grecs: et des Dithyrambes chantés au bouc de E. Jodelle Poëte Tragiq* (1553, Little Book of Follies to Janot the Parisian. Plus a Few Greek Epigrams and Dithyrambs Sung to the Goat of E. Jodelle, Poet of Tragedies). Strongly influenced by the saucy writings of the Roman love poet Catullus and various racy pieces assembled in the *Greek Anthology* (the sixteen-book opus comprised of short Greek poems written on various topics between the seventh century B.C. and the tenth century A.D.), this collection of twenty-nine "sornettes / Et . . . mignardes chansonnettes" (playful words and wanton little songs) came out anonymously in April and, as the author had expected, attracted immediate official disapproval. That reception notwithstanding, the book was as widely read as other morally daring works of the day. Moreover, its mixture of earthiness and brash humor exposed a side of the poet that coincides with his playful *galliard* spirit, an amalgam of Gallic sensuality, audacity, and wit that found its most poignant expression in future rebuttals to his Huguenot detractors. Coincidentally, these same detractors pointed to the *Livret de folastries* as grounds for their condemnations, citing the overall eroticism of the work and, specifically, the approval of paganism implied in the

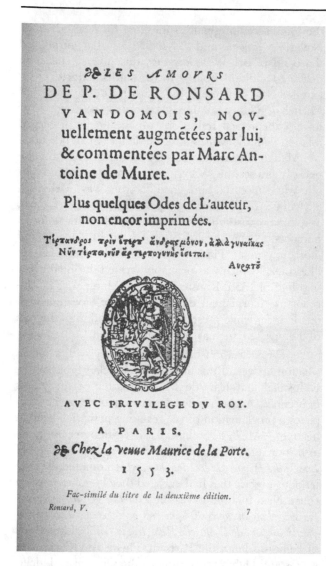

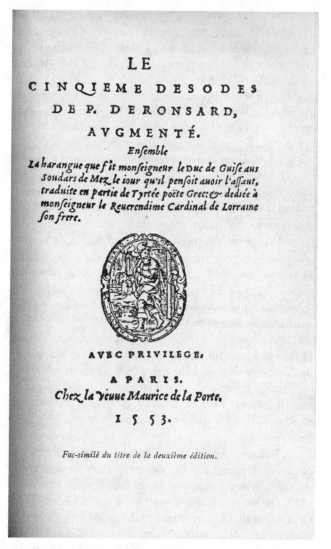

Title pages for works originally published together in 1552 under the title Les Amours de P. de Ronsard Vandomoys. Ensemble Le cinquiesme de ses Odes (*from* Œuvres Complètes, *edited by Paul Laumonier, Isidore Silver, and Raymond Labègue, 1914–1975; Thomas Cooper Library, University of South Carolina*)

"Dithyrambes," a Bacchanalian song evoking the Brigade's mock sacrifice of a goat in celebration of the successful debut of the tragedy, *Cléopâtre captive* (Captive Cleopatra), by a group newcomer, Etienne Jodelle.

In May 1553 a second edition of *Les Amours* was separately published in which Ronsard's tribute to his love for Cassandre then embraced 220 sonnets in all (of which 39 were new) and four odes, including the first published version of his reconciliation poem to Saint-Gelais, his famous carpe diem piece "Mignonne, allons voir si la rose" (Darling, let us see if the rose . . .), and "Les Isles fortunées" (The Isles of Fortune), providing the latest roster of Brigade associates. Furthermore, the volume offered extensive textual commentaries by the humanist lawyer, Marc-Antoine Muret, who had

greatly impressed Ronsard with his lectures on Catullus and his recently published collection of Latin love verses. Ronsard hoped to improve reception of his *canzoniere* by elucidating the obscure literary and mythological references that had frustrated readers of the initial version. Finally, before health problems and an outbreak of the plague in Paris prompted a retreat to his recently acquired provincial priory of Mareuil-lès-Meaux and ultimately to Vendôme, Ronsard oversaw the separate publication of a revised version of *Le Cinquiesme Livre des Odes*. Here the poet continued his effort to mend relations with Saint-Gelais by suppressing the attacks levied against him in the first edition. The revised work also introduced the earliest elegies and pieces in other poetic genres. Most notable

among the former is the "Elégie à J. de la Péruse," a tribute to the tragedy writer and poet, Jean Bastier de La Péruse, whom Ronsard includes in his Brigade.

Ronsard's success and productivity grew considerably in the three-year period from 1554 through 1556. His rising prestige was signaled, early in 1554, both by his acquisition of a royal privilege granting him the singular right to "faire imprimer les oeuvres par luy ja mises en lumiere, & autres qu'il composera & escrira cy apres" (to have printed his formerly published works, and others he will compose and write hereafter) and by his appointment as "poète ordinaire du Roy" (staff poet of the King) shortly after Henri II learned of the Franciade project and heard the poet praised by Pierre Lescot, chief architect of the Louvre palace. In the course of the same year Ronsard produced two major collections: *Le Bocage . . . , dedié à P. de Paschal, du bas païs de Languedoc* (1554, The Grove . . . Dedicated to P. de Paschal, from the Low Country of Languedoc) and *Les Meslanges* (Mixtures). The first work (printed and published in November 1554) was dedicated to Pierre de Paschal, the royal historiographer whose name appeared in the early descriptions of the Brigade and in whom the poet vainly hoped to find a biographer to sing his praise; the second (likewise printed that November, though dated 1555) was devoted to Jean Brinon, a magistrate in the Parliament of Paris whose generosity toward the poets, painters, and musicians of the day precipitated his financial ruin and death at a young age. Together the two works incorporated 99 new poems of multiple types, including familiar forms such as odes, sonnets, and elegies, and rarely or never attempted genres such as epitaphs, *voeux* (wishes), and "odelettes," a term Ronsard used to designate his early *chansons* (songs) as to avoid association with the "chansons vulgaires" (vulgar songs) of the prior poetic generations, which had been denounced in *La Deffence et illustration de la langue françoyse.*

Notable among the pieces of the 1554 *Bocage* are the ode "A Pierre de Pascal," presenting an autobiography of the Pléiade leader through 1550, and eight assorted "epitaphs" attesting to the poet's growing obsession with human mortality. The eight poems from *Livret de folastries* republished in the same collection indicate Ronsard's willingness to continue to defy his critics. Most remarkable in the *Meslanges* are the many sensuous love poems for Cassandre inspired by Ronsard's readings of Henri Estienne's recently published *Anacreontica,* a collection of tantalizing verses by the Greek lyric poet, Anacreon (sixth century B.C.), and his imitators in late antiquity. Among these poems the *Elegie à Janet peintre du Roi* (Elegy to Janet, the King's Painter) has received the greatest critical attention as an example of Ronsard's mastery of *ekphrasis,* the represen-

tation in words of a work of visual art (here an imaginary portrait of Cassandre by the royal painter, François Clouet), and as evidence of his occasional ambivalence toward the relative merits of painting and poetry within the contemporary *paragone* (competitive comparison) over the hierarchy of the arts.

Ronsard was even more productive in 1555. In January the third edition of his *Quatre Premiers Livres des Odes* appeared. Besides adding twenty-one new pieces to the collection, he dedicated the work to the king, thereby signaling the central place of Henri II in its conception. This latest version was designed to prod the monarch to fulfill his pledge to subsidize the Franciade enterprise. In the prefatory ode "Au Roy" (To the King), for example, Ronsard insists that he is ready to build Henri's "nef" (boat), a metaphor for the epic, "Pourvue que l'on [lui] baille estoffes pour le faire" (provided one supplies him the stuff to do it). In other instances, notably in the seven new odes of book 3, he extols the monarch, his immediate family, mistress, and closest political allies in magnificent verse. To further advance his point, he repeats the theme of inevitable death to underscore the power of poetry—and his epic, in particular—to immortalize any subject. This rhetoric obtains in most of the family odes as well as in the four new epitaphs added to book 4 and in his much cited ode, "Quand je suis vint ou trente mois" (When I am twenty or thirty months . . .), wherein a lamentation against approaching death culminates in a surprise acceptance of that degeneration when regarded as the price for loving Cassandre.

The second edition of *Les Meslanges,* published in March 1555, featured two new pieces, both of which concerned the dedicatee of the collection: a prefatory "odelette" and an epitaph, "Sur le tombeau de Jan Brinon" (On the Tomb of Jean Brinon), lamenting the death of his benefactor during the printing of the book. The edition was otherwise remarkable because, for the first time and in order to underscore his continuing wish to create the foremost heroic epic of France, the author had appended the phrase "Vers heroïques" (heroic verses) to the titles of the four pieces composed in alexandrine meter, the twelve-syllable line found in most poems accorded elevated importance. For the first time, too, Ronsard openly acknowledged his debt to Anacreon by inserting the Greek author's name into the titles of sixteen pieces in the collection.

In April or May 1555 Ronsard is believed to have discovered his second major love interest: Marie, a fifteen-year-old girl with chestnut-colored hair of modest social rank from the small town of Bourgueil, located then in the province of Anjou. The following July or September the fruits of this encounter were published in the *Continuation des Amours* (Continuation of the Loves). The col-

Liuret de folaſtries,

A Ianot Pariſien.

Plus, quelques Epigrames grecs:
& des Dithyrambes chan-
tés au Bouc de E. Iodélle.
Poëte Tragiq.

*Nam caſtum eſſe decet pium poëtam
Ipſum, verſiculos nihil neceſſe eſt.*

Catul.

Auec Priuilege.
A PARIS.
Chez la veufue Maurice de la porte.
1 5 5 3.

Fac-similé du titre de la première édition.

Title page for the work Ronsard published anonymously that was strongly
influenced by the Roman poet Catullus (from Œuvres complètes,
edited by Paul Laumonier, Isidore Silver, and Raymond
Lebègue, 1914–1975; Thomas Cooper Library,
University of South Carolina)

lection embraced 99 pieces, including 70 new sonnets (58 in alexandrines), 5 odes, and 5 pieces from the 1553 edition of *Livret de folastries,* renamed "Gayetez" (gaieties). As conveyed by its contents and opening sonnet addressing another Pléiade principal, Pontus de Tyard, the work constituted the next stage in Ronsard's love poetry. It filled the space between *Les Amours,* whose mythology and Petrarchan spirituality had made the author "trop obscur au simple populaire" (too obscure to the simple people), and the *Livret de folastries,* for whose eroticism Ronsard had been denounced as "parlant trop bassement" (speaking too lowly). By contrast, the love staged in the *Continuation des Amours* is at once human and spiritual: human, insofar as it originates in

a deliberate choice rather than a fateful glance and because both lover and beloved are as open to sensual pleasure as they are susceptible to illness and jealousy; spiritual, insofar as the physical enjoyment experienced at the beginning of the relationship is ultimately supplanted by the sublimated desire of a poet frustrated by Marie's decision to reject him for loving her too much. Ronsard otherwise achieves a medial sensibility throughout the collection by minimizing the abstruse mythology and by inserting only his more modest *folastries,* henceforth called *gayetez* to diminish the suggestiveness of the original title.

The last major work Ronsard published in 1555 was *Les Hymnes* (Hymns), published in late October or early November. Although Ronsard had previously produced five poems labeled *hymnes*—beginning with the minor *Hymne de France* (1549, Hymn of France)—the eleven pieces designated as such in this collection afford his clearest sense of the genre. Modeled after the hymns of the third century B.C. Hellenistic bard Callimachus and the *Hymni naturales* (Natural Hymns) of the fifteenth-century neo-Latin poet Marullus, the majority of these poems employ alexandrines in rhyming couplets deployed in a tripartite structure enclosing the moralized examination of a lofty subject drawn from science, philosophy, theology, mythology, politics, or history. Thus, the *Hymnes* of 1555 were intended for a more elite public than the *Continuation.* Leading that audience as dedicatee of the book, the proem, and four subsequent hymns was Ronsard's latest patron, Odet de Coligny, cardinal of Châtillon. He was a member of the powerful Coligny-Châtillon family whose principals included Anne de Montmorency, the constable of France; his brother, Gaspard de Coligny, the marshal of France; and their nephews, Admiral Gaspard II de Coligny and Colonel-General François de Coligny. Other readers targeted were the author's allies and mentors Morel, Paschal, Dorat, and Saint-Gelais. Always politically prudent, Ronsard also dedicated a piece to Charles, cardinal of Lorraine, Ronsard's former classmate from the Collège de Navarre some twenty-two years earlier who now enjoyed a strong influence over the royal coffers as Henri II's principal domestic minister and a head of the house of Guise.

As indicated by the opening poem of *Les Hymnes,* "Hymne du treschrestien roy de France Henri II. de ce nom" (Hymn to the Most Christian King, Henry II, of That Name), the king was likewise a main object of Ronsard's attention, as he continued to hope that Henri might yet be persuaded to award him ecclesiastical preferments that would enable him to concentrate fully on "La Franciade." In *Ronsard's* Hymnes: *A Literary and Iconographical Study* (1997), Philip Ford argues that the collection is broadly conceived to convince the monarch that poems are worthier of his treasure than buildings and paintings. Ford ascribes a related rhetorical goal to the selection of poem topics and the arrangement of the book. Ronsard thus sought to prove his value to Henri by explaining not only all the mysteries of the earthly and celestial worlds—represented in the first and last five hymns, respectively—but also those of the medial realm that links them: the strange domain evoked in the pivotal sixth hymn, "Les Daimons" (Demons).

The pursuits and achievements of 1556 resembled those of the preceding twelve months. Still anxious about his precarious social station—a sentiment that intensified as political and religious contentions spread throughout the country—Ronsard continued his search for patrons and church benefices. In the first regard he strengthened his ties to the court and Charles de Lorraine. While journeying with the royal entourage in early August 1556, for example, Ronsard joined the cardinal for a dinner that included reassuring reminiscences about their boyhood days at the Collège de Navarre. Shortly thereafter, Ronsard wrote a poignant description of the occasion in his "Epitre de Pierre de Ronsard, à tresillustre prince Charles, Cardinal de Lorraine" (Epistle of P. de Ronsard to the Most Illustrious Prince Charles, Cardinal of Lorraine), published in *Le Second livre des Hymnes* (The Second book of Hymns) later in the year. His attempts to attain an important ecclesiastical appointment were less successful, especially as he lost his newly acquired priory of Saint-Jean-de-Côle at the end of August. The same epistle to Charles records that interventions on the poet's behalf by the cardinal and the king's sister, Marguerite, were unable to reverse the injustice. To add to his tribulations, his older brother, Claude de Ronsard, died that September, leaving the succession of the family estate in disarray and both Ronsard and his surviving brother, Charles, burdened with debts.

Such distractions notwithstanding, the poet wrote and published two important poetry sequels between mid August and November 1556. In addition to his epistle to the cardinal, *Le Second livre des Hymnes* (The Second Book of Hymns), dedicated to Marguerite de France, included three new hymns and an elegy to the royal counselor and abbot of Mureaux, Chrétophle de Choiseul. *Nouvelle Continuation des Amours* (1556, New Continuation of the Loves) included 61 new poems: 25 sonnets, 21 chansons, 8 odes, 4 elegies, 2 blazons, and a dialogue. Like the preceding *Hymnes* and *Continuation des Amours,* the new collections were broadly conceived to solidify the author's success with two different audiences: the social elite, in the case of the conceptually complex hymns, and the average French courtier, in the case of the emotionally turbulent love poems.

In other regards, however, these volumes were unlike their predecessors. Different from the work it succeeded, for example, *Le Second livre des Hymnes* intoned Ronsard's sternest reproaches yet to neglectful patrons, especially Henri II. He also again emphasized mythology in the collection. Following the "Hymne de l'Eternité" (Hymn to Eternity), another Marullus-inspired philosophical poem, the author evokes mythological subjects retrieved from the writings of the third-century-B.C. Alexandrian poet, Apollonius Rhodius, and his first-century-A.D. Latin imitator, Valerius Flaccus, for "Hymne de Calaïs, et de Zetes" (Hymn to Calais and Zetes) and "Hymne de Pollux et de Castor" (Hymn to Pollux and Castor). While advancing overarching messages about good and bad patrons, both poems demonstrated Ronsard's mastery of heroic topics such as those he hoped to incorporate in the promised epic of Francus. *Le Second livre des Hymnes* is also notable for introducing the name Pléiade to denote the fraternity of seven premier Brigade poets of which Ronsard was the self-proclaimed leader. The reference occurs at the end of the collection, in the concluding "Elegie . . . à Chrétophle de Choiseul, abbé de Mureaux" (Elegy to Chrétophle de Choiseul, Abbot of Mureaux), as he invites the Nogent poet Rémy Belleau, a Brigade member since 1553, to join the Pléiade. Ronsard's wider point is that poetic fertility still abounds in France and merits the support of those who rule her.

The distinctions of the *Nouvelle Continuation des Amours* are equally apparent. Six types of poems make up the collection, twice as many as in *Continuation des Amours.* The large number of chansons in the volume is likewise remarkable. Ronsard's enthusiasm for the genre may have been whetted by the revival of Marullus style songs by Jean-Antoine de Baïf in his *Les Amours* (1552). Because of its rustic charm, the form was also well suited to portraying a relationship with a country girl such as Marie de Bourgueil. The last point underscores another difference between the collections. Whereas the poet of the *Continuation des Amours* evoked three additional objects of his affection—Cassandre, a certain "Janne" (changed to "Anne" in 1557), and an upper-class Marie reportedly encountered in Paris—Ronsard in the new book focuses almost exclusively on his relationship with the provincial Marie. This new volume affords the first clues about the girl's family name, deduced to be "Dupin" from the poet's claim to love or see "un pin" (a pine tree) in Bourgueil in the sonnets "J'ayme la fleur de Mars" (I love the flower of Mars) and "Si quelque amoureux passe en Anjou" (If some lover passes in Anjou). The *Nouvelle Continuation* also offers one of Ronsard's most candid reflections on the goals of his lyrical enterprise. In the poem "A son livre" (To His Book), appended as an epilogue, he not only

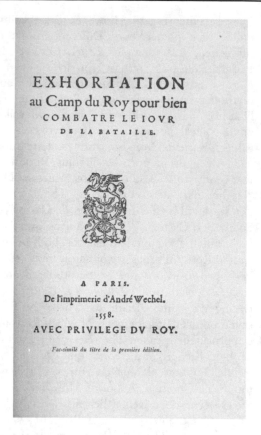

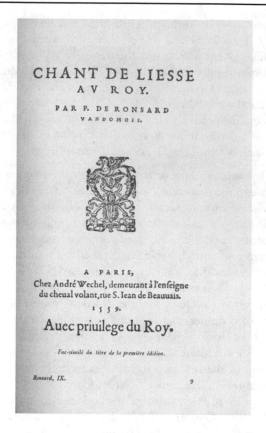

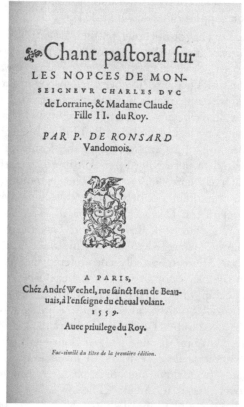

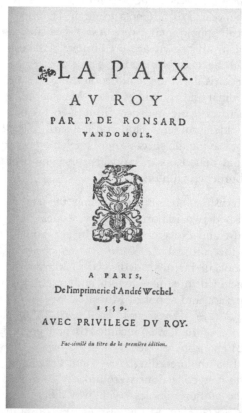

Title pages for pamphlets made up mainly of occasional poems Ronsard wrote in his capacity as the official court poet of Henri II (from Œuvres complètes, edited by Paul Laumonier, Isidore Silver, and Raymond Lebègue, 1914–1975; Thomas Cooper Library, University of South Carolina)

reiterates his intent to write "d'un beau stille bas, / Populaire & plaisant" (in a pretty low style, popular and pleasant) when singing of love but also claims to follow the first-century-B.C. Roman poets Tibullus, Ovid, and Catullus when doing so.

The two years that followed the appearance of the *Nouvelle Continuation* were difficult ones for the poet. From November 1556 until summer 1558, Ronsard wrote little. For a variety of possible reasons—ranging from a depression caused by the king's continued indifference toward the Franciade project to the financial distractions he endured upon the death of his older brother, Claude, both of which prompted another retreat to the Vendôme region—the only work he produced was a combined edition of the *Continuation* and *Nouvelle Continuation,* published in September 1557.

The year following his return to court, between summer 1558 and summer 1559, was productive, as Ronsard authored eight separate poetic pamphlets comprised mostly of occasional poems. For most critics these poems are inferior to the those published in and before 1556 for their overall lack of intellectual depth, formal refinement, and sincerity. Michel Dassonville, the author of the five-volume work *Ronsard: Etude historique et littéraire* (1968–1990, Ronsard: An Historical and Literary Study), has described the poetry assembled in the eight pamphlets as the hasty result of the "servitude" that attended Ronsard's duties as official court poet and, starting in late fall 1558, as Henri II's "Conseiller & Aumosnier ordinaire" (staff counselor and chaplain), a post to which he was appointed following Saint-Gelais's death in October of that year.

Compounding the difficulties of these years was the death of Henri II on 10 July 1559, after a jousting accident that interrupted the festivities surrounding the June weddings of his sister, Marguerite, to Emmanuel-Philibert, Duke of Savoie, and his eldest daughter, Elizabeth of France, to King Philip II of Spain. Ronsard's personal and professional hopes were deeply shaken by the event. Not only did he lose the royal patron whose favor he had so long labored to secure, but also the vacuum left by Henri's death intensified contentions between the Catholic and Huguenot factions at court, complicating Ronsard's ongoing effort to walk the line between the houses of Guise and Coligny-Châtillon.

In this anxious time Ronsard hastened to assemble and publish an assortment of verses written in the months just prior to the accident. Clearly, he perceived an advantage in heightening his visibility during the transition to the reign of Henri II's feeble fifteen-year-old son, François II, crowned at Reims on 18 September 1559, and his pretty sixteen-year-old queen, Marie Stuart, daughter of King James V of Scotland and Marie de Guise—hence, titular queen of Scotland and

niece to the heads of the house of Guise. Printed during the second half of 1559, the resulting collection of sixty-five new poems (plus an epigram by Du Bellay and four pieces by Louis des Masures, a minor figure in the Brigade) was called *Le Second livre des meslanges* (The Second Book of Mixtures), a title that indicated its diverse contents as well as capitalized on the lingering success of the first *Meslanges*. In this volume Ronsard allots abundant space to complaints against his life as a poet of the court. As expressed in a sonnet to Henri II's counselor general of finance, Jean du Thier, he especially resented his need to "tousjours les riches supplier" (always beseech the rich). Ronsard articulated this sentiment most poignantly near the start of the book, in the "Complainte contre Fortune" (Complaint against Fortune), a *discours* addressed to Odet de Coligny in which the poet imagines leaving court for the wilds of Brazil in order to regain his poetic freedom and the pleasures of a simple life. Also significant was the sequence of sixteen Petrarchan-style love sonnets involving a sixteen-year-old blonde named Sinope, whom Paul Laumonier in *Ronsard poète lyrique* (1923, Ronsard the Lyric Poet) has identified as the Marie from Paris first evoked in *Continuation des Amours*. These and other sensual love poems in the collection were doubtless intended to garner public favor at a time when Ronsard's prospects for future royal deference seemed uncertain.

Despite the sad events at the beginning of the decade—the mortal stroke suffered by his close friend, Joachim du Bellay, on New Year's Day 1560, and the massacre of Protestants at Amboise that March, following a thwarted Huguenot conspiracy targeting the Guises—Ronsard's fortunes soon changed for the better. By the end of September he had not only been awarded the archdiaconate of Château-du-Loir and the prebend of Saint-Julien-du-Mans but also had earned the recognition of Marie Stuart, who counted him among her favorite poets. Moreover, François II confirmed Ronsard's position as royal counselor and chaplain and renewed his privilege to publish all of his works. Ronsard then moved rapidly to produce the first collective edition of his most important writings from the preceding two decades.

Les Œuvres de P. de Ronsard gentilhomme vandomois (Works of P. de Ronsard, Gentleman of Vendôme), which included twenty-four new pieces, was printed in four volumes defined by poetic genre, between 29 November and 2 December 1560. Volume one consisted of two books of *Amours*: the first featured most of the Cassandre poems (sonnets, chansons, and elegies such as "Elegie à Janet") supplemented by three new pieces and the Muret commentaries of 1553; the second book presented the sonnets and songs for Marie and Marie's Parisian alter ego, Sinope, enhanced by a new set of commentaries by Belleau. The latter book also added five recently written poems, the most notable of which was "Le Voyage de Tours, ou les Amoureux Thoinet et Perrot" (The Voyage to Tours, or the Lovers, Tony and Pete), dedicated to Jérôme L'Huillier, another Brigade associate and a rising figure at court. This bucolic eclogue in 346 alexandrine verses is based largely on the idylls of Theocritus and stages Ronsard and his friend Baïf as the shepherds, Perrot and Thoinet, on a journey from La Possonnière to the island of Saint-Cosme (site of Ronsard's future priory near Tours). There they attend a spring wedding ceremony at which they chance upon their respective beloveds, Marie (Marion) and Francine, who in turn become the foci of much spirited poetic pining.

In volume two Ronsard united and reorganized the five previously published books of *Odes,* adding several generically related pieces originally located in other collections. In book 1, for example, he inserted "Ode à Michel de l'Hospital," formerly of the *Cinquiesme livre des Odes,* to assemble all the Pindaric works in one section; the remaining four books gained odes that had first appeared in *Les Amours, Continuation des Amours,* and *Nouvelle Continuation,* the first and second *Bocage,* and the first and second *Meslanges.* Only one new ode was added to the volume, a piece celebrating the accomplishments of André Thevet, a contemporary explorer, naturalist, and chaplain to Catherine de Médicis. At the same time, Ronsard moved some poems previously included in the Odes volumes to volume three, titled *Les Poëmes* (The Poems). This third multipart volume ranges from elegies, epistles, and epitaphs to *blazons, gayetez,* and sonnets. Among its fifteen new pieces, "Elegie au Seigneur l'Huillier" (Elegy to Lord L'Huillier) and the "Elegie à Pierre l'Escot" (Elegy to Pierre Lescot) best show Ronsard's attitude toward his service to two conflicting masters, the Muses and his courtly patrons, since entering public life in the mid 1540s, especially during the difficult years 1556–1559. The two books comprising volume four are hymns drawn from *Les Hymnes* of 1555 and 1556 as well as a few qualified poems from other sources, notably the pamphlets *L'Hymne de tresillustre Prince Charles Cardinal de Lorraine* (1559, Hymn for the Most Illustrious Prince Charles Cardinal of Lorraine and *Suyte de l'Hymne de tres-illustre Prince Charles Cardinal de Lorraine* (1559, Continuation of the Hymn for the Most Illustrious Prince Charles Cardinal of Lorraine).

As 1560 ended, France was again shaken by the death of her monarch when, on 5 December, François II succumbed to the complications of an ear infection. The first consequence for Ronsard was that he was soon deprived of the favor he had gained in the circle of his admirer, Marie Stuart. Divested of the French crown

by her mother-in-law, Catherine de Médicis, the young widow was obliged to return to Scotland in mid August 1561. A second consequence was that Ronsard was drawn into a new level of controversial political engagement as France came under the nearly three-year regency of the Italian-born Catherine while awaiting the majority of her second eldest son, the future Charles IX.

Whereas Henri II and François II had adopted the policy of Huguenot suppression favored by Charles de Lorraine, Ronsard's patron during the preceding five years, Catherine took the position of tolerance toward Reformers advocated by her adviser, Michel de l'Hospital, a protector to the poet since 1550. Notwithstanding his own orthodox Catholic leanings, Ronsard remained true to his charge as poet of the royal household and Catherine's policy. He willingly considered the Protestant concerns voiced by former benefactors such as Odet de Coligny and leading humanist intellectuals such as Théodore de Bèze. This disposition explains his readiness to write an elegy for a Huguenot playwright in *Théâtre de J. Grévin,* a poem in which Ronsard provides one of his clearest statements on the difference between real poets—such as Jacques Grévin and himself—and mere "versificateurs" (versifiers).

In late summer and fall of 1561 Ronsard attended several sessions of the Colloquy of Poissy, which was held to facilitate a dialogue that might lead to a doctrinal compromise between Catholics and Protestants. In the spirit of the colloquy, he soon composed his *Institution pour l'adolescence du Roy treschrestien Charles neufviesme de ce nom* (Instruction for the Adolescence of the Most-Christian King, Charles the Ninth of That Name), a didactic epistle published as a pamphlet in January 1562. Like other contemporary poems of royal instruction, Ronsard's letter was foremost a reminder to the boy king about the virtues gained in maintaining a proper balance between Raison (reason) and Cuider (belief), a word he used to mean deceptive imagination, the source of irrational opinions. Ronsard, however, also cautioned Charles to keep a vigilant eye on those who might be swayed by the "curieux discours d'une secte nouvelle" (curious discourses of a new sect)—a likely allusion to the speeches of Bèze, whose "harangue" Ronsard had heard in person at a meeting of the colloquy on 9 September 1561.

Despite Poissy and other measures taken to reconcile the religious rivals, the quarrels were never satisfactorily resolved, and shortly after the massacre of Protestants instigated by Lorraine's brother, François, Duke of Guise, at Wassy in March 1562, religious war broke out in earnest, with Louis de Bourbon, prince of Condé heading the Huguenot forces against the Catholic "Triumvirs": François, Anne de Montmorency, and

Jacques d'Albon de Saint-André. The violence on the battlefield also spawned further civilian massacres, and in more than one instance, Ronsard's Protestant critics accused the poet of taking an active part in the killing, although no proof has survived to substantiate the charges. Indeed, Ronsard continued to promote Catherine's policy of moderation, albeit with personal reservations. In June 1562 he wrote and published *Discours des miseres de ce temps* (Discourse on the Miseries of This Time), his famous 236-verse pamphlet to the queen mother in which he reassured her, at a point of when she seemed hesitant to act, that she could still "en commandant, les mettre tous d'accord" (by taking command, bring them all into accord).

In his heart, however, Ronsard was fundamentally allied with the Catholic Church and the defenders of French national sovereignty. As the Reformers wreaked increasing havoc throughout Vendôme and continued to resist conciliation–even signing the 20 September 1562 Treaty of Hampton Court with England by which Condé agreed to give Elizabeth I the Protestant-occupied port city of Le Havre in exchange for troops and funds–he began to lean more openly toward the hard line of the Guises than the conciliatory politics of Catherine. In October he composed his next polemical pamphlet to the queen, *Continuation du discours des miseres de ce temps* (Continuation of the Discourse on the Miseries of This Time), at 448 verses nearly twice as long as *Discours des miseres de ce temps,* in which his appeals to Bèze and Coligny for a restoration of doctrinal reason gave way to accusations that the Huguenots had committed "malices cruelles" (cruel acts of malice) and scourges tantamount to those inflicted by the "sauterelles" (locusts) envisioned in St. John's account of the Apocalypse.

As Louis de Condé laid siege to Paris in late November and early December 1562, Ronsard wrote a long poem of 844 alexandrines, *Remonstrance au peuple de France* (Remonstrance to the People of France), which was published in January 1563. In addition to taking all of France to task for providing "le Turc, le Juif, le Sarrasin" (the Turk, the Jew, the Saracen) with examples of the worst "erreurs du Christien son voisin" (errors of his Christian neighbor), Ronsard reaffirms the mystery of Holy Communion. He entreats the prince of Condé and other honorable noblemen led into the heresy of Martin Luther or Jean Calvin to respect their allegiance to the monarchy and, above all, to return to the fold of "ce grand Dieu qui bastit tout de rien" (that great God who built all from nothing).

Although the first religious civil war ended when Catherine and Condé signed the Peace of Amboise on 19 March 1563, a treaty that secured relative concord for the next three years, Ronsard that spring was

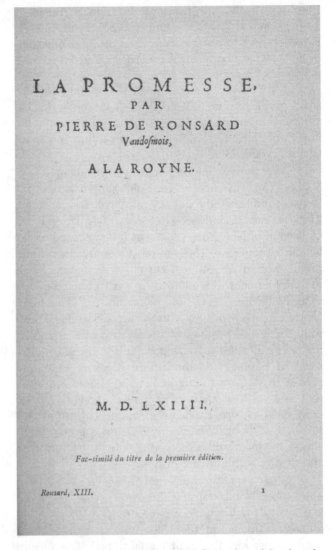

Title page for the allegorical satire in which Ronsard complains about the unfulfilled promises made to the royal poet (from Œuvres complètes, *volume 13, edited by Paul Laumonier, Isidore Silver, and Raymond Lebègue, 1914–1975; Thomas Cooper Library, University of South Carolina)*

plunged into a lingering personal dispute. Piqued at Ronsard's support of the Catholic cause, Huguenots published *Response aux calomnies contenues au Discours et Suyte du Discours sur les Miseres de ce temps* (1563, Response to the Calumnies Contained in the Discourse and Continuation of the Discourse on the Miseries of This Time), a collection of three versified pamphlets attacking everything from Ronsard's poetics to the origins of his partial deafness, imputed to a venereal disease he had acquired in pursuit of a hedonistic lifestyle. By May 1563 Ronsard had written and published his reply, *Responce de P. de Ronsard Gentilhomme Vandomois, aux injures et calomnies, de je ne scay quels Predicans, et Ministres de Genève*

(Response from P. de Ronsard, Vendôme Gentleman, to the Injuries and Calumnies of Some or Another Preachers and Ministers of Geneva). In the 176 alexandrine verses of the poem, Ronsard presented a striking portrayal of his critic as a venom-vomiting "Lou-garou" (werewolf) as well as a reasoned defense of the church; a thoughtful account of his daily activities, including his amorous diversions; and a persuasive justification of his poetics of "libre contrainte" (free constraint) and "gaillardise" (youthful audacity).

After a royal ban on libel was ordered on 10 September 1563 by thirteen-year-old King Charles IX, Ronsard published the nonpolemical collection *Les Trois Livres du Recueil des nouvelles Poësies* (1564, Three Book Collection of New Poetry), in which he gathered pieces he had written since 1561. In most regards, the volume reveals Ronsard's genuine return to prior interests, with the predominant tone defined by what Laumonier has called "la Muse légère ou même folâtre" (the lighthearted or even playful Muse). Central to that mood were the lyrical poems introducing two new objects of the poet's affections: Isabeau de la Tour, a cousin and maid of honor of Catherine de Médicis, whom he evokes in the concluding sonnets of the collection as well as in at least eight other sonnets, songs, and elegies; and Genèvre, explicitly mentioned in two elegies of the third book, a lady whose name is presumed to allude, by anagram, to the young wife of the translator and treatise author, Blaise de Vigenère.

Other verses in the *Recueil des nouvelles Poësies* were more sober. Notable among these poems are "Elegie sur le despart de la Royne Marie retournant à son royaume d'Ecosse" (Elegy on the Departure of Queen Mary Returning to Her Realm of Scotland) and "Compleinte à la Royne mère du Roy" (Complaint to the Queen Mother of the King), in which Ronsard couples praises for Catherine's skill in guiding the ship of state during the recent troubles with renewed complaints about his life as a poet of the court. In the hymns of the "IIII Saisons de l'an" (Four Seasons of the Year), Ronsard mixes scientific and philosophical discussions with burlesque mythological and allegorical references. These hymns also offered further thoughts on the nature of poetry. His most famous reflection appears in "Hymne de l'Automne" (Hymn of the Fall), in which he submits that the true poet must hide divine verities under a "fabuleux manteau" (fabulous mantle) of obscure mythological imagery in order to avoid the scorn of the "vulgaire" (incompetent vulgar reader). With the prefatory prose "Epistre au lecteur" (Epistle to the Reader), Ronsard offered a final response to the Huguenot pamphleteers—especially his former friend, Jacques Grévin, who had joined forces with Florent Chrestien to write and publish, in September 1563, some of the most scathing

personal attacks against the Pléiade leader. Doubtless wary of the royal interdiction against libel, Ronsard in his letter focuses less on denouncing the political and theological errors of his critics than on decrying their ignorance of poetry. They are mere "Poëtastres" (ignorant poets) who could never comprehend the goals, challenges, and achievements of a divinely anointed poet like himself.

In the three years from 1564 through 1566 Ronsard remained principally engaged in fulfilling his duties as royal poet, accompanying young Charles IX and his mother at various stages of their two-year journey to visit and consolidate the kingdom, contributing to the various court festivals along the way. At the king's invitation, he also briefly joined the royal delegation at the Bayonne conference where, in summer 1565, the French attempted to reconcile the Spanish to Catherine's domestic policy of accommodation with the Protestants. Ronsard acquired additional church privileges through the intercession of the queen mother, including his most cherished benefice, the priory of Saint-Cosme-lez-Tours. On 22 November 1565, the date of the king's official entrance into Tours, Ronsard had the honor of hosting at the priory the king, his mother, and the future Henri III.

In January 1564 Ronsard published a pamphlet addressed to the queen mother titled *La Promesse . . . à la Royne* (The Promise), a 282-verse allegorical satire presenting a dream dialogue in which the poet admonishes Promise for failing to deliver the rewards he had properly earned during his fifteen years of service to the crown. He also wrote verses for the royal entertainments at the castle of Fontainebleau and the Guises' seigneury at Bar-le-Duc. These curious works were combined with several recent political pieces—including elegies to the queen of England and her suitor, Robert Dudley, composed at Catherine's request after the signing of the Treaty of Troyes that sought to repair Anglo-French relations strained by the first religious war—to comprise the *Elegies, Mascarades et Bergeries* (Elegies, Masquerades, and Bergerettes), dedicated to Elizabeth I and published in July or August 1565. Also published in 1565 was *Le Proces* (The Trial), a 274-verse poem whose dedicatee and target was Charles de Lorraine, whom he indicts in an imaginary trial for supporting the likes of the Tuileries architect Philibert de l'Orme while ignoring the remunerations due to Pléiade members such as Baïf, Belleau, Du Bellay, and himself. These words were the last Ronsard wrote to or about his former schoolmate and benefactor.

In mid June 1565 Ronsard met an acquaintance of Marguerite de France (now de Savoie), Alphonse Delbene, an aspiring young poet of Italian descent with whom he and others collaborated on the poetic memorial for the recently deceased philologist Adrien Turnebe. Ronsard dedicated *Abbregé de l'Art poëtique François* (Summary of the French Art of Poetry) to Delbene. Purportedly written in only three hours and published shortly thereafter, the prose treatise stands as Ronsard's most extensive—albeit disjointed—reflection on the theory and practice of writing poetry in French. Of particular interest is Ronsard's opening reminder about the theological origins of poetry: "la Poësie n'estoit au premier aage qu'une Theologie allegoricque" (originally poetry was just an allegorical theology). In apparent disagreement with his long-asserted principle of copious diversity, Ronsard later pays deference to Horace's warnings against creative grotesquerie, asserting that the inventions of the poet should remain "bien ordonnées & disposées" (well ordered and disposed) in order to avoid becoming "mille formes monstrueueses sans ordre ny liayson" (a thousand monstrous forms, without order or connection).

In September 1566 an ill Ronsard took a leave from his official court duties in Paris and returned to La Possonnière. The retreat afforded him an opportunity to prepare the second edition of his collected works, before the expiration of his latest royal privilege. Published in early April 1567, *Les Œuvres* (The Works) consisted of six volumes, the first four of which were arranged in much the same fashion as the 1560 edition. The principal differences were the addition to volume three (*Les Poëmes*) of an independent book of sonnets to diverse people and one devoted entirely to epitaphs (an indication of the aging Ronsard's growing preoccupation with the theme of death), and the creation of additional volumes for elegies (volume five) and discourses (volume six). Among the fourteen previously unpublished poems were two important elegies to Marie Stuart: "Elegie à la Royne: Je n'ay voulu, Madame que ce livre" (Elegy to the Queen: Madam, I did not wish that this book), which had served as preface to the personalized copy of the *Elegies, Mascarades et Bergeries* that he sent to Marie on the occasion of her 29 July 1565 marriage to Henry Steward, Lord Darnley; and "Bien que le trait de vostre belle face" (Although the line of your beautiful face"), an ekphrastic elegy evoking a François Clouet portrait of the queen dressed in white mourning following the death of François II in which the author signals his continuing concern for the contentious relations between the verbal and pictorial arts.

By the time the second war of religion broke out in September 1567 Ronsard had already rejoined the court and accompanied King Charles, of whom he was especially fond, during the royal retreat from Ronceaux to Meaux and back to Paris. Shortly thereafter came news of the death of Anne de Montmorency, killed in battle against the Huguenots at Saint-Denis on 11 November 1567. In tribute to the constable's memory, the poet composed the "Epitaphe de tres puissant Seigneur Anne duc de Montmorancy" (Epitaph for the Most-Powerful Lord Anne, Duke of Montmorency), published within weeks as part of the Tombeau, or poetic memorial, assembled in his honor.

Ronsard spent much of 1568 and 1569 in rustic retreat in Touraine. Distressed by the rigors of court life, the effects of a "fièvre quarte" (recurring high fever), and the renewed escalation of religious violence (a third war began at the end of September 1568, only six months after the conclusion of the second war), he found particular solace in cultivating his Saint-Cosme gardens. He wrote "Hydre deffaict" (Defeated Hydra) for inclusion in Dorat's *Peanes sive Hymni* (Paeans or Hymns), a collection of poems praising Henri d'Anjou's victory over the Protestants at the battle of Moncontour, and worked on the poems published as *Le Sixiesme Livre des Poëmes* and *Le Septiesme Livre des Poëmes* (Sixth and Seventh Books of Poems). Although conceived as a continuation of the poems published in volume three of *Les Œuvres,* these new poems were published apart and each under a separate cover in August 1569. The two books introduced a total of sixty poems in a wide array of forms and on a broad range of topics, indicating Ronsard's continuing poetic vitality at a time when stress, illness, and age (he was then nearly forty-five years old) had eroded his physical strength and reportedly caused his hair to gray prematurely.

The twenty-two new pieces of *Le Sixiesme Livre* were primarily devoted to philosophical and autobiographical topics. Many were also cast as confidential communications to close friends and neighbors, including Belleau; Baïf; his recently appointed personal secretary, Amadis Jamyn; and Jean Dutreuilh de Belot, the dedicatee of the book and the royal counselor and master of requests at whose Bordeaux home Ronsard had been warmly received on his journey to Bayonne in 1565. The book also presented some of Ronsard's most intimate reflections on life and death, as well as a daring but serious-minded commentary on prophecy in *Le Chat* (The Cat), a poem that ascribes powers of divination to felines and a host of God's other animal, vegetable, and mineral creations.

The thirty-eight new pieces of *Le Septiesme Livre* continued the frank personal tone of the preceding volume. The seventh book differed from the sixth, however, in the emphasis it gives to Petrarchan-style love verses, twenty-eight in all, or about three-quarters of the collection. The object of the poet's affections has yet to be identified, for despite allusions to Genèvre and to Cassandre, twenty-six of these poems refer only to "Mignonne" (darling), "Maîtresse" (mistress), or "Madame." Critics generally believe that Ronsard was

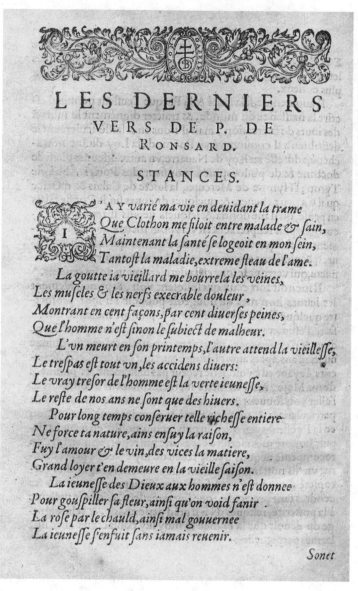

First page from Ronsard's last collection, which was distributed at his memorial service (Harlingue/Roger-Viollet/Getty Images)

either writing on behalf of an unidentified patron or alluding to one or more of the unnamed Touraine ladies who visited him during his retreat.

In the last months of 1569 Ronsard not only acquired the Vendôme priory of Croixval and other benefices but also recovered his health. Soon after returning to court around the beginning of 1570, he met two ladies whose names he evoked in love verses published eight years later: "Astrée" (Françoise Babou de La Bourdaisière, and later d'Estrées, mother to Henri IV's future mistress, Gabrielle d'Estrées) and "Hélène" (Hélène de Surgères, a lady-in-waiting to Catherine de Médicis). Throughout most of 1570 and 1571, however,

Ronsard was principally engaged in writing "La Franciade": the long-awaited epic he had at last begun in earnest, with the young new king's enthusiastic support, during his Saint-Cosme retreat of 1568. By September 1571 he had completed the manuscript for the fourth and, as it turned out, final book of the story. In the same 1570–1571 period Ronsard also wrote "Amours d'Eurymedon et de Callirée" (Loves of Eurymedon and Callirhoe), six poems of mixed genres that provide an allegorical portrayal of Charles IX's (Eurymedon's) affections for his court mistress, Anne d'Atri d'Aquaviva (Callirhoe). These poems were first published in the 1578 version of *Les Œuvres*.

In February and March 1571 Ronsard joined Dorat to prepare the Parisian festivities honoring Charles's marriage to Elisabeth of Austria the preceding November. Ronsard commemorated the king's entrance into Paris on 6 March 1571 with nine poems subsequently included in Simon Bouquet's *Bref et sommaire recueil de . . . la joyeuse . . . Entrée de Charles IX* (1572, Brief and Summary Anthology of . . . the Joyous . . . Entrance of Charles IX). Seven of these pieces were epigrams intended to serve as inscriptions on various artworks displayed for the occasion. Ronsard was also assembling the third collective edition of his *Œuvres,* published in May 1571, which added twenty-nine new pieces, the majority of which were poems of circumstance such as the six "supper" sonnets praising the royal finance secretary, Nicolas de Neufville, Lord of Villeroy, and three recent epitaphs. Among the latter, the tribute to the twenty-six-year-old secretary of state and close friend of Charles IX, Claude de l'Aubespine, merits particular attention for its especially gloomy inscription of the ancient *nascentes morimur* (born-to-die) theme.

On 13 September 1572, less than a month after the St. Bartholomew's Day massacre of Protestants that precipitated a fourth religious war lasting until the following summer, Ronsard formally released his *Quatre premiers livre[s] de la Franciade* (First Four Book[s] of the Franciade) and dedicated it to Charles IX. As the title reveals, the author intended the version then published to be but the first installment of the twenty-four-volume opus he had originally proposed in the *Ode de la Paix au Roi* of 1550. In November he petitioned his religious chapter in Tours for a leave of absence in order to devote more time to the project. However, apart from making editorial modifications and eventually providing an alternate preface to the reader (published posthumously in 1587), Ronsard was to publish nothing more of his heroic history of the French monarchy, a work which, in his own mind and according to the theory laid out in *La Deffence et illustration de la langue francoyse,* should have constituted the crowning achievement of his career.

By the beginning of 1573 Ronsard had produced a fourth version of his collected works, which was distinguished by the inclusion of the *Franciade* bearing the first round of authorial corrections and amendments. In January he composed a sonnet honoring the dramatist Robert Garnier, that immediately joined the front matter of Garnier's recent tragedy, *Hippolyte* (1573, Hippolite). Ronsard's only other published work in 1573 was "La Nymphe de France parle" (The Nymph of France Speaks), an allegorical ode subsequently appended to Dorat's *Magnificentissimi spectaculi* (Most Magnificent

Spectacles), in which he praises the political and artistic achievements of Catherine de Médicis and her sons.

Ronsard began 1574 with a pair of minor poems of circumstance: the ode "Homere, il suffisoit assez" (Homer, It Was Quite Sufficient) for Jamyn's translation of the *Iliad* and the prefatory sonnet "Le vieil cothurne d'Euripide" (Euripides' Old Cothurn) for Garnier's *Cornelie.* The sudden death of Charles IX on 30 May 1574, however, prompted Ronsard to greater efforts. Then only a few months away from his fiftieth birthday, he had lost the most generous and amicable monarch he had ever served and once again faced the challenge of gaining the support of a new king. Henri III was to be the fourth royal master of his career and, in this instance, one who (like the Henri before him) already had a favorite poet: the Pléiade leader's friend and now rival, Philippe Desportes, whose neo-Petrarchan love poetry quickly won over a court that continued to prefer the style of Saint-Gelais. After organizing and overseeing the July publication of *Le Tombeau du feu Roy Tres-Chrestien Charles IX. Prince tres-debonnaire, tres vertueux & tres-eloquent* (The Tomb of the Late Most-Christian King Charles IX, Most-Kind Prince, Most-Virtuous and Most-Eloquent), to which he contributed the initial epitaph, a sonnet, and a Latin quatrain, Ronsard hastened to compose *Discours au Roy, après son retour de Pologne en l'année LMDLXXIIII* (Discourse to the King after His Return from Poland in the Year 1574), in which he offered Henri his political wisdom along with his poetic talent. At the author's request, the original document, which eventually became public in a pamphlet dated 1574, was delivered by the king's sister Marguerite de Valois on the occasion of Henri's entrance into Lyon on 6 September of the same year.

Ronsard devoted much of the next three-and-a-half years to preparing the substantially revised and expanded fifth edition of his collected works while continuing to discharge his official poetic duties in response to the necessities of the moment. The most important poems of circumstance from the period are his sixteen lyrics written in memory of the king's mistress, Marie de Clèves, who died in childbirth on 30 October 1574. These poems appeared under the title "Vers et Stances sur la mort de Marie" (Verses and Stanzas on the Death of Marie), coming after his poems for Marie de Bourgueil in the second book of *Amours* published the new edition of *Les Œuvres.* Other works of significance are *Les Estoilles à Monsieur de Pibrac* (1575, The Stars, to Monsieur de Pibrac), a seven-piece pamphlet that presented his last verses for Charles IX along with two poems of praise for Ronsard written by the king himself, and *Le Tombeau de tres-illustre Princesse Marguerite de France Duchesse de Sayoye* (The Tomb of the Most-Illustrious Princess Marguerite de France, Duchess of Savoie), commemo-

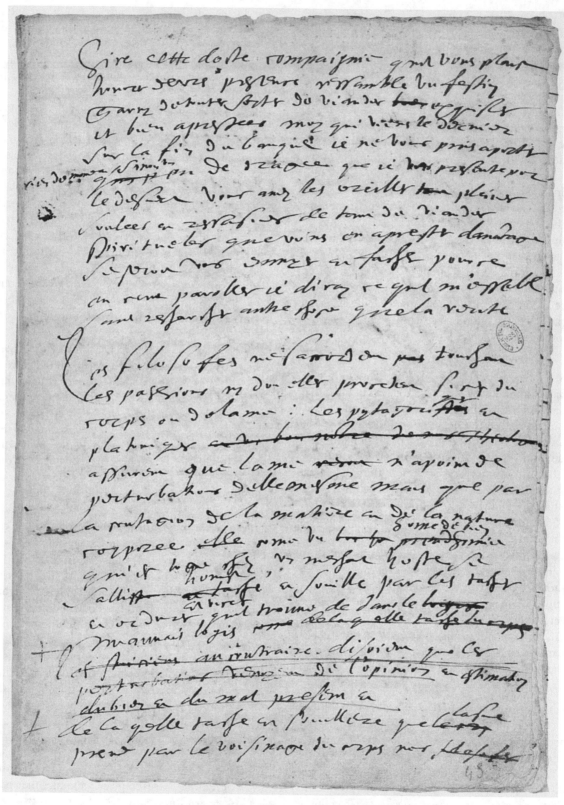

Page from Ronsard's manuscript for a discourse first published as "De la joie et de la tristesse" (Of Joy and Sadness) in the December 1924
issue of Mercure de France *(Bibliothèque nationale de France)*

rating his inveterate protectress after her death on 18 September 1574, which includes a vivid retrospection on his service to the house of Valois since his days as a page to the dauphin François. His lesser accomplishments affirmed his allegiance to the new regime. These compositions included *Estreines au Roy Henry III* (New Year's Gift to King Henri III) published in pamphlet form in early 1575, a set of three masquerades and three sonnets celebrating Henri's entrance into Paris in February 1575 that he later included in *Les Œuvres,* and three philosophical speeches in prose personally delivered before the king at meetings of the recently constituted Palace Academy in the course of 1576. He also contributed pieces to the works of his friends, notably an encomiastic quatrain for Louis Le Jars's 1576 *Lucelle;* a four-verse "epigram" for the 1577 edition of Jamyn's *Œuvres poétiques*); and an epitaph for inclusion in the *Tumulus* (Tomb) of his Pléiade colleague, Belleau, who died in Paris in March 1577.

Augmented by 238 new pieces, multiple revisions to poems from the past, and a seventh volume devoted to the *Franciade,* the fifth edition of *Les Œuvres* was published on 6 February 1578. By far the most noteworthy additions were those Ronsard introduced among the *Amours* of volume one. They included not only "Amours d'Eurymedon et de Callirée" and his verses "Sur la mort de Marie" but also "Sonnets et Madrigals pour Astrée" (Sonnets and Madrigals for Astrée), a seventeen-poem Petrarchan salute to Françoise d'Estrées (presumably written on behalf of the lady's suitor, Béranger du Gast, before October 1575) and most importantly the two-book "Sonnets pour Hélène." Composed during the three or four years following the poet's first encounter with Hélène de Surgères in 1570, "Sonnets pour Hélène" includes 111 sonnets, 2 chansons, a madrigal, an anagram, and a set of *stances* (stanzas). Although scholars have differed in their willingness to attribute the magnitude of this effort to any sincere affection Ronsard may have felt toward the queen's lady-in-waiting, they broadly agree that a principal motivation was the Pléiade leader's desire to defend his reputation against the growing popularity of Desportes. No doubt striving to surpass his rival, Ronsard restaged the conventional neo-Petrarchan image of an aloof and often cruel beloved, subverting the tradition by identifying his poet-lover with himself at a point when the experiences of his life had taught him to challenge the idea of suffering for love. Ever committed to promoting his poetic prestige, he likewise took the opportunity to remind his lady of the honor she received by becoming the object of so many rhymes. All of these effects are wittily woven together, along with a reprise of the carpe diem theme so common in the early *Amours,* in the most quoted poem of the Helen sequence, "Quand vous serez bien vieille, au soir à la chandelle" (When you are very old, in the evening beside the candle).

During the final eight years of his life Ronsard was markedly less engaged in matters of the court. Although a frequent traveler between Paris—where he resided at the College of Boncourt with Jean Galland, the principal of the school and a close friend since the mid 1570s—and his priories of Saint-Cosme or Croixval, the poet suffered from recurrent fevers, gout, and other pains of aging that kept him away from the social spotlight. It was an exception, then, when he elected to join Dorat and Baïf in organizing the sumptuous ballet marking the marriage, in September 1581, of Anne de Joyeuse, admiral of France, to Marguerite de Vaudémont-Lorraine (sister of the queen, Louise de Lorraine), though the extraordinary wage he collected for his efforts (two thousand *écus*) may account for the decision. His diminished presence in society notwithstanding, during the months following the appearance of the fifth edition of *Les Œuvres,* Ronsard's praises were enthusiastically sung by several writers of the new generation, including Henri III's secretary, Clovis Hesteau, and the Angevin poet Pierre Le Loyer. In 1582 Ronsard was further honored with a dedication in Jean Le Bon's *De l'Origine et invention de la rhyme* (On the Origin and Invention of Rhyme) and by the inclusion of fifty-seven of his poems in Gervais Mallot's *La Muse chrestienne* (The Christian Muse), an anthology celebrating the greatest French poets of the day. From the seclusion of one of her English prisons Marie Stuart also remembered her faithful admirer by sending him an ornately decorated vase in early 1583.

The new edition of *Les Œuvres* published on 4 January 1584 was Ronsard's final major achievement. The basis for more than one modern version of Ronsard's complete works, this sixth and last collective edition produced under authorial supervision shows extensive and meaningful structural revisions. Scholar and editor Isidore Silver, agreeing with Jacques du Perron in his "Oraison funèbre" (1586, Funerary Oration), contends that these formal modifications reveal Ronsard's wish to leave his best to posterity. More than any of the preceding versions of *Les Œuvres,* the sixth edition demonstrated Ronsard's commitment to produce a wholly royal edition of his writings—an intention most clearly signaled in his new design for volume four. Not only did the fourth volume include a two-part *Bocage Royal* (Royal Grove), honoring alternately Henri III and Catherine de Médicis, but also it presented a series of "Eclogues & Mascarades" (Eclogues and Masquerades) and elegies which, while including again many of the same poems from the fourth volume of the 1578 edition, opened here with dedications to the king's younger brother, François de France, Duke of Anjou (for the eclogues), and his brother-in-law, Anne de Joyeuse (for the elegies). With the exception of the *Amours* of volume one, the other volumes were similarly dedicated, in whole or substantial part, to members of the house of Valois and closely affiliated princely lines (notably the house of Guise): the *Odes* of volume two to Henri II; the *Franciade,* newly transferred to volume three (from the seventh volume it had occupied in 1578), to Charles IX; the *Hymnes* of volume five to Marguerite de France; the *Poëmes* and *Epitaphes* of volume six to Marie Stuart and Charles de Lorraine, respectively; the *Discours des miseres de ce temps* (Discourses on the Miseries of This Time) of volume seven to Catherine de Médicis.

The 1584 *Œuvres* also introduced thirty-two new pieces, primarily poems of circumstance commemorating events of concern to the royal family since 1578. Examples include "Mascarade. Aux Dames" (Masquerade. To the Ladies), four "Cartels" (satirical letters), and "Epithalame de Monseigneur de Joyeuse" (Epithalamium for My Lord de Joyeuse), all written in connection with Ronsard's involvement in the Joyeuse nuptials of 1581 and subsumed into the freshly conceived fourth volume. Similar verses of the moment may be found in volume six among the epitaphs—a section entirely absent from the preceding edition in which Ronsard reluctantly acceded to his royal master's wishes by including three poems lamenting two court favorites killed in duels in April 1578. One of the most interesting additions was "Prognostiques sur les miseres de nostre temps" (Prognostications on the Miseries of Our Time)—a poem included in the *Discours des miseres* of volume seven—in which Ronsard shows not only his late-life confidence in the prophetic powers of poetry but also his pessimism about the future of the nation. In the years since his first *Discours* of 1563, France had suffered the ravages of six different religious wars, the horrors of the St. Bartholomew's Day Massacre, and now under Henri III, shameful moral corruptions at court—all "signes" (signs) in which the poet reads ominous evidence: "Dieu qui tout ordonne . . . / . . . nous donne / De son courroux, & qu'il est irrité / Contre le Prince, ou contre la Cité, / Où le peché s'enfuit devant la peine" (God who commands all . . . gives us his anger and is irritated at the Prince, or the City [i.e., nation], where sin [is allowed to] flee from punishment).

To manage his social and poetic affairs in the months before his death Ronsard relied heavily upon the assistance of admiring friends such as Galland and Claude Binet, an acquaintance since 1570 who became Ronsard's personal secretary and confidant during the last three years of his life and, ultimately, his sole contemporary biographer. Although increasingly limited by declining health, Ronsard continued to travel back and forth between Paris and his provincial benefices, and while at Croixval in September 1584, he even began work on a seventh edition of *Les Œuvres.* However, the "prince of poets, poet of princes" died in his bed at the priory of Saint-Cosme at two in the morning on 28 December 1585.

At Ronsard's request, the seventh edition of *Les Œuvres* was completed and published posthumously by Galland and Binet at the end of 1586 (though with a title-page date of 1587). This last edition consisted of ten volumes because the eclogues, elegies, and epitaphs each came to occupy separate volumes and introduced 27 poems and three prose texts that the bedridden author dictated to his assistants. These final works included a new hymn, "De Mercure" (On Mercury), dedicated to Binet, four poems first published in the first edition of Binet's *Vie de Ronsard* (1586, Life of Ronsard), and the new preface for the *Franciade.* Among the epitaphs, Galland and Binet inserted seven poems derived from *Les Derniers vers* (1586, Last Verses), a collection of nine poems (six sonnets, a *stances,* and two epitaphs for the poet himself) dictated during Ronsard's last weeks and first distributed in pamphlet form by Binet to the overflowing crowd that had gathered at the College of Boncourt to hear Galland's oration for the poet's memorial service on 24 February 1586. The poem "Pour son Tombeau" (For His Tomb) from this little book is often cited as a testimony to the author's never-ending commitment to fashioning his image as the Gallic Apollo, the quintessential purveyor of ancient Greek culture into Renaissance France: "Ronsard repose icy qui hardy és enfance / Détourna d'Helicon les Muses en la France, / Suivant le son du luth & les traits d'Apollon" (Here lies Ronsard who, bold in his youth, brought the Muses from Helicon into France, following the sound of the lute and the tracks of Apollo.)

Bibliography:
Paul Laumonier, *Tableau chronologique des œuvres de Ronsard* (New York: Burt Franklin, 1969).

Biographies:
Claude Binet, *La Vie de P. de Ronsard* (1586), edited by Paul Laumonier (Geneva: Slatkine, 1909);
Morris Bishop, *Ronsard Prince of Poets* (Ann Arbor: University of Michigan Press, 1940);
Raymond Lebègue, *Ronsard l'homme et l'oeuvre* (Paris: Boivin, 1950);
Gustave Cohen, *Ronsard sa vie et son oeuvre,* third edition (Paris: Gallimard, 1956);
Michel Dassonville, *Ronsard: Etude historique et littéraire,* 5 volumes (Geneva: Droz, 1968–1990);
Michel Simonin, *Pierre de Ronsard* (Paris: Fayard, 1990).

References:

Remy Balleau, *Commentaire au second livre des Amours de Ronsard,* edited by Marie-Madeleine Fontaine and François Lecercle (Geneva: Droz, 1986);

Roberto E. Campo, *Ronsard's Contentious Sisters: The Paragone between Poetry and Painting in the Works of Pierre de Ronsard* (Chapel Hill, N.C.: NCSRLL, 1998);

Campo, "Ronsard's Eutrapelian *Gaillardise,*" *Neophilologus,* 87 (2003): 529–551;

Terence Cave, ed., *Ronsard the Poet* (London: Eyre Methuen, 1973);

Philip Ford, *Ronsard's* Hymnes: *A Literary and Iconographical Study* (Tempe, Ariz.: Medieval and Renaissance Texts and Studies, 1997);

Claudine Jomphe, *Les théories de la disposition et le Grand Oeuvre de Ronsard* (Paris: Champion, 2000);

Kenneth R. W. Jones, *Pierre de Ronsard* (New York: Twayne, 1970);

Paul Laumonier, *Ronsard poète lyrique* (Paris: Hachette, 1923);

Jacques Lavaud, ed., *Sonnets pour Hélène* (Paris: Droz, 1947);

Marc-Antoine de Muret, *Commentaires au premier livre des Amours de Ronsard,* edited by Jacques Chomarat, Marie-Madeleine Fragonard, and Gisèle Mathieu-Castellani (Geneva: Droz, 1985);

Marcel Raymond, *L'Influence de Ronsard sur la poésie française (1550–1585),* 2 volumes (New York: Burt Franklin, 1971);

François Rouget, "Ronsard en Protée: Le poète et ses doubles (Orphée, Protée, l'abeille et le jardinier)," in *Les figures du poète Pierre de Ronsard,* edited by Marie-Dominique Legrand (Nanterre: Centre des Sciences de la Littérature, 2000);

Isidore Silver, *The Intellectual Evolution of Ronsard: I. The Formative Influences* (St. Louis: Washington University Press, 1969);

Frances A. Yates, *The French Academies of the Sixteenth Century* (London: Warburg Institute, 1947).

Mellin de Saint-Gelais

(1490? – 14 October 1558)

Gerald Seaman
Ripon College

BOOKS: *Sangelais, Œuvres de luy tant en composition que translation ou allusion aux Auteurs Grecs et Latins* (Lyon: Pierre de Tours, 1547).

Collections: *Œuvres poétiques de Mellin de Sainct-Gelais* (Lyon: Antoine de Harsy, 1574);

Œuvres poétiques de Mellin de Sainct-Gelais (Lyon: Benoist Rigaud, 1582);

Œuvres poétiques de Mellin de Sainct-Gelais (Paris: Guillaume de Luynes, 1656);

Œuvres poetiques de Mellin de Sainct-Gelays. Nouvelle Edition. Augmentées d'un très-grand nombre de Pièces Latines et Francises (Paris: Coustelier, 1719);

Œuvres complètes de Melin de Sainct-Gelays, 3 volumes, edited by Prosper Blanchemain (Paris: Paul Daffis, 1873);

Sonnets, edited by Luigia Zilli (Geneva: Droz, 1990);

Œuvres poétiques françaises, 2 volumes, edited by Donald Stone Jr. (Paris: Société des Textes Français Modernes, 1993, 1995).

The poetry of Mellin de Saint-Gelais has not occupied a prominent place in French literary history. On some levels the marginal place of Saint-Gelais in the canon is understandable and deserved. His poetry often lacks substance and gravitas; it is frequently thematically repetitive and stylistically inconsistent; and, in only a minority of cases, is it worthy of sustained contemplation. Such a critique, although broadly accurate, is too easily dismissive of Saint-Gelais's importance, for the Pléiade, and more specifically Joachim du Bellay through the *Deffence et Illustration de la Langue Francoyse* (1549, Defense and Illustration of the French Language), thought Saint-Gelais important enough to make him a subject of a vigorous and obliquely personal attack—an attack that accounts, perhaps more than anything else, for Saint-Gelais's marginal place in the canon of French literature in the twenty-first century. But in its directness and severity, the attack from the Pléiade also underscored the scale of Saint-Gelais's political and poetic dominance in the courtly environment of mid-sixteenth-century France.

Mellin de Saint-Gelais (drawing by François Clouet; Château de Chantilly, Musée Condé)

Saint-Gelais himself, even without the help of the Pléiade, was also partly responsible for the obscure place of his works in French literary history. Like a good courtier, he wrote not for posterity but for a noble audience whom his poetry was intended primarily to please; moreover, he consciously avoided publication of his work during his lifetime. As a result, his presence in the historical record has been diminished, and the full appreciation of his literary production has been hindered. Posthumous efforts to reassemble and reconstitute his œuvre from manuscripts, books, and fragments have faced multiple difficulties. Scholars have had to contend with false attributions and are aware that what remains of Saint-Gelais's work is not definitive and is almost certainly incomplete.

At the courts of the French kings François I and Henri II and prior to the rise of the Pléiade poets, no poet aside from Clément Marot held greater sway than Saint-Gelais—a fact that in some ways accounts for his historical fate. Considering the poet's family origins, his high standing at court was not surprising or accidental. Mellin was descended from an illustrious line of French nobles whose roots in Lusignan are traceable to the early Middle Ages. The castle at Lusignan is said to be haunted by the serpentine fairy Mélusine, in whose name one may detect a faint echo of Mellin's. Mellin was also at times called Merlin, an appellation that underscored his universal learning and further linked him to legendary tales and chivalric folklore.

Saint-Gelais was advantaged at court, furthermore, by his connection to Octavien de Saint-Gelais, Bishop of Angoulême, a poet himself and a man who, in his younger days, was a courtier in high esteem at the court of King Charles VIII of France. The exact familial relationship between Mellin and Octavien, who referred to each other as nephew and uncle, is not clear. Scholars contend that Mellin was almost certainly Octavien's illegitimate son, probably born in 1490, prior to his father's entry into religious orders, and there is much to support this claim. As biographer H.-J. Molinier notes, no record of Mellin's actual parents exists; genealogies of the day list Mellin as Octavien's illegitimate son; and, toward the end of his life, Mellin admitted to his illegitimate birth (though without naming his father) in a letter to the Pope.

Under Octavien's tutelage at the Episcopal palace in Angoulême, Saint-Gelais was educated in Latin, Greek, theology, philosophy, mathematics, and astrology. He learned to ride horseback and perform feats of arms; he was trained in music and singing and, most relevant to his later life as a courtier poet, he became skilled in stringed instruments, particularly the lute. Octavien de Saint-Gelais, however, died at the age of thirty-four and Mellin subsequently left Angoulême to continue his education at the University of Poitiers where, scholars believe, he stayed until setting out for Italy around the age of twenty. Though there is no convincing record of Saint-Gelais's journey, it is supposed that, while in Italy, he became familiar with Italian tastes and trends, learned to read and speak the language, acquired a love for literature and the arts, and felt the literary influence of Italian luminaries such as Francesco Petrarca, Giovanni Boccaccio, Dante Ali-

ghieri, and Lodovico Ariosto. Basing his claim on these assumptions, Molinier has called Saint-Gelais the primary and most active agent of Italian influence on French literature in the sixteenth century.

When King Louis XII died on the first of January 1515, the succession of his son-in-law the duke of Valois was propitious for Saint-Gelais. Son of Charles d'Orléans, Count of Angoulême, the duke of Valois as king took the name François I and later became Mellin's first patron. With origins in Angoulême in common, the two shared at least a geographic and social connection, and they may have been linked even more closely. The king's birth, in 1494, shortly after Mellin's, could suggest that the two young men from illustrious Angoulême families may have had deeper childhood ties.

With the reign of the new king beginning, the moment was ripe for changes in French poetry. Along with Jean and Clément Marot, the French court readily accommodated Saint-Gelais and his Italian and neo-Latin influence, even as it cast aside the remains of late-medieval poetic traditions and the turgid exercises of the *grands rhétoriqueurs*, whose search for stylistic refinement and structural complexity led to pedantic and artificial poetry.

Reputed to be handsome and blond, Saint-Gelais was known at court for his ability to combine poetic improvisation with song and musical accompaniment on the lute or the guitar. Some titles of his extant works, in many cases labeled "Chansons" (Songs), show a connection between Saint-Gelais's poetry, voice, and stringed instruments. On one level, such poems demonstrate the central importance of music to Saint-Gelais's self-conception as a poet and to his definition of the poetic enterprise. In this sense he stands out as significant among other sixteenth-century poets. It can be said probably of him alone that song and musical instruments were devices that not only facilitated the creation of poetic beauty but also awakened and adorned what the poet believed to be unmediated self-expression. His titles include: "Legger chappitre: pour le luth, à double repos" (A Light Piece for Lute), "Pour la guitterre" (For the Guitar), and "Sur une Guiterne espaignole rompue et puis faicte r'habiller par Monseigneur d'Orleans, estant mallade" (On a Broken Spanish Guitar Repaired by Monseigneur d'Orleans, While Sick). His poem "Sur un luth" (On a Lute) begins with these lines:

O luth, plus estimé present
Que chose que j'aye à present,
Luth, de l'honneste lieu venu
Où mon coeur est pris et tenu,
Luth, qui responds à mes pensées
Si tost qu'elles sont commences

(O lute, a more esteemed gift
Than anything I currently possess,
Lute, that comes from the honest place
Where my heart resides,
Lute, that responds to my thoughts
As soon as they have begun).

From his earliest successes at court, Saint-Gelais's talent was related not simply to the creation of a poem as a purely verbal composition but was also and more importantly directed toward the expression of a kind of three-part harmony created by the combination of the words of the poem with the song of the poet's voice and with the accompanying music of the strings. This harmony defined him as a poet throughout his career. Musical settings of some of his works, arranged by Renaissance composers such as Clément Janequin and Pierre Attaignant, still exist, though they are not now well known. Nonetheless, even at the end of his life, the poet's talent and relationship with his lute were legendary. According to the eighteenth-century commentator Prosper Blanchemain, on his deathbed Saint-Gelais called one last time for his lute and, in the grips of a fever, sang and played a final composition in Latin.

Throughout his life, Saint-Gelais was known to be an epicurean, and both his relationship to the court and his otherwise high noble station may have provided him with a nearly unlimited ability to experience the best the period had to offer. Like Octavien before him, however, Mellin decided to enter religious orders and was eventually named chaplain to Henri II, François I's son and heir apparent, who was born on 31 March 1518. In his connection to the royal court, Saint-Gelais also performed a variety of other duties, among them revising and correcting the king's own verse and extolling the virtues and singing the praises of the king and of other members of the nobility. Though a chaplain, Saint-Gelais was fundamentally and ineluctably a courtier and, in this role of royal bard, he apparently was as frequently called upon to animate the festivities of the French court as he was to carry out his spiritual functions in the service of the king's son. For his efforts, Saint-Gelais was richly rewarded. Already abbot of La Fresnade, Mellin in 1532 was named head abbot of Reclus en Brye, a prosperous abbey founded by Saint Bernard in 1142. A few years later, no later than 1536, Saint-Gelais was named warden of the royal library at the chateau de Blois and ostensibly charged with the collection and oversight of all the published materials in France. After the reconstruction of the medieval Château de Fontainebleau (begun in 1528), the royal library and its contents were moved there from Blois at the order of François I. In 1544 Mellin was appointed royal librarian at Fontainebleau, and in that capacity he was charged with bringing together, augmenting, and pro-

tecting the nation's literary treasure and heritage. In Molinier's estimation, the success of Saint-Gelais in this enterprise was instrumental in laying the foundation for the modern Bibliothèque nationale.

Because of Saint-Gelais's role at court, there is a ceremonial and occasional quality to some of his writing. In certain instances, this writing is directed to specific individuals for obvious reasons, as can be seen in a title such as "A Mademoiselle de Tallard, le jour de ses nopces" (To Mademoiselle Tallard, on her Wedding Day), a poem that reads like a personal note. Other such poems stand as invocations for the staging of different royal events. Examples of these include "Pour une partie d'armes Au Roy" (For a Contest at Arms, To the King)—which might have been declaimed before the competition began—and "Au festin que le Cardinal de Lorraine feit aux Roynes et le lendemain des nopces, un masque vestu en Amphion, merchant devant les douze masques servans, vestuz en six sortes, de six différentes nations, deux à deux, accompaignez de douze dames vestues de mesme, eulz arrivant pres de la Royne, luy dict ce qui s'ensuit" (At the Feast that the Cardinal of Lorraine held for the Queens and the Day after the Wedding, a Masked Person Dressed as Amphion, Walking in Front of Twelve Masked Servants, Dressed in Six Styles, from Six Different Nations, Two by Two Accompanied by Twelve Ladies Similarly Dressed, Them Arriving by the Queen, Tells Her What Follows Here). This latter and excessively long title records an almost theatrical set of stage directions for a masquerade procession involving Cathérine de Médicis and Marie Stuart. The poem itself provides a kind of script for this procession; it frames and accompanies the feast while at the same time it celebrates the participants in the various ranks. The length of the title indicates that Saint-Gelais likely did not prepare this item for publication but rather intended it only for performance at a specific event. A final poem in this idiom, titled "Inscription de trois cloches mises en une eglise de St. Denis dont l'une avoit nom Marie, l'autre Denis et la tierce Jean, à la requeste du Viconte d'Orbée" (Inscription on Three Bells set in the Church of St. Denis, of which One was Named Marie, another Denis, and the third Jean, at the Request of the Viconte d'Orbée), attempts to give voice to inanimate objects and fails to communicate any significance beyond Saint-Gelais's debt to his patron. While none of these ceremonial and occasional poems contains significant literary value, they do possess a provocative historical and anthropological quality, providing an illumination on the people and on their times.

Saint-Gelais also composed a small corpus of sonnets and is considered, if not the first, at least among the first poets in France to employ this poetic form. As expected from the works of a courtier poet, some of Saint-Gelais's sonnets celebrated important events in the history of the royal household. Examples of these titles include "Sonnet mis en le Petrarque de feu Monseigneur le duc d'Orleans" (Petrarchan Sonnet about the Duke of Orleans), about François I's deceased third son, Charles; "Sonnet en la naissance de Monseigneur le duc de Bretaigne qui fut après l'ecclipse du soleil en janvier, l'an 1544" (Sonnet on the Occasion of the Birth of the Duke of Brittany, which was after the January 1544 Eclipse of the Sun), written for the birth of François II, the first son of Henri II; "Du Roy Henry au commencement de son regne" (Of King Henry at the Beginning of His Reign); and "De Monsieur le Dauphin" (Of the King's Heir), also written for Henri II. Significantly, Saint-Gelais also wrote two sonnets about other poets: one about his friend and fellow court poet Marot and another about Pierre de Ronsard, who succeeded Sanit-Gelais at court and was in some respects his poetic rival. The "Sonet [sic] à Clement Marot," particularly notable because it connects Saint-Gelais's vocation as a poet with his station as a courtier, begins:

D'un seul malheur se peult lamenter celle
En qui tout l'heur des astres est comprins;
C'est, o Clement, que tu ne fus espris
Premier que moy de sa vive estincelle

(One grief alone can the lady lament
In whom all the light of the heavens is contained;
That is, O Clement, that you were not smitten
By her vital flame before I was).

In this self-referential poem about poets, their subject of a beautiful lady, and their poetic challenge to exalt and immortalize her, Saint-Gelais effects a gesture of humility and praise that simultaneously touches upon Marot, the lady, and himself:

Peussé-je au moins mettre en toy de ma flamme
Ou toy en moy de ton entendement
Tant qu'il suffit à louer telle Dame,
Car estans tels nous faillons grandement

(Would it that I had at least been able to inject my passion
    into you
Or you your intelligence into me
In such a way that would suffice to praise this Lady,
For as we are, we are greatly deficient).

While recording the positive traits of each poet—his own "flamme" (passion) and Marot's "entendement" (intelligence)—Saint-Gelais also underscores the limits of their separate capacities for expressing the virtues of the lady. Equally helpless before the poem, Marot and Saint-Gelais are two halves of an idealized poetic whole,

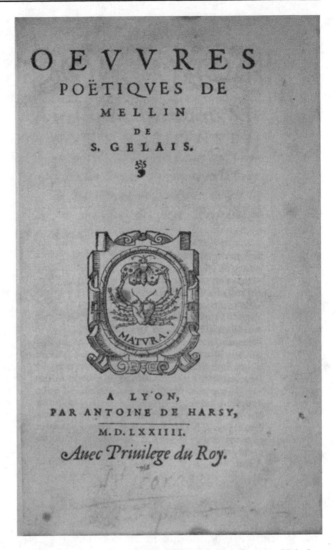

Title page for the first collection of Saint-Gelais's poetry, published sixteen years after his death (Douglas H. Gordon Collection, University of Virginia Library)

and the poem is about them more than it is about any real or figurative lady. The professional dependencies of Marot and Saint-Gelais, their poetic and artistic relationship, thus lie at the heart of this sonnet. The poets are in this sense partnered in a mutual quest for the unattainable, one which joins them as poets in ways that are unspoken, profound and, apparently, long lasting.

The emphasis of the poem, however, is on the bond of the two court poets and not necessarily on the personal bond between the two men. For Saint-Gelais the courtier, his affiliation with Marot as a poet in the political setting of the court was the crucial aspect of their relationship, and there is almost nothing personal in the sonnet. Indeed, in a reworked version of the sonnet, written after Marot's death and at a time when another great poet, Ronsard, was ascending at the

French court, Saint-Gelais simply substituted Ronsard's name for Marot's in the third line—"C'est, o Ronsard, que tu ne fus espris" (That is, O Ronsard, that you were not smitten)—leaving the rest of the sonnet virtually untouched. The political expediency of such a substitution should not be underestimated; it illustrates much that is true about Saint-Gelais himself and about the social dynamics of poetry and the royal court during his lifetime.

In the decade prior to the 1549 publication of Du Bellay's *Deffence et Illustration de la Langue Francoyse,* Saint-Gelais was considered a leading humanist and one of the most important intellectuals in France. In addition to Marot, another great author of the period, François Rabelais, was one of Saint-Gelais's intellectual companions and perhaps one of his friends. Some think it possible that Rabelais's well-known episode about the utopian "abbaye de Thélème" (abbey of Thélème) in *Gargantua* (1534) is in no small measure indebted to his relationship to Saint-Gelais, whose epicurean tendencies might have made him an excellent abbot of an abbey where the ladies and gentlemen eat, drink, work, and sleep whenever it suits them. Most scholars believe, moreover, that the enigmatic prophecy that closes the Thélème episode—written in "le stille est de Merlin le Prophète" (the style of Merlin the prophet)—is a direct citation of Mellin, since the verses of the prophecy also appear in the 1574 compilation of Saint-Gelais's works, *Œuvres poétiques de Mellin de Sainct-Gelais* (The Poetic Works of Mellin de Saint-Gelais).

On the eve of the publication of the *Deffence et Illustration de la Langue Francoyse,* several authors praised Saint-Gelais publicly and cited his work as among the most honorable in France. Jacques Peletier du Mans was among these authors, as was Thomas Sebillet, whose 1548 *Art poétique français* (Art of French Poetry) ratified Saint-Gelais's status as an author "tant dous que divin" (as sweet as he is divine) and listed him along with Marot as worthy of imitation in almost every genre. As scholars such as Donald Stone Jr. have pointed out, precise passages of Du Bellay's *Deffence et Illustration de la Langue Francoyse* respond directly to Sebillet, seeking to discredit his assertions about Saint-Gelais and to assert differing views on the poetry that Sebillet so esteems. Where Saint-Gelais deserves credit as a leader and an innovator, for instance in the use of the sonnet in France (a form praised by the *Deffence et Illustration de la Langue Francoyse*), Du Bellay gives him none and, in fact, overlooks him entirely. Where Saint-Gelais is considered a model of greatness, Du Bellay sees in him an example of poetic imperfection, limited depth, and questionable skill.

Du Bellay challenges directly Sebillet's choice in *Art poétique français* of two of Saint-Gelais's odes, "Laissez la verde couleur" (Leave the Green Color) and "O combien est heureuse" (O How Happy), as examples of French lyric poetry at its finest. In marked and acerbic contrast, Du Bellay judges these same works to be unworthy of such praise and goes so far as to associate them with any variety of "chansons vulgaires" (vulgar songs). Du Bellay not only denigrates Saint-Gelais the poet but also explicitly separates Saint-Gelais's work from what he and the other poets of the Pléiade consider to be lyric poetry that is worthy of the name.

Because the *Deffence et Illustration de la Langue Francoyse* became a seminal document in the literary history of France, its critique of Saint-Gelais has shaped his literary legacy. The long-term historical effect of the *Deffence et Illustration de la Langue Francoyse* was to create the marginal place that Saint-Gelais eventually occupied in the evolving French literary canon, but it did not do so easily or immediately. At the time of the *Deffence et Illustration de la Langue Francoyse,* Saint-Gelais was firmly established at the French court, and his importance as a poet had only grown since the death of Marot in 1544. Nothing in the *Deffence et Illustration de la Langue Francoyse* could have diminished or altered in an immediate way the political and social stature of Saint-Gelais, a man who had been at the side of King Henri II since his birth. One sign of Saint-Gelais's maturity and place in the universe of French poetry and nobility is that he did not reply in kind to Du Bellay. In the remaining ten years of Saint-Gelais's life, however, a kind of quarrel between new and old schools ensued. If Saint-Gelais participated in this quarrel, he did so largely from the side, leaving the dispute to others, such as Barthélemy Aneau and Guillaume des Autels, a fact that may suggest he viewed the matter with a measure of personal ambivalence.

Du Bellay and the Pléiade were apparently also ambivalent and conflicted about Saint-Gelais. Even as they contested the quality of his poetry in the *Deffence et Illustration de la Langue Francoyse,* they also later acknowledged him as one of their precursors: Saint-Gelais wrote sonnets and odes; he brought an Italian and neo-Latin influence to French poetry; and he cited, paraphrased, and reworked poems from ancient sources, just as the Pléiade poets did. Equally important, Saint-Gelais confidently occupied a place at the royal court—the center of political, social, and artistic power—a place that the members of the Pléiade coveted. He was also the royal librarian, and so must have wielded both real and perceived power over all textual production in France. Royal librarian, poet to the king, chaplain to Henri II, and a favorite of the court for almost forty years, Saint-Gelais was a venerable and imposing fixture in French culture and society, one that Du Bellay and the Pléiade could neither sidestep nor sweep aside, despite their artistic principles and youthful enthusiasm. Viewing the court poet from this perspective, it is understandable that, in the first edition of *Olive et quelques autres oeuvres poëticques* (Olive and Other Poetic Works), published the same year as the *Deffence et Illustration de la Langue Francoyse,* Du Bellay solicited first the approbation of a reader such as Saint-Gelais, followed by such writers as Ronsard and Maurice Scève. Shortly after the publication of the *Deffence et Illustration de la Langue Francoyse,* Du Bellay also composed an ode in praise of Saint-Gelais, a gesture that apparently reconciled his poetic and aesthetic judgments with the indisputable literary and political realities of the French court.

Some scholars contend that Ronsard—who eventually eclipsed Saint-Gelais as court poet—at one time feuded bitterly with the older writer. If true, the two later reconciled, as is shown not only by Saint-Gelais's revised sonnet but also by two odes by Ronsard. When Ronsard first broke upon the literary scene, however, he was openly critical of some of the poetic modes that were most closely associated with Saint-Gelais. First, Saint-Gelais wrote most often as a courtier and not often as an intellectual. Attuned to the close circle of his courtly supporters, his work was at times gallant and slightly frivolous. Related to this, Saint-Gelais did not circulate his poems to a wider audience nor did he compile them for publication so that they could face the trials of history, as Ronsard believed that true poets should. In making this critique, Ronsard attempted to redefine the historical subject matter of poetry and the intellectual status and importance of the poet in France. He eventually succeeded in doing so, but not before being openly and harshly ridiculed at court by Saint-Gelais who, it is said, read some of Ronsard's first odes aloud to the king in a mockingly theatrical manner. Young and somewhat insolent, Ronsard mocked Saint-Gelais in return, speaking in a derogatory way of a certain kind of "Mellinized verse." Like Du Bellay, Ronsard discovered that Saint-Gelais was too powerful politically to challenge and to unseat. Ronsard likely could not have supplanted Saint-Gelais at court had he not reconciled with the king's chaplain and the court's most favored poet.

In Paris on 14 October 1558, after suffering from a fever and enduring a relatively brief but painful illness, Saint-Gelais died. His funeral was attended by King Henri II, high-ranking members of the nobility, Ronsard and his disciples, and France's leading intellectuals. Saint-Gelais was buried in the church of Saint-Thomas du Louvre, near the entry to the choir, in a spot marked by a Latin inscription with his name and the date of his death. Following his death, Saint-Gelais was deeply mourned by many, including Ronsard and Du Bellay. In the twenty-five years after Saint-Gelais's passing, a variety of posthumous compilations of his works were produced. In each subsequent century, at least one collection of Saint-Gelais's work has appeared. He has never entirely ceased to draw the attention of literary scholars, though in the twenty-first century he is one of the sixteenth century's lesser-studied authors.

Saint-Gelais's dominance at the courts of kings François I and Henri II; the critique of his work in the *Deffence et Illustration de la Langue Francoyse;* the later ambivalence of the Pléiade; and his relationship to Ronsard—these are the principal features of the author's literary life. Because they have lingered longest in the collective memory, these features have defined Mellin de Saint-Gelais in the history of French literature. Lines from Ronsard's 1584 *Bocage Royal* (Royal Grove) illustrate and summarize these important features and nicely detail their origins in the courtier poet Saint-Gelais:

> Saint-Gelais qui estoit l'ornement de notre age,
> Qui, le premier en France, a ramené l'usage
> De sçavoir chatouiller les aureilles des rois
> Par un luth marié aux douceurs de la vois
>
> (Saint-Gelais, who was the ornament of our age
> Who first brought back to France the skill
> Of knowing how to flatter the ears of kings
> With a lute accompanied by the sweetness of his voice).

Biography:

H.-J. Molinier, *Mellin de Saint-Gelays (1490?–1558): Etude sur sa Vie et sur ses Œuvres* (Paris: Librairie Alphonse Picard et Fils, 1910).

References:

August Becker, *Mellin de Saint-Gelais, eine kritische Studie* (Wien: Hölder-Pichler-Tempsky, 1924);

Yvonne Bellengier, *La Pléiade: La poésie en France autour de Ronsard* (Paris: Nizet, 1988);

Henry Chamard, *Histoire de la Pléiade,* 4 volumes (Paris: Henry Didier, 1939–1963);

Donald Stone Jr., *Mellin de Saint-Gelais and Literary History* (Lexington, Ky.: French Forum, 1983);

Stone, "Saint-Gelais and the Epigrammatic Mode," in *Pre-Pléiade Poetry,* edited by Jerry C. Nash (Lexington, Ky.: French Forum, 1985), pp. 31–34;

Le Trésor d'Orphée productions: Mellin de Sainct Gelais et ses musiciens, 31 March 2005 <http://tresordorphee.free.fr/mellin.htm>;

Luigia Zilli, "A propos de quelques sonnets de Mellin de Saint-Gelais," in *Le Sonnet à la Renaissance des origines au XVIIe siècle,* edited by Yvonne Bellenger (Paris: Amateurs de Livres, 1988), pp. 135–146.

Papers:

Manuscript versions of Mellin de Saint-Gelais's works are located primarily in Paris, at the Bibliothèque nationale.

Maurice Scève

(1502? – 1564?)

JoAnn DellaNeva
University of Notre Dame

BOOKS: *Délie, Object de plus haulte vertu* (Lyon: Printed by Sulpice Sabon for Antoine Constantin, 1544); excerpts translated by Richard Sieburth as *Emblems of Desire: Selections from the "Délie" of Maurice Scève* (Philadelphia: University of Pennsylvania Press, 2003);

Saulsaye, Eglogue de la vie solitaire (Lyon: Printed by Jean de Tournes, 1547);

La Magnificence de la superbe et triumphante entrée de la noble et antique cité de Lyon faicte au Treschrestien Roy de France Henry deuxiesme de ce nom, et à la Royne Catherine son Espouse (Lyon: Printed by Guillaume Roville, 1549);

Microcosme (Lyon: Printed by Jean de Tournes, 1562).

Editions and Collections: *Délie object de plus haulte vertu,* edited by Eugène Parturier (Paris: STFM, 1916);

Oeuvres poétiques complètes, edited by Bertrand Guégan (Paris: Garnier, 1927);

Le Opere minori di Maurice Scève, edited by Enzo Giudici (Parma, Italy: Guanda, 1958);

The "Délie" of Maurice Scève, edited by I. D. McFarlane (Cambridge: Cambridge University Press, 1966);

Oeuvres poétiques complètes, 2 volumes, edited by Hans Staub (Paris: Union Générale d'Editions, 1971);

Oeuvres complètes, edited by Pascal Quignard (Paris: Mercure de France, 1974);

Microcosme, edited by Giudici (Cassino, Italy: Garigliano, 1976; Paris: Vrin, 1976);

Délie: Object de plus haulte vertu, edited by Françoise Joukovsky (Paris: Dunod, 1996);

The Entry of Henry II into Lyon: September 1548. A Facsimile, edited by Richard Cooper (Tempe, Ariz.: Medieval & Renaissance Texts and Studies, 1997);

Délie object de plus haulte vertu, 2 volumes, edited by Gérard Defaux (Geneva: Droz, 2004).

Edition in English: *Sixty Poems of Scève,* edited and translated by Wallace Fowlie (New York: Swallow Press, 1949).

OTHER: Juan de Flores, *La Déplourable fin de Flamette, elegante invention de Jehan de Flores espaignol, traduicte*

Maurice Scève (from Jean-Pierre Attal, Maurice Scève, 1963; Thomas Cooper Library, University of South Carolina)

en langue françoyse, translated anonymously by Scève (Lyon: Printed by François Juste, 1535);

"Le Sourcil," "La Larme," "Le Front," "La Gorge," and "Le Soupir," in *Hecatomphile: Blasons du corps femenin* (N.p., 1536);

Etienne Dolet, ed., *Recueil de vers latins et vulgaires de plusieurs poëtes françoys composés sur le trepas de feu monsieur le Daulphin,* contributions by Scève (Lyon: Printed by François Juste, 1536);

Psalmes du Royal Prophete David, translated by Scève (Lyon: Printed by Etienne Dolet, 1542?).

Maurice Scève is a pivotal figure in the history of French lyric poetry of the Renaissance. In some ways his work resembles that of earlier sixteenth-century figures such as Jean Lemaire de Belges or Clément Marot, who sometimes wrote in the flamboyant, playful, and highly rhetorical style of the *Grands Rhétoriqueurs,* the school of French poetry that was dominant near the turn of the century. In other ways, however, Scève's sophisticated poems anticipate the elegant, classical style and lofty ambitions of the premier school of French Renaissance poetry, the Pléiade. As the head of what came to be known as the Ecole lyonnaise (Lyonnais School) of poetry, Scève, along with his compatriots Louise Labé and Pernette du Guillet, enjoyed great fame and respect in the middle decades of the sixteenth century, only to be overshadowed by the achievements of the Pléiade poets Joachim du Bellay and Pierre de Ronsard. Still, Scève's *Délie, Object de plus haulte vertu* (1544, Delie, Object of Highest Virtue; excerpts translated as *Emblems of Desire: Selections from the "Délie" of Maurice Scève,* 2003) has long been recognized as a masterpiece of French Renaissance verse because of its rich imagery, dense structure, learned textual echoes, and expansive and sometimes novel vocabulary.

Little is known of Scève's life, including the dates of his birth and death. What can be documented is that he was born into a prominent Lyonnais family and that his father was an influential city magistrate. Scève is believed to have had three sisters who became local celebrities for their learning and writing; they each appear to have been the recipient of poems by Marot praising their accomplishments. Somewhat more is known about Scève's cousins Jean and Guillaume Scève, who were celebrated humanists, poets in their own right, and literary patrons. Maurice Scève probably took minor orders in his youth and was well versed in Latin, Greek, Italian, and Spanish. Some of his education certainly took place in Avignon during the 1530s. His humanist studies earned him the title "docteur," and his erudition was renowned.

Scève's first brush with fame was reportedly his discovery in 1533 of the tomb of Laura, the beloved of the fourteenth-century Italian poet Petrarch (Francesco Petrarca) in an Avignon chapel. The story is recounted in great detail in the dedication to Scève in an edition of Petrarch's love poetry published by the Lyonnais printer Jean de Tournes in 1545. Accounts contemporaneous with the discovery, however, make no mention of Scève's role, leading some critics to suggest that Jean de Tournes's version is a myth meant to explain Scève's predilection for Petrarch and to suggest the figurative unearthing of the Italian's rhymes as the prime source for Scève's love poetry. Whether it was fact or fiction, Jean de Tournes's account of Scève's discovery helped to establish the phenomenon of French Petrarchism by reinforcing the connection between Petrarch's Italian love poetry and France and helping French readers to realize that Laura was a Frenchwoman and that Petrarch had lived most of his life in their native land.

Scève first seems to have tried his hand at literature within two years of his alleged discovery by translating from Spanish a romance by Juan de Flores that was itself based on the story "La Fiammetta" (1343) by Petrarch's friend, the Italian writer Giovanni Boccaccio. Scève's translation, *La Déplourable fin de Flamette* (Fiammetta's Deplorable End), was published anonymously in Lyon in 1535. The text is significant because it includes a *huitain* (eight-line poem) that Scève reworked and placed in the *Délie,* published nearly ten years later. It also demonstrates some of the stylistic idiosyncracies and turns of phrase that reappear in that work.

Scève's next recorded literary endeavor was his participation in what came to be known as the "Concours des Blasons Anatomiques" (Contest of Anatomical *Blasons*). A *blason* is a poem that describes an object in minute detail, usually focusing on a single aspect—in this case, a part of the female body. The "contest" was launched by Marot in 1535, while he was in exile in Ferrara, Italy. Marot wrote an epigram on the "beau tetin" (beautiful breast) and sent it to the French royal court, in effect inviting other poets to write their own anatomical *blasons* in competition with each other. Many poets took advantage of this opportunity to showcase their talent. According to Marot, the best of the lot was a poem by a then-unknown Lyonnais, Scève, "Le Sourcil" (The Eyebrow). Scève wrote four other *blasons:* "La Larme" (The Tear), "Le Front" (The Brow), "La Gorge" (The Bosom or Neckline), and "Le Soupir" (The Sigh); all were published in 1536 as an appendix to the 1534 French translation of Leon Battista Alberti's *Hecatomphile.* While such poems might seem to be mere exercises, they allowed Scève to develop a stock of imagery to describe the ideal feminine form, and he used some of these formulae in the *Délie.* The contest also brought Scève considerable renown in poetic circles; most important, it brought him to the attention of Marot, who at that time reigned as the prince of French poets. By participating in the contest Scève demonstrated that he was willing to enter into direct competition with the best poets of his era, including Marot. After returning from Ferrara in early 1537, Marot spent considerable time in Lyon; there he frequented the literary circles of which Scève had become an integral part.

Shortly after this literary competition, Scève engaged in another project along with some of the best poets of his day. This occasion, however, was not a lighthearted one like the "Concours des Blasons" but the somber "Tombeau du Dauphin" (The Dauphin's

SAVLSAYE

EGLOGVE,
DE LA VIE SO-
LITAIRE.

A LYON,
Par Ican de Tournes.
1547.

Title page for Scève's poem in which shepherds in the Lyonnais countryside debate the merits of the solitary life (from Scève's Oeuvres poétiques complètes, *edited by Bertrand Guégan, 1927; Thomas Cooper Library, University of South Carolina)*

Poetic Memorial) mourning François, eldest son of King François I, who died suddenly and somewhat mysteriously in 1536 while the court was in Lyon. The "Tombeau" (an anthology honoring the life and death of a celebrated figure) was organized by the French humanist Etienne Dolet and published under the title *Recueil de vers latins et vulgaires de plusieurs poëtes françoys composés sur le trepas de feu monsieur le Daulphin* (1536, Collection of Latin and Vernacular Verse by Several French Poets Composed on the Death of the Late Dauphin); Scève contributed almost a third of the material in the volume, including five Latin poems, two French epigrams, and a long eclogue in French titled "Arion." The mythological allusions and classical resonances of "Arion" betray Scève's humanist background, while its style and theme are reminiscent of the work of the

Grands Rhétoriqueurs, especially Jean Lemaire de Belges, as well as of the manner of Marot.

Moreover, the *tombeau* bears witness to the importance of the literary circles that flourished in Renaissance Lyon, especially Dolet's Sodalitium Lugdunense (Lyonnais Sodality). Various learned groups had formed by the mid 1530s: some were centered around such humanists as Dolet and Guillaume Scève; others were attached to the workshops of celebrated publishers such as Sebastien Gryphe (Gryphius); still others evolved in the private homes of cultivated patrons, particularly women. Dolet's Sodalitium dedicated itself to composing in Neo-Latin, and Dolet was a prime promoter of Ciceronian purity who urged his countrymen to rival the Italians by forsaking vernacular literary endeavors in favor of an excellent Neoclassical style. By 1541, however, Dolet had determined that the French could best rival Italian literary achievement by writing strictly in the vernacular—an idea that Du Bellay reiterated at the end of the decade in *La Deffence et Illustration de la Langue Francoyse* (1549; translated as *The Defence and Illustration of the French Language,* 1939). Scève was affiliated with Dolet's group, as well as with that of his cousin, and may also have frequented private salons. In these settings he developed his mastery of both Latin and vernacular poetry and found a forum in which to exchange his early verse.

According to tradition, as well as certain clues in his poetry, 1536 was the year Scève fell in love and began to compose the poems that eventually formed his masterpiece. *Délie, Object de plus haulte vertu* constitutes the first French *canzoniere,* a sustained sequence of poems dedicated to a single mistress; the prototype of the genre was Petrarch's *Rime sparse* (circa 1366–1374, Scattered Rhymes). Unlike Petrarch's work, which is composed of various lyric forms, Scève's *canzoniere,* after a single *huitain* dedicated to the lady Délie, consists solely of *dizains.* The *dizain* is a ten-line epigram with ten syllables per line, forming a perfect square of one hundred syllables. The invariability of poetic form in the *Délie* produces a tightness of structure not present in Petrarch's collection. While Petrarch was at liberty to describe certain events or emotions at greater length simply by using a longer form, such as the *canzone* (song), Scève limits himself to the boundaries of the *dizain,* eschewing even the comparatively longer Italian sonnet form that had recently been introduced into France by Marot and Mellin de Saint-Gelais in favor of the native French epigram. Such limitations contribute to the dense style of what Scève calls his "durs Epygrammes" (harsh epigrams), which contrasts with Petrarch's more leisurely approach and *dolcezza* (sweet style).

Moreover, Scève's sequence of 449 *dizains* is interrupted by 50 woodcuts or "emblems." The first is placed after the fifth poem; thereafter, one follows every ninth poem. The emblems are set within geometrical frames such as circles, rectangles, and ovals and depict mythological or classical characters, biblical scenes, or tableaus of everyday domestic life. Most have no direct connection to the theme of love. Each woodcut incorporates a motto that surrounds the scene and is normally reworked in some form in the *dizain* that follows it—the "gloss" poem—usually as the *pointe* or "punch line" in verse 10. The origin of these woodcuts remains a mystery: it is not known whether Scève found them ready-made or had them commissioned for his work. (Emblem books were popular in France and Italy at this time and usually had a didactic or moralizing purpose.) In any case, the emblem and motto add a visual dimension not only to the poem they immediately precede but sometimes also to the remainder of the *neuvaine* (sequence of nine poems) they introduce.

Early critics took the spacing of the emblems, dividing the poems into groups of nine, as evidence that Scève attributed a hidden meaning to the structure of the *Délie*. One formula describes the structure as "5 + $(3^2 \times 7^2) + 3 = 449$" and notes the traditional significance of the numbers 3, 7, and 9. Such theories became suspect in the light of later work demonstrating that the placement of the emblems may have been simply practical, reflecting the publisher's need to print both emblems and poems in an efficient manner in the original edition. Further support for the argument that the structure of the *Délie* has no numerological foundation is the fact that several poems are misnumbered in the first edition, suggesting that numbering was not a significant consideration for Scève. Yet, patterns of verbal and thematic repetition continue to intrigue critics who maintain that discerning the structure of the *Délie* is key to understanding its meaning.

While the emblems render Scève's *canzoniere* unique in the French Petrarchist tradition, it must be stressed that the *Délie*, like Petrarch's *Rime sparse,* is primarily, though not exclusively, a collection of love poems. The beloved lady's name is an unusual one in French and evokes several connotations. First, Délie is the French equivalent of Delia, the name bestowed by the Roman poet Tibullus on his beloved. Moreover, it evokes the goddess born on the isle of Delos: Diana, the sister of Apollo, god of the sun and poetry. The virgin goddess Diana, as Scève explains in *dizain* XXII, has several manifestations: identified with the Greek deity Artemis, she is alternately depicted as the moon, a huntress, and, through her association with Hecate, goddess of the underworld ("Diana of the crossroads"). Scève exploits each of these associations in his poetry,

making especially significant use of moon and night-time imagery. Just as Diana is fiercely protective of her virginity and does not hesitate, as the hapless Actaeon discovered, to punish those who threaten it, so, too, Délie is often depicted as chaste and as cruel in her refusals of the poet's love. Furthermore, because Renaissance authors often used language play in their poetry, the *Délie* has also been taken as an anagram of *L'Idée* (the Idea) and thus as a key to a Neoplatonic reading of the text, which sings of idealized love and beauty; this interpretation has, however, been discredited. Other critics have seen in the name a form of the verb *délier* (to untie) and thus a means of suggesting many themes and images of linking, including the ties of the marriage bond or the unbinding of the soul from the body in the moment of death.

Although Petrarch's *Rime sparse* has an obvious narrative component in which time is marked by several anniversary poems commemorating the beginning of love and the death of the lady Laura, Scève's *canzoniere* is decidedly less linear and rarely develops a plot or story line. Still, certain narrative moments in the text allow the reader to discern the thin outline of a story. The love of the poet for his lady is sudden and fatal, beginning when his eye meets hers. There are exchanges of love tokens, absences and returns, physical encounters, and periods of intense jealousy at the thought of a rival. But unlike Laura, Délie does not die in the course of the sequence; thus, there is here nothing comparable to the single most important narrative event of the *Rime sparse*. Laura's death has a profound effect on the poet/lover of the *Rime sparse,* generating moments of religious anxiety that are foreshadowed earlier in the sequence by several penitential poems and that betray the influence of St. Augustine's *Confessions* (397–401), the prototypical autobiography, which relates the saint's conversion from sin to salvation. But the *Délie* is not a narrative, and the theme of conversion is not explicitly pursued by Scève. Because Délie, in effect, lives eternally in the confines of the book, the poet may sing of his love continuously. In contrast to Petrarch's final hymn to the Virgin Mary, the last *dizains* of the *Délie* do not turn Scève's human passion into a vehicle that leads him to Christian salvation. While there may be a struggle between passion and the pursuit of a higher, ennobling desire, Scève does not discount the value of his terrestrial love even in his final poem.

Still, Petrarch's influence is visible throughout the *Délie*. Scève begins his *canzoniere* with a subtle homage to the *Rime sparse* by referring to his own "jeunes erreurs" (youthful errors), an echo of the "giovenile errore" of Petrarch's first sonnet. Similarly, he ends his poetic sequence with a quotation from Petrarch's *I Trionfi* (The

Title page for Scève's masterpiece, a collection of 449 love poems that is considered the first French canzoniere *(from Scève's* Oeuvres poétiques complètes, *edited by Bertrand Guégan, 1927; Thomas Cooper Library, University of South Carolina)*

appear all the more brilliant with respect to his illustrious poetic rival.

Petrarch is not the only source Scève exploits in the *Délie.* The work is a complex tissue of multiple strands taken from earlier texts, including works by Petrarch's Italian imitators and by several of Scève's French predecessors, classical literature, the Bible, and liturgical writings. Of these sources, one of the most significant is the poetry of Marot. Just as Scève rewrote Petrarch's poems in an effort to outshine his historically, geographically, and linguistically distant Italian master, he engaged in an intertextual dialogue with his more immediate French rival, the chief poet of the preceding generation. A case in point, noted by Gérard Defaux in the introduction to his 2004 edition of the *Délie,* is *dizain* XVII, which includes several Marotic echoes. The dialogue with Marot, like that with Petrarch, serves not only to affiliate Scève with prestigious literary traditions of the past but also—and principally—to differentiate the *Délie* from its textual models. According to Defaux, Scève rewrites or "corrects" Marot in part because Marot did not adequately differentiate himself from Petrarch. Marot's Petrarchism, as evidenced largely by his translation, rather than imitation, of six Petrarchan sonnets, is penitential and otherworldly in nature. In contrast, Scève's rewriting of Marot and Petrarch stresses a profoundly secular vision of love.

Religious imagery is, however, not absent from the *Délie,* which from its first *dizain* evokes the language of Christian liturgy and prayer. Many critics have found here a distinctly spiritual message, conveyed by images and themes that have their root in the Judeo-Christian tradition. Several *dizains* make explicit use of biblical imagery, especially Old Testament stories such as that of the brazen serpent (CXLIII) or the plague of darkness (CXXIX). Some have found it hardly coincidental that, according to the evangelical humanist and Bible translator Jacques Lefèvre d'Etaples, the name Christ appears in the Epistles of St. Paul 449 times—the number of *dizains* in the *Délie.* Still others have found in Scève's descriptions of Délie echoes of prayers and poems in honor of the Virgin Mary, just as one can find them in Petrarch's descriptions of Laura and Dante's descriptions of Beatrice. Yet, some critics claim that while Petrarch and Dante used such Christian elements to help turn their human love into a love of God, Scève does not renounce his passion for Délie but engages in an idolatrous worship of his lady, who constitutes, he declares in *dizain* I, the "Idole de ma vie" (Idol of my life).

The seemingly contradictory nature of the love experience described in the *Délie* has also been discerned by critics addressing the role of Neoplatonism in the text. Intellectuals in sixteenth-century Lyon were

Triumphs). In between, Scève twice alludes to his poetic master: first as a "Tuscan" (CCCLXXXVIII) and then as a "Tuscan Apollo" (CCCCXVII), reminding the reader that Petrarch had fashioned himself as the alter ego of the god of poetry in pursuit of his Laura—a female embodiment of the poetic laurel, much like the nymph Daphne, who was chased by the ardent Apollo. *Dizain* CCCCXVII likewise establishes a comparison between Scève's love story and Petrarch's via the image of the Rhône River, which passes through Lyon as well as through Avignon, the site of Petrarch's love affair. Moreover, many *dizains* include close verbal echoes of Petrarch's poems or recall his distinctive imagery. Nevertheless, Scève is not a mere imitator but a persistent rewriter of Petrarch's legacy, eager to revise and rework his inherited material in a way that will make him familiar with the Neoplatonic theory espoused by the Italians Marsilio Ficino and Leone Ebreo, and Ebreo's Neoplatonic dialogues were translated by Pontus de Tyard and published in Lyon shortly after the *Délie* appeared. There is no doubt that Scève borrowed considerable imagery from Neoplatonism, such as the notion of the transmigration of the soul from lover to beloved in a kiss. But few critics today would argue that the *Délie* is unambiguously Neoplatonic in its depiction of the love experience, and several have emphasized the physical or anti-Platonic quality of the text. In these ways Scève's love poetry has defied easy or consistent interpretation by critics, some of them viewing it as spiritual, Platonic, and edifying and others seeing it as terrestrial, erotic, and profoundly human.

Few readers of the *Délie* would disagree, however, that Scève's portrayal of his love owes a great deal to the Petrarchan tradition and to the *fin amors* (noble love) of the medieval troubadours. Both traditions are predicated on the inaccessibility of the beloved, who is usually a married woman, and the consequent frustration of the poet/lover. Délie, like her medieval and Petrarchist counterparts, is aloof and unattainable, as distant as the moon. Nevertheless, the poet never ceases to praise her many accomplishments and gifts. She is, of course, beautiful and virtuous, and some poems hint at her musical talent. Several describe one or more of her features, using stock epithets such as "mains yvoirines" (ivory-like hands) or "levres coralines" (coral-like lips). Because she is married to another, "Délie" is most likely a *senhal* (code name) used to hide her true identity, thereby keeping her reputation clean and the poet/lover safe from harm—though the lovers are not always successful in achieving these goals.

Although the *Délie* is essentially a love story and advertises itself as a repeated retelling of the fatal encounter between lover and beloved, it is by no means monotonous; instead, it embraces the rhetorical virtue of variety in theme, style, and versification, if not in genre. While the *dizain* is the sole poetic form employed, Scève varies the internal structure of the poems by dividing his ten verses into syntactic units of different lengths. Some poems consist of two sentences, dividing the *dizain* unevenly into units of six and four verses; others might be divided into syntactic combinations of four/six, eight/two, two/eight, four/four/two, four/two/ four, or two/two/two/two/two. In some cases, such as *dizain* LXXVII, Scève forgoes internal divisions altogether, so that the structure of his poem mimics a solid, impenetrable block. As for thematic variety, some *dizains* do not treat the subject of love at all but—as is also the case in Petrarch's *canzoniere*—refer to historical or political events. Many poems are steeped in classical mythological imagery; others are allegories that have a distinctly medieval air; and a few recall the tradition of the medieval debate. Some poems are anecdotal, recounting a particular event that occurred in the course of the love affair. Others are narrative vignettes in the playful style of the *Greek Anthology* that depict a dialogue in which the usually silent Délie participates. Many evoke the geographical features of Lyon and the surrounding countryside. Indeed, Lyon is the perfect locale for love, Scève implies. Not only is it dominated by a hill, Mont Fourvière, dedicated to Venus (the name was mistakenly thought to be derived from the Latin *Forum Veneris*), but it is also the privileged meeting point of two rivers: the virile Rhône and the docile Saône, whose respective masculine and feminine grammatical genders reinforce the image of an erotic encounter.

Because Scève grounds his love story in the actual landscape of Lyon, it has been tempting for readers to try to find the real lady behind the figure of Délie. Nearly all critics have agreed that Scève's true love was Du Guillet, herself an important poet of the Lyonnais school. Du Guillet, who was approximately twenty years Scève's junior, married around 1538 and died at the age of twenty-five within a year of the publication of the *Délie*. Lending credence to this identification is the fact that several of Du Guillet's posthumously published poems correspond to verses in the *Délie* by using identical vocabulary, similar or inverted imagery, and the like. Also, Du Guillet frequently describes her beloved as a learned, eloquent poetic master from whom she wishes to learn more about their common craft, and this description certainly fits the erudite Scève. Moreover, Du Guillet appears to pun on Scève's name in some poems, further hinting that he is the man about whom she is writing and, by implication, that she is the beloved Scève praises in his poetry. Still, Délie's portrayal is far too complex to allow her simply to be identified with Du Guillet.

In the years immediately following the publication of the *Délie*, Scève contributed preliminary poems to the works of other writers—most notably, Marguerite de Navarre—suggesting the high esteem in which he was held. During this period Jean de Tournes dedicated two important Italian works to Scève: the edition of Petrarch's *Rime sparse*, with the prefatory letter recounting the discovery of Laura's tomb, in 1545 and Dante's *Divina Commedia* in 1547. During these same years Scève wrote *Saulsaye, Eglogue de la vie solitaire* (1547, The Willow Grove, Eclogue of the Solitary Life). In this short work, whose sources include Virgil's eclogues and the Italian Renaissance writer Jacopo Sannazaro's *Arcadia* (1504), the idyllic Lyonnais countryside is populated by shepherds who debate the virtues of "the solitary life." The simple style of the poem contrasts vividly with the dense and rich—even obscure—verses of the *Délie*.

MAGNIFICENCE
DE LA SVPERBE ET TRIVMPHANTE
entree de la noble & antique Cité de Lyon fai-
éte au Treschreſtien Roy de France
Henry deuxieſine de ce
Nom,

Et à la Royne Catherine ſon Eſpouſe le X X I I I.
de Septembre   M. D. XLVIII.

A LYON: Chés Guillaume Rouille à l'Eſcu de Veniſe.

Title page for Scève's account of the official entry into Lyon in 1548 of the newly crowned king, Henri II, and his Italian queen, Catherine de Médicis. Scève was one of the organizers of the ceremonies (from Paul Ardouin, La Délie de Maurice Scève et ses cinquante emblèmes, *1982; Thomas Cooper Library, University of South Carolina).*

In 1548 Scève, in collaboration with several artisans, was charged with overseeing the pageantry and ceremony for the official entry into Lyon of the newly crowned king, Henri II, and his Italian queen, Catherine de Médicis. Soon after the events, Scève wrote a detailed account of the festivities that was published the following year and quickly translated into Italian. While this work has no real literary merit, it is important for its detailed descriptions and documentary value. It also offers further evidence of Scève's familiarity with the themes and images of antiquity, many of which were integral parts of the royal entry into the city.

Scève produced another significant piece of writing early in his career, though the exact date of this composition is disputed. It was his translation of two psalms, published perhaps as early as 1542 or as late as 1549. In this endeavor he once again followed the initiative of Marot. While biblical translation was most often associated with the Evangelical movement, Scève's

translations need not be taken as a sign of Reformist sympathies: when the texts were republished in 1557, he dedicated them to a Roman Catholic cardinal. In the early 1550s Scève continued to write preliminary poems for the works of his literary associates and, along with many other well-known figures, composed a sonnet in honor of his compatriot Labé on the occasion of the publication of her works in 1555. Scève continued to enjoy respect and fame within Lyonnais literary circles, but his reputation beyond the confines of that city was less glorious. In his *Art Poétique François* (1548, The Art of French Poetry) Thomas Sebillet places Scève third after Marot and Saint-Gelais in his list of exemplary French poets. Du Bellay, in his *La Deffence et illustration de la langue francoyse,* published the following year, is even more severe in his carefully phrased criticism of Scève's obscurity, which he couches in terms of things he has heard others say. Yet, Du Bellay went on to write three poems in honor of Scève, including one that describes Du Bellay's homecoming through the streets of Lyon at the end of his self-imposed exile in Rome in 1557. Nevertheless, the learned allusions of the *Délie,* coupled with the stylistic density and tortured syntax that seem to be the almost inevitable by-products of his economically structured *dizains,* led many Renaissance readers to malign Scève's difficult verses in the 1550s.

Scève's last important work, *Microcosme* (Microcosm), was published in 1562 but had probably been completed by 1559. It is his contribution to the domain of "scientific poetry," a serious, philosophical, and learned genre characterized by encyclopedic content and almost epic proportions. The work is divided into three books; each of the first two consists of 1,000 lines, while the final book features an additional 3-line coda or signature for a total of 3,003 twelve-syllable verses. This expansiveness stands in striking contrast to the tight structure of the *dizains* of the *Délie.* In *Microcosme* Scève has abandoned Petrarchism and love lyrics in favor of poetry on a grand scale, reminiscent of Virgil's *Aeneid* or—in light of its tripartite structure—Dante's *Divina Commedia.*

The hero of Scève's "epic" is the first man, Adam, who is treated as a microcosm of the world. Scève's primary source material is the Book of Genesis, but classical motifs are intertwined with biblical ones throughout this text no less than in the *Délie.* The first book of the *Microcosme* is the story of God's creation of Adam and Eve and their life in Eden, including their own sin and the murder of their son Abel by his brother, Cain. Book 2 recounts a prophetic dream sent to Adam that describes the future technological achievements of humanity, future nations in various geographical areas, and scientific and artistic achievements such as arithmetic and writing. The final book, in which Adam tells

Eve a story, delves further into humanity's future technical and scholarly accomplishments, touching on such subjects as astronomy and architecture, and ends with an exaltation of human greatness and dignity. Through labor, initially designed as punishment for Adam's sin, his descendants will realize these astounding accomplishments. Thus, while punishable, Adam's sin is, nevertheless, a *felix culpa* (happy fault), because it leads to growth and prosperity on Earth, as well as to salvation in heaven when that sin is redeemed by Christ.

Scève's *Microcosme* is, thus, a hymn to the advances made possible through human endeavors. In the best Renaissance humanist tradition, a central component of this progress is the growth of knowledge. Scève gives considerable attention to the development of the literary arts, from the beginnings of writing to the invention of specific genres, and makes Adam the first poet. He also describes the physical sciences, showing how human beings conquer time and space through geography and navigation and the discovery of a workable measure of time. The agricultural arts are praised, along with such mundane accomplishments as the perfection of hunting and fishing skills. Scève's index of human achievements is truly encyclopedic in scope, and to express himself on such a variety of topics he does not hesitate to forge new words and otherwise cultivate an expansive vocabulary—perhaps even more so than in the *Délie*.

Evidence suggests that the *Microcosme* was a posthumous publication. V.-L. Saulnier demonstrates that the original edition includes far too many typographical errors—particularly misspellings of learned, esoteric vocabulary—for Scève to have seen the work to completion. Instead, Saulnier surmises, the proofreading was left to someone without Scève's vast erudition. Defaux, however, in the introduction to his edition of the *Délie,* points to other evidence that Scève was alive in June 1563. In any case, the second edition of the *Délie,* published in 1564, certainly postdates the death of its author and stands as a lone testament to Scève's enduring reputation in the second half of the sixteenth century; by all other measures, his influence was on the wane long before the 1560s. By the time Etienne Pasquier published the 1610 edition of his *Les Recherches de la France,* he was justified in saying that Scève's *Délie* had died along with its author: it was no longer read, owing to its overarching obscurity.

In short, Maurice Scève had quietly disappeared from the Lyonnais literary scene, and no one marked his passing in any form that has survived. Scève and his *Délie, Object de plus haulte vertu* remained virtually unknown, and certainly unread, for more than three hundred years; they were resurrected in the twentieth century, thanks in large measure to the efforts of

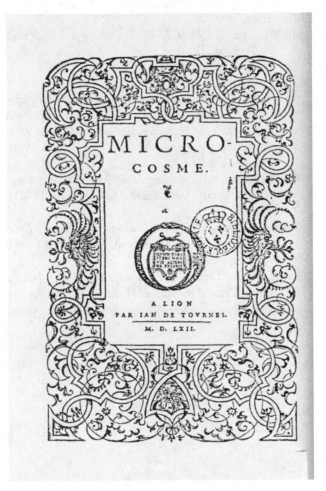

Title page for Scève's three-thousand-line poem, in which the sin of Adam in Eden leads to the scientific and technological achievements of the human race (from Paul Ardouin, La Délie de Maurice Scève et ses cinquante emblèmes, *1982; Thomas Cooper Library, University of South Carolina)*

Eugène Parturier and I. D. McFarlane, who produced scholarly editions of the text in 1916 and 1966, respectively. These books permitted a reevaluation of Scève's work by the modern academic community, which has resulted in a proliferation of further editions and studies of this first French *canzoniere* and other Scevian texts. Scève's important contributions to French Renaissance literature are now widely recognized, and he is routinely accepted as a canonical author. He is especially appreciated for the openness with which he confronts the vicissitudes of love, the pangs of jealousy, and the depths of forbidden desire. Far from lamenting the complexity of Scève's allusion-rich verses, modern readers have commended his innovative use of wide-ranging source material and have, it seems, been far more eager than his contemporaries to embrace the challenge of reading this difficult but rewarding poet.

References:

Paul Ardouin, *La Délie de Maurice Scève et ses cinquante emblèmes, ou, Les noces secrètes de la poésie et du signe: esquisse d'un plan raisonné* (Paris: Nizet, 1982);

Jean-Pierre Attal, *Maurice Scève: Un tableau synoptique de la vie et des oeuvres de Maurice Scève et des événments artistiques, littéraires et historiques de son époque. Une suite iconographique accompagnée d'un commentaire sur Maurice Scève et son temps. Une étude sur l'écrivain* (Paris: Seghers, 1963);

Gérard Defaux, "(Re)visiting *Délie*: Maurice Scève and Marian Poetry," *Renaissance Quarterly,* 54 (2001): 685–739;

JoAnn DellaNeva, *Song and Counter-Song: Scève's 'Délie' and Petrarch's 'Rime'* (Lexington, Ky.: French Forum Monographs, 1983);

Jean de Tornes, Preface to Francesco Petrarca, *Il Petrarca* (Lyon: Printed by Jean de Tournes, 1545);

Lance Donaldson-Evans, "'Love Divine, All Loves Excelling': Biblical Intertextualities in Scève's *Délie,*" *French Forum,* 14 (1989): 5–15;

Doranne Fenoaltea, *"Si haulte architecture": The Design of Scève's 'Délie'* (Lexington, Ky.: French Forum Monographs, 1982);

Jerry C. Nash, *The Love Aesthetics of Maurice Scève* (Cambridge: Cambridge University Press, 1991);

Etienne Pasquier, *Les Recherches de la France* (Paris: Printed by L. Sonnius, 1610);

François Rigolot, *Poétique et onomastique: L'Exemple de la Renaissance* (Geneva: Droz, 1977);

V.-L. Saulnier, *Maurice Scève* (Paris: Klincksieck, 1948);

Cynthia Skenazi, *Maurice Scève et la pensée chrétienne* (Geneva: Droz, 1992);

Hans Staub, *Le Curieux désir: Scève et Peletier du Mans poètes de la connaissance* (Geneva: Droz, 1967).

Thomas Sebillet

(1512 – November 1589)

Bernd Renner
Brooklyn College and the Graduate Center, The City University of New York

BOOKS: *Art Poétique François. Pour l'instruction de's ieunes studieus, & encor peu avancé'z en la Pöe'sie Françoise,* anonymous (Paris: Arnould L'Angelie or Gilles Corrozet, 1548);

L'Iphigene d'Euripide poete tragic: Tourné de grec en françois par l'auteur de l'Art Poétique, anonymous (Paris: Gilles Corrozet, 1549)–preface translated by Bernard Weinberg as "Thomas Sebillet. Preface to Euripides' *Iphigenia*," in *Critical Prefaces of the French Renaissance* (Evanston, Ill.: Northwestern University Press, 1950), pp. 141–144;

Contramours. L'Anteros ou Contramour de Messire Baptiste Fulgose, jadis duc de Gennes. Le Dialogue de Baptiste Platine, gentilhomme de Cremonne, contre les folles amours. Paradoxe contre l'amour (Paris: Martin, 1581);

Advis civils contenans plusieurs beaux et utiles enseignemens, tant pour la vie politique que pour conseils, et gouvernemens des Estats Republiques. Traduicts puis nagueres en François de l'Italien de Messire Francisque Lotin, gentilhomme de Volterre, au territoire Florentin (Paris: Jean Richer, 1584).

Edition: *Art poétique français* in *Traités de poétique et de rhétorique de la Renaissance,* edited by Francis Goyet (Paris: Le Livre de poche classique, 1990), pp. 37–183.

OTHER: Two poems on the death of Pierre de Ronsard, in Claude Binet, *Discours de la vie de Pierre de Ronsard* (Paris: Gabriel Buon, 1586), p. 99;

Nine quatrains celebrating the 1549 entry of Henri II into Paris, edited by V. L. Saulnier, in "Sebillet, Du Bellay, Ronsard: L'Entrée de Henry II à Paris et la révolution poétique de 1550," *Les Fêtes de la Renaissance,* volume 1, edited by Jean Jacquot (Paris: Editions du CNRS, 1956), pp. 41, 47–53.

SELECTED PERIODICAL PUBLICATIONS–UNCOLLECTED: *Discours de M^e Th. Sibilet, advocat au Parlement, sur les affaires de l'année 1589,* in Lewis Thorpe, *French Studies,* 3 (1949): 256–266;

"Thome Sibilleti," in Harry Redman Jr., "New Thomas Sebillet Data," *Studi Francesi,* 13 (1969), pp. 204–205.

Thomas Sebillet's significance as a literary figure is almost exclusively based on his first work, *Art Poétique François* (The Art of French Poetry), published anonymously in 1548. This treatise was the first original publication in French that considered poetry as being distinct from rhetoric, a development for which Jacques Peletier du Mans's 1541 translation of Horace's *Ars Poetica* (Art of Poetry) paved the way. Traditionally, poetry had been classified under the rubric of a "art de seconde rhétorique" (second rhetoric) and was essentially regarded as a craft with strict rules of rhythm and versification. Mastery of these rules used to be the only prerequisite for becoming what the authors of Renaissance poetic treatises, which flourished in the wake of Sebillet's groundbreaking work, would pejoratively call a "rimailleur" (rhymester) or "versificateur" (versifier). The school of the Grands Rhétoriqueurs poets of the fifteenth and early sixteenth centuries attests to the subordinate status of poetry that Sebillet's influential text helped to alter. Sebillet's ideas–especially his belief in "divine inspiration" and the concept of "inventio" as the key elements of a poem and his endorsement of the imitation of classical models–anticipated those formulated in the much better known Pléiade manifesto, Joachim du Bellay's *La Déffence et illustration de la langue françoyse* (Defense and Illustration of the French Language), which was a direct reply to Sebillet published the following year.

Little is known about Sebillet's life, especially prior to the publication of his famous treatise. He was born in 1512, most likely in Paris, studied law, and became an attorney at the Parlement de Paris (Parliament of Paris). According to Etienne Pasquier, who was grateful to Sebillet for inspiring him to take up writing, the attorney enjoyed poetry much more than legal speeches. Pasquier was one of the many illustrious friends and acquaintances with whom Sebillet was in

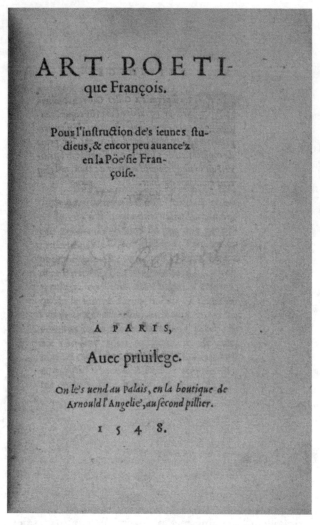

Title page for Thomas Sebillet's anonymous first book, in which he elevated poetry as an art, above its traditional status as a type of rhetoric (Douglas H. Gordon Collection, University of Virginia Library)

supplanting medieval Latin—the elevation of a national literature to the heights of the classical and Italian models was indispensable to the transfer of power and learning *(translatio imperii et studii)* and served as a justification of France's prominent position in Europe. Sebillet's treatise was also a reaction to the arrogance of a group of young poets led by Ronsard and Du Bellay, the Brigade, which later became known as the Pléiade. The poets of the Brigade had begun to invade the scene dominated until then by the *marotiques,* or followers of Clément Marot; they rejected the native French literary heritage, with the exception of the medieval allegory *Roman de la rose* (Romance of the Rose), in order to stake their claim to the legacy of the revered Ancients. Sebillet, however, defended the French heritage, particularly the *marotiques,* citing their works as positive proof of the capacity of the French language and letters to equal the Greek, Latin, and Italian models.

The conflict between Sebillet's vision and that of the Brigade poets was more personal and political than it was theoretical, for both poetics agreed on the theory of imitation and the importance of divine inspiration in poetic creation—both thus elevating poetry above all other forms of literature and, consequently, glorifying the divine persona of the poet himself. The concept of divine fury, as it was also known, raised an important contradiction that Sebillet faced and that, at the same time, is indicative of the intermediate position that his treatise occupied in the transition between poetry as an "art of second rhetoric" and as an independent genre far superior to rhetoric and its formal constraints: he had to justify writing a manual of the rules of poetry (*art* here signifies *artifice,* the rules of a craft), whose orientation seemed similar to the preceding handbooks of "second rhetoric," while claiming at the same time that the factor that sets apart the mere "rhymester" from the true poet is his unteachable divine inspiration or enthusiasm (from the Greek *en-theos,* signifying the presence of the divine in the poet's very nature). The short answer to this dilemma, which became much clearer in the more elitist Pléiade's theoretical writings, is that even the inspired poet needs to have sound knowledge of the rules and mechanics of the creative process to produce truly superior work. The rare combination of nature and learning distinguishes the true poet, further underscoring his outstanding position in human society.

In the first paragraph of his text Sebillet actually excuses himself for his choice of the term "art," with its connotation of artifice, and goes on to justify it via a bark-and-sap metaphor—referring respectively to "art" and "nature"—insisting on the necessary presence of both elements. The first book of the treatise is extremely technical, as Sebillet concentrates on the teachable aspects of poetry such as style, rhyme

contact, especially during the second half of his life: Pierre de l'Estoile, Michel de l'Hospital, Joachim du Bellay, Antoine Loisiel, Hugues Salel, and Pierre de Ronsard are the most important figures among them. Pasquier's regard for Sebillet might be best illustrated by the fact that he published the sixth volume of his *Recherches de la France* (French Pursuits), which included critical remarks about the *Art Poétique François,* seven years after his friend's death.

In 1548 Sebillet was largely unknown in the literary world, which might be one reason for the anonymous publication of his treatise. The impact of this first *Art Poétique François* was not only literary but also political. At a time when the formation of the French nation was inextricably tied to the assertion of the potential of the vernacular language—French had become the official administrative language of the country in 1539,

schemes, metrics, pronunciation, and conjugation. In the second book he differs markedly from the preceding handbooks of rhetoric, however, by providing models for imitation and discussing the different poetic genres available to the future poet, many of which stem from the French medieval tradition—for instance, Alain Chartier and Jean de Meung—and from the practice of contemporary poets such as Marot, Mellin de Saint-Gelais, and Maurice Scève, precisely the French models whom Du Bellay later argued against. The other main controversial issue was the value of the exercise of translation, praised by Sebillet as an excellent means to enrich the vernacular but rejected by Du Bellay in favor of the more liberal imitation.

The quarrel between the rival schools, which lasted several years, began when the Brigade rushed to publish Du Bellay's *Défence et illustration de la langue française* attacking Sebillet for his praise of French literary models. The promptness of this reaction was also because of another event that underlined the importance of poetry in the political and ideological project of heightening the glory of France: Sebillet was chosen, probably as early as February 1549, to compose the poems celebrating the entry of King Henri II into Paris on 16 June of the same year. Royal entries were highly prestigious events, and the appointment of the official poet and deputy to the main organizer of the festivities, Jean Martin, a well-known translator and secretary of the Cardinal of Lenoncourt, was a political decision. For his services Sebillet was paid the handsome sum of 25 *écus soleil* on 17 August, according to Philippe Macé's payroll preserved in the National Archives. Their rival's appointment bothered Ronsard and Du Bellay to the point that they offered their own celebratory verses of the event: the former's "Avant-entrée du roi treschrestien" (Prelude to the Entry of the Most Christian King) and the latter's "Prosphonématique au roy tres-chrestien Henry II" (Prosphonematic for the Most Christian King Henry II).

The appointment of Sebillet might be explained in part by the fact that Henri II's official court poet was François Habert, whose poetry was indebted to the Grands Rhétoriqueurs tradition that had been praised in the *Art Poétique François*. For the occasion Sebillet composed nine rather conservative celebratory quatrains of mediocre quality that were displayed on the monuments erected for the festivities: several arches and one obelisk. Furthermore, the verses had the main function of glossing and explaining the Greek and Latin inscriptions, which were either quotes or paraphrases from classical authors such as Homer and Virgil or verses composed most likely by Jean Salmon Macrin, the most distinguished neo-Latin poet of the time. The poems juxtaposed the classical past with the glorious French present and future and exalted the exploits of Henri, and his predecessor François I, by turning the French kings into worthy successors of classical heroes, an undertaking in tune with one of the main themes of the entry, the celebration of the "Gallic Hercules."

In the preface to *L'Iphigene d'Euripide poete tragic* (1549, The Iphigenia by the Tragic Poet Euripides), Sebillet retorted bluntly to Du Bellay's criticism from the *Défense et illustration de la langue française* as well as his further attacks in the second preface to his *L'Olive* (1550, Olive). Sebillet's translation of Euripides' work was his second publication, as there is no trace of the French grammar that he had announced in the last sentence of book 1 of the *Art Poétique François*. *L'Iphigene* is more an imitation than merely a translation, however, as Sebillet attempted to illustrate the technical and ideological principles that he had established in the *Art Poétique François* by using the various meters and poetic genres that he had defined there. Ronsard joined the quarrel in his preface to the *Odes* (1550), and Bartélemy Aneau came to Sebillet's defense in his *Quintil horacien* (1550, Horatian Quintil), a point-by-point criticism of *Défence et illustration de la langue française*. Aneau's text accompanied the *Art Poétique François* in all six republications that the text underwent in the sixteenth century (1551, 1555, 1556, 1564, 1573, and 1576).

Tempers calmed down quickly after the publication of Aneau's work, however. In a 1552 New Year's poem to Robert de La Haye, an associate of Sebillet at the *parlement* and an admirer of the Pléiade, Du Bellay praised his former adversary. The artistic superiority of the Pléiade poets had been firmly established by then, and Sebillet was simply no longer seen as a worthy opponent. In 1552 Du Bellay published a translation of the fourth book of the *Æneid,* in which he declared that he was not ashamed at having changed his mind and included an introductory sonnet by Sebillet, thus acknowledging the validity of his former rival's endorsement of translation. Du Bellay further honored Sebillet by dedicating sonnet 122 of *Les Regrets* (1558, Regrets) to him. He also praised the attorney's translation of Euripides' *Iphigenia.*

Probably toward the end of 1549, Sebillet traveled to Italy with his friend Denis Lambin and Lambin's protector, the Cardinal François de Tournon. Traveling to Rome was a required rite of passage for all men of letters of the period, and Sebillet was no exception. Upon his return in 1550, he undertook his work on the *Contramours* (Anti-Love), as he notes in the preface to this text that was not published until 1581. This second major translation project provided French versions of Baptiste Fulgose's *Anteros* (Anti-eros) and Baptiste Platine's *Dialogue contre les folles amours* (Dialogue against Mad Love).

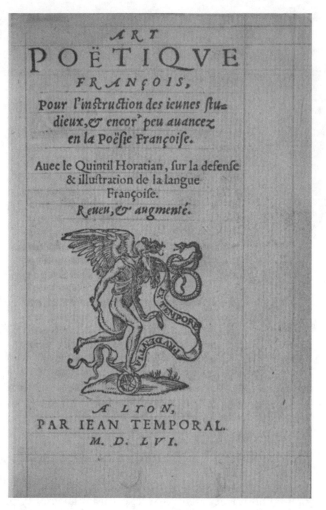

Title page for one of six sixteenth-century reprints of Sebillet's treatise that included Bartélemy Aneau's criticism of Joachim du Bellay's Défense et Illustration de la langue française *(Douglas H. Gordon Collection, University of Virginia)*

There is hardly any trace of Sebillet's activities in the following two decades. His literary career evidently stagnated, partially because of his bad luck in choosing protectors. Jean Brinon, the dedicatee of *L'Iphigene* who was the king's counselor at the parlement as well as a musician, poet, and rich patron of letters, died young. Henri II was not as devoted to promoting the cause of literature as his father, and two other possible patrons, the Cardinal de Tournon and Michel de l'Hospital, were consumed by their various duties on the international and domestic scenes. So Sebillet kept his post at the parlement and worked as a translator. Most of the texts that he produced are lost; a few are preserved in manuscript form at the Bibliothèque Nationale de France (National Library of France).

Sebillet's first marriage to Madeleine Le Roy, the widow of the Parisian merchant draper Jean Choffart,

on 15 May 1570, documented in the National Archives, makes it possible to pick up his tracks again. A 1573 document attests to a sum of money owed by the couple, and the belated recording of the marriage contract (31 August 1574), shortly before Madeleine's death, leads to the assumption that Sebillet tried to put order into his financial situation. A second marriage occurred on 9 September 1575, to Claude Hervé, another widow. The new marriage contract, recorded on 1 December 1575, shows that Sebillet was rather well-off financially at that time, as he made generous provisions for his new wife, who survived him and remarried in 1591.

During the 1580s, the last decade of his life, Sebillet became more and more concerned by the political turmoil of the era. He composed two poems for Claude Binet's *Discours de la vie de Pierre de Ronsard* (Discourse on the Life of Pierre de Ronsard) in 1586, but his most important late writings were political in nature: *Advis civils contenans plusieurs beaux et utiles enseignemens, tant pour la vie politique que pour conseils, et gouvernemens des Estats Republiques* (1584, Civil Advice Containing Several Beautiful and Useful Teachings, as Much for Political Life as for the Government of Republics) and *Discours de Me Th. Sibilet, advocat au Parlement, sur les affaires de l'année 1589* (Discourse of Mr. Th. Sebillet, Lawyer of Parliament, on the Affairs of the Year 1589), which was first published in 1949 in *French Studies*. He was evidently deeply involved in politics as he and Pierre de L'Estoile, according to the latter's account, were sent to prison during the upheavals of the Catholic League, whose executive committee, known as *les Seize* (The Committee of the Sixteen) after 1587, kept a close watch on Sebillet. He was released from prison in 1589, an experience that motivated him to write the passionate discourse that calls for the restoration of order and virtue under a Catholic monarch. The speech was delivered in October or November 1589, shortly before his death, which occurred in late November of that year.

Thomas Sebillet's significant contribution to Renaissance letters has long been overshadowed by Du Bellay's manifesto in particular and the Pléiade poets' overwhelming achievements in general. The Parisian attorney, however, began the process of liberating poetry from the constraints of rhetoric and, by extension, played an important role in the political, cultural, and ideological struggles of his time. The success of his initiative is manifest in the many poetic treatises that were published in its wake—not only works by Du Bellay and Bartélemy Aneau, but also Claude de Boissière's *Art poétique reduict et abregé* (1554, Art of Poetry Reduced and Abridged), which was published with Sebillet's treatise from 1556 onward; Jacques Peletier du Mans's *L'Art poétique* (1555, The Art of Poetry); Antoine Fouquelin's *La rhétorique française* (1555, French Rhetoric); and finally Ronsard's *Abbrégé de l'Art poétique Français* (1565, Summary of the Art of French Poetry). Moreover, Boissière's and Ronsard's texts were little more than rewritings of Sebillet's, which serves as the ultimate proof of the considerable influence exerted by the first *Art Poétique François*.

References:

Ehsan Ahmed, "Du Bellay, Sebillet, and the Problematic Identity of the French Humanist," *Neophilologus,* 75 (1991): 185–193;

Grahame Castor, *Pléiade Poetics* (Cambridge: Cambridge University, 1964);

Perrine Galand-Hallyn and Fernand Hallyn, eds., *Poétiques de la Renaissance. Le modèle italien, le monde franco-bourguignon et leur héritage en France au XVIe siècle* (Geneva: Droz, 2001);

Yves Le Hir, "Sur un manuscrit inédit de Thomas Sébillet," *Bibliothèque d'Humanisme et Renaissance,* 54 (1992): 477–480;

Kees Meerhoff, "Antoine Fouquelin et Thomas Sebillet," *Nouvelle Revue du XVIe Siècle,* 5 (1987): 59–77;

Meerhoff, "Paratexte et intertexte à propos d'un sonnet liminaire de Thomas Sebillet," in *Du Bellay,* edited by Georges Cesbron (Angers, France: Presses de l'Université d'Angers, 1990), pp. 353–368;

Harry Redman, "New Thomas Sebillet Data," *Studi Francesi,* 13 (1969): 201–209;

Richard Regosin, "Language and Nation in 16th-Century France: The *Arts poétiques,*" in *Beginnings in French Literature,* edited by Freeman G. Henry (New York: Rodopi, 2002), pp. 29–40;

François Rigolot, "Le Sonnet et l'épigramme, ou: L'Enjeu de la 'superscription,'" in *Pre-Pléiade Poetry,* edited by Jerry C. Nash (Lexington, Ky.: French Forum, 1985), pp. 97–111;

V. L. Saulnier, "Sebillet, Du Bellay, Ronsard: L'Entrée de Henry II à Paris et la révolution poétique de 1550," in *Les Fêtes de la Renaissance,* volume 1, edited by Jean Jacquot (Paris: Editions du CNRS, 1956), pp. 31–59.

Papers:

The major collections of Thomas Sebillet's papers are at the Bibliothèque Nationale de France and National Archives, both located in Paris.

Jean de Sponde

(1557 – 18 March 1595)

Jessica L. Wolfe
University of North Carolina, Chapel Hill

BOOKS: *Méditations sur les pseaumes XIIII. ou LIII., XLVIII., L. et LXII., avec un Essay de quelques poèmes chrestiens* (N.p. [La Rochelle], 1588);

Advertissement Au Roy, ou sont deduictes les Raisons d'Estat, pour lesquelles il ne luy est pas bien seant de changer de Religion, anonymous (La Rochelle, 1589); republished as Sponde in Simon Goulart, *Mémoires de la Ligue contenant le évenemens le plus remarquables depuis 1576, jusqu'à la paix accordée entre le roi de France & le roi d'Espagne, en 1598,* volume 5, edited by Claude-Pierre Goujet (Amsterdam: Arkstée & Merkus, 1758);

Response d'un Catholique, Apostolique, Romain à la Confession de Foy d'un Protestant de Reformation (Chartres: Claude Cottereau, 1593);

Déclaration des principaux motifs qui induisent le sieur de Sponde, conseiller et maistre des requestes du Roy, à s'unir à l'Eglise catholique apostolique et romaine, adressée à ceux qui en sont séparez (Chartres: Claude Cottereau, 1593; revised and enlarged, Melun, 1594);

Response du feu sieur de Sponde Conseiller et Maistre des Requestes du Roy Au Traicté des marques de l'Eglise faict par Th[eodore] de Bèze, edited by Florimond de Raemond (Bordeaux: S. Millanges, 1595).

Editions and Collections: *Œuvre poétique,* edited by Marcel Arland (Paris: Delamain & Boutelleau, 1945);

Sonnets et stances de la mort. Gravures sur cuivre par Jean Deville (Paris: P. Seghers, 1946);

Stances et sonnets de la mort, edited by Alan Martin Boase (Paris: J. Corti, 1947);

Poésies, edited by François Ruchon and Boase (Geneva: P. Cailler, 1949);

Les amours et la mort: stances et sonnets (Paris: GLM, 1949);

Jean de Sponde et ses Méditations sur les psaumes, edited by Ruchon (Geneva: Droz, 1951);

Méditations, avec un essai de poèmes chrétiens, edited by Boase (Paris: José Corti, 1954);

La response d'un Catholique, edited by Giuseppe Antonio Brunelli (Catania: Castorina, 1967);

Oeuvres littéraires, suivis d'Ecrits apologétiques avec des Juvénilia, edited by Boase (Geneva: Droz, 1978);

D'Amour et de mort: poésies complètes, edited by James Sacré (Paris: La Différence, 1989);

Méditations sur les pseaumes, edited by Sabine Lardon (Paris & Geneva: H. Champion, 1996).

Editions in English: *Sonnets on Love and Death,* translated by Robert Nugent (Painesville, Ohio: Lake Erie College, 1962; Westport, Conn.: Greenwood Press, 1979);

Poems of Love and Death, translated by Gilbert Farm Cunningham (Edinburgh: Oliver & Boyd, 1964);

Sonnets of Love and Death, translated by David Slavitt (Evanston, Ill.: Northwestern University Press, 2001).

OTHER: "In Theatrum Musicum," in Orlando di Lassus, *Theatrum Musicum Orlandi de Lassus, aliorumque praestantissionum musicorum selectissimas cantiones sacras* (Geneva: S. Goulart, 1580);

"In A. Turnebi Adversariorum libros quaedam observationes," in *Adriani Turnebi Adversariorum tomi III: Auctorum loci, qui in his sine certa nota appellabantur, suis locis inserti, auctoribusq[ue] suis adscripti sunt* (Basel: Thomas Guarinus, 1581);

"A Paschal de L'Estocart rare et tresexcellent musicien," in Paschal de L'Estocart, *Le Premier Livre des Octonaires de la Vanité du Monde* (Geneva: Eustace Vignon, 1582);

"Au Roy de Navarre, Sonnet," "A mon cher ami et tresexcellent Musicien Paschal de L'Estocart," and "Hic bonus orbi nervus," in Pascal de L'Estocart, Clément Marot, and Théodore de Bèze, *Cent cinquante pseaumes de David, mis en rime françoise par Clément Marot et Th[éodore] de Bèsze, et mis en musique à quatre, cinq, six, sept et huit parties par Paschal de L'Estocart* (Geneva: Eustace Vignon, 1583);

"Sur la Canelle," in Jean de la Goutte, *La Canelle, les Larmes, et Sonnets de I. de la Goutte* (Tours: Claude Montrœil & Jean Richer, 1591);

398

Dedicatory epistle, in Jacques Faye, Sieur d'Espeisses, *Recueil des remonstrances faites en la cour de Parlement de Paris, aux ouvertures des plaidoiries,* edited by Sponde (La Rochelle: Jerome Haultin, 1591; revised and enlarged by Sponde, 1592);

Fifty-five poems, in *Recueil de diverses poésies, tant du feu sieur de Sponde, que des sieurs Du Perron, de Bertaud, de Porchères, et autres non encor imprimées,* edited by Raphaël Du Petit Val (Rouen: Raphaël Du Petit Val, 1599; revised and enlarged, 1600); revised as *Premier recueil de diverses poésies,* (1604); revised as volume 2 of *Le Temple d'Apollon ou nouveau recueil des plus excellents vers de ce temps* (1611);

"Stances du Sacré Banquet," in *L'Academie des modernes poètes françois remplie des plus beaux vers que ce siècle reserve à la postérité* (Paris: Antoine du Breuil, 1599);

"Miracle d'Amour en la Guérison d'une Dame Mourante," in *Les muses françoises ralliées de diverses pars,* edited by Sieur Despinelle (Paris: Mathieu Guillemot, 1599);

"Hymne à Saincte Geneviève," in *Le Parnasse des plus excellens poëtes de ce temps,* edited by Sieur Despinelle (Paris: Mathieu Guillemot, 1607).

TRANSLATIONS: Pythagoras, "Fragmenta Politica," in *Aristotelis Politicorum Libri octo, ex Dion[ysius] Lambini et P[ietro] Victorii interpretationib[us],* edited and translated by Theodor Zwinger (Basel: Eusebius Episcopius, 1582);

Aristotelis Organum Graeco-latinum, novissime conversum et emendatum, nec non Annotationculis marginalibus utillissimis illustratum (Basel: Oporinus, 1583);

Homeri quae extant omnia, Ilias, Odyssea, Batrachomyomachia, Hymni, poemata aliquot, cum latina versione omnium quae circumferuntur emendatiss. Aliquot locis iam castigatiore, perpetuis item justisque in Iliada simul et Odysseam Jo. Spondani, . . . commentariis. Pindari quinetiam Thebani epitome Iliados latinis versib. et Daretis Phrygii de Bello trojano libri, a Corn. Nepote eleganter latino versi carmine. Indices Homeri textus et commentariorum locupletissimi (Basel: Eusebius Episcopius, 1583);

Hesiodi Ascræi Opera et Dies (La Rochelle: Jerome Haultin, 1592).

The poetry, scholarship, and devotional writings of Jean de Sponde are steeped in the political and religious tensions of late-sixteenth-century France. Sponde's brief life was marked profoundly by the Wars of Religion (1562–1598), and his entire oeuvre is a response to the violence, dissent, and factionalism of these turbulent years. Active after the great achievements of poets of the Pléiade such as Pierre de Ronsard and Joachim du Bellay, Sponde expresses a new, more

eclectic classicism in his poetry and prose, one less reliant on the generic and rhetorical models favored by the previous generation. Best known in the twentieth century for his anguished, highly mannered *Sonnets et stances de la mort* (1946, Sonnets and Stanzas of Death), a collection that earns him frequent comparison to late-sixteenth- and early-seventeenth-century poets such as John Donne, Luis de Góngora, and Giambattista Marini, Sponde was recognized in his own time as an accomplished scholar whose monumental edition of Homer, with its original, often topical commentary, marks a watershed moment in the history of classical scholarship. Yet, he was even more famous—or perhaps infamous—in his own time for his conversion to Catholicism, an event precipitated either by prudence or conscience, according to conflicting accounts, and which initiated a pamphlet war that began shortly before Sponde's death and persisted for several years afterward.

Born in 1557 in the village of Mauléon en Soule, Sponde was the youngest of the children born to Enécot de Sponde and Catherine d'Ohix, daughter of the royal bailiff and the second of Enécot's three wives. Located between Pau and Bayonne in the Béarn region, Mauléon en Soule was a predominantly Basque-speaking area during the sixteenth century, and Sponde probably learned the language as a child. Although the town itself was predominantly Catholic, it belonged to the Diocese of Oloron, whose bishop from 1533 to 1550 was Gérard Roussel, an Erasmian evangelical and former disciple of the reformed theologian Jacques Lefèvre d'Etaples, who may have aroused the intellectual sympathies of Enécot de Sponde before his son's birth. It is not known precisely when Enécot de Sponde, who is identified in a 1541 document as the general vicar of Roger d'Aspremont, an apostolic secretary and abbot of the monastery of Saint-Sever, converted to Protestantism. Jean de Sponde, after his own apostasy, repeatedly described himself as baptized Catholic but raised in the heretical Protestant faith, so his father's conversion can tentatively be dated to sometime between 1557 and the end of 1560, when the elder Sponde assumed the position of secretary to Jeanne d'Albret, Queen of Navarre. The niece of François I and mother of Henri de Navarre (the future King Henri IV), D'Albret converted in December 1560 and subsequently oversaw a state-sponsored Reformation in the Béarn, outlawing Mass and requiring participation in reformed services.

By 1563, when Sponde was seven years old, the Wars of Religion came to the Béarn, and Mauléon became an island of Catholic sympathies in the otherwise predominantly Huguenot territories of southwestern France. In 1568, by which time Sponde's mother had died, his father was brought before an inquest led

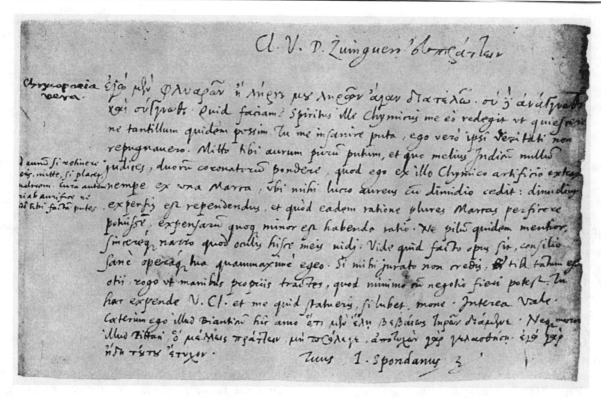

Letter from Jean de Sponde to Theodor Zwinger, who included Sponde's translation of Pythagoras's "Fragmenta Politica" in his 1582
edition of Aristotle's Politics (from Sponde, Poésies, edited by François Ruchon and Alan Martin Boase, 1949;
Thomas Cooper Library, University of South Carolina)

by Jean de Ferrière, an emissary from the Bordeaux parliament. While Enécot de Sponde was not accused outright of heresy, he was formally admonished for his three marriages, especially his third and final marriage to his brother-in-law's widow, Sauvade de Osta, a union that produced at least three additional children, including Henri de Sponde, the future bishop of Palmiers. By the time of his father's inquest, Jean de Sponde had been sent to the Collège de Béarn, a school in nearby Orthez established by D'Albret in Lescar, near Pau, in 1566 but then relocated temporarily to Orthez after the outbreak of civil war in the region. The staunchly Protestant outlook of the school must have attracted the Sponde family: when asked at his inquest why he had sent several sons to study at Orthez, Enécot de Sponde replied that he wished his sons to be instructed with greater piety in matters of religion. D'Albret played an instrumental role in securing Sponde a place at the college, instructing the school's director in a 1571 letter to keep an eye on the son of her friend and loyal counselor and secretary. After D'Albret's death in 1572, her son Henri de Navarre continued to assist both the elder and the younger Sponde, appointing them to various political offices and, in 1580, granting the Sponde family a house near Orthez with the understanding that it was to be kept ready to receive his majesty.

Sponde appears to have spent between four and five years at Orthez, an academy modeled upon the Collège de Genève, from whence hailed several of the school's more prominent lecturers. According to scholar Alan Martin Boase in Vie de Jean de Sponde (1977, Life of Jean de Sponde), Sponde studied Greek with Robert Constantin, a disciple of the classical scholar Julius Caesar Scaliger, and then with Constantin's successor Claude de la Grange, who was elected professor of Greek and rhetoric at Orthez in 1571. Another figure who undoubtedly influenced Sponde during his time at Orthez was Lambert Daneau, the rector of the school between 1571 and 1579 and lecturer in theology at the Académie de Genève from 1572 onward. In 1571, when Sponde was attending Orthez, Daneau published a French translation of Hesiod's Works and Days, the Greek georgic poem that Sponde translated into Latin two decades later.

Little is known of Sponde's whereabouts between his departure from Orthez and 1579, when he was given 240 livres tournois (pounds) by Henri de Navarre in order to pursue his studies. In autumn 1579 Sponde traveled to Geneva armed with letters of introduction provided by his father in order to meet prominent scholars such as Théodore de Bèze, whom Sponde's father probably met in 1563 when he traveled to

Geneva to recruit Protestant pastors able to speak Gascon for his native region.

By autumn 1580 Sponde was residing in Basel, another Protestant town but one not entirely sympathetic to the strict Calvinism of Geneva. The Protestant dissident Sébastien Castellion fled to Basel in the 1540s after he was repudiated by Jean Calvin and Bèze for his defense of the freedom of the will and his advocacy of religious toleration. The legacy of tolerance in Basel was based on the enduring influence of Castellion, who died in Basel in 1563, as well as that of the Dutch theologian Desiderius Erasmus, who died there three decades earlier. Sponde's first known publication, a dedicatory poem titled "In Theatrum Musicum," appeared in Orlando di Lassus's *Theatrum Musicum* (1580, Theater of Music). On 26 November 1580 Sponde presented editor Thomas Guarinus with a supplement of critical notes, "In A. Turnebi Adversariorum libros quaedam observationes" (Certain Observations on Adrian Turnebus's Books of Adversaria), which were published in a new edition of the prominent Hellenist's *Adversariorum* (1581). In these notes Sponde reveals his intent to edit the works of Homer, a project he completed only two years later, in 1583, at the age of twenty-five.

In April 1581 Sponde matriculated at the University of Basel, where he joined the circle of an eminent group of scholars including Theodor Zwinger, Thomas Erastus, and the jurist François Hotman. Zwinger, who since the 1560s had been working on a collected Greek-Latin edition of Aristotle, solicited from Sponde an annotated Latin translation of the political fragments of the Greek philosopher Pythagoras to be included in Zwinger's 1582 edition of Aristotle's *Politics*. Sponde sent his translation of Pythagoras's "Fragmenta Politica" to Zwinger on 24 August 1582, the ten-year anniversary of the Saint Bartholomew's Day Massacre. The fragments, collected from the writings of various classical and late-antique authors such as Iamblichus and Stobaias Stobaios, were perhaps intended as an antidote to the ongoing religious strife in France, since Pythagoras's political maxims envision a tranquil, communalistic polity governed with justice and harmony.

Sponde may have first conceived of the idea of composing meditations on the Psalms during the summer of 1582. In August he wrote to his half brother Henri, then a student at the Collège de Genève, and recounted how he was gripped by a poetic fury while rereading and translating the Psalms: "je ne sais quelle fureur poétique m'a tout de suite m'envahi" (I know not what poetic fury suddenly overcame me), Sponde writes, "à ce point que je n'ai pu retenir ma plume" (to the point that I could no longer hold my pen). During this period, Sponde composed the dedicatory epistle "A

Paschal de L'Estocart rare et tresexcellent musicien" (To Paschal de L'Estocart Rare and Very Excellent Musician) for L'Estocart's *Le Premier Livre des Octonaires de la Vanité du Monde* (1582, The First Book of Octets on the Vanity of the World). Several additional dedicatory poems by Sponde appear in *Cent cinquante pseaumes de David* (1583, One Hundred and Fifty Psalms of David), a collection of the Psalms translated some years earlier by Bèze and Clément Marot, newly set to music by L'Estocart.

On 20 January 1583, while still in Basel, Sponde signed the dedication to his annotated translation of the six treatises on logic *Aristotelis Organum* (Aristotle's *Organon*). The following month, on 1 February 1583, Sponde sent the printer Episcopius the manuscript of his edition of Homer, printed later that spring as *Homeri quae extant omnia* (All the Extant Works of Homer) and dedicated to Henri de Navarre. Sponde based his edition on the Greek text discovered two decades earlier in Geneva by the French printer and editor Henri Estienne; the Latin prose translation is not Sponde's work but that of Andreas Divus, whose translations of the *Iliad* and the *Odyssey* were first published in Venice in 1537 and reprinted in both Paris and Leyden the following year. Sponde's edition of Homer also includes untranslated Greek texts of the "Homeric Hymns" and the "Batrachomyomachia" (Battle of the Frogs and the Mice), both commonly but erroneously attributed to Homer during the sixteenth century; it also includes Dares Phrygius's "De Bello Troiano" (On the Trojan War) and several other post-Homeric accounts of the fall of Troy. As Jean Jehasse in *La Renaissance de la Critique* (2002, The Renaissance of Criticism) and Christiane Deloince-Louette in *Sponde: commentateur d'Homère* (2001, Sponde: Commentator on Homer) have noted, Sponde's prolegomena and his extensive commentary represent Homer as a divinely inspired poet whose works reveal, albeit enigmatically, a monotheistic theology and a proto-Protestant attitude toward divine providence. Deeply informed by his reading of patristic writers including Augustine, Clement of Alexandria, and Lactantius, Sponde's commentary is filled with theological discussions of the Homeric underworld, of pagan rituals of prayer and supplication, and of archaic Greek notions of sin, fate, and divine favor. Sponde's prolegomena, titled "De Origine et Dignitate Poeticae" (On the Origin and Dignity of Poetry), offers a general defense of poetry on ethical and political grounds as well as a specific defense of Homer; its arguments are usefully summarized and analyzed by Deloince-Louette as well as by Franck L. Schoell in his article "Un Humaniste français oublié, Jean de Sponde" (A Forgotten French Humanist, Jean de Sponde).

Title page for Sponde's edition of Homer's works, in which he presented the ancient writer as a sacred and moral poet (from Poésies, edited by François Ruchon and Alan Martin Boase, 1949; Thomas Cooper Library, University of South Carolina)

(Agamemnon) and prudence (Odysseus), and he extracts from Homer a consistent theory of limited monarchy, finding both Agamemnon and Zeus to uphold the model of a single, divinely appointed ruler who relies upon his counselors for advice and humbly acknowledges the borrowed and contingent nature of his political authority.

Late in 1583 Sponde left Basel and traveled to Pau, near his native Mauléon. He was probably appointed Master of Requests by Henri de Navarre during this voyage, for in December 1583, while visiting Geneva, he signed his name in the *album amicorum* (book of friends) of Grégoire Amann de Gratz as "regis Navarrae consiliarius" (counselor to the king of Navarre). Little else is known of Sponde's whereabouts between the 1583 appearance of his edition of Homer and the summer of 1587, when, on 28 July, Sponde received a *Frais de Voyages,* a paid royal commission to release and deliver various Huguenot prisoners who had been captured in battle the previous month. Sponde may have endured during the intervening years the first of the four imprisonments to which he alludes in later writings.

Most critics agree that Sponde probably composed his twenty-six "Sonnets d'Amour" (Sonnets of Love) and their companion poems (three *chansons,* or songs, and one *elégie*) during the mid 1580s, though none of these works was published until two years after his death, in *Recueil de diverses poésies* (1599, Collection of Diverse Poems), an anthology assembled by Raphaël Du Petit Val. Probably assembled with the assistance of Sponde's fellow poet Hubert Laugier de Porchères, several of whose poems are also included in the anthology, the 1599 *Recueil* was almost certainly a reprinting of an earlier volume of the same name, no longer extant except for a privilege dated 4 February 1597. This collection, which was reprinted under various titles in 1600, 1604, and 1611, contains fifty poems attributed to Sponde, including both of his sonnet sequences, the twenty-six sonnets composing the *Sonnets d'Amour* and the twelve sonnets composing his *Sonnets de la Mort.* Boase in *Vie de Jean de Sponde* dates the "Sonnets d'Amour" to either 1586–1587 or 1590–1591, depending on whether one regards them as addressed to the poet's wife, Anne Legrand, whom he married on 30 May 1588 in La Rochelle. Reprinted in seven separate anthologies in the three decades after Sponde's death, including *L'Academie des modernes poëtes François* (1599) and *Le Parnasse des plus excellens poëtes de ce temps* (1607), the poems vary in order from one collection to another, and it is uncertain which order, if any, was intended by the poet. As Gilbert Shrenck observed in his essay "La Structure 'Délicate' des *Sonnets d'amour* de Jean de Sponde" (The "Delicate" Structure of Jean de Sponde's

Despite his efforts to recuperate Homer as a sacred and moral poet, Sponde resists for the most part the allegorical interpretations of the Homeric gods offered by Renaissance mythographers such as Giovanni Boccaccio in his *De genealogia deorum gentilium* (1350–1374, Genealogy of the Pagan Gods), Natale Comes in his oft-printed *Mythologiae* (1551, Mythographia), or Jean Dorat, the poet and Hellenist whose lectures on the allegorical meanings of Homer's *Odyssey* influenced earlier sixteenth-century poets such as Ronsard and Du Bellay. By contrast Sponde periodically acknowledges the incompatibility between pagan and Christian religious beliefs, and he condemns the anthropomorphism and immorality of the Homeric gods, who are subject to human passions and injuries. Nonetheless, Sponde regards Homeric heroes as models of moral and political virtues such as magnanimity

Sonnets of Love), modern editors continue to vary the order in which Sponde's love poetry is printed, a practice that enables different editors of Sponde's work to posit either stability or dynamism, coherence or disorder, in the narrative structure of the poems. The numbers used by Boase and Ruchon in their editions of Sponde's poetry are commonly accepted.

Like much sixteenth-century French Petrarchan lyric, Sponde's "Sonnets d'Amour" are dominated by antitheses: spiritual and earthly love, constancy and vicissitude, vision and blindness, speaking and writing. Sponde's love poetry reveals a fondness for cosmological metaphors; yet, unlike his predecessors in the Pléiade, Sponde often imagines the cosmos as unstable and disorderly, governed by the haphazard collision of atoms (sonnet III) or subject to an inconstancy refracted by the emotional turmoil of love. In some of the finest poems in the sequence, Sponde invokes the cosmological theories of pre-Socratic philosophers such as Empedocles and Heraclitus to demonstrate how love provides harmony and constancy in a discordant, turbulent world. In the opening sonnet the strife that governs the four elements is counterbalanced by the "justes contrepoids" (just counterweight) of love, while in sonnet III, Sponde distinguishes the constancy of his love from the sensual, disorderly love that resembles "Le monde d'Epicure en atomes réduit" (Epicurus's World Reduced to Atoms).

A more unconventional conceit governs sonnet XIII, which invokes Archimedes' claim that he could move the entire universe if he could find a stable point from which to operate his lever: the "solidité' (solidity) of the poet's heart provides such a location, for it remains steadfast even when moved, and "prend son assurance en l'inconstance même" (draws its stability even from inconstancy). Here, as in sonnets XVIII and XXVI, love promises to reconcile the "deux contraires" (two contraries) of constancy and flux at combat within the lover's soul. In sonnet XVIII the lover's mind remains fixed even as it "passe / De travail en travail par tant de mouvements" (passes from concern to concern with so many movements), while sonnet XXVI contrasts the poet-lover to the Halcyon, a bird who waits for a calm sea to build his nest. Halcyon-like, the lover patiently awaits this "paix" (peace) amidst the turbulent waves of love, but unlike the bird, whose calm sea comes but once a year, "celui de mon âme y sera pour jamais" (that [peace] of my soul will be there forever).

Like sonnet XXVI, sonnet X uses the conceit of water to represent the mutability that surrounds yet does not affect the constant lover, depicting the poet as a reef that remains steadfast in the ocean's waves. Such constancy in adversity is celebrated throughout Sponde's work as a Stoic, Christian, and Petrarchan virtue; yet, sonnet XIX turns this commonplace inside out. In the opening line the poet contemplates "le dormant de ce fleuve" (this stagnant river), its languor a reminder that the course of a river, whose "peine" (toil) ends in "repos" (repose), little resembles the course of love, which involves all "peine" and "non point du repos" (nothing of repose).

Invoking metaphors common to Petrarch and his sixteenth-century French imitators, the "Sonnets d'Amour" often represent their narrator's internal strife in terms of what sonnet X terms a "guerre d'amour" (war of love). Six sonnets in the sequence draw their conceits from ancient military history. Sonnet XII, for example, invokes the military tactics of Fabius Maximus, better known as "Cunctator" (delayer) for his evasion of Hannibal's armies, as a model for the prudent lover who resists surrender to the violence of love. In sonnet XVI the valor and perseverance of Numantia inspire the poet to pursue a similar ethics of courage, rather than cunning, to achieve victory in love. Forever vigilant against the assaults of passion, Sponde's constant lovers inhabit an adversarial universe: sonnet XIV describes the "bouclier d'Ajax" (shield of Ajax) that arms the poet-lover against "une armée d'ennuis" (an army of troubles), while sonnet XVII depicts his soul as ravaged by a "guerre civile" (civil war) waged between reason and the senses, a conflict that must be solved in the Roman manner:

> Faisons comme dans Rome: à ce peuple mutin
> De mes sens inconstans, arrachons-les en fin!
> Et que nostre raison y plante son Empire.
>
> (Let's do as the Romans do: let us finally uproot
> this mob of my inconstant senses!
> And let our reason plant its empire there.)

Representing the lover's spiritual turmoil as a confrontation between mob and ruler, sonnet XVII reworks the paradox first voiced in sonnet V that love produces both war and peace, effecting both harm and cure. In sonnet V, Sponde likens the lover tormented by the "mille chagrins" (thousand cares) occasioned by the absence of his beloved to the mythological figure of Acteon torn apart by his dogs, an allusion that casts the poet as both predator and prey in his internal struggle between stability and change.

For Sponde, poetry offers only limited assistance in controlling the inconstancy of human passions and the natural world. Sonnet VI unravels a contrast between speech and writing in which the "témoins muets" (mute witnesses) of the written word are the appropriate medium through which to depict a terrestrial love subject to change and absence, while the immediacy of speech is preserved for the "plus fermes plaisirs" (firmer pleasures) of heavenly love. The impoverished power of poetry also serves as the principal motif of *L'Elegie,* which opens with the poet's lament that his verse is languishing ("Vous languissez, mes vers") and which, according to Boase, in his biography, reveals a poet fearful of the intensity of his own poetic inspiration. Critics almost unanimously assume that the three *chansons* printed alongside the "Sonnets d'Amour" in Du Petit Val's 1597 anthology—"Comment pensez-vous que je vive" (How Do You Think I Live), "O doux object de mes desirs" (O Sweet Object of My Desire), and "Un bien qu'on desire tant" (A Good that One Desires So Much)—are among Sponde's earliest works by virtue of their relative lack of originality and technical skill.

The critical consensus is that Sponde wrote his *Méditations sur les pseaumes* (Meditations on the Psalms) during 1586–1587, years in which France suffered from plague, famine, and escalating religious turmoil. Presented to Henri de Navarre in 1588 and printed that same year in La Rochelle as *Méditations sur les pseaumes XIIII. ou LIII., XLVIII., L. et LXII,* this sole edition of Sponde's four prose meditations was only rediscovered in 1950. While these poems were already known to twentieth-century scholars, having been printed in the 1599 *Recueil* and subsequent anthologies, Boase's discovery of the 1588 edition has prompted scholars to explore the affinities between Sponde's sonnets and stanzas on death and his prose works. Their recovery has shed new light on the spiritual outlook and the style of Sponde's poetry, particularly since the 1588 edition of the meditations also comprises fifteen of Sponde's religious poems under the subtitle *Essay de quelques poëmes chrestiens* (Essay of Several Christian Poems), poems now commonly referred to as the *Stances et sonnets de la Mort* (Stanzas and Sonnets of Death).

Two works, Terence Cave's *Devotional Poetry in France c. 1570–1613* (1969) and Michel Jeanneret's *Poésie et Tradition Biblique au XVIᵉ Siècle. Recherches stylistiques sur les paraphrases des psaumes de Marot à Malherbe* (1969, Poetry and Biblical Tradition in the Sixteenth Century: Stylistic Research on the Paraphrases of the Psalms from Marot to Malherbe) are particularly helpful for understanding Sponde's meditations in their intellectual and religious contexts, while Sabine Lardon's *L'écriture de la méditation chez Jean de Sponde* (1998, The Writing of Meditation in Jean de Sponde) and the introduction to her 1996 edition of the meditations offer thorough discussions of the textual history and argumentative style of Sponde's text. Like many critics, Jeanneret attributes the tensions and anxieties of Sponde's meditations to the discord and doubt aroused by the Counter-Reformation and the French

Religious Wars, events that disturbed social and political harmony and disrupted the calm classicism of the Pléiade. Francis Higman in his essay "The *Méditations* of Jean de Sponde: A Book for the Times" argues that the meditations are best understood in their specific political context as texts dedicated to Henri de Navarre and offered to him as advice and consolation to a ruler during a difficult time.

The psalm-meditation was a popular genre among late-sixteenth-century Huguenot writers, and like many meditations of the period, Sponde's are penitential. In spite of the Calvinist de-emphasis of discussions of the self (Catherine Randall writes on the effects of Calvin's proscription against introspection on Protestant meditational literature in her essay "A Protestant Poetics of Process: Reformation Rhetorics of the Self in Sponde, de Bèze, and d'Aubigné"), Sponde's meditations offer frequent admissions of personal sins and encourage similar self-examination on the part of the reader. Bèze, whom Sponde met and befriended in Geneva, wrote eight meditations on the seven penitential psalms during the 1550s or early 1560s, revising them for d'Albret a decade later and finally publishing them as *Chrestiennes Méditations* (1582, Christian Meditations). Bèze's psalm meditations, as well as those of Philippe Duplessis-Mornay in *Discours et méditations chrestiennes* (1586, Christian Discourses and Meditations), almost certainly influenced the style of Sponde's meditations, written in a dense and difficult prose marked by sudden shifts in emotional register and punctuated by frequent antitheses, question marks, exclamations, ellipses, and other syntactical ruptures and dislocations that accentuate the tense and disharmonious relationship between God and the sinner and between the celestial and terrestrial worlds.

Yet, unlike most contemporary psalm-meditations, which offer close paraphrases of their scriptural texts, Sponde's meditations are loosely organized, even digressive; Cave compares them to sermons in that they offer a tissue of wide-ranging biblical allusions held together by a forceful, personal, first-person voice. Several critics who have studied Sponde's *Méditations,* including Lardon, Jeanneret, and Josiane Rieu in *Jean de Sponde, ou, La cohérence intérieure* (1988, Jean de Sponde, or Interior Coherence), regard the abrupt changes in tone, the habitual use of paradox, and the various discursive shifts that Rieu terms a "rhétorique du renversement" (rhetoric of reversal) as expressions of Sponde's fundamental theological concerns: his desire to demonstrate the profound disparity between the wretchedness of the sinner and the glory of God, as well as his desire to depict the possibility for that sinner to experience sudden attacks of conscience brought about by the intervention of divine grace.

For sixteenth-century Protestants, meditations offered to replace the Catholic practice of auricular confession; as spiritual exercises, they demand the concentration of all one's intellectual faculties on God and away from the vanities of earthly life. Accordingly, one of the dominant motifs of Sponde's *Méditations* is the inconstancy and transitoriness of man and the mortal world, a theme expressed by means of an oft-changing stream of metaphors comparing human nature to Proteus, a coursing stream, crumbling ruins, and a boat rocked by angry waves. By contrast, stability and harmony are to be found only in God. Sponde's first meditation, on Psalm 14, thus opens with an opposition between the pride of man and his weakness and misery: "Rien de si miserable que l'homme, mais rien de si superbe" (There is nothing so miserable as man, but nothing so proud), Sponde writes, going on to describe man's body and soul as so delicate that "la moindre durté, le moindre desordre peuvent nuire" (the least difficulty, the least disorder can destroy him). In the second meditation, on Psalm 48, Sponde shifts his focus to man's intellectual limitations, arguing that the human mind is incapable of understanding either the magnitude of the cosmos or the "grandeur incompréhensible" (incomprehensible grandeur) of divine grace.

Critics of the *Méditations* detect a spiritual progression toward greater faith and submission to God in the last two meditations, a narrative structure that prompts Pascale Blum-Cluny to argue that Sponde's text is modeled rhetorically and thematically on the Book of Job in his essay "Les *Méditations sur les Pseaumes* de Sponde: De David à Job, La Transgression d'un modèle" (Sponde's Meditations on the Psalms: From David to Job, the Transgression of a Model). Turning away from the persistent, anguished interrogation of divine mysteries that characterizes the first two meditations, the third attacks hypocrisy and idolatry with righteous indignation, while the narrator of the fourth and final meditation oscillates between despair over "ces combats contre ma chair" (these struggles against my flesh) and a calm confidence in God's mercy best exemplified by Sponde's image of the "echelle de ma foi qui touche au Ciel" (ladder of my faith that reaches to Heaven). Such a metaphor repairs the loss of correspondence between Earth and heaven lamented by the earlier meditations, and several critics cite this passage as evidence that Sponde ultimately rejects the radical and essential disparity between fallen humanity and God that characterizes the Protestantism of Calvin and Bèze.

Yet, as both Rieu and Lardon acknowledge, Sponde does not explicitly deviate from Calvinist theology in the *Méditations* so much as leave unresolved certain key theological debates, such as whether and how the freedom of the will is compatible with divine grace,

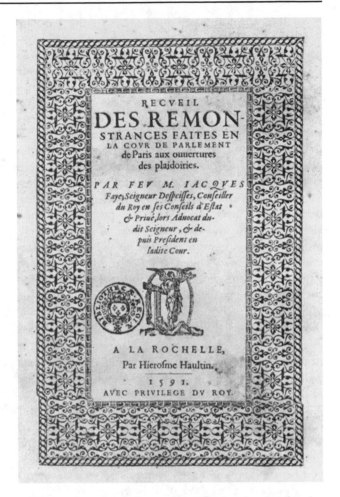

Title page for a work by Jacques Faye d'Espeisses for which Sponde wrote a dedicatory epistle (from Poésies, *edited by François Ruchon and Alan Martin Boase, 1949; Thomas Cooper Library, University of South Carolina)*

whether that grace is irresistible as well as indispensable to salvation, and whether God predestined man's fall or simply had foreknowledge of it. Sponde's use of paradox provides one means of resistance to the resolution of such theological mysteries, while another means is supplied by his demand that God silence his vain theological speculations. After considering whether God's grace is granted equally to all, Sponde dismisses the question by imploring God, "ne me respon point mais chastie-moy de silence" (do not respond to me but chastise me with silence). While the critical consensus is that the meditations voice many key arguments and sentiments of Calvinist theology, many of these critics also acknowledge that the meditations are inclusively, and not exclusively, Calvinist, detecting the influence of authors as varied and heterodox as Aristotle, the late-fifteenth-century monk and heretic Girolamo Savonarola, and the Italian mystic and occult philosopher Giordano Bruno, who resided in Geneva between 1581 and 1583.

The poems printed in the 1588 edition of the *Méditations* as the *Essay de quelques poèmes chrestiens* comprise three lyric poems, or *stances,* titled "Stances de la Cène" (Stanzas on the Communion), "Autre Poeme Sur le Mesme Subject" (Another Poem on the Same Subject), and "Stances de la Mort" (Stanzas on Death), followed by twelve sonnets collectively titled the "Sonnets sur le Mesme Subject" (Sonnets on the Same Subject) in the 1588 edition but now commonly referred to as the *Sonnets de la Mort.* It is uncertain whether Sponde composed these poems at the same time as his meditations. While most critics find a great deal of thematic unity between the meditations and the poems published alongside them, the *Stances et sonnets de la Mort* were probably composed some years before their publication, since Sponde apologizes in his 1588 dedication to Henri de Navarre for sending him the poems again, "estimant que vous ne leur fairiez point plus mauvais visage qu'autres-fois" (hoping that you will not regard them in a worse light than before).

A majority of critics also find strong thematic correspondences between the stanzas and the sonnets as well as within the group of twelve sonnets. Both groups of poems are dominated by an alienation from worldly pleasures, a *taedium vitae* or ennui both caused and cured by the promise of death and eternal life. Yet, while the *Stances et sonnets de la Mort* depict death as the final port that brings hope and tranquility to the Christian believer, an attitude that reveals Sponde's debts to Seneca's *De Brevitate Vitae* (On the Brevity of Life), the poems also depict the challenges of adhering to the proper capitulation to mortality advocated by Seneca, the Stoic Roman philosopher whose prescription that one must learn how to live by learning how to die courses through contemporary works such as Duplessis-Mornay's *Excellent discours de la vie et de la mort* (1576, Excellent Discourse on Life and Death) and Michel de Montaigne's early neo-Stoic *Essais* (1580, Essays). Wrestling with the Senecan paradox that one must withdraw from life in order to live well, Sponde's narrators move between two competing attitudes toward death, resignation and resistance, a struggle that reveals the difficulty of cultivating the twin virtues of Senecan constancy and Christian patience. According to Susan Hills in her essay "'Stances de la Mort' and 'Autres sonnets sur le mesme sujet': Losing to the Angel," the poems enact the various errors and misconceptions about death to which humans are subject, from suicidal despair, to forgetfulness of death, to a cynical indifference to life provoked by the recognition of death's inevitability.

The spiritual conflicts of the *Stances et sonnets de la Mort* are registered through the dominant images and rhetorical strategies of the poems, from allusions to military combat and the cosmic strife of the elements to a dialectical tension between the terrestrial and celestial worlds expressed by means of paradox, interrogative formulas, and abrupt shifts in points of view. The first word of the opening sonnet—"Mortels" (mortals)—urges readers to contemplate their mortality, yet, by the end of the poem Sponde complicates this message of memento mori by voicing a paradox: "Un oubly d'une mort / Vous montre un souvenir d'une eternelle vie" (A forgetfulness of death / Shows you remembrance of eternal life). The second sonnet similarly moves from an initial resignation toward death toward a subtle defiance of it, a shift underscored by the repetition of the opening half line, "Mais si faut-il mourir," in the final line of the poem, which concludes that the recognition of mortality need not entail a withdrawal from mortal life: "Vivez, hommes, vivez, mais si faut-il mourir" (Live, men, live, but yes, one must die).

The next three sonnets assume a moralistic, almost mocking tone, admonishing the presumption and vanity of human aspirations and designs, showing in sonnet III that the grand human edifices and empires fall to dust, in sonnet IV the emptiness of rivalries over "Throsnes débattus" (contested thrones) and similarly false honors, and in sonnet V the futility of pursuing "désirs orgueilleux" (proud desires) that leave one unprepared for death. Echoing the first sentence of Seneca's *De Brevitate Vitae,* the opening lines of sonnet VI observe how men deceive themselves by complaining that life is too short but also by longing too eagerly for death. Both this sonnet and the next offer the consolation that mortal life is an "ombre" (shadow), a realm fraught with illusions and conflicts that are resolved only through death.

Sonnet VIII compares the narrator's impatient longing for the celestial world and his inability to reach that world to an arrow shot into the air that climbs but then falls back to Earth. "C'est le train de nos jours" (This is the story of our life), laments the poet, concluding the sonnet by comparing the flux of mortal life to an arrow whose feathers are blown every which way by the wind of worldly vicissitudes: "Que ta vie et de Plume, et le monde de Vent" (Your life is a feather, and the world is wind). Typical of Sponde's use of paradox and interrogation—six of its fourteen lines end in question marks—sonnet IX again chastises worldly vanity, inveighing against "les fumées de la Court" (the smoke of the court) in an admonitory voice that Cave finds indebted both to the satirical voice of Du Bellay's *Les Regrets* (1558, The Regrets) and to the vehement, anti-Ciceronian *style coupé* (cropped style) favored by Sponde's meditations and by contemporary prose stylists such as Montaigne and Justus Lipsius.

Sonnet X focuses upon the inconstancy of mortal life and the accompanying unpredictability of death.

Comparing his feeble body to a flowing river advancing inexorably toward its end, the poet laments the "sablon de mes jours" (the sand of my days), an image that evokes both the sand of an hourglass and the sandy banks of a river, which shift and erode with the winds of life. While sonnet X ends with the discomfiting observation that God conceals from us the hour of our death, sonnet XI opens by asking the question begged by the end of the previous sonnet, "Et quel bien de la Mort?" (And what good comes of Death?). The answer provided is that by untying "ces nœuds si beaux" (these beautiful knots) between body and soul, death resolves the conflicts and tensions of mortal life, leading to the paradox of the final tercet of the poem: "Pour vivre au Ciel il faut mourir plutôt ici" (To live in heaven one must first die on Earth).

Opening with an image of being besieged by "le Monde" (the world), "la Chair" (the flesh), and "l'Ange" (the Devil), the poet in the twelfth and final sonnets seeks refuge from the triple agents of temptation and despair in the stable trinity of God's "nef" (ship), "appuy" (prop), and "oreille" (ear), divine supports that, paradoxically, offer the sinner hope only through despair and constancy only through spiritual tumult. Critics disagree as to whether the declaration of faith in the final sonnet reconciles the antitheses and tensions of mortal life, or whether the sequence ends where it began, with a *psychomachia* (spiritual battle) that remains unresolved until death. In his essay "Jean de Sponde: Et quel bien de la Mort?" (Jean de Sponde: And What Good Is Death?), Jean-Claude Carron detects a chiastic structure in the *Sonnets de la Mort,* in which the first six sonnets are reflected in mirror image in the final six, while Mario Richter in "Sponde: Sonnets de la mort, X" perceives a progression toward greater introspection and faith from the opening sonnets, which address and exhort the reader, to the final sonnets, dominated by a first-person narrative. Critics also disagree as to whether and to what extent the *Sonnets de la Mort* posit a Calvinist theology: while various critics detect Calvin's Christology (in sonnet X) and his doctrine of irresistible grace (in sonnet XII), Cave argues that the sonnets bear no clear mark of either Calvinism or Catholicism.

By contrast, "Stances de la Cène" and the companion poem "Autre poeme sur le mesme Subject" (Another Poem on the Same Subject) are almost universally interpreted as upholding a rigorously Calvinistic belief in Consubstantiation, representing Communion as a ritual in which the believer's feeble and sinful body "n'en prend visiblement que le visible signe" (takes visibly only the visible sign) of Christ's body, while his soul receives Christ invisibly. The first of the two *stances* on the Eucharist begins with a penitential apostrophe to

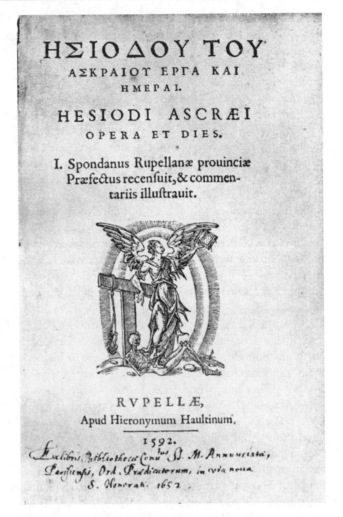

Title page for Sponde's Latin translation of Hesiod's Work and Days *(from* Poésies, *edited by François Ruchon and Alan Martin Boase, 1949; Thomas Cooper Library, University of South Carolina)*

the poet's soul, preparing him for the act of Communion in which he "embrasse estroictement ce Corps" (tightly embraces this body) of Christ. Yet, the conceit of Communion as an amorous union between sinner and Christ abruptly turns as Sponde asks God why he must eat the flesh he adores: "Seray-je son meurtrier, seray-je son tombeau?" (Will I be His murderer? Will I be His tomb?). Sponde presents Communion as an act of both love and hate that pits flesh against spirit and reminds the believer of his sinfulness even as it promises redemption from that sin. Communion is described as an incomprehensible mystery, a paradox: through Communion, Christ dwells in the sinner whose very sins are responsible for his sacrifice.

One persistent critical debate about Sponde's poetry is whether and to what extent the poems ultimately reconcile the spiritual tensions and paradoxes they voice, a debate manifest in the disagreement regarding whether to classify Sponde as Mannerist or Baroque, terms whose overlapping and flexible definitions encompass Sponde's rhetorical excess, wit, and preoccupation with inconstancy. Two influential studies by Jean Rousset, *La Littérature de l'Age Baroque en France* (1953, Literature of the Baroque Age in France) and *L'Intérieur et L'Extérieur* (1968, The Interior and the Exterior), define Sponde as "pré-Baroque," arguing that, typical of the generation of poets active between 1580 and 1625, he is too desirous of immutability to qualify as Baroque. In the latter work, Rousset distinguishes Sponde's pessimistic, macabre attitude toward the impermanence of earthly things, or what Rousset terms his "inconstance noire" (dark inconstancy), from the "inconstance blanche" (light inconstancy) of seventeenth-century Baroque writers who delight in the dynamic, Protean aspects of humanity and the natural world. Rousset's argument is echoed by André Baïche, who in *La naissance du baroque français. Poésie et image de la Pléiade à Jean de la Ceppède* (1976, The Birth of the French Baroque: Poetry and Image from the Pleiad to Jean de la Ceppède) attributes Sponde's emergent Baroque style to his neo-Stoic preoccupation with constancy, and by Gisèle Mathieu-Castellani, who in *Les Thèmes Amoureux dans la poésie française (1570–1600)* (1975, Themes of Love in French Poetry) regards Sponde as a poet who seeks refuge in unity and stability yet also points to the poems' multiple points of view, their thematic emphasis on metamorphosis, and their rhetorical dislocations as evidence of Sponde's Baroque outlook. In *Une Poétique de crise: Poètes baroques et mystiques (1570–1660)* (1996, A Poetics of Crisis: Baroque and Mystical Poets) Michèle Clément looks to Sponde's reliance upon scholastic philosophical terms such as *essence, abstrait, suject,* and *nature des choses* (essence, abstract, subject, nature of things) as further evidence of his status as a Baroque poet, a category she regards as intimately related to the mystical spirituality of contemporary poets such as Jean de La Ceppède and Jean de la Croix. On the other side, Marcel Raymond and Marc Bensimon regard Sponde as Mannerist, while Rieu, following Eugénie Droz, identifies his principal influence, like that of Guillaume du Bartas, as the "style Navarrais" (Navarre style) that predominated at the courts of D'Albret and Henri IV.

On 12 September 1589 while in La Rochelle, a few weeks after the assassination of King Henri III, Sponde anonymously published *Advertissement Au Roy, ou sont deduictes les Raisons d'Estat, pour lesquelles il ne luy est pas bien seant de changer de Religion* (Advertisement to the King, in Which Are Presented the Political Reasons Why It Is Not Fitting That He Change Religion). Highly critical of the king's betrayal of the Protestant cause, the treatise warns that Henri IV's imminent conversion, which was not made public until July 1593,

will exacerbate political strife by fostering "division par la désunion de vous-même" (division by your own disunion). Sponde indicts Henri IV both as an imprudent ruler whose conversion will fail to ensure political tranquility and as a man subject to a wavering conscience. These criticisms are driven home by Sponde's epigraph: "Toutes les autres vertues combattent, mais la seule constance triomphe" (All the other virtues combat each other, but constancy alone triumphs).

By November 1589 Sponde had arrived in Paris, where he became ill and was then imprisoned along with Jacques Canaye, a counselor of Henri IV and fellow Huguenot. Sponde probably wrote "Sur sa Fièvre" (On His Fever) at this time, though it is uncertain whether the poem alludes to the poet's physical illness, to the feverish political unrest of the moment, or both. After his release from prison and a brief stay in Tours, Sponde returned to La Rochelle sometime before December 1590, when he began serving as lieutenant general of that city. Shortly after the new year, Jacques Faye, Sieur d'Espeisses's *Recueil des Remonstrances* (Collection of Remonstrances) was printed by the Haultin press at La Rochelle with a dedicatory epistle by Sponde addressed to the author, who had died the previous September. Several occasional poems by Sponde also probably date from the period between 1589 and 1592, most notably "Sur la Canelle" (On Cinnamon), printed as an introductory epistle to a 1591 pamphlet commemorating the death of Jean de la Goutte, who died at the Battle of Ivry in March 1590. Written before Goutte's death, the poem is an extended series of puns on variations of the subject's name—*Goutte* (Gout), *goût* (taste, odor, drop), and *égout* (sewer)—as well as on the term *can[n]elle,* which means spigot or tap as well as cinnamon.

Also dating from this period are seven *stances,* three of which Sponde almost certainly wrote to celebrate the love affair between Henri IV and his mistress Gabrielle d'Estrées, who met in November 1591. Probably composed between May 1592, when Sponde left La Rochelle for the royal court, and January 1593, when the poet was imprisoned at Orléans, these three poems were first printed in Du Petit Val's *Recueil de diverses poésies* and reprinted in later editions of that volume as well as in Antoine du Breuil's anthology *Academie des modernes poètes françois* (1599, Academy of Modern French Poets). Another *stance* from this period also first printed in 1597, "Ma belle languissoit dans sa funeste couche" (My dear languishes on her fatal couch), depicts a dying female lover who is cured by love. A different version of the poem, missing its two final stanzas, was printed in Mathieu Guillemot's *Les muses françoises ralliées de diverses pars* (1599, The French Muses Rallied Together from Diverse Parts) under the title "Miracle d'Amour en la Guérison d'une Dame Mourante" (Miracle of Love in the Cure of a Dying Woman). Sponde also wrote two poems, "Stances B.D.F." and "Sur la Mort du B.D.F." (On the Death of B.D.F.), both addressed to his friend and fellow poet Belesbat du Fay, who died in 1592 and whose works were anthologized with Sponde's in the *Recueil de diverses poésies*.

Sponde also renewed his scholarly work in the early 1590s. His Greek-Latin edition of Hesiod's *Opera et Dies* (Works and Days) was printed in 1592; in his dedication to Achille de Harlay, dated 1 May 1592, Sponde explains that he sought refuge from the turbulent atmosphere of La Rochelle in Hesiod's poetry, gazing down at the turmoil from "Halcyonios illos in rustica malacia nidos spectaveris" (the rustic calm of the Halcyon's nest) afforded by *Opera et Dies*. With its vision of a Golden Age unsullied by war or corruption, Hesiod's georgic poem offers Sponde an antidote to France's political ills by advocating quiet living and earnest agricultural labor: "Iam furens in sese Gallia, nisi se rusticationi rursum mancipaverit, quando tandem conquiescet" (Already in fury against herself, when will France finally find repose if not by liberating herself through agriculture).

Sponde's dream of tranquil rusticity was shattered in 1593, when he was imprisoned for the fourth and final time in Orléans. The incarceration may have been the catalyst for Sponde's conversion to Catholicism, at least according to Jean de Boysseul, the author of *La Confutation des Déclarations de Jean et de Henri de Sponde* (1598, The Confutation of the Declarations of Jean and Henri de Sponde) which attacks Sponde and his half brother for converting out of fear rather than the stirrings of conscience. Sponde's first written justification of his apostasy, the *Response d'un Catholique* (Response of a Catholic), was published in autumn 1593. This work was followed later the same year by Sponde's *Déclaration des principaux motifs qui induisent le sieur de Sponde, conseiller . . . l'Eglise catholique apostolique et romaine* (1593, Declaration of the Principal Motives Which Induced Mr. Sponde, The King's Counselor and Master of Requests, to Join the Apostolic Roman Catholic Church) and was reprinted in 1594 with a dedication to King Henri IV and a preface in which Sponde defends his conversion as an act of conscience. Sponde explains that "j'ay longtemps debattu en mon esprit" (I debated a long time in my soul) between the two faiths, and he refutes the accusation that he was driven to convert because of the king's own conversion, which was announced publicly on 25 July 1593.

It is possible that Jacques Davy du Perron, the cardinal whose persuasive force enticed King Henri IV toward Catholicism, also had a hand in Sponde's conversion. The two men had met in 1592; after their meeting, Sponde wrote that he intended to prepare him-

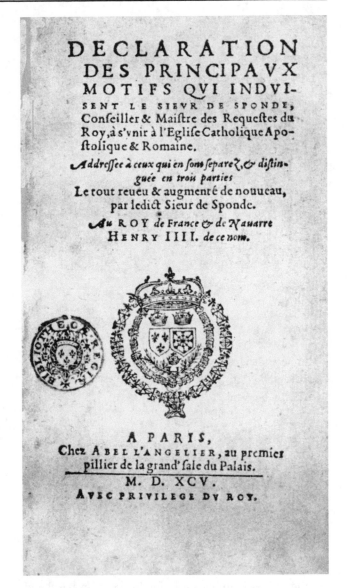

Title page for the first Paris edition of the work in which Sponde defended his conversion to Catholicism (from Poésies, *edited by François Ruchon and Alan Martin Boase, 1949; Thomas Cooper Library, University of South Carolina)*

self better for his next encounter with the man whom contemporary reformers dubbed "Monsieur le Convertisseur" (Mister Converter). Yet, while Sponde's poems and meditations dating from the 1580s are commonly acknowledged to indicate a thoroughly Protestant sensibility, it is possible that his disenchantment with Protestantism began even before these works were composed. In a bitter letter to Sponde dated 25 July 1584, Bèze reproached the young poet for betraying him and warns him that "vous ne tromperez pas le Seigneur" (you cannot betray God). Although it is uncertain that Bèze's allusion is to Sponde's alienation from the Protestant faith, it is certainly possible that Sponde's ques-

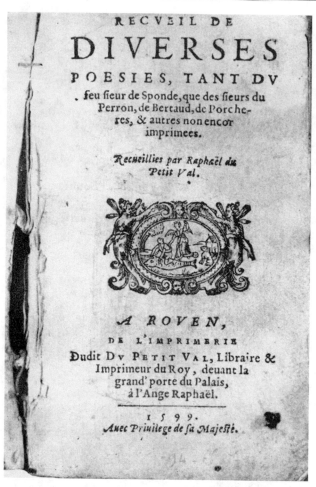

RECVEIL DE
DIVERSES
POESIES, TANT DV
feu fieur de Sponde, que des fieurs du
Perron, de Bertaud, de Porche-
res, & autres non encor
imprimees.

*Recueillies par Raphaël du
Petit Val.*

A ROVEN,
DE L'IMPRIMERIE
Dudit Dv Petit Val, Libraire &
Imprimeur du Roy, deuant la
grand' porte du Palais,
à l'Ange Raphaël.

1599.
Auec Priuilege de fa Majefté.

Title page for a collection that includes Sponde's "Sonnets d'Amour"
(from Poésies, *edited by François Ruchon and Alan Martin Boase,*
1949; Thomas Cooper Library, University
of South Carolina)

tioning of that faith began during his years in Basel and Geneva.

From the opening of the *Déclaration des principaux motifs,* Sponde attacks the central tenets of Protestant theology, suggesting that his conversion was indeed motivated by conviction, not fear. He argues that, despite the reformers' cry of *sola scriptura* (Scripture alone), many points of Protestant doctrine, such as justification by faith alone and the doctrine of election, cannot be located anywhere in Scripture. Sponde appeals throughout to the authority of the Roman Catholic Church and its councils, refuting the common Protestant argument that the Holy Spirit fled the church of Rome during the early Christian period and now resides in Geneva. In the third section of the *Déclaration des principaux motifs,* Sponde takes on Calvin directly, attacking the Genevan reformer's repudiation of the real presence of Christ in the Eucharist and criticizing Calvin's excessive emphasis upon the sinfulness of

humankind and the wrathfulness of God. Sponde argues that the Lord "aime l'unité, et s'esloigne de la division" (loves unity, and distances himself from faction) and fallen humanity is still "naturellement capable de raison" (naturally capable of reason).

At some point before Sponde wrote his preface to the revised 1594 edition of the *Déclaration des principaux motifs,* he returned to his native Béarn because of the death of his father, who was murdered by a band of Catholic Ligueurs, or militant Catholics, in a riot that probably took place on 8 August 1594. For the brief remainder of his life, Sponde appears to have stayed close to home, revising his editions of Homer and Hesiod and preparing an edition of Seneca for which he obtained a privilege but probably never completed; no extant manuscript of the work remains. After a particularly harsh winter in the Pyrenees, Sponde succumbed to pleurisy and died on 18 March 1595.

Sponde left his final work—a response to Bèze's *De Veris et Visibilibus Ecclesiae Catholicae notis tractatio* (1579), translated into French as *Traité des vrayes, essencielles et visibles marques de la vraye Eglise Catholique* (1592, Treatise on the True, Essential, and Visible Signs of the True Catholic Church)—unfinished at his death. *Response au Traicté des Marques de l'Eglise* (Response to the Treatise on the Signs of the Church) was printed posthumously in *Response du feu sieur de Sponde Conseiller et Maistre des Requestes du Roy Au Traicté des marques de l'Eglise faict par Th[eodore] de Bèze* (1595, Response of the Deceased Master de Sponde, Counselor and Master of Requests to the King, to Theodore de Bèze's Treatise on the Signs of the Church), which included several tributes and funeral elegies to the recently deceased author. The editor of the treatise, Florimond de Raemond, dedicated the work to Cardinal du Perron, praising him in the dedicatory epistle as the agent of Sponde's conversion. In more than eight hundred pages of prose densely packed with metaphors and antitheses, Sponde refutes seventy-two separate points of doctrine promulgated by Bèze; he also offers sweeping indictments of Protestant theology, including the argument that Protestantism undermines political stability by transforming the kingdom of heaven from "une pure and simple monarchie" (a pure and simple monarchy) into "la plus embrouillée Démocratie que fust jamais" (the most chaotic Democracy that ever existed). Despite its forceful, often indignant tone, *Response au Traicté des Marques de l'Eglise* almost never exhibits the viciousness typical of much sixteenth-century polemic, instead reflecting a spirit of charity, tolerance, and skeptical tranquility perhaps influenced by the later writings of Erasmus or by the *Essays* of Montaigne.

The pamphlet war between the critics and defenders of Sponde's conversion began shortly before his death with the publication of Pierre de la Primaudaye's *Examen de la Responce de Sponde catholique apostolique romain* (1595, Examination of the Response of Sponde, Apostolic Roman Catholic) and continued until the end of the century with similar attacks written by Etienne Bonnet, Bernard Sonis, Boysseul, and Raymond Tholoze, to name but a few. Many of these "anti-Sponde" treatises feature outrageous, and presumably groundless, calumnies against the poet, including the oft-repeated account that Sponde poisoned his wife and impregnated a serving girl while residing in La Rochelle. Several defenses of Sponde also appear during the same period, including Henri de Sponde's *Défense de la déclaration du feu Sieur de Sponde contre les cavillations des ministres Bonnet et Sonis* (1597, Defense of the Declaration of Master Sponde against the Cavillations of the Ministers Bonnet and Sonis), written two years after Henri followed his brother's footsteps and converted to Catholicism. After these debates died down, Sponde slid into almost complete obscurity except for his edition of Homer, which profoundly influenced George Chapman's translation of Homer, the first complete English translation of the *Iliad* and *Odyssey,* which Chapman finished in 1616. Only with the scholarship of Droz, Boase, and Ruchon during the 1940s and 1950s did Sponde begin to attract renewed attention along with other minor French poets of the period such as La Ceppède, Jacques de Constans, and Jean-Baptiste Chassignet. Since the 1950 rediscovery of Jean de Sponde's meditations, which contribute to a modern understanding of Protestant devotional literature, he has also come to be appreciated as a masterful prose stylist, a quality that has earned him a place alongside major prose writers of the period such as Bèze, Duplessis-Mornay, and Montaigne.

Biographies:

François Ruchon and Alan Martin Boase, *La vie et l'œuvre de Jean de Sponde* (Geneva: Cailler, 1949);

Boase, *Vie de Jean de Sponde* (Geneva: Droz, 1977).

References:

André Baïche, *La naissance du baroque français. Poésie et image de la Pléaide à Jean de la Ceppède,* Publications de L'Université de Toulouse-Le Mirail, Series A, volume 31 (Toulouse: Publications de L'Université de Toulouse-Le Mirail, 1976), pp. 122–131, 245–255;

Marc Bensimon, "La porte étroite: essai sur le maniérisme (Le Greco, Saint Jean de la Croix, Sponde, Chassignet, d'Aubigné, Montaigne)," *Journal of Medieval and Renaissance Studies,* 10, no. 2 (1980): 255–280;

Théodore de Bèze, *Chrestiennes Méditations,* edited by Mario Richter (Geneva: Droz, 1964);

Pascale Blum-Cluny, "Les *Méditations sur les Pseaumes* de Sponde: De David à Job, La Transgression d'un modèle," *Nouvelle Revue du XVIᵉ Siècle,* 10 (1992): 69–80;

Alan Boase, "Des débuts d'un humaniste," in *Mélanges à la mémoire de Franco Simone: France et Italie dans la culture européene,* 4, no. 9 (1983): 221–226;

Jean-Claude Carron, "Jean de Sponde: Et quel bien de la Mort?" *French Studies,* 31 (April 1977): 129–138;

Terence Cave, "Poetry of Sin, Sickness and Death," *Devotional Poetry in France c. 1570–1613* (Cambridge & London: Cambridge University Press, 1969), pp. 171–183;

Michèle Clément, *Une Poétique de crise: Poètes baroques et mystiques (1570–1660),* Bibliothèque Littéraire de la Renaissance, series 3, volume 34 (Paris: H. Champion, 1996);

Christiane Deloince-Louette, *Sponde: commentateur d'Homère* (Paris: H. Champion, 2001);

Eugénie Droz, "Les années d'études de Jean et Henri de Sponde," *Bibliothèque d'humanisme et renaissance,* 9 (1947): 141–150;

Laura G. Durand, "Sponde and Donne: Lens and Prism," *Comparative Literature,* 21 (Autumn 1969): 319–336;

Robert Griffin, "Jean de Sponde's 'Sonnet de la Mort' XII: the World, the Flesh, and the Devil," *Romance Notes,* 9 (Autumn 1967): 102–106;

Griffin, "The Presence of Saint Paul in the Religious Works of Jean de Sponde," *Bibliothèque d'humanisme et renaissance,* 27 (1965): 644–652;

Francis Higman, "The *Méditations* of Jean de Sponde: A Book for the Times," *Bibliothèque d'humanisme et renaissance,* 28 (1966): 564–582;

Susan Hills, "'Stances de la Mort' and 'Autres sonnets sur le mesme sujet': Losing to the Angel," *French Forum,* 4 (January 1979): 69–85;

Michel Jeanneret, *Poésie et Tradition Biblique au XVIᵉ Siècle. Recherches stylistiques sur les paraphrases des psaumes de Marot à Malherbe* (Paris: José Corti, 1969), pp. 400–417, 440–452;

Jean Jehasse, "Sponde et Homère," in *La Renaissance de la Critique: l'essor de l'humanisme érudit de 1560 à 1614* (Saint-Etienne: Université de Saint-Etienne, 1976; revised and enlarged, Paris: H. Champion, 2002), 465–469;

Sabine Lardon, *L'écriture de la méditation chez Jean de Sponde* (Paris: H. Champion, 1998);

Gisèle Mathieu-Castellani, *Les Thèmes Amoureux dans la poésie française (1570–1600)* (Paris: Klincksieck, 1975), pp. 490–501;

Catherine Randall, "A Protestant Poetics of Process: Reformation Rhetorics of the Self in Sponde, de Bèze, and d'Aubigné," in *The Rhetorics of Life-Writing in Early Modern Europe: Forms of Biography from Cassandra Fedele to Louis XIV,* edited by Thomas F. Mayer and D. R. Woolf (Ann Arbor: University of Michigan Press, 1995), pp. 223–241;

Mario Richter, *Jean de Sponde: e la lingua poetica dei protestanti nel cinquecento* (Milan: Cisalpino-Goliardica, 1973);

Richter, "Sponde: Sonnets de la mort, X," *Bibliothèque d'Humanisme et Renaissance,* 38 (1976): 73–76;

Josiane Rieu, *Jean de Sponde, ou, La cohérence intérieure* (Paris: H. Champion, 1988);

Jean Rousset, "La châine des sonnets," *L'Intérieur et L'Extérieur. Essais sur la poésie et sur le théâtre au XVIIᵉ Siècle* (Paris: José Corti, 1968), pp. 22–26;

Rousset, *La Littérature de l'Age Baroque en France. Circé et le Paon* (Paris: José Corti, 1953);

Daniel Russell, *Emblematic Structures in French Culture* (Toronto: University of Toronto Press, 1995), pp. 225–236;

Franck L. Schoell, "L'Hellénisme Français en Angleterre à la fin de la Renaissance," *Etudes sur l'humanisme continental en Angleterre à la fin de la Renaissance* (Paris: Edouard Champion, 1926), pp. 151–177;

Schoell, "Un Humaniste français oublié, Jean de Sponde," *Revue du Seizième Siècle,* 12 (1925): 361–400;

Gilbert Shrenck, "La Structure 'Délicate' des *Sonnets d'amour* de Jean de Sponde," in *Poétique et Narration: Mélanges offerts à Guy Demerson,* edited by François Marotin and Jacques-Philippe Saint-Gerand, Bibliothèque Franco Simone, no. 22 (Paris: H. Champion, 1993), pp. 255–265.

Papers:

Letters written by and to Jean de Sponde are in the Bibliothèque nationale (Collection Dupuy), Paris; Archives de La Rochelle (Registres Bion and Bounyn); Bibliothèque publique and Bibliothèque Universitaire, Basel; Bibliothèque publique and Musée de la Réformation (Archives Tronchin), Geneva. Additional documents pertaining to Sponde's life are located in the Archives des Pyrenées Atlantiques and the Archives des Basses Pyrenées (Chambre des comptes de Navarre), Pau.

Odet de Turnèbe

(23 October 1552 – 20 July 1581)

Catherine E. Campbell
Cottey College

BOOK: *Les Contens* (Paris: Felix le Mangnier, 1584); republished as *Les Déguisez, Comédie françoise, avec l'esplication des proverbes & mots difficiles par Charles Maupas* (Blois: Gauché Collas, 1626); translated by Donald A. Beecher as *Satisfaction All Around* (Ottawa: Carleton University Press, 1979).

Edition: *Les Contens,* edited by Norman B. Spector (Paris: Librairie Marcel Didier, 1961).

OTHER: "La Puce d'Odet de Tunrèbe, Advocat en la cour de Parlement" and three other poems, *La Puce de Ma Dame des Roches* (Paris: Abel L'Angelier, 1582);

Epistolae Arnulphi episcopi Lexoviensis nunquam antehac in lucem editae, edited by Turnèbe (Paris: J. Richer, 1585).

Often considered the best playwright of the French Renaissance on the basis of a single surviving comedy, Odet de Turnèbe is one of the few playwrights known and studied by scholars of sixteenth-century French literature. Celebrated as the finest example of social comedy of the French Renaissance, Turnèbe's play, *Les Contens* (1584, The Happy Ones; translated as *Satisfaction All Around,* 1979), portrays bourgeois manners and preoccupations in contemporary Paris. With its complex and comic love intrigue, critics regard the play as the most socially realistic and best crafted of the popular comedic imitations of the period.

Odet de Turnèbe was born on 23 October 1552, son of Madeleine Clément and the humanist scholar Adrien de Turnèbe (or Turnebu), a reader in Greek at the Collège Royal. In 1552 his father became director of the royal printing press, specifically in charge of printing works in Greek. A few years later Adrien de Turnèbe left the press to devote himself to teaching and his scholarly pursuits. He translated dozens of Greek and Latin texts, wrote copious commentaries on authors, including Aristotle and Cicero, and edited the works of Plato, Sophocles, and an array of Greek poets. Such a prodigious output combined with the scholarly environment appar-

ently had an effect on the young Odet, who seems also to have had an aptitude for languages.

Odet was fourteen when his father died, and the following year the young man published two Latin pieces by his father that were based on Plutarch. At fifteen he was a student at the Collège of Lisieux in Paris. At twenty he became a student at the law school in Toulouse. He was accepted into the Parlement of Paris soon thereafter and participated in the "Grands Jours" (Great Days) of Poitiers. These were a kind of irregular assize court in which a commission of the Parlement of Paris, selected and sent at short notice by the king, had full power to hear and determine all cases, especially those in which seignorial rights had been abused. (This institution fell into disuse at the end of the seventeenth century, allegedly resulting in deleterious effects on the social and political welfare of the French provinces.)

Turnèbe became a vital member of the salon in Poitiers led by the Dames des Roches, Madeleine and her daughter, Catherine. He dedicated to Catherine des Roches twelve sonnets on the destruction of the fortress at Lusignan after the siege in 1574 under the title "Sonets sur les ruines de Luzignan" (Sonnets on the Ruins of Lusignan), which were later included in the Dames des Roches's collection *La Puce* (1582, The Flea). These twelve poems alternate in form between alexandrines and decasyllables, like those of his model Joachim du Bellay in his *Les Premier Livre des antiquitez de Rome* (1558, The First Book of The Antiquities of Rome). A connection is made between the *Roc* (fortress or rock) of Lusignan and the name of the dames des *Roches,* which also means "rocks."

Turnèbe also contributed four other poems to *La Puce* that were related to its main subject: an ode of two hundred octosyllabic lines in French titled "La Puce d'Odet de Turnèbe, Advocat en la cour de Parlement" (The Flea of Odet de Turnèbe, Advocate in the Court of Parliament) and three sonnets, one each in Italian, Spanish, and Portuguese. Like many pieces in the collection that included work by Etienne Pasquier and several other distinguished lawyers, Turnèbe's poems show much punning on the flea reportedly seen by Pasquier on Cathe-

Title page for Odet de Turnèbe's comedy of mistaken identities that was published three years after his death (from Les Contens, *edited by Norman B. Spector, 1961; Porter Henderson Library, Angelo State University)*

of the Cour des monnaies (Court of the Currencies). Originally a subdivision of the chamber that audited the royal finances, the Cour des monnaies was elevated in 1551 to the role of sovereign court. Established to supervise the twenty or so mints of France, to repress the mint workers' temptations to fraud and larceny, and to ensure that the coins' official size, shape, and decoration corresponded to the officially mandated content of precious metal, the Cour des monnaies eventually became the government's principal adviser on highly technical issues of monetary policy. Also, in addition to preventing counterfeiting, this body took over supervision of all aspects of the precious metal industry, including goldsmithing, gilding, and money changing. Indeed, a major part of the business consisted of regulating the precious-metal content, not of coins, but of plate, jewelry, gilding, and gold thread. The body worked hard to confine the precious-metal trades to a limited number of public, established shops in the larger cities of France. Shortly after his appointment to the Cour des monnaies, Turnèbe died on 20 July 1581 of a high fever lasting five days, at the age of twenty-eight.

His major work, *Les Contens,* was published posthumously, three years after Turnèbe's death. While there is no direct indication of when this play was written, internal evidence suggests that the date of composition probably falls between 1577 and 1581. There are two references to military victories that happened in 1576 at Issoire and Maestrich. Other references to historical events lead scholar Aulotte to deduce that it was written in late 1580 or early 1581, which gave Turnèbe no time to publish it before his death, if he had so desired.

This acclaimed comedy of the French Renaissance uses the traditional structure of five acts of more or less equal length (the third act being somewhat shorter than the others) with both a prologue and epilogue. Written in prose, it tells the story of Geneviefve, a young girl being courted by three men—Eustache, preferred by her mother Louise because of his good family; Basile, her neighbor, also from a good family; and Rodomont, a braggart soldier. Basile has tried every way possible to ingratiate himself with Louise and finally asks advice from his servant Antoine, who suggests that he disguise himself as Eustache and spend the night with the girl. Geneviefve's mother will then have to accept their union as a fact. To help him in his plan, Basile consults Françoise, an old woman, a hypocrite, known for being an arranger of love affairs. She agrees to help Basile by getting Louise out of the house, by making Geneviefve amenable to the idea, and by redirecting the attentions of Eustache.

Françoise begins by working on Eustache. While praising the beauty and virtue of the young girl, the old woman seemingly lets slip that Geneviefve is infected by a cancer that is eating at her breast. Eustache is so horrified

rine's breast. Based on Turnèbe's contribution to this volume, critics, notably Robert Aulotte, have decided that Turnèbe was in love with Catherine, but Anne R. Larsen disagrees in her essay "Chastity and the Mother-Daughter Bond: Odet de Turnèbe's Response to Catherine des Roches." Whereas Catherine des Roches provides a powerful endorsement of chastity, Larsen argues that Turnèbe's play shows a "diabolical engagement with the contemporary polemics on sex, marriage, and women's nature." She contends that Turnèbe may have taken this position only to be in opposition to Des Roches.

After returning to Paris, Turnèbe had published *Poemata,* another of his father's texts, and prepared an edition of the Latin letters of Arnoul, bishop of Lisieux from 1141 to 1181, which was published posthumously as *Epistolae Arnulphi episcopi Lexoviensis nunquam antehac in lucem editae* in 1585. In 1581 he obtained the post of first president

that he gives up Geneviefve and vows to oppose his father's further actions in favor of their marriage. Until then he passes the time with a prostitute, Alix, obtained for him by Saucisson, a local procurer and parasite.

Rodomont, however, has overheard the conversation between Basile and Françoise and decides to take advantage of Geneviefve before his rival can have her. He plans to borrow Eustache's clothes first and go to Geneviefve. He goes to Eustache's home to do so, but Basile has already taken the clothes. Eustache proposes that the soldier borrow instead those of his cousin René, which are very similar. Because the play takes place during carnival, costumes are common, but no real reason is given for Basile and Rodomont borrowing Eustache's clothes except to use as costumes. En route to René's home, Rodomont is arrested by three policemen representing his creditors.

Basile goes to see Geneviefve, and all goes very well indeed until the unexpected return of Louise. She sees her daughter in a compromising position with a young man who, by the clothing, she takes to be Eustache. Upset by this discovery, she locks them in and goes to her brother, demanding revenge. Girard, Eustache's father, learns of his son's actions and promises that the lovers will marry. Not happy with this solution, Louise demands that Eustache die. Happily, Antoine, the valet, knows everything that has happened and helps Basile escape, replacing him with the prostitute Saucisson procured earlier, dressing her in the borrowed clothes.

Girard, upset by Louise's demands, encounters Eustache and reprimands him for his conduct. Initially, the young man thinks his father is referring to the prostitute, but on learning that Geneviefve is the lady in question, he does his best to persuade his father that nothing has happened and that Girard is the victim of a trick. Louise arrives and takes everyone to Geneviefve's room, where she finds Alix dressed as a man. Rodomont arrives, and Louise, no longer able to marry her daughter to Eustache, proposes the soldier instead. However, Rodomont knows what the girl has been up to and renounces her, leaving the way free for Basile, who now has Louise's blessing.

The comedy is a curious mix of naive license and refined gallantry, depending on who is speaking. Each of the suitors presses his case with appropriate words and terminology. Each act except the last ends on a note of suspense. In act 3, for example, the audience is left wondering whether or not Louise has discovered the treachery going on in the closed room.

Although *Les Contens* is similar in some respects to the Italian play *I Contenti*, it is not a translation of Girolamo Parabosco's work, published in Venice in 1560. Instead, it is an original play with a truly original character, Françoise. She is all things to all people, changing to fit the situation in which she finds herself. Françoise is a French adaptation

of a Spanish character type inaugurated in 1499 by the Spanish author Fernando de Rojas. In his twenty-one-act dialogue/play titled *La Celestina,* the title character is a bawd and a go-between, arranging meetings between lovers, and sacrificing virtue for self-interest and greed. Translated into French in 1527 and again in 1578, the work was quite popular in France. Like her Spanish predecessor La Celestina, Françoise is seemingly pious, while arranging clandestine meetings and acting as a procuress. She works her wiles on behalf of lovers, regardless of the morality involved. Although the character of the procuress had already appeared in several other French and Italian plays, Françoise is the best delineated of the group. The other characters in Turnèbe's play are conventional ones—young lovers, old drunkards, tricky valets, a braggart soldier, a parasite-procurer, and a merchant.

Structurally, Turnèbe's play is faithful to the three unities—unity of action, place, and time—especially that of time. The hours are scrupulously marked by allusions to church services, meals, positions of the sun, ringing of bells, and direct mentions of time. The plot takes place in only one location—a street or public square. Louise's and Girard's houses are both located there, but not next-door to each other. Two or three alleys open on the square as well, providing places for people to overhear conversations without being observed. Patrick Dandrey has made much of the setting of this play, arguing that the playwright's conception of space imposes the unity of time. He also argues that the comedy must be considered trivial, because it extends the street and never really leaves it. He calls the space of the play a *carrefour comique* (comic crossroad), because the street is a space both vague and specific, a meeting place in which the contrast between the private nature of some conversations and the public nature of the street adds to the comedy of the play. The street remains the primary motivater of action—a place where people meet, observe each other, spy on each other, plot, decide, open their hearts, and burst into threats; a place of scandal, then of reconciliation; a place to be seen, where the only privacy can be found in corners and angles. As is necessitated by these unities, much of the action takes place offstage and is narrated after the fact. The play is a comedy of intrigue, of character, of manners, and especially of carnival. Since it is set during that season, the costumes referred to are not an affectation but an integral part of the celebration.

There is no record that Turnèbe's play was ever presented, although there is nothing inherent in it that makes it impossible to stage. In the preface to the first edition, Turnèbe's friend Pierre de Ravel states that the work was written only for entertainment purposes. However, Larsen has proposed that the play was written to parody the play by Catherine des Roches titled *Tragicomedie de Tobie* (1579) and the relationship between Catherine and her mother, Madeleine. Unlike the attachment between the Des Roches women, the bond between Louise and Geneviefve is anything but strong. Moreover, the idea of chastity, espoused by the mother, is ignored by the daughter. In his conception of Geneviefve, Turnèbe breaks with the social norm, making her a willing participant in her own seduction. As Larsen states, "The mother-daughter dyad, so powerfully integral to . . . the lives of the Dames de Roches, is deliberately broken up in *Les Contens*."

The prologue to the play is addressed to "Dames" (ladies) only, an unusual strategy for the time. Laced with double entendres and hints about insatiable sexual appetites, Turnèbe's preface blatantly appeals to the chauvinism of the males in the audience, while it relegates women to the role of lusty, giggling simpletons. The prologue is neither apologetic nor polemic, nor even moral. Instead it aims only to present the author's wish that the audience be satisfied and content with the play that has as its base love in all its forms.

The first edition of *Les Contens* was published in 1584, dedicated to M. de Salut, an adviser to the king. In 1626 the play was reprinted with the title *Les Déguisez, Comédie françoise . . . par Charles Maupas* (The Disguised Ones, French Comedy by Charles Maupas). No indication was given of the original author. The later edition included a small glossary by Maupas, the editor and commentator, for use by his students. Viollet-le-Duc included the play in volume seven of his *Ancien Théâtre français* (1856, Old French Theatre). Edouard Fournier also chose it for his collection, *Théâtre français au XVIème et au XVIIème siècles* (1871, French Theatre of the Sixteenth and Seventeenth Centuries). The critical edition of *Les Contens*, prepared by Norman B. Spector in 1961, includes an extensive introduction and notes.

In his study of French Renaissance comedy, Aulotte argued that Turnèbe was better able than any of his contemporaries to make his play an integrated comedy in which the characters, the plot, and the vivid portrayal of sixteenth-century customs all contribute to the success of the whole. The characters presented in *Les Contens* are as recognizable as types seen in modern society as they were familiar to their Renaissance audiences. Admittedly, there are several drawn from the traditional repertoire for comedies—lovers faced with a parental obstacle, wise and/or foolish servants, the procuress, the braggart soldier, the greedy merchant, the unfaithful wife—but Turnèbe treats these types with greater insight and depth than is usually found in other comedies of the era. The character of Louise is particularly human, for she sincerely loves her daughter and wants only the best for her. While Françoise may be original, Louise is the most sincere, displaying none of the hypocrisy seen by the procuress. Though she serves as the obstacle to love (a role usually held by a father), her intentions are good.

Turnèbe created a story full of plot twists, multiple disguises, and a satisfying conclusion—the ending hoped for by most of the major characters (except, perhaps, Louise) and by the audience as well. The action moves steadily forward without languishing or stumbling. The society presented by Turnèbe is vividly and accurately painted. Although slightly satiric in this portrayal, Turnèbe's goal is not to satirize, but rather to amuse and reassure.

Turnèbe earned a place in French literature, not because he was able to adapt theatrical conventions to his times or because he used the first elements of mannerism. Instead he merited it because, in a time when the style was to reject medieval farce in favor of Italianate comedies, he kept contact with the *comedia erudita* (learned comedy) espoused by humanists. At the same time he reinforced the national tradition of farce in the situations, actions, and especially language of his play.

Like many playwrights of the French Renaissance, Odet de Turnèbe has been neglected. Despite being acclaimed by some scholars, he is often overlooked in discussions of the literature of his era. Any influence that he might have had on writers who followed him has not been studied. He remains, however, an intriguing figure.

References:

Robert Aulotte, *La Comédie française de la Renaissance et son chef-d'oeuvre "Les Contens" d'Odet de Turnèbe* (Paris: Sedes, 1984);

G. Cavalucci, *Odet de Turnèbe* (Naples: Pironti / Paris: Margraff, 1942);

Patrick Dandrey, "La comédie, espace 'trivial': A propos des 'Contens', d'Odet de Turnèbe," *Revue d'histoire du théâtre,* 36 (1984): 323–340;

Marina Eaton, *Les "Contents" of Odet de Turnèbe: A Critical Study* (Ann Arbor, Mich.: University Microfilms International, 1973);

Marie-Madeleine Fontaine, "Les *Antiquitez* chez les dames des Roches: les *Sonets sur les ruines de Luzignan* d'Odet de Turnèbe (1579)," *Oeuvres et Critiques,* 20 (1995): 197–208;

Anne R. Larsen, "Chastity and the Mother-Daughter Bond: Odet de Turnèbe's Response to Catherine des Roches," in *Renaissance Women Writers: French Texts/American Contexts,* edited by Larsen and Colette H. Winn (Detroit: Wayne State University Press, 1994), pp. 172–188;

Jules Lemaître, "Les 'Contens' d'Odet de Turnèbe," *Revue des Cours et Conférences* (20 May 1893): 150–158;

Norman B. Spector, "Odet de Turnèbe's 'Les Contens' and the Italian Comedy," *French Studies,* 13 (October 1959): 304–313.

Pontus de Tyard

(1521? – 23 September 1605)

Frederic J. Baumgartner

Virginia Polytechnic Institute and State University

BOOKS: *Les erreurs amoureuses* (Lyon: Jean de Tournes, 1549);

Continuation des erreurs amoureuses (Lyon: Jean de Tournes, 1551);

Solitaire premier ou prose du Muses & de la fureur poetique plus quelques vers liriques (Lyon: Jean de Tournes, 1552);

Solitaire second, ou, Prose de la musique (Lyon: Jean de Tournes, 1555);

Les erruers amoureuses, augmentées d'une tierce partie (Lyon: Jean de Tournes, 1555);

Discours du temps, de l'an et de ses parties (Lyon: Jean de Tournes, 1556);

Ephemerides octavae spherae (Lyon: Jean de Tournes, 1556);

L'Univers, ou discours des parties & de la nature du monde (Lyon: Jean de Tournes, 1557); republished as *Le Premier Curieux* (Paris, 1578);

Mantice, ou discours de laverité de divination par astrologie (Lyon: Jean de Tournes, 1558);

Les Oeuvres Poétiques de Pontus de Tyard, Seigneur de Bissy: a scavoir, Trois livres des Erreurs Amoureuses (Paris: Galiot du Pré, 1573);

De Coelestibus asterismis poematium ad Petrum Ronsardum (Paris: Galiot du Pré, 1573);

Homilies, ou discours sur l'orasion dominicale (Paris: Mamert Patisson, 1585);

Douze fables de fleuves ou fontaines (Paris: Jean Richer, 1586);

Homilies, ou discours sur la passion de nostre Sauveur (Paris: Mamert Patisson, 1586);

Homilies sur la dignité de la croix (Paris: Mamert Patisson, 1586);

Tumuli duo (Dijon? 1594);

Extrait de la genealogie de Hughes surnommé Capet, roy de France (Paris: Mamert Patisson, 1594);

De recta nominum impositione (Lyon: Jacob Roussin, 1603);

Les advis du diacre Agapet à L'Empereur Justinian (Rouen: Jean Osmont, 1604).

Editions and Collections: *Les Discours philosophique* (Paris: Abel L'Angelier, 1587);

Pontus de Tyard (drawing by Bernard Salomon; from Maurice Scève, edited by Jean-Pierre Attal [Paris: Pierre Seghers, 1963], Thomas Cooper Library, University of South Carolina)

Oeuvres poétiques, edited by Charles Marty-Laveaux (Paris: Lemerre, 1875);

The Universe of Pontus de Tyard, edited by John Lapp (Ithaca, N.Y.: Cornell University Press, 1950);

Oeuvres Poétiques complètes, edited by John Lapp (Paris: Libraire Marcel Didier, 1966);

Mantice: Les Discours de la vérité de la divination par astrologie, edited by Sylviane Bokdam (Geneva: Droz, 1990).

OTHER: *Leon Hebrieu De l'amour,* translated by Tyard (Lyon: Jean de Tournes, 1551).

Pontus de Tyard was a Burgundian poet, philosopher, and prelate, whose verses in French secured his inclusion in the literary circle known as the Pléiade. His dialogues, also in French, cover a wide range of philosophical and scientific topics and reveal sympathy toward heliocentrism and opposition to astrology. Named a bishop by Henri III, he was active in that king's Palace Academy and supported him and Henri IV against the Catholic League (La Ligue).

Tyard was born at Bissy-sur-Fley in Burgundy (in the modern department of Saône-et-Loire) into a prominent noble family that claimed its status dated to the time of Philip IV. The precise date of his birth is unknown, largely because the family library and records were destroyed when the château of Bissy burned in 1636, but it was either in 1521 or 1522. Biographer Abel Jeandet has argued for 1521 based on Tyard's will and the testimony of five contemporaries, while Kathleen Hall, assessing the same evidence in her 1958 essay "En quelle année naquit Pontus de Tyard?" (In What Year was Pontus de Tyard Born?), proposes 1522.

The family name was spelled Tyart until Pontus's time, and later generations often used Thyard. Pontus always spelled it Tyard. As Burgundians, the family remained in service to the dukes of Burgundy even after the duchy's reunion with France in 1477, and Pontus's uncle, Claude de Tyard, served as maréchal des logis (sergeant in mounted arms) and ambassador to the Holy See for Emperor Charles V. His mother, Jeanne de Ganay, was the niece of Jean Ganay, chancellor to Louis XII. His father, Jean de Tyard, had the office of royal lieutenant general of the baillage of Mâcon. As second son of an illustrious noble family, Pontus was destined for a career in the church. Little is known of his early years, but in 1537 he was at the University of Paris, which he later called the "nourrice de la vertu et les arts" (nurturer of all virtues and arts). How long he was there remains uncertain, but what evidence there is suggests his stay was brief. He gained a good knowledge of classical Latin, but little Greek. His knowledge of Italian became strong enough to read widely in it, but his Spanish never progressed beyond being able to understand simple phrases. His first ecclesiastical appointment was as a canon in the cathedral chapter of Mâcon. When he received the office is unknown, but his father's will written in 1552 referred to Pontus by that title. In 1553 Pope Julius III named him a papal protonotary, the title he used when witnessing his older brother's marriage contract in May 1553.

Tyard received his literary education close to home. Burgundy and Lyon, with access to Italy and with their large Italian communities, were centers of French Renaissance culture and literature during his formative years. He was a disciple of Maurice Scève and Louise Labé, the most illustrious members of the Lyonnais school, and was supposedly close to Pernette du Guillet, whose knowledge of languages made her famous in her era. Tyard and she were about the same age. Scève, Labé, and Du Guillet drew heavily from Petrarch in their poetry, and Scève, "le prince des italienistes" (prince of the Italianists), claimed to have discovered the tomb of Petrarch's beloved Laura in Avignon. In his first published poems, Tyard acknowledged his debt to Scève.

Tyard began writing poetry in 1543, according to his second cousin Guillaume des Autelz in his *Chant lyrique* (1561, Lyrical Song). Des Autelz was an important poet in his own right, who was eight years Tyard's junior and grew up as his companion. Tyard verified this date in his collected poems printed in 1573, where he stated he had begun writing the poems thirty years before. In late 1549 he published the first book of *Les erreurs amoureuses* (The Errors of Love). Written to and about a mysterious Pasithée, the poems were Petrarchan in both their style and idea of spiritual love. According to a story by Homer, Pasithée was the fourth Grace whom Juno offered as a bride to Hypnos, and the use of her name was not unique to Tyard among Renaissance poets.

Who Tyard's Pasithée was has never been established, but she almost certainly was neither Louise Labé nor Pernette du Guillet, as has been conjectured based on Tyard's calling Pasithée a writer of verses. (The two portraits of Pasithée in *Les erreurs amoureuses* do not fit Labé's description, although it is possible that Tyard intended them as an ideal type of female beauty.) What Tyard and his cousin Des Autelz wrote about her suggests she was eighteen years of age when Tyard's first poems were written and from a noble family, likely of higher standing than the Tyard family. She was married, probably to an older man, as Tyard hinted in one of his poems. That fact would not have prevented a spiritual love between the lady and her poet-lover, nor does it seem that Tyard would have objected to a physical love despite his being a cleric. On the contrary, Tyard suggested that there was a physical side to their relationship:

Amy (dit-elle en visage amoureux)
Je mettray fin à tes jours langoureux,
Pour commencer tes bien-heureuses nuits.

(Friend [she said lovingly, with an amorous look]
I will put an end to your languishing days
So to begin your blissful nights.)

Les erreurs amoureuses included many sonnets, which later prompted Tyard to claim priority among French poets in introducing the form to French literature, although literary historians are more inclined to give recognition to Mellin de Saint-Gelais, who composed in the sonnet form a generation before Tyard. Petrarch's works and the Neoplatonic ideal of spiritual love were chief influences on Tyard's poems, although they include hints of sexual attraction to Pasithée. Italian influences abound in Tyard's work, including several French words created from Italian ones. In *Les erreurs amoureuses,* Tyard used the poetic form called the *sestine* (sestina) for the first time in French, although it originally appeared among medieval poets of Provence.

The publication of *Les erreurs amoureuses* established Tyard as a notable poet and led to his inclusion in the Brigade, later known as the Pléiade. The original Pléiade was a group of seven poets from the third century B.C. in Alexandria, corresponding to the seven stars of the Pleiades constellation. Pierre de Ronsard is credited with using the term for the first time in 1557 for himself, Etienne Jodelle, Antoine de Baïf, Joachim du Bellay, Jean de La Péruse, Tyard, and Des Autelz. The membership was not precisely defined, and others, especially Rémy Belleau and Jacques Peletier du Mans, appeared on the list soon after La Péruse died, and Des Autelz was dropped. Ronsard has always been regarded as the leader of the group, but Du Bellay's *La Deffense et illustration de la langue françoyse* (1549, Defense and Illustration of the French Language) served as its manifesto. Du Bellay aimed to break with earlier traditions of French poetry and ennoble the French language by imitating the Ancients. To achieve that goal he recommended the use of Greek and Latin poetic forms in French and the creation of new words based on Greek and Latin. Du Bellay's ideal was a poet so well versed in ancient literature that he would be able to convert it into an new and rich poetic language in the vernacular.

Tyard was sympathetic to that ideal and demonstrated it effectively in his poetry, but his inclusion in the Pléiade has been regarded as somewhat tenuous because his corpus of poetry is small in comparison to the other members of the group and his contacts with them were also limited, except for Peletier du Mans, who came often to Bissy. The Pléiade was centered first at the Collège de Coqueret in Paris and then at the French court, while Tyard spent most of his time at Bissy, where he gained a reputation as a congenial host. His later poetry, however, is regarded as showing the influence of Ronsard, and he wrote several verses in his

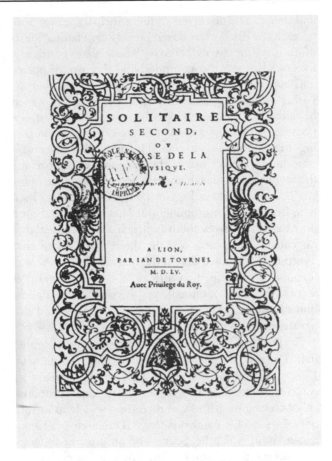

Title page for Tyard's second work, in which Pasithée, the young woman who figures in several of his books, learns about poetry and music through discourse (from Paul Ardoin, La Délie de Maurice Scève et ses cinquante emblèmes [Paris: A.-G. Nizet, 1982]; Thomas Cooper Library, University of South Carolina)

praise. In the *De Coelestibus asterismis poematium ad Petrum Ronsardum* (1573, Poems on Heavenly Bodies and Constellations for Pierre Ronsard) he described Ronsard and Du Bellay as most favored by the Muses. Ronsard reciprocated nearly as effusively, but Du Bellay seems not to have thought so highly of Tyard.

In 1551 Tyard published the *Continuation des erreurs amoureuses* (Continuation of the Errors of Love), which included more love poems to Pasithée, and in the same year, his French translation of Leo Hebraeus's *Dialoghi di amore* (Dialogue of Love). Three years later he published *Les erreurs amoureuses, augmentées d'une tierce partie* (1555, The Errors of Love, augmented with a Third Part). Pasithée remained the focus of these later books of *Les erreurs,* and she appeared in a somewhat different guise in *Solitaire premier ou prose du Muses & de la fureur poetique plus quelques vers liriques* (First Solitary or Prose of the Muses & the Poetic Fury plus some Verse Lyrics) printed in 1552, in which Tyard instructs her on poetry and music. The title refers to the principal speaker, Solitaire, in the discourses. Based heavily on Platonic ideals of beauty, the two discourses show that Tyard was interested in the theory underlying the arts of poetry and music. He was a musical humanist in that he wished to restore classical musical forms. Like Ronsard he intended that his poems be sung but was disappointed that so few musicians were capable of composing the appropriate music. The two discourses also introduced Tyard's use of the dialogue, which became the literary form for which he is best known. One of his characters in them is Le Curieux (The Curious One), who became more prominent in later dialogues. Based on what Tyard states about him, it has been argued that his cousin Des Auletz was the model for Le Curieux. Tyard once lamented that in the dialogue format he was forced to include such phrases as "Il dit" (he says) or "Il a continue" (he continued), yet the dialogue did allow him to interject dramatic tension and even heated disagreements into his work.

The introduction of Le Curieux demonstrated that Tyard's interests had taken another direction by 1552. Probably together with Peletier du Mans, who was a committed astrologer, he was making astronomical observations at Bissy and reading widely in astronomy. In 1556 his *Discours du temps* (Discourse on Time), appeared, in which he, Scève, and an unnamed theologian debate the nature of time and the entomology of the days and months. About the same time he acquired a copy of Nicolaus Copernicus's *De revolutionibus orbium celestium* (1543, On the Revolutions of the Heavenly Spheres) and made extensive notes in it. The notes in his copy, which is now in the Bibliothèque municipale of Vienna, reveal that he studied the book with a critical eye. He made the corrections in the text of about half of the items noted on the errata page, which indicates a zeal for proper understanding of the work. Tyard's skill as an astronomer is clear in his marginal notes, especially in the star tables appended to *De revolutionibus orbium celestium*. He worked through the tables and made the changes necessary to correct them to his own day, which, based on those corrections, was 1557. He was certainly one of the best observational astronomers in sixteenth-century France.

In 1557 Tyard published the dialogue *L'Univers, ou discours des parties & de la nature du monde* (The Universe, or Discourse on the Parts and the Nature of the World). When it was republished in 1578, it was given the title by which it is now called, *Le Premier Curieux* (The First Curious One), from its principal character. Tyard placed himself in the dialogue as a moderator between the free-thinking Le Curieux and a conservative theologian, Hieromnime. Tyard defends the use of French as a language for philosophy against the latter, who is

depicted as thinking that the vernacular was fit only for humorous tales and romances. Tyard indicated that he wished to further Du Bellay's program of making the French language more illustrious as laid out in Du Bellay's *Deffense et illustration de la langue françoyse*. The topics in *L'Univers* are far ranging. Tyard involved himself in the Querelles des femmes (Quarrels of Women), the debate over the intellectual and artistic capacities of women coming down firmly on the side of virtues of womanhood, citing as examples his own Pasithée, Louise Labé, Pernette du Guillet, and Marguerite de Navarre. Tyard was also well informed about the lands that the Europeans were exploring overseas, another subject he treats in *L'Univers*. He was fascinated by what he had heard of the lifestyles and cultures of their peoples, although his sources were not always accurate, nor his understanding of them always correct.

The dialogue format also provided Tyard the opportunity to write at great length on scientific matters: he has Le Curieux deliver a strong case for a challenge to traditional opinion, has Hieromnime defend it, and, then presents himself as the moderator between them. This pattern is most clear in regard to heliocentrism, where Le Curieux speaks enthusiastically of Copernicus's theory and, as depicted, comes closest to anyone in sixteenth-century France to accepting its truth. The character Tyard concludes that discussion by commenting that the courses of the stars will never be known for certain and astronomers will always find new hypotheses to explain them, thus revealing a tendency toward skepticism about the ability of the human mind to have certain knowledge. Such a habit of mind became much more pronounced in the writing of Michel de Montaigne.

Tyard's next dialogue, *Mantice* (1558), is devoted to a debate over astrology. A new character, Mantice, probably modeled after Peletier du Mans, makes the case for prediction by the stars, while Hieromnime objects that humans have free will and Le Curieux contends that fortune determines fate. The character Tyard, while moderating among these opinions, largely supports Le Curieux, since cause and effect in divination by the stars is too complicated and confused to be true. The author demonstrates a thorough knowledge of the literature on astrology and its principles and methods.

Tyard's productivity in the decade after 1549 was remarkable, but in the next fifteen years he published for certain only a poem dedicated to Ronsard and *Ephemerides octavae spherae* (1556, Star Tables of the Eight Spheres). The new book was essentially an updated version of Copernicus's tables. His scholarly existence at Bissy continued into the 1560s, but toward the end of that decade he was drawn into life at the court.

Title page for Tyard's last revised edition of the three books of Erreurs amoureuses (*from* Oeuvres Poétiques complètes, *edited by John Lapp, 1966; Thomas Cooper Library, University of South Carolina*)

Whether he was summoned or went there on his own is unclear, but his contacts with the court were not entirely absent previously. Henri II had named him a royal almoner with an pension of 200 livres, and Henri's mistress, Diane de Poitiers, had commissioned him to write a set of sonnets that probably were intended as accompanying descriptions for murals or tapestries she was having made for her château of Anet. They were published in 1586 as *Douze fables de fleuves ou fontaines* (Twelve Fables of Rivers and Fountains) at the insistence of a friend.

By 1569 Tyard had become a regular at the court of Charles IX and Catherine de Médicis. He joined the circle of poets and scholars centered in the salon of Catherine de Retz, and it is generally agreed that she is the new Pasithée to whom he dedicated his *Oeuvres poetiques* (1573, Poetic Works), a new edition of the three books of *Erreurs amoureuses,* with some new verses. His relationship with this tenth Muse is clearly that of patron and client, and while he brusquely dismisses the first Pasithée, there is no hint of the passion that he had

felt for her. He dedicated a second edition of the first *Solitaire* to Catherine de Retz, published also in 1573.

Tyard's standing at the court significantly improved with the succession in 1575 of Henri III, an enigmatic monarch who was more knowledgeable in philosophy, science, and the arts than any other French king. Tyard served as reader to him on such topics for a three-year period ending in 1578. He also was active in the two academies established in this era by Henri III and Antoine de Baif, Académie du Palais and Académie de poésie et musique, where poetry, music, philosophy, and science were discussed—serving as a philosophical theorist, to use Frances Yates's term in *The French Academies in the Sixteenth Century* (1947). Giordano Bruno participated in the Palace Academy for a time, and Yates argued that his works reveal the influence of Tyard's philosophical views. In the new 1578 edition of *L'Univers,* retitled *Le Premier Curieux,* Tyard described his duties as royal reader and praised Henri for his knowledge and support of scholarship.

Henri in 1578 appointed Tyard bishop of Chalons-sur-Saône in Burgundy. Tyard had never been ordained a priest, which was quickly remedied, and he departed the court to take possession of the see. His formal entry into the city disappointed the city authorities in its simplicity and lack of ostentation. Despite the lack of previous commitment to his clerical career, he became a conscientious bishop dedicated to reforming his clergy and people. Most of his publications from then on were religious, largely collections of his homilies. As a bishop he was also a political leader, and he became active in politics at both the local and national levels. He served as the leader of the clergy of the province of Lyons to the Assembly of Clergy in 1579 and speaker for the First Estate for the Estates of Burgundy in 1587.

Still Tyard found the time in 1587 to produce a new edition of all of his discourses. The great comet of 1577 had given rise to intense speculation as to what great evils it foreshadowed, and he appears pleased to show that none had come true. He also wrote that he had tested Aristotle's belief that fire spontaneously generated salamanders by putting one in a fire and watching it roast to death.

Tyard's loyalty to Henri III and the crown is obvious in its preface to the new edition of his discourses. By 1585 the Catholic League, dedicated to preventing the Huguenot Henri de Navarre from succeeding to the throne, had become powerful in Chalons-sur-Saône. The leaguers objected to the king's policy toward Henri de Navarre, and that quickly put them at loggerheads with their bishop, who is credited with keeping the city loyal to the king in 1585 during an attempted coup by the league. Three years later Tyard served as a deputy for the clergy to the Estates of Blois, where he was one of the few to support the king. His stand made him unwelcome in Chalons-sur-Saône, and he had to take up residence at his house at Bragny-sur-Sâone, north of Mâcon. Henri III's summery execution of Henri, duc de Guise, and Charles, cardinal de Guise in late 1588 led in turn to his own assassination in August 1589.

Tyard gave his support to Henri de Navarre, and recognizing that his politics made it impossible for him to serve as bishop, he resigned his office to a nephew in 1589. The leaguers sacked Bissy in 1591, and in 1594 they killed his favorite nephew, heir of his older brother, and his wife in a raid on their château. Tyard wrote an elegy for the couple that revealed his great loss. After Henri IV announced his intention to convert to Catholicism in early 1594, he summoned Tyard to instruct him in Catholic theology, but the leaguers, who still controlled Burgundy, refused him a safe-conduct. That same year Henri and the Pope accepted Tyard's resignation of his bishopric, and he retired to Bragny, where he spent his last years mostly doing translations from Latin into French. He died there on 23 September

1605. The belief that he was buried in the church at Bragny persists, although there is no tomb or plaque with his name on it in the building to support this idea.

Pontus de Tyard, the last of the Pléiade, lived long enough to see their style of writing fall into disrepute. François de Malherbe sharply criticized them for their extravagance, and the French classicists ignored them. The rise too of French rationalism in philosophy and science led to the dismissal of Tyard's works in those topics, as his skepticism no longer was welcome. In 1784 Gaspard-Pontus de Thyard lamented the fact that his contemporaries had become indifferent to his namesake and all of the Pléiade. Only in 1875, with the publication of *Oeuvres poétiques,* did Tyard again come to the attention of scholars. Since then Tyard has the subject of biographers, and his works have appeared in several modern editions. His work in astronomy has been the object of the most attention, as historians of science have found him to be an important intermediary between Copernicus and Galileo.

Biographies:

Abel Jeandet, *Pontus de Tyard* (Paris: Aubry, 1860);

Sylviane Baridon, *Pontus de Tyard (1521–1605)* (Milan: Viscontea, 1953).

References:

Frederic Baumgartner, "Skepticism and the French Reception of Copernicanism to 1630," *Journal for the History of Astronomy,* 17 (1985): 77–89;

Sylvian Bokdam, "La Poésie astronomique de Pontus de Tyard," *Bibliothèque d'Humanisme et Renaissance,* 48 (1986): 653–670;

Roberto Campo, "Tyard's Graphic Metamorphoses: Figuring the Semiosic Drift in the Douze Fables de fleuves ou fontaines," *Renaissance Quarterly,* 54 (2001): 776–800;

Jean-Claude Carron, *Discours de l'errance amoureuse: Une Lecture du canzoniere de Pontus de Tyard* (Paris: Vrin, 1986);

Françoise Charpentier, "La Poétique de Pontus de Tyard entre Scève et la Pléiade," in *Intellectual Life in Renaissance Lyon,* edited by Philip Ford and Gillian Jondorf (Cambridge: Cambridge French Colloquia, 1993), pp. 173–191;

Robert Griffin, "Pontus de Tyard's 'Le Curiuex' and the Forbidden Fruit," *L'Esprit Créateur,* 12 (1972): 214–225;

Kathleen Hall, "En quelle année naquit Pontus de Tyard?" *Revue des sciences humaines,* new series, facsimile 91 (1958): 133–139;

Hall, *Pontus de Tyard and His Discours Philosophiques* (Oxford: Oxford University Press, 1963);

Hall, "Pontus de Tyard and His 'Disgrace,'" *L'Esprit Createur,* 5 (1965): 102–109;

Margaret Harp, "The Château Anet as Artistic Inspiration," *Quidditas: Journal of the Rocky Mountain Medieval and Renaissance Association,* 19 (1998): 27–47;

Eva Kushner, "L'Atelier de Pontus de Tyard," in *Les Voies de l'invention aux XVIe et XVIIe siècles: Etudes génétiques,* edited by Bernard Beugnot and Robert Melançon (Montréal: Université de Montréal, 1993), pp. 105–114;

Kushner, "L'Evolution du sacré chez Pontus de Tyard," *Renaissance and Reformation/Renaissance et Reforme,* 11 (1987): 59–66;

Kushner, "Pontus de Tyard devant le pouvoir royal," in *Culture et pouvoir au temps de 'l'humanisme de la Renaissance* (Geneva: Slatkine, 1978), pp. 340–361;

Kushner, "Pontus de Tyard, poète lyrique," *Renaissance and Reformation/Renaissance et Reforme,* 13 (1989): 185–198;

J. C. Lapp, "The Identity of Pontus de Tyard's 'Curieux,'" *Modern Language Notes,* 62 (1947): 468–471;

Lapp, "Pontus de Tyard and the Science of His Age," *Romanic Review,* 38 (1947): 16–22;

Emmanuel Mère, *Pontus de Tyard, ou l'univers d'un curieux* (Paris: Editions Hérode, 2003);

François Rouget, "La Poétique de Pontus de Tyard dans les Vers liriques (1555) et les Nouvell'Oeuvres poetiques (1573): De la célébration lyrique aux adieux à la poésie," *Nouvelle Revue du XVIe Siècle,* 15 (1997): 277–299;

V. L. Saulnier, "Maurice Scève et Pontus de Tyard: Deux notes sur le Petrarquisme de Pontus," *Revue de littérature comparée,* 22 (1948): 267–272;

Cathy Yandell, "L'Amour ou féminim?: Ronsard and Pontus de Tyard Speaking as Women," in *Ronsard: Figure de la variété,* edited by Colette Winn (Geneva: Droz, 2002);

Margaret Young, *Guillaume des Autelz: A Study of His Life and Works* (Geneva: Droz, 1961).

Jacques Yver
(1520? – 1570?)

Margaret Harp
University of Nevada, Las Vegas

BOOK: *Le Printemps d'Yver contenant cinq histoires, discourues par cinq journees, en une noble compagnie, au chasteau du printemps* (Paris: Printed by Jean Ruelle, 1572); translated by Henry Wotten as *Courtlie Controversie of Cupids Cautels: Conteyning fiue tragicall histories, very pithie, pleasant, pitiful, and profitable: discoursed vppon wyth arguments of loue, by three gentlemen and two gentlewomen, entermedled with diuers delicate sonets and rithmes, exceeding delightfull to refresh the yrkesomnesse of tedious tyme. Translated out of French as neare as our English phrase will permit* (London: Printed by Francis Coldock & Henry Bynneman, 1578).

Editions: "Le Printemps d'Yver," in *Les Vieux Conteurs Français: Rev. et corr. sur les éditions originales, accompagnés de notes et précédés de notices historiques, critiques et bibliographiques,* edited by Paul L. Jacob (Paris: Desrez, 1841), pp. 619–654;

"Le Printemps," in *Conteurs français du XVIe siècle,* edited by Pierre Jourda, Bibliothèque de la Pléiade, volume 177 (Paris: Gallimard, 1965), pp. 1135–1274;

Le Printemps d'Yver contenant cinq histoires discourues par cinq journées en une noble compagnie au château du Printemps (Geneva: Slatkine, 1970).

Jacques Yver is known for a single book: *Le Printemps d'Yver* (1572, The Spring of Yver), a collection of five short stories with a framing narrative. Yver's stories are reminiscent of the seventy-two stories in *L'Heptaméron* (1559; translated as *The Heptameron,* 1894), by Marguerite de Navarre, the sister of King François I, which was itself modeled after Giovanni Boccaccio's Italian story collection, the *Decameron* (1350). *L'Heptaméron* was highly popular for its purportedly true tales of the risks and tragedy of passionate love, and Yver's book, in which three gentlemen and three noblewomen spin tales to distract each other from the horrors of the recent Third War of Religion and to rejoice in the 1570 truce of St.-Germain, provides an intriguing continuation of this theme. Yver was also a skilled poet: the excellence of the poems of various genres found throughout *Le Printemps d'Yver* has led some

critics to speculate that the work was meant as an introduction to a collection of Yver's poetry.

A member of the upper bourgeoisie who held the title of Seigneur of Plaisance and of la Bigottière, Yver was born in the Poitou town of Niort, probably in 1520. The multiple subtle references to Greek and Latin mythology throughout *Le Printemps d'Yver* indicate that he received an excellent classical education. He studied law in Poitiers between 1542 and 1545. The vivid portrayal of Italy and areas along the Rhine in *Le Printemps d'Yver* indicates first-hand knowledge of those areas, but no record of Yver's travels exists. Literary devices and textual references in *Le Printemps d'Yver* suggest that he began writing it in his youth; in his epilogue he calls it "le gage éternal de ma folle jeunesse" (the everlasting token of my mad youth).

Yver became mayor of Niort in 1556; the office had previously been held by several members of his family. Passages in *Le Printemps d'Yver* critical of the king's actions during the religious wars suggest that Yver had Protestant leanings, and accounts exist of his brother, Joseph, joining in the pillaging of local Catholic churches. Nineteenth-century literary critics went so far as to claim that Yver fought on the Protestant side under Louis de Bourbon, first Prince of Condé, and Admiral Gaspard de Coligny, but there is no proof of his having had military experience. Until the twentieth century, Yver was presumed to have been a victim of the August 1572 St. Bartholomew's Day Massacre, an orchestrated mass killing of Protestants by Catholics throughout France at the time of the wedding of the Protestant Henri de Navarre—the future King Henri IV—and Marguerite de Valois, the Catholic sister of King Charles IX. This belief in the author's martyrdom fueled interest in the work: readers saw Yver's reflections on the futility and tragedy of the religious wars in his gloomy opening ode, "Complainte sur les misères de la guerre civile" (Plaint of the Miseries of the Civil War), as a prescient forewarning of the massacre and, perhaps, of his own death. More recently, scholars have argued that Yver died in 1571 or, perhaps, as early as 1570. Yver evidently completed *Le Printemps d'Yver* shortly before he died. It was published in 1572 by his brother, Joseph, and sister,

Marie, and they added introductory sonnets alluding to Yver's death. Yver's introductory epistle to his readers alludes to a subsequent work that he hopes will be yet more worthy of their time. No such work is known to exist either in published or manuscript form, leaving it unclear whether this reference was a mere convention or evidence of a lost piece of writing.

From his opening pages Yver establishes parallels between his work and ancient and recent texts. He is the first French writer to emulate the narrative structure of Marguerite de Navarre's *L'Heptaméron*: in the wake of calamity, genteel folk gather to distract themselves by debating points of love and honor between men and women as represented in stories that they swear to be true and accurate. The listeners respond to the stories, rarely persuaded by the moral they are intended to show. Like Marguerite de Navarre, Yver has an equal number of men and women protagonists. A full third of his work consists of descriptions of the six friends, their activities, and, most important, their discussions. Hence, the framing of the stories plays a significant role for the reader.

Le Printemps d'Yver could be categorized as a response to the Pléiade poet Joachim du Bellay's call for authentic, if not original, French literature in his *La Deffence et Illustration de la Langue Francoyse* (1549; translated as *The Defence and Illustration of the French Language*, 1939). In his prologue Yver explains that *Le Printemps d'Yver* is an attempt to demonstrate the validity of French without resorting to borrowing from other languages, particularly Italian. Yver uses both original and standard metaphors for the modeling of French on other languages: using others' thread and needles to weave new cloth, roosting on eggs laid by others, and eating the crumbs that fall from the table of the rich. Yet, Yver, like Du Bellay, presents a paradox: while claiming to create an original work, he borrows freely from Italian authors. His characters' discussions of Neoplatonic love are patterned closely on those in Pietro Bembo's *Gli Asolani* (1505; translated, 1954), and the plots of several tales are based on Matteo Bandello's *Novelle* (1554–1573). Written more than a decade before the outbreak of the religious wars, *La Deffence et Illustration de la Langue Francoyse* has always been considered a nationalistic work—a plea for French unity, at least on the linguistic level. Yver's evocation of it calls his readers back to this moment of a comparatively orderly and peaceful France.

Yver also borrows devices from Guillaume de Lorris and Jean de Meun's thirteenth-century allegory, the *Roman de la Rose* (Romance of the Rose), the quintessential work on love. For example, rather than identifying by name the three gentlemen who are visiting the château of the three ladies, he gives them the allegorical titles Bel-Accueil (Beautiful-Greeting), Fleur-d'Amour (Flower-of-Love), and Ferme-Foy (Firm-Faith)—names that would certainly have reminded contemporary readers of the medieval romance. The ladies are virtually anonymous: the eldest is identified simply as "La Dame" (The Lady), and the reader learns only the given names of La Dame's daughter and niece—Marie and Marguerite, two of the most common names possible. By describing five days of leisurely pursuits Yver also replicates the fanciful atmosphere of the *Roman de la Rose,* which is described as a *songe* (dream). The refined atmosphere of the lively dialogues links *Le Printemps d'Yver* to Baldassare Castiglione's *Il Cortegiano* (1528; translated as *The Book of the Courtier,* 1561), which was tremendously popular in France, and it may well have influenced Stefano Guazzo's *La Civil Conversazione* (1574; translated as *The Civile Conversation,* 1581, 1586).

Le Printemps d'Yver also documents folklore traditions of sixteenth-century France. It is the only text that preserves songs to accompany traditional Poitou dances, known as *branles;* Yver includes five such pieces of varying length and meter. The stanzas consist of verses of no more than eight syllables and offer multiple rhyming combinations. The songs of courtship, love, and seduction reinforce the themes of the tales. Playful in tone, they most resemble the poems in Pierre de Ronsard's *Livret de Folastries* (1553, Little Book of Follies). Yver presents four of the *branles* in an idyllic pastoral setting: playing flutes and bagpipes, local villagers arrive spontaneously, early in the morning, to entertain the château's inhabitants; Yver says that they appear as angels from a village paradise. The residents come down from their rooms, half asleep and half dressed, to listen and eventually to join in the revelry. Claiming to fear that the colloquial language will be difficult for the non-Poitevin to understand, Yver translates the lyrics of the songs he best remembers; hence, the text does not repeat the authentic *branles* nor even all that are supposedly sung. This adaptation simultaneously presents the songs but veils them from the larger French public; in this way Yver cleverly underscores that this world is not that of the reader. The first four *branles* serve as an interlude between the second and third stories, breaking the tragic tone established in the first two stories. The fifth appears at the end of Ferme-Foy's narration of the final story. It is a duet sung by the newly married couple whose infidelities are depicted in the tale. Happily reconciled, they tell of their present joy and deep love in alternating stanzas of the *branle*. With the husband and wife each singing eight stanzas, Yver balances the masculine and feminine points of view and thus provides a fitting closing device to this work about disputes between the sexes.

Dedicating his book to the demoiselles of France, Yver proclaims that he follows all writers in hoping to "louer le bien et blâmer le mal" (praise the good and condemn the bad) but that he also wishes to emphasize the gracious, virtuous, and well-educated young women who serve as the most worthy of subjects for a writer. A substantial number of women made up the reading public of this period, and such a dedication was relatively commonplace. Nonetheless, Yver's announced intention to write both for and about women reinforces the themes of love, marriage, and the role of women in society as they are presented in the tales. It is noteworthy, too, that Yver refers to the demoiselles of France in general, specifying neither their region nor their faith. During this moment of truce Yver offers an image of national unity in which his protagonists are defined only by their genders, not by their political leanings.

The word *Printemps* (Spring) in the title has multiple references; the most obvious is a playful juxtaposition with Yver's name, which is a homonym of *hiver* (winter). Spoken aloud, the title can be heard as "Printemps divers," or diverse/diverting spring–a subtle reference to the many genres, narrations, and themes in the collection. *Printemps* evokes, as well, rebirth, nascent love, and beauty, and these themes are broached, if not maintained, in all of the stories. Yver emphasizes that the five days of storytelling take place not only during a moment of military peace at the height of spring but also during the Christian season of Pentecost. A commemoration of the descent of the Holy Spirit on the disciples, Pentecost is associated with special graces of enlightenment and with devotions demonstrating joy and celebration, such as an end to fasting. The consistently witty banter of Yver's storytellers, even while recounting tales of woe, reinforces the celebratory atmosphere.

Printemps is also the name of the residence where the stories are told; it is, thus, a physical incarnation of this season of political and spiritual hope. The château Printemps continues the motif of a refined and luxurious household established by François Rabelais in *Gargantua* (1534) with the idyllic Abbaye de Thélème and continued by Claude de Taillemont in *Discours des Champs faëz, à l'honneur, & exaltation de l'amour, & des Dames* (1553, Discourse of the Enchanted Fields, in Honor and Exultation of Love and of Ladies). Each of these three narratives depicts an abode that has every elegant and rich Italianate architectural feature and is surrounded by productive gardens and farmland. Resembling the spectacular château Lusignan in Poitou, Printemps is described as surpassing the splendor of the sultan of Ultibie's palace, which itself "annihilait la gloire des pyramides du Caire" (annihilates the glory of the pyramids of Cairo). Such exotic and multiple comparisons occur in Yver's descriptions of the house throughout *Le Printemps d'Yver*. Further to persuade the reader of the otherworldly nature of the château Printemps, Yver declares that it is one of the many châteaux, fortresses, and churches that, according to local legend, the fairy Mélusine constructed in one night throughout the Poitevin region. Evocation of Mésuline establishes a

theme of female ambiguity: Mésuline was a beautiful fairy who built these structures in tribute to her human husband. But she hid a terrible secret: for having killed her father, she was condemned to turn into a serpent one night a week. Her disappearances on these evenings awakened her husband's jealousy, and he burst in on her during one of her transformations. She fled, destroying all of the buildings. Yver does not repeat this legend, which would have been well known to his readers, but its theme of secrets and suspicion between lovers fits in well with the tales about to be told. As Printemps is a château that has escaped Mésuline's fury, as well as the ravages of war, the reader is convinced of its singular atmosphere. (The château Lusignan, the model for Printemps, was destroyed by Louis de Bourbon, Duke of Montpensier in renewed religious warfare in 1574.)

According to Yver, the château Printemps is a terrestrial paradise whose perfection is enhanced by the beauty and virtue of its inhabitants. The women are described as having been formed by God rather than born to human beings. The noblewoman and her daughter and niece are perfect hostesses who devote themselves to games, music, and rich foods; in short, they personify the women of France to whom Yver dedicates his stories. It becomes evident that the three hostesses relish the five days of sustained storytelling not only for diversion but also–and tellingly–for cathartic reasons. The narrator explains that the women had recently returned to the château:

> je peux bien assurer que, entre tous les François, les habitants du pays de Poitou retournèrent avec extrême joie en leurs désolées maisons, pensant entrer en nouveaux ménages . . . si qu'après s'être accommodés tellement quellement selon que la nécessité pouvoit permettre, n'eurent rien en plus singulière recommandation, que de s'entrevoir les uns les autres, conter et communiquer entre eux leurs pertes et se consoler par la pratique d'un devoir d'amitié en leur commune misère.

> (I can surely attest that of all the French, it was those of Poitou who returned to their ravaged houses with extreme joy, thinking to enter new homes . . . after being lodged hither and yon as necessity permitted and who had no more compelling recommendation than to meet with each other, to tell and communicate between themselves their losses and to console each other by practicing the duty of friendship in their common suffering.)

The telling of tales confers order on a unique kind of misfortune: the chaos of war. The preoccupation in all of the stories with the hazards of fate, betrayal, suicide, and the violent ends of seemingly perfect lovers betrays the trauma of the vagaries of war, particularly a civil war. Whereas the storytellers of the *Decameron* and *L'Heptaméron* are faced with natural disasters—the plague and a flood, respectively—this group has survived a strictly human-made catastrophe.

The elaborate ceremony with which the characters order their entertainment and dining extends to their spiritual exercises. Unlike Marguerite's storytellers, who are Catholics—albeit with evangelical leanings—and attend daily mass, Yver's six provincial nobles are not specified as either Catholic or Protestant but simply as Christians who begin their day with a prayer. Since no mention is made of the mass, one might infer that they are Protestants; but if so, they are certainly not partisan ones. In his opening description of the storytellers' daily routine, Yver emphasizes that their practice of faith is most valuable for lending order to daily life: they "présenté à Dieu leur première oeuvre concernant le devoir de piété et de dévotion requise, non-seulement requise pour le bon règlement d'une famille bien instituée, mais selon le tribut que doivent tous chrétiens" (presented to God their first task concerning the duty of requisite piety and devotion, not only necessary for the good rule of a well-ordered family but according to the tribute that all Christians owe). This generic but sincere reference to the practice of faith reinforces the carefully neutral religious tone of the text. Yver maintains a rhetorical truce to parallel the military one, reserving heated disputes for the storytellers' discussions of love.

La Dame, a widow, does not often engage in the debates but provides order to the gatherings. She serves as arbiter, designating each day's storyteller with the ceremonial passing of a laurel branch encircled with flowers. When all of the tales have been told, she promises to give a long discussion of Platonic love on the following day. Since the narrative ends with that day, the discussion is not included. La Dame does, however, provide a brief discussion of love as a moral virtue. Her role is similar to that of Oisille, the oldest storyteller and organizer of the stranded travelers in *L'Heptaméron*. The other participants are young unmarried men and women who represent the future of France. While none have the verve or complexity of the raconteurs in *L'Heptaméron,* their joyful attitudes reflect the optimism of what, in reality, turned out to be a brief moment of peace. The seventh participant in *Le Printemps d'Yver* is the unnamed narrator, presumably Yver himself; an intimate of the others, he reports what is said by the rest but rarely offers his own comments.

Yver's stories, while few in number compared to Marguerite de Navarre's seventy-two, are more cohesive in their intent. The storytellers aim to determine whether women or men are at fault in the misfortunes of love. But some of the tales contradict the moral they purportedly impart, and the storytellers admit as much. Hence,

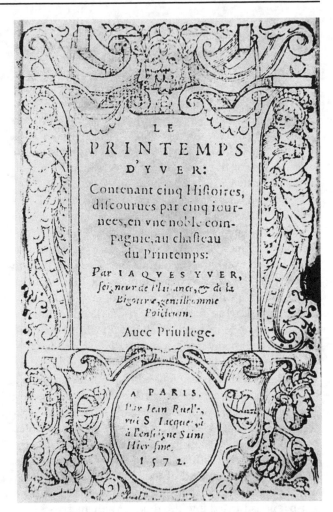

Title page for Jacques Yver's only known work, published posthumously, in which six aristocratic ladies and gentlemen gather at a château during a truce in the Wars of Religion and tell stories to try to show which sex is at fault in the misfortunes of love (Microform Collection, Thomas Cooper Library, University of South Carolina)

despite the tragic elements of some of the tales, the narrators' ironic tone reveals that they are meant to amuse as much as to instruct.

The first tale, like the subsequent ones, is preceded by a lengthy description of the storytellers and their discussions. The first day's preface, a mixture of narration, poetry, and prose, maintains a relatively somber tone that evokes the anxious atmosphere created by the religious wars. La Dame sings the heartrending "Complainte sur les misères de la guerre civile" (Plainte of the Misery of the Civil War), which offers striking images of the ravages of war while making pointed and doleful accusations against the king, Charles IX. The final lines declare that by showing his strength with sword and cannon, the king is only burying his name under the rubble of France. Contemporary readers saw in the ode a forewarning of the type of massacre in which they believed that Yver died.

Recognizing the pall she has cast over her guests, La Dame concludes with the hopeful "Hymne pour le bienviennement de la paix" (Hymn for the Happy Arrival of Peace). Bel-Accueil lauds his hostess by exclaiming that her songs have left their hearts to both break and rejoice at the same time. Fleur-d'Amour adds that the most striking aspect of her first song is that it kept the rest of the company speechless, as they are all prone to chatter.

Fleur-d'Amour then offers the tragic story of Perside and Eraste, set in early-sixteenth-century Greece, as proof that women's inconstancy is at the root of the conflict between men and women. The story is not persuasive, however, as the beautiful and virtuous Perside chooses to die rather than succumb to the desires of her husband's rival. Perside's heroism, rather than Eraste's, is highlighted: while Eraste is imprisoned and summarily executed, Perside dresses herself as a knight to draw the arrows of the enemy army and dies a heroic death.

Marie tries to respond to this opening salvo, as she calls it, with a tale intended to demonstrate men's blame in love's misfortunes. Before she can do so, Bel-Accueil intervenes with a cautionary fable intended to prove the Turks' claim that women may not enter heaven because of their provocative natures. An Egyptian woman faced with assault by two angels persuades them to let her go ahead of them to heaven, where she will meet them. She then rises quickly, escaping their grasp, and is turned into the moon. With angels serving as the villains, the fable is a retooling of the fifth story of the first day in L'Heptaméron: the well-known tale of the ferrywoman of Coulon, who outwits two monks who attempt to rape her. By replacing the monks with angels, Yver sidesteps an attack on Catholicism.

The motifs of Marie's story contrast with this mythic fable. Two prosperous bourgeois families in the German town of Mayence in the sixteenth century hope to expand their wealth through the marriage of their children, Fleurie and Herman. The two do love each other, and their happiness is seemingly sealed. But the villainous Ponifre, obsessed with Fleurie, drugs and rapes her. Having no memory of the attack, Fleurie is horrified when she discovers that she is pregnant. Believing that she has betrayed him, Herman marries another woman, and they have a child. Fleurie, Herman, and Ponifre eventually die tragically. True love endures, however, as their offspring marry and live happily. The concluding discussion of this second tale offers more interest than do the others, as the storytellers directly confront the issue of rape: the culpability of the attacker, the shame of the victim, and the consequences of the resulting pregnancy.

In advance of the third story, Bel-Accueil attributes lovers' unhappiness to the vagaries of fortune, with neither the man nor the woman being the responsible party. Yet, he announces in his introduction that dissimulation and hypocrisy are the most dangerous evil for any relationship, whether of individuals or nations. Against the backdrop of the Italian Wars of 1494 to 1559 he presents the incarnation of this vice of "Beau-Semblant" (Fair Seeming): the Italian prince Adilon, an eager adversary of the French in Pope Julius II's army. In Mantua, Adilon falls in love with the beautiful Clarinde; but she is in love with d'Alègre, a French knight who was taken hostage during the battle of Ravenna and whom Adilon has befriended. In a jealous rage Adilon gives d'Alègre a poisoned apple. Struck by the fruit's beauty, d'Alègre offers it to Clarinde. As Clarinde lies dying, d'Alègre hunts down Adilon and stabs him in the heart. He then returns to Clarinde's side, and the two express their eternal love. Overcome with grief and with guilt for inadvertently poisoning his lover, d'Alègre dies of a broken heart beside her.

The story is replete with baroque imagery: Yver details the savagery of the battle of Ravenna, as well as the physical effects of Clarinde's poisoning, Adilon's stabbing, and d'Alègre's death, the last of which is presented through a metaphor: "Ainsi, quand un canon ne peut vomir le feu et le fer qui guerraient dans ses entrailles, force lui est de crever et se rompre en pièces. Or tel fut la glorieuse fin de notre chevalier françois, pour être tant oppressé de diverses passions qu'il ne les put digérer" (As when a cannon cannot vomit the fire and iron which was warring in its insides, it is forced to split and break up in pieces. Thus was the glorious end of our French knight, for being so oppressed with various passions that he could not digest them). It is obvious that d'Alègre's death was far from glorious, and Bel-Accueil's ironic commentary belies the tragic elements of the tale. Bel-Accueil concludes with a return to his original premise, the vagaries of fortune, with an inventory of historical and mythological examples of haphazard good and bad luck. The conversational tone and philosophical subject matter of this epilogue are strikingly similar to Michel de Montaigne's Essais (translated as The Essayes, or, Morall, politike and millitarie discourses of Lo. Michaell de Montaigne, 1603), the first edition of which was published eight years after Le Printemps d'Yver.

In the fourth tale Marguerite protests Bel-Accueil's denial of free will and claims to show with her story that the vice of envy, which can afflict both sexes, is at the root of unhappiness in love. William the Conqueror would have remained happily with his true love, Viergine, if not for the machinations of the embittered and defeated king of Denmark. As in the story of Clarinde and d'Alègre, Yver adds sufficient twists to a seemingly straightforward tale of thwarted love to cause the reader to question its tragic elements. William falls in love with Amire, a Danish princess, on seeing her portrait and writes her an impassioned letter declaring his love. In a scene reminiscent of *Tristan et Iseult,* however, during his voyage to meet her William drinks from a fountain whose waters evoke hatred, and his love turns to revulsion. Arriving in Denmark, he meets the exiled Turkish princess Viergine, and they immediately fall in love. Forced to return to England, he writes Viergine a love letter similar to his first letter to Amire. This story is distinctive because the doomed couple do marry and have a happy relationship before falling victim to the treachery of English nobles and the Danes. Yver takes great liberties with English history in this convoluted tale while also maintaining a highly cynical stance in regard to enduring love. Romantic love is described alternately as a plague or as a scorpion bite from which one rarely recovers.

The outcomes of these four tales are certainly not happy: all of the principal protagonists die from broken hearts, suicide, execution, or extraordinary accidents. They are also unsatisfactory because none offers sufficiently persuasive lessons on whether men or women are at the root of their mutual discontent in the realm of love.

Ferme-Foy provides a tiebreaker of sorts with a tongue-in-cheek tale of woe of two best friends who each sleep with the other's wife. Despite this betrayal the young couples end up reconciled and happy, creating a bond of history but also of friendship. This story contrasts with the four tales that precede it in several respects. First, the principal couple is not a love match but a pair of French *chevaliers errants* (knights-errant), Claribel and Floradin, who met while attending school in Padua. Second, while the first, third, and fourth stories are set in foreign courts decades or even centuries in the past, these protagonists live in the present and are natives of the Poitou region. Hence, they resemble their narrator, and his listeners may well know them. Third, both young men willingly submit to the practicality and profitability of arranged marriages; there is no question of grand passion or absolute fidelity. And yet, these arranged marriages lead to love and esteem between the husbands and wives, much as in several of Marguerite de Navarre's tales of roving husbands.

Claribel and Floradin are so preoccupied with themselves that they remain oblivious to the military strife surrounding them. Most significantly, they are indifferent to the religious principles at stake in the civil war. In a telling scene the two young men travel together through the countryside, each keeping handy both a Catholic Book of Hours and a Protestant psalter.

As they pass through alternately Protestant- or Catholic-controlled checkpoints, they pull out the appropriate text to ensure their safety. The reader also has the impression that, like all good courtiers, they simply wish to please everyone they encounter. As their route mostly takes them through Catholic-held territory, one might assume that they are Catholic. Yver does not, however, reveal their religious convictions, and it is likely that they have none; for them, faith would appear to be but a partisan position in the current civil war, rather than a matter of the spiritual state of their souls. It is clear that Yver does not wish to engage in religious debate. One might assume that he wished to avoid the censors, but certainly such discussions would have detracted from the burlesque tone of this final tale, with its jocular asides and ribald comments made directly to the reader. This tone reflects the tenor of the frame story of *Le Printemps d'Yver.*

In the closing *branle* Claribel and his wife, Marguerite, sum up their feelings about each other and the love they share. Claribel makes a plea for enjoying passionate love before death extinguishes it:

> Belle, reprenons ore l'ère
> De nos amours,
> Et aux combats de cette guerre
> Passons nos jours.
> Las! Quand une froide pâleur
> Nous cache en terre,
> Le feu de l'amour le meilleur
> Perd sa chaleur.

> (My beauty, let us once again take up the era
> Of our love,
> And in the battles of this war
> Spend our time.
> Alas! When a cold pallor
> Hides us in the ground,
> The best love's fire
> Loses its heat.)

Marguerite evokes eternal love:

> Ami, la gaillarde jeunesse
> Et l'amour fol,
> Fuyant la temblante vieillesse
> D'un même vol; Plutôt donc dessous la mer
> Le feu s'abaisse,
> Qu'on nous voie désaffamer
> De nous aimer

> (Friend, bold youth
> And mad love
> Flee trembling old age
> In the same way; Better that fire slip away below the sea
> Than for us to be seen quenched
> In our love for each other).

These verses reflect the preoccupation with love–both carnal and emotional–of all of the storytellers and its primacy for them over other earthly concerns.

In his concluding ode, "Congé à son Livre" (Farewell to His Book), Yver says that he is loath to let his work go forth: "Demeure un peu, demeure; où vas-tu, mon enfant?" (Stay a bit, stay; where are you going, my child?). Yver's concern with the public's reception of his book reveals a modern sensibility and anticipates Montaigne's view of the *Essais* as an extension of himself.

Le Printemps d'Yver concludes with three brief memorial poems signed "J. Th."–presumably Jean Tharon, a minor nobleman who owned one of the most extensive private libraries in France during this period and was a friend and patron of writers. Tharon's first memorial, a quatrain, is addressed to Yver and states that the author will be immortal as long as his work lives. The following sonnet reinforces this motif by claiming that Yver's book provides him with a strong enough shield to disappoint Death and its force. By depicting Yver as a warrior, the sonnet reinforces the theme of war that is found throughout the stories. The last words of the concluding four-line poem form an anagram of Yver's name: "J'acquiers vye" (I obtain life). In later editions this anagram appeared as frequently as did Yver's formal name.

Yver's work was immediately successful: the collection went through at least twenty editions in the three decades after its initial publication, and by 1635 ten more editions had appeared. Early critics praised *Le Printemps d'Yver* for its accounts of battles that occurred in 1570 in Poitou and Saintonge, the areas that experienced the most intense military conflict during the religious wars. These references are of less interest today and do not appear to offer any historical insights. Later critics have seen in *Le Printemps d'Yver* a portrait of attitudes toward love, war, and morals, and, most significantly, of the varying relationships between men and women in prosperous provincial society in the late sixteenth century.

Le Printemps d'Yver spawned imitations both in France and in England. Bénigne Poissenot modeled his *L'Esté* (1583, The Summer), a collection of raucous stories told by three down-and-out French university students, on *Le Printemps d'Yver*. Albeit engaging, its lack of female storytellers makes for more superficial analyses of the relationships between men and women than those in *Le Printemps d'Yver*, and it was less widely read. In 1578 Henry Wotten produced an English translation of Yver's work titled *Courtlie Controversie of Cupids Cautels*. With his use of "cautels" (precautions) Wotten emphasizes the practical moral lessons offered by these diverting tales. The plots of several anonymous English plays of the Elizabethan era, including *Faire Em* (circa 1591) and *Solimon and Perseda* (1599), are based partly on Yver's stories by way of Wotten's translation. It can be argued that Yver's influence extends indirectly to William Shakespeare, whose *King John* (performed circa 1594–1596) and *Henry IV* (performed circa 1596–1597) include passages alluding to characters from these plays.

Unlike *L'Heptaméron*, *Le Printemps d'Yver* offered contemporary readers a clear, practical moral of a truce between the sexes during a fleeting moment of military truce. This clever, erudite, and well-written text met the need of a late-sixteenth-century public starving for nuance and refinement in the midst of horror. Both male and female readers could appreciate the multiple thematic dichotomies that Yver establishes in the first short-narrative collection to appear since Marguerite de Navarre's work. They could easily relate to the descriptions of conflicts between men and women against a backdrop of war and peace, while savoring the witty manner in which the stories are told. While not a great piece of literature, *Le Printemps d'Yver* is a pleasing and at times thought-provoking work for all periods and deserves the renewed critical interest it has received since the late twentieth century. In his preface Jacques Yver describes the religious wars as a "douloureuse maladie de France" (painful sickness of France) marked by a "fièvre frénétique" (frenetic fever). *Le Printemps d'Yver* offered a salutary medicine to its victims, if not a cure, and the narrative skill with which its stories are told, if not the originality of the tales themselves, merits continued attention.

References:

Michel Jeanneret, "Le Cadre et le miroir (sur quelques transformations du système narrative dans les recueils de nouvelles au XVIe siècle)," in *"D'Une fantastique bigarrure": Le Texte composite à la Renaissance,* edited by Jean-Raymond Fanlo (Paris: Champion, 2000), pp. 19–27;

Gabriel-A. Pérouse, *Nouvelles françaises du XVIe siècle: Images de la vie du temps* (Geneva: Droz, 1977), pp. 191–226;

Jerome Schwartz, "Structures dialectiques dans le *Printemps* de Jacques Yver," *French Review,* 57, no. 3 (1984): 291–299.

Checklist of Further Readings

Baumgartner, Frederic. *France in the Sixteenth Century.* New York: St. Martin's Press, 1995.

Bellenger, Yvonne. *La Pléiade: La poésie en France autour de Ronsard.* Paris: Libraire Nizet, 1988.

Bellenger. *Le temps et les jours dans quelques recueils poétiques du XIVe siècle.* Paris: Champion, 2002.

Berriot-Salvadore, Evelyne. *Les femmes dans la société française de la Renaissance.* Geneva: Droz, 1990.

Boriaud, Jean-Yves. *La Littérature française du XVIe siècle.* Paris: Armand Colin, 1995.

Burke, Peter. *Popular Culture in Early Modern Europe.* New York: Harper & Row, 1978.

Castor, Grahame. *Pléiade Poetics: A Study in Sixteenth-Century Thought and Terminology.* Cambridge: Cambridge University Press, 1964; revised and translated into French by Yvonne Bellenger as *La poétique de la Pléiade.* Paris: Champion, 1998.

Cave, Terence. *The Cornucopian Text: Problems of Writing in the French Renaissance.* Oxford: Clarendon Press, 1979.

Cave. *Recognitions: A Study in Poetics.* Oxford: Clarendon Press, 1988 / New York: Oxford University Press, 1988.

Christin, Olivier. *Une révolution symbolique: l'iconoclasme huguenot et la reconstruction catholique.* Paris: Les Editions de Minuit, 1991.

Cottrell, Robert. *The Grammar of Silence: A Reading of Marguerite de Navarre's Poetry.* Washington, D.C.: Catholic University of America Press, 1986.

Dauphiné, James, and Béatrice Périgot, eds. *Conteurs et romanciers de la Renaissance. Mélanges offerts à Gabriel-André Pérouse.* Paris: Champion, 1997.

Davis, Natalie Zemon, and Arlette Farge, eds. *Renaissance and Enlightenment Paradoxes,* volume 3 of *A History of Women,* edited by Georges Duby and Michelle Perrot. Cambridge, Mass.: Belknap Press of Harvard University, 1994.

Demerson, Guy. *La Notion de genre à la Renaissance.* Geneva: Editions Slatkine, 1984.

Dubois, Claude-Gilbert. *La poésie du XVIe siècle.* Talance: Presses universitaires de Bordeaux, 1999.

Fumaroli, Marc. *L'âge de l'éloquence: Rhétorique et "res literaria" de la Renaissance au seuil de l'époque classique,* second edition. Paris: Albin Michel, 1994.

Gadoffre, Gilbert, and Jean Céard. *La révolution culturelle dans la France des humanistes: Guillaume Budé et François Ier.* Geneva: Droz, 1997.

Galland-Hallyn, Perrine, and Fernand Hallyn, eds. *Poétiques de la Renaissance.* Geneva: Droz, 2001.

Goyet, Francis, ed. *Traités de poétique et de rhétorique de la Renaissance: Sebillet, Aneau, Peletier, Fouquelin, Ronsard.* Paris: Libraire générale française, 1990.

Grafton, Anthony. *Commerce with the Classics: Ancient Books and Renaissance Readers.* Ann Arbor: University of Michigan Press, 1997.

Gray, Hanna. "Renaissance Humanism: The Pursuit of Eloquence," *Journal of the History of Ideas,* 24 (1963): 497–514.

Greene, Thomas M. *The Light in Troy: Imitation and Discovery in Renaissance Poetry.* New Haven: Yale University Press, 1982.

Grenblatt, Stephen. *Renaissance Self-Fashioning, from More to Shakespeare*. Chicago: University of Chicago Press, 1980.

Jourda, Pierre, ed. *Conteurs français du XVIᵉ siècle*. Paris: Gallimard, 1965.

Knecht, Robert Jean. *French Renaissance Monarchy: Francis I and Henry II*. New York: Longman, 1996.

Knecht. *The French Wars of Religion, 1559–1598*. New York: Longman, 1996.

Knecht. *Renaissance Warrior and Patron: The Reign of Francis I*. Cambridge: Cambridge University Press, 1994.

Knecht. *Un prince de la Renaissance. François Ier et son royaume*. Paris: Editions Fayard, 1998.

La Croix du Maine, François Grudbe, and Antoine Du Verdier. *Les bibliothèques françoises de la Croix du Maine et de Du Verdier, sieur de Vauprivas*, 6 volumes, edited by Jean Antoine Rigoley de Juvigny. Paris: Saillant & Nyon, booksellers, Michel Lambert, printer, 1772–1773.

Laplanche, François. *L'Écriture, le Sacré et l'Histoire, érudits et politiques protestants devant la Bible en France au XVIIᵉ siècle*. Amsterdam: Holland University Press, 1986.

Lazard, Madeleine. *Les aventures de Fémynie: Les femmes sous la Renaissance*. Paris: Editions Fayard, 2001.

Lazard. *La comédie humaniste au XVIᵉ siècle et ses personnages*. Paris: Presses universitaires de France, 1978.

Lazard. *Images littéraires de la femme à la Renaissance*. Paris: Presses universitaires de France, 1985.

Lazard. *Le Théâtre en France au XVIᵉ siècle*. Paris: Presses universitaires de France, 1980.

Lechner, Joan Marie. *Renaissance Concepts of the Commonplaces; An Historical Investigation of the General and Universal Ideas Used in All Argumentation and Persuasion with Special Emphasis on the Educational and Literary Tradition of the Sixteenth and Seventeenth Centuries*. New York: Pageant Press, 1962.

Mathieu-Castelani, Gisèle. *Mythes de l'Eros baroque*. Paris: Presses universitaires de France, 1981.

Mathieu-Castelani. *Rhétorique des passions*. Paris: Presses universitaires de France, 2000.

Mazouer, Charles. *Le Théâtre français de la Renaissance*. Paris: Champion, 2002.

Meerhoff, Kees. *Rhétorique et poétique de la Renaissance: Du Bellay, Ramus et les autres*. Leiden: Brill, 1986.

Miernowski, Jan. *Le dieu néant: Théologies négatives à l'aube des temps modernes*. Leiden: Brill, 1998.

Miernowski. *Signes dissimilaires: La quête des noms divins dans la poésie française de la Renaissance*. Genève: Droz, 1997.

Millet, Olivier. *Calvin et la dynamique de la parole; étude de rhétorique réformée*. Paris: Champion, 1992.

Mourgues, Odette de. *Metaphysical, Baroque and Précieux Poetry*. Oxford: Clarendon Press, 1953.

Pérouse, Gabriel A. *Nouvelles françaises du XVIᵉ siècle. Images de la vie du temps*. Geneva: Droz, 1977.

Rebhorn, Wayne A. *Renaissance debates on rhetoric*. Ithaca, N.Y.: Cornell University Press, 2000.

Reynier, Gustave. *Le roman sentimental avant l'Astrée*. Paris: Colin, 1908.

Rigolot, François. *Erreur de la Renaissance: perspectives littéraires*. Paris: Champion, 2002.

Rigolot. *Poésie et Renaissance*. Paris: Seuil, 2002.

Rubin, David Lee, ed. *Poésie française du premier 17ᵉ siècle*. Tübingen: G. Narr, 1986.

Schmidt, Albert-Marie, ed. *Poètes du XVIᵉ siècle*. Paris: Gallimard, 1964.

Sommers, Paula. *Celestial Ladders: Readings in Marguerite de Navarre's Poetry of Spritual Ascent*. Geneva: Droz, 1989.

Stone, Donald, Jr. *France in the Sixteenth Century: A Medieval Society Transformed*. Englewood Cliffs, N.J.: Prentice-Hall, 1969.

Stone. *French Humanist Tragedy: A Reassessment*. Manchester: Manchester University Press, 1974.

Tripet, Arnaud. *Entre humanisme et rêverie: études sur les littératures française et italienne de la Renaissance au Romantisme*. Paris: Champion, 1998.

Weber, Henri. *La création poétique en France au XVIᵉ siècle*. Paris: Nizet, 1955.

Contributors

Ehsan Ahmed . . . . *Michigan State University*

Frederic J. Baumgartner. . . . . *Virginia Polytechnic Institute and State University*

Barbara C. Bowen. . . . . *Vanderbilt University*

Catherine E. Campbell . . . . *Cottey College*

Roberto E. Campo . . . . *University of North Carolina–Greensboro*

Megan Conway. . . . . *Louisiana State University–Shreveport*

James Herbert Dahlinger, S.J. . . . . *Le Moyne College*

JoAnn DellaNeva. . . . . *University of Notre Dame*

Lance K. Donaldson-Evans . . . . *University of Pennsylvania*

Isabelle Fernbach. . . . . *University of California, Berkeley*

Russell Ganim. . . . . *University of Nebraska–Lincoln*

Margaret Harp . . . . *University of Nevada, Las Vegas*

E. Bruce Hayes . . . . *University of Kansas*

Gillian Jondorf. . . . . *University of Cambridge*

Judy Kem. . . . . *Wake Forest University*

Virginia Krause . . . . *Brown University*

Anne R. Larsen. . . . . *Hope College*

Kathleen P. Long. . . . . *Cornell University*

Ellen Loughran . . . . *Gallaudet University*

Karin Maag . . . . *H. Henry Meeter Center, Calvin College and Calvin Theological Seminary*

Eric MacPhail . . . . *Indiana University*

Scott M. Manetsch. . . . . *Trinity Evangelical Divinity School*

Julia A. Nephew . . . . *Elmhurst College*

Marie-Thérèse Noiset . . . . *University of North Carolina at Charlotte*

Dora E. Polachek. . . . . *Binghamton University, State University of New York*

Bernd Renner . . . . *Brooklyn College and the Graduate Center, The City University of New York*

Régine Reynolds-Cornell . . . . *Agnes Scott College*

Robert B. Rigoulot . . . . *University of Illinois at Springfield*

Mary Santina. . . . .

Gerald Seaman . . . . *Ripon College*

Emily Thompson . . . . *Webster University*

Danielle Trudeau. . . . . *San José State University*

Jessica L. Wolfe . . . . *University of North Carolina, Chapel Hill*

Thomas L. Zamparelli. . . . . *Loyola University New Orleans*

Elizabeth Chesney Zegura. . . . . *University of Arizona*

Cumulative Index

Dictionary of Literary Biography, Volumes 1-327
Dictionary of Literary Biography Yearbook, 1980-2002
Dictionary of Literary Biography Documentary Series, Volumes 1-19
Concise Dictionary of American Literary Biography, Volumes 1-7
Concise Dictionary of British Literary Biography, Volumes 1-8
Concise Dictionary of World Literary Biography, Volumes 1-4

Cumulative Index

DLB before number: *Dictionary of Literary Biography,* Volumes 1-327
Y before number: *Dictionary of Literary Biography Yearbook,* 1980-2002
DS before number: *Dictionary of Literary Biography Documentary Series,* Volumes 1-19
CDALB before number: *Concise Dictionary of American Literary Biography,* Volumes 1-7
CDBLB before number: *Concise Dictionary of British Literary Biography,* Volumes 1-8
CDWLB before number: *Concise Dictionary of World Literary Biography,* Volumes 1-4

Cumulative Index

Cumulative Index

J

K

M

ISBN 0-7876-8145-8

90000

9 780787 681456